T0396558

Springer International Handbooks of Education

The Springer International Handbooks of Education series aims to provide easily accessible, practical, yet scholarly, sources of information about a broad range of topics and issues in education. Each Handbook follows the same pattern of examining in depth a field of educational theory, practice and applied scholarship, its scale and scope for its substantive contribution to our understanding of education and, in so doing, indicating the direction of future developments. The volumes in this series form a coherent whole due to an insistence on the synthesis of theory and good practice. The accessible style and the consistent illumination of theory by practice make the series very valuable to a broad spectrum of users. The volume editors represent the world's leading educationalists. Their task has been to identify the key areas in their field that are internationally generalizable and, in times of rapid change, of permanent interest to the scholar and practitioner.

More information about this series at http://www.springer.com/series/6189

Susen R. Smith

Editor

Handbook of Giftedness and Talent Development in the Asia-Pacific

Volume 2

With 71 Figures and 89 Tables

 Springer

Editor
Susen R. Smith
GERRIC, School of Education
University of New South Wales
Sydney, NSW, Australia

ISSN 2197-1951   ISSN 2197-196X (electronic)
ISBN 978-981-13-3040-7   ISBN 978-981-13-3041-4 (eBook)
ISBN 978-981-13-3042-1 (print and electronic bundle)
https://doi.org/10.1007/978-981-13-3041-4

This Springer imprint is published by the registered company Springer Nature Singapore Pte Ltd.
The registered company address is: 152 Beach Road, #21-01/04 Gateway East, Singapore 189721, Singapore

This handbook is dedicated to my husband Raymond John Smith, my daughter Sheridan Hewson-Smith, and my grandsons Lawson and Zak, all of whom are the lights of my life. Your unwavering support, encouragement, joy of learning, creativity, exploration, exceptionality, and capacity to find love and laughter in the midst of unimaginable sadness nurture my soul every day. Thank you will never be enough, but love always will be!

Foreword

No one has ever accused Americans of being overly deferential to citizens of other countries or of being reluctant to place their country squarely in the centre of the universe. This is as true in the field of education as it is in many other arenas, even if international comparisons of educational achievement do not lend support to claims of American superiority.

However, one area in which we Yanks can claim a reasonable degree of primacy is the field of gifted education. Although many in this field cite the brilliant, if odious, Englishman Sir Frances Galton as the *fons et origo* of the construct of giftedness, that is a tenuous link (VanTassel-Baska, 2016). For gifted education, in a form we can recognise as such, was sprung upon the world sometime in the second decade of the twentieth century by Lewis M. Terman and other American educators and psychologists (Warne, 2019). Indeed, gifted education can rightly be considered an American export.

Thus, for many, if not most, educators in the USA, American gifted education is gifted education. One might even claim that gifted education is *as American as apple pie* (the first printed recipe for which, by the way, was produced by that great *American* poet Geoffrey Chaucer; Eschner, 2017). The idea that: (a) some students are gifted, although most are not; (b) gifted students require curricular and instructional modifications that other students do not; and (c) these modifications should occur in full-time or part-time segregated settings—all of these foundational axioms of our field sprang, like amber waves of grain, directly from American soil. And, since discourse in this field is still dominated by American educators (although volumes such as this one are making that less and less the case), in order to be considered gifted, students everywhere must pretty much conform to American conceptions of what constitutes giftedness (ignoring the fact that there is anything but a consensus in this country as to how to define the construct).

Moreover, the three foundational axioms cited above are usually regarded as universal, at least in the USA. That is, the prevailing belief is that gifted students are gifted students irrespective of where they live. Do a roundup of conceptions of giftedness and you will quickly realise that few of our ways of thinking about giftedness take sociocultural contexts into consideration.

I was disabused of this notion of universality and absolute American hegemony with respect to the discourse around gifted education when I was invited a number of years ago to participate in a conference in Seoul, South Korea, that focused on under-represented populations of gifted students. I was one of ten invited speakers, each of us hailing from a different country. As the conference unfolded and more of us spoke, it became quite clear to me that giftedness is anything but universal, that the construct is profoundly shaped by the various cultures in which it is created, and that there is no such thing as giftedness divorced from a specific context.

For example, it became clear that, whereas in the USA giftedness is typically, if not unanimously, regarded as something that one is blessed with by virtue of inborn and acquired characteristics and that gifted students are more or less passive recipients of, well, a gift, educators in some other countries regard it as something altogether different. In some cultures, for example, giftedness is not thought of as something with which some students are blessed, but rather as something that students can earn through hard work. In addition, there are countries and cultures in which the construct is meaningless; the culture has not seen a need to create the category of gifted students, for whatever reasons. And it was striking to learn from a Russian educator that, in that country, the construct of socio-economic status, which we regard as indispensable in discussions of under-represented groups of gifted students, was relatively unfamiliar since it was incoherent in the classless society that the Soviet Union purported to be.

All of which brings me to the volume at hand. Susen Smith has made a significant contribution to the field of gifted education by conceiving of, carefully editing, and contributing to the *Giftedness and Talented Development in the Asia-Pacific, Springer International Education Handbook*. This is a very ambitious project in at least two respects. First, Susen adopts an appropriately expansive view of what constitutes the "Asia-Pacific". As she writes, "The Asia-Pacific region is defined by countries being in or near the Pacific Ocean that encompass East Asia, South Asia, Southeast Asia, Oceania, and the Americas." This chunk of the world's geography comprises the majority of the people living on Earth and, more important, encompasses a diversity of cultures in which we can see the construct of giftedness play out in its various sociocultural contexts.

Second, as even a quick glance at the table of contents reveals, the range of topics included herein is impressive: Socialcultural conceptions and perceptions; Social and emotional needs and learning processes; Identifying and nurturing diversely gifted and talented students; Assessment, pedagogy, and curricula; Diverse dimensions of gifted education; and Educational contexts, transitions, and community engagement. These would be sufficient to provide the outline for a comprehensive course on gifted education or even the framework for a degree program in this field. The overlay of such an exhaustive array of areas of scholarship onto the book's vast geographical reach allows for the consideration of perennial issues within the field in contexts that, in some cases, to me at least, are novel and productive of new ideas and practices.

This is not a slim volume. Its heft may be sufficient to make even the most resolute Luddite long for a compact e-reader. Moreover, it is not necessarily a book that one would read in order from beginning to end, although that approach would yield many valuable insights. Rather, it is a source of ideas that one will want to keep handy, to dip into when one's thinking needs a jolt of fresh thinking.

Some books zoom into and out of our lives, quickly read (or not) and then consigned to a place on one's bookshelf, gathering dust over the years. Others become long-time companions, continuing to challenge our thinking and to broadening our knowledge. This book is one of the latter.

Teachers College, Columbia University   James H. Borland
New York, NY, USA

References

Eschner, K. (2017). Apple pie is not all that American. *The Smithsonian.* Retrieved from https://www.smithsonianmag.com/smart-news/why-apple-pie-linked-amer ica-180963157/

VanTassel-Baska, J. (2016). Sir Francis Galton: The Victorian polymath (1822–1911). *APAPsychNet.* Retrieved from https://psycnet.apa.org/record/2013-37318-002

Warne, R. T. (2019). An evaluation (and vindication?) of Lewis Terman: What the father of gifted education can teach the 21st century. *Gifted Child Quarterly, 63,* 3–21. https://doi.org/10.1177/0016986218799433

James H. Borland, PhD, is Professor of Education in the Department of Curriculum and Teaching at Teachers College, Columbia University, New York, NY, where he directs the graduate programs in the education of gifted students. The author of numerous books, book chapters, journal articles, and miscellanea, Borland is also editor of the Education and Psychology of the Gifted series of Teachers College Press. He was editor of the section on 'Teaching, Learning, and Human Development' of the American Educational Research Journal from 1993 to 1995 (with two Teachers College colleagues), and he has served on the editorial boards of the Gifted Child Quarterly, Roeper Review, and Journal of Secondary Gifted Education. He has won two Paper of the Year awards from the Gifted Child Quarterly (with Lisa Wright and with Lisa Wright and Rachel Schnur) and has twice won the Award for Excellence in Research from the Mensa Education and Research Foundation. He has lectured and consulted on the education of gifted students across the USA and abroad, undertakes staff development programs for teachers of the gifted; develops and evaluates programs for the gifted; and provides media consultancies and appearances.

Preface

Welcome to the first ever handbook on giftedness and talent development for the Asia-Pacific region! The Asia-Pacific region is defined by countries being in or near the Pacific Ocean that encompass East Asia, South Asia, Southeast Asia, Oceania, and the Americas. Experts in academia and practice in the field were invited to contribute and, ultimately, over 60 submissions derived from over a hundred authors from 18 nations: Australia, Canada, Chile, China/Taiwan/Hong Kong, Japan, South Korea, Malaysia, Mexico, New Zealand, Peru, Philippines, Singapore, Thailand, United Arab Emirates, the UK, and the USA. The handbook evolved from the inaugural *GERRIC Gifted Education Forum for Talent Enhancement* in Australia in 2015. It deals with critical issues for an important group of students; addresses a number of gaps in the current understandings of gifted education in the region; traverses substantial intellectual, empirical, and theoretical terrain; and draws on past and present research literature.

All invitees were requested to provide abstract submissions on a proposed chapter that incorporated an overview of the current research on their topic, their own research, and implications for future research and practice. These were double-blind peer reviewed in phase one. Phase two incorporated double-blind peer review of chapters, and phase three involved editing by the editor and section editors reviewing and preparing separate parts of the handbook. These peer-review processes ensured higher quality of chapters, especially as many came from authors whose native language was not English. The chapters derive from the authors' own research, wider recent research, theories, discourse, and practice and reflect the cultural, educational, linguistic, and ethnic diversity emanating from the Asia-Pacific and Pacific-rim nations.

The handbook represents a comprehensive overview of contemporary research and practice in the Asia-Pacific region that has not been highlighted elsewhere. While the list of authors reflects esteemed experts in the field, and many have already contributed significantly to other publications or handbooks in the past, the process also targeted emerging scholars who are not widely published in such handbooks, such as doctoral candidates or postdoctoral fellows or early career academics, but are nevertheless significant contributors to gifted education in their own countries.

Another aspect of the handbook is the focus on collaborative and multi-disciplinary partnerships. While individual submissions were accepted from contributors in various stages of their careers, contributions that involved inter-country partnerships and mentorships by senior academics of early career and postgraduate researchers were particularly encouraged. Hence, authors from other countries such as Britain, Germany, Sweden, Egypt, and UAE co-authored chapters. Additionally, the process promoted networking across universities, education sectors, gifted education associations, and disciplines to encourage a foundation for future collaborative projects. It is noteworthy that PhD candidates, Endeavour Fellowship scholarships, and University Postdoctoral grants for inter-country research also evolved from the handbook process.

The handbook differs from other handbooks or monographs in the gifted education field as it highlights contemporary sociocultural issues rather than adopt the traditional approach of focusing on conceptions, identification, curriculum, programs, and the like. Nevertheless, as the aforementioned foci are important, they are incorporated into one or more of the six parts of the handbook that emanated from the author guidelines combined with the collated chapter themes, though some chapters crossed more than one part: (1) Socialcultural Conceptions and Perceptions; (2) Social and Emotional Needs and learning Processes; (3) Identifying and Nurturing Diversely Gifted and Talented students; (4) Assessment, Pedagogy, and Curricula; (5) Diverse Dimensions of Gifted Education; and (6) Educational Contexts, Transitions, and Community Engagement.

Besides esteemed experts who have contributed to the handbook, many of the contributors have never collaborated on a project of this nature, and many are new to the field or are from other fields altogether. This author diversity ensured that a unique collation of contemporary research and practice on giftedness and talent development in the Asia-Pacific region was produced that is not highlighted in other handbooks in the field, nor across fields. While there are other international handbooks in gifted education, they often do not include many experts from the Asia-Pacific nations. For example, in recent times, new handbooks in gifted education have been published, such as the *SAGE Handbook of Gifted and Talented Education*, the *APA Handbook of Giftedness and Talent*, and the *Handbook of Giftedness in Children: Psychoeducational Theory, Research, and Best Practices.* However, they do not focus on the issues most prevalent in the Asia-Pacific region and usually only include one or two chapters from the Asian, Australasian, or South American part of the world, if any. In addition, new Australasian books have been published on gifted education recently, but they only tell part of the narrative of the Asia-Pacific regions and rim countries rather than a comprehensive overview from this diverse region. Taken together, I view this handbook as complementary to past and current publications; therefore, it is also of international importance. Indeed, this handbook builds on the prolific work emanating from other parts of the world, such as Britain, Europe, and the USA.

The chapters in the Asia-Pacific handbook extend current gifted education research on selected topics and include: sociocultural concepts of giftedness, talent development, differentiated pedagogy and curriculum, and life of extraordinary people. Some original foci include: seeking intuitive theories, Social-Emotional Learning (SEL), youth scholarship, wisdom, spirituality, ethics, popular culture, dynamic pedagogy, STEM/STEAM, mindfulness, career choices, transitions, and community partnerships. Coverage of topics also includes: innovations in technology, theoretical growth, critical arguments, and recommendations that may inform future research and practice. The handbook has a stronger focus on pedagogy that could assist researchers, academics/educators/specialists, postgraduate students, families, advocates, teachers/practitioners, and other stakeholders to support gifted students in practice.

Thank you to all involved in this project. This monumental task could not have been achieved without the collegiality shared amongst us. I was blessed to work with such a dedicated range of experts in the field, many of whom I eagerly reference in my research, and many of whom I am honoured to have met throughout my career. Initially, thank you to all the authors; your work is unique and exceptional and I am delighted to showcase it in this handbook. While not all invitees were able to provide a chapter, many did contribute to the advisory or review boards. Reviewers also came from additional Pacific-rim countries, such as, Brazil, Columbia, and Uraguay. Thank you especially to each of the section editors (in order from Part I to Part VI): Roger Moltzen, Rhoda Myra Garces-Bacsal, Sheyla Blumen, Maria Leonor Conejeros-Solar, James Watters, Seokhee Cho, and Selena Gallagher whose role involved editing and reviewing the chapters with me in the final stages to ensure acceptance of higher quality manuscripts. So, my sincere thanks are extended to everyone who contributed to the peer-review, editing, and writing process. I greatly appreciate your generosity of time and expertise which helped to ensure the quality that the handbook deserved.

The Springer production team also added to the quality of the chapters with their ongoing support and finalising of chapters. Thank you to the Editor Nick Melchior and Reference Editorial team's Audrey Wong-Hillmann, Sindhu Ramachandran, Mokshika Gaur, Madhivathani Madhi Maran, and Mary Antony in particular. Nick you were there right from the beginning and encouraged me when I almost gave up at the start. Your enthusiasm for the project reassured me to take the original project from a small volume to double its size for an international handbook. Thank you also to my virtual Springer colleagues, Audrey, Sindhu, Mokshika, and Madhi who provided almost weekly support over the last two plus years and, beyond everything else, helped me come to terms with the differences between Springer formatting and APA formatting! I appreciated our email and Skype interchanges which added that personal touch to an otherwise lonely endeavour. I also thank sincerely my mentors Margaret Ivanyi, my principal when I first started teaching all those years ago; Professor Andrew Martin and Professor Iva Strnadova from the UNSW, Australia; and Professor James Borland from Columbia University, USA, without whose guidance, genuine joy of learning, exceptional expertise, critical discourse, and encouragement this project would never have evolved.

Last, but by no means least, a heartfelt thank you to my husband Mr. Raymond Smith and daughter Sheridan, whose love, encouragement, proofing, technical expertise, referencing, understanding, and other immeasurable support during this very difficult transition was so invaluable. Thank you for giving up all those wonderful recreation moments and family memories to support me in this momentous endeavour.

Thank you to all who contributed in some way, if, in my error, I have failed to mention you. This was a first-time process for me as an editor-in-chief, so I'm sure I can be forgiven if my inexperience reflects in this inaugural handbook. Nonetheless, I do believe that the handbook content should inform pre-service education programs in gifted education, in-service professional learning programs, familial support, and future research and practice in this region of the world and beyond. Thank you all for your enthusiasm and commitment to this collaborative project and to gifted education in particular. I look forward to seeing this ambitious volume online for easier access and in print and also to see how it contributes to supporting you in your role as nurturers of talent development in children and youth in your part of the world.

January 2021   Susen R. Smith
                                                                          Editor-in-Chief

Contents

Susen R. Smith
GERRIC, School of Education
University of New South Wales
Sydney, NSW, Australia

Dr. Susen Smith is a GERRIC Senior Research Fellow and Senior Lecturer in Gifted and Special Education at the School of Education, University of NSW, Australia, where she teaches in the Master in Gifted Education program and supervises PhD students. She has four decades of leadership, teaching, and research experience from pre-K to adult education. Her research and practice interests include: differentiating curriculum and pedagogy for diverse student needs in multi-disciplinary contexts, gifted underachievement and indigeneity, twice-exceptionalities, social-emotional learning, academic engagement, enrichment, education for sustainability, and community outreach programs. Susen is published internationally and is on the editorial boards of the *Gifted Child Quarterly, Roeper Review, International Journal for Talent Development and Creativity,* and the *Australasian Journal of Gifted Education*. She has been a visiting scholar to Columbia University, Imperial College London, CUNY, National Taipei University of Education, and the Hong Kong Institute of Education; has acquired many competitive research grants; is widely published; and keynoted at national and international conferences. She has been an academic adviser for educational departmental policies and programs for decades in addition to having on-going advisory board and association memberships. Susen chaired the inaugural national *GERRIC Gifted Futures Forum for Talent Enhancement* in Australia and has organised

regional, national, and world conferences and many
gifted education outreach enrichment programs across
several universities in Australia and internationally, such
as the *TalentEd* program and the *2eMPower* project. She
created the *Model of Dynamic Differentiation* (MoDD)
for supporting student diversity across the learning continuum, provides professional learning across Australia
and internationally, and is Editor of the first ever *Handbook of Giftedness and Talent Development in the Asia-
Pacific*, in the series *Springer International Handbooks
of Education.* E-mail: susen.smith@unsw.edu.au

Section Editors

Part I: Sociocultural Conceptions

Professor Roger Moltzen Division of Education, The University of Waikato, Hamilton, New Zealand

Part II: Social and Emotional Needs and Learning Processes

Associate Professor Rhoda Myra Garces-Bacsal College of Education, Special Education Department, United Arab Emirates University, Al Ain, United Arab Emirates

Part III: Identifying and Nurturing Diversely Gifted and Talented Students

Professor Sheyla Blumen Department of Psychology, Pontificia Universidad Católica del Perú, Lima, Peru

Professor Maria Leonor Conejeros-Solar Escuela de Pedagogía, Pontificia Universidad Católica de Valparaíso, Viña del Mar, Chile

Part IV: Assessment, Pedagogy, and Curriculum

Associate Professor James Watters Faculty of Education, Queensland University of Technology, Brisbane, QLD, Australia

Part V: Diverse Dimensions of Gifted Education

Professor Seokhee Cho St. John's University, Queens, Queens, NY, USA

Part VI: Educational Contexts, Transitions, and Community Engagement

Dr. Selena Gallagher Cairo American College, Cairo, Egypt

International Advisory Board Members

Usanee Anuruthwong Bangkok, Thailand

Susan Assouline Iowa City, IA, USA

Sheyla Blumen Lima, Peru

Linda E. Brody Baltimore, MD, USA

Seokhee Cho Queens, NY, USA
ChungCheongbuk-Do, South Korea

Bonnie Cramond Athens, GA, USA

David Yun Dai Albany, NY, USA

James R. Delisle Kent, OH, USA

Françoys Gagné Montréal, QC, Canada

Miraca U. M. Gross Sydney, NSW, Australia

E. Jean Gubbins Storrs, CT, USA

Jae Yup Jared Jung Sydney, NSW, Australia

Leonie Kronborg Frankston, VIC, Australia

Chin-hsieh Lu Taipei, Taiwan

C. June Maker Tucson, AZ, USA

Andrew J. Martin Sydney, NSW, Australia

Roger Moltzen Hamilton, Waikato, New Zealand

John Munro East Melbourne, VIC, Australia

Kyungbin Park Seongnam-si, Gyeonggi-do, South Korea

Paula Olszewski-Kubilius Evanston, IL, USA

Susana Graciela Pérez Barrera Montevideo, Uruguay

International Review Board Members

Contributors

Dale Albanese Center for Creativity and Innovation Studies, National Chengchi University, Taipei, Taiwan

Lindsey Anderson Javits Project, College of Charleston, Charleston, SC, USA

Susan G. Assouline Belin-Blank Center, College of Education, University of Iowa, Iowa City, IA, USA

Amy Price Azano Virginia Tech, Blacksburg, VA, USA

Abu Yazid Abu Bakar Faculty of Education, Universiti Kebangsaan Malaysia, Bangi, Malaysia

Daniel Patrick Balestrini University of Regensburg, Regensburg, Germany

Nadine Ballam University of Waikato, Hamilton, New Zealand

Michelle Bannister-Tyrrell School of Education, University of New England, Armidale, NSW, Australia

Aranzazu M. Blackburn Brisbane, QLD, Australia

Sheyla Blumen Department of Psychology, Pontificia Universidad Católica del Perú, Lima, Peru

Eunjoo Boo Seoul National University, Seoul, South Korea

Linda E. Brody Johns Hopkins University Center for Talented Youth, Baltimore, MD, USA

Emma C. Burns School of Education, University of New South Wales, Sydney, NSW, Australia

Carolyn M. Callahan University of Virginia, Charlottesville, VA, USA

Ana Karen Camelo-Lavadores Universidad Autónoma de Yucatán, Mérida, Yucatán, México

Wei-Ren Chen Department of Special Education, National Chiayi University, Chiayi City, Taiwan

Terence Titus Chia Centre for Research in Pedagogy and Practice, Office of Education Research, National Institute of Education, Singapore, Singapore

T. W. Chiang Gaterac Limited, Sheung Wan, Hong Kong, China

Seokhee Cho St. John's University, New York, NY, USA

Maria Leonor Conejeros-Solar Escuela de Pedagogía, Pontificia Universidad Católica de Valparaíso, Viña del Mar, Chile

Bonnie Cramond The University of Georgia, Athens, GA, USA

David Yun Dai University at Albany, State University of New York, Albany, NY, USA

Gabriela de la Torre García PAUTA, Institute of Nuclear Sciences, Universidad Nacional Autónoma de México UNAM, Mexico City, México

James R. Delisle Kent State University, Kent, OH, USA

Carmel Diezmann Faculty of Education, Queensland University of Technology, Brisbane, QLD, Australia

Ann Easter Gifted Education Consultancy Services, Aotearoa, New Zealand

Joyce J. Y. Fung Center for Advancement in Inclusive and Special Education, Faculty of Education, University of Hong Kong, Hong Kong, China

Françoys Gagné Université du Québec à Montréal (UQAM), Montréal, QC, Canada

Selena Gallagher Cairo American College, Cairo, Egypt

Rhoda Myra Garces-Bacsal College of Education, Special Education Department, United Arab Emirates University, Al Ain, United Arab Emirates

Susanne Garvis University of Gothenburg, Gothenburg, Sweden

María Paz Gómez-Arízaga Universidad de Los Andes, Santiago, Chile

Payal Goundar UNSW, Sydney, NSW, Australia

Anne Grant Deakin University, Melbourne, VIC, Australia

Miraca U. M. Gross GERRIC, School of Education, University of New South Wales, Sydney, NSW, Australia

E. Jean Gubbins University of Connecticut, Storrs, CT, USA

Rashea Hamilton Washington Student Achievement Council, Olympia, WA, USA

Peta K. Hay GERRIC/School of Education, The University of New South Wales, Sydney, NSW, Australia

Lesley Henderson Flinders University, Adelaide, SA, Australia

Takeo Higuchi Idea-Marathon Institute (IMS Institute), Tokyo, Japan

Jenny Horsley Victoria University of Wellington, Wellington, New Zealand

Gail Fischer Hubbard Prince William County Public Schools, Manassas, VA, USA

Takuya Iwata The University of Georgia, Athens, GA, USA
NIC International College, Osaka, Japan

Jane Jarvis Flinders University, Adelaide, SA, Australia

Jae Yup Jung GERRIC/School of Education, The University of New South Wales, Sydney, NSW, Australia

Daehyun Kim Torrance Center for Creativity and Talent Development, University of Georgia, Athens, GA, USA

Eunhyang Kim Gachon University, Seongnam-si, Gyeonggi-do, South Korea

Kyung Hee Kim The College of William & Mary, Williamsburg, VA, USA

Youngmin Kim Korea Advanced Institute of Science and Technology, GIFTED, Daejeon, South Korea

Yun-Kyoung Kim Seoul National University, Seoul, South Korea

Tay T. R. Koo The University of New South Wales, Sydney, NSW, Australia

Leonie Kronborg Faculty of Education, Monash University, Clayton, VIC, Australia

Carly Lassig Queensland University of Technology, Brisbane, QLD, Australia

Jeongkyu Lee The Korea Foundation for the Advancement of Science, Seoul, South Korea

Jihyun Lee School of Education, The University of New South Wales, Sydney, NSW, Australia

Seon-Young Lee Seoul National University, Seoul, South Korea

Youngju Lee Korea Advanced Institute of Science and Technology, GIFTED, Daejeon, South Korea

Chin-hsieh Lu Department of Special Education, National Taipei University of Education, Taipei, Taiwan

Ann Lupkowski-Shoplik Belin-Blank Center, College of Education, University of Iowa, Iowa City, IA, USA

Min Ma Central University of Finance and Economics, Beijing, China

C. June Maker Department of Disability and Psychoeducational Studies, The University of Arizona, Tucson, AZ, USA

Marcella Mandracchia Adelphi University, New York, NY, USA

Andrew J. Martin School of Education, University of New South Wales, Sydney, NSW, Australia

D. Betsy McCoach University of Connecticut, Storrs, CT, USA

Salvatore Sal Mendaglio University of Calgary, Calgary, AB, Canada

Azra Moeed Victoria University of Wellington, Wellington, New Zealand

Roger Moltzen Division of Education, The University of Waikato, Hamilton, New Zealand

Anne-Marie Morrissey Deakin University, Melbourne, VIC, Australia

John Munro Faculty of Education and Arts, Australian Catholic University, East Melbourne, VIC, Australia

Paula Olszewski-Kubilius Center for Talent Development, School of Education and Social Policy, Northwestern University, Evanston, IL, USA

Ananda Kumar Palaniappan Tunku Abdul Rahman University College, Kuala Lumpur, Malaysia

Kyungbin Park Gachon University, Seongnam-si, Gyeonggi-do, South Korea

Donna Pendergast Griffith University, Brisbane, QLD, Australia

Pamela Peters University of Connecticut, Storrs, CT, USA

Shane N. Phillipson Faculty of Education, Peninsula Campus, Monash University, Frankston, VIC, Australia

Margaret Plunkett School of Education, Federation University, Churchill, VIC, Australia

Jeb Puryear ACS-Cobham International School, Hersham, UK

Tracy Riley Massey University, Palmerston North, New Zealand

Janice I. Robbins The College of William and Mary, Williamsburg, VA, USA

Karen B. Rogers University of St. Thomas, Minneapolis, MN, USA

Jennifer Rowley The University of Sydney, Sydney, NSW, Australia

Lara Walker Russell Javits Project, College of Charleston, Charleston, SC, USA

Jiyoung Ryu Korea Advanced Institute of Science and Technology, GIFTED, Daejeon, South Korea

Pedro Antonio Sánchez-Escobedo College of Education, Universidad Autónoma de Yucatán, Mérida, Yucatán, México

Shozo Saegusa Shujitsu University, Okayama, Japan

Robert Arthur Schultz University of Toledo, Toledo, OH, USA

Del Siegle University of Connecticut, Storrs, CT, USA

Susen R. Smith GERRIC, School of Education, The University of New South Wales, Sydney, NSW, Australia

Julia Steinbach University of Regensburg, Regensburg, Germany

Heidrun Stoeger University of Regensburg, Regensburg, Germany

Rena F. Subotnik American Psychological Association, Washington, DC, USA

Julie Dingle Swanson College of Charleston, Charleston, SC, USA

Liang See Tan Centre for Research in Pedagogy and Practice, Office of Education Research, National Institute of Education, Singapore, Singapore

Jing Yi Tan Centre for Research in Pedagogy and Practice, Office of Education Research, National Institute of Education, Singapore, Singapore

Geraldine Townend GERRIC/School of Education, The University of New South Wales, Sydney, NSW, Australia

Angel Alberto Valdés-Cuervo Instituto Tecnológico de Sonora, Ciudad Obregón, Sonora, México

Joyce VanTassel-Baska The College of William and Mary, Williamsburg, VA, USA

Wilma Vialle University of Wollongong, Wollongong, NSW, Australia

Russell Walton Learning Development, University of Wollongong, Wollongong, NSW, Australia

Janna Wardman University of Auckland, Auckland, New Zealand

James Watters Faculty of Education, Queensland University of Technology, Brisbane, QLD, Australia

Myra Wearne NSW Department of Education, North Sydney Demonstration School, Waverton, NSW, Australia

Melinda Webber Faculty of Education and Social Work, The University of Auckland, Auckland, New Zealand

Cara Wienkes Belin-Blank Center, College of Education, University of Iowa, Iowa City, IA, USA

Sally Windsor University of Gothenburg, Gothenburg, Sweden

Denise Wood Charles Sturt University, Bathurst, NSW, Australia

Catherine Wormald Faculty of Social Sciences, School of Education, University of Wollongong, Wollongong, NSW, Australia

Frank C. Worrell University of California Berkeley, Berkeley, CA, USA

Jing-Jyi Wu Center for Creativity and Innovation Studies, National Chengchi University, Taipei, Taiwan

Jenny Yang St. John's University, New York, NY, USA

Ming-Jen Yu Center for Creativity and Innovation Studies, National Chengchi University, Taipei, Taiwan

Allan H. K. Yuen Centre for Information Technology in Education (CITE), University of Hong Kong, Hong Kong, China

Faculty of Education, The University of Hong Kong, Hong Kong, China

Yew Chung College of Early Childhood Education, Hong Kong, China

Mantak Yuen Center for Advancement in Inclusive and Special Education, Faculty of Education, University of Hong Kong, Hong Kong, China

María Alicia Zavala Berbena Universidad De La Salle Bajío, León, México

Yong Zhao University of Kansas, Lawrence, KS, USA

Albert Ziegler University of Erlangen-Nuremberg, Nuremberg, Germany

Part IV

Assessment, Pedagogy, and Curriculum

Assessment, Pedagogy, and Curriculum: Part IV Introduction

34

James Watters

Contents

Abstract

In Part IV the focus is on assessment, pedagogy, and curriculum for gifted students within a variety of educational contexts, from early childhood to university. The chapter begins with some discourse on the gifted curriculum and pedagogy, by tapping into curriculum and pedagogic ideologies. I examine each chapter's foci in this section, by exploring the overall question: What is the purpose of schooling for gifted students? However, do these chapters answer this question? I would suggest no, but they go part way to highlighting the key issues in the Asia-Pacific Rim countries when the researchers are researching to inform practice and educators within these countries are endeavouring to teach and assess gifted students' holistic needs in order to frame their learning as effectively as possible for potential to thrive.

Keywords

Gifted · Assessment · Pedagogy · Curriculum · Mathematics · Science · Technology · Early years schooling · Tertiary · Inquiry-oriented learning

J. Watters (✉)
Faculty of Education, Queensland University of Technology, Brisbane, QLD, Australia
e-mail: j.watters@qut.edu.au

© Springer Nature Singapore Pte Ltd. 2021
S. R. Smith (ed.), *Handbook of Giftedness and Talent Development in the Asia-Pacific*,
Springer International Handbooks of Education,
https://doi.org/10.1007/978-981-13-3041-4_78

Chapters in this part of the handbook address the broad topic of pedagogy and curriculum. Interestingly, although not exclusively, many of the chapters tend to focus on some aspect of mathematics, science, or technology. In the chapters, initiatives are described that cover the early years of schooling through to tertiary students from a range of countries in the Indo-Pacific Region, that are Australia, China, Hong Kong, Korea, New Zealand, Taiwan, and the USA.

A Perspective on Curriculum

Before discussing the themes that emerge in the chapters that contribute to this section, I take the liberty of presenting some dimensions of curriculum that are salient to the discussion of the chapters. Curriculum is a very broad topic which in its most general sense can be considered as any learning experience or opportunity that a student is exposed to as part of his or her development. In the narrowest sense, curriculum can be interpreted as the syllabus laid down by governing bodies and policymakers within an educational jurisdiction. Of course, a lot happens between the mandated curriculum developed by policymakers and what teachers adopt or students experience. Cutting across this dimension are the influences of social, cultural, and political norms that set boundaries around individual teachers and systems—the so called *hidden curriculum*. The well-documented attitudes of many teachers to the gifted and the stereotypes they adopt of the gifted can be considered a contribution to this hidden curriculum. Another dimension is to consider the purpose of curriculum or for that matter, schooling. Here, I turn to the work of Schiro (2013) who identifies four curriculum ideologies: *Scholarly Academic, Learner-Centred, Social Efficiency,* and *Social Reconstruction*. These represent the primary focus of curricula, but in many instances a blend of ideologies can be perceived in programs. These ideologies do not direct pedagogical practices, but are aligned with beliefs about the purpose of schooling. Understanding the ideology informing programs is important as curriculum prioritises what is important in learning and what should be taught.

Schiro argues that the *Scholarly Academic* ideologues believe that the primary purpose of schooling is for students to acquire "accumulated important knowledge that has been organised into the academic disciplines found in universities" (p. 4). The focus is on helping students acquire cutting edge knowledge by focusing on traditional knowledge domains. The *Learner-Centred* ideology views students as unique individuals and aims to nurture their development and growth (Schiro, 2013 p. 26). The emphasis is to help students grow in harmony with their own unique, intellectual, social, emotional, and physical attributes. Learning is grounded in the interaction of the learner with other students, teachers, ideas, and the environment. The *Social Efficiency* curriculum ideology asserts that students should be taught the requisite skills that enable them to contribute to society and lead meaningful lives (Schiro, 2013, p. 90). Helping learners to develop skills and practices to be competent in their daily life and workplace is the main theme in this ideology. In one sense the focus is on productive career development. *Social Reconstruction* focuses on education as a means by which to eliminate economic and social injustices or disadvantage in order to create a better society. Students are taught the knowledge, skills, and values so that they may be informed and empowered to shape the world for the common good. The natural order of development in the child is the most significant and scientifically defensible basis for determining what should be taught.

A reader could argue that any program targeting opportunities for gifted students has elements of a *Learner-Centred* ideology but most gifted programs focus on students acquiring advanced knowledge and hence reflect a *Scholarly Academic* ideology. The arguments for providing gifted education programs invariably rely on developing economic prosperity and assume that the gifted will be major contributors through eminence in their careers. This argument is grounded in a *Social Efficiency* ideology. The chapters in this section draw primarily on these three ideologies. There is one exception, that being the chapter by Cho et al. which focuses on empowering gifted students in English-speaking countries whose first language is not English and hence illustrates a *Social Reconstructionist* ideology.

Pedagogy

The curriculum describes what is important in learning but not how learning should be nurtured. While all students should be challenged by the taught curricula gifted students are less likely to tolerate content that is not challenging. The teaching or pedagogical practices adopted will be influenced somewhat by curriculum ideology in particular *Social Reconstruction* where action learning approaches may predominate. In contrast, transmission models of teaching in which content is delivered may be more common in *Scholarly Academic* curricula. The pedagogical practices advocated for the gifted are cross-disciplinary and inquiry-oriented (e.g., vanTassel-Baska, 2015).

While pedagogy should be driven by theoretical frameworks around learning, curriculum as described before reflects our perspectives on what education should achieve for gifted students. What is the purpose of schooling for gifted students? To answer this question, I now examine how the chapters in this section align with the curriculum ideologies discussed.

Introductions to the Individual Chapters

The majority of chapters in Part IV focus on issues of curriculum and in this reflection the underlying processes, assumptions, and ideology are examined.

The ▶ Chap. 39, "Nurturing Mathematical Talents of Young Mathematically Gifted English Language Learners", by Seokhee Cho', Marcella Mandracchia, and Jenny Yang focuses on a potentially marginalised group of students. Gifted English learners are often immigrant or possible refugee students whose potential is constrained by the challenge of fitting into an English language schooling system. The authors highlight the underrepresentation of gifted students from non-English backgrounds in gifted education programs. They argue a contributing factor could be their disadvantaged environments and lack of English language competence. This program would appear to represent an amalgam of *Scholarly Academic* and *Social Reconstruction* ideologies. The ultimate goal is to equip disadvantaged students with the knowledge and skills of traditional mathematics. The authors emphasise the importance of empowering students to engage with mathematics using a strength-based philosophy. The focus is role played by language in learning mathematics. Many of these gifted students may have had limited exposure to formal mathematical ideas when young and lack the language to express mathematical ideas. For those students potentially gifted in mathematics, language may thus be a constraint. Through culturally responsive pedagogy, they support language development using scaffolding strategies in preparatory or transition programs. This program aligns well with a *Social Reconstruction* focus as it attempts to empower marginalised students.

In ▶ Chap. 40, "Online Learning for Mathematically Talented Students: A Perspective from Hong Kong", the authors Joyce Fung, Mantak Yuen, and Allan Yuen presuppose that gifted students would be able to successfully capitalise on online learning opportunities. The assumption they explore is that gifted students are autonomous, self-regulated learners who are highly motivated, self-efficacious, and good time managers. Hence a pedagogical approach that provides access to differentiated mathematics programs may provide an avenue to extend mathematically gifted students. The advantage of online courses where feedback is immediate is acknowledged as an important contribution to student motivation. They explore their proposition by examining an online mathematics course in Hong Kong, acknowledging that perhaps cultivating autonomous learners may not be a priority. Their findings based on a survey design raise questions about the extent that students will engage autonomously in learning through online tools. Not surprisingly, they found that course design is a significant contributor to student willingness to engage. However, the support provided by teachers in fostering a sense of self-efficacy mediated the effect of course design and teacher support on self-regulated learning. The principles behind the course explored appears to be those that "add depth to the normal curriculum" which implies a somewhat *Scholarly Academic* approach.

Jenny Horsley's and Azra Moeed's ▶ Chap. 35, "How Do Teachers Meet the Academic Needs of High-Ability Students in Science?" has a focus on science education in New Zealand and explores how teachers can generate students' interest in science—particularly students of high-academic ability—which is a topic requiring further investigation. In this chapter, the focus is on identification of gifted students who excel academically in science. The emphasis on science and academic achievement in science represents a *Scholarly Academic* ideology. This is not surprising as the authors address general responses to New Zealand policy. Like most developed countries, curricular is driven by an economic imperative that sees eminence in science and related disciplines as fuel for economic growth. The purpose of schooling is for students to be equipped with the knowledge to engage in 'cutting-edge science and technological innovation'. The authors profile a preliminary study that explored the ways that teachers identified and met the academic needs of their high-ability students in junior high school. Identification was driven by measures of achievement in content. Programming focused on acquisition of the knowledge and skills of science. They also report student perceptions of their experiences in science. Their findings revealed limited opportunities for experiences advocated for gifted students. They also highlight a common problem that identification and/or selection of students for support and extension are often based on invalid assessments such as performance on language tests as a selection criterion for placement in programs for those who are potentially gifted in science. Insights into how teachers in New Zealand are attempting to adapt national curricular priorities into regular classroom programs are provided in this chapter.

The focus of ▶ Chap. 43, "Differentiation of Instruction for Gifted Learners: Collated Evaluative Studies of Teacher Classroom Practices", by Joyce VanTassel-Baska, Gail Hubbard, and Janice Robbins is on pedagogical practices. The assumption is that curricula are mandated and the goal is to ensure that students acquire the formal knowledge that enables them to progress into advanced professional careers, a blend of *Scholarly Academic* and *Social Efficiency* ideologies. However, a *Learner-Centred* focus is evident in the importance attributed to ensuring the development of self-directed learning that enables gifted students to understand and act on issues in the real world. The chapter reports an observational study using a standardised observation protocol (*William and Mary Classroom Observation Scale-Revised* [COS-R]) to support data collection from 329 classrooms in the United States. This instrument helped to focus observations on the prevalence of best-practice teaching approaches. The study provides compelling evidence that effective differentiation for gifted students is not common practice. Practices that are more widely used relate to setting high expectations, encouraging student expression, and providing opportunities for independent or group learning. However, the authors deemed these practices as 'basic building blocks' for differentiation. Helping students to set goals and monitoring learning were less common despite the research evidence that goal setting and feedback are among the most powerful contributors to effective learning. Observations of high-level questioning, critical thinking, and argument building were seen in less than half of the classes. Interestingly, the study found that high school teachers were more effective in differentiating instruction. Brought into question is the level of professional in-servicing that teachers receive. Although anecdotal evidence, there is widespread delivery of programs intended to upskill teachers in many countries, the effectiveness is questionable. Even with effective programs, they report the willingness or capability of teachers to implement programs effectively can be constrained by personal factors such as self-efficacy or contextual factors such as competing agendas and school cultures.

The June Maker and Myra Wearne ▶ Chap. 41, "Engaging Gifted Students in Solving Real Problems Creatively: Implementing the Real Engagement in Active Problem-Solving (REAPS) Teaching/Learning Model in Australasian and Pacific Rim Contexts", provides an interesting insight into a program and philosophy that bridges the curriculum ideologies described previously while adopting teaching approaches that gifted children value. The underpinning argument is that if teachers can engage students in real-world abstract problems that are meaningful, learning will follow. The learning outcomes include formal knowledge as mandated by curricula which echo the *Scholarly Academic* world view as well as a *Learner-*

Centred focus that enables students to engage in self-satisfying learning in their passion areas. The authors explicitly state this blending of ideologies in their introduction "educators must achieve a balance in which they facilitate the learning of required content while also teaching in ways that engage students in authentic learning experiences that are linked to their interests and passions". This approach has implicitly informed a teaching model called *Real Engagement in Active Problem Solving* (REAPS). The teaching approach has been grounded in what has been described as a 'Prism of Learning', developed in Thailand and tested in a number Pacific Rim countries as well as Europe. The emphasis in the program is to provide students with a differentiated learning experience in which the focus is on macro concepts and themes which are abstract, complex and seemingly cross-disciplinary in contrast to a "tightly structured one consisting of only discipline-based concepts and skills". The approach addresses the needs of all children with less able ones exploring a problem from a personal perspective, while the more able students had to examine the problem from a social-political perspective. The chapter provides a significant advancement on the Maker model in so far as it elaborates on those components central to differentiation for the gifted.

The ▶ Chap. 38, "Fostering and Developing Talent in Mentorship Programs: The Mentor's Perspectives", by Liang See Tan, Jing Yi Tan, and Terence Chia also reports on pedagogical practices. They explore the role of mentoring gifted students and provide an interesting perspective on the purpose of educating gifted students. While the authors acknowledged that the students in their program will acquire advanced understandings, the use of mentors whose role is "to develop nuanced understandings in an area of expertise and to stimulate thinking in the area of mentee interest... [and] to induct and enculturate those who are new to the community" suggests a *Social Efficiency* ideology. They argue that the role of mentors is to address broader issues related to the cognitive, social, and emotional needs of the gifted and talented. Mentors also help to connect students with essential social networks within the targeted academic community, in short to "align learning in school and at the workplace". As the authors reveal, the ideal role of mentors as expert guides to enculturate novices depends on the selection of the mentor. Some appear to see their role as purveyor of knowledge. This equips students with knowledge of the social norms of their future professional community. This chapter provides an extensive review of the literature on mentoring and attributes of good mentors.

Jiyoung Ryu, Youngju Lee, Youngmin Kim, Payal Goundar, Jihyun Lee, and Jae Yup Jung provide insights into a policy-driven inquiry-oriented strategy adopted in Korea in an attempt to make science and mathematics more engaging for young students by employing a STEAM education model. In their ▶ Chapter 37, "STEAM in gifted education in Korea", is an acronym for the educational methods of Science, Technology, Engineering, Arts, and Mathematics that incorporates the arts with STEM (Science, Technology, Engineering, and Mathematics) subjects. The motives are clearly aligned with enhancing economic outcomes for Korea and represent a *Social Efficiency* ideology. The inclusion of arts is supposed to enhance the focus on creativity although the authors do not explain how this is achieved. The teaching approach involves three phases: presentation of a situation, creative design, and emotional connection. These phases align with real-world problem finding, designing an investigation into a meaningful problem and metacognitive reflection on the process. Problems as real-world problems are intended to provide a platform for learning across the traditional domains of science while incorporating aspects of mathematics, technology, and engineering where appropriate. Opportunities exist for teachers specialised in different STEAM areas to teach the same topic to the students. The program is designed as a general approach to teaching across the STEM domains, but has been extended to meet the needs of gifted students through extension, out of school, research programs run by the *Korea Foundation for the Advancement of Science, and Creativity*, and partnerships with industry. Evaluation studies have suggested improvements in cognitive and noncognitive outcomes.

In ▶ Chapter 36, "Why Is It So? Interest and Curiosity in Supporting Students Gifted in Science", Watters reflects a concern that to confront the challenges of a world facing major problems of sustainability, we as educators of gifted children need to capitalise on their strengths to help them solve the problems they will inherit. The future needs creative and passionate scientists and engineers to fix the globe. Thus, the underpinning ideology is grounded in *Social Efficiency*. Given the apparent decline in interest in science and technology around the world, the first challenge is to generate a passion for science and related domains of knowledge among students, and particularly the gifted. Hence, this chapter focuses on the alignment between curiosity, interest, and engagement in learning science to attract the most highly able students to pursue careers in science and related fields including the trades. In this chapter the constructs of curiosity and interest are unpacked and how these can be fostered through the establishment of learning opportunities that provide for student autonomy and differentiated learning opportunities are illustrated.

Chin-hsieh Lu and Wei-Ren Chen present an interesting ▶ Chap. 42, "Attuned Pedagogy: The Artistry of Differentiated Instruction from a Taiwanese Cultural Perspective", that highlights how traditional cultural educational practices can be thwarted by imported models. The concept of differentiation has been popularised across many countries—predominately in the US research—as an approach to supporting gifted students. Lu and Chen draw attention to the millennial old practice of *Yin Cai Shi Jiao* (因材施教) which they translate as *Attuned Pedagogy*. They define *Attuned Pedagogy* as the "mutual construction of the professional relationship between teachers and students as the artistry of differentiation based on the Taiwanese experience". The proposition is that giftedness is a multi-dimensional phenomenon rather than a set of characteristics defined in terms of constructs such as intelligence, thinking styles, passions, and aptitudes. Thus, the fundamental goal of education is to perceive and understand each child holistically and help to fully develop them as persons. They further argue that *Attuned Pedagogy* promotes students' talent while transforming teachers by mutual construction. The implication the authors draw is that effective teachers of the gifted must also be effective learners. The challenge facing gifted education in Taiwan is the implementation of policies advocating differentiation and consequently the marginalisation of effective cultural practices that embody *Yin Cai Shi Jiao*. In a study of highly effective master teachers of the gifted, Lu and Chen identify three essential principles and four praxis strategies of *Attuned Pedagogy*. These principles can be applied to define the attributes of effective differentiation. A widely expressed concern among teachers confronted with policies on differentiation is how to do it. The authors in this chapter provide clear insights into the approach that Chinese teachers have used for centuries.

Conclusion

In Part IV, some insights into the raft of approaches adopted to support gifted students were provided. It is pleasing to see a number of initiatives are driven by respective government policies suggesting some prioritisation of gifted education. It is also pleasing to see a number of the authors reflected on specific programs that have been implemented in more than one country.

References

Schiro, M. (2013). *Curriculum theory: Conflicting visions and enduring concerns*. Thousand Oaks, CA: Sage.

VanTassel-Baska, J. (2015). The integrated curriculum model. In H. E. Vidergor & C. R. Harris (Eds.), *Applied practice for educators of gifted and able learners* (pp. 169–197). Rotterdam, Netherlands: Sense Publishers.

James (Jim) Watters, PhD, is an Adjunct Professor in Education at the Queensland University of Technology (QUT). Jim draws on over 30 years of experience as a science teacher and science teacher educator. His particular interest has been in the education of students gifted in science and mathematics (more recently rebadged as STEM). Jim has run enrichment programs, provided professional development, advised government on policy, supervised graduate students in gifted education, taught pre-service and in-service teachers in gifted education courses, and published internationally in-gifted education. He has a strong commitment to apply research to practice.

How Do Teachers Meet the Academic Needs of High-Ability Students in Science?

35

Jenny Horsley and Azra Moeed

Contents

Abstract

Eminent scientist and passionate orator Sir Paul Callaghan aspired for New Zealand to concentrate on cutting-edge science and technological innovation. Underpinning this vision is a need to nurture and develop talented science students and to retain them in higher science studies. However, retaining students in science study is proving challenging. Therefore, identifying how teachers can sustain students' interests in science—particularly students of high-academic ability—is a topic requiring further investigation. An overview of international initiatives in science education for those with high-academic ability is provided in this chapter, in addition to reporting New Zealand research involving four teachers and 53 high-ability students from each teacher's science class. Findings revealed that while these high-ability students identified motivating and exciting learning experiences in their science classes, their learning was

J. Horsley (✉) · A. Moeed
Victoria University of Wellington, Wellington, New Zealand
e-mail: jenny.horsley@vuw.ac.nz; azra.moeed@vuw.ac.nz

© Springer Nature Singapore Pte Ltd. 2021
S. R. Smith (ed.), *Handbook of Giftedness and Talent Development in the Asia-Pacific*,
Springer International Handbooks of Education,
https://doi.org/10.1007/978-981-13-3041-4_33

limited to science content knowledge and some procedural knowledge and skills and not on understanding how scientific knowledge is created and how science works. Importantly, given the emphasis on gifted students requiring an understanding of the philosophy of the 'nature' of science, these students provided no evidence of a nuanced understanding of the nature of science, that is, how science works. The example study identifies high-ability students' perceptions of what teachers say and do that motivate them in science classes. Similarly, identifying what teachers perceive they do to support their high-ability science students will benefit not only students, but also other teachers and communities that aspire to foster students capable of performing in cutting-edge science and innovation.

Keywords

Science · High ability · High-academic ability · Gifted and talented · Nature of science (NoS)

The aims in this chapter are to:
1. Identify evidence-informed strategies to support effective teaching and learning of high-ability students in science.
2. Identify high-ability students' perceptions of what teachers say and do that motivate them in science classes.
3. Identify what teachers perceive they do to support their high-ability science students.
4. Assist teachers and communities that aspire to foster students capable of performing in cutting-edge science and innovation to engage with practice.
5. Consider future directions for research into science teaching and learning for high-ability students.

Introduction

Sir Paul Callaghan is renowned as New Zealand's greatest physicist. A Fellow of the Royal Society, he specialised in nanotechnology and magnetic resonance. Just days before his passing, Sir Paul spoke of his interest in science that emerged after hearing Nobel Chemist Alan MacDiarmid speak. According to Callaghan, MacDiarmid:

> ... resonated with New Zealanders. He touched audiences. I realised people were interested in science but there was a framework in which you had to operate to make it interesting, to tell them stories, to give them a thought about where we're going in the future, what the possibilities for our country are. (MacDonald, 2012, para 38)

Despite this recognised interest in science, both nationally and internationally, students who can opt out of studying science are choosing to do so (Education Counts, 2015; Goodrum, Druhan, & Abbs, 2011; Kennedy, 2014; Kennedy, Lyons, & Quinn, 2014; Kennedy et al., 2016). This makes it increasingly important that teachers can attract and retain students' interest in science subjects and, more particularly, retain those students who demonstrate, or are capable of demonstrating, high-academic ability in the subject.

The focus of this chapter is science education for high-ability students and includes a study of science teaching and learning in four New Zealand schools, as experienced by a purposive sample of high-ability students from a range of state and independent schools, and their science teachers. The schools were either secondary schools or middle schools that included lower secondary. With New Zealand schools required by the Ministry of Education (2017a) to report on how they address the needs of high-ability (or more globally labelled 'gifted and talented') students, this study aimed to determine how this requirement translated to classroom practice and how teachers were supported to meet the needs of these students. Throughout the chapter, we use the phrase 'high-academic ability' rather than the term 'gifted and talented'. The reason for this is that high-academic ability is a subset of 'gifted and talented', and we are focused on student learning in one domain—science—hence our focus on high-academic ability. To refer to the more global phrase 'gifted and talented' is to consider a very wide range of characteristics aligned to conceptions of giftedness. For example, Borland (2008) states that theories of giftedness require research that ought to include identification related to "ability, cognitive and personality structures" (p. 110). In this chapter, we focus solely on academic ability—a subset of the cognitive structure. Literature to identify components of this ability in relation to high-achieving science students cites the need for these students to have access to mentors and to receive ". . . pacing, optimal instructional conditions, and ability grouping" (VanTassel-Baska & MacFarlane, 2008, p. 583). Taber has identified that "an individual student will often have a very uneven profile of existing knowledge, understanding and skills . . ." (2016, p. 2), suggesting that not all high-ability students will demonstrate high-academic ability across all aspects of all domains. Further, Taber (2007) advises a pragmatic approach to selecting the terminology that is used to describe these students, suggesting that terms such as 'gifted', 'talented', 'highly able', and 'high academic' vary according to educational contexts. He recommends that in relation to science, those students whom:

> we should consider as high-academic or gifted learners [are] those students who, given appropriate support, are able to either: achieve exceptionally high levels of attainment in all or some aspects of the normal curriculum demands in school science . . . or undertake some science-related tasks at a level of demand well above that required at that curricular stage. (p. 7).

Therefore, we have focused our research on those students of high-academic ability in just one domain, that of science.

New Zealand's National Administration Guideline (NAG) (iii)c requires:

> . . . school boards, through their principal and staff, to use good quality assessment information to identify students who have special needs (including gifted and talented), and to develop and implement teaching and learning strategies to meet the needs of these students. (Education Review Office [ERO], 2008, p. 1)

Although NAG (iii)c does not detail how teachers ought to plan to meet these students' needs, both international and national literature provide a range of recommendations to describe what effective practice can look like (e.g., Colangelo et al., 2010; Taber, 2016; VanTassel-Baska, MacFarlane, & Feng, 2008; Wardman & Hattie, 2012). While identification of, and programming for, high-ability science students has been considered internationally (e.g., Taber, 2016; Taber & Riga, 2007; Taber, Sumida, & McClure, 2017), it has received little attention in Australasia—that is, Australia and New Zealand—and surrounding islands.

Literature also identifies that there have been different rates of development in identification and programming across Asia (Chan, 2018; Hui et al., 2018; Ibata-Arens, 2012). In 2004, Cho reported that any special provisions designed to support gifted and talented students in Korea were perceived as a "threat to the healthy development of public education" (p. 119). The practice of not providing for these learners removed opportunities for high-ability students to receive individual tuition commensurate with their academic learning needs. As a result, the rate of progress was slowed in terms of developing programs for students of high-academic ability, in a nation that chose instead to implement practices aimed at equalising the education offered to students (Cho, 2004). In a later report, Ibata-Arens (2012) suggested that while gifted policies and national practices had been developed in some Asian countries—including Korea, China, and Singapore—Japan had been much slower to follow suit.

New Zealand schools' definitions of high-ability students ought to relate to the school context and to a school's approach to delivering the national curriculum. In practice, it appears that there is still some progress to be made, with an ERO (2008) report finding that only 42% of the 315 schools reviewed were meeting the needs of high-ability students. Those schools considered to be in the 42% were using either enrichment, acceleration, or a combination of both.

However, with a national mandate to identify and report on these students and a great deal of choice in how identification is determined, there exists a challenge for teachers to identify those students who are, or who have the potential to be, students of high-academic ability and, more specifically, high-ability science students. Well-known education researcher, John Hattie (2011), drew on his visible learning research when asked for his views on gifted education and whether he perceived they had changed over time. He responded "I [also] wonder why so many gifted students do not become gifted adults: have we got the selection correct?" (Hattie, 2011, p. 16). Borland (2008) suggests that the wide choice given to those tasked with identifying gifted students is the reason for the challenge, as there is no agreement as to "what this construct, giftedness, is, how it reveals itself, or what it is composed of" (p. 262). Sternberg (2010) contributes to the argument by stating that:

> Assessments of giftedness need to measure not only g[ifted]-based abilities, but also, creative and practical abilities, and in the ideal case, wisdom-based abilities as well. (p. 328)

Taber et al. (2017) take a pragmatic view of giftedness and advocate for all students who are legally required to attend a school to receive the kind of educational experiences that will make a substantive contribution to the development of their knowledge, skills, and understandings. They emphasise the need for learning experiences to be sufficiently challenging and the outcome to be considerable new learning. Hattie's (2011) views are similar in that he says that all students should be challenged by the taught curricula and argues that gifted students are less likely to tolerate content that is not challenging. Given the purpose statement of the New Zealand Ministry of Education, "We shape an education system that delivers equitable and excellent outcomes" (2019, para 1), there is an obvious argument for ensuring classroom programs provide opportunities for all learners to experience curricula that will enable them to develop to their full potential. The need to produce equitable outcomes in our classrooms means that a tension exists between teachers providing a curriculum that will challenge *all* students while delivering greater challenge for high-ability students. Challenge for gifted students is especially important given that research has identified that a lack of engagement for high-ability learners may lead to boredom (Preckel, Götz, & Frenzel, 2010) and underachievement (Rubenstein, Siegle, Reis, McCoach, & Burton, 2012). How then does this dilemma impact the delivery of science education for high-ability students?

Current Issues in Science Education

Both nationally and internationally, the modern curricular focus is on students developing an understanding of science ideas, developing procedural skills, and an understanding about the nature of science (NoS). Developing NoS understanding is learning about how science works and the epistemology of the discipline. However, living in a world in which science plays a major part for making everyday living simple, for example, providing food for the world, quality health care and ways of moving around the world, it is important that *all* citizens are scientifically literate. The current science curriculum in New Zealand states:

> In **science**, students explore how both the natural physical world and science itself work so that they can participate as critical, informed, and responsible citizens in a society in which science plays a significant role. (Ministry of Education, 2007, p. 17)

This more recent goal of science education—for all to become scientifically literate citizens capable of making informed decisions that affect their everyday lives— reduces the emphasis on science education for those who continue in science. It is said that until recent times, science curricula were designed to meet the needs of a minority of school students who would carry on in further education in science and seek employment in science-related areas (Millar, 2006; Millar & Osborne, 1998; Osborne & Dillon, 2008). Although it is desirable for high-ability students to have greater understanding of NoS, there is little research that says these students are developing a better understanding of NoS in New Zealand or elsewhere (Taber, 2007). Current evidence suggests that although NoS was a focus for the previous curriculum, *Science in the New Zealand Curriculum* (Ministry of

Education, 1993), there was little evidence that this was achieved (ERO, 2012). To address this, the present *New Zealand Curriculum* (Ministry of Education, 2007) has made the NoS strand an overarching strand. Teachers are expected to develop programs that will support students to understand science ideas, develop skills, and understand how science itself works. To make the complex task of helping students to develop a functional understanding of NoS more manageable, five science capabilities for citizenship have been proposed in New Zealand science education (Bull, 2015; Hipkins & Bull, 2015). These are:

- Gather and interpret data.
- Use evidence.
- Critique evidence.
- Interpret representations.
- Engage with science (Ministry of Education, n.d., para 3).

The capabilities are underpinned by ideas similar to the requirements of the Framework for K–12 Standards (National Research Council, 2012; Osborne, 2014) in the United States. Osborne (2014) proposes that these standards provide a strong representation of the current understanding of NoS as a social and cultural practice.

When we consider issues pertaining to science for high-ability students, there are two related factors that are critical in attracting and keeping these students interested and with an aspiration that they become future creators of scientific knowledge and innovation. First, consideration needs to be given to how educators are attracting and keeping students interested and engaged in science. Teachers argue that they do practical work to enthuse and engage students and there is research evidence that this does happen (Moeed, 2015). Second, there is a need for a curriculum that provides appropriate challenge and leads to students constructing new understandings and making significant progress in their science learning (Taber, 2016). This science learning would include understanding how scientific knowledge is created, theorised, critiqued, defended, and communicated. There is little evidence that current science education is achieving this (Duschl & Grandy, 2013; Lederman & Lederman, 2004). In sum, engaging students in hands-on practical activities may lead to engagement, situational interest, and short-term motivation (Abrahams, 2009; Hampden-Thompson & Bennett, 2013; Moeed, 2016; Palmer, 2004, 2009). One would expect that all students learn science by engaging in practical work; however, there is little evidence of this (Abrahams & Millar, 2008; Osborne, 2015). Importantly, high-ability students need to engage in authentic science investigations (inquiry) to develop an understanding of the empirical nature of science investigation (Lederman & Lederman, 2004).

Identification of High-Ability Students in Science

The task of identifying students who are gifted or talented can be extremely challenging. With a narrower focus on high-academic ability, it can be expected that identification and subsequent programming will be easier to achieve.

However, it seems this is not necessarily true in relation to identifying science students of high-academic ability (Horsley & Moeed, 2017). In general, identifying students for inclusion in special gifted and talented programs—whether they are in class or withdrawal activities—is reliant on the use of some form or other of identification tools. Some Asian countries, for example, test and then use intelligent quotients (IQ) to identify giftedness, suggesting that an IQ of 130+ indicates giftedness (Ibata-Arens, 2012). However, this single means of identification appears less frequently in international literature with a range of tools available to teachers identifying high-ability students (Assouline, Ihrig, & Mahatmya, 2017; Tyler-Wood, Mortenson, Putney & Cass, 2000; Warne, 2012). While much has been written on the range of tools available to teachers identifying high-ability students, there is less written about specific tools to aid the identification of high-ability science students. However, there is some alignment between tools recommended for identification of gifted students per se and effective practice for meeting the needs of high-ability students in science. This includes the use of above-level (also recognised as out-of-level, off-grade, or off-level) testing (Warne, 2012) which involves the use of a test that was normed on older children, with the (younger) child who is being assessed. This testing is well used in parts of the United States where teachers may screen students for 'giftedness' using tests that are two grade levels above the student's class level. A comparable example would be the administration of the New Zealand Year 6 *Progressive Achievement Test* (PAT) in English to a Year 4 student whom teachers/parents/the student perceive to be gifted in English. Debate exists around which percentile ought to be used to identify students, with Reis and Renzulli (1982) advocating for a wider and more inclusive selection, as they perceive that under the right conditions, for example, a classroom program that provides the opportunity for students to demonstrate task commitment and creativity, where they have also demonstrated average ability will lead to more students achieving to their potential and demonstrating high-academic ability or giftedness.

The idea of employing a wider and more inclusive selection process has also been considered in a number of other studies (Assouline et al., 2017; Tyler-Wood et al., 2000). An American study conducted by Assouline et al. (2017) aimed to identify high-achieving rural students in science and mathematics and increased the potential size of the Iowa talent pool they were selecting by using the 85th percentile—rather than the more frequently used 95th percentile (Lupkowski-Shoplik & Swiatek, 1999; Swiatek, 2007)—to identify high-achieving STEM (Science, Technology, Engineering, Mathematics) students. Assouline et al. (2017) invited teachers to use standardised grade-level data to identify high-achieving students in mathematics and science, at or above the 85th percentile. The identified students sat standardised mathematics and science tests two levels above their grade level in addition to completing a self-report survey relating to their motivation and engagement. The self-report survey measured students' broad psychosocial attributes. Following on from identification, the researchers provided a 12-week extracurricular out-of-school science program. Results from this study suggested that a more inclusive approach to identifying potentially high-ability students had resulted in a greater proportion of appropriately qualified students identified for the science program than would have been selected if the usual 3–5% of students had been selected.

Although some Asian countries are now considering wider methods of identification to include arts subjects (Chan, 2018), some still rely on IQ to identify giftedness (Ibata-Arens, 2012). However, across Asia practice varies, suggesting a disparate approach to identifying and providing for high-ability students (Hui et al., 2018).

Additional testing to augment the data from standardised testing may include not only psychosocial testing as used by Assouline et al. (2017), but also other forms of psychological testing. For example, Stumpf, Mills, Brody, and Baxley (2013) advocate for spatial testing to be used alongside standardised testing in STEM subjects. They argue that while a spatial test has limited relevance as a predictor of performance in many fields, it is *critically* important in STEM fields.

In addition to standardised testing and various forms of psychological testing, behavioural characteristics that support scientific inquiry may also form part of the identification process. Those characteristics or indicators that relate to scientific inquiry include curiosity, enthusiasm, and interest, coupled with a student's ability to clearly articulate his or her interpretation of data (Renzulli, Siegle, Reis, Gavin, & Reed, 2009). Taber and Riga (2007) suggest using behavioural characteristics to identify high-ability students in science, while also highlighting the need for these students to have a strong understanding of NoS (Gilbert & Newberry, 2007; Taber, 2016).

Clearly, there is also a need for teacher observation to be one of the criteria in identifying high-academic ability students in science. Given that indicators relating to behavioural characteristics (e.g., curiosity, enthusiasm, and interest) are recommended as part of the identification process (Taber & Riga, 2007), careful observation by teachers to record when they see these behaviours will support them to identify their most able science students.

When identifying high-ability students in science, the important considerations emerging from the literature are that the process is transparent (i.e., it is clear what measures are being used; Lupkowski-Shoplik & Swiatek, 1999; Swiatek, 2007) and that the test is valid and fit for purpose Assouline et al. 2017 (i.e., if STEM students are being identified, the testing needs to have a connection to STEM subjects; Assouline et al., 2017) and that the purpose for testing aligns with program content to support the learning of high-ability students (i.e., if high-ability students in physics are being identified, then it is logical to assume that the differentiated program being provided will be in physics; Assouline et al., 2017).

Once high-ability learners in science have been identified, the next step in supporting them to achieve success in science is dependent on the content of the program, which needs to include opportunities for deepening the science experience of these students; this is most important between the ages of 11 and 22 (Adams & Pierce, 2008).

Content for High-Ability Students in Science

Providing content to deepen science learning for high-ability students is an important next step following on from identification. The critical importance of high-ability science students having a *functional knowledge of science*

(VanTassel-Baska et al., 2008) includes the need for these students to have access to high-level content knowledge, alongside opportunities to demonstrate their understanding of the NoS (Gilbert & Newberry, 2007). Empowering high-ability students to think about the world through a scientific lens is a key role in the effective education of these students and will hopefully help to retain their interest in science. Coupled with this idea is the need to provide these students with skills to enable them to become knowledge producers, alongside gaining specific scientific skills that include observation, experimentation, and measurement (Kaplan, McComas, & Manzone, 2016; VanTassel-Baska et al., 2008). High-ability students in science also require opportunities to develop authentic enquiries, ensuring they do so in depth and level to demonstrate their understanding of complex ideas.

Shin, Levy, and London (2016) identified the importance of role modelling in order to retain students within STEM subjects. This study found that exposure to role models had a positive impact on STEM students' academic sense of belonging, although it is often difficult to locate such individuals willing to provide this modelling. Further, opportunities to experience 'real-world' internships in laboratories or other research places such as hospitals enable high-ability students to experience 'authentic' science (VanTassel-Baska & MacFarlane, 2008). Observing role models who are scientists assists these students to experience first-hand authentic inquiry and impacts positively on the student's sense of belonging to the field of scientific study.

While the essential role of content to provide opportunities for engaging in scientific thinking, creativity, and reasoning for high-ability students in science is well established in literature (e.g., Kind & Osborne 2017; Osborne, 2014), one New Zealand study conducted with high-ability science students and their teachers found that the content did not specifically include opportunities to engage in practical work as a means of encouraging authentic scientific inquiry (Horsley & Moeed, 2017). Furthermore, it did not appear that these high-ability students were engaging in authentic scientific inquiry that enabled them to come up with their own questions to investigate. Similarly, VanTassel-Baska and Macfarlane (2008) identified that school organisation may inhibit opportunities for these students to become fully engaged in science, with rigid timetables impacting on laboratory experiences that require longer than the traditional time period. They suggest that 'most' teachers rely "heavily on textbook worksheets and canned experiments for conveying science" (p. 580).

Reliance on worksheets was not evident in a study involving two groups of gifted mathematics and science students (a control and an effect group). Students in the effect group were provided with a differentiated curriculum that exposed them to higher-level thinking skills and more real-life laboratory experiences (Tyler-Wood et al., 2000). These lessons were reinforced in their science and mathematics classes. Assessment results after two years and again at the conclusion of secondary school showed that the students in the effect group who had received the differentiated curriculum (i.e., more laboratory experiences and greater high-level thinking skills) gained higher scores in standardised testing than those who were in the control group.

Since the late 1960s, some Asian countries have offered high-ability students access to science learning in specialised STEM secondary schools (Chan, 2018). In recent years, these schools have modelled themselves after similar establishments in western counties, such as those found in the United States. Once again, the availability of these schools varies across Asia, as does provision in general, for these high-ability students. Chan suggests that, overall, the preference throughout this region is for enrichment rather than acceleration, citing the densely packed curriculum as a barrier to acceleration.

One program that can be described as 'enrichment' is available in New Zealand and internationally and can be offered to high-ability students in science. The CREST (*Creativity in Science and Technology*) program is made available in New Zealand by the Royal Society. CREST projects require students to research and investigate creative and innovative science and technological solutions to practical problems. According to Taber and Cole (2010), "CREST can be a valuable contribution to schools' programs for meeting the needs of their gifted students in science and technology" (p. 117). Additionally, some universities offer enrichment opportunities for students to attend science extension and enrichment programs. Participation in these appears to be either due to student interest or teacher selection (University of Otago, n.d.). A further option for enriching science students is through participation in Physics, Chemistry, and Biology Olympiads. These competitions are held annually and are an international "competition for teams of four young people from around the world". The New Zealand team is "selected, trained and coordinated as a collaboration between the universities and high schools" (University of Canterbury, n.d., para 1). Teachers are required to register interested students, and once again, how teachers determine whose names are submitted appears to be based on student interest or teacher selection. Following registration, selection for training camps is made following a test that has been designed around student understanding of Year 12 (NCEA Level 2) chemistry, biology, or physics (para 3).

While the components of effective science education for high-ability science students include the need for high-level content, authentic science experiences, coupled with a clear understanding of NoS, it is also important that these students are exposed to role modelling that may encourage them to continue to study science. Given that Australia, New Zealand, and Asia have a number of eminent science citizens, it would seem that there is a possibility for role modelling and mentoring to occur.

High-Ability Science Education: A New Zealand Perspective

One recent study investigated how New Zealand secondary school science teachers identify and make provision for their high-ability students (Horsley & Moeed, 2017). This study invited teacher recipients of a university *Teacher Excellence Award* to identify their high-ability science students. The award is given to top graduates of an initial teacher education program in one large university and is based on a grade point average (GPA). Each of the participant teachers held at least one degree in science, and one of them had also attained a PhD. The teachers ($N = 4$) (from four different schools, which included independent and state schools) were within the first three years of commencing their teaching career, and each identified high-ability science students ($N = 53$) across their years 6 to 9 classes. These high-ability students were invited to complete an anonymous survey that considered both science and high-academic ability. The four science teachers also helped to arrange a focus group interview with five or six of their identified high-ability students. The focus group provided an opportunity for the lead researcher to follow up on survey responses, and she also interviewed each of the teachers to gain their perspectives on how they identified and met the needs of their high-ability students. The research was conducted in 2017 and was informed by a constructivist theory of learning, underpinned by the idea of knowledge being personally constructed by the learner who makes connections between new ideas and prior knowledge.

Teacher Perceptions: Identification of High-Ability Students in Science

Data revealed that the teachers had developed their own means of identifying their most able students, using observations and their individual nuanced understandings of what they ought to look for when identifying these students:

> I've kept track of all their results of all their assessments . . . but it was mainly based on their assessment results and a couple I threw in just because I thought they were pretty talented, but they just hadn't really pushed themselves. (Sam, 2017)
> Consistently high marks in tests, often accelerated in one or more subjects. (Beth, 2017)

Educators in schools in New Zealand are required to have a policy pertaining to the provisions they make for their gifted and talented students (Ministry of Education, 2017b, n.p.). Interestingly, none of the teacher participants had sighted their school's gifted policy. They each said that they used the school's *Progressive Achievement Tests* (PAT; PATs are a series of standardised tests developed specifically for use in New Zealand—for further details, see http://www.nzcer.org.nz/tests/pats) as a guide for identifying high-ability students. Commonly, schools use these standardised tests in primary school from Year 3 and at entry level to secondary school to assess students' mathematics, listening comprehension, punctuation, grammar, reading comprehension, and reading vocabulary. The teachers in this study were able to access the results of the PAT mathematics and English results, with two teachers—Sam and James—reporting that their schools streamed Year 9 (the first year of secondary school) classes based on these test results.

In addition to using standardised testing to identify high-ability students, a couple of the teachers also referred to behavioural characteristics they observed. Beth—who, in addition to having a graduate diploma in teaching, holds a PhD in physics and is a certified clinical psychologist—used PAT results, but gave priority to "students who are curious and creative, thoughtful learners, ask questions often. . ."

(2017). She explained that her school encouraged students to participate in science activities beyond the classroom, providing the following example, "They are keen to learn, often involved in out-of-class science activities such as Olympics, science fairs, enjoy going to science related talks at Royal Society" (Beth, 2017). James preferred to use behavioural characteristics to identify his high-ability students rather than relying on PAT scores. Included in his criteria were student responses to questioning, how quickly they answer questions and their conveyed understanding of conceptual ideas.

Although she used them as a guide, Jane, the fourth teacher, was concerned about using PAT tests to identify across her classes as she taught several students who had learning disabilities such as dyslexia, dyscalculia, and dyspraxia. She perceived that these students typically scored lower than others because they found reading (a component of PAT tests) challenging:

> I think behaviour issues have got in the way of their learning quite a bit and have resulted in lower outcomes and so while they are a challenging class, we also have some high-ability individuals in the class and in general, apart from maybe two or three students, they are probably higher ability than what their PATs show. (2017)

While each of the four teachers had their own way of identifying their high-ability students, identification appeared to have occurred through an ad hoc approach, perhaps due to the lack of familiarity with school policy that ought to have framed the way in which students can be identified. The use of behavioural characteristics and standardised testing (PAT) aligns with recommendations in the literature (Assouline et al., 2017; Lupkowski-Shoplik & Swiatek, 1999; Swiatek, 2007; Warne, 2012). However, it is important to note that none of the PAT tests were a *science test*. These teachers were using English and mathematics tests to identify high-academic ability in science, a method that is likely to disadvantage those students who may be outstanding in science, but weak in mathematics. Following on from describing how they identified these students, each of the teachers discussed the content they provided for their high-ability learners.

Students and Teacher Perceptions: Content for High-Academic Ability in Science

Both students and teachers were asked to describe their experiences in science, including activities they enjoyed and those they did not. In terms of what they enjoyed, most student responses referred to practical activities, with comments including:

> I really enjoyed dissecting the heart as it was not only interesting but also very educational and made my passion for science even greater.
> I enjoyed learning about the eye and how it works. We are halfway through our 'Matter Matters' topic, and I'm really liking it.
> Completing chemistry and physics practicals.
> Practicals and working through the text book at my own pace and given pages to complete.

While students enjoyed dissecting and chemistry and physics practicals, a few students believed that they had received little opportunity to experience practical work. They claimed that such work comprised worksheets that 'science wasn't a big thing' at school and that other than astronomy their school did not do any science. A number of students commented that prior to their current year of study they had no previous experience of practical work in science.

In terms of what these high-ability students perceived they learned in science, it appeared that most learning related to conceptual understanding of science content or to learning specific procedures. NoS understanding was evident in just two responses; one student said he had conducted an investigation, provided observations, and had offered an explanation: "I learnt that you don't need light in order to grow a seed, because the process of germination happens underground with no light".

The teacher participants in this study described how they planned to meet the needs of their most able students and how they identified evidence of learning. Sam described how he aimed to differentiate his practice, providing options for his students:

> ….the start-up questions, sometimes they're easy, sometimes they lead into something else. Sometimes they're *excellence*∗ questions because I feel that we didn't do well enough in the previous lesson and need to revise it. (2017)

The terms *Achieved, Merit*, and *Excellence* in our context align with levels of achievement. Although coined for assessment, these terms are being used extensively to talk about assessment grades students achieve and have become a way of talking about teaching and learning. Briefly, an *Achieved* grade indicates that a student can describe things, a *Merit* grade means they can explain, and gaining an *Excellence* means they can discuss their responses in a more thoughtful manner. Generally:

Achieved (A) for a satisfactory performance.
Merit (M) for a very good performance.
Excellence (E) for an outstanding performance.
Not achieved (N) if students do not meet the criteria of the standard (NZQA, 2017, n.p.).

James (2017) felt confident that he was meeting the needs of his high-ability students:

> I probably pitch my lessons towards the top end . . . I am trying my best to differentiate my lessons. Sometimes unconsciously, and too much. As a perfectionist and high achiever, myself, I often unconsciously pitch the content to the level that I think I would be happy with, which is higher than the mainstream standard. I bring in anecdotes that demonstrate that theory is interesting and thought-provoking. This often satisfies the *top* students but confuses the majority. But on the other hand, as a beginner teacher, I am not very good at differentiation. Most of the times I do not have heaps of extension material for the gifted and talented due to time constraint in planning.

Jane (2017) perceived that she provided opportunities for her high-ability students to learn and excel as they aim towards gaining scholarships in Year 13, "I need to ask those questions and have those discussions. Not just to extend them but to keep them curious and interested in wanting to learn more".

Sam (2017) described how he used students' natural curiosity in planning to meet the needs of his most able students:

> I guess the talented ones, the ones that I know can do things, like they usually jump straight to the more difficult ones [tasks] and I like spending time with them, getting them to work out how to solve it and maybe just give them a hint ... At other times, when I'm going over something on the board, I will just take it a little bit further and I'll be linking it to other things and other topics that they otherwise wouldn't know. Linking it to next year's mathematics umm, and saying, I'll just show this, you don't have to know this but I'll just show you it anyway ... that works to raise their curiosity.

The teachers each commented on the time they felt they needed to differentiate for student learning, with James (2017) suggesting that his focus on the 'top end' students meant that he was less likely to meet the needs of his other students. Beth (2017), who is in her third year of teaching, said that she is only now managing to find time to create planning that she felt met the needs of her high-ability students:

> Until last year most planning I did was give them more challenging work sometimes. This year I have definitely managed to plan for them and it is so good to see them blossom.

Student participants were asked to describe what they felt they had learned from practicals in science classes. The responses proved interesting because while some students were able to describe what they had observed, it was unclear what they had learnt:

> This experiment made it a lot easier to picture how the different organs in a creature relate to one another. It highlighted how each organ fits with the next and showed how every animal and creature differs from others as well.

As this student's response shows, they were able to carry out an investigation, make observations, and offer an explanation. Other students gave responses that showed they were 'doing' science and learning science ideas:

> I enjoyed dissecting the cow's eyeball for the light and sight topic. Although it was disturbing I got to not only learn the different parts of the eye and where they are and how they work, I also got to feel what they feel like and see how it looks in a real-life object. We used enzymes from potatoes to watch peroxidase break down into water and oxygen.

And one student claimed he learned the value of patience:

I learnt that patience will go a long way in any science class, especially Chemistry. And that higher level science experiments can be both educational and entertaining in the right context.

Students proffered advice for those who aimed to achieve at the very highest level in science and for those who were teaching them, suggesting that teachers need to:

Actually give a damn and remember that they're [students] there to learn, not there to mess around. At the highest possible level, likely it would be best to allow students to partake of their own investigations, limitedly, so they find something that interests THEM, so they will put more effort into it.

One student identified the importance of 'teacher passion' for the subject they teach, "Have a teacher that inspires the students to learn and someone that has a passion for the topic and the job".

Students also identified the effect of teachers not considering the pace of the learning, describing this as a potential barrier to their success, ". . .by getting taught the subject really quickly and having a teacher who doesn't teach to our needs".

This pivotal role of the teacher in providing a classroom in which learners are prepared to take risks is highlighted in many student comments. Some participants mentioned shyness and an unwillingness to ask questions as a potential barrier. "[I'm] too afraid to ask for help . . . feeling shy . . . don't understand and too shy to ask".

Others made the following suggestions for high-aspiring science students:

Don't just think about it in class and don't think it has to be applied to questions only, the possibilities are endless.
I think doing all of the work set in class as well and making sure you do some work outside of school as well is extremely important when wanting to achieve highly. In science, it's especially important to make sure you fully understand the concepts and so memorising definitions and understanding them is key as well.
Pay attention and learn how to correctly answer questions because most of your mark comes from how you answer the question.
Make sure they understand concepts.

The students were also asked if they had experienced acceleration and/or enrichment during their schooling. Clearly, many were confused as to what enrichment entailed, with one student responding to the question asking about enrichment by stating, "In our science class, if we do really well in class, then we get small rewards like Chocolate and Fossils".

Others, however, could describe examples of acceleration:

. . . making higher level classes (e.g., Year 13 subjects whilst in Year 12).
High achieving students can do upper years' work out of class.
Year 12 students are able to take Year 13 scholarships, some talented Year 11 students end up in Year 12 calculus classes.

Some Reflections on Research on High-Academic Ability Students in Science

The above are only preliminary findings of a small study in NZ; however, the wider research both supports and conflicts with the findings. In this study, there was evidence of a disconnect between student and teacher perceptions of what was being taught and what was learned. What was evident was the teachers' willingness to do all they could within a limited time, to prepare lessons to support all their students, including those they perceived to be their most able. Taber (2016) has identified that this agenda of ensuring "all students (and especially young people who are legally required to attend school) are entitled to provision that is genuinely educative in the sense of supporting them to significantly develop their knowledge, understanding and skills" (p. 1) is fundamental to developing gifted learners and a key principle that is contingent upon the teacher having the time and capabilities to "enable genuine progress" (p. 1). Regardless of any perceived challenges in meeting the needs of their high-academic ability students, each of the teachers in this study spoke of their willingness to support their high-achieving students. Student responses suggest that they were not always cognisant of this—some felt that they weren't even learning science!

Clearly, scientific knowledge and understanding were perceived to be a strength for each teacher as 'science' teaching was the domain in which they were accepted for their study in the initial teacher education program. Furthermore, Beth held a PhD in physics, and James described himself as "a perfectionist and high achiever" (James, 2017), suggesting that at least two of the participant teachers had personal experience of high-academic success. Seminal work by Mills (2003) identified that teachers who were considered to be 'exceptional teachers of gifted students' often held advanced degrees in the subject they taught. Mills also identified that these teachers had similar personalities to their students, suggesting that:

> teachers who are judged to be highly effective in working with gifted students prefer abstract themes and concepts, are open and flexible, and value logical analysis and objectivity. Results suggest that teacher personality and cognitive style may play a role in his or her effectiveness in teaching gifted students. (p. 272)

Identifying teachers with strong qualifications and the disposition to teach high-ability students in science is undoubtedly a key component in findings ways to continue to engage and retain our most able students in this field. A study to identify how many science teachers hold advanced degrees in the subject, coupled with investigation into teachers' personality and cognitive style, can be one means of identifying those who have the potential to be considered "exceptional teachers of gifted [science] students".

While literature cites the importance of high-academic science students having a mentor or role model (Shin et al., 2016; VanTassel-Baska & MacFarlane, 2008), that was not something students identified in this study. Similarly, opportunities for these students to experience 'real-world' internships in laboratories or other research places were also not evident in this study, and ways to make opportunities such as these available to all interested science students quite clearly require further consideration in Australasia and Asia. Possibly, opportunities such as CREST had not yet arisen as these students who were in the lower level of secondary or middle school and CREST is most often accessed towards the end of secondary schooling. However, opportunities to experience science outside the classroom were mentioned by Beth who suggested that her high-ability students, ". . . are keen to learn, often involved in out-of-class science activities such as Olympics, science fairs, enjoy going to science related talks at Royal Society" (Beth, 2017). These opportunities align well with the findings of Adams and Pierce (2008) who recommend that the most significant time for providing opportunities for deepening the science experience of these students is between the ages of 11 and 22.

It is likely that the perceived differences between the student and teacher perceptions occurred through the initial identification process as it is possible that not all of these students were correctly identified as those of high-academic ability. Identification methods varied between teachers which one could expect with the freedom New Zealand schools have been given to identify these learners. Perhaps most important was the finding that the identification process for each teacher was underpinned by data gained from PATs that were not science tests. At one stage in the study, teacher Sam queried why some students gained 'excellence' in one subject and not in others. The answer to Sam's query is similar to the rationale behind using science testing to gauge students' ability in science rather than using English or mathematics tests: students are not necessarily gifted or demonstrating high-academic ability in all domains. As Taber (2016) identified, students' knowledge, understanding, and skills may not be consistent across domains. Therefore, using an English or mathematics test to assess student ability in science is akin to gauging how fast a cheetah can run by observing a sheep walk.

Hattie (2011) has also questioned how students are identified as 'gifted', asking why there is an apparent lack of gifted students being identified later in life as gifted adults. Borland (2008) expressed concern around identification practices, suggesting that issues arise through the wide choice given to those charged with identifying these students. In this study, it appeared that not only did identification practices vary, but none was informed by official Ministry of Education policy. This finding aligns with much of the Australasian and Asian literature pertaining to identification practices (Chan, 2018; ERO, 2008; Hui et al., 2018; Ibata-Arens, 2012).

Implications and Future Directions for Gifted Students in Science Education

Internationally, science education for those of high-academic ability has received some attention (e.g., Cho, 2004; Sumida, 2013; Wang & Tsai, 2016; Watters & Diezmann, 2002). However, the evident paucity of Australasian and Asian research relating to high-ability science students provides an opportunity for further investigation. In particular, more research is needed to support teachers to identify and then to provide appropriate content to teach to these high-ability students. In light of the priority given to STEM subjects in New Zealand, Australia and elsewhere, along with the recognised needs of high-ability students in science, it is imperative that further research is carried out with some urgency.

While the teachers in the Horsley and Moeed (2017) study indicated willingness to meet the needs of their high-ability students, they identified the additional time this required and the possible negative impact this may have had on other learners. Interestingly—and at odds with the teachers in this study—international literature (Millar, 2006; Osborne & Dillon, 2008) has identified that the more recent goal of science education—for all to become scientifically literate citizens—is more likely to *reduce* the emphasis on science education for those who continue in science, including those of high-academic ability. While the New Zealand study revealed teachers' lack of awareness of procedures and protocols within their school that were aimed at meeting the needs of high-ability students, it also showed that the small sample of excellent science teachers were aware of the needs of these students and were doing their best to support them within the constraint of available time. These constraints include the need for teachers to balance time for national policies, curriculum, assessment requirements, and parental expectations, as well as trying to undertake professional learning, including engaging with the recommendations from the research literature in the field (Hui et al., 2018).

Science teaching in New Zealand primary schools is constrained by non-specialist teachers who feel they do not have enough science knowledge to teach and lack in confidence (Anderson & Moeed, 2017). Additionally, teachers are required to support the individual needs of a diverse array of students (ERO, 2016, para 5) who—as the teachers in this study identified—may have typical, special, or the unique needs of gifted students. So, how do teachers support the high-academic ability students in science? One initiative to support teaching of science is provided by the Royal Society of New Zealand. This society provides a science teacher fellowship program where primary teachers spend six months in a science research organisation and return back to schools as leaders. Program review has identified that there has been some impact in improving science teaching in those schools (Anderson, 2013; Anderson & Moeed, 2017).

In the many countries that constitute the Asia-Pacific region, science education is considered important and provision of quality science education has primacy (e.g., Sumida, 2013; Taber, 2016). Based on the review of the wider research literature and the study reiterated in this chapter, several key messages have emerged for teachers and those who aspire to facilitate high academic success through science teaching. These include the importance of:

(a) Finding and using the school's policies or procedures to support identification of, and provision for, students of high-academic ability in science.
(b) Ensuring those methods used to identify student learning needs in science are appropriate for the domain in which teachers are identifying high-academic ability (i.e., if students are being identified for advanced science study, the identification measures ought to relate to science).

(c) Ensuring the taught curriculum includes access to high-level content, coupled with opportunities to demonstrate understanding of NoS.
(d) Providing opportunities for authentic science learning, that is, working in laboratories and with role models and mentors.

Additionally, the high-ability science students in this study recognised the importance of having teachers who "actually give a damn. . ." and who ". . .inspires the students to learn … someone that has a passion for the topic and the job" while allowing students to ". . .find something that interests *them*, so they will put more effort into it". This aligns with the findings of an earlier study that identified high-ability students' beliefs about those factors that facilitated their academic success (Horsley, 2012). Notably, students have identified the essential role of the teacher in facilitating environments that engender student interest and high-academic success (e.g., this was a major finding in Hattie's 2011 meta-analyses), valuing those teachers who are in the role because they *want* to be there. Undoubtedly, the essential role of enthusiastic and quality teachers is a key message for educators.

With Australia, New Zealand, and Asia having a number of eminent science citizens, it would seem that there is a possibility for role modelling and mentoring to occur, and anecdotal evidence suggests that in places this may be occurring with some universities providing open days that allow students to experience science in a 'real' laboratory. However, what is not clear is how accessible these days are to all students who aspire to continue to study science.

Further research is also needed to gauge outcomes for those who are identified as students of high-academic ability in science and to identify whether teaching practice is indeed producing academic outcomes that facilitate high academic success in STEM subjects that may eventually lead to eminence that emulates their role models/mentors in the field.

Conclusion

While in this chapter we have considered the lack of research within Australasia that addresses the provisions that high-ability science students require, and the variation of practice throughout Asia, opportunities that we would hope would encourage these students to be retained in STEM subjects have also been identified. Clearly, the opportunity to work beside a mentor in an authentic experience is one to be considered more widely. So too is the importance of a curriculum that provides students with opportunities to be both 'hands-on' and 'minds-on' in science and to have some autonomy over what they study. Importantly, the students in this study recognised the role teachers play in their success, particularly commenting on those who inspired student learning while demonstrating their own passion for the subject. Similarly, this emulates Sir Paul Callaghan's first experience with being inspired towards science endeavours in which he eventually became eminent in his field (MacDonald, 2012).

Identification of high-ability students in science is problematic, and having the time to prepare and deliver an appropriate curriculum to these students—without compromising their learning or that of others—is also difficult. The current decline in students choosing to study science beyond the compulsory level needs urgent attention. Supporting motivated teachers to not only identify students using appropriate tools, but also to provide a curriculum that is commensurate with students' learning ability is of critical importance if we aim to attract high-academic ability students to continue with science in secondary school and, later, to interest them and encourage them to choose science-related careers.

Cross-References

- ▶ Assessment, Pedagogy, and Curriculum: Part IV Introduction
- ▶ Australian Teachers Who Made a Difference: Secondary Gifted Student Perceptions of Teaching and Teacher Effectiveness
- ▶ Being of Like-Mind: Giftedness in the New Zealand Context
- ▶ Differentiation of Instruction for Gifted Learners: Collated Evaluative Studies of Teacher Classroom Practices
- ▶ Engaging Gifted Students in Solving Real Problems Creatively: Implementing the Real Engagement in Active Problem-Solving (REAPS) Teaching/Learning Model in Australasian and Pacific Rim Contexts
- ▶ Gifted Education in the Asia-Pacific: From the Past for the Future – An Introduction
- ▶ Highly Able Students in International Schools
- ▶ Learning from International Research Informs Academic Acceleration in Australasia: A Case for Consistent Policy
- ▶ Put Them Together and See How They Learn! Ability Grouping and Acceleration Effects on the Self-Esteem of Academically Gifted High School Students
- ▶ Some Implications for the Future of Gifted Education in the Asia-Pacific
- ▶ STEAM in Gifted Education in Korea
- ▶ The Lives and Achievements of Four Extraordinary Australians: A Master, a Maker, an Introspector, and an Influencer
- ▶ Why Is It So? Interest and Curiosity in Supporting Students Gifted in Science

References

Abrahams, I. (2009). Does practical work really motivate? A study of the affective value of practical work in secondary school science. *International Journal of Science Education, 31*(17), 2335–2353. https://doi.org/10.1080/09500690802342836

Abrahams, I., & Millar, R. (2008). Does practical work really work? A study of the effectiveness of practical work as a teaching and learning method in school science. *International Journal of Science Education, 30*(14), 1945–1969. https://doi.org/10.1080/09500690701749305

Adams, C. M., & Pierce, R. L. (2008). Science, elementary. In J. A. Plucker & C. M. Callahan (Eds.), *Critical issues and practices in gifted education* (pp. 563–578). Waco, TX: Prufrock Press.

Anderson, D. (2013). Leading change in primary science: Experiences of primary science teacher fellows who have raised the profile of science in their schools. *Journal of Educational Leadership, Policy and Practice, 28*(2), 15–27.

Anderson, D., & Moeed, A. (2017). Working alongside scientists. *Science & Education, 1* 1–28.

Assouline, S. G., Ihrig, L. M., & Mahatmya, D. (2017). Closing the excellence gap: Investigation of an expanded talent search model for student selection into an extracurricular STEM program in rural middle schools. *The Gifted Child Quarterly, 61*(3), 250–261. https://doi.org/10.1177/0016986217701833

Borland, J. H. (2008). Identification. In J. A. Plucker & C. M. Callahan (Eds.), *Critical issues and practices in gifted education* (pp. 261–301). Waco, TX: Prufrock Press.

Bull, A. (2015). *Capabilities for living and lifelong learning: What's science got to do with it?* Wellington, New Zealand: New Zealand Council for Educational Research.

Chan, W. (2018). Gifted education in Asia. In S. Pfeiffer, E. Shaunessy-Dedrick, & M. Foley-Nicpon (Eds.), *APA handbook of giftedness and talent* (pp. 71–84). Washington, DC: American Psychological Association. https://doi.org/10.1037/0000038-005

Cho, S. (2004). Gifted and talented education in Korea: Its problems and visions. *KEDI Journal of Educational Policy, 1*(1), 119–127.

Colangelo, N., Assouline, S. G., Marron, M. A., Castellano, J. A., Clinkenbeard, P. R., Rogers, K., ... Smith, D. (2010). Guidelines for developing an academic acceleration policy: National work group on acceleration. *Journal of Advanced Academics, 21*(2), 180–203. https://doi.org/10.1177/1932202X1002100202

Diezmann, C. M., & Watters, J. J. (2002). Summing up the education of mathematically gifted students. In Proceedings 25th Annual Conference of the Mathematics Education Research Group of Australasia, pages 219–226, Auckland. Retrieved from https://pdfs.semanticscholar.org/d7f9/f247713fd073e2b8c5555cf58c2b370fa7e9.pdf

Duschl, R. A., & Grandy, R. (2013). Two views about explicitly teaching nature of science. *Science & Education, 22*(9), 2109–2139. https://doi.org/10.1007/s11191-012-9539-4

Education Counts. (2015). *PISA 2015: The science context for PISA*. Retrieved from http://www.educationcounts.govt.nz/publications/series/2543/pisa-2015/pisa-scientific-literacy-report

Education Review Office. (2008). *Schools' provision for gifted and talented students*. Wellington, New Zealand: Author. Retrieved from http://www.ero.govt.nz/National-Reports/Schools-Provision-for-Gifted-and-Talented-Students-Good-Practice-June-2008

Education Review Office. (2012). *Science in the New Zealand curriculum: Years 5 to 8*. Wellington, New Zealand. Retrieved from http://www.ero.govt.nz/publications/science-in-the-new-zealand-curriculum-years-5-to-8/

Education Review Office. (2016). *Education diversity in New Zealand state schools*. Wellington, New Zealand. Retrieved from http://www.ero.govt.nz/footer-upper/news/ero-insights-term-1/ethnic-diversity-in-new-zealand-state-schools/

Gilbert, J. K., & Newberry, M. (2007). The characteristics of the gifted and exceptionally able in science. In K. Taber (Ed.), *Science education for gifted learners* (pp. 15–31). Abingdon, Oxon: Routledge.

Goodrum, D., Druhan, A., & Abbs, J. (2011). *The status and quality of year 11 and 12 science in Australian schools*. Report prepared for the Office of the Chief Scientist. http://www.science.org.au/reports/documents/Year-1112-Report-Final.pdf.

Hampden-Thompson, G., & Bennett, J. (2013). Science teaching and learning activities and students' engagement in science. *International Journal of Science Education, 35*(8), 1325–1343. https://doi.org/10.1080/09500693.2011.608093

Hattie, J. (2011). Q & A. *Tall Poppies*, March.

Hipkins, R., & Bull, A. (2015). Science capabilities for a functional understanding of the nature of science. *Curriculum Matters, 11*, 117–133. https://doi.org/10.18296/cm.0007

Horsley, J. (2012). Teacher catalysts: Characteristics of teachers who facilitate high academic success. *Australasian Journal of Gifted Education, 21*(1), 23–31.

Horsley, J., & Moeed, A. (2017). If only I had time. *New Zealand Science Review, 74*(2), 36–44.

Hui, N. N. A., He Wu, J. M., Kuo, C. C., Tan, A. G., Lyu, L., & Chan, L. K. (2018). Gaps and goes in policy, practice, and research of gifted education in China, Hong Kong, Singapore, and Taiwan. In J. K. Kennedy & J. C.-K. Lee (Eds.), *Routledge international handbook of schools and schooling in Asia* (pp. 555–569). London, England: Routledge.

Ibata-Arens, K. C. (2012). Race to the future: Innovations in gifted and enrichment education in Asia, and implications for the United States. *Administrative Sciences, 2*(1), 1–25.

Kaplan, S. N., McComas, W. F., & Manzone, J. A. (2016). Teaching science and gifted students. *International Perspectives on Science Education for the Gifted: Key Issues and Challenges, 27*, 27–42.

Kennedy, D. (2014). The role of investigations in promoting inquiry-based science education in Ireland. *Science Education International, 24*(3), 282–305. Retrieved from http://www.icaseonline.net/sei/september2013/P3.pdf

Kennedy, J. P., Lyons, T., & Quinn, F. (2014). The continuing decline of science and mathematics enrolments in Australian high schools. *Teaching Science, 60*(2), 34–46. Retrieved from http://www.growingtallpoppies.com/wp-content/uploads/2015/07/Continuing-Decline-of-Science-by-Kennedy-Lyons-Quinn.pdf

Kennedy, M. J., Wagner, D., Stegall, J., Lembke, E., Miciak, J., Alves, K. D., . . . Hirsch, S. E. (2016). Using content acquisition podcasts to improve teacher candidate knowledge of curriculum-based measurement. *Exceptional Children, 82*(3), 303–320. https://doi.org/10.1177/0014402915615885

Kind, P., & Osborne, J. (2017). Styles of scientific reasoning: A cultural rationale for science education? *Science Education, 101*(1), 8–31. https://doi.org/10.1002/sce.21251

Lederman, N. G., & Lederman, J. S. (2004). Revising instruction to teach nature of science. *The Science Teacher, 71*(9), 36–39.

Lupkowski-Shoplik, A., & Swiatek, M. A. (1999). Elementary student talent searches: Establishing appropriate guidelines for qualifying test scores. *The Gifted Child Quarterly, 43*, 265–272. https://doi.org/10.1177/001698629904300405

MacDonald, N. (2012). Sir Paul Callaghan: Kiwi visionary looks back on life. The dominion post. Retrieved from http://www.stuff.co.nz/dominion-post/news/6636553/Sir-Paul-Callaghan-Kiwi-visionary-looks-back-on-life

Millar, R. (2006). Twenty first century science: Insights from the design and implementation of a scientific literacy approach in school science. *International Journal of Science Education, 28*(13), 1499–1521. https://doi.org/10.1080/09500690600718344

Millar, R., & Osborne, J. (1998). *Beyond 2000. Science education for the future*. London, England: Nuffield Foundation.

Mills, C. J. (2003). Characteristics of effective teachers of gifted students: Teacher background and personality styles of students. *The Gifted Child Quarterly, 47*(4), 272–281.

Ministry of Education. (2007). *The New Zealand curriculum*. Wellington, New Zealand: Learning Media.

Ministry of Education. (2017a). The National Administration Guidelines (NAGs). Retrieved from https://education.govt.nz/ministry-of-education/legislation/nags/

Ministry of Education. (2017b). *Legislation*. Retrieved from https://education.govt.nz/ministry-of-education/legislation

Ministry of Education (2019). About us: Tā mātou kaupapa – Our purpose. Retrieved from https://education.govt.nz/our-work/our-role-and-our-people/.

Ministry of Education. (n.d.). *Science online: Science capabilities for citizenship*. Retrieved from http://scienceonline.tki.org.nz/Science-capabilities-for-citizenship

Ministry of Education (MoE). (1993). *Science in the New Zealand curriculum*. Wellington, New Zealand: Learning Media.

Moeed, A. (2015). Investigating science investigation: A robust case study design. *International Journal of Teaching and Case Studies, 6*(4), 303–319. https://doi.org/10.1504/IJTCS.2015.074599

Moeed, A. (2016). Novelty, variety, relevance, challenge and assessment: How science investigations influence the motivation of year 11 students in New Zealand. *School Science Review, 97*(361), 75–81.

National Research Council. (2012). *A framework for K–12 science education: Practices, crosscutting concepts, and core ideas.* Washington, DC: Committee on a Conceptual Framework for New K–12 Science Education Standards, Board on Science Education, Division of Behavioral and Social Sciences and Education.

New Zealand Qualifications Authority (NZQA). (2017). Qualify for the future world. Retrieved from https://www.nzqa.govt.nz/qualifications-standards/qualifications/ncea/under standing-ncea/how-ncea-works/standards/

Osborne, J. (2014). Teaching scientific practices: Meeting the challenge of change. *Journal of Science Teacher Education, 25*(2), 177–196. https://doi.org/10.1007/s10972-014-9384-1

Osborne, J. (2015). Practical work in science: Misunderstood and badly used? *School Science Review, 96*(357), 16–24. Retrieved from https://pdfs.semanticscholar.org/ba9c/4c63d00002d887e7abdaf9fa12ab81b529a7.pdf

Osborne, J., & Dillon, J. (2008). *Science education in Europe: Critical reflections* (Vol. 13). London, England: The Nuffield Foundation.

Palmer, D. (2004). Situational interest and the attitudes towards science of primary teacher education students. *International Journal of Science Education, 26*(7), 895–908. https://doi.org/10.1080/0950069032000177262

Palmer, D. H. (2009). Student interest generated during an inquiry skills lesson. *Journal of Research in Science Teaching, 46*(2), 147–165. https://doi.org/10.1002/tea.20263

Preckel, F., Götz, T., & Frenzel, A. (2010). Ability grouping of gifted students: Effects on academic self-concept and boredom. *British Journal of Educational Psychology, 80*(3), 451–472. https://doi.org/10.1348/000709909X480716

Reis, S. M., & Renzulli, J. S. (1982). A case for a broadened conception of giftedness. *Phi Delta Kappan, 63*(4), 619–620. Retrieved from https://gifted.uconn.edu/wp-content/uploads/sites/961/2015/02/Broadened_Conception_Giftedness.pdf

Renzulli, J. S., Siegle, D., Reis, S. M., Gavin, M. K., & Reed, R. E. S. (2009). An investigation of the reliability and factor structure of four new scales for rating the behavioral characteristics of superior students. *Journal of Advanced Academics, 21*(1), 84–108. https://doi.org/10.1177/1932202X0902100105

Rubenstein, L. D., Siegle, D., Reis, S. M., McCoach, D. B., & Burton, M. G. (2012). A complex quest: The development and research of underachievement interventions for gifted students. *Psychology in the Schools, 49*(7), 678–694. https://doi.org/10.1002/pits.21620

Shin, J. E. L., Levy, S. R., & London, B. (2016). Effects of role model exposure on STEM and non-STEM student engagement. *Journal of Applied Social Psychology, 46*(7), 410–427. https://doi.org/10.1111/jasp.12371

Sternberg, R. J. (2010). Assessment of gifted students for identification purposes: New techniques for a new millennium. *Learning and Individual Differences, 20*(4), 327–336. https://doi.org/10.1016/j.lindif.2009.08.003

Stumpf, H., Mills, C. J., Brody, L. E., & Baxley, P. G. (2013). Expanding talent search procedures by including measures of spatial ability: CTY's spatial test battery. *Roeper Review, 35*(4), 254–264. https://doi.org/10.1080/02783193.2013.829548

Sumida, M. (2013). Emerging trends in Japan in education of the gifted: A focus on science education. *Journal for the Education of the Gifted, 36*(3), 277–289. https://doi.org/10.1177/0162353213493534

Swiatek, M. A. (2007). The talent search model: Past, present, and future. *The Gifted Child Quarterly, 51*(4), 320–329. https://doi.org/10.1177/0016986207306318

Taber, K. S. (2007). *Science education for gifted learners.* Abingdon, Oxon: Routledge.

Taber, K. S. (2016). The nature of science and the teaching of gifted learners. In K. Taber & M. Sumida (Eds.), *International perspectives on science education for the gifted* (pp. 2–11). Oxford, UK: Routledge.

Taber, K. S., & Cole, J. (2010). The CREST awards scheme: Challenging gifted and talented students through creative STEM project work. *School Science Review, 92*(339), 117–126.

Taber, K. S., & Riga, F. (2007). In K. Taber. (Ed.), *Science education for gifted learners* (pp. 15–31). Oxfordshire: Routledge.

Taber, K. S., Sumida, M., & McClure, L. (Eds.). (2017). *Teaching gifted learners in STEM subjects: Developing talent in science, technology, engineering and mathematics*. Abingdon, Oxon: Routledge.

Tyler-Wood, T. L., Mortenson, M., Putney, D., & Cass, M. A. (2000). An effective mathematics and science curriculum option for secondary gifted education. *Roeper Review, 22*(4), 266–269. https://doi.org/10.1080/02783190009554050

University of Canterbury. (n.d.). Chemistry Olympiad. Retrieved from https://www.canterbury.ac.nz/science/schools-and-departments/phys-chem/chemistry/chemistry-olympiad/

University of Otago. (n.d.). New Zealand marine studies centre: Science extension and enrichment. Retrieved from https://www.otago.ac.nz/marine-studies/learning/science-extension/otago062394.pdf

VanTassel-Baska, J., & MacFarlane, B. (2008). Secondary science. In J. A. Plucker & C. M. Callahan (Eds.), *Critical issues and practices in gifted education* (pp. 579–593). Waco, TX: Prufrock Press.

VanTassel-Baska, J., MacFarlane, B., & Feng, A. (2008). A cross-cultural study of exemplary teaching: What do Singapore and the United States secondary gifted class teachers say? *Gifted and Talented International, 21*, 38–47. https://doi.org/10.1080/15332276.2006.11673474

Wardman, J., & Hattie, J. (2012). Administrators' perceptions of full-year acceleration at high school. *Australasian Journal of Gifted Education, 21*(1), 32–41.

Warne, R. T. (2012). History and development of above-level testing of the gifted. *Roeper Review, 34*(3), 183–193. https://doi.org/10.1080/02783193.2012.686425

Jenny Horsley, PhD, is a senior lecturer in the School of Education, Victoria University of Wellington where she lectures in initial teacher education programs. Her research focuses on high-ability learners and initial teacher education. Jenny was the inaugural recipient of the Cognition-Fulbright Scholar Award that enabled her to travel to Johns Hopkins Center for Talented Youth where she researched successful strategies for engaging high-academic ability minority students.

Azra Moeed, PhD, is an associate professor in the School of Education, Victoria University of Wellington where she lectures in science teacher education programs. Her research interests are in teaching and learning science, particularly in practical work and science investigation. Earlier in her career Azra has taught science in primary and secondary schools and was responsible for establishing and teaching in an accelerated learning program for able learners in a New Zealand secondary school.

Why Is It So? Interest and Curiosity in Supporting Students Gifted in Science

James Watters

Contents

Abstract

Interest, curiosity, or a *passion-to-know* feature in many models of giftedness. Gagné (2013) incorporates 'needs, interests, and passion' as motivational catalysts and *psychological energy* as a driver for talent development in his Differentiated Model of Giftedness. In his three-ring conception of giftedness, Renzulli (1986) highlights *task commitment,* defined as the energy brought to bear on a particular task, as one important attribute of giftedness. This conception is analogous to the work of other theorists, for example, Alex Luria (1966), who identified aspects of intellectual functioning termed 'attention/arousal', and Csikszentmihalyi (2002) who conceptualised the notion of 'flow' to represent a state of concentration or complete absorption in a task. The attribute generating this energy has been described as epistemic curiosity or the need to know—why is

J. Watters (✉)
Faculty of Education, Queensland University of Technology, Brisbane, QLD, Australia
e-mail: j.watters@qut.edu.au

© Springer Nature Singapore Pte Ltd. 2021
S. R. Smith (ed.), *Handbook of Giftedness and Talent Development in the Asia-Pacific,*
Springer International Handbooks of Education,
https://doi.org/10.1007/978-981-13-3041-4_34

it so? All these theories more or less coalesce and explain the desire for gifted students to engage at length and in depth with complex integrated problems. Gifted students are curious, but opportunities to exploit their curiosity in formal classrooms are rare. Although inquiry/enquiry learning is strongly advocated in policy, research evidence suggests that it is rarely adopted in mainstream classes. This state of affairs conflicts with the research on inquiry-based approaches that have shown the benefits for gifted students in undertaking investigations into ill-defined problems. Such investigations also provide opportunities for students to capitalise on their creative traits to make connections among existing ideas to solve novel problems. The outcome is invariably new knowledge. Opportunities for students in science classes to negotiate novel and interesting learning tasks are infrequent, and thus, for many gifted students, learning school science is boring. The focus in this chapter will be on the alignment between curiosity, interest, and engagement in inquiry learning in science and proposes that science education needs to capitalise on student curiosity if it is to be successful in attracting the most highly able to pursue careers in science.

Keywords

Gifted in science · Inquiry learning · Investigations in science · Epistemic curiosity · Interest · STEM · Mathematical investigations

It is not the possession of truth, but the success which attends the seeking after it, that enriches the seeker and brings happiness to him. Max Planck (1858–1947) (Nobel Prize in Physics, 1918)

The aims in this chapter are to:
1. Highlight the importance of affect in meeting the needs of intellectually gifted students.
2. Provide an overview of inquiry approaches that engage students in learning science.
3. Argue that effective science teaching for gifted students should be based on three principles: an authentic approach to the discipline, a constructivist view of how students learn science, and opportunities for active learning.
4. Highlight the gaps and hence the need for further research into the importance of motivation and sense of well-being for gifted students engaged in learning science and mathematics.

A Personal Reflection: Science Project Class

My first exposure to gifted students occurred in my beginning years of teaching. I entered teaching as a career-change, mature-age candidate with a substantial background in scientific research. The school I began teaching at had a vertical curriculum structure, and considerable flexibility was provided in designing and delivering units of study. I was responsible for teaching Years 7–10 in chemistry, biology, and behavioural science. My Year 10 chemistry class had students that ranged in age from 13 to 15 given the vertical curriculum which meant some were very advanced and highly committed and others were taking the unit to meet career entry requirements. I also was in charge of a timetabled science project unit. It was the science project unit that introduced me to gifted students, highly able, and talented students (Watters, 1985). The term gifted never passed the lips of any of the teachers, students, administrators, or parents. The critical attribute was passion and interest in science. Students were nominated by other science teachers and parents provided a supporting letter. Students were interviewed and the main focus was whether they felt committed to a semester of independent study. The approach adopted was project-based in which students designed and carried out an original research project on a topic of their choosing. The students were provided with support to identify an expert mentor in a local hospital, institution, or university who willingly provided guidance. There were few formal lessons other than seminar sessions where students reported back to the group on their progress at regular intervals. In many instances, projects became a passion absorbing all available spare time. Parents often became involved to ferry students to research sites and to meet with mentors.

Some participants had learning difficulties and would now be described as having twice exceptionality. For example, one girl was diagnosed with dyslexia and considered by many teachers as a poor student. However, advocacy by the Head of Department who recognised her talents in biology enabled her to join the project class. Her deep understanding of ecology and passion for studying native wildlife was clearly evident, and her limitations were accommodated through the use of then primitive computer technology. With minor accommodations, these students with twice exceptionalities excelled.

Success was evident in the number of awards achieved by students at local science fairs, national competitions, and even international competitions. The career destinations of these students were never systematically monitored, but some have become significant research scientists, while others chose non-science careers. The point of this reflection is that by providing challenging, motivating, and sustained opportunities for pupils to engage in meaningful problem-based and thematic investigations, students demonstrated interest, commitment, and exceptional achievement. Learning had been enhanced by the chance to engage in solving these challenges in the company of like-minded peers with the support of mentors and a tolerant teacher. The content and specific strategies had been less important than the experience of a shared journey of discovery in science and engineering. Unknowingly, many of the principles of gifted education—complexity, abstract ideas, productive thinking skills, knowledge production, self-directed learning, and deep insight into the culture of science—were adopted. For me, as the sole teacher, the experience resonated with what Csikszentmihalyi (2002) described as an optimal experience and Coleman (2014) has reported in other teachers of the gifted. I was not the 'sage on stage' but in what McWilliam (2009) terms the 'Meddler in the Middle' whose role was to challenge and provoke students and when necessary console them.

Contribution of Independent Investigatory Experiences to Academic and Socio-emotional Satisfaction for Gifted Students in Science

There is concern that many students who potentially could contribute to solving major environmental, population, and technical issues facing contemporary society are turning away from school science (Kennedy, Lyons, & Quinn, 2014). The former Australian Chief Scientist in a position paper on the future of *Science, Technology, Engineering, and Mathematics* (STEM) in Australia argued that building a skill base in the sciences, particularly is essential to meet the emerging challenge of developing an economy for the twenty-first century (Office of the Chief Scientist, 2013). Calls have been made to reform science teaching to make it more engaging and relevant for students of all capabilities as an understanding of science and processes of science permeates all aspects of society. A specific question that is addressed in this chapter is *why do some intellectually gifted students reach peak performances at school and others do not?* To address this question, I explore the role played by non-cognitive and environmental effects central to a raft of theoretical perspectives on the development of talent including the Differentiated Model of Giftedness and Talent (Gagné, 2013) and the Munich model (Heller, Perleth, & Lim, 2005). Motivation is a central non-cognitive factor that explains students' engagement and persistence with a task.

   Any one model of gifted education is not endorsed in this chapter, but the issue of fostering talent by focusing on the provision of opportunities for students to pursue their passions will be examined. The chapter commences with a brief overview of the current status of school science, and I argue the need to align school science with current authentic practices of science. The disjunction between school science and practices and epistemologies of science leads to an analysis of why students are disengaged from school science and consequently why some are disinterested in pursuing a career in science. Thus, a discussion of theories that relate to engagement and commitment that underpin a student's sense of academic and social well-being is provided. Attention then turns to the role with examples that inquiry learning plays in supporting intellectually gifted students in science. My argument is that these independent investigatory experiences contribute to both academic and social-emotional, satisfaction both of which predict overall academic performance. Learning through investigations is not new, but my intention is to provide an alternative theoretical lens framed around interests, curiosity, and negotiated learning to examine its benefits as a pedagogical approach for intellectually gifted students in learning science.

Science: A Key Learning Area

Globally there are assertions that there is a shortfall in recruitment of talented students into the sciences. Such claims are often disputed although in some specialist areas in some countries there are shortages of skilled scientists. The *National*

Innovation and Science Agenda Report (2015), while acknowledging the potential of Australians to be innovative, identified that only 9% of Australian small-to-medium-sized businesses brought a new idea to market in 2012–2013—one of the lowest rates in the developed world. A contribution to this situation is the widely acknowledged loss of interest in school science studies globally (Global Science Forum, 2008; Osborne, 2008) and in Australia (Kennedy et al., 2014). The Australian government like many others has embarked on initiatives to build capacity in the *Science, Technology, Engineering, and Mathematics* (STEM) domains. The National STEM School Education Strategy 2016–2026 is supported by all Australian Education Ministers and focuses on teaching science and mathematics through purposeful investigations of real-life problems and contexts (Australian Academy of Science, 2017a; Education Council, 2015). Although building economic capacity is high on the policy agenda, there are other reasons for engaging students in science. An important goal of science education is to equip the citizen with a sound understanding of the nature of science so that they are able to distinguish pseudo-science, misinformation, and conflicting views of natural phenomena and to have confidence in the process of science. Osborne and Dillon (2008) along with many other science educators have argued:

> that science education for all can only be justified if it offers something of universal value for all rather than the minority who will become future scientists. For these reasons, the goal of science education must be, first and foremost, to offer an education that develops students' understanding both of the canon of scientific knowledge and of how science functions. (Osborne & Dillon, p. 7)

Epistemological Assumptions in the Teaching of Science

The public perception of science is often that it is elitist, obscure, and unethical and involves accumulation of facts that stems from a misunderstanding of the nature of science (Boulter, 1999) and is influenced by the politicised media (Hmielowski, Feldman, Myers, Leiserowitz, & Maibach, 2013). These beliefs even impact gifted students as Schommer and Dunnell (1997) have suggested that poorly developed beliefs about the nature of science may contribute to intellectually gifted students' underachievement. Thus, teaching practices need to address the nature of scientific knowledge as much as the canonical content. It is through authentic practices, such as inquiry into everyday phenomena rather than the transmission of facts that more mature epistemological beliefs may develop and a more humanistic understanding of science is achieved (Aikenhead, 2006).

Both the Australian and New Zealand curricula, in line with curricular goals across the globe, emphasise the necessity of engaging students with learning experiences based on inquiry processes that are commensurable with the way science is practised (Australian Curriculum and Assessment Reporting Authority [ACARA], 2016; Ministry of Education, 2014). Despite these goals, science teaching adopts a naïve epistemology and hence is often conducted in ways that fail to reflect how scientists undertake their scientific investigations. This situation has been attributed to the pressure of high-stakes testing and accountability (Donnelly & Sadler, 2009; Judson, 2010). As a result, those students highly able or gifted in science who have no problem remembering details, rules, or laws of science are often deprived of opportunities to apply this knowledge through interest-driven investigations. Hence, the role of inquiry science—investigations or practical work—is central to the teaching of science for all students, but especially those with interests and the capability to explore phenomena in original and creative ways. Unfortunately, in many instances, practical work in science equates to students following recipes without an opportunity to pursue curiosity and plan, implement, record, or interpret interesting phenomena (e.g., West, 2007).

Affective variables particularly related to science learning receive little attention from both researchers and curricula. It has been often stated that children are born scientists displaying enthusiasm to explore the world, test ideas, and generate conclusions (e.g., Chaillé & Britain, 1997; Cook, Goodman, & Schulz, 2011). However, numerous studies have shown that by early adolescence, students are no longer inquisitive and have lost their drive to explore and make sense of the world (e.g., Fortus, 2014). This observation is disturbing as interest at the onset of secondary school is a major predictor of interest at the end of school (Sadler, Sonnert, Hazari, & Tai, 2012). Whether considered gifted or not, students' attitudes are mediated by the nature of the classroom learning environment and school culture (e.g., Eddles-Hirsch, Vialle, Rogers, & McCormick, 2010; Fraser, 2012; Hattie, 2009). Studies comparing the effect of school culture, peers, and parents show interesting results. In secondary schools that adopted democratic processes, such as providing choice and autonomy, students maintained or increased levels of interest and set mastery goals (Vedder-Weiss & Fortus, 2012). These authors also found that in classrooms where mastery-oriented goal setting was encouraged, students viewed peers as more focused on achieving a sense of deep understanding of science. Analysis of TIMSS data reveals that attitudes to science of Australian students are particularly related to achievement in science, but moderated apparently by peer relationships (Papanastastasiou & Zembylas, 2004) which may inhibit exceptional performance. Although most of this research has not specifically examined gifted students, the findings are applicable to the gifted and reinforce the importance of relationships and positive affective experiences as contributors to talent development. As suggested by Krapp and Prenzel (2011), failure to acknowledge the role of affect in learning is a contributor to falling engagement with science careers among "students with high potential" (p. 42).

Gifted students are often characterised by their encyclopaedic knowledge of certain topics and their capacity to readily absorb and assimilate information. However, giftedness is also manifested through a person's behaviour in novel situations. The characteristics often found in gifted students in science are given in Table 1 (Watters & Diezmann, 2003). Passion, interest, and curiosity are recurring themes. Gifted students may have developed a warehouse of conceptual and procedural knowledge in science, but can they use that knowledge? Considering the way

Table 1 Characteristics of students gifted in science

Characteristic	Explanation
Seek meaning and explanation of phenomena.	A passion for exploration and finding out about things—epistemic curiosity. They possess a questioning nature. They tend to read scientific or factual books—dictionaries—rather than fiction. They prefer to watch documentaries or nature programs on TV. Personal drive or disposition to engage in long-term explorations.
An awareness of the complexities of the world and sensitivity to the environment including life and death.	Gifted children are sensitive to their environment and seek to organise it, structure it and understand its complexity.
Often categorise natural phenomena in abstract ways.	Sorting out items: the scientifically gifted child may sort on the basis of composition, whereas less-able students would sort on use, shape, colour or surface features.
Often exhibit intensive interest in particular areas of science and persist in exploring these areas and understanding concepts.	Younger students may explore dinosaurs or astronomy to the extreme, well beyond the interest level of peers. In high school, they display persistence and willingness to work beyond ordinary schedules often in the face of physical discomfort.
Will engage in collection of materials—stamps, insects and objects.	A passion to accumulate as much information about classes of objects as is possible. Collecting allows for investigation, persistence and commitment.
Are tinkers wanting to pull objects apart and reassemble.	Intrinsic interest in how things work and a desire to discover for themselves. This behaviour reveals a strong investigative nature. They will often build their own instruments to conduct investigations.
Passionate interest in the origins of things.	Represents the child's need to explain where they come from leading to an understanding of past and future.
Builders and constructors, puzzle solvers, detailed artistic representations, well-developed sense of space.	The scientifically gifted often have strong visualisation skills and in adulthood often reason through diagrams and spatial models. Evident in the search for patterns in phenomena.
Will gravitate towards people who are expert in fields of interest.	They seek like minds and mentors who are able to satisfy their insatiable appetite
Often anxious and single-minded in explaining their ideas.	They assume that others are interested in what they are and wish to share their interests.

Source: Compiled from multiple sources: Rakow (1988), Roeper (1988), Watters and Diezmann (1997)

science is traditionally taught, there are few opportunities to be exposed to new situations or problems where they are able to apply knowledge or seek knowledge relevant to novel situations (Lyons, 2006; Rennie, Goodrum, & Hackling, 2001).

Implementing inquiry-based learning in regular classrooms is challenging for teachers. Navigating high-stakes testing, mandated standards and limiting timetables constrains opportunities for engaging in extended inquiry (Wideen, O'Shea, Pye, & Ivany, 1997). Tests reward the right answer, standards direct what must be learnt in canonical form, and inquiry requires flexibility in timetabling and resourcing. Investigating open-ended problems frequently results in idiosyncratic solutions contrary to expectation. It is these circumstances that provide the richness of learning as students argue, debate, and challenge each other's findings and interpretations.

However, such opportunities for long-term investigations suitable for gifted students are generally implemented, if at all, through extracurricular activities such as pull-out programs, extension classes, lunchtime clubs, science fairs, or competitions. Classroom-initiated investigations and inquiry programs are generally short term and infrequent. There is much research that suggests that teaching practices in general education classrooms are repetitive, unchallenging, and restrictive for gifted students. In a study of Australian senior schooling practices, Goodrum, Druhan, and Abbs (2012) found that 73% of science students indicated that they spend every lesson copying notes from the teacher, while 65% never or seldom have choice in pursuing areas of interest. Where more engaging pedagogy was practised, attitudes were more positive. For example, there is evidence from multiple countries that laboratory-based inquiry experiences have a positive influence on the students' attitudes towards science and their achievement in science knowledge (Acar Sesen & Tarhan, 2013; Adesoji & Raimi, 2004; Freedman, 1997; Potvin & Hashi, 2014; Wolf & Fraser, 2008). Furthermore, Gallagher and Gallagher (2013) have provided evidence that problem-based inquiry learning environments encourage more students to reveal academic potential. However, school science is rarely implemented in ways that typify genuine science (Watters & Diezmann, 2003). It is understandable that gifted students and indeed all students are disengaging from science. To compound the challenges of offering an inquiry approach are issues related to the confidence of many teachers, especially those in the primary years, to implement inquiry approaches (Gillies & Nichols, 2015).

Commitment, Curiosity, and Engagement

In his three-ring conception of giftedness, Renzulli (1986, 1999) proposed an interaction among three clusters of traits contributes to the human potential for creative productivity. He describes *task commitment*, defined as the energy brought to bear on a particular task, as one important cluster. The others are *above average ability* and *creativity*. My focus in this chapter is on the aspect of task commitment. The conception of task commitment is congruent with the work of other theorists, for example, Luria (1966), who identified aspects of intellectual functioning termed 'attention/arousal', and Csikszentmihalyi (2002) who conceptualised the notion of 'flow' to represent a state of concentration or complete absorption in a task. The attribute generating this energy has been described by others as *epistemic curiosity* or the need to know (Berlyne, 1954; Litman, Hutchins, & Russon, 2005).

Engagement with any task is influenced by the level of interest and value in the task (Linderman, Durik, & Hall, 2018). Tasks are valuable if they are novel events that have high information content which involves uncertainty as there is a lack of information about what preceded the event and what will follow the event. The task may also have properties that are hidden or have not yet been noticed (Berlyne, 1954). The consequence of engaging in such tasks contributes to both cognitive and affective satisfaction (de Brabander & Martens, 2014). Learning occurs when students engage in these tasks because they have high relative cognitive value for them (Diezmann & Watters, 2000) and are within the student's *Zone of Proximal Development* [ZPD] (Vygotsky, 1978). Novel and challenging tasks are engaging because they drive curiosity and generate interest. Both the concepts of curiosity and interest have been well studied over the past 30 years, but little research has examined these concepts in the context of gifted education. Gifted students are curious, but opportunities to exploit their curiosity in formal classrooms are rare. So, what do we know about curiosity and interest that may lead to gifted students— or for that matter all students—engaging in learning?

Curiosity is the desire to learn something that leads to an intrinsically rewarding experience (Litman, 2005). There have been multiple theories to explain curiosity, but contemporary models suggest that when individuals encounter novel, complex, or ambiguous experiences, they may find that there are discrepancies between what they know and what they do not know, in other words a knowledge gap (Loewenstein, 1994). The magnitude of the knowledge gap stimulates a desire to find out, to learn. However, if the knowledge gap is perceived to be too great, anxiety may be induced and avoidance behaviour may be adopted, while if there is no knowledge gap, the learner becomes bored and alternative sources of stimuli are sought. At the optimal level, when a learner is exposed to a novel task or problem that she or he feels is within their capacity to solve they are cognitively aroused. At this point, if we accept Vygotsky's (1978) notion of the role of the Zone of Proximal Development, then a more knowledgeable peer, teacher, or social environment that fosters rich discussions may help to bridge the knowledge gap.

Litman and colleagues (Litman et al., 2005; Litman & Jimerson, 2004) summarise the competing processes in terms that curiosity is driven by a feeling of deprivation and/or a feeling of interest. Humans seek to understand events in terms of cause and effect. In contrast, the feeling of interest involves positive emotional states of joy brought on by learning new information, whereas feelings of deprivation involve some degree of tension related to uncertainty. This feeling of interest in finding out something new has been termed epistemic curiosity or a desire for intellectual enrichment (Berlyne, 1954; Litman et al., 2005). The extent to which these processes dominate depends on the perceived level of knowledge that a learner has related to the task. Litman (2005) has attempted to explain curiosity in terms of *liking* and *wanting*. He argues that "wanting is influenced by a variation in deprivation states, the presence of learned incentives for rewards, and the anticipated potential for a given stimulus to satisfy one's desire based on past experience" (p. 803). He proposes that liking may be related to the "cognitive and perceptual interpretability" (p. 803) of some stimulus, in other words the potential for being able

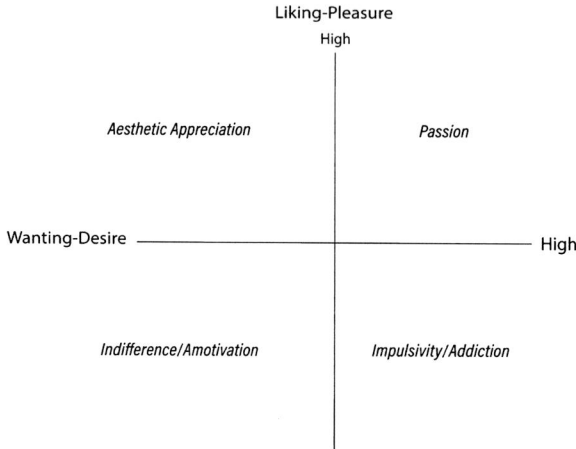

Fig. 1 Wanting-liking model of curiosity. This figure illustrates potential behaviours resulting from levels of wanting and pleasure

to understand. The interaction of these processes leads to a variety of behaviours as is illustrated in Figure 1. Both high levels of a desire to know and high levels of pleasure obtained from engaging are manifested as a passion or intense commitment to engaging in a task. Such tasks have high cognitive value. The learner seeks to attain mastery as there is enjoyment in being able to master the task. Perhaps, this state of pleasure in the task is represented by the state of flow conceptualised by Csikszentmihalyi (2002). Curiosity is manifested as aesthetic appreciation if there is high interest and pleasure in partaking in an experience, but engaging does not lead to any specific rewards. Intense cravings, addiction, or morbid curiosity is seen when there is some reward, but the experience may not involve pleasure. Finally, a low sense of reward and a low sense of pleasure lead to indifference, apathy, and lack of motivation to engage.

Interest determines how students select and persist in engaging with phenomena (Hidi, 1990). Interest is aroused through perceptions of novelty, complexity, surprisingness, or incongruity. Murphy and Alexander (2002) provided evidence that interest predicts learning achievement. The prevailing theoretical framework proposes that two forms of interest—namely, *individual* interest and *situational* interest—are involved (Hidi, 1990). *Individual interest* describes a person's long-term involvement or engagement with a domain of knowledge, whereas *situational interest* is sparked by immediate contextual events (Hidi & Harackiewicz, 2000). According to Hidi (1990), people process interesting information in ways different to how they process information that lacks interest. Further elaboration is provided by Hidi and Renninger (2006) who describe the evolution of interest in four phases: (1) triggered situational interest, (2) maintained situational interest, (3) emerging (or less-well-developed) individual interest, and (4) well-developed individual interest. Hence, engagement and learning occur when students perceive tasks have high cognitive value and are within the student's Zone of Proximal Development [ZPD] (Vygotsky, 1978). The cognitive value of tasks can be reduced by teachers' practices. For example, Diezmann (2005), in the context of mathematical investigations, applied the work of Henningsen and Stein (1997) to demonstrate that complex tasks are often oversimplified by teachers. The way a task is presented and the level of intervention by the teacher eliminates the intrinsic value that may be associated with the task. Unnecessary scaffolding occurs when all students receive hints and clues rather than only those who need this support.

Negotiated Learning

Academic achievement and development of full potential are dependent on a strong sense of social-emotional well-being (Gray & Hackling, 2009), and a poor sense of well-being is strongly associated with underachievement among gifted students (Blaas, 2014). Well-being is a state of mind in which the individual feels that they are in a state of harmony and balance with themselves, life experiences, and their environment (Dodge, Daly, Huyton, & Sanders, 2012). For gifted students, balance can be achieved when they are able to face challenges commensurate with their intellectual and emotional resources. In this section, the conditions for achieving a sense of well-being by drawing on aspects of theories of motivation will be explored.

Gifted students are often perfectionists, for some this is healthy although for others it may be problematic. In discussing aspects of perfectionism, Silverman (2007) argues that "the extent of joy it is possible to experience is directly related to the intensity of the struggle in which one engaged to reach his or her goal . . . perfectionists are capable of ecstatic heights" (p. 234). Successful achievements are accompanied by a feeling of *emotional enjoyment*. Students exhibiting productive perfectionistic tendencies enjoy the challenge of a difficult task. *Engagement* is an important construct in understanding underachievement among gifted students (Landis & Reschly, 2013). Students are likely to engage and achieve if their perceptions of their ability, the meaningfulness of tasks, and the support of the environment are aligned (Rubenstein, Siegle, Reis, McCoach, & Burton, 2012; Sulkowski, Demaray, & Lazarus, 2012). In other words, there is a sense of connect-edness with the task and class (or school) environment. The social world of gifted students is complex, but the consensus is that access to 'like minds' is important in developing *positive relationships*. When possible, gifted students will seek out those with similar interests and abilities. For example, drawing on social synchrony theory, Farmer and Farmer (1996) found that gifted students in heterogeneous classrooms spontaneously associated with others who were also gifted. There is compelling evidence to support ability grouping (Steenbergen-Hu, Makel, & Olszewski-Kubilius, 2016; Vogl & Preckel, 2014). Failure to achieve positive relationships and social rejection have profound effects on gifted students compared to non-gifted peers (e.g., Peairs, 2011). Positive *identity development* is a critical aspect of a sense of well-being. An individual's identity is manifested not only in the way in which the person perceives himself or herself, but also in the way the person evaluates his or her abilities. Gifted students often reject their giftedness and moderate their public identity in their learning and extracurricular environments so as to be perceived to be more socially acceptable (Gross, 1998; Jung, Barnett, Gross, & McCormick, 2011; Luus & Watters, 2012). Finally, a sense of *accomplishment* occurs when a person achieves something that is important, valued, and challenging. For many gifted students, classroom experiences are boring and disengaging as they are taught content that they have long understood. There is limited diagnostic assessment or acknowledgment of what they already know. A strategy that draws on the principles of mastery learning includes (e.g., Guskey, 2010) "effective enrichment activities that provide valuable, challenging experiences . . . [and] should enable successful learners to explore in greater depth a range of related topics that keenly interest them" (p. 56). Novel and interesting topics provide challenges, which are important motivators that satisfy the need for achievement and sense of self-efficacy (Lens & Rand, 2000; Phillips & Lindsay, 2006).

Self-Determination Theory (SDT) can be seen to greatly assist in understanding student motivation in the school environment and, therefore, their engagement in formal education. The issue facing educators when students begin their formal education at around the age of five is what that student values; therefore, what intrinsically motivates them has been predetermined by their culture and familial upbringing (Ryan & Deci, 2000). Fundamentally, the psychological needs and sense of well-being can be achieved, given opportunities for positive relationships with peers and teachers, a sense of competence in being successful in solving complex problems and choice or autonomy in prioritising learning opportunities. Relatedness, competence and autonomy became the three basic psychological needs identified by Ryan and Deci in self-determination theory. Wenzel and Brophy (2015) suggest that a positive self-esteem may also feature as a basic need. Self-esteem can be enhanced by associating with supportive people including peers and teachers.

All these theories coalesce and explain the need for gifted students to engage at length and in depth with complex novel problems independently or within compatible social groupings. The factors that contribute to engagement in learning science by gifted students are complex and multiple and, in many cases, not unlike those that impact all students, especially in the early adolescent years. Studies of mainstream high school students in the United States have shown that students will engage if the perceived challenge of the task and their own skills are aligned, the content was relevant, and the learning environment was under their control (Shernoff, Czikszentmihalyi, Schneider, & Shernoff, 2003). It would be expected, given their characteristics, that similar conditions are necessary to engage the gifted student. However, much of the emphasis in supporting gifted students focuses on cognitive strategies (e.g., Maker & Schiever, 2010) with less focus on affective and environmental factors. To maximise achievement, the social-emotional dimension of human development demands consideration. Thus, an effective teacher needs to identify and design relevant learning experiences that capitalise on students' interests to engage them in learning, to effectively set goals, and to apply their knowledge and skills. In the domain of science, such experiences involve processes of inquiry learning in ways that simulate the authentic practices of science. During inquiry, student social interaction is high, and therefore, students must work in a risk-free environment (Brewer & Daane, 2002) where they are encouraged to ask questions, share ideas, and engage in dialogue. The establishment of a powerful learning environment addresses the needs of gifted students while also providing effective opportunities for all students.

Inquiry Learning in Science

Inquiry learning is not new and has been advocated in policy for many years. Inquiry learning promotes opportunities for students to plan, carry out, and interpret novel investigations into phenomena (Scanlon, Anastopoulou, & Kerawalla, 2012). It fosters higher-order thinking skills, such as critical and creative thinking, and encourages social learning. Clearly, implementation is sporadic in Australia given the findings of Goodrum et al. (2012). Inquiry finds its modern roots in Dewey's belief that learning science best occurs through practical engagement in natural learning places (Herman & Pinard, 2015). The history of inquiry learning extends back much further. Pestalozzi in the eighteenth century promoted inquiry-based learning where there was opportunity for children to explore their interests. It was at a Pestalozzi-inspired school in Aarau that Einstein attributes his capacity to develop 'thought experiments' (Isaacson, 2007). Hands-on activities, investigations, and inquiry learning are often used interchangeably to define a process in which students either individually or in collaboration with others identify problems, pose questions, generate hypotheses, design strategies to solve these questions or test hypotheses, and investigate a problem by collecting data either through direct experimental manipulation of variables or by interpreting existing data sets. Conclusions are reached and disseminated following analysis and interpretation of data. More often than not, inquiry learning opportunities are far more structured than suggested by this definition (Ireland, Watters, Lunn-Brownlee, & Lupton, 2014). Multiple labels have been applied from problem-based learning (Neufeld & Barrows, 1974), project-based learning, design-based learning (Barron & Darling-Hammond, 2008), and challenge-based learning (Johnson, Smith, Smythe, & Varon, 2009). A notable, and widely used model in Australian primary schools is *Primary Connections* developed by the Australian Academy of Science (Australian Academy of Science, 2017b) and based on the 5Es instructional model (Bybee, 1997). The program provides a scaffold to support teachers to integrate conceptual learning and inquiry learning. Evaluations of the program indicate that a model incorporating an inquiry-based approach had a positive impact on student learning outcomes in science and the literacies of science (Dawson, 2009). Research on problem-based learning by VanTassel-Baska and her colleagues has shown the benefits for gifted students in undertaking investigations into ill-defined problems (e.g., VanTassel-Baska, 2012). Procedural guidelines exist for most of these approaches which assume that students will investigate some meaningful problem with scaffolding from their teachers and peers (e.g., Barell, 2007; Kuhlthau, Maniotes, & Caspari,

2012; Larmer, Mergendoller, & Boss, 2015). Implementing effective inquiry learning relies on more than selecting problems, but also the classroom environment is a significant contributor.

De Corte, Verschaffel, and Masui (2004) provide a window into learning environments that differentiates learning opportunities, boosts creativity, acknowledges the need for autonomy, and leads to productive outcomes. They argue:

> a powerful learning environment is characterized by a good balance between discovery and personal exploration, on the one hand, and systematic instruction and guidance, on the other, always taking into account individual differences in abilities, needs, and motivation among learners. (p. 370)

Such classes are characterised by student planning and conducting investigations, rich conversations, dialogical interactions, negotiated learning, and flexibility, and teachers who listen to the needs and interests of students (Watters & Diezmann, 2016). The more-able students have opportunities to explore problems of their choosing, having demonstrated mastery of core content requirements. Through dialogical interactions, they are encouraged to engage in reasoned argument, consider alternative explanations and to reach consensus on interpreting data (Gillies, 2016). The extent that students gifted in science have opportunities to undertake investigations strongly determines motivational and epistemological prerequisites of self-regulatory strategy use (Neber & Schommer-Aikins, 2002). Less-able students are still engaged but often require more scaffolding. In essence, inquiry, discussion, and critical thinking become ways of knowing.

Technology also plays an important role in facilitating powerful learning experiences. Technology operationalises the real-world enabling students to research topics of contemporary interest, to manage data, and to communicate findings. Hunter (2014) has described how Nina, a teacher of a middle year's gifted class in New South Wales, implemented inquiry learning using technology to accelerate learning. Further evidence of the potential of technology emerged from a study of how four gifted Year-6 students engaged in science in a one-to-one laptop class in Queensland (Knights, 2017). The students became more actively engaged, self-reflective, and developed a strong sense of competence and self-regulation. Self-regulated learners have a strong sense of identity which has been directly linked to high academic achievement (Pintrich & Schunk, 2002).

Several approaches to inquiry learning in science can be identified. These include structured, guided, and open inquiry. In both structured and guided inquiry, the teacher plays a significant role in both identifying and planning the problem (Ireland et al., 2014). However, open inquiries foster opportunities for students to experience uncertainties, ambiguities, and the social nature of scientific work and knowledge. Here, the teacher plays a very different role, where she or he engages in dialogical knowledge-building processes that are at the core of science.

Through these complex investigations, students develop in context a range of key scientific and mathematical processes and skills such as problem finding, problem posing, constructing hypotheses, explaining, justifying, predicting, and representing, together with quantifying, coordinating, and organising data. Students become *mathematically* literate by generating, and interpreting information that is represented in multiple forms such as diagrams, charts, tables, and graphs. They become *scientifically* literate by engaging in hypothesis testing and evaluation of evidence, and they become *technologically* literate through the use of tools relevant to information or data gathering. These processes and associated understandings are essential for effective participation in a knowledge-based society. They become technologically literate through the use of calculators, the Internet, and various word processing, spread-sheeting, and presentation technologies. Powerful learning environments will meet the needs of many gifted in science and engage those who are not necessarily as gifted, but will need basic literacies of science to cope with an ever-changing technological world (Ireland et al., 2014).

Attention now turns to two cases of inquiry conducted in a mixed-ability class over an extended period of weeks. *Terraforming Mars* is a topic of contemporary interest with a number of planned voyages to Mars to be conducted in the next decade. Creek Watch capitalised on younger children's concerns about their local environment and the implications of pollution.

Case 1: Terraforming Mars – Year 8. Over a period of eight weeks (90–135 min per week), I introduced students in a Grade 8 science class of 32 boys (approx. 13-year-olds) to a program of inquiry science in which they explored a common problem (Watters & Ginns, 1999). A broad plan of action, consisting of three phases, was developed. In Phase 1, it was decided to introduce students to open-ended, independent inquiry by engaging them in problem-solving activities and the use of problem identification and problem-solving techniques. Students were accustomed to a traditional strict teacher-directed approach to instruction, and thus, the purpose of Phase 1 was to encourage risk-taking and foster greater argument and discussions than they were used to. In Phase 2, they were introduced to a problem by way of being presented with a scenario. The scenario referred to a futuristic newspaper item, dated 28 February 2035, that suggested travel to Mars was now much easier and migration to the planet would be an attractive possibility, considering the large population on Earth. The newspaper item included an advertisement inviting interested groups to tender for the construction of a biosphere to support the establishment of a colony on Mars. They were required then to pose a problem to solve, plan, and implement the investigation. Students had to identify their particular problem, speculate on solutions, consider the efficacy of the question, develop and implement these solutions or experiments, and reflect on the outcomes. In Phase 3, which lasted for about four weeks, students worked independently (as groups) on their projects. Finally, the students, were given the opportunity to evaluate each other's products of the investigation, as well as the processes in which they were engaged.

Two significant findings emerged from the inquiry program. First, interest, meaningfulness, and engagement by all students were substantial. As one student reflected, "in the first two terms it was more of a case of learn the science exam material and now it is more like learning for our own knowledge—and what we're taught we remember" ... "we are interested". Learning was seen as about "learning to think" and "learning to learn". Although it was perceived as "friendlier—laidback" it was "it's learning to learn—we still had to put in the hard work".

Second, spontaneous differentiation occurred. Those students with passion and ability in science gained considerable depth of understanding of the specifics of certain classes of animals by personal research. Students seen to be less able engaged in more practical activities and achieved substantial outcomes by designing and constructing model buildings, taking into account perceived environmental conditions.

The study highlighted the importance of three main issues. First, the formation of a community of learners was developed which facilitated the higher ability students and also contributed to enhanced performances of lower ability students. Second, an open-ended inquiry approach afforded opportunities for capable students to grapple with more sophisticated ideas and processes. Third, classroom discourse was structured to encourage the development of 'scientific talk' for the students. These contributed to enhanced engagement, interest, and a sense of well-being which was acknowledged by both the students and their regular teacher.

Case 2: Creek Watch – Year 5. Students in four Year-5 classes (9- to 10-year-olds) were taught by their regular teachers and developed mathematical models to assess the quality of water in a creek that ran through the school yard (English & Watters, 2009). The lessons ran over four sessions of 40–60 minutes across 3–4 weeks. They engaged with core ideas in biological science and environmental studies and brought the lens of mathematics to understand the interrelationships between water quality and biodiversity. They were presented with a scenario that increased urban development in the western suburbs of Brisbane that was threatening the quality of the local environment. In particular, suburban runoff was impacting water quality and visible signs such as rising salinity and blue-green algal blooms that are becoming more prevalent. The local community was offering a prize for the group that developed the best system that described the most important criteria in establishing the total quality of a creek. Students were required to investigate the presence of macro-invertebrates, the type and quantity of fish (native and exotic), and the concentration of various chemicals in the water. The teacher provided support in the form of technical resources and water-bug identification charts, but was not involved in any direct teaching. For example, students were provided with the appropriate resources to analyse for levels of nitrogen and oxygen and were able to measure water turbidity and pH.

The investigation concluded with students preparing and presenting a report that linked science and mathematics. Students were confronted with concepts in both mathematics and science well beyond what was expected in Year 5. However, confronting an authentic problem that impacted their own neighbourhood challenged them to go beyond expectations and successfully generate novel solutions. The richness of discussions and debate and diversity of solutions were typical of the characteristics of powerful learning environments.

Concluding Comments

The aim in this chapter was to argue the case that inquiry learning contributes to both academic and social-emotional satisfaction. Investigations capitalise on students' interest and curiosity about their environment and scientific events that are meaningful. The focus taken was to examine conditions that contribute to student motivation. In the context of teaching science, how teaching can support gifted students to pursue their interests and engagement in learning and to achieve a sense of well-being were explored in this chapter. The argument centres on the importance of engagement in learning and avoidance of underachievement. Inquiry approaches that explore natural phenomena challenge the gifted student in science and capitalises on the innate epistemic curiosity that characterises humans. A novel complexing situation provides scope to develop conceptual understanding to engage in abstract thinking and generate creative solutions. However, just as important are negotiations around choice of direction, ability to choose and work with like minds, and to achieve success that contributes to psychological well-being. Balancing academic achievement and well-being contributes to engagement and commitment. A focus on gifted student well-being is in its infancy in the Australian context. Emerging research is broadening the field of view to accommodate affective dimensions in supporting gifted students (Baker, 2018; Wright-Scott, 2018).

The cases reported in this chapter are provided by way of examples. In both cases, the focus was on establishing a learning experience where students had to make decisions, work collaboratively, explore complex novel situations, discuss findings, and self-regulate learning. None was ostensibly designed with gifted students in mind. Given the scope of this chapter, these cases were deliberately chosen to exemplify whole of class strategies that do address the needs of gifted students in science, but also stretches the less-able or less-interested student. Cases 1 and 2 were research projects where I as a researcher taught a class or supported a teacher to implement a new approach. The context was artificial, but nevertheless the experiences for students were successful. My personal beginning experience represented an authentic program that was core business to the school. However, adopting inquiry approaches can be challenging (Ireland, Watters, Brownlee, & Lupton, 2012; Quigley, Marshall, Deaton, Cook, & Padilla, 2011). Inquiry approaches to learning assume that teachers are well-prepared to engage in inquiry themselves—a position that is challengeable given the pre-service educational courses most have experienced. Teachers on the whole have had limited experiences in scientific research or opportunities to generate knowledge themselves through inquiry. A reconceptualisation of the role of the teacher from 'sage on stage' to 'being a manager of learning and provoker of thinking' is a seminal step in implementing inquiry learning, especially for the gifted in science who probably know more than the teacher.

First, extended problem explorations provide students with opportunities to engage in deep learning through the identification of a problem, collection of data, exploration of multiple strategies, communication of solutions, and reflection on the outcomes of the investigation. Second, due to their open-ended nature, teachers can capitalise on the use of investigations to provide opportunities for students with a range of scientific abilities and interests. Individuals can contribute their specialised knowledge or skills to the task. For example, one student may undertake and record data within an investigation, while another student may capitalise on their communications skills and prepare and present reports. Third, investigations are collaborative as students are working at the cutting edge of knowledge, and there is necessity to work together which builds effective relationships. Fourth, open-ended investigations provide powerful learning environments that are engaging, meaningful, and productive which contribute to students' sense of well-being. Fifth, from a teacher's perspective, it provides an opportunity to gauge the ability of the student and to identify those gifted students who may be underachieving or disengaged. The final consideration is assessment. Given the high-stakes assessment regimes that distort teaching practices (Polesel, Rice, & Dulfer, 2014), teachers are expected to assess students against national standards. Academically gifted students achieve well beyond these mandates. A detailed discussion of assessment is beyond the scope of this chapter; however, what inquiry approaches provide is a case of authentic assessment that documents what students can produce and not just reproduce.

The Australian National STEM School Education Strategy 2016–2026 (Education Council, 2015) and the New Zealand Curious Minds government initiative (https://www.curiousminds.nz) have as their central goal the enhancement of STEM education in the national interest. These strategy documents are rife with platitudes about enhancing student interest in STEM. Although it is important that all members of society are well grounded in these domains, the ultimate responsibility for innovation and advancement in these fields lies in the hands of those gifted students currently in the school systems. In preparing this review, it became evident that little research has been conducted specifically on the issues of curiosity, engagement, and the elements that feature in models of giftedness postulated by gifted educationalists, such as Renzulli and Gagné. Much of the research involves students of broad ability; thus a plethora of potential avenues for future research exist (Brusic & Steinmacher, 2015; Zoller, 2011). Further avenues for research include the effect of high-stakes testing that prioritises performance-oriented learning on gifted students (Scot, Callahan, & Urquhart, 2009), the efficacy of inquiry-based teaching for gifted students (Robinson, Dailey, Hughes, & Cotabish, 2014), the optimal balance of inquiry learning and explicit instruction for gifted students (Housand & Reis, 2008; Machtinger, 2014), and what effective structures and policies schools can adopt to acknowledge how gifted education and inclusive education can be achieved (Pérez & Beltrán, 2012).

In this chapter, I have argued that it is important to recognise the importance of affect and to encourage students to engage in learning through inquiry into topics of personal interest. However, affect is only one part of the story. A question posed at the beginning of this chapter was why do some intellectually gifted students reach peak performances at school and others do not? The research cited and personal experiences reflected on only provide some clues. The decision to engage with learning science and pursuing careers in science is influenced by many factors. The evidence from qualitative studies conducted not specifically with gifted students suggests a process of negotiation and renegotiation of choice often involving consideration of social relationships (Holmegaard, 2015). In Holmegaard's analysis of decision-making by Danish secondary students, they were able to carefully articulate their interests, but they also related how they considered making choices about subjects in a way that was both culturally and socially acceptable to family and friends. The implications for educational policy makers and teachers are that educational experiences including learning approaches such as inquiry must be linked with constructing images of what it means to be a scientist and explore the nature of science as a human endeavour.

In concluding, I refer back to the opening quote by the eminent physicist, Nobel Prize winner and father of quantum theory, Max Planck. The pursuit of science should bring happiness, and it will only be when school science provides those experiences that the gifted will engage for their own satisfaction and possibly through science careers for the benefit of society. It is noteworthy that Albert Einstein was a friend and colleague of Max Planck. The title of this chapter borrows from an Australian Broadcasting Corporation (ABC) television program of the 1960s hosted by Julius Sumner Miller. Julius Sumner Miller often asked, 'Why is it so?' and through interesting demonstrations engaged a generation of pupils. He also was a friend and admirer of Einstein. I conclude with the words widely attributed to Einstein 'I have no special talent. I am only passionately curious'.

Cross-References

▶ Assessment, Pedagogy, and Curriculum: Part IV Introduction
▶ Australian Teachers Who Made a Difference: Secondary Gifted Student Perceptions of Teaching and Teacher Effectiveness
▶ Being of Like-Mind: Giftedness in the New Zealand Context
▶ Differentiation of Instruction for Gifted Learners: Collated Evaluative Studies of Teacher Classroom Practices
▶ Engaging Gifted Students in Solving Real Problems Creatively: Implementing the Real Engagement in Active Problem-Solving (REAPS) Teaching/Learning Model in Australasian and Pacific Rim Contexts
▶ Gifted Education in the Asia-Pacific: From the Past for the Future – An Introduction
▶ How Do Teachers Meet the Academic Needs of High-Ability Students in Science?
▶ Highly Able Students in International Schools
▶ Learning from International Research Informs Academic Acceleration in Australasia: A Case for Consistent Policy
▶ Put Them Together and See How They Learn! Ability Grouping and Acceleration Effects on the Self-Esteem of Academically Gifted High School Students
▶ Some Implications for the Future of Gifted Education in the Asia-Pacific
▶ STEAM in Gifted Education in Korea
▶ The Lives and Achievements of Four Extraordinary Australians: A Master, a Maker, an Introspector, and an Influencer

References

Acar Sesen, A. B., & Tarhan, L. (2013). Inquiry-based laboratory activities in electrochemistry: High school students' achievements and attitudes. *Research in Science Education, 43*(1), 413–435. https://doi.org/10.1007/s11165-011-9275-9

Adesoji, F. A., & Raimi, S. M. (2004). Effects of enhanced laboratory instructional technique on senior secondary students' attitude toward chemistry in Oyo Township, Oyo State, Nigeria. *Journal of Science Education and Technology, 13*(3), 377–385. https://doi.org/10.1023/B: JOST.0000045465.81437.3b

Aikenhead, G. S. (2006). *Science education for everyday life: Evidence-based practice.* New York, NY: Teachers College Press.

Australian Academy of Science [AAS]. (2017a). *Schools.* Retrieved from https://www.science.org.au/learning/schools

Australian Academy of Science [AAS]. (2017b). *Primary Connections.* Retrieved from https://primaryconnections.org.au/

Australian Curriculum and Assessment Reporting Authority [ACARA]. (2016). F–10 Curriculum, science v8.3. Retrieved from ACARA website http://www.australiancurriculum.edu.au/science/curriculum/f-10?layout=1

Baker, G. (2018). *Gifted adolescent wellbeing: Case study of an Australian immersion* (Unpublished PhD thesis). Queensland University of Technology, Brisbane, Australia.

Barell, J. (2007). *Problem based learning: An inquiry approach* (2nd ed.). Thousand Oaks, CA: Corwin Press.

Barron, B., & Darling-Hammond, L. (2008). How can we teach for meaningful learning? In L. Darling-Hammond, B. Barron, P. D. Pearson, A. H. Schoenfeld, E. K. Stage, T. D. Zimmerman, G. N. Cervetti, & J. L. Tilson (Eds.), *Powerful learning: What we know about teaching for understanding* (pp. 34–144). San Francisco, CA: Jossey-Bass.

Berlyne, D. E. (1954). A theory of human curiosity. *British Journal of Psychology, 45*, 180–191.

Blaas, S. (2014). The relationship between social-emotional difficulties and underachievement of gifted students. *Australian Journal of Guidance and Counselling, 24*(2), 243–255. https://doi.org/10.1017/jgc.2014.1

Boulter, D. (1999). Public perception of science and associated general issues for the scientist. *Phytochemistry, 50*(1), 1–7. https://doi.org/10.1016/S0031-9422(98)00455-5

Brewer, J., & Daane, C. J. (2002). Translating constructivist theory into practice in primary-grade mathematics. *Education, 123*(2), 416–421.

Brusic, S. A., & Steinmacher, J. G. (2015). Creating the curious classroom. *Children's Technology & Engineering, 19*(3), 24–28.

Bybee, R. W. (1997). *Achieving scientific literacy: From purposes to practices.* Portsmouth, NH: Heinemann.

Chaillé, C., & Britain, L. (1997). *The young child as scientist: A constructivist approach to early childhood science education.* London, England: Longman.

Coleman, L. J. (2014). Being a teacher. *Journal for the Education of the Gifted, 37*(1), 56–69. https://doi.org/10.1177/0162353214521495

Cook, C., Goodman, N. D., & Schulz, L. E. (2011). Where science starts: Spontaneous experiments in preschoolers' exploratory play. *Cognition, 120*(3), 341–349. https://doi.org/10.1016/j.cognition.2011.03.003

Csikszentmihalyi, M. (2002). *Flow: The classic work on how to achieve happiness* (Revised Ed.) London, England: Rider.

Dawson, V. (2009). *Science is primary: A review of Primary Connections Stage 3 2006–2008.* Canberra, ACT: Australian Academy of Science. Retrieved from Australian Academy of Science website https://primaryconnections.org.au/about/history/research-and-evaluation/science-is-primary.pdf

de Brabander, C. J., & Martens, R. L. (2014). Towards a unified theory of task-specific motivation. *Educational Research Review, 11*, 27–44. https://doi.org/10.1016/j.edurev.2013.11.001

De Corte, E., Verschaffel, L., & Masui, C. (2004). The CLIA-model: A framework for designing powerful learning environments for thinking and problem solving. *European Journal of Psychology of Education, 19*(4), 365–384. https://doi.org/10.1007/bf03173216

Diezmann, C. M. (2005). Challenging mathematically gifted primary students. *Australasian Journal of Gifted Education, 14*(1), 50–57.

Diezmann, C. M., & Watters, J. J. (2000). Catering for mathematically gifted elementary students: Learning from challenging tasks. *Gifted Child Today, 23*(4), 14–19. https://doi.org/10.4219/gct-2000-737

Dodge, R., Daly, A. P., Huyton, J., & Sanders, L. D. (2012). The challenge of defining wellbeing. *International Journal of Wellbeing, 2*(3), 222–235. https://doi.org/10.5502/ijw.v2i3.4

Donnelly, L. A., & Sadler, T. (2009). High school science teachers' views of standards and accountability. *Science Education, 93*(6), 1050–1075. https://doi.org/10.1002/sce.20347

Eddles-Hirsch, K., Vialle, W., Rogers, K. B., & McCormick, J. (2010). "Just challenge those high-ability learners and they'll be all right!". The impact of social context and challenging instruction on the affective development of high-ability students. *Journal of Advanced Academics, 22*(1), 106–128. https://doi.org/10.1177/1932202X1002200105

Education Council. (2015). *National STEM school education strategy a comprehensive plan for science, technology, engineering and mathematics education in Australia*. Canberra, ACT: Education Council. Retrieved from http://www.educationcouncil.edu.au/site/DefaultSite/filesystem/documents/National%20STEM%20School%20Education%20Strategy.pdf

English, L. D., & Watters, J. J. (2009). Mathematically modelling in the early school years. In B. Sriraman, V. Freiman, & N. Lirette-Pitre (Eds.), *Interdisciplinarity, creativity, and learning* (pp. 177–204). Charlotte, NC: Information Age Publishing Inc.

Farmer, T. W., & Farmer, E. M. Z. (1996). Social relationships of students with exceptionalities in mainstream classrooms: Social networks and homophily. *Exceptional Children, 62*(5), 431–450. https://doi.org/10.1177/001440299606200504

Fortus, D. (2014). Attending to affect. *Journal of Research in Science Teaching, 51*(7), 821–835. https://doi.org/10.1002/tea.21155

Fraser, B. J. (2012). Classroom learning environments: Retrospect, context and prospect. In B. J. Fraser, K. G. Tobin, & C. J. McRobbie (Eds.), *Second international handbook of science education* (pp. 1191–1239). New York, NY: Springer.

Freedman, M. P. (1997). Relationship among laboratory instruction, attitude toward science, and achievement in science knowledge. *Journal of Research in Science Teaching, 34*(4), 343–357. https://doi.org/10.1002/(SICI)1098-2736(199704)34:4<343::AID-TEA5>3.0.CO;2-R

Gagné, F. (2013). The DMGT: Changes within, beneath, and beyond. *Talent Development and Excellence, 5*(1), 5–19.

Gallagher, S. A., & Gallagher, J. J. (2013). Using problem-based learning to explore unseen academic potential. *Interdisciplinary Journal of Problem-Based Learning, 7*(1), 111–131. https://doi.org/10.7771/1541-5015.1322

Gillies, R. M. (2016). Dialogic interactions in the cooperative classroom. *International Journal of Educational Research, 76*, 178–189. https://doi.org/10.1016/j.ijer.2015.02.009

Gillies, R. M., & Nichols, K. (2015). How to support primary teachers' implementation of inquiry: Teachers' reflections on teaching cooperative inquiry-based science. *Research in Science Education, 45*(2), 171–191. https://doi.org/10.1007/s11165-014-9418-x

Global Science Forum. (2008). *Encouraging student interest in science and technology studies*. Paris, France: OECD. https://doi.org/10.1787/9789264040892-en

Goodrum, D., Druhan, A., & Abbs, J. (2012). *The status and quality of year 11 and 12 science in Australian schools*. Canberra, ACT: Australian Academy of Science. Retrieved from Australian Academy of Science website https://www.science.org.au/files/userfiles/support/reports-and-plans/2015/year11and12report.pdf

Gray, J., & Hackling, M. (2009). Wellbeing and retention: A senior secondary student perspective. *Australian Educational Researcher, 36*(2), 119–145. https://doi.org/10.1007/BF03216902

Gross, M. U. M. (1998). The 'me' behind the mask: Intellectually gifted students and the search for identity. *Roeper Review, 20*(3), 167–175. https://doi.org/10.1080/02783199809553885

Guskey, T. R. (2010). Lessons of mastery learning. *Educational Leadership, 68*(2), 52–57. Retrieved from http://www.ascd.org/publications/educational-leadership/oct10/vol68/num02/Lessons-of-Mastery-Learning.aspx

Hattie, J. (2009). *Visible learning: A synthesis of over 800 meta-analyses relating to achievement.* Abingdon, UK: Routledge.

Heller, K. A., Perleth, C., & Lim, T. K. (2005). The Munich model of giftedness designed to identify and promote gifted students. In R. J. Sternberg & J. E. Davidson (Eds.), *Conceptions of giftedness* (pp. 147–170). Cambridge, UK: Cambridge University Press.

Henningsen, M., & Stein, M. K. (1997). Mathematical tasks and student cognition: Classroom-based factors that support and inhibit high-level mathematical thinking and reasoning. *Journal for Research in Mathematics Education, 28*(5), 524–549. https://doi.org/10.2307/749690

Herman, W. E., & Pinard, M. R. (2015). Critically examining inquiry-based learning: John Dewey in theory, history, and practice. In P. Blessinger & J. M. Carfora (Eds.), *Inquiry-based learning for multidisciplinary programs: A conceptual and practical resource for educators* (pp. 43–63). Bingley, UK: Emerald Publishing Group.

Hidi, S. (1990). Interest and its contribution as a mental resource for learning. *Review of Educational Research, 60*(4), 549–571. https://doi.org/10.3102/00346543060004549

Hidi, S., & Harackiewicz, J. (2000). Motivating the academically unmotivated: A critical issue for the 21st century. *Review of Educational Research, 70,* 151–179. https://doi.org/10.3102/00346543070002151

Hidi, S., & Renninger, K. A. (2006). The four-phase model of interest development. *Educational Psychologist, 41*(2), 111–127. https://doi.org/10.1207/s15326985ep4102_4

Hmielowski, J. D., Feldman, L., Myers, T. A., Leiserowitz, A., & Maibach, E. (2013). An attack on science? Media use, trust in scientists, and perceptions of global warming. *Public Understanding of Science, 23*(7), 866–883. https://doi.org/10.1177/0963662513480091

Holmegaard, H. T. (2015). Performing a choice-narrative: A qualitative study of the patterns in STEM students' higher education choices. *International Journal of Science Education, 37*(9), 1454–1477. https://doi.org/10.1080/09500693.2015.1042940

Housand, A., & Reis, S. M. (2008). Self-regulated learning in reading: Gifted pedagogy and instructional settings. *Journal of Advanced Academics, 20*(1), 108–136. https://doi.org/10.4219/jaa-2008-865

Hunter, J. L. (2014, March). *High possibility classrooms: Technology integration in action.* Paper presented at the Society for Information Technology & Teacher Education International Conference, Jacksonville, FL. https://www.learntechlib.org/p/131231

Ireland, J., Watters, J. J., Lunn Brownlee, J., & Lupton, M. (2014). Approaches to inquiry teaching: Elementary teacher's perspectives. *International Journal of Science Education, 36*(10), 1733–1750. https://doi.org/10.1080/09500693.2013.877618

Ireland, J. E., Watters, J. J., Brownlee, J., & Lupton, M. (2012). Elementary teacher's conceptions of inquiry teaching: Messages for teacher development. *Journal of Science Teacher Education, 23*(2), 159–175. https://doi.org/10.1007/s10972-011-9251-2

Isaacson, W. (2007). *Einstein: His life and universe.* New York, NY: Simon & Schuster.

Johnson, L. F., Smith, R. S., Smythe, J. T., & Varon, R. K. (2009). *Challenge-based learning: An approach for our time.* Austin, TX: The New Media Consortium. Retrieved from https://eric.ed.gov/?id=ED505102

Judson, E. (2010). Science education as a contributor to adequate yearly progress and accountability programs. *Science Education, 94*(5), 888–902. https://doi.org/10.1002/sce.20396

Jung, J. Y., Barnett, K., Gross, M. U. M., & McCormick, J. (2011). Levels of intellectual giftedness, culture, and the forced-choice dilemma. *Roeper Review, 33*(3), 182–197. https://doi.org/10.1375/ajgc.21.1.85

Kennedy, J. P., Lyons, T., & Quinn, F. (2014). The continuing decline of science and mathematics enrolments in Australian high schools. *Teaching Science, 60*(2), 34–46. Retrieved from http://www.growingtallpoppies.com/wp-content/uploads/2015/07/Continuing-Decline-of-Science-by-Kennedy-Lyons-Quinn.pdf

Knights, A. (2017). *Through the LCD glass: Investigating the experiences of gifted students in a one- to-one laptop classroom* (Master of Education Thesis). Queensland University of Technology.

Krapp, A., & Prenzel, M. (2011). Research on interest in science: Theories, methods, and findings. *International Journal of Science Education, 33*(1), 27–50. https://doi.org/10.1080/09500693.2010.518645

Kuhlthau, C. C., Maniotes, L. K., & Caspari, A. K. (2012). *Guided inquiry design: A framework for inquiry in your school.* Santa Barbara, CA: ABC-CLIO.

Landis, R. N., & Reschly, A. L. (2013). Reexamining gifted underachievement and dropout through the lens of student engagement. *Journal for the Education of the Gifted, 36*(2), 220–249. https://doi.org/10.1177/0162353213480864

Larmer, J., Mergendoller, J., & Boss, S. (2015). *Setting the standard for project-based learning: A proven approach to rigorous classroom instruction.* Alexandria, VA: ASCD.

Lens, W., & Rand, P. (2000). Motivation and cognition: Their role in the development of giftedness. In K. A. Heller, F. J. Mönks, R. J. Sternberg, & R. F. Subotnik (Eds.), *International handbook of giftedness and talent* (pp. 193–202). Oxford, UK: Elsevier Science.

Lindeman, M., Durik, A., & Hall, G. (2018). Sometimes less is more: The role of subjective task experience in self-generated value interventions. *Social Psychology of Education, 21*(2), 371–381. https://doi.org/10.1007/s11218-017-9417-7

Litman, J. (2005). Curiosity and the pleasures of learning: Wanting and liking new information. *Cognition and Emotion, 19*(6), 793–814. https://doi.org/10.1080/02699930541000101

Litman, J., Hutchins, T., & Russon, R. (2005). Epistemic curiosity, feeling-of-knowing, and exploratory behaviour. *Cognition and Emotion, 19*(4), 559–582. https://doi.org/10.1080/02699930441000427

Litman, J. A., & Jimerson, T. L. (2004). The measuremThe measurement of curiosity as a feeling-of-deprivationent of curiosity as a feeling-of-deprivation. *Journal of Personality Assessment, 82*, 147–157.

Loewenstein, G. (1994). The psychology of curiosity: A review and reinterpretation. *Psychological Bulletin, 116*, 75–98. https://doi.org/10.1037/0033-2909.116.1.75

Luria, A. R. (1966). *Higher cortical functions in man.* New York, NY: Basic Books.

Luus, S., & Watters, J. J. (2012). Gifted early adolescents' negotiating identity: A case study of self-presentation theory. *Australasian Journal of Gifted Education, 21*(2), 19–32.

Lyons, T. (2006). Different countries, same science classes: Students' experiences of school science in their own words. *International Journal of Science Education, 28*(6), 591–613. https://doi.org/10.1080/09500690500339621

Machtinger, E. T. (2014). Using a combined approach of guided inquiry & direct instruction to explore how physiology affects behavior. *American Biology Teacher, 76*(9), 595–600. https://doi.org/10.1525/abt.2014.76.9.5

Maker, C. J., & Schiever, S. W. (2010). *Curriculum development and teaching strategies for gifted learners* (3rd ed.). Austin, TX: Pro-Ed.

McWilliam, E. L. (2009). Teaching for creativity: From sage to guide to meddler. *Asia Pacific Journal of Education, 29*(3), 281–293. https://doi.org/10.1080/02188790903092787

Ministry of Education. (2014). The New Zealand Curriculum online: Science. Retrieved from The New Zealand Curriculum Online website http://nzcurriculum.tki.org.nz/The-New-Zealand-Curriculum/Science

Murphy, P. K., & Alexander, P. A. (2002). What counts? The predictive powers of subject-matter knowledge, strategic processing, and interest in domain-specific performance. *Journal of Experimental Education, 70*(3), 197–214. https://doi.org/10.1080/00220970209599506

National Science and Innovation Agenda. (2015). *National innovation and science agenda report.* Canberra, ACT: Commonwealth of Australia. https://www.industry.gov.au/national-innovation-and-science-agenda-report

Neber, H., & Schommer-Aikins, M. (2002). Self-regulated science learning with highly gifted students: The role of cognitive, motivational, epistemological, and environmental variables. *High Ability Studies, 13*(1), 59–74. https://doi.org/10.1080/13598130220132316

Neufeld, V. R., & Barrows, H. S. (1974). The "McMaster Philosophy": An approach to medical education. *Journal of Medical Education, 49*(11), 1040–1050.

Office of the Chief Scientist. (2013). *Science, technology, engineering and mathematics in the national interest: A strategic approach*. Canberra, ACT: Australian Government. Retrieved from http://www.chiefscientist.gov.au/wp-

Osborne, J. (2008). Engaging young people with science: Does science education need a new vision? *School Science Review, 89*(328), 67–74.

Osborne, J., & Dillon, J. (2008). *Science education in Europe: Critical reflections*. London, England: Nuffield Foundation. Retrieved from Nuffield Foundation website http://www.nuffield foundation.org/science-education-europe

Papanastasiou, E. C., & Zembylas, M. (2004). Differential effects of science attitudes and science achievement in Australia, Cyprus, and the USA. *International Journal of Science Education, 26*(3), 259–280. https://doi.org/10.1080/0950069022000038277

Peairs, K. F. (2011). *The social world of gifted adolescents: Sociometric status, friendship and social network centrality* (Doctoral dissertation). Duke University, Ann Arbor, MI.

Pérez, L. F., & Beltrán, A. J. (2012). Can systemic education end up limiting the gifted person's autonomy? *High Ability Studies, 23*(1), 93–95. https://doi.org/10.1080/13598139.2012.679102

Phillips, N., & Lindsay, G. (2006). Motivation in gifted students. *High Ability Studies, 17*(1), 57–73. https://doi.org/10.1080/13598130600947119

Pintrich, P. R., & Schunk, D. H. (2002). *Motivation in education: Theory, research, and applications*. Upper Saddle River, NJ: Merrill-Prentice Hall.

Polesel, J., Rice, S., & Dulfer, N. (2014). The impact of high-stakes testing on curriculum and pedagogy: A teacher perspective from Australia. *Journal of Education Policy, 29*(5), 640–657. https://doi.org/10.1080/02680939.2013.865082

Potvin, P., & Hasni, A. (2014). Interest, motivation and attitude towards science and technology at K–131 levels: A systematic review of 12 years of educational research. *Studies in Science Education, 50*(1), 85–129. https://doi.org/10.1080/03057267.2014.881626

Quigley, C., Marshall, J. C., Deaton, C. C. M., Cook, M. P., & Padilla, M. (2011). Challenges to inquiry teaching and suggestions for how to meet them. *Science Educator, 20*(1), 55–61. Retrieved from https://files.eric.ed.gov/fulltext/EJ940939.pdf

Rakow, S. J. (1988). The gifted in middle school science. In P. Brandwein & A. H. Passow (Eds.), *Gifted young in science* (pp. 141–154). Washington, DC: National Science Teachers Association.

Rennie, L. J., Goodrum, D., & Hackling, M. (2001). Science teaching and learning in Australian schools. *Results of a National Study Research in Science Education, 31*(4), 455–498. https://doi.org/10.1023/A:1013171905815

Renzulli, J. S. (1986). The three-ring conception of giftedness: A developmental model for creative productivity. In R. J. Sternberg & J. E. Davidson (Eds.), *Conceptions of giftedness* (pp. 53–92). New York, NY: Cambridge University Press.

Renzulli, J. S. (1999). What is this thing called giftedness, and how do we develop it? A twenty-five year perspective. *Journal for the Education of the Gifted, 23*(1), 3–54. https://doi.org/10.1177/016235329902300102

Robinson, A., Dailey, D., Hughes, G., & Cotabish, A. (2014). The effects of a science-focused STEM intervention on gifted elementary students' science knowledge and skills. *Journal of Advanced Academics, 25*(3), 189–213. https://doi.org/10.1177/1932202X14533799

Roeper, A. (1988). The early environment of the child: Experience in a continuing search for meaning. In P. Brandwein & A. H. Passow (Eds.), *Gifted young in science* (pp. 121–139). Washington, DC: National Science Teachers Association.

Rubenstein, L. D., Siegle, D., Reis, S. M., McCoach, D. B., & Burton, M. G. (2012). A complex quest: The development and research of underachievement interventions for gifted students. *Psychology in the Schools, 49*(7), 678–694. https://doi.org/10.1002/pits.21620

Ryan, R. M., & Deci, E. L. (2000). Self-determination theory and the facilitation of intrinsic motivation, social development, and well-being. *American Psychologist, 55*(1), 68–78. https://doi.org/10.1037/0003-066X.55.1.68

Sadler, P. M., Sonnert, G., Hazari, Z., & Tai, R. (2012). Stability and volatility of STEM career interest in high school: A gender study. *Science Education, 96*(3), 411–427. https://doi.org/10.1002/sce.21007

Scanlon, E., Anastopoulou, S., & Kerawalla, L. (2012). Inquiry learning reconsidered: Contexts, representations and challenges. In K. Littleton, E. Scanlon, & M. Sharples (Eds.), *Orchestrating inquiry learning* (pp. 7–30). London, England: Routledge.

Schommer, M., & Dunnell, P. A. (1997). Epistemological beliefs of gifted high school students. *Roeper Review, 19*, 153–156. https://doi.org/10.1080/02783199709553812

Scot, T. P., Callahan, C. M., & Urquhart, J. (2009). Paint-by-number teachers and cookie-cutter students: The unintended effects of high-stakes testing on the education of gifted students. *Roeper Review, 31*(1), 40–52. https://doi.org/10.1080/02783190802527364

Shernoff, D. J., Csikszentmihalyi, M., Shneider, B., & Shernoff, E. S. (2003). Student engagement in high school classrooms from the perspective of flow theory. *School Psychology Quarterly, 18*(2), 158–176. https://doi.org/10.1521/scpq.18.2.158.21860

Silverman, L. K. (2007). Perfectionism: The crucible of giftedness. *Gifted Education International, 23*(3), 233–245. https://doi.org/10.1177/026142940702300304

Steenbergen-Hu, S., Makel, M. C., & Olszewski-Kubilius, P. (2016). What one hundred years of research says about the effects of ability grouping and acceleration on K–12 students' academic achievement. *Review of Educational Research, 86*(4), 849–899. https://doi.org/10.3102/0034654316675417

Sulkowski, M. L., Demaray, M. K., & Lazarus, P. J. (2012). Connecting students to schools to support their emotional well-being and academic success. *Communiqué, 40*(7), 1, 20–22.

VanTassel–Baska, J. (2012). Curriculum issues. *Gifted Child Today, 36*(1), 71–75. https://doi.org/10.1177/1076217512465289

Vedder-Weiss, D., & Fortus, D. (2012). Adolescents' declining motivation to learn science: A follow- up study. *Journal of Research in Science Teaching, 49*(9), 1057–1095. https://doi.org/10.1002/tea.21049

Vogl, K., & Preckel, F. (2014). Full-time ability grouping of gifted students. *The Gifted Child Quarterly, 58*(1), 51–68. https://doi.org/10.1177/0016986213513795

Vygotsky, L. S. (1978). *Mind in society.* Cambridge, MA: Harvard University Press.

Watters, J. J. (1985). Science research project: An experience in discovery learning. *Australian Science Teachers Journal, 31*, 35–38.

Watters, J. J., & Diezmann, C. M. (1997). Optimizing activities to meet the needs of young children gifted in mathematics and science. In P. Rillero & J. Allison (Eds.), *Creative childhood experiences: Integrating science and math through projects, activities, and centers.* Washington, DC: ERIC/CSMEE.

Watters, J. J., & Diezmann, C. M. (2003). The gifted student in science: Fulfilling potential. *Australian Science Teachers Journal, 49*(3), 46–53.

Watters, J. J., & Diezmann, C. M. (2016). Engaging elementary students in learning science: An analysis of classroom dialogue. *Instructional Science, 44*(1), 25–44. https://doi.org/10.1007/s11251-015-9364-7

Watters, J. J., & Ginns, I. S. (1999, July). *Development of a learning community in a science classroom.* Paper presented at the Annual Meeting of the Australasian Science Education Research Association, (8–11 July), Rotorua, New Zealand.

Wentzel, K. R., & Brophy, J. E. (2015). *Motivating students to learn* (4th ed.). London, England: Taylor & Francis.

West, A. (2007). Practical work for the gifted in science. In K. S. Taber (Ed.), *Science education for gifted learners* (pp. 172–181). London, England: Routledge.

Wideen, M., O'Shea, T., Pye, I., & Ivany, G. (1997). High-stakes testing and the teaching of science. *Canadian Journal of Education, 22*(4), 428. https://doi.org/10.2307/1585793

Wolf, S. J., & Fraser, B. J. (2008). Learning environment, attitudes and achievement among middle-school science students using inquiry-based laboratory activities. *Research in Science Education, 38*(3), 321–341. https://doi.org/10.1007/s11165-007-9052-y

Wright-Scott, K. (2018). *The social-emotional well-being of the gifted child and perceptions of parent and teacher social support* (Unpublished PhD thesis). Queensland University of Technology, Brisbane, Australia.

Zoller, U. (2011). Science and technology education in the STES context in primary schools: What should it take? *Journal of Science Education and Technology, 20*(5), 444–453. https://doi.org/10.1007/s10956-011-9306-3

James (Jim) Watters, PhD, is an Adjunct Professor in Education at the Queensland University of Technology (QUT). Jim draws on over 30 years of experience as a science teacher and science teacher educator. His particular interest has been in the education of students gifted in science and mathematics (more recently rebadged as STEM). Jim has run enrichment programs, provided professional development, advised government on policy, supervised graduate students in gifted education, taught pre-service and in-service teachers in gifted education courses, and published internationally in-gifted education. He has a strong commitment to apply research to practice.

STEAM in Gifted Education in Korea

37

Jiyoung Ryu, Youngju Lee, Youngmin Kim, Payal Goundar, Jihyun Lee, and Jae Yup Jung

Contents

J. Ryu (✉) · Y. Lee · Y. Kim
Korea Advanced Institute of Science and Technology, GIFTED, Daejeon, South Korea
e-mail: jryu01@kaist.ac.kr; creativity@kaist.ac.kr; entedu@kaist.ac.kr

P. Goundar
UNSW, Sydney, NSW, Australia
e-mail: z5023632@unsw.edu.au

J. Lee
School of Education, The University of New South Wales, Sydney, NSW, Australia
e-mail: jihyun.lee@unsw.edu.au

J. Y. Jung
GERRIC/School of Education, The University of New South Wales, Sydney, NSW, Australia
e-mail: Jae.Jung@unsw.edu.au

© Springer Nature Singapore Pte Ltd. 2021
S. R. Smith (ed.), *Handbook of Giftedness and Talent Development in the Asia-Pacific*,
Springer International Handbooks of Education,
https://doi.org/10.1007/978-981-13-3041-4_35

Abstract

Developing an education system that caters for a diverse range of learners while keeping up with the ever-changing demands of a global twenty-first century society is a feat that countries worldwide are grappling with. The South Korean education system in the past decade has seen an upheaval in the agenda set for Korean students in preparation for an economy that will require further creativity and innovation to remain viable. Gifted education in particular has seen significant investment in the further expansion and development of specialised programs and curriculum, with the most recent government plan for the promotion of gifted and talented education (2013–2017) focusing on the utilisation of the STEAM education model. STEAM is an acronym for the educational methods of *Science, Technology, Engineering, Arts, and Mathematics*, that incorporates the arts with STEM (*Science, Technology, Engineering, and Mathematics*) subjects. The STEAM pedagogy is based on the belief that students' knowledge and skills of STEM subjects can be further enhanced through the arts by developing students' capacity for creativity and innovation while they try to solve real-life problems or design and make science-related products (Ministry of Science and Technology [MEST], 2011a). The second basic plan to foster and support the human resources in science and technology (MEST, 2011–2015). With a range of studies identifying positive relationships between gifted education and STEAM education (An & Yoo, 2015; Kwon, Heo, & Yang, 2015; Lee, Kim, & Moon, 2013), the journey of how South Korea has incorporated STEAM education within gifted education and the ramifications makes for a significant case to explore. Hence, the current status of STEAM education for gifted students in South Korea is presented in this chapter.

Keywords

STEAM · Gifted education · Science · Technology · Mathematics · Gifted students

The aims in this chapter are to:
1. Define STEAM from a South Korean perspective.
2. Describe how STEAM education integrates gifted education in South Korea.
3. Provide some implications for STEAM for gifted students in South Korea.

Introduction of STEAM Education in Gifted Education in South Korea

The Korean government introduced gifted education in the public school system in 2003, after the government passed the Gifted Education Promotion Act in 2002. Since the introduction, the Korean Department of Education reviews and renews both the gifted education programs and curriculum every five years. A discussion of STEAM education in South Korea, that incorporates provisions for gifted students, will be provided in this chapter.

Gifted Education in Korea

In Korea, gifted students are catered for within education institutions in four distinct ways: primary school-based gifted enrichment classes, education departmental gifted education centres, university gifted education centres, and special high schools (Korea Educational Development Institute [KEDI], 2018).

Gifted Enrichment Classes Within Primary Schools

Gifted classes for students in Years 5 and 6 are offered within public primary schools. They are typically arranged as an after-school enrichment program or extra-classes on Saturdays, with a disciplinary focus of mathematics and science. This approach to upper-primary gifted education started in Korea in 2003. The Department of Education requires schools providing gifted education to have at least 100 hours of instruction per year for a typical class of about 20 gifted students.

Gifted Education Centres

Gifted education centres are established outside of the school program and operated by the Education Department of the City Counsel for Years 5 and 6 gifted students. The class structure and requirements are the same as those in the gifted classes within a public primary school (i.e., at least 100 hours of classes for a class size of about 20 students, offered on Saturday). However, there is only one gifted education centre per municipal area, and therefore, admission to the gifted education centres tends to be considered as more competitive and more attractive for parents and students alike.

University-Run Gifted Education Centres

Currently, there are 27 university-run gifted education centres for students in Year 6–8, which is funded by the Department of Science, Information and Communication Technologies (KEDI, 2018). Gifted teachers in the university-run gifted education centres are typically university lecturers or higher degree program students. Many Korean parents consider the university-run gifted education centres as highly relevant for their children's future education, and thus, it is a popular option for highly able students to apply.

High Schools for Gifted Students

Perhaps the most widely known form of gifted education provision in Korea is high schools for gifted students. This type of high school only caters for students in Years 10–12. There are two types of high schools that are officially regarded as gifted schools: *Gifted High Schools* and *Science High Schools* (Choi & Hong, 2009). There are only eight Gifted High Schools across all provinces of Korea, and they are the Korean Science Gifted High School, Seoul Science High School, Kyung-Gi Science High School, Daejeon Science High School, Daegu Science High School, Kwang-Joo Science High School, Sejong Arts and Science Gifted School, and Incheon Arts and Science Gifted School (KEDI, 2018). While these eight schools are considered specifically *Gifted High Schools*, the inclusion of 'Science' within the school names also indicates a strong focus on science education. Students living in any part of Korea can apply to any of these Gifted High Schools. Admission to such High Schools is highly competitive, with only a 10% success rate.

On the other hand, admission to *Science High Schools* is slightly less competitive than admission to the *Gifted High Schools*. There are 20 Science High Schools in Korea, and the application is open only to local students living in the cities and provinces where the school is located (KEDI, 2018). Due to this residential limitation, students in other cities or other provinces cannot apply to out-of-city or out-of-province Science High Schools.

Selection of Students in Gifted Classes and Gifted Schools in Korea

Typical admission processes across different types of gifted education programs and gifted schools involve a three-stage application. For gifted classes within a primary school and the government-run gifted centres, the (1) first stage of application is through documents that students put together. The required documents include teacher recommendation letter, teacher observation logs, student personal essay, and school report cards. Once students pass the first application process, the (2) second stage is to sit in an academic aptitude test targeted to assess problem-solving and critical thinking skills. The test is developed by the Korean Institution of Educational Evaluation. The (3) third and final stage requires an interview with gifted teachers, with much of the interview content determined by each school and each centre (KEDI, 2018). The interview content ranges from asking about scientific knowledge or personal experiences to asking the applicants to conduct laboratory work as part of the interview.

Admission to university-run gifted education centres has a similar process, with: (1) the initial submission of relevant documents; (2) sitting a test for problem-solving and critical skills; followed by (3) an interview. The difference is that students are admitted for specific majors (mathematics, science, ICT and invention, which are classes where students make actual products based on their own creative ideas), and the test itself is developed within each university gifted education centre (KEDI, 2018).

Both *Gifted High Schools* and *Science High Schools* have the same three-stage admission procedure. Students are allowed to apply to multiple gifted high schools, but the date of the testing in the second phase of the admission process is set as the same date across all Gifted High Schools, requesting students to choose one high school. This second stage of the admission process, which is scholastic aptitude testing, is the most competitive procedure for admission with only 10% of students being selected in this process. Many gifted students apply to one of the eight Gifted High Schools (listed above) first (typically the admission deadline is in April with the admission result announcement in August). Then, those who are not admitted to the Gifted High Schools tend to apply to a Science High School (typically admission deadline is in September with the admission result announcement in November).

Current Trends of Gifted and STEAM Education in Korea

As described above, most of the gifted programs and gifted schools have a strong curriculum focus on science and mathematics. In Korea, gifted students are considered to be those who have a high ability in science and mathematics. In the 2010 government report, *Future Korea with Creative Human Resource and Advanced Scientific Technology*, the Korean Ministry of Education defined six national core tasks, and one of them was to foster the world-class development of science-related human resources. In order to cater for this core task, adjustments were made to all gifted and talented classes, which include the system-wide adoption of STEAM curriculum and programs. STEAM is an acronym for the educational methods combining Science, Technology, Engineering, Arts, and Mathematics, which essentially incorporates Arts Education with STEM (Science, Technology, Engineering and Mathematics) subjects. Arts Education in the Korean curriculum refers to a raft of skills and practices that requires the design and implementation of new and innovative ideas, through Music, Dance, Visual Arts (painting and sculpture), Writing, and Drama and Oral Presentation (Peak et al., 2011, pp. 8–9). It was believed that there would be a significant synergy in learning when Arts Education and STEM subjects are taught simultaneously; students can utilise scientific knowledge and innovation in creating their arts work while they can use imagination and special-visual effects that might have been learned in Arts classes into the development of science projects.

Arguably, creativity is one of the core components in STEAM education. The construct of creativity is defined as "the optimal interaction among personal, process, social, and environment factors by which an individual or group produces an idea or product that is judged to be novel and appropriate by experts of a relevant context". This definition is an adaptation of Plucker et al. (2004) from their "meta-analysis of 30 refereed journal articles" (Lassig, 2009, p. 230). Creativity occurs naturally in both Arts and STEM domains where students are encouraged to take new, even non-conventional, perspectives on planning and designing investigations in the STEAM classes. Further, the promise that STEAM curriculum and programs held in nurturing creative human resource development, flexible ideas, a defiant mind, and integrated thinking, required special provisions

Table 1 Numbers and percentages of students enrolled in the gifted programs in Korean public schools by the focused subject areas in the 2017 Korean school system

Math	Science	STEAM	ICT	Invention	Liberal arts	Language	Music	Arts	Sports	Others
13,172 (12.1%)	16,900 (15.5%)	54,396 (49.8%)	5,193 (4.8%)	4,563 (4.2%)	4,096 (3.7%)	2,232 (2%)	1,934 (1.8%)	1,679 (1.5%)	579 (0.5%)	4,522 (4.1%)

Source: KEDI (2018)

be made for gifted students (Ministry of Education Science, and Technology, 2010). The government plan for the promotion of gifted and talented education for the period of 2013–2017 has stressed the need to focus on creative human resource development, highlighting the important role STEAM education can play in supporting this goal. With strong governmental support, STEAM education has evolved into the premier pedagogy for gifted and talented students to support their high abilities and creative minds in Korea.

The number of students enrolled in the gifted programs in the Korean public schools (Table 1) suggests a positive reception of the STEM subjects including STEAM among the gifted students in Korea. According to the 2017 Korean school system database, the majority (86.4%) out of a total of 109,226 students who were identified as gifted in Korea were taking STEM or STEAM-related classes (KEDI, 2018). In contrast, only about 13.60% of the gifted students in Korea were taking non-STEM subject areas such as liberal arts, language, music, arts, and sports.

Currently, the Department of Education in Korea provides gifted teachers with the STEAM curriculum manuals and guidelines and support materials for teacher training on STEAM curriculum. Within the Government's framework, teachers who are interested in the development of the STEAM curriculum and program design the curriculum for their own students. Gifted High Schools and Science High Schools have implemented STEAM subjects in all classes (see Table 2). The Gifted Education Centres across the country, which are managed by selective universities and the government offices of Education (at the Metropolitan and Provincial levels) in Korea, also have implemented STEAM-based programs in the majority of their classes: 73.1% classes (1,358 out of 1,857) run by the Department of Education and 61.45% classes (518 out of 843) organised and offered at universities. As of 2017, a total of 3,315 general gifted classes are offered at the regular elementary, middle and high schools in Korea, with 2,288 classes (69%) having STEAM-based classes. Overall, across all gifted education providers, 71.2% classes (4,575 out of 6,426) have implemented STEAM-based gifted programs, showing the fluid merging of STEAM programs within gifted education (KEDI, 2018).

Table 2 Numbers and percentages of STEAM curriculum coverage in the gifted education schools and centres in Korea

	Gifted High Schools and Science High Schools	Gifted education centres run by Department of Education	Gifted education centres run by university	Gifted classes in regular schools	Total
Number of classes using STEAM	411	1,358	518	2,288	4,575
Total number of classes	411	1,857	843	3,315	6,426
%	100%	73.13%	61.45%	69.02%	71.20%

Source: KEDI (2018)

Why STEAM in South Korea?

The introduction of the STEAM programs in Korean education in 2011 originated as a concept for all and not just for gifted students. The introduction of STEAM strategic plans into elementary and middle schools (2011) and then into high schools (2018) was in response to startling international student assessment results that indicated a lack of interest and enjoyment for STEM-based subjects. In the *Program for International Student Assessment* (PISA), Korean students ranked 55th out of 57 PISA participating countries in interest for science and ranked 43rd and 27th out of 50 countries for confidence in mathematics and science, respectively (OECD, 2007). Nearly identical results were found in the *Trends in International Mathematics and Science Study* (TIMSS), with Korean students ranked 43rd and 29th out of 50 TIMSS participating countries for enjoyment in mathematics and science, respectively, in spite of their rank at 2nd in mathematics achievement and 4th in science achievement in the eighth-grade results (Mullis, Martin, & Foy, 2008).

These international comparative results attracted much attention from the Korean government to take appropriate actions to increase the students' intrinsic engagement in mathematics and science. Efforts centred on ensuring that there was enthusiasm to learn these subjects at the tertiary level and for students to choose STEM-related careers (Ministry of Education, Science and Technology, 2011a, 2011b). Accordingly, the Korean government opted for reform in educational curriculum and teaching pedagogy that would encourage students to question, wonder, and actively engage with STEM subjects in a genuine manner. The adoption of STEAM pedagogy was considered as the best solution for correcting the misalignment between current STEM teaching pedagogy and low student interest, engagement, and motivation.

STEAM Curriculum at the Policy Level

With all Korean schools required to follow the national curriculum set by the Ministry of Education, introducing STEAM through the national curriculum has allowed for large-scale dissemination of the pedagogy. To support such a large-scale adoption, the Korean government published a guideline illustrating the essential elements of STEAM education programs (Korea Foundation for the Advancement of Science and Creativity [KOFAC], 2016). The aim of this guideline is to help STEAM program developers and teachers to understand the main purpose, basic concepts, and learning standards of STEAM education and to be able to develop and evaluate their own STEAM programs.

It is suggested in the first element of the STEAM education guideline that teachers will need to understand the main purpose of STEAM education and assess whether the utilisation of a STEAM education program will be appropriate for their students and for their class. Considerations as to the learning dispositions of students, that is, whether students would have the capacity to integrate the disciplines within STEAM, are necessary in addressing the first element. Currently, such evaluation by teachers has led to the expansion of STEAM education for gifted and talented students, particularly when the teachers find the STEAM program relevant to address the needs of the students seeking intellectually challenging tasks in the school curriculum (KOFAC, 2017a).

The second element of the STEAM education guideline requires teachers to ensure that the STEAM education program follows the notions of: increasing students' interest; making connections to real-world problems; and cultivating thinking abilities to integrate knowledge and information from various academic subjects (KOFAC, 2017a). In the Korean government's guidelines of STEAM classes (KOFAC, 2017a), the aim is for students to experience successful problem-solving cases, gaining a sense of accomplishment, while also developing resilience and perseverance in the face of adversity, according to the guidelines. The student-centred curriculum development and implementation can provide continuous motivation for students and a keen sense of interest in science and science-related subjects.

In the third element that focuses on the learning standards of STEAM, the steps involved in designing lessons that adopt a STEAM pedagogy are essentially defined. The *learning standard* of the STEAM education program acts as perhaps the most beneficial element for teacher instruction in how to develop a STEAM education program. With clear steps and guiding questions, the *learning standard* element provides concrete support in developing a STEAM education program. The element is broken down into further three sub-elements and centres on the *presentation of situations*, *creative design*, and *emotional connection*. These three sub-elements of learning standards of STEAM education are believed to be the cornerstones of STEAM education (KOFAC, 2017b).

- *Presentation of situations*: Teachers are expected to provide a scenario for students to be able to utilise their own real-life situations. They set up the investigation by introducing a real-world problem for students to work on. At this stage, the STEAM teachers are expected to stimulate students' initial curiosity and interest as well as understanding of the issues at hand.
- *Creative design*: Students develop ideas and plans to solve the problem presented. Students' ideas come to life as they start to implement their ideas by designing a product to solve the problem.
- *Emotional connection*: Students think through their challenges in creating and designing new products. This sub-element encourages program planning that allows students to reflect on their project and engage in emotional connections (such as joy, interest, and feeling challenged) to their product development.

The final element concentrates on the *evaluation of STEAM education*, ensuring teachers are thinking as to how students are presented with opportunities for reflection and use of metacognition throughout the STEAM education program. Also, teachers evaluate whether their own STEAM classes were able to provide opportunities for students to experience success through idea generation, problem-solving or product development (Kang & Kim, 2014; Kim & Choi, 2012).

As shown in Table 3 below, the guidelines and specific elements of the STEAM education program encapsulate the outlined purpose, concept, learning standards, and evaluation. Questions to ask for each specific element are also presented to serve

Table 3 Guideline and specific elements of the STEAM educational program in South Korea

Category	Specific element	Questions to ask	
Purpose of STEAM	Nurturing talents for integration	Is the class appropriate for the purpose of nurturing talents for integration?	
Concept of STEAM education	Increasing students' interest	Is the class designed to increase the students' interest in scientific technology?	
	Connection to the real world	Is the theme related to scientific technology in the real world?	
	Cultivation of integrated thinking abilities	Is the program designed to cultivate the integrated thinking abilities of students?	
Learning standards of STEAM	Presentation of situations	Connection to the real world	Does the class present problematic contexts for students to solve in the real world?
		Interest and immersion	Is it a specific context that can arouse the interest of students and is appropriate for their level?
	Creative design	Creativity	Is the process of creative design clearly revealed for the students to think about how they will solve the problem?
		Focusing on students	Is the class made up of activities focusing on play and experiences, and is there a process for the students to personally devise and think about the issues at hand?
		Results (ideas)	Is the class designed for various results (or ideas) to be presented by each student (or group) as a result of creative design?
		Use of tools	Is the class designed for students to solve problems using devices from the real world?
	Emotional connection	Solving problems	Are the contents presented in the context presentation step for students to feel the joys of success in solving a problem?
		Learning through cooperation	Is the class designed for students to solve problems through cooperation in coming up with their results?
		Spirit of challenge	Is the class guided for students to challenge new tasks through the process of solving problems?
Evaluation of STEAM education	Detailed perspective	Is it made to evaluate the experience of success for students having solved the problem?	
		Are various results (ideas) analysed in the evaluation of the students?	
		Is the aim to conduct not a results-focused evaluation but rather an evaluation focusing on the process and its steps?	

Source: KOFAC (2016, pp. 33–34)

as teachers' self-questioning and a checklist. An example of a STEAM topic along with descriptions of how it corresponds to the specific elements of the STEAM curriculum planning was drawn from the KOFAC document (2016) and presented in Table 4.

Table 4 Example of a STEAM curriculum

Target	Year 8; Subject areas: Korean, Technology, Science and Mathematics class.	
Theme	Become an environment expert in my village.	
Goal	Reading about environmental issues in our hometown. Raising humanities knowledge through reading Newspaper in Education (NIE). Raising environmentalist that engage with their local community by developing science and technology knowledge through 'question solving process – SW training'.	
Learning standards of STEAM	Presentation of situations	Read environment-related book called '7 mysterious things to save the earth' and present a question that connects book's topic and with a relevant issue impacting the local community. Collect data related to the environmental issue impacting the local community through NIE.
	Creative design	Question analysis through NIE. New idea for solution plan using technical problem solving, divergent thinking and convergent thinking method. Reconstruction of concrete idea by storytelling and pre-sketch. Environmental factor analysis and setting problem-solving variable through concepts in mathematics and science textbooks. Realise related theory, data, problem-solving variable with Scratch, and produce creative environmental improving invention simulation program.
	Emotional touch	Problem-solving accomplishment experienced in the process of invention hypothesis through analysing related data. A sense of challenge and accomplishment through making an environment improving simulation program with Scratch. Through dividing a group into Scratch production and data analysis teams, effective labour distribution and cooperation are required.
Evaluation	Coding linear function with a variable. Environment tour preparation: and feedback on other groups' project. Each group manages exhibition booth: environment tour. After the environment tour, brainstorm and share any improvement ideas. Project final confirmation and examination of goal attainment.	

Source: KOFAC (2017b). 2017 STEAM Best practices for middle schools

Models of STEAM Education

In order to incorporate the STEAM curriculum within schools, the Ministry of Education of Korea has suggested three general models of STEAM classrooms. They are broadly divided into: *classes within a STEAM subject*, *classes across multiple STEAM subjects*, and *STEAM learning in afterschool programs* (KOFAC, 2016). It is expected that students not only cultivate science-related knowledge, but also learn how to connect the knowledge from other STEAM subject areas.

- *Classes within a STEAM subject* emphasise gaining knowledge and skills of one specific STEAM subject while linking it to learning about other STEAM subjects. For instance, a science teacher in a science-focused STEAM class would present a lesson about, for example, water evaporation. The science teacher will focus on scientific aspects of water evaporation, while presenting potential applications and implications about water evaporation from the mathematical, technological, or artistic point of view, during the science lesson. Thus, the teacher in one subject area (e.g., science) presents how learning about the same topic can occur across different STEAM subject areas. Studies on integrated science, technology, and engineering education showed the positive effects on students' content knowledge (Yoon, Dyehouse, Lucietto, Diefes-Dux, & Capobianco, 2014) as well as attitudes towards STEAM subjects (Becker & Park, 2011; Stohlmann, Moore, & Roehrig, 2012).
- *Classes across multiple STEAM subjects* encourage topic-based learning across multiple STEAM subjects. In this model, teachers specialised in different STEAM areas are involved and teach the same topic to the students. For example, a science teacher may teach the topic of water evaporation from the scientific point, a technology teacher may introduce how technology can control and manage water evaporation in a technology class, and an art teacher may ask the students to draw a picture representing water evaporation in an art class. The curriculum is developed, managed, and implemented by teachers in multiple STEAM subjects through this integrated education model. Students can choose a topic and learning about the topic takes place across the classrooms of multiple subject areas. The aim of this model is that students make the connections from what they have learned in various STEAM subject areas.
- *STEAM in an after-school program* classes focus on hands-on activities and creating a product during after-school or Saturday gifted classes. Students are asked to solve a STEAM-related problem that may occur in the real world, such as preventing cyber bullying under the main title of 'digital world'. This type of after-school program is seen as an enrichment program. The STEM enrichment program in particular is known to improve students' science concepts and knowledge (Cotabish, Dailey, Robinson, & Hughes, 2013), and academic achievement across different subject domains such as mathematics, science, and reading (Kendricks, Nedunuri, & Arment, 2013; Olivarez, 2014). Existing educational curriculum can be marginally changed to create a project-based learning program

or reconstructed to develop separate STEAM-based programs for after-school activities.

- *STEAM Research and Education (R & E) Program* offers opportunities for high school students to engage in STEAM education beyond typical classroom settings. *The Korea Foundation for the Advancement of Science and Creativity* (KOFAC) sponsors this program throughout schools by funding up to 130 student projects per year. The program is designed to offer high school students' opportunities to conduct research on real-life applications. Previous studies have shown that application of scientific knowledge and skills to solve real-life problems contributed to the improvement of students' science achievement as well as academic engagement, civic responsibility, and resilience in learning (Newman, Dantzler, & Coleman, 2015). Students identify a real-life problem that they want to investigate, define research questions, design a research methodology to answer the research questions, and submit their research proposal to the KOFAC. The completed research projects are shared at the STEAM R & E Festival, which takes place once a year. Examples of KOFAC-funded research topics include 'biodegradation of synthetic plastics using chicken feathers' Keratin', 'effective road traffic signs' 'angle on the road considering a driver's judgment time', and 'development of eco-friendly material using a spider-web' (KOFAC, 2017b).
- *Outreach Programs* offer STEAM education through a partnership with business industry providers, university and research institutes, and government-funded research centres to provide students with science- and technology-related experiences. The program scheme was established in 2013 and about 10 organisations are currently involved to offer STEAM outreach programs to high school students in Korea. In this scheme, research mentors of the partnership organisation develop the STEAM education programs. Previous research indicates that such STEM-related outreach programs have helped to improve students' cognitive skills, design skills, engineering skills (Baran, Canbazoglu Bilici, Mesutoglu, & Ocak, 2016), as well as increasing interest in STEM careers (Wyss, Heulskamp, & Siebert, 2012). Within Korea, students tend to enjoy and be satisfied with STEAM outreach programs that they attended, specifically on the aspect of being exposed to various science-related careers (KOFAC, 2017a).

STEAM Program Topics

The *Korea Foundation for the Advancement of Science and Creativity* (KOFAC) suggests three types of programs that the schools may adapt and develop further: integrated STEAM-related subjects program, advanced product utilisation, and future occupations.

- *Integrated STEAM-related subjects program* is centred on the topic in a subject with cooperation of teachers and on-site professionals outside of the schools. An example topic would be 'making bio-art with neurons'; students learn about the role and functions of neurons in a human body, and then, use an application called

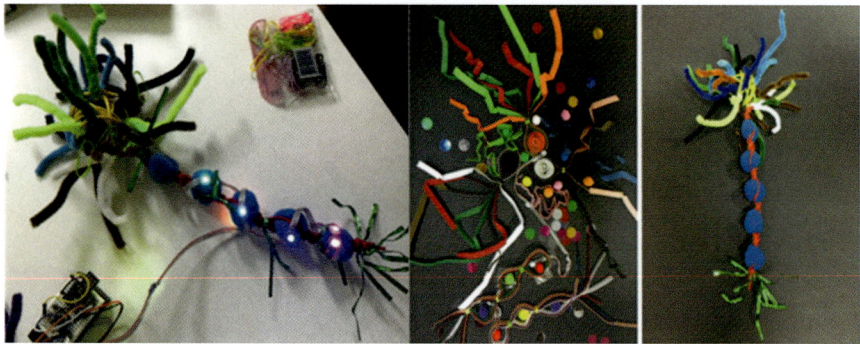

Fig. 1 An example of a STEAM project in the integrated STEAM-related subjects. (Source: KOFAC (2017b). Making bio-art with neurons)

'neural network simulator' to simulate how real neurons and related nerves create their own stories and establish an appropriate nervous system accordingly. Furthermore, LED lights, bread board, electric wires, steel wires, threads, or other materials are used to make various structures of a neuron (see Fig. 1). In this model, the learning focus is for students to be able to make connections across different STEAM areas.

- In *advanced product utilisation,* students will have the opportunity to be exposed to and use equipment, products, and applications that are based on advanced technological development. An example is elementary students' 'making smart name tags to protect pets'. Students create pet necklaces with near-field communication (NFC) stickers that can enable the cognition of relevant information, and then, interlock the necklace with a smartphone's NFC application. Through this activity, the students have a hands-on, real-world experience about how the advanced technology can solve a real-life problem.

- *Future occupations program* sets a STEAM-related future job as a topic. Students are exposed to the most advanced types of technology such as *Artificial Intelligence* (AI) or the *Internet of Things* (IoT) and learn about the applications. An example topic would be 'personalised smart car designer'. Students would collect information about smart cars on their own, select a specific role of smart cars, conduct research on high-tech and forthcoming technology, and think about various jobs that are related to smart cars and new technology such as light or autoregulation developers. These activities focusing on future jobs provide opportunities for the students to predict what future technology may look like and how it can be developed and impact professions of the future.

Teacher Development for STEAM Education

The STEAM education in Korean schools started with teacher training in STEAM, which was established and supported by the *Korea Foundation for the Advancement of Science and Creativity* (KOFAC). Since 2011, the KOFAC has taken the role of developing and imparting STEAM curriculum and STEAM-related projects to STEAM participating schools. Further, the KOFAC founded the training centres for STEAM teachers with various training programs.

In-Service STEAM Teacher Training Program

The in-service STEAM teacher training program offers three levels of training sessions: entry, basic, and advanced levels (KOFAC, 2015).

- *Entry-level training.* Since 2012, more than 50,000 teachers completed the entry-level STEAM training, which included 15 hours of online training on the fundamental philosophies and national policies of STEAM, the basic components and key elements of STEAM education and real STEAM application lessons. Teachers who complete the entry level of STEAM education can participate in the basic level.
- *Basic-level training.* Teachers need to complete 15 hours of online training, trying to improve their competency to use STEAM in their classrooms. Teachers are trained to become familiarised with STEAM content and also to understand and evaluate the STEAM curriculum. Teachers can apply the STEAM curriculum in their classes after completing the basic level. By 2015, there have been 103,858 teachers who participated in the basic level online training (KOFAC, 2015).
- *Advanced-level training.* Teachers who complete both entry and basic levels of STEAM training can participate in the advanced level. The advanced-level training has multiple components: 10 hours of online training, 40 hours of on-site training at the Teacher Training Center for Cutting-edge Science run by KOFAC, 5 hours of field training and 5 hours of attendance in STEAM fairs and exhibitions (KOFAC, 2015). In the advanced level, teachers are engaged in collaborative peer learning in experiencing and learning about updated technology and science knowledge and skills to build STEAM curriculum with other teachers. Also, the training covers the curriculum development to design how to link STEAM education to after-school programs or school curriculum. It is expected that teachers, who completed the advanced level, would be able to create their own STEAM related content for their students. As of 2017, a total of 3,262 teachers have completed the advanced level, and most of them continue to participate in teacher-led study groups on STEAM programs. Currently, 1,117 teacher-led study groups exist in Korea (Ministry of Education, 2017), and their STEAM curriculum designs are available on the KOFAC homepage (http://steam.kofac.re.kr) for others to use. In addition, the Ministry of Education has designated STEAM leader schools as STEAM exemplary schools to assist STEAM programs in other schools. There are 166 STEAM leader schools across the country, and among them, 52 schools have been provided with special teacher training in developing curriculum for creative and integrative education.

Overseas Professional Development for Teachers

Efforts to further expand the professional development of Korean teachers beyond localised STEAM pedagogy knowledge has been seen in the KOFAC provision of overseas training programs for Korean teachers to learn about STEAM education programs outside Korea. As of 2017, 166 teachers have visited STEAM educational institutions, STEAM related schools, science institutions, and research centres in the USA, England, Germany, Finland, Canada, and the Netherlands through the KOFAC program.

The purpose of this overseas training program for the teachers is to look at how educational institutions in other developed countries are using, applying, and developing STEAM education. The teachers are expected to apply what they learn overseas to their own STEAM curriculum and program in South Korean schools when they finish their overseas visitation. In alignment with the general purpose of STEAM education, teachers are to learn about various teaching and learning strategies to increase students' interest and enjoyment in STEAM-related subjects. The previous participants have formed the teachers' research society, aided through financial support from the Ministry of Education of Korea to exchange and share knowledge and skills and further develop their specialty in STEAM education.

Engagement with the Education Community

Attempts at wider engagement of STEAM education with the education community include the sharing of developed STEAM curriculum with the general public through the KOFAC website (http://steam.kofac.re.kr). An annual STEAM conference is also held to promote the teachers' development of STEAM curriculum. At the annual conference, teachers across the elementary, middle, and high school levels present their STEAM curriculum to other teachers as well as the general audience. Moreover, the conference provides an opportunity for teachers to converse with others to exchange opinions or improve their own ideas. The STEAM curriculum presented in the past conference is also publicly available to the general audience through the KOFAC STEAM website.

With a steady stream of initiatives and programs supporting teacher development in implementing STEAM education, teachers who have completed the advanced level indicate that they recognise the necessity of STEAM education and believe that STEAM education has helped their students in the areas of problem-solving and convergent thinking skills (Kim, Lee, & Kim, 2016a). However, it also important to acknowledge the difficulties faced by teachers when implementing new pedagogies that are as complex as STEAM. Research shows that the application of STEAM education is still seen as difficult for many Korean teachers, due to insufficient time to develop understandings across STEAM subjects (Kang et al., 2018). The classroom application of STEAM subjects was also seen as a challenge along with some school leaders' relative lack of understanding of the benefits of STEAM education (Kim et al., 2016b).

Research on the Impact of STEAM on Gifted Education

Research that examined the STEAM education for gifted students in mathematics and science has in general reported positive results. A study on mathematically gifted elementary students noted the positive effect that STEAM education has played on enhancing creative problem-solving skills in mathematics and creative behaviours (Lee, Kim, & Moon, 2013). By developing and applying a STEAM program for mathematically gifted elementary students, students showed high satisfaction in learning mathematical concepts and activities, and their creativity and problem-solving skills were enhanced (Lee, Baek, & Lee, 2013).

Studies on project-based STEAM programs for scientifically gifted elementary students in Korea showed a positive impact on the students' creative problem-solving skills (e.g., Kang & Kim, 2014). Another study conducted to evaluate the effectiveness of a science-focused STEAM program over four weekends for scientifically gifted elementary students showed a positive effect on students' science research ability and self-regulated learning strategies (Kwon, Heo, & Yang, 2015). A study based on a longer period of intervention, that is, over four months, for elementary gifted students demonstrated that the students' ability and skills in the areas of creativity, problem-solving, thoughtfulness, convergence, and communication were enhanced as a result of the application of a STEAM education program (Kim & Moon, 2016). Further, a result of improvement in creative problem-solving skills was shown in the robot programming-based STEAM for gifted middle school classes (Lee, 2015). An intervention study conducted outside of Korea also reported similar findings. Robinson et al. (2014) reported an increased achievement level of gifted elementary students on the measures of science process skills, science concepts, and science content knowledge after STEM-classes focused on science content, inquiry-based instruction, technological applications, and differentiated instruction.

Other research studies have also highlighted the benefits of STEAM education for gifted students not only in the realm of cognitive ability but also in the affective characteristics, such as interest and attitude towards creative development (An & Yoo, 2015). In a study of the effect of STEAM education, students who had STEAM education (6,236 students) showed higher interests, self-efficacy, and self-concept on mathematics and science than students who did not have STEAM education (3,160 students; Kang et al., 2018). Also, students who had STEAM education showed higher scores in self-directed learning skills, interest in science, and creative-convergent thinking skills (Jung et al., 2014).

Further research has established how the education system has catered for STEAM within gifted education. Positive results associated with STEAM education and gifted education have come in the form of improved cognitive (Kwon et al., 2015; Lee et al., 2013) and non-cognitive skills (An & Yoo, 2015) including attitudes towards STEM subjects, career outlooks on STEM-related jobs, and STEAM curriculum and classroom satisfaction among the gifted and talented students who have participated in STEAM education. For example, researchers have found that a mathematics-focused STEAM program for gifted middle school students improved students' math-related career orientation and STEAM competencies (Yang & Yoo, 2017). Further, attending a biology-based STEAM program, scientifically gifted middle school students showed improvement in divergent thinking skills (Seo, 2015) as well as high satisfaction on the classes which dealt with the topics related to enhancement of human behaviours in real-life settings (Kang & Seo, 2013).

Conclusion

Initially, STEAM pedagogy was introduced to Korean mainstream education as a way of combatting a lack of interest and enthusiasm shown by the Korean students towards STEM subjects. Over the years, it has evolved to becoming the premier pedagogy for gifted and talented students to support and nourish their high abilities and creative minds. With the third master plan for the promotion of gifted and talented education (2013–2017), STEAM education now plays an important role in supporting gifted education in Korea.

It is also seen as the necessity for the country to continue to build future generations with strong aptitudes and interest in the *Information Technology* (IT) industry areas. STEAM was progressively introduced by the government at a number of levels through the education system, ranging from initiatives at the policy, school, teacher, and community levels. While the implementation of the pedagogy has shown successful student achievement and positive results in improving problem-solving skills and attitudes towards creativity (Kang & Kim, 2014; Kim & Choi; 2012; Lee et al., 2013), and self-efficacy and self-esteem of students within STEM-related subjects (Lee & Choi, 2017; Lee & Lee, 2014), further support at the school level is required to ensure the sustainability of STEAM education as an integrated teaching pedagogy (Kim et al., 2016a). There is still a long way to go in order to ensure STEAM can be an effective approach for gifted and talented students.

In general, STEAM education is still used restrictively, in that the gifted students only receive STEAM education 2–3 hours per week in gifted programs. STEAM, by the nature of its content (incorporating at least a couple of subject areas), cannot be taught or implemented by a single teacher or an expert in a classroom. In order for STEAM education to be continuously used in gifted classes in future, STEAM education may need to be directed towards encouraging students to discover various problems in daily activities on their own and experiencing and conducting independent research activities. Moreover, considering that the gifted programs in regular schools in South Korea are normally conducted after school or on weekends, the availability of team-teaching depending on the teachers' major fields, along with various administrative and financial supports, will continue to be a vital factor to see more expansion of the STEAM curriculum in Korean classrooms.

While the Korean government has offered a range of opportunities to address the needs of teachers in implementing the STEAM pedagogy, there is still insufficient time and administrative support available to thoroughly utilise the provisions. Along with the development of STEAM curriculum and three levels of the STEAM teacher training, more training may be needed for schools to learn about and create possible STEAM applications and models for the future curriculum. While the current state of STEAM within gifted education is still evolving in the Korean education landscape, further research will be required to understand the long-term impact that the STEAM pedagogy has on gifted and talented students. If the research provides an indication of long-term benefits of STEAM education, the future prospects of its application may hold a significant promise for gifted education in Korea.

Cross-references

► Assessment, Pedagogy, and Curriculum: Part IV Introduction
► Creative and Gifted Education in Korea: Using the CATs Model to Illustrate How Creativity Can Grow into Innovation
► Differentiation of Instruction for Gifted Learners: Collated Evaluative Studies of Teacher Classroom Practices
► Gifted Education in the Asia-Pacific: From the Past for the Future – An Introduction
► Highly Able Students in International Schools
► Leadership Development of Gifted Adolescents from a Korean Multicultural Lens
► Learning from International Research Informs Academic Acceleration in Australasia: A Case for Consistent Policy
► Some Implications for the Future of Gifted Education in the Asia-Pacific
► The Lives and Achievements of Four Extraordinary Australians: A Master, a Maker, an Introspector, and an Influencer
► The Predictors of the Decisions by Gifted Students to Pursue STEM Careers: The Case of Brazilian International Students in Australia
► Why Is It So? Interest and Curiosity in Supporting Students Gifted in Science

References

An, H., & Yoo, M. (2015). Analysis of research trends in STEAM education for the gifted. *Journal of Gifted and Talented Education, 25*, 410–420. https://doi.org/10.9722/JGTE.2015.25.3.401
Baran, E., Canbazoglu Bilici, S., Mesutoglu, C., & Ocak, C. (2016). Moving STEM beyond schools: Students' perceptions about an out-of-school STEM education program. *International Journal of Education in Mathematics, Science and Technology, 4*(1), 9–19. https://doi.org/10.1 8404/ijemst.71338
Becker, K., & Park, K. (2011). Effects of integrative approaches among science, technology, engineering, and mathematics (STEM) subjects on students' learning: A preliminary meta-analysis. *Journal of STEM Education: Innovations & Research., 12*(5 & 6), 23–37. https://doi.org/10.4236/ce.2015.68071
Choi, K. M., & Hong, D. S. (2009). Gifted education in Korea: Three Korean high schools for the mathematically gifted. *Gifted Child Today, 32*(2), 42–49. https://doi.org/10.4219/gct-2009-883

Cotabish, A., Dailey, D., Robinson, A., & Hughes, G. (2013). The effects of a STEM intervention on elementary students' science knowledge and skills. *School Science and Mathematics, 113*, 215–226. https://doi.org/10.1111/ssm.12023

Jung, J. S., Min, Y. K., Park, C. D., Lim, S. M., You, J. H., Kim, H. B., … Park, J. Y. (2014). *Study on developing evaluation tools of STEAM education*. Seoul, South Korea: KOFAC.

Kang, H., & Kim, T. (2014). The development of the STEAM project learning program for creative problem-solving of the science gifted in elementary school. *Journal of Gifted/Talented Education, 24*, 1025–1038.

Kang, H., & Seo, H. (2013). The development and application of a life science-based STEAM program for middle school science gifted students. *Korean Science Education Society for the Gifted, 5*, 162–173.

Kang, N. H., Lim, S. M., Byun, S. Y., Lee, J. K., Lee, E. K., Seo, Y. S., & Oh, K. C. (2018). *The effect of STEAM projects: Year 2017*. Seoul, South Korea: KOFAC.

Kendricks, K. D., Nedunuri, K. V., & Arment, A. R. (2013). Minority student perceptions of the impact of mentoring to enhance academic performance in STEM disciplines. *Journal of STEM Education, 14*(2), 38–46. https://search.proquest.com/docview/1355441588?accountid=27828

Kim, G., & Choi, S. (2012). The effects of the creative problem-solving ability and scientific attitude through the science-based STEAM program in the elementary gifted students. *Journal of Korean Elementary Science Education, 31*, 216–226. https://doi.org/10.15267/keses.2012.31.2.216

Kim, M., & Moon, D. (2016). The effect of invention-based STEAM education program on STEAM literacy of the gifted in invention of elementary school. *Journal of Korean Practical Arts Education, 29*, 77–93.

Kim, Y., Lee, Y., & Kim, K. (2016a). An analysis on the perceptions and educational needs of elementary and secondary school teachers for the advanced STEAM professional development. *Journal of Korean Practical Arts Education, 22*, 51–70.

Kim, Y., Lee, Y., & Kim, Y. (2016b). An analysis of school administrators' perceptions of STEAM education. *Journal of Korean Practical Arts Education, 22*, 85–101.

Korea Educational Development Institute (KEDI). (2018). *2018 Statistical yearbook of gifted education in Korea, SM 2019-01*. Seoul, South Korea: Gifted Education Research Centre.

Korea Foundation for the Advancement of Science and Creativity (KOFAC). (2015). *STEAM for future talent*. Seoul, South Korea: KOFAC.

Korea Foundation for the Advancement of Science and Creativity (KOFAC). (2016). *Introduction to STEAM education*. Seoul, South Korea: KOFAC.

Korea Foundation for the Advancement of Science and Creativity (KOFAC). (2017a). *The effect of STEAM projects: Year 2016 analysis*. Seoul, South Korea: KOFAC.

Korea Foundation for the Advancement of Science and Creativity (KOFAC). (2017b). 2017 STEAM R & E lists. STEAM education website. https://steam.kofac.re.kr.

Kwon, S., Heo, S., & Yang, Y. (2015). Effects of self-regulatory learning strategies embed into STEAM programs on science gifted elementary students' scientific inquiry ability. *The Korean Journal of Thinking & Problem Solving, 11*, 45–63.

Lassig, C. J. (2009). Promoting creativity in education from policy to practice: An Australian perspective. In *Proceedings of the seventh ACM conference on creativity and cognition* (pp. 229–238). ACM. https://doi.org/10.1145/1640233.1640269

Lee, G., & Choi, J. (2017). The effects of STEAM-based mathematics class in the mathematical problem-solving ability and self-efficacy. *Journal of Elementary Mathematics Education in Korea, 21*, 663–686.

Lee, H. (2015). *The effect of STEAM-based robot programming education on the creative problem-solving skills of secondary information gifted students*. Master's thesis, Graduate School of Korea National University of Education, Korea.

Lee, M. S., Kim, M. S., & Moon, E. S. (2013). The effect of STEAM instruction on math creative problem-solving ability and creative attitude in elementary math gifted students. *The Journal of the Korean Society for the Gifted and Talented, 12*, 75–94.

Lee, S., Baek, J., & Lee, J. (2013). The development and the effects of educational program applied on STEAM for the mathematical prodigy. *Education of Primary School Mathematics, 16*(1), 35–55. https://doi.org/10.7468/jksmec.2013.16.1.035

Lee, Y., & Lee, H. (2014). The effects of engineering design and scientific inquiry-based STEAM education programs on the interest, self-efficacy and career choices of middle school students. *Journal of Research in Curriculum and Instruction, 18*, 513–540.

Ministry of Education. (2017). *The plan of STEAM education (2018–2022)*. Sejong, South Korea: MOE.

Ministry of Education, Science and Technology. (2010). Future Korea with creative human resources, and advanced science and technology, 2011 Korea government resolution. Seoul, South Korea: MEST.

Ministry of Education, Science and Technology. (2011a). *The second basic plan to foster and support the human resources in science and technology (2011–2015)*. Seoul, South Korea: MEST.

Ministry of Education, Science and Technology. (2011b). *The 2009 revised science curriculum*. Seoul, South Korea: MEST.

Mullis, I. V. S., Martin, M. O., & Foy, P. (with Olson, J. F., Preuschoff, C., Erberber, E., Arora, A., & Galia, J.). (2008). *TIMSS 2007 International Mathematics Report: Findings from IEA's trends in international mathematics and science study at the fourth and eighth grades*. Chestnut Hill, MA: TIMSS & PIRLS International Study Centre, Boston College.

Newman, J. L., Dantzler, J., & Coleman, A. N. (2015). Science in action: How middle school students are changing their world through STEM service-learning projects. *Theory Into Practice, 54*(1), 47–54. https://doi.org/10.1080/00405841.2015.977661

OECD. (2007). *PISA 2006 Science competencies for tomorrow's world* (Analysis) (Vol. 1). Paris, France: OECD Publications.

Olivarez, N. (2014). *The impact of a STEM program on academic achievement of eighth grade students in a South Texas middle school*. Doctoral dissertation, Texas A & M University. http://hdl.handle.net/1969.6/417.

Peak, Y. S., Park, H. J., Kim, Y. M., No, S. K., Park, J. Y., Lee, J. Y., … Han, H. S. (2011). Direction of STEAM education in Korea. *Journal of Learner-Centered Curriculum and Instruction, 11*, 149–171.

Plucker, J. A., Beghetto, R. A., & Dow, G. T. (2004). Why isn't creativity more important to educational psychologists? Potentials, pitfalls, and future directions in creativity research. *Educational Psychologist, 39*, 83–96. https://doi.org/10.1207/s15326985ep3902_1

Robinson, A., Dailey, D., Hughes, G., & Cotabish, A. (2014). The effects of a science-focused STEM intervention on gifted elementary students' science knowledge and skills. *Journal of Advanced Academics, 25*(3), 189–213. https://doi.org/10.1177/1932202X14533799

Seo, H. (2015). *Effects of STEAM-based educational program on the creative thinking ability of scientifically gifted students*. Master's thesis, Graduate School of Kongju National University, Korea.

Stohlmann, M., Moore, T. J., & Roehrig, G. H. (2012). Considerations for teaching integrated STEM education. *Journal of Pre-College Engineering Education Research, 2*(1), 28–34. https://doi.org/10.5703/1288284314653

Wyss, V. L., Heulskamp, D., & Siebert, C. J. (2012). Increasing middle school student interest in STEM careers with videos of scientists. *International Journal of Environmental and Science Education, 7*, 501–522. Retrieved from https://files.eric.ed.gov/fulltext/EJ997137.pdf

Yang, Y., & Yoo, M. (2017). The effect of mathematics-based STEAM program using big data on the creative problem-solving abilities, mathematics career orientation and STEAM core competencies of middle school gifted students. *Journal of Gifted/Talented Education, 27*, 607–629.

Yoon, S., Dyehouse, M., Lucietto, A. M., Diefes-Dux, H. A., & Capobianco, B. M. (2014). The effects of integrated science, technology, and engineering education on elementary students' knowledge and identity development. *School Science and Mathematics, 114*, 380–391. https://doi.org/10.1111/ssm.12090

Jiyoung Ryu is currently working as a Deputy Director at KAIST (*Korea Advanced Institution of Science and Technology*) GIFTED (*Global Institution of Talented Education*). She holds a master's degree in educational psychology (Harvard University) and a doctoral degree in gifted education (Columbia University). Her research interests span education and social/psychological adjustment of economically disadvantaged gifted students, and STEAM education for gifted students.

Youngju Lee is a senior researcher at KAIST GIFTED. She holds a master's degree in child development and a doctoral degree in school psychology. Her research interests are teacher training for gifted teachers and STEAM Education.

Youngmin Kim is a senior researcher at KAIST GIFTED. He holds a doctoral degree in engineering education. He is interested in STEAM education for gifted students and teacher training of gifted teachers.

Payal Goundar is a PhD candidate in the School of Education at the UNSW, Sydney, Australia. Her primary research focus is in the area of actionable knowledge and examining its relevance to critical and creative thinking paradigms of science learning in the classroom.

Jihyun Lee is an associate professor in the School of Education at the UNSW, Sydney, Australia. Her area of research is what to measure and how to best measure non-cognitive constructs in the context of international large-scale assessments and national assessments. During her employment at *Educational Testing Service* (ETS), she worked on the NAEP and PISA questionnaire development, and she continues to research on survey features (e.g., response categories, survey responding behaviours) in measuring non-cognitive constructs. She received a PhD in Measurement and Applied Statistics from Columbia University and a Master in Human Development from Harvard School of Education. She recently held a visiting research position as a TJA fellow at the OECD where she examined the PISA questionnaire features for middle- and low-income countries.

Jae Yup Jung is an associate professor in the School of Education at the UNSW, Sydney, Australia. His primary research focus is on the decision-making of adolescents (including gifted adolescents) on topics such as careers, university entrance, and friendships, usually incorporating motivational and cultural perspectives.

Fostering and Developing Talent in Mentorship Programs: The Mentor's Perspectives

38

Liang See Tan, Jing Yi Tan, and Terence Titus Chia

Contents

L. S. Tan (✉) · J. Y. Tan · T. T. Chia
Centre for Research in Pedagogy and Practice, Office of Education Research, National Institute of Education, Singapore, Singapore
e-mail: liangsee.tan@nie.edu.sg; liangsee@gmail.com; jingyi.tan@nie.edu.sg; terence.chia@nie.edu.sg

© Springer Nature Singapore Pte Ltd. 2021
S. R. Smith (ed.), *Handbook of Giftedness and Talent Development in the Asia-Pacific*,
Springer International Handbooks of Education,
https://doi.org/10.1007/978-981-13-3041-4_36

Abstract

The pivotal role of the mentor in the lives of talented youth has long been recognised in the field of high ability studies, and the significance of mentorship in developing talented youth is frequently discussed with a tenacious view of how mentoring can benefit mentees. Very often, researchers assume that successful experts in their respective domains of work are also competent mentors. Recently, there have also been increasing demands to provide adolescents with diverse learning capacity with more opportunities to be mentored. As a result, there is pressure to expand mentoring programs in schools and research communities. The role of mentors in fostering talents and some of the implications will be highlighted in this chapter. Scientific researchers' understandings of the nature, process, and significance of mentoring will be examined through the reiteration of findings from focus group discussions and professional learning workshops. We posit that these understandings among the scientists are the key elements of quality mentoring experiences for both the mentor and mentee. We note the importance of preparing both the mentor and mentee before the engagement of the mentoring relationship and that it is essential to engage the scientists in examining their intentions and assumptions about the learning needs and personal goals of their mentees. Based on the review of the literature and findings, we suggest directions for future research and make recommendations for practice and policy.

Keywords

Mentorship · Talented adolescent · Talent development · Secondary education · Tertiary education

The aims in this chapter are to:
1. Highlight the pivotal role of mentors in fostering talents in science.
2. Examine the issues and assumptions about mentoring in the literature.
3. Unpack the implications on the shifting landscape in engaging mentors.
4. Emphasise the importance of examining mentors' perspectives about nurturing talents, nuances in mentors' thinking about the work they do, and their capacity to mentor.
5. Discuss the potentials and possibilities of the mentoring relationships.

Introduction

In the field of high ability studies, the pivotal role of the mentor in the lives of gifted and talented youth has long been recognised. Researchers often assume that successful experts in their respective domains of work are also competent mentors and there is generally a tenacious view of how mentoring can benefit mentees. Due to the increasing demands to provide more opportunities for adolescents who are keen on learning more about the scientific world to be mentored, there is tremendous pressure to expand mentoring programs among schools and research communities. There are reasons for us to be concerned about the pressure on the use of expertise in the intellectual communities. We note the importance of preparing both the mentor and mentee before the engagement of the mentoring relationship and that it is essential to engage scientists in examining their intentions and assumptions about the learning needs and personal goals of their mentees. We posit that the nuances in the mentors' thinking about the work they do is the key element of quality mentoring experiences for both the mentor and mentee.

The pivotal role of mentors in fostering talents and the assumptions about the capacity of mentors will be highlighted in this chapter. The shifting landscape in the engagement of mentors will also be unpacked and the importance of examining mentors' beliefs about nurturing talents and their capacity to mentor will be emphasised. Scientific researchers' understandings of the nature, process, and significance of mentoring will be examined through the reiteration of findings from focus group discussions and professional learning workshops. Finally, the potentials and possibilities of mentoring relationships in science will be discussed.

Review of the Pivotal Role of Mentors in Fostering Talents

The unique and pivotal role of mentoring in developing gifts into talents (Assouline & Lupkowski-Shoplik, 2005; Casey & Shore, 2000; Feldhusen, 2005; Jarvin & Subotnik, 2015), and the relationship between mentor and mentee has been documented in the literature of gifted education (Little, Kearney, & Britner, 2010; Olszewski-Kubilius, Subotnik, & Worrell, 2016; Pleiss & Feldhusen, 1995; Subotnik & Rickoff, 2010). Dating back to its roots, the term 'mentor' originates from Homer's epic poem, *The Odyssey* (Anderson & Shannon, 1988). In this Greek mythology, a mentor was an admired provider of advice and a guardian to an entire royal household. Pleiss and Feldhusen (1995) point out that the role of mentor is complex. We cannot understand the mentor merely as an equivalent of teacher. Instead, they are the role models and heroes in the lives of talented adolescents. Very often, mentoring is a channel to develop nuanced understandings in an area of expertise and to stimulate thinking in the area of mentee interest. It is also a means to induct and enculturate those who are new to the community. It serves as a window to the world of practice and immerses the gifted and talented in disciplinary thinking. Hence, mentorship does not imply an internship, an apprenticeship, or a casual haphazard relationship in which the student spends time with a knowledgeable adult (Boston, 1979).

Mentoring is an effective pedagogical practice in meeting the cognitive, social, and emotional needs of the gifted and talented. Talented adolescents typically have an above-average level of confidence and perseverance in their intellectual pursuits. These fast-minded youth need adults to be their intellectual peers. Engaging these adolescents, who are advanced in specific domains, in mentorship is a way to facilitate and develop their potential into talents (Ellingson, Haeger, & Feldhusen, 1986; Grybek, 1997). In his seminal study, Bloom (1984, 1985a, b) interviewed 120 individuals who achieved excellence in sports, arts, mathematics, chess, and science and who grew to be talented in highly customised learning environments nurtured by a personal mentor (1985b). He concluded that mentors are essential for talented individuals to achieve eminence. Gagné's (2003, 2004, 2007) *Differentiated Model of Giftedness and Talent* (DMGT) states that giftedness is perceived as potential and a gift that needs to be transformed into talents through a developmental process that is catalysed by mentors, parents, teachers, and peers. A mentor-paced program is typically recommended to develop the fullest potential of academically talented adolescents (Ellingson et al., 1986; Lupkowski, Assouline, & Vestal, 1992; Stanley, 1978). For example, university Professor of Chemistry and Nobel Laureate, Glenn Seaborg (1991) who served as Chairman of Science Service for 25 years, noted the impressive level of excellence these talented adolescents achieved with the involvement of committed mentors in contributing to the fostering of talents:

> Science Service sponsors the annual Westinghouse Science Talent Search for high school seniors, ... of these 2000 finalists, five have won the Nobel Prize; two, the Fields Medal (highest honor in the field of mathematics); eight have won MacArthur Foundation Fellowships; 51 have been named Sloan Fellows; and 28 have been elected to the National Academy of Sciences. Seventy percent of those who are old enough have earned a PhD or an M.D. (p. 7)

For a long time, research on mentorship for gifted adolescents has primarily focused on one of the following lines of inquiry:

(a) The effectiveness of mentoring based on interviews and biographical materials of eminent individuals in specific domains of talent (e.g., Bloom, 1985; Feldman, 1986; Goertzel, Goertzel, & Goertzel, 1978).
(b) Justifications on the significance of mentorship at the conceptual level (e.g., Gagné, 2003; Grassinger, Porath, & Ziegler, 2010; Pleiss & Feldhusen, 1995).
(c) Principles and forms of mentorship practices (e.g., Assouline & Lupkowski-Shoplik, 2005; Clasen & Clasen, 1997; Ellingson et al., 1986; Stanley, 1978; Stoeger, Hopp, & Zeigler, 2017; Subotnik, Edmiston, Cook, & Ross, 2010).

More recently, Sahin's (2014) quantitative study found that mentorship with a focus on creative thinking increased the creative thinking scores of both gifted and non-gifted students. When comparing the gifted and non-gifted experimental groups, there was a statistically significant difference in favour of the gifted group ($d = 0.33$).

Casey and Shore (2000) argued that not only do mentors contribute to the cognitive growth of the talented adolescents, but they also facilitate gifted adolescents' affective and social development. A study conducted by Little et al. (2010) showed that besides increases in students' perceived research skills and job competence in a pre/post survey, mentoring is a social process that involves developing relationships between the mentor and mentee. In their study, students from a three-week summer mentorship program for talented adolescents reported positive relationships with mentors who were approachable, friendly, and engaging, particularly when they felt that their mentor spent a great deal of time with them. Hence, mentorship is a dynamic and shared relationship in which values, attitudes, passions, and traditions are passed from one person to another and internalised (Boston, 1976).

We agree with scholars in the field of gifted education and talent development (e.g., Olszewski-Kubilius et al., 2016; VanTassel-Baska, 2000) that the mentoring of talented adolescents into professional or practitioner communities is a long-term goal in catering for the advanced development of talented adolescents in domain-specific giftedness that might inspire these youth for eminence. Given the importance of mentoring in the nurturing of gifted and talented students (Jarvin & Subotnik, 2015; Subotnik & Rickoff, 2010), we argue that it is necessary for researchers, practitioners, and policy-makers to clearly delineate learning objectives when connecting the mentors and mentees who are gifted and talented.

Issues and Assumptions About Mentoring in the Literature

The nature of mentorship relationships is diverse and complex. Grassinger et al. (2010) analysed the mentoring literature on gifted individuals and concluded that there can never be a universally shared approach to mentoring. Rather, an ideal of mentoring may exist from which varied meanings are derived as mentors and mentees individually sense-make, guided by their own subjective experiences. The ideal that they put forth, based on a collection of literature, is as follows:

> Mentoring of gifted individuals is a relatively chronologically stable dyadic relationship between an experienced mentor and a less experienced gifted mentee, characterised by mutual trust and benevolence, with the purpose of promoting learning, development, and, ultimately, progress in the mentee. (Grassinger et al., 2010, p. 30)

Appropriate Use of Opportunities for Mentoring

Mentoring can also be idiosyncratic and context-bound and mentors may not hold the same beliefs or motivating factors within the process of mentoring. Notably, there are two possible reasons to engage talented adolescents in mentorship programs: (a) the exceptional (top 1:10,000, SD +3.7) and extreme (top 1:100,000, SD +4.3) intellectual capacity of talented adolescents who are way beyond the typical standard and (b) when the learning needs of the highly gifted (top 1:1000, SD +3.0) exceed what schools can provide (Gagné, 2007). When the development of these talented adolescents hits a roadblock or comes to a plateau, mentorship programs allow them to explore new learning opportunities in a 'ceilingless' environment

(Purcell, Renzulli, McCoach, & Spottiswoode, 2001). While the former is based on the diagnosis and assessment of a specific domain of talent with the aim of focusing intensely on the area of talent and interest, the latter aims to expose these adolescents to advanced knowledge. This suggests that only those who are intellectually and socially ready might benefit from a mentorship program. As intellectual thresholds differ, the aims of mentorship programs could be differentiated (Gagné, 2007), and the expectations of the mentoring process and outcomes should be practical and realistic (Subotnik & Rickoff, 2010). It seems the suitability of such an opportunity is dependent on nuances such as the capacity and readiness of talented adolescents. Researchers (Clasen & Clasen, 2003; Reilly, 1992) have underscored the importance of readiness of talented adolescents to be engaged in mentorship programs and stressed that schools must exhaust possible opportunities and resources in schools before considering mentorship. Hence, mentorship programs should not be a convenient way to address boredom among talented adolescents. If mentoring is the gold standard to foster talents (Bloom, 1984), there is a need to emphasise and value the critical role of expert mentoring and the tacit knowledge they demonstrate and share with talented adolescents (Subotnik & Rickoff, 2010). With that, the probability of implementing successful mentorship programs may increase.

Putting Theory into Practice on Mentoring

In practice, there are numerous and varied definitions of the term 'mentor' in different domains of expertise (Grassinger et al., 2010). Similar to the literature on adult mentoring at the workplace (e.g., Burlew, 1991; Dominguez & Hager, 2013; Merriam, 1983), the mentoring process for talented adolescents is connected with three key theories, namely, developmental, learning, and social. Developmental theories depict the mentoring relationship as one that is mutual and progressive in stages (Burlew, 1991; Dominguez & Hager, 2013; Merriam, 1983). The developmental theories emphasise the importance of matching the mentor's and mentee's developmental needs, and inherent in its conceptualisation is the belief of a mentor who is able to provide quality learning experiences (Dominguez & Hager, 2013; Subotnik et al., 2010). However, it is naive to assume that all experts, even without going through an induction about mentorship, are able to perform the role. Mentors act as facilitators to guide mentees who ideally play a more active role in their learning. Hence, mentors' beliefs about mentoring talented adolescents drive the quality of the mentorship. The goal is to provide greater exposure and the advanced skills, as well as to stimulate advanced intellectual capacity to the talented adolescents. The social theorists go a step further and posit that, as role models, mentors not only disseminate information and develop their mentees' capabilities, but are also bridges between their mentees and key social networks (Dominguez & Hager, 2013; Subotnik et al., 2010; Zukerman, 1967). Mentors are the catalysts in building social capital (Chariker, Zhang, Pani, & Rouchka, 2017; Zuckerman, 1968). In short, to mentor talented adolescents is to provide intellectual stimulation so that talented adolescents can chart new frontiers to advance knowledge and practices that benefit humanity.

While mentorships vary greatly in description and implementation, based on the working knowledge of the first author and narratives of mentorship programs in the literature (Clasen & Clasen, 2003; Grassinger et al., 2010; Subotnik & Rickoff, 2010), some of the characteristics include the following:

(a) Clear delineation of objectives of the program.
(b) Assessment of suitability of mentors and mentees.
(c) Careful pairing and matching of mentors and mentees.
(d) Appropriate training to prepare mentors and mentees.
(e) Suitable planning and sufficient duration of the mentoring programs.
(f) Measures to promote the quality of the relation of mentor and mentee.
(g) Sufficient communication and monitoring of the progress of mentorship.
(h) Availability of feedback channels during and at the end of the mentorship.
(i) Assessment of the satisfaction level of mentors and mentees.

Altruism in Mentoring

Although the potential of a successful, long-term relationship between mentor and mentee can be a productive and meaningful experience, mentorship has its impediments and challenges (Clasen & Clasen, 2003; Grassinger et al., 2010; Subotnik & Rickoff, 2010). Subotnik and Rickoff (2010) studied the participants in Westinghouse and found that despite their talent, drive, and opportunities for early exposure to eminence in science and related fields, a good number of participants did not continue to make use of the opportunities and grow their talent after high school. These findings suggest two key understandings about mentorship: (a) although mentorship is an effective intervention for those who take it, it is surely not the silver bullet in educating talented adolescents and (b) the quality of experiences in mentorship matters.

In a study of mentorship programs for adolescents who are talented in science, Quek (2005) found that the highly ranked important qualities of effective mentors are: "genuine interest in mentee as an individual, well-versed in his field, and passion for the subject/field" (p. 199). Other frequently cited qualities of a good mentor included: "knows when to help and when to let mentee work independently [and] creates opportunities to give mentee more exposure in the field" (p. 199). In highlighting the elements of "trust and benevolence" (p. 30), Grassinger et al.'s (2010) definition introduces altruism as a key area of mentoring. Altruism entails feeling sympathy, empathy, and an inclination to help others in need. Presuming external motivations are not all that drive all mentors to mentor, it would seem logical to suppose that an internal motivation driving some mentoring relationships could be altruism. While the number of studies that explore the effects of altruism in mentoring relationships is limited, the ones that have paint a positive picture. Hu, Baranik, and Wu (2014) found only four studies on the relationship between having "altruistic-related personality traits" (p. 220) and mentoring. The studies' findings suggest that having an altruistic personality trait is predictive of engaging in mentoring (Allen, 2003; Chun, Sosik, & Yun, 2012). Hu et al. (2014) also found that mentors' sense of altruism could improve mentees' perception of received support from mentors. However, their finding is limited to adult mentees who hold dissimilar "values, beliefs, attitudes and personality" (p. 220) to their mentors.

Understanding Mentoring from the Mentors' Points of View

During a mentorship, the mentor assumes several interlocking roles: teacher, expert, guide, advisor, friend, and role model (Clasen & Clasen, 2003). While a mentorship program brings the mentor and mentee into a relationship, the success of such a relationship is largely dependent on the quality of the experiences within the program. The expertise and scholarship of mentors are necessary, but not sufficient, to ensure the success of mentorship. Currently, the narratives in the literature on mentoring talented adolescents paint the roles that mentors play as ideal, but in practice, mentors might not always have the knowledge and skills to facilitate an effective mentoring relationship. What exactly do we need to ensure successful mentorship? Since mentorship programs are typically established with research institutions outside the context of schools and gifted education programs, perhaps the literature on mentoring from the organisational and management points of view (e.g., Allen, Poteet, & Burroughs, 1997; Grima, Paillé, Mejia, & Prud'Homme, 2014), particularly from the mentor's perspective, could shed light on research in mentoring talented adolescents.

Willingness, Enthusiasm, and Intrinsic Rewarding Experiences

Motivations for mentoring could affect the quality of mentoring experiences for both the mentor and mentee. A few studies (e.g., Allen, Poteet, Russell, & Dobbins, 1997; Ragins & Scandura, 1999) have described the variations in the perspectives and willingness of mentors based on their level of experience in mentoring. However, these studies seldom look into how this variability directly affects the mentor's experience and/or perspective of mentoring. A study conducted by Allen et al. (1997) briefly explored this, and they found that one's previous experience as a mentor and/or a protégé was positively correlated to his or her "greater willingness to mentor" (Allen, Poteet, & Burroughs, 1997, p. 71) and fewer perceived barriers to mentoring. However, this study merely looked at whether or not mentors had mentoring experience—it did not address differences in the number of mentees the mentor has mentored or the number of years of experience as a mentor. There is thus much room for further investigation in these areas.

Being Empathetic and Sensitive to the Cognitive and Social Needs of Talented Adolescents

Allen et al. (1997) investigated mentor-mentee attraction and found the following compelling factors: (a) mentees' talent, ability, and desire to learn; (b) perceived mentee need—whether a mentee's needs are able to stimulate a mentor's desire to help; and (c) perceived mentee similarity in interest and beliefs. Talented adolescents are driven and advanced in specific talent domains, but they are not adults. Little et al. (2010) reported positive relationships with mentors who are approachable, friendly, and engaging, particularly when they felt that their mentor spent a great deal of time with them. Based on an understanding of the cognitive and affective characteristics of talented adolescents, it seems that they need mentors with the following traits: patience, good communication, problem-solving skills, creativity, flexibility, strong integrity, and a sense of humour.

In addition, if mentors can recognise the cognitive needs of talented adolescents, they will be able to create conditions for 'flow' (Csikzentmihayli, Rathunde, & Whalden, 1993) and be more equipped to prepare the learning environment for optimal learning experiences in which student becomes entirely engrossed in learning that is enjoyable, challenging, and rewarding. Instead of routine learning and practice, these mentors are capable of providing constructive feedback and gauging the shifting needs of talented adolescents under their tutelage.

Experience in Managing Mentor-Mentee Relationships

Despite the increasing proliferation of mentoring literature in andragogy (e.g., Kardos & Johnson, 2010; Lozinak, 2016), few studies on mentoring talented adolescents have focused on the pre-requisites of how such mentoring relationships occur, and one of these pre-requisites is the matching of mentors with mentees. Ragins and Scandura (1999) examined how prior experience with mentoring, as mentee and/or mentor, influences a mentor's perceived costs and benefits from a mentoring relationship and, consequently, their intentions to mentor. They found that mentors who had prior experience as mentees were more likely to perceive benefits and fewer costs than mentors who did not have prior experience as mentees. We posit that this is the case for mentors who lack experience in mentoring as well.

There is the need to examine mentor/mentee matching and the nature of the mentoring experiences to ascertain the quality of mentoring (Kardos & Johnson, 2010). One of the functions of a mentor is to possess skills that supplement the weaknesses of the mentees (Lozinak, 2016); it is a problem when the learning needs of mentees and the mentoring capacity of mentors do not converge. Bozeman and Feeney (2008) viewed mentoring using the social exchange theory and suggested that there should be a fit between the mentor and mentee in these aspects: preferences, endowments, and content knowledge. An example of an acceptable mentor-mentee fit is when the mentor has the knowledge preferred by the mentee, perceives value in passing down the knowledge to a mentee who has the capabilities to understand the knowledge, and in return, the mentors receive benefits of training someone, gaining in both leadership skills and social capital. This suggests the importance in matching mentors' mentoring capacity to mentees' learning needs in order to have an efficient mentor-mentee relationship.

Outcomes of Mentoring for Mentors

Allen et al. (1997) also explored the outcomes of mentoring and found that mentors often perceive more advantages rather than disadvantages in mentoring. One major advantage mentors derive from mentoring is that they are able to develop professionally themselves, while one major cost mentors perceive is the time taken away from their job to mentor. Anchored on social exchange theory, Grima et al. (2014) explained that instrumental advantages for mentors include an increase in the mentor's social capital and organisational recognition, whereas psychosocial advantages include intrinsic emotions, such as satisfaction and pride in mentees' learning and progress, and possibly even a resurgence of professional satisfaction through vicariously experiencing the mentee's development.

Unpacking the Implications on Current Practice and Contexts of Mentoring in Singapore

In the following section, we will share some of the practices and features in mentoring in the Singapore context.

Instrumental Nature of Mentoring Relationships Shaped by Performance-Based Mentoring Programs

In order to align learning in school and at the workplace, mentoring has become a means to socialise tertiary students in Singapore. These mentorships are an avenue for students to meet one of the graduation criteria by completing a final-year project-cum-report or preparing students for one of the examination papers. The relationship between mentor and mentee is shaped by the demands and outcomes required of high-stakes learning such as the H3 paper in the *General Certificate of Education* (GCE) 'A' Level examination or the final-year project. Given the structure and desired outcomes of the education system in Singapore, the mentor and mentee face challenges that include managing expectations, inadequate sessions for meeting due to limited time, communicating with each other, and managing time for research. Specific issues mentors face include: knowing how to motivate students or structure the learning process for students. In

Singapore, mentorship programs observe strict timeframes and there are specific deliverables for the mentors and mentees. Despite students' desire to be exposed to a wider range of scientists and scientific methods, the association with possible high-stakes outcomes in Singapore could result in the relationship between the mentor and mentee becoming transactional in nature. Transactional in this sense refers to the mentoring relationship being predominantly career-oriented (e.g., to fulfil organisational obligations).

Ambiguous Understanding and Use of Mentorship as Pedagogic Practice

With organisations institutionalising mentoring programs, mentoring has become part of a professional's job scope. Where it used to be domain experts experienced in mentoring who became mentors in the past, it might not necessarily be the case now. It is unclear if professionals working in organisations who partner with schools to provide mentoring programs or internships are trained in mentoring. Several issues arise because of this shift from a more organically formulated mentoring to an institutionalised mentoring program. First, the organisational communication of what is needed of a mentor might be unclear, which means that there might be divergent goals for both mentor and mentee within the mentoring program, right from the start (Subotnik & Rickoff, 2010). Second, professionals nominated to be mentors might not always be willing and ready to mentor talented adolescents. As discussed in previous sections, there are specific competencies and attributes that mentors should possess to develop the cognitive needs of talented adolescents (Assouline & Lupkowski-Shoplik, 2005; Clasen & Clasen, 1997). Beyond cognitive development, studies (e.g., Jen, 2017; Silverman, 1997) have pointed out that talented adolescents may be prone to idiosyncrasies in their "asynchronous development" (Jen, 2017, p. 227) of affective and cognitive abilities. This means that on top of developing their mentees' intellectual talents, mentors should also be well equipped to handle mentees' social-emotional needs in the course of mentoring, for the holistic development of talent in talented adolescents (Grassinger et al., 2010).

In the following section, we present three case studies that illustrate some of the conceptions of mentoring and issues faced by three mentors when mentoring talented adolescents as part of institutionalised mentoring programs.

Qualitative Case-Study Research on Mentoring

This section provides a description of three interviews conducted to explore mentors' perspectives of mentoring. The study recruited participants from a pool of scientists who attended a workshop on mentoring. Three volunteers responded to the call for participation. This recruitment method allowed for the selection of cases that met a predetermined set of criteria—the participants are currently mentors and have attended professional learning workshops related to mentoring. All three interviewees have different levels of mentoring experience and research areas, with one in computer science, the second in biology, and the last in materials research. They reported a range of mentoring experience with one having mentored at least 60 mentees in four years, another having mentored at least 79 mentees in five years, and the last having at least 10 years of experience and having won several awards for mentoring. All three scientists reported engaging in face-to-face mentoring and at times, e-mentoring via email or instant messaging. The reported profile of mentees includes students from secondary schools, polytechnics, junior colleges, and universities. Among the secondary school and junior college students, there were a large number of scientifically talented students.

One-on-one semi-structured interviews were undertaken with each scientist. Some example interview questions included: 'Why do you choose to mentor?' and 'How do you see your relationship with your mentee(s)?' Interview notes were taken by two note-takers during each interview session. The interview notes were peer-checked and sent back to the scientists for fact-checking before they were used for analysis. Information gathered from the interviews were synthesised, coded, and tabulated into a table according to the mentors' perceptions of the nature, processes, and outcomes of mentoring. The coding process was an inductive one and used broad categories (e.g., nature, process, and significance) to generate specific codes (e.g., goals, willingness), allowing for an easier comparison of the qualitative responses (e.g., Anfara, Brown, & Mangione, 2002; Patton, 2002) across the three male informants. The research team then analysed each mentor's responses individually, which enabled the formation of a holistic idea of each mentor's conception of mentoring and the research team had regular discussions as a form of peer checking. Using thematic analysis, the research team then engaged in further discussions to compare across the three mentors' perceptions and surfaced themes supported by theoretical underpinnings from the mentoring literature (e.g., Fereday & Muir-Cochrane, 2006). In the analysis and discussion of thematic findings, the participants are known by pseudonyms of Paul (had the least number of years of experience), Peter and Patrick (had the most number of years of experience).

Findings and Discussion: What Factors Affect Mentors' Mentoring?

Grima et al. (2014) illustrated that mentoring benefits fall under two broad components: psychosocial and instrumental. Under these two components, which are posited as advantages of mentoring for mentors, are factors such as "rejuvenation and rewarding experience [psychosocial and] improved job performance and recognition by others" (instrumental; Grima et al., 2014, p. 473). Our analyses further expand the conceptualisation of the two broad components to include more dimensions (see Table 1). The dimensions are framed with this question in mind: what factors affect mentors' mentoring?

Table 1 Psychosocial and instrumental factors affecting mentors' mentoring

Dimensions		Sample quotes
Psychosocial	Goals	"When I first started out right, students right, I just wanted some extra hands for my research". "When I mentor students, I feel younger myself, in many ways". "There are a lot of people with potential that I can guide".
	Willingness	"When I mentor, I feel younger myself". "In some cases, I didn't have a choice".
	Mentor-mentee matching	"I learnt that it is more productive to learn from people who are interested and want to learn". "I must choose students who fit in my team and who have passion". "You can get someone with very good grades and just lousy but generally I get...One of them is extremely, damn good. She won competitions but her grades are bad".
	Perceived mentee capacity	". . .can't expect them to do bachelor's level work or master's level work, it's unfair to them". "If I let students carry out their own ideas, I believe students can find something unexpected too".
Instrumental	Improved job performance	"A student's input gave me fresh insight into how my model might work". "One student pointed out a flaw in my proposal that I did not notice". "They try out new things I haven't tried yet".
	Recognition by others and building social capital	". . .connections between different batches of students are very important because they each recommend good students to me". ". . .keeping good contacts and reputation as a mentor helps".

Psychosocial Factors Affecting Mentors' Mentoring

Goals: How do mentors' goals affect their plan of action in mentoring?
According to Grassinger et al. (2010), mentoring allows for the pursuit of a range of educational goals including psychosocial, career-related, developing individual orientation, and strengthening goal commitment and motivation. In line with Grassinger et al. (2010) supposition that different types of mentors would focus on different goals, our analyses indicated that all three mentors, Paul, Peter, and Patrick, had different goals set for their mentees. The mentor with fewer years of experience seemed to focus mainly on psychosocial and career-related goals for himself and for his mentees. These included helping mentees be "exposed to scientific thinking" (Paul), teach "management skills" (Peter), to "help them be ethical" (Paul) and "figure out their soft skills" (Peter). Specifically, for Peter, he shared that if some of his mentees were going to become his staff in future, he would need to train these

mentees to be good workers in the workplace. Conversely, Patrick seemed to focus on developing individual orientation ('let them [mentees] carry out ideas that they want to do'), on top of psychosocial and career-related goals. In prioritising the development of his mentees' individual interests and talents, Patrick was the only mentor to customise projects that furthered both his work and his mentees' interests. Interestingly, Patrick was also the only mentor to have mentees who were able to interest a business partner and translate their work into a research partnership. Patrick's case exemplifies Grassinger et al.'s (2010) idea that with experience, a knowledgeable mentor is able to determine the best goals to bring about success, given the appropriate selection of actions and situations to achieve these goals.

Willingness: What are the motivations driving mentors' decisions to mentor? As mentioned, Allen et al. (1997) looked into individual reasons for why mentors chose to mentor, categorising reasons into either other-focused reasons (e.g., a desire to pass information on to others, a desire to build a competent workforce, for the benefit of the organisation) or self-focused reasons (e.g., gratification seeing others succeed/grow, to increase personal learning, pride). Looking into the motivations behind Paul, Peter, and Patrick as mentors, we find that Paul seems to be driven mainly by other-focused reasons such as "there are a lot of people with potential I can guide". On the other hand, Peter and Patrick were driven by both other-focused and self-focused reasons, such as "they [mentees] have a positive reputation that they give to me and themselves" (Peter) and "working with students helps me think deeper about what I do" (Patrick). By deriving self-beneficial reasons for mentoring, Peter and Patrick seemed to have had greater clarity in the outcomes they would like to develop in mentors. For Peter, it was for his mentors to become "good workers", while Patrick envisioned mentees becoming accomplished in their specific field of scientific interest. This is in contrast to Paul who struggled with the idea of "imparting values" to mentees and reported simply trying "to give advice" and "help them [mentees] along". Indeed, by viewing mentees as a reflection of themselves and their work, Peter and Patrick were seemingly motivated to develop in mentees not just skills, and knowledge, but characteristics and beliefs that they valued in themselves as professionals. According to Anderson and Shannon (1988), this is important as a mentor must undertake both the professional and personal role if one were to be a "true mentor" (p. 40).

Matching of mentor-mentee interests: How does mentor-mentee matching benefit both mentors and mentees? Studies have indicated the importance of mentor-mentee matching in areas such as personality (e.g., Menges, 2015), goal orientations (e.g., Egan, 2005), and demographic factors like gender (e.g., Weinberg & Lankau, 2011), and race (e.g., Campbell & Campbell, 2007). Yet few studies have mentioned the matching of mentor-mentee by skill set or by interest. Subotnik and Rickoff (2010) argue that a good match of interests will enable mentees to glean 'tacit knowledge about the field' as mentors provide professional advice. Likewise, Peter and Patrick espoused the importance of a match between the mentor and mentee in terms of skills and interest respectively. For Peter, having talented youths with a set of skills that is useful to him was so important that he "had to fight for her [mentee] to get into" the mentoring program which she did not qualify for as the program recruited students based on grades. Patrick emphasised a need "to really share the same or similar interests. . .so that the mentoring and work done is useful and relevant for both parties". This way, mentees were able to help him out with his projects, and he was able to "springboard students to other platforms". Both Peter and Patrick shared that they had tapped on their professional networks to recruit suitable candidates. This availability of external connections is also key to being a mentor and is further elaborated later in the findings.

Perceived mentee capacity: How do the way mentors perceive mentees' capacity to learn affect the way they choose to mentor? Another factor that has been mentioned in the mentoring literature is mentors' beliefs about their mentees. Specifically, Allen et al. (1997) found that mentors highly valued factors such as high capacity/ability, a strong work ethic, and openness/willingness to learn from mentees, among others. Of interest is how mentors perceive talented youths' capacities to learn affect the way they choose to mentor. For Paul, he adopted a more structured approach to mentoring such as providing mentees with literature, crafting project ideas, setting hypotheses, and keeping track of timelines for mentees. His reasons being that talented youths "won't know what to look for" in the literature, "might have interesting ideas but they tend not to work" and "do not have the level of educational background" to think beyond their grade level. To be fair, Paul mentioned that time tends to be a constraint as some mentoring programs can be as short as three months; and in other cases, he does allow for projects that are more "open-ended" (2017). In contrast, Patrick entrusted mentees with an idea that he did not have time to carry out despite them not having background knowledge. He did this by teaching and setting tasks that were needed in the project such as "measuring certain aspects" of his project. The mentors illustrate a difference in mentoring that could be influenced by certain assumptions mentors hold of mentees. As Searby (2009) argues, while assumptions may be helpful in sense making, it is vital to also recognise and explore assumptions of both mentee and mentor even before either party enters into a mentoring relationship.

Instrumental Factors Affecting Mentors' Mentoring

Improved job performance: How does mentoring benefit me as a professional? An instrumental benefit for professionals to mentor is the improvement of job performance. It is explained in Feldman's (1988) work that with mentees learning new knowledge, they support their mentors and that support allows the mentors to maintain their competences or even possibly develop new competencies. Apart from the learning benefits mentees gain from being mentored, mentors themselves can also learn from the mentorship and benefit in the form of improvement in performance (Dobrow, Chandler, Murphy, & Kram, 2012; Eby & Lockwood, 2005). Based on the literature on mentor's instrumental benefits for mentoring, specifically with regard to job performance, our interviews also revealed similar findings, but vary in the extent to which it improves performance. One mentor (Peter) indicated that mentees are 'extra hands for my [his] research', and he is able to achieve more now, with mentees supporting him in the work that he could not do due to workload and a lack of time. Another mentor (Patrick) revealed that apart from having "students [mentees] to help him with the project" which "he did not have time to carry out", mentees help him "think deeper about what they [mentors] do", whereby one of his mentees "pointed out a flaw in his research proposal". Analysing data from Peter and Patrick, work performance in the former increased in greater breadth, where one is able to accomplish more tasks with more hands, while the latter increases the breadth as well as deepens the mentor's professional thinking. Though both mentors increased in work performance, how mentors get mentees to support them in their work affects what mentees learn. Engaging mentees with wider breadth allows mentees to learn in breadth, while supporting mentees in depth, deepens learning for the mentees.

Recognition by others and building social capacity: How does mentoring affect my profession? As described by social exchange theory, mentorship for adults is perceived as a balanced relationship of exchange (Grima et al., 2014), whereby both mentor and mentee benefit from one another. Grima et al. (2014) further elaborated that as the mentee gains recognition within the organisation, the mentor is recognised and gains a reputation for nurturing mentees who could give back to the organisation. Similarly, from our findings, the best example shows that Patrick seems to develop the scientific interest of his mentees and helps them gain some form of professional traction in the field. Professional traction in the field was further elaborated as "awards and achievements his mentees accomplished" (Patrick). In alignment with the literature on the enhancement of mentors' professional image when mentees progress within the organisation, our findings also showed that Patrick was recognised for his mentorship by being awarded the best mentor and presented his practices on mentorship to his organisation. Recognition by others in this aspect of mentorship can be seen as a reflection of how one mentors that translates to how mentees would progress in the organisation.

Alongside being recognised by others, mentorship creates opportunities for mentors to improve their position in the organisation, such as creating bonds of friendship that can be useful to the mentor (Chariker et al., 2017; Grima et al., 2014). Building social capital is seen in Patrick where he forged a friendship with his mentees and formed school partnerships with school teachers. As Patrick keeps close contact with his mentees after they have completed the mentoring program, "they [mentees] recommend good students to him". In addition, by fostering good relations with school teachers and acquiring a reputation as a mentor, "teachers are more inclined to recommend good students to good mentors". Our findings suggested that being recognised as a mentor has spillover effects on building social capital, and one is more likely to have a larger social capital when accompanied with a reputation as a competent mentor.

While some previous research (Chun et al., 2012; Grassinger et al., 2010; Hu et al., 2014) highlighted the importance of altruism as a prompt for the professional expert's involvement as a mentor, the few narratives in this small study did not provide any information on relationships between altruism and associated characteristics, such as empathy with their mentees.

Potentials and Possibilities of Mentoring Relationships: Implications for Future Practice and Research

In this chapter, the research literature combined with the aforementioned narratives we gathered revealed some issues and assumptions about mentoring from the mentors' perspectives. Each informant perceived the mentor-mentee dyad relationship from somewhat different perspectives. Their perspectives on motivation to mentor, empathy towards talented adolescents, experience in managing mentor-mentee relationships, and outcomes of mentoring were based on their mentees' learning needs, while their capacity seems to determine how they interacted and reciprocated with each other. These mentors' perspectives suggest the benefits or potential and possibilities of mentoring relationships.

Clasen and Clasen (2003) warned that the proliferation of mentorships beyond the schools to meet the needs of a wide variety of students comes with increased potential risks and they suggested designing liability and risk management policies within the mentorship program. A mentorship program for talented adolescents should foreground the purpose to both mentors and mentees. Clarity of objectives helps to delineate policy regarding the mentorship. The written policy regarding mentorships should include selection and screening of mentors, procedures in monitoring, and evaluating the programs, as well as the intended outcomes of mentoring.

Although it is imperative to have meticulously designed mentorship structure, process, and outcome, it is more meaningful for both schools and organisations or individual mentors to be commissioned to foster a culture for holistic mentoring. Organisations that coordinate such mentorship programs could create dialogic space for exploration and discussion among potential mentees as well as mentors in action. Such discussions on philosophical aspects of mentoring help both mentors and mentees to construct and deconstruct their personal belief systems about mentoring and the purposes of mentoring. For example, mentors who showed the significance of developing a sense of personal authority, based on their dream of himself/herself as a mature adult among the mentees, is described to be the mentee's conscious and unconscious projection of his/her adult-self (Alderfer, 2014). Mentors, who support and facilitate the realisation of the mentee's dream, will foster the development of the mentee's dream by believing in him/her.

Psychosocial advancement is one of the key features in mentorship (Subotnik, 2015). Mentors who see mentoring as a way to socialise and guide mentees into a new aspect of mentoring by acquainting them with its values, customs, resources, and cast of mind (Krutetskii, 1976) play the essential role of modelling. During mentorship, mentees view their mentors as role models; however, if mentors could describe and demonstrate the errors mentors have made and learned from there, in the eyes of mentees, the mentors are their heroes (Pleiss & Feldhusen, 1995).

Organisations that host mentorship programs might consider inviting experienced mentors to articulate their personal reflections and share with the mentor-to-be. Levinson's *Career Stage or Life Stage Theory* (Levinson, Darrow, Klein, Levinson,

& McKee, 1978) suggests that as mentors have long walked and progressed on the paths on which the mentees are just beginning to embark, the mentees are able to relate to their mentors as individuals who have made mistakes and become who they are now due to learning from their mistakes. Sharing concrete reflections as examples might just encourage more experts to become mentors or begin the journey of mentoring on their own.

Besides the recommendations for the practical implementation of mentorship programs, we would like to suggest some key issues for future research. While there is a body of literature on the theoretical underpinnings of mentorship (Gagné, 2003, 2004; Grassinger et al., 2010) and seminal work on the outcomes of mentoring (e.g., Bloom, 1985; Feldman, 1986; Goertzel et al., 1978), the learning environment and the way potential mentors of different talent communities respond could be vastly different after three decades. Factors such as the intensive use of technology, availability of a larger pool of mentors, and evolving demands of mentors' work in the talent domains may contribute to this changing mentoring landscape. Hence, it would be pertinent to explore how mentoring has continued to change in its many forms, processes, and outcomes across the variety of talent domains (e.g., e-mentoring, group mentoring).

Moreover, research on mentorship might tease out nuances of such mentoring practices. Since mentorship is a pedagogical practice to engage talented adolescents who are more specialised and advanced than their peers, research on mentorship could distinguish the appropriate form, process, and effect of mentorship, especially when mentees' learning hits a blockade in school. Additionally, although Little et al.'s (2010) research points to the limited effects of short-term mentorship, it is critical to investigate the ideal duration and examine the facilitative conditions of mentorship attachment for talented adolescents in different domains of talents (Gagné, 2007). The findings we presented in this chapter suggest research on mentorship should take multiple perspectives of the tripartite relationship. Further research could explore the quality of interaction between the mentor and mentee in both the contexts of dyads and group mentoring. In addition, investigating the culture of mentoring in a range of talent domains would contribute empirically to the practice of mentorship.

Conclusion

In this chapter, we highlighted the pivotal role of mentors in developing talents in science, examined the issues and assumptions about mentoring talented adolescents in the literature and unpacked the implications on the instrumental use of mentorship that can result in shifting the landscape to engage mentors as a beneficial pedagogical practice. Combined with the research literature, the narratives from our interaction at a workshop, and interviews with the mentors suggest mentoring is a demanding role regardless of the career phases and professional status of an individual mentor. Apart from careful selection and invitation to mentors with dispositions and capacity to mentor, mentors need orientation on both the cognitive and social-emotional needs of talented adolescents regardless of the scholarship and professional experience of mentors. Hence, planning, implementing, monitoring, and evaluating mentorship programs require much thought when matching the mentor-mentee dyad or group mentoring to avoid disappointment in the mentoring relationship for both mentors and mentees.

Cross-References

▶ A Counselling Framework for Meeting the Needs of Gifted Students in Malaysia
▶ Assessment, Pedagogy, and Curriculum: Part IV Introduction
▶ Creativity Talent Development: Fostering Creativity in Schools
▶ Creative and Gifted Education in Korea: Using the CATs Model to Illustrate How Creativity Can Grow into Innovation
▶ Differentiation of Instruction for Gifted Learners: Collated Evaluative Studies of Teacher Classroom Practices
▶ Engaging Gifted Students in Solving Real Problems Creatively: Implementing the Real Engagement in Active Problem-Solving (REAPS) Teaching/Learning Model in Australasian and Pacific Rim Contexts
▶ Gifted Education in the Asia-Pacific: From the Past for the Future – An Introduction
▶ Leadership Development of Gifted Adolescents from a Korean Multicultural Lens
▶ Some Implications for the Future of Gifted Education in the Asia-Pacific
▶ STEAM in Gifted Education in Korea
▶ The Lives and Achievements of Four Extraordinary Australians: A Master, a Maker, an Introspector, and an Influencer
▶ The Predictors of the Decisions by Gifted Students to Pursue STEM Careers: The Case of Brazilian International Students in Australia

References

Alderfer, C. P. (2014). Clarifying the meaning of mentor–protégé relationships. *Consulting Psychology Journal: Practice and Research, 66*(1), 6–19. https://doi.org/10.1037/a0036367
Allen, T. D. (2003). Mentoring others: A dispositional and motivational approach. *Journal of Vocational Behavior, 62*(1), 134–154. https://doi.org/10.1016/S0001-8791(02)00046-5
Allen, T. D., Poteet, M. L., & Burroughs, S. M. (1997). The mentor's perspective: A qualitative inquiry and future research agenda. *Journal of Vocational Behavior, 51*(1), 70–89. https://doi.org/10.1006/jvbe.1997.1596
Allen, T. D., Poteet, M. L., Russell, J. E., & Dobbins, G. H. (1997). A field study of factors related to supervisors' willingness to mentor others. *Journal of Vocational Behavior, 50*(1), 1–22. https://doi.org/10.1006/jvbe.1995.1525
Anderson, E. M., & Shannon, A. L. (1988). Toward a conceptualization of mentoring. *Journal of Teacher Education, 39*(1), 38–42. https://doi.org/10.1177/002248718803900109

Anfara, V., Brown, K., & Mangione, T. (2002). Qualitative analysis on stage: Making the research process more public. *Educational Researcher, 31*(7), 28–38. https://doi.org/10.3102/0013189X031007028

Assouline, S., & Lupkowski-Shoplik, A. (2005). *Developing math talent: A guide for educating gifted and advanced learners in math*. Waco, TX: Prufrock Press, Inc..

Bloom, B. S. (1984). The 2 sigma problem: The search for methods of group instruction as effective as one-to-one tutoring. *Educational Researcher, 13*, 4–16. https://doi.org/10.2307/1175554

Bloom, B. S. (1985a). *Developing talent in young people*. New York, NY: Ballantine Books.

Bloom, B. S. (1985b). Generalisations about talent development. In B. S. Bloom (Ed.), *Developing talent in young people* (pp. 507–549). New York, NY: Ballantine Books.

Boston, B. (1979). The mentor and the education of the gifted and talented. In J. H. Orloff (Ed.), *Beyond awareness: Providing for the gifted child* (pp. 36–41). Proceedings of the Fourth Annual Northern Virginia Conference on Gifted/Talented Education, Northern Virginia Council for Gifted/Talented Education, Falls Church, VA.

Boston, B. O., & ERIC Clearinghouse on Handicapped and Gifted Children, R. V. (1976). *The Sorcerer's Apprentice: A Case Study in the Role of the Mentor*. ERIC Document: ED126671

Bozeman, B., & Fenney, M. K. (2008). Mentoring matching: A "goodness of fit" model. *Administration & Society, 40*(5), 465–482. https://doi.org/10.1177/0095399708320184

Burlew, L. D. (1991). Multiple mentor model: A conceptual framework. *Journal of Career Development, 17*(3), 213–221. https://doi.org/10.1007/BF01322028

Campbell, T. A., & Campbell, D. E. (2007). Outcomes of mentoring at-risk college students: Gender and ethnic matching effects. *Mentoring & Tutoring: Partnership in Learning, 15*(2), 135–148. https://doi.org/10.1080/13611260601086287

Casey, K. M. A., & Shore, B. M. (2000). Mentors' contributions to gifted adolescents' affective, social, and vocational development. *Roeper Review, 22*(4), 227–230. https://doi.org/10.1080/02783190009554043

Chariker, J. H., Zhang, Y., Pani, J. R., & Rouchka, E. C. (2017). Identification of successful mentoring communities using network-based analysis of mentor-mentee relationships across Bobel laureates. *Scientometrics, 111*(3), 1733–1749. https://doi.org/10.1007/s11192-017-2364-4

Chun, J. U., Sosik, J. J., & Yun, N. Y. (2012). A longitudinal study of mentor and protégé outcomes in formal mentoring relationships. *Journal of Organizational Behavior, 33*(8), 1071–1094. https://doi.org/10.1002/job.1781

Clasen, D. R., & Clasen, R. E. (1997). Mentoring: A time-honoured option for education of the gifted and talented. In N. Colangelo & G. Davis (Eds.), *Handbook of gifted education* (2nd ed., pp. 218–229). Boston, MA: Allyn & Bacon.

Clasen, D. R., & Clasen, R. E. (2003). Mentoring the gifted and talented. In N. Colangelo & G. Davis (Eds.), *Handbook of gifted education* (3rd ed., pp. 254–267). Boston, MA: Allyn & Bacon.

Csikzentmihayli, M., Rathunde, K., & Whalden, S. (1993). *Talented teenagers: The roots of success and failure*. New York, NY: Cambridge Press.

Dobrow, S. R., Chandler, D. E., Murphy, W. M., & Kram, K. E. (2012). A review of developmental networks: Incorporating a mutuality perspective. *Journal of Management, 38*(1), 210–242. https://doi.org/10.1177/0149206311415858

Dominguez, N., & Hager, M. (2013). Mentoring frameworks: Synthesis and critique. *International Journal of Mentoring and Coaching in Education, 2*(3), 171–188. https://doi.org/10.1108/IJMCE-03-2013-0014

Eby, L. T., & Lockwood, A. (2005). Protégés' and mentors' reactions to participating in formal mentoring programs: A qualitative investigation. *Journal of Vocational Behavior, 67*(3), 441–458. https://doi.org/10.1016/j.jvb.2004.08.002

Egan, T. M. (2005). The impact of learning goal orientation similarity on formal mentoring relationship outcomes. *Advances in Developing Human Resources, 7*(4), 489–504. https://doi.org/10.1177/1523422305279679

Ellingson, M. K., Haeger, W. W., & Feldhusen, J. F. (1986). The Purdue Mentor Programme: A university-based mentorship experience for G/C/T children. *Gifted Child Today, 9*(2), 2–5. https://doi.org/10.1177/107621758600900201

Feldhusen, J. F. (2005). Giftedness, talent, expertise, and creative achievement. In R. J. Sternberg & J. E. Davidson (Eds.), *Conceptions of giftedness* (2nd ed., pp. 64–79). New York, NY: Cambridge University Press.

Feldman, D. (1988). *Managing careers in organizations*. Glenview, IL: Scott Foresman & Company.

Feldman, D. H. (1986). *Nature's gambit*. New York, NY: Basic Books.

Fereday, J., & Muir-Cochrane, E. (2006). Demonstrating rigor using thematic analysis: A hybrid approach of inductive and deductive coding and theme development. *International Journal of Qualitative Methods, 5*(1), 80–92. https://doi.org/10.1177/160940690600500107

Gagné, F. (2003). Transforming gifts into talents: The DMGT as a developmental theory. In N. Colangelo & G. A. Davis (Eds.), *Handbook of gifted education* (3rd ed., pp. 60–74). Boston, MA: Allyn & Bacon.

Gagné, F. (2004). Transforming gifts into talents: The DMGT as a developmental theory. *High Ability Studies, 15*(2), 119–147. https://doi.org/10.1080/1359813042000314682

Gagné, F. (2007). Ten commandments for academic talent development. *Gifted Child Quarterly, 51*(2), 93–118. https://doi.org/10.1177/0016986206296660

Goertzel, M. G., Goertzel, V., & Goertzel, T. G. (1978). *300 eminent personalities*. San Francisco, CA: Jossey-Bass.

Grassinger, R., Porath, M., & Ziegler, A. (2010). Mentoring the gifted: A conceptual analysis. *High Ability Studies, 21*(1), 27–46. https://doi.org/10.1080/13598139.2010.488087

Grima, F., Paillé, P. H., Mejia, J., & Prud'Homme, L. (2014). Exploring the benefits of mentoring activities for the mentor. *Career Development International, 19*(4), 469–490. https://doi.org/10.1108/CDI-05-2012-0056

Grybek, D. D. (1997). Mentoring the gifted and talented, preventing school failure. *Alternative Education for Children and Youth, 41*(3), 115–118. https://doi.org/10.1080/10459889709603278

Hu, C., Baranik, L. E., & Wu, T. (2014). Antidotes to dissimilar mentor-protégé dyads. *Journal of Vocational Behavior, 85*(2), 219–227. https://doi.org/10.1016/j.jvb.2014.07.002

Jarvin, L., & Subotnik, R. F. (2015). Academic talent development in North America and Europe. *Asia Pacific Education Review, 16*, 297–306. https://doi.org/10.1007/s12564-015-9370-0

Jen, E. (2017). Affective interventions for high-ability students from 1984–2015: A review of published studies. *Journal of Advanced Academics, 28*(3), 225–247. https://doi.org/10.1177/1932202X17715305

Kardos, S. M., & Johnson, S. M. (2010). New teachers' experiences of mentoring: The good, the bad, and the inequity. *Journal of Educational Change, 11*(1), 23–44. https://doi.org/10.1007/s10833-008-9096-4

Krutetskii, V. A. (1976). *The psychology of mathematical abilities in school children*. Chicago, IL: University of Chicago Press.

Levinson, D. J., Darrow, C. N., Klein, E. B., Levinson, M. H., & McKee, B. (1978). *The seasons of a man's life*. New York, NY: Knopf.

Little, C. A., Kearney, K. L., & Britner, P. A. (2010). Students' self-concept and perceptions of mentoring relationships in a summer mentorship programme for talented adolescents. *Roeper Review, 32*, 189–199. https://doi.org/10.1080/02783193.2010.485307

Lozinak, K. (2016). Mentor matching does matter. *Delta Kappa Gamma Bulletin, 83*(1), 12–24.

Lupkowski, A. E., Assouline, S. G., & Vestal, J. (1992). Mentors in math. *Gifted Child Today, 15*(3), 26–31. https://doi.org/10.1177/107621759201500307

Menges, C. (2015). Toward improving the effectiveness of formal mentoring programs: Matching by personality matters. *Group & Organization Management*. Prepublished April 13, 2015, https://dx.doi.org/10.59601115579567

Merriam, S. (1983). Mentors and protégés: A critical review of literature. *Adult Education Quarterly, 33*(3), 161–173. https://doi.org/10.1177/074171368303300304

Olszewski-Kubilius, P., Subotnik, R. F., & Worrell, F. C. (2016). Aiming talent development toward creative eminence in the 21st century. *Roeper Review, 38*, 140–152. https://doi.org/10.1080/02783193.2016.1184497

Patton, M. (2002). *Qualitative research & evaluation methods* (3rd ed.). Thousand Oaks, CA: Sage.

Pleiss, M. K., & Feldhusen, J. F. (1995). Mentors, role models, and heroes in the lives of gifted children. *Educational Psychologist, 30*(3), 159–169. https://doi.org/10.1207/s15326985ep3003_6

Purcell, J. H., Renzulli, J. S., McCoach, D. B., & Spottiswoode, H. (2001). The magic of mentorships. *Parenting for High Potential, 27*, 22–26.

Quek, C. G. (2005). *A national study of scientific talent development in Singapore.* Unpublished doctoral thesis. Center for Gifted Education, College of William and Mary.

Ragins, B. R., & Scandura, T. A. (1999). Burden or blessing? Expected costs and benefits of being a mentor. *Journal of Organizational Behavior, 20*(4), 493–509. https://doi.org/10.1002/(SICI)1099-1379(199907)20:4<493:AID-JOB894>3.0.CO;2-T

Reilly, J. (1992). When does a student really need a professional mentor? *Gifted Child Today, 15*(3), 2–8. https://doi.org/10.1177/107621759201500301

Sahin, F. (2014). The effectiveness of mentoring strategy for developing the creative potential of the gifted and non-gifted students. *Thinking Skills and Creativity, 14*, 47–55. https://doi.org/10.1016/j.tsc.2014.07.002

Seaborg, G. T. (1991). *A nation at risk revisited.* Lawrence Berkeley Laboratory, University of California. Retrieved from https://escholarship.org/uc/item/37m3m9v0

Searby, L. (2009). "But I Thought. ..." An examination of assumptions in the mentoring relationship. *Adult Learning, 20*(1–2), 10–13. https://doi.org/10.1177/104515950902000103

Silverman, L. K. (1997). The construct of asynchronous development. *Peabody Journal of Education, 72*(3–4), 36–58. https://doi.org/10.1080/0161956X.1997.9681865

Stanley, J. (1978). Educational non-acceleration: An international tragedy. *Gifted Child Today, 1*(3), 2–5.

Stoeger, H., Hopp, M., & Zeigler, A. (2017). Online mentoring as an extracurricular measure to encourage talented girls in STEM (science, technology, engineering, and mathematics): An empirical study of one-on-one versus group mentoring. *Gifted Child Quarterly, 61*(3), 239–249. https://doi.org/10.1177/0016986217702215

Subotnik, R. F. (2015). Psychosocial strength training: The missing piece in talent development. *Gifted Child Today, 38*(1), 41–48. https://doi.org/10.1177/1076217514556530

Subotnik, R. F., Edmiston, A. M., Cook, L., & Ross, M. D. (2010). Mentoring for talent development, creativity, social skills, and insider knowledge: The APA Catalyst Programme. *Journal of Advanced Academics, 21*(4), 714–739. https://doi.org/10.1177/1932202X1002100406

Subotnik, R. F., & Rickoff, R. (2010). Should eminence based on outstanding innovation be the goal of gifted education and talent development? Implications for policy and research. *Learning and Individual Differences, 20*, 358–364. https://doi.org/10.1016/j.lindif.2009.12.005

VanTassel-Baska, J. (2000). Curriculum policy development for secondary gifted programs: A prescription for reform coherence. *NASSP Bulletin, 84*(615), 14–29. https://doi.org/10.1177/019263650008461503

Weinberg, F. J., & Lankau, M. J. (2011). Formal mentoring programs: A mentor-centric and longitudinal analysis. *Journal of Management, 37*(6), 1527–1557. https://doi.org/10.1177/0149206309349310

Zukerman, H. (1967). Nobel laureates in science: Patterns of productivity, collaboration, and authorship. *American Sociological Review, 23*(3), 391–403. https://doi.org/10.2307/2091086

Zuckermam, H. (1968). Nobel laureates in the United States: A sociological study of scientific collaboration. Doctoral Dissertation, Columbia University.

Liang See Tan is a Senior Research Scientist, the Assistant Dean (School Partnerships) at Office of Education Research, and also the Program Director, Teacher Professionalism and Learning at the Centre for Research in Pedagogy and Practice, National Institute of Education, Singapore. She began as a teacher in the regular classroom and later in the gifted education program. She received a PhD from Nanyang Technological University and graduated from Purdue University with Master of Science in education. She taught high school for 16 years and was the Head of its Gifted Education Department before joining the NIE. She has published book chapters and journal papers and serves as a reviewer for international peer-reviewed journals. She is the principal investigator of several projects in the area of curriculum innovation and teacher professional learning and development. Liang See's research interests include academic emotion, motivation, and student outcomes, teacher learning and teacher agency in the area of curriculum differentiation for high ability learners and talent development.

Jing Yi Tan is a Research Assistant in the Centre for Research in Pedagogy and Practice, Office of Education Research, National Institute of Education. She graduated from Singapore Management University with a Bachelor's Degree in Social Sciences in 2016 and has since been developing research knowledge and skills in the field of education. She is currently working on a two-year project that focuses on characterising professional learning communities in Singapore.

Terence Titus Chia is a Research Assistant under the Centre for Research in Pedagogy and Practice, Office of Education Research, National Institute of Education. He graduated and received his Bachelor of Psychology Degree from James Cook University Singapore in 2016. He is currently working on a two-year project that focuses on the characterisation and contextualisation of professional learning communities in Singapore.

Nurturing Mathematical Talents of Young Mathematically Gifted English Language Learners

39

Seokhee Cho, Marcella Mandracchia, and Jenny Yang

Contents

Abstract

English Learners (ELs) are the fastest-growing segment of the school-age population in the USA and across the world. Yet, they are the least represented in gifted programs. Research studies on gifted ELs mainly focus on how to increase the number of gifted ELs placed in the gifted education program. Few studies are

S. Cho (✉) · J. Yang
St. John's University, New York, NY, USA
e-mail: chos1@stjohns.edu; yangj1@stjohns.edu

M. Mandracchia
Adelphi University, New York, NY, USA
e-mail: mmandracchia@adelphi.edu

© Springer Nature Singapore Pte Ltd. 2021
S. R. Smith (ed.), *Handbook of Giftedness and Talent Development in the Asia-Pacific*,
Springer International Handbooks of Education,
https://doi.org/10.1007/978-981-13-3041-4_38

available on how to provide equitable education to the gifted ELs. The study presented in this chapter uses *Recognition, Expectation, and Differentiation* (RED) as a theoretical framework for creating preparatory/transitional programs for gifted ELs. Exemplary preparatory programs—that is, the Javits Project HOPE and Javits Project BRIDGE—for nurturing mathematical talent of gifted ELs, with sample scaffolding strategies, are provided. Scaffolding strategies for developing receptive language skills, productive language skills, and metacognitive skills are also presented. Examination of the effects of *Mentoring Mathematical Minds* (M^3) program, developed by Gavin, Casa, Adelson, Carroll, Sheffield, and Spinelli (2007), on mathematics achievement and English proficiency development of the *Mathematically Promising ELLs* (MPELLs) demonstrated significant mathematical gains and language proficiency for intervention group students. Qualitative analyses of instructional behaviours of the treatment teachers with high and low fidelity with their students supplemented evidence that students' achievement gains in mathematics may be from creating safe, supportive, but challenging environments with challenging mathematics content and scaffolding language and metacognitive skills developing within the M^3 units. Implications for educational practices and future research are discussed.

Keywords

English learners · Mathematics · Gifted · Scaffolding strategies · Preparatory program

The aims in this chapter are to:
1. Address the issue of developing mathematical talent of gifted English learners.
2. Provide theoretical frameworks for nurturing mathematical talent of gifted English learners.
3. Guide teachers on how to create safe, supportive, but challenging environments for gifted English learners with receptive, productive, and metacognitive scaffolding strategies.
4. Present research findings on the effects of accelerated and enriched mathematics curriculum with scaffolding mathematics achievement and English proficiency.

Introduction

How to recognise and cultivate the talents of gifted *English Learners* (ELs) is a global issue, since many countries are experiencing an increase in immigration for various reasons including for employment, for study, or as refugees. Globally, migration in various directions has increased continuously from 1900 to 2015 (Connor & Lopez, 2016). ELs represent more than 4.4 million students in K–12 public schools in the USA (National Center for Education Statistics [NCES], 2014).

As of 2012–2013, approximately 21% of school-aged children in the USA spoke a language other than English at home (NCES, 2014). This percentage is projected to be more than 40% by 2030 (Thomas & Collier, 2001). In Asian countries, the number of students with limited educational language proficiency is also growing steadily. In South Korea, recently, the number of children from multicultural families has reached 41,000 in 2011 (Han & Han, 2013). Children from multicultural families are born between spouses of Koreans and foreign residents with different cultural backgrounds and languages. Hence, Korean multicultural families, especially where mothers are not native Korean speakers, have rapidly increased from 8.4% in 2003 to 11.9% of all new families in 2006 (Han & Han, 2013). In Hong Kong, there are "700,000 new Chinese immigrant children, which is one-tenth of the total population of Hong Kong" in 2002 (Zhang & Ting, 2011, p. 49). During the last 60 years, Australia and New Zealand have adopted a qualification system to encourage the selection of highly skilled migrants, thereby increasing the percentage of *English Language Learners* (ELLs) every year (Winkelmann, 2001). Many of these immigrant children's education within these different countries and contexts are impacted by cultural difference, economic disadvantage, language differences, and limited language proficiency (Han & Han, 2013; Zhan, 2005; Zhou & Kim, 2006).

With lack of the second or third language as a barrier to participation in and access to the education system, ELs are disproportionately underrepresented in gifted education programs (Brulles, Castellano, & Laing, 2011; García & Frede, 2010; Harris, Plucker, Rapp, & Martínez, 2009; Harris, Rapp, Martínez, & Plucker, 2007; Plucker, Burroughs, & Song, 2010). The excellence gap between gifted ELs and their English-speaking gifted peers continues to widen (Finn, 2014a, b). It is critical to recognise and nurture the academic talents of gifted ELs more systematically (Bianco & Harris, 2014; Marshall, McGee, McLaren, & Veal, 2011; Olszewski-Kubilius & Clarenbach, 2012; Walsh, 2013).

The majority of students in gifted education programs in the USA represent the dominant culture (Donovan & Cross, 2002). Under-representation of gifted ELs in gifted education programs may be a result of their disadvantaged environments. Many gifted ELs may have had limited exposure to intellectual stimuli when younger. Lack of exposure to learning experiences or intellectual stimuli may have been caused by economic poverty, ineffective childcare by parents, the low value placed on education, low awareness of the right to an education, disregard for knowledge and skills, lack of verbal interaction, provision of inappropriate information to questions, or low value on social success (Banks, 1993; Lee, Yoo, Yeo, & Kim, 2011).

Teachers and parents can begin to cultivate talent in young students by engaging their interests in different knowledge domains. Once a student starts to exhibit superior abilities in a specific field, their talent can be further developed through intense learning opportunities (Gagné, 2010; Subotnik, Olszewski-Kubilius, & Worrell, 2012). Teachers and parents have the responsibility to recognise talented students and provide them with resources and access to information to refine their talents (Siegle et al., 2016). In addition, teachers and parents must nurture students' interests and intrinsic motivation to learn, as this self-generated desire to achieve exceptional talent is the central force behind talent development. Ultimately, it is the individual who has to actively seize and utilise the opportunities available to them to develop their talents to the maximum extent (Subotnik et al., 2012).

Science, Technology, Engineering, and Mathematics (STEM) talents of ELs are the least recognised and nurtured in school settings. Given the continued growth of students learning English as a new language, their chronic academic under-performance (National Center for Education Statistics, 2016) and low participation rate in STEM and gifted programs is alarming.

The workforce in STEM has grown 669% from 1950 to 2000, whereas the workforce as a whole only grew by 130% (Lowell & Regets, 2006 as cited in Varma & Frehill, 2010). Job growth in STEM occupations is projected to be 22% between 2012 and 2022 (U.S. Bureau of Labor, 2014). However, there is a gap between the number of job opportunities and the number of minority students who matriculate in STEM fields.

Research studies on gifted ELs mainly focus on the identification process, but few studies focus on how schools should provide an equitable education for gifted ELs (Blackburn, Cornish, & Smith, 2016; Peters, Matthews, McBee, & McCoach, 2014). The "general dearth of evidence of effective practices and activities" (USDOE, 2007, p. 8) is especially seen in STEM fields. Without challenging and nurturing interventions for gifted ELs, they will not be ready for, nor seek, nor have an interest in developing their high potential to their maximum.

Theoretical Frameworks for Developing Preparatory Programs for Gifted ELs

Identifying and placing more ELs into gifted programs does not guarantee their talent development (Siegle et al., 2016). Gifted ELs need support and challenge for intense learning and practice. Few models are available on how to nurture the mathematical talent of gifted ELs (Blackburn et al., 2016). One model found for nurturing talent development of gifted ELs is Bianco and Harris' (2014) strength-based *Response To Intervention* (RTI) model. Echevarria, Vogt and Short's (2010) *Sheltered Instruction Observation Protocol* (SIOP) for comprehensible input for ELs and culturally responsive pedagogy (Gay, 2010; Paris, 2012) is used to provide scaffolding supports for ELs' English language acquisition needs. However, these approaches do not differentiate for enrichment and acceleration for their needs as gifted students.

One of the recommended practices for under-represented gifted students is to provide a preparatory/transitional program for accessibility to more under-represented gifted and help them stay in gifted education programs (Baldwin, 1994; Borland & Wright, 1994; Cho, Yang, & Mandracchia, 2015; Siegle et al., 2016). In this chapter, a conceptual model for preparatory/transitional programs for gifted ELs based on the RED model is presented. The RED is a model to improve the achievement of gifted ELs by modifying classroom practices through promoting their perception of their own competency and increase the perceived value of initiating and completing tasks (Eccles, 2006; Eccles, O'Neill, & Wigfield, 2005). RED is an acronym that stands for the three most compelling components that have an impact on student achievement and motivation: recognition, expectation, and differentiation. The aims of the RED model are to recognise and take advantage of strengths and identify and compensate for weaknesses in schools, families, and communities so that students can become more confident about their capacity, develop their mastery goals, be more passionate, have an intense engagement with tasks, and persevere with challenges when completing tasks.

The RED model is developed based on the dual-view of motivation (Eccles, 2006; Eccles et al., 2005). The dual-view of motivation is summarised into the two questions of 'Can I?' and 'Do I want to do it?'. 'Can I?' is related to *expectancy*, which includes attribution, confidence, self-efficacy, and self-concept. 'Do I want to do it?' is related to the sources of *value*, which include interest in tasks (e.g., intrinsic motivation), importance or usefulness (e.g., extrinsic motivation, performance goal, mastery goal), or trade-off or cost of doing the task. Studies have found different consequences for different sources of motivation especially for gifted students (e.g., Siegle & McCoach, 2005). If any individual answers 'Yes' to the two questions, then it is highly likely that they will take opportunities and commit themselves to the tasks.

Recognition of Strengths

Recognition of their strengths motivates the individual to excel more (Bianco & Harris, 2014). Upon recognition of a gifted EL's strengths, educational interventions should be implemented to maximise those strengths. Then, their efforts and improvements through the educational intervention should be rewarded. Criterion-referenced evaluation is useful to recognise individual student's strengths and provide feedback on their work in relation to the standards. The information from the criterion-referenced evaluation will also be very informative for differentiation of curriculum and instruction. Teachers can also be informed about what the students need to master and what they are already advanced in (Bianco & Harris, 2014).

Recognition is generally viewed as an extrinsic motivator, but recognition for their efforts and improvement in comparison with the learning goals or with their starting point, not with their classmates, is what will develop their intrinsic motivation (Dweck, 2007). Feedback on their work should be individually provided, rather than in comparison to a group for the recognition to contribute to the development of intrinsic motivation.

Expectations from Parents and Teachers

It is necessary to challenge gifted ELs with high expectations from parents and teachers. However, deficit thinking is prevalent among educators and community members for gifted EL students (Ford, 2011; Frasier, 1997). Expectations, as communicated schoolwide and in the classroom, can and do influence student achievement (Brophy, 1983; Brophy & Good, 1970; Good, 1987; Wineburg, 1987). Cotton (1989) reviewed several studies on the relationship between teacher expectations and student achievement and found that teacher expectations and accompanying behaviours have a very real effect on student performance, accounting for five to ten per cent of achievement outcomes. Communicating low expectations has more power to limit student achievement than communicating high expectations to raise student performance (Ford, 2010). Younger children are more susceptible to the effects of expectations than are older children. Long-Mitchell (2011) found some teachers treat students with low expectations in ways likely to inhibit their growth (e.g., expose them to less learning material and material that is less interesting, giving them less time to respond to questions and communicating less warmth and affection to them).

It was also found that different ethnic groups in different countries have different expectations about their students' achievements, resulting in different ratios of low-performing children with low-income. Tucker (2016) claimed that most of the Asian countries have less low-performing children with low income, because these countries expect all children to perform at high levels. Yamamoto's and Holloway's (2010) review of studies on parental expectations and children's academic performance found that Asian parents expected their children could improve their performances whether their children already performed high or not, whereas European American parents' expectations are based on their children's past achievement or based on their children's innate abilities.

Children with limited English proficiency may not be challenged in mathematics. Classroom environments with high expectations of gifted ELs should stimulate them and encourage them to achieve as much as they can, rather than protecting them from failure (Cotton, 1989). To stretch students' minds, Maker and Nielson (1995) suggest that classrooms should: be learner-centred (rather than teacher- or content-centred); promote independence (rather than dependence); be open to students' new ideas and innovations; exercise acceptance rather than judgement; focus on complexity rather than simplicity; vary grouping options (rather than have one general grouping technique); and use flexible (rather than rigid or chaotic) class structures. When expecting the gifted EL to perform outstandingly, these environmental conditions should be maintained.

Differentiation of Curriculum and Instruction

Differentiation is critical for gifted EL students to feel 'Yes, I can' and 'I want to do'. Differentiation is a process for teachers to enhance the match between learners' unique learning needs and various curriculum components. Content, teaching methods, learning activities, and student products can be modified to address the needs of individual students to maximise their learning (Tomlinson, 1999; Tomlinson et al., 2003). Through differentiation in complexity, depth, pacing, and breadth, teachers can provide individual students with learning experiences of optimum difficulty (Maker & Schiever, 2010). To meet the unique needs of gifted ELs, such as limited English vocabulary, weak academic content knowledge, and inexperienced skills, comprehensible input (Krashen, 1982) should be provided.

Comprehensible input follows Vygotsky's (1978) *Zone of Proximal Development* (ZPD) theory, which claims that students will progress to the next stage of knowledge and skill acquisition when learning materials require knowledge and skills, which are slightly above their mastery level. At the same time, gifted ELs need challenges in other aspects such as logical reasoning, creativity, and problem-solving. A differentiated classroom offers a variety of learning options designed to tap into different readiness levels, interests, and learning profiles (Maker & Schiever, 2010).

Goals of differentiation for gifted ELs are to intensely build content knowledge and skills and to improve English proficiency so that they may enter and be successful in the traditional advanced gifted education programs available. Program activities need to be moved from enrichment activities initially to accelerative experiences eventually (Ford & Grantham, 2012; Olszewski-Kubilius & Thomson, 2010). Through the many forms of differentiation, students will have more choice, which will contribute to increased expectancy and value of engaging in certain tasks. Providing diverse options in terms of topics, methods, and products or providing open-ended tasks where students can choose issues, methods, or form of products will allow students to pursue their interests (Maker, & Schiever, 2010).

Exemplary Preparatory Program for Nurturing Mathematical Talent of Gifted ELs

Preparatory programs for under-represented gifted students have been implemented through several Javits grant projects (e.g., Project LIVE, Project HOPE, Project BRIDGE, Project U-Star Plus), but are not practised in schools widely. The Hong Kong government provides a six-month full-time initiation program for young immigrant children before they enter regular schools. It provides schools with resources that can be used for a supplementary program, extracurricular activities, and orientation sessions (Education Bureau, The Government of the Hong Kong Special Administrative Region, 2018). Even though it is not specifically for gifted students, similar arrangements can be made for children with high potential.

These preparatory/transitional programs are well aligned with a new innovative talent development paradigm (Peters et al., 2014; Siegle et al., 2016; Subotnik et al., 2012). Peters et al. (2014) suggest creating a gifted education program based on the needs of the community or the school and then identify those who would benefit the most from the program. To identify students for the preparatory gifted program, the local norm of the target student group may be used (Lohman, 2005). These preparatory programs take different forms and many supplement schooling with afterschool, summer, and weekend courses. Preparatory gifted programs for the under-represented are designed to improve students' academic competency in consideration of their needs, strengths, and current achievement levels, based on the belief that talent development requires intense learning, practice, and experiences. It was found that Minority gifted students who participated in preparatory types of educational programs were better prepared to enter advanced and accelerated programs later. In addition, they were potentially less negatively influenced by their peers and received support for their goals and aspirations (Baldwin, 1994; Borland & Wright, 1994; Cho et al., 2015; Grantham, 2002; Olszewski-Kubilius, 2007; Olszewski-Kubilius & Thomson, 2010).

The Javits Project HOPE and Javits Project BRIDGE attempted to create preparatory mathematics programs for gifted ELs. With Project HOPE conducted in 2009–2014, Cho et al. (2015) had the 3rd Grade Mathematically Promising ELs learn advanced mathematics curriculum for three consecutive years until they completed Grade 5. Project BRIDGE in 2017–2022 will extend the Project HOPE program for gifted ELs in Grades K for three consecutive years until they complete Grade 2. Both Project HOPE and Project BRIDGE implement an enriched and advanced mathematics program with language scaffolding strategies for gifted ELs, but in different grades. These programs were developed and implemented based on the RED model.

Selected Base Curriculum: M^2 and M^3, the Enriched and Advanced Mathematics Curriculum

Considering gifted EL students' unique needs, *Mentoring Young Mathematicians* (M^2) and *Mentoring Mathematical Minds* (M^3) were selected for gifted ELs. M^2 and M^3 are a series of eight to twelve curriculum units designed for grades K–2 and grades 3–5 respectively. M^2 and M^3 units have several other features that can be effectively utilised for teaching mathematics to Mathematically Promising ELs. These programs employ an enriched and accelerated approach to learning (Gavin et al., 2007; Gavin, Casa, Firmender, & Carroll, 2013) with four key characteristics: important and advanced mathematics, a depth of understanding and complexity, differentiated instruction, and communication (see Gavin, Casa, Adelson, Carroll, & Sheffield, 2009; Gavin et al., 2013, for detailed descriptions). Each lesson has 'Think Deeply' questions and a mathematician's journal that students use to develop and organise their mathematical reasoning. These questions are based on a student-centred inquiry approach to encourage students to make sense of a 'big idea' or concept through four stages of problem-solving: problem presentation, learning new concepts, using learning concepts to solve problems, and summarising. Students express their mathematical reasoning through writing in their student journals and verbally presenting ideas to small or large groups. These opportunities not only stimulate dialogue but also foster conceptual understanding. To address differentiated instruction, each lesson provides 'Think Beyond Cards' for students who are ready for additional challenges and 'hint cards' for struggling students who need assistance with understanding the concept and/or a catalyst for jump-starting the self-inquiry process. Using the pre-assessment unit tests, teachers can determine who is ready for more challenges and who needs more support (Gavin et al., 2009, 2013).

Recognise students' strengths and talents. Project HOPE provided a mathematics enrichment supplementary program to gifted ELs in Grade 3 during the afterschool hours for three consecutive years. The top 25% of ELs in Grade 3 in each school were selected as Mathematically Promising ELs based on their mathematics classroom behaviours to participate in the advanced mathematics program. Teachers were trained on the observational checklist and recommended students who were eligible. Students' peers also nominated. No test score was used for selection of gifted ELs (Cho et al., 2015). Selected students gathered together during the afterschool hours and learnt the advanced and enriched mathematics program M^3 for about 100 hours a year. In these homogenous classes of gifted ELs during the afterschool hours, students should have felt that their talents were being recognised as much as their strengths. The simple rhetoric of teachers, such as 'our mathematicians', aimed to motivate and improve students' mathematical problem-solving.

Expectations: Create Safe and Supportive, but Challenging Environments

Gifted ELs should be expected to be active problem-solvers participating in classroom activities and discussions, and they should be allowed to take risks to make mistakes while being challenged with problems rather than being protected (Levitt, 2001; Reeve, 2006). To encourage gifted ELs to be active problem-solvers, the classroom environment needs to be supportive, warm, and structured (LeClair, Doll, Osborn, & Jones, 2009; Maker & Nielson, 1995). As indicated by a focus group with the teachers of Project HOPE, the environment was safe and their feelings were valued (Mandracchia, 2015). The idea that students can speak about their ideas and feelings in an unobtrusive setting allowed for a safe classroom climate. Students must be able to feel supported, receive gentle discipline, and feel as if the teacher can relate to them. Therefore, the positive teacher-student rapport helped students develop their capacity for independent action and responsibility (Grasha, 1994).

Removal of affective filters is another currently recommended practice for ELs. Krashen (1982) stated that there were several 'affective' variables that influence the acquisition of a second language. The hypothesis of the affective filter comprises that the environment for learning must be low-anxiety where motivation, self-confidence, and self-image must be in good standing. If the environment causes high anxiety, and low self-esteem, the context raises the affective filter, which forms a 'mental block' that impedes comprehensible input from being used. In this example study, teachers made pedagogical connections within the context in which they are teaching. Winn and Johnson (2011) suggested teachers should effectively develop an inclusive environment for diverse learners by asking pertinent questions, such as:

- How can I honour my students' backgrounds and experiences to help them become better?

- How can I teach in a culturally responsive way if I don't share the cultural identities with my students?
- How can I move beyond a heroes-and-holidays approach to culturally relevant pedagogy?
- How can I draw on what I already know about good instruction to make my classroom more culturally relevant?
- How can I create culturally responsive assessments?

Once teachers have internalised and applied these pedagogical ideas, students' achievements, as well as self-efficacy, has the potential to improve (Winn & Johnson, 2011).

While most teachers already set ground rules for classroom behaviour—be on time, listen, and follow directions, share, and take turns—gifted ELs' active participation in classroom discussion requires more specialised norms. For young students, this means explicit teaching and a repeated reminder of the rules until students have internalised them. Firm establishment of rules for respectful discourse can help build students' confidence in talking about how they think. Chapin, O'Connor, and Anderson (2009) have suggested the following list of students' rights and obligations for building supportive classroom cultures. As speakers, we will:

- Talk loud enough for others to hear.
- Turn to talk to the class.
- Share different ideas.
- Explain our ideas.
- Agree and disagree with ideas, not with each other.

As listeners, we will:

- Ask speakers to speak up.
- Show speakers we are listening.
- Listen to understand.
- Ask questions to make sense of the ideas.
- Think carefully about speakers' ideas.

When ELs make mistakes, they are less afraid of being ridiculed or dismissed and more open to constructive criticism from their teachers and peers. To further reduce the anxiety that ELs may experience in public speaking, the teacher can structure partner talk or small group talk as a preparation time for students to practise what they will say. By giving ELs the extra time to think and practise, teachers build in extra support in the classroom to help build students' confidence for future participation (Chapin et al., 2009).

In fact, the intervention group teachers of Project HOPE, during their focus group discussions, mentioned safe environment frequently as a critical factor, which resulted in higher achievement of gifted ELs (Mandracchia, 2015). One participating teacher told the authors that:

> when students first came to the class, they stared at each other without saying much. I was not sure whether I could actually teach them at all. After one-month implementation of the program (during the afterschool hours), they talk a lot. I cannot believe they are the same students that I met in the first session. (Cho et al., 2015)

Gifted ELs, being in a homogenous group of all gifted ELs without native speakers who may overwhelm ELs with their fluent English, might have felt safe and supported and wanted to share their ideas and thoughts for challenging problems even though their language was not proficient yet. By infusing culturally responsive pedagogy into the classroom, students' cultural backgrounds and differences can be recognised as students' assets rather than deficits (Gay, 2010; Nieto, 2003).

Differentiate to Support with Receptive and Productive Language Scaffolding Strategies

The classroom dialogue should be comprehensible and supportive for ELs. Mathematically gifted ELs, by definition, have limited vocabulary and unmastered language skills of the dominant language. Critical to their development are language scaffolding strategies, which can be categorised into two types: receptive and productive scaffolding strategies. Receptive scaffolding strategies may include presenting new important vocabulary with sounds, pictures, and their native languages, or the use of a glossary, word banks, and visual aids. Productive scaffolding strategies include sentence frames, sentence starters, and word drops which support students' writing (Donnelly & Roe, 2010). Below are examples of these receptive and productive scaffolding strategies to support gifted ELs for their comprehension and written and oral expression.

Various receptive scaffolds have been developed to support gifted ELs through the Lesson 1.1: *Measuring the Space Shuttle Flight* from the Mentoring Young Mathematicians (M^2) curriculum on measurement. M^2's focus on discourse in mathematics poses a formidable challenge to gifted ELs in Grade K. Our goal is to adapt the curriculum based on strategies that are best practice for all students and provide additional language support for gifted ELs (Cho, Jo, & Hulse, 2018). What follows is a sample of these flexible, high-yield scaffolds that teachers can adapt to help their students meet and exceed the standards of mathematical literacy.

Explicit teaching of mathematics vocabulary is coupled with repetitive opportunities for students to use the new words with peers and the teacher (Feldman & Kinsella, 2008). In the example below, we will show how the teacher can guide students to examine the key aspects of academic vocabulary in a whole-class discussion setting:

T: You measured how far your space shuttle flew, and then you measured how far your partner's space shuttle flew. Please hold up your tapes (direct students to stand next to their partners).

T: Can you look at your tape? And then look at your partner's tape. What do you notice?

S: They have different lengths.

T: Would someone like to come up with their partner and show us their tapes (select a pair of students with a longer and shorter tape to come to the front of the room)?

T: Do you see any difference between Sandra's and James' tapes?

S: Sandra's tape is long. James' tape is short.

T: When we compare different lengths, you can say "Sandra's tape is longer than James' tape." "James' tape is shorter than Sandra's." They look like words that we have learned before. I am trying to think back.... can someone help me?

S: Longer is almost like long. And you add "er" at the end.

T: Very good. "Longer" and "shorter" look like "long" and "short", but their ends are different with extra letters, "er" (highlight the "er" endings in longer and shorter")?

T: Can we say, "My hair is longer"?

S: No, you can't.

T: Then, when can you use "longer" or "shorter"?

S: You can say "My hair is longer than my brother's" (write students' examples on the board, circle the sentences with the correct usage of the words "long" and "longer"; illustrate the syntax or the rules of grammar).

T: Oh, I see, so we can use "longer" when we are looking at two people's hair, like yours and your brother's. When do we use the word "long"?

S: When you are only talking about one person's hair.

T: Correct. We use "long" when we are looking and talking about one thing. We use "longer" when we compare two things (direct students to compare their tapes against their partner's).

T: Now let's compare your tape with your partners. Talk to each other about who has a longer tape, and who has a shorter tape. Write down your answers.

Productive scaffolding strategies include the use of sentence frames, sentence starters, and graphic organisers, examples of which are below.

Sentence frames. Sentence frames are used to scaffold students' writing with some necessary words already provided and a small range of options to complete the sentences (Kinsella, 2012). They may be accompanied by a word bank of relevant vocabulary that students have learned. For example:

My partner and I _____the _____ of our tapes.
My tape is _____ than my partner's.
Word bank: measured, compared, length, longer, shorter.

Sentence starters. Sentence starters, like sentence frames, provide a partial frame for students to express their ideas. However, sentence starters provide the first few words that begin the sentence, and the student must complete the rest independently. This type of support should be used for open-ended questions and is more suited for students with a higher level of language proficiency. Sentence starters can also be used to help students sequence a series of events. For example:

First, my partner and I _____.
Next, we _____.
Finally, we_____.
After comparing the tapes, I _____.

Graphic organisers. Graphic organisers are visual and graphic displays that can be used to help students connect a newly learnt concept to prior knowledge at the summarising phase of the problem-solving. Types of graphic organisers include concept maps, story maps, word drop, and foldables. The teacher can either provide the graphic organiser to students to partially complete or allow students to construct independently. The level of support given should be differentiated based on students' abilities (August, Fenner, & Bright, 2014). In the example below, word drop is used to help students make connections between key vocabulary and concepts learnt from previous lessons, including length and measurement. Word drop can be used on an individual basis, or as a tool to facilitate classroom discussion. It can be text or visual-based or a mixture of both.

Differentiate to Challenge with Metacognitive Scaffolding Strategies

Research has shown that students who communicate and reason about mathematics problems show a greater potential for understanding the concepts that underlie the problems (Ball & Bass, 2000; Cobb, Boufi, McClain, & Whitenack, 1997; Krashen, 1982; Stein, Grover, & Henningsen, 1996). Gifted ELs can think at a deeper level and grasp new concepts. Metacognitive scaffolding strategies, such as Talk moves or 6W higher order thinking questions, support students' critical thinking and problem-solving processes during the discussions.

Talk Moves. To assist ELs, teachers can prompt students with talk moves (Chapin et al., 2009). Talk Moves can be used to facilitate gifted ELs to become active problem-solvers and improve their discourse competency as well. Talk Moves allow students to move from being passive learners to active problem-solvers. Chapin et al. (2009) developed Talk Moves, such as 'revoice', 'restate', 'agree/disagree and why', 'add-on', 'wait time', and 'partner talk'. These particular strategies were infused into Project HOPE as part of the *Mentoring Mathematical Minds* (M^3) curriculum developed by Gavin et al. (2009). In the Project HOPE, these talk moves were used to: "(a) explicitly validate ELs' reasoning; (b) invite ELs to share, justify, or clarify thinking that positioned ELs as competent problem solvers; and (c) invite peers to respond to an EL's idea in ways that positioned the idea as important and/or mathematically justified" (Turner, Dominguez, Maldonado, & Empson, 2013, p. 199). Furthermore, *Talk Moves* helped gifted ELs to understand critical mathematical content, since the ELs had to participate in behaviours, such as: "(a) explaining a solution strategy: (b) justifying an idea; (c) making a mathematical connection or claim; and (d) evaluating the idea of a peer" (Turner et al., 2013, p. 209). Therefore, the gifted ELs were becoming agentive problem-solvers. *Revoicing*, as Moschkovich (1999) stated, enables the teacher to restate the ideas to the class in a different way and demonstrate that the contributions of the students are valued. Restate allows for the students to repeat what their classmate has stated in their own way to build their own linguistic competencies as well as mathematical competencies. Other strategies such as agree/disagree and why allowed students to evaluate ideas and add pertinent information needed to the response. These Talk Moves can be integrated with *6W questions* not only to allow the gifted ELs to actively participate in the classroom discourse, but also to organise and rationalise their reasoning during the classroom discussions. Talk Moves can be used by teachers to provide structured opportunities for students to speak out their reasoning processes as below (Chapin et al., 2009). To help students clarify and share their own thoughts:

- Will you share that with the class?
- Can you say more?
- So, are you saying...?

To help students orient to the thinking of others:

- Who can say that again?
- Who can put that into their own words?
- Can someone repeat what they heard (student's name) say?
- Tell us what your partner said. Will you share that with the class?

To help students deepen their own reasoning:

- Why do you think that?
- How did you get that answer?
- Why did you think that would work?
- Can you show us?
- What makes you think that? Can you say that again?

To help students engage with the reasoning of others:

- What do you think about (student's name) just said?
- Do you agree or disagree...and why?
- Who can add on to what (student's name) said?

Outcomes of Programs

Cho et al. (2015), Mandracchia (2015), Napolitano (2016), and Yang (2012) found that the teaching of enriched and advanced mathematics to gifted ELs in a safe, supportive but challenging environment with recognition of their strengths and cultural background, using language scaffolding and Talk Moves, resulted in significantly higher gains in mathematics achievement of gifted EL students. The M^3 program implementation for one year to intervention Mathematically Promising ELLs (MPELLs, $n = 86$) was found to result in significant more gains than for control MPELLs ($n = 85$). Treatment teachers attended five days of professional development provided by the program development team. The treatment group students were grouped into classes of eight to ten, and the instructions were given in a self-contained setting during afterschool hours.

Hierarchical linear modelling (HLM) was used to find and examine differences between: (a) treatment and control groups (level 1); (b) the same groups (treatment or control) in different schools (level 2); and (c) the same groups (treatment or control) in the same school (level 3). HLM analyses found significant difference at level 1, which indicated that treatment groups demonstrated significantly higher gains in mathematics achievement than the control groups ($d = 0.63$). There was no significant difference at level 2, which indicated that treatment groups from different schools performed similarly, and so did the control groups. There was also no significant difference at level 3, which means that in schools that had multiple treatment or control groups, the students from the same type of groups performed similarly. English proficiency of the treatment group was significantly higher than that of the control group ($F (1,190) = 8.03, p = 0.005$; Cho, Yang, & Mandracchia, 2014).

Qualitative analyses of instructional behaviours of the treatment teachers with high and low fidelity with their students supplemented evidence that students' achievement gains in mathematics may be more from the instructional and language scaffolding strategies used by the teachers than from curriculum. Their teachers used language scaffolding strategies as well as embodied the curriculum's strategies, such as Talk Moves, whereas the comparison group teachers did not. The fidelity and belief based on these ideas of culturally responsive pedagogy were, therefore, essential to its implementation. Without the marriage of strategies (culturally responsive pedagogy, affective filter, comprehensible input, Talk Moves, and scaffolding strategies), the gifted ELs would not be able to progress in their mathematical problem-solving. These strategies allowed the gifted ELs to have a clear pathway towards fostering their critical and creative thinking skills in these programs (Cho et al., 2014).

Implications for Future Educational Practices

The children of immigrants "carry on their young shoulders the dreams of families and communities who hope their children will gain the language and the skills for full participation in an English-speaking world" (Olsen, 2014, p. 4). In the USA the *Every Student Succeeds Act*, the main federal education law, has required states and districts to report the number of their students performing at the advanced academic level and to include advanced-achievement data for specific student groups, including English-language learners since 2016.

Focusing on how to identify and place more ELs into the gifted education program does not seem to be a solution for helping gifted EL students to excel academically. Erwin and Worrell (2012) found that those ethnically diverse students persist with low achievement even after they are placed in academically talented summer programs as gifted students. They claim that the use of multiple indicators and without the use of strict cut-off scores more ethnically diverse students may be identified and placed into gifted education programs. However, placement has not resulted in reducing the achievement gap among ethnic/racial groups in the academically talented summer program. Similar results may be expected for gifted ELs if gifted ELs are placed in gifted education programs without building habits of intense learning, confidence, and a strong foundation of knowledge and skills in advance.

Many Mathematically Promising ELs, without preparatory or transitional programs, may not immediately succeed in gifted education programs. They may struggle, persist with low achievement, and eventually drop out of gifted programs. However, they can flourish if their talents are recognised at a young age and they are placed in preparatory programs and are provided with advanced content, but with enough scaffolding in terms of inquiry, thinking skills, and language acquisition (Briggs, Reis, & Sullivan, 2008; Olszewski-Kubilius, Lee, Ngoi, & Ngoi, 2004). High expectations of gifted ELs with recognition of their cultures as assets through culturally responsive pedagogy will elevate their motivation for intense learning and practice. Providing a safe environment for risk taking while they are trying to express their ideas and thoughts is also critically needed, especially for gifted ELs.

With preparatory programs, gifted EL students have opportunities to develop habits of intense learning and practice, confidence, and the foundation of knowledge and skills. Siegle et al. (2016) also proposed a model of identification and talent development for gifted students, which includes pre-identification and placing under-represented students into preparation/transitional programs before formal identification and intervention. As Olszewski-Kubilius and Clarenbach (2012) and Siegle et al. (2016) suggest, creating and placing gifted ELs into preparatory programs need to be more widely practised alongside the provision of supplemental programs and an extension to their learning hours beyond regular school hours to equalise their learning opportunities.

Implications for Future Research

For future research, more studies should be conducted to understand how ELs either excel academically or struggle and drop out of high schools. Current research studies that focus on problems and possible modifications of identification practices of gifted ELs may need to be continued. However, the problem of underachievement of gifted ELs is complex and not fully understood. Surprisingly, many gifted ELs in the USA are born and raised in the USA, but they still remain and are identified as ELs in schools. Over 70% of the 3rd Grader ELs who participated in the Project HOPE were born and raised in the US for seven years and attended US schools for more than three years (Cho et al., 2015). These types of students have been described as Long-Term ELs. Long-Term ELs are students who have been categorised to have *Limited English Proficiency* for more than six years, and do not show progress towards reaching a threshold of adequate English language skills. As a result, they continue to struggle academically (Olsen, 2014; Perez, 2011). Olsen (2014) summarised the characteristics of Long-Term ELs as having habits of non-engagement, learned passivity, and invisibility in school; wanting to attend college despite significant gaps in academic preparation; and being discouraged and tuned-out learners, ready to drop out of high school. These learning characteristics of Long-Term ELs imply that it is possible for young gifted ELs to remain as Long-Term ELs due to low motivation and development of negative learning habits. It is also worthwhile to note that they still want to attend college showing high expectations for their own education.

Depending on the language proficiency level and age of gifted ELs, effective approaches for improving the achievement of gifted ELs and for stopping the development of negative learning habits may vary. Depending on the culture and value of the family and community, service delivery models for preparatory programs may take different approaches as well. Eng and Cho (2012) found Hispanic children who spent more time with their parents had lower achievement. These findings are contrary to what can be observed among Asian families. Asian parents including Koreans and Taiwanese children who spent more time with their parents had higher achievement (Cho & Campbell, 2011). It is necessary to further investigate why similar lengths of family time bring about different achievement outcomes for different ethnic groups and how each ethnic's family values and culture can be better understood and utilised to help children's achievement improve.

In terms of research design, spillover effects of a supplemental and longitudinal enrichment program for gifted ELs need to be carefully examined. The effects of the enrichment supplemental program were significant in the first year of the Project HOPE (Cho et al., 2015), but were not in years two and three. The intervention teachers' practices of teaching advanced mathematics curriculum and language-scaffolding strategies during the afterschool hours may have spilled over to comparison students during their teaching mathematics to all students during regular school hours. To prevent spillover effects, assigning different schools in the same district, rather than classes in the same school, to intervention or comparison groups is recommended. When schools are used for intervention or comparison groups, hierarchical linear modelling analyses can be used to tease out the school effects as in the study by Yang (2012).

Conclusion

Gifted ELs should have equitable representation in gifted programs. However, it is not enough to have equitable representation. It is critical that preparatory/transitional programs are provided to prepare them to succeed in gifted education programs where they will be placed after identification. Preparatory/transitional programs which integrated three essential components of the RED (Recognise strengths, efforts, and improvement; Expect High; and Differentiate) model have been found to be quite effective for developing academic competence of gifted ELs.

The preparatory/transitional programs identified promising ELs based on teacher recommendations without testing and an implemented challenging mathematics curriculum with scaffolding in language and instruction. Scaffolding strategies were selected to facilitate the development of not only receptive and productive language skills, but also metacognitive skills. As a result, those who participated in the preparatory/transitional programs achieved significantly higher than comparison group students.

Scaffolding for gifted or promising English learners should hone into the factors of being student-centred, accepting, and open to students' ideas. Furthermore, it needs to be flexible in terms of grouping and class structures. This flexibility within the instructor themselves calls for modelling metacognitive skills, which align with the behaviours that ELs need to gain for success. This will support ELs to become autonomous learners and courageous enough to take risks.

High motivation for and persistence with challenging tasks can be developed and maintained only when the instructor has instituted a safe and positive environment through recognition of their strengths, efforts, and improvement and through high expectations with trust. Without the indelible, positive relationship between the ELs and the instructor, persistence when faced with challenges and frustration may not occur nor be maintained. Lack of intensive learning is one of the weaknesses of ELs. High motivation and persistence will enable ELs to be engaged in the intensive learning, which will result in improved competency in academic subjects and language proficiency. In return, this will give ELs more eligibility for gifted education programs.

These preparatory/transitional programs may not function if instructors are reluctant to challenge their students fearing that ELs may be deterred by the difficulty or complexity of the assignment. Instructors should be prepared to scaffold their instructions for gifted ELs and present more challenging tasks frequently, since the gifted ELs need to build language skills, metacognitive skills, as well as academic content knowledge. Preparatory/transitional programs become imperative across the world, as there are rapidly growing immigrants and education language learners. They need recognition, high expectations, challenges, and support appropriately differentiated to their unique needs. Without these aspects, ELs cannot take ownership of their own learning, which leads to future academic as well as career success.

Cross-References

▶ A Model for Growing Teacher Talent Scouts: Decreasing Underrepresentation of Gifted Students
▶ Assessment, Pedagogy, and Curriculum: Part IV Introduction
▶ Differentiation of Instruction for Gifted Learners: Collated Evaluative Studies of Teacher Classroom Practices
▶ Engaging Gifted Students in Solving Real Problems Creatively: Implementing the Real Engagement in Active Problem-Solving (REAPS) Teaching/Learning Model in Australasian and Pacific Rim Contexts
▶ Highly Able Students in International Schools
▶ Gifted Education in the Asia-Pacific: From the Past for the Future – An Introduction
▶ Identifying Underrepresented Gifted Students: A Developmental Process
▶ Online Learning for Mathematically Talented Students: A Perspective from Hong Kong

▶ Some Implications for the Future of Gifted Education in the Asia-Pacific
▶ STEAM in Gifted Education in Korea
▶ The Lives and Achievements of Four Extraordinary Australians: A Master, a Maker, an Introspector, and an Influencer
▶ Underachievement and the Quest for Dignity: Contemporary Perspectives on a Timeless Issue

References

August, D., Fenner, D., & Bright, A. (2014). *Scaffolding instruction for English language learners: A resource guide for mathematics*. Washington, DC: American Institute for Research. https://doi.org/10.1177/001698629403800206

Baldwin, A. Y. (1994). The seven plus story: Developing hidden talent among students in socio-economically disadvantaged environments. *The Gifted Child Quarterly, 38*(2), 80–84. https://doi.org/10.1177/001698629403800206

Ball, D. L., & Bass, H. (2000). Interweaving content and pedagogy in teaching and learning to teach: Knowing and using mathematics. In J. Boaler (Ed.), *Multiple perspectives on mathematics teaching and learning* (pp. 83–104). Westport, CT: Ablex Publishing.

Banks, J. A. (1993). Approaches to multicultural curricular reform. In J. A. Banks & C. A. M. Banks (Eds.), *Multicultural education: Issues and perspectives* (2nd ed.). Boston, MA: Allyn & Bacon.

Bianco, M., & Harris, B. (2014). Strength-based RTI: Developing gifted potential in Spanish-speaking English language learners. *Gifted Child Today, 37*, 169–176. https://doi.org/10.1177/1076217514530115

Blackburn, A. M., Cornish, L., & Smith, S. R. (2016). Gifted English language learners: Global understandings and Australian perspectives. *Journal for the Education of the Gifted, 39*(4), 338–360. https://doi.org/10.1177/0162353216671834

Borland, J. H., & Wright, L. (1994). Identifying young, potentially gifted, economically disadvantaged students. *The Gifted Child Quarterly, 38*(4), 164–171. https://doi.org/10.1177/001698629403800402

Briggs, C. J., Reis, S. M., & Sullivan, E. E. (2008). A national view of promising programs and practices for culturally, linguistically, and ethnically diverse gifted and talented students. *The Gifted Child Quarterly, 52*(2), 131–145. https://doi.org/10.1177/0016986208316037

Brophy, J. E. (1983). Research on the self-fulfilling prophecy and teacher expectations. *Journal of Educational Psychology, 75*, 631–661. https://doi.org/10.1037/0022-0663.75.5.631

Brophy, J. E., & Good, T. L. (1970). teachers' communication of differential expectations for children's classroom performance: Some behavioral data. *Journal of Educational Psychology, 61*, 365–374. https://doi.org/10.1037/h0029908

Brulles, D., Castellano, J. A., & Laing, P. C. (2011). Identifying and enfranchising gifted English language learners. In J. A. Castellano & A. D. Frazier (Eds.), *Special populations in gifted education: Understanding our most able students from diverse backgrounds* (pp. 305–313). Waco, TX: Prufrock Press.

Chapin, S., O'Connor, C., & Anderson, N. (2009). *Classroom discussions: Using math talk to help students learn, Grades K–6*. Sausalito, CA: Math Solutions.

Cho, S., & Campbell, J. (2011). Differential influences of family processes for scientifically talented individuals' academic achievement along development stages. *Roeper Review, 33*(1), 33–45. https://doi.org/10.1080/02783193.2011.530205

Cho, S., Jo. S. M. & Hulse, N. (2018). *Effects of the project BRIDGE program on mathematically promising young language learners' motivation and confidence*. Presented at the Biannual conference of the European Council for High Abilities, August 9–12, Dublin, Ireland.

Cho, S., Yang, J., & Mandracchia, M. (2014, April). *The effect of an advanced math curriculum on the math achievement and English proficiency of mathematically promising English language learners*. Paper presented at the AERA, Philadelphia, Pennsylvania.

Cho, S., Yang, J., & Mandracchia, M. (2015). Impact of mentoring mathematical minds program to promising English language learners. *Journal of Advanced Academics, 26*, 112–142.

Cobb, P., Boufi, A., McClain, K., & Whitenack, J. (1997). Reflective discourse and collective reflection. *Journal for Research in Mathematics Education, 28*(3), 258–277. Retrieved from http://jwilson.coe.uga.edu/EMAT7050/Students/Dwyer/749781.pdf

Connor, P., & Lopez, G. (2016). "5 facts about the US rank in worldwide migration." Pew Research Center. Retrieved on 14 Jan 2017, from http://www.pewresearch.org/fact-tank/2016/05/18/5-facts-about-the-u-s-rank-in-worldwide-migration/

Cotton, K. (1989). *Expectations and students outcomes. CLOSE-UP #7*. Portland, OR: Northwest Regional Educational Laboratory.

Donnelly, W. B., & Roe, C. (2010). Using sentence frames to develop academic vocabulary for English learners. *The Reading Teacher, 64*, 131–136. Retrieved from https://www.lowell.k12.ma.us/cms/lib/MA01907636/Centricity/Domain/489/Using_Sentence_Frames.pdf

Donovan, M. S., & Cross, C. T. (Eds.). (2002). *Minority students in special and gifted education*. Washington, DC: Academy Press.

Dweck, C. (2007). *Mindset: The new psychology of success*. New York, NY: Ballantine Books.

Eccles, J. S. (2006). A motivational perspective on school achievement: Taking responsibility for learning, teaching, and supporting. In R. J. Sternberg & R. F. Subotnik (Eds.), *Optimizing student success with the other three Rs: Reasoning, resilience, and responsibility* (pp. 199–224). Greenwich, CT: Information Age.

Eccles, J. S., O'Neill, S. A., & Wigfield, A. (2005). Ability self-perceptions and subjective task values in adolescents and children. In K. Anderson Moore & L. H. Lippman (Eds.), *What do children need to flourish?* (pp. 237–249). New York, NY: Springer.

Echevarria, J., Vogt, M., & Short, D. J. (2010). *Making content comprehensible for elementary English learners: The SIOP model*. Upper Saddle River, NJ: Pearson.

Eng, N., & Cho, S. (2012, April). *Family processes, beliefs about intelligence, and openness as predictors of English learners' creative problem solving*. Paper presented at the annual conference of the American Educational Association, Vancouver, Canada.

Erwin, J. O., & Worrell, F. C. (2012). Assessment practices and the underrepresentation of minority students in gifted and talented education. *Journal of Psychoeducational Assessment, 30*(1), 74–87.

Feldman, K., & Kinsella, K. (2008). Narrowing the Language Gap: The case for explicit vocabulary instruction. In L. Denti & G. Guerin (Eds.), *Effective practice for adolescents with reading and literacy challenges* (pp. 3–24). New York, NY: Routledge.

Finn, C. (2014a). Gifted, talented, and underserved. *National Affairs, 18*, 50–62.

Finn, C. (2014b). No (gifted) child left behind. *Hoover Institution Journal*. http://www.hoover.org/publications/defining-ideas/article/169261

Ford, D. Y. (2010). Underrepresentation of culturally different students in gifted education: Reflections about current problems and recommendations for the future. *Gifted Child Today, 33*(3), 31–35. https://doi.org/10.1177/107621751003300308

Ford, D. Y. (2011). *Multicultural gifted education* (2nd ed.). Waco, TX: Prufrock Press.

Ford, D. Y., & Grantham, T. C. (2012). Using the NAGC gifted programming standards to create programs and services for culturally and linguistically different gifted students. In S. L. K. Johnsen (Ed.), *NAGC pre-K-grade 12 gifted education programming standards: A guide to planning and implementing high-quality services* (pp. 45–70). Waco, TX: Prufrock Press.

Frasier, M. M. (1997). Gifted minority students: Reframing approaches to their identification and education. In N. Colangelo & G. A. Davis (Eds.), *Handbook of gifted education* (pp. 498–515). Needham Heights, MA: Allyn & Bacon.

Gagné, F. (2010). Motivation within the DMGT 2.0 framework. *High Ability Studies, 21*, 81–99. https://doi.org/10.1080/13598139.2010.525341

García, E. E., & Frede, E. C. (2010). *Young English language learners: Current research and emerging directions for practice and policy.* New York, NY: Teachers College Press.

Gavin, M. K., Casa, T. M., Adelson, J. L., Carroll, S. R., & Sheffield, L. J. (2009). The impact of advanced curriculum on the achievement of mathematically promising elementary students. *The Gifted Child Quarterly, 53,* 188–202. https://doi.org/10.1177/0016986209334964

Gavin, M. K., Casa, T. M., Adelson, J. L., Carroll, S. R., Sheffield, L. J., & Spinelli, A. M. (2007). Project M3: Mentoring mathematical minds: A research-based curriculum for talented elementary students. *Journal of Advanced Academics, 18,* 566–681. https://doi.org/10.4219/jaa-2007-552

Gavin, M. K., Casa, T. M., Firmender, J. M., & Carroll, S. R. (2013). The impact of advanced geometry and measurement curriculum units on the mathematics achievement of first-grade students. *The Gifted Child Quarterly, 57,* 71–84. https://doi.org/10.1177/0016986213479564

Gay, G. (2010). *Culturally responsive teaching: Theory, research, and practice* (2nd ed.). New York, NY: Teachers College Press.

Good, T. L. (1987). Two decades of research on teacher expectations: Findings and future directions. *Journal of Teacher Education, 38,* 32–47. https://doi.org/10.1177/002248718703800406

Grantham, T. (2002). Underrepresentation of gifted education. *Roeper Review, 24*(2), 50–51.

Grasha, A. F. (1994). A matter of style: The teacher as expert, formal authority, personal model, facilitator, and delegator. *College Teaching, 42*(4), 142–149. Retrieved from http://www.montana.edu/gradschool/documents/A-Matter-of-STyle-Grashab.pdf

Han, T.-H., & Han, K. S. (2013). Major issues and challenges of gifted children from multicultural families. *Journal of Gifted/Talented Education, 23*(3), 453–477.

Harris, B., Plucker, J., Rapp, K., & Martínez, R. (2009). Identifying gifted and talented English language learners: A case study. *Journal for the Education of the Gifted, 32*(3), 368–393. Retrieved from https://files.eric.ed.gov/fulltext/EJ835865.pdf

Harris, B., Rapp, K., Martínez, R., & Plucker, J. (2007). Identifying English language learners for gifted and talented programs: Current practices and recommendations for improvement. *Roeper Review, 30,* 26–29. https://doi.org/10.1080/02783193.2007.11869221

Kinsella, K. (2012). Cutting on the same wavelength. *Language Magazine, 12,* 18–23.

Krashen, S. D. (1982). *Principles and practice in second language acquisition.* Oxford, UK: Permagon Press Inc.

LeClair, C., Doll, B., Osborn, A., & Jones, K. (2009). English language learners' and non-English language learners' perceptions of the classroom environment. *Psychology in the Schools, 46*(6), 568–577.

Lee, J., Yoo, K. J., Yeo, S., & Kim, A. (2011). *Exploring cases and support plans for disadvantaged gifted students.* Seoul, Korea: Korean Educational Development Institute.

Levitt, K. E. (2001). An analysis of elementary teachers' beliefs regarding teaching and learning of science. *Science Education, 86*(1), 1–22. https://doi.org/10.1002/sce.1042

Lohman, D. F. (2005). The role of nonverbal ability tests in identifying academically gifted students: An aptitude perspective. *The Gifted Child Quarterly, 49,* 111–138. https://doi.org/10.1177/001698620504900203

Long-Mitchell, L. A. (2011). High-achieving black adolescents' perceptions of how teachers impact their academic achievement. In J. A. Castellano & A. D. Frazier (Eds.), *Special populations in gifted education: Understanding our most able students from diverse backgrounds* (pp. 99–123). Waco, TX: Prufrock Press.

Lowell, B. L., & Regets, M. (2006). *A half-century snapshot of the STEM workforce, 1950 to 2000 (STEM workforce data project whitepaper No. 1).* Washington, DC: Commission on Professionals in Science and Technology.

Maker, C. J., & Schiever, S. W. (2010). *Curriculum development and teaching strategies for gifted learners* (3rd ed.). Austin, TX: Pro-Ed.

Maker, J., & Nielson, A. (1995). *Curriculum development and teaching strategies for gifted learners* (2nd ed.). Austin, TX: Pro-Ed.

Mandracchia, M. (2015). *The effects of a challenging math curriculum and teacher as a facilitator on mathematically promising English language learners* (Unpublished doctoral dissertation). St. John's University, New York, NY.

Marshall, S. P., McGee, G. W., McLaren, E., & Veal, C. (2011). Discovering and developing diverse STEM talent: Enabling academically talented urban youth to flourish. *Gifted Child Today, 34*(1), 16–23. https://doi.org/10.1177/107621751103400107

Moschkovich, J. (1999). Supporting the participation of English language learners in mathematical discussions. *For the Learning of Mathematics, 19*(1), 11–19. Retrieved from http://www.jstor.org/stable/40248284.

Napolitano, K. (2016). *How classroom discourse and interaction patterns influence mathematically promising English language learners' experience in mathematics* (Unpublished doctoral dissertation). St. John's University, New York, NY

National Center for Education Statistics. (2014). *Digest of education statistics*. Washington, DC: Author.

National Center for Education Statistics. (2016). *Digest of education statistics*. Washington, DC: Author.

Nieto, S. (2003). Profoundly multicultural questions. *Educational Leadership, 60*(4), 6–10.

Olsen, L. (2014). *Meeting the unique needs of long term English language learners: A guide for educators*. Washington, DC: National Education Association.

Olszewski-Kubilius, P. (2007). Working with promising learners from poverty: Lessons learned. In J. VanTassel-Baska & T. Stambaugh (Eds.), *Overlooked gems: A national perspective on low-income promising learners* (pp. 43–46). Washington, DC: National Association for Gifted Children.

Olszewski-Kubilius, P., & Clarenbach, J. (2012). *Unlocking emerging talent: Supporting high achievement of low-income, high-ability students*. Washington, DC: National Association for Gifted Children.

Olszewski-Kubilius, P., Lee, S. Y., Ngoi, M., & Ngoi, D. (2004). Addressing the achievement gap between minority and non-minority children by increasing access to gifted programs. *Journal for the Education of the Gifted, 28*, 127–158. https://doi.org/10.1177/016235320402800202

Olszewski-Kubilius, P., & Thomson, D. (2010). Gifted programming for poor or minority urban students: Issues and lessons learned. *Gifted Child Today, 33*(4), 58–64. https://doi.org/10.1177/107621751003300413

Paris, D. (2012). Culturally sustaining pedagogy: A needed change in stance, terminology, and practice. *Educational Researcher, 41*(3), 93–97.

Perez, L. E. (2011). *Long-Term English learner experiences: Discovering pathways to success* (Unpublished doctoral dissertation). University of California, San Diego, CA. Retrieved from http://jerome.stjohns.edu:81/login?url=https://search-proquest-com.jerome.stjohns.edu/docview/862553575?accountid=14068

Peters, S., Matthews, M. S., McBee, M. T., & McCoach, B. (2014). *When addressing underrepresentation IS the goal. Beyond gifted education: Designing and implementing advanced academic programs* (pp. 157–181). Waco, TX: Prufrock Press, Inc.

Plucker, J., Burroughs, N., & Song, R. (2010). *Mind the (other) gap! The growing excellence gap in K–12 education*. Bloomington, IN: CEEP. Retrieved from http://ceep.indiana.edu/mindthegap/

Reeve, J. (2006). Teacher as facilitators: What autonomy-supportive teachers do and why the students benefit. *The Elementary School Teacher, 106*(3), 225–236.

Siegle, D., Gubbins, E. J., O'Rourke, P., Langley, S. D., Mun, R. U., Luria, S. R., . . . Plucker, J. A. (2016). Barriers to underserved students' participation in gifted programs and possible solutions. *Journal for the Education of the Gifted, 39*(2), 103–131. https://doi.org/10.1177/0162353216640930

Siegle, D., & McCoach, D. B. (2005). *Motivating gifted students*. Waco, TX: Prufrock Press.

Stein, M. K., Grover, B. W., & Henningsen, M. A. (1996). Building student capacity for mathematical thinking and reasoning: An analysis of mathematical tasks used in reform classrooms.

American Educational Research Journal, 33(2), 455–488. https://doi.org/10.3102/00028312033002455

Subotnik, R. F., Olszewski-Kubilius, P., & Worrell, F. C. (2012). A proposed direction forward for gifted education based on psychological science. *The Gifted Child Quarterly, 56*(4), 176–188. https://doi.org/10.1177/0016986212456079

Thomas, W., & Collier, V. (2001). *A national study of school effectiveness for language minority students. Long-term academic achievement.* Washington, DC: National Center for Bilingual Education. Retrieved from http://cmmr.usc.edu/CollierThomasExReport.pdf

Tomlinson, C. A. (1999). *The differentiated classroom: Responding to the needs of all learners.* Alexandria, VA: Association for Supervision and Curriculum Development.

Tomlinson, C. A., Brighton, C., Hertberg, H., Callahan, C., Moon, T., Brimijoin, K., ... Reynolds, T. (2003). Differentiating instruction in response to student readiness, interest, and learning profile in academically diverse classrooms: A review of literature. *Journal for the Education of the Gifted, 27*(2–3), 119–145. https://doi.org/10.1177/016235320302700203

Tucker, M. (2016, February 29). Asian countries take the U.S. to school. Next America: Higher Education. *The Atlantic.* Retrieved from https://www.theatlantic.com/education/archive/2016/02/us-asia-education-differences/471564/

Turner, E., Dominguez, H., Maldonado, L., & Empson, S. (2013). English learners' participation in mathematical discussion: Shifting positioning and dynamic identities. *Journal of Research in Mathematics Education, 44*(1), 199–234. https://doi.org/10.5951/jresematheduc.44.1.0199

U.S. Bureau of Labor. (2014). STEM 101: Intro to tomorrow's jobs. Retrieved 16 Jan 2018. https://www.bls.gov/careeroutlook/2014/spring/art01.pdf

U.S. Department of Education. (2007). *Report of the academic competitiveness council (ED 496649).* Washington, DC: Author.

Varma, R., & Frehill, L. M. (2010). Special issue on science and technology workforce. *American Behavioral Scientist, 53*(7), 943–948. https://doi.org/10.1177/0002764209356229

Vygotsky, L. (1978). *Interaction between learning and development.* Cambridge, MA: Harvard University Press.

Walsh, K. (2013, February, 26). Is STEM education in high school a lost cause? WashingtonExec. Retrieved from http://www.washingtonexec.com/2013/02/is-stem-education-in-high-school-a-lost-cause/

Wineburg, S. S. (1987). The self-fulfillment of the self-fulfilling prophecy. *Educational Researcher, 16*, 28–37. https://doi.org/10.3102/0013189X016009028

Winkelmann, R. (2001). *Immigration policies and their impact: The case of New Zealand and Australia.* Bonn, Germany: Institute for the Study of Labor.

Winn, M. T., & Johnson, L. P. (2011). *Writing instruction in the culturally relevant classroom. Campaign for Educational Equity.* New York, NY: Teachers College.

Yamamoto, Y., & Holloway, S. D. (2010). Parental expectations and children's academic performance in sociocultural context. *Educational Psychology Review, 22*, 189–214. https://doi.org/10.1007/s10648-010-9121-z

Yang, J. (2012). *The impact of accelerated and enriched curriculum, general intellectual ability, English proficiency level, gender, students perception of teacher goal orientation and teacher challenge on the math achievement of high-ability English language learners* (Unpublished doctoral dissertation). St. John's University, New York, NY.

Zhan, M. (2005). Assets, parental expectations, and involvement and children's educational performance. *Children and Youth Services Review, 28*, 961–975. Retrieved from http://citeseerx.ist.psu.edu/viewdoc/download?doi=10.1.1.463.9354&rep=rep1&type=pdf

Zhang, K. C., & Ting, C. L. M. (2011). The education of new Chinese immigrant children in Hong Kong: Challenges and opportunities. *British Journal of Learning Support, 26*(2), 49–55.

Zhou, M., & Kim, S. (2006). Community forces, social capital, and educational achievement: The case of supplementary education in the Chinese and Korean immigrant communities. *Harvard Educational Review, 76*(1), 1–29. https://doi.org/10.17763/haer.76.1.u08t548554882477

Seokhee Cho, PhD, is a Professor at the School of Education and Director of the Center for Creativity and Gifted Education, St. John's University, New York. She has been conducting two consecutive five-year Javits Grant Projects funded by US DOE on teaching mathematics to mathematically promising English learners and teaching science to twice exceptional high school students from 2009 to 2019. Her 12 books and about 200 articles focus on creativity and gifted education. She has been the Director of the National Research Center for Gifted Education in Korea for 20 years. She is currently an Editorial Board Member of the *Gifted Child Quarterly, Gifted Education International, Turkish Journal of Giftedness and Education* and J*ournal of Gifted/ Talented Education* (Korean).

Marcella Mandracchia, EdD, received her doctorate in instructional leadership from St. John's University. She works at Adelphi University as the Assistant Director of Assessment in the School of Education. She also currently works at Hostos Community College in the Teacher Education Department and Queens College in the Department of Linguistics and Communication Disorders as an Adjunct Assistant Professor. She also currently works as an Adjunct Associate Professor in the Department of Curriculum and Instruction at St. John's University. She teaches courses on instructional technology, research methods, human relations and communications, introduction to education and early childhood education and TESOL education.

Jenny Yang, EdD, received her doctoral degree in instructional leadership from St. John's University. She received her bachelor's and master's degrees at Stony Brook University in Biochemistry and Education, respectively. She is currently an Adjunct Professor at St. John's University in Queens, NY, USA.

Online Learning for Mathematically Talented Students: A Perspective from Hong Kong

40

Joyce J. Y. Fung, Mantak Yuen, and Allan H. K. Yuen

Contents

J. J. Y. Fung (✉) · M. Yuen
Center for Advancement in Inclusive and Special Education, Faculty of Education, University of Hong Kong, Hong Kong, China
e-mail: joycejyfung@gmail.com; mtyuen@hku.hk

A. H. K. Yuen
Centre for Information Technology in Education (CITE), University of Hong Kong, Hong Kong, China

Faculty of Education, The University of Hong Kong, Hong Kong, China

Yew Chung College of Early Childhood Education, Hong Kong, China
e-mail: hkyuen@hku.hk; allan.yuen@yccece.edu.hk

© Springer Nature Singapore Pte Ltd. 2021
S. R. Smith (ed.), *Handbook of Giftedness and Talent Development in the Asia-Pacific*,
Springer International Handbooks of Education,
https://doi.org/10.1007/978-981-13-3041-4_39

Abstract

In developed countries in the Asia-Pacific region, many subjects in the school curriculum are now available in e-learning formats for target groups such as gifted learners or students with learning difficulties. In order to accomplish the objectives of these online courses, the research literature indicates that students need a high degree of self-regulation, self-efficacy, and the ability to make effective use of social support. Social support usually comes in the form of advice, encouragement, and feedback from more knowledgeable others. In addition, the design features and structure of online courses can significantly affect students' motivation, engagement, and achievement. The potential influence of these variables on gifted students' online learning in mathematics and how these variables may interact will be discussed in this chapter. A study conducted in Hong Kong is used as an example that examined mathematically gifted students' self-regulation and self-efficacy in relation to online course design and social support. The 374 participating students undertook an online mathematics course specifically designed for high achievers and completed self-reporting questionnaires. Structural Equation Modelling (SEM) was used to investigate the direct relationships that exist between online self-regulated learning and social support, self-efficacy, and course design. In the findings it was suggested that course design and support from teachers, parents, and peers may influence online self-regulated learning, with self-efficacy acting as a mediator. Implications for designing and implementing online mathematics programs, and for more effectively supporting gifted students' online learning are discussed in this chapter.

Keywords

Mathematically talented students · Online learning · e-learning · Self-efficacy · Self-regulated learning · Social support

The aims in this chapter are to:
1. Explore the factors influencing online learning.
2. Review the characteristics of mathematically gifted students and how online learning can benefit them.
3. Outline an example of an online mathematics course for gifted students in Hong Kong.
4. Provide some implications for designing, teaching and supporting online mathematics courses for gifted students.

Introduction

In this digital world, various forms of online learning play an essential role in contemporary education. Online or e-learning is by definition very broad, but largely entails accessible learning through technology and the Internet that is an additional educational resource or educational context that complements traditional classroom teaching and learning (Morgan, 2015). Online learning can be undertaken individually or in a group format with or without teacher or peer facilitation.

While there are commercially produced online programs and applications, many schools use *Learning Management Systems* (LMS) that enable teachers to upload learning tasks tailored to meet the goals of local curricula, provide a level of social interactivity, and can be embedded within classroom practices. Teachers can organise teaching notes and assignments, boost collaboration, and foster better communication using these online systems. Many subjects in the school curriculum, including mathematics, are now available in e-learning formats for specific target groups. For example, on the Internet one can find websites such as *Coursera* and *Khan Academy* offering online courses in various subjects. The *EPGY Mathematics* course offered by Stanford University is very popular worldwide; and an interactive online course called *My Maths* is widely subscribed to by both primary and secondary schools. Apart from these, many school teachers use learning management systems, such as *Google Classroom* and *Course Kit* which are provided by *Google Education* to meet the goals of local curricula. Teachers can organise teaching notes and assignments, boost collaboration, and foster better communication using these systems (Morgan, 2015).

Online courses and other forms of e-learning have thus provided many new opportunities for differentiation of teaching approaches and curriculum content according to students' aptitudes and rates of learning (Thomson, 2010; Westwood, 2018). In order to engage successfully in such online courses, students must not only be talented in the particular subject, but must also have a high level of self-regulation (Artino & Stephens, 2007). Along with intrinsic motivation (Artino & Stephens, 2007), self-efficacy in computer skills (Pellas, 2014), Internet navigation ability (Wang, Shannon, & Ross, 2013) and, in this case, mathematical capability are also needed for studying online effectively (Shen, Cho, Tsai, & Marra, 2013).

It has been stated in previous writings that in most learning and teaching contexts, gifted students tend to use more self-regulatory strategies and self-monitoring than average students (Fung, 2015; Tortop, 2015) and exhibit higher expectations of success (Clark, 2013; Gross, 2006). It may be anticipated that these strengths can predispose gifted students to work very successfully in an independent learning situation, such as online courses and using e-learning materials.

Factors Influencing Online Learning

Online learning is now an additional resource or an alternative to traditional classroom instruction and can be effective in engaging students' interests and active involvement (e.g., Fazal & Bryant, 2019; Lee, 2019). While students who are learning online may need initial teaching of new concepts and skills and ongoing support from their teacher, parents, or peers during the learning process, online learning is also a type of independent learning that places a premium on students' abilities to plan ahead, set goals, use appropriate strategies, seek information, and monitor their own performance (Wang et al., 2013).

Common findings which emerged from research into online learning suggest that three factors are extremely important: (a) self-efficacy in the specific skills involved in that topic and in computer skills (Shen et al., 2013); (b) course design (Garrison & Cleveland-Innes, 2005); and (c) social support (McInnerney & Roberts, 2004). A review by Li and Irby (2008) found that students' self-discipline, time management, and organisation skills significantly affected their engagement in online learning. These are all areas of performance that can be monitored, managed, and improved where necessary by appropriate teaching and opportunities for practice. They are described in more detail in the following sections.

Self-Regulation

Self-regulated learning means that performance is controlled by the learner rather than through direction or scaffolding from a teacher (Gaeta & Martha, 2013; Stoeger & Zeidner, 2019). Many writers emphasise the importance of all students developing self-regulation as a major step towards greater autonomy in learning (Artino, 2008; Cavanaugh, 2007; DiPietro, Ferdig, Black, & Preston, 2008; Dykman & Davis, 2008). It is important that teachers recognise their role in encouraging this type of autonomy in learners.

Having reviewed the research, Ormrod (2000) concluded that in order to promote students' self-regulated learning, teachers should ensure that students are taught strategies that facilitate attention-to-task, self-monitoring, self-evaluation, and self-correction. Students need time to work independently, to plan ahead, solve problems, and reflect upon their own progress, while receiving encouraging and constructive feedback from the teacher when necessary. In online learning, it has been found that students who use self-regulation strategies are more confident in navigating course materials and are superior in their performance and attainment (Wang et al., 2013).

There are of course, marked individual differences in learners' ability to self-regulate (Zumbrunn, Tadlock, & Roberts, 2011). Very young learners do not have sufficient experience to develop strong self-regulation and self-monitoring; and 'novices' of any age are quite different from 'experts' when managing themselves while learning new skills or studying new material (Usher & Pajares, 2008). There are also differences in self-regulation associated with intellectual ability—with gifted students reportedly using more self-regulation than typical learners or those with disabilities (Regan & Martin, 2014; Shepherd, 2010; Stoeger & Zeidner, 2019).

There are obviously many factors that influence how effectively students develop self-regulation for learning. Studies over many years (e.g., Lynch & Dembo, 2004; Zimmerman, 2008a) have suggested that successful self-regulation requires students to have self-efficacy, high motivation, time-management skills, and the ability to call upon and use available assistance and resources.

There are also some indications that the cultural background within which individuals develop can influence the extent to which they are encouraged (or not encouraged) to develop autonomy in their own learning (Boyer, 2012). In some cultures, encouraging learner autonomy in school is not a priority goal in education, and students are expected to learn mainly from direct teaching in a fairly lockstep manner rather than through their own independent efforts (Watkins & Biggs, 2001). That type of learning environment does nothing to foster self-regulation and is unsuitable for gifted and talented students as it inhibits their self-regulation by lack of personal control of learning (Allan, 2006). In contrast, it is worth noting that online learning offers an opportunity for these teachers to promote more self-regulated learning through scaffolding skill development during the learning process (Anderton, 2006).

The education system in Hong Kong is an example of a setting in which parental and community expectations may indirectly encourage self-regulation in students. For example, many studies have reported on the high academic achievement of Chinese students in mathematics (e.g., Chen & Stevenson, 1995; Zhang et al., 2016). Possible reasons for this academic excellence include high parental expectations (Chen & Stevenson, 1995), an emphasis on high achievement evident in the education system, and classroom teaching practices (Stevenson & Lee, 1996). The prevailing philosophy of education in Hong Kong is to invest maximum effort in studies in order to do well in life beyond school. Chinese students are expected to be hardworking and self-disciplined, and they become self-regulated because they recognise it as the way to succeed (Bandura, 1997).

Ho (2004) investigated self-regulated learning in Hong Kong students as compared to students in other countries. In Ho's study, a positive and mutually supportive relationship between self-regulated learning and academic achievement was found; and in particular, self-efficacy and self-control were found to be the most important influences associated with achievement. Ho suggested that there is thus a clear reason to ensure that all students in Hong Kong are helped to develop self-regulation and to show initiative in their approach to learning. Participating in online courses is one possible way of encouraging such development.

Self-Efficacy

Another key factor strongly associated with successful online learning is self-efficacy (DiBenedetto & Bembenutty, 2013; Wang, 2010; Wang et al., 2013). Self-efficacy is best described as the belief one holds about one's own capability to achieve certain goals. Self-efficacy and self-regulation are attributes that are closely related and mutually supportive—the better self-regulated one becomes, the more likely it is that one will feel increasingly efficacious in a specific field (Constantine, Fernald, Robinson, & Courtney, 2019).

Various experiences and types of support are regarded as essential for increasing students' self-efficacy. According to Bandura (1997), self-regulation and self-efficacy are attributes that affect students' learning and achievement. Bandura theorised that there are four main influences on self-efficacy: performance accomplishments (recognising one's own successes); modelling (observation and copying the behaviours of others); social persuasion (verbal support and encouragement from others); and emotional support. These sources are important for developing both self-regulation and self-efficacy in all learning contexts, including the use of technology. Empirical studies have found that these sources of self-efficacy are also related to developing mathematical self-efficacy (Shen et al., 2013; Wang et al., 2013). These researchers reported that among the four sources of self-efficacy, *performance accomplishments* are most influential in the mathematics domain. According to Zimmerman, Bandura, and Martinez-Pons (1992), high-ability students have stronger self-efficacy perceptions than less successful students—almost certainly because they are able to recognise their successes much more frequently and receive more positive teacher feedback than their less-competent peers. However, authentic self-efficacy requires the student to be able to recognise genuine success. This often requires an external evaluator. High-ability students, particularly perfectionists, need some modulation of learning through honest and effective feedback which in most instances is provided by a knowledgeable teacher (Benny & Blonder, 2016).

Mathematical self-efficacy is an individual's perception of his or her own abilities in this subject. This type of self-efficacy is constructed over time by building confidence in one's understanding of mathematics concepts, developing fluency in computation skills, and by successfully completing a wide variety of mathematical tasks.

Closely associated with mathematics self-efficacy is intrinsic enjoyment of the subject. This can be observed readily in an individual's ongoing pleasure in the process of learning that motivates the student to engage more deeply (Skaalvik & Skaalvik, 2006). Students who enjoy mathematics and have high self-efficacy tend to be more attentive and to persist longer when facing challenges (Bandura, 1997; Pintrich & Zusho, 2002). When students are working independently online, being persistent in the face of challenge is particularly important.

Finally, 'computer self-efficacy' is a term that has been coined in the literature to describe beliefs about one's capability in using a computer and its associated applications (Compeau & Higgins, 1995). Learners should have confidence and competence in using *Information and Communication Technology* (ICT) tools to engage with online courses; and most students today possess these skills and probably regard themselves as 'computer literate' (Kolikant, 2010).

Course Design

A key factor that appears to influence online learners' acquisition of self-regulation is course design. According to Song and Hill (2007), 'design' refers here to the construction of an online learning course to include the appropriate sequence of content, learning activities, explanations, feedback, and links to necessary resources. In the case of gifted learners, the course must present content that is perceived by the learner to be of interest and value, and that presents sufficient challenge to stimulate deep thought (Chen, Dai, & Zhou, 2013; Lubinski, Benbow, & Kell, 2014; Morgan, 2015).

The resources associated with an online course are usually embedded within the program or can be located easily online by following hyperlinks and conducting searches. An online course should enable participants to access all necessary resources swiftly and easily (Hiemstra, 1994), because frustration and disengagement can occur if learners have difficulty following instructions, conducting searches, or locating resources. If the system is structured clearly and resources are accessed readily, students can feel empowered to search, make choices, and find solutions (Dee-Lucas, 1999). A positive correlation has been reported between course design and learners' self-efficacy (Ibrahim & Callaway, 2012; Zundans-Fraser & Lancaster, 2012).

The effective design of an online course can be a key to participants' engagement and motivation (Akdemir & Koszalka, 2008). In an ideal situation, course structure should be flexible enough to be matched to any learners' current aptitudes and be capable of encouraging independent learning (Garrison, 1997). For example, some courses, such as the *Khan Academy*, *iMath* and *MyiMaths* allow participants to select specific topics and omit others (i.e., a form of curriculum compacting), which is particularly appropriate for gifted students who learn at a faster pace (Clark, 2013). Ideally, a well-designed online course for gifted learners in mathematics should also incorporate learning tasks that encourage students' creativity and ingenuity when solving problems (Chen et al., 2013; Lubinski et al., 2014; Renzulli, 2005).

In addition to providing challenging tasks, it is important also to ensure that different types of learning activities are included to maintain interest and motivate and challenge gifted students (Clark, 2013; Diezmann & Watters, 2000; House, 1987). Online mathematics courses should be structured to promote enjoyment as well as provide appropriate cognitive challenges to academically engage students (Gavin, 2003). It is said that gifted students usually prefer open-ended and non-routine problems that provide opportunities for high-level thinking and mathematical reasoning (Clark, 2013; Gagné, 1985; Lubinski et al., 2014).

Social Support

While it might be imagined that social support is not a major influence in online learning, the independence of online learning appears to involve only a computer and a student. However, effective learning requires authentic and constructive feedback. Normally, a teacher will diagnose student learning problems and provide guidance to the student struggling with a problem. Hence, as Bandura (1997) pointed out many years ago, an individuals' development of self-efficacy in any context relies to a large extent on positive verbal support, feedback, and emotional encouragement from others. Availability of this type of social support is still very much required for fostering self-efficacy and ongoing engagement in online learning.

Much of the literature suggests a direct link between social support and successful online self-regulated learning (e.g., Fung, Yuen, & Yuen, 2018; Song & Hill, 2007). Findings from several studies have suggested that ICT represents a medium for learning that yields best results when it also involves regular guidance and input from a teacher (Slavin, Lake, & Groff, 2009; Zaranis, 2016; Zaranis & Synodi, 2017). Support from teachers, parents, and peers is important to enhance online learning as instructional assistance and feedback from others can help talented learners recognise their own accomplishments and strengthen their self-regulation and self-efficacy (Liu et al., 2018; Muratori et al., 2006; Sun & Hui, 2007).

After interviewing gifted and average students, Zimmerman and Martinez-Pons (1986) determined that social assistance from peers, teachers, and knowledgeable adults seems to be essential for developing students' self-regulation. Examples of social assistance can include encouragement and conveying realistic expectations from teachers and parents (Song & Hill, 2007). While teachers can obviously support a student in acquiring deeper conceptual understanding in a subject—and peers may also assist with explanations and examples—parents may not have the knowledge or skills to do this, so for online learning, tools such as chatrooms and supportive discussion groups are often needed to provide immediate feedback. It has been noted that students who are capable of self-regulation usually know when they should seek guidance and feedback from others (Zumbrunn et al., 2011), and seeking assistance and support from knowledgeable others when necessary is certainly an essential aspect of online learning.

Characteristics of Mathematically Gifted Students

Students who are gifted in mathematics often demonstrate a remarkable depth of understanding and concept development that extends far beyond simply being efficient at computation (Rotigel, 2000). They can 'reason mathematically' and they prefer to learn as much as possible about how and why mathematical ideas operate (Sheffield, 1994). In other words, their desire is to develop what Skemp (1976) referred to as 'relational understanding' rather than remaining at the 'instrumental level' concerned only with mastering arithmetic. Gifted students in mathematics are reported to have the ability to see patterns and think abstractly, and to transfer mathematical principles to unfamiliar problems and situations (Singer, Sheffield, Freiman, & Brandl, 2016). It has been found that students who are talented in mathematics can use analytical, deductive, and inductive reasoning when they are faced with complex and difficult problems (Sheffield, 1994). Students who enjoy mathematics and have high mathematics self-efficacy are reported to persist more when faced with challenging problems to solve (Bandura, 1997; Pintrich & Zusho, 2002).

Many learners who are deemed later to be mathematically gifted actually demonstrate unusual interest in mathematical concepts during the preschool period. Even at this young age, they may exhibit an ability to understand and manipulate number relationships (Rotigel & Fello, 2004). Heid (1983) pointed out that these mathematically gifted young students have the ability to see relationships among concepts even without teachers' instructions, and they are more independent than their peers in satisfying their curiosity.

Krutetskii (1976) suggested that, "some persons have inborn characteristics in the structure and functional features of their brains which are extremely favourable to the development of mathematical abilities" (p. 361). If this is true, then it appears that at a neurological level some students already have the potential to develop more mathematical ability than others. Suitable stimulation and guidance are then essential to nurture their mathematical talent. Johnson (2000) advocates that mathematically gifted students need the mainstream mathematics curriculum to be differentiated to match their thirst for knowledge and their faster rate of learning. Online learning courses are one way of providing this type of differentiation (Wallace, 2005).

Whether or not mathematical ability is innate, the literature has shown that nurturing (effective teaching) is also extremely important (Koshy, Ernest, & Casey, 2009). Some mathematically gifted students become bored in the classroom because the learning tasks are not challenging, they already understand the content being taught and the pace of instruction is too slow for them (Goetz, Preckel, Pekrun, Hall, & Lüdtke, 2007). Studies have tended to find that the mathematics curricula taught in too many classrooms are highly repetitive, geared only to an instrumental level of learning, and lack depth and creativity (Rotigel & Fello, 2004). What is known now of the characteristics of mathematically gifted students suggests that they need opportunities to cover a more challenging mathematics curriculum in greater depth and at a faster pace. The manner in which mathematics is presented to gifted students should strive to maintain their motivation and maximum cognitive engagement. Online resources and programs offer obvious pathways to meet this need (Chen et al., 2013).

Online Learning for Mathematically Talented Students

The tendency for mathematically gifted students to be self-motivated and independent in their engagement with the subject means that online learning is potentially a valuable means of matching curriculum content to each student's interests, ability, and learning rate. The online platform is ideal for delivering mathematics programs that are well designed and appropriately differentiated. In Hong Kong, the Gifted Education Section of the Education Bureau and the Hong Kong Academy is offering online courses for gifted students.

Online mathematics materials need to stimulate students' interests to investigate and solve problems (Yeh, Cheng, Chen, Liao, & Chan, 2019). These materials have the great benefit of being able to depict real-life problems in multimedia formats (e.g., video, virtual reality, or animation). The use of interactive multimedia can optimise cognitive engagement by holding students' full attention, ensuring active participation, and providing immediate feedback (Susila, Muslim, & Syahrial, 2018). When students are fully engaged in learning in this way, they often go beyond the requirements of a set task and are keen to meet the challenges and obstacles that the learning process may present (Andersen & Cross, 2014; Trowler, 2010).

Well-designed online mathematical materials can also provide a learner with immediate feedback and links to relevant resources such as data banks, statistical tables, graphing functions, and formulae. At the other end of the ability scale, motivating online programs can also provide students with learning disabilities—for example, those with twice-exceptionalities—with much needed exercises for practice to enhance fluency in computational skills (Westwood, 2018).

An Example of an Online Mathematics Course in Hong Kong

In Hong Kong, mathematics is regarded as a core subject from kindergarten through secondary education. In this technological age, ability in mathematics is regarded as extremely important for employment and for entry to tertiary studies. In recent years, students in Hong Kong have demonstrated consistently high performance in mathematics within international studies of achievement (Martin, Mullis, Foy, & Olson, 2008; Mullis, 2012). Gifted students within this high-achieving population are now growing up in a digital world and online learning plays a role in their education (Chen et al., 2013).

The Gifted Education Section of the Education Bureau developed an online mathematics course that is tailor-made for talented students. The course is delivered in an online platform so that the students can access it from their schools or their own homes. Each year, around 1000 students who are talented in mathematics participate in this course.

The course consists of three levels: Level 1—junior secondary level algebra, number theory, geometry, combinatorics, and probability; Level 2 and 3—senior secondary level algebra, number theory, geometry, combinatorics, probability, and complex number. Each level consists of reading texts, graphics, animations, reference links, exercises, quizzes, and an end-of-level test. The course allows participants to choose the sequence of chapters to learn and they must complete all tasks and obtain the passing mark in the End-of-Level Test in order to enter the next level. Only three attempts are allowed for each End-of-Level Test. Students who failed all three attempts will not be able to enter the next level. However, according to the course structure, the participants must follow a tight schedule to complete the course in one year. This arrangement may not be flexible enough for busy Hong Kong students. Some participants may give up attempting the tests and quit the course if the test dates clash with school activities or school examinations. It seems that if the course could be delivered in a more flexible way, the participants could engage more with the course content. The course provider could allow the participants to join the course at any time and at any level. A pre-test can be given to the potential participants to determine which level is suitable for them to join. Moreover, the learning sequence of this online course is restricted, which means the participants are not allowed to skip any content. This design contradicts the idea of allowing flexibility of learning among gifted students (Van Tassel-Baska & Stambaugh, 2005). Thus, the course designer can make provision for the students to choose the learning sequence according to their own interests and abilities.

In the study reported briefly here, the authors investigated the extent to which self-regulation is involved in completing this course, and looked specifically at the variables of self-efficacy, course design, and support for learning (Fung, 2015). The aims of the study were to:

- Obtain a better understanding of the strategies used by mathematically gifted students to engage successfully in self-regulated learning in an online context.
- Explore how course design can support the engagement of learners.
- Deepen our understanding of how teacher support, parent support, and peer support may influence student engagement in online courses.
- Explore the degree to which mathematics enjoyment, mathematics self-efficacy, and computer self-efficacy are predictors of online self-regulated strategies used in mathematically gifted students.

The proposed framework underpinning this study had three key elements: personal factors, environmental factors, and behavioural factors (Fig. 1).

Personal factors were gender, age, and educational level. Participants' mathematical self-efficacy and enjoyment were treated as personal factors and operated as independent variables that may influence learning and motivation. *Environmental factors* included the online course itself and the available social support from parents, teachers, and peers. These factors were treated as independent variables that may influence learning. *Behavioural factors* in online learning include the use of self-regulated learning strategies that reflect the autonomy of the learner.

Online self-regulated learning strategies can be categorised into six dimensions: goal setting, environmental structuring, task strategies, time management, help

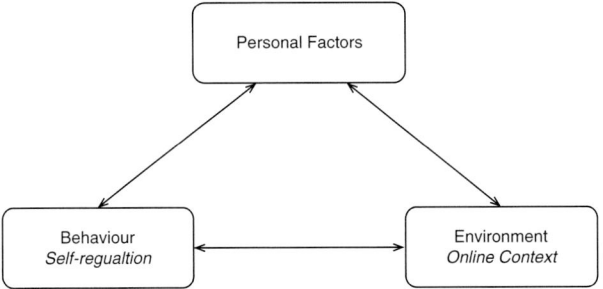

Personal factors: gender, age, grade, mathematics self-efficacy, mathematics enjoyment, and computer self-efficacy
Environment: online context includes the online course and social support (parents, teachers, and peers)
Behavour: demonstrate the use of online self-regulated learning strategies

Fig. 1 Triadic reciprocal determinism of self-regulated learning strategies used by gifted students in the online context

seeking, and self-evaluation. All six dimensions were considered as dependent variables that may be influenced by personal factors and environmental factors.

Figure 2 depicts a model that suggests the relationships among these variables and the contributions they make to self-regulated learning.

Given the importance of self-efficacy as discussed above, it was hypothesised that self-efficacy would perhaps mediate the impact of social support and course design on the development of self-regulated learning. In this study, the authors investigated five interrelated issues:

- Is self-efficacy significantly and positively related to self-regulated online learning in this group of students?
- Is social support significantly and positively related to self-regulated online learning?
- Is the design of a specific mathematics online course significantly and positively related to self-regulated learning?
- Does self-efficacy mediate the influence of social support on self-regulated learning?
- Does self-efficacy mediate the influence of course design on self-regulated learning?

The 374 participants (of potentially 1400 students) were all nominated by their schools as high-achievers in mathematics and were enrolled in the online mathematics course. The students came from school years Primary 4 to Secondary 3 (age range 9–15 years; mean age = 12.2; 51.6% male, 48.4% female). The self-reporting 5-point Likert scaled questionnaires used in this study were used and validated in previous studies and were presented to participants and completed online. All students were required to complete the following questionnaires transcribed into the Chinese language: *Online Self-Regulated Learning Questionnaire (OLSQ)*

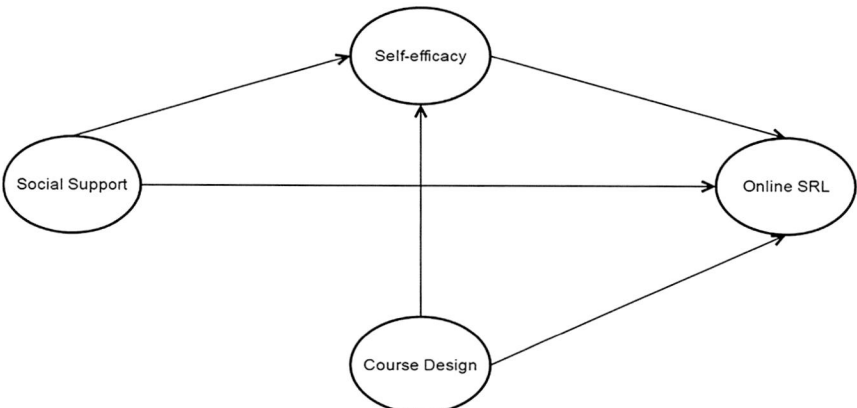

Fig. 2 Model of self-efficacy, social support and course design in relation to online self-regulated learning

(Barnard, Lan, To, Paton, & Lai, 2009; Appendix 1); *Social Support Scale for Online Learning (SSSOL)* specifically constructed for this study (Appendix 2); *Design of Online Course Scale (DOCS)* also specifically constructed for this study (Appendix 3); and a questionnaire containing items from the *Self-Efficacy Scale for Mathematically Talented Online Learners (SESMTOL*; Fast et al., 2010) with added items from the research literature to measure mathematics enjoyment (Adelson & McCoach, 2011), and computer self-efficacy adapted from Compeau and Higgins (1995; Appendix 4). The factorial structure of the Chinese questionnaire scales were evaluated by Confirmatory Factor Analysis (CFA) using SPSS version 22 and AMOS version 20.

Self-Efficacy, Social Support, and Course Design Were Found to Be Keys to Supporting Online Self-Regulated Learning: Brief Analysis and Findings

Using the data collected from the participants, *Structural Equation Modelling* (SEM) was used to investigate: (a) the direct relationship of social support to online self-regulated learning, self-efficacy to online self-regulated learning, and course design to online self-regulated learning; (b) the indirect relationship of social support and online self-regulated learning via the mediating effect of self-efficacy; and (c) the indirect relationship of course design and online self-regulated learning via the mediating effect of self-efficacy. To improve the model fit, several error covariances were added, based on the modification indices. The goodness-of-fit indices then fit the data adequately (Fig. 3). The results indicated a Normed Fit Index (NFI) =0.826, a Comparative Fit Index (CFI) =0.910 and a Root Mean Square Error of Approximation (RMSEA) =0.048. All parameters were standardised and were significant ($p < 0.001$), indicating that the hypothesised direct and indirect paths were significant. Hence, it was suggested that social support may have a direct influence on online self-regulated learning; and the causal relationship between social support and online self-regulated learning was mediated significantly by self-efficacy but the effect was low.

The findings in this study help to dispel notions that gifted and talented learners do not require social support during learning processes (Johnson, 2000) and can learn completely independently from online resources. In the findings, it was suggested that social support from teachers played a role in maintaining students' motivation and persistence in the mathematics course, and also helped reinforce their self-efficacy beliefs. It was not surprising that the students reported more support from teachers than from parents or from peers, but all three stakeholders contributed in varying degrees to the students' overall success. Teachers were able to model effective ways of working online, answer students' questions, clarify difficult mathematical concepts, and offer encouragement. Peers often provided support mainly by sharing ideas and helping to clarify any points of confusion through discussion.

Course design in terms of structure, resources, and nature of tasks also proved to be important, because it helped to generate positive and reinforcing relationships among course content, self-efficacy, and self-regulation. Resources and learning

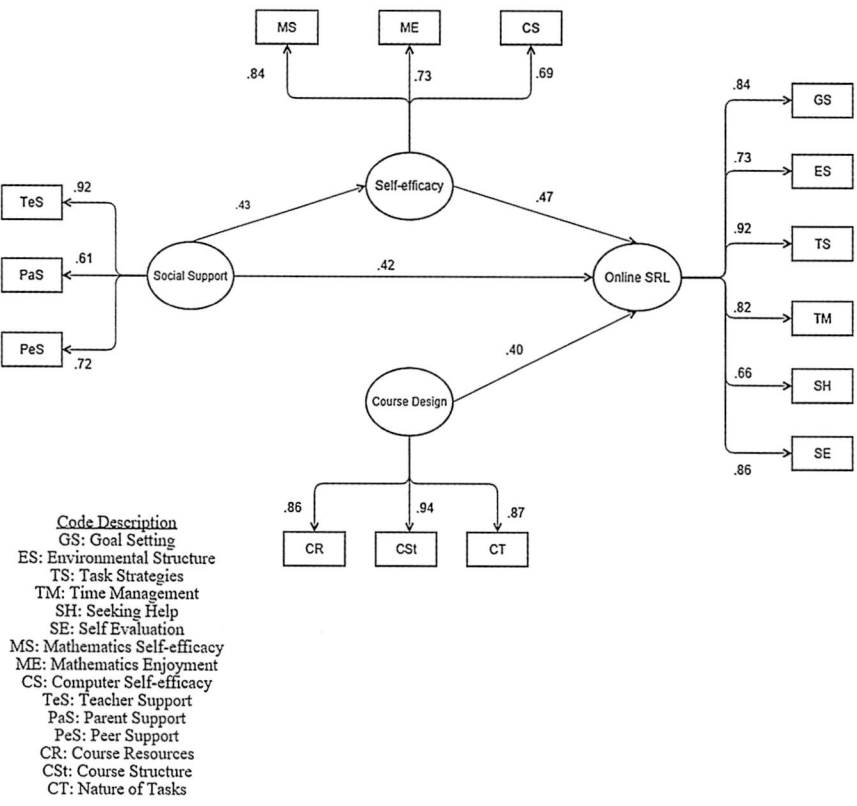

Fig. 3 The structure model of self-efficacy, social support and course design in relation to online self-regulated learning

tasks that are well designed arouse and maintain learners' motivation, and can enhance mathematics self-efficacy, computer self-efficacy, and enjoyment (Fung, 2015). Self-efficacy appears to play a role in mediating the relationship between social support and self-regulated learning, and also between course design and self-regulated learning in this sample of mathematically talented students in Hong Kong.

Implications for Future Practice

There were limitations to the study presented here, such as only about a fifth of the possible participants responded to the questionnaires and nearly half the participants were primary school age, the findings cannot be generalised to any particular cohort, and the forced response design of the questionnaires may have impacted the findings. Hence, in tentatively interpreting the findings from the study, four implications can be relevant for educators, specifically in the field of gifted education. The first implication is related to developing thoughtfully designed online courses for mathematically gifted students and the second is related to promoting online learning in schools. The third is related to designing online courses which can support online self-regulated learning, while the fourth implication addresses the teacher's role in promoting online self-regulated learning.

Online Course Design Should Match the Needs of Mathematically Gifted Students

Gavin (2003) claimed that mathematically gifted students usually need separate learning programs that enable flexibility in ability grouping and a more rapid learning pace, as gifted learners can work more abstractly (Bicknell & Holton, 2009), solve problems more quickly (Sriraman, 2003), and produce more creative or innovative responses. Additionally, there should be sufficient problems at each stage to allow gifted students to satisfy their curiosity about the current topic (Rotigel & Fello, 2004). A 'spiral curriculum' in which topics are frequently revisited (which is often recommended for average students (e.g., Liu, 2017) is often redundant with gifted students since they may already know the content and usually do not need repetition (Rotigel & Fello, 2004). They need a curriculum that adds depth and breadth to the normal curriculum and allows them to move forward at a faster rate. In particular, they benefit from problems and tasks that present a genuine cognitive challenge (Diezmann & Watters, 2002). Where possible, appropriate use should be made of animations, visual displays, video clips and models embedded in the online course (Bonk & Zhang, 2006), and linking mathematical concepts and processes with real life (Lindwer et al., 2003).

Promoting Online Learning in School

Fung, Yuen, and Yuen (2014) reviewed relevant literature in this field and found strong evidence supporting the value of online learning as a contemporary medium for advancing mathematical development in all students. Online learning can allow students to engage actively and creatively in their own learning at all age and ability levels. For most students, this can occur within the school day and also at home. The extant research literature suggests that this form of active learning is effective in motivating students to engage in mathematics and maximises their cognitive engagement in mathematical reasoning (Fung et al., 2014). Since online learning in mathematics has the potential to greatly enrich and extend mathematics education, school leaders have a responsibility to promote the approach to teachers. There is also a pressing need to provide relevant training for teachers and to ensure that the school has the necessary resources and ICT infrastructure (Yuen, Law, & Wong, 2003). Relevant training for teachers in this context can include digital and information literacy (Kereluik, Mishra, Fahnoe, & Terry, 2013), integration of ICT in teaching and development of appropriate pedagogical practices such as promoting the *flipped classroom* (Roehl, Reddy, & Shannon, 2013).

Developing Courses to Support Online Self-regulated Learning

In the context of online learning, Howland and Moore (2002) have indicated that students who have higher self-regulation for learning generally have more positive perceptions of online courses and also achieve more positive academic outcomes. According to Fung et al. (2018), course design has a direct influence on facilitating and maintaining self-regulated learning.

The appropriate design of an online course is a critical factor to ensure participants' active engagement with the course content and to maintain their motivation (Akdemir & Koszalka, 2008; Ibrahim & Callaway, 2012). Students who are highly motivated to learn are more likely to engage cognitively with the content and retain what they learn (Radosevich, Vaidyanathan, Yeo, & Radosevich, 2004). Self-regulation can be encouraged when the design of an online course requires students to plan ahead, consider alternative paths, reflect upon their decisions and actions and monitor their own progress (Zundans-Fraser & Lancaster, 2012). Online courses could also have effective ways of providing feedback to a student and encouraging self-correction. For example, when a student makes an error or appears not to understand a process, the program can already have self-correction or feedback within it to links that take the student to more detailed explanations and provide additional examples. *Adaptive Learning* (AL) as found through proprietary software is relevant here, for example, *Smart Sparrow*. A peer feedback system can also be embedded in the online program so that students can learn from each other (Wanchid, 2013). Such embedded feedback may be in the form of grades, aural responses for correct answers, electronic rubrics or checklists, feedback statements, correct answers, or students monitoring and self-evaluating their own progress, all of which would support the teacher's provision of direct feedback verbally to the student (Archer, 2010; Atkinson & Lim, 2013).

The Role of Teachers in Promoting Online Self-Regulated Learning

In the Hong Kong study, teacher support was found to have a greater effect than parent support and peer support on students' online self-regulated learning (Fung et al., 2018). It is important therefore, in the preservice and in-service training of teachers, to help teachers to understand their key role in facilitating and supporting students who are engaging in online learning. In particular, teachers can discuss openly with students the real value of self-regulation when working online and can model effective ways of working independently, reflecting on one's progress, self-correcting, and seeking outside help when necessary.

Self-regulation is not necessarily an innate attribute for working with technology, but it can be taught and improved through appropriate intervention and encouragement (Lee, McInerney, & Liem, 2010; Schunk & Greene, 2019; Zimmerman, 2008b). According to Zimmerman (2002), self-regulated learning can be processed effectively in three stages: forethought and planning, performance control, and self-reflection. In the forethought and planning stage, teachers can instruct their students about effective approaches and guide them to plan for their learning (Fung, 2015). In the performance control stage, teachers can support their students in the use of different strategies to accomplish their learning tasks and give feedback to them (Fung, 2015). In the final reflection stage, teachers can encourage their students to self-evaluate (Fung, 2015). Self-reflection can give students insights for improvement and goal planning for future learning.

Fung (2015) suggested the development of an online platform for gifted students to organise and keep records of their learning in the form of learning profiles. In this way, students can plan for the learning programs they will join, monitor the progress of their learning, record important remarks, and evaluate their own performances. In the portfolio, students can reflect on whether they have reached specific learning goals, evaluate the strategies they have used, and consider what strategies they need to keep or change in the future.

Implications for Future Research

It was suggested in the study described here, that gifted students in Hong Kong did use self-regulation when engaged in online learning, and they displayed better self-regulated strategies than average students in this situation (Fung, 2015). Future research could explore how well gifted students in other countries compare to Hong Kong students in self-regulated online learning in mathematics. It would also be useful to explore gifted students' online self-regulated learning strategies when studying other subjects—such as language, history, or geography. For example, to what extent do the same variables influence and enhance their performances?

Future research could also investigate in more detail how designers of gifted education programs can incorporate resources and learning tasks into online courses to produce optimum learning outcomes and at the same time enhance students' self-efficacy. The importance of self-efficacy in learning has been recognised for many years (Bandura, 1997; Wang et al., 2013) and was also found in the Hong Kong sample. Self-efficacy can be a mediator between course design and self-regulated learning, and also a mediator between social support and self-regulated learning. Researchers may explore what features of teachers' support practices and feedback are most effective in encouraging students' self-efficacy and self-regulation.

Previous researchers (e.g., Schunk & Zimmerman, 2008; Wang & Holcombe, 2010; You, & Kang, 2014) have suggested that motivation is an important factor influencing self-regulated learning. For example, students can be motivated by their teachers, parents, and peers to learn and to persevere in their studies. In fact, teacher immediacy and presence in an online course can motivate the engagement of students (Baker, 2010). Students can also be motivated by well-designed curricular materials and online courses. The ultimate goal should be that students become self-motivated, rather than depending on external sources. Self-motivation is a strong indication of a learner becoming autonomous and self-regulated (Lehmann, Hähnlein, & Ifenthaler, 2014; Zimmerman, 2004). In future studies, the interplay of motivation with self-regulated learning, self-efficacy, social support, and course design, especially in relation to teacher, parent, or peer support, could be investigated.

Conclusion

Online learning has become a valuable medium for encouraging independent learning in all students. This mode of learning is particularly appropriate for gifted students because it represents one important means of differentiating curriculum to allow individuals to progress at their own faster rate and pursue their own interests. Certain variables contribute to a student's ability to do well in online learning—these include the design of the course, self-regulation, self-efficacy, computer self-efficacy, and the availability of social support in the form of advice and feedback from more knowledgeable others. The potential influence these variables have on gifted students' online learning in mathematics and suggestions for improving course design were provided in this chapter. The need to increase teachers' skills for encouraging students' self-regulation and autonomy was also stressed.

Cross-References

▶ Assessment, Pedagogy, and Curriculum: Part IV Introduction
▶ Creativity Talent Development: Fostering Creativity in Schools
▶ Differentiation of Instruction for Gifted Learners: Collated Evaluative Studies of Teacher Classroom Practices
▶ Engaging Gifted Students in Solving Real Problems Creatively: Implementing the Real Engagement in Active Problem-Solving (REAPS) Teaching/Learning Model in Australasian and Pacific Rim Contexts
▶ Fostering and Developing Talent in Mentorship Programs: The Mentor's Perspectives
▶ Gifted Education in the Asia-Pacific: From the Past for the Future – An Introduction
▶ Motivational Issues in Gifted Education: Understanding the Role of Students' Attribution and Control Beliefs, Self-Worth Protection and Growth Orientation
▶ Self-Regulated Learning for High-Ability and High-Achieving Students in Mixed-Ability Classrooms Throughout the Asia-Pacific
▶ Some Implications for the Future of Gifted Education in the Asia-Pacific
▶ STEAM in Gifted Education in Korea
▶ The Lives and Achievements of Four Extraordinary Australians: A Master, a Maker, an Introspector, and an Influencer

Appendix 1

Online Self-Regulated Learning Questionnaire (OLSQ) Original

Instructions: Please read each statement and then circle the number which best shows how you feel.

SD = Strongly Disagree. D = Disagree. U=Undecided. A = Agree. SA = Strongly Agree.

			SD	D	U	A	SA
	Goal Setting						
1	I set standards for my assignments in online courses.	(1)	1	2	3	4	5
2	I set short-term (daily or weekly) goals as well as long-term goals (monthly or for the semester).	(2)	1	2	3	4	5
3	I keep a high standard for my learning in my online courses.	(3)	1	2	3	4	5
4	I set goals to help me manage studying time for my online courses.	(4)	1	2	3	4	5
5	I don't compromise the quality of my work because it is online.	(5)	1	2	3	4	5
	Environment Structuring						
6	I choose the location where I study to avoid too much distraction.	(6)	1	2	3	4	5
7	I find a comfortable place to study.	(7)	1	2	3	4	5
8	I know where I can study most efficiently for online courses.	(8)	1	2	3	4	5
9	I choose a time with few distractions for studying for my online courses.	(9)	1	2	3	4	5
	Task Strategies		1	2	3	4	5
10	I try to take more thorough notes for my online courses because notes are even more important for learning online than in a regular classroom.	(10)	1	2	3	4	5
11	I read aloud instructional materials posted online to fight against distractions.	(11)	1	2	3	4	5
12	I prepare my questions before joining in the chat room and discussion.	(12)	1	2	3	4	5
13	I work extra problems in my online courses in addition to the assigned ones to master the course content.	(13)	1	2	3	4	5
	Time Management						
14	I allocate extra studying time for my online courses because I know it is time-demanding.	(14)	1	2	3	4	5
15	I try to schedule the same time everyday or every week to study for my online courses, and I observe the schedule.	(15)	1	2	3	4	5
16	Although we don't have to attend daily classes, I still try to distribute my studying time evenly across days.	(16)	1	2	3	4	5
	Help Seeking						
17	I find someone who is knowledgeable in course content so that I can consult with him or her when I need help.	(17)	1	2	3	4	5
18	I share my problems with my classmates online so we know what we are struggling with and how to solve our problems.	(18)	1	2	3	4	5
19	If needed, I try to meet my classmates face-to-face.	(19)	1	2	3	4	5
20	I am persistent in getting help from the instructor through e-mail.	(20)	1	2	3	4	5

(continued)

			SD	D	U	A	SA
	Self-evaluation						
21	I summarize my learning in online courses to examine my understanding of what I have learned.	(21)	1	2	3	4	5
22	I ask myself a lot of questions about the course material when studying for an online course.	(22)	1	2	3	4	5
23	I communicate with my classmates to find out how I am doing in my online classes.	(23)	1	2	3	4	5
24	I communicate with my classmates to find out what I am learning that is different from what they are learning.	(24)	1	2	3	4	5

Barnard et al., (2009)

Appendix 2

Social Support Scale for Online Learning (SSSOL)

Teacher Support Subscale
- My teacher instructs me on the content of the online learning course. (Instructional assistance)
- My teacher is a role model for me to engage in online learning. (Modelling)
- My teacher encourages me to engage in online learning. (Verbal encouragement)
- My teacher comforts and supports me when I encountered difficulties. (Emotional support)

Parent Support Subscale
- My parent helps me with the content of the online learning course. (Instructional assistance)
- My parent is a role model for me to engage in online learning. (Modelling)
- My parent encourages me to engage in online learning. (Verbal encouragement)
- My parent comforts me when I encountered difficulties. (Emotional support)

Peer Support Subscale
- My peers help me with the content of the online learning course. (Instructional assistance)
- My peers are role models for me to engage in online learning. (Modelling)
- My peers encourage me to engage in online learning. (Verbal encouragement)
- My peers comfort me when I encountered difficulties. (Emotional support)

Appendix 3

Design of Online Course Scale (DOCS)

Resources Subscale
- The online course includes a variety of learning resources. (text, animations, games, etc.)
- The online course is rich in learning content. (notes, examples, answer key, etc.)
- The online course includes help facilities. (forum, email, etc.)

Structure Subscale
- The learning instructions are clear and easy to understand.
- The user interface is easy to use.
- I am allowed to choose the learning sequences for different topics.
- I am allowed to skip some content.
- I am allowed to learn at any time.

Nature of Tasks Subscale
- There are various types of learning tasks. (exercises, tests, etc.)
- The learning tasks are challenging.
- The learning tasks encourage creativity.

Appendix 4

Self-Efficacy Scale for Mathematically Talented Online Learners (SESMTOL)

Mathematics Self-Efficacy
- I'm sure that I can learn everything that is taught in mathematics.
- I'm sure that I can do even the hardest work set in my math class.
- Even if a new topic in math is difficult I'm sure that I can learn it.
- I'm sure that I can figure out the answers to any problems my teacher gives me in math class.

Mathematics Enjoyment
- I enjoy studying math.
- I enjoy doing math puzzles.
- I enjoy playing math games.

Computer Self-Efficacy

- I could complete a job using the platform of the online course if someone shows me how to do it first.
- I could complete a job using the platform of the online course if I could call someone for help if I got stuck.
- I could complete a job using the platform of the online course if I had just the built-in help facility for assistance.
- I could complete a job using the platform of the online course if I had used a similar online platform before.

References

Adelson, J. L., & McCoach, D. B. (2011). Development and psychometric properties of the Math and Me Survey: Measuring third through sixth graders' attitudes toward mathematics. *Measurement and Evaluation in Counseling and Development, 44*(4), 225–247. https://doi.org/10.1177/0748175611418522

Akdemir, O., & Koszalka, T. A. (2008). Investigating the relationships among instructional strategies and learning styles in online environments. *Computers & Education, 50*(4), 1451–1461. https://doi.org/10.1016/j.compedu.2007.01.004

Allan, G. M. (2006). *Responsibility for learning: students' understandings and their self reported learning attitudes and behaviours* (Masters dissertation, Queensland University of Technology, Brisbane, Australia). Retrieved from https://eprints.qut.edu.au/16209/1/Gary_Allan_Thesis.pdf

Andersen, L., & Cross, T. L. (2014). Are students with high ability in math more motivated in math and science than other students? *Roeper Review, 36*(4), 221–234. https://doi.org/10.1080/02783193.2014.945221

Anderton, B. (2006). Using the online course to promote self-regulated learning strategies in pre-service teachers. *Journal of Interactive Online Learning, 5*(2), 156–177.

Archer, J. C. (2010). State of the science in health professional education: Effective feedback. *Medical Education, 44*(1), 101–108. https://doi.org/10.1111/j.1365-2923.2009.03546.x

Artino, A. R. (2008). Promoting academic motivation and self-regulation: Practical guidelines for online instructors. *TechTrends, 52*(3), 37–45. https://doi.org/10.1007/s11528-008-0153-x.32

Artino, A. R., & Stephens, J. M. (2007, October). *Motivation and self-regulation in online courses: A comparative analysis of undergraduate and graduate students.* In Annual meeting of the Association for Educational Communications and Technology, Anaheim, CA.

Atkinson, D., & Lim, S. L. (2013). Improving assessment processes in higher education: Student and teacher perceptions of the effectiveness of a rubric embedded in a LMS. *Australasian Journal of Educational Technology, 29*(5), 651–666. https://doi.org/10.14742/ajet.526

Baker, C. (2010). The impact of instructor immediacy and presence for online student affective learning, cognition, and motivation. *Journal of Educators Online, 7*(1), 1–30. https://doi.org/10.9743/JEO.2010.1.2

Bandura, A. (1997). *Self-efficacy: The exercise of control.* New York, NY: Freeman.

Barnard, L., Lan, W. Y., To, Y. M., Paton, V. O., & Lai, S. L. (2009). Measuring self-regulation in online and blended learning environments. *The Internet and Higher Education, 12*, 1–6. https://doi.org/10.1016/j.iheduc.2008.10.005

Benny, N., & Blonder, R. (2016). Factors that promote/inhibit teaching gifted students in a regular class: Results from a professional development program for chemistry teachers. *Education Research International, 2016*, 1–11. https://doi.org/10.1155/2016/2742905

Bicknell, B., & Holton, D. (2009). Gifted and talented mathematics students. In R. Averill & R. Harvey (Eds.), *Teaching secondary school mathematics and statistics: Evidence-based practice* (pp. 173–185). Wellington, New Zealand: NZCER Press.

Bonk, C. J., & Zhang, K. (2006). Introducing the R2D2 model: Online learning for the diverse learners of this world. *Distance Education, 27*(2), 249–264. https://doi.org/10.1080/01587910600789670

Boyer, W. (2012). Cultural factors influencing preschoolers' acquisition of self-regulation and emotion regulation. *Journal of Research in Childhood Education, 26*(2), 169–186. https://doi.org/10.1080/02568543.2012.657923

Cavanaugh, C. (2007). Effectiveness of K–12 online learning. In M. Moore (Ed.), *Handbook of distance education* (2nd ed., pp. 157–168). Mahwah, NJ: Lawrence Erlbaum.

Chen, C., & Stevenson, H. W. (1995). Motivation and mathematics achievement: A comparative study of Asian-American, Caucasian-American, and East-Asian High school students. *Child Development, 66*(4), 1215–1234. https://doi.org/10.2307/1131808

Chen, J., Dai, Y. D., & Zhou, Y. (2013). Enable, enhance, and transform: How technology use can improve gifted education. *Roeper Review, 35*(3), 166–176. https://doi.org/10.1080/02783193.2013.794892

Clark, B. (2013). *Growing up gifted: Developing the potential of children at school and at home.* Boston, MA: Pearson/Allyn & Bacon.

Compeau, D. R., & Higgins, C. A. (1995). Application of social cognitive theory to training for computer skills. *Information Systems Research, 6*(2), 118–143. Retrieved from https://www.jstor.org/stable/23011006

Constantine, J., Fernald, J., Robinson, J., & Courtney, M. B. (2019). *Best practices guide-book: Supporting students' self-efficacy.* Barbourville, KY: Bluegrass Center for Teacher Quality.

Dee-Lucas, D. (1999). Hypertext segmentation and goal compatibility: Effects on study strategies and learning. *Journal of Educational Media and Hypermedia, 8*(3), 279–314. Retrieved from https://www.learntechlib.org/primary/p/10812/

DiBenedetto, M. K., & Bembenutty, H. (2013). Within the pipeline: Self-regulated learning, self efficacy, and socialization among college students in science courses. *Learning and Individual Differences, 23*, 218–224. https://doi.org/10.1016/j.lindif.2012.09.015

Diezmann, C. M., & Watters, J. J. (2000). Catering for mathematically gifted elementary students: Learning from challenging tasks. *Gifted Child Today, 23*(4), 14–19. https://doi.org/10.4219/gct-2000-737

Diezmann, C. M., & Watters, J. J. (2002). The importance of challenging tasks for mathematically gifted students. *Gifted and Talented International, 17*(2), 76–84. https://doi.org/10.1080/15332276.2002.11672991

DiPietro, M., Ferdig, R. E., Black, E. W., & Preston, M. (2008). Best practices in teaching K–12 online: Lessons learned from Michigan Virtual School teachers. *Journal of Interactive Online Learning, 7*(1), 10–35. Retrieved from https://www.ncolr.org/jiol/issues/pdf/7.1.2.pdf

Dykman, C. A., & Davis, C. K. (2008). Online education forum: Part two–teaching online versus teaching conventionally. *Journal of Information Systems Education, 19*(2), 157–164. Retrieved from https://www.learntechlib.org/p/105722/

Fast, L. A., Lewis, J. L., Bryant, M. J., Bocian, K. A., Cardullo, R. A., Rettig, M., & Hammond, K. A. (2010). Does math self-efficacy mediate the effect of the perceived classroom environ-ment on standardized math test performance? *Journal of Educational Psychology, 102*(3), 729–740. https://doi.org/10.1037/a0018863

Fazal, M., & Bryant, M. (2019). Blended learning in middle school math: The question of effectiveness. *Journal of Online Learning Research, 5*(1), 49–64. Retrieved from https://files.eric.ed.gov/fulltext/EJ1208816.pdf

Fung, J., Yuen, M., & Yuen, A. H. K. (2014). Self-regulation in learning mathematics online: Implications for supporting mathematically gifted students with or without learning difficulties. *Gifted and Talented International, 29*(1–2), 113–123. https://doi.org/10.1080/15332276.2014.11678434

Fung, J. J., Yuen, M., & Yuen, A. H. (2018). Validity evidence for a Chinese version of the online self-regulated learning questionnaire with average students and mathematically talented stu-dents. *Measurement and Evaluation in Counseling and Development, 51*(2), 111–124. https://doi.org/10.1080/07481756.2017.1358056

Fung, J. Y. (2015). *Exploring the self-regulated learning strategies of mathematically gifted students in an online context* (Doctoral dissertation). University of Hong Kong Faculty of Education, Hong Kong, China.

Gaeta, G., & Martha, L. (2013). Learning goals and strategies in the self-regulation of learning. *US-China Education Review A, 3*(1), 46–50.

Gagné, R. (1985). *The conditions of learning* (4th ed.). New York, NY: Holt, Rinehart & Winston.

Garrison, D. R. (1997). Self-directed learning: Toward a comprehensive model. *Adult Education Quarterly, 48*(1), 18–33. https://doi.org/10.1177/074171369704800103

Garrison, D. R., & Cleveland-Innes, M. (2005). Facilitating cognitive presence in online learning: Interaction is not enough. *The American Journal of Distance Education, 19*(3), 133–148. https://doi.org/10.1207/s15389286ajde1903_2

Gavin, M. K. (2003). Meeting the needs of talented elementary math students. *Understanding Our Gifted, 16*(1), 19–22. Retrieved from https://eric.ed.gov/?id=EJ975947

Goetz, T., Frenzel, A. C., Pekrun, R., Hall, N. C., & Lüdtke, O. (2007). Between-and within-domain relations of students' academic emotions. *Journal of Educational Psychology, 99*(4), 715–733. Retrieved from https://psycnet.apa.org/doiLanding?doi=10.1037%2F0022-0663.99.4.715

Gross, M. U. M. (2006). Exceptionally gifted children: Long-term outcomes of academic acceleration and non-acceleration. *Journal for the Education of the Gifted, 29*(4), 404–429. Retrieved from https://files.eric.ed.gov/fulltext/EJ746290.pdf

Heid, M. K. (1983). Characteristics and special needs of the gifted student in mathematics. *Mathematics Teacher, 76*, 221–226.

Hiemstra, R. (1994). Self-directed learning. In T. Husen & T. N. Postlethwaite (Eds.), *The international encyclopedia of education* (2nd ed.). Oxford, UK: Pergamon Press.

Ho, S. C. (2004). Self-regulated learning and academic achievement of Hong Kong secondary school students. *Education journal, 32*(2), 87–107. Retrieved from https://www.fed.cuhk.edu.hk/~hkcisa/articles/Ho_2004_ej_v32n2_87-107.pdf

House, P. (Ed.). (1987). *Providing opportunities for the mathematically gifted K–12*. Reston, VA: National Council of Teachers of Mathematics.

Howland, J. L., & Moore, J. L. (2002). Student perceptions as distance learners in internet-based courses. *Distance Education, 23*(2), 183–195. https://doi.org/10.1080/0158791022000009196

Ibrahim, M., & Callaway, R. (2012). Assessing the correlations among cognitive overload, online course design, and student self-efficacy. In P. Resta (Ed.), *Proceedings of Society for Information Technology & Teacher Education International Conference 2012* (pp. 463–470). Chesapeake, VA: AACE.

Johnson, D. T. (2000). *Teaching mathematics to gifted students in a mixed-ability classroom.* Reston, VA: Council for Exceptional Children.

Kereluik, K., Mishra, P., Fahnoe, C., & Terry, L. (2013). What knowledge is of most worth: Teacher knowledge for 21st century learning. *Journal of Digital Learning in Teacher Education, 29*(4), 127–140. https://doi.org/10.1080/21532974.2013.10784716

Kolikant, Y. B. D. (2010). Digital natives, better learners? Students' beliefs about how the Internet influenced their ability to learn. *Computers in Human Behavior, 26*(6), 1384–1391. https://doi.org/10.1016/j.chb.2010.04.012

Koshy, V., Ernest, P., & Casey, R. (2009). Mathematically gifted and talented learners: Theory and practice. *International Journal of Mathematical Education in Science & Technology, 40*(2), 213–228. https://doi.org/10.1080/00207390802566907

Krutetskii, V. A. (1976). *The psychology of mathematical abilities in school children*. Chicago, IL: University of Chicago Press.

Lee, J. Q., McInerney, D. M., & Liem, G. A. (2010). The relationship between future goals and achievement goal orientations: An intrinsic-extrinsic motivation perspective. *Contemporary Educational Psychology, 35*(4), 264–279. https://doi.org/10.1016/j.cedpsych.2010.04.004

Lee, Y. (2019). Promoting students' motivation and use of SRL strategies in the web-based mathematics learning environment. *Journal of Educational Technology Systems, 47*(3), 391–410. https://doi.org/10.1177/0047239518808522

Lehmann, T., Hähnlein, I., & Ifenthaler, D. (2014). Cognitive, metacognitive and motivational perspectives on preflection in self-regulated online learning. *Computers in Human Behavior, 32*, 313–323. https://doi.org/10.1016/j.chb.2013.07.051

Li, C. S., & Irby, B. (2008). An overview of online education: Attractiveness, benefits, challenges, concerns and recommendations. *College Student Journal, 42*(2), 449–458. Retrieved from https://eric.ed.gov/?id=EJ816925

Lindwer, M., Marculescu, D., Basten, T., Zimmermann, R., Marculescu, R., Jung, S., & Cantatore, E. (2003, March). Ambient intelligence visions and achievements: Linking abstract ideas to real-world concepts. In *Proceedings of the conference on Design, Automation and Test in Europe-Volume 1* (p. 10010). IEEE Computer Society. https://doi.org/10.1109/DATE.2003.1253580

Liu, J. (2017). A project-based spiraling curriculum model of supporting learning Eeficiency and engagement on modified flipped class. *Revista de la Facultad de Ingeniería, 32*(7), 417–425. Retrieved from https://www.researchgate.net/publication/321007994_A_project-based_spiraling_curriculum_model_of_supporting_learning_efficiency_and_engagement_on_modified_flipped_class

Liu, R.-D., Zhen, R., Ding, Y., Liu, Y., Wang, J., Jiang, R., & Xu, L. (2018). Teacher support and math engagement: Roles of academic self-efficacy and positive emotions. *Educational Psychology, 38*(1), 3–16. https://doi.org/10.1080/01443410.2017.1359238

Lubinski, D., Benbow, C. P., & Kell, H. J. (2014). Life paths and accomplishments of mathematically precocious males and females four decades later. *Psychological Science, 25*(12), 2217–2232. https://doi.org/10.1177/0956797614551371

Lynch, R., & Dembo, M. (2004). The relationship between self-regulation and online learning in a blended learning context. *The International Review of Research in Open and Distributed Learning, 5*(2), 1–16. https://doi.org/10.19173/irrodl.v5i2.189

Martin, M., Mullis, I., Foy, P., & Olson, J. (2008). *TIMSS 2007 international mathematics report*. Chestnut Hill, MA: IEA.

McInnerney, J. M., & Roberts, T. S. (2004). Online learning: Social interaction and the creation of a sense of community. *Journal of Educational Technology & Society, 7*(3), 73–81.

Morgan, H. (2015). Online instruction and virtual schools for middle and high school students: Twenty-first century fads or progressive teaching methods for today's pupils? *The Clearing House, 88*(3), 72–76. https://doi.org/10.1080/00098655.2015.1007909

Mullis, I. (2012). *TIMSS 2011 international results in mathematics*. Boston, MA: TIMSS & PIRLS International Study Center.

Muratori, M., Stanley, J., Ng, L., Ng, J., Gross, M., Tao, T., & Tao, B. (2006). Insights from SMPY's greatest former child prodigies: Drs. Terence ("Terry") Tao and Lenhard ("Lenny") Ng reflect on their talent development. *Gifted Child Quarterly, 50*(4), 307–324. https://doi.org/10.1177/001698620605000404

Ormrod, J. E. (2000). *Educational psychology: Developing learners* (3rd ed.). Upper Saddle River, NJ: Merrill-Prentice Hall.

Pellas, N. (2014). The influence of computer self-efficacy, metacognitive self-regulation and self-esteem on student engagement in online learning programs: Evidence from the virtual world of Second Life. *Computers in Human Behavior, 35*, 157–170. https://doi.org/10.1016/j.chb.2014.02.048

Pintrich, P. R., & Zusho, A. (2002). The development of academic self-regulation: The role of cognitive and motivational factors. In A. Wigfield & J. S. Eccles (Eds.), *Development of achievement motivation* (pp. 249–284). San Diego, CA: Academic.

Radosevich, D. J., Vaidyanathan, V. T., Yeo, S. Y., & Radosevich, D. M. (2004). Relating goal orientation to self-regulatory processes: A longitudinal field test. *Contemporary Educational Psychology, 29*(3), 207–229. https://doi.org/10.1016/S0361-476X(03)00032-8

Regan, K. S., & Martin, P. J. (2014). Cultivating self-regulation for students with mild disabilities. *Intervention in School and Clinic, 49*(3), 164–173. https://doi.org/10.1177/1053451213496163

Renzulli, J. S. (2005). The three-ring conception of giftedness: A developmental model for promoting creative productivity. In R. J. Sternberg & J. E. Davidson (Eds.), *Conceptions of giftedness* (2nd ed., pp. 246–279). New York, NY: Cambridge University Press. https://doi.org/10.1017/CBO9780511610455.015

Roehl, A., Reddy, S. L., & Shannon, G. J. (2013). The flipped classroom: An opportunity to engage millennial students through active learning strategies. *Journal of Family & Consumer Sciences, 105*(2), 44–49. https://doi.org/10.14307/JFCS105.2.12

Rotigel, J. V. (2000). *Exceptional mathematical talent: Comparing achievement in concepts and computation* (Unpublished doctoral dissertation). University of Pennsylvania, Indiana, PA.

Rotigel, J. V., & Fello, S. (2004). Mathematically gifted students: How can we meet their needs? *Gifted Child Today, 27*(4), 46–51. https://doi.org/10.4219/gct-2004-150

Schunk, D. H., & Greene, J. A. (2019). *Handbook of self-regulation of learning and performance* (2nd ed.). New York, NY: Routledge.

Schunk, D. H., & Zimmerman, B. J. (2008). Motivation: An essential dimension of self-regulated learning. In D. H. Schunk & B. J. Zimmerman (Eds.), *Motivation and self-regulated learning: Theory, research, and application* (pp. 111–139). New York, NY: Routledge.

Sheffield, L. J. (1994). *The development of gifted and talented mathematics students and the National Council of Teachers of Mathematics Standards (RBDM9404)*. Storrs, CT: University of Connecticut, The National Research Center on the Gifted and Talented. Retrieved from https://nrcgt.uconn.edu/research-based_resources/sheffiel/

Shen, D., Cho, M. H., Tsai, C. L., & Marra, R. (2013). Unpacking online learning experiences: Online learning self-efficacy and learning satisfaction. *The Internet and Higher Education, 19*, 10–17. https://doi.org/10.1016/j.iheduc.2013.04.001

Shepherd, T. L. (2010). *Working with students with emotional and behavior disorders*. Upper Saddle River, NJ: Pearson Education.

Singer, F. M., Sheffield, L. J., Freiman, V., & Brandl, M. (2016). *Research on and activities for mathematically gifted students* (pp. 1–41). New York, NY: Springer International Publishing. https://doi.org/10.1007/978-3-319-39450-3_2

Skaalvik, E. M., & Skaalvik, S. (2006). *Self-concept and self-efficacy in mathematics: Relation with mathematics motivation and achievement*. In Proceedings of the International Conference on Learning Sciences, Bloomington, IN. Retrieved from http://www.findarticles.com

Skemp, R. (1976). Relational understanding and instrumental understanding. *Mathematics Teaching, 77*, 20–26. Retrieved from https://eric.ed.gov/?id=EJ154208

Slavin, R. E., Lake, C., & Groff, C. (2009). *What works in teaching maths?* York, UK: Institute for Effective Education, University of York. https://doi.org/10.4135/9781483377544.n1

Song, L., & Hill, J. R. (2007). A conceptual model for understanding self-directed learning in online environments. *Journal of Interactive Online Learning, 6*(1), 27–42. Retrieved from https://eric.ed.gov/?id=EJ1092260

Sriraman, B. (2003). Mathematical giftedness, problem solving, and the ability to formulate generalisations: The problem-solving experiences of four gifted students. *Journal of Secondary Gifted Education, 14*(3), 151–165. https://doi.org/10.4219/jsge-2003-425

Stevenson, H. W., & Lee, S. Y. (1996). The academic achievement of Chinese students. In M. H. Bond (Ed.), *The handbook of Chinese psychology* (pp. 124–142). Hong Kong, China: Oxford University Press.

Stoeger, H., & Zeidner, M. (2019). Self-regulated learning in gifted, talented, and high-achieving learners. *High Ability Studies, 30*(1–2), 1–8. https://doi.org/10.1080/13598139.2019.1601326

Sun, R. C. F., & Hui, E. K. P. (2007). Building social support for adolescents with suicidal ideation: Implications for school guidance and counselling. *British Journal of Guidance and Counselling, 35*(3), 299–309. https://doi.org/10.1080/03069880701384452

Susila, H., Muslim, S., & Syahrial, Z. (2018). Interactive multimedia to enhance students' engagement. In *Proceedings of the 1st International Conference on Science and Technology for an Internet of Things*. European Alliance for Innovation (EAI). Retrieved from https://eudl.eu/doi/10.4108/eai.19-10-2018.2281286

Thomson, D. L. (2010). Beyond the classroom walls: Teachers' and students' perspectives on how online learning can meet the needs of gifted students. *Journal of Advanced Academics, 21*(4), 662–712. https://doi.org/10.1177/1932202X1002100405

Tortop, H. S. (2015). A comparison of gifted and non-gifted students' self-regulation skills for science learning. *Journal for the Education of Gifted Young Scientists, 3*(1), 42–57. Retrieved from https://www.researchgate.net/publication/280741719_A_Comparison_of_Gifted_and_Non-Gifted_Students_Self-regulation_Skills_for_Science_Learning_Indexed_in_EBSCO_DOAJ

Trowler, V. (2010). Student engagement literature review. *The Higher Education Academy, 11*(1), 1–15. https://doi.org/10.4324/9780429025648-3

Usher, E. L., & Pajares, F. (2008). Self-efficacy for self-regulated learning: A validation study. *Educational and Psychological Measurement, 68*(3), 443–463. https://doi.org/10.1177/0013164407308475

Van Tassel-Baska, J., & Stambaugh, T. (2005). Challenges and possibilities for serving gifted learners in the regular classroom. *Theory Into Practice, 44*(3), 211–217. Retrieved from https://eric.ed.gov/?id=EJ692318

Wallace, P. (2005). Distance education for gifted students: Leveraging technology to expand academic programs. *High Ability Studies, 16*(1), 77–86. https://doi.org/10.1080/13598130500115288

Wanchid, R. (2013). The use of self-correction, paper-pencil peer feedback and electronic peer feedback in the EFL writing class: Opportunities and challenges. *Academic Journal of Interdisciplinary Studies, 2*(3), 157. https://doi.org/10.5901/ajis.2013.v2n3p157

Wang, C., Shannon, D., & Ross, M. (2013). Students' characteristics, self-regulated learning, technology, self-efficacy, and course outcomes in online learning. *Distance Education, 34*(3), 302–323. https://doi.org/10.1080/01587919.2013.835779

Wang, C. H. (2010). *Students' characteristics, self-regulated learning, technology self-efficacy, and course outcomes in web-based courses* (Unpublished doctoral dissertation). Auburn University, Auburn, AL

Wang, M. T., & Holcombe, R. (2010). Adolescents' perceptions of school environment, engagement, and academic achievement in middle school. *American Educational Research Journal, 47*(3), 633–662. Retrieved from https://www.researchgate.net/publication/250185085_Adolescents%27_Perceptions_of_School_Environment_Engagement_and_Academic_Achievement_in_Middle_School

Watkins, D. A., & Biggs, J. B. (Eds.). (2001). *Teaching the Chinese learner: Psychological and pedagogical perspectives*. Hong Kong, China: Comparative Education Research Centre, University of Hong Kong.

Westwood, P. (2018). *Inclusive and adaptive teaching* (2nd ed.). London, England: Routledge.

Yeh, C. Y., Cheng, H. N., Chen, Z. H., Liao, C. C., & Chan, T. W. (2019). Enhancing achievement and interest in mathematics learning through Math-Island. *Research and Practice in Technology Enhanced Learning, 14*(5), 1–19. Retrieved from https://telrp.springeropen.com/articles/10.1186/s41039-019-0100-9

You, J. W., & Kang, M. (2014). The role of academic emotions in the relationship between perceived academic control and self-regulated learning in online learning. *Computers & Education, 77*, 125–133. https://doi.org/10.1016/j.compedu.2014.04.018

Yuen, A. H., Law, N., & Wong, K. C. (2003). ICT implementation and school leadership: Case studies of ICT integration in teaching and learning. *Journal of Educational Administration, 41*(2), 158–170. https://doi.org/10.1108/09578230310464666

Zaranis, N. (2016). The use of ICT in kindergarten for teaching addition based on Realistic Mathematics Education. *Education and Information Technologies, 21*(3), 589–606. https://doi.org/10.1007/s10639-014-9342-8

Zaranis, N., & Synodi, E. (2017). A comparative study on the effectiveness of the computer assisted method and the interactionist approach to teaching geometry shapes to young children. *Education and Information Technologies, 22*(4), 1377–1393. https://doi.org/10.1007/s10639-016-9500-2

Zhang, Q., Barkatsas, T., Law, H.-Y., Leu, Y.-C., Seah, W., & Wong, N.-Y. (2016). What primary students in the Chinese Mainland, Hong Kong and Taiwan value in Mathematics learning: A comparative analysis. *International Journal of Science and Mathematics Education, 14*(5), 907–924. https://doi.org/10.1007/s10763-014-9615-0

Zimmerman, B. J. (2002). Becoming a self-regulated learner: An overview. *Theory Into Practice, 41*(2), 64–70. https://doi.org/10.1207/s15430421tip4102_2

Zimmerman, B. J. (2004). Sociocultural influence and students' development of academic self-regulation: A social-cultural perspective. In D. M. McInerney & S. Van Etten (Eds.), *Big theories revisited* (Research on sociocultural influences on motivation and learning) (Vol. 4, pp. 139–164). Greenwich, CT: Information Age.

Zimmerman, B. J. (2008a). Investigating self-regulation and motivation: Historical background, methodological developments, and future prospects. *American Educational Research Journal, 45*(1), 166–183. https://doi.org/10.3102/0002831207312909

Zimmerman, B. J. (2008b). Goal setting: A key proactive source of academic self-regulation. In D. H. Schunk & B. J. Zimmerman (Eds.), *Motivation and self-regulated learning. Theory, research and applications* (pp. 267–295). New York, NY: Lawrence Erlbaum.

Zimmerman, B. J., Bandura, A., & Martinez-Pons, M. (1992). Self-motivation for academic attainment: The role of self-efficacy beliefs and personal goal setting. *American Educational Research Journal, 29*(3), 663–676. https://doi.org/10.3102/00028312029003663

Zimmerman, B. J., & Martinez-Pons, M. (1986). Development of a structured interview for assessing student use of self-regulated learning strategies. *American Educational Research Journal, 23*, 614–628. https://doi.org/10.3102/00028312023004614

Zumbrunn, S., Tadlock, J., & Roberts, E. D. (2011). *Encouraging self-regulated learning in the classroom: A literature review.* Richmond, VA: Virginia Commonwealth University.

Zundans-Fraser, L., & Lancaster, J. (2012). *Enhancing the inclusive self-efficacy of pre-service teachers through embedded course design.* Education Research International. Retrieved from https://www.researchgate.net/publication/258385209_Enhancing_the_Inclusive_Self-Efficacy_of_Preservice_Teachers_through_Embedded_Course_Design

Joyce J. Y. Fung, EdD, is a member of the Centre for Advancement of Inclusive and Special Education at the University of Hong Kong. She has extensive experience in mathematics education and online teaching and learning for secondary students. Her research interests are in gifted education, talent development, and online self-regulatory learning.

Mantak Yuen, PhD, is an Associate Professor and Director of the Centre for Advancement of Inclusive and Special Education in the University of Hong Kong. His research interests are in students' life skills and career development, students' connectedness to schools, talent development, and inclusive education.

Allan H. K. Yuen, PhD, is Associate Professor and Director of the Centre for Information Technology in Education in the Faculty of Education at the University of Hong Kong, Pokfulam, Hong Kong, China. His particular expertise is in the areas of technology adoption and pedagogical innovations, especially those related to e-learning.

Engaging Gifted Students in Solving Real Problems Creatively: Implementing the Real Engagement in Active Problem-Solving (REAPS) Teaching/Learning Model in Australasian and Pacific Rim Contexts

41

C. June Maker and Myra Wearne

Contents

C. J. Maker (✉)
Department of Disability and Psychoeducational Studies, The University of Arizona, Tucson, AZ, USA
e-mail: junemaker@hotmail.coml

M. Wearne
NSW Department of Education, North Sydney Demonstration School, Waverton, NSW, Australia
e-mail: myra.janes@det.nsw.edu.au

© Springer Nature Singapore Pte Ltd. 2021
S. R. Smith (ed.), *Handbook of Giftedness and Talent Development in the Asia-Pacific*,
Springer International Handbooks of Education,
https://doi.org/10.1007/978-981-13-3041-4_40

Abstract

We believe that engaging students in solving problems they perceive as real and relevant in their lives, combined with differentiation, is an effective way to nurture giftedness and talent in all domains while also discovering hidden talents and providing a setting for developing all students' strengths, interests, and passions. In this chapter, we describe a teaching model made up of three other evidence-based teaching models with a common goal of enhancing students' ability to think creatively, critically, and collaboratively while learning essential content-related ideas and skills. We demonstrate the model's comprehensiveness as a way to: differentiate the curriculum for all levels of learners and children with varied types of abilities, inclusive of gifted students; outline the guiding paradigms of thinking that led to its creation; give an overview of the evidence-based models that form the framework and methods of teaching that make up *Real Engagement in Active Problem-Solving* (REAPS); describe ways it has been implemented in Australasian and Pacific Rim contexts; provide examples from classrooms in Korea, Australia, China, and New Zealand; introduce a long-term, whole-school collaboration to improve the model and test its effectiveness; and summarise results of research.

Keywords

Student engagement · Curriculum differentiation · Creative problem-solving · Teaching gifted students · Implementing and sustaining innovations

The aims in this chapter are to:
1. Spark the interest of educators in learning more about REAPS.
2. Instil confidence in implementing a model such as this in a different environment and culture.
3. Provide a roadmap that can be followed in other journeys to try a new approach, sustain it and evaluate its effectiveness.
4. Inspire collaboration among educators in the Australasian and Pacific Rim region.
5. Demonstrate the value of collaboration between researchers and practitioners.
6. Infect readers with our enthusiasm for the learning journey.

Student Engagement in Learning

Student engagement is essential for in-depth, lasting learning (Jang, Kim, & Reeve, 2016; Lee, 2014; Martin, Martin, & Evans, 2017; Watt et al., 2017; Zhou & Ren, 2017). Engagement is associated with many positive outcomes such as test scores, retention, and graduation (Parsons, Malloy, Parsons, Peters-Burton, &

Burrowbridge, 2016). Teachers and researchers alike have noted that when students recognise what they are learning is relevant for their lives, both now and in the future, learning is connected to authentic, real-world situations and what they are learning is something that they are passionate about, students will be engaged in that learning (Beckett et al., 2016; Reeve, 2012; Shernoff, Csikszentmihalyi, Schneider, & Shernoff, 2003).

Gifted students often have well-developed and specific interests (Delisle, 2012; Little, 2012) and may have achieved high levels of understanding in their areas of interest and passion (Fredricks, Alfeld, & Eccles, 2010). Engaging them is particularly challenging at times (Little, 2012). To add to the challenges for educators, in the current educational and political contexts, curriculum standards have been developed at local, state, national, and international levels in most Pacific Rim countries; teachers are judged on their ability to teach these standards, and students are assessed on their ability to learn the content considered to be important. Thus, educators must achieve a balance in which they facilitate the learning of required content while also teaching in ways that engage students in authentic learning experiences that are linked to their interests and passions. Programs and curricula for gifted students are not excluded from these requirements; often the standards gifted students are expected to reach are even higher than those for other students.

Theoretical Perspectives

Paradigms: Talent Development and Differentiation

In the past, the dominant paradigm guiding development of programs for gifted students was the gifted child paradigm (Dai & Chen, 2013). In this way of thinking, giftedness is general and stable over one's lifetime, and gifted children's thinking and behaviour are qualitatively different from the thinking and behaviour of other children. Students often were served in pull-out programs, special schools, and special classes designed to cater to their educationally different needs. However, two different paradigms have emerged over the past several years: *talent development* and *differentiation*. These two ways of thinking about giftedness and talent have been integrated as the paradigms guiding the development of the *Real Engagement in Active Problem Solving* (REAPS) teaching model. In the *talent development* paradigm, giftedness is seen as domain-specific rather than general; the methods teachers and others need to employ to develop talent differ across domains and developmental stages, and motivation plays an important part in talent development. Most importantly, talent evolves over time. Talents are grown through developmentally appropriate, interest-based learning experiences, and resemble what professionals in a domain may be engaged in doing.

The *differentiation* paradigm also is important as a guiding thought system. From this perspective, giftedness is seen within the context of the school or classroom setting and is influenced by culture, customs, and other factors (Dai & Chen, 2013). The purpose of differentiation is to develop a better match between the needs and characteristics of individual students and classroom instruction in school settings.

A variety of student needs is considered, including interests, abilities, learning preferences, thinking styles, and affective characteristics.

Prism of Learning

From these perspectives, the *Prism of Learning* was developed by Maker and Anuruthwong (2003) based on Anuruthwong's experiences in Thailand and Maker's experiences in a variety of cultural and national perspectives, including indigenous people and people of various economic levels in the USA, Australia, Hong Kong, and Taiwan and in Europe (France, Turkey) and South America (Chile). The Prism has similarities to other theories of domain-specific giftedness within the talent development paradigm, such as *Multiple Intelligences* (Gardner, 1983) and the *Theory of Successful Intelligence* (Sternberg, 1997). However, it is unique in several aspects because of Maker and Anuruthwong's research and practice.

A prism is used as a metaphor for the theory (Fig. 1). In the Prism of Learning, the white light that comes into one side of the prism is a challenge, interest, perplexing situation, or goal one is passionate about, often labelled 'a problem'. This 'problem', combined with the motivation to solve it, is perhaps the most important factor in activating general capabilities (memory, creativity, intuition, metacognition, and reasoning/logic) that are important components of and seen in all specific abilities (auditory, bodily, emotional, linguistic, mathematical, mechanical-technical, scientific, social, spiritual, and visual-spatial). General capabilities, although seen in all

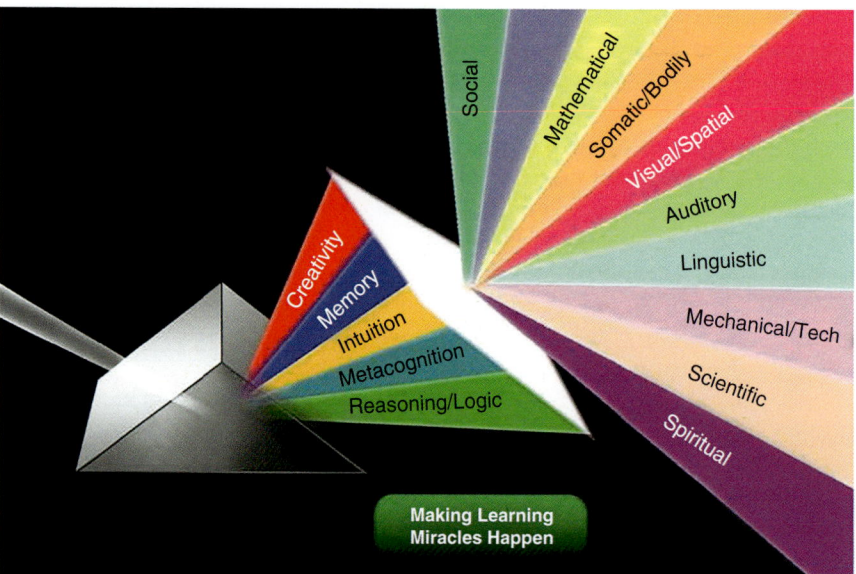

Fig. 1 The Prism of Learning

specific abilities, are expressed differently in different domains. The 10 specific abilities are the domains in which giftedness is expressed and identified. Although specific abilities are seen as separate domains, they are not seen as intelligences, and are related. Some are more closely related than others, such as visual-spatial being closely related to mechanical-technical and social being closely related to emotional. Scientific ability also is closely related to both visual-spatial and mechanical-technical abilities (Maker & Anuruthwong, 2003).

Development of general capabilities and specific abilities is facilitated or inhibited by the physical and dynamic environments, which include all aspects of the learning context and are the essential elements in the differentiation of both process and learning environment dimensions of the curriculum (Maker & Schiever, 2010). The dynamic environment, for instance, is composed of factors such as learning experiences, the amount of freedom students are given to choose what and how they will learn, problems they are encouraged to engage in solving, thinking processes students are asked to use, and questions teachers ask. To provide freedom to design differentiated instruction in content and product dimensions of the curriculum (Maker & Schiever, 2010), learning goals are expressed as macro concepts such as change, sustainability, and interdependence and skills such as decision-making, communication, leadership, creativity, and critical thinking rather than specific facts, and isolated content-related skills, such as letter recognition, computation, and spelling.

The Prism of Learning is the overall framework for the REAPS model and is an important way to integrate the three evidence-based models that form the model. One of the most important aspects of the Prism is the definition of the specific domains of talent for teachers to recognise as they guide students in choosing and solving problems. Another is its usefulness as a way to view the different dimensions of the curriculum and integrate them within the REAPS model: content, process, products, and learning environment.

Talent Development and Differentiation Using the Real Engagement in Active Problem-Solving (REAPS) Model

In 2004, Maker (Maker & Zimmerman, 2008) was asked to design professional development for Korean teachers of mathematics and science and to facilitate teachers' understanding of innovative ways to develop children's abilities. With a team consisting of graduate students from several countries and a scientist with experience in helping medical professionals learn better ways to control diseases in developing countries, Maker developed a teaching approach in which three evidence-based teaching models with a similar emphasis on problem-solving were combined: *Problem-Based Learning* (PBL; Gallagher, 1997, 2015; Gallagher & Gallagher, 2013), *Discovering Intellectual Strengths and Capabilities while Observing Varied Ethnic Responses* (DISCOVER; Maker, 2005), and *Thinking Actively in a Social Context* (TASC; see Fig. 2; Wallace, 2008; Wallace, Maker, Cave, & Chandler, 2004).

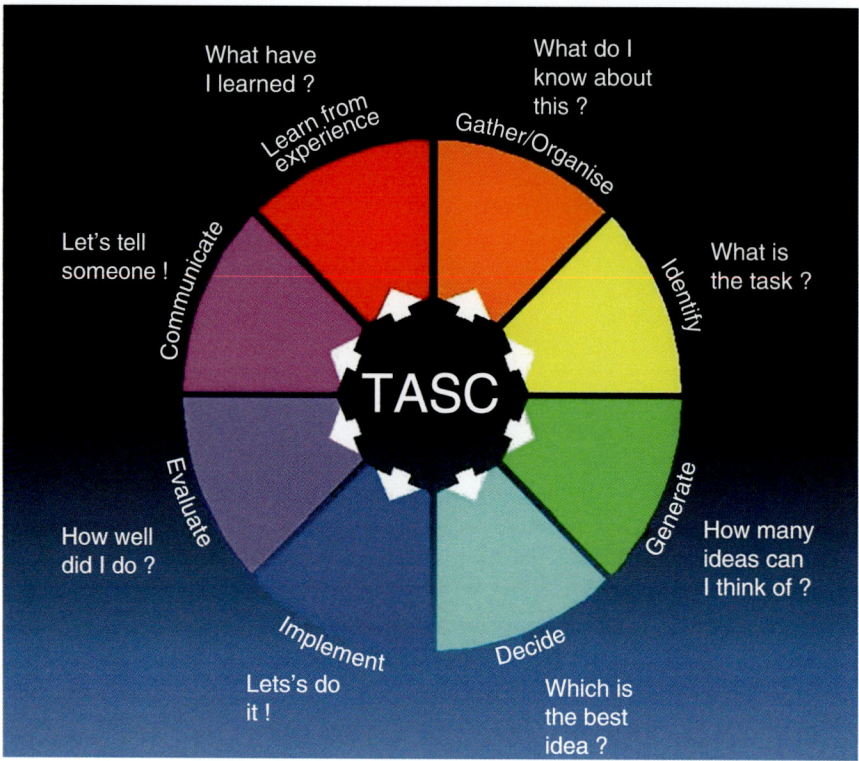

Fig. 2 Thinking Actively in a Social Context

All three evidence-based teaching models had strengths, but were missing components important in talent development and differentiation of instruction. For example, PBL provided the structure for selecting problem situations that were authentic, solved from multiple points of view, and derived from the cultural and environmental contexts, but were missing guidelines for assisting students in the process of solving those problems. DISCOVER had guidelines for structuring various types of problems, ranging from closed to open-ended, so students can develop academic skills and knowledge as well as creative and critical thinking, but similar to PBL, did not have methods for solving complex, open-ended problems. TASC provided an easy-to-follow process with clear steps, progressing through divergent and convergent thinking, that can be used by both individuals and groups: *gather and organise* information about the task or problem; *identify* the task or problem; *generate* ideas for solving the problem; *decide* on the best solution; *implement* the solution; *evaluate* the implementation; *communicate* the solution to others; and *reflect* on learning. Each step of TASC includes developing many ideas and perspectives and then making decisions about which of the ideas to incorporate into the problem-solving process. However, the TASC model did not have guidelines for selecting or structuring the problems for students to solve.

The TASC problem-solving process, unlike others, was designed to be recursive, with emphasis on returning to earlier steps when needed and included some steps not a part of problem-solving systems often used by professionals. TASC was specifically designed for educational settings. In all the models, emphasis was placed on selecting complex challenges with the potential for developing talents in specific domains and for developing general capabilities needed across all domains. The models are flexible enough to be appropriate for students at many levels of development.

All three models had evidence of effectiveness with gifted students and, when combined, provided specific ways to implement all the principles of differentiation of content, process, products, and learning environments recommended by Maker and Schiever (2010) to make the curriculum more appropriate for gifted students (Maker, Zimmerman, Alhusaini, & Pease, 2015a). In general, PBL is the most important model for implementing content differentiation principles (abstractness, complexity, variety, organisation for learning value, study of people, study of methods). It is most effective when teachers can work within a curriculum consisting of macro concepts and themes rather than a tightly structured one consisting of only discipline-based concepts and skills. TASC and DISCOVER provide a framework for the implementation of process principles (higher levels of thinking, open-endedness, discovery, evidence of reasoning, freedom of choice, group interaction, pacing, variety). When combined, all models provide guidance in implementing product principles (real problems, real audiences, transformation, variety, self-selected formats, and appropriate evaluation) and learning environment principles (learner-centred, encouraging independence, openness, acceptance, complexity, variety, flexibility, and high mobility). More information about these principles and ways the models are used to implement them can be found in the article by Maker et al. (2015a) as well as the Maker and Schiever book on teaching models (2005).

Since its introduction in the Korean teachers' institute, REAPS has been implemented in different contexts, including the following:

- Korean students in a special high school (Jo & Ku, 2011).
- Navajo students in high (Maker, 2016), middle, and elementary school programs in Arizona (Reinoso, 2011).
- Regular classrooms in an elementary school in a multicultural area in Arizona (Maker, Zimmerman, Gomez-Arizaga, Pease, & Burke, 2015b).
- An elementary school in Saudi Arabia (Alhusaini, Maker, & Alamiri, 2015).
- An elementary school in a multicultural area in Australia (Wu, Pease, & Maker, 2015).
- Across several schools in the Catholic School system in Sydney, Australia.
- In two high schools with high percentages of Māori students in New Zealand (Riley, Webber, & Sylva, 2017; Webber, Riley, Sylva, & Scobie-Jennings, 2018).
- Most recently, in elementary, middle, and high schools in China.

We will focus on the implementation of REAPS in Pacific Rim and Australasian contexts, but will include a synthesis of research from the other projects.

Implementing REAPS in Korea

The first implementation of REAPS was in elementary, middle, and high schools in programs for students gifted in mathematics and science in Seoul, Korea. The 40 teachers who attended the institute were expected by their government to implement some aspect of the model in their classrooms. They developed teaching units prior to returning to their country. Teachers chose problems with a science focus, and integrated mathematics into the analysis of data and presentation of results. Two teachers in a special high school for students gifted in mathematics and science developed three ill-structured problems with conflicting hypotheses that could be defended through arguments. The gifted students then selected the hypothesis they believed was correct and used personal experiences as well as real-time data to develop their arguments. They presented these data in discussions and debates. For example, one problem was the following:

> A typhoon occurred in the Pacific Ocean near the equator and is moving towards the northwest. This typhoon is turning to the northeast at 25 to 30 degrees of latitude. The path looks like a parabolic orbit. The northeastward path of the typhoon is well explained by the prevailing westerly winds, but the northwestward path of the typhoon in low latitude is not clear because the trade winds between 0 and 30 degrees of latitude blow toward the southwest. Why is the typhoon moving northward at low latitudes? Please, explain this movement with scientific evidence, such as real-time data or experimental data. (Jo & Ku, 2011, pp. 266, 267)

Students were given information about websites where they could find data to support their hypotheses. For example, if they needed to know surface temperature data for water in Korea, they could go to the Korean Ocean Research and Development Institute. If students needed data about magnetic storms, they could find it on websites of the *National Aeronautics and Space Administration* (NASA). Teachers created a web-based environment where students could share their hypotheses and also held classroom debates. In their article (Jo & Ku, 2011), the teachers described four different hypotheses, data used to support them, objections expressed by students who presented other hypotheses, and counter-objections of students who presented the original hypothesis. From the examples in the article, one can see that students' thinking was advanced, and that they were behaving as real scientists during their investigations. Their thoughtfulness was evident.

Data on student beliefs about their creativity and self-regulation were collected before and after REAPS was used for one semester in physics, biology, earth science, and chemistry. Results of the teachers' research are reported in the final section of this chapter; more information about the program and research can be found in their article (Jo & Ku, 2011).

Implementing REAPS in Australia

Beginning in 2013, REAPS was implemented in a multicultural primary school (K-6) in New South Wales (NSW) with an enrolment of 800+ students. Students are transient and diverse in language background (58 different languages), educational experiences, academic ability, social and emotional capabilities, and physical ability. In this school, located 10 min from the Sydney Central Business District in an affluent northern suburb, many of the students have tertiary educated parents who have high expectations for both academic results and future-focused learning. The school has a long-standing partnership with the Education Faculty of a nearby university and shares a common goal of bridging educational practice and theory. It attracts aspirational teachers, employs a high percentage of early career teachers, and experiences a high level of transience in its teaching population.

The *NSW Education Standards Authority* (NESA, 2012a), whose role is to ensure that all NSW Government and non-Government schools meet the Education Act, promotes the differentiation of content, process, product, learning environment, and assessment when meeting the needs of diverse student groups. Similarly, the NSW Institute of Teachers (NESA, 2012b) requires teachers to provide evidence that their teaching activities incorporate differentiated strategies that meet the specific learning needs of students across the full range of abilities and use relevant teaching strategies to develop knowledge, skills, problem-solving, and critical and creative thinking. As part of the school's commitment to aligning practice with these requirements, the faculty and administration have developed a strong identification and provision program to support students who are gifted, have a disability or speak English as a second or additional language. Since 2015 (NSW Department of Education, 2017), all schools are required to capture data from every classroom about the provisions of personalised learning and support that have been put in place for students with a disability. From our experiences, the pressure to provide differentiated learning opportunities to students has never been greater and teachers and administrators have sought to find models of curriculum delivery that can meet the needs of students in the most efficient and effective manner possible.

Challenges in Differentiation at the School

Previous efforts to differentiate student learning at the school have included a combination of conceptual programming, collaborative planning, support through withdrawal (pull-out programs), learning support officers, acceleration, and Personal Interest Projects. While these provisions have been successful, they have required significant levels of additional work by classroom teachers. In particular, the design of Personal Interest Projects to extend gifted students in their areas of talent or interest has resulted in teachers having to develop up to 14 unique interest projects and seek suitable subject-specific mentors to work with their students. Projects have lacked consistency in complexity and challenge; because of the lack of criteria for designing and evaluating these projects, some students were not engaged in critical and creative thinking or in problem-solving. The REAPS model was seen as an important way to differentiate the curriculum for all students as described in the following section.

REAPS as a Method for Differentiation

The REAPS was initially implemented in seven classrooms with students ranging in age from six to twelve years. Classrooms had students of mixed ability and clusters of students identified as gifted. After completing two REAPS projects based on the *Science* and *Human Society and Its Environment* (HSIE) syllabi, teachers reported they had been able to use REAPS to differentiate for student ability, both gifted students and those with additional learning needs, in the areas of content, process, and product. Implementation of REAPS was then expanded in 2014 to include an additional mixed-ability class at each level, thus implementing the model with 12 classes, all of which included a cluster of gifted students.

Based on our collaborative and collegial support of REAPS in action in the participating school, there were a number of constructive outcomes as well as concerns that teachers expressed. Teachers reported that they could readily embed effective differentiation strategies into the REAPS model without extensive changes to the overall process. Thoughtful assigning of stakeholder groups was one successful strategy. One Year-3 teacher reported that her lower ability group was required to design a functional school playground from the perspective of a child while her more able cluster of gifted students was required to design the playground from the perspective of the local council. The gifted students then had to take into account regulations, aesthetics, heritage requirements, and safety.

In sharing the results of our collaboration, we noted that the use of grouping as a differentiation strategy at times involved a problem being broken down and its different components analysed. For example, a Year-2 class considering the concept of transformation and interdependence through the subject area of science, more specifically weather, considered the problem of keeping the school safe. The teacher grouped her gifted students together and gave them more challenging weather conditions (cyclones), which required in-depth research above the students' general knowledge. The group with lower abilities examined sun safety because they had first-hand experience in this area. Lower ability groups were provided more resources, such as fact sheets, while gifted students were expected to conduct independent research. The same teacher noted that she did not always use ability groups when conducting REAPS investigations. When she grouped according to personal interest and passion, the differentiation was less evident, but appeared to be offset by increased engagement and peer support resulting from student choice.

Process differentiation was reported by some teachers through the use of mixed-ability groups. We noticed that gifted students were at times appointed as the leader of a mixed-ability group in which they were challenged to articulate their thinking about the task demands and the associated complexities. One Year-5 teacher reported grouping students with learning difficulties with students who were gifted in social domains and who enjoyed the challenge of facilitating the learning of others. These students worked with the teacher to facilitate the group's success in each step of the problem-solving process.

The teachers indicated that the open-ended nature of the *gather and organise* step of TASC, when paired with high expectations for sophisticated sorting of information and open-ended (DISCOVER Type VI) prompting questions provided an appropriate level of challenge and complexity for gifted students. Similarly, use of other types of prompting questions, scaffolds, and guided instruction for students with additional learning needs allowed these students to access the task at an entry point that was meaningful and allowed for success. Twice-exceptional students often benefited from both of these provisions. A Year-1 teacher reported differentiation at the *gather and organise* step using multimodal information such as videos and articles. Students with low literacy skills watched videos to gather information while students with highly developed literacy skills read complex written texts. A Year-6 teacher reported differentiating for high- and low-ability students during this step by varying the level of information provided to each group. When solving the problem of providing protection from earthquakes, her lower ability group was given lots of information about building structures and warning systems, while the higher ability groups were required to research and find much of that information themselves.

Students in the school demonstrated varying depths of understanding of the complexities of a problem when *identify*ing the task, and clear differences appeared between students as they participated in the *generate* step with more novel and complex ideas documented in groups containing gifted students. Use of the TASC process gave these students freedom to demonstrate their understanding of big ideas and to think laterally and deeply about possible solutions. Individualised support was required across all ability levels for students with learning needs because of their social and emotional capacities, thus enabling students' gifts and strengths to manifest as talents that could readily transfer to social and workplace settings.

We observed that differentiation at the *decide* step of the problem-solving process ranged from teachers providing students with criteria for evaluation and then guiding them through the decision-making process to communication of higher expectations for gifted students, who were required, with some facilitation, to design their own criteria that reflected the complexities of the problem and multiple stakeholder perspectives. Students' choice featured strongly in the *implement* step with students having freedom to explore areas of personal interest, strength, or giftedness when developing their solutions. Students' choice was important in maintaining engagement, particularly in light of reduced use of Personal Interest Projects. Clustering students during REAPS with like-minded peers who not only possessed similar ability levels, but also had similar strengths in ability domains or areas of interest became important. Students with abilities in the mechanical-technical, scientific, or visual-spatial domains were noticeably more likely to design and build a model, whereas groups with abilities in social, emotional, and linguistic domains often chose to prepare films or deliver strong verbal presentations. Incompatible grouping led to difficulties when students were required to reach consensus about the format of their solutions.

A Year-5 teacher reported that at the *implement* step a useful strategy was to encourage students to use their particular skills or passions in engineering, design, or logic, or other areas so they understood they had the freedom to make choices. This same teacher reported that questioning could be used as a means of differentiation when students were implementing their solutions. For example, when designing structures to provide protection against a flood, she asked questions such as "Your building is waterproof and can cope with a flood, but what about the force of a tsunami? How will your building survive this? In the video of a tsunami we saw that even concrete buildings were broken from the force..." or "What if your building was also in an earthquake zone?" "What materials would be available to you if you were poor and lived on this island?" These twists were methods for increasing complexity.

Only one teacher reported a flexible learning environment as a strategy used to differentiate during implementation of REAPS. This teacher noted that Year-1 students could sit anywhere and use the equipment they wanted/needed and that the teacher was easily available as a resource. Although no other teachers reported providing learning environments important in differentiation, observers noted that the environments in all classrooms were flexible, open, varied, promoted independence of thinking, and allowed movement around the classroom. Some photos of classrooms showed children working in their groups at computers, sitting or lying on the floor, writing on the whiteboard, recording ideas on large sheets of paper or working individually as they created a model. Students also were permitted to record their videos outside when appropriate and could go to the library or computer lab to access information.

Professional Learning and REAPS

Prior to students engaging in REAPS, their classroom teachers participated in a five-day professional learning workshop. They were actively engaged in solving a real-world environmental problem followed by a facilitated programming session in which they were guided in the selection and development of a REAPS problem and case study. Teachers' first-hand immersion in the problem-solving process was important in developing their understanding of the model prior to incorporating it into their teaching and learning programs.

During the year following the professional development workshop, not all implementing teachers had completed the intensive training, so the teachers who had not attended the workshop were provided with a one-hour professional learning workshop. Teachers were given an overview of REAPS. They received planning documents, and the teachers leading the workshop presented and discussed student work samples. During this school year, some teachers also participated in a REAPS action learning project. Initial professional learning in this project included teacher immersion in the use of the REAPS model followed by identification of an age appropriate student problem, designing a case study, and participation in a five-week action learning process. Teachers met each week to talk about their implementation of REAPS with discussions focusing on challenges encountered, benefits perceived, and changes observed in student behaviour and learning.

While the five-day immersion workshop was the most valuable professional learning for REAPS, observation of teachers by experts and provision of feedback about implementation was highly valued by teachers. These observation and feedback sessions occurred at least once each year of implementation. For example, one Year-6 teacher who received feedback following an observation of her class participating in REAPS shifted her practice. The students had been solving a problem about earthquake protection in the Solomon Islands and the observer suggested that engagement would be higher if the problem were local and identified by students. She then changed her methods based on this feedback, and the following REAPS problem facilitated by this teacher was determined by her students. She posed a problematic situation of population increases in the local area, the school's physical confinement, and provision of facilities for school children. From this case study, students determined they would solve the problem of reconfiguring available playground space to allow for a growing population. The teacher reported higher and more meaningful engagement from all students. A Year-2 teacher reported receiving feedback after a classroom observation that she was trying to do too many things at once and that this did not really allow for deep, long discussions. She subsequently changed her practice to limit key or contributing question/s to one main idea per session.

When asked about the benefits of classroom observations and feedback as a form of professional learning, a Year-5 teacher, said:

> I had unpacked all we had done so far to give the students a big picture of their projects before sending them off to begin their models. I was worried they (observers) might think this was a waste of time as it took a while, but Randy said that this was very useful as it allowed the students to ground their work in the purpose of the task/bring it back to the original problem we were trying to solve. Following this feedback, I have continued to unpack where the lesson sits on the TASC wheel, where it sits in terms of the overall purpose. I try to do this for all my lessons, not just REAPS. (Personal communication from a teacher to the second author, 2016)

REAPS as an Identification Tool

As principal, the second author can attest that, in the school, multiple tools are used to identify gifted students, including information from teacher and parent nomination forms, standardised achievement testing, standardised cognitive, IQ and psychometric assessments, and academic test scores. Shortly after the introduction of

REAPS at the school, the faculty agreed that REAPS provided another means by which a student could be identified as gifted due to the fact that abilities and talents often became more pronounced during REAPS investigations.

Students' gifts and talents were particularly pronounced in the intellectual, creative, social, and affective domains. Teachers noticed that some students, who had previously tested in the average range in academic tasks, displayed advanced reasoning and judgement abilities when required to develop criteria for solutions. These students were able to identify and synthesise multiple stakeholder objectives in areas of commonality and could create criteria that placated the needs of many stakeholders while prioritising a key stakeholder group. Teachers also reported that the creative abilities of some students were more pronounced during problem-solving activities. A previously unidentified student with learning difficulties demonstrated advanced problem-solving abilities when he generated a novel solution to enable swimming in an unsafe river in the local area. The student used his knowledge of forces and his creative abilities to design underwater waterfalls that slowed the current of the river making it safer for swimmers and local residents.

The third area in which teachers reported seeing students' giftedness was in the area of influence and social abilities. Some students demonstrated superior abilities when leading groups of students in problem-solving tasks. Teachers noticed that these students had the ability to intuitively recognise areas of confusion and hesitation in others and were seen to have mastered skills in encouraging their peers and capitalising on individual and group strengths. These skills were not readily apparent in highly structured or individual tasks.

Challenges and Changes in Direction During Implementation of REAPS

By 2017, all classes across the school were implementing REAPS whether or not a class included students identified as gifted. With REAPS now being used as one of the ways students could be identified as gifted, all students needed to be exposed to this model of learning so that possible gifts or talents could be discovered. Agreement was reached among teachers, administrators, and parents that all students had the right to receive quality teaching and to engage in learning that focused on the development of critical and creative thinking skills, problem-solving skills, and skills in communicating and collaborating. These were essential in the delivery of a future-focused education.

Throughout 2016 and early 2017, discussions took place between staff and administrators about the complexities and challenges of using REAPS to teach conceptual units given the increased levels of mandated content in the new NSW Science, Geography, and History syllabi. Teachers reported that on many occasions the success criteria for REAPS, if the focus were to remain on the use of critical and creative thinking skills to solve problems, differed and often contradicted the success criteria for meeting the mandated content and assessment requirements of the syllabi. Teachers and administrators in the school acknowledged both as important. Together they decided that the twenty-first-century skills developed through REAPS were important and valued in their own right and that teachers would have the freedom to choose when and where to use REAPS when planning for teaching and learning. One REAPS project was required to take place each year in every class. When REAPS could be used to meaningfully engage with the Science, History, and Geography syllabi, teachers could choose to use it; however, flexibility in choosing the subject area now existed. In 2017, three out of the seven grades continued to align their REAPS investigations to conceptual units in the previously used curriculum areas. Others explored more student-identified problems. Examples included years 5 and 6 solving the problem of stereotypes in teenage magazines. Teachers were able to create strong links to the English syllabus. Year-1 students solved the problem of playground loneliness, with links to the NSW Personal Development, Health, and Physical Education syllabus.

Teachers and administrators in the school understood that the criteria for deciding on a REAPS project would at times be the development of creative and critical thinking skills, problem-solving skills, and communication and collaboration skills and at other times as the means for delivering mandated content. Communication of the purpose of using REAPS to students will be important moving forward so they can determine the appropriate level of emphasis they should place on creativity versus demonstration of deep understanding of specific ideas identified in the syllabus.

In this school, parental support for this style of learning, despite an acknowledged lack of transparency, was high. In interviews, parent and community meetings, and open days, parents articulated their understanding of the need to develop skills in critical and creative thinking, problem-solving, collaboration, and communication. Time spent supporting students in working collaboratively was valued by all stakeholders and they understood and accepted that time spent on REAPS was an investment in the future.

From the authors' perspectives, research on REAPS has been ongoing and challenging. Results and studies in progress are reported in the final section of this chapter. In this section, the focus is on ways REAPS has been implemented in Asian and Pacific Rim countries.

Implementing REAPS in New Zealand

REAPS was implemented in a *Teacher-Led Innovation Fund* (TLIF) inquiry funded by the Ministry of Education in two high schools with high percentages of Māori (i.e., people indigenous to New Zealand) and Pasifika (i.e., people indigenous to the Pacific Islands) students in a low-income rural area on the north island (Riley et al., 2017; Webber et al., 2018). New Zealand has a founding bicultural document called *The Treaty of Waitangi* signed in 1840 by early British settlers and representatives of some of the indigenous people of the country. Three key principles of this treaty are mandated in legislation (*protection, partnership, and participation*) and the education system is obligated to demonstrate how it values and protects the rights of indigenous children by following these three principles. Like those in many other countries, however, New Zealand's indigenous people have not experienced effective culturally responsive teaching methods, which has led to lower school performance, lower qualifications after leaving school, and fewer life choices than students from other cultural groups (Webber et al., 2018). However, an increasing recognition that changes must be made to meet the needs of this important population has led to system-wide educational initiatives designed to facilitate the success of the indigenous Māori population. An important educational policy is *Ka Hikitia: culture is important*. Teachers must know, respect, and value 'where students are' and where they come from and must build on what they bring with them (New Zealand Ministry of Education, 2017).

The TLIF project had three important goals consistent with the Treaty of Waitangi, the initiatives of the Ministry of Education and the purposes of REAPS: increase engagement and achievement of Māori and Pasifika boys; identify gifted potential in Māori and Pasifika boys as they were engaged in REAPS; and adapt and localise an evidence-based, international curriculum delivery model. In one school, REAPS was implemented in all beginning Year-9 science classes (90 students), and in the other, with 20 identified gifted students in years 8 and 9. In the beginning science classes, students were randomly assigned to groups of three or four within their classes. They worked together to solve the problem of the decline of seagrass in a local harbour and its effect on snapper populations from the perspectives of important stakeholders: the district council, the Ministry of Fisheries, the local iwi (i.e., indigenous people), a land-care trust, and an international dairy company (Riley et al., 2017). In the other school, gifted students worked on the problem of the decline in the pipi population in another harbour along with local iwi groups and regionally based scientific communities and organisations, resulting in their experiencing important connections with others concerned about the same problem (Webber et al., 2018).

Teachers involved at both schools planned together, creating their teaching units and a Google site for students to use as a guide as they progressed through the problem-solving process and followed the steps in the TASC model. Over the 10-week period, teachers provided scaffolding and support to supplement on-line resources; students also collected data during fieldwork at the sites. Students at both schools presented their findings and solutions to community groups. Their presentations were evaluated by teachers, peers, and community members (Riley et al., 2017; Webber et al., 2018). Riley and her colleagues concluded that certain principles of differentiation (Maker & Schiever, 2010; Maker et al., 2015a), when applied to all learners, may increase engagement and help teachers identify potential: "the complexity of localised content, thinking processes, open-endedness, group interactions, and the development of a variety of self-selected products derived from real problems and delivered to appropriate audiences" (Riley et al., 2017, p. 14).

Three aspects of this project stand out as different from the implementation of REAPS in other countries described in this chapter and important for implementation in other settings: (a) emphasis on localising the model, especially by involving community leaders and members in deciding on the problems to be solved, having students work alongside iwi and scientists in the problem-solving, and having students present solutions to local community members; (b) studying the model's effectiveness in identifying talents in students previously unrecognised, especially Māori and Pasifika boys; and (c) focusing, on implementation of culturally responsive teaching through REAPS (Riley et al., 2017; Webber et al., 2018). The first aspect has been described in the previous section, and the second aspect (results) will be included in the following section. The third aspect of implementation of REAPS in New Zealand schools is an example of its potential for use in other cultures and contexts and is described in this section.

One important way to increase culturally responsive teaching is through *Place-Based Education* (PBE; Smith, 2002; Webber & Macfarlane, 2017). PBE fits easily with REAPS, especially with the *Problem-Based Learning* (PBL) model, in which students solve real-life problems important in their lives and in their communities. In PBE, learning is connected to local phenomena and students' lived experiences so that students, teachers, and schools are engaged intimately with their local setting, thus encouraging responsibility and accountability. PBE develops love for the environment, the *place* where they are living—its history, its biodiversity, and the ways people respond to the natural and social environment, both now and in the past. In this way of teaching, the depth of knowledge possessed by indigenous people, their values, their beliefs, and their practices are seen as integral to the shared responsibility of all those who live in a particular place. In their article, Webber and her colleagues (2018) describe the aspects of REAPS and its implementation in the Ruamano project that are responsive to the Treaty of Waitangi, which includes the ways PBE is part of REAPS. Readers are encouraged to refer to this research and the research of Riley and her colleagues (2017) for more information about the implementation of REAPS in the Ruamano Project.

Implementing REAPS in China

The REAPS in China is in its beginning stage. An aspect of the setting important in this context is that documented professional learning is required each year for teachers to maintain their certification, and they must participate in authorised programs, not simply programs organised at the school level. A faculty member at the Beijing Institute for Education is responsible for professional development for the Ministry of Education, and his projects include schools and educators from all regions of China. The current Chinese Educational Reform movement is towards student-centred learning, so REAPS fits well with the direction of movement of professional development programs sponsored by the government (X. Yu, personal communication, October 25, 2017).

The REAPS has been introduced in two different ways in different regions of China. In the first introduction, students from the school in NSW visited schools in China, and at one of the schools, located in Jinan within the Shandong province, the principal of the NSW School facilitated a session in which Chinese and Australian students worked together in teams to solve a problem that was common to the two countries. The use of REAPS to explore air pollution in both Sydney and Jinan highlighted the validity and universality of this approach. Although language differences prevented them from working in international teams, both groups of students used the TASC wheel to simultaneously explore the problem of air pollution. The process was seen to be culturally appropriate to both groups and a range of abilities were evident in both cohorts throughout the process. While the Chinese students were not interviewed about the experience, Australian students reported feeling a deeper sense of connection to their Chinese counterparts after having shared the problem-solving experience and were positive about the prospect of future problem-solving initiatives. Students were engaged and excited, and teachers were interested in learning more. Staff from both countries agreed that this was a model that catered to the learning needs of their students and that offered possibilities for future collaboration.

In the second introduction of REAPS, a workshop sponsored by the *Beijing Institute of Education* (BIE), faculty from the Institute and teams of teachers from different elementary, middle, and secondary schools near Beijing participated in a six-day workshop in which they solved the problem of plastic waste in Beijing from the perspective of stakeholder groups: China Environmental Protection Foundation, Beijing Concerned Residents' Association, Beijing Municipal Commission of Tourism Development, Department of Resource Conservation and Environmental Protection, China Petroleum and Chemical Industry Federation, and the China Plastics Processing Association. All stakeholder groups were real except the residents' association. All the teachers and BIE faculty members were immersed in solving the problem. Perhaps even more importantly, they were excited to be participating in a teacher workshop in which they experienced the teaching model they were learning from the point of view of a learner. How to use the model was being demonstrated for them.

During the workshop, the first day was spent explaining the theoretical framework of the Prism of Learning and how it was used as a way to integrate the three teaching models that make up REAPS. Emphasis was placed on problem-solving and the need for creatively solving problems using the three component models. An interactive atmosphere was encouraged, facilitated by a full-time translator who had worked with the workshop leaders for a day prior to the professional development process. While they were involved in solving the problem, teachers were encouraged to ask questions; after each step, the workshop leaders reviewed important aspects of the process. After teachers communicated their solutions to the group and reflected on their learning, they spent two additional days working together in content-area groups to develop case studies and teaching plans to implement in their schools. When teachers returned to their schools, students were involved in solving the following problems: (a) water shortage in Beijing (secondary science); (b) students who are not interested in reading (elementary Chinese language); and (c) designing an area of their classroom for reading with groups working on different aspects of the design, using measurement, cost, and other mathematical concepts (elementary mathematics).

Faculty who participated in the workshop provided follow-up assistance to teachers as they implemented their REAPS teaching units. Teachers and BIE faculty are connected with each other and the workshop leaders through an online chat group in which they share ideas, support each other, and share materials. Teachers will communicate their results and future plans as the project progresses. No other publications are available at this time, but readers are encouraged to contact the first author or the Beijing Institute of Education (Professors Zhou, Yuru and Yu, Xin) for more information.

Research on REAPS

In this section, we will present a summary of research studies of various aspects of the REAPS model. Readers are invited to refer to the publications referenced for additional details.

Creativity and Problem-Solving

Researchers and teachers studied creativity and problem-solving in different ways; however, results are similar: use of Real Engagement in Active Problem-Solving can enhance students' creativity and problem-solving. In Korea, students' creativity was measured using a self-report questionnaire in which students were asked to tell how they had used fluency, flexibility, elaboration, and originality in solving problems (Jo & Ku, 2011). Examples of items are the following: "I consider various solutions to solve the problem", and "I am trying to solve the problem beyond what I know" (p. 271). Pre-post paired t-tests showed that students made significant gains ($p = 0.021$) in self-perception of creativity as a result of their participation in the classes.

In Saudi Arabia, a post-test only design was used to assess changes in creativity of elementary students who participated in REAPS and those who did not participate. Students in both groups were in the same schools, and the classrooms were selected because of their similarities in student backgrounds, age, and ability (Alhusaini et al., 2015). Using the *Test of Creative Thinking – Drawing Production* (TCT-DP; Urban & Jellen, 1996), a non-verbal, cross-cultural test of general creativity (Urban & Jellen, 1996), researchers found that creativity of students in the classrooms in which REAPS was implemented (M = 28.52) was significantly higher ($p = 0.0001$) than creativity of students in classrooms in which their teachers did not implement the model (M = 17.09). In contrast, using the TCT-DP during the initial implementation of the model in Australia, no significant differences ($p = 0.095$) were found in the level of creativity of students who participated in classrooms in which REAPS was used for short (4 months) and long (10 months) periods of time (Alhusaini, 2016). Interestingly, this difference may be a reflection of the overall differences in teaching methods in use at the two schools. Perhaps, all the teachers in the NSW school, regardless of their implementation of REAPS, were developing general creativity in their students.

However, consistent with the guiding paradigm in which giftedness is viewed as domain-specific, Alhusaini (2016) found that although the duration of exposure to REAPS at the school in Australia did not have an impact on general creativity, it did have an impact on students' creative problem-solving in science. Administering the *Test of Creative Problem-Solving – Science* (TCPS-S; Maker, Jo, Alfaiz, & Alhusaini, 2017) when teachers in Australia began using REAPS and again at the end of the school year (4 months' exposure for some students and 10 months' exposure for others), and controlling for pre-test scores, Alhusaini found greater gains in creative problem-solving in science of students who participated in REAPS for a longer period of time ($N = 115$, $M = 80.36$ and $SD = 32.26$) than in those who participated for a shorter period ($N = 245$, $M = 64.63$ and $SD = 28.00$). The effect size was small: 0.6%, $F(1, 357) = 20.84$, $p = 0.001$, $\eta^2 = 0.06$. Aspects of creative problem-solving that were affected most by different durations were generating ideas, adding details to ideas (from the TCT-DP), and finding problems (from the TCPS-S).

Another aspect of creative problem-solving is student beliefs about self-regulation (Jo & Ku, 2011). When they responded to items such as, "I have the confidence to solve the problem" (p. 271), in the paired t-test comparisons, high school students in Korea demonstrated a significant positive change ($p = 0.000$).

Understanding the Complexity of Concepts and Their Interrelationships

An important component in talented students' development of expertise (Sternberg, 1999) is their in-depth understanding of content and how ideas are related, not just their accumulation of factual information. Researchers have found, for instance, that experts in a domain have a more hierarchical and interconnected knowledge base than novices (Bransford, Brown, & Cocking, 2000; Chi, Feltovich, & Glaser, 1981). Thus, experts are able to access their knowledge and apply it in diverse situations as well as to access it quickly and efficiently (Bransford et al., 2000). The REAPS research team first studied students' development of expertise by having students complete concept maps before and after each teaching unit in the *Full Option Science System* (FOSS) curriculum. In one study (Zimmerman, Maker, Gomez-Arizaga, & Pease, 2011), students completed concept maps before and after the earth materials teaching unit. Students clearly increased in their content understanding as demonstrated by the changes in their concept maps from pre-test to post-test using two different scoring systems. Students' maps showed a significant increase in the number of accurate relationships they identified across all methods of scoring and both teaching times ($p = 0.0005, 0.0001, 0.003, 0.0006$) and understanding of the complexity of these relationships (total scores) with one scoring method ($p = 0.0042$) and convergence or similarity to an expert's map using the other scoring method ($p = 0.047$ and 0.0001). Researchers concluded that the use of REAPS enhanced the teacher's ability to teach the FOSS Earth Materials unit and at the same time meet Arizona State Standards in science and other non-science standards such as art, through building models of their solutions to problems. Tan, Erdimez, and Zimmerman (2017) also found that repeated use of concept maps increased students' understanding of the complexity of concepts and their interrelationships, leading to the use of concept maps in evaluating the implementation of REAPS in Australia.

As a result of experiences with concept mapping and two scoring systems, Zimmerman, Alfaiz, and Maker (2019) and Alfaiz, Pease, Maker, and Zimmerman (2019) merged two, scoring systems to create one that could be used, easily and would yield information helpful in determining students' levels of expertise and understanding of the complexity of concepts and their interrelationships. This scoring system was used to analyse the first set of concept maps from comparison and implementation classrooms when the REAPS model was introduced in the school in Australia (Zimmerman & Maker, 2017). Although the time between pre-test and post-test was only four months, significant differences were found between concept maps of students in implementation ($N \sim 228$) and comparison classrooms ($N \sim 512$). Concept map scores for students from implementation classrooms were significantly higher on the post-tests for cross links ($p = 0.023$) and examples ($p = 0.000$) but not propositions and hierarchy. Proposition scores were higher in the comparison group ($p = 0.007$) and differences in hierarchy scores were not significant ($p = 0.167$). Concept maps are considered to be effective measures of student gains in conceptual thinking that is an important goal of REAPS, so ongoing studies are being conducted.

Student Perceptions

An important measure of effectiveness of any teaching model is the way students perceive it. Four studies have been completed in which student perceptions of REAPS experiences have been included. Two included interviews and analysis of children's drawings, one in Arizona with six students from one classroom (Gomez-Arizaga, Bahar, Maker, Zimmerman, & Pease, 2016) and one in Australia with 46 students from six classrooms (Wu et al., 2015). Researchers and teachers in New Zealand conducted focus groups with students at both schools. Teachers in Korea included two areas of student perceptions in their research (Jo & Ku, 2011).

In the two studies of elementary children's perceptions, researchers found that students were challenged and motivated, and they enjoyed the thinking and hands-on activities. Students' drawings of themselves in both programs during REAPS often showed student-centred experiences, independent learning, and active participation (Gomez-Arizaga et al., 2016; Wu et al., 2015). Most of the students in Arizona (96%) described their experiences in the class as 'fun', 'cool', 'neat', and 'exciting' (Gomez-Arizaga et al., 2016, p. 440). Most importantly, words of enjoyment were followed by descriptions of the ways their classes had helped them learn new and exciting things. For example, one student in Arizona said, "It's fun learning about rocks and minerals and also water and how we could conserve it" (p. 441). A student in Australia said, "I feel having fun, having the best day ever. I can do lots of projects that are very fun" (Wu et al., 2015, p. 111). In Arizona, 76% of students described opportunities to *do* things as their favourite aspects of the program. For instance, one boy said, "I like building models because you get to think and have a bunch of ideas" (p. 441). Similarly, in the program in Australia, 45% of the students talked about processes as being their most favourite things during REAPS, such as, "…generating ideas. After you generate, you use the process of elimination to figure out what is best". Another student in Australia said, "It's quite hard, because there are lots of steps you have to do" (Wu et al., 2015, p. 113). In Australia, 24% of the students described solving real problems as the part of REAPS they liked most. One said, "Finding out about the world, researching, finding out solutions about the problem" (Wu et al., 2015, p. 113). Another 25% described working together as their most favourite part of REAPS. "Our ideas, how we are going to persuade others to do fun things and how we get to work on a team, not just get others' ideas. We learned from other people's presentations" (Wu et al., 2015, p. 113).

In the study of perceptions of students in Australia (Wu et al., 2015), researchers identified several themes in student answers to all of the questions and in their drawings: *topic, process, activity, collaboration*, and *support*. *Topic* was an area of study such as global warming, saving endangered species; *process* included the kinds of thinking and learning processes students used (watching, thinking, observing, investigating, designing); specific *activities* they engaged in such as designing models; *collaboration* with others; and *support*, which included being given choices, time, and materials. Two domains of positive effects were frequently described by students across all questions: *positive emotions* and *interpersonal skills*. For instance, positive emotions were expressed in most students' responses. They valued the interpersonal skills they developed, even though they disliked arguments and unevenly distributed tasks (Wu et al., 2015). High school students in Korea believed that during their REAPS classes, they engaged in discussions frequently and their interest in science increased (Jo & Ku, 2011).

In New Zealand, students identified collaboration—working in groups or with their teacher—as an important aspect of REAPS. Working with others for a purpose was not only meaningful but also supportive (Riley et al., 2017). Similar to the younger children in Australia and Arizona, Māori boys appreciated the hands-on experimentation and its authenticity: "Cos you actually know it's true, cos we actually found it out ourselves" (Riley et al., 2017, p. 12). Webber and her colleagues (2018) concluded from their analysis of student perceptions expressed during focus groups that student engagement resulted from two related aspects of the implementation of REAPS: connectedness to the local environment and experiential, hands-on learning. For example, students commented that their project was motivating because it was about 'our ocean', and others remembered how they had personally experienced the decline in the pipi population, so they could easily connect with the problem as well as the scientific methods employed to study it. Students demonstrated their understanding of these methods when they suggested additional studies needed to continue the research: testing water quality, studying the mangroves, studying the pH levels of the water, finding out what kinds of chemicals were in the water from the local refinery, and the kinds of substances in the water that keep the pipi alive, and the kinds of substances that make them die or get sick.

From the studies cited, one can see that students developed creative thinking and problem-solving, increased their understanding of the complexity and interrelationships of ideas, made important connections between their communities (with both people and the environment) and their learning in school, and were highly engaged in their learning. They had fun even though the work and personal relationships were challenging, and they valued both activities and learning gained from their experiences. Students were able to articulate perceptions demonstrating that their views of REAPS classes and programs were aligned with the purposes of the model. Student perceptions and gains demonstrated that teachers were able to integrate important elements of and were effective in their use of REAPS. They also were able to differentiate content, processes, products, and learning environments in ways consistent with guiding paradigms and best practices in the field.

In New Zealand, in addition to focus groups with students, focus groups and interviews were held with teachers and community members (Riley et al., 2017; Webber et al., 2018). At one school, all three teachers identified, engagement in learning as the greatest change in their students, specifically noting the involvement of Māori boys. They identified: increased attendance; greater involvement with peers; having more creative ideas for solutions; and higher quality in student work as evidence of their perceptions. Teachers also noted the students' involvement with the scientific aspects of the problem. Perhaps most importantly, given the objectives of the project, teachers noted that they had identified several students as gifted through their participation in the REAPS experiences. One of the teachers said 'abilities surfaced'. In their report to the Ministry of Education, project directors concluded they had identified three Māori boys as gifted through the school's usual process. Project directors noted they would not have recognised these boys prior to their involvement in REAPS (Riley et al., 2017). Teacher perceptions were supplemented by assessments showing large shifts in the achievement of Māori boys. For instance, in the school's testing, one Māori boy was identified for the top mathematics group and two Māori boys were identified for the top English group.

When teachers reflected on their use of REAPS, they believed the model had been effective and they would use it again. They thought the structure was important, and they had learned the value of being facilitators, amazed at the ability of their students to 'run with it' on their own. Teachers believed they needed more time for collaboration, needed to include more New Zealand vocabulary and Māori concepts, would benefit from having speakers from stakeholder groups during the students' problem-solving process, and that to be sustainable as a practice, new staff would need to access professional development on use of the model (Riley et al., 2017).

In evaluations of student presentations and surveys completed about their perceptions of aspects of the REAPS implementation in which they were involved, community members emphasised the importance of students' engagement with the local community, both now and in the future. For example, many said student engagement in conservation efforts was the greatest benefit for students and the community. Others noted that the inclusion of stakeholder groups allowed students to look at the problem from other perspectives, take into account all points of view, and challenge some of the theories behind proposed solutions. They noted that these students will be the future stewards of the local environment.

Studies in Progress

At this time, several studies are in progress. More studies of teacher and administrator perceptions are important, as is the level of fidelity of implementation of REAPS. All are being investigated in related studies. In a study of teacher perceptions, data were collected at the NSW school through interviews with teachers and administrators; teachers were asked questions similar to the questions asked of students. Data have been analysed and a manuscript is in progress (Pease & Maker, 2017). In a study of teaching effectiveness, teachers were observed by the expert who developed the model, the teacher who implemented it for five years in his classroom in Arizona and an administrator at the school. Observers wrote extensive notes about how curriculum principles in content, process, product, and learning environment were being implemented in the classrooms. They drew diagrams of the classroom environments and took photographs of both the environments and students as they were engaged in various activities. Afterwards, observers asked teachers about their instructional objectives, shared notes, and invited teachers to add their own comments. After observations and discussions with teachers, each evaluator completed a checklist of teacher behaviours important for curriculum differentiation for gifted students in the dimensions of content, process, product, and learning environment and important in the implementation of the model. Each teacher was rated on a scale of 0–6 with 0 indicating no evidence of a behaviour and 6 indicating excellent evidence. Comments were made in each section to support ratings. All ratings were combined and each teacher was given an overall score by each observer on the level of fidelity of implementation of the model (Maker & Pease, 2017). Qualitative data on teacher practices were analysed and practices of teachers at high levels of fidelity of implementation were described. In three other studies in progress, these ratings of teacher implementation are being used to place teachers in implementation groups so student gains can be analysed according to the level of fidelity of implementation. A design such as this is necessary if all teachers in a school setting are implementing a model and researchers wish to determine the degree to which the model has contributed to student gains (Azano et al., 2011). Investigations in progress include continued examination of students' understanding of the complexity of concepts and their interrelationships (Zimmerman, Maker, & Pease, 2017), creative problem-solving in science (Alfaiz, 2019), and creative problem-solving in mathematics (Maker, Wu, & Pease, 2017).

Parent perceptions of REAPS also are important, as seen in the focus group and survey responses of community members in the *Ruamano Project* in New Zealand;

some interviews have been conducted in Australia in which parents were asked questions similar to the questions asked of children, teachers, and administrators. To date, however, not enough parent interviews have been conducted to begin analysis of their content. One challenge in this research is to find parents who believe they are knowledgeable enough to talk about the model, both due to their participation in projects at school and their children's willingness to talk about their experiences. Recent innovations at the school will make a difference. Student expositions are now being held for each grade level, in which students present their solutions and their problem-solving processes to the community, attended mainly by parents.

Future Directions in Research

One area of importance for future research is student engagement. Although the studies of student perceptions have shown that students are engaged in and challenged during REAPS problem-solving experiences, researchers have not studied engagement in depth. Because student engagement is a complex construct including interacting cognitive and affective factors, a study focusing on these factors and based on recently developed theories would be valuable in the implementation of models such as REAPS in which increasing engagement of students of all levels of ability, especially those who are gifted, is an important goal and has been identified by parents, teachers, administrators, and community members as an important result of REAPS implementation.

Another important area of research is to continue studies of the effectiveness of REAPS by comparing student gains in classrooms in which it is used with student gains in classrooms in which it is not used. Although this type of research is difficult because of teachers' desire to implement an exciting new approach and administrators' desire to provide all students with similar experiences, the results would be useful to others considering implementation of REAPS.

Case studies of the implementation of the model similar to the ones in preparation by Riley (in press) describing how REAPS was introduced in two small, rural communities with high percentages of Māori and Pacifica students would be valuable. In a teacher-led innovation project, community support was gained and local leaders were engaged in choosing the problems students would solve. Although such involvement may not be considered essential in other contexts, the journey from conception and introduction of an innovation to its widespread use and/or sustainability is important to document. Across the Australasian and Pacific Rim countries, sharing experiences, challenges, and successes in contexts as different as Beijing, China, Sydney, Australia, and Dargaville, New Zealand, can be beneficial to everyone, both those who document their experiences and those who read about them.

Implications for Practice: Links with the Wider Community

For practice, we believe we have developed some practical ways to differentiate curricula; however, continuing to document and expand these methods is an important future direction. Continuing to share with others implementing REAPS would benefit all of us. An important direction in the school in Australia is to continue to allow and encourage more student voice and choice in their REAPS experiences. At the beginning of the project, we all believed in the value of connecting the REAPS problems to the school's conceptual curriculum and the NSW syllabus for the Australian Curriculum. However, as the project developed, we saw that by doing this, we were limiting the amount of student choice in that teachers selected the problems to be solved. Although we did not realise it at the time, this requirement also limited some of the students' creativity and choices in both the solutions proposed and the methods of presenting those solutions. For instance, teachers were asking students to include in their presentations and evaluations ways their solutions demonstrated that they had learned and applied certain content knowledge and skills. When teachers were given the choice of connecting or not connecting problems to the curriculum and were encouraged to involve students in choosing problems to solve, the pressure to connect to the curriculum was reduced, and teachers began to see that students were *learning* important content *through* solving problems as well as *applying* content they had learned previously. Student engagement was noticeably higher when they chose problems that affected their lives and were seen as important for them to solve together. This practice also leads to identifying natural links in content and between content of the problem-solving experiences and expertise of people in the community.

To link with the wider community, we have been thinking of connections we already have made as well as connections we would like to make. For instance, our second author took a delegation of students to China and facilitated a group experience in which students from both countries followed the TASC problem-solving model to solve a problem they had identified. They reported their results to each other at each step, and the similarities were evident. Our first author and the expert teacher with the REAPS team conducted a six-day teacher workshop in China, and teachers in and near Beijing are implementing REAPS in their schools. We would like to organise both on-site and web-based problem-solving projects in which students participating in REAPS in Australia and China are connected. Such a project would facilitate connections among both teachers and students, leading to increased understanding of the global nature of many of our challenges. Similarly, indigenous populations of students in Australia and New Zealand can be connected through web-based, group problem-solving experiences in which they can discover and develop their strengths, create solutions for local and international problems and enhance their understanding of their role as indigenous people in shaping and preserving both our current and future world.

Conclusions

Writing this chapter has been an occasion for reflecting on the journey we have taken together over the past four years, what we have learned about introducing a new teaching approach, supporting teachers and administrators in implementing it, and sustaining it over time. We came to the partnership with different experiences, different skills, and different positions in educational settings but with a shared goal of making learning relevant, exciting, productive, and fun for all learners, inclusive of gifted students, through strength-based attitudes and methods. We continued that perspective into the writing of this chapter. For example, a researcher cannot understand the day-to-day mentoring and support needed to put into place and sustain a new teaching approach in the same way that the principal of that school can understand it. A principal has an understanding of the general attitudes of children, teachers, and parents, but does not have time to interview them in a consistent way, so these perceptions can be analysed and published. Often, administrators are not encouraged to publish what they have learned.

Together, in the writing of this chapter and the discussions that ensued during the writing process, we have gained more depth in our individual perspectives of REAPS and its value as well as our shared perspective. Some of the principles we have attempted to illustrate in this chapter are as follows: (a) engagement is essential for learning; (b) use of a practical evidence-based model can simplify the process of differentiation to meet the needs of students of different ability levels as well as to identify gifted students who may be missed by traditional methods; (c) a strength-based perspective is valuable for all students; (d) any teaching model needs to evolve over time; (e) the context of the school, which includes parent perspectives, teacher skills and attitudes, and the needs of students must be at the forefront of both the decision to implement a particular model and its evolution over time; (f) researchers must continually revisit their methods and instruments, making modifications to fit the context, the purpose, and the results of research; and (g) collaboration among researchers, leaders, and practitioners at all levels both enhances the experience of implementing educational innovations and increases the potential of the innovation to be accepted and sustained.

Cross-References

▶ Differentiation of Instruction for Gifted Learners: Collated Evaluative Studies of Teacher Classroom Practices
▶ Gifted and Talented Aboriginal Students in Australia
▶ Gifted Education in the Asia-Pacific: From the Past for the Future – An Introduction
▶ How Do Teachers Meet the Academic Needs of High-Ability Students in Science?
▶ Identifying Gifted Learning in the Regular Classroom: Seeking Intuitive Theories
▶ Motivational Issues in Gifted Education: Understanding the Role of Students' Attribution and Control Beliefs, Self-Worth Protection and Growth Orientation
▶ Nurturing Mathematical Talents of Young Mathematically Gifted English Language Learners
▶ Place-Based Gifted Education in Rural Schools
▶ Self-Regulated Learning for High-Ability and High-Achieving Students in Mixed-Ability Classrooms Throughout the Asia-Pacific
▶ Some Implications for the Future of Gifted Education in the Asia-Pacific
▶ Supporting Australian Gifted Indigenous Students' Academic Potential in Rural Settings
▶ Teachers' Knowledge and Understandings of Twice Exceptionality Across Australia
▶ The Development of Mana: Five Optimal Conditions for Gifted Māori Student Success
▶ Why Is It So? Interest and Curiosity in Supporting Students Gifted in Science

References

Alfaiz, F. S. (2019). *The association between the fidelity of implementation of the Real Engagement in Active Problem Solving (REAPS) model and student gains in creative problem solving in science* (Unpublished doctoral dissertation). The University of Arizona, Tucson, AZ.

Alfaiz, F. S., Pease, R., Maker, C. J., & Zimmerman, R. (2017). *Culturally responsive assessment of physical science skills and abilities: Development, field testing, and implementation.* Manuscript submitted for publication.

Alfaiz, F. S., Pease, R., & Maker, C, J. (2019). Culturally responsive assessments of physical science skills and abilities: Development, field testing, and implementation. Manuscript submitted to the Journal of Advancee Academics. Department of Disability and Psychoeducational Studies, University of Arizona, Tucson, AZ, USA.

Alhusaini, A. A. (2016). *The effects of duration of exposure to the REAPS model in developing students' general creativity and creative problem solving in science* (Unpublished doctoral dissertation). University of Arizona, Tucson, AZ.

Alhusaini A. A., Maker, C. J., & Alamiri, F. Y. (2015). *Adapting the REAPS model to develop students' creativity in Saudi Arabia: An exploratory study.* Unpublished manuscript, Jeddah University, Jeddah, Saudi Arabia.

Azano, A., Missett, T. C., Callahan, C. M., Oh, S., Brunner, M., Foster, L. H., & Moon, T. R. (2011). Exploring the relationship between fidelity of implementation and academic achievement in a third-grade gifted curriculum a mixed-methods study. *Journal of Advanced Academics, 22*(5), 693–719. https://doi.org/10.1177/1932202X11424878

Beckett, G. H., Hemmings, H., Maltbie, C., Wright, K., Sherman, M., & Session, B. (2016). Urban high school student engagement through CincySTEM iTest projects. *Journal of Science Education Technology, 25*, 995–1007. https://doi.org/10.1007/s10956-016-9640-6

Bransford, J., Brown, A. L., & Cocking, R. R. (2000). *How people learn: Brain, mind, experience, and school* (Expanded ed.). Washington, DC: National Academy Press.

Chi, M. T. H., Feltovich, P., & Glaser, R. (1981). Categorization and representation of physics problems by experts and novices. *Cognitive Sciences, 5*(2), 121–152. https://doi.org/10.1207/s15516709cog0502_2

Dai, D. Y., & Chen, F. (2013). Three paradigms of gifted education: In search of conceptual clarity in research and practice. *Gifted Child Quarterly, 57*(3), 151–168. https://doi.org/10.1177/0016986213490020

Delisle, J. R. (2012). Reaching those we teach: The five Cs of student engagement. *Gifted Child Today, 35*(1), 53–67. https://doi.org/10.1177/1076217511427513

Fredricks, J. A., Alfeld, C., & Eccles, J. (2010). Developing and fostering passion in academic and nonacademic domains. *Gifted Child Quarterly, 54*(1), 18–30. https://doi.org/10.1177/0016986209352683

Gallagher, S. A. (1997). Problem-based learning: Where did it come from, what does it do, and where is it going? *Journal for the Education of the Gifted, 20*(4), 332–362. https://doi.org/10.1177/016235329702000402

Gallagher, S. A. (2015). The role of problem based learning in developing creative expertise. *Asia Pacific Education Review, 16*, 225–235. https://doi.org/10.1007/s12564-015-9367-8

Gallagher, S. A., & Gallagher, J. J. (2013). Using problem-based learning to explore unseen academic potential. *Interdisciplinary Journal of Problem-Based Learning, 7*(1), 111–131. https://doi.org/10.7771/1541-5015.1322

Gardner, H. (1983). *Frames of mind: The theory of multiple intelligences.* New York, NY: Basic Books.

Gomez-Arizaga, M. P., Bahar, A. K., Maker, C. J., Zimmerman, R. H., & Pease, R. (2016). How does science learning occur in the classroom? Students' perceptions of science instruction during implementation of the REAPS model. *Eurasia Journal of Mathematics, Science, and Technology Education, 12*(3), 431–455. Retrieved from https://www.ejmste.com/download/how-does-science-learning-occur-in-the-classroom-students-perceptions-of-science-instruction-during-4499.pdf

Jang, H., Kim, E., & Reeve, J. (2016). Why students become more engaged or disengaged during the semester: A self-determination theory dual-process model. *Learning and Instruction, 43*, 27–38. https://doi.org/10.1016/j.learninstruc.2016.01.002

Jo, S., & Ku, J. (2011). Problem based learning using real-time data in science education for the gifted. *Gifted Education International, 27*(3), 263–273. https://doi.org/10.1177/026142941102700304

Lee, J.-S. (2014). The relationship between student engagement and academic performance: Is it a myth or reality? *The Journal of Educational Research, 107*(3), 177–185. https://doi.org/10.1080/00220671.2013.807491

Little, C. A. (2012). Curriculum as motivation for gifted students. *Psychology in the Schools, 49*(7), 695–705. https://doi.org/10.1002/pits.21621

Maker, C. J. (2005). *The DISCOVER project: Improving assessment and curriculum for diverse gifted learners* (Senior scholars series monograph). Storrs, CT: National Research Center on the Gifted and Talented.

Maker, C. J. (2016). Recognizing and developing spiritual abilities through real-life problem solving. *Gifted Education International, 32*(3), 271–306. https://doi.org/10.1177/0261429415602574

Maker, C. J., & Anuruthwong, U. (2003). *The miracle of learning.* Featured Speech presented at the World Conference on the Gifted and Talented, Adelaide, Australia.

Maker, C. J., Jo, S.-M., Alfaiz, F. S., & Alhusaini, A. A. (2017). *The Test of Creative Problem Solving in Science: Construct and concurrent validity.* Manuscript submitted to Creativity Research Journal. Department of Disability and Psychoeducational Studies, University of Arizona, Tucson, AZ, USA.

Maker, C. J., & Pease, R. (2017). *What do effective teachers do when implementing the REAPS model to differentiate instruction in a general education classroom?* Manuscript in preparation.

Department of Disability and Psychoeducational Studies, University of Arizona, Tucson, AZ, USA.

Maker, C. J., & Schiever, S. W. (2005). *Teaching/learning models in education of the gifted* (3rd ed.). Austin, TX: Pro-Ed.

Maker, C. J., & Schiever, S. W. (2010). *Curriculum development and teaching strategies for gifted learners* (3rd ed.). Austin, TX: Pro-Ed.

Maker, C. J., Wu, I.-C., & Pease, R. (2017). *The relationship between teachers' fidelity of implementation of the Real Engagement in Active Problem Solving (REAPS) model and student gains in creative mathematical problem solving.* Manuscript in preparation. Department of Disability and Psychoeducational Studies, University of Arizona, Tucson, AZ, USA

Maker, C. J., & Zimmerman, R. (2008). Problem solving in a complex world: Integrating DISCOVER, TASC and PBL in a teacher education project. *Gifted Education International, 24*(2–3), 160–178. https://doi.org/10.1177/026142940802400305

Maker, C. J., Zimmerman, R., Alhusaini, A., & Pease, R. (2015a). Real Engagement in Active Problem Solving (REAPS): An evidence-based model that meets content, process, product, and learning environment principles recommended for gifted students. *APEX: The New Zealand Journal of Gifted Education, 19*(1), 1–24. https://doi.org/10.21307/apex-2015-006

Maker, C. J., Zimmerman, R., Gomez-Arizaga, M., Pease, R., & Burke, E. (2015b). Developing real-life problem solving: Integrating the DISCOVER problem matrix, problem based learning, and thinking actively in a social context. In H. Vidergor & R. Harris (Eds.), *Applied practiced for educators of gifted and able learners*. Rotterdam, Netherlands: Sense Publishers.

Martin, T. G., Martin, A. J., & Evans, P. (2017). Student engagement in the Caribbean region: Exploring its role in the motivation and achievement of Jamaican middle school students. *School Psychology International, 38*(2), 184–200. https://doi.org/10.1177/0143034316683765

New South Wales Department of Education. (2017). National disability data collection. Retrieved from https://education.nsw.gov.au/teaching-and-learning/disability-learning-and-support/perso nalised-support-for-learning/national-disability-data-collection

New South Wales Education Standards Authority. (2012a). Differentiated programming. Retrieved from https://syllabus.nesa.nsw.edu.au/support-materials/differentiated-programming/

New South Wales Education Standards Authority. (2012b). Teacher accreditation teacher practice. Retrieved from http://educationstandards.nsw.edu.au/wps/portal/nesa/teacher-accreditation/pro ficient-teacher/evidence

New Zealand Ministry of Education. (2017). The Māori education strategy: Ka Hikitia – Accelerating 2013–2017. Retrieved from https://www.education.govt.nz/ministry-of-education/overall-strate gies-and-policies/the-maori-education-strategy-ka-hikitia-accelerating-succes s-20132017/

Parsons, S. A., Malloy, J. A., Parsons, A. W., Peters-Burton, E. E., & Burrowbridge, S. C. (2016). Sixth-grade students' engagement in academic tasks. *The Journal of Educational Research, 111*(2), 232–245. https://doi.org/10.1080/00220671.2016.1246408

Pease, R., & Maker, C. J. (2017). *Teachers' perceptions of the Real Engagement in Active Problem Solving (REAPS) model.* Manuscript in preparation.

Pease, R. & Maker, C. J. (2017). *at the end of the reference, add the following:* Department of Disability and Psychoeducational Studies, University of Arizona, Tucson, AZ, USA.

Reeve, J. (2012). A self-determination theory perspective on student engagement. In S. Christenson, A. Reschly, & C. Wylie (Eds.), *Handbook of research on student engagement* (pp. 149–172). New York, NY: Springer. https://doi.org/10.1007/978-1-4614-2018-7

Reinoso, J. (2011). Real-life problem solving: Examining the effects of alcohol within a community on the Navajo nation. *Gifted Education International, 27*(3), 288–299. https://doi.org/10.1177/026142941102700306

Riley, T., Webber, M., & Sylva, K. (2017). Real Engagement in Active Problem Solving for Māori boys: A case study in a New Zealand secondary school. *Gifted and Talented International, 32*(2), 75–86. https://doi.org/10.1080/15332276.2018.1522240

Shernoff, D. J., Csikszentmihalyi, M., Schneider, B., & Shernoff, E. S. (2003). Student engagement in high school classrooms from the perspective of flow theory. *School Psychology Quarterly, 18*(2), 158–176. https://doi.org/10.1521/scpq.18.2.158.21860

Smith, G. A. (2002). Place-based education: Learning to be where we are. *Phi Delta Kappan, 83*(8), 584–594. https://doi.org/10.1177/003172170208300806

Sternberg, R. J. (1997). *Successful intelligence*. New York, NY: Plume.

Sternberg, R. J. (1999). Intelligence as developing expertise. *Contemporary Educational Psychology, 24*(4), 359–375. https://doi.org/10.1006/ceps.1998.0998

Tan, S., Erdimez, O., & Zimmerman, R. (2017). Concept mapping as a tool to develop and measure students' understanding in science. *Acta Didactica Naponcensia, 10*(2), 109–122. https://doi.org/10.24193/adn.10.2.9

Urban, K., & Jellen, G. (1996). *Test for creative thinking – Drawing production (TCT-DP)*. Lisse, Netherlands: Swets & Zeitlinger.

Wallace, B. (2008). The early seedbed of the growth of TASC: Thinking actively in a social context. *Gifted Education International, 24*(2–3), 139–155. https://doi.org/10.1177/026142940802400303

Wallace, B., Maker, C. J., Cave, D., & Chandler, S. (2004). *Thinking skills and problem-solving: An inclusive approach*. London, UK: David Fulton Publishers.

Watt, H. M. G., Carmichael, C., & Callingham, R. (2017). Students' engagement profiles in mathematics according to learning environment dimensions: Developing an evidence base for best practice in mathematics education. *School Psychology International, 38*(2), 166–183. https://doi.org/10.1177/0143034316688373

Webber, M., & Macfarlane, A. (2017). The transformative role of tribal knowledge and genealogy in indigenous student success. In L. Smith & E. McKinley (Eds.), *Indigenous handbook of education* (pp. 1–25). Australia: Springer. Retrieved from https://link.springer.com/referenceworkentry/10.1007/978-981-10-1839-8_63-1

Webber, M., Riley, T., Sylva, K., & Scobie-Jennings, E. (2018). The Ruamano project: Raising expectations, realising community aspirations and recognising gifted potential in Māori boys. *The Australian Journal of Indigenous Education*. Retrieved from https://doi.org/10.1017/jie.2018.16

Wu, I.-C., Pease, R., & Maker, C. J. (2015). Students' perceptions of Real Engagement in Active Problem Solving. *Gifted and Talented International, 30*(1–2), 106–121. https://doi.org/10.1080/15332276.2015.1137462

Zhou, M., & Ren, J. (2017). A self-determination perspective on Chinese fifth-graders' task disengagement. *School Psychology International, 38*(2), 149–165. https://doi.org/10.1177/0143034316684532

Zimmerman, R., Alfaiz, F. S., & Maker, C. J. (2017). *Culturally responsive assessments of life science skills and abilities: Development, field testing, and implementation.* Manuscript submitted for publication.

Zimmerman, R., & Maker, C. J. (2017). *Students' understanding of the complexity of concepts and their interrelationships in REAPS and comparison classrooms.* Manuscript in preparation.

Zimmerman, R. H., Maker, C. J., Gomez-Arizaga, M. P., & Pease, R. (2011). The use of concept maps in facilitating problem solving in earth science. *Gifted Educational International, 27*(3), 274–287. https://doi.org/10.1177/026142941102700305

Zimmerman, R. H., Maker, C. J., & Pease, R. (2017). *Fidelity of implementation of the Real Engagement in Active Problem Solving (REAPS) model and student gains in understanding the complexity of concepts and their interrelationships.* Manuscript in preparation.

Zimmerman, R. H., Maker, C. J., & Alfaiz, F.S. (2019). Culturally responsive assessments of life science abilities: Development, field testing, and implementation. Manuscript submitted to the Journal of Advanced Academics. Department of Disability and Psychoeducational Studies, University of Arizona, Tucson, AZ, USA.

Zimmerman, R. H. & Maker, C. J. (2017). *add the following at the end of the reference:* Department of Disability and Psychoeducational Studies, University of Arizona, Tucson, AZ, USA.

Zimmerman, R. H., Maker, C. J., & Pease, R. (2017). add the following at the end of the reference: Department of Disability and Psychoeducational Studies, University of Arizona, Tucson, AZ, USA.

C. June Maker   has been active in the *National Association for Gifted Children* (NAGC) and the *World Council for Gifted and Talented Students* (WCGTS). She is associate editor of *Gifted and Talented International* (GTI) and serves on editorial boards for journals in education of the gifted, special education and general education in the USA and other countries, such as The *Gifted Child Quarterly* (GCQ). She is an internationally known writer, researcher, teacher educator, consultant and keynote speaker, and has published many books and articles. In 2015, she received the International Research Award from WCGTS and a Doctor of Letters Degree from Western Kentucky University.

Myra Wearne   has worked as both a teacher and an educational leader in South Western and Northern Sydney. She has engaged in multiple projects aimed at bridging the gap between educational theory and practice and is a passionate advocate for educational research in school settings.

Attuned Pedagogy: The Artistry of Differentiated Instruction from a Taiwanese Cultural Perspective

Chin-hsieh Lu and Wei-Ren Chen

Contents

Abstract

Differentiated instruction has been a framework of effective teaching and a main indicator of professional standards of gifted teachers in Taiwan. However, practically, there are significant disparities between the theoretical expectations and practical implementations regarding curriculum modification, teaching strategies, and demanded resources. Before the advocacy of the concept of differentiated instruction, *attuned pedagogy* was a very similar idea to differentiated instruction and has been a common language used to describe the goal of effective teaching in Taiwan and in the Chinese culture. Based on the perspective of the culture-sensitive research paradigm, the purpose of this chapter is to delineate the ideal of attuned pedagogy and suggest *attuned pedagogy* as the artistry of differentiated

C.-h. Lu (✉)
Department of Special Education, National Taipei University of Education, Taipei, Taiwan
e-mail: chinlu50@gmail.com

W.-R. Chen
Department of Special Education, National Chiayi University, Chiayi City, Taiwan
e-mail: cweiren@ms36.hinet.net

© Springer Nature Singapore Pte Ltd. 2021   917
S. R. Smith (ed.), *Handbook of Giftedness and Talent Development in the Asia-Pacific*,
Springer International Handbooks of Education,
https://doi.org/10.1007/978-981-13-3041-4_41

instruction for cultivating giftedness when we face the challenges of intellectual diversity. In this chapter, a review of the challenges of differentiated instruction in Taiwan will be provided. Then based on the studies of master gifted teachers in elementary schools, three essential principles of attuned pedagogy will be proposed: uniqueness not individuality, intimate relationships, and matching the curve of variation. The four recurrent themes regarding the praxis of attuned pedagogy include: inspiring volition to discipline the minds, following student's natural tendency to find the sweet spot; moderating in-between to trigger potential; and leaving space to attune personalised connections. Accordingly, the goal of gifted education is to transform giftedness in context. With the long-term purpose of gifted education being to build the student's learning potential and guide harmony in diversification, the task of gifted educators has to be rooted in wisdom based on professional knowledge and judgement.

Keywords

Attuned pedagogy · Differentiated instruction · Giftedness · Master gifted teachers · Artistry · Cultural-historical perspective

The aims in this chapter are to:
1. Review the challenges of differentiated instruction in Taiwan.
2. Explain attuned pedagogy as the artistry of differentiated instruction for cultivating intellectually diverse giftedness.
3. Propose three essential principles and four strategies of attuned pedagogy as the artistry of differentiation.
4. Provide suggestions for further research and practice regarding attuned pedagogy.

Introduction: Striving for Rightness of Good Fit

While gaining more knowledge of the concept of giftedness, we recognise more the dynamic interconnected nature of human potential and its developmental, environmental, and interactional complexity. Striving for understanding of the diversity of gifted students and the rightness of good educational fit to maximise individual student success has been the ultimate goal of gifted education. For decades, differentiated instruction has become a common shared language term in general schooling practice and in gifted education to help maximise student success. Global educators advocate for accomplished successful differentiation in the current climate of standardised curricula and testing.

Differentiating teaching is a broad term that encompasses differentiating instruction, differentiating the curriculum, differentiating assessment, and differentiating learning. The focus in this chapter is on differentiating instruction. As Tomlinson (2001) emphasised, differentiated instruction progresses from whole class teaching to flexible grouping, from passive acceptance to active adjustment and from *whether* to respond to *how* to respond. Hence, differentiating instruction, for many teachers, first requires a paradigm shift.

For teachers in Taiwan, the challenge to implement the concept of differentiated instruction is not a paradigm shift from whole class teaching to differentiated instruction, rather a paradigm shift regarding what *rightness of good fit* means: that is, to *dynamically and efficiently fit teaching to a student's unique needs*. It is to fully understand that differentiated instruction is not a new concept at all (Maker, 1982; Smith, 2015a, 2015b; Tomlinson, 2017), and the highest misconception is to assume that teachers do not differentiate without understanding the concept of differentiated instruction.

Before the advocation of the concept of differentiated instruction, *Yin Cai Shi Jiao* (因材施教) was a very similar idea to differentiated instruction and has been a common language used to describe the goal of *effective* teaching in Taiwan and in Chinese culture. In Chinese culture, the best fit of the adjustment decisions during the procedure for enhancing individual student's learning is what counts as *Yin* (因, attuned), which "closely follows the course of the context that its dynamism is continuously renewed" (Jullien, 2004, p. 184). For the purpose of discussions, attuned pedagogy will be used as *Yin Cai Shi Jiao* in this chapter.

Smith and Lu (2015) pointed out that over the past century, the conceptual foundation of gifted education has evolved due to the diverse contributions of researchers in the field. With the understanding of the complex interrelationship of the nature and nurture of giftedness, research has moved the focus from gifted individuals to gifted students, then to gifted learners, and gifted behaviour so aspects of the conception of giftedness tends to be more confluent now. Persson (2012) borrowed and integrated concepts from multiple disciplines and concluded that gifted education is dominated by American cultural influences. Dai and Chen (2014) restructured the field of gifted education into three paradigms: (1) the *gifted child*, (2) *talent development*, and (3) *differentiation*, and elaborated the continuities and discontinuities of the three paradigms. They suggested that the articulation of the paradigms' properties may make the relevance and significance of a particular line of research clearer to the community of gifted education practitioners. However:

> the best paradigm can only really work if all the parts are integrated into the process and if the design itself is structured with a dynamic that has inherent flexibility, is responsive to change and refinement, and maintains acutely aware, balanced cultural sensitivity that stands firm against ethnocentricity and dominance. (Persson, 2012, p. 49)

Though attuned pedagogy is a similar concept to differentiated instruction, it is constructed based on a different philosophy of human beings (Lu, 2015b) and culture. Attuned pedagogy practitioners hold a different perspective regarding what counts as effectiveness of teaching. In *Toward a Psychology of Being*, Maslow (1968) stated:

> When the philosophy of man changes, then everything changes, not only the philosophy of politics, of economics, of ethics and values, of interpersonal relations, and of history itself, but also the philosophy of education, of psychotherapy, and of personal growth, the theory of how to help men become what they can and deeply need to become. (p. 189)

Based on the perspective of the cultural-sensitive research paradigm, the purpose in this chapter is to delineate the idea of *attuned pedagogy* and suggest attuned pedagogy as the artistry of differentiated instruction for cultivating giftedness when we face the challenges of intellectual diversity. Supporting teachers helps them to: contribute to the best practice of differentiated instruction; free their wisdom (Trotman, 2010); make their professional judgements visible; and recognise the value of their professional contribution. The ultimate goal of this chapter is to propose attuned pedagogy as an alternative perspective to differentiated instruction and to liberate the wise educator for the best practice of differentiated instruction to eventuate. First, the challenges of differentiated instruction and attuned pedagogy in Taiwan will be reviewed in this chapter. Then, based on the studies of master elementary school teachers of gifted students, we will propose the idea of attuned pedagogy and discuss the praxis of attuned pedagogy. Finally, we will conclude with a reiteration of cultivating giftedness in the cultural-historical perspective of the artistry of teaching (Eisner, 2002).

The Challenges of Differentiated Instruction as Attuned Pedagogy in Taiwan

Theoretically, differentiated instruction has been an emerging issue in Taiwan's gifted education. However, practically, there are significant disparities between the theoretical expectation and the practical implementation regarding curriculum modification, teaching strategies, and associated resources (Chen, Chen, & Pan, 2008). In a survey on resource room teachers for the intellectually gifted in Taipei City by Chen et al. (2008), gifted education teachers pointed out that the support in terms of additional relevant resources is most critical in implementing effective differentiation, such as sufficient time and resources and the support from parents and administrators.

A comparative study on the differentiated curriculum of gifted education between Taiwan and China (Huang, 2014) also pointed out that there was still room for improvement in professional development and empirical studies of differentiated curriculum of gifted education although relevant policies have been made in Taiwan. The use of the concept of differentiated instruction does provide very helpful perspectives and strategies for teaching gifted children. As mentioned above, in Chinese culture, the best fit of the adjustment decisions during the procedure for enhancing the individual's learning within context is what counts as attuned pedagogy. However, while emphasising the practice of differentiated instruction, attuned pedagogy can become insignificant, or the wrong strategies may be used.

Constructing the competences of differentiated instruction in teaching for Taiwan's teachers not only involves learning a new concept or practice or just changing the thinking process of teaching. It is, however, more profoundly a social-cultural process of "paradigmatic thinking" from the perspective of "mind in society" (Bruner, 1996; Haste, 2008; Vygotsky, 1978). "Knowing is what is shared within discourse, within a textual community" (Bruner, 1996, p. 57).

Based on a series of individual interviews and informal observations during professional workshops (Lu, 2015a), we identified three challenges of attuned pedagogy while implementing differentiated instruction in Taiwan that will be discussed based on the cultural-historical perspective (Bruner, 1996; Haste, 2008): *discourse, identity,* and *culture.*

Discourse. For every effective teacher, it is impossible to teach students without accordance with the student's aptitude or characteristics. In responding to the individual student, assisting and guiding each student to develop their unique potential have always been an important goal for effective teaching. Effective teachers always find their ways to accommodate unique differences under the constraints of classroom situations without extra administrative or parent support nor professional training. In the last decade, while academic researchers actively advocated the concept of differentiated instruction for the effective teaching for gifted and talented students, the strategies related to differentiated instruction have been gradually accepted and applied in Taiwan. Differentiated instruction has become the professional index of effective teaching, and a common language used by the community of teaching has become the most important index for a qualified teacher. In the Taiwanese teaching certificate program and academic conferences of education, differentiated instruction became the major issue. In a professional development course that we worked on with the Department of Education, Taipei City Government, most of the teachers and principals reported that they are proud of using differentiated instruction as the main teaching approach and are using all the new strategy terminologies related to differentiated instruction, such as learning stations, different groupings, tiering, and teaching models, and the like (Lu, 2015a). There are many projects and programs funded by the Taiwanese government to support professional development and measure the impact of differentiated instruction. It seems that for those who accepted and implemented differentiated instruction, differentiated instruction has been a professional language. For those who did not really understand or implement the concept of differentiated instruction, the terms differentiated instruction and associated language are used for political correctness.

In our professional development workshops, when the teachers talked regarding the concept of differentiated instruction and how they dealt with the diversities of gifted students, many teachers responded directly, "It is not a problem at all. Of course, attuned pedagogy!" Some teachers said, "every child is different, how could we not attune to student's difference?" And some teachers asked, "What is the difference between differentiated instruction and attuned pedagogy?" With further inquiries, we found that most of the teachers took differentiated instruction as attuned pedagogy (Lu, 2015a). While interpreting the concept of differentiated instruction, teachers tended to take the idea of attuned pedagogy as the concept of differentiated instruction or perceived these two as totally different concepts. Obviously, there should be some similarities between differentiated instruction and attuned pedagogy, and of course, there might be some uniqueness in each concept. However, without professional recognition or systematic discussions or training, we observed that teachers tended to see differentiated instruction as a new strategy of teaching and attuned pedagogy has become a weak folklore idea and not a professional criterion. Gradually, attuned pedagogy has faded out. It dissipated and then almost disappeared among the community of general and gifted education, while the concept of differentiated instruction has been more widely accepted.

Identity. Tomlinson (1995) has proposed a continuum of differentiated instruction from micro to macro differentiation in which macro differentiation is the best practice. Macro differentiation is more proactive, more fluid, more open, and more dependent on teacher coaching. It requires an articulated philosophy that promotes respect for student difference, planned assessment/compacting, planned variation of content/process/product, and use of flexible groups, individual goal setting based on developmental growth and relevant grading, and mentoring. Micro differentiation is more reactive, more fixed, more closed, and more dependent on students' responses. Micro differentiation focuses on adjusting questions in discussions, occasional exceptions for pacing, grading and grouping, extended work that is more dependent on students' decisions.

In terms of differentiated instruction, shifting from whole classroom teaching to differentiated instruction, for most of the teachers, the problem originates in *how*. They need more strategies for grouping students appropriately based on students' abilities, learning preferences and interests. They need to know how to use instruments or pre-assessments for making proper decisions for instructional planning. Teachers need effective teaching strategies to scaffold acceleration or enrichment or self-directed learning (Smith, 2015a, 2015b). However, in terms of attuned pedagogy—the best practice for teaching to unique student needs from a Taiwanese perspective—the problem originates from *when* more than *how*. The major differences between the levels of good practices for differentiated instruction and attuned pedagogy lie in their respective concepts of *timing*. When we interviewed teachers of gifted children regarding their teaching strategies for attuned pedagogy, every teacher told us "incidental" which means they depend more on the context, especially "good timing" for addressing or changing student's learning (Lu, 2015a). Teachers tend to attune their teaching more to a student's learning needs based on their personal judgements within the context. Apparently, without systematic pre-assessment or planning, it is more like micro level differentiation. In other words, it is not evidence-based, nor scientific, but practice-based. Somehow, attuned pedagogy is mistaken as the micro level of differentiated instruction, and teachers need to be trained to implement differentiation at the macro level. In terms of scientific or evidence-based teaching, we observed in our study (Lu, 2015a) that most of the teachers who used effective attuned pedagogy—that is, the artistry of differentiated instruction—were considered as needing lots of professional training sessions on macro differentiated instruction. The end result being that many teachers who we interviewed felt very frustrated and some of them retired sooner than needing to or earlier than expected.

Jackson (1996) mentioned that in teaching, as in every professional field, there are masters who are well recognised and who serve as models in the community. The profession as a whole can learn much from the masters or experts in the profession. However, we believe that many of the masters fade out of their profession if their practices do not fit the focus or the trend of the time. Dewey (1929) said loss of the experts or masters is a huge waste in every profession and "the only way by which we can prevent such waste in the future is by methods which enable us to make an analysis of what the gifted teacher does intuitively, so that something accruing from his work can be communicated to others" (pp. 10–11). William James (1899/2008) pointed out over a hundred years ago that it is much like the science of war if teaching is based only on the science of psychology. He said:

> I cannot too strongly agree with my colleague, Professor Münsterberg, when he says that the teachers' attitudes toward the child, being concrete and ethical, is positively opposed to the psychological observer's, which is abstract and analytic. Although some of us may conjoin the attitudes successfully, in most of us they must conflict. (p. 13)

James (1899/2008) emphasised that:

> the worst thing that can happen to a good teacher is to get a bad conscience about her profession because she feels herself hopeless as a psychologist. Teachers are overworked already. Every one adds a jot or a little of unnecessary weight to their burden is a foe of education. (p. 13–14)

Culture. Education does not exist in a cultural vacuum. Bruner (1996) emphasised that if we are true educators, we must first understand the people who we want to influence the people who we want to educate. Teachers' cultural beliefs are deep-rooted in their daily life and influenced by their perspectives of education, their personal goals, and what they believe is success. He said:

> Education is not just about conventional school matters like curriculum or standards or testing. What we resolve to do in school only makes sense when considered in the broader context of what the society intends to accomplish through its education investment in the young. How one conceives of education, we have finally come to recognise, is a function of how one conceives of the culture and its aims, professed and otherwise. (Bruner, 1996, p. X)

The ideal of *Yin Cai Shi Jiao* proliferated deeply in the Chinese culture of education. This ideal means that teaching should be in accordance with students' dispositions and it offered Chinese teachers an avenue to pursue teaching excellence. It was derived from the *Collective Commentaries on the Analects* (Zhu Xi, 1130~1200), was a common language to describe the ideal of Confucius' teaching, and has been the highest goal of teaching for a thousand years in Chinese culture. Hence, it is expected that this ideal should be explicitly or implicitly represented in teaching practice. However, it is a challenge to understand or represent a folklore language from a contemporary professional perspective without over simplifying the ideal. For our professional discussion regarding the idea of *Yin Cai Shi Jiao*, we use the concept of *attuned pedagogy* to delineate the ideal in this chapter, but do not intend to define or interpret the whole ideal of *Yin Cai Shi Jiao*. The purpose in this chapter is to define the concept and the praxis of attuned pedagogy and to provide an alternative perspective of differentiated instruction from the cultural-historical perspective. As mentioned above, attuned pedagogy is more a folklore language than a professional concept. The idea of 'teaching according to a student's disposition' can be interpreted in many different ways at different times. How can we consolidate the concept of attuned pedagogy?

Persson (2012) borrowed and integrated concepts from multiple disciplines and concluded that gifted education is dominated by American cultural influences. The foundation of gifted education in Taiwan has grown from the American pot, both theoretically and practically. Taiwan has implemented pull-out gifted programs since 1984, and the national curriculum standards were issued in 2008. Before the curriculum and professional standards were promoted, it was a big challenge for good teachers to maximise gifted students' learning under the pressure of coaching for testing and lack of learning motivation without sufficient support from administration or parents or sufficient knowledge of differentiated strategies (Wu, 2013).

Teaching gifted children is highly personal and dependent on teachers' personal philosophy and professional judgement (Lu, 2015a). Such a diverse teacher background has resulted in a diverse array of gifted programs in Taiwan and very extreme styles of teaching. While the ideal of attuned pedagogy was gradually replaced by differentiated instruction, there are master gifted teachers who hold the perspective of attuned pedagogy and live up to the philosophy in their good practice. Before the advocation of differentiated instruction, master teachers were always the teachers from whom their peers sought professional advice, and they were also the ones who served as models when there were outside visitors. Hence, after the advocacy of differentiated instruction, they are the ones who can explain their teaching without confounding it with the concept of differentiated instruction, and they are easily recognised as examples or masters for other teachers.

> In teaching as in several other things, it does not matter much what your philosophy is or is not. It matters more whether you have a philosophy or not. And it matters very much whether you try to live up to your philosophy or not. The only principles of teaching which I thoroughly dislike are those to which people pay only lip service. (Polya, cited in Jackson, 1996, p. 113)

Those master teachers have gained insights of attuned pedagogy accrued from their life-long teaching and are the masters of attuned pedagogy. The term of *master teacher* rather than *expert teacher* used in this chapter implies that the teachers practise what they believe is good teaching of attuned pedagogy.

As Trotman (2010) reminded us, "the implications for professional educational practice might simply be construed as letting go" (p. 164). Training teachers to implement theories or strategies for responding to the diversity of student's needs is important to gifted education (Dai & Chen, 2014; Tomlinson, 2017). Understanding how the master teachers have taught efficiently to respond to individual differences would enrich and redefine the concept of differentiated instruction from the teacher's perspective. With a series of studies, we redefine *education as cultivation* based on Chinese traditional literature (Lu, 2015b; Yen, 2015) and investigate the master gifted teachers' insights regarding attuned pedagogy to enlighten our perspective of attuned pedagogy. As Lave (1996) pointed out, educational research rarely focuses on great teachers' teaching. Lave said:

Research on learning is mostly research on "instruction", on depersonalized guidelines for the teaching of specific lesson-like things in school settings [in order to improve learning]. The "teaching" that "learning research" is research *on* has little recognisable relationship to the creative, productive work that arouses admiration for great teachers. Yet it seems likely that most people who devote their lives to education do so in part because they have been deeply affected by one or more. (p. 158)

Based on official evaluations by the Ministry of Education and peer recommendations, we invited 15 master gifted elementary school teachers who are the masters of attuned pedagogy to participate in a series of studies (Lu, 2015a). We invited these teachers to talk about their insights or philosophy regarding attuned pedagogy in seven focused group sessions, in-depth personal interviews, and classroom observations. For discussions, we will use the *master teacher* in place of the *master gifted teachers of attuned pedagogy*. At the same time, we informally interviewed and observed three novice and three experienced teachers to glean a deeper understanding of the differences between personal and professional judgements regarding the concept of attuned pedagogy. Based on this three-year study, we analysed the practical professional reasoning of the master teachers and constructed a prototype of attuned pedagogy.

Seemingly, the master teachers set the same plan, outcomes, and assessments for every student and then attuned their teaching according to the individual student's unique aptitude during the process of learning without a proactive plan based on pre-assessment or clear grouping strategies for differentiated instruction. It seems their teaching focused more on personal interaction and is at the micro level according to the continuum of differentiated instruction (Tomlinson, 1995). The main question of the study was how the master teachers defined the concept of attuned pedagogy. The questions of the focused group interviews, in-depth interviews, and classroom teachers had five foci: What are the master teacher's views and expectations for gifted students? How did the master teachers plan for attuned pedagogy? How did they attune to every student' aptitude in the classroom teaching based on their personal judgement? How did they maximise student's personal learning with attuned pedagogy? How did the master teachers know their teaching was effectively attuned? Based on the analyses, we defined three essential principles and four praxis strategies of attuned pedagogy and will discuss in detail in the following.

Attuned Pedagogy: The Artistry of Differentiated Instruction

The greatest challenge for teachers in implementing differentiated instruction is ensuring the effectiveness of teaching and learning, which, in this chapter's context, is also called the *artistry* of differentiated instruction. Every educator of gifted students should recognise that every gifted student is unique and harbours diverse potential (Smith, 2017). Each gifted child's ability is constantly developing (Gagné, 2009, 2013). The context of classroom learning is dynamically changed through the interactions between teacher and student and resources and instruction (Smith,

2009a, 2015a). This means that effective differentiated instruction relies on teachers' perspectives and professional judgement as Tomlinson (1999, 2003, 2017) previously emphasised. Teachers' judgement helps to make differentiation dynamically and efficiently match individual student's needs, which is the artistry of enacting multiplicitly, flexibly, and continuously in a classroom. Smith proposed the *Model of Dynamic Differentiation* (MoDD), (2009a, 2015a, 2017) for an explanation of the dynamicity of differentiated teaching and learning. In other words, the dynamicity of interacting multiplicitly, flexibly, and continuously in a classroom is the essence of the artistry of differentiated instruction.

As Chen (2014) pointed out, *multiplicity* indicates that the teacher provides diverse avenues to make students' learning visible and meaningful. *Flexibility* refers to orchestrating flexible interactions which make learning happen in a constructive atmosphere, such as providing unique opportunities for personal needs. *Continuity* implies designing prolonged learning experiences by a wide range of educational services so that students continuously enjoy investigating their interest areas. The question is how to develop this kind of dynamicity for the artistry of differentiated instruction? As Smith and Lu (2015) pointed out, diverse differences are leading the dynamics of gifted education, and the more we understand the diversity of learners, the more we tend to differentiate for individual differences with more strategies and toolkits. However, at the end of every teacher professional development workshop, every teaching toolkit, and every exploration of theoretical foundations for best practices of differentiated instruction, there is always a reminder: *every child is unique* (Smith & Lu, 2015). There is always another reminder about differentiation: *it depends* on a variety of interrelated factors. There is always another reminder: *start small.* Artistry is very personal. Obviously, we need the language to discuss what artistry means or how to develop it in our teaching and learning.

From a scientific paradigm and regarding effective teaching, we talk more about strategies rather than great teachers (Lave, 1996). It is very challenging to talk about the great teacher because "the art of teaching grew up in the classroom and out of inventiveness and sympathetic observation" (James, 1899/2008). Jackson (1996) emphasised that the teacher develops a more or less adequate understanding of how [every child] behaves in recurring learning situations. However, this kind of understanding is more extensive and more accurate for some students than for others. Rubin (1989) also pointed out that:

> inspired teaching comes not merely from a command of content and method, but also from a conditioned instinct for guiding learning. Contextual clues frequently influence instructional decisions, but it is reaching back into experience, the tacit interpretation of earlier encounters similar to the present, and the inferring of potential solutions that serve as the spring-head of intuition. (p. 32)

The artistry of attuned pedagogy is supported by the aesthetic feeling of *rightness of fit* (Eisner, 2002) within diversification, elasticity, and continuation. In the Chinese culture, the way to attain the *rightness of fit* for students' needs within diversification, elasticity, and continuation is also called attuned pedagogy. However, as mentioned above, attuned pedagogy holds a very different philosophy from differentiated instruction regarding the concept of efficiency. Differentiated instruction focuses more on the self-efficacy of the means-to-an-end relationship. It requires individual measures, which are directly planned, instrumental, and selective. Regarding the rightness of fit, the master teachers' concern is not the concept of self-efficacy but more of efficiency. They are concerned more about how to assist students to succeed under the conditions of uncertainty with the least resistance. As the French sinologist Jullien (2004) concluded, "attuned [is more] a logic of processivity" (p. 130) than a logic of means to an end. Based on the understandings of Lao-zi, Jullien (2004) provides a very clear interpretation of the concept of efficiency in Chinese culture:

> The qualities peculiar to efficiency stem from the fluidity and continuity of a process: efficiency opens up efficacy to an aptitude that has no need of the concrete in order to operate. Proceeding, as it does, from a comprehensive system, it requires neither a goal nor effort. And given that, instead of being willed, it stems from the conditions implied in a situation, it never suddenly proves inadequate or misdirected. It belongs not so much to the domain of action (and events) as to that of happening-and-accomplishment. Whereas efficacy can be localised and its results are therefore directly perceptible, efficiency rightly passes unperceived, since particular effects relate to it only indirectly, and do not affect it. (p. 133)

Efficiency of attuned pedagogy has three essential principles that are merged from the studies of master teachers: (a) everyone is unique, (b) intimate relationships, and (c) matching the curve of variation.

Uniqueness not individuality. The complexity of human nature is not logically structured nor ordered (Scheffler, 1985). However, in order to effectively differentiate for students' differences, strategies are sought to achieve this outcome with assessments that will elaborate the outcomes immediately. Originating from the perspective of means to an end, differentiation requires structured procedures to make teaching more effective. Based on this perspective, we will tend to reduce the "problem" of education to questions like "what potential does the student have?" and "how is this potential to be realised most efficiently?" (Scheffler, 1985, p. 14). The main concern regarding differentiated instruction is to reduce teaching to identifying individual differences and responding to their differences accordingly, without considering students' personal best goals (Martin, 2011).

To master teachers, every gifted child is a small universe within. One of the most important concepts that master teachers use to describe gifted students is *every student is unique*. The concept of uniqueness is not the same as individuality. That students differ from each other is obvious, but how are differences defined? In the last century, abundant knowledge about individual differences and the ways to address differences in terms of academic achievement, learning style, interest, or expertise has been gained (Gardner, 1983; Renzulli, 1978; Tomlinson, 1995). Differentiation requires a standard, an instrument, or an assessment to identify, address, and compare the differences between students. In other words, individual difference is defined by a standard or an assessment task. While everything is uncertain and complicated by student-teacher interactions, from the perspective of efficacy, taking every student as an individual case is not an efficient way of educating students.

What did master teachers say? We cannot see the uniqueness of every student just by "gathering the petals of the flower" (Tagore, cited in Scott, 2009). Master teachers of attuned pedagogy tend to see every student as a human being and tend not to describe them in term of categories, such as learning style, intelligence, or personality. It is not because they do not have the vocabularies but because it is not proper. One of the master teachers said, "When we classify a student into different categories, we will lose the possibilities of the student" (Lu, 2015a, p. 20). "When we call for educating the whole child, how could we define students into a list of characteristics?" They appreciate the uniqueness whenever students are in different contexts, such as in a whole class, a small group, or individually. Teacher Cai said, "It is not the size of the class or the group, the core of differentiated instruction is set in the mindset of teachers" (Lu, 2015a, p. 28). In a focused group interview, master teachers used metaphors, such as universe, onion, or a flower to interpret what they perceive as a gifted student (Lu, 2015a).

Master teachers understand the uniqueness of every student in the classroom context like connoisseurs. Eisner (2002) believed that, just like music, connoisseurs can only cultivate the advanced music appreciation level upon full exercise of one single music expression mode based on varied experience, while teachers shall accumulate abundant experiences of classroom teaching, so they can recognise important aspects of teaching praxis and *perceive* students as an integration rather than identify and classify students. Eisner (2002) stressed, "if the main way [of teaching] is identification" and "turning a blind eye", then, no matter how many years it takes, it will do nothing to cultivate ability. To cultivate ability, human behaviours and details need to be carefully explored and perceived. "Watching is necessary but basically a task, and the real achievement is to understand and discern" (p. 223). Master teachers aim to understand and discern the uniqueness of every student rather than classifying them into different categories.

Intimate Relationship. From the time of Confucius to the master teachers we interviewed, the view is that close relationships between teachers and students are essential for teaching in Chinese culture. In order to appreciate wine or art, we must first be able to truly see the arts or taste the wine, and after we grasp their common characteristics of different varieties, we can appreciate the uniqueness of the wine or the art. In order to appreciate the uniqueness of every student, we have to truly be with the students. It requires teachers to build intimate professional relationships between themselves and the students. Understanding or knowing (Polanyi, 1979) is a personal participation, a responsible act that requires personal commitments and trusteeship. To master teachers, being attuned means an intuitive consideration or sensitivity to every aspect, especially every subtle change of a student's situation. Understanding is established through personal, emotional, and practical interaction and ends with new articulated understanding. As Eisner (2002) emphasised, practical educational aesthetics is building *relationships* echoed in the dynamic learning context.

With the personal (but professional) intimacy and trusteeship, the master teachers see the complexity of each little universe inside the student. As William James (1899/2008) said:

> We gain confidence in respect to any method which we are using as soon as we believe that it has theory as well as practice at its back. Most of all, it fructifies our independence, and it reanimates our interest, to see our subject at two different angles, to get a stereoscopic view, so to speak, of the youthful organism who is our enemy, and while handling him with all our concrete tact and divination, to be able, at the same time, to represent to ourselves the curious inner elements of his mental machine. Such a complete knowledge as this of the pupil, at once intuitive and analytic, is surely the knowledge at which every teacher ought to aim. (p. 11)

During long, daily-based, close interaction with students, master teachers become acquainted with each one of their students (Jackson, 1996) and plan and adjust teaching based on these understandings. They construct the immersive "stereoscopic view" of children (James, 1899/2008), an intuitional and holistic perception of children based on the personal commitment and trusteeship and also an appreciation of insights to gifted children in life and development. By integrating the immersive 'stereoscopic view' into the classroom contexts, all master teachers object to comparing students or categorising students' abilities, but tend to personalise every element they perceive during the teaching process.

Following the Curve of Contextual Changes. The processes and effectiveness of differentiated instruction are found to bond contextually, socially, and culturally (Tomlinson, 2017). The more strategies available or being implemented do not necessarily mean the teaching would or should go smoothly without variations (Eisner, 2002; Jackson, 1996). There is always something unexpected happening in the classroom. The biggest challenge of differentiated instruction is making professional judgements appropriately based on every student's needs and the dynamics of context (Smith, 2017; Tomlinson, 2017). Furthermore, it is assumed that the more strategies or models available to teachers, the easier it is for teachers to differentiate (Dixon, Yssel, McConnell, & Hardin, 2014; Heacox, 2002). Researchers and educators are trying to propose more strategies or models to reduce the loading of teachers' work and reduce the risk of personal judgements (Dixon et al., 2014; Heacox, 2002). In contrast, attuned pedagogy relies on and appreciates teachers' personal judgements. Artistic teaching and qualitative judgement are required to understand and discern characteristics that appear in both contexts and behaviours. The proper ways needed for responding to student's needs seem more personal, but this does not make the understanding subjective (Eisner, 2002).

While recognising the variation and uncertainty of the classroom, master teachers see variation in the classroom as the opportunity for teaching and learning (Lu, 2015a). Instead of being focused on the stable elements in the context, master teachers look for variations and grasp them for teaching. Giftedness has the dynamic nature of multiple dimensions and fulfilment; hence, for master teachers, variation is the opportunity to discover and understand all the possibilities of gifted children. Variation is the opportunity to keep the teaching and learning fluid and alive, like an artist creates according to qualitative features, such as rhythms, rhymes, atmospheres, and the like. Based on qualitative judgement, master teachers can interpret gifted children and consider all gifted students as persons of great potential, to observe students' uniqueness with their own experience and knowledge and cultivate gifted children to be complete and unique learners by means of learning activities. This kind of personal judgement is established based on the intimate contact with 'a hidden reality' (Polanyi, 1979). Polanyi (1979) said it is:

> a contact that is defined as the condition for anticipating an indeterminate range of yet unknown (and perhaps yet inconceivable) true implications. It seems reasonable to describe this fusion of the personal and the objective as Personal Knowledge. Personal knowledge is an intellectual commitment, and as such inherently hazardous. (p. iv)

As Tomlinson (2003) pointed out, differentiation is a way of thinking, believing, and attitudinal rather than practice or pedagogy, and Smith (2009a, 2017) proposed an ecological systemic and holistic view of differentiation as a dynamic interconnected process, of which differentiated instruction is only one aspect of differentiation. In terms of the dynamics of differentiation then—such as multiplicity, flexibility, and continuity—attuned pedagogy as the art of mastering changes is the artistry of differentiated instruction. The master teachers are the artists of teaching who:

> can grasp a situation and—depending on the nature of the learners, the social context, the intended instructional outcomes, and the particular conditions that prevail—make enlightened choices regarding the most appropriate subject matter, the right objectives, and the best pedagogy. (Rubin, 1989, p. 31)

The Praxis of Attuned Pedagogy

As mentioned above, attuned pedagogy is a kind of professional judgement that bridges between tacit and explicit knowledge in which teachers draw on clues, a sense of pattern, or underlying conditions based on an intimately close professional relationship between students and teachers. Master teachers of attuned pedagogy are the masters who are aware of the changes in the classroom context, can grasp the implications of the changes and can make the best out of the changes for student's learning. The critical question is how the master teachers implement it efficiently; in other words, what is the logic of processivity regarding the efficiency of attuned pedagogy? Based on the analyses of the master teacher studies (Lu, 2015a), four recurrent themes emerged: (a) inspiring volition, (b) following natural tendencies, (c) moderate in-between, and (d) leaving space. Although every master teacher emphasised that the four themes are intertwined and are all closely related with each other dynamically in the teaching context, they are worth distinguishing for delineating the concept of attuned pedagogy. Each of the themes of efficient attuned pedagogy will be discussed individually:

Inspiring volition to discipline the mind. "The human understanding is no dry light but receives infusion from the will and affections" (Bacon, 1620/2019). The challenge of educating gifted children is always the nonrational of meaning making not a matter of authority, textual, or pedagogic. In "the culture of education", Bruner (1996) emphasises that "learning to be a scientist is not the same as learning science: it is learning a culture, with all the attendant non-rational meaning making that goes with it" (p. 132). Likewise, educating a child to fulfil his or her potential is very different from educating a child based on his or her identified giftedness. Teacher Siou said that:

educating a gifted child is cultivating the child's mind regardless how gifted he or she is. Teaching a child with giftedness, obviously, we have to identify what gifted means and how gifted the child is and put a lot of effort in to deal with the concept of giftedness. It is very ironic that in [professional training] it takes us so much time to learn the new concepts of gifted education, but does not leave us enough time to really understand the child's mind in our classrooms. (Lu, 2015a, p. 26)

Lu said it is wrong to assume that it is easy to teach gifted students since they are so smart. "Yes, gifted students are smart enough or capable to do whatever they are asked to do. However, it is only when he or she thinks that it is meaningful" (Lu, 2015a, p. 30). Teacher Siou said it is not a question of motivation. It is a question about "why do I learn this for"? For something to be considered as essential for master teachers regarding educating gifted children, it must fall within the bounds defined by belief and volition.

Taking mathematics learning as the platform, the purpose of Teacher Cai's teaching is developing children's habits of minds. She is concerned with how students think about mathematics, how they see the beauty of mathematics and, more than that, their character formation. Regarding the most important thing of teaching mathematics, Teacher Cai said:

When conducting "inquiry-based mathematics learning", in addition to understanding children's cognitive development and being familiar with mathematical knowledge, teachers shall not be satisfied with imparting knowledge but adopt "the method of discovery" for teaching, to enable gifted students to feel how mathematical principles are discovered and created in person like "mathematicians". Only in this way, students who are willing to think, [can have their creativity, confidence, and being able to show] initiative to explore problems ... cultivated. (Lu, 2015a, p. 33)

The most important thing for educating gifted students is making them 'fall in love' with learning and devote themselves to what they are learning. The question is not what kind of professionals they will become in the future but why they learn? It is a determined mind, not just a kind of motivation. Without purposeful learning, fine tuning to students' learning needs would not be efficient. "As long as students find [the task] meaningful to them, everything goes one by one. It is like putting together a jigsaw puzzle. Purposes and volition are the keys to bringing every piece together." Teacher Siou said, "there is nothing that can be done in the world without volition.

With strong commitment, gifted students would be able to accomplish everything" (Lu, 2015a, p. 24). Personal volition is purposively striving and consciously building up as a habit of mind over time. Teacher Cai emphasises disciplining students' minds is the best way to build up students' personal volition. As the saying goes, "the jade must be chiselled before it can be considered a gem". One cannot become useful without being cultivated. A jade cannot be made into anything if it is not cut and polished. Disciplining children's minds is necessary for making the best out of them, to cultivate their potential. This point is very similar to the concept of 10,000 hours practice for making perfect.

As Bruner (1996) said, "good science teachers place the emphasis on lived science making, rather than upon the achieved remains of already accomplished science" (p. 127). That is to say, good teaching shall pay more attention to the living process of discipline construction from beginning to end and not only enable students to explain the accomplished knowledge. Master teachers are concerned with the living discipline construction process and enlightening gifted children to sustain their passions in the area of interest.

Following the natural tendency to find the sweet spot. As mentioned above master teachers of attuned pedagogy focus on personal long-term purposes to drive students' passions. It is not only a kind of motivation for one unit or one area. It is not to fit individual differences or teachers' personal views but to guide the students based on the dynamic nature of students' unique ability and the context. The goal of education is to develop every student into a complete person in his or her current situation during the process, respecting every child's natural tendency to fully become himself or herself and grow to the highest level one can approach. What does natural tendency mean? Gadamer (1979) suggested that humans are not blindly obedient to the prescribed rules of a society. In everyday life, we always seek to be better and strive towards being the best of ourselves.

How do master teachers see students' natural tendencies? Master teachers always use 'disposition' to describe the uniqueness of gifted children. They consider all the students as special individuals with unlimited potential and emphasise teachers' guidance to support what gifted students need. But when being asked for their opinions about how bright a gifted student is or what their potential could be, it is not a simple question for master teachers to answer, and they usually have to make detailed lists of the long-term goals of each student. However, through careful observation of these teachers' adjustment in classroom teaching and analysis of subsequent interviews, we found that, in their minds, they have different levels of understanding towards each student, from being willing to devote to the student's learning to focusing on the student's learning performance; the combinations of all the students are varied (Lu, 2015a). Students' giftedness or natural tendency is not a set of characteristics or traits, but their learning potential is continuously unfolding through their interactions with the context (Lu, 2015a; Yen, 2015) and cannot be separated from the context or categorised by single characteristics. That is why master teachers do not preset groups before class; rather they structure the curriculum design to guide each student through the learning process in a whole class or smaller grouping contexts as they evolve within the teaching and learning contexts.

To master teachers, the most efficient way for developing the gifted child's potential is to see every student's giftedness as a continually evolving universe.

In fact, master teachers do not underestimate the importance of accomplished knowledge; they stress the importance of following students' natural learning tendencies for finding the sweet spot of effective teaching. Based on the strategic mechanism of flexibility, Teacher Ching said, "let every student find the position to exercise his or her talents . . . until where he or she can develop, and students usually go beyond your expectations" (Lu, 2015a, p. 25). To make certain to let the students love mathematics, Teacher Ching specifically and precisely points out:

> I will not tell any child's parents that your child can solve only one problem or your child can solve three problems, each child will be enlightened at different times in different classes. I will not presuppose how many problems each student can solve . . . , but I do consider the children, and I would think of the tools students can use and how to let students begin the master teachers' formulas in the simplest and the funniest way. . . (Lu, 2015a, p. 27)

Moderating in-between to trigger potential. Jackson (1996) pointed out that teaching is an opportunistic process, which means that neither the teacher nor the students can predict exactly what will happen next. He emphasised that outcomes may be unintended, and unexpected opportunities for achieving educational goals are constantly emerging. Master teachers who we interviewed did plan lessons, but they kept their plan open to seize upon the unexpected opportunities and used them to his/her and his/her student's advantage. And most of them actually looked forward to the occurrence of unexpected events. As Teacher Ching said, her students always surprised her, and to improvise with them is the most wonderful moment in her teaching. They see the path of teaching more closely resembles "the flight of a butterfly than the flight of a bullet" (Jackson, 1996, p. 167). For master teachers, potential is circumstantial. It exists in the context and has to be exploited from the context. They recognised that the best strategy for exploiting potential is to rely on the inherent potential of the situation and be carried along by it as it evolves (Jullien, 2004). Master teachers tended to be careful not to impose upon the course of student development any predetermined plan but ensure they are following the course that it is bound to take.

How do the master teachers trigger gifted students' potential in context? Master teachers enjoy *giving a hint* to different students and *guiding* them according to their subtle differences. Giving a hint to students enables students to *comprehend* knowledge, as well as enables teachers to express the key points of the learning content that they guide students to comprehend. This part involves many indescribable details. How do we know that students need to be given a hint? How do we give a hint? How do we judge that students have comprehended knowledge? How do we guide students? All of the above require the control of the details of situations, namely, the incidental teaching frequently mentioned by master teachers. This opportunity cannot be grasped unless there is an overall understanding of students' learning. Such teaching is incidental, but not arbitrary. It is master teachers' displays of the art of teaching in their precise understanding of subjects and students.

Not staying with the instructional plan, but staying closely to the students' or teacher's improvisation seems random. However, Teacher Cai believes that, "the students will tell you in all kinds of methods", namely, students' eyes, diaries, or notes, assignments, their gestures in class, parents' memorandum, or student's attitude towards assignments or learning activities. Confronting students with expressive faces in classroom teaching and continuously communicating with students' parents and other class teachers every day in the school, teachers *soak in* the information related to gifted students' learning continually. Teacher Cai said that, through constant contact with students every day, gifted teachers' understandings about students' abilities are hard to be specifically described or standardised just like in interest inventories, learning style questionnaires, or intelligence tests. It is more like "a feeling continuously accumulated in teaching and real" (Lu, 2015a, p. 27). As James (1899/2008) said, to be excellent teachers:

> We must have an additional endowment altogether, a happy tact and ingenuity to tell us what definite things to say and do when the pupil is before us. That ingenuity in meeting and pursuing the pupil, that tact for the concrete situation, though they are the alpha and omega of the teacher's art, are things to which psychology cannot help us in the least. (p. 14)

Leaving space to attune personalised connections. Taking every student's unique needs and leaving time and space to perceive students as a whole are critical to attuned pedagogy. Leaving space(留白 liu bai) is one of the Chinese painting techniques that allows the artist and the viewer to meander and elaborate in their inner world (Wu, 2018). Master teachers use this concept to describe how they connect to students personally. We all understand how busy teachers are in daily classroom life. They never have time to complete everything. Things just keep coming and pushing. Time is the most precious resource every teacher needs. Being attuned to every student requires lots of personal time and energy, especially building professional personal relationships. In between the structured classroom context and gifted children's educational needs, master teachers leave space purposely to allow them to attune to students' unique needs.

Leaving space is trying not to do something that interferes with students' personal pace and developmental understandings. To many teachers, especially principals in Taiwan, leaving space looks like teachers are not doing their job. To master teachers, however, this is the strength of respect, giving gifted students a good opportunity to see themselves and others. In panel discussions and in-depth interviews, many master teachers simultaneously mentioned that sometimes they are confused about how to guide gifted students well and begin to think they are not good teachers (Lu, 2015a). In class, all master teachers shall face all situations in the teaching field by themselves. Master teachers are aware that they may be unwittingly filling students' minds with knowledge or adult life experiences that may become the cage imprisoning their abilities. Hence, for master teachers, the problem is not how much to teach, but what and when not to teach, and the trust in students and keenness to self-limitations, to know when and where to stop. What master teachers always say to students is "what do you think" and "can you tell me why?" Teacher Miao provides space for free expression in classroom memorandums, and Teacher Ann gives students the preparation time after brainstorming. For master teachers, teaching constantly remains open, to provide the degree of freedom and discover all the possibilities of teaching and students' learning within this openness. Teacher Miao said, "careful observation, reflection, communication, adaptation, intervention, and diversified supports" (Lu, 2015a, p. 28).

Leaving space extends the elasticity of time and space, and teachers and students can freely call on each other to express their understandings, passion, care, and empathy, for it becomes control if without any awareness of care. That is to say, potential identification is the immersive integration of understanding rather than the classification of students; and potential development is the continuous construction in daily interaction rather than the script of instructional planning. Letting go of control, *attuned pedagogy* can be performed, and the reason why these teachers give up control is because they believe in the power of education and the uniqueness and potential of gifted students' learning.

The Goals of Attuned Pedagogy: Transforming Giftedness in Context

As Dewey and Dewey (1973) pointed out, each child has a strong individuality and every child must have a chance to show what she or he truly is, so that the teacher can find out what she or he really needs to make her or him a complete human being. A truly scientific education can develop only when "every student has an opportunity to express himself [or herself], to show what are his [or her] particular qualities, the teacher will have the material on which to base her [or his] plans of instruction" (Dewey & Dewey, 1973, p. 102). If the purpose of education is to make students complete human beings or to be the best of themselves or to reach their full potential, the question regarding effective differentiated instruction in gifted teaching is what it means to be 'a complete human being' or the best version of each gifted student.

Cultivating a complete competent *junzi*. Regarding the purpose of gifted education, master teachers are concerned with the ultimate goal of human development. The fundamental goal of gifted education is to perceive and understand gifted children *holistically* and help students to be fully developed persons as far as possible. As Lu (2015b) points out, becoming a *junzi* is the meme of Chinese education, a Chinese Confucian idea of supreme goodness, and the way which supreme goodness was achieved by Confucian scholars. The essential question that concerned Chinese philosophers was how people can realise the potential of humanity and the meaning of life. Scholars were advised to cultivate the self to become a *junzi*. In the *Analects,* Confucius said:

Cultivated junzi do not compete. (You might object by saying) do not they clearly do so in the case of archery? But before ascending (to shoot) they bow and defer to one another. And (after shooting) they descend and drink together. Such is the competition of the cultivated *junzi.* (Legge, 1893)

Archery was not intended to merely elicit particular behaviours or skills. The goal is to instill certain sensibilities, attitudes, and dispositions in the practitioner that is beyond knowledge or merely skill practicing (Lu, 2015b). Potential or giftedness is a multidimensional and compounded concept rather than a set of characteristics analysed with intelligence, thinking styles, interests, and aptitudes. Ultimately, educators are concerned about what kind of person we hope the child will become. Obviously, what master teachers aim to cultivate is not just a scientist, but a scientist of balanced development, a healthy organism, and a person fully displaying the value of human potential. May (1982) considered the human as a potential with certain structures. "The daimonic is the urge in every being to affirm itself, assert itself, perpetuate and increase itself...But these are the reverse side of the same assertion which empowers our creativity" (p. 123).

The key point of cultivating a complete competent *junzi* is to encourage students to go deep into the discipline and inner self. Master teachers truly believe in the power of education, and they strive to arouse and activate students' feelings and interests and encourage students for self-transformation. Hart (2010) stressed the transformation of the deep power of education. Transformation means surpassing the current form, and it is a movement towards integrality of "ability, inclination, and sensitivity" (Tishman, 2018) and an advance to diversification and uniqueness, so that we will become more special and move towards unification and sharing. With master teachers' eclectic guidance, students are able to cultivate themselves personally as well as connect their unique potential with human concerns.

In one of the early master studies, Chen (2014) explored the operational curricula of an art teacher's responsive pedagogies that focused on the differentiation aspects for those identified as artistically talented in an elementary school in Taiwan. In this qualitative study, the art teacher's responsive pedagogies were discussed in light of Confucian heritage. To some extent, the art teacher's pedagogy reflected the concept of nurturing a *junzi*, who has *Cai De Jian Bei* (才德兼備, both talent and virtue). The concept of giftedness as rooted in Chinese culture draws on the social responsibility of giftedness. The community-based art projects designed by the teacher aimed to cultivate students' sensitivity to human concerns. Likewise, Smith (2009b) proposed education for eco-engagement as a component of the *Model of Dynamic Differentiation* (MoDD) which reinforces the community engagement and the social sensitivities during differentiated teaching and learning. Through guided discovery, the teacher helped students make connections between their *Zh* (substance; intrinsic traits) and *Wen* (refinement; disciplined knowledge or dispositions; Chen, 2014). The art teacher played the role of connoisseur in personalising guidance to bridge different class elements with the individual students' unique readiness levels, interests, and learning profiles. She was not only attuned to multiple dimensions of the students' 'artistic selves' (Walsh, 2002), but she also integrated the students' unique potentials into a cooperative effort of *He Er Bu Tong* (和而不同, harmony but not uniformity).

Mutual transformation. How can attuned pedagogy not be confined to teachers' control but lead gifted children through dynamic integration between individuality and sociality? While differentiated instruction defines the artistry of teaching in accordance with the triangulated relationship between student seeking, teacher responding, and curriculum modification (Tomlinson, 2003), we propose that attuned pedagogy is defined by the mutual construction of the professional relationship between teachers and students as the artistry of differentiation based on the Taiwanese experience. Laying the learning path of exploration, orientation, and continuation synchronously, gifted students can be transformed, as well as teachers, through the process of attuned pedagogy. In fact, every teacher has the sense of educational mission and every master who is willing to reflect will face the complexity and positivity of classroom teaching. Master teachers are the mediators of the cultural transmission and at the same time they need courage to redefine the educational structure. Master teachers are great learners themselves in understanding students' developmental potential in imaginative, creative, and complete ways and enabling their teaching to become the palace to self-fulfilment (Eisner, 2002; Schwab, 1983).

Attuning to students provides the room to grow professionally for master teachers, on the one hand that can assist student development and, on the other hand, promoting self-development, which is the process that is the most inspiring and powerful. On the surface, achieving the curriculum and unit purposes and evaluation indexing are deserved targets. However, in attuning to gifted students' unique needs, master teachers reconcile the cognitive differences of *giftedness* within the school community, and with the teachers, parents, and the students, and then transform the differences to the willing goals the school community strives for. It is not a simple task but an opportunity to conduct creative transformation between teachers and students.

The mutual transformation experiences between teachers and students are very similar to the relationship of forgetting both yourself and the external world between viewers and artworks referred to by Armstrong (2000). Normally, viewers can see relations between parts by noticing details to further seize the whole as the whole, taking no account of the instrumental goal. There is no reaching and nothing to do with trying to reach a destination, but there is a lingering caress, and as a result, mutual absorption or learning and the possibility of mutual creation may eventuate. If teachers are compared to viewers and students are artworks, attuned pedagogy promotes students' talent while transforming teachers by mutual construction. That is, teaching benefits teachers' learning as well as students' learning.

Self-cultivation. *Junzi* is a powerful meme that inspires both Chinese students and teachers to achieve the complete human being. Among the many paths to *junzi* described in Chinese culture, self-cultivation is the most important meaning of Confucianism-influenced modern education. To comprehend the Chinese way of cultivating giftedness, the methods of self-cultivation by which to achieve a complete competent junzi must be examined. As we mentioned above, every student is unique. To master teachers, self-cultivation is the only way to grasp the insight of any field. As teacher Anna said, "they are the best learners which means they can educate themselves with mentors' supports" (Lu, 2015a, p. 27). How do students learn to be self-cultivated? To gifted students, staying with mentors who love to learn, especially their teacher in the elementary level, is the most efficient way.

Teacher Cai said, "we have to be a good learner if we want the gifted students to be good learners" (Lu, 2015a, p. 21). We are not sure if Gandhi really said, "If we could change ourselves, the tendencies in the world would also change. As a man changes his own nature, so does the attitude of the world change towards him. ... We need not wait to see what others do" (Morton, 2011), but it is still a proper interpretation regarding self-cultivation.

Implications for Research and Practice: Professional Development on Attuned Pedagogy

Only by truly understanding students, can teachers reconcile and balance the dynamic rhythmicity of teaching and learning, know which professional relationship is best for effective differentiated interaction with all students, and discern how to achieve effective results. Developing the expertise of attuned pedagogy would enable teachers to imagine and characterize the reality of teaching gifted students, testing their intuition, and developing an advanced perceptiveness and sensitivity to what is essential in the discovery of best-fit teaching and learning for students (Moustakas, 1990; Trotman, 2010). In this chapter, we proposed that attuned pedagogy is the artistry of differentiated instruction and we delineated the concept and practice of attuned pedagogy based on the study of master teachers' teaching. We will gain more insights if we can investigate more of how to make skilled teachers of differentiated instruction become more efficient artists and masters in their teaching practice to assist in building the theoretical foundation for professional development.

Practically. The dynamic process of attuned pedagogy is a continuous interconnected whole that is hard to be divided into many separate steps. So, attuned pedagogy is a process with all details together that will vary according to personnel, resources, and context and is much more than pondering skills and using strategies separately (Smith, 2015). Attuned pedagogy is about the attuned relationship between the teacher and the students, with students self-reflecting on their own growth and the teacher intuiting to the students' needs and nurturing them developmentally. Likewise, Tomlinson (2014) emphasised, "in differentiated classrooms, teachers ensure that students compete against themselves as they grow and develop more than they compete against one another, always moving toward—and often beyond—designated content goals (p. 3)."

Practically, we constantly use the 'teaching as an art' metaphor to reinforce 'education as an aesthetic process' (Eisner, 2000). Metaphorically, attuned pedagogy is like an 'art' and, for gifted educators in Taiwan, attuned pedagogy is the art of teaching that helps make the best out of every student. For developing this kind of artistry, we need to "have an additional endowment altogether, a happy tact, and ingenuity to tell us what definite things to say and do when the pupil is before us" (James, 2008, p. 123). This ingenuity, the master teacher's art, is a kind of personal knowledge which cannot be trained by psychology principles or strategies, but can be guided by experienced and wise mentors. How to bridge teachers' personal experiences into professional judgement will be essential for cultivating master teachers of attuned pedagogy.

Theoretically. Theoretically, it is difficult to define the artistic experience or philosophy of teaching that is based on scientific method. While Tomlinson (1995) proposed the continuum of differentiated instruction, the first indicator of macro-differentiation is the "articulated philosophy of student differences." It is assumed that teachers believe in and "want to focus on the child" (Tomlinson, 1995, p. 79), their individual needs, and bring out the best in every student, but do they focus on the whole child? Are teachers aware of the need to articulate their own philosophy of student differences, are they attuned to their students' individual needs, and do they then change their level of differentiated instruction according to the student's developmental phase?

Based on the holistic view of every child, the continuum of instrumental, ego-generated, and receptive mode regarding the artistic teaching process of differentiation may provide a framework for further professional development and research on attuned pedagogy (Deikman, 2000; Dewey, 1934; Hart, 2001). The novice teachers of differentiated instruction are mostly at the state of the instrumental mode, where their focus is on the instruments of the teaching strategies, resources, and evaluation tools of differentiated instruction. Novice teachers—like most novice artists—are still learning to use their tools or instruments and cannot yet balance their understanding of the student's needs with the student's uniqueness and strengths. Conversely, experienced teachers are just like master artists who are skilled at using their tools, who can gradually become attuned to the student's uniqueness, strengths, and potential and teach accordingly. Most experienced teachers are able to describe their differentiated strategies or understand their students based on their professional knowledge and understandings. While the masters of attuned pedagogy (like most great artists) might use the same teaching strategies (that can be likened to a master artist's favourite tools) for years, the importance is becoming familiar with every way to use their strategies (or artist's tools) effectively within varying contexts with varying students for varying outcomes (producing artful masterpieces in the interim). The differences of differentiating instruction for supporting gifted students between the novice, the skilled, and the master are due to what they see as the holistic child. As the master teacher said: "Every child is different in his/her own way."

What we do depends on how and what we see. As mentioned above, master teachers construct a 'stereoscopic view' of children (James, 1899/2008), an intuitional and holistic perception of students based on the intimate professional relationship. How do master teachers develop this kind of tact for the classroom context? It requires an artistic receptive mode (Deikman, 2000) that welcomes the intuitive flash of appreciation absorbed when teaching and being able to recognise the beauty of every child. While there are a set of gifted characteristics that can be defined in terms of constructs, such as intelligence, thinking styles, passions, and aptitudes, there are other modes that involve a more receptive, open-ended, intuitive recognition of the student's needs—just like most great artists do when producing a great work of art. With this mode of mind, we may be able to shift our attention from the normally dominant categories of gifted characteristics and be more open to the possibility for intuition, insight, and imagination of the whole child. With the artistic receptive mode, the teachers can intuitively accrue from their experience, which can be communicated to others and recognised by their community, so others will gain more insights regarding the artistry of differentiation.

Conclusion: The Art of Differentiated Instruction

In the Chinese culture, teaching is neither a profession nor a job and education is a mission of cultivating a better human being and making a better world. While the world is constantly changing and human beings are constantly developing, master teachers *attune* to the changes rather than try to control the changes. Attuned pedagogy is the art of mastering changes for the ultimate goal of effective education.

The fundamental goal of gifted education is to perceive and understand each child holistically and help to fully develop them as persons. Thus, effective teachers of the gifted must also be effective learners because effective teaching is a 'mutually constructive' process between teachers and students. This is the millennial practice of Yin Cai Shi Jiao (因材施教) in Chinese culture which we translate as *Attuned Pedagogy*, the artistry of differentiation, based on the Taiwanese experience. However, the challenge of gifted education in Taiwan is the implementation of policies advocating differentiation and, consequently, the marginalisation of effective cultural practices that embody attuned pedagogy

A widely expressed concern among teachers confronted with policies on differentiation is how to do it in the context of their classrooms, schools, and culture. In this chapter, we present three essential principles and four praxis strategies of Attuned Pedagogy to help guide differentiating teaching and learning more effectively for gifted students. There are master teachers who are concerned about student potential development in various cultural contexts, such as: those breaking through the teaching pattern of one-size-fits-all and basing their teaching on the concepts of differentiated instruction in heterogeneous classes of general education (Tomlinson, 2017); those teacher communities of learning who scaffold students within the learning culture of mutual cooperation and investigation in Japan (Sato, 2008); and the gifted master teachers who practice attuned pedagogy as reiterated in this chapter. Such teachers observe students' uniqueness within various kinds of contexts and attempt to develop students' potential. More importantly, they recognise that potential would be enhanced or reduced if the contexts have been changed. Their practices reflect the connotations of their social cultures, like deep ploughing of *gifted education pedagogy* (Hertzog, 2005) in various cultural soils to respond to all the students' need for challenges in the learning context, including those individuals who have shown excellent learning potential.

The concept of differentiation has been advocated for decades across many countries as an effective approach to support gifted students. The artistry of differentiated instruction from a Taiwanese cultural perspective is one of the effective approaches that teachers have used for centuries. If we can appreciate the best practices of differentiated instruction in different cultures, we may revive the diversity of cultural practices and bring out the best version of every student worldwide. As Geertz (1983) pointed out, "We need, in the end, something rather more than local knowledge. We need a way of turning its varieties into commentaries one upon another, the one lighting what the other darkens" (Geertz, 1983, p.233).

By reviewing the practical education language in our cultural heritage, we find the artistry of attuned pedagogy makes learning alive and varies with different people, times, and places, but the fundamental things remain the same. For example, potential development and cultivation become clear in the master teachers' minds. Provided this goal or purpose is mastered, any strategy in favour of differentiation can be conducted. Thus, teachers do not use special skills, strategies, or fixed models, but build learning potential through guidance of harmony in diversification with long-term purposes. In terms of attuned pedagogy, the task of the educator has to be rooted in a wisdom that, "unites knowledge, imagination, and the good" (Scheffler, 1985, p. 12).

Cross-References

- ▶ Assessment, Pedagogy, and Curriculum: Part IV Introduction
- ▶ Bricolage and the Evolution of Giftedness and Talent in Taiwan
- ▶ Creativity Talent Development: Fostering Creativity in Schools
- ▶ Differentiation of Instruction for Gifted Learners: Collated Evaluative Studies of Teacher Classroom Practices
- ▶ Engaging Gifted Students in Solving Real Problems Creatively: Implementing the Real Engagement in Active Problem-Solving (REAPS) Teaching/Learning Model in Australasian and Pacific Rim Contexts
- ▶ Exploring Diverse Perceptions of Wise Persons: Wisdom in Gifted Education
- ▶ Fostering and Developing Talent in Mentorship Programs: The Mentor's Perspectives
- ▶ Gifted Education in the Asia-Pacific: From the Past for the Future – An Introduction
- ▶ In Search of an Explanation for an Approach-Avoidance Pattern in East Asia: The Role of Cultural Values in Gifted Education
- ▶ Some Implications for the Future of Gifted Education in the Asia-Pacific
- ▶ Spirituality and Giftedness: Threading the Path of Identity
- ▶ The Development of Mana: Five Optimal Conditions for Gifted Māori Student Success
- ▶ The Lives and Achievements of Four Extraordinary Australians: A Master, a Maker, an Introspector, and an Influencer

References

Armstrong, J. (2000). *Move closer: An intimate philosophy of art*. New York, NY: Farrar, Straus, & Giroux.

Bacon, F. (2019). *Novum Organum*. New York, NY: P. F. Collier & Son. (Original work published 1902).

Bruner, J. (1962). *On knowing: Essays for the left hand*. Cambridge, MA: Harvard University Press.

Bruner, J. (1996). *The culture of education*. Cambridge, MA: Harvard University Press.

Chen, W.-R. (2014). Cultivating a Jian Zi: Exploring an art teacher's responsive pedagogy for the development of art talent in Taiwan. *Gifted Education International, 33*(1), 18–33. https://doi.org/10.1177/0261429414548967

Chen, J., Chen, C., & Pan, Y. (2008). A study on differentiated instruction in Taipei elementary gifted education. *Journal of Gifted Education, 8*(2), 1–22.

Dai, D. Y., & Chen, F. (2014). *Paradigms of gifted education: A guide to theory-based, practice-focused research*. Waco, TX: Prufrock Press.

Deikman, A. (2000). Service as knowing. In T. Hart, P. Nelson, & K. Puhakka (Eds.), *Transpersonal knowing: Exploring the horizon of consciousness* (pp. 303–318). Albany: State University of New York Press.

Dewey, J. (1929). *The sources of a science of education*. New York, NY: Liveright. Retrieved from https://archive.org/details/sourcesofascienc009452mbp/page/n5

Dewey, J., & Dewey, E. (1973). *Schools for tomorrow*. New York, NY: Dutton.

Dewey, J. (2005). *Art as experience*. NY: Perigee Books.

Dixon, F. A., Yssel, N., McConnell, J. M., & Hardin, T. (2014). Differentiated instruction, professional development, and teacher efficacy. *Journal for the Education of the Gifted, 37*(2), 111–127.

Eisner, E. W. (2002). *The arts and the creation of mind*. New Heaven, CT: Yale University Press.

Gadamer, H. (1979). Practical philosophy as a model of the human sciences. *Research in Phenomenology, 9*, 74–85.

Gagné, F. (2009). Debating giftedness: Pronat vs. Antinat. In L. V. Shavinina (Ed.), *International handbook on giftedness* (pp. 155–198). Dordrecht, The Netherlands: Springer.

Gagné, F. (2013). The DMGT: Changes within, beneath, and beyond. *Talent Development and Excellence, 5*, 5–19.

Gardner, H. (1983). *Frames of mind: The theory of multiple intelligences*. New York, NY: Basic Books.

Geertz, C. (1983). Local Knowledge. NY: Basic Books.

Hart, T. (2001). *From information to transformation: Education for the evolution of consciousness*. NY: Peter Lang Publishing, Inc.

Hart, L. (2010). *On the wings of self-esteem: A companion for personal transformation*. Oakland, CA: Uplift.

Haste, H. (2008). Constructing competence: Discourse, identity, and culture. In I. Plath, I. Graudenz, & H. Breit (Eds.), *Kultur-Handlung-Demokratie* (pp. 109–134). Wiesbaden, Germany: VS Verlag für Sozialwissenschaften.

Heacox, D. (2002). *Differentiating instruction in the regular classroom: How to reach and teach all learners*. Minneapolis, MN: Free Spirit Publishing.

Hertzog, N. B. (2005). Equity and access: Creating general education classrooms responsive to potential giftedness. *Journal for the Education of the Gifted, 29*(2), 213–257. https://doi.org/10.1177/016235320502900205

Huang, R. (2014). *A comparative study on the differentiated curriculum of gifted education between Taiwan and China* (Unpublished master thesis). National University of Taipei, Taiwan.

Jackson, P. W. (1996). *Life in classrooms*. New York, NY: Teachers College, Columbia University.

James, W. (1899/2008). *Talks to teachers on psychology and to students on some of life's ideals*. New York, NY: Holt. (Original work published 1899).

Jullien, F. (2004). *A treatise on efficacy: Between Western and Chinese thinking* (J. Lloyd, Trans.). Honolulu, HI: University of Hawaii. (Original work published 1996).

Lave, J. (1996). Teaching as learning, in practice. *Mind, Culture & Activity, 3*(3), 149–164. https://doi.org/10.1207/s15327884mca0303_2

Legge, J. (1893). *The Chinese classics.* Oxford, UK: Oxford University Press. Retrieved from https://ctext.org/zh?en=on

Lu, C. H. (2015a). *Individuating: Teachers' praxis of connoisseurship of gifted children's potential* (National Science Council Report, No. NSC 101-2410-H-152-014-MY2). Taipei, Taiwan: National Taipei University of Education, Department of Special Education.

Lu, C. H. (2015b). The Chinese way of goodness. In S. Hsu & Y.-Y. Wu (Eds.), *Education as cultivation in Chinese culture* (pp. 45–62). Singapore, Singapore: Springer.

Maker, J. C. (1982). *Curriculum development for the gifted.* Rockville, MD: Aspen.

Martin, A. (2011). Personal best approaches to academic development: Implications for motivation and assessment. *Educational Practice and Theory, 33*(1), 93–99. https://doi.org/10.7459/ept/33.1.06

Maslow, A. H. (1968). *Toward a psychology of being.* New York, NY: Van Nostrand.

May, R. (1982). *The courage to create.* New York, NY: Bantam Books.

Morton, B. (2011, August 29). Falser words were never spoken. *The New York Times.* https://www.nytimes.com/2011/08/30/opinion/falser-words-were-never-spoken.html

Moustakas, C. E. (1990). *Heuristic research: Design, methodology, and applications.* Newbury Park, CA: Sage.

Persson, R. S. (2012). Cultural variation and dominance in a globalized knowledge-economy: Towards a culture-sensitive research paradigm in the science of giftedness. *Gifted and Talented International, 27*(1), 15–48. https://doi.org/10.1080/15332276.2012.11673603

Polanyi, M. (1979). *Personal knowledge towards a post-critical philosophy.* London, UK: Routledge.

Renzulli, J. S. (1978). What makes giftedness? Re-examining a definition. *Phi Delta Kappan, 60,* 180–184, 261.

Rubin, L. (1989). The thinking teacher: Cultivating pedagogical intelligence. *Journal of Teacher Education, 40,* 31–34. https://doi.org/10.1177/002248718904000607

Sato, M. (2008). Philosophy on the restoration of schools in Japan: The vision, principles and activity system of the learning community. *E-Journal of All India Association for Educational Research.* Retrieved from http://www.aiaer.net/ejournal/vol20208/3.htm

Scheffler, I. (1985). *Of human potential: An essay in the philosophy of education.* Boston, MA: Routledge & Kegan Paul.

Schwab, J. J. (1983). The practical 4: Something for curriculum professors to do. *Curriculum Inquiry, 13*(3), 239–265. https://doi.org/10.1080/03626784.1983.11075885

Scott, J. (Ed.). (2009). *Bengali flower: 50 selected poems from India and Bangladesh by Rabindranath Tagore.* Newark, NJ: Unique Art & Gifts Publishing.

Smith, S. R. (2009a). A dynamic ecological framework for differentiating the primary curriculum. *Gifted and Talented International, 24*(2), 9–20. https://doi.org/10.1080/15332276.2009.11673526

Smith, S. R. (2009b). Differentiated education for eco-engagement: Supporting teachers and challenging gifted students through community service projects. In D. Wood (Ed.), *The gifted challenge: Challenging the gifted* (pp. 79–89). Mudgee, NSW: NSW Association of Gifted and Talented Children: Lynx Printing.

Smith, S. (2015a). A dynamic differentiation framework for talent enhancement: Findings from syntheses and teacher perceptions. *Australasian Journal of Gifted Education, 24,* 59–72.

Smith, S. R. (2015b). Differentiating teaching for sustainability for diverse student learning. In N. Taylor, F. Quinn, & C. Eames (Eds.), *Educating for sustainability in primary schools: Teaching for the future* (pp. 65–87). Rotterdam, The Netherlands: Sense Publishers.

Smith, S. R. (2017). Model of dynamic differentiation (MoDD): Innovation education for talent development. In T. S. Yamin, K. W. McCluskey, T. Lubart, D. Ambrose, K. C. McCluskey, & S. Linke (Eds.), *Innovation education* (pp. 41–66). Ulm, Germany: The International Centre for Innovation in Education (ICIE).

Smith, S. R., & Lu, C. H. (2015). Nurturing interdisciplinary interconnections to enhance theoretical talent development: Using metaphor to reflect on Ambrose's insights for gifted education. *International Journal for Talent Development and Creativity, 3,* 77–92.

Tishman, S. (2018). *Slow looking: The art and practice of learning through observation.* New York, NY: Routledge.

Tomlinson, C. A. (1995). Deciding to differentiate instruction in middle school: One school's journey. *Gifted Child Quarterly, 39*(2), 77–87. https://doi.org/10.1177/001698629503900204

Tomlinson, C. A. (1999). *The differentiated classroom: Responding to the needs of all learners.* Alexandria, VA: ASCD.

Tomlinson, C. A. (2001). *How to differentiate instruction in mixed ability classroom* (2nd ed.). Alexandria, VA: ASCD.

Tomlinson, C. A. (2003). *Fulfilling the promise of the differentiated classroom: Strategies and tools for responsive teaching.* Alexandria, VA: ASCD.

Tomlinson, C. A. (2017). *How to differentiate instruction in academically diverse classrooms* (3rd ed.). Alexandria, VA: ASCD.

Trotman, D. (2010). Liberating the wise educator: Cultivating professional judgment in educational practice. In A. Craft, H. Gardner, & G. Claxton (Eds.), *Creativity, wisdom and trusteeship: Exploring the role of education.* New York, NY: Sage.

Vygotsky, L. S. (1978). *Mind and society: The development of higher mental processes.* Cambridge, MA: Harvard University Press.

Walsh, D. (2002). Constructing an artistic self: A cultural perspective. In L. Bresler & C. Thompson (Eds.), *The arts in children's lives: Context, culture, and curriculum* (pp. 101–111). Dordrecht, The Netherlands: Kluwer Academic Publishers.

Wu, W. T. (2013). The 40th anniversary of gifted education in Taiwan (III): Confusion and enlightenment. *Gifted Education Quarterly, 128,* 7–14.

Wu, R. (2018). Xie Yi painting: A Chinese cultural therapy. In D. Scharff (Ed.), *Psychoanalysis and psychotherapy in China* (Vol. 2, pp. 1–36). New York, NY: Routledge.

Yen, H.-C. (2015). Human nature and learning in ancient China. In S. Hsu & Y.-Y. Wu (Eds.), *Education as cultivation in Chinese culture* (pp. 19–43). Singapore, Singapore: Springer.

Chin-hsieh Lu PhD is a professor from the Department of Special Education, National Taipei University of Education (NTUE) in Taiwan. She was the president of the Chinese Association of Gifted Education from 2012 to 2016. For the past 5 years, Professor Lu and her colleagues have been developing and studying ways to implement a differentiated instruction and design-based learning (UbD+DBL) model with gifted children and teachers. Her research interests focus on curriculum design, disadvantage, and differentiation models, while her publications mainly focus on assessment and curriculum design for gifted students and conceptual foundations of giftedness from the cultural-historical perspective.

Wei-Ren Chen PhD is an assistant professor from the Department of Special Education, National Chiayi University (NCU) in Taiwan. He received his doctoral degree in Curriculum and Instruction from the University of Illinois at Urbana, Champaign. Since 2013, Professor Chen has worked with his team members to design a professional development project that guided teachers to generate curriculum based on design-based learning as a way of implementing gifted pedagogy in general education. His research focuses on curriculum differentiation and teacher professional learning in the field of gifted education. With an interest in the arts, he loves to explore aesthetic qualities in teaching, learning and life.

Differentiation of Instruction for Gifted Learners: Collated Evaluative Studies of Teacher Classroom Practices

43

Joyce VanTassel-Baska, Gail Fischer Hubbard, and Janice I. Robbins

Contents

J. VanTassel-Baska (✉) · J. I. Robbins
The College of William and Mary, Williamsburg, VA, USA
e-mail: jlvant@wm.edu; jirobb@wm.edu

G. F. Hubbard
Prince William County Public Schools, Manassas, VA, USA
e-mail: gfhubbard@aol.com

© Springer Nature Singapore Pte Ltd. 2021
S. R. Smith (ed.), *Handbook of Giftedness and Talent Development in the Asia-Pacific*,
Springer International Handbooks of Education,
https://doi.org/10.1007/978-981-13-3041-4_45

Abstract

In this chapter the focus is on research findings from multiple evaluation studies on the teacher use of differentiated practices for gifted learners that have implications for best practice in gifted education internationally. Research questions centred on what specific differentiation practices were employed with gifted learners and distinctions found between levels of teaching and content areas. Using the *Classroom Observation Scale-Revised* (COS-R) with 329 teachers in six different school districts in four states in the Eastern United States, we report data on differentiation practices that suggest that teachers of the gifted as well as regular classroom teachers underutilise these practices, do not match them to instructional purposes and fail to implement them as effectively as possible to have an impact on gifted student learning. Moreover, the lack of consistent use of flexible grouping practices to support instructional goals was apparent in the majority of regular classroom contexts. Findings also suggested that teachers who were using differentiated practices were using them at least somewhat effectively, suggesting that some teachers were successful in implementing best practice strategies. The results of these multiple studies also revealed that middle school classrooms were less effective in the use of differentiation for the gifted than either elementary or high schools. A comparison of results by subject area showed that mathematics classrooms were the most successful in implementing differentiation practices for the gifted. Implications from the study suggest that more careful attention needs to be paid to the use of specific differentiation practices found in the research literature and taught in model university gifted education training programs. A model of classroom organisation and delivery is also presented in the chapter to provide direction for program design and development. This model illustrates the relationship of teacher behaviours to learning outcomes for students. The chapter concludes with a set of recommendations for practitioners on improving differentiation practices in classrooms for gifted learners.

Keywords

Acceleration · Differentiation · Classroom observation · Higher level thinking · Instructional grouping · Instructional strategies · Professional development · Teacher behaviours

The aims in this chapter are to:
1. Illustrate what differentiated strategies are effective with gifted learners, enumerating 26 behaviours in six categories.
2. Suggest that classroom observation is a viable data source for evaluating the use of differentiation in classrooms.

3. Provide data that show that differentiation use varies by teacher, level of schooling and subject area.
4. Show that there is a commonality among specific differentiation strategies that are used and not used in current practice.
5. Demonstrate that teachers at the high school level are more effective in the use of differentiation strategies than elementary or middle school teachers.
6. Show how mathematics teachers are the most effective in the use of differentiation in comparison to English, science or social sciences peers.
7. Show how the *William and Mary Classroom Observation Scales-Revised* works as an instrument designed for observing key aspects of differentiation practices, including curriculum planning and delivery, accommodation to individual differences, materials and strategy utilisation, critical thinking strategies, creative thinking strategies, and analysis and inquiry strategies.
8. Argue that schools actively employ multiple approaches to improve the use of effective differentiation practices through targeted professional development, monitoring of classroom instruction, employment of standards as a checklist, incorporating differentiation into annual school improvement plans, and assessing gifted student advanced learning benchmarks.

Introduction

When we consider the development of programs and services for gifted learners, the term 'differentiation' is often used to encapsulate how we envision those programs and services. Often the nature of the service and even the area in which it is offered is less critical than is the use of materials and strategies that promote the use of higher level thinking skills and processes that will move gifted students towards self-directed learning and enable them to understand and act on issues and problems in the real world (VanTassel-Baska, 2017). An equally important goal is to provide these students with advanced academic opportunities and preparation for college and careers in a broad array of professional fields. Because programs for gifted students seek to satisfy these goals, there is a need to ensure that differentiation of instruction is occurring at all levels of schooling in gifted programs (Dixon, Yssel, McConnell, & Hardin, 2014).

Purpose of the Evaluation Study

In the United States, education is primarily the responsibility of state government. States vary in their procedures for administering gifted programs. Some states mandate gifted identification and services, some mandate identification but not services, and other states provide 'discretionary' programs in this area. The majority of states do require state plans, however, that include procedures for identification. Fewer states specify the nature of programming in these plans, leaving decisions about models and differentiation practices to individual districts.

With the National Association for Gifted Children Pre-K to Grade 12 Gifted Programming Standards (Johnsen, 2012) in place in the United States, it was important to examine the use of differentiation practices and the performance of teachers in districts that have strong gifted education programs and services in place at all levels. Given access to multiple modalities of professional development and the use of in-district training opportunities, are teachers taking advantage of these opportunities and converting them into differentiation practices in their classrooms to the benefit of both gifted and non-gifted learners? In this chapter, the purpose of the study was to examine the prevalence and effectiveness of differentiation practices in selected classrooms across K–12 in six districts in the Eastern United States, all of which have well-established programs for the gifted. Many of these programs have been in place for 30 years or more.

This collated evaluation study is of interest to Asia-Pacific educators because of its approach to methodology, using observed teacher behaviours in the classroom, rather than self-reports, and compiling those observations across schools and districts. Moreover, the evaluation study sought to specify what classroom-based instructional practices are used by teachers who have participated in professional development in gifted education. Both in Asian-Pacific countries and in the United States, educators in gifted education are seeking to increase the use of differentiation in classrooms in order to enhance the learning of gifted students. Thus, studies that focus on specific instructional practices of teachers are of interest.

Review of Relevant Literature

The following brief review of the literature focuses on recent studies of teacher use of differentiation, and more distally, on selected studies of professional development aimed at enhancing the use of differentiation.

Effective differentiation for gifted learners is highly dependent on the quality of teaching that is provided in their classrooms. Studies of common characteristics of teachers of the gifted have revealed traits such as high intelligence, passion, humour and flexibility (Gentry, Steenbergen-Hu, & Choi, 2011). Mills (2003) studied the characteristics of exceptional teachers of the gifted, reporting that subject matter expertise, coupled with passion for the subject, were the most critical factors in respect to effective student learning. These studies certainly can inform our selection of teachers to work with the gifted. However, most schools work with existing staff members in differentiating instruction for this population, generally providing professional development for teachers assigned to classes which include gifted learners.

Studies have shown that teachers have a strong impact on their students' learning and that gifted students are particularly influenced by their teachers' attitudes and actions (Croft, 2003; Roberts, 2006). Researchers have noted that teachers of the gifted demonstrate particular characteristics and competencies and use a range of teaching practices to achieve optimal learning experiences for their gifted students (Chan, 2001; Knopfelmacher & Kronborg, 2003; Kronborg, 2017; Kronborg & Plunkett, 2013; Maker & Schiever, 2010). One study at least has suggested that students have a preference for greater choice in their own activities as a prevailing approach to be used by their instructors (Kanevsky, 2015).

Some studies have focused on the competencies of trained versus untrained teachers of the gifted, demonstrating the skill set of teaching for higher order thinking to be more in evidence among trained teachers and thus more aligned with the needs of these students in the classroom (e.g., see Hansen & Feldhusen, 1994). Others have shown that training in differentiation can positively impact the increased use of differentiation of regular classroom teachers over time (e.g., VanTassel-Baska et al., 2008). Yet, despite positive outcomes being reported from such studies, the problem with the lack of fidelity of implementation remains large as seen in other studies across decades that have shown limited use of differentiation in regular classrooms that include gifted students (e.g., see Westberg, Archambault, Dobyns, & Salvin, 1993; Westberg & Dauost, 2003) and an attitudinal mindset of teachers as being apologetic, but having no time to differentiate effectively for this population (Farkas & Duckett, 2008). From these research studies, it is evident that training alone is not the sole solution to effective differentiation.

Recent studies have also been mixed in their findings related to the role of professional development in changing the instructional practices of teachers who work with the gifted (see Jolly & Jarvis, 2018). One small-scale study (Peters & Jolly, 2018) reports no differences, regardless of the degree of training in gifted education instructional practices, among Australian teachers. The authors agree that classroom observations of actual practice might have presented a different picture than teacher self-reports did in their study. On the other hand, Kronborg and Plunkett's (2012, 2013) studies of Australian pre-service teachers and teachers who have completed gifted education coursework report positive changes in attitudes and teacher competencies when working with gifted students.

Yet, Miller's (2009) study of 60 Australian elementary teachers, 65% of whom had received 12 hours of professional development in gifted education, suggests that regardless of the level of professional development, teacher beliefs about giftedness in students were the same. In another study of primary classrooms (Lassig, 2009), this was particularly true, related to the use of instructional grouping and acceleration, the two best researched differentiation approaches that may be employed in regular classrooms to accommodate the gifted. Even though teachers improved in their attitudes towards the gifted in the Lassig study, their use of instructional grouping and acceleration as positive and important differentiation strategies was not impacted.

In a cross-cultural comparison of teachers in specialised high schools for the gifted, Singapore teachers used significantly more differentiated strategies at a deeper level of implementations than their American counterparts (VanTassel-Baska et al., 2008). In a follow-up qualitative study, Singapore teachers attributed their increased implementation of differentiation to the practicum portion of their training, which allowed for continuing dialogue with more experienced teachers of the gifted in their subject areas (VanTassel-Baska, MacFarlane, & Feng, 2006). These studies would suggest that more focused and in-depth professional development may make a difference in the effective use of differentiation skills.

Several researchers have concluded that until teachers engage in professional learning in gifted education, there is no change or any improvement in attitudes towards the gifted nor any awareness or consciousness of gifted students' academic or educational needs (Geake & Gross, 2008; Kronborg & Plunkett, 2012; Lassig, 2009; Pedersen & Kronborg, 2014; Plunkett & Kronborg, 2011). While it would appear that professional development must be concerned about changing teacher attitudes, Guskey (2000) has strongly suggested in his research that classroom practice changes precede and influence changes in teacher attitudes.

Reviews of research in general education on the use of differentiation to promote student growth have also delivered mixed results. A recent study in the Netherlands (Deunk, Doolaard, & Smale, 2015) selected only 26 studies for review out of over 1000, based on several rigorous methodological criteria. Of these selected studies, only three were not from the United States. The studies that were assessed neither present a consistent nor cohesive picture of differentiation applied in classroom practice. In this climate of uncertainty about what is happening in classroom differentiation practices, the current study focuses on what teachers are actually doing in their classroom routines and the extent to which differentiation is a part of such routines.

Most of the literature available on how to enhance effective teaching of gifted learners, including best practice standards, suggests the need to have teachers trained in specific strategies and materials that elicit high-level performance of gifted students in classroom work (Johnsen, 2012; Roberts, Inman, & Robins, 2018; VanTassel-Baska & Little, 2017). Moreover, policy research advocates for the need for effective teacher preparation as well (Olszewski-Kubilius & Clarenbach, 2014; Plucker, Hardesty, & Burroughs, 2013; Wyner, Bridgeland, & Dilulio, 2007) to address the excellence gap and the socio-economic gap among gifted students. Of greatest importance is the assurance that these students have exposure to higher level thinking in the modes of both critical and creative thought. Gifted programs must employ systems of implementation that ensure fidelity in the use of such strategies as well as training teachers annually in how to apply them by level of schooling and content area.

Method of This Study

Sample

In the United States, elementary schools usually include students in kindergarten and in grades 1 through 5. Students in grades 6 through 8 attend middle school, and students in grades 9 through 12 are considered high school students. In this sample, the levels of schooling correspond to these designations.

To ensure a representative picture of gifted students and learning opportunities for them at school sites, the researchers observed classes at 57 schools in six districts across all levels (elementary, middle, and high) and in all of the core subject areas of English/language arts, mathematics, science, and social sciences. Elementary and middle school sites were purposively selected, based on several criteria, including geography within the district and Title I status of the school at elementary level. At the high school level, two districts did not have the high school as a part of the evaluation parameters. Two to four high school sites were observed in the other four districts.

To ensure clarity, key subject designations for Australian Curriculum, English, Mathematics (math), Science (science), Humanities, and Social Sciences (social sciences), have been used (Australian Government Department of Teaching and Learning, 2018). These designations are also commonly used for the four core subjects in the United States, although English may be designated as English/Language Arts.

The breakdown of content areas included the following: 120 English/language arts classes, 100 mathematics classes, 56 science classes, and 47 social sciences classes. Table 1 displays the school district breakdowns by number of schools, observations and subject area designations.

Observation time in each class ranged from 30 to 60 min, depending on the length of a given lesson. In most instances, at least one full lesson was observed. In the case of some secondary classrooms, where there was block scheduling, the observation time often was longer, encompassing an hour or more.

Instrumentation: The Use of the COS-R

One way to study the prevalence of classroom differentiation for the gifted is to observe classrooms 'up close and personal' through formal observations. The purpose of classroom observation is to gain firsthand knowledge of the instruction being provided for gifted learners at all relevant school grade levels. The focus of observations is not on the evaluation of individual teachers, but on the prevalence of best practice instructional behaviours for advanced students in these classrooms. The *William and Mary Classroom Observation Scales-Revised* (COS-R), the classroom observation instrument used in this study, contains 26 different research-based, best practice instructional strategies, divided into six subscales (VanTassel-Baska et al., 2003). It was not expected that all instructional behaviours listed on the form would be seen during any one observation. Having at least 30 minutes per observation, however, captured a snapshot of overall instructional practices within a given classroom.

Technical Adequacy of the COS-R

The analyses in three studies showed that overall the COS-R scale was highly reliable (alpha 0.91 to 0.93; VanTassel-Baska, Quek, & Feng, 2006). The subscale

Table 1 Districts ($N = 6$) observed with the COS-R by number and level of school, number of observations and core content areas

School district	Number of schools ($N = 57$)			Number of observations ($N = 329$)			Core content area ($N = 323$)[a]			
	Elementary ($N = 34$)	Middle ($N = 13$)	High ($N = 10$)	Elementary ($N = 168$)	Middle ($N = 84$)	High ($N = 77$)	English ($N = 120$)	Mathematics ($N = 100$)	Science ($N = 56$)	Social sciences ($N = 47$)
A	7	2	2	24	7	17	19	13	9	5
B	5	1	0	16	4	0	2	5	5	7
C	8	3	2	57	35	28	45	31	25	21
D	4	1	0	9	1	0	4	3	1	2
E	8	2	2	56	27	24	41	40	13	8
F	2	4	4	6	10	8	9	8	3	4
Total	**34**	**13**	**10**	**168**	**84**	**77**	**120**	**100**	**56**	**47**

[a]Core content areas only: some observations occurred in non-core areas and are not reported

reliability for all the clusters averaged above 0.70. Based on a content validity assessment by four scholars in gifted education, the scale achieved an intra-class coefficient of 0.98. Inter-rater reliability was assessed in four studies, with results suggesting a range of 0.87–0.89 across trained raters. A recent analysis of structured observation tools (Farah & Chandler, 2018) included a review of the COS-R as a teacher observation tool to assess differentiation and found it to meet all criteria used to determine appropriateness of use in classrooms, including evidence of validity, reliability, inter-rater reliability, and standardised administrative procedures for use (VanTassel-Baska, 2004; VanTassel-Baska, Quek, & Feng, 2005).

The scale has been used in the United States in multiple federally funded Javits Project studies to help document teacher growth. The use of differentiated content-based curriculum, tied to state and national standards, has demonstrated important learning gains for gifted learners across several years in various subjects (e.g., see Kim, VanTassel-Baska, Bracken, Feng, & Stambaugh, 2014; Little, Feng, VanTassel-Baska, Rogers, & Avery, 2007; VanTassel-Baska, 2018; VanTassel-Baska, Bass, Ries, Poland, & Avery, 1998; VanTassel-Baska, Bracken, Feng, & Brown, 2009; VanTassel-Baska, Zuo, Avery, & Little, 2002). Most of these smaller scale studies (i.e., six school districts and 35 classrooms on average) also collected data on teacher growth in the use of differentiation strategies in the classroom, finding that significant growth occurred. Yet the focus of the reported findings in journals often was on student growth, obtained through pre–post analyses of student achievement, using quasi-experimental designs.

In spite of best practice calls for the use of off-level measures to assess gifted student learning gains, there is little indication that gifted education programs systematically assess such gains using appropriate learning measures (Avery & VanTassel-Baska, 2001; VanTassel-Baska, 2006). In the absence of student impact data, evaluators often rely on the quality of the instructional experience as a proxy method for investigating program effectiveness. Classroom observation then becomes the tool for investigating those classroom-based experiences. In fact, some studies have used teacher effectiveness data as the main determinant of student progress (e.g., see Sanders & Horn, 1998).

Inter-Rater Reliability

The same three observers examined teacher use of differentiation across the span of the evaluation studies' data collection efforts. One of the observers was the first author of the COS-R. The other two were experienced administrator/practitioners in gifted education. All three went through a training session on the form and assessed each other's ratings in two of the districts by discussing and comparing each other's scores in order to reach 100% consensus in the process. After reaching such consensus, raters then independently assessed teachers on the form in all of the districts studied. Each reviewer independently reached the 1.00 confidence level for inter-rater reliability. In each district, however, ratings were still discussed for consonance across raters in selected teacher classrooms.

Standards of Use for the COS-R

Classroom observation provides a nexus between the input variables of the teacher and his or her students and the process of instruction itself, a process that combines instructional intent (goals and objectives), curriculum resources and materials, instructional and assessment strategies and classroom management skills within a delimited period of time. In meeting the needs of the gifted learner, the observer focuses on three dimensions of practice: good teaching in general, key elements of educational reform, and differentiation for high-ability learners. Use of the COS-R form allows researchers to probe several areas of instruction: curriculum planning and delivery, use of specific materials and strategies, accommodation for individual differences, critical thinking strategies, creative thinking strategies, and analysis and inquiry strategies. These categories represent best practice in teaching in general as well as best practice for gifted learners in particular (e.g., see NAGC Standards; Johnsen, 2012; VanTassel-Baska, 2012).

The COS-R captures both the frequency of individual teacher behaviours and the effectiveness of those behaviours. Both dimensions are reported in the analyses in this chapter. The presence of a given behaviour was rated along a 3–1 scale, with 3 being 'effective', 2 being 'somewhat effective' and 1 being 'ineffective'. The 'not observed' category (N/O) indicates the behaviour was not attempted or used in the observed lesson. Expanded definitions for each rating are found on the COS-R form itself and comprise statements about the degree of use of the strategy in the classroom lesson observed. A copy of the *Classroom Observation Scale-Revised* (COS-R), used in the study, has been included as Appendix A.

Data Analysis

Basic statistics were used to obtain numerical scores on the COS-R instrument for each school and then each district studied. Frequencies were tallied, and means were computed by item and item clusters or categories, using the MS Excel program. These data were then collated across a district to show the overall picture of differentiation in that particular district. For this study, the data were collated across six districts to show broader patterns in the use of differentiation on a common tool.

Computing overall categorical mean scores on the form was done by eliminating consideration of the 'not observed' category in the calculation of effectiveness. Thus, all mean scores reflect only teachers who were using the behaviour and receiving a rating on it. Both item frequency percentages and categorical effectiveness means are recorded in the chapter to provide specificity to the behaviours noted or not noted in the observations. Categorical means were calculated as means of means, derived from item mean scores.

Expectations for frequency of use of specific strategies may vary, depending on the level, subject, and group of learners observed. In general, it would be expected that higher level thinking strategies, such as critical thinking, creative thinking, and inquiry, would be employed in some form in every classroom observed (VanTassel-Baska et al., 2006). Moreover, evidence of accommodations for gifted learners, such as sub-grouping, individual conferencing, and/or use of differentiated materials or assignments, would be expected. Absence of the use of any of these strategies suggests the lack of a routine for working with gifted learners that should be a hallmark of effective practice. High percentages of 'not observed' ratings (i.e., over 50%) in a category, moreover, may indicate a problematic lack of frequency in the use of a set of differentiated practices at the level of classroom, school, and district. This also may be a critical factor in analysing effectiveness at grade levels and in different content areas.

Expectations for teachers of gifted learners would be that the mean scores in the areas observed would be at the 2.5+ rating level, signifying that, for these behaviours, teachers were in the range of effectiveness. In the 2.0–2.5 range, teachers would be perceived as having a satisfactory use of the behaviours, although not yet effective as described on the form itself. Mean ratings below 2.0 would suggest that the strategy was being used ineffectively, calling into question the teacher's capacity to sustain specific differentiated practices (VanTassel-Baska et al., 2006).

Through these onsite visits, researchers were able to see how classroom implementation functioned by school and level (i.e., elementary, middle, and high) in a gifted program. A total of 329 classrooms were observed in six different districts, using the COS-R instrumentation administered by trained observers. Class size ranged from 4 to 32 in the observed classrooms, with secondary classrooms typically being larger and more aligned with class size figures for the district. Smaller classes were observed at the elementary level when the pull-out grouping model was employed.

Findings

The following findings were computed on 329 observations across elementary, middle and high school classrooms. Findings were reported by 'observed' and 'not observed' teacher behaviours within categories to determine frequency percentages by COS-R item. In all, 10 out of 26 differentiation strategies were used in over 50% of classrooms observed.

Strategy Use Findings

Data were analysed within and across the six categories defined in the COS-R. The first category of instructional behaviour, entitled *curriculum planning and delivery*, includes five items. The first two items on the form focused on high expectations and application of new knowledge and were observed in 96% and 93% of classrooms, respectively, and generally at an 'effective' or 'somewhat effective' level. Encouraging student expression was observed in 81% of classrooms. Items that focused on the use of metacognition in the classroom were rated lower across all schools and levels. The item on 'planning, monitoring, and assessing their learning' was observed in only 38% of classrooms, and the item that asked students to 'reflect on what they had learned' was observed in only 19%. The lower ratings on metacognitive activities were troubling in that the general district curriculum in all the contexts studied stressed the importance of teaching these skills as does best practice literature in gifted education.

The teacher behaviours in the second category, entitled *materials and strategy utilization,* were limited in use across the school sites observed. The deliberate use of differentiated materials for the gifted in the classrooms was not widely evident and noted for only 40% of the classrooms observed. Only slightly more than half of the classrooms (54%) used any discernible instructional grouping approach. The use of models of thinking was evident in only 22 (7%) classrooms. Yet more than half of the classrooms observed (61%) employed instructional approaches such as concept mapping or graphic organisers. Because of the wide range of 'not observed' for items (39%–93%), the overall mean score may not be useful in understanding particular teacher behaviours in this category.

The category *accommodations for individual differences* includes four factors related to student grouping and instructional practices in support of individual needs and readiness. Such teaching behaviours were in evidence across the majority of classes in respect to discovering ideas through structured activities or questions (76%). Slightly over 81% of the classrooms demonstrated opportunities for independent or group learning to promote depth in understanding content. This latter instructional strategy is intended to encourage students to find meaning for themselves rather than to parrot back pre-digested subject matter. Its widespread use was seen as very positive. Less positive were the findings that less than half (45%) of the classrooms observed encouraged multiple interpretations of events and only 46% accommodated individual differences through conferencing, different assignments, or choice of materials.

In the category dealing with *critical thinking strategies*, only one of the four items was observed in over half of the classes, that of encouraging students to judge or evaluate situations, positions, or issues (68%). Engaging students in comparing and contrasting ideas was less in evidence, seen in only 41% of classrooms. In only 137 (42%) classrooms was there evidence of moving students from concrete to abstract ideas, a critical indicator for engaging in higher level thinking. Student synthesis of information within or across disciplines was observed only in a minority of classrooms (21%).

Most of the items in the category on *creative thinking strategies* were infrequently observed. The solicitation of diverse ideas was observed in 40% of classrooms. Only 16% of classrooms showed evidence of an exploration of diverse viewpoints to reframe ideas, yet the provision of opportunities to develop and elaborate these ideas was apparent in 49% of the classrooms. Only 17% of the classes encouraged open-mindedness from students.

The final category, *analysis and inquiry strategies*, focuses on several behaviours that promote higher level thinking and reasoning in students through deliberate teacher behaviours. The specific behaviours of using inquiry processes to encourage higher level learning were observed in 58% of classrooms, while encouraging students to draw inferences from data and represent them in appropriate forms was seen in 40% of classrooms. The majority of classrooms (64%) used activities that encouraged analysis of text, use of models or other symbolic sources. The use of higher level questions was also evident in almost half of classrooms (49%), yet building argument was observed in only 37%. These last two skills are prominently featured in the preparation for *Advanced Placement* (AP) and *International Baccalaureate Diploma Program* (IB) classwork in most subjects and in the relevant content standards required that lead up to that level of work at secondary levels of learning.

Table 2 reports the frequency of use by items and categories on the COS-R.

District Variations

Individual districts, however, showed variation in some of the categories that are worth noting. In District C, for the category of *Critical Thinking Strategies*, only one of the four items was observed in over half, of the classrooms ($N = 32$ or 68%), the item dealing with 'encouraging students to evaluate situations, problems, or issues', while in District F, almost 75% of critical thinking skill strategies were used in over half of the classrooms observed. Thus, it is fair to say that the variation by district on the employment of critical thinking skills was as great as the variation by teacher.

At the district level, again significant variation occurred in the cluster on creative thinking. District C showed a positive variation from other districts in the use of two of the *creative thinking strategies*. In 84% of the classrooms, teachers provided opportunities for students to develop and elaborate on their ideas. In 62% of classrooms, teachers deliberately solicited diverse thoughts from students about a topic, issue, or idea. However, open-mindedness and tolerance of imaginative thought were still encouraged in only 29% of classrooms. Finally, there was limited evidence of promoting 'diverse points of view to reframe ideas', observed in only 18% of classrooms.

In some districts, there was variation within the category of *analysis and inquiry* also worth noting. In District A, for example, the use of *analysis and inquiry* was mixed, depending on the item. Evidence for the use of 'analysis of text, models, or other symbolic sources' was found in 75% of classrooms observed. In 59% of classrooms, the use of an inquiry process was in evidence and the use of higher level questions was seen. However, fewer classrooms elicited inferences (39%) and engaged in the process of building argument (29%).

Effectiveness Findings

While it is useful to know what specific differentiation strategies were being used or not used in the districts studied, it was also important to consider how effective teachers were at using the specific differentiation strategies that were employed. Consequently, the researchers analysed the ratings of effectiveness by item, category,

Table 2 Number and percentages of differentiated teaching behaviours across districts observed and not observed by COS-R items and categories ($N = 329$)

Categories on the COS-R	Observed		Not observed	
Curriculum planning and delivery	*Number*	*Percentage*	*Number*	*Percentage*
1. High expectations	316	**96**	13	3
2. Application of new knowledge	305	**93**	24	7
3. Planning, monitoring or assessing learning	124	38	205	**62**
4. Expressing thoughts	266	**81**	63	19
5. Reflection	62	19	267	**81**
Materials and strategy utilization[a]	*Number*	*Percentage*	*Number*	*Percentage*
6. Differentiated materials use	117	40	178	**60**
7. Sub-grouping for instruction	160	**54**	135	46
8. Models for thinking	22	7	273	**93**
9. Evidence-based strategies for higher level thinking	179	**61**	116	39
Accommodations for individual differences	*Number*	*Percentage*	*Number*	*Percentage*
10. Independent and/or group learning	265	**81**	64	19
11. Accommodation for individual/sub-group differences	151	46	178	**54**
12. Multiple interpretations	147	45	182	**55**
13. Self-discovery of ideas	249	**76**	80	24
Critical thinking strategies	*Number*	*Percentage*	*Number*	*Percentage*
14. Evaluating situations, etc.	224	**68**	105	32
15. Comparing and contrasting	136	41	193	**59**
16. Generalising from concrete to abstract	137	42	192	**58**
17. Synthesis or summary of information	70	21	259	**79**
Creative thinking strategies	*Number*	*Percentage*	*Number*	*Percentage*
18. Many diverse thoughts	132	40	197	**60**
19. Application of diverse points of view	53	16	276	**84**
20. Use of open-mindedness and imagination	56	17	273	**83**
21. Elaboration of ideas	160	49	169	**51**
Analysis and inquiry strategies[a]	*Number*	*Percentage*	*Number*	*Percentage*
22. Inquiry process	172	**58**	123	42
23. High-level questions	145	49	150	**51**
24. Analysis of text, models and symbols	188	**64**	107	36
25. Building argument in multiple forms	108	37	187	**63**
26. Draw inferences	117	40	178	**60**

[a]Form differences did not allow total calculations of items in these categories

and district to determine if teachers' practices with differentiation in all of its manifestations were 'effective', 'somewhat effective' or 'ineffective'.

For *curriculum planning and delivery*, the overall effectiveness rating was 2.35, clearly in the range of the 'somewhat effective' use of the strategy. Teachers appeared to have routinised some of these items into their teaching repertoire. However, most lessons observed were whole class, thus rendering the ratings lower than if there had been an attempt to differentiate by the level of the learner. Overall district ranges for this category were 2.08–2.65.

In the *materials and strategy utilization* category, the rating was 2.23, with a range of 1.84–2.46, suggesting that the teachers observed were 'somewhat effective' in dealing with the differentiation behaviours in this cluster. Of special interest was the effectiveness rating for Item #16 on the use of materials. The rating for the specific item was 2.32 overall, but in two districts, mean scores were in the effectiveness range of 2.40 and 2.46, suggesting more effective use of differentiated materials.

The overall effectiveness mean score for classrooms observed in the category of *Accommodation for Individual Differences* yielded a 2.32 score, indicating that teachers using strategies in this category were 'somewhat effective' in their implementation. Of particular interest in this category was Item #11, related to providing for individual and/or group differences. Although it was used by less than 50% of observed teachers, it was found to be at the effectiveness rating level of 2.42, suggesting that teachers using the strategy were close to being effective in the 46% of classrooms where the strategy was observed.

In the category of *Critical Thinking Strategies*, judged by the researchers to be one of the most important categories of observation because of its focus on core skills used in most training in this area of higher level learning, the mean score for effectiveness was 2.36. This category, therefore, was rated within the 'somewhat effective' range when strategies were implemented. It should be noted that in several of the high school classrooms observed, especially AP and IB classes, teachers were rated as 'effective' (2.5–3.0) in their use of several of the item-based strategies in this cluster. Some of the elementary programs at grades 4 and 5 also yielded higher effectiveness means for items in this category. Yet, mean scores across districts varied from 2.06 to 2.74, suggesting that some districts were implementing the strategies at a high effectiveness level, while others appeared to be more limited in their capacity to do so.

Even lower in overall effectiveness ratings were those items related to *creative thinking strategies*, the second pillar in the use of higher level thinking strategies with the gifted and other learners. The mean score effectiveness in this category was 2.21, indicating that the strategies were 'somewhat effective' in the classrooms where they were employed. No district reached the 'effective' level of implementation of these strategies (i.e., the range was 1.97–2.42), a concern for both gifted and non-gifted populations, as the items in this category are basic elements for the successful instruction of innovative thinking in all content areas.

Finally, in the category of *analysis and inquiry strategies*, the effectiveness score for observed classrooms was 2.42, indicating that teachers observed using the behaviours were close to the effectiveness range in implementing the indicators (i.e., 2.5–3.0). Three districts did have ratings in the effectiveness range for this category. District C scored at 2.55, District D at 2.75, and District F at 2.67, demonstrating effective use of many of the strategies evaluated. Again, as seen in

Table 3 Effectiveness means by category and by district

District	Curriculum planning and delivery	Materials and strategy utilization	Accommodations for individual differences	Critical thinking strategies	Creative thinking strategies	Analysis and inquiry strategies	Total
A	2.36	2.20	2.17	2.24	2.22	2.24	**2.24**
B	2.08	1.84	2.18	2.29	1.97	2.03	**2.07**
C	2.50	2.46	2.48	2.50	2.42	2.55	**2.49**
D	2.09	a	2.33	2.06	2.05	2.75	**2.26**
E	2.40	2.40	2.33	2.33	2.27	2.30	**2.34**
F	2.65	a	2.42	2.74	2.33	2.67	**2.56**
Total	**2.35**	**2.23**	**2.32**	**2.36**	**2.21**	**2.42**	**2.32**

[a]The COS-R form used in Districts D and F did not include the *materials and strategy utilization* category

other categories, districts varied in their use of these strategies, ranging from 2.03 to 2.75. As with the categories on critical and creative thinking, the skills emphasised in this category are critical to instilling the type of higher level thinking required on AP and IB examinations as well as other evidence of higher level thinking students must produce when they graduate from high school and matriculate to a tertiary institution.

Table 3 shows the mean effectiveness scores by category and district.

Sub-analysis of Effectiveness by Level of Schooling

A sub-analysis was conducted by disaggregating results on the COS-R by elementary, middle, and high school ratings for effectiveness. The total number of classroom observations by level may be seen in Figure 1 which shows the effectiveness means by category and by school level.

It is striking to note that these mean scores showed very little deviation from the 'somewhat effective' level, with the exception of the middle school level where the *materials and strategy utilization* effectiveness rating was below 2.0. These results suggest that where teachers were using differentiated teaching behaviours, they were in the range of 'somewhat effective' to 'effective' in that use in all categories and at all levels, with the middle school exception noted above. These data were also comparable across districts.

In general, the highest mean scores for observed behaviours by level were for high school observations, with the exception of the category of *accommodations for individual differences*, where elementary level effectiveness mean scores were higher. Although the average of most behavioural categories was above a 2 rating of 'somewhat effective', it is apparent that middle schools consistently were rated lower than all other levels of schooling on each of the categories on the form.

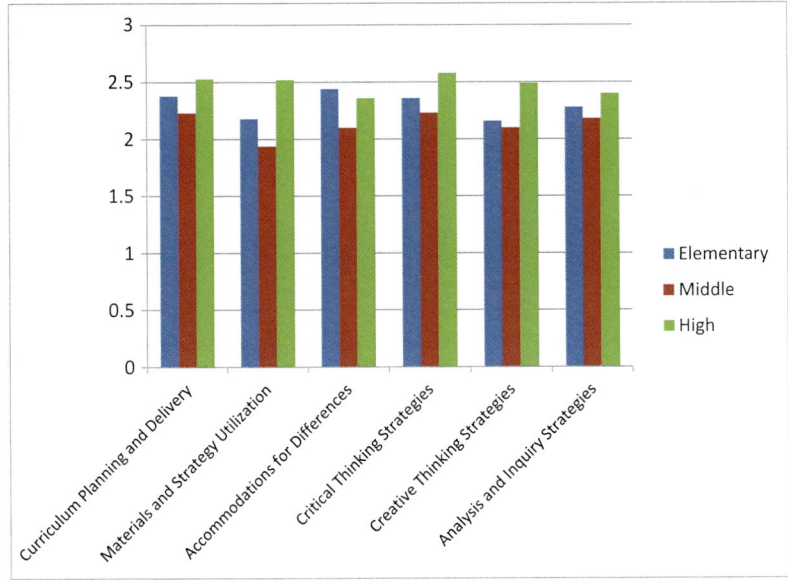

Fig. 1 Effectiveness by category and by level (3=Effective, 2=Somewhat Effective, 1=Not Effective) (Elementary Level N=168 Middle School Level N=84 High School Level N=77)

Sub-analysis of Effectiveness by Subject Area

The data were also disaggregated by subject area (see Fig. 2). Sample sizes for science and social sciences classrooms were smaller than for the two core areas of English and mathematics. English had the largest number of rated observations, followed by mathematics, and then science, and finally the social sciences. The differences in observations may be accounted for by how many classrooms were identified as having gifted learners in them where a program or service was supposed to be occurring. All districts provided programs in English and mathematics. Very few did so in science or in social sciences. Therefore, these classes often did not differentiate instruction routinely for gifted students even if there was a cluster group of these students in the classroom.

Figure 2 shows the results of effectiveness mean scores of classroom observations by subject area and category. In all categories, observed behaviours were above 2.00 for all subjects. This suggests that teachers who used differentiated behaviours were 'somewhat effective' to 'effective' in that use in each of the four core subject areas.

Variations were still noted by content area, however. Mathematics classrooms exceeded all other subjects in the effectiveness of use of differentiated strategies with the exception of *analysis and inquiry strategies* where English was stronger. Since more English and mathematics classes were observed (116 and 98 respectively), the pattern of use of strategies was easier to discern within and across them.

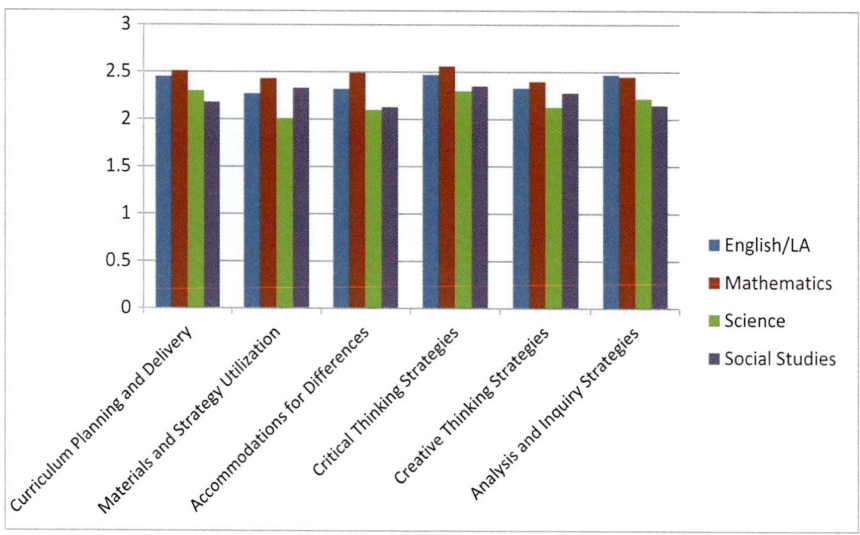

Fig. 2 Effectiveness Means by Category and by Subject Area (3=Effective, 2=Somewhat Effective, 1=Not Effective) English N=116; Mathematics N=98; Science N=55; Social Sciences N=45∗. (∗District D elementary level observation forms were not available for calculation)

Limitations of the Evaluation Study

An important limitation of this evaluation study is that it represents a collation of six different evaluation studies done across a period of four years. As such, it does not follow the standard model for conducting research where research questions are focused on a single phenomenon at one point in time, and where there is a single source of data for determining teacher or program efficacy. Rather the data collected on classroom practice in the use of differentiation constituted one of five data sources for rendering evaluation recommendations. Other sources included focus groups with parents, students, teachers and administrators, interviews with program leadership, document and curriculum, review, and NAGC program standards accreditation review. The preponderance of evidence from these other sources substantiated the findings from the COS-R as reported on in this chapter. However, these other sources of evidence were not included in the study findings reported in this chapter.

Because the data were collected across six different evaluation sites, the resulting compilation of scores on the COS-R must be viewed in light of that process. No tests of significance were run by item or item clusters as most differences noted between items and clusters on the form were prima facie significant and found so in individual district analyses. Differences between districts on given items were also significant and are noted by discussing the greatest variations on specific items. No other statistical analyses were run.

Because data highlighting teacher training in gifted education were unavailable, we were not able to disaggregate data by level of teacher preparation. Therefore, we cannot make inferences about the relationship of individualised teacher training to the behaviours noted in classrooms. This reality makes it difficult to offer specific suggestions for follow-up efforts in professional development.

Another limitation of the study was the uneven distribution of numbers of classrooms observed at given levels. Effectiveness data were generated by using means generated only for those behaviours evident in the classrooms observed. Consequently, the actual number of teachers represented by effectiveness means was masked. Thus a 3.00 score might have been obtained for a category in one district as a result of three teachers performing at the highest level. Conversely, 20 teachers may have obtained a 2.00 mean in a category in another district, representing the mean for that category across all classrooms in that district.

Finally, researchers observed each teacher only once, offering a snapshot of instruction in each teacher's classroom. Therefore, there was no way to know whether their behaviours, and consequently COS-R ratings, would have differed if these teachers were observed more than once over time.

Discussion of Findings

What can be said about commonalities among the most used differentiation strategies? It may be fair to say that they are the most general approaches to differentiation such as using various forms of instructional grouping, for example, or asking students to express themselves. Items of this sort are really behavioural precursors to a deeper level of differentiation that probes the nature of a task demand and its challenge and complexity. Thus, the items most often observed in these classrooms are the basic building blocks for differentiation of curriculum to occur. They are necessary but insufficient components on their own to suggest that differentiation is occurring.

On the other hand, the teacher behaviours that were more limited in frequency of use (used in fewer than 50% of classrooms) ranged from metacognitive behaviours that target self-awareness in learners to higher level thinking skills that elevate learning. Often, they were the more specific types of skills related to thinking such as synthesis or inferencing. Moreover, the range of non-use of these behaviours was often wide. For example, the use of models of thinking was *not observed* in 93% of classrooms, while the elaboration of ideas and higher level questions were *not observed* in 51% of classrooms, suggesting that teachers were selective in deciding which higher level skills may be applied or were ignorant in the absence of such skills in their teaching.

Other skills not observed frequently in these studies were those associated with effective grouping of the gifted for instruction and the use of differentiated materials found to be effective with gifted learners. Lower ratings for science and the social sciences, especially in the area of *Accommodation for Individual Differences*, may be explained in part because of the lack of effective instructional grouping for program delivery. In many of the districts, only English and mathematics classes were grouped in any way. In some cluster group settings, no instructional differentiation was used, thereby negating the effectiveness of the grouping delivery model employed. Given the research that has been conducted in the last 25 years on the importance of using instructional grouping with the gifted (e.g., see Steenbergen-Hu, Makel, & Olszewski-Kubilius, 2016) and employing materials that have demonstrated gifted student gains in both subject matter skills and critical thinking (e.g., see VanTassel-Baska, 2018), it is disheartening to find districts not employing these research-based practices routinely in classrooms with gifted learners (i.e., cluster groupings and special class settings).

Many strategies that are markers of differentiated practice clearly were not evident in many classrooms and schools across the districts studied. Especially of concern, as noted earlier, was the paucity of skills that employed higher level thinking as the core element. In *critical thinking strategies*, only one item was observed above the 50% level. No *creative thinking strategies* were observed above the 50% level. In *analysis and inquiry strategies*, only 2 out of 5 strategies were observed in at least 50% of classrooms. The limited use of these skills suggests that gifted programs in these six districts are not delivering effective gifted instruction consistently across classrooms and levels. These findings were also consistent with an earlier analysis of 20 school district evaluations that used the same instrumentation where teachers were observed to be using limited critical and creative thinking skills (see VanTassel-Baska, 2006).

Discussion of Effectiveness Findings

Where differentiated behaviours were observed, teachers were rated as 'somewhat effective' to 'effective' in their practice, indicating movement towards effectiveness in the use of differentiation strategies appropriate for gifted learners. These findings suggest that numbers of teachers in the six observed districts are demonstrating important skills in working with gifted learners, but that many more teachers, who have responsibility for these classes, are not employing the strategies at a level that would more likely ensure a positive effect on gifted student learning. Suprayogi, Valcke, and Godwin (2017) found that teachers' self-efficacy, beliefs, experience, professional development, and certification, along with classroom size, all contributed to their ability to differentiate effectively in the classroom. Suprayogi et al.'s research supports the findings in our study in respect to understanding that multiple variables influence teacher behaviours. These may include the learning environment, student readiness, pressure to address lower level state standards, and teacher preparation, including content knowledge, and pedagogical skill. Consequently, it is not surprising to find teachers at variable levels of efficacy in differentiating for gifted learners.

At a deeper level, it is suggested in the data that the teacher selection process for working with the gifted in these districts may need to be improved. Too many of the districts' 'grandfathers in' existing staff members participate in planned in-service sessions that are said to equate with university level coursework. Some of these staff members neither wish to participate in such work nor do they emerge from it able to work effectively with gifted learners. Moreover, the content and scope of these district in-service opportunities are often not at a level or extensive enough to be considered comparable to more formalised university work (Johnsen, 2012). Of greatest concern in this area of professional development, however, is that attendance at in-service on any aspect of gifted education is not mandatory for teachers. Thus, a broad range of limited teacher expertise in the use of differentiated curriculum, instruction, and assessment is common. In other parts of these evaluation studies, administrators reported on the levels of professional development that teachers selected and received, with the majority always favouring Level I activities that translated into 1–6 hours of training at the local level, while fewer than 10% of teachers participated in Level III coursework in gifted education equal to 12 hours of college credit.

Closely aligned to this *laissez faire* practice of teacher choice in preparation for working with the gifted is the belief that all teachers can work with gifted learners successfully if they receive some form of training, regardless of its scope or depth. Teacher preparation is a combination of qualities—ability, applied intelligence, developed skill, interest, and motivation—all necessary to be effective with the gifted population (Kyriakides, Christoforidou, Panayiotou, & Creemers, 2017; Valiandes & Neophytou, 2018). According to the US program standards for practitioners, at least 12 hours of university coursework should be completed before teachers are endorsed to work with gifted learners (see Johnsen, 2012). The final aspect of training in any gifted education program that has been nationally accredited involves teachers in a practicum where they apply their skills under supervision. Without this piece, there is little evidence of effectiveness that can be assumed. As noted in the cross-cultural Singapore study, the practicum experience was the most significant in sealing teachers' understanding of differentiation techniques (see VanTassel-Baska et al., 2006).

Another troubling belief related to differentiation of instruction for the gifted is that the strategies to achieve differentiation are the same for all gifted learners, thus taking a reductionist view of how differentiation may be applied to classroom practice (Coleman, Gallagher, & Job, 2012; Coleman & Johnsen, 2013). This belief can be highly damaging for students. Many students who cannot handle acceleration are subjected to it because it is appropriate for some gifted students in some areas of learning. This is especially true in mathematics where gifted students, who may be strong in verbal areas, are placed in accelerated mathematics classrooms, often without support for their needs which require more teaching and learning in mathematical concepts (see Assouline, Colangelo, VanTassel-Baska, & Lupkowski-Shoplik, 2015).

On the other hand, lack of discrimination in helping students choose their path to differentiation may be problematic as well. Frequently differentiation is seen as an endless array of choices students may make in activities, projects, materials, and the like. Although choice may be a part of the process, it hardly should dominate the thinking of quality differentiation (see VanTassel-Baska & Little, 2017). For example, appropriate choices for a twice exceptional child rarely match what is needed for a more typical gifted learner (see Baska & VanTassel-Baska, 2018). Guidance in making such choices at an individual level, based on ability, skill level, and interest is still required.

Findings in this study also suggest that differentiation requires more specialised attention by grade level and subject area. Teachers need to understand that critical reading in English and advanced problem solving in mathematics, for example, both require critical thinking, and that activities and projects in each area need to focus on creative opportunities as well as other more convergent tasks. Vertical planning is essential to build coherent programs for gifted learners within and across levels of schooling. The same process must be applied to content area development. The careful acquisition of advanced content skills is an essential part of all students' learning in schools. For the gifted learner, it requires a tailored scope and sequence model of learning that acknowledges the need for advanced instruction (e.g., see Hughes, Kettler, Shaughnessy-Dedrich, & VanTassel-Baska, 2014).

In our study's results, it was also suggested that the use of differentiation strategies differs by level of schooling. High school classrooms observed used strategies more effectively than any other level of schooling. Elementary classrooms appeared to be best attuned to making accommodations for individual differences. Middle school classrooms were rated the lowest of the three levels in all categories of differentiation. These findings may suggest the need for schools and districts to differentiate professional development programs by level of schooling as well as by teacher, in order to accommodate the differences that continue to emerge across classrooms and schools in the Asia-Pacific as well as in the United States (see Jolly & Jarvis, 2018).

Vertical planning and the development of curriculum scope and sequence models for gifted learners in core subject areas would ameliorate this problem by situating middle schools as the fulcrum point for continued advanced opportunities for the gifted. Yet many districts continue to emphasise the middle school years as a time for all students and teachers to concentrate on the affective domain, rather than as a time where advanced student learning is a central consideration for instructional decision making, based on level of proficiency attained in core areas. Although evidence for the effectiveness of accelerative approaches to learning for gifted students continues to grow in the gifted literature (e.g., see Assouline, Colangelo, & VanTassel-Baska, 2015), with the exception of mathematics, applications of acceleration in the classrooms observed at middle school levels was still scant.

Variations in effective use of differentiated strategies were also noted by content area. Our analyses showed that mathematics classes used more higher level thinking skills than other subjects, although English used more analysis and inquiry. Since more English and mathematics classes were observed (120 and 100 respectively), a clear pattern of strategy use was easier to discern within and across them. In all categories, however, observed behaviours were above 2.00 for all subjects and ranged up to 3.00 in a given district by category. Thus, teachers, who were observed using differentiated behaviours, were 'somewhat effective' to 'effective' in that use in each of the four core subject areas. This finding suggests that all subject areas may be adapted to using differentiation strategies effectively for the gifted learner, with appropriate examples and models of practice provided. Much of the professional development literature also suggests that differences in effective use of strategies often can be best seen and changed by subject area applications in professional development (e.g., see Kennedy, 1999).

Problems related to the use of differentiation appeared to be common across all the districts in the sample. The specific skills being addressed in a given classroom ranged from analysis to evaluation, but higher level skills rarely governed classroom activities. Across all of the districts, the use of higher level thinking was not a routine part of daily instruction in a majority of classrooms. The full-scale evaluation studies conducted (of which the classroom observation data were a part) suggested that teachers and other stakeholders have a limited understanding of what a differentiated classroom may look like. Focus group data, collected from administrators, teachers, students, and parents, suggested that these stakeholder groups either had no knowledge of differentiation use (usually parents) or understood it at a more general level (administrators viewing group work and independent research as evidence of its use). Students focused on the type of rapport the teacher built with them, not the specific strategies employed. The teachers generally believed they were using differentiation practices as defined by the use of higher level skills, providing choice, and organising students for group work. Thus, each stakeholder group had a different concept of what differentiation was.

More unique problems with differentiation use occurred if teachers were unfamiliar with a text or problem selection or with how to differentiate, given a specific instructional grouping pattern. The difficulty appeared to arise from the specific choices made by the teacher in the selection of materials or on how to organise students to address complex assignments effectively. Such problems suggest the need for professional development that is not only general to the district but also specific to the needs of individual teachers. For example, workshops in critical thinking in subject areas may be augmented by specific topics such as 'effective use of specific mathematics materials to teach thinking' or 'using cluster grouping to differentiate for gifted learners in reading'.

Decision Making About Instructional Practice

Observers found that the absence of appropriate attention to clustering or grouping gifted learners together within a classroom hampered the ability of teachers to differentiate instruction in other ways. In many classrooms, whole group instruction dominated, with the use of one lesson plan for all learners, regardless of their designation as gifted. In cases where the lesson plan was derived from materials selected by district content specialists, the lessons were frequently not advanced enough for gifted learners. At all levels, mathematics classrooms were an exception to this, with advanced opportunities in evidence in most of the mathematics classrooms, regardless of level. Some of the most inspired teaching, in fact, was seen in mathematics classrooms.

The evidence further suggested that teachers who work with gifted learners in well-defined programs appear to be more effective in their use of differentiated teaching behaviours. For example, teachers who are working with gifted learners at grades 4 and 5 in cluster-grouped or self-contained delivery systems in reading and mathematics as well as in high school AP and IB programs use differentiation to a greater extent and more effectively than other teachers observed. This pattern was discernible across districts as well as within districts.

Instructional practice at the secondary level appears to be dominated by subject specialist decisions or program-based requirements (such as AP, IB) related to materials and instructional focus rather than by what works with gifted learners.

Discussions with teachers and program staff suggested that these programs dominate the training and materials decisions made in the gifted program. In several cases, AP and IB teachers were not trained in gifted education, but only in the prescribed training for the relevant program they were to teach. This rendered them somewhat less prepared to focus sharply on issues of differentiation even though the level of the material taught called for the use of higher level thinking strategies. Results still suggested, however, that high school teachers as a group were the most effective. These teachers may have been able to parlay their content skills into instruction that accommodated the needs of gifted learners more readily than teachers at other levels. Studies have suggested that content knowledge is an essential precursor to using critical thinking strategies effectively (e.g., Mills, 2003).

Teachers' decisions to differentiate critical and creative thinking for gifted learners often have resulted in the use of tiered activities or rotating learning stations, or both (e.g., see Tomlinson, 2017). These approaches do allow for all students to use higher level activities, with gifted learners employing greater complexity and more abstraction in their work. Products for advanced learners, for example, would call for written and graphic representations organised around a macro-concept, such as change, or a theme, such as oppression.

Finally, many classroom teachers appear to need professional development in how to use gifted materials in a differentiated way, how to plan for cluster groups of gifted learners in the classroom and how to assess differentiated instruction as well as deliver it. Moreover, the professional development offered should be more closely linked to the expectations for use of materials and strategies in the classroom. For example, implementation of research-based materials and training in specific models and strategies should be a priority for teacher in-service sessions if the goal is to elevate the use of higher level thinking. Studies of appropriate differentiated materials for use in classrooms have been conducted systematically over the past 20 years (see Gavin, Casa, Adelson, Carroll, & Sheffield, 2009; Kim et al., 2014; Stambaugh, 2007; Stambaugh & VanTassel-Baska, 2018; VanTassel-Baska, 2018; VanTassel-Baska, Avery, Little, & Hughes, 2000) and include recommendations for professional development models that aid fidelity of implementation.

Implications for Instructional Practice

Providing effective instruction for gifted learners requires appropriate instructional grouping, thoughtful assignment and training of teachers, a focus on the needs of and benefits to gifted students and evidence of the use of effective differentiation practices as seen on the COS-R form and its supporting studies reiterated above.

In those districts where instructional grouping was employed, cluster grouping was the prevalent classroom organisation for serving gifted students at the K-3 primary level. Where the instructional grouping was a cluster group within a given classroom, differentiated instructional strategies directed towards the needs of gifted learners were rarely observed. Such cluster grouping also did not employ acceleration of content.

Certain classroom teachers in cluster-grouped classrooms used differentiated instructional strategies effectively. These were teachers who had been carefully selected and trained to work with gifted students. This was especially the case if a gifted resource teacher provided consistent support. However, with the exception of mathematics, even when the instruction was effective, evidence of acceleration of content was rare.

At the upper elementary level, the instructional group was usually composed of identified gifted students and advanced learners. This was the case in special classes with replacement curriculum or in pull-out groups with supplemental curriculum. While these classes often focused on English or mathematics, science or social sciences classes were sometimes offered. Differentiated instructional strategies and advanced curriculum materials were frequently observed in these classes. The specialised curriculum materials used were generally research-based products in each of the content areas.

Although some cluster grouping occurred at the middle school level in several districts, honours classes were the more common form of instructional grouping. If the honours classes had a defined curriculum with an established scope and sequence, acceleration of curriculum was sometimes observed. Mathematics was the subject area in which such advanced curricula were most frequently present. Advanced reading selections were sometimes used in English classrooms, but advanced curricula beyond the readings were less frequently observed. Such specialised, advanced curriculum documents were even less common in science and social sciences classes.

Honours class were also a common form of instructional grouping in grades 9 and 10 and less frequently offered in grades 11 and 12. The issues for honours classes at the high school level were similar to those of honours classes at the middle school level. No learning plan had been designed for the gifted students in these classes, nor did teachers use differentiated strategies consistently. Honours classes tended to have a wide range of levels of effective practice at all levels from middle to high school.

In high school AP and IB classes, the most frequent type of grouping for gifted students, the required syllabi comprised the curriculum. This meant that the curriculum was accelerated and enriched in all subject areas offered. While the use of effective differentiated instructional strategies was not universal, effective differentiation for advanced and gifted learners was frequently observed.

Table 4 includes a synthesis of the role of grouping, teacher assignment, student needs, and benefits and evidence of differentiation in the six districts where classrooms were observed.

These classroom observation findings then clearly have implications for providing training and professional development that will ensure that regular classroom teachers and those who work with the gifted have the skill sets they need to work effectively with differentiation strategies. Effective professional development for teachers of the gifted must focus on specific needs based on teachers'

Table 4 Role of grouping, teacher assignment, student needs and benefits and evidence of differentiation on gifted program delivery

Grouping model	Teacher assignment	Needs of/benefits to advanced students	Observed evidence of differentiation
Elementary school level			
Cluster grouping within a given class	Classroom teacher with or without targeted training	The needs of the cluster group are rarely recognised. Lessons focus on whole class instruction.	Specific materials for advanced learners are rarely observed. Strategies directed to the academic needs of advanced learners are rarely observed.
Cluster grouping within a given class (4–6 identified students in one class)	Classroom teacher with targeted training with support from gifted resource teacher	The academic needs of the cluster group are recognised.	Specific materials for advanced learners are sometimes observed. Strategies directed to the academic needs of advanced learners are sometimes observed. Acceleration of content is rarely observed.
Special class grouping Replacement curriculum (organising instruction with advanced learners at a grade level)	Classroom teacher with targeted training	The academic needs of advanced students are recognised.	Specific materials for advanced learners are often observed. Strategies directed to the academic needs of advanced learners are often observed. Advanced thinking skills are frequently observed. Acceleration of content is frequently observed.
Special class grouping Replacement curriculum (organising instruction with advanced learners or identified gifted students at a grade level)	Classroom teacher with targeted training and support from gifted resource teacher	The academic needs of advanced students are recognised.	Specific materials for advanced learners are often observed. Strategies directed to the academic needs of advanced learners are often observed. Advanced thinking skills are frequently observed. Acceleration of content is frequently observed.
Pull-out class grouping Supplemental curriculum (organising	Gifted resource teacher	The academic needs of advanced	Specific materials for advanced learners are often observed.

(continued)

Table 4 (continued)

Grouping model	Teacher assignment	Needs of/benefits to advanced students	Observed evidence of differentiation
instruction with identified gifted students at a grade level)		students are recognised.	Strategies directed to the academic needs of advanced learners are often observed. Advanced thinking skills are frequently observed. Acceleration of content is frequently observed.
Middle School Level			
Cluster grouping within a given class	Classroom teacher	The needs of the cluster group are rarely recognised. Lessons focus on whole class instruction.	Specific materials for advanced learners are rarely observed. Strategies directed to the academic needs of advanced learners are rarely observed.
Honours class	Classroom teacher	The academic needs of advanced students are sometimes recognised.	Acceleration of content is sometimes observed if the class has a structured curriculum. Advanced thinking skills are sometimes observed.
High school level			
Honours classes	Classroom teacher	The academic needs of advanced students are sometimes recognised.	Acceleration of content is sometimes observed if the class has a structured curriculum. Advanced thinking skills are sometimes observed.
Advanced class with established advanced curriculum (advanced placement [AP]; international baccalaureate diploma program [IB])	Classroom teacher with specific training in AP or IB	The academic needs of advanced students are frequently recognised.	Acceleration of content is always observed. Advanced thinking skills are frequently observed.

experience (i.e., novice or veteran) and familiarity with gifted learners. The nature of the training may need to be differentiated accordingly, distinguishing between the needs of teachers ready to move to advanced strategies versus those still requiring basic support in the ideas of differentiation (Dall'Alba & Sandberg,

2006). This suggests that teachers move through developmental stages in their ability to gain efficacy in implementation of classroom instruction (Brody & Hadar, 2015). Therefore, training needs to be ongoing and closely focused on stages of teacher development in strategy utilisation to support higher level thinking for all learners.

Recommendations to Developers of Gifted Education Programs

In this chapter we have reported on the compilation of data collected from six districts on the prevalence and effectiveness in the use of differentiated strategies for the gifted in order to provide insight into what needs to happen in practice for stronger differentiation to occur. In the spirit of what this study represents, it seems appropriate then to render a few final recommendations to developers of gifted programs:

- Design a process for monitoring classroom behaviour in differentiation, using a model such as the COS-R. If district administrators routinely examined classroom practice with a focus on higher level thinking, then insights would emerge about teacher effectiveness and professional development needs.
- Ensure that international or national standards, such as the NAGC Gifted Education Programming Standards for curriculum planning and instruction, are used for planning and implementing programs. If these standards were used as a checklist, it would create an awareness of what is missing from instructional practice.
- Select a few core differentiation behaviours to include in an annual plan for school improvement so the behaviours are the focus of expectations for all teachers. If the school focuses on differentiation, especially higher level thinking skills, as a legitimate pathway to improvement in learning for all, then student learning progress is more likely. For example, a principal may select the skill of 'inferencing' as a focus for teacher professional development as a part of an annual school improvement plan.
- Employ higher level questions that probe understanding. The use of proverbs, mathematics problems, or current issues may be the basis for framing questions, such as 'What does this mean? How do you know?' Such questions, if used routinely, elevate discussions and on-going dialogue in the classroom from teacher to student, student to student, and student to teacher.
- Provide professional development on differentiation, based on needs demonstrated by classroom teachers. If such professional development were available locally and based on specific identified areas of needed improvement, positive change in teacher behaviours may result. For example, it can also be helpful for the professional development to be offered within different content areas. This means that 'drawing inferences from the literature' or 'inferring pathways for problem solutions' may be titles for workshops.
- Assess gifted student learning as a register of progress on the use of differentiation behaviours by teachers. If gifted students are demonstrating successful advanced learning as seen in daily work, portfolios, and

performance-based assessments, then the evidence would suggest that teachers are differentiating effectively. Student outcomes then are an additional approach to monitor teacher differentiation use and effectiveness.

Conclusion

A compilation study of classroom teacher behaviours that revealed both the frequency of use and effectiveness of use of differentiation in classrooms that included gifted learners in six districts across the Eastern United States was described in this chapter. The findings from the observations of 329 classrooms presented a portrait of the under-utilisation of differentiated strategies and materials. At the same time, the study suggested that teachers who employ these strategies are using them with some effectiveness, opening up the question of why such strategies of higher level thinking are not being routinely applied in classrooms with gifted students. More work on teacher selection, preparation, and administrative support is required to ensure that teachers are addressing gifted student needs effectively.

Cross-References

► Assessment, Pedagogy, and Curriculum: Part IV Introduction
► Attuned Pedagogy: The Artistry of Differentiated Instruction from a Taiwanese Cultural Perspective
► Australian Teachers Who Made a Difference: Secondary Gifted Student Perceptions of Teaching and Teacher Effectiveness
► Engaging Gifted Students in Solving Real Problems Creatively: Implementing the Real Engagement in Active Problem-Solving (REAPS) Teaching/Learning Model in Australasian and Pacific Rim Contexts
► Gifted Education in the Asia-Pacific: From the Past for the Future – An Introduction
► Highly Able Students in International Schools
► Learning from International Research Informs Academic Acceleration in Australasia: A Case for Consistent Policy
► Nurturing Mathematical Talents of Young Mathematically Gifted English Language Learners
► Online Learning for Mathematically Talented Students: A Perspective from Hong Kong
► Put Them Together and See How They Learn! Ability Grouping and Acceleration Effects on the Self-Esteem of Academically Gifted High School Students
► Some Implications for the Future of Gifted Education in the Asia-Pacific
► Teaching Gifted Education to Pre-service Teachers: Lessons Learned

Appendix A

> **The William and Mary Classroom Observation Scales-Revised**
> *Joyce VanTassel-Baska, Ed.D.,Linda Avery, Ph.D.,Jeanne Stuck, Ph.D.,Annie Feng, Ed.D.,*
> *Bruce Bracken, Ph.D.,Dianne Drummond, M.Ed.,Tamra Stambaugh, M.Ed.*

School_____Subject_____Level_____Number of students_____

Directions: Please employ the following scale as you rate each of the checklist items. Rate each item according to how well the teacher characteristic or behaviour was demonstrated during the observed instructional activity. Each item is judged on an individual, self-contained basis, regardless of its relationship to an overall set of behaviours relevant to the cluster heading.

3 = Effective	2 = Somewhat effective	1 = Ineffective	N/O = Not observed
The teacher evidenced careful planning and classroom flexibility in implementation of the behaviour, eliciting many appropriate student responses. The teacher was clear and sustained focus on the purposes of learning.	The teacher evidenced some planning and/or classroom flexibility in implementation of the behaviour, eliciting some appropriate students responses. The teacher was sometimes clear and focused on the purposes of learning.	The teacher evidenced little or no planning and/or classroom flexibility in implementation of the behaviour, eliciting minimal appropriate student responses. The teacher was unclear and unfocused regarding the purpose of learning.	The listed behaviour was not demonstrated during the time of observation. (NOTE: There must be an obvious attempt made for the certain behaviour to be rated 'ineffective' instead of 'not observed'.)

General teaching behaviours

Curriculum planning and delivery	3	2	1	N/O
The teacher...				
1. set high expectations for student performance.				
2. incorporated activities for students to apply new knowledge.				
3. engaged students in planning, monitoring or assessing their learning.				
4. encouraged students to express their thoughts.				
5. had students reflect on what they had learned.				

Comments:

Differentiated teaching behaviours

Materials and strategy utilization	3	2	1	N/O
The teacher...				
6. showed evidence of using program-relevant differentiated materials for the gifted in mathematics, science, social studies or language arts. (circle which subject applied)				
7. used cluster, pull-out, self-contained or advanced class grouping to target gifted learners for instruction. (circle one or more)				
8. used models of thinking to promote deeper conceptual understanding and advanced content learning.				
9. employed evidence-based instructional strategies, such as graphic organisers, to enhance student higher level thinking.				

Comments:

Accommodations for individual differences	3	2	1	N/O
The teacher...				
10. provided opportunities for independent or group learning to promote depth in understanding content.				
11. accommodated individual or sub-group differences (e.g., through individual conferencing, student or teacher choice in material selection and task assignments).				
12. encouraged multiple interpretations of events and situations.				
13. allowed students to discover key ideas individually through structured activities and/or questions.				
Comments:				

Critical thinking strategies	3	2	1	N/O
The teacher...				
14. encouraged students to judge or evaluate situations, problems or issues.				
15. engaged students in comparing and contrasting ideas (e.g., analyze generated ideas).				
16. provided opportunities for students to generalise from concrete data or information to the abstract.				
17. encouraged student synthesis or summary of information within or across disciplines.				
Comments:				

Creative thinking strategies	3	2	1	N/O
The teacher...				
18. solicited many diverse thoughts about issues or ideas.				
19. engaged students in the exploration of diverse points of view to reframe ideas.				
20. encouraged students to demonstrate open-mindedness and tolerance of imaginative, sometimes playful solutions to problems.				
21. provided opportunities for students to develop and elaborate on their ideas.				
Comments:				

Analysis and inquiry strategies	3	2	1	N/O
The teacher...				
22. employed the inquiry process to stimulate high-level learning.				
23. asked high-level questions that encouraged students to think and ask their own questions.				
24. employed activities that required analysis of text, use of models or other symbolic sources.				
25. employed activities that required students to build argument orally, visually, in written form or by using models and symbols.				
26. asked students to collect and draw inferences from data and represent findings in a relevant form.				
Comments:				
Additional Comments:				

Scales used with permission of Prufrock Press, Waco, Texas, USA.

References

Assouline, S., Colangelo, N., & VanTassel-Baska, J. (2015). *A nation empowered: Evidence trumps the excuses that hold back America's brightest students* (Vol. 1). Iowa City, Iowa: University of Iowa, the Connie Belin and Jacqueline N. Blank International Center for Gifted Education and Talent Development.

Assouline, S., Colangelo, N., VanTassel-Baska, J., & Lupkowski-Shoplik, A. (2015). *A nation empowered: Evidence trumps the excuses that hold back America's brightest students* (Vol. 2). Iowa City, Iowa: University of Iowa, the Connie Belin and Jacqueline N. Blank International Center for Gifted Education and Talent Development.

Australian Government Department of Teaching and Learning. (2018). Retrieved from http://www.education.gov.au/australian-curriculum-0.

Avery, L., & VanTassel-Baska, J. (2001). Investigating the impact of gifted program evaluation at state and local levels: Problems with traction. *Journal for the Education of the Gifted, 25*(2), 153–176. https://doi.org/10.1177/016235320102500204

Baska, A., & VanTassel-Baska, J. (2018). *Interventions for special needs gifted learners.* Waco, TX: Prufrock Press.

Brody, D. L., & Hadar, L. L. (2015). Personal professional trajectories of novice and experienced teacher educators in a professional development community. *Teacher Development, 9*(2), 246–266. https://doi.org/10.1080/13664530.2015.1016242

Chan, D. W. (2001). Characteristics and competencies of teachers of gifted learners: The Hong Kong teacher perspective. *Roeper Review, 23*, 197–202. https://doi.org/10.1080/02783190109554098

Coleman, M. R., Gallagher, J. J., & Job, J. (2012). Developing and sustaining professionalism within gifted education. *Gifted Child Today, 35*(1), 27–36. https://doi.org/10.1177/1076217511427511

Coleman, M. R., & Johnsen, S. K. (2013). *Implementing RtI with gifted students.* Waco, TX: Prufrock Press.

Croft, L. J. (2003). Teachers of the gifted: Gifted teachers. In N. Colangelo & G. A. Davis (Eds.), *Handbook of gifted education* (3rd ed., pp. 558–571). Boston, MA: Allyn and Bacon.

Dall'Alba, G., & Sandberg, J. (2006). Unveiling professional development: A critical review of stage models. *Review of Educational Research, 76*(3), 383–412. https://doi.org/10.3102/00346543076003383

Deunk, M., Doolaard, S., & Smale, A. (2015). *Differentiation within and across classrooms: A systematic review of studies into the cognitive effects of differentiation practices.* Groningen, The Netherlands: GION.

Dixon, F. A., Yssel, N., McConnell, J. M., & Hardin, T. (2014). Differentiated instruction, professional development, and teacher efficacy. *Journal for the Education of the Gifted, 37*(2), 111–127. https://doi.org/10.1177/0162353214529042

Farah, Y. N., & Chandler, K. L. (2018). Structured observation instruments assessing instructional practices with gifted and talented students: A review of the literature. *Gifted Child Quarterly, 62*(3), 276–288. https://doi.org/10.1177/0016986218758439

Farkas, S., & Duckett, A. (2008). *High achieving students in the era of NCLB: Results from a national teacher survey.* Washington DC: Fordham Foundation.

Gavin, M. K., Casa, T. M., Adelson, J. L., Carroll, S. R., & Sheffield, L. J. (2009). The impact of advanced curriculum on the achievement of mathematically promising elementary students. *Gifted Child Quarterly, 53*(3), 188–202. https://doi.org/10.1177/0016986209334964

Geake, J. G., & Gross, M. U. M. (2008). Teachers' negative affect toward academically gifted students: An evolutionary psychology study. *Gifted Child Quarterly, 52*, 217–231. https://doi.org/10.1177/0016986208319704

Gentry, M., Steenbergen-Hu, S., & Choi, B. (2011). Student-identified exemplary teachers: Insights from talented teachers. *Gifted Child Quarterly, 55*, 111–125. https://doi.org/10.1177/0016986210397830

Guskey, T. R. (2000). *Evaluating professional development.* Thousand Oaks, CA: Corwin Press.

Hansen, J., & Feldhusen, J. (1994). Comparison of trained and untrained teachers of gifted students. *Gifted Child Quarterly, 38*(3), 115–121. https://doi.org/10.1177/001698629403800304

Hughes, C., Kettler, T., Shaughnessy-Dedrich, E., & VanTassel-Baska, J. (2014). *A teacher's guide to using the common core state standards with gifted and advanced learners in the English/ language arts*. Waco, TX: Prufrock Press.

Johnsen, S. (Ed.). (2012). *The preK–12 program standards in gifted education*. Waco, TX: Prufrock Press.

Jolly, J. L., & Jarvis, J. M. (Eds.). (2018). *Exploring gifted education: Australian & New Zealand perspectives*. Abington, Oxon: Routledge.

Kanevsky, L. (2015). Do high ability learners enjoy learning alone "or" in groups? It depends. *International Journal of Special Education, 30*(2), 32–43.

Kennedy, M. (1999). Form and substance in mathematics and science professional development. *NISE Brief, 3*(2), 1–7.

Kim, K. H., VanTassel-Baska, J., Bracken, B. A., Feng, A., & Stambaugh, T. (2014). Assessing science reasoning and conceptual understanding in the primary grades using standardized and performance-based assessments. *Journal of Advanced Academics, 25*(1), 47–66. https://doi.org/ 10.1177/1932202X14520946

Knopfelmacher S., & Kronborg, L. (2003). Characteristics, competencies and classroom strategies of effective teachers of gifted and talented students. *Proceedings of the 9th National Conference of the Australian Association for the Education of the Gifted and Talented (AAEGT)*.

Kronborg, L. (2017). Gifted education in Australia and New Zealand. In S. Pfeiffer's (Ed.), *APA handbook of giftedness and talent* (pp. 85–96). Washington, DC: American Psychological Association.

Kronborg, L., & Plunkett, M. (2012). Examining teacher attitudes and perceptions of teacher competencies required in a new selective high school. *Australasian Journal of Gifted Education, 21*(2), 33–46.

Kronborg, L., & Plunkett, M. (2013). Responding to professional learning: How effective teachers differentiate teaching and learning strategies to engage highly able adolescents. *Australasian Journal of Gifted Education, 22*(2), 52–63.

Kyriakides, L., Christoforidou, M., Panayiotou, A., & Creemers, B. (2017). The impact of a three-year teacher professional development course on quality of teaching: Strengths and limitations of the dynamic approach. *European Journal of Teacher Education, 40*(4), 465–486. https://doi. org/10.1080/02619768.2017.1349093

Lassig, C. J. (2009). Teachers' attitudes towards the gifted: The importance of professional development and school culture. *Australasian Journal of Gifted Education, 18*(2), 32–42.

Little, C., Feng, A., VanTassel-Baska, J., Rogers, K., & Avery, L. (2007). A study of curriculum effectiveness in social studies. *Gifted Child Quarterly, 51*(3), 272–284.

Maker, C. J., & Schiever, S. (2010). *Curriculum development and teaching strategies for gifted learners* (3rd ed.). Austin, TX: Pro-ed.

Miller, E. M. (2009). The effect of training in gifted education on elementary classroom teachers' theory-based reasoning about the concept of giftedness. *Journal for the Education of the Gifted, 33*(1), 65–105. https://doi.org/10.1177/016235320903300104

Mills, C. J. (2003). Characteristics of effective teachers of gifted students: Teacher background and personality styles of students. *Gifted Child Quarterly, 47*, 272–281. Retrieved from http://www. gifted.gr/documents/useful-documents/Effective_teacher.pdf

Olszewski-Kubilius, P., & Clarenbach, J. (2014). Closing the opportunity gap: Program factors contributing to academic success in culturally different youth. *Gifted Child Today, 37*, 103–110. https://doi.org/10.1177/1076217514520630

Pedersen, F., & Kronborg, L. (2014). Challenging secondary teachers to examine beliefs and pedagogy when teaching highly able students in mixed-ability health education classes. *Australian Journal of Gifted Education, 23*(1), 15–27.

Peters, S. J., & Jolly, J. L. (2018). The influence of teacher training on the frequency of gifted education instructional practices. *The Australian Educational Researcher*, (2), 45. https://doi. org/10.1007/s13384-018-2060-4

Plucker, J. A., Hardesty, J., & Burroughs, N. (2013). *Talent on the sidelines. Excellence gaps and America's persistent talent underclass*. Storrs, CT: University of Connecticut, Center for Education Policy Analysis.

Plunkett, M., & Kronborg, L. (2011). Learning to be a teacher of the gifted: The importance of examining opinions and challenging misconceptions. *Gifted and Talented International, 26*(1–2), 33–46. https://doi.org/10.1080/15332276.2011.11673587

Roberts, J., Inman, T., & Robins, J. (2018). *Introduction to gifted education.* Waco, TX: Prufrock Press.

Roberts, J. L. (2006). Teachers of secondary gifted students: What makes them effective? In A. Dixon & S. Moon (Eds.), *Handbook of secondary gifted education* (pp. 567–580). Waco, TX: Prufrock Press.

Sanders, W. L., & Horn, S. P. (1998). Research findings from the Tennessee value-added assessment system (TVAAS) database: Implications for educational evaluation and research. *Journal of Personnel Evaluation in Education, 12*(3), 247–256. https://doi.org/10.1023/A:1008067210518

Stambaugh, T. (2007). *Effects of the Jacob's Ladder Reading Comprehension Program on reading comprehension and critical thinking skills of third, fourth, and fifth grade students in Title I schools* (Unpublished doctoral dissertation). William & Mary, Williamsburg, VA.

Stambaugh, T., & VanTassel-Baska, J. (2018). *Jacob's ladder reading comprehension program: Socio-emotional intelligence.* Waco, TX: Prufrock Press.

Steenbergen-Hu, S., Makel, M., & Olszewski-Kubilius, P. (2016). What 100 years of research says about the effects of ability grouping and acceleration on K–12 students' academic achievement: Findings of two second-order meta-analyses. *Review of Educational Research, 86*(4), 849–899. https://doi.org/10.3102/0034654316675417

Suprayogi, M. N., Valcke, M., & Godwin, R. (2017). Teachers and their implementation of differentiated instruction in the classroom. *Teaching & Teacher Education, 67,* 291–301. https://doi.org/10.1016/j.tate.2017.06.020

Tomlinson, C. A. (2017). *How to differentiate instruction in academically diverse classrooms* (3rd ed.). Alexandria, VA: Association for Supervision and Curriculum Development (ASCD).

Valiandes, S., & Neophytou, L. (2018). Teachers' professional development for differentiated instruction in mixed-ability classrooms: Investigating the impact of a development program on teachers' professional learning and on students' achievement. *Teacher Development, 22*(1), 123–138. https://doi.org/10.1080/13664530.2017.1338196

VanTassel-Baska, J., Avery, L., Struck, J., Feng, A., Bracken, B., Drummond, D., & Stambaugh, T. (2003). *The William and Mary classroom observation scales-revised (COS-R).* Williamsburg, VA: Center for Gifted Education.

VanTassel-Baska, J. (2004). Assessing classroom practice: The use of a structured observation form. In J. VanTassel-Baska & A. X. Feng (Eds.), *Designing and utilizing program evaluation for gifted program improvement* (pp. 87–107). Waco, TX: Prufrock Press.

VanTassel-Baska, J. (2006). A content analysis of evaluation findings across 20 gifted programs: A Clarion call for enhanced gifted program development. *Gifted Child Quarterly, 50*(3), 199–215. https://doi.org/10.1177/001698620605000302

VanTassel-Baska, J. (2012). Analyzing differentiation in the classroom: Using the COS-R. *Gifted Child Today, 35*(1), 42–48. https://doi.org/10.1177/1076217511427431

VanTassel-Baska, J. (2017). Considerations in curriculum for the gifted. In S. Pfeiffer's (Ed.), *APA handbook of giftedness and talent* (pp. 349–370). Washington, DC: American Psychological Association.

VanTassel-Baska, J. (2018). Achievement unlocked: Effective curriculum interventions with low-income students. *Gifted Child Quarterly, 62*(1), 68–82. https://doi.org/10.1177/0016986217738565

Van-Tassel-Baska, J., Avery, L. D., Little, C. A., & Hughes, C. E. (2000). An evaluation of the implementation of curriculum innovation: The impact of William and Mary units on schools. *Journal for the Education of the Gifted, 23,* 244–272. https://doi.org/10.1177/016235320002300201

VanTassel-Baska, J., Bass, G., Ries, R., Poland, D., & Avery, L. (1998). A national pilot study of science curriculum effectiveness for high ability students. *Gifted Child Quarterly, 42,* 200–211.

VanTassel-Baska, J., Bracken, B., Feng, A., & Brown, E. (2009). A longitudinal study of enhancing critical thinking and reading comprehension in Title I classrooms. *Journal for the Education of the Gifted, 33*(1), 7–37. https://doi.org/10.1177/016235320903300102

VanTassel-Baska, J., Feng, A., Brown, E., Bracken, B., Stambaugh, T., French, H., & Bai, W. (2008). A study of differentiated instructional change over three years. *Gifted Child Quarterly, 52,* 297–312. https://doi.org/10.1177/0016986208321809

VanTassel-Baska, J., Feng, A., MacFarlane, B., Heng, M., Teo, C., Wong, L., . . . Khong, B. (2008). A cross-cultural study of teachers' instructional practices and beliefs. *Journal for the Education of the Gifted, 31*(3), 338–363. https://doi.org/10.4219/jeg-2008-770

VanTassel-Baska, J., & Little, C. (Eds.). (2017). *Content-based curriculum for high-ability learners* (3rd ed.). Waco, TX: Prufrock Press.

VanTassel-Baska, J., MacFarlane, B., & Feng, A. (2006). A cross-cultural study of exemplary teaching: What do Singapore and the United States secondary gifted class teachers say? *Gifted and Talented International, 21*(2), 38–47. https://doi.org/10.1080/15332276.2006.11673474

VanTassel-Baska, J., Quek, C., & Feng, A. X. (2005). *Classroom observation scales-revised: Users' manual.* Retrieved from https://education.wm.edu/centers/cfge/_documents/resources/cosrmanualrevised.pdf

VanTassel-Baska, J., Quek, C., & Feng, A. X. (2006). The development and use of a structured teacher observation scale to assess differentiated best practices. *Roeper Review, 19*(2), 84–92. https://doi.org/10.1080/02783190709554391

VanTassel-Baska, J., Zuo, L., Avery, L., & Little, C. (2002). A curriculum study of gifted student learning in the language arts. *Gifted Child Quarterly, 46*(1), 30–43. https://doi.org/10.1177/016235329301600204

Westberg, K. L., Archambault, F. X., Dobyns, S. M., & Salvin, T. J. (1993). The classroom practices observation study. *Journal for the Education of the Gifted, 16*(2), 120–146. https://doi.org/10.1177/016235329301600204

Westberg, K. L., & Daoust, M. E. (2003). The results of the replication of the classroom practices survey in two states. *National Research Center on the Gifted and Talented (NRCGT) Newsletter, 1*, 3–8.

Wyner, J. S., Bridgeland, J. M., & Dilulio, J. J. (2007). *Achievement trap: How America is failing millions of high-achieving students from low-income families.* Washington, DC: Jack Kent Cooke Foundation.

Joyce Van Tassel-Baska, PhD, is the Jody and Layton Smith Professor Emerita of Education and founding director of the Center for Gifted Education at The College of William and Mary in Virginia where she developed a graduate program and a research and development center in gifted education. Formerly, she initiated and directed the Center for Talent Development at Northwestern University. She has also served as a state, regional, and local director of gifted programs and as a high school teacher of the gifted. She has published widely including 30 books and more than 600 refereed journal articles, book chapters, and scholarly reports. She has received national and international awards for her work. Her major research interests are on the talent development process and effective curricular interventions with the gifted.

Gail Fischer Hubbard   served as supervisor of gifted education for Prince William County Public Schools, Virginia, for 26 years. Before she entered administration, she was a high school gifted education resource teacher for a decade. She has served as the president or chairperson of several Virginia organisations for the gifted. She received her AB from Bryn Mawr College and her master of arts in teaching from Harvard University. Her major research interests are in classroom differentiation for gifted learners and in the education of gifted students in rural settings.

Janice Robbins,   PhD, is an adjunct assistant professor at the College of William and Mary as well as at Rutgers University. Dr. Robbins has served as acting Director of the Center for Gifted Education and Director of Project Civis at William and Mary. She was formerly Curriculum Chief for the United States Department of Defense schools worldwide as well as district coordinator of gifted programs and school principal at the elementary and secondary levels. Dr. Robbins has authored several curriculum books and journal articles and supports teacher and administrator professional development for numerous school districts. Her particular areas of research and teaching are in gifted education, creativity, inquiry, and online learning.

Part V

Diverse Dimensions of Gifted Education

Diverse Dimensions of Gifted Education: Part V Introduction

Seokhee Cho

Contents

Abstract

The authors of the chapters in Part V address diverse dimensions of gifted education including the conceptual evolution of gifted education and talent development, counselling, teaching for creativity, trends and challenges of creativity development, professional development of teachers in disadvantaged schools, and rural gifted girls in Asia-Pacific countries.

Keywords

Gifted education · Counselling · Creativity · Professional development · Disadvantage · Popular culture

The aims in this chapter are to:
1. Address the dynamic influence of sociocultural conditions on gifted education through human interactions.
2. Demonstrate diversity in varied dimensions within the gifted education field by sociocultural contexts.

S. Cho (✉)
St. John's University, New York, NY, USA
e-mail: chos1@stjohns.edu

© Springer Nature Singapore Pte Ltd. 2021
S. R. Smith (ed.), *Handbook of Giftedness and Talent Development in the Asia-Pacific*,
Springer International Handbooks of Education,
https://doi.org/10.1007/978-981-13-3041-4_79

3. Compare policies and practices in creativity education among countries in Asia-Pacific regions.

Introduction

While each chapter addresses a different dimension of gifted education, the authors of each discuss the changes in, conflicts with, or effects on the dimension influenced by sociocultural conditions where students and educators reside. The variety in the content of the chapters is replicated in the diversity of the contributing authors, being from Australia, Mainland China, Taiwan, Hong Kong/Macau, Japan, Malaysia, and South Korea. Though multi-cultural in context, Australia has primarily a western culture with individual-oriented values, whereas other countries represented in this section have been influenced by collectivism or Confucianism.

These chapters can be read with the framework of sociocultural theory in mind, which asserts that the role of culture and social contexts are central to human learning and development. According to the sociocultural theories, individuals are socially, culturally, and historically situated and these contexts influence their under-standings, beliefs, and actions (Vygotsky, 1978). As learning does not occur in a fixed static circumstance, it is shaped by dynamic sociocultural contexts and human interactions. However, it should also be noted that human beings have not only been influenced by the environment but have changed and improved the environment by coping with their circumstances and challenges. The chapters mirror the diversity in the varied dimensions found within the gifted education field. Hence, it would be easier to get insights if the chapters are read keeping this diversity and the interaction between the human and the sociocultural conditions in mind.

Introduction to the Individual Chapters

In ▶ Chap. 45, "A Counselling Framework for Meeting the Needs of Gifted Students in Malaysia" Abu Yazid Abu Bakar and Linda Brody describe a counselling model developed as a part of the gifted education system in Malaysia which uses the holistic approach developed through collaboration between *Universiti Kebangsaan Malaysia* and the *Centre for Talented Youth (CTY)* at the *Johns Hopkins University*, USA, in 2009. The authors reiterated that counselling should be individualised to meet the requirements of each student and support the holistic talent development of its students. In the chapter, the authors describe and discuss the framework and guiding principles of counselling initiatives for gifted learners in the Malaysian context. Since it is still in the beginning stage of the counselling services, the authors briefly describe their findings on the students' psychosocial and emotional concerns, their perceptions of the counselling services they have received, and the common issues faced by gifted students in current local educational settings. However, there is no report of systematic research on the effects of the counselling services yet. It would be interesting to learn how their sociocultural environment created different concerns and issues and whether the counselling services based on this framework was effective for the gifted students.

Dale Albanese, Ming-Jen Yu, and Jing-Jyi Wu, in ▶ Chap. 46, "Bricolage and the Evolution of Giftedness and Talent in Taiwan", discuss how the concept of gifted education and talent development evolved going through conflicts between traditional values based on meritocracy and the demand to meet the new wave of producing creative human resources. The authors describe how the sociocultural context of Taiwan influenced the practices of educational policies on the identification of gifted-ness and talent development. Confucianism emphasises meritocracy and harmony among members of the society and in life. Meritocracy perpetuated exam-based identification of giftedness and talent in the academic/intellectual domains. Harmony requires individuals not to be revolutionary. The Taiwanese government initiated the increase of economic competitiveness by opening up the identification of giftedness and talent in other areas than the academic/intellectual domains. Hence, it encouraged competition and contests for the identification and development of talents in various fields. However, the authors were not sure about the effects of the educational policies. The Taiwanese government's efforts to nominally aspire to moving away from examination-based education and toward a more inclusive appreciation of diverse abilities have been met with controversy and resulted, paradoxically, in increased pressure for students. The challenges that the Taiwanese government and people face in their efforts to recognise and develop talent in various fields can be quite similar to those in other Asian countries under Confucian influence, such as South Korea, Japan, China and Hong Kong. The effects of interweaving traditional values and new educational reform that resulted in a bricolage are effectively delineated by the authors. The question is how to take advantage of the Confucian influence—if it is not possible to eliminate its influence—for the identification and development of talent in other areas than the intellectual or the academic?

The next chapter has a focus on creativity. In Carly Lassig's ▶ Chap. 47, "Creativity Talent Development: Fostering Creativity in Schools", she presents students' perceptions of the formal educational environment which is either nurtur-ing or inhibiting creativity talent development. The author claims that individuals' creative processes and outcomes are developed within the external constraints of a particular educational program, including limitations posed by task demands and assessment criteria or teachers' instructions. Lassig suggests replacing discrete creative thinking skill programs and packages with a curriculum that has creativity infused throughout. In her study, students reported that their educational environ-ment needed favourable conditions for creativity development, such as: (a) opportunities, (b) autonomy, (c) structure, (d) challenge, (e) stimuli, (f) congruous physical conditions, (g) like minds, (h) experts, (i) cognitive support, and (j) affective support. Meanwhile, (a) curriculum constraints, (b) lack of time, (c) pressure, (d) distractions, (e) lack of resources, and (f) negative social interactions were reported as nonfavourable conditions for creativity development in schools. This author brings into question how teachers and administrators can achieve both goals (meeting accountability while also facilitating creativity development) when there are constraints of curriculum, time, and resources.

▶ Chapter 48, "Creative and Gifted Education in Korea: Using the CATs Model to Illustrate How Creativity Can Grow into Innovation" is Kyung Hee Kim's and Jeongkyu Lee's. The authors used the model of CATs (Climates, Attitudes and Thinking skills) to analyse and evaluate the recent Korean education efforts for creative and gifted education. Kim's CATs model uses such a natural analogy: (a) CATs model cultivating climates 4S (*sun, storm, soil* and *space)*; (b) nurturing the 4S attitudes; and (c) applying ION (Inbox, Outbox and Newbox) thinking skills. The 4S climates nurture the 4S attitudes, which enable ION thinking skills. Based on the CATs model, the authors evaluated Korean creative and gifted education, which has been under the influence of Confucianism with a high value on academic success, filial piety, social hierarchy, and social conformity. The authors reported that Korean creative and gifted education tried to cultivate the Sun climate in various ways. However, they also claim that these policies and investment efforts on research and development have not achieved its intended outcomes due to the values cherished by Confucianism. Kim and Lee suggest specific strategies on how to cultivate students' creativity based on the CATs Model. However, they have not provided either qualitative or quantitative data used for the evaluation of the students' creativity and the effects of Korean government's policies or investments for creativity development. While the students' anecdotal responses seem to support the benefits of using the CATs model in practise, it is still not clear whether these strategies will help Korean students and educators cope with the negative influences of Confucianism or whether they will need some other mechanism to counteract the traditional influence of Confucianism?

In gifted education, collaborations between researchers across different countries have become more common in the last two decades. The ▶ Chap. 49, "Trends and Challenges of Creativity Development Among Selected Asian Countries and Regions: China, Hong Kong/Macau, Japan, Malaysia, and South Korea", by Bonnie Cramond, Kyung Hee Kim, T.W. Chiang, Takeo Higuchi, Takuya Iwata, Min Ma, and Ananda Kumar Palaniappan is illustrative of such collaboration. The authors compared creativity development in several countries which are under Confucian influence through the perspectives of scholars from each society. One perspective was clear and that is the conflict between their efforts to develop creativity for economic competitiveness and their traditional value of collectivism. For example, the government may take initiatives to promote creative industries as a marketing strategy, but not on creativity as a culturally valued characteristic. These societies emphasise harmony and conformity over independence and non-conformity, which reflect Confucian values and norms. Individuals are celebrated for their creative achievements, and they report that the education curricula have attempted to incorporate creative teaching practices. In addition, high-stakes testing pressures have inhibited creativity development in these societies. For assessment of creativity, all of these societies use both translated versions of the *Torrance Tests of Creative Thinking* (TTCT) and their own respective assessments. These authors claim that due to the collectivistic values, the individual's unique thoughts and expressions are not celebrated. Interestingly, the authors have reported an irony that South Korea has been the most successful at innovation, according to the Bloomberg Innovation Ranking worldwide for the last several years. Does this report imply that, contrary to the overall claim of these authors on the negative influence of Confucianism, can creativity be effectively developed in that context? Then, what would be the mechanism that enabled the creativity development?

There has been much research on creativity, but less on how to develop creativity itself. Takeo Higuchi, Shozo Saegusa, and Daehyun Kim endeavour to address this within the Japanese university context. Their chapter is entitled ▶ Chap. 50, "Using the Idea-Marathon System (IMS) in University Education and Creativity Development". The authors relate specific strategies to nurture the creativity of Japanese college students by fusing self-reflection, idea generation, and journal writing. This system was created by Takeo Higuchi who found that it helped students develop both creativity and good study habits. When taught to college freshmen in Business Administration, graphs on the changes in students' idea generation, curiosity, intellectual interest, love of learning, and better cooperation among groups were visually inspected and the number of ideas generated and their final performance assessment were found to be improved. Faculty support (i.e., weekly communication cards with students) was found to be critical for students to maintain their motivation for the IMS writing regimen. The authors claim the IMS to be good for students to help their innate creative talents grow by engaging in self-reflection and encouraging written and visual expression. This chapter shows creativity development requires persistent use of self-reflection, idea generation and journal writing to develop the habit of these behaviours with the support and guidance of experts.

Teaching and learning for gifted students in rural contexts can present both benefits and hindrances to talent development. Denise Wood's ▶ Chap. 51, "Rural Adolescent Gifted Girls: Exploring the Impact of Popular Culture on Their Talent Development" focuses on Australian adolescent gifted girls. She presents findings on how rural gifted girls perceive giftedness and talent from popular culture which they interact with and are influenced by every day. It was found that rural girls' responses to popular culture do not present gifted women with a positive perspective on giftedness, nor did it portray the effort and work that may go into talent development. The author developed a theoretical model on talent development of rural gifted girls, informed by Gagné's *Differentiating Model of Giftedness and Talent*, and gender specific talent development models. In the model, Wood identifies important influences from individual interactions of adolescent girls with popular culture, aspirational thinking and action and interactions with other people and places. The author suggested that if these influences are balanced within the life of a girl, they offer the support she needs to counteract the impact of popular culture on her vision of how a girl or woman can be, or what she can do. In this chapter, the author provided details on how popular culture can negatively influence the talent development of gifted rural girls. However, how to neutralise the negative influences from popular culture is relatively general. To verify the validity of the model, further research on how aspirational thinking and action and interactions with other people and places can be effectively utilised to overcome the negative influences of popular culture may need to be conducted.

In the final chapter in Part V, ▶ Chap. 52, "A Model for Growing Teacher Talent Scouts: Decreasing Underrepresentation of Gifted Students", Julie Dingle Swanson, Lara Walker Russell, and Lindsey Anderson present a professional development model developed in the USA through a Javits Grant project. In Title 1 schools, many students think that they are gifted and talented. The authors recognise that the values of a culture contribute to the identification and development of giftedness and talent. Many gifted and talented students from disadvantaged families are hard to recognise, resulting in the limited provision of resources for them. These authors believe that teachers can open access and opportunity for diverse learners from disadvantaged families. So, well-informed teachers are the most needed for children in poverty. The authors created the model of talent development that consists of three primary components: (a) cultural influences, (b) psychology of learning, and (c) powerful curriculum and instruction that utilises the *Integrated Curriculum Model* with student-driven inquiry. Research-based approaches used to advance professional learning of teachers, including whole group, small group, fidelity observations, and differentiated teacher learning are shared. The chapter concludes with a discussion of a framework for growing student talent through focused teacher development and the implications for the adoption of such a framework in the field, and potential directions for further research.

Conclusion

There are many foci in gifted education that are difficult to place under the one umbrella topic area and Part V includes many of these foci, hence, this section is titled *Diverse Dimensions*. However, the one constant binding the chapters together is the authors' steeping their work in their socioculturally based contexts. While the authors in this section reiterated many issues, such as underrepresentation and gender concerns, they also provided models, frameworks, and strategies for enhancing creativity and talent development, while also providing recommendations for translating theory into practice through teacher professional learning.

References

Vygotsky, L. S. (1978). *Mind in society: The development of higher psychological processes.* Cambridge, MA: Harvard University Press.

Seokhee Cho, PhD, is a Professor at the School of Education and Director of the *Center for Creativity and Gifted Education*, St. John's University, New York. She has been conducting two consecutive five-year Javits Grant Projects funded by US DOE on teaching mathematics to mathematically promising English learners and teaching science to twice-exceptional high school students from 2009 to 2019. Her 12 books and about 200 articles focus on creativity and gifted education. She has been the Director of the *National Research Center for Gifted Education* in Korea for 20 years. She is currently an Editorial Board Member of the *Gifted Child Quarterly, Gifted Education International, Turkish Journal of Giftedness and Education*, and *Journal of Gifted/ Talented Education* (Korean).

A Counselling Framework for Meeting the Needs of Gifted Students in Malaysia

45

Abu Yazid Abu Bakar and Linda E. Brody

Contents

Abstract

Gifted education has yet to be considered as one of the mainstream paradigms in the Malaysian national education system. Even though local initiatives for gifted learners were in existence in Malaysia as early as the 1960s, such efforts were short-lived due to a lack of a clearly defined curriculum, as well as limited training, leadership, and resources. Recently, however, interest in promoting programs to serve the learning needs of students with high academic potential has been reignited. In particular, the collaborative effort that begun in 2009 between Universiti Kebangsaan Malaysia and the Center for Talented Youth (CTY) at the Johns Hopkins University, USA, resulted in the development of a

A. Y. A. Bakar (✉)
Faculty of Education, Universiti Kebangsaan Malaysia, Bangi, Malaysia
e-mail: yazid3338@ukm.edu.my

L. E. Brody
Johns Hopkins University Center for Talented Youth, Baltimore, MD, USA
e-mail: lbrody1@jhu.edu

© Springer Nature Singapore Pte Ltd. 2021
S. R. Smith (ed.), *Handbook of Giftedness and Talent Development in the Asia-Pacific*,
Springer International Handbooks of Education,
https://doi.org/10.1007/978-981-13-3041-4_47

national program to serve gifted learners known as PERMATApintar™. At present, this program includes four main components: (1) talent search, (2) school holiday program, (3) residential college, and (4) pre-matriculation. In addition, the administration of the PERMATApintar™ program has decided to provide counselling services as one of the strategies to support the holistic talent development of its students. In this chapter a description and discussion of the framework, and guiding principles of counselling initiatives for gifted learners in the Malaysian context, particularly in the PERMATApintar™, will be provided. Concomitantly, an elaboration of the research findings on the students' psychosocial and emotional concerns, their perceptions of the counselling services they have received and the common issues faced by gifted students in current local educational settings will be presented in this chapter.

Keywords

Counselling · Gifted students · Malaysian education · Psychosocial services

The aims in this chapter are to:
1. Explain the psychosocial and emotional learning needs of gifted students.
2. Share information on special schools and programs for gifted students.
3. Reiterate the development of gifted students' education in Malaysia.
4. Compare counselling initiatives in two specific special programs of gifted students in the United States and Malaysia.
5. Present the conceptual framework of counselling provisions for Malaysian gifted students.

Introduction

The important role that psychosocial adjustment plays in talent development has been gaining much recognition, along with an increased understanding that many positive psychological traits that affect achievement can be cultivated, particularly if students are placed in settings that meet their personal and educational needs (Neihart, Pfeiffer, & Cross, 2016; Subotnik, Olszewski-Kubilius, & Worrell, 2011; VanTassel-Baska, Cross, & Olenchak, 2009). A debate continues, however, over whether gifted students exhibit psychological and personal characteristics that make them particularly prone to having social and emotional problems or whether their exceptional abilities enhance their resilience to experiencing psychological difficulties.

Webb et al. (2005) suggested that these two views are not incompatible, but may describe different populations. That is, the belief that gifted students have special social and emotional challenges as a result of their exceptional abilities may have been influenced by clinicians who see students who are seeking help for their problems, while the suggestion that most gifted students are resilient is based on research on high functioning students in selective academic programs, that specifically attempt to address the academic, social, and emotional needs of the participants (Cross & Andersen, 2016; Cross, Cassady, Dixon, & Adams, 2008; Cross & Cross, 2018; Lee, Olszewski-Kubilius, & Thompson, 2012; Neihart et al., 2016). A review of the literature on the psychosocial adjustment needs of gifted students and a description of how two centres, one in the United States and the other in Malaysia, have added counselling components to their academic programs in order to address these needs more specifically will be reiterated in this chapter.

Psychological Risk Factors

Although there is little evidence that gifted students experience social and emotional difficulties in greater numbers than other students, researchers and clinicians have long pointed to personal characteristics that may be risk factors for gifted students when they are present in excess and/or when there is a poor fit between student's needs and his or her learning environment (Neihart et al., 2016).

One thought is that gifted students may be prone to exhibiting enhanced sensitivities to stimuli, a concept that derives from Dabrowski's (1964) *Theory of Positive Disintegration* (Mendaglio, 2008; Probst & Piechowski, 2012). This characteristic can be associated with great passion for, and exceptional achievement in, a domain, but it can also lead to inappropriate behaviour and psychological difficulties when frustration and failure to achieve personal goals result (Webb et al., 2005). On the other hand, finding ways for students who exhibit intense curiosity and passion for a domain, such as in mathematics or the arts, to pursue it in deep and challenging ways, can relieve frustration and allow them to achieve at the highest levels (Brody, 2013; Subotnik & Jarvin, 2005).

There have also been studies linking gifted individuals to certain psychological types based on Jung's (1971) theory. In particular, some researchers have found a preponderance of introverts among gifted populations (e.g., Sak, 2004), a characteristic that is not, in itself, a negative trait and can correlate with deep thinking and high achievement (Mills, 1993). However, if introversion leads to a withdrawal from social situations, social and emotional problems may develop, while exposure to peers who share students' interests can help introverted students connect to others like themselves and improve their social interaction (Brody, 2007; Mickenberg & Wood, 2009).

A persons' self-concept is the view they have of themselves, their understanding of their strengths, weaknesses, and capabilities. It relates to self-efficacy, which is the confidence in one's own ability to complete tasks, control outcomes, and achieve goals (Bandura, 1993). The degree to which a student fits into his or her academic and social environments can influence their social and academic self-concepts, and this can influence their achievement, motivation, and social and emotional adjustment (Mendaglio, 2012). Much of the research in this area has examined the impact of special programs for gifted students on the participants' self-concepts. The results have been mixed with regard to academic self-concept with some studies finding 'big-fish-little-pond effect', that is, that a student's view of his or her academic competence can decrease in the face of greater competition (Marsh, 1984), while other studies have found no change in academic self-concept as a result of participating in rigorous academic programs (Preckel, Rach, & Scherrer, 2016). Some studies have even found an increase in academic self-concept in supportive and rigorous academic programs (e.g., Makel, Lee, Olszewski-Kubilius, & Putallaz, 2012). With regard to students' social self-concepts, the research literature reports more consistently positive results when students are placed in special programs with opportunities to connect to peers who share their interests and abilities (e.g., Preckel et al., 2016).

The importance of feeling in control of one's ability to achieve a goal is also reflected in the work of Dweck (2006) who outlined two mindsets: a 'fixed' one that attributes achievement to innate ability and a 'growth' mindset that fosters the idea that achievement is cultivated through effort. Students with fixed mindsets are less likely to recognise setbacks as temporary, which can lead to fear of failure and depression, while those with growth mindsets are more likely to take control and change situations that contribute to depression (Dweck, 2006). Attributing high achievement to being smart rather than to working hard encourages the fixed mindset and can contribute to problems when students are faced with challenges that they have difficulty overcoming (Siegle & Langley, 2016).

Mindsets can also be linked to perfectionism and much has been written about the relationship between giftedness and perfectionism (e.g., Spiers Neumeister 2016; Greenspon, 2012; Parker & Adkins, 1995). Perfectionism can be healthy when it motivates a student to do his or her best, but it can cross a line into a danger zone when it interferes with productive achievement and causes psychological distress. Unhealthy perfectionism can result in procrastination and failure to turn in assignments not perceived as perfect enough, behaviour that can also result in poor grades, and a despondence for failing to live up to expectations. Low self-esteem, social isolation, anxiety, and depression can be consequences of unhealthy perfectionism. There is little evidence that gifted students, as a group, are more perfectionistic than other students, but students who consistently earn top grades because work is too easy for them can be at risk of exhibiting unhealthy perfectionistic behaviour when demands become more rigorous (Spiers Neumeister, Williams, & Cross, 2009). On the other hand, placement in a rigorous academic environment has been shown to reduce unhealthy perfectionism among the participants (Spiers Neumeister, Williams, & Cross, 2007).

Asynchronous development is a common characteristic among gifted students, particularly if they are exceptionally gifted or twice exceptional (Silverman, 2012). Typically, the term pertains to students whose cognitive abilities are much more advanced than their social-emotional development, although it also describes those who exhibit strong abilities in one or more content areas and significantly lesser abilities in others. When social and emotional maturity lags behind cognitive abilities and interests, it can make academic placement and finding a compatible peer group difficult (Cross, 2016). In the cognitive domain, there is evidence that students who excel in verbal areas experience more social difficulties than those whose gifts are in mathematics, possibly because it may be easier to find a peer group that participates in and enjoys mathematically-related activities (Brody & Benbow, 1986; Lee et al., 2012). Looking back on their development, mathematicians have suggested that their participation in special programs and competitions with intellectual peers was an important part of their social and emotional development during their middle and high school years (Brody, 2013).

Finally, if any of these characteristics result in a certain level of social isolation, it can interfere with the development of social skills. Clearly, extreme shyness, lack of empathy, severe introversion, or having a disability that impacts social development makes the development of social skills much more difficult. Even students with lesser challenges may fail to develop adequate social skills if they lack positive experiences interacting with peers as a consequence of their high abilities (Cross, 2016).

The Need to Belong

The psychological literature teaches us the importance of individuals having a sense of belonging to the other people in their lives (e.g., Maslow, 1943). Thus, the psychosocial development of gifted students can depend a great deal on them feeling at ease in their home and school environments, in their communities and among their peers. When students struggle to find the support they need, psychosocial issues can result. It is likely that adjustment problems are further exacerbated when unsupportive environments overlap with any of the personal risk factors described above (Neihart et al., 2016).

A supportive family that reinforces a child's positive sense of self, holds realistic expectations, and provides opportunities for talent development seems essential for optimal social and emotional adjustment (Hermann & Lawrence, 2012; Olszewski-Kubilius, Lee & Thompson, 2014). Olszewski-Kubilius (2016) cautions against parents being overly invested in their child's success; instead, they must allow them to have the autonomy, independence, and psychological and emotional space to develop their own identities. Unfortunately, well-intentioned parents can develop unrealistic academic expectations that can contribute to their child's emotional distress, but they can also be instrumental in providing important resources such as access to special educational opportunities (Olszewski-Kubilius, 2016).

The role of schools in the psychosocial development of gifted students is crucial, leading Cross (2013) to conclude, "I have come to believe that the most pervasive threat to the mental health of gifted students is the mismatch between the school's curriculum and the student's academic needs" (p. 79). Unfortunately, this mismatch occurs often when schools fail to provide sufficient accommodations for gifted students, and it can lead to students hiding their advanced abilities (Coleman, 2012; Cross, Coleman, & Stewart, 1993). In addition, a lack of access to intellectual peers remains an issue for gifted students in many school settings. On the other hand, out-of-school opportunities have been shown to fill some of the voids for some students. Participants in special programs that bring gifted students together in supportive atmospheres with peers attribute much satisfaction to the feeling of belonging that these programs offer (e.g., Brody & Muratori, 2015; Mickenberg & Wood, 2009; Olszewski-Kubilius, 2007).

The community beyond the school can also negatively impact a gifted learner who is sensitive about not fitting in. For example, communities where athletics are more valued than academics can cause issues for non-athletic gifted students, and a lack of role models for high achievement can negatively affect students eager to pursue higher education goals. Students who live in rural areas with fewer resources and those who live in disadvantaged urban neighbourhoods without role models may be particularly at risk of feeling isolated and uncomfortably at odds with the values embraced by their communities (Stambaugh & Wood, 2015; VanTassel-Baska, 2010).

Special Schools and Programs

As educators have become aware of the unique academic, social, and emotional needs of gifted students, there has been an increase in opportunities designed to meet these needs. For example, full-time high schools, such as the state-supported residential high schools in the United States (Cross & Frazier, 2010; Roberts & Alderdice, 2015), the PERMATApintar™ College in Malaysia, and the Nazarbayev Intellectual Schools in Kazakhstan, offer students an advanced curriculum in the company of peers who are also advanced in their abilities and content knowledge. Similarly, special early college entrance programs are designed to provide students who enrol in college at younger-than-typical ages with considerable social and emotional support in the company of same-age peers (Brody & Muratori, 2015; Dai & Steenbergen-Hu, 2015).

There are also part-time outside-of-school options for students who wish to supplement their school programs including online courses, summer programs, academic competitions, and extracurricular activities. These opportunities can offer intellectual challenge, the chance to probe topics of interest in depth and/or to assume leadership roles, access to intellectual peers, and numerous psychosocial benefits (VanTassel-Baska, 2007). Stanley (2005) coined the concept of a 'smorgasbord' of educational options, from which students may choose those supplemental opportunities most appropriate for meeting their own needs. Research has shown that a combination of the right supplemental experiences can have an impact much like attending full-time specialised high schools (Olszewski-Kubilius, 2010).

If we revisit the psychosocial risk factors that were outlined earlier, we can see that many can be addressed through participation in special programs for gifted students. When an extreme intensity about something translates into wanting to focus on a topic in depth, advanced courses, internships and competitions can offer that option in environments with other students who share that interest. Academic rigour can help students re-evaluate perfectionistic tendencies and can promote a growth mindset when students realise that they are not the most talented person in the room and must work hard to achieve at a high level. Being with intellectual peers can promote a feeling of belonging, help introverts connect to others, and encourage the development of social skills. And, when asynchronous development is the concern, selection from the smorgasbord of programmatic options to address specific strengths and weaknesses can facilitate optimal talent development. However, gifted students may need access to knowledgeable counsellors to help them identify appropriate programs and services to meet their unique academic and psychosocial needs (Brody, 2007).

Gifted Education in Malaysia

The Malaysian Education Act 550 outlines six paradigms of the national education system namely: the pre-school, elementary, secondary, post-secondary, higher, and special education. Thus, other paradigms of education—for instance, gifted education—are not considered as mainstreams, and gifted students are not given considerable attention towards their holistic growth. As such, the direction of Malaysian gifted education programming—especially in school environments—has never been officially established, and the effort to design appropriate curriculum for this population of students has never become a national agenda at the ministerial level (Bakar & Ishak, 2016; Bakar & Zakaria, 2018).

Nonetheless, the non-existence of a gifted education policy in the Malaysian educational system (Bakar, 2017; Bakar & Ishak, 2010) does not mean that the educational provision for local populations of gifted students is being totally discounted from the system. In fact, over a period of three decades (1960s–1990s), the Ministry of Education has intermittently introduced special programs for selected highly able students to skip grades and therefore complete their elementary education early. As an illustration, the introduction of the 'Express Class System' in 1962 gave such students the opportunity to accelerate their elementary education. However, the program development has been sporadic and had no specific plan to help the students cope with their secondary and tertiary education at a younger age. Unsurprisingly, the program came to a halt in the 1970s. Likewise, the introduction of 'Level One Assessment System' in 1996 was a similar acceleration effort to shorten the elementary education of academically gifted students. Nevertheless, this transformational effort was also short-lived due to factors such as lack of instruction, training, leadership, and resources. Further exertions to champion the progress of educational provision for local gifted students were later conducted mostly by researchers in public universities and non-governmental organisations like the *National Association for Gifted Children, Malaysia* (NAGCM), and Malaysian MENSA Society (Bakar & Ishak, 2016; Bakar & Zakaria, 2018; Ishak & Bakar, 2017).

Since then, the scenario of Malaysian gifted education has been constantly evolving. An initial move was set in 2006 through a recommendation put forward by the Ministry of Education's Planning and Research Department. The recommendation emphasised the necessity to institute a special school for gifted students or at least the formation of gifted classes in the normal school system in order to realise the nation's vision to become an industrialised country by 2020. The recommendation was later realised with the establishment of two local gifted students' programs—PERMATApintar™ at the Universiti Kebangsaan Malaysia and PERMATA Insan at the Universiti Sains Islam Malaysia—in 2009 and 2010, respectively. Later, the Ministry of Education launched the Malaysian Educational Blueprint 2013–2025 that outlines the initiative to constitute a future national strategy of gifted education, in which the ministry is hoping to formulate an effective gifted education program to be implemented in all schools nationwide by 2025. All these developments show that Malaysia has started to focus attention on educating its population of gifted students (Bakar & Ishak, 2016; Ishak & Bakar, 2017).

Both PERMATApintar™ and PERMATA Insan established their 'laboratory' schools for gifted students in 2011 and 2015, respectively. As local pioneer programs and centres of excellence in gifted education, the holistic aim for these educational institutions was to develop comprehensive educational programs to foster positive growth of the nation's population of gifted students in terms of physical, emotional, spiritual, intellectual, and social aspects (Bakar, 2016; Bakar & Zakaria, 2018; Ishak & Bakar, 2014). Both programs focus on a differentiated learning approach based on the *National Education Philosophy* (NEP), which balanced the development of students' intellectual, social, spiritual, physical, and emotional growth as displayed in Figure 1. As a model of education for local gifted students, both programs incorporate the integration of high school curriculum injected with a higher education syllabus and balanced with the curriculum for international-level education (Bakar & Ishak, 2016; Ishak & Bakar, 2017).

Captions/Figures

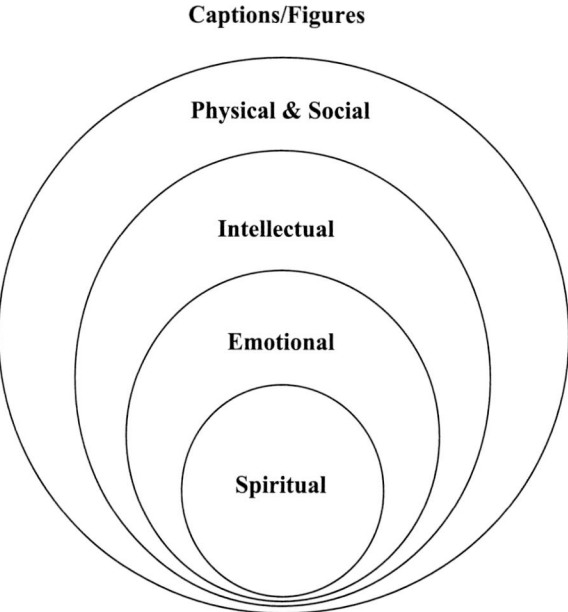

Fig. 1 PERMATApintar™ and PERMATA Insan Program's development framework

The establishment of these programs was a sign of commitment from the Malaysian government to revamp its national policy on gifted education that in return should benefit the country in the long run. As such, both programs' main target is to develop a new generation of talents—a pool of well-balanced students equipped with the right knowledge, skills, and attitudes—which the nation can tap into in many years to come.

Counselling Initiatives at the Johns Hopkins Center for Talented Youth (CTY)

Gifted education in the United States is not mandated at the national level; rather identifying and serving gifted students is left to the domain of local schools, school systems, and/or states. The result is an inconsistent pattern, whereby some gifted students have access to highly advanced and appropriately challenging educational programs, while others lack the opportunities in their schools or communities that allow them to excel to the full extent of their abilities (Plucker & Peters, 2016). In addition, while most middle and high schools in the United States have counsellors who advise students on choices among the school's offerings and try to be aware of any social and emotional difficulties their students face, few school counsellors have special training in the needs of gifted students, counsellors in large schools have difficulty getting to know their students well, and it is extremely rare for any counsellors to see it as their role to identify outside-of-school opportunities that advanced students may pursue to develop their talents. Consequently, gifted students who lack adequate options for meeting their academic, social, and emotional needs within their schools, and who are unaware of outside programs that can fill the voids, may fail to achieve their full potential, and psychosocial difficulties may result (Reis & McCoach, 2000).

The mission of the *Center for Talented Youth* (CTY) at the Johns Hopkins University is to offer a variety of outside-of-school programs and services that gifted students can utilise to augment their school offerings (Brody, 2009). CTY's assessments: help students gain insight into their cognitive strengths and weaknesses; residential summer programs provide access to challenging coursework not available in their schools and opportunities to interact with peers who share their interests and abilities; online courses offer advanced content to students throughout the year; and family programs expose students to new topics that may evolve into stronger areas of interest. The positive academic and psychosocial effects of these CTY offerings, as well as those of other out-of-school programs that offer a sense of belonging, challenging content and interaction with intellectual peers, have been documented in the research literature (e.g., Lee, Olszewski-Kubilius, Makel, & Putallaz, 2015; Mickenberg & Wood, 2009).

Several counselling initiatives complement CTY's programmatic offerings and are intended to help students understand their needs and find options for addressing them. Currently, CTY offers three counselling programs that each serve a different pool of students, all of whom are considered at risk in some way for not having their needs met in typical school situations. The *Study of Exceptional Talent* (SET) serves students with extremely advanced academic abilities, many of whom need to have access to above-grade-level work and struggle to find age peers at their intellectual level; the *Diagnostic and Counselling Centre* (DCC) focuses primarily, though not exclusively, on the needs of twice-exceptional students, that is, students with high abilities but who struggle academically due to some learning difficulty; and the CTY Scholars program provides counselling and programmatic options to traditionally underserved low-income students who may lack the resources they need to excel academically (Brody, 2009).

The SET evolved from the pioneering work of the late Professor Julian Stanley at Johns Hopkins University, who founded the *Study of Mathematically Precocious Youth* (SMPY) in 1971 and CTY in 1979 (Stanley, 2005). SMPY was established to:

> find [more] youths who reason exceptionally well mathematically and to provide the special, supplemental accelerative smorgasbord of educational opportunities they sorely need and richly deserve for their own optimal development and the good of society. (Stanley, 2005, p. 9)

Stanley and the SMPY researchers used above-grade-level, domain-specific aptitude tests to assess the full extent of students' abilities and evaluated a variety of intervention strategies to serve the students they identified. In spite of all the students that SMPY worked with exhibiting high mathematical abilities, the students were found to be a heterogeneous group in other ways with a range of unique characteristics and needs, leading SMPY to believe that counselling them should be as individualised as possible and that numerous accelerative options and out-of-school activities and programs be considered for meeting their needs. Stanley and the SMPY staff encouraged CTY to offer academic residential summer programs that would bring students together with like-minded others in a rigorous learning environment and also recommended other opportunities, such as academic competitions and early college entrance programs, with this goal in mind (Stanley, 2005).

The SET was established at CTY in 1991 as a continuation of the SMPY's efforts to study and serve exceptionally advanced students. After students qualify for SET by achieving a qualifying score on the SAT administered several years earlier than is typical, the SET's counsellors work to determine each student's individual profile of abilities, personal characteristics, goals, and interests, as well as their academic and psychosocial needs. To meet those needs, the counsellor evaluates their school options, advocates for accelerated placement when necessary, and suggests out-of-school possibilities. Students are encouraged to find ways to explore their interests in depth. In addition, providing opportunities for SET students to interact with their intellectual peers is an important consideration, since psychosocial issues for gifted students can often be avoided if students feel that they belong to a compatible peer group. The SET has been successful in helping students who attend all kinds of schools create the learning environments that they need to achieve their full potential by supplementing the school offerings (Brody, 2007). The SET is an approach that educators and parents can emulate in their efforts to serve gifted students (Brody, 2017).

Concern that the CTY was seeing an increasing number of students who exhibited high abilities, but were also struggling academically, and specific interest in this population by Johns Hopkins researchers (Brody & Mills, 1997; Fox, Brody, & Tobin, 1983), led to the founding of the CTY's *Diagnostic and Counselling Centre* (DCC) in 1997. Though the DCC offers a variety of assessment and counselling services, its focus continues to be on conducting psychoeducational assessments of twice-exceptional children in an effort to diagnose any underlying causes of their academic and/or psychosocial issues and to provide recommendations to help them be successful in challenging educational environments (Brody & Mills, 2004). Depending on the individual student's needs, recommendations may include changes in school placement and remediation of skills. However, there is also a strong emphasis on implementing accommodations, such as using technology (computers, calculators, recorders), providing additional time on tests and for completion of tasks, and permitting alternate ways of showing content mastery that can help twice-exceptional students excel in advanced classes. Many of these students, especially those with ADHD or those on the Autism Spectrum, also warrant special help with organisation, study skills, and social skills and/or may benefit from therapy (Brody & Mills, 2004).

Another CTY population that has warranted special attention includes students from low-income and traditionally underserved backgrounds. These students often lack the support and resources they need to achieve their full potential, particularly if they are the first person in their family to aspire for college education, attend schools that lack advanced course offerings, and/or are unable to connect to a peer group that is motivated to excel (Plucker & Peters, 2016; VanTassel-Baska, 2010). In response to this recognised need, CTY established the CTY Scholars program in 2004. This 4-year scholarship and advising program is used to encourage eligible CTY high school students from low-income and underrepresented backgrounds aspire to achieve at top levels. The students receive financial support to participate in the CTY summer and online programs, as well as ongoing advice from a CTY counsellor who recommends other opportunities for talent development and helps them apply to college. Many of the graduates have enrolled in some of the most selective colleges and universities in the United States (Kasahara, 2017).

All of CTY's counselling efforts involve getting to know each student's individual characteristics and needs well and recommending the strategies and program opportunities that can meet those needs. Assessments, including above-grade-level tests for students who hit the ceiling on in-grade tests and psychoeducational assessments for students with learning difficulties to identify the underlying causes of their difficulties, are essential for identifying strengths and weaknesses. Students' personality traits, interests, goals, and social and emotional adjustment should also be assessed and factored into decision-making. In an effort to meet each student's needs, many options should be considered, including accelerative strategies that can make school offerings more challenging, extracurricular activities and summer programs that can extend learning and provide access to peers with similar interests, and accommodations for gifted students with learning disabilities that allow them to excel in challenging learning environments (Brody, 2017).

Of course, some students exhibit more serious mental health issues and must be referred to a medical professional and/or therapist for treatment. Anyone working with gifted students should be aware of this possibility. But for many gifted students who are at risk of social and emotional problems because they feel ill at ease from not fitting into their current academic and social environment, addressing their needs by creating more compatible environments that support their educational needs can do much to enhance their emotional adjustment as well. This reason for environmental differentiation is the rationale that led to the establishment of the CTY, and it also permeates the CTY's counselling efforts; that is, students are urged to access appropriately challenging coursework in supportive environments in the company of intellectual peers who share their interests. This orientation also influenced the development of the holiday and other programs and is reflected in part in the counselling model at PERMATApintar™ College in Universiti Kebangsaan Malaysia (UKM).

Counselling Strategies at the PERMATApintar™ College, UKM

The PERMATApintar™ College was founded after realising that many of the nation's most gifted minds are only able to nurture their potential by pursuing advanced courses abroad, thereby losing one of the nation's most precious resources. Research has indicated that at least one in 10,000 children possesses a gifted mind, one in 100,000 is identified as highly gifted, and one in 1,000,000 is identified as exceptionally gifted (Tidwell, 1980). With 3.5 million school-going children in Malaysia, a very important resource was left untapped. The selected students are chosen from across the country based on three tests (UKM1, UKM2, UKM3) specially developed by a team of experts from the Universiti Kebangsaan Malaysia. Two of the tests (UKM1 and UKM2) are available online while the third is a competency-based test that assesses students' knowledge and skills in mathematics, science, research, communication, presentation, emotional intelligence, and creativity (Bakar & Ishak, 2016).

Students who are eventually enrolled into the PERMATApintar™ College are committed to a 2-year intensive program and are technically students of the UKM, bound and governed by the University's rules. Through this program, the students' natural abilities (giftedness) are nurtured into talents through a suitable system of learning that hones their potential. This learning approach provides the students with a more challenging mode of study befitting the child's intellect, while enabling a shorter route for the students to pursue their tertiary education (Bakar & Ishak, 2016; Ishak & Bakar, 2017).

The introduction of counselling services in the Malaysian educational system began around 1960s, with an initial focus on vocational guidance. Since gifted education is yet to be recognised as a mainstream component of the national education system, studies on the implementation of counselling services for the gifted students' population in school are limited. In fact, research in the area of counselling and guidance for gifted students have been extremely rare and far between (Bakar, 2016; Ishak & Bakar, 2014). At present, studies on the counselling and guidance needs of Malaysian gifted students are still in their infancy. Indeed, there is little literature describing the psychological issues and counselling needs of Malaysian gifted students. Moreover, school counselling provisions in Malaysia have never been targeted for the population of students with specific needs, such as gifted students. The possible reasons for this are as follows:

(a) School counsellors are trained to be generalists and are not exposed to any gifted education topics; thus, they have no specific skills or knowledge to work with gifted students.
(b) There is no specific framework within the local education system to guide counsellors in working with gifted students.
(c) The counsellor training programs provided by Malaysian higher education institutions do not specifically incorporate the necessary aspects of gifted students (developmental psychology of individuals, their characteristics, idiosyncrasies, and psychological issues; Bakar, 2014).

However, the basic data on the existence of such a counselling service that fulfils the needs of this group of students in the school environment are relevant (Bakar, 2016; Ishak & Bakar, 2014).

Shore and Delcourt (1996) suggested that any programs developed for gifted learners must have clear objectives and be tailored to their specific and unique needs. Treffinger (1998), on the other hand, proposed that the development of any gifted education programs require comprehensive services based on sound philosophical, theoretical, and empirical supports. Kettler (2011), in addition, postulated that three essential elements, which are the grouping of students, curriculum and instruction, and guidance and counselling, must exist in any gifted programs within school environments to ensure their effectiveness. Furthermore, Davis and Rimm (1998) stated that the need for counselling and guidance increases with the intellectual capability of an individual, and Bee (1999) found that students with high intellectual abilities would normally face self-adjustment problems in comparison to their peers. Findings of the works mentioned imply that a community of gifted students living and learning together will require systematic psychological, and social-emotional support, especially in terms of counselling and guidance provision (Bakar, 2016; Bakar & Ishak, 2014; Brody, 2007; Wood, 2010).

As advocated by the *American School Counsellor Association* (ASCA), school counsellors are called to proactively serve all students; thus, to best meet the needs of all students, counsellors must be aware of the strengths and challenges inherent to a variety of students (Bailey, 2007), including the gifted ones. Therefore, having a good provision of counselling and guidance at school and providing the necessary training to the school counsellors would be the initial steps towards providing better services to gifted students and their families (Bakar, 2017; Ishak & Bakar, 2010). Thus, when the PERMATApintar™ College opened its door in 2011, the need to establish a provisional guide of effective counselling service for the students was extensively discussed, in order to ensure the success of the whole program (Bakar, 2016; Bakar & Zakaria, 2018).

While there are many studies on best practices in the literature, studies on best practices by school counsellors for the population of gifted students are scarce. According to Wood (2010), school counsellors play a vital role in meeting the needs of gifted students, but they may not know how best to serve this unique population of students. This is because, up to now, there has been a lack of structured, standardised, and empirically tested best practices of counselling and guidance for gifted students. A majority of researchers in the field of gifted education share the opinion that the provision of counselling and guidance services for gifted students is not only critical, but it has to be specifically tailored to meet the unique needs of this population (Mahoney & Lyddon, 1988; Ryan, 1999, 2001; VanTassel-Baska, 2005, 1990; Wood, 2010). Zaffrann and Colangelo (1977), Peterson (2006) and Wood (2010) insinuated that gifted students require a differentiated counselling and guidance method, which involves creative approaches that take into consideration the students' unique affective and cognitive development. These approaches should be varied from one student to another, depending on his or her specific needs. In other words, the approach chosen should be individualised and meet the requirements of each student. In addition, Mahoney and Lyddon (1988) and Ryan (1999, 2001) recommended that gifted students should be afforded specialised counselling and guidance services in order to develop their abilities and talents. Specifically, the 'specialised' counselling and guidance approach for gifted students should take into consideration the counsellor's role, personality, the therapeutic environment, and the theoretical framework and strategic approaches; for instance, humanistic, cognitive, or behavioural methods may be used in counselling and guidance sessions (VanTassel-Baska, 1990, 2005; Wood, 2010).

Hence, continuous and ongoing research work has been carried out at PERMATApintar™ College in order to establish effective counselling services for the students. In its initial study of 560 students, the researchers found that only 30% of the students surveyed would talk to teachers and peers if they had a personal problem, whereas another 60% preferred to solve their personal problems themselves. Surprisingly, only 7% would willingly turn to counsellors for help while only 3% of the students chose to share problems with their parents. Another significant finding of this recent study was that female students may have a higher tendency to seek help compared to male students. The researcher also found that career counselling and academic guidance—particularly pertaining to college/university information search, career path advice, and enhancement of study skills—are the most preferred types of service, while family counselling is the least preferred (Bakar, 2014; Ishak & Bakar, 2010).

Consequently, taking into account the Johns Hopkins University Centre for Talented Youth's (CTY) counselling initiatives model as well as findings from continuous studies conducted within its compound (Bakar, 2016; Bakar & Zakaria, 2018) counselling researchers at PERMATApintar™ College, Universiti Kebangsaan Malaysia, have developed a conceptual framework of gifted students' counselling service strategies that is relevant to the local Malaysian context. They have adapted the provisional concept of 'differentiated' and 'specialised' service, combined it with the 'one-size-does-not-fit-all' approach, and derived

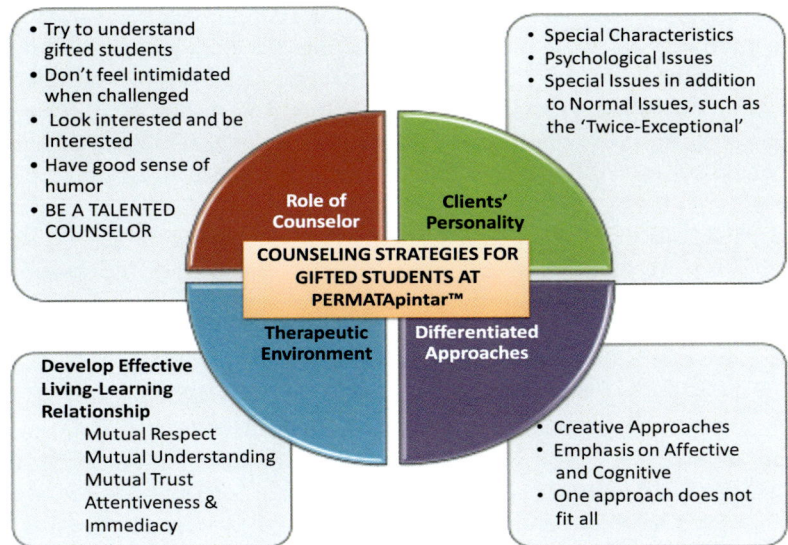

Fig. 2 A conceptual framework of counselling strategies at PERMATApintar™ College

a conceptual framework that comprises four main components (refer Fig. 2). Specifically, it is stressed in this framework that in order to develop a holistically conducive helpful relationship for the gifted students, it is essential for the counsellor to understand their own role and their clients' special traits, skills, and issues. In addition, the counselling environment must be therapeutically supportive where the relationship is built on mutual respect, understanding, and trust between both counsellor and client. Finally, the approach itself must be unique and individualised; thus, an assessment is proposed as the starting point of the whole process. Concurrently, the framework is somewhat aligned with ideas proposed by Zaffrann and Colangelo (1977) and Peterson (2006) which suggest that school counsellors, who are keen to provide services to gifted students, must take into consideration five elements, namely: the students' profile and issues being presented, the working therapeutic environment, the interventions proposed, the termination process, and the follow-up process.

Conclusion

In summary, the development of the counselling strategies framework that evolved from the collaborative affiliation between the PERMATApintar™, Universiti Kebangsaan Malaysia and the John Hopkins Center for Talented Youth (CTY) serves as concrete evidence that Malaysia is serious about ensuring the well-being of the nation's future generation. Even though gifted education is not yet inserted into the mainstream educational paradigm, it does not prevent local researchers from continuing to carry out studies in this field, as the potential for expanding the study in this area is considerably boundless. If the proposed framework could be accepted by the broader counselling community in Malaysia, especially among the practitioners in school settings, it would be a beneficial contribution not only to the local field of counselling and guidance, but also to the Malaysian national paradigm of gifted education as a whole.

Nonetheless, the challenges ahead are considerably numerous, ranging from whether Malaysian school counsellors are ready to deliver such 'differentiated' services to how much exposure do the counsellors have to such a 'specialised' approach. Moreover, it should also be worth exploring whether local counsellor education programs are capable of accommodating such approaches in their curriculum. It is also relevant to debate what roles should be assumed, by parties like the Malaysian Counselling Association, the Malaysian Board of Counsellors, and the Ministry of Education in accommodating such a transition by providing clear justifications and directions. Until the establishment of a clear and well-documented policy, research activities in counselling, and guidance provision for local gifted students should continuously be explored.

Cross-References

▶ Australian Teachers Who Made a Difference: Secondary Gifted Student Perceptions of Teaching and Teacher Effectiveness
▶ Diverse Dimensions of Gifted Education: Part V Introduction
▶ Fostering and Developing Talent in Mentorship Programs: The Mentor's Perspectives
▶ Gifted Education in the Asia-Pacific: From the Past for the Future – An Introduction
▶ More than Passion: The Role of the Gifted Education Coordinator in Australasian Schools
▶ Sociocultural Perspectives on the Talent Development Megamodel
▶ Some Implications for the Future of Gifted Education in the Asia-Pacific
▶ Trends and Challenges of Creativity Development Among Selected Asian Countries and Regions: China, Hong Kong/Macau, Japan, Malaysia, and South Korea

References

Bailey, C. L. (2007, October 11–14). *Social and emotional needs of gifted students: What school counselors need to know to most effectively serve this diverse student population?* Paper presented at the 2007 Association for Counselor Education and Supervision Conference, Columbus, OH.
Bakar, A. Y. A. (2014). *Perkhidmatan kaunseling untuk pelajar pintar dan berbakat* (Doctoral thesis). Faculty of Education, Universiti Kebangsaan Malaysia.
Bakar, A. Y. A. (2016). Counseling and guidance for Malaysian gifted students: A conceptual framework. *Journal for the Education of Gifted Young Scientists, 4*(1), 21–29. Retrieved from https://dergipark.org.tr/en/pub/jegys/issue/37319/430598

Bakar, A. Y. A. (2017). Developing gifted and talented education program: The Malaysian experience. *Creative Education, 8*, 1–11. Retrieved from https://m.scirp.org/papers/73302

Bakar, A. Y. A., & Ishak, N. M. (2010). Counselling issues of gifted students attending a school holiday residential program: A Malaysian experience. *Procedia-Social and Behavioral Sciences, 7*, 568–573. https://doi.org/10.1016/j.sbspro.2010.10.076

Bakar, A. Y. A., & Ishak, N. M. (2014). Depression, anxiety, stress, and adjustments among Malaysian gifted learners: Implication towards school counseling provision. *International Education Studies, 7*(13), 6–13. https://doi.org/10.5539/ies.v7n13p6

Bakar, A. Y. A., & Ishak, N. M. (2016). *Pendidikan pintar dan berbakat di Malaysia*. Bangi, SGR: UKM Press.

Bakar, A. Y. A., & Zakaria, Z. (2018). Counseling services for gifted students in Malaysia: A qualitative exploration. *International Journal of Engineering and Technology (UAE), 7*(2), 66–69. https://doi.org/10.14419/ijet.v7i2.10.10957

Bandura, A. (1993). Perceived self-efficacy in cognitive development and functioning. *Educational Psychologist, 28*, 117–148. https://doi.org/10.1207/s15326985ep2802_3

Bee, H. (1999). *The growing child: An applied approach* (2nd ed.). New York: Longman.

Brody, L. E. (2007). Counseling highly gifted students to utilize supplemental educational opportunities: Using the SET model. In J. L. V. T. Baska (Ed.), *Serving gifted learners beyond the traditional classroom* (pp. 123–143). Waco, TX: Prufrock Press.

Brody, L. E. (2009). The Johns Hopkins talent search model for identifying and developing exceptional mathematical and verbal abilities. In L. V. Shavinina (Ed.), *International handbook on giftedness* (pp. 999–1016). New York, NY: Springer.

Brody, L. E. (2013). The promise of mathematical precocity. In S. B. Kaufman (Ed.), *The complexity of greatness* (pp. 275–292). New York, NY: Oxford University Press.

Brody, L. E. (2017). Meeting the individual needs of students by applying talent search principles to school settings. In J. A. Plucker, A. N. Rinn, & M. C. Makel (Eds.), *From giftedness to gifted education: Reflecting theory in practice* (pp. 43–64). Waco, TX: Prufrock Press.

Brody, L. E., & Benbow, C. P. (1986). Social and emotional adjustment of adolescents extremely talented in verbal or mathematical reasoning. *Journal of Youth and Adolescence, 15*, 1–19.

Brody, L. E., & Mills, C. J. (1997). Gifted children with learning disabilities: A review of the issues. *Journal of Learning Disabilities, 30*(3), 282–296. https://doi.org/10.1177/002221949703000304

Brody, L. E., & Mills, C. J. (2004). Linking assessment and diagnosis to intervention for gifted students with learning disabilities. In T. Newman & R. J. Sternberg (Eds.), *Students with both gifts and learning disabilities* (pp. 73–93). New York, NY: Kluwer Academic Publishers.

Brody, L. E., & Muratori, M. M. (2015). Early entrance to college: Academic, social, and emotional considerations. In S. G. Assouline, N. Colangelo, & J. L. VanTassel-Baska (Eds.), *A Nation empowered* (pp. 153–167). Iowa City, IA: University of Iowa.

Coleman, L. J. (2012). Lived experience, mixed messages, and stigma. In T. L. Cross & J. R. Cross (Eds.), *Handbook for counselors serving students with gifts and talents* (pp. 371–392). Waco, TX: Prufrock Press.

Cross, J. R. (2016). Gifted children and peer relationships. In M. Neihart, S. I. Pfeiffer & T. L. Cross (Eds.), *The social and emotional development of gifted children* (2nd ed., pp. 41–54). Waco, TX: Prufrock Press.

Cross, T. L. (2013). *Suicide among gifted children and adolescents*. Waco, TX: Prufrock Press.

Cross, T. L., & Andersen, L. (2016). Depression and suicide among gifted children and adolescents. In M. Neihart, S. I. Pfeiffer, & T. L. Cross (Eds.), The social and emotional development of gifted children (2nd ed., pp. 79–90). Waco, TX: Prufrock Press.

Cross, T. L., Cassady, J. C., Dixon, F. A., & Adams, C. M. (2008). The psychology of gifted adolescents as measured by the MMPI-A. *The Gifted Child Quarterly, 52*, 326–339. https://doi.org/10.1177/0016986208321810

Cross, T. L., Coleman, L. J., & Stewart, R. A. (1993). The social cognition of gifted adolescents: An exploration of the stigma of giftedness paradigm. *Roeper Review, 16*, 37–40. https://doi.org/10.1080/02783199309553532

Cross, T. L., & Cross, J. R. (2018). *Suicide among gifted children and adolescents* (2nd ed.). Waco, TX: Prufrock Press.

Cross, T. L., & Frazier, A. D. (2010). Guiding the psychosocial development of gifted students attending specialized residential STEM schools. *Roeper Review, 32*, 32–41. https://doi.org/10.1080/02783190903386868

Dabrowski, K. (1964). *Positive disintegration*. Boston, MA: Little, Brown.

Dai, D. Y., & Steenbergen-Hu, S. (2015). Special class for the gifted young: A 34-year experimentation with early college entrance programs in China. *Roeper Review, 37*(1), 9–18. https://doi.org/10.1080/02783193.2014.975882

Davis, G. A., & Rimm, S. A. (1998). *Education of the gifted and talented* (4th ed.). Boston, MA: Allyn & Bacon.

Dweck, C. S. (2006). *Mindset*. New York, NY: Ballantine Books.

Fox, L. H., Brody, L., & Tobin, D. (Eds.). (1983). *Learning disabled/gifted children: Identification and programming*. Baltimore, MD: University Park Press.

Greenspon, T. S. (2012). Perfectionism: A counselor's role in a recovery process. In T. L. Cross & J. R. Cross (Eds.), *Handbook for counselors serving students with gifts and talents* (pp. 597–613). Waco, TX: Prufrock Press.

Hermann, K. M., & Lawrence, C. (2012). Family relationships. In T. L. Cross & J. R. Cross (Eds.), *Handbook for counselors serving students with gifts and talents* (pp. 393–407). Waco, TX: Prufrock Press.

Ishak, N. M., & Bakar, A. Y. A. (2010). Counseling for gifted students: Implication for a differentiated approach. *International Journal of Learning, 17*(6), 377–392. https://doi.org/10.18848/1447-9494/CGP/v17i06/47102

Ishak, N. M., & Bakar, A. Y. A. (2014). Counseling services for Malaysian gifted students: An initial study. *International Journal for the Advancement of Counselling, 36*(4), 372–383. https://doi.org/10.1007/s10447-014-9213-4

Ishak, N. M., & Bakar, A. Y. A. (2017). Identification of young gifted learners: The Malaysian experience. *Journal for the Education of Young Gifted Scientists, 5*(2), 71–81. https://doi.org/10.17478/JEGYS.2017.57

Jung, C. G. (1971). *Psychological types*. Princeton, NJ: Princeton University Press.

Kasahara, E. (2017). *The Johns Hopkins CTY Scholars Program 2017 annual report*. Baltimore, MD: Center for Talented Youth.

Kettler, T. (2011). Grouping and instructions for gifted students. *Gifted Child Today, 34*, 62–63.

Lee, S.-Y., Olszewski-Kubilius, P., Makel, M. C., & Putallaz, M. (2015). Gifted students' perception of an accelerated summer program and social support. *The Gifted Child Quarterly, 59*(4), 265–282. https://doi.org/10.1177/0016986215599205

Lee, S.-Y., Olszewski-Kubilius, P., & Thomson, D. T. (2012). Academically gifted students' perceived interpersonal competence and peer relationships. *The Gifted Child Quarterly, 56*, 90–104. https://doi.org/10.1177/0016986212442568

Mahoney, M. J., & Lyddon, W. J. (1988). Recent development in cognitive approaches to counseling and psychotherapy. *The Counseling Psychologist, 16*, 190–234. https://doi.org/10.1177/0011000088162001

Makel, M. C., Lee, S.-Y., Olszewski-Kubilius, P., & Putallaz, M. (2012). Changing the pond, not the fish: Following high ability students across different educational environments. *Journal of Educational Psychology, 104*, 778–792. https://doi.org/10.1037/a0027558

Marsh, H. W. (1984). The big-fish-little-pond effect on academic self-concept. *Journal of Educational Psychology, 79*, 280–295.

Maslow, A. H. (1943). A theory of human motivation. *Psychological Review, 50*, 370–396.

Mendaglio, S. (Ed.). (2008). *Dabrowski's theory of positive disintegration*. Tucson, AZ: Great Potential Press.

Mendaglio, S. (2012). Self-concept of gifted students: A multitheoretical perspective. In T. L. Cross & J. R. Cross (Eds.), *Handbook for counselors serving students with gifts and talents* (pp. 297–313). Waco, TX: Prufrock Press.

Mickenberg, K., & Wood, J. (2009). *Alumni program satisfaction and benefits of CTY summer programs* (Technical Report No. 29). Baltimore, MD: Johns Hopkins Center for Talented Youth.

Mills, C. J. (1993). Personality, learning style, and cognitive profiles of mathematically talented students. *European Journal for High Ability, 4*, 70–85. https://doi.org/10.1080/0937445930040108

Neihart, M., Pfeiffer, S. I., & Cross, T. L. (Eds.). (2016). *The social and emotional development of gifted children* (2nd ed.). Waco, TX: Prufrock Press.

Olszewski-Kubilius, P. (2007). The role of summer programs in developing the talents of gifted students. In J. L. VanTassel-Baska (Ed.), *Serving gifted learners beyond the traditional classroom* (pp. 13–32). Waco, TX: Prufrock Press.

Olszewski-Kubilius, P. (2010). Special schools and other options for gifted STEM students. *Roeper Review, 32*, 61–70. https://doi.org/10.1080/02783190903386892

Olszewski-Kubilius, P. (2016). Optimal parenting and family environments for talent development In M. Neihart, S. I. Pfeiffer & T. L. Cross (Eds.). The social and emotional development of gifted children (2nd ed., pp. 205–215). Waco, TX: Prufrock Press.

Olszewski-Kubilius, P., Lee, S.-Y., & Thomson, D. (2014). Family environment and social development in gifted students. *The Gifted Child Quarterly, 58*, 199–216. https://doi.org/10.1177/0016986214526430

Parker, W. D., & Adkins, K. K. (1995). Perfectionism and the gifted. *Roeper Review, 17*, 173–176. https://doi.org/10.1080/02783199509553653

Peterson, J. S. (2006). Addressing counseling needs of gifted students. *Professional School Counseling, 10*(1), 43–51. https://doi.org/10.1177/2156759X0601001S06

Plucker, J. A., & Peters, S. J. (2016). *Excellence gaps in education*. Cambridge, MA: Harvard Education Press.

Preckel, F., Rach, H., & Scherrer, V. (2016). Self-concept changes in multiple self-concept domains of gifted students participating in a summer residential school. *Gifted and Talented International, 31*, 88–101. https://doi.org/10.1080/15332276.2017.1304781

Probst, B., & Piechowski, M. (2012). Overexcitabilities and temperament. In T. L. Cross & J. R. Cross (Eds.), *Handbook for counselors serving students with gifts and talents* (pp. 53–73). Waco, TX: Prufrock Press.

Reis, S. M., & McCoach, D. B. (2000). The underachievement of gifted students: What do we know and where do we go? *The Gifted Child Quarterly, 44*(3), 152–170. https://doi.org/10.1177/001698620004400302

Roberts, J. L., & Alderdice, C. (2015). State residential STEM schools: A model for accelerated learning. In S. G. Assouline, N. Colangelo, & J. L. VanTassel-Baska (Eds.), *A Nation empowered* (pp. 137–151). Iowa City, IA: University of Iowa.

Ryan, J. J. (1999). Behind the mask: Exploring the need for specialized counseling for gifted females. *Gifted Child Today, 22*(5), 14–17. https://doi.org/10.1177/107621759902200505

Ryan, J. J. (2001). Specialized counseling: The social-emotional needs of gifted adolescents. *Tempo Newsletter, 21*(1), 6–7–17–18.

Sak, U. (2004). A synthesis of research on psychological types of gifted adolescents. *Journal of Secondary Gifted Education, 15*, 70–79. https://doi.org/10.4219/jsge-2004-449

Shore, B. M., & Delcourt, M. A. B. (1996). Effective curricular and program practices in gifted education and the interface with general education. *Journal for the Education of the Gifted, 20*, 138–154.

Siegle, D., & Langley, S. D. (2016). Promoting optional mindsets among gifted children. In M. Neihart, S. I. Pfeiffer & T. L. Cross (Eds.), The social and emotional development of gifted children (2nd ed., pp. 269–281). Waco, TX: Prufrock Press.

Silverman, L. K. (2012). Asynchronous development: A key to counseling the gifted. In T. L. Cross & J. R. Cross (Eds.), *Handbook for counselors serving students with gifts and talents* (pp. 261–279). Waco, TX: Prufrock Press.

Speirs Neumeister, K. (2016). Perfectionism in gifted students. In M. Neihart, S. I. Pfeiffer, & T. L. Cross (Eds.), The social and emotional development of gifted children (2nd ed., pp. 29–39). Waco, TX: Prufrock Press.

Speirs Neumeister, K. L., Williams, K. K., & Cross, T. L. (2007). Perfectionism in gifted high school students: Responses to academic challenge. *Roeper Review, 29*, 11–18. https://doi.org/10.1080/02783193.2007.11869219

Speirs Neumeister, K. L., Williams, K. K., & Cross, T. L. (2009). Gifted high school students' perspectives on the development of perfectionism. *Roeper Review, 31*, 198–206. https://doi.org/10.1080/02783190903177564

Stambaugh, T., & Wood, S. M. (Eds.). (2015). *Serving gifted students in rural settings*. Waco, TX: Prufrock Press.

Stanley, J. C. (2005). A quiet revolution: Finding boys and girls who reason exceptionally well mathematically and/or verbally and helping them get the supplemental educational opportunities they need. *High Ability Studies, 16*(1), 5–14. https://doi.org/10.1080/13598130500115114

Subotnik, R. F., & Jarvin, L. (2005). Beyond expertise. In R. J. Sternberg & J. E. Davidson (Eds.), *Conceptions of giftedness* (pp. 343–357). New York, NY: Cambridge University Press.

Subotnik, R. F., Olszewski-Kubilius, P., & Worrell, F. C. (2011). Rethinking giftedness and gifted education: A proposed direction forward based on psychological science. *Psychological Science in the Public Interest, 12*, 3–54. https://doi.org/10.1177/1529100611418056

Tidwell, R. (1980). A psycho-educational profile of 1,593 gifted high school students. *The Gifted Child Quarterly, 24*(2), 63–68. https://doi.org/10.1177/001698628002400204

Treffinger, D. J. (1998). From gifted education to programming for talent development. *Phi Delta Kappan, 79*, 752–755.

VanTassel-Baska, J. L. (1990). *A practical guide to counseling the gifted in a school setting*. Reston, VA: The Council for Exceptional Children.

VanTassel-Baska, J. L. (2005). Gifted programs and services: What are the nonnegotiables? *Theory Into Practice, 44*(2), 90–97.

VanTassel-Baska, J. L. (Ed.). (2007). *Serving gifted learners beyond the traditional classroom*. Waco, TX: Prufrock Press.

VanTassel-Baska, J. L. (Ed.). (2010). *Patterns and profiles of promising learners from poverty*. Waco, TX: Prufrock Press.

VanTassel-Baska, J. L., Cross, T. L., & Olenchak, F. R. (Eds.). (2009). *Social-emotional curriculum with gifted and talented students*. Waco, TX: Prufrock Press.

Webb, J. T., Amend, E. R., Webb, N. E., Goerss, J., Beljan, P., & Olenchak, F. R. (2005). *Misdiagnosis and dual diagnoses of gifted children and adults*. Scottsdale, AZ: Gifted Potential Press.

Wood, S. (2010). Best practices in counseling the gifted in school: What's really happening. *The Gifted Child Quarterly, 54*(1), 42–58. https://doi.org/10.1177/0016986209352681

Zaffrann, R. T., & Colangelo, N. (1977). Counseling with gifted and talented students. *The Gifted Child Quarterly, 21*, 305–321.

Abu Yazid Abu Bakar, PhD, is a senior lecturer at the Faculty of Education, Universiti Kebangsaan Malaysia. He holds a bachelor degree in psychology from the University of Michigan, Ann Arbor, USA, a master's degree and a doctorate degree in counselling from Universiti Kebangsaan Malaysia and a postgraduate certification in gifted education from the University of New South Wales, Australia. He was a former research fellow at PERMATApintar™ program, Universiti Kebangsaan Malaysia, and he has been actively writing and presenting papers on the Malaysian gifted education scenario at international and local conferences.

Linda E. Brody, Ed.D., directs the *Study of Exceptional Talent* (SET) and the *Diagnostic and Counseling Center* (DCC) at the Johns Hopkins University *Center for Talented Youth* (CTY). SET offers counselling to academically advanced students and studies their progress over time, while the DCC provides psychoeducational assessments and counselling, with an emphasis on serving twice-exceptional students. She earned her doctorate at Johns Hopkins, focusing on gifted education, counselling and learning disabilities. Her research interests include studying special populations of gifted students and evaluating strategies that facilitate talent development, especially acceleration.

Bricolage and the Evolution of Giftedness and Talent in Taiwan

46

Dale Albanese, Ming-Jen Yu, and Jing-Jyi Wu

Contents

D. Albanese (✉) · M.-J. Yu · J.-J. Wu
Center for Creativity and Innovation Studies, National Chengchi University, Taipei, Taiwan
e-mail: dalealbanese@gmail.com; mingjenyu@mail.nsysu.edu.tw; jjwu@nccu.edu.tw

© Springer Nature Singapore Pte Ltd. 2021
S. R. Smith (ed.), *Handbook of Giftedness and Talent Development in the Asia-Pacific*,
Springer International Handbooks of Education,
https://doi.org/10.1007/978-981-13-3041-4_48

Abstract

Discourse in Taiwan regarding talent development reflects anxiety, both from a government seeking to increase economic competitiveness and a populous striving for individual success amidst uncertainty. Identification and development of giftedness and talent within the mainstream education system has predominantly focused on academic and intellectual giftedness and talent in select areas of the arts and sports, overlooking other potential. At the same time, efforts to reform Taiwan's education, which nominally aspire to moving away from examination-based education and towards a more inclusive appreciation of diverse abilities, have been met with controversy and resulted, paradoxically, in increased pressure for students. To help understand this paradox and further illuminate processes for social change, a sociocultural understanding of how Taiwanese society defines success and identifies and develops giftedness and talent is developed in this chapter. We argue that education in Taiwan is influenced by both meritocracy and a preference for harmonising rather than strictly revolutionary creativity and further posit such harmonising creative work a bricolage. We then discuss how these characteristics have shaped the evolution of Gifted and Talented Education (GATE) in Taiwan, both in mainstream education reform and GATE development, and in informal bricolage work on the margins, focusing in part on the role of competitions and contests in GATE and research. Finally, we close with a discussion of the implications of these findings and conceptual approach for understanding the evolution of GATE in Taiwan and other Confucian-influenced societies, along with methodological implications. Responding to calls to employ diverse methods of inquiry and simultaneously think methodologically and philosophically in education research, this chapter is itself a bricolage and thus affords a novel perspective on processes relevant to the evolution of giftedness and talent in Taiwan, as well as on the work of educational research in general.

Keywords

Competitions · Bricolage · Meritocracy · Talent · Education reform

The aims in this chapter are to:
1. Develop a sociocultural understanding of giftedness and talent in Taiwan, informed by preferences for meritocracy and harmonising creativity.
2. Demonstrate how these preferences have shaped the evolution of gifted and talented education and education reform.
3. Employ the concept of bricolage to illuminate processes of change overlooked within mainstream academic research.
4. Explain the rise of educational competitions and contests as an example of bricolage that satisfies both the logic of meritocracy and an understanding of social change afforded by harmonising creativity.

5. Argue for both the importance of context-sensitive, culturally informed interpretations of educational phenomena and the adoption of diverse methodological practices in educational research.

Introduction: Mapping Gifted and Talented Education in Taiwan

Friction at the Margins

At age 15, Zhou Yi-xun is working in a paid internship position with an app development company in Taipei, where he moved on his own across the island from Kaohsiung. He obtained this position only after receiving attention for performance in competitions. In a news segment for the Public Television System's (2017) Youth News series on Makers, he is praised by his supervisor as a natural problem solver, more so than most recent university engineering graduates. Zhou regularly participates in international innovation competitions, relishing the chance to work with talented individuals from around the world; experiences, he says, offer global perspectives and new ways of thinking. He dreams of being an entrepreneur and wants to develop an international app platform that will benefit and connect would-be entrepreneurs. Fresh from a two-month program in the 'Maker Kingdom' of Silicon Valley, he is sure of his talent and potential. Specifically, he would like to move to China, which he calls 'a new paradise for entrepreneurs'.

Zhou's parents worry for him. His early interest in coding and web design, pursued late into nights, caused his grades to slip. Both parents and teachers advised him to focus on his classes instead. His parents cite his intelligence and decent grades and express their wish that he would graduate from a good high school and study at *National Taiwan University* (NTU, Taiwan's top-ranked school). They worry about his future, viewing a university degree a necessity for work and a middle school education a significant detriment. They are concerned also for his safety as, young and alone, he plots a trajectory from Kaohsiung to Taipei and then China.

Presented in a news segment as a young, ambitious 'Maker' with great potential, Zhou ends the piece with an admonishment for other students: please, do not follow my footsteps. He says he has faced discrimination while walking this unconventional road and believes many judge him wasteful for not studying high school.

Anxiety and Talent Cultivation in Taiwan

Taiwanese today exhibit anxiety over a perceived talent crisis. Taiwan is burdened with a sluggish economy, stagnant wages, a declining birth rate, and rising social inequality (Lee, 2008) in the face of the complex challenges of dynamic global industrial competition, longstanding geopolitical insecurity, and pressing global issues, from climate change to technological development. Concerned government policy discourse regarding a need to retain local talent and attract foreign talent (e.g., Executive Yuan, 2017), develop alternative education options (K–12 Education Administration, 2015), and cultivate creativity and entrepreneurship (Ministry of Education, 2003) all reflect this anxiety.

Not wholly unfounded, this shortage of talent is supported by international research. For example, the Oxford Economics (2012) 'Global Talent 2021' report (2012) predicts that, of 46 countries in the modelling exercise, Taiwan will face the most acute talent shortage by 2021. Expressing this concern at an Executive Yuan news conference in November 2017, Prime Minister William Lai identified talent as one of the nation's 'five industrial shortages', proposing immigration of talented workers from New Southbound Policy nations as a key solution (Lee, 2017). To this end, the National Development Council (2016) announced a series of reforms to attract migrants, ranging from simplifying visa, employment, and residency procedures to offering finance, tax, and insurance incentives. These policies directly equate 'high-level talent' with the overall 'competitiveness of a country'.

This issue is exacerbated by a trend that has emerged in recent years of young Taiwanese moving to China for work (Z.-L. Chen, 2017). Policies in China seek to exploit both a dearth of job opportunities and low wages, such as financial incentives for young Taiwanese entrepreneurs to develop in Fujian (Z.-L. Chen, 2017) and compensation from individual universities double those available to academics at domestic schools (Yang, 2016). Some academics and members of the public view targeted relaxation of employment rules and other financial incentives for Taiwanese as a nefarious effort to subvert Taiwanese politics and the local economy (Chung & Chin, 2017). Taiwan's status is precarious. China maintains a constant military threat—as shown in military deployment planning (Easton, 2017) and a recent increase in air force encirclement drills (Reuters, 2017)—has increased efforts to persuade Taiwan's diplomatic allies to switch recognition (Gao, 2018) and pursues economic and cultural integration as annexation strategies (Rowen, 2016). Within this context, anxiety about the perceived leveraging of promised youth job security for political aims is understandable.

Reflecting both this subtext of anxiety and the logic of human capital development, which seeks to translate education into productive capacity, the development of giftedness and talent has long been a core motivation of education reform. Both historical (Morris, 1996) and contemporary (K–12 Education Administration, 2015) reform efforts explicitly link education and national competitiveness. However, the evolution of Gifted and Talented Education (GATE) is marked by paradox. Efforts in the mainstream academic system predominantly focus on the development of intellectual and academic capacities in STEM areas or select subjects such as music, dance, theatre, or fine arts (Wu, 2013) and occur within a meritocratic social and cultural context that over-emphasises ranking based on performance on standardised assessment (Chou & Ching, 2012). While ostensibly aspiring to accommodate all students' needs and nurture a range of diverse abilities, a cultural predisposition for identifying and rewarding high achievers often overlooks and thus fails to develop giftedness and talent outside traditional academic areas.

Towards a Sociocultural Understanding of Giftedness and Talent in Taiwan

What are dominant understandings of giftedness and talent in Taiwan, how have these understandings changed over time, and how do the relevant drivers of such change influence the nurturing of giftedness and talent, both within formal and informal educational contexts? Within this chapter, we argue that answering such questions requires socioculturally informed understandings of the local context.

We think with two salient cultural features, namely: (1) meritocracy (So, 2015) inherited from Confucian thought and practice and (2) a harmony model of creativity (Sundararajan & Raina, 2015), characterised by the conjunction of incremental, evolutionary creativity with potentially revolutionary alternative practices from the margins so that they mutually subsist within and co-constitute, rather than outright subvert, society. We further propose Levi-Strauss' (1967) concept of the bricolage as a metaphor to help illuminate our research journey and explain the paradoxical co-existence of a mainstream, meritocratic system that values achievement on standardised assessments of intellectual ability and the stated goals of education reform to diversify recognition and development of talent and routes to success. In our conception, both education practitioners, desiring to identify and nurture giftedness and talent traditionally overlooked by the mainstream system and those overlooked are bricoleurs, working within and sometimes actively harnessing the limitations of a system dominated by meritocratic thinking to overcome sociocultural constraints and achieve their goals. To demonstrate an example of educational mechanisms both developed outside of, and yet in dialogue with, mainstream education, we present the educational competitions and contests as sites of bricolage. Still underrepresented in scholarship on GATE, competitions and contests simultaneously satisfy the logic of meritocratic achievement while inducing reconsiderations of success, potentially widening the scope of identification and development of giftedness and talent.

In this chapter, we first elaborate on the sociocultural connections to meritocracy and the harmony model of creativity and further posit harmonising creative work as bricolage. We then engage these characteristics in discussing the evolution of GATE in Taiwan, both in mainstream education reform and GATE development and in informal bricolage work on the margins, focusing in part on the role of competitions and contests in GATE and research. Finally, we close with a discussion of practical and methodological implications of this exploration and conceptual approach for understanding the evolution of GATE in Taiwan and Confucian-influenced societies in general.

This work utilises data from popular discourse, such as online media and news, government-supported research and policy documents, academic publications, and diverse first-hand experiences in relevant education arenas. In this way, this chapter is itself an example of research as bricolage (Kincheloe, 2005) and researcher as bricoleur (Steinberg, 2006) and thus a response to the call for both "diverse inquiry methods [in the] fragmented, porous, contested field" of gifted and talented education (Ambrose, 2016, p. 133) and "way[s] of thinking methodologically and philosophically together" (Jackson & Mazzei, 2012, p. vii).

Sociocultural Components of Giftedness and Talent in Taiwan

Confucianism, *Keju* and Meritocracy

Though employing diverse and oft-contested interpretations, public figures have evoked Confucianism in name as a guiding philosophy of bureaucratic governance and ideals for social relations for over two millennia (Li, 2012). Within various discourses, such as cross-cultural psychology (e.g., Kim, 2007), Confucian thought is regularly maligned for prescribing subjugation to authority, resulting in obedience and limited independent thought. This does not necessarily follow for all interpretations of Confucian teachings and scholars have attributed misconceptions to cultural misunderstandings (e.g., Chan, 1999). This criticism, in part, arises from the hierarchical nature of the Confucian worldview. In terms of education, Confucius encouraged diligent, reflective practice as the path to learning (Hwang, 2012), yet at the same time valued "spontaneous interest" (Hwang, 2012, p. 117) as the most efficient way to learn, saying "To prefer it is better than to only know it. To delight in it is better than merely to prefer it" (from *The Analects*, quoted in Hwang, 2012, p. 117). Yet, one result of idealising "spontaneous interest", according to Hung (2016, p. 94), is a "hierarchical view of knowledge [and] belittlement of laborious knowledge". Hung argues that in the hierarchical Chinese social structure, spontaneity belongs to the *junzi*, or superior person, who sits above those who toil.

The result is paradox: the conjunction of both a lofty ideal (the elite *junzi*) and universal effort. Effort is "the ultimate factor that differentiates … achievement" (Stevenson, Lee, Chen, Kato, & Londo, 1994, p. 128). The flip side of this effort focus is an inherent element of exclusion, particularly within contexts of structural inequality—if you do not succeed, it is because you did not expend the correct effort. While *junzi,* society's elite recipients of recognition and honours may no doubt possess great talent, resources afforded by class and upbringing may also afford the privilege of idealised spontaneity. These Confucian values manifest in meritocratic mechanisms for educational and professional mobility in both contemporary Taiwan and China, universalising aspirations towards exclusive heights.

This paradox also helps explain the functional conflation of giftedness and talent in Taiwanese society. Formal definitions of giftedness employed within policy and research in Taiwan and other Confucian-influenced societies are largely western imports (Ibata-Arens, 2012), yet practice and discourse in Taiwan exhibit a degree of conceptual and functional overlap of giftedness and talent. In Mandarin, talent (*rencai*) has been used to describe individuals with superior domain-specific abilities, while someone with innate genius may be considered a heaven-endowed talent (*tiancai*). Yet, it is understood that even heaven-endowed talents wither without development, hence a Confucian emphasis on self-cultivation and deliberate practice (Zhang, 2017). The language of the Ministry of Education (MOE) K–12 Education Administration (2015) *Mid-term Plan for Gifted Education Quality Development* demonstrates an embrace of such paradox: exclusive and universal. Outlining gifted education goals and strategies, MOE evokes the need to cultivate young "sprouts [as] future talent" (p. 1) by expanding access to gifted education resources in a systematic, comprehensive and equitable manner and diversifying measurements and indicators to look for and nurture creativity, leadership ability, and civic care. The policy plan, an engagement between historical (holistic self-cultivation) and contemporary (education for national competitiveness) values, justifies expansion of gifted education with a universal proscription for talent cultivation.

Common to talent and giftedness is how they are identified, both historically and contemporarily. The *keju* (Imperial Examination) system is the most conspicuous marker of Confucian-influenced bureaucracy and served to both identify ability and cultivate talent, as aspirants prepared for the tests as the primary mechanism for upward social movement (Zhang, 2017). In the *keju* system, progress through the ranks of bureaucracy involved achieving top scores in a series of standardised examinations, and to have produced a *jinshi*—advanced scholar or palace graduate—was a source of great pride for a locality. The entrenchment of elite power with ostensibly objective mechanisms for acquiring such power is demonstrative of what Elliot (2012) calls 'the real China Model'. The *keju* system did not provide equal access to social mobility (Elman, 2013; Liu, 2016). Rather, it was the purview of elites "as the linguistic and academic requirements were unattainable for the majority of peasants" (Liu, 2016, p. 24). Ostensibly, one practical upshot of this meritocratic system was a refining of talent and knowledge upward through imperial bureaucracy. A strong emphasis on form and presentation in the *keju* established outstanding literary ability as a primary indicator of talent and potential future success, while continual success within society was contingent both upon novel practical applications of scientific and philosophical knowledge as well as the formal presentation of such knowledge. Elite education has thus been long associated with language and heaven-endowed, yet further cultivated talent with examinations.

Within contemporary education in both China and Taiwan, many parents, students, and educators feel that 'one exam determines your whole life' (*yi shi ding zhongshen*). This may seem most true in China, where the *gaokao* examination system is still the sole gatekeeping mechanism for domestic university admission. Within Taiwan, even with the introduction of multiple paths to higher education in the 1990s, scores on standardised examinations still play a dominant role in admissions and placement in high schools and universities (Chou & Ching, 2012) and thus upward educational mobility. In professional spheres, an elaborate *Civil Service Entrance Examination* (CSEE) system, with tests primarily requiring reproduction of transmitted knowledge, is used to staff Taiwan's bureaucracy (So, 2015), while competitive ranking through standardised assessment is at the core of some promotion schemes for local officials in China (Zhou, 2007).

Sociologist and British politician Michael Young (1958, 1994) proposed the concept of meritocracy to describe a political philosophy whereby power within the political structure is accessed by demonstrating intellectual talent and personal achievement. According to Kim and Choi (2017), many scholars "have reported evidence that the initial concept of meritocracy primarily emerged in Asia first [and] argued that the concept of merit initially started in China and came to the West via Confucian texts" (Kim & Choi, 2017, p. 112). So (2015) argues that meritocracy in

Taiwan has evolved with the CSEE system and "has contributed to a top-down state-building approach [and culture of] hiring-by-examination" (p. 312).

Several other recent examples of meritocratic practice in Taiwan, here from academia, include the following: (a) the Ministry of Science and Technology Einstein and Columbus Program grants (Ministry of Science & Technology, 2017a, 2017b) for identifying and rewarding young scholars creating research sufficiently ground-breaking to garner international attention; (b) the recently announced Yushan Scholars program from the Executive Yuan (2017)—named after Taiwan's highest mountain peak—which, beginning in 2018, is intended to help retain and attract higher education talent with financial incentives and is a partial response to Taiwan's relatively low faculty salaries as compared to other places in Asia; and (c) the MOE Aim For the Top University Project, which distributed NT $10 billion over 10 years to a dozen top-tier schools to increase their international rankings and scholastic excellence.

The preceding examples all fit within the logic of tournament theory (Connelly, Tihanyi, Crook, & Gangloff, 2014), as developed in the management literature, whereby motivation is understood as a partial function of "reward structures ... based on relative rank rather than absolute levels of output" (Connelly et al., 2014, p. 16). The 500 domestic and 500 international Yushan Scholars would receive bonuses of up to NT $5 million (roughly US$170,000) each year based on salary and rank, far outpacing the average academic in Taiwan (W.-H. Chen, 2017). Within the Aim for the Top University Project, MOE distributed the awards unevenly even across this select group of 'top' schools (e.g., with a ratio of 15:1 for National Taiwan University and National Chengchi University). Policy-makers present accolades to top performers as efforts to cultivate, attract, or retain talent. Ostensibly, in such a system the vast majority, forever only aspirants, may also strive harder with eyes upward.

In this way, meritocracy produces a feedback loop, what social psychologists call system justification (Jost & Banaji, 1994), whereby "individuals are motivated to justify and rationalise existing social arrangements, defending and bolstering the status quo simply because it exists" (Godfrey, Santos, & Burson, 2017, p. 1). In Taiwan, the belief in the objectivity of standardised tests and the democratic ideals of equal access they represent—and thus the manoeuvering to justify the system despite contrary evidence in the form of increased inequality (Lee, 2008)—is still pervasive.

The meritocratic emphasis on ranking for social mobility has several implications for our understanding of GATE in Taiwan. Success within mainstream social institutions is tied to competition for top scores and positions within top institutions (Mao, 2018). Society, and thus parents and students, overvalue success on standardised tests and other forms of competition (Chou & Yuan, 2011). Education practitioners and policy-makers face pressure to accommodate demands to both: (a) equitably develop diverse talents and (b) prepare students for standardised examinations and other competitions. Teacher-centred education is still common in most schools, with classes focusing on knowledge acquisition in preparation for tests in traditional academic subjects (Chou & Ching, 2012). Highly motivated and talented students overlooked in non-traditional academic areas are legion (Chou & Ching, 2012; Gao, 2010), while inexperienced graduates often lack desired workplace skills and initiative (Ministry of Education, 2010). While Taiwan has been the site of rapid social change in the past century (Morris, 2004), cultural change does not necessarily follow the same pace (e.g., Moskowitz, 2008). Our sociocultural understanding of GATE in Taiwan considers how entrenched cultural forces perpetuate competition, both in standardised tests and novel focus areas for giftedness and talent cultivation.

Harmonising Creativity in Social Change

Is he not a man of complete virtue, who feels no discomposure though men may take no note of him? *The Confucian Analects*, Book 1, Chapter 1, Line 3 (Legge, 1893)

The preceding quote from Confucius reflects one aspect of the virtue of the learned person ('man [*sic*] of complete virtue'): equanimity when gifts go unrecognised. While entrenched meritocratic values may result in institutional bottlenecks and exclusionary practices, Taiwanese society does not stand still. Sundararajan and Raina (2015) argue from an indigenous psychology perspective that western conceptions of revolutionary creativity—with an emphasis on field-changing breakthroughs and crowd-defiance—are misfits for understanding creative practice and ideals in Chinese-influenced cultural contexts. To Sundararajan and Raina (2015), Gardner's (1996) attribution of "revolutionary ideas [to a] Western European culture" (p. 143) that is "heroic and epoch-making" (p. 156) typifies a "widely accepted view" (Sundararajan & Raina, 2015, p. 4) both dismissive of a lesser evolutionary creativity, which fosters incremental change and is seen as the purview of Chinese culture, and blind to conjunctive revolutionary creative forces of social change in non-western cultures, often located at the individual level. As "creativity and conformity are not necessarily mutually exclusive terms" (p. 12), they offer a harmony model of creativity, whereby "a both/and perspective … capitalizes on the dialectic interplay of the two opposing forces" (p. 11), both social evolution and personal revolution. This model is informed by the metaphysical belief that "life itself…thrives on the preservation, rather than the dissolution, of the tension between old and new" (Sundararajan & Raina, 2015, p. 12).

While institutional novelty is typically incremental, and thus evolutionary, revolutionary breakthrough is possible at the individual level. Both Needham (1956) and Chang (1963) hold that Taoist handling of paradox, discovery, and spontaneity foster conditions conducive to creativity, such that contributed to significant scientific discoveries in China historically outpacing the west. Taoism and Chan Buddhism both emphasise "a combination of effortlessness, accuracy, and speed [in] spontaneity" (Sundararajan & Raina, 2015, p. 10) applicable to discovering novel recombination of features of present reality, replete with limits and potentials. The romanticised hermits of Chinese history, with their many "lasting contributions in Chinese philosophy, scholarship, poetry, music, painting, the art of tea, medicine, geography, health sciences, and more" (p. 6), achieve personal creative break-throughs in self-transcendence (e.g., "development of consciousness"; p. 9) while remaining peripheral to, and thus distinct from, the mainstream. They are only then able to contribute something novel to the co-construction of an evolving totality of society. Truly creative (both novel *and* appropriate) contributions need not wholly subvert mainstream systems, but may instead co-exist distinct within a collective whole.

Conflict resolution, here between traditional academic emphases and educational values within the formal system and the growing awareness of and need for diverse forms of giftedness and talent, is marked by a strategy of "obey publicly and defy privately" (Hwang, 2000, p. 172 cited in Sundararajan & Raina, 2015). Mainstream institutional authorities adopt policies that both delimit and facilitate change, especially when broadly worded. Enacting change, stakeholders on the outside adjust the presentation (language and logic) of their private, revolutionary discoveries to fit within these limits, aware the whole must adjust to their presence as they do to other elements of the whole. In this way, a co-constructed harmonious social sphere endures, characterised not by subservience to convention but ideally "perpetuation of . . . tension between innovation and convention" (Sundararajan & Raina, 2015, p. 13) as the elements continually reconstitute each other, their friction a perpetual harmonising.

The Evolutionary Creativity of the Marginal Bricoleur

Given this context, we propose that Levi-Strauss' (1967) bricolage is an apt conceptual metaphor for understanding the harmonising creativity potential borne of the meeting between the mainstream and the margins. Bricolage refers to the work of a bricoleur, French for handyperson, who makes use of available tools at hand for task completion (Kincheloe, 2005).

Scholars have employed bricolage as a conceptual metaphor in diverse fields, including organisational and management theory (Boxenbaum & Rouleau, 2011; Duymedjian & Rüling, 2010; Miner, Bassoff, & Moorman, 2001), entrepreneurship (Davidsson, Baker, & Senyard, 2017; Phillips & Tracey, 2007), social enterprises (Molecke & Pinkse, 2016), gastronomy (Rao, Monin, & Duran, 2005), design thinking (Louridas, 1999), and financial innovation (Engelen, Erturk, Froud, Leaver, & Williams, 2010). Phillips and Tracey (2007) call for research on the role of bricolage at the institutional level as "there is little research on how actors creatively tinker with techniques from rival [institutional] categories infused with competing logics" (Rao et al., 2005, p. 317). In addition, qualitative researchers have adopted and developed bricolage as a research methodology (Denzin & Lincoln, 1994; Kincheloe & Berry, 2004; Tobin & Steinberg, 2006), with implications for critical, self-reflexive knowledge production (Berry, 2006; Steinberg, 2006).

In this chapter, we follow Garud and Karnoe (2003, p. 278) in employing the connotations of "resourcefulness and improvisation on the part of the involved actors" in the face of environmental constraints. In their study on technological entrepreneurship, a bricolage approach is contrasted to breakthrough strategies, mirroring Sundararajan and Raina's (2015) contrasting views of western conceptions of revolutionary creativity marked by heroic, field-changing creations and the harmonious integration of revolutionary personal discoveries into evolutionary processes of social change. Faced with the constraints of an education system and meritocratic society, creative education practitioners and individuals whose talents and potential remain unsupported by the mainstream system continue to cultivate themselves and leverage available resources to achieve their goals. Further, the GATE landscape may be conceived of as a bricolage, a work in progress reflecting an assemblage of stakeholders with diverse motivations and needs operating within and pushing the boundaries of past constraints.

Evolution of GATE in Taiwan

Education Reform and Persistent Examination Focus

Widespread public education in Taiwan began during the Japanese period (1895–1945), with primary education a part of colonial assimilation efforts (e.g., the creation of a Japanese speaking population; Morris, 2004), later extending through universities—Japan established Taiwan's first university, Taipei Imperial University, which later became National Taiwan University, Taiwan's top university today. During Nationalist rule, marked by the establishment of martial law in 1949, public education continued to expand, constructing a 'new national character' through Sinicisation (Tu, 2007). Seeking political and economic stability in an emerging role as part of the global manufacturing chain, government education focused on the development of human capital, eventually earning Taiwan status as one of 'Asia's four little tigers' (Morris, 1996). The lifting of martial law (Wu, 1987) resulted in a process of relaxation of regulations and paved the way for a liberalisation of education for teachers, students, and the system as a whole (Tu, 2007). Subsequent reform reflects further adoption of key features of capitalism: human capital, modernisation, increased privatisation, and development of specialised workforce competencies (Chou & Ching, 2012). We can, thus, understand education reform as a series of ideological transitions—earlier focused on constructing national identity and later promoting economic competitiveness—to realise modern individualistic ideals. Central to the logic of the latter ideology is broadening the reach of education to cultivate desired talent for mobilisation in a globalising economic system.

The government established a cabinet-level committee, the Council on Education Reform, in 1994, to carry out reform. As an idealised figure whose credentials afforded necessary political clout and public favour (Kwok, 2017), the Executive Yuan appointed Taiwan's first Nobel Laureate (the 1986 Nobel Prize in Chemistry) and Academia Sinica academician Lee Yuan-Tseh to chair the committee, composed of many western trained academics. With the goals of improving the quality of and access to education for a wider range of society, the committee focused on continuing deregulation and the empowering of education practitioners (Chou & Ching, 2012). During this reform era, MOE moved from a single examination system to a diversified entrance system, allowing students to enter university through a variety of means, including proficiency examinations, admissions applications and school recommendations (Chou & Ching, 2012; Ministry of Education, 2005). During this period, the *Basic Academic Competence Test* was broadly implemented, and many colleges and universities began using a combination of examinations and alternative enrolment processes to recruit students.

These reform initiatives have been met with substantial controversy, marked by miscommunication between schools, parents, and the government and the growing socio-economic gaps between urban and rural areas (Chou & Ching, 2012). The transition to a diversified entrance system intended to increase educational access and decrease pressure on students brought new pressure to not only perform academically but also gain experience and present aptitude in a range of other areas, such as through volunteering, extra-curricular activities and participation in international competitions, now crucial to admission to better universities (Chou & Ching, 2012). The rapid rise of cram schools, discussed in detail below, attests to this phenomenon. Meanwhile, entrance examinations have still remained a near universal requirement for Taiwanese students, with the enrolment rate for the College Entrance Examination exceeding 90% among 18–21-year-olds not in junior colleges or graduate schools, an increase from 82.02% in 2006 and 40.90% in 1996 (Chang Chien, Lin, & Chen, 2013). While there is regular public discussion and even research on adjusting admissions criteria, such as the development of comprehensive creativity indicators for university admissions (Chan, Lin, & Hsieh, 2008), exam performance in traditional academic subjects is still a primary criterion.

Cram Schools and Reform Paradox

The nature of Taiwan's pervasive shadow education (Chou & Ching, 2012) is demonstrative of the limitations of reform in moving away from examination-oriented education. Cram schools (*buxiban* and *anqinban*) are ubiquitous in Taiwan. While the diversified entrance system was meant to release steam from the 'pressure cooker'—a common term for junior high school in Taiwan when 'one exam [really would] determine your whole life'—the demand for test-prep-focused cram schools has risen. Nowadays, with some starting years before formal education begins, many Taiwanese students attend private classes after school, in some cases lining up on school grounds to be led by cram school teachers to one of the outlets for competing companies encircling public schools. The number of registered cram schools has risen from 5,891 in 2001 (Chou & Ching, 2012) to 18,022 in 2017 (Kaohsiung City Government Education Bureau, 2017), a majority of which are for elementary (45%) and junior high school (15%) students (Kaohsiung City Government Education Bureau, 2017).

Chou and Yuan (2011) attribute the paradoxical rise in demand for supplementary private education after moving away from a single entrance examination system to a predominant focus on entrance to 'star schools' (Xu, 2007). Many students report feeling that they must attend exam-focused cram schools, as well as being obliged to complete regular classes, so they face increased stress while fast-paced rote learning strategies influence educational attitudes (Chou & Ching, 2012).

While reform efforts like diversifying entrance mechanisms theoretically provide greater access and choice, they are also open to co-option by meritocratic values that may perpetuate or even exacerbate inequality. According to Chou and Ching (2012, p. 164), costs for a month in any given subject averaged US$80, with many children attending classes for multiple subjects. Given that as of 2015, the average monthly income per person was roughly NT $51,000 (or US$1,700; Directorate General of Budget, Accounting and Statistics, 2016), a hypothetical dual-working-parent family with two children each enrolled in three subjects would, based on the conservative 2012 rates, spend up to 14% of their monthly income on cram schools. In truth, wealth disparity means that many families earn much less than this, so cram schools are either a greater burden or not an option. Despite the significant financial burden, parents feel obligated to send their children to cram schools, as they feel it is their responsibility to ensure their children 'never lose at the starting line' (*buyao shu zai qipao dian*).

As evidence of the demand for examination performance, it is telling that the vast majority of cram schools (80% in 2010, Chou & Ching, 2012) are focused on traditional intellectual subjects found in standardised examinations: Chinese, English, mathematics, and science. At the same time, there has been a small increase in cram schools focusing on arts, crafts, and other non-academic skills (2,197 in 2003 to 2,773 in 2017, Kaohsiung City Government Education Bureau, 2017), such as graphic design, coding, or sports.

Upward academic mobility is still a selling point of cram schools regardless of subject, as students applying directly to particular colleges under the diversified entrance system may need to attend interviews, demonstrate efficacy in specific talents, or present portfolios of work. Advertisements for cram schools often boast of top-score earners who have been through their programs and justify their costs in terms of tangible achievement gains in particular subjects or on specific tests (Chou & Yuan, 2011). Interestingly, there were only two registered cram schools devoted to preparing students to retake the College Entrance Examination (X.-Y. Chen, 2017), perhaps a function of the ballooning university numbers during the relatively recent and rapid expansion of higher education (Chan & Lin, 2015) and Taiwan's declining birth rate (Chou, 2014).

Formal Gifted and Talented Education in Taiwan

Seen as a strategy for translating human capital into economic growth, GATE in Taiwan preceded widespread education reform. Wu (2013) describes five stages of GATE in Taiwan over the past four decades: (a) dawning (before 1973); (b) experimentation (1973–1983); (c) promotion (1984–1994); (d) establishment (1995–2005); and (e) transformation (2006–2016).

The *dawning* stage began with the 1962 call for the development of gifted education at the 4th National Conference on Education. This resulted in MOE sponsored trial programs in several elementary and junior high schools in 1969 and 1970, which focused on mathematics, science, and Chinese (Stevenson et al., 1994). The first gifted education in fine arts began in 1968 in a private school, and it was another decade before public pilot programs began (Stevenson et al., 1994).

The *experimentation* stage (Wu, 2013) began with the formal adoption of categories of giftedness imported from the framework of The Marland Report (Marland, 1972), the first formal definition of giftedness as presented to the US Congress by the US Commissioner of Education in 1972. This definition included academic and intellectual talent, as well as leadership ability, visual and performing arts, creative or productive thinking, and psychomotor ability. Taiwan adopted similar language in 1973, but in practice retained emphasis on academic and intellectual skills. This period saw a six-year experimental project in elementary schools, as well as the first program evaluations, elementary-level gifted summer camps, dance classes, and creative education programs.

The *promotion* stage (Wu, 2013) began with the passing of the Special Education Act in 1984 (later amended in 1997, 2009, and 2013; Ministry of Justice, 2014) and included a section on gifted education, with categories of gifted education potentially eligible for resource assistance, including artistic, creative, and leadership abilities, as well as 'other special abilities' (as opposed to psychomotor abilities in the Marland Report; 1972), and enshrined GATE in all levels of education (Wu & Kuo, 2016). Programs in junior and senior high schools also expanded during this period, and by 1994, mechanisms were established for providing International Mathematical Olympiad participants special enrolment opportunities. In 1994, the National Science Council also began a comprehensive five-year research project on strategies for GATE development.

The *establishment* stage (Wu, 2013) is marked by the formation of the Taipei Gifted Education Development Association in 1995, Chinese Gifted Education Association in 1998, and the publication of the 1999 *White Paper on Taipei City Gifted Education*, the first *Gifted Education Research* journal in 2001 (2012 name changed to *Gifted Education Forum*), the *White Paper on Creativity* in 2003, and finally MOE's establishment of the *National University of Science and Technology Youth Class* with six public high schools.

Finally, the stage of *transformation* (Wu, 2013) is most notable for an emerging association of GATE with creative education, as seen in the preliminary research for the *White Paper on Creative Education* and subsequent action plans (Wu & Albanese, 2013), which emphasised a need for pedagogical change to harness universal creative potential. Further, the Special Education Act was amended in 2009, as arts education became the purview of the Arts Education Act rather than a part of gifted education (Wu, 2013). During this period, the *White Paper on Gifted Education* (Ministry of Education, 2009) called for a diversification of gifted education to both create more equitable access and cover a broader range of abilities, while ascribing the cultivation of social responsibility and service to the realm of gifted education.

Based on the overviews of formal giftedness education referenced above and found in policy papers, we identify several key features reflecting the sociocultural understanding of GATE in Taiwan developed in this chapter. These include: (a) a persistent focus on merit ('credentialism'; Wu & Kuo, 2016, p. 46) and traditional intellectual and academic skills, despite adoption of policy language covering diverse areas (Wu & Kuo, 2016); (b) policy with broadly interpretable definitions of giftedness, with 'giftedness in other special abilities' evolving to include skills in sports, games, and computers (Ministry of Education, 2009); (c) incremental implementation with pilot programs (Wu, 2013); (d) stated intention to leverage efforts in gifted education to reach everyone in the education system, such as with policies calling for promotion of flexible, student-centred learning (K–12 Education Administration, 2015) or expansion of creative education (Wu & Albanese, 2013); and (e) the conjunction of giftedness, creativity, and talent in later policy and practice (Ministry of Education, 2009, 2013).

Reconceptualising Talent in the Mainstream System

As we have argued, understandings of giftedness and talent are historically and contemporarily entangled with meritocratic values. A predominant feature of relevant policy development is a deference to academic prestige in developing and justifying implementation of new policy. We see this reflected in the recent development of the *White Paper on Cultivation of Talent* (Ministry of Education, 2013), with plans reaching to 2023. With a public that considers economic security and social stability the purview of the government, education reform is historically highly politicised (Chou & Ching, 2012; Kwok, 2017). Faced with criticisms reflecting public anxieties surrounding economic insecurity (e.g., youth unemployment, shifting landscape for jobs, pension reform, general economic stagnation), the Executive Yuan established a reform committee to produce the white paper, again asking Lee Yuan-Tseh to chair a committee of academics. This paper (Ministry of Education, 2013) defined ideally talented individuals as (paraphrasing): possessing sufficient professional knowledge and skills, communicative and cooperative capabilities, and basic civic literacy, enabling engagement and co-creation of an open, civilised society in its various dimensions. Key focus competency areas include global mobility (including language and international vision), employability, innovation, interdisciplinary abilities, information competency and civic competence. The paper directly articulates urgent cultivation of talent for diverse industries as a key to bolstering national competitiveness and addressing challenges such as youth unemployment.

Two aspects of this policy are particularly noteworthy for this study: the process of development and definition. First, in terms of process, when faced with complex challenges and public pressure, the government utilised a committee of scholars to construct a definition with little input from current GATE scholars and practitioners. An Academia Sinica Academician and Nobel Prize Winner, Lee Yuan-tseh is a veteran in the education reform arena and typifies the meritocratic reverence for elite scholars. The policies put forth in such reform initiatives, while likely well-intended, are informed by perspectives of academicians themselves epitomising intellectual and academic achievement and accolades, such as Li's Nobel Prize. One implication of offering reform discretion to academicians is a potential disconnect between intended ideals and practical applications and results. Uhlmann and Cohen (2007) show that higher rates of self-perceived objectivity can in fact result in greater bias, as self-scrutinising and self-monitoring behaviours are reduced. Valuing personal objectivity as academics, committee efforts appeal to meritocratic values of objectivity to continue to identify giftedness and talent with achievement indicators in traditional intellectual and academic realms, functionally reifying existing academic emphases, and potentially overlooking possible limitations and unintended consequences of reform efforts, such as the rise of cram schools in the decades following the 1994 reform.

Second, the white paper definition covers a broad range of competencies. We argue this allows practitioners to tailor the language and intentions of their particular initiatives to fit within the framework and receive resources. Thus, the formal system sets new benchmarks that can be interpreted broadly, opening the doors to experimentation from enterprising bricoleurs, who may gain access to a wider set of concepts to integrate into their GATE bricolages.

This tendency of MOE to employ academic research to guide policy towards broad goals meant to increase inclusivity can also be seen in several other initiatives from the past two decades. These include: (a) the emergence of six action plans for creativity education implemented over six years from research in the *White Paper on Creative Education* (Ministry of Education, 2003; Wu & Albanese, 2013); (b) the subsequent *Creativity and Imagining the Future in Education* project (Ministry of Education, 2011); and (c) the three new acts governing experimental education of 2014 (Ministry of Education, 2015), which created mechanisms for publicly approved experimental education (T. Chen, 2017), such as with charter schools, alternative schools like Waldorf schools and non-school organisations, like the Taipei City Government Department of Cultural Affairs run Taipei Media School. The language of relevant policy papers for each of these cases represents a broadly conceived policy effort from the central government. They outline initiatives intended to be implemented in part with collaborative academic pilot programs, in an incremental, evolutionary manner. At the same time, they also contain language encouraging the development of distinct local initiatives. We argue that administrators may view these initiatives as opportunities to increase their school reputations, in turn offering teachers the chance to exercise novel educational practice. Thus, the conditions are present for education practitioners and students to act as bricoleurs.

'Naughty' Bricoleurs: Redefining Talent from the Margins

In our sociocultural understanding of GATE in Taiwan, government policies, in part informed by eminent academics and motivated by political considerations and social concerns, articulate guidelines that delimit conceptions. These operate as both boundaries and guideposts, and the institutional weight and sociocultural heritage behind these structures often result in incremental, evolutionary change. The other element of Sundararajan and Raina's (2015) harmony model of creativity often overlooked when examining only the mainstream social system is the concurrent exploration and discovery, revolutionary at the individual level. We argue that given that understandings of heaven-endowed giftedness and talent require cultivation

(Zhang, 2017), these smaller scale creative acts, themselves insufficient to revolutionise the system, can still affect change in the way giftedness and talent are conceived by society by serving as alternative models of success. Outside of the mainstream system, examples abound of individuals who forged their own paths to success, though often at significant sacrifice to the extent social relations and identities are constructed based on the wishes of parents. Like Mr. Zhou from our introduction (Public Television System, 2017), we conceive of these creative individuals who are forced to grapple with systemic constraints as bricoleurs.

One such bricoleur at the heart of an initiative to create a platform that fosters recognition of alternative learning experiences is Ozzie Su. Inspired to create art from a young age, Su was fortunate to grow up with a family who supported his pursuit of his interests even though aspiring artists are often considered 'difficult' children among Taiwanese parents (Su & Chen, 2016). Appreciating opportunities to pursue his own interests, he perceived mainstream education and social values as limiting and saw rampant neglect and ultimately replacement of individual interests with unquestioned social values. Su had a vision of gathering those who did not quite fit to encourage society to actively question what we mean by education and success (Su & Chen, 2016) with a learning 'utopia' for 'ages 1–99' (Za Share, 2018b). Moving from the life of an artist into the unknown as an event organiser, Su opened the doors to the *Naughty Education Fest* at the Huashan 1914 Creative Park in Taipei in May 2015. He gathered groups and organisations involved in alternative education, with Su, a mainstream educational outsider, spending NT $7 million of his own funds (W. Chen, 2017). The term 'naughty' (*bu tai guai*, literally 'not very well-behaved') was chosen in an attempt to reappropriate and celebrate a commonly disparagingly used term for someone exhibiting any behaviour not adhering to mainstream academic or social values (Su & Chen, 2016)—for example, not completing homework, playing video games, or even socialising with friends instead of studying.

Within two days, 25,000 visitors attended, free of charge, to learn about educational innovation efforts from 250 exhibitors (Za Share, 2016). Building on this success, in 2016, Su organised *Za Share-Expo for Innovative Education*, this time a ticketed event showcasing 160 organisations involved in educational innovation in Asia, including several from the mainstream education system in Taiwan (Za Share, 2018a). Over 17,000 visitors attended over two days (Za Share, 2016), including, as witnessed by the present authors, representatives from MOE. In October 2017, a third iteration, titled *Za Share-Expo for Innovative Education in Asia*, included 120 organisations with over 50 lectures and workshops over three days, notably drawing from education practitioners from all areas, not necessarily from the ranks of the "'successful personages' as defined by traditional society" (W. Chen, 2017). Su envisions this platform as a new mode of learning: Za Share. The name, literally 'miscellaneous school' or 'miscellaneous learning' in Chinese, but the Romanisation for miscellaneous, ZA, invokes everything from Z to A. Su's encouragement to learn from anything at hand and of interest (Za Share, 2018b) reflects the bricolage nature of these non-mainstream educational endeavours.

Adopting the lens of a harmony model of creativity (Sundararajan & Raina, 2015), we see how the tension between the limitations of extant formations and novel creations may drive social change. We believe that the success of initiatives like Su's has the potential to reconfigure social conceptions of talent by publicly identifying new markers of success. The understanding of the social landscape for GATE we propose here includes the conjunction of conservative approaches of mainstream educational authorities and the introduction of creative ideas from outside voices.

Competitions and Contests as Bricolage

Competitions and Contests Satisfying Meritocratic Logic

According to Wu and Kuo (2016), identification of giftedness is conceived of as a competition, with a 'winner-takes-all' effect, whereby those identified have access to better resources and more opportunities for academic and career success. This competition for resource access is governed by standardised tests as scores are presumed to be more objective. The practice, however, excludes "culturally diverse and socioeconomically disadvantaged students" (Wu & Kuo, 2016, p. 37), as familiarity with mainstream culture and access to private resources, such as coaching through cram schools, is not distributed evenly in Taiwan.

Competition played a role in the earliest methods of identifying giftedness in contemporary Taiwanese education, as in addition to high scores in mathematics, or science (top 1% of the class), general intelligence (IQ) or creativity tests, performance in a national or international competition, such as a mathematics contest or science fair, was one way of fulfilling requirements of being identified as gifted early on in Taiwan (Stevenson et al., 1994). Only after drawing the attention of and receiving a recommendation from a teacher would a committee of teachers and administrators convene and notify the local education bureau, who in turn initiated further screening and placement. A national law delineated explicit requirements regarding GPA and IQ, which relied on comparative rank (e.g., IQ test scores two standard deviations above the mean). Overall, GATE in formal education is mainly for students with high general abilities, talents in traditional academic domains, or students with fine arts, music, dance, drama, or sports potential, while identification "highly relies on...objective test scores" in conjunction with additional criteria, such as recommendations, documentation of learning characteristics, and excellent academic performance (Wu & Kuo, 2016, p. 36). This reflects both local cultural beliefs in elitism and talent development and western emphases on creativity and multiple assessments (Wu & Kuo, 2016).

Competitions and contests have risen in popularity in Taiwan in recent years. In addition to international Science and Mathematical Olympiads, competitions are used in a wide array of educational arenas, including nursing (Chiu et al., 2010), creativity, and entrepreneurship (Feng, 2013), green energy (Wang, Chang, Huang, & Chu, 2010), and the knowledge economy (Yang & Hsu, 2007). Innovation competitions have also recently become popular in many countries around the world as tools for education, particularly in the sciences and technology (Feng, 2013). For example, MOE recently hosted an applied computer systems competition for 128 teams from 27 schools, a majority of which were technology universities (Wu & Chung, 2017).

Mainstream institutional stakeholders, including MOE and the *Ministry of Economic Affairs* (MOEA), have also recently increased support for the use of competitions as criteria for identifying talent. For this study, we asked MOE for information regarding how Taiwan has performed in international competitions. MOE prepared and provided an unpublished 37-page report (Ministry of Education, 2017) entitled *International Achievements: International Rankings and International Competitions*. The materials included indicate how MOE conceives of Taiwan's achievements in this area. While dominated by performance in international sports competitions, the document also lists Taiwan's scores participating in the *Progress of International Reading Literacy Study* (PIRLS; International Association for the Evaluation of Educational Achievement, 2018), OECD-run *Programme for International Student Assessment* (PISA; Organisation for Economic Co-operation and Development, 2018), *Trends in International Mathematics and Science Study* (TIMSS; International Association for the Evaluation of Educational Achievement, 2018), and *International Civic and Citizenship Education Study* (ICCS; International Association for the Evaluation of Educational Achievement, 2018).

The MOE report began by saying they started the 'Nurturing Talent in the Arts and Design Project' in 2005 in order to nurture talent in the arts and design through internationalisation. The project allocated budget to encourage students to participate in international competitions and contests or for MOE to sponsor competitions. As achievements, MOE notes that in the 12 years of hosting the Asia University administered 'Project to Encourage Students to Participate in International Arts and Design Competitions', 701 participants have received awards with a value of over NT$480 million (roughly US$16 million). Taiwan boasts three gold award recipients in international design contests, two silver awards and 18 bronze awards, while 68 have received awards of excellence or been nominated (Ministry of Education, 2017). Calling it an "outstanding performance" (p. 1), the 91 award-winning products receiving a total of NT$4.87 million. The report also cites Taiwanese students' performances in Germany's *iF World Design Award* and *Red Dot Design Award*, with 133 products on iF Design Top 100 lists between 2004 and 2016 (third behind South Korea with 188 and Germany with 168), and the presence of six Taiwanese universities in the top 15 performing universities in the Asia-Pacific region within the Red Dot Design Award. A breakdown of subsidies for participation in design competitions from 2012 to 2016 indicated 385 recipients received NT $16.71 million for competing in product (224), graphic (51), craft (4), visual communications (56), and digital animation (13) design competitions. From this, we understand that MOE is concerned with Taiwan's international reputation and considers performance on international competitions as an indicator of general educational quality.

Conceptions of the role of international competitions in GATE from mainstream policy stakeholders reflect both an idealised stated goal of providing access to unique opportunities for students and underlying realities of motivations based on pursuit of economic competitiveness or international merit. In policy language, participation in international competitions is viewed as a learning mechanism for students to gain international perspective, a major competency area discussed in the *White Paper on Cultivation of Talent* (Ministry of Education, 2015). Locally hosting international competitions in order to increase exchange opportunities for gifted students is also a stated goal in the recent white paper regarding gifted education (K–12 Education Administration, 2015). It is clear that MOE is willing to spend significant public education funds on these activities in the name of cultivating giftedness and talent. However, success in these areas seems to be measured by securing placement in international competitions, while exposing only the premier performers to potential educational benefits, again reflecting meritocratic values. As we have seen above, MOE proudly notes achievements in international competitions that bolster an international reputation, with millions spent on select students. Besides reputation, economic gain is the other desired form of competitiveness. In 2014, the then R.O.C. Premier Jiang Yi-huah publicly lambasted the 'leaking' of NT$15.7 billion in public funds over six years on strategies to capitalise on patents under the Executive Yuan's Industrialisation of Inventions and Patents policy, a major thrust of which was to promote and subsidise participation in international competitions and contests. Premier Jiang lamented that no such returns had materialised (Wu, 2017). His criticism reveals a conception of performance on international competitions and contests, and education in general, as tools for economic growth and competitiveness.

Recently, various educational authorities have also integrated competitions and contests into enrolment criteria for high schools and universities. Under the Basic Education Act, all students are entitled to a high school education, yet schools and the counties with oversight discretion in the implementation of basic education utilise the legal flexibility in admissions criteria to differentiate their student populations. Many counties offer bonus points on non-exam-based admissions for performance in international competitions (Wu, 2017). Many private science and technology-based universities have also created mechanisms to subsidise faculty and student participation in international invention competitions in pursuit of reputation, finances (via patents), and high rankings. Thus, competitions and contests are seen as a part of a survival strategy within Taiwan's competitive university landscape, particularly as they face declining student populations and imminent downsizing, either through university closures or mergers (X.-W. Chen, 2017). It remains to be seen how pervasive this practice becomes and to what degree it presents opportunities for talented individuals who may not have excelled in traditional academic areas or functions as another marker of elitism.

Academic Interest in Competitions and Contests

To ascertain research interest in the area of competitions and contests in education, we searched for keywords in local databases of: (a) master's theses and doctoral dissertations, (b) Ministry of Science and Technology (MOST)-funded research projects, and (c) Taiwan Social Sciences Citation Index (TSSCI) journals. Using Chinese, we searched for combinations of 'student(s)' and 'competition(s)' or 'contest(s)'. The reader should note that there is no ambiguity in Chinese between a competitive event (*jingsai*) and the activity or condition of competing (*jingzheng*). Further, Chinese does not pluralise nouns.

Our search of doctoral dissertations and master's theses returned 43 doctoral dissertation abstracts with a combination of 'student(s)' and 'competition(s)', while 16 contained 'student(s)' and 'contest(s)', and only one title contained 'student(s)' and 'contest(s)'. For master's theses, we found 1,032 theses with 'student(s)' and 'competition(s)' in the abstracts (with 87 with the same in the titles) and 925 with 'student(s)' and 'contest(s)' in the abstracts (with 43 in titles).

MOST, which helps set research agendas through funding and whose research results often inform policy and action initiatives, has supported 153 projects with 'competition(s)' or 'contest(s)' in the title, but only 14 of those also included 'student(s)', indicating that while there have been a decent number of studies in other areas, the vast majority are not explicitly related to education. The link between competitions and contests and education has not thoroughly been established within MOST research discourse. Regarding journal publications, scholars have published 49 articles in TSSCI journals with 'students' and 'competitions' or 'contests' in either the title or abstracts.

This indicates to us that although competitions and contests are increasingly important educational activities for identifying talent, academics have yet to begin seriously investigating the phenomenon. The higher numbers of master's theses may be a reflection of the numbers of master's students overall. Taiwan has over 150 colleges and universities, almost all of which have master's programs, and each year over 24,000 students graduate from master's programs (Ministry of Education Department of Statistics, 2017). Further up the academic merit-ladder, however, there are still very few studies in this area.

Of note, however, is that the start of interest in this area, in both doctoral dissertations and master's theses, coincides with the 1994 education reform, which moved away from the single entrance examination system. This indicates a potential expansion of competitions and contests, and research on this novel phenomenon occurred at a time where the academic and intellectually focused entrance examination no longer wholly monopolised the definition of talent and success and mainstream educational policy began aspiring to meet a more diverse set of needs and abilities.

Competitions Switching on the 'Lights of Taiwan'

While competitions and contests fulfil the logic of achieving merit and are employed to identify and assist highly talented individuals based on ranking, they can also serve as sites for individuals to develop and demonstrate talents not recognised within the mainstream educational system. In this section, we introduce several 'Lights of Taiwan', showing how the bestowing of such a title of success is related to award recognition.

The public lauding of an individual as a 'Light of Taiwan' (*Taiwan zhiguang*) typically follows international recognition in the context of contests, competitions, or awards. These individuals, newly held in popular esteem and praised by the government, are often from among those whose talents went unrecognised and unsupported by schools and yet managed to develop their gifts independently or with support from informal educational mechanisms. For example, in 2017, at the age of 13, Chiang Ching-Liang became the youngest student ever admitted to the New York University and the first Taiwan-educated junior high student to become accepted to a top-tier school (You & Wu, 2017). Chiang, certified by Mensa International with an IQ of 160, was precocious from an early age. A voracious reader, Chiang won numerous piano and violin competitions, and was autodidactic. Chiang's mother cited negative feedback in schools as reasons for self-directed preparation for international English examinations and the Scholastic Assessment Tests and completion of advanced placement courses before gaining admittance, both to NYU and the world of public esteem as a 'Light of Taiwan'.

The case of another 'Light of Taiwan', Wu Pao-Chun, demonstrates talent in areas outside of formal education. Growing up the youngest of eight in an impoverished single-parent family, Wu's passion for baking garnered him the title of Master Baker at the 2010 Bakery Masters competition in Paris. Continually enhancing the commercial success of his brand and the development of his craft, Wu applied in 2014 to enrol in the National Chengchi University Executive MBA (EMBA) program in Taiwan, only to be rejected because of national regulations stipulating that a university degree was needed for enrolment. Wu had only completed junior high school. A case was made to either make an exception or adjust the rules. To keep this light in Taiwan, even the President at the time called for a rule change. MOE did end up changing the rule to open admissions to winners of major international competitions, but ultimately Wu chose to enrol in an EMBA program at the National University of Singapore, graduating in 2016. The policy, though, is now in place as an opportunity for others perhaps likewise overlooked by the formal education system.

This second case is an excellent example of how individual creative breakthroughs through self-cultivation from a marginal bricoleur can influence the mainstream system by appealing to its own meritocratic logic, demonstrating a harmonising creativity. Wu's case represents someone who achieved success by realising revolutionary personal potential, honed by self-cultivation, and all despite the mainstream educational system that did not acknowledge his area of talent. After achieving merit outside the formal system, reform-minded academics and policy-makers argued for a legal change. The government then enacted substantive legal changes with the potential to shift the optics regarding progress in developing talent and giftedness. Given the anxiety to retain talent in Taiwan, change was introduced in the form of expanding mechanisms for enrolment, demonstrating not a deliberate, premeditated policy response informed by consideration of theory or best practices, but a circumstantial reaction to an encounter with a marginal element (i.e., a successful baker without a high school diploma ready to benefit from an EMBA program) able to satisfy mainstream meritocratic logic.

Diverse Talents Developed and Identified in Competitions

Wu's is a unique case. While not everyone can achieve a top rank in an international event, a growing number of competitions and contests are intentionally designed to provide opportunities to develop and display non-traditional talent and skills. One such example is the *Intelligent Ironman Creativity Contest* (IICC), which emerged initially as a Taiwanese contest from an MOE sponsored creative education project in 2004 where it was a highlight of a creative education exhibition (Wu, 2009). The first international IICC contest took place in 2005 and participation has continued to grow in the 13 iterations since then. The contest is immensely popular among high school and vocational high school students in Taiwan, as well as teams from abroad. In 2006, 1,138 teams with over 6,000 students participated, while in 2012, there were over 12,000 participants in 2,000 teams with international participants from over six countries (Wu & Fan, 2011). IICC staff indicated (personal communication, December 14, 2017) that in 2017, 8,124 students in 1,354 teams participated, with international teams from Vietnam, Indonesia, South Korea, Malaysia, Singapore, Hong Kong, Japan, Chile, and Nigeria. The majority of students from Taiwan came from vocational high schools (119), yet the participation from regular high schools (25) indicates that IICC is attractive to students beyond STEM as well.

The contest was designed for team members to develop and exercise intelligence, endurance, and creativity in collaborative, project-based team settings (Fan et al., 2016). The completion of a creative team project, done over a consecutive 72-hour period in a closed room, is preceded by the gathering of resources in earlier stages, acquired by answering questions in mathematics, science, technology, and even the social sciences and arts. The better teams perform in earlier stages, with more resources acquired for the final push. Thus, the contest focuses on traditional academic talent, as well as team-work, presentation, aesthetics, and creativity skills (Fan et al., 2016).

The IICC is just one example of an increasing number of educational contests in Taiwan. Depending on the intentions of organisers and practices of facilitators, contests may be designed to necessitate exercising both traditional academic skills and demonstrating diverse talents. Fulfilling the logic of the meritocratic system, parents and educators may be inclined to see value in student participation. While only a select few may win these competitions—and thus as an educational mechanism they are open to similar critiques of perpetuating inequality—the evaluation of alternative talents and skills within these competitions may carve out more space for further formal and informal social validation.

Assembling Bricolage Understandings of Giftedness and Talent

In this chapter, we developed a sociocultural understanding of giftedness and talent that engaged concepts of meritocracy and harmonising creativity in assemblages of elements of the sociocultural context. This bricolage recognises *keju* heritage, rank-based comparisons, individual and national competitiveness, imported knowledge systems, and economic imperatives in conjunction with desires for equitable flourishing and nurturing of diverse gifts and talents, individual creativity, and self-cultivation. These elements find new purchase in society through their mutual tensions, and the educational landscape is continually reconstituted between incremental social evolutions and self-transcendent personal revolutions. We believe that this bricolage approach to inquiry offers insight into the present constraints and opportunities of the education system, while also drawing attention to relevant phenomena and stakeholders, facilitating unique encounters between elements of complex processes of social change.

Implications and Orientations for Future Research and Practice

Harmonising Creativity Across the Region. Both Taiwan's case and this approach may have implications for other contexts as well, particularly several contemporary East Asian societies that present similar disjuncts between policy and practice. As shown already, official policy definitions of giftedness in Taiwan closely mirror the Marland Report (Marland, 1972), while assessment and practice adapt theory from western academia (e.g., Gardner, 1983; Sternberg, 1999). Hong Kong employs a similar definition for giftedness (Tommis, 2013), though hews even closer to the Marland Report, as does South Korea, where gifted education laws and policies from 2000 and 2002 established gifted programming throughout the education system (Kim, Shim, & Hull, 2009; Lee, Kang, & Lee, 2016). In China, the definition of 'supernormal' (*chaochang*) students dominates GATE discourse. The term emerged from the establishment of the Special Class for the Gifted Young at the University of Science and Technology in Hefei, Anhui Province, in 1978 by three Chinese-American Nobel Prize winners in physics, Yang Chen-Ning, Samuel C. C. Ting, and Tsung-Dao (T.-D.) Lee (Shi, 2005). Supernormal is employed to describe children with superior performance or potential relative to normal children as determined by the statistical measurement of cognitive, non-cognitive, creativity, and domain-specific talents (Zhang, 2017), with a predominant focus on IQ and academic performance, particularly in science and mathematics. Japan is an outlier among contemporary Confucian-influenced societies for its relatively less comprehensive gifted education programming and policy, in part due to a cultural aversion to perceived elitism (Ibata-Arens, 2012).

Throughout the region, giftedness and talent cultivation is associated with development of human capital as a key to international competitiveness, whether via scientific progress or economic prowess (Ibata-Arens, 2012). Further, though broad definitions adapted from western academia designate cultivation of diverse abilities as GATE objectives in theory, stakeholders in these systems consistently engage with sociocultural heritage that emphasises competition and traditional, exam-based measures of intelligence and academic performance (Sriraman & Lee, 2016; Wu & Albanese, 2013; Zhang, 2017).

Future research may consider exploring how aspects of local sociocultural contexts in other Confucian-influenced societies interact with GATE efforts, particularly when such efforts involve the transfer and translation of GATE policy and knowledge across unique sociocultural contexts. Future research that strives to create socioculturally informed understandings of the evolution of GATE in various national and administrative contexts may help illuminate historical social change and offer insight into how to more effectively direct such change towards intended development goals. Practitioners and participants may benefit from reconsidering their position as essential co-constitutive parts of an evolving GATE landscape.

Researcher as Bricoleur. We also believe that this chapter serves as a case of employing bricolage in the process of discovering how things fit and creating knowledge about those connections. Discoveries were made by assembling and verifying data points from diverse areas, including news and popular media, government statistics and policy papers, academic publications and a wide range of first-hand experiences in both formal and informal education research and practice. For example, our third author has over 50 years in the field of educational psychology and has led numerous MOE and MOST commissioned research projects and advised and evaluated countless competitions and contests, while our other two authors have both conducted research on and served as judges for competitions. We hope that our exercise in bricolage and use of data marginalised in traditional academic discourse will help encourage others to broaden the search for authoritative voices and accept more diverse sources. The interrogation of authority is central to critical methodologies (Darian-Smith & McCarthy, 2017) and concerns of epistemic violence and oppression (Dotson, 2011), and epistemic marginalisation and inequality (Go, 2017). Steinberg (2006) presents a moving case for embracing the construction of knowledge as a bricoleur in such a way that it enables the illumination of previously unseen phenomenon and broadcasting of unheard voices.

We are aware our authority as researchers is derived in part from our merit, as is the authority of this publication, and recognise those most convinced of their objective authority may indeed be blind to their own biases (Uhlmann & Cohen, 2007). By exploring and referencing primarily academic sources, and from within the limited scope of top-tier journals (Chou, 2014), scholarship may perpetuate the limited concerns of previous authority, leaving unilluminated, whether by interest-serving intention or unintentional omission, phenomena beyond the light of established concepts and theory. We have shown in this chapter that academic discourse is regularly employed to promote political, economic, and other ideological concerns within education in ways that affect students' growth and potential.

As long as mainstream academic discourse and educational practice in Taiwan remain blind to salient sociocultural features and marginal educational phenomena, it is little wonder that the answers for Taiwan's gifted education and talent development and education reform yield paradox, uncertainty, and anxiety. Fortunately, the bricoleurs can feel their way over the boundaries, for recognising and manipulating such limits and constraints is the bricoleur's *modus operandi*.

Limitations

Naturally, there are limitations, both to the bricolage approach and this chapter. To overcome the focus on a singular subject or limitations of a single method or theory (Kincheloe & Berry, 2004), the use of bricolage is inherently multidisciplinary and multitheoretical (Kincheloe, 2005). Yet this subjects it to concerns of interdisciplinarity (e.g., Friedman, 1998) and epistemological relativism (e.g., McLaren, 2001). However, the continued use and development of bricolage as a methodology within various fields attests to its potential for making substantive knowledge contributions. Specific to this chapter, in presenting a novel perspective, we acknowledge that many aspects of the phenomena described have yet to be substantiated with extensive empirical support in academic literature. We acknowledge a need for further research on the roles of competitions and contests and the strength of the salience of the concepts employed in this sociocultural understanding of GATE in Taiwan.

Further, a critical reading of this chapter is warranted. For instance, we acknowledge a tenor of methodological nationalism (Darian-Smith & McCarthy, 2017) that treats the nation as a stable container for homogenous subjects. Taiwan has experienced waves of historical colonisation and immigration, and the creative results of rebalancing tensions have had painful, violent ends for many (Morris, 2004), far from the standard sense of harmonious. Changing demographics in Taiwan today are imbued with creative tension speaking to what it means to be Taiwanese and how the government and society may better acknowledge, reflect, and accommodate a range of identities and experiences. The framing of this chapter is not intended to essentialise any particular form of Taiwanese identity nor over-ascribe the pervasiveness of any particular philosophical heritage (e.g., Confucian or Chinese), while the treatment of government, education system, or society as cohesive wholes is not intended to negate the myriad disjunctions between assembled elements of the aggregated conceptual containers. We hope that the philosophical underpinnings of the harmony model of creativity, with its embrace of both/and logic, will enable readers to appreciate and utilise these tensions as necessary aspects of this co-creative meaning making process in which we are engaged. Despite these limitations, we believe we still offer contributions with the potential to stimulate further research and action.

Conclusion

We believe that interrogating the motivations and sociocultural attributes of GATE initiatives is essential at this time as new technologies begin to disrupt educational and occupational landscapes. The perceived global reach of neoliberal capitalism proscribes the nurturance and deployment of talent for both collective economic competitiveness and cultivation of modern identity. Yet, at the same time, substantive changes to ways of life are imminent around the world and vulnerability is on the rise; reduced security and increased instability visit us unequally. According to McKinsey Global Institute (2017), with current technology, nearly half of work activities worldwide can potentially be automated, while a third of tasks in 60% of jobs are potentially automatable (p. 21). Does this mean more diverse work tasks (Susskind in Mahdawi, 2017) or jobs are characterised by creativity, unpredictability, and complex relationships (Ford, 2015)? How will we respond to this creativity and complexity tomorrow?

Education is at the forefront of this response, whatever form it takes. Scholars, practitioners, and policy-makers are indeed working hard to adapt to changing global and local challenges and opportunities. In Taiwan, rising socio-economic inequality makes the need to reach diverse learners all the more imperative. Efforts to move away from exam-based achievement in traditional academic areas as primary criteria for the identification of ability and to open pathways to success and further development of gifts and talents must still reckon with meritocracy. As we argue in this chapter, policy intentions and the realities of practice are not yet, nor may they ever be, fully aligned. We offer an exploration of Taiwan as an example of how the engagement of educational reforms and initiatives with local sociocultural conditions is a crucial component of the outcomes of those efforts. The stakes are high, as it is children who bear the burden of our shortcomings. As part of the effort to create and think with new paradigms in GATE research and practice appropriate for the realities of the twenty-first century (Dai, 2016), we hold that much can be gained from moving towards and working with socioculturally informed understandings of complex phenomenon.

Cross-References

- ► Attuned Pedagogy: The Artistry of Differentiated Instruction from a Taiwanese Cultural Perspective
- ► Creative and Gifted Education in Korea: Using the CATs Model to Illustrate How Creativity Can Grow into Innovation
- ► Diverse Dimensions of Gifted Education: Part V Introduction
- ► Engaging Gifted Students in Solving Real Problems Creatively: Implementing the Real Engagement in Active Problem-Solving (REAPS) Teaching/Learning Model in Australasian and Pacific Rim Contexts
- ► Exploring Diverse Perceptions of Wise Persons: Wisdom in Gifted Education
- ► Fostering and Developing Talent in Mentorship Programs: The Mentor's Perspectives
- ► Gifted Education in the Asia-Pacific: From the Past for the Future – An Introduction
- ► In Search of an Explanation for an Approach-Avoidance Pattern in East Asia: The Role of Cultural Values in Gifted Education
- ► Sociocultural Perspectives on the Talent Development Megamodel
- ► Some Implications for the Future of Gifted Education in the Asia-Pacific
- ► The Lives and Achievements of Four Extraordinary Australians: A Master, a Maker, an Introspector, and an Influencer
- ► Trends and Challenges of Creativity Development Among Selected Asian Countries and Regions: China, Hong Kong/Macau, Japan, Malaysia, and South Korea

References

Ambrose, D. (2016). From the editor's desk. *Roeper Review, 38*(3), 133–135.
Berry, K. S. (2006). Research as bricolage: Embracing relationality, multiplicity and complexity. In K. Tobin & J. L. Kincheloe (Eds.), *Doing educational research: A handbook* (pp. 87–116). Rotterdam, The Netherlands: Sense Publishers.

Boxenbaum, E., & Rouleau, L. (2011). New knowledge products as bricolage: Metaphors and scripts in organizational theory. *Academy of Management Review, 36*(2), 272–296.

Chan, C.-Y., Lin, S.-Y., & Hsieh, P.-H. (2008). Constructing a system of indicators for choosing potentially creative students. In C.-Y. Chan (Ed.), *Feng hu wu yu: Ministry of Education Advisory Office "creative education medium-term plan" implementation record* (pp. 258–283). Taipei, Taiwan: Ministry of Education. (Chinese).

Chan, S. (1999). The Chinese learner: A question of style. *Education + Training, 41*(6/7), 294–304.

Chan, S.-J., & Lin, L.-W. (2015). Massification of higher education in Taiwan: Shifting pressure from admission to employment. *Higher Education Policy, 28*(1), 17–33.

Chang, C. Y. (1963). *Creativity and Taoism: A study of Chinese philosophy, art & poetry.* New York, NY: The Julian Press.

Chang Chien, C., Lin, L., & Chen, C. (2013). The main features and the key challenges of the education system in Taiwan. *Higher Education Studies, 3*(6), 1–14. Retrieved from https://files.eric.ed.gov/fulltext/EJ1079213.pdf

Chen, T. (2017, November 21). What is experimental about experimental education? *CommonWealth.* Retrieved from https://opinion.cw.com.tw/blog/profile/352/article/6332

Chen, W. (2017, October 11). Helping kids who don't like to study find value: "Za Share School" initiates a donation project. *United Daily News.* Retrieved from https://udn.com/news/story/7266/2749716. (Chinese).

Chen, W.-H. (2017, August 11). Academic talent: MOE plan aims to retain top academics. *Taipei Times.* Retrieved from http://www.taipeitimes.com/News/taiwan/archives/2017/08/11/2003676312

Chen, X.-W. (2017, November 23). With less than 100,000 new university students by 2028, Executive Yuan will assist private schools to merge or close. *United Daily News.* Retrieved from https://udn.com/news/story/7314/2835325. (Chinese).

Chen, X.-Y. (2017, January 16). After 20 years promoting education reform, cram schools have tripled? *Global Views Monthly.* Retrieved from https://www.gvm.com.tw/article.html?id=36384. (Chinese).

Chen, Z.-L. (2017, July 16). Mainland attracting Taiwanese youth at any cost. *China Times.* Retrieved from http://www.chinatimes.com/newspapers/20170716000659-260301. (Chinese).

Chiu, Y. W., Weng, Y. H., Lo, H. L., Shih, Y. H., Hsu, C. C., & Kuo, K. N. (2010). Impact of a nationwide outreach program on the diffusion of evidence-based practice in Taiwan. *International Journal for Quality in Health Care, 22*(5), 430–436. https://doi.org/10.1093/intqhc/mzq049

Chou, C. P. (Ed.). (2014). *The SSCI syndrome in higher education. A local or global phenomenon.* Rotterdam, The Netherlands: Sense Publishers.

Chou, C. P., & Ching, G. (2012). *Taiwan education at the crossroad.* New York, NY: Palgrave Macmillan.

Chou, C. P., & Yuan, J. K. S. (2011). Buxiban in Taiwan. *The Newsletter: International Institute for Asian Studies, 56,* 15. Retrieved from http://www.iias.asia/article/buxiban-taiwan

Chung, L.-H., & Chin, J. (2017, November 18). Brain drain a Chinese ploy, academics say. *Taipei Times.* Retrieved from http://www.taipeitimes.com/News/taiwan/archives/2017/11/18/2003682484

Connelly, B. L., Tihanyi, L., Crook, T. R., & Gangloff, K. A. (2014). Tournament theory: Thirty years of contests and competitions. *Journal of Management, 40*(1), 16–47. https://doi.org/10.1177/0149206313498902

Dai, Y. D. (2016). Envisioning a new century of gifted education: The case for a paradigm shift. In D. Ambrose & R. J. Sternberg (Eds.), *Giftedness and talent in the 21st century: Adapting to the turbulence of globalization* (pp. 45–63). Rotterdam, Netherlands: Sense Publishers.

Darian-Smith, E., & McCarthy, P. C. (2017). *The global turn: Theories, research designs, and methods for global studies.* Oakland, CA: University of California Press.

Davidsson, P., Baker, T., & Senyard, J. M. (2017). A measure of entrepreneurial bricolage behavior. *International Journal of Entrepreneurial Behavior & Research, 23*(1), 114–135. https://doi.org/10.1108/IJEBR-11-2015-0256

Denzin, N. K., & Lincoln, Y. S. (Eds.). (1994). *Handbook of qualitative research*. Thousand Oaks, CA: SAGE.

Directorate General of Budget, Accounting and Statistics. (2016). *National accounts yearbook 2015*. Taipei, Taiwan: Chinese Statistical Association.

Dotson, K. (2011). Tracking epistemic violence, tracking practices of silencing. *Hypatia, 26*(2), 236–257. https://doi.org/10.1111/j.1527-2001.2011.01177.x

Duymedjian, R., & Rüling, C.-C. (2010). Towards a foundation of bricolage in organization and management theory. *Organization Studies, 31*, 133–151. https://doi.org/10.1177/0170840609347051

Easton, I. (2017). *The Chinese invasion threat: Taiwan's defence and American strategy in Asia*. North Charleston, SC: CreateSpace Independent Publishing.

Elliot, M. (2012, November 13). The real China model. *The New York Times*. Retrieved from http://www.nytimes.com/2012/11/14/opinion/the-real-china-model.html

Elman, B. (2013). *Civil examinations and meritocracy in late Imperial China*. Cambridge, MA: Harvard University Press.

Engelen, E., Erturk, I., Froud, J., Leaver, A., & Williams, K. (2010). Reconceptualizing financial innovation: Frame, conjuncture and bricolage. *Economy and Society, 39*(1), 33–63.

Executive Yuan. (2017, August 18). Yushan project to raise salaries for academics and researchers. Retrieved from https://english.ey.gov.tw/News_Hot_Topic.aspx?n=5974542AF70162DA&sms=E5F898FDED22FAB8

Fan, H.-L., Chang, P.-F., Albanese, D., Wu, J.-J., Yu, M.-J., & Chuang, H.-J. (2016). Multilevel influences of transactive memory systems on individual innovative behavior and team innovation. *Thinking Skills and Creativity, 19*, 49–59. https://doi.org/10.1016/j.tsc.2015.11.001

Feng, H. Y. (2013). A case study on creativity, innovation and entrepreneurship education of the university in Taiwan. *Active citizenship by knowledge management & innovation: Proceedings of the Management, Knowledge and Learning International Conference 2013* (pp. 679–684). ToKnowPress. Retrieved from http://www.toknowpress.net/ISBN/978-961-6914-02-4/papers/ML13-305.pdf

Ford, M. (2015). *Rise of the robots: Technology and the threat of a jobless future*. New York, NY: Perseus.

Friedman, S. S. (1998). (Inter)Disciplinarity and the question of the women's studies PhD. *Feminist Studies, 24*(2), 301–325. Retrieved from https://www.jstor.org/stable/3178699

Gao, C. (2018, September 10). Is the US ready to stand up for Taiwan against China? *The Diplomat*. Retrieved from https://thediplomat.com/2018/09/is-the-us-ready-to-stand-up-for-taiwan-against-china/

Gao, P. (2010, July 01). Gifted, in many ways. *Taiwan Today*. Retrieved from https://taiwantoday.tw/news.php?post=22519&unit=12,29,33,45

Gardner, H. (1983). *Frames of mind*. New York, NY: Basic Books.

Gardner, H. (1996). The creators' patterns. In M. A. Boden (Ed.), *Dimensions of creativity* (pp. 143–158). Cambridge, MA: The MIT Press.

Garud, R., & Karnoe, P. (2003). Bricolage versus breakthrough: Distributed and embedded agency in technology entrepreneurship. *Research Policy, 32*(2), 277–300. https://doi.org/10.1016/S0048-7333(02)00100-2

Go, J. (2017). Decolonizing sociology: Epistemic inequality and sociological thought. *Social Problems, 64*(2), 194–199. https://doi.org/10.1093/socpro/spx002

Godfrey, E. B., Santos, C. E., & Burson, E. (2017). For better or worse? Sixth-grade system-justifying beliefs predict self-esteem and behavioral trajectories across early adolescence. *Child Development*. Advanced online publication. https://doi.org/10.1111/cdev.12854

Hung, R. (2016). A critique of Confucian learning: On learners and knowledge. *Educational Philosophy and Theory, 48*(1), 85–96. https://doi.org/10.1080/00131857.2015.1084220

Hwang, K.-K. (2000). Chinese relationalism: Theoretical construction and methodological considerations. *Journal for the Theory of Social Behaviour, 30*, 155–178. https://doi.org/10.1111/1468-5914.00124

Hwang, K.-K. (2012). *International and cultural psychology. Foundations of Chinese psychology: Confucian social relations*. New York, NY: Springer Science + Business Media.

Ibata-Arens, K. C. (2012). Race to the future: Innovations in gifted and enrichment education in Asia, and implications for the United States. *Administrative Sciences, 2*(1), 1–25. https://doi.org/10.3390/admsci2010001

International Association for the Evaluation of Educational Achievement. (2018). IEA studies. Retrieved from https://www.iea.nl/iea-studies

Jackson, A. Y., & Mazzei, L. A. (2012). *Thinking with theory in qualitative research: Viewing data across multiple perspectives*. London, UK: Routledge.

Jost, J. T., & Banaji, M. R. (1994). The role of stereotyping in system-justification and the production of false consciousness. *British Journal of Social Psychology, 33*, 1–27. https://doi.org/10.1111/j.2044-8309.1994.tb01008.x

K–12 Education Administration. (2015). *Ministry of Education K–12 Education Administration mid-term plan for gifted education quality development: The first 5-year plan (2015–2019)*. Taipei, Taiwan: Ministry of Education. Retrieved from http://www.ttsh.tp.edu.tw/file.php?id=215

Kaohsiung City Government Education Bureau. (2017). *All cities and counties short-term tutorial center information and management system*. Kaohsiung City Government Education Bureau. Retrieved from http://bsb.edu.tw/afterschool/register/statistic_city.jsp

Kim, C. H., & Choi, Y. B. (2017). How meritocracy is defined today? Contemporary aspects of meritocracy. *Economics and Sociology, 10*(1), 112–121. https://doi.org/10.14254/2071-789X.2017/10-1/8

Kim, K. H. (2007). Exploring the interactions between Asian culture (Confucianism) and creativity. *The Journal of Creative Behavior, 41*(1), 28–53. https://doi.org/10.1002/j.2162-6057.2007.tb01280.x

Kim, K. H., Shim, J. Y., & Hull, M. (2009). Korean concepts of giftedness and the self-perceived characteristics of students selected for gifted programs. *Psychology of Aesthetics, Creativity, and the Arts, 3*(2), 104–111. https://doi.org/10.1037/a0013324

Kincheloe, J. L. (2005). On to the next level: Continuing the conceptualization of the bricolage. *Qualitative Inquiry, 11*(3), 323–350. https://doi.org/10.1177/1077800405275056

Kincheloe, J. L., & Berry, K. S. (Eds.). (2004). *Rigour and complexity in educational research: Conceptualizing the bricolage*. London, UK: Open University Press.

Kwok, K.-H. (2017). *When education meets politics in Taiwan: A game theory perspective (1994–2016)*. Rotterdam, The Netherlands: Sense Publishers.

Lee, H.-F. (2017, November 11). Immigrants key to labor shortage: Lai. *Taipei Times*. Retrieved from http://www.taipeitimes.com/News/front/archives/2017/11/11/2003682047

Lee, J., Kang, B., & Lee, D. (2016). Law for gifted and talented education in South Korea: Its development, issues, and prospects. *Turkish Journal of Giftedness and Education, 6*(1), 14–23.

Lee, Y. F. (2008). Economic growth and income inequality: The modern Taiwan experience. *Journal of Contemporary China, 17*(55), 361–374. https://doi.org/10.1080/10670560701809577

Legge, J. (1893). *The Chinese classics*. Oxford, UK: The Clarendon Press.

Levi-Strauss, C. (1967). *The savage mind*. Chicago, IL: University of Chicago Press.

Li, J. (2012). *Cultural foundations of learning: East and West*. Cambridge, MA: Cambridge University Press.

Liu, Y. (2016). Origins of meritocracy in China. In Y. Liu (Ed.), *Higher education, meritocracy and inequality in China* (pp. 11–34). Singapore, Singapore: Springer Science+Business Media.

Louridas, P. (1999). Design as bricolage: Anthropology meets design thinking. *Design Studies, 20*(6), 517–535. Retrieved from http://www0.dmst.aueb.gr/louridas/pubs/louridas-bric.pdf

Mahdawi, A. (2017, June 26). What jobs will still be around in 20 years? Read this to prepare your future. *The Guardian*. Retrieved from https://www.theguardian.com/us-news/2017/jun/26/jobs-future-automation-robots-skills-creative-health

Mao, C.-J. (2018). A global-local mixture of educational reform policy in Taiwan: Taking school choice policy as an example of unevenness of educational opportunity, Chapter 5. In J. McLeod, N. Sobe, & T. Seddon (Eds.), *World yearbook of education 2018: Uneven space-times of education: Historical sociologies of concepts, methods and practices*. Retrieved from Taylor & Francis Group. https://www.taylorfrancis.com/books/e/9781315363806

Marland, S. P., Jr. (1972). *Education of the gifted and talented: Report to the Congress of the United States by the U.S. Commissioner of Education and background papers submitted to the U.S. Office of Education* (2 vols). Washington, DC: U.S. Government Printing Office. (Government Documents Y4.L 11/2: G36).

McKinsey Global Institute. (2017). *A future that works: Automation, employment, and productivity.* New York, NY: McKinsey & Company. Retrieved from https://www.mckinsey.com/global-themes/digital-disruption/harnessing-automation-for-a-future-that-works

McLaren, P. (2001). Bricklayers and bricoleurs: A Marxist addendum. *Qualitative Inquiry, 7*(6), 700–705.

Miner, A. S., Bassoff, P., & Moorman, C. (2001). Organizational improvisation and learning: A field study. *Administrative Science Quarterly, 46*, 304–337. https://doi.org/10.2307/2667089

Ministry of Education. (2003). *White paper on creative education.* Taipei, Taiwan: Ministry of Education. (Chinese).

Ministry of Education. (2005). Multi-opportunities for school entrance. Retrieved from https://english.moe.gov.tw/cp-32-14685-F097F-1.html

Ministry of Education. (2009). *White paper on gifted education.* Taipei, Taiwan: Ministry of Education. (Chinese).

Ministry of Education. (2010). *The intelligent Taiwan: Manpower cultivation project (Forming part of the "i-Taiwan 12 Projects").* Taipei, Taiwan: Ministry of Education. Retrieved from https://english.moe.gov.tw/cp-32-14541-6CF3A-1.html

Ministry of Education. (2011). *Imagining the future and creativity in education project.* Taipei, Taiwan: Ministry of Education. Retrieved from http://www.edu.tw/plannews_detail.aspx?sn=501&pages=2. (Chinese).

Ministry of Education. (2013). *Ministry of Education white paper on cultivation of talent.* Taipei, Taiwan: National Academy for Educational Research. Retrieved from http://www.naer.edu.tw/ezfiles/0/1000/attach/5/pta_2189_2524507_39227.pdf

Ministry of Education. (2015, January 29). *Three acts governing experimental education – A new lease for education development.* Ministry of Education. Retrieved from https://www.edu.tw/news_Content.aspx?n=9E7AC85F1954DDA8&s=C5AC6858C0DC65F3

Ministry of Education. (2017). International performance (international evaluations and international competitions). Unpublished report. (Chinese)

Ministry of Education Department of Statistics. (2017). *Statistics categories.* Taipei, Taiwan: Ministry of Education Department of Statistics. Retrieved from https://stats.moe.gov.tw/. (Chinese).

Ministry of Justice. (2014). *Special Education Act.* Taipei, Taiwan: Ministry of Justice. Retrieved from https://law.moj.gov.tw/LawClass/LawAll.aspx?PCode=H0080027

Ministry of Science and Technology. (2017a). The pilot directions for MOST grant for the Columbus program. Retrieved from https://www.most.gov.tw/most/attachments/9b1cca56-7f17-42a3-a0e0-347d49ec2d30

Ministry of Science and Technology. (2017b). The pilot directions for MOST grant for the Einstein program. Retrieved from https://www.most.gov.tw/most/attachments/4c368c9a-f7ef-4400-8443-b29f862f43ae

Molecke, G., & Pinkse, J. (2016). Accountability for social impact: A bricolage perspective on impact measurement in social enterprises. *Journal of Business Venturing.* Advanced online publication. https://doi.org/10.1016/j.jbusvent.2017.05.003

Morris, A. D. (2004). Taiwan's history: An introduction. In D. K. Jordan, A. D. Morris, & M. L. Moskowitz (Eds.), *The minor arts of daily life: Popular culture in Taiwan* (pp. 3–31). Honolulu, HI: University of Hawai'i Press.

Morris, P. (1996). Asia's four little tigers: A comparison of the role of education in their development. *Comparative Education, 32*(1), 95–109. https://doi.org/10.1080/03050069628948

Moskowitz, M. L. (2008). Message in a bottle: Lyrical laments and emotional expression in Mandopop. *The China Quarterly, 194*, 365–379. https://doi.org/10.1017/S0305741008000428

National Development Council. (2016, October 19). *Foster Taiwan's environment for retraining talent* (Policy statement). Taipei, Taiwan: National Development Council. Retrieved from https://www.ndc.gov.tw/en/cp.aspx?n=A362E58882219C90&s=ED6734C130D6F33E&upn=6010885C37FF6856

Needham, J. (1956). *Science and civilization in China, vol. 2: History of scientific thought*. Cambridge, UK: Cambridge University Press.

Organisation for Economic Co-operation and Development. (2018). PISA: Programme for International Student Assessment. Retrieved from http://www.oecd.org/pisa/

Oxford Economics. (2012). *Global talent 2021: How the new geography of talent will transform human resource strategies*. Oxford, UK: Oxford Economics. Retrieved from http://www.oxfordeconomics.com/my-oxford/projects/128942

Phillips, N., & Tracey, P. (2007). Opportunity recognition, entrepreneurial capabilities and bricolage: Connecting institutional theory and entrepreneurship in strategic organization. *Strategic Organization, 5*(3), 313–320. https://doi.org/10.1177/1476127007079956

Public Television System. (2017, April). *Youth straight talk, No. 11*. Taipei, Taiwan: Public Television System. Retrieved from https://www.facebook.com/ptsyouthnews/videos/1666327750330287/

Rao, H., Monin, P., & Duran, R. (2005). Border crossing: Bricolage and the erosion of categorical boundaries in French gastronomy. *American Sociological Review, 70*, 968–991. https://doi.org/10.1177/000312240507000605

Reuters. (2017, December 19). PLA planes fly around Taiwan again. *Taipei Times*. Retrieved from http://www.taipeitimes.com/News/front/archives/2017/12/19/2003684229

Rowen, I. (2016). The geopolitics of tourism: Mobilities, territory and protest in China, Taiwan, and Hong Kong. *Annals of the American Association of Geographers, 106*(2), 385–393. https://doi.org/10.1080/00045608.2015.1113115

Shi, J.-N. (2005). Recent development in research on and education of supernormal children in Mainland China. *Gifted Education, 97*, 17–22. (Chinese).

So, B. W. Y. (2015). Exam-centred meritocracy in Taiwan: Hiring by merit or examination? *Australian Journal of Public Administration, 74*(3), 312–323. https://doi.org/10.1111/1467-8500.12139

Sriraman, B., & Lee, K. (2016). The Hobbesian trap in contemporary India and Korea. In D. Ambrose & R. J. Sternberg (Eds.), *Giftedness and talent in the 21st century: Adapting to the turbulence of globalization* (pp. 137–146). Rotterdam, Netherlands: Sense Publishers.

Steinberg, S. R. (2006). Proposing a multiplicity of meanings: Research bricolage and cultural pedagogy. In S. Steinberg & K. Tobin (Eds.), *Doing educational research: A handbook* (pp. 111–132). Rotterdam, The Netherlands: Sense Publishers.

Sternberg, R. J. (1999). The theory of successful intelligence. *Review of General Psychology, 3*(4), 292–316. https://doi.org/10.1037/1089-2680.3.4.292

Stevenson, H. W., Lee, S., Chen, C., Kato, K., & Londo, W. (1994). Education of gifted and talented students in Mainland China, Taiwan, and Japan. *Journal for the Education of the Gifted, 17*(2), 104–130. https://doi.org/10.1177/016235329401700203

Su, Y.-C., & Chen, H.-T. (2016). Naughty focal person. In Y.-C. Su, H.-T. Chen, & CommonWealth Education Media & Publishing Co., Ltd. (Eds.), *Naughty Generation: Not rebellious and definitely not treacherous, instead just persisting in being well-behaved by being myself* (pp. 12–66). Taipei, Taiwan: CommonWealth Education. (Chinese).

Sundararajan, L., & Raina, M. K. (2015). Revolutionary creativity, East and West: A critique from indigenous psychology. *Journal of Theoretical and Philosophical Psychology, 35*(1), 3–19.

Tobin, K., & Steinberg, S. (2006). *Doing educational research: A handbook*. Rotterdam, The Netherlands: Sense Publishers.

Tommis, S. (2013). Gifted education in the Hong Kong special administrative region. *Journal for the Education of the Gifted, 36*(3), 259–276. https://doi.org/10.1177/0162353213492701

Tu, C.-S. (2007, January 10). *Taiwan's educational reform and the future of Taiwan*. Paper presented at the London School of Economics and Political Sciences, London, UK. Retrieved from http://english.moe.gov.tw/content.asp?culItem=7045&mp=2

Uhlmann, E. L., & Cohen, G. L. (2007). "I think it, therefore it's true": Effects of self-perceived objectivity on hiring discrimination. *Organizational Behavior and Human Decision Processes, 104*(2), 207–223.

Wang, Y.-H., Chang, M. C., Huang, Y.-Y., & Chu, Y.-M. (2010). Investigate the senior high school students' understandings toward green energy after participating the innovation competition. In *Technology Education Curriculum Reform and Development Symposium* (pp. 100–110).

Wu, B.-E. (2017, July 16). *Jiang Yi-Huah's not happy! Executive Yuan duped into leaking NT $15.7 billion over six years to patent exhibitions*. Taipei, Taiwan: North American Intellectual Property Corporation. Retrieved from http://www.naipo.com/Portals/1/web_tw/Knowledge_Center/Editorial/publish-186.htm. (Chinese).

Wu, J.-J. (2009). Planting the seeds of creative education in Taiwan: Some examples of down-to-earth programs. *The International Journal of Arts Education, 7*(1), 153–156. Retrieved from https://ed.arte.gov.tw/uploadfile/periodical/2272_01530166.pdf

Wu, J.-J., & Albanese, D. L. (2013). Imagination and creativity: Wellsprings and streams of education – The Taiwan experience. *Educational Psychology, 33*(5), 561–581.

Wu, J.-J., & Fan, H.-L. (2011). The policy and practice of creative education in Taiwan. *Journal of Chinese Creativity, 2*(1), 5–28.

Wu, P.-H., & Chung, J. (2017, December 23). Students' fish robot wins gold. *Taipei Times*. Retrieved from http://www.taipeitimes.com/News/taiwan/archives/2017/12/23/2003684492

Wu, W.-T. (1987). Gifted education in Taiwan. *Educational Perspectives, 26*, 10–14.

Wu, W.-T. (2013). The 40th anniversary of gifted education in Taiwan (I): A retrospection. *Gifted Education Quarterly, 126*, 1–11. (Chinese).

Wu, W.-T., & Kuo, Y.-L. (2016). Gifted and talented education in Taiwan: A 40-year journey. In D. Y. Dai & C. C. Kuo (Eds.), *Gifted education in Asia: Problems and prospects* (pp. 33–50). Charlotte, NC: Information Age Publishing.

Xu, M.-Z. (2007). 12–year compulsory education: Stop, listen and watch. *NPF Commentary*. National Policy Foundation. Retrieved from http://www.npf.org.tw/2/2254. (Chinese).

Yang, C.-H., & Hsu, M.-J. (2007). *Creative economy and personnel training* (Report No. 095-001). Taipei, Taiwan: National Policy Foundation. Retrieved from https://www.npf.org.tw/2/1871. (Chinese).

Yang, O. (2016, January 8). Universities in China offering doubled salaries to attract Taiwanese professors. *The News Lens*. Retrieved from https://international.thenewslens.com/article/34093

You, K.-H., & Wu, L. (2017, July 10). 13-year-old Taiwanese student becomes youngest admitted by NYU. *Focus Taiwan*. Retrieved from http://focustaiwan.tw/news/aedu/201707100015.aspx

Young, M. D. (1958). *The rise of the meritocracy*. Piscataway, NJ: Transaction Publishers.

Young, M. D. (1994). Meritocracy revisited. *Society, 31*(6), 87–89.

Za Share. (2016). Naughty Education Fest. Retrieved from http://zashare.weebly.com/2015naughty.html

Za Share. (2018a). Learn to be, not taught to fit. Retrieved from https://zashare.org/expo/2016

Za Share. (2018b). Make education different. Retrieved from https://zashare.org/about

Zhang, Z. (2017). Gifted education in China. *Cogent Education, 4*(1), 1364881. https://doi.org/10.1080/2331186X.2017.1364881

Zhou, L.-A. (2007). Governing China's local officials: An analysis of promotion tournament model. *Economic Research Journal, 7*, 36–50.

Dale Albanese is a PhD candidate in the Department of Education at National Chengchi University in Taiwan and an adjunct faculty instructor for the Long Island University (LIU) Global College China Center in Hangzhou, China. He has published co-authored articles in Educational Psychology and Thinking Skills and Creativity. In the past, he has taught for LIU's Comparative Religion and Culture program in Taiwan, India, and Thailand, and was a recipient of a Fulbright English Teaching Assistantship in Taiwan in 2007, where he has since resided.

Ming-Jen Yu obtained his PhD in 2018 from the Graduate Institute of Technology, Innovation, and Intellectual Property Management at National Chengchi University (NCCU) in Taiwan, where he was also an affiliate of the Center for Creativity and Innovation Studies at NCCU. He is currently an Assistant Professor in the Si-Wan College of National Sun Yat-sen University. His recent publications can be found in *Thinking Skills and Creativity* (SSCI) and *Journal of Technology Management* (TSSCI). He was a judge of the Intelligent Ironman Creativity Contest in Taiwan in 2015 and has been commissioned by the Yilan County Government in Taiwan to review academic studies related to the Yilan International Children's Folklore and Folkgame Festival.

Dr. Jing-Jyi Wu obtained his PhD in educational psychology from the University of Minnesota and taught at US universities before returning to Taiwan to eventually chair the National Chengchi University (NCCU) Department of Psychology. He is currently the Endowed Chair in Creativity at NCCU's Center for Creativity and Innovation Studies. Author and editor of 20 books, much of his work has focused on creativity, innovation, and entrepreneurship. Dr. Wu was once a theatre artist of La MaMa Theatre in New York and was co-founder and artistic director of Taiwan's influential Lanling Theatre Workshop.

Creativity Talent Development: Fostering Creativity in Schools

47

Carly Lassig

Contents

Abstract

How do we prepare gifted students to be leaders who can tackle the complex social, environmental, medical, political, technological, economic, and ethical challenges in our globalised society? International rhetoric about the importance of developing creativity in twenty-first century education in our current global climate often stands in stark contrast to educational systems that still emphasise performativity, standardised curricula, and testing. Creativity has been conceptualised as a continuum with four forms of creativity: Big-C (eminent) creativity, Pro-c (professional) creativity, little-c (everyday) creativity, and mini-c (intrapersonal) creativity. Educational creativity (ed-c) as an additional form of creativity, useful for discussions on creativity in education, is proposed in this chapter. Creativity's relationship to intelligence and giftedness is also discussed in relation to two major schools of thought, namely, creativity as an essential

C. Lassig (✉)
Queensland University of Technology, Brisbane, QLD, Australia
e-mail: cj.lassig@qut.edu.au

© Springer Nature Singapore Pte Ltd. 2021
S. R. Smith (ed.), *Handbook of Giftedness and Talent Development in the Asia-Pacific*,
Springer International Handbooks of Education,
https://doi.org/10.1007/978-981-13-3041-4_49

component of intelligence/giftedness and creativity as a domain of intelligence/giftedness. The development of creativity has been largely the purview of stand-alone creativity training programs, which have been popular in gifted education and talent development programs. However, it is argued that teaching for creativity needs to be infused throughout the curriculum using empirical research of how education can develop students' creative capacity. Findings from the literature about how creativity can be fostered in schools, as well as original research on environmental influences on students' creativity, as reported by young people themselves in research conducted with students in selective secondary schools in Australia will be presented in this chapter. Understanding how highly creative students are creative to varying degrees, depending on how environments support or inhibit creativity, has practical implications for students, teachers, school administrators, teacher education, and educational policy regarding how we can foster creative engagement and development of creative intelligence in schools.

Keywords

Creativity · Intelligence · Gifted · Students · School

The aims in this chapter are to:
1. Overview the significance of creativity in the twenty-first century.
2. Highlight tensions between creativity and the current educational culture of performativity and standardisation.
3. Conceptualise creativity and its relationship to intelligence and giftedness.
4. Delineate different forms of creativity and propose *educational creativity* (*ed-c*) as an addition to the continuum of creativity.
5. Review current literature on how creativity can be fostered in schools.
6. Present original research on student perspectives of how the school environment can support or inhibit creativity.
7. Present practical implications of research on fostering creativity for students, teachers, schools, teacher education, and educational policy.

Introduction

Globally, we face increasingly complex social, environmental, medical, political, technological, economic, and ethical challenges. We require a twenty-first century education system that matches twenty-first century demands if we are to support young people to thrive personally and to contribute successfully to society (Ambrose, 2016). A key capacity for facing these challenges and thriving in our current society is creativity. Creativity enables individuals "to live with complexity and uncertainty" (Lucas, 2001, p. 42). It is promoted as important for preparing students for careers in the unforeseeable future, many of which may not yet exist

(Runco, 2016). Related to this is the view that attracting creative talent contributes to global economic competitiveness for industries and governments (Florida, 2012; Harris & Ammermann, 2016; Hartley, 2003). However, arguably, creativity's importance for personal development and well-being is equally important. Creativity empowers individuals to learn new knowledge and discover new possibilities and experiences, engage socially and educationally, manage the challenges and complexities of everyday life, contribute to their personal expression and self-actualisation, and enrich their lives through making and experiencing creativity in cultural artefacts (Craft, 2005, 2011; Harris & Ammermann, 2016; Maslow, 1968; Richards, 2007; Rogers, 1961; Ward, Smith, & Vaid, 1997).

Within the landscape of education, the flow-down effect of global interest in creativity is that creativity has begun moving from the periphery to the core (Craft, 2005), including in Australia (Harris & de Bruin, 2017). This can be seen in various policy and curricular documents internationally. For example, the United Nations Educational, Scientific, and Cultural Organisation's (2016) *Education 2030: Framework for Action* emphasises that quality education requires fostering creativity and problem-solving skills, alongside developing foundational knowledge and skills. In Australia, *critical and creative thinking* is listed as a general capability in the national curriculum (Australian Curriculum, Assessment and Reporting Authority, n.d.), and the 2008 Melbourne Declaration on Educational Goals for Young Australians noted that an aim of education is "to support all young Australians to become … confident and creative individuals" (Ministerial Council on Education, Employment, Training, and Youth Affairs, 2008, p. 8). Similarly, in other parts of the Asia-Pacific region, creativity is being increasingly highlighted in policy and curriculum reform. For example, Singapore has had the *Thinking Schools, Learning Nation* framework since 1997 and later identified *21st Century Competencies* that underpin their education, including critical and inventive thinking (Ministry of Education, 2015); Taiwan's Ministry of Education published the *White Paper on Creative Education* proposing six strategies for developing creativity in education with funding for projects until 2011 (Ministry of Education, 2002); China's *National Medium- and Long-term Talent Development Plan (2010–2020)* includes an increased focus on developing students' creative thinking and abilities (Pang & Plucker, 2013); and creativity is one of the "priority generic skills" in Hong Kong's curriculum reforms (Education Commission, 2006, p. 13).

Recognition of the educational value of creativity in many contexts often fails to go beyond rhetoric, however, largely due to the tension teachers face with implementing creativity alongside other competing educational priorities (Burnard & White, 2008). Teachers report not specifically teaching students how to be creative; it remains on the periphery rather than central to learning and achievement (Forster, 2012). There is a crossroad of competing agendas: performativity and creativity (Craft & Jeffrey, 2008; Davies, Newton, & Newton, 2017).

Currently, there is a significant emphasis on standardised curriculum and high-stakes testing in Western culture (Pfeiffer & Thompson, 2013). Similarly, in Eastern culture, schools have a highly competitive exam focus and the Confucian emphasis on collectivism, conformity, and rote learning (Cheng, 2004, 2010; Kim, 2007).

Internationally, standardisation and performativity are exemplified by the *Programme for International Student Assessment* (PISA), in which educational quality is measured by student performance in reading, mathematics, and science. Problem-solving is assessed within these domains and a collaborative problem-solving test component is also being trialled (Organisation for Economic Co-operation and Development, 2018), but problem-solving is only one component of creativity. The Asian region scores very highly in PISA. The 2015 top four countries in overall mean scores across the three domains were all from Asia: (1) Singapore, (2) Hong Kong, (3) Japan, and (4) Macao (OECD, 2018). Performativity in Australia is also encapsulated by judgments and comparisons of schools on the basis of student results in the *National Assessment Program Literacy and Numeracy* (NAPLAN), an annual assessment for students in Years 3, 5, 7, and 9 of the basic skill domains of reading, writing, and mathematics. A focus on performativity whereby judgements and comparisons are a measure of quality (Ball, 2003) has led schools down a path of centralised curricula and high-stakes standardised testing of concrete outcomes. A focus on creativity requires embracing teacher and adolescent autonomy and focusing on encouraging creative processes in teaching and learning.

Increasing achievement levels and developing young people's creativity are both justifiable aims from the perspective of ensuring high-quality education that equips students with the necessary knowledge and skills for their lives. There is even evidence to suggest that teaching for creativity improves student achievement (Forster, 2012; Schacter, Thum, & Zifkin, 2006). However, a tension arises from balancing these agendas of performativity and creativity when translating policy into practice. For example, complex thinking (such as creativity) may not be assessable through standardised testing, but that does not mean we should not teach and value such skills (Baer, 2016). "Not everything that can be counted counts, and not everything that counts can be counted" (Cameron, 1963, p. 13). On the other hand, the PISA is reportedly proposing to do just that: an advisory group has been established to develop an assessable definition of creativity and recommendations for assessing creative thinking (Lucas, 2017). Researchers are continuing to explore opportunities for assessing creative potential, including multifaceted assessments, such as the *Evaluation of Potential Creativity* (EPoC; Barbot, Besançon, & Lubart, 2016), and the creativity multifaceted test battery structure for assessing scientific and artistic creativity (Agnoli, Corazza, & Runco, 2016). A challenge for education is nurturing creativity while developing core curriculum knowledge and skills.

Conceptualising Creativity

Given the diverse understandings and beliefs of its nature, it is important in discussions of creativity to be explicit about how it is defined. The definition of creativity underpinning this chapter is that creativity is the confluence and interaction among person, process, and environment by which an individual or group produces an outcome that is novel and appropriate, as defined within the relevant context. This definition is an adaptation of Plucker, Beghetto, and Dow's (2004) widely accepted definition and considers the role of the *Four Ps* of creativity identified by Rhodes (1961): person, process, product, and press (environment). However, it is also acknowledged that conceptions of creativity are culturally dependent and may differ. For example, in Western culture, creativity is often focused on radical 'conceptual ruptures' that result in surprisingly new outcomes, while in Eastern culture, being creative is considered a gradual process of progressive adaptations, rearrangements, and improvements (Celik & Lubart, 2016; Tam, Phillipson, & Phillipson, 2014).

A Continuum of Creativity

Everyone has the potential to be creative in different ways and at different levels. It is not expected that people are creative all the time or in all domains. Creativity has previously been categorised as falling into four types: *Big-C, Pro-c, little-c*, and *mini-c* creativity (Kaufman & Beghetto, 2009). This is known as the Four C Model of creativity.

Big-C research that focuses on unquestionable, eminent creativity throughout history characterises creativity as a rare phenomenon. Big-C has also been referred to as *high creativity* (Craft, 2001) and *Historical Creativity* (*H-Creativity*) (Boden, 2004). Since the creativity or impact of some eminent work is often not appreciated during the life of its creator (Csikszentmihalyi, 1996), many studies are conducted posthumously. Studying eminent creators is the most straightforward approach because of their visibility and distinction. Common examples of Big-C creativity include the work of Einstein, Picasso, Mozart, Dickinson, and Ghandi.

Professional creativity, known as Pro-c, recognises the creativity of people with high levels of expertise who have made a significant creative achievement in their particular domain (Kaufman & Beghetto, 2009). For example, the late Anna Craft achieved Pro-c success with her research and publications on creativity in education and is perhaps best known for her work on possibility thinking. The work of most Pro-c creators might be virtually forgotten over time; however, some contributions remain significant, and a select few might be later recognised for their genius (Kaufman & Beghetto, 2009).

People's everyday creativity is often referred to as little-c creativity (Beghetto & Kaufman, 2007b; Craft, 2001). Little-c refers to creativity used to engage in and manage everyday life activities and adapt to change (Beghetto & Kaufman, 2007b; Craft, 2001, 2005; Hennessey & Amabile, 2010). It involves the production of a novel outcome that is appropriate (useful, valuable, or meaningful) to other people in a particular social context (Beghetto & Kaufman, 2007b; Craft, 2001). This context is more localised than that of Big-C or Pro-c creativity. For example, an original song by young people in a rock band deemed creative by those in their community can be classed as little-c creativity.

The notion of mini-c or intrapersonal creativity encompasses an individual's personal learning experiences and focuses more on processes than products (Beghetto & Kaufman, 2007b). An example of mini-c creativity includes connections a student makes to develop new understandings of related scientific concepts. Mini-c is similar to the concept of *personal creativity* (Runco, 2003, 2007a, 2007b) and *Psychological Creativity* (*P-Creativity*), which refers to ideas that are original in an individual's mind, even if others have also thought of the ideas (Boden, 2004). Notions similar to mini-c and little-c are also found in the work of Maslow (1970) and Rogers (1961), who viewed creativity as essential to our everyday adaptation to and shaping of our world, and as part of self-expression and self-actualisation.

Through research with highly creative secondary school students, this author contends that the Four C Model of creativity can be expanded to better capture students' creativity for educational purposes, including for learning and achievement. Just as Big-C and little-c do not sufficiently encapsulate creativity by professionals (Pro-c), little-c and mini-c are inadequate to account for all forms of creativity by young people, particularly in their roles as students. Thus, a new form of creativity is proposed: *ed-c* or *educational creativity.*

Ed-c refers to creativity for learning or achievement in formal educational environments (e.g., schools, universities). In this form of creativity, individuals' creative processes and outcomes are developed within the external constraints of a particular educational body, including limitations posed by task demands, assessment criteria, or teachers' instructions. These constraints and limitations are a key point of difference from little-c. The resulting outcomes of ed-c differ from work typically presented by peers. Ed-c, like little-c, is a form of interpersonal creativity, meaning the outcome must be creative to someone other than just the creator. For students in formal educational environments, the judges of creativity are usually teachers, external examiners of assessments, or fellow students.

Mini-c creativity is arguably the origin of all creative endeavours (Beghetto & Kaufman, 2007a, 2007b). That is, there is a developmental continuum of creativity beginning with mini-c creativity, which might develop into higher levels of creativity (Beghetto & Kaufman, 2007a, 2007b). Within the continuum of creativity, mini-c, little-c, and ed-c creativity are particularly relevant to school students. A comparison of these is presented in Table 1.

Table 1 Student creativity: mini-c, little-c and ed-c

	Mini-c	Little-c	Ed-c
Form of creativity	Intrapersonal creativity that is part of formal or informal learning and other life experiences.	Interpersonal, everyday creativity that is novel and valuable to someone other than the creator.	Interpersonal creativity for learning and achievement in formal education.
Who it affects	Creator.	Creator + audience in everyday context.	Creator + audience in the educational context.
Example creative outcome	Experimentation with drawing manga (Japanese comics).	Self-initiated paintings for home or friends.	Digital art series for a visual art assessment.
Example judge of creativity	Creator (student).	Family, friends.	Teachers, external examiners.

Mini-c can be demonstrated in a range of activities and tasks inside and outside school. Little-c is evident in everyday life and in personal interests and activities. Ed-c is exhibited in educational tasks in school; extracurricular activities with a formal structure of evaluating progress, ability, or achievement (e.g., debating); or other formal extracurricular activities outside school (e.g., private music lessons). Ed-c is always created within the external constraints of an educational environment; this is not necessarily the case with mini-c and little-c. The continuum of creativity from mini-c through to Big-C implies the developmental nature of creativity, with even eminent creators beginning with mini-c ideas; therefore, it is important to nurture creativity from an early age.

Creativity, Intelligence, and Giftedness

Definitions and theories of giftedness highlight different relationships with creativity (Bucik & Neubauer, 1996; Gagné, 2009; Guilford, 1959; Heller, 2005; Renzulli, 1999). These theories reveal two perspectives about creativity in relation to intelligence and giftedness: (a) creativity as a necessary capacity for intelligence/giftedness and (b) creativity as a type or domain of intelligence/giftedness. The Three-Ring Conception of giftedness states that high levels of creativity are required, along with above-average ability and high levels of task motivation, for all gifted behaviour (Renzulli, 1999). Creativity is also seen as a component of intelligence in theories such as the Structure of Intellect model (Guilford, 1959) and Berlin Model of Intelligence Structure (Bucik & Neubauer, 1996); however, these models do not explicitly state that high levels of creativity are a requirement for high levels of intelligence. Alternatively, theories such as the *Differentiated Model of Giftedness and Talent* (DMGT; Gagné, 2009) and *Munich Model of Giftedness* (Heller, 2005; Perleth & Heller, 1994) define creative ability as a domain of giftedness or talent (comparable to domains such as intellectual or psychomotor ability). Similarly, creativity has been viewed as a type of intelligence, along with analytical intelligence and practical intelligence, in the *Theory of Successful Intelligence* (Sternberg, 1999). This theory has since evolved into the *Wisdom, Intelligence, Creativity, Synthesised* (WICS) model, which proposes that future gifted leaders are those who demonstrate a synthesis of creativity, analytical, and practical intelligence and wisdom in making decisions and implementing ideas (Sternberg, 2005; Sternberg, Jarvin, & Grigorenko, 2011).

Multidimensional conceptions of giftedness that include creativity are more inclusive and are essential for education that is responding to the challenges of the twenty-first century. Although definitions that include creativity as a domain of giftedness have been established for some time now, schools often still use relatively narrow conceptions of giftedness as analytical intelligence when identifying students. Students who are creatively gifted (who may or may not be gifted in other domains) are often not well supported by schools. Even gifted education programs, which often have a goal of developing creative thinking, do not necessarily provide the same opportunities for creatively gifted students to accelerate their creative development as they typically do for students who are gifted in subject domains (Kim, Kaufman, Baer, & Sriraman, 2013). Therefore, although pedagogies to develop analytical intelligence are well established in gifted education, a greater focus is still needed on how to develop creative intelligence within the current education system.

Education for Creativity

Creativity was once viewed as an entirely innate and an unteachable ability demonstrated only by geniuses (Galton, 1892). However, Guilford, in his presidential address to the American Psychological Association in 1950, contested this perception and raised many important questions surrounding creativity, which motivated a surge of interest in this field of research. Particularly pertinent for exploring creativity in education were Guilford's following questions: "Why is there so little apparent correlation between education and creative productiveness? How can we discover creative promise in our children and our youth? How can we promote the development of creative personalities?" (Guilford, 1950, pp. 444–445). It is now widely accepted that creative ability can be stimulated and taught, at least to some extent.

Developing creativity has long been a goal of many gifted education and talent development programs. Traditionally, it has been common to draw on discrete creative thinking skill programs and packages. However, such programs are often isolated, add-on tasks that are not necessarily linked to the core curriculum (Beghetto & Kaufman, 2014). Two meta-analyses of the effectiveness of creativity training programs concluded that well-designed creativity training can be effective (Ma, 2006; Scott, Leritz, & Mumford, 2004), although the results were more positive for non-gifted students than gifted students (Scott et al., 2004). This supports the assertion that creativity can be taught; however, not all creativity training programs are successful. To be most effective, creativity training should: (a) be based on a strong and valid cognitive approach; (b) be conducted over an extended period; (c) be challenging and teach a variety of discrete cognitive skills and heuristics; (d) illustrate application in authentic contexts; and (e) include time for practice in relevant, complex and authentic contexts (Scott et al., 2004). The importance of these criteria for success may explain why previous studies have shown that many creative training programs produce mixed results and limited transferability from the specific context of the training task (e.g., Clapham, 1997; Cropley, 1997; Dow & Mayer, 2004; Nickerson, 1999; Rose & Lin, 1984). Scott et al.'s (2004) meta-analysis findings imply that one-off, context-free creative thinking activities often used in school are not likely to contribute to enhancing student creativity. The movement towards 'naturalising creativity' means that creativity is now seen as an inherent part of learning and meaning making, rather than a special process to use in special tasks (Dai, 2016). However, there is uncertainty among teachers about approaches to developing, recognising, and assessing creativity (Harris & de Bruin, 2017). Therefore, while selected creativity training programs might have a place in education, creativity development needs to be infused throughout education. This requires an understanding of how to establish the optimal environment to foster creativity.

Fostering Creativity: A Synthesis of the Literature

The school environment is an important consideration for encouraging and enhancing creativity. It is generally agreed that education in schools can influence creative development positively when learning is more authentic and student-centred and goes beyond a focus on reproduction of particular knowledge or skills to students developing their own contexts, knowledge, and strategies for engaging in creative challenges (Beghetto & Plucker, 2006). However, a traditional, formal, teacher-centred classroom, where all learning goals are exogenously defined by mandated policy and curricula, leaves little room for creativity (Beghetto & Plucker, 2006).

In relation to the general classroom environment, open and flexible classroom situations that provide some choice in learning have been known for some time to be more supportive of creative development than traditional classrooms (Giaconia & Hedges, 1982; Haddon & Lytton, 1968, 1971; Halpin, Goldenberg, & Halpin, 1990; Horwitz, 1979). One reason for this is that a traditional classroom is unlikely to provide an appropriate person-environment fit given the psychological characteristics commonly observed in children and adolescents being creative (e.g., being unconventional and individualistic). Creativity requires an environment that encourages independent, autonomous learning (Amabile, 1996), which occurs in a challenging environment with high expectations (Craft, Cremin, Hay, & Clack, 2014; Davies et al., 2013). The use of some constraints and obstacles can also be viewed as 'anchors' to aid creativity (Haught-Tromp, 2016), particularly if provided in a nurturing environment for students (Sternberg & Lubart, 1995). However, a demanding environment should not create excessive stress or constraints for students, as negative stress prevents optimal brain function (Lucas, 2001). Moreover, if creativity is seen as a ubiquitous capacity, it should be fostered across all curriculum areas, including opportunities for cross-curricular creativity (Craft, 2005; Harris, 2016; Harris & de Bruin, 2017; Soh, 2017).

Teachers can have one of the most significant influences on the development of students' creativity. Although there is no single, unequivocal, or incontrovertible approach guaranteed to enhance creativity, some pedagogical recommendations for teachers to facilitate their students' creativity across all learning include:

- Establishing authentic, meaningful and relevant learning tasks (e.g., Beghetto & Kaufman, 2014; Craft, 2000, 2005; Craft et al., 2014; Cremin, Burnard, & Craft, 2006; Davies et al., 2013; Harris, 2016; Jeffrey & Craft, 2004).
- Promoting student autonomy and shared ownership of learning (e.g., Beghetto & Kaufman, 2014; Craft, 2011; Craft et al., 2014; Cremin et al., 2006; Davies et al., 2013; Harris, 2016; Harris & de Bruin, 2017; Jeffrey & Craft, 2004; McWilliam, 2008; Schacter et al., 2006).
- Stretching students' imaginations (e.g., Beghetto & Kaufman, 2014; Craft, 2000, 2005, 2011; Craft et al., 2014; Cremin et al., 2006; Jeffrey & Craft, 2004).
- Fostering curiosity, question-posing, and problem-posing (e.g., Craft, 2000; Harris, 2016; Harris & de Bruin, 2017; Jeffrey & Craft, 2004; Schacter et al., 2006; Soh, 2017).

- Encouraging possibility thinking (e.g., Craft, 2000, 2005; Cremin et al., 2006; Jeffrey & Craft, 2004).
- Modelling creativity (e.g., Beghetto & Kaufman, 2014; Harris, 2016; Harris & de Bruin, 2017; Jeffrey & Craft, 2004; Soh, 2017).
- Accessing external spaces and establishing external creative partnerships and mentor for student creativity (e.g., Davies et al., 2013; Harris, 2016; Harris & de Bruin, 2017).
- Building relevant knowledge and skills (e.g., Boden, 2001; Harris, 2016; McWilliam, 2008; Soh, 2017).
- Using play as a stimulus for imagination and creativity (e.g., Craft, 2000; Cremin et al., 2006; Davies et al., 2013).
- Teaching creative thinking strategies and techniques explicitly (e.g., Beghetto & Kaufman, 2014; Forster, 2015; Schacter et al., 2006).
- Teaching students to think metacognitively about their creativity (e.g., Beghetto & Kaufman, 2014; Schacter et al., 2006).
- Adopting liberal-democratic rather than conservative-autocratic teaching methods (e.g., Ng & Smith, 2004).

These suggestions for pedagogical practices to enhance creativity are based on the work of researchers from early childhood through to tertiary education settings.

In addition to utilising specific pedagogies to enhance creativity, teachers can create conditions that contribute to a positive affective climate for creativity, such as:

- Providing open, flexible physical spaces, and a range of resources (e.g., Craft, 2000; Cremin et al., 2006; Davies et al., 2013; Harris, 2016).
- Allowing sufficient, flexible time for creativity (e.g., Craft, 2000, 2005; Cremin et al., 2006; Davies et al., 2013; Harris & de Bruin, 2017).
- Encouraging intrinsic motivation for creativity, for example, by incorporating students' interests into their learning (e.g., Beghetto & Kaufman, 2014; Craft et al., 2014; Harris, 2016; Lucas, 2001; Runco, 2003; Schacter et al., 2006).
- Creating a climate of psychological safety and mutual respect (e.g., Craft et al., 2014; Davies et al., 2013; Harris & de Bruin, 2017; Lucas, 2001).
- Promoting risk-taking, facing uncertainties, and being persistent in overcoming obstacles and failure (e.g., Craft, 2000, 2011; Harris, 2016; Harris & de Bruin, 2017; McWilliam, 2008; Schacter et al., 2006).
- Welcoming and encouraging original ideas, flexible thinking, and multiple perspectives (e.g., Harris & de Bruin, 2017; Schacter et al., 2006; Soh, 2017).
- Recognising and valuing creative thinking and diverse creative expressions (e.g., Beghetto & Kaufman, 2014; Craft, 2000; Harris, 2016; Schacter et al., 2006; Soh, 2017).

In these strategies, it is recognised that affective support, in addition to cognitive support, is important in the fostering of student creativity.

In addition to teachers, peers are influential. They can be negative in their influence when there is peer pressure to conform to group norms (Craft, 2005; Cropley, 2006; Runco, 2003; Torrance, 1968), which has been said to begin around the time of the 'fourth-grade slump' (Runco, 1999; Torrance, 1968). This pressure to conform can inhibit students' willingness to take risks and their confidence in openly displaying unconventional ideas and behaviours (Amabile, 1996). However, although young people may conform to peer pressures externally, internally they are still forming their own ideas (Claxton, Pannells, & Rhoads, 2005), allowing for the possibility that some of their creative ideas are never expressed. Many of the afore-mentioned pedagogies and conditions created by teachers might assist in reducing students' feelings of needing to conform and celebrate nonconformity instead.

Peers can also play a positive role in creativity. For example, opportunities for collaboration are important for creativity (Beghetto & Kaufman, 2014; Davies et al., 2013; Harris, 2016; Harris & de Bruin, 2017; Soh, 2017), with shared decision-making encouraging students to support and build on each other's ideas. In implementing collaborative creativity in education, it is important to consider the social, emotional, and cognitive components that facilitate collective success (Craft, 2008b). Collaborations not only with peers but also with teachers, community members, industry professionals, and other role models all have the potential to play a role in creating a supportive environment for creativity. Another consideration is that the permeation of online environments offers increasing potential for creative collaboration with people anywhere in the world. Unfortunately, the value of collaborative creativity at school can be overshadowed by a focus on competition or individual student achievement (Craft, 2008a).

A Gap in Creativity Research: An Example Australian Study

Data Collection and Analysis

The majority of literature on how the educational environment can affect creativity is studies of teachers' beliefs and experiences (e.g., Bereczki & Kárpáti, 2018; European Commission, 2009; Harris, 2016) and researcher observations of class-rooms (e.g., Richardson & Mishra, 2018; Schacter et al., 2006; Soh, 2017). Studies of young people's creativity typically use standardised measures or tests and the interpretations of adults, without seeking the perspectives of the young people themselves. A gap in creativity research is the perspectives of creative young people of school age. Therefore, a study was conducted by the author to uncover high school students' experiences of how their creativity was supported and enhanced, as well as how it was inhibited or suppressed, within and beyond the school environ-ment. This research was a grounded theory study of 20 high-ability high school students: 10 students from a selective arts school and 10 students from a selective science, mathematics, and technology school. Both were International Baccalaureate (IB) schools. The schools' target populations are students who demonstrate high academic ability (many have been identified as gifted) and interest and potential in one or more of the schools' specialist areas. Researching creativity at schools with students who have interests and abilities in diverse domains was designed to surmount the false dichotomy of creativity for the arts and innovation for science/technology. Therefore, the schools offered a unique context for studying the diverse creative experiences of high-ability students. The findings from this study contribute to existing research on environmental influences on creativity, offering a new student voice perspective.

Data were analysed using grounded theory methods from Corbin and Strauss (2008, 2015) and Charmaz (2006, 2014): concepts were grounded in the data and not drawn from existing theory; data collection and analysis were conducted concurrently using the constant comparative method; theoretical sampling and saturation were used; and recording and developing theory included memo writing and diagramming, which culminated in theory development. In presenting excerpts from the data, pseudonyms are used. As a study that valued student voice, the researcher did not assign pseudonyms; participants developed them instead. The school pseudonyms were also created by participants based on the researcher's prompt to create a name that they felt represented their school. The students from the arts school chose *Whimsical High School* (WHS); the students from the science, mathematics and technology school chose *Nerdopolis High School* (NHS).

Fostering Creativity: Student Perspectives—Some Findings

This section presents findings on how the environment can affect creativity, as experienced and reported by the students themselves. The environment includes sociocultural and physical aspects of the macro-environment (e.g., the educational milieu), as well as students' micro-environments (e.g., home and school). Conditions that positively or negatively influenced the establishment of an environment for creativity can be divided into three categories: supportive environmental conditions for creativity, inhibiting environmental conditions for creativity, and contingent conditions that can either support or inhibit creativity.

A favourable environment for creativity comprised the following main supportive environmental conditions: (a) opportunities, (b) autonomy, (c) structure, (d) challenge, (e) stimuli, (f) congruous physical conditions, (g) like minds, (h) experts, (i) cognitive support, and (j) affective support. Table 2 outlines these environmental conditions, the key properties that support creativity and representative examples of each condition.

The influence of a supportive environment on student creativity can be viewed as a matrix (Fig. 1). One continuum scales from having all identified supportive environmental conditions to having none; the other continuum ranges from having high to low levels of these supportive environmental conditions (e.g., high levels of autonomy to low levels of autonomy). Supportive environments had: (a) high levels of all or many supportive environmental conditions; (b) high levels of a few supportive environmental conditions important for a task or domain (e.g., high levels

Table 2 Environmental conditions supporting creativity

Environmental condition	Properties	Example
Opportunities	Tasks valuing creativity; time	We get opportunities to put, to submit our work into competitions outside of school. We have opportunities to work with people outside of our school who come into our school. . . . I reckon we have a lot of opportunities. . . . the extra-curricular stuff that happens at our school, is created by us. (PeterPan, WHS)
Autonomy	Task, intellectual, environmental autonomy	A lot of the time, creativity comes from autonomy. (CandleJack, WHS)
Structure	Structure without excessive constraints	It's really a threshold between being informative and being, not being restrictive, in that there's things you need, you can't just like walk into a lesson and say, 'Go for it!'. But you can't talk the whole lesson about concepts and not let any freedom happen. (PatrickBateman, WHS)
Challenge	Intellectual rigour, complexity, higher-order thinking	Well, when I first went to do it [the IB], I thought it wouldn't help at all because it is such a strict, hard thing to deal with. But I think that in that it requires you to be creative, otherwise you wouldn't think of the different ways they want to think. (TuathaDuOrothrim, NHS)
Stimuli	Exposure to new outcomes, people, places and experiences	I think one of the most significant things a person can do to enhance their [sic] own creativity is to immerse themselves in the creativity or ideas of others. To be exposed to new ideas, and perspectives other than their [sic] own in order to draw inspiration and fuel their [sic] own creativity. (Ma'at, NHS)
Congruous physical conditions	Ritual versus change; internal versus external locations; sound; lighting; comfort; resources	I think you need to have a physical state that can actually tell your body, 'Hey, it's time to be creative', and your mind goes back into that mindset of uninhibited imagination. . . . to trigger my mind into 'getting into the zone'. It is a psychosomatic effect where physically being in the same situation where you were last creative can trigger that same mindset. (DaVinci, WHS)

(continued)

Table 2 (continued)

Environmental condition	Properties	Example
Like minds	Like-minded in creativity, interests, abilities, personality	We have a good network of people, and so, therefore, you don't have to be afraid to be creative. . . . how we can be creative at this school is we accept each other's creativity. . . . and originality and imagination. (PeterPan, WHS)
Experts	Experts in the field; teachers working in industry; mentors	Generally the teachers themselves are actually working within the industry, and they themselves have, bring their experience to whatever they might say. . . . Yeah, mainly it's just them bringing their way of thinking and their experience to what you do, and using it to help you improve it by suggesting new ways of thinking about things. (UltraShiny, WHS)
Cognitive support	Open to creative ideas; feedback; creative teaching; encouraging creative learning; teacher-student collaboration	And the teachers, like, oh wow, I can't think of the word, they kinda [sic] promote learning creatively... They have a big influence on me to be creative, 'cause [sic] the way that you learn best in those subjects is to learn creatively. . . . they encourage me to learn creatively. (Hippopotamus, NHS)
Affective support	Acceptance; trust; high expectations; recognition; encouragement	Environment-wise, it's pretty much, they've nailed it... You don't feel as restricted...they're [teachers and peers are] very, generally really accepting of what, of how people practise their art or whatever. (UltraShiny, WHS)

of structure and cognitive support for a mathematics problem-solving task); or (c) low to average levels of many or all of these environmental conditions that collectively created a supportive environment for creativity.

An unfavourable context for creativity was established by inhibiting environmental conditions. The following major inhibiting environmental conditions were identified from student reports: (a) curriculum constraints, (b) lack of time, (c) pressure, (d) distractions, (e) lack of resources, and (f) negative social interactions. The main properties and representative examples of these conditions are presented in Table 3.

A matrix can similarly be used to illustrate how inhibiting environments influenced students' creativity (Fig. 2). The range of all to no identified inhibiting environmental conditions form one continuum; the second continuum spans between having high and low levels of these inhibiting environmental conditions

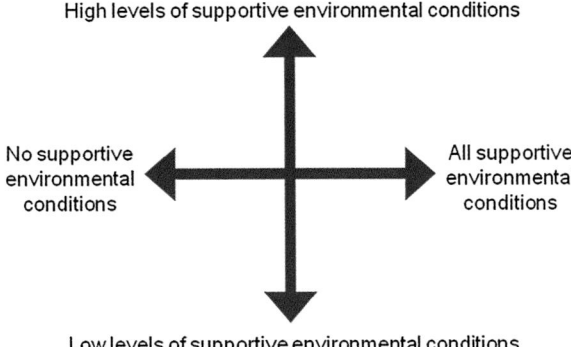

Fig. 1 Supportive environment matrix

(e.g., high levels of pressure to low levels of pressure). An inhibiting environment for creativity usually had: (a) high levels of all or many inhibiting environmental conditions; (b) high levels of a few inhibiting environmental conditions that strongly impacted on a task or domain (e.g., high levels of negative social interactions and distractions in a collaborative creativity task); or (c) low or average levels of many or all of these conditions that collectively formed an inhibiting environment for creativity.

In this study, there were also environmental conditions that emerged as having the potential to either support or inhibit creativity, contingent on the individual or situation. These two conditions—extrinsic motivation and the educational milieu—are presented in Table 4, with supportive and inhibiting examples of each.

Findings in this study also indicated that extrinsic motivation supported creativity when it complemented existing intrinsic motivation, motivated the adolescents to do a creative task in which they were otherwise unmotivated, or supplemented other supportive environmental conditions (e.g., interest in a task). Extrinsic motivation appeared to inhibit creativity when it undermined supportive environmental conditions (e.g., existing intrinsic motivation) or reinforced or added inhibiting environmental conditions (e.g., limited time). An educational milieu positively influenced creativity when it promoted creative dispositional conditions (e.g., celebrating intellectual ability), introduced supportive environmental conditions (e.g., grouping like minds), or decreased inhibiting environmental conditions (e.g., addressing a lack of resources). Conversely, creativity was negatively influenced when an environmental milieu reinforced inhibiting environmental conditions or added new inhibitors (e.g., more pressure to be creative; less time to be creative) or when it undermined or reduced supportive environmental conditions (e.g., reduced opportunities for creativity).

Although all students were creative given the right situation, some students needed substantially higher levels of support from environmental conditions, as suggested in this study. For example, simply having opportunities for creativity was sometimes enough for highly creative students, but was insufficient for others. These other students usually required high levels of supportive environmental conditions in addition to opportunity.

Table 3 Environmental conditions inhibiting creativity

Environmental condition	Properties	Example
Curriculum constraints	Strict and inflexible curriculum and assessment; creativity not valued	What the teachers, um, say to us, not to discredit the IB or anything, they say, 'IB doesn't like creativity'. And what they mean about that is they don't like original thought and they don't, they prefer you stick by the structure and the way that they work. (PeterPan, WHS)
Lack of time	Lack of time for creative pursuits; lack of time for ideation, incubation and production	As far as time is a factor, it's [the IB has] stopped me from doing as much artistically as I'd want to. Um, and I think it also, 'cause [sic] I don't have as much free time as I did beforehand, then it stops me from, um, accessing that little, the extra bit of the mood [to be creative]. (Orange, WHS)
Pressure	School or extracurricular activity workload; stressful situations; social pressure	Situations when I'm getting very stressed, like, I'm not creative in any way and I can't, like I'll keep coming back to the same idea even though I know it's wrong and won't work. (TuathaDuOrothrim, NHS)
Distractions	Physical; social	I can't work in my room because there are magazines in my room. There's [sic] so many distractions in my room. There's always music playing and it's always this big distraction. So, and there's a phone in my room, so I can't be in my room. (Hippopotamus NHS)
Lack of resources	Lack of required materials/ environments; lack of social supports; lack of intellectual stimuli	I was home-schooled for most of my life … I didn't have friends I could see everyday and bounce things off. (GLaDOS, NHS)
Negative social interactions	Lack of support; disrespect; judgement; criticism	People who don't respect your ideas. Like, it's okay to not agree with some other ideas, but to disrespect them I don't think is appropriate. Like, you can disagree and that's fine, but if you say, like, 'That's stupid', it doesn't really help anything. … I had another English teacher who rewrote all my sentences in her own words. And I was, like, what's the point? That's all my originality and creativity translated into your words, it's just not the same. (GLuck, NHS)

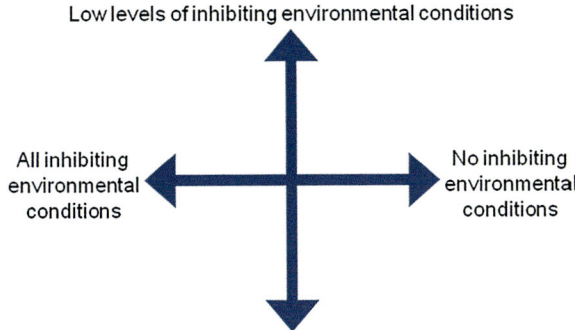

Fig. 2 Inhibiting environment for creativity matrix

Table 4 Environmental conditions that can support or inhibit creativity

Environmental conditions	Supportive/ inhibiting	Example
Extrinsic motivation	Supportive	A friend of a few different people from WHS ... wanted to start up a magazine. ... she wanted me to do some graphic design ... I said yes because I'm really poor, and I would like some money. (PatrickBateman, WHS)
	Inhibiting	I find that one of the scariest things about being creative within a school environment is the worry that you will be penalised for it. Often it feels like teachers or assignments want you to be creative, as long as you come up with what they are thinking of. (AnOptimisticVole, NHS)
Educational milieu	Supportive	I'd been the smartest kid in my school my entire life, until I came here, and now I'm average. And I've never been average, ever! ... I was like, this is the stupidest thing I've ever heard of, like, I have to work harder to get the same mark I would if I did nothing. But now, looking back, I think it was so worth it. 'Cause [sic] even though I'll probably get the same mark as I would at another school and my work's like a thousand times harder, it's not about the marks. It's about you and what you've become, and not so much what you know, but who you've become and how you think, and, like, how you learn. ... To be creativity, creative, you do have to think. ... by making kids think it really, like, it helps with their creativity. (GLuck, NHS)
	Inhibiting	Last year I think it was the Year of Creativity and... it's like they [the government] think creativity is this new energy that will power our nation and take us to new heights (laughs) and, that bugs me! Like, just being creative, I don't think it, forced creativity ridiculously annoys me! And sometimes that's what WHS makes you do. (Kate, WHS)

An environment is not categorically supportive or unsupportive of creativity; it can be supportive or inhibiting to varying extents. It can also depend on the student, task, and domain. In this study, creativity resulted when the right equilibrium or person-environment fit was found. However, what was considered a supportive environment for one student could be an inhibiting environment for another.

Young people have less choice about the contexts to which they are exposed (e.g., they are required to attend school). Furthermore, they can also be susceptible to pressure to conform from the media, parents, and peers if they have often not yet developed a strong sense of self (Cropley, 2006). Therefore, providing a supportive environment or climate for creativity is particularly important for students.

The findings of this study contribute to a currently limited body of empirical studies about how creativity is supported or inhibited in the school environment, according to students themselves. The research supported many existing findings about physical and social conditions in the school environment that can have a positive or negative influence on student creativity. Many of these findings relate not only to school environments, but also to other home and social situations.

Research and/or Practice: Implications and Future Directions

As a researcher of student voice, an initial consideration is the potential implications of creativity research for young people. The participants in the example study of student creativity presented here reported that they found it a valuable experience to have opportunities to reflect on their creativity. Findings about creativity development can provide a foundation for students to self-assess how their own creativity may be influenced by different environments.

In terms of teacher practice, research findings about learning environment influences on student creativity can provide empirical evidence to guide teachers' evaluations of how their classrooms may be supporting or inhibiting creativity. For example, creative role models or mentors can contribute to a supportive environment for creativity. Teachers who capitalise on their own creativity can become role models for their students. Creativity researchers can play an important role in directly assisting teachers to support creativity and address common barriers to creativity (Beghetto, 2010).

Education for creativity, including creativity programs within gifted education and talent development programs, should provide opportunities for creativity in all domains/subjects and in transdisciplinary tasks. The environments and pedagogies used should be based on empirical research about what supports the development of student creativity, including considerations such as: providing both cognitive support (e.g., creative teaching, encouraging creative learning, explicit teaching of creative thinking strategies, collaborating) and affective support (e.g., respect, trust, high expectations, acceptance and recognition of creativity); balancing autonomy and structure/constraints; finding time and space for creativity; optimising physical conditions and resources/stimuli; and students accessing like minds, role models and experts/mentors. An interesting future direction would be further research with young people in other contexts to see if the findings are consistent with the study exampled in this chapter.

Creativity can be an intrinsically enjoyable and spontaneous process. However, often it takes hard work and effort to be creative. Therefore, in an era of 'raising standards', it seems paradoxical and counterproductive to 'dumb down' creativity with extrinsically motivated, isolated generic creative thinking programs. Teaching for creativity without meaningful, authentic content and contexts does not promote creativity as an integral part of learning and life.

Implementing education for creativity requires in-service and pre-service teacher education. Like their students, current and future teachers would benefit from understanding their own creativity and recognising how they use it in their lives and teaching, which might provide a real and personal foundation from which they can teach for creativity. It is important for teachers to understand how the learning environments they create communicate their values and priorities to students (Beghetto & Kaufman, 2014). In addition, introducing teachers to the different forms of student creativity—mini-c, little-c, and ed-c—may have implications for how they identify, perceive, and encourage creativity in their students. In particular, the focus on ed-c supports teachers to recognise how creativity can be encouraged within the educational system and balanced with the competing priority of performativity.

An additional educational consideration is policy. Creativity has been embedded in policy and curricular documents around the world; however, these policies lack clear definitions of, and consistent discourse about, creativity. Simply adding the word 'creativity' to policy and hoping for creativity to be developed in current educational systems is insufficient (McWilliam & Haukka, 2008). We cannot rely on impromptu or accidental creative experiences to foster lifelong creative capacity. It would be beneficial to further clarify creativity and how it can be developed in policy and curricula based on shared conceptions and empirical research, a process to which students can contribute.

A practical direction of future research is evaluating how the preliminary empirical findings presented here can enhance understandings of creativity and contribute to creating more supportive contexts for creativity in schools. Another valuable research opportunity would be investigating the applicability of student voice research findings about how education can support or inhibit creativity in diverse educational environments, as well as in other cultures.

Conclusion

Rhetoric abounds espousing creativity's importance for individuals, for social and environmental issues, for advancement of society and for the economy. All students are capable of creativity, albeit at different levels (mini-c, little-c, and ed-c); therefore, all students deserve to have this important capacity developed. Moreover, students who demonstrate creative giftedness require talent development opportunities to focus on and accelerate their creative development, in line with the opportunities presented to students who are gifted in other domains.

Although the importance of creativity in education has been established, the current emphasis on standardisation and performativity presents challenges for prioritising students' creativity development. Findings from the literature and the empirical study presented in this chapter offer some evidence for how environmental conditions can be promoted to positively influence student creativity. Our lives, by necessity, are full of boundaries and constraints. However, it would be unfortunate if we allowed standardised curricula and assessments that are imposed in educational contexts to standardise or constrain creative young people's thinking.

Cross-References

► Bricolage and the Evolution of Giftedness and Talent in Taiwan
► Creative and Gifted Education in Korea: Using the CATs Model to Illustrate How Creativity Can Grow into Innovation
► Diverse Dimensions of Gifted Education: Part V Introduction
► Engaging Gifted Students in Solving Real Problems Creatively: Implementing the Real Engagement in Active Problem-Solving (REAPS) Teaching/Learning Model in Australasian and Pacific Rim Contexts
► Fostering and Developing Talent in Mentorship Programs: The Mentor's Perspectives
► Gifted Education in the Asia-Pacific: From the Past for the Future – An Introduction
► Some Implications for the Future of Gifted Education in the Asia-Pacific
► The Lives and Achievements of Four Extraordinary Australians: A Master, a Maker, an Introspector, and an Influencer
► Trends and Challenges of Creativity Development Among Selected Asian Countries and Regions: China, Hong Kong/Macau, Japan, Malaysia, and South Korea
► Using the Idea-Marathon System (IMS) in University Education and Creativity Development

References

Agnoli, S., Corazza, G. E., & Runco, M. A. (2016). Estimating creativity with a multiple-measurement approach within scientific and artistic domains. *Creativity Research Journal, 28*(2), 171–176. https://doi.org/10.1080/10400419.2016.1162475

Amabile, T. M. (1996). *Creativity in context*. Boulder, CO: Westview Press.

Ambrose, D. (2016). Twenty-first century contextual influences on the life trajectories of creative young people. In D. Ambrose & R. J. Sternberg (Eds.), *Creative intelligence in the 21st century* (pp. 21–48). Rotterdam, The Netherlands: Sense Publishers.

Australian Curriculum, Assessment and Reporting Authority. (n.d.). Critical and creative thinking. Retrieved from https://www.australiancurriculum.edu.au/f-10-curriculum/general-capabilities/critical-and-creative-thinking/

Baer, J. (2016). Creativity and the common core need each other. In D. Ambrose & R. J. Sternberg (Eds.), *Creative intelligence in the 21st century: Grappling with enormous problems and huge opportunities* (pp. 175–190). Rotterdam, The Netherlands: Sense Publishers.

Ball, S. J. (2003). The teacher's soul and the terrors of performativity. *Journal of Education Policy, 18*(2), 215–228. https://doi.org/10.1080/0268093022000043065

Barbot, B., Besançon, M., & Lubart, T. (2016). The generality-specificity of creativity: Exploring the structure of creative potential with EPoC. *Learning and Individual Differences, 52*, 178–187. https://doi.org/10.1016/j.lindif.2016.06.005

Beghetto, R. A. (2010). Creativity in the classroom. In J. C. Kaufman & R. J. Sternberg (Eds.), *The Cambridge handbook of creativity* (pp. 447–463). New York, NY: Cambridge University Press.

Beghetto, R. A., & Kaufman, J. C. (2007a). The genesis of creative greatness: Mini-c and the expert performance approach. *High Ability Studies, 18*(1), 59–61. https://doi.org/10.1080/13598130701350668

Beghetto, R. A., & Kaufman, J. C. (2007b). Toward a broader conception of creativity: A case for 'mini-c' creativity. *Psychology of Aesthetics, Creativity, and the Arts, 1*(2), 73–79. https://doi.org/10.1037/1931-3896.1.2.73

Beghetto, R. A., & Kaufman, J. C. (2014). Classroom contexts for creativity. *High Ability Studies, 25*(1), 53–69. https://doi.org/10.1080/13598139.2014.905247

Beghetto, R. A., & Plucker, J. A. (2006). The relationships among schooling, learning, and creativity: "All roads lead to creativity" or "you can't get there from here"? In G. Kaufman & J. Baer (Eds.), *Creativity and reason in cognitive development* (pp. 316–332). New York, NY: Cambridge University Press.

Bereczki, E. O., & Kárpáti, A. (2018). Teachers' belief about creativity and its nurture: A systematic review of the recent research literature. *Educational Research Review, 23*, 25–56. https://doi.org/10.1016/j.edurev.2017.10.003

Boden, M. A. (2001). Creativity and knowledge. In A. Craft, B. Jeffrey, & M. Leibling (Eds.), *Creativity in education* (pp. 95–102). London, England: Continuum.

Boden, M. A. (2004). *The creative mind: Myths and mechanisms* (2nd ed.). London, England: Routledge.

Bucik, V., & Neubauer, A. C. (1996). Bimodality in the Berlin model of intelligence structure (BIS): A replication study. *Personality and Individual Differences, 21*(6), 987–1005. https://doi.org/10.1016/S0191-8869(96)00129-8

Burnard, P., & White, J. (2008). Creativity and performativity: Counterpoints in British and Australian education. *British Educational Research Journal, 34*(5), 667–682. https://doi.org/10.1080/01411920802224238

Cameron, W. B. (1963). *Informal sociology: A casual introduction to sociological thinking*. New York, NY: Random House.

Celik, P., & Lubart, T. (2016). When east meets west. In V. P. Glăveanu (Ed.), *The Palgrave handbook of creativity and culture research* (pp. 37–55). London, England: Palgrave Macmillan.

Charmaz, K. (2006). *Constructing grounded theory*. London, UK: SAGE Publications.

Charmaz, K. (2014). *Constructing grounded theory (2nd ed.)*. London, UK: SAGE Publications.

Cheng, V. M. Y. (2004). Progress from traditional to creativity education in Chinese societies. In S. Lau, A. H. H. Hui, & G. Y. C. Ng (Eds.), *Creativity: When east meets west* (pp. 137–167). Singapore: World Scientific Publishing.

Cheng, V. M. Y. (2010). Tensions and dilemmas of teachers in creativity reform in a Chinese context. *Thinking Skills and Creativity, 5*, 120–137. https://doi.org/10.1016/j.tsc.2010.09.005

Clapham, M. M. (1997). Ideational skills training: A key element in creativity training programs. *Creativity Research Journal, 10*(1), 33–44. https://doi.org/10.1207/s15326934crj1001_4

Claxton, A. F., Pannells, T. C., & Rhoads, P. A. (2005). Developmental trends in the creativity of school-age children. *Creativity Research Journal, 17*(4), 327–335. https://doi.org/10.1207/s15326934crj1704_4

Corbin, J., & Strauss, A. L. (2008). *Basics of qualitative research: Techniques and procedures for developing grounded theory* (3rd ed.). Thousand Oaks, CA: SAGE Publications.

Corbin, J., & Strauss, A. L. (2015). *Basics of qualitative research: Techniques and procedures for developing grounded theory* (4th ed.). Thousand Oaks, CA: SAGE Publications.

Craft, A. (2000). *Creativity across the primary curriculum: Framing and developing practice*. London, England: Routledge.

Craft, A. (2001). 'Little c' creativity. In A. Craft, B. Jeffrey, & M. Leibling (Eds.), *Creativity in education* (pp. 45–61). London, England: Continuum.

Craft, A. (2005). *Creativity in schools: Tensions and dilemmas*. London, England: Routledge.

Craft, A. (2008a). *Creativity in the school*. Retrieved from the Beyond Current Horizons Web site: http://www.beyondcurrenthorizons.org.uk/wp-content/uploads/ch3_final_craft_creativityinschool_20081218.pdf

Craft, A. (2008b). Studying collaborative creativity: Implications for education. *Thinking Skills and Creativity, 3*(3), 241–245. https://doi.org/10.1016/j.tsc.2008.09.006

Craft, A. (2011). *Creativity and education futures: Learning in a digital age*. London, England: Trentham Books.

Craft, A., Cremin, T., Hay, P., & Clack, J. (2014). Creative primary schools: Developing and maintaining pedagogy for creativity. *Ethnography and Education, 9*(1), 16–34. https://doi.org/10.1080/17457823.2013.828474

Craft, A., & Jeffrey, B. (2008). Creativity and performativity in teaching and learning: Tensions, dilemmas, constraints, accommodations and synthesis. *British Educational Research Journal, 34*(5), 577–584. https://doi.org/10.1080/01411920802223842

Cremin, T., Burnard, P., & Craft, A. (2006). Pedagogy and possibility thinking in the early years. *Thinking Skills and Creativity, 1*, 108–119. https://doi.org/10.1016/j.tsc.2006.07.001

Cropley, A. J. (1997). Fostering creativity in the classroom: General principles. In M. A. Runco (Ed.), *The creativity research handbook* (Vol. 1, pp. 83–114). Cresskill, NJ: Hampton Press.

Cropley, A. J. (2006). Creativity: A social approach. *Roeper Review, 28*(3), 125–130. https://doi.org/10.1080/02783190609554351

Csikszentmihalyi, M. (1996). *Creativity: Flow and the psychology of discovery and invention*. New York, NY: Harper Collins Publishers.

Dai, D. Y. (2016). Envisioning a new century of gifted education: The case for a paradigm shift. In D. Ambrose & R. J. Sternberg (Eds.), *Giftedness and talent in the 21st century: Adapting to the turbulence of globalization* (pp. 45–63). Rotterdam, The Netherlands: Sense Publishers.

Davies, D., Jindal-Snape, D., Collier, C., Digby, R., Hay, P., & Howe, A. L. (2013). Creative learning environments in education: A systematic literature review. *Thinking Skills and Creativity, 8*, 80–91. https://doi.org/10.1016/j.tsc.2012.07.004

Davies, L. M., Newton, L. D., & Newton, D. P. (2017). Creativity as a twenty-first-century competence: An exploratory study of provision and reality. *Education 3–13*. https://doi.org/10.1080/03004279.2017.1385641

Dow, G. T., & Mayer, R. E. (2004). Teaching adolescents to solve insight problems: Evidence for domain specificity in creativity training. *Creativity Research Journal, 16*(4), 389–402. https://doi.org/10.1080/10400410409534550

Education Commission. (2006). Progress report on the education reform (4). Retrieved from https://www.e-c.edu.hk/doc/en/publications_and_related_documents/education_reform/Progress%20Report%20(Eng)%202006.pdf

European Commission. (2009). *Creativity in schools in Europe: A survey of teachers*. Retrieved from https://ec.europa.eu/jrc/en/publication/eur-scientific-and-technical-research-reports/creativity-schools-survey-teachers-europe

Florida, R. (2012). *The rise of the creative class, revisited*. New York, NY: Basic Books.

Forster, J. (2012). Creativity: The hub of real achievement. *Gifted Education International, 28*(3), 281–299. https://doi.org/10.1177/0261429411435108

Forster, J. (2015). Creativity and achievement: Words and wishes, waste or wisdom. *Australasian Journal of Gifted Education, 24*(1), 52–58.

Gagné, F. (2009). Building gifts into talents: Detailed overview of the DMGT 2.0. In B. MacFarlane & T. Stambaught (Eds.), *Leading change in gifted education: The festschrift of Dr Joyce VanTassel-BaskA*. Waco, TX: Prufrock Press.

Galton, F. (1892). *Hereditary genius: An inquiry into its laws and consequences*. London, England: Macmillan.

Giaconia, R. M., & Hedges, L. V. (1982). Identifying features of effective open education. *Review of Educational Research, 52*(4), 579–602. https://doi.org/10.3102/00346543052004579

Guilford, J. P. (1950). Creativity. *American Psychologist, 5*(9), 444–454. https://doi.org/10.1037/h0063487

Guilford, J. P. (1959). Three faces of intellect. *The American Psychologist, 14*(8), 469–479. https://doi.org/10.1037/h0046827

Haddon, F. A., & Lytton, H. (1968). Teaching approach and the development of divergent thinking abilities in primary schools. *British Journal of Educational Psychology, 38*(2), 171–180. https://doi.org/10.1111/j.2044-8279.1968.tb02002.x

Haddon, F. A., & Lytton, H. (1971). Primary education and divergent thinking abilities – Four years on. *British Journal of Educational Psychology, 41*(2), 136–147. https://doi.org/10.1111/j.2044-8279.1971.tb02245.x

Halpin, G., Goldenberg, R., & Halpin, G. (1990). Are creative teachers more humanistic in their pupil control ideologies. *Journal of Creative Behavior, 7*(4), 282–286. https://doi.org/10.1002/j.2162-6057.1973.tb01099.x

Harris, A. (2016). *Creativity and education.* London, England: Palgrave Macmillan.

Harris, A., & Ammermann, M. (2016). The changing face of creativity in Australian education. *Teaching Education, 27*(1), 103–113. https://doi.org/10.1080/10476210.2015.1077379

Harris, A., & de Bruin, L. R. (2017). Training teachers for twenty-first century creative and critical thinking: Australian implications from an international study. *Teaching Education.* https://doi.org/10.1080/10476210.2017.1384802

Hartley, D. (2003). New economy, new pedagogy? *Oxford Review of Education, 29*(1), 81–94. https://doi.org/10.1080/0305498032000045377

Haught-Tromp, C. (2016). Facilitating creative thinking in the 21st century: When constraints help. In D. Ambrose & R. J. Sternberg (Eds.), *Creative intelligence in the 21st century: Grappling with enormous problems and huge opportunities* (pp. 107–117). Rotterdam, The Netherlands: Sense Publishers.

Heller, K. A. (2005). The Munich model of giftedness and its impact on identification and programming. *Gifted and Talented International, 20*(1), 30–36. https://doi.org/10.1080/15332276.2005.11673055

Hennessey, B. A., & Amabile, T. M. (2010). Creativity. *Annual Review of Psychology, 61*, 569–598. https://doi.org/10.1146/annurev.psych.093008.100416

Horwitz, R. A. (1979). Psychological effects of the "open classroom". *Review of Educational Research, 49*(1), 71–85. https://doi.org/10.3102/00346543049001071

Jeffrey, B., & Craft, A. (2004). Teaching creatively and teaching for creativity: Distinctions and relationships. *Educational Studies, 30*(1), 77–87. https://doi.org/10.1080/0305569032000159750

Kaufman, J. C., & Beghetto, R. A. (2009). Beyond big and little: The four c model of creativity. *Review of General Psychology, 13*(1), 1–12. https://doi.org/10.1037/a0013688

Kim, K. H. (2007). Exploring the interactions between Asian culture (Confucianism) and creativity. *Journal of Creative Behaviour, 41*(1), 28–53. https://doi.org/10.1002/j.2162-6057.2007.tb01280.x

Kim, K. H., Kaufman, J. C., Baer, J., & Sriraman, B. (2013). Introduction to creatively gifted students are not like other gifted students: Research, theory, and practice. In K. H. Kim, J. C. Kaufman, J. Baer, & B. Sriraman (Eds.), *Creatively gifted students are not like other gifted students: Research, theory, and practice* (pp. 1–2). Rotterdam, The Netherlands: Sense Publishers.

Lucas, B. (2001). Creative teaching, teaching creativity and creative learning. In A. Craft, B. Jeffrey, & M. Leibling (Eds.), *Creativity in education* (pp. 35–44). London, England: Continuum.

Lucas, B. (2017, November 22). *The power of creative thinking.* Retrieved from https://www.thersa.org/discover/publications-and-articles/rsa-comment/2017/11/the-power-of-creative-thinking

Ma, H. (2006). A synthetic analysis of the effectiveness of single components and packages in creativity training programs. *Creativity Research Journal, 18*(4), 435–446. https://doi.org/10.1207/s15326934crj1804_3

Maslow, A. H. (1968). *Toward a psychology of being.* New York, NY: Van Nostrand Reinhold.

Maslow, A. H. (1970). *Motivation and personality* (2nd ed.). New York, NY: Harper & Row Publishers.

McWilliam, E. (2008). *The creative workforce: How to launch young people into high-flying futures.* Sydney, NSW: University of New South Wales Press.

McWilliam, E., & Haukka, S. (2008). Educating the creative workforce: New directions for twenty-first schooling. *British Educational Research Journal, 34*(5), 651–666. https://doi.org/10.1080/01411920802224204

Ministerial Council on Education, Employment, Training and Youth Affairs. (2008, December). Melbourne declaration on educational goals for young Australians. Retrieved from http://scseec.edu.au/site/DefaultSite/filesystem/documents/Reports%20and%20publications/Publications/National%20goals%20for%20schooling/National_Declaration_on_the_Educational_Goals_for_Young_Australians.pdf

Ministry of Education. (2002). *White paper on creative education.* Taipei, Taiwan: Ministry of Education.

Ministry of Education. (2015). Education system. Retrieved from https://www.moe.gov.sg/education/education-system/

Ng, A. K., & Smith, I. (2004). Why is there a paradox in promoting creativity in the Asian classroom? In S. Lau, A. H. H. Hui, G. Y, & C. Ng (Eds.), *Creativity: When east meets west* (pp. 87–112). Singapore, Singapore: World Scientific Publishing.

Nickerson, R. S. (1999). Enhancing creativity. In R. J. Sternberg (Ed.), *Handbook of creativity* (pp. 392–430). Cambridge, UK: Cambridge University Press.

Organisation for Economic Co-operation and Development. (2018). PISA 2015 results in focus. Retrieved from http://www.oecd.org/pisa/pisa-2015-results-in-focus.pdf

Pang, W., & Plucker, J. A. (2013). Recent transformations in China's economic, social, and education policies for promoting innovation and creativity. *Journal of Creative Behaviour, 46*(4), 247–273. https://doi.org/10.1002/jocb.17

Perleth, C., & Heller, K. A. (1994). The Munich longitudinal study of giftedness. In R. F. Subotnik & K. D. Arnold (Eds.), *Beyond Terman: Contemporary longitudinal studies of giftedness and talent* (pp. 77–114). Norwood, NJ: Ablex Publishing Corporation.

Pfeiffer, S. I., & Thompson, T. L. (2013). Creativity from a talent development perspective: How it can be cultivated in schools. In K. H. Kim, J. C. Kaufman, J. Baer, & B. Sriraman (Eds.), *Creatively gifted students are not like other gifted students* (pp. 231–256). Rotterdam, The Netherlands: Sense Publishers.

Plucker, J. A., Beghetto, R. A., & Dow, G. T. (2004). Why isn't creativity more important to educational psychologists? Potentials, pitfalls, and future directions in creativity research. *Educational Psychologist, 39*(2), 83–96. https://doi.org/10.1207/s15326985ep3902_1

Renzulli, J. S. (1999). What is this thing called giftedness, and how do we develop it? A twenty-five year perspective. *Journal for the Education of the Gifted, 23*(1), 3–54. https://doi.org/10.4219/jeg-1999-561

Rhodes, M. (1961). An analysis of creativity. *Phi Delta Kappan, 42*, 305–310. Retrieved from www.jstor.org/stable/20342603

Richards, R. (2007). Everyday creativity: Our hidden potential. In R. Richards (Ed.), *Everyday creativity and new views of human nature: Psychological, social, and spiritual perspectives* (pp. 25–53). Washington, DC: American Psychological Association.

Richardson, C., & Mishra, P. (2018). Learning environments that support student creativity: Developing the scale. *Thinking Skills and Creativity, 27*, 45–54. https://doi.org/10.1016/j.tsc.2017.11.004

Rogers, C. R. (1961). *On becoming a person: A therapist's view of psychotherapy.* London, England: Constable & Company.

Rose, L. H., & Lin, H. T. (1984). A meta-analysis of long-term creativity training programs. *Journal of Creative Behavior, 18*(1), 11–22. https://doi.org/10.1002/j.2162-6057.1984.tb00985.x

Runco, M. A. (1999). Fourth grade slump. In M. A. Runco & S. R. Pritzker (Eds.), *Encyclopaedia of creativity* (Vol. 1, pp. 743–744). San Diego, CA: Academic.

Runco, M. A. (2003). Education for creative potential. *Scandinavian Journal of Educational Research, 47*(3), 317–324. https://doi.org/10.1080/00313830308598

Runco, M. A. (2007a). *Creativity: Theories and themes, research, development and practice*. San Diego, CA: Elsevier Academic Press.

Runco, M. A. (2007b). To understand is to create: An epistemological perspective on human nature and personal creativity. In R. Richards (Ed.), *Everyday creativity and new views of human nature: Psychological, social, and spiritual perspectives* (pp. 91–107). Washington, DC: American Psychological Association.

Runco, M. A. (2016). We must prepare for the unforeseeable future. In D. Ambrose & R. J. Sternberg (Eds.), *Creative intelligence in the 21st century* (pp. 65–73). Rotterdam, The Netherlands: Sense Publishers.

Schacter, J., Thum, Y. M., & Zifkin, D. (2006). How much does creative teaching enhance elementary school students' achievement? *The Journal of Creative Behavior, 40*(1), 47–72. https://doi.org/10.1002/j.2162-6057.2006.tb01266.x

Scott, G., Leritz, L. E., & Mumford, M. D. (2004). The effectiveness of creativity training: A quantitative review. *Creativity Research Journal, 16*(4), 361–388. https://doi.org/10.1080/10400410409534549

Soh, K. (2017). Fostering student creativity through teacher behaviors. *Thinking Skills and Creativity, 23*, 58–66. https://doi.org/10.1016/j.tsc.2016.11.002

Sternberg, R. J. (1999). The theory of successful intelligence. *Review of General Psychology, 3*(4), 292–316. https://doi.org/10.1037/1089-2680.3.4.292

Sternberg, R. J. (2005). WICS: A model of giftedness in leadership. *Roeper Review, 28*(1), 37–44. https://doi.org/10.1080/02783190509554335

Sternberg, R. J., Jarvin, L., & Grigorenko, E. L. (2011). *Explorations in giftedness*. Cambridge, NY: Cambridge University Press.

Sternberg, R. J., & Lubart, T. I. (1995). *Defying the crowd: Cultivating creativity in a culture of conformity*. New York, NY: The Free Press.

Tam, C. S. Y., Phillipson, S. N., & Phillipson, S. (2014). Creativity in Hong Kong: Current contexts and issues. *Australasian Journal of Gifted Education, 23*(1), 28–38.

Torrance, E. P. (1968). A longitudinal examination of the fourth grade slump in creativity. *The Gifted Child Quarterly, 12*, 195–199. https://doi.org/10.1177/001698626801200401

United Nations Educational, Scientific and Cultural Organization. (2016). *Education 2030: Incheon declaration and framework for action for the implementation of sustainable development goal 4* (Report No. ED-2016/WS/28). Retrieved from http://unesdoc.unesco.org/images/0024/002456/245656E.pdf

Ward, T. B., Smith, S. M., & Vaid, J. (1997). Conceptual structures and process in creative thought. In T. B. Ward, S. M. Smith, & J. Vaid (Eds.), *Creative thought: An investigation of conceptual structures and processes* (pp. 1–27). Washington, DC: American Psychological Association.

Carly Lassig, PhD, is a lecturer at the Queensland University of Technology. Her teaching and research areas include inclusive education, gifted education, differentiation, and creativity. Carly has consulted on national policy and curricula and provided inclusive and gifted education professional development programs and mentoring for school and university educators from Australia and developing countries in the Asia-Pacific region. She was the Vice President of the Queensland Association for Gifted and Talented Children. She is currently on the editorial panel of the *Australasian Journal of Gifted Education*.

Creative and Gifted Education in Korea: Using the CATs Model to Illustrate How Creativity Can Grow into Innovation

48

Kyung Hee Kim and Jeongkyu Lee

Contents

K. H. Kim (✉)
The College of William & Mary, Williamsburg, VA, USA
e-mail: kkim@wm.edu

J. Lee
The Korea Foundation for the Advancement of Science, Seoul, South Korea
e-mail: counsel2u@kofac.re.kr

© Springer Nature Singapore Pte Ltd. 2021
S. R. Smith (ed.), *Handbook of Giftedness and Talent Development in the Asia-Pacific*,
Springer International Handbooks of Education,
https://doi.org/10.1007/978-981-13-3041-4_50

Abstract

In the research-based CATs (Climates, Attitudes, and Thinking skills) model (Kim, 2016, 2017, 2019), we propose how individuals can develop creativity into innovation. We used this model as the basis for analysing and evaluating the recent Korean education efforts for creative and gifted education. The CATs model includes three steps and metaphors of natural phenomenon and acronyms are used to illustrate these three steps, that are: (a) cultivating climates uses the 4S metaphors of *sun, storm, soil* and *space*; (b) nurturing the 4S creative attitudes; and (c) applying ION (Inbox, Outbox, and Newbox) creative thinking skills. The 4S climates nurture the 4S attitudes, which enable ION thinking skills. For these three steps of climate, attitudes, and creative thinking, metaphorically: *sun* characterises inspiration and encouragement; *storm* includes high expectations and challenges; *soil* comprises diverse resources, experiences and viewpoints; and *space* represents thinking deeply and freely. How Korean education inhibits or fosters creativity, even though significant educational efforts have attempted to cultivate the 4S climates for its gifted students, will be explored in this chapter.

Keywords

Korean education · Creative economy · Creativity and character education · Creative climate · Creative attitude · Creative thinking · Creative personality

The aims in this chapter are to:
1. Provide a model of three steps from creativity to innovation.
2. Illustrate the four climates that nurture creative attitudes.
3. Detail the four attitudes that enable creative thinking skills.
4. Explain how Korean education stifles (or fosters): inspirational and encouraging sun climates and the sun attitudes; high-expectation-holding and challenging stormy climates and the stormy attitudes; resources-, experiences-, and viewpoints-diverse soil climates and the soil attitudes; and deep- and free-thinking space climates and space attitudes.

Introduction

Nurturing creativity can enable the transformation of potential into exceptional outcomes and giftedness into innovation (Torrance, 2002). In the research-based CATs model (Kim, 2016, 2019), we illustrate how creativity in thought can grow into an innovative outcome; a unique and useful outcome (ranging between small *i*nnovation and big *I*nnovation). The *i*nnovation, with a lower case 'i' is personal self-actualisation. However, *I*nnovation with a capital 'I' is the self-actualisation that has global impact.

Based on the CATS model, in order to nurture creativity into innovation, first, creative **C**limates are cultivated, then creative **A**ttitudes are nurtured and, finally, creative **T**hinking **s**kills are applied to achieve an innovation. Korean creative and gifted education are discussed within the CATs model after a brief introduction to creative climates, attitudes, and thinking skills.

The CATs Model

All individuals are born curious and unique with an innate capacity for creativity, but their creative attitudes and thoughts can either be nurtured or squashed by their climates (e.g., families, schools, organisations, societies, or cultures). This chapter uses metaphors, which are part of creative thinking skills to provide visualisations of the points being made (Ambrose & Sternberg, 2012; Marin, Reimann, & Castaño, 2013; Smith & Lu, 2015). For example, like producing high-quality apples that require bright, warm sunlight, fierce storms, nutrient-diverse soil, and open space, producing innovations require the interactions between four distinct learning environments, are represented as metaphors (Kim, 2016, 2019; see Fig. 1):

1. An inspirational and encouraging *sun* climate.
2. A high-expectation-holding and challenging *storm* climate.
3. Resource-, experience-, and viewpoint-diverse *soil* climate.
4. A deep- and free-thinking *space* climate.

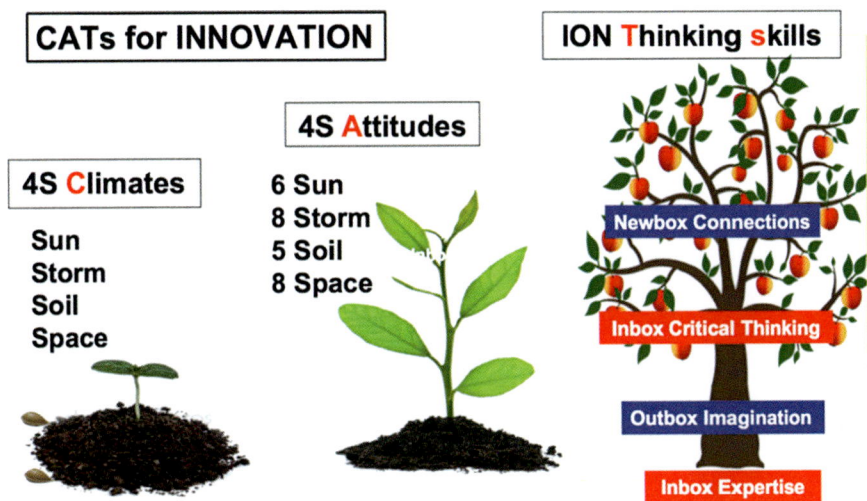

Fig. 1 CATs for Innovation: Creative Climates, Attitudes, and Thinking skills (Inbox, Outbox, & Newbox: ION; Kim, 2019)

Creative attitudes are characteristics shared by all notable innovators, which enable them to use their creative minds (e.g., Kwang & Rodrigues, 2002; Simonton, 2000). Researchers have identified creative attitudes that predict individuals' innovations better than their IQs do (Kwang & Rodrigues, 2002; Simonton, 2000). In the CATS model, these creative attitudes are categorised as sun, storm, soil, and space *attitudes* (4S attitudes), which in turn are nurtured by the sun, storm, soil, and space *climates* (4S climates), respectively (Kim, 2016).

Sun attitudes nurtured by the sun climate include being (e.g., Kim, 2016, 2019, in press):

- Optimistic: seeing positive outcomes regardless of circumstances.
- A big-picture thinker: projecting vision beyond the here and now to construct a meaningful life in the big world.
- Curious: insatiably seeking new information with childlike wonder.
- Spontaneous: being flexible and immediately acting on opportunities.
- Playful: approaching situations in exploratory ways and treating challenges as fun games.
- Energetic: deriving energy and motivation from curiosity impulses and passions.

Storm attitudes nurtured by the storm climate include being (e.g., Kim, 2016):

- Independent: making decisions free from others' influences.
- Self-disciplined: delaying instant gratification and avoiding distractions.
- Diligent: being meticulously hard-working.
- Self-efficacious: accurate self-confidence on specific strengths.
- Resilient: thriving on challenges and failures.
- Risk-taking: leaving secure situations for uncertain rewards.
- Uncertainly accepting: being excited about ambiguous things and the unknown.
- Persistent: continuous commitment to goals.

Soil attitudes nurtured by the soil climate include being (e.g., Kim, 2016):

- Open-minded: delaying judgment and considering different viewpoints.
- Bicultural: embracing new cultures while retaining their cultural identities.
- Mentored: learning from experts' frankly honest feedback.
- Complexity-seeking: thinking in shades of grey rather than in black and white.
- Compassionate: empathising with others and improving the world.
- Resourceful: finding and using resources and opportunities.

Space attitudes nurtured by the space climate include being (e.g., Kim, 2016):

- Empathic: expressing and understanding the feelings of others.
- Self-reflective: analysing their feelings, thoughts, and experiences.
- A daydreamer: trying out a series of unrealistic or futuristic thoughts.
- Autonomous: being intrinsically motivated to become the best at what you love.

- Nonconforming: choosing to differ from mainstream thought or behaviour.
- Gender-bias-free: rejecting gender stereotypes.
- Defiant: challenging existing norms, traditions, hierarchies, or authorities.

Creativity relies upon a solid foundation of expertise or know-how, that is, a thorough mastery of the existing knowledge and skills, regardless of fields (e.g., Kim, 2016; Mumford, Hester, & Robledo, 2010). In the CATs model, creative thinking consists of *inbox, outbox*, and *newbox* (*ION*) thinking (e.g., Kim, 2016). Creative thinking *inbox* expertise is developed through at least 10 years of deep immersion and dedication to comprehending and applying in-depth content knowledge and skills in their chosen field (Fig. 2), which is facilitated by individuals' storm attitudes, such as being self-disciplined, diligent, and persistent (Simonton, 2009). Individuals often start accumulating expertise early and spend about 10,000 hours of solitary and purposeful practice by age 20, with a clear and specific goal to improve (Ericsson, 2014).

Based on the expertise in their chosen subject, individuals must be able to use their *outbox* imagination to go beyond their existing knowledge and skills (Cropley, 2006; Kim, 2016; Zhong, Dijksterhuis, & Galinsky, 2008). Outbox imagination uses fluent, flexible, and original thinking skills to imagine something unique by challenging the norm, the status quo or unjust stereotypes or hierarchies, instead of conforming to uniformity or standardisation (e.g., Kim, 2016; see Fig. 3). These skills are facilitated specifically by the individuals' sun attitudes, such as big-picture thinking and curious and playful attitudes; and space attitudes, such as daydreaming, nonconforming, and defiant attitudes (Kim, 2016). Without outbox imagination, experts can only reinvent the wheel. With outbox imagination, individuals can combine the wheel with something else, or extend the wheel or its use, or create something completely new or extraordinary.

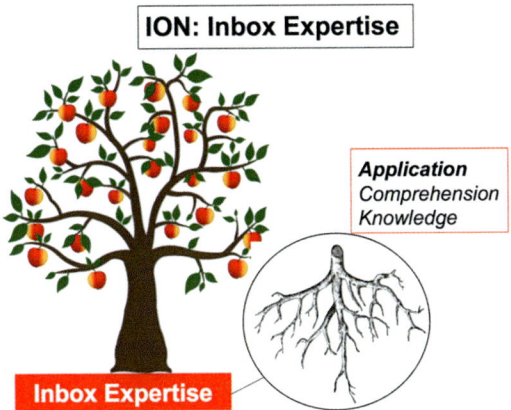

Fig. 2 ION (Inbox, Outbox & Newbox) Thinking: Inbox Expertise by Knowledge, Comprehension, and Application (Kim, 2019)

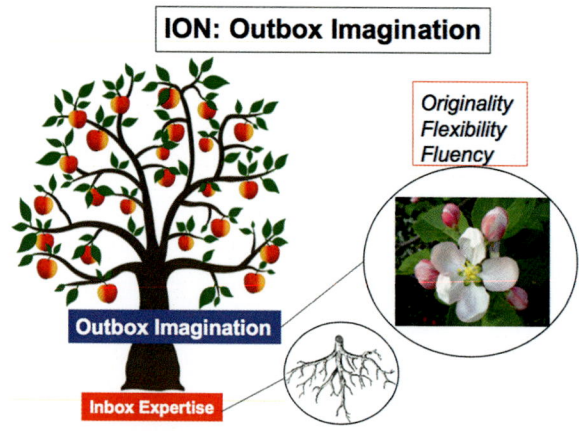

Fig. 3 ION (Inbox, Outbox & Newbox) Thinking: Outbox Imagination by Fluency, Flexibility, and Originality (Kim, 2019)

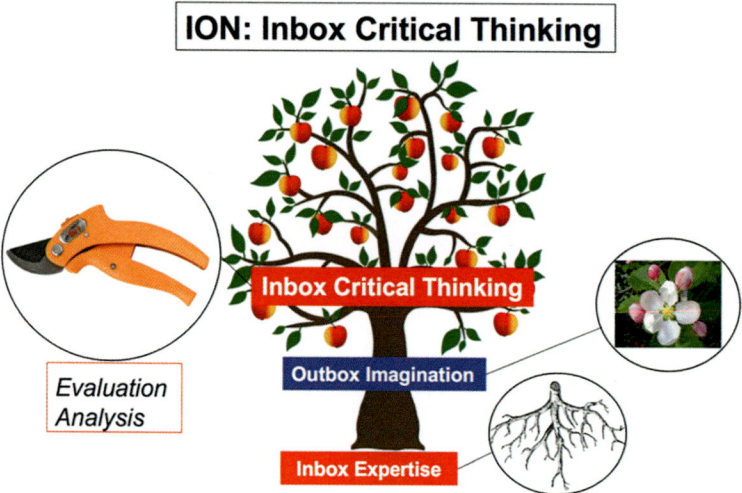

Fig. 4 ION (Inbox, Outbox & Newbox) Thinking: Inbox Critical Thinking by Analysis and Evaluation (Kim, 2019)

Inbox critical thinking is critically analysing and evaluating what is unique for its *useful*ness (see Fig. 4). Critical thinking is facilitated by an individuals' soil attitudes, such as being open-minded (Mezias & Starbuck, 2003) and complexity-seeking (Haller & Courvoisier, 2010) and being mentored (Cropley, 2006; Torrance, 2002).

Newbox connections consist of combining and synthesising seemingly irrelevant ideas together. Newbox connections also include refining and improving the synthesis through a balanced process of elaboration and simplification (Fig. 5). Newbox

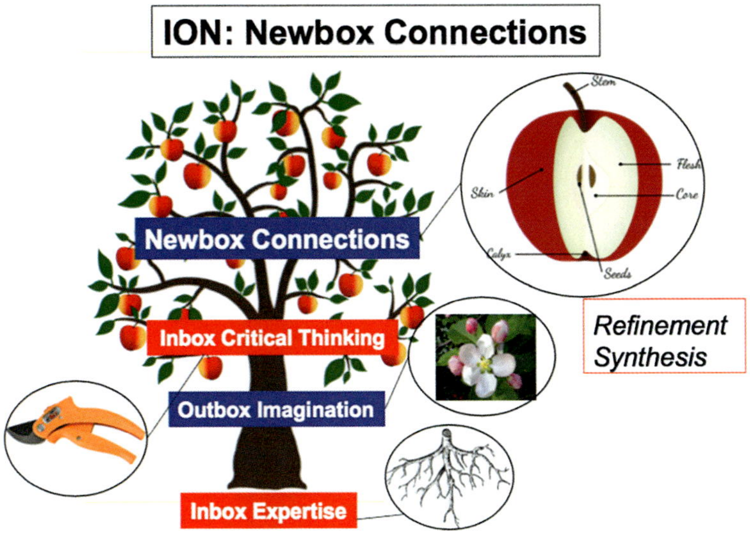

Fig. 5 ION (Inbox, Outbox & Newbox) Thinking: Newbox Connections by Synthesis and Refinement (Kim, 2019)

connections are based on inbox expertise, then outbox imagination and then inbox critical thinking (e.g., Kim, 2016; Sriraman & Dickman, 2017; Tabach & Friedlander, 2013), and are facilitated by all of the metaphors of the sun, storm, soil, and space attitudes. Inbox thinkers with only storm and soil attitudes tend to become technicians, and outbox thinkers with only sun and space attitudes tend to become frustrated dreamers (Kim, 2016). Thus, innovation results from a whole-brain creative process, moving between inbox and outbox thinking (e.g., Badzakova-Trajkov, Häberling, & Corballis, 2011; Chávez-Eakle, Graff-Guerrero, García-Reyna, Vaugier, & Cruz-Fuentes, 2007; Gonen-Yaacovi, Levy, Urbanski, & Volle, 2013; Jaušovec, 2000; Kowatari et al., 2009; Lindell, 2011; Shobe, Ross, & Fleck, 2009).

Asian Cultural Values

In order to understand the background of Korean education, one must look into the four critical values of Asian culture that have shaped Korean education—Asian culture has been built on Confucianism and a test-centric meritocracy (Kim, 2009, 2016, in press; Kim, Lee, Chae, Andersen, & Lawrence, 2011; Park & Shin, 2006):

- Academic success: Achieving high test-scores by mastering rote information.
- Filial piety: Being a good son or daughter by achieving high socio-economic family status.
- Social hierarchy: Obeying authority.
- Social conformity: Thinking and acting like others.

Additionally, Korea's historical legacies have influenced Korean education, such as Japanese colonisation (Son, 2013), fear of Communism and North Korea since the Korean War (Son, 2013), and heavy dependence on the American academic community and English language (Kang, 2006).

Academic Success

A high-stakes test produces a test score that greatly impacts an individual's potential opportunities. High-stakes, standardised testing justifies meritocracy, which is the belief that hard work and effort alone lead to success and the word *standardised* implies uniformity and fairness for everyone (Au, 2009, 2011). The world's first high-stakes standardised tests began with China's civil service tests system over 1400 years ago (Elman, 2009; Suen & Yu, 2006). The purpose was to channel its ambitious, smart young men to a single-minded focus on academic success so they would not challenge the social hierarchy (Elman, 2009; Suen & Yu, 2006). Extremely high socio-economic rewards for those who passed the tests, and scant opportunities for those who did not, have built a cultural obsession with test scores and a disregard for alternative pursuits. Millions of men purchased and memorised previously successful test answers and other written knowledge to prepare for the tests. They spent all their time memorising the tests, leaving them no time for other work, and so depended on their families' financial support (e.g., Chun, 2013; Elman, 2009; Hawkins, 2008; Marginson, 2011; Suen & Yu, 2006; Yuan-kang, 2009). Although the test system officially ended in 1905, this obsession has infiltrated every aspect of Asian life (in China, Japan, Korea, Singapore, and Taiwan). Commonly called *exam hell*, the cultural obsession with achieving high test scores via rote memorisation and private tutoring is still evident today (e.g., Chun, 2013; Elman, 2009; Kim, 2007, 2008, 2009, 2011, 2016, in press; Li & Wu, 2011; Mack-Cozzo, 2002; Marginson, 2011; Park & Chung, 2012; Suen & Yu, 2006; Yang & Shin, 2008).

Exam hell's test-centric education has resulted in Asian students' high scores on international assessments including the PISA, TIMSS, and PIRLS (e.g., Lee, 2009; Mullis, Martin, & Foy, 2008; National Center for Education Statistics, 2016; OECD, 2015). It has also resulted in high IQ test-scores (e.g., Barrow & Rouse, 2006; Lynn & Meisenberg, 2010; Rushton & Jensen, 2005). Through emphasising the importance of higher education, test-centric education has contributed to dramatic economic growth in Asian countries since the 1980s (e.g., Hahm, 2003; Hawkins, 2008; Marginson, 2011).

Filial Piety

The Asian students' common goal is to achieve high socio-economic family status, which is usually achieved by their high-test scores and high-ranking university entrance scores. Achieving these goals determines their filial piety, the most essential Asian value and thus their self-worth (Bang & Montgomery, 2013; Mack-Cozzo,

2002; Marginson, 2011; Yang & Shin, 2008). Achieving a high-ranking university entrance score enables students to repay the debt they owe their parents for sacrificing their time and money on test preparations (Bong, 2008; Hwang, 1999; Kim, 2007; Kim et al., 2011; Liu, 2003; Yang & Shin, 2008). Students who fail to gain admission into a high-ranking university buy more chances by entering expensive preparatory institutions to prepare for the following year's tests (Koyama, Matsushita, Ushijima, Jono, & Ikeda, 2014; Ono, 2007). The socio-economic rewards of high-ranking universities pay off across their careers if their families can afford for them to repeatedly take these tests for years while doing nothing but test preparations (Ono, 2007). Over 60% of the students at the highest-ranking universities have attended these institutions, which are unaffordable for low-income families. Thus, it seems that the students who have access to the most high-paying, highly respected jobs have bought their way in, not necessarily earned it (Ono, 2007).

Upon entrance to their dream university, students' studying is over. The socio-economic rewards of university education depend not on their efforts within their university, but the prestige of their university relative to its peers. University ranking becomes their social status, and alumni connections become their ladder to socio-economic success in the steep occupational hierarchy following university (Mack-Cozzo, 2002; Marginson, 2011; Ono, 2007; Yang & Shin, 2008). The significant economic rewards for entering high-ranking universities become even greater in later career stages. The majority (e.g., in Japan 63%) of companies' top executives are graduates of the top 10 universities (Ono, 2007, 2008). These are much higher than the percentages (e.g., 10%) of the Fortune 100 companies' executives who are Ivy League university graduates in the USA (Cappelli & Hamori, 2004).

Because Asian students are under extreme pressure for high test scores, their parents, especially mothers, push them to memorise information, leaving little time for exploring, questioning, or discussing (e.g., Chan & Chen, 2008; Entrich, 2015; Marginson, 2011; Park & Chung, 2012; Suen & Yu, 2006; Yang & Shin, 2008). Viewing humanity through the lens of winners and losers, Asian students not only in Asia, but also in other countries, may cheat to avoid becoming losers (e.g., Bartlett & Fischer, 2011; Bong, 2008; Friedman, 2010; Kim & Park, 2003; Lim, 2011; Schroth, 2012; Suen & Yu, 2006). It is also thought that those who feel filial piety cheat even more to become 'good' daughters or sons (Bong, 2008).

Social Hierarchy

Asian test-centric meritocracy has emphasised *effort*, implying that anyone can succeed entirely by focused effort and that higher achievers deserve respect due to their effort, which has fostered a rigid top-down hierarchy and blind respect for authority (e.g., Kim, 2007, 2009, 2016, in press; Kim & Lee, 2010; Kim et al., 2011; Park, 2010). Higher achievers' deservingness and lower achievers' un-deservingness are unintended consequences of a test-centric meritocracy (e.g., Anderson, 2015; Bang & Montgomery, 2013; Booher-Jennings, 2008; Wiederkehr, Bonnot, Krauth-Gruber, & Darnon, 2015; Yang & Shin, 2008). This disguises social inequality by conditioning lower achievers to blame themselves for their lack of effort (e.g., Booher-Jennings, 2008; Hawkins, 2008; Marginson, 2011). Moreover, lower achievers value the test-centric meritocracy even more than higher achievers because lower achievers often come from lower socio-economic family backgrounds and must rely on schooling to climb the social hierarchy ladder to success (Wiederkehr et al., 2015).

Because of the extraordinary socio-economic rewards for entering high-ranking universities, Asian families have spent disproportionately on test-preparations, such as private courses and tutoring to compete against their children's peers, which has solidified social inequality in Asian countries (e.g., Chun, 2013; Entrich, 2015; Hawkins, 2008; Kim & Lee, 2010; Marginson, 2011; Ono, 2007). Although lower socio-economic families cannot afford higher socio-economic families' expensive private courses and tutoring, they refuse to give up the competition. Higher socio-economic families spend more than lower socio-economic families, but lower socio-economic families spend higher percentages of their incomes, which have placed enormous burdens and psychological stress on lower socio-economic families (Jones, 2011; Kim & Lee, 2010; Marginson, 2011; Tan et al., 2016). The costs are so burdensome that Asian families often cannot afford more than one child, leading to Asians' low fertility rate (Anderson & Kohler, 2013; Jones, 2011; Koo, 2007; Liu, 2012; Tan et al., 2016).

Social Conformity

Asian countries have been ruled by conforming elites who best memorise past knowledge, pass the one-chance exam, and then maintain the status quo for themselves (e.g., Chun, 2013; Elman, 2009; Hawkins, 2008; Kim, 2007, 2009, 2011, 2016, in press; Mack-Cozzo, 2002; Marginson, 2011; Suen & Yu, 2006; Yuan-kang, 2009). Test-centric education forces social conformity by: rewarding conforming students who follow the standards the authority has created; forcing students to learn exactly what and how (rote learning); selecting conforming students for universities and graduate schools; and turning teachers into technicians who follow exact scripts for both the content and methodology (e.g., Chun, 2013).

Asians tend to be collectivists who value an individual's ability to fit in with the groups and the groups' interests more than they value an individual's uniqueness (e.g., Barkema, Chen, George, Luo, & Tsui, 2015; Kim, 2007, 2009, 2016, in press; Kim et al., 2011; Miron-Spektor, Paletz, & Lin, 2015; Noriko, Fan, & Dusen, 2001). The uniformity of test-centric education inhibits original thinkers, considering them antisocial because they are curious and dare to question what others just accept (e.g., Kim, 2007, 2009, 2016, in press; Kim et al., 2011; Mack-Cozzo, 2002). By the time Asian students finish schooling under this standardised, mass production, test-centric education, many of them not only think and behave alike but also are easily controlled by the hierarchy (Mack-Cozzo, 2002).

Korean Creative and Gifted Education

The Korean government has led Korean education based on the nation's industrial needs. Its main focus has been on science and technology education to rebuild and modernise the nation since Japanese Colonisation and the Korean War (e.g., Choi, 2014; Jung & Mah, 2014; Park, 2010). Hence, creative and gifted education is now centred around Science, Technology, Engineering, and Mathematics (STEM; Choi, 2014; Jung & Mah, 2014). The government enacted the Law for Promotion of Gifted and Talented Education in 2000 (Lee, Kang, & Lee, 2016; Yeo, 2016). To add *creativity* to STEM education for gifted students, the government has changed the Association for Supporting Science and Technology into the *Korea Foundation for the Advancement of Science and Creativity* (KOFAC), and gifted education emphasised creativity afterwards, especially since 2009 (KOFAC, 2017; The Korea Ministry of Education, 2016). One of the main goals of gifted education has been to foster creativity among future leaders (Jung & Mah, 2014). In addition to 24 STEM-specialised high schools for gifted students, and due to the increasing emphasis on the English language because individual competence in English is closely linked to academic and occupational success (Koo, 2007), the government has established 31 foreign language-specialised high schools.

There are gifted programs in both regular schools and outside schools, but all are held outside regular school hours (Lee et al., 2016). For example, one type of outside program is the *Invention* gifted program that nurtures creativity through primary/middle school students' inventing based on their strengths and interests (Lee, 2016). The selection criteria for inclusion in the invention gifted education programs is a multistep process and includes teacher recommendations, IQ, academic achievement test scores, creativity test scores, aptitude test scores, and performance assessment (Lee, 2016). The performance assessment measures *invention* principles, problem-discovering, and problem-solving that are different from the selection criteria for other gifted programs which are solely test-based (Lee, 2016). Yet, *invention gifted education* focuses on gifted programs' short-term results, and gifted students' performance improvements are judged mainly by measurable results (Lee, 2016). When teachers focus on a narrow framework or a fragmented set of task-oriented activities for creating new ideas or products, rather than a deep or continuous process of developing expertise, students only invent items by adding miscellaneous functions to their inventions (Lee, 2016).

Sun Climate and Attitudes

Big-Picture Thinking and Optimistic Attitudes

Innovators are inspired by big ideas followed their curiosities in their chosen topics, such as envisioning *changing the world* (e.g., Kim, 2016; Thrash, Maruskin, Cassidy, Fryer, & Ryan, 2010; Walsh, 2013). These big ideas help their minds transcend concrete constraints and recognise patterns or relationships among the seemingly unrelated, often leading to innovation (e.g., Kim, 2016; Polman & Emich, 2011; Shavinina, 2004). Innovators extend their compassion to the wider world, as they overcame their challenges and form different perspectives in life (Lim & DeSteno, 2016; Simonton, 2004, 2008, 2009; Torrance, 2002). Their compassion for humanity often drove their creative endeavour, and their passion was strengthened by compassion for others' needs, which inspired their big-picture goals and facilitated creative thinking (Grant, 2008; Polman & Emich, 2011). Thus, international studies report that nations pursuing visionary goals or ideals produce more innovations than nations pursuing selfish interests or narrow goals (Brewer & Venaik, 2011; Taylor & Wilson, 2012).

Korean creative and gifted education aims to cultivate an inspirational and encouraging *sun* climate by nurturing students' big-picture thinking and optimistic attitude, through celebrating or promoting creative achievements or stories of innovations, and by helping students to generate and implement new ideas (KOFAC, 2018). However, extreme pressures and fears associated with high-stakes testing push students to focus on test scores and short-term results, rather than creativity that requires development over a long period of time (e.g., KOFAC, 2017; Yang & Shin, 2008). Traditionally, Koreans commonly say, 'Your arm bends in (i.e., the skin is nearer than the shirt)'. This saying may indicate that test-centric education and overemphasis on filial piety encourages students to serve only family and in-group members who inhibit their visionary or big-picture thinking (e.g., Bong, 2008; Hwang, 1999; Kim, 2016). Additionally, fewer Korean students indicate their optimistic attitude than their peers among PISA-participating countries; for example, they are not very satisfied with life (Kim, in press).

Curious Attitude

Innovation begins with curiosity, and innovators ask countless questions because they approach situations and problems with a beginner's mind. Their curious impulses and prior knowledge enable them to find details that others miss, which expedites their creative process toward innovation and leads to even more questions (Tamdogon, 2006). Innovators do not give up, and their curiosity ignores social restrictions and conventions, and allows them to find new options and opens them to new possibilities (Plucker, Beghetto, & Dow, 2004; Rueda, Posner, & Rothbart, 2005; Simonton, 2008).

However, because most test questions measure lower-level thinking skills, such as memorisation and comprehension, students earn high test scores by memorising facts and pieces of knowledge without application of higher-level thinking, thereby stifling natural curiosities and the joy of learning (Flake et al., 2006). As a result, Korean students report little curiosity or motivation for learning the tested subjects, despite their high-test scores (e.g., Kim, in press; Mullis, Martin, Foy, & Arora, 2012; Mullis, Martin, & Loveless, 2016; OECD, 2004, 2015, 2016). Additionally, even after Korean students have spent enormous sums of money and years of practice to learn English, a tested subject, many of them can barely speak it, because they have merely memorised English vocabulary and grammatical rules to obtain high scores (e.g., Kines, 2012; Mack-Cozzo, 2002).

High-scoring Korean students reported their curious attitudes and teachers' provision of learning encouragement less than their low-scoring peers among 70 PISA-participating countries (Kim, in press). For example, high-scoring Korean students reported their less frequent participation in: (a) investigations to test ideas; (b) opportunities to explain their ideas; and (c) practical experiments in the laboratory. High-scoring Korean students less frequently reported that their teachers nurtured students' curious attitudes by showing them how science can be a tool for interacting with the real world, or explaining the relevance of science concepts to students' lives, or how a scientific idea can be applied to many different phenomena (Kim, in press).

Love for Reading

To fulfil their insatiable curiosities, innovators grow up with a love for reading as a favourite leisure activity. Reading habits start at home before formal schooling (Mol & Bus, 2011) and exposure to fiction such as classic fables, fairy tales, nursery rhymes, and fantasy books increases the uniqueness of later creations (Torrance & Safter, 1999). Reading books maintains a healthy mind (Bavishi, Slade, & Levy, 2016). A relaxed state of mind that is stress-free and distraction-free is vital for both deep thought and the creative process, which can be achieved while reading a book (Csikszentmihali, 1996). One's mind is passive when watching television which reduces imagination, but reading a book increases imagination, as one visualises images and thoughts and creates a world in which anything is possible. Reading both fiction and nonfiction can increase imagination and compassion, but reading fiction requires greater effort for imagination and compassion (e.g., Bavishi et al., 2016; Kim, 2016; Mumper & Gerrig, 2017).

Curiosity promotes more curiosity, and reading becomes a critical tool that innovators use for their entire lives (Simonton, 2009). They also develop a love for learning and self-education rather than just formal schooling. Innovators do not attain high levels of formal schooling; they deepen their expertise by self-education through reading to develop and fulfil their passion (Simonton, 2009).

However, in test-centric education, students read only for the tests, not for pleasure, and students' reading interests are squelched by focusing on memorisation of basic facts and details rather than experiencing or creating meaningful interactions with the written word (Davis & Willson, 2015; Miller, 2015). This approach influences students to consider reading a required or boring chore, fuelling dislike and avoidance of reading. An 18-year longitudinal study found that reading among Korean gifted students tends to decrease as they move up through elementary, middle, and high school while their self-study hours increase (Cho, Ahn, Han, & Park, 2008).

Storm Climate and Attitudes

Self-Efficacious and Persistent Attitudes

Doing a task or activity for a reward, rather than doing it for enjoyment, tends to decrease learning (De Jesus, Rus, Lens, & Imaginário, 2013; Luh & Lu, 2012). Little autonomous motivation leads to little opportunity to develop a strength or passion, which prevents persistence (Luh & Lu, 2012).

Innovators build self-efficacy (true self-confidence), which is self-knowledge of what one is specifically good at, by gradually accomplishing challenging tasks on their own through real-world activities, projects, and career explorations, and by learning their strengths (Lane, Lane, & Kyprianou, 2004; Prat-Sala & Redford, 2010; Richardson, 2007). Innovators are autonomously engaged in learning and developing strengths, which become their passion and eventually they devote all of their energy to their passion (e.g., Hammond, Neff, Farr, Schwall, & Zhao, 2011; Luh & Lu, 2012; Simonton, 2008; Winner, 2003). Innovators are committed to their goals and persist over time (Beghetto, 2006; Hsu, Hou, & Fan, 2011; Lane et al., 2004; Prat-Sala & Redford, 2010; Richardson, 2007).

The biggest difference between innovators and non-innovators is that innovators persisted even when they experience challenges, setbacks or failures, and their passion for their chosen field compels them to be persistent and committed (Ericsson, Charness, Feltovich, & Hoffman, 2006; Simonton, 2009). The creative process is a journey riddled with anxiety, frustration, and failures, but innovators persist until they achieve a final creation while their minds continue learning through failures (e.g., Amireault, Godin, & Vézina-Im, 2013; Simonton, 2008, 2009). Their persistence continues even after their final creation; they constantly think about and improve their creations, which leads to other creations (e.g., Ericsson, Nandagopal, & Roring, 2005). Innovators produce more creations than non-innovators do, which increases the probability for one of their creations to be recognised as an innovation, and a quantity of ideas or creations increases the quality of ideas or creations (Kim, 2006, 2016; Kim, Cramond, & Bandalos, 2006; Nijstad, De Dreu, Rietzschel, & Baas, 2010; Paulus, Kohn, & Arditti, 2011; Putman & Paulus, 2009; Rietzschel, Nijstad, & Stroebe, 2007; Torrance, 2000). Their persistence helps them overcome bad luck, lack of resources, and all possible excuses (Simonton, 2008).

Korean creative and gifted education aims to cultivate a high-expectation-holding and challenging *storm* climate by nurturing students' self-efficacious and persistent attitudes (KOFAC, 2018). In order to foster creativity among future leaders in STEM fields, the admission criteria for the STEM-specialised gifted high schools includes interviews, observations, and creativity assessments, in addition to students' GPA. The criteria include gifted students' interests in pursuing a STEM career, but exclude a medical career due to many parents' medical career preference for their children (Choi, 2014). However, despite the criteria for identifying future leaders in the STEM fields, these gifted schools have been criticised for just being college-preparatory schools for prestigious universities that produce future medical students based on parent's career preferences rather than student' interests, instead of promoting future leaders in the STEM fields (Choi, 2014; Seo, Kwak, Jung, & Son, 2007). Moreover, students' performance, progress, and achievements are assessed mainly by test scores. This limited view of students' performance may inhibit gifted students' opportunities to discover what they love to do and develop their self-efficacy (Kim, 2016, 2017; Lee, 2016). As a result, high-scoring Korean students less frequently report setting high expectations for themselves less frequently and lower levels of self-efficacious attitudes than their low-scoring peers among the PISA-participating countries (Kim, in press). For example, high-scoring Korean students less frequently reported that they can easily: (a) identify the scientific concepts associated with the disposal of garbage; (b) recognise the scientific concepts underlying a newspaper report on a health issue; (c) discuss how new evidence can lead them to change their understanding about the possibility of life on Mars; or (d) interpret the scientific information provided on the labelling of food items, than their low-scoring PISA peers (Kim, in press). Additionally, high-scoring Korean students less frequently reported their motivation for learning science or higher education, such as their intentions to work in science-related occupations at age 30 than their low-scoring PISA peers (Kim, in press).

Risk-Taking Attitude

Presenting different ideas may challenge the status quo, which invites resistance because new ideas often conflict with others' interests or result in rejection (e.g., Janssen, 2004). Creativity requires taking risks and innovators are optimistic and adventurous and are willing to risk the negative feelings that can accompany mistakes or failures in pursuit of their passions (e.g., Hsu et al., 2011; Qian, Plucker, & Shen, 2010; Saeidi & Khaliliaqdam, 2013; Schwebel, 2009; Treffinger, Young, Selby, & Shepardson, 2002). Innovators who take high risks may be more successful than those who take low risks (Marade, Gibbons, & Brinthaupt, 2007).

However, with preparation starting at an early age for the *one*-chance university-entrance test, Korean students' anxiety is extreme—including gifted students. Failing the test makes both students and their parents consider themselves losers, brings shame on the family, and lowers their own expectations (e.g., Choi, 2014; Jung & Mah, 2014; Koyama et al., 2014; Mack-Cozzo, 2002; Marginson, 2011; Yang & Shin, 2008). Fear of failure in test-centric education increases students' test anxiety and physical illness, especially for disadvantaged students and girls, thereby decreasing their test performance (e.g., Jones, 2007; Sung, Chao, & Tseng, 2016). Students develop little tolerance of failure and become risk-averse, considering a mistake as a permanent mark of shame (e.g., Choi, 2014; Chun, 2013; Eum & Rice, 2011; Jung & Mah, 2014; Mack-Cozzo, 2002; Marginson, 2011; Yang & Shin, 2008; Yuan-kang, 2009).

Soil Climate and Attitudes

Open-Minded and Complexity-Seeking Attitudes

Creativity requires diverse human interactions and influences, and educational and social resources, opportunities, and experiences. An open-minded attitude, such as embracing different people, perspectives, ideas, and viewpoints that are *radically* different from their own and recognising how others arrive at their conclusions have the strongest relationship with creativity among all of the creative attitudes (Li et al., 2015).

Innovators nurture their complexity-seeking attitudes by welcoming new experiences and conflicting viewpoints, instead of right-and-wrong or good-or-bad thinking (Haller & Courvoisier, 2010; Kim, 2016; Tadmor, Galinsky, & Maddux, 2012). They often grow up around people who agree with each other on fundamental values, but are different from one another in personality, attitudes, interests, and other values. Innovators have opposite views to others on many issues and often *agree to disagree*. Agreeing to disagree, or considering multiple perspectives, is more conducive to creativity development than their socio-economic backgrounds or even the warmth and encouragement they receive. They constantly question how things are, learn new things and change their ingrained beliefs (Mezias & Starbuck, 2003).

Korean creative and gifted education aims to cultivate a resources-, experiences-, and viewpoints-diverse *soil* climate. The government has played a critical role in planning curriculum, training teachers, and providing facilities and funds to foster creativity among gifted students (Jung & Mah, 2014). The government has (KOFAC, 2018):

- Provided new curricula for preservice-teachers.
- Supported teachers' professional development and networking.
- Developed online platforms, such as Crezone, to share information among students, teachers, and parents.
- Provided entrepreneurs with consulting services to commercialise their products.
- Built science museums, libraries, and community centres to provide resources for creativity development.

In order to educate mathematically- and scientifically-minded high school students, the government has tried to provide excellent science education for gifted students. In some of the STEM-specialised high schools, many students are on government scholarships (Seo et al., 2007). These schools focus on the students' research abilities and require students to take research courses that are guided by universities and research centres (Jung & Mah, 2014). The government has supported these schools by providing excellent educational facilities and inviting science and technology experts to educate gifted students (Jung & Mah, 2014).

However, one view is that Korean gifted education has failed to cultivate the diverse viewpoints of students. Korean schools have little autonomy because the Korean central government controls all schools, both public and private (e.g., Cho,

2018). The government pays the salaries of public and private school teachers, and both public and private schools must use the national curriculum (Alexander & Kim, 2017). The Korean Ministry of Education monitors the educational system and develops the curriculum with exclusive power, including school textbooks, educational content, goals, objectives, evaluation, and guidelines (Lee & Misco, 2014). The Korean Ministry of Education controls gifted education, and local governments do not have much control over policies or securing funds for gifted education, and thus implementing gifted education programs can be inflexible (Lee et al., 2016). Students are usually taught with government-generated textbooks and by national curriculum standards that only represent one perspective by the government, though there are options to access texts from different publishing companies (Cho, 2018).

Cross-Pollination and Resourceful Attitude

Most people habitually use either more inbox or more outbox thinking, but both inbox and outbox thinking are required for innovation. Thus, innovators often cross-pollinate not only between inbox and outbox thinking but across different fields between different thinkers by boundary-crossing. Cross-pollination (i.e., leveraging others' strengths) illustrates how new ideas are built on others' ideas through formal and informal interactions by networking, getting feedback, collaboration, and win-win competition. Innovators' boundary-crossing and cross-pollination often lead to Big I (Innovation). Many artistic innovators have science or engineering backgrounds and many scientific innovators have art backgrounds, that can differentiate science Nobel laureates from other scientists (Kim, 2016).

Although Korean education has provided students—including gifted students—teachers, and parents with various resources and experiences, it has been unable to promote cross-pollination because test-centric education is too competitive and too test-scores-oriented with a single preoccupation to prepare students for university entrance tests (e.g., Choi, 2014; Koo, 2007; Seo et al., 2007). Schools are compelled to depend on rote lecturing, and students have few opportunities for group work or discussions to learn or collaborate with others. Moreover, test-centric education has prevented collaboration among students, teachers, and schools by instigating competition instead. Schools emphasise individual excellence at the expense of collaboration, which fosters competition rather than compassion and collaboration (e.g., Bang & Montgomery, 2013; Yang & Shin, 2008). Students view the world as an arena of cutthroat competition within which to beat their peers (Kim, 2016; Yang & Shin, 2008). As a result, Korean students tend to report their exhibition of resourceful attitudes and cross-pollination attributes less than PISA peers. For example, fewer Korean students have reported that they cooperated with peers or enjoyed seeing peers succeed (Kim, in press). As the Koreans' common saying goes 'It hurts when my peers prosper' (Turning green with envy), the competitive culture demands that students outpace their peers, which stifles the consideration of diverse viewpoints for critical thinking that innovations require. The laser-sharp focus on test scores based on the narrowly defined notion of success in Korean education prevents many students from realising their full potential (Alexander & Kim, 2017). Thus, one of the most important efforts Korean gifted education must make is to prevent negative side effects from extreme educational competitions among parents and children (Lee et al., 2016). Privileging competition over cooperation is also related to ignoring others in need. For example, Korean people are less likely to donate money to charity, volunteer their time, or help strangers than those not experiencing exam hell (Charities Aid Foundation, 2016, 2017).

Korean students—including gifted students—have no time to engage in non-tested subjects or extracurricular activities, play sports, interact with peers, get a real-life job or experience, or learn real-life skills, because they focus only on tested subjects and activities, for university entrance (Bang & Montgomery, 2013; Choi, 2014; Koo, 2007; Seo et al., 2007; Won & Han, 2010; Yang & Shin, 2008). For example, compared to their low-scoring PISA peers, high-scoring Korean students less frequently reported their rote learning was supplemented with diverse experiences or practical work experiences, such as outside school work (Kim, in press). This not only narrows students' thinking, but gives them few opportunities for expressing their individuality and cross-pollinating across different subjects or fields. This further eliminates their motivation to learn while intensifying their anxiety (e.g., Kim, 2008; Looney, 2009). Students' single-minded focus makes it difficult to imagine a different world, opportunity or skill they may be missing (Bang & Montgomery, 2013; Won & Han, 2010; Yang & Shin, 2008). This single-mindedness can prevent students from developing complex and critical thinking that innovation developments require.

Space Climate and Attitudes

Self-Reflective and Daydreaming Attitudes

Active, outdoor play strengthens children's imagination, emotional health, and resilience while allowing them to stumble, falter, trip, fall, fail, bounce back, and try again early and often instead of being afraid (e.g., Dowdell, Gray, & Malone, 2011; Janssen, 2016; Kim, 2016). These early experiences are key to later innovations. Being outdoors and connecting to nature can facilitate individuals' self-reflection and daydreaming as well as their emotional health and mental or physical energy (e.g., Berman, Jonides, & Kaplan, 2008; Capaldi, Dopko, & Zelenski, 2014; Dowdell et al., 2011; Kim, 2016, in press; Nisbet, Zelenski, & Murphy, 2009, 2011; Ryan et al., 2010; Tam, 2013). Moreover, being allowed to think differently can enable outbox thinking, forming unique perspectives and ideas. Daydreaming can facilitate creative processes, especially when individuals are unable to solve a problem after persistently working on it for a long time (Dijksterhuis & Meurs, 2006; Dijksterhuis & Nordgren, 2006; Sio & Ormerod, 2009).

However, Korean students worry about their test scores and suffer from severe test-related stresses, having little time for deep thoughts or imagination (e.g., Huan, See, Ang, & Har, 2008; Kim, 2016; Lee & Larson, 2000). Spending their entire day studying in school and then in private courses or tutoring to prepare for tests leaves them little time for play or being outdoors (Kim, 2016; Shin et al., 2012). Their need for play, sleep, or psychological and emotional well-being are ignored beginning in early childhood (e.g., Kim, 2016, in press; Lee & Larson, 2000; Yang & Shin, 2008). This not only deprives them of time for deep thoughts or imagination, but may cause high rates of clinical depression (Huan et al., 2008; Lee & Larson, 2000). Significant percentages of students report suicidal ideations, instead of imagination (Korea National Statistics Office, 2008), and suicide is the leading cause of death among Korean students generally (e.g., Ahn & Baek 2013; Economist, 2011; Korea National Statistics Office, 2008; Lee, 2011; New York Times, 2013; Roberts, 2014; Shin et al., 2016; Suen & Yu, 2006; Wang, 2015; Yonngong, 2015).

Nonconforming Attitude

Innovators are like eagles who are content without a flock, and this ability to be alone enables the formation of unique perspectives and ideas. Thus, few innovations or innovators survive in societies that force conformity and suppress self-expression and uniqueness (Chua, Roth, & Lemoine, 2015; Gelfand et al., 2011; Rinne, Steel, & Fairweather, 2012, 2013). Innovation requires outbox thinking to go beyond current knowledge, which requires original thinking. Original thinking is thinking differently from others, deviating from the norm or challenging the status quo (Guildford, 1986; Sternberg & Kaufman, 2010; Torrance, 2002; Torrance & Safter, 1999). Therefore, original thinking is one of the best predictors of innovation (Guilford, 1986; Nijstad et al., 2010; Torrance, 2000, 2002; Torrance & Safter, 1999). However, the space climate that allows students to think deeply and behave differently from others is the one that Korean education does not aim to cultivate. The Ministry of Education has explicitly aimed at creativity and character education since 2009; yet, this in fact discourages students' nonconforming thoughts and behaviours in the name of *character education* that encourages social conformity (Kim et al., 2011; KOFAC, 2018). Character education emphasises students' self-restraint, suppression of emotions, predictable actions and filial piety that encourage conformity and respect for authority (Kim et al., 2011; KOFAC, 2018). Test-centric education generates students' uniformity and conformity, which discourages the uniqueness that is required for innovation. As a result, Korean students can tend to report their exhibition of space attitudes less than their PISA peers, and even less than other Asian students. Compared to their PISA peers from other countries, for example, high-scoring Korean students less frequently reported that their teachers provided students with opportunities to think differently and nurtured students' nonconforming attitudes, such as: (a) having a class debate about investigations; (b) allowing students to design their own experiments; (c) requiring students to argue about science questions; and (d) asking students to draw conclusions from their own experiments, than their low-scoring PISA peers (Kim, in press). The uniformity and conformity of standardised-testing can result in students replicating others and having little original imagination. This pressure to conform has been so deeply ingrained in Koreans' minds for generations that they view original thinkers as troublemakers or antisocial outcasts (e.g., Kim, 2016, in press; Kim et al., 2011). As a Korean common saying goes, 'the nail that stands up must be hammered', which indicates that exam hell results in standardised mass-production of students who not only think alike, but also police their own and others' nonconforming thoughts and behaviours. However, it is suggested in the research that societies that force conformity and suppress individuality and originality are less creative and produce fewer innovations (Chua et al., 2015; Gelfand et al., 2011; Kurman, Liem, Ivancovsky, Morio, & Lee, 2015; Rinne et al., 2012, 2013; Tellis, Prabhu, & Chandy, 2009).

Social Inequality

Gaps in racial/ethnic representations have been persistent in the USA gifted/talented education programs. For example, Black, Hispanic, and Native American students are 66% less likely to be identified as gifted than Asian and White students (Hodges, Tay, Maeda, & Gentry, 2018). Asian American students had the greatest likelihood of being identified as gifted and were 173.6% more likely to be identified as gifted than White students. However, after taking into consideration academic achievement and socio-economic status (measured by students who were eligible for free or reduced lunch), all demographic groups of students were more likely to be identified as gifted than White students (Warne, Anderson, & Johnson, 2013). The gaps among racial/ethnic groups are predicted by the differences in: (a) students' academic achievements and (b) their families' socio-economic backgrounds, such as parental education and income among the groups (Erwin & Worrell, 2012; Warne et al., 2013). Differences in families' socio-economic backgrounds explain students' academic preparations or achievements (Warne et al., 2013). This indicates that students who are identified as gifted in the USA system are students who are already academic achievers and are from high socio-economic family backgrounds.

Similarly, Korean gifted education has been criticised for increasing gaps in educational opportunities between the higher-SES elites and others (Park, 2010). In the time of industrialisation between the 1960s and 1980s, the Korean government used its centralised power to engage individuals in government-led economic development (Lee, 2012) and to implement education policies for social integration (Park, 2010). Since the 1990s, Korean education policies have been increasingly influenced by the elites who can afford expensive private tutoring and education (e.g., Choi, 2014; Kwon, 2009; Park, 2010). The Korean government once outlawed private tutoring to reduce burdens on low-income families (Kim & Lee, 2010; Park, 2010), but the elites persuaded policymakers in their favour. Parents of gifted high school students tend to earn much higher incomes and are more educated than parents of other high school students (Korean Educational Development Institute [KEDI], 2007; Kwon, 2009). Pledging to establish another gifted high school has become one of the most popular agenda items among Korean politicians running in an election (Park, 2010). Korean politics is dominated by the elitists including family-owned, large business conglomerates, and their rights and freedom are placed above those of the others (Koo, 2007; Son, 2013). Economic gaps have widened since the 1997–1998 financial crisis, and more mid-SES families have become lower-SES families (C. J. Lee, 2005). What is remarkable about Korean parents' educational zeal is their exceptionally high aspiration for upward mobility by means of education, which is shared by families of all socio-economic classes (Koo, 2007; C. J. Lee, 2005). Educational competition has intensified and is expensive in terms of time and money (Koo, 2007), and families have to pay for school transportation and food services, in addition to private tutoring and education (Alexander & Kim, 2017). This has become an enormous burden for lower SES families and has restricted social mobility through education, so education is becoming a mechanism for SES reproduction rather than for societal mobility (e.g., Koo, 2007; C. J. Lee, 2005; Park, 2010). As a result, Korean students tend to negatively perceive high-achieving peers and attribute their achievement mainly to families' socio-economic backgrounds, such as parents' financial support and private tutoring and education (Oh et al., 2015).

Defiant Attitude

Textbooks present neither alternate perspectives of Korean history, culture, or social issues, nor big-picture perspectives to contribute to future world peace and social justice as global citizens (Lee & Misco, 2014). Textbooks are mainly aimed at strengthening the Korean government's and elites' centralised power, above the others' rights and freedoms, by claiming to: (a) prevent Japanese reinvasions; (b) eliminate Communist perspectives and reunify South and North Korea; and (c) maintain Confucian values (e.g., Lee & Misco, 2014; Moon & Koo 2011; Zhao, Hoge, Choi, & Lee, 2007). As a result, dissenters from the government are considered pro-Communists and pro-North Koreans who jeopardise national security, and hierarchical top-down administrations are pervasive in schools (Cho, 2018; Lee & Misco, 2014). Teaching students critical thinking skills, such as social justice and equity, the right to dissent from the government, and the importance of egalitarian relationships, is extremely difficult (Cho, 2018). Korean students act in subservient ways to authority, rather than nurture a defiant attitude, while ignoring the needs of those *beneath* them (e.g., Hawkins, 2008; Kim et al., 2011), and their outbox imagination becomes stifled (e.g., Kim, in press; Song, 2017a, b). Closed social hierarchies unknowingly stifle a defiant attitude, and consequently creative thinking, especially outbox imagination. Individuals in societies who value hierarchies often expect authoritarian figures to make decisions instead of taking their own initiatives, using free and equal discussions or debates or challenging top-down decisions (Pellegrini & Scandura, 2008).

Research and Practice: Implications and Future Directions

Torrance's longitudinal studies (2002) found that students identified as creatively gifted out-achieved academically gifted students in adulthood. However, many creatively gifted students remain unidentified because of the threshold IQ score needed for most USA gifted programs before creativity is even considered (Kim & VanTassel-Baska, 2010; Renzulli, 2005; Torrence, 2002). In a study by Kim and VanTassel-Baska (2010), the use of the IQ score as the primary identifier of giftedness eliminated up to 80% of the most highly creative students from consideration for Korean gifted programs. Guignard et al. (2016) found that creative potential between gifted ($IQ \geq 130$) and non-gifted ($IQ < 130$) French children did not differ. Further, a Hong Kong study (Chan & Yuen, 2014) reported no difference found in fostering students' creativity between teachers of gifted students and teachers of other students. Thus, teacher training on fostering creativity in gifted students seems to be necessary. Additionally, this lack of recognition of creativity in students suggests that more research is needed to highlight creativity in policies and identification processes for gifted education programs.

The recent Korean gifted education's identification of gifted students and its focus on fostering their creativity is remarkable compared to the lack of focus on creativity in recent USA gifted education. Only 21 USA states include creativity in their definitions of giftedness, which is a decrease from 27 states in 2010, which, in turn, was a decrease from 30 states in 2000 (Luria, O'Brien, & Kaufman, 2016). In contrast, 44 USA states include academics and 34 states include intelligence (National Association for Gifted Children [NAGC], 2015). Moreover, only nine states require a program/service for creativity, whereas such a program/service is required by 33 states for academics and 22 states for intelligence (NAGC, 2015). Although Korean gifted education has not tried to foster the deep- and free-thinking *space* climate, it has tried to foster: (a) the inspirational and encouraging *sun* climate; (b) high-expectation-holding and challenging *storm* climate; and (c) resources-, experiences-, and viewpoints-diverse *soil* climate. However, mainly due to the traditional focus on test-scores, gifted education has been unsuccessful in fostering students' sun attitudes (e.g., the big-picture thinking, optimistic and curious attitudes), storm attitudes (e.g., self-efficacious, persistent and risk-taking attitudes), soil attitudes (e.g., open-minded, complexity-seeking, and resourceful attitudes) and space attitudes (e.g., self-reflective, daydreaming, nonconforming, and defiant attitudes). As a result, Korean gifted students have difficulty in developing their ideas and in thinking imaginatively (e.g., Lee, 2016). Korean students' high-test scores have cost them their individuality and creativity (e.g., Kim et al., 2011; Kim in press; Kurman et al., 2015; Miron-Spektor et al., 2015; Ng, 2000; Niu & Sternberg, 2001, 2002, 2003; Noriko et al., 2001; Nouri et al., 2015). This may have contributed to few Korean innovators becoming Nobel Laureates (Kim, 2016). In addition, only a few Korean technology patents and scientific publications have been commercialised or received international recognition (Song, 2017a, b). Korean companies often copy products from the West and make them more useful because they infrequently produce something unique (Kim, 2016).

An innovation requires: (a) mastery of or expertise in what one loves to do, which the storm climate and storm attitudes can facilitate; (b) original imagination for unique ideas to solve a problem or improve something, which the sun and space climates and sun and space attitudes can facilitate; (c) deeper inbox critical thinking to check unique ideas for usefulness, which the soil climate and soil attitudes can facilitate; and (d) newbox synthesis and refinement for a unique and useful creation, which addressing all 4S climates and 4S attitudes can facilitate.

To cultivate the sun climate and nurture students' sun attitudes, educators can inspire students to focus on big-picture goals or ideals and optimism, rather than selfish interests or narrow goals and short-term results and pessimism. They can also spark students' natural curiosities and nurture the joy of learning and reading and exploring topics, rather than memorising facts and pieces of knowledge without application (Kim, 2016, in press). Educators can also provide students with many opportunities to think about new ideas and inventions in real-life situations (Lee, 2016).

To cultivate the storm climate and nurture students' storm attitudes, educators can motivate students to find a topic of interest and develop a strength that can become their passion, rather than focusing on test scores and other measurable results. Teachers can also teach students to learn from mistakes and failures, rather than considering a mistake a permanent mark of shame (Kim, 2016, in press). An innovation requires mastery of or expertise in what one loves to do for at least 10 years duration. Having their own specialised area will provide students with a starting point for carving out an area of interest and promote further development toward expertise (Lee, 2016). Although much more time is needed to develop expertise in any area of interest than is available in any schools, gifted education can still build a good foundation for such development (Lee, 2016).

To cultivate the soil climate and nurture students' soil attitudes, educators can provide students with multiple or conflicting viewpoints and help them practice how to agree to disagree (Kim, 2016, in press). Textbooks can appeal to students and present logical evidence and realistic facts from multiple perspectives. Teachers can help students solve open and complex problems related to real-life and future problems and implement effective cross-pollination processes. They can stimulate discussion, debate and cooperation (Kim, Roh, & Cho, 2016). Educators can also encourage students to engage in non-tested subjects or extracurricular activities, such as sports and volunteer experiences, and job experiences. Additionally, gifted education cannot just aim to produce inventors or engineers, nor be a pipeline for STEM careers, but foster creativity in all areas (Kim, 2016; Lee, 2016).

To cultivate the space climate and nurture students' space attitudes, educators can encourage students to think differently from others, daydream, and challenge the status quo, rather than to conform and respect authority (Kim, 2016, in press). In textbooks, alternate and big-picture perspectives as global citizens can be presented. Indeed, school leaders can build on the textbook usage by recommending other resources and nurturing a democratic school community where intellectual diversity is shared. Educators can teach students how to critically analyse: (a) social injustice to help students to actively participate in social actions; (b) conflicting beliefs and ideologies; (c) particular views in the textbooks and other resources; and (d) how to diplomatically challenge authority (Kim, 2016, in press).

Conclusion

Korean education has begun to foster creativity in gifted students; however, without cultivating all of the 4S climates to nurture students' 4S attitudes, Korean students might become bored and boring technicians who enact the dreams of those from other countries, without fulfilling dreams of their own. If Korean students are to become true innovators who enrich Korean society with their endeavours, then the Korean Ministry of Education needs to ensure that students experience all of the 4S climates and attitudes—rooted in nutrient-diverse soil resources, experiences, and viewpoints; warmed by sun inspirations and encouragement; setting high expectations and goals based on storm challenges; and nurtured by the space of thinking deeply and freely— to cultivate their innate creativity.

Cross-References

▶ A Model for Growing Teacher Talent Scouts: Decreasing Underrepresentation of Gifted Students
▶ Bricolage and the Evolution of Giftedness and Talent in Taiwan
▶ Creativity Talent Development: Fostering Creativity in Schools
▶ Diverse Dimensions of Gifted Education: Part V Introduction
▶ Engaging Gifted Students in Solving Real Problems Creatively: Implementing the Real Engagement in Active Problem-Solving (REAPS) Teaching/Learning Model in Australasian and Pacific Rim Contexts
▶ Gifted Education in the Asia-Pacific: From the Past for the Future – An Introduction
▶ Identifying Underrepresented Gifted Students: A Developmental Process
▶ Leadership Development of Gifted Adolescents from a Korean Multicultural Lens
▶ Sociocultural Perspectives on the Talent Development Megamodel
▶ Some Implications for the Future of Gifted Education in the Asia-Pacific
▶ STEAM in Gifted Education in Korea
▶ Trends and Challenges of Creativity Development Among Selected Asian Countries and Regions: China, Hong Kong/Macau, Japan, Malaysia, and South Korea
▶ The Career Decisions of Gifted Students: An Asian-Pacific Perspective
▶ Using the Idea-Marathon System (IMS) in University Education and Creativity Development
▶ Underachievement and the Quest for Dignity: Contemporary Perspectives on a Timeless Issue

References

Ahn, S.-Y., & Baek, H.-J. (2013). Academic achievement-oriented society and its relationship to the psychological well-being of Korean adolescents. In C.-C. Yi (Ed.), *The psychological well-being of East Asian youth* (Vol. 2, pp. 265–279). Dordrecht: Springer. https://doi.org/10.1007/978-94-007-4081-5_13

Alexander, N. A., & Kim, H. (2017). Adequacy by any other name: A comparative look at educational spending in the United States and the Republic of Korea. *Journal of Education Finance, 43*(1), 65–83. Retrieved from https://eric.ed.gov/?id=EJ1169323

Ambrose, D., & Sternberg, R. J. (Eds.). (2012). *How dogmatic beliefs harm creativity and higher level thinking.* New York, NY: Routledge.

Amireault, S., Godin, G., & Vézina-Im, L. (2013). Determinants of physical activity maintenance: A systematic review and meta-analyses. *Health Psychology Review, 7*, 55–91. https://doi.org/10.1080/17437199.2012.701060

Anderson, K. T. (2015). The discursive construction of lower-tracked students: Ideologies of meritocracy and the politics of education. *Education Policy Analysis Archives, 23*(110), 1–30. https://doi.org/10.14507/epaa.v23.2141

Anderson, T. M., & Kohler, H.-P. (2013). Education fever and the east Asian fertility puzzle: A case study of the low fertility in South Korea. *Asian Population Studies, 9*, 196–215. https://doi.org/10.1080/17441730.2013.797293

Au, W. (2009). *Unequal by design: High-stakes testing and the standardization of inequality.* New York, NY: Routledge.

Au, W. (2011). Teaching under the new Taylorism: High-stakes testing and the standardization of the 21st century curriculum. *Journal of Curriculum Studies, 43*, 25–45. https://doi.org/10.1080/00220272.2010.521261

Badzakova-Trajkov, G., Häberling, I. S., & Corballis, M. C. (2011). Magical ideation, creativity, handedness, and cerebral asymmetries: A combined behavioural and fMRI study. *Neuropsychologia, 49*, 2896–2903. https://doi.org/10.1016/j.neuropsychologia.2011.06.016

Bang, H., & Montgomery, D. (2013). Wisdom and ego-identity for Korean and American late adolescents. *Journal of Cross-Cultural Psychology, 44*, 807–831. https://doi.org/10.1177/0022022112466941

Barkema, H. G., Chen, X.-P., George, G., Luo, Y., & Tsui, A. S. (2015). West meets east: New concepts and theories. *Academy of Management Journal, 58*, 460–479. https://doi.org/10.5465/amj.2015.4021

Barrow, L., & Rouse, C. E. (2006). The economic value of education by race and ethnicity. *Economic Perspectives, 30*(2), 14–27.

Bartlett, T., & Fischer, K. (2011). The China conundrum. The Chronicle Retrieved from http://chronicle.com/article/The-China-Conundrum/129628/

Bavishi, A., Slade, M. D., & Levy, B. R. (2016). A chapter a day: Association of book reading with longevity. *Social Science & Medicine, 164*, 44–48. https://doi.org/10.1016/j.socscimed.2016.07.014

Beghetto, R. A. (2006). Creative self-efficacy: Correlates in middle and secondary students. *Creativity Research Journal, 18*, 447–457. https://doi.org/10.1207/s15326934crj1804_4

Berman, M. G., Jonides, J., & Kaplan, S. (2008). The cognitive benefits of interacting with nature. *Psychological Science, 19*, 1207–1212. https://doi.org/10.1111/j.1467-9280.2008.02225.x

Bong, M. (2008). Effects of parent-child relationships and classroom goal structures on motivation, help-seeking avoidance, and cheating. *Journal of Experimental Education, 76*, 191–217. https://doi.org/10.3200/JEXE.76.2.191-217

Booher-Jennings, J. (2008). Learning to label: Socialization, gender, and the hidden curriculum of high-stakes testing. *British Journal of Sociology of Education, 29*, 149–160. https://doi.org/10.1080/01425690701837513

Brewer, P., & Venaik, S. (2011). Individualism–collectivism in Hofstede and GLOBE. *Journal of International Business Studies, 42*, 436–445. https://doi.org/10.1057/jibs.2010.62

Capaldi, C. A., Dopko, R. L., & Zelenski, J. M. (2014). The relationship between nature connectedness and happiness: A meta-analysis. *Frontiers in Psychology, 5*(976), 1–15. https://doi.org/10.3389/fpsyg.2014.00976

Cappelli, P., & Hamori, M. (2004). *The path to the top: Changes in the attributes and careers of corporate executives, 1980–2001.* NBER working paper 10507. Cambridge, England: National Bureau of Economic Research (NBER).

Chan, J., & Chen, Y. (2008). Processes and outcomes of encouraging universities to implement creative studies colleges. In J. Chan (Ed.), *Creative education programs in Taiwan: Development and implementation* (pp. 244–257). Taipei: Ministry of Education.

Chan, S., & Yuen, M. (2014). Creativity beliefs, creative personality and creativity-fostering practices of gifted education teachers and regular class teachers in Hong Kong. *Thinking Skills and Creativity, 14*, 109–118. https://doi.org/10.1016/j.tsc.2014.10.003

Charities Aid Foundation. (2016). CAF world giving index 2016. Retrieved from https://www.cafonline.org/about-us/publications/2016-publications/caf-world-giving-index-2016

Charities Aid Foundation. (2017). CAF world giving index 2017. Retrieved from https://www.cafonline.org/about-us/publications/2017-publications/caf-world-giving-index-2017

Chávez-Eakle, R. A., Graff-Guerrero, A., García-Reyna, J. C., Vaugier, V., & Cruz-Fuentes, C. (2007). Cerebral blood flow associated with creative performance: A comparative study. *NeuroImage, 38*, 519–528. https://doi.org/10.1016/j.neuroimage.2007.07.059

Cho, H. (2018). Crafting a third space: Integrative strategies for implementing critical citizenship education in a standards-based classroom. *Journal of Social Studies Research, 42*, 273–285. https://doi.org/10.1016/j.jssr.2017.07.001

Cho, S., Ahn, D., Han, S., & Park, H. (2008). Academic developmental patterns of the Korean gifted during the 18 years after identification. *Personality and Individual Differences, 45*, 784–789. https://doi.org/10.1016/j.paid.2008.08.007

Choi, K. M. (2014). Opportunities to explore for gifted STEM students in Korea: From admissions criteria to curriculum. *Theory Into Practice, 53*(1), 25–32. https://doi.org/10.1080/00405841.2014.862117

Chua, R. Y., Roth, Y., & Lemoine, J.-F. (2015). The impact of culture on creativity how cultural tightness and cultural distance affect global innovation crowdsourcing work. *Administrative Science Quarterly, 60*, 189–227. https://doi.org/10.1177/0001839214563595

Chun, A. (2013). De-societalizing the school: On the hegemonic making of moral persons (citizenship) and its disciplinary regimes. *Critique of Anthropology, 33*, 146–167. https://doi.org/10.1177/0308275X13478222

Cropley, A. (2006). Dimensions of creativity: Creativity, a social approach. *Roeper Review, 28*, 125–130. https://doi.org/10.1080/02783190609554351

Csikszentmihali, M. (1996). *Creativity: Flow and the psychology of discovery and invention.* New York, NY: Harper Perennial.

Davis, D. S., & Willson, A. (2015). Practices and commitments of test-centric literacy instruction: Lessons from a testing transition. *Reading Research Quarterly, 50*, 357–359. https://doi.org/10.1002/rrq.103

De Jesus, S. N., Rus, C. L., Lens, W., & Imaginário, S. (2013). Intrinsic motivation and creativity related to product: A meta-analysis of the studies published between 1990–2010. *Creativity Research Journal, 25*, 80–84. https://doi.org/10.1080/10400419.2013.752235

Dijksterhuis, A., & Meurs, T. (2006). Where creativity resides: The generative power of unconscious thought. *Consciousness and Cognition, 15*(1), 135–146. https://doi.org/10.1016/j.concog.2005.04.007

Dijksterhuis, A., & Nordgren, L. F. (2006). A theory of unconscious thought. *Perspectives on Psychological Science, 1*(2), 95–109. https://doi.org/10.1111/j.1745-6916.2006.00007.x

Dowdell, K., Gray, T., & Malone, K. (2011). Nature and its influence on children's outdoor play. *Journal of Outdoor and Environmental Education, 15*(2), 24–35. https://doi.org/10.1007/BF03400925

Economist. (2011). Exams in South Korea: The one-shot society. *The Economist.* Retrieved from http://www.economist.com/node/21541713

Elman, B. A. (2009). Civil service examinations (Keju). In *Berkshire encyclopedia of China* (pp. 405–410). Great Barrington, MA: Berkshire.

Entrich, S. R. (2015). The decision for shadow education in Japan: Students' choice or parents' pressure? *Social Science Japan Journal, 18*, 193–216. https://doi.org/10.1093/ssjj/jyv012

Ericsson, K. A. (2014). Expertise. *Current Biology, 24*, 508–510. https://doi.org/10.1016/j.cub.2014.04.013

Ericsson, K. A., Charness, N., Feltovich, P. J., & Hoffman, R. R. (Eds.) (2006). The Cambridge handbook of expertise and expert performance. New York, NY: Cambridge University Press.

Ericsson, K. A., Nandagopal, K., & Roring, R. W. (2005). Giftedness viewed from the expert performance perspective. *Journal for the Education of the Gifted, 28*, 287–311. https://doi.org/10.4219/jeg-2005-335

Erwin, J. O., & Worrell, F. C. (2012). Assessment practices and the underrepresentation of minority students in gifted and talented education. *Journal of Psychoeducational Assessment, 30*, 74–87. https://doi.org/10.1177/0734282911428197

Eum, K., & Rice, K. G. (2011). Test anxiety, perfectionism, goal orientation, and academic performance. *Anxiety, Stress and Coping, 24*, 167–178. https://doi.org/10.1080/10615806.2010.488723

Flake, M. A., Benefield, T. C., Schwartz, S. E., Bassett, R., Archer, B., Etter, F., ... Kahan, E. (2006). A firsthand look at NCLB. *Educational Leadership, 64*(3), 48–52. Retrieved from http://www.ascd.org/publications/educational-leadership/nov06/vol64/num03/A-Firsthand-Look-atNCLB.aspx

Friedman, P. (2010). China's plagiarism problem. Forbes.com. Retrieved from http://www.forbes.com/2010/05/26/china-cheating-innovation-markets-economy-plagiarism.html

Gelfand, M. J., Raver, J. L., Nishii, L., Leslie, L. M., Lun, J., Lim, B., ... Yamaguchi, S. (2011). Differences between tight and loose cultures: A 33-nation study. *Science, 332*, 1100–1104. https://doi.org/10.3389/fnhum.2013.00465

Gonen-Yaacovi, G., Levy, R., Urbanski, M., & Volle, E. (2013). Rostral and caudal prefrontal contribution to creativity: A meta-analysis of functional imaging data. *Frontiers in Human Neuroscience, 7*(465), 1–22. https://doi.org/10.3389/fnhum.2013.00465

Grant, A. M. (2008). Does intrinsic motivation fuel the prosocial fire? Motivational synergy in predicting persistence, performance, and productivity. *Journal of Applied Psychology, 93*, 48–58. https://doi.org/10.1037/0021-9010.93.1.48

Guignard, J., Kermarrec, S., & Tordjman, S. (2016). Relationships between intelligence and creativity in gifted and non-gifted children. *Learning and Individual Differences, 52*, 209–215. https://doi.org/10.1016/j.lindif.2015.07.006

Guilford, J. P. (1986). *Creative talents: Their nature, uses, and development*. Buffalo/New York, NY: Bearly Limited.

Hahm, C. (2003). Law, culture, and the politics of confucianism. *Colombia Journal of Asian Law, 16*(2), 254–301.

Haller, C. S., & Courvoisier, D. C. (2010). Personality and thinking style in different creative domains. *Psychology of Aesthetics, Creativity, and the Arts, 4*, 149–160. https://doi.org/10.1037/a0017084

Hammond, M. M., Neff, N. L., Farr, J. L., Schwall, A. R., & Zhao, X. (2011). Predictors of individual-level innovation at work: A meta-analysis. *Psychology of Aesthetics, Creativity, and the Arts, 5*, 90–105. https://doi.org/10.1037/a0018556

Hawkins, J. (2008). Myth or reality? Assessing the validity of the Asian model of education. *Harvard International Review, 30*(3), 52–56. Retrieved from www.jstor.org/stable/42763600

Hodges, J., Tay, J., Maeda, Y., & Gentry, M. (2018). A meta-analysis of gifted and talented identification practices. *Gifted Child Quarterly, 62*, 147–174. https://doi.org/10.1177/0016986217752107

Hsu, M. L. A., Hou, S., & Fan, H. (2011). Creative self-efficacy and innovative behavior in a service setting: Optimism as a moderator. *Journal of Creative Behavior, 45*, 258–272. https://doi.org/10.1002/j.2162-6057.2011.tb01430.x

Huan, V. S., See, Y. L., Ang, R. P., & Har, C. W. (2008). The impact of adolescent concerns of their academic stress. *Educational Review, 60*, 169–178. https://doi.org/10.1080/00131910801934045

Hwang, K.-K. (1999). Filial piety and loyalty: Two types of social identification in Confucianism. *Asian Journal of Social Psychology, 2*, 163–183. https://doi.org/10.1111/1467-839X.00031

Janssen, I. (2016). Estimating whether replacing time in active outdoor play and sedentary video games with active video games influences youth's mental health. *Journal of Adolescent Health, 59*, 517–522. https://doi.org/10.1016/j.jadohealth.2016.07.007

Janssen, O. (2004). How fairness perceptions make innovative behavior more or less stressful. *Journal of Organizational Behavior, 25*, 201–215. https://doi.org/10.1002/job.238

Jaušovec, N. (2000). Differences in cognitive processes between gifted, intelligent, creative, and average individuals while solving complex problems: An EEG study. *Intelligence, 28*, 213–237. https://doi.org/10.1016/S0160-2896(00)00037-4

Jones, B. (2007). The unintended outcomes of high-stakes testing. *Journal of Applied School Psychology, 23*, 65–86. https://doi.org/10.1300/J370v23n02_05

Jones, R. (2011). *Education reform in Japan*. Paris, France: OECD.

Jung, H., & Mah, J. S. (2014). The role of the government in science and technology education of Korea. *Science, Technology and Society, 19*, 199–227. https://doi.org/10.1177/0971721814529877

Kang, J. I. (2006). Academic dependency: Western-centrism in Korean political science. *Korea Journal, 46*(4), 115–135.

Kim, A. E., & Park, G.-S. (2003). Nationalism, Confucianism, work ethic and industrialization in South Korea. *Journal of Contemporary Asia, 33*(1), 37–49. https://doi.org/10.1080/00472330380000041

Kim, K. H. (2006). Can we trust creativity tests? A review of The Torrance Tests of Creative Thinking (TTCT). *Creativity Research Journal, 18*, 3–14. Retrieved from http://citeseerx.ist.psu.edu/viewdoc/download?doi=10.1.1.587.3752&rep=rep1&type=pdf

Kim, K. H. (2007). Exploring the interactions between Asian culture (Confucianism) and creativity. *Journal of Creative Behavior, 41*, 28–54. https://doi.org/10.1002/j.2162-6057.2007.tb01280.x

Kim, K. H. (2008). Underachievement and creativity: Are gifted underachievers highly creative? *Creativity Research Journal, 20*, 234–242. https://doi.org/10.1080/10400410802060232

Kim, K. H. (2009). Cultural influence on creativity: The relationship between Asian culture (Confucianism) and creativity among Korean educators. *Journal of Creative Behavior, 43*, 73–93. https://doi.org/10.1002/j.2162-6057.2009.tb01307.x

Kim, K. H. (2011). The creativity crisis: The decrease in creative thinking scores on the Torrance tests of creative thinking. *Creativity Research Journal, 23*, 285–295. https://doi.org/10.1080/10400419.2011.627805

Kim, K. H. (2016). *The creativity challenge: How we can recapture American innovation*. Amherst, NY: Prometheus Books.

Kim, K. H. (2017). Creativity crisis update: How high-stakes testing stifles innovation. Retrieved from https://www.creativitypost.com/article/the_2017_creativity_crisis_update_how_high_stakes_testing_has_stifled_innov

Kim, K. H. (2019). Demystifying creativity: What creativity isn't and is? *Roeper Review, 41*, 119–128. https://doi.org/10.1080/02783193.2019.1585397

Kim, K. H. (In press). Creativity crisis update: U.S. follows Asia in pursuing high test scores over learning. *Roeper Review*.

Kim, K. H., Cramond, B., & Bandalos, D. L. (2006). The latent structure and measurement invariance of scores on the Torrance tests of creative thinking –figural. *Educational and Psychological Measurement, 66*, 459–477. https://doi.org/10.1177/0013164405282456

Kim, K. H., Lee, H., Chae, K., Andersen, L., & Lawrence, C. (2011). Creativity and Confucianism among American and Korean educators. *Creativity Research Journal, 23*, 357–371. https://doi.org/10.1080/10400419.2011.621853

Kim, K. H., & VanTassel-Baska, J. (2010). The relationship between creativity and behavior problems among underachievers. *Creativity Research Journal, 22*, 185–193. https://doi.org/10.1080/10400419.2011.627805

Kim, M. K., Roh, I. S., & Cho, M. K. (2016). Creativity of gifted students in an integrated math-science instruction. *Thinking Skills and Creativity, 19*, 38–48. https://doi.org/10.1016/j.tsc.2015.07.004

Kim, S., & Lee, J.-H. (2010). Private tutoring and demand for education in South Korea. *Economic Development and Cultural Change, 58*, 259–296. https://doi.org/10.1086/648186

Kines, S. W. (2012). The viability of English television programs inside of South Korean class-rooms. *Journal of International Education Research, 8*, 183–196. https://doi.org/10.19030/jier.v8i3.7100

Koo, H. (2007). The changing faces of inequality in South Korea in the age of globalization. *Korean Studies, 31*, 1–18. https://doi.org/10.1353/ks.2008.0018

Korea Educational Development Institute (KEDI). (2007). For the institutional improvement of the special purpose high schools, we have to find them a right place. Seoul, South Korea: Author.

Korea Foundation for the Advancement of Science & Creativity (KOFAC). (2018). What we do. Retrieved from https://www.kofac.re.kr/?page_id=1784.

Korea Foundation for the Advancement of Science (KOFAC). (2017). The Korea Ministry of Education's policy for fostering creativity in students. Seoul, South Korea: Author.

Korea Ministry of Education. (2016). *The Korea Ministry of Education.* Retrieved from http://english.moe.go.kr/sub/info.do?m=020101&s=english

Korea National Statistics Office. (2008). *Statistics on the causes of death.* Retrieved from http://www.kostat.go.kr

Kowatari, Y., Lee, S. H., Yamamura, H., Nagamori, Y., Levy, P., Yamane, S., & Yamamoto, M. (2009). Neural networks involved in artistic creativity. *Human Brain Mapping, 30*, 1678–1690. https://doi.org/10.1002/hbm.20633

Koyama, A., Matsushita, M., Sshijima, H., Jono, T., & Ikeda, M. (2014). Association between depression, examination-related stressors, and sense of coherence: The ronin-sei study. *Psychiatry and Clinical Neurosciences, 68*, 441–447. https://doi.org/10.1111/pcn.12146

Kurman, J., Liem, G. A., Ivancovsky, T., Morio, H., & Lee, J. (2015). Regulatory focus as an explanatory variable for cross-cultural differences in achievement-related behavior. *Journal of Cross-Cultural Psychology, 46*, 171–190. https://doi.org/10.1177/0022022114558090

Kwang, N. A., & Rodrigues, D. (2002). A big-five personality profile of the adaptor and innovator. *Journal of Creative Behavior, 36*, 254–268. https://doi.org/10.1002/j.2162-6057.2002.tb01068

Kwon, Y. G. (2009). *An analysis on the occupations of the parents in foreign language high schools and independent high schools.* Seoul, South Korea: Democratic Labor Party.

Lane, J., Lane, A. M., & Kyprianou, A. (2004). Self-efficacy, self-esteem and their impact on academic performance. *Social Behavior and Personality: An International Journal, 32*, 247–256. https://doi.org/10.2224/sbp.2004.32.3.247

Lee, C. J. (2005a). Korean education fever and private tutoring. *KEDI Journal of Educational Policy, 2*(1), 99–107.

Lee, S.-J. (2005b). Democratization and polarization in Korean society. *Asian Perspective, 29*(3), 99–125.

Lee, J. (2009). Universals and specifics of math self-concept, math self-efficacy, and math anxiety across 41 PISA 2003 participating countries. *Learning and Individual Differences, 19*, 355–365. https://doi.org/10.1016/j.lindif.2008.10.009

Lee, J. (2011). South Korean students' 'year of hell' culminates with exams day. *CNN.* Retrieved from http://www.cnn.com/2011/11/10/world/asia/south-korea-exam.

Lee, J., Kang, B., & Lee, D. (2016). Law for gifted and talented education in South Korea: Its development, issues, and prospects. *Turkish Journal of Giftedness and Education, 6*(1), 14–23.

Lee, J. B. (2012). Ethnic nationalism and multiculturalism in Korea. *Multicultural Education Review, 5*(1), 199–215.

Lee, L., & Misco, T. (2014). All for one or one for all: An analysis of the concepts of patriotism and others in multicultural Korea through elementary moral education textbooks. *Asia-Pacific Education Researcher, 23*, 727–734. https://doi.org/10.1007/s40299-013-0146-1

Lee, M., & Larson, R. (2000). The Korean 'examination hell': Long hours of studying, distress, and depression. *Journal of Youth and Adolescence, 29*, 249–271. https://doi.org/10.1023/A:1005160717081

Lee, S. (2016). Identifying and developing inventive talent in the Republic of Korea. *Gifted Child Today, 39*(1), 40–50. https://doi.org/10.1177/1076217515613384

Li, C., & Wu, J. (2011). The structural relationships between optimism and innovative behavior: Understanding potential antecedents and mediating effects. *Creativity Research Journal, 23*, 119–128. https://doi.org/10.1080/10400419.2011.571184

Li, W., Li, X., Huang, L., Kong, X., Yang, W., Wei, D., . . . Liu, J. (2015). Brain structure links trait creativity to openness to experience. *Social Cognitive and Affective Neuroscience, 10*, 191–198. https://doi.org/10.1093/scan/nsu041

Lim, D., & DeSteno, D. (2016). Suffering and compassion: The links among adverse life experiences, empathy, compassion, and prosocial behavior. *Emotion, 16*, 175. https://doi.org/10.1037/emo0000144

Lim, L. (2011). Plagiarism plague hides China's scientific ambition. NPR. Retrieved from http://www.npr.org/2011/08/03/138937778/plagiarism-plague-hinders-chinas-scientific-ambition

Lindell, A. K. (2011). Lateral thinkers are not so laterally minded: Hemispheric asymmetry, interaction, and creativity. *Laterality: Asymmetries of Body, Brain and Cognition, 16*, 479–498. https://doi.org/10.1080/1357650X.2010.497813

Liu, J. (2012). Does cram schooling matter? Who goes to cram schools? Evidence from Taiwan. *International Journal of Educational Development, 32*, 46–52. https://doi.org/10.1016/j.ijedudev.2011.01.014

Liu, Q. (2003). Filiality versus sociality and individuality: On Confucianism as "Consanguinitism". *Philosophy East & West, 53*, 234–250. https://doi.org/10.1353/pew.2003.0015

Looney, J. (2009). *Assessment and Innovation in Education*. OECD Education Working Paper No. 24. Retrieved from http://www.oecd.org/edu/43338180.pdf

Luh, D.-B., & Lu, C.-C. (2012). From cognitive style to creativity achievement: The mediating role of passion. *Psychology of Aesthetics, Creativity, and the Arts, 6*, 282–288. https://doi.org/10.1037/a0026868

Luria, S. R., O'Brien, R. L., & Kaufman, J. C. (2016). Creativity in gifted identification: Increasing accuracy and diversity. *Annals of the New York Academy of Sciences, 1377*(1), 44–52. https://doi.org/10.1111/nyas.13136

Lynn, R., & Meisenberg, G. (2010). National IQs calculated and validated for 108 nations. *Intelligence, 38*, 353–360. https://doi.org/10.1016/j.intell.2010.04.007

Mack-Cozzo, J. B. (2002). If you think we have problems. . . Japan's inferior university system. *The American Enterprise, 13*(6), 46–47.

Marade, A. A., Gibbons, J. A., & Brinthaupt, T. M. (2007). The role of risk-taking in songwriting success. *Journal of Creative Behavior, 41*, 125–149. https://doi.org/10.1002/j.2162-6057.2007.tb01285.x

Marginson, S. (2011). Higher education in East Asia and Singapore: Rise of the Confucian model. *Higher Education, 61*, 587–611. https://doi.org/10.1007/s10734-010-9384-9

Marin, A., Reimann, M., & Castaño, R. (2013). Metaphors and creativity: Direct, moderating, and mediating effects. *Journal of Consumer Psychology, 24*, 290–297. https://doi.org/10.1016/j.jcps.2013.11.001

Mezias, J. M., & Starbuck, W. H. (2003). What do managers know, anyway? A lot less than they think. But now, the good news. *Harvard Business Review, 81*(5), 16–17.

Miller, R. (2015). Learning to love reading: A self-study on fostering students' reading motivation in small groups. *Studying Teacher Education, 11*(2), 103–123. https://doi.org/10.1080/17425964.2015.1045771

Miron-Spektor, E., Paletz, S. B., & Lin, C. C. (2015). To create without losing face: The effects of face cultural logic and social-image affirmation on creativity. *Journal of Organizational Behavior, 36*, 919–943. https://doi.org/10.1002/job.2029

Mol, S. E., & Bus, A. G. (2011). To read or not to read: A meta-analysis of print exposure from infancy to early adulthood. *Psychological Bulletin, 137*, 267–296. https://doi.org/10.1037/a0021890

Moon, R. J., & Koo, J. W. (2011). Global citizenship and human rights: A longitudinal analysis of social studies and ethnics textbooks in the republic of Korea. *Comparative Education Review, 55*, 574–599. https://doi.org/10.1086/660796

Mullis, I. V. S., Martin, M. O., & Foy, P. (2008). TIMSS 2007 international mathematics report: Findings from IEA's trends in international mathematics and science study at the fourth and eighth grades. Chestnut Hill, MA: TIMSS and PIRLS International Study Center, Boston College with Olson, J.F., Preuschoff, C., Erberber, E., Arora, A., & Galia, J.

Mullis, I. V. S., Martin, M. O., Foy, P., & Arora, A. (2012). TIMSS 2011. Chestnut Hill, MA: TIMSS and PIRLS International Study Center, Boston College.

Mullis, I. V.S., Martin, M. O., & Loveless, T. (2016). TIMSS 2015. Chestnut Hill, MA: TIMSS and PIRLS International Study Center, Boston College.

Mumford, M. D., Hester, K. S., & Robledo, I. C. (2010). Scientific creativity: Idealism versus pragmatism. *Gifted and Talented International, 25*, 59–64. https://doi.org/10.1080/15332276.2010.11673550

Mumper, M. L., & Gerrig, R. J. (2017). Leisure reading and social cognition: A meta-analysis. *Psychology of Aesthetics, Creativity, and the Arts, 11*, 109–120. https://doi.org/10.1037/aca0000089

National Association for Gifted Children. (2015). *2014–2015 state of the states in gifted education: Policy and practice data.* National Association for Gifted Children and the Council of State Directors of Programs for the Gifted.

National Center for Education Statistics. (2016). *Program for International Student Assessment (PISA): PISA 2009 results.* Retrieved from http://nces.ed.gov/surveys/pisa/pisa2009highlights.asp

New York Times. (2013). Asia's college exam mania. *New York Times.* [Editorial Board]. Retrieved from http://www.nytimes.com/2013/11/07/opinion/asias-college-exam-mania.html?_r=0

Ng, A. K. (2000). *Why Asians are less creative than westerners.* Upper Saddle River, NJ: Prentice Hall.

Nijstad, B. A., De Dreu, C. K. W., Rietzschel, E. F., & Baas, M. (2010). The dual-pathway to creativity model: Creative ideation as a function of flexibility and persistence. *European Review of Social Psychology, 21*, 34–77. https://doi.org/10.1080/10463281003765323

Nisbet, E. K., Zelenski, J. M., & Murphy, S. A. (2009). The nature relatedness scale: linking individuals' connection with nature to environmental concern and behavior. *Environment and Behavior, 41*, 715–740. https://doi.org/10.1177/0013916508318748

Nisbet, E. K., Zelenski, J. M., & Murphy, S. A. (2011). Happiness is in our nature: Exploring nature relatedness as a contributor to subjective Well-being. *Journal of Happiness Studies, 12*, 303–322. https://doi.org/10.1007/s10902-010-9197-7

Niu, W., & Sternberg, R. J. (2001). Cultural influences on artistic creativity and its evaluation. *International Journal of Psychology, 36*, 225–241. https://doi.org/10.1080/00207590143000036

Niu, W., & Sternberg, R. J. (2002). Contemporary studies on the concept of creativity: The east and the west. *Contemporary Studies, 36*, 269–288. https://doi.org/10.1002/j.2162-6057.2002.tb01069.x

Niu, W., & Sternberg, R. J. (2003). Societal and school influences on student creativity: The case of China. *Psychology in the Schools, 40*, 103–114. https://doi.org/10.1002/pits.10072

Noriko, S., Fan, X., & Dusen, L. (2001). A comparative study of creative thinking of American and Japanese college students. *The Journal of Creative Behavior, 35*, 24–36. https://doi.org/10.1002/j.2162-6057.2001.tb01219.x

Nouri, R., Erez, M., Lee, C., Liang, J., Bannister, B. D., & Chiu, W. (2015). Social context: Key to understanding culture's effects on creativity. *Journal of Organizational Behavior, 36*, 899–918. https://doi.org/10.1002/job.1923

Oh, H., Sutherland, M., Stack, N., Badia Martín, M. D. M., Blumen, S., Nguyen, Q. A.-T., ... Ziegler, A. (2015). A cross-cultural study of possible iatrogenic effects of gifted education programs: Tenth graders' perceptions of academically high performing classmates. *High Ability Studies, 26*(1), 153–166. https://doi.org/10.1080/13598139.2015.1044080

Ono, H. (2007). Does "examination hell" pay off? A cost-benefit analysis of "Ronin" and college education in Japan. *Economics of Education Review, 26*, 271–284. https://doi.org/10.1016/j.econedurev.2006.01.002

Ono, H. (2008). Training the nation's elites: National-private sector differences in Japanese university education. *Research in Social Stratification and Mobility, 26*, 341–356. https://doi.org/10.1016/j.rssm.2008.08.002

Organisation for Economic Co-operation and Development (OECD). (2004). First results from PISA 2003: *Executive summary.* OECD Publishing. Retrieved from https://www.oecd.org/edu/school/programforinternationalstudentassessmentpisa/34002454.pdf

Organisation for Economic Co-operation and Development (OECD). (2015). *PISA 2015 results in focus.* OECD.org. The organisation for economic co-operation and development. Retrieved from https://www.oecd.org/pisa/pisa-2015-results-in-focus.pdf

Organisation for Economic Co-operation and Development (OECD). (2016). *In memorization a good strategy for learning mathematics? PISA in focus.* OECD Publishing. Retrieved from http://www.oecd-ilibrary.org/education/is-memorisation-a-good-strategyfor-learning-mathematics_5jm29kw38mlq-en

Park, C.-M., & Shin, D. C. (2006). Do Asian values deter popular support for democracy in South Korea? *Asian Survey, 46*, 341–361. https://doi.org/10.1525/as.2006.46.3.341

Park, J-M., & Chung, J. (2012). *Military discipline for "soldiers" on Korea exam's front line.* Retrieved from http://www.reuters.com/article/2012/11/05/us-korea-exam id USBRE8A408 Q20121105.

Park, S.-Y. (2010). Crafting and dismantling the egalitarian social contract: The changing state society relations in globalizing Korea. *Pacific Review, 23*, 579–601. https://doi.org/10.1080/09512748.2010.522247

Paulus, P. B., Kohn, N. W., & Arditti, L. E. (2011). Effects of quantity and quality instructions on brainstorming. *Journal of Creative Behavior, 45*(1), 38–46. https://doi.org/10.1002/j.2162-6057.2011.tb01083.x

Pellegrini, E. K., & Scandura, T. A. (2008). Paternalistic leadership: A review and agenda for future research. *Journal of Management, 34*, 566–593. https://doi.org/10.1177/0149206308316063

Plucker, J. A., Beghetto, R. A., & Dow, G. T. (2004). Why isn't creativity more important to educational psychologists? Potentials, pitfalls, and future directions in creativity research. *Educational Psychologist, 39*, 83–96. https://doi.org/10.1207/s15326985ep3902_1

Polman, E., & Emich, K. J. (2011). Decisions for others are more creative than decisions for the self. *Personality and Social Psychology Bulletin, 37*, 492–501. https://doi.org/10.1177/0146167211398362

Prat-Sala, M., & Redford, P. (2010). The interplay between motivation, self-efficacy, and approaches to studying. *British Journal of Educational Psychology, 80*, 283–305. https://doi.org/10.1348/000709909X480563

Putman, V. L., & Paulus, P. B. (2009). Brainstorming, brainstorming rules and decision making. *Journal of Creative Behavior, 43*, 23–39. https://doi.org/10.1002/j.2162-6057.2009.tb01304.x

Qian, M., Plucker, J. A., & Shen, J. (2010). A model of Chinese adolescents' creative personality. *Creativity Research Journal, 22*, 62–67. https://doi.org/10.1080/10400410903579585

Renzulli, J. S. (2005). The three ring conception of giftedness: A developmental model for promoting creative productivity. In R. J. Sternberg & J. E. Davidson (Eds.), *Conceptions of giftedness* (pp. 246–279). Cambridge, England: Cambridge University Press. https://doi.org/10.1017/CBO9780511610455.015

Richardson, J. T. (2007). Motives, attitudes and approaches to studying in distance education. *Higher Education, 54*, 385–416. https://doi.org/10.1007/s10734-006-9003-y

Rietzschel, E. F., Nijstad, B. A., & Stroebe, W. (2007). Relative accessibility of domain knowledge and creativity: The effects of knowledge activation on the quantity and originality of generated ideas. *Journal of Experimental Social Psychology, 43*, 933–946. https://doi.org/10.1016/j.jesp.2006.10.014

Rinne, T., Steel, G. D., & Fairweather, J. (2012). Hofstede and Shane revisited the role of power distance and individualism in national-level innovation success. *Cross-Cultural Research, 46*, 91–108. https://doi.org/10.1177/1069397111423898

Rinne, T., Steel, G. D., & Fairweather, J. (2013). The role of Hofstede's individualism in national level creativity. *Creativity Research Journal, 25,* 129–136. https://doi.org/10.1080/10400419.2013.752293

Roberts, D. (2014). *China exam system drives student suicides.* Retrieved from http://www.bloomberg.com/news/articles/2014-05-15/china-exam-system-drives-student-suicides

Rueda, M. R., Posner, M. I., & Rothbart, M. K. (2005). The development of executive attention: Contributions to the emergence of self-regulation. *Developmental Neuropsychology, 28,* 573–594. https://doi.org/10.1207/s15326942dn2802_2

Rushton, P. J., & Jensen, A. R. (2005). Thirty years of research on race differences in cognitive ability. *Psychology, Public Policy, and Law, 11,* 234–294. https://doi.org/10.1037/1076-8971.11.2.235

Ryan, R. M., Weinstein, N., Bernstein, J., Brown, K. W., Mistretta, L., & Gagné, M. (2010). Vitalizing effects of being outdoors and in nature. *Journal of Environmental Psychology, 30,* 159–168. https://doi.org/10.1016/j.jenvp.2009.10.009

Saeidi, M., & Khaliliaqdam, S. (2013). The effect of socio-affective strategies on students test anxiety across different genders. *Theory and Practice in Language Studies, 3,* 269–274. https://doi.org/10.4304/tpls.3.2.269-274

Schroth, R. A. (2012). The plagiarism plague, America. National Catholic Weekly. Retrieved from http://americamagazine.org/node/150525

Schwebel, M. (2009). Jack London: A case study of moral creativity. *Creativity Research Journal, 21,* 319–325. https://doi.org/10.1080/10400410903297329

Seo, H.-A., Kwak, Y.-S., Jung, H.-C., & Son, J.-W. (2007). Teachers' perceptions of management of science high schools. *Journal of the Society for the International Gifted in Science, 1,* 125–134.

Shavinina, L. V. (2004). Explaining high abilities of Nobel laureates. *High Ability Studies, 15,* 243 254. https://doi.org/10.1080/1359813042000314808

Shin, H.-Y., Kim, K., Lee, C., Shin, H., Kang, M., Lee, H.-R., & Lee, Y.-J. (2012). High prevalence of vitamin D insufficiency or deficiency in young adolescents in Korea. *European Journal of Pediatrics, 171,* 1475–1480. https://doi.org/10.1007/s00431-012-1746-0

Shin, H.-Y., Lee, J.-Y., Song, J., Lee, S., Lee, J., Lim, B., . . . Huh, S. (2016). Cause-of-death statistics in the Republic of Korea, 2014. *Journal of Korean Medical Association, 59,* 221–232. https://doi.org/10.5124/jkma.2016.59.3.221

Shobe, E. R., Ross, N. M., & Fleck, J. I. (2009). Influence of handedness and bilateral eye movements on creativity. *Brain and Cognition, 71,* 204–214. https://doi.org/10.1016/j.bandc.2009.08.017

Simonton, D. K. (2000). Creativity: Cognitive, personal, developmental, and social aspects. *American Psychologist, 55,* 151–158. https://doi.org/10.1037/0003-066X.55.1.151

Simonton, D. K. (2004). *Creativity in science: Chance, logic, genius, and Zeitgeist.* Cambridge, England: Cambridge University Press.

Simonton, D. K. (2008). Creativity and genius. In O. P. John, R. W. Robins, & L. A. Pervin (Eds.), *Handbook of personality: Theory and research* (3rd ed., pp. 679–698). New York, NY: GuilfordPress.

Simonton, D. K. (2009). *Genius 101. The psych 101 series.* New York, NY: Springer.

Sio, U. N., & Ormerod, T. C. (2009). Does incubation enhance problem solving? A meta-analytic review. *Psychological Bulletin, 135*(1), 94–120. https://doi.org/10.1037/a0014212

Smith, S. R. & Lu, C. H. (2015). Nurturing interdisciplinary interconnections to enhance theoretical talent development: Using metaphor to reflect on Ambrose's insights for gifted education. *International Journal for Talent Development and Creativity, 3,* 77–92. Retrieved from https://www.unsworks.unsw.edu.au/permalink/f/a5fmj0/unsworks_modsunsworks_37966

Son, H. (2013). Alternative future scenarios for South Korea in 2030. *Futures, 52,* 27–41. https://doi.org/10.1016/j.futures.2013.06.005

Song, J. (2017a). Rules and conformity frustrate south Korean tech start-ups: Concern is growing that the country could lose its cutting edge. Financial Times. Retrieved from https://www.ft.com/content/77650312-f24c-11e6-95ee-f14e55513608

Song, J. (2017b). South Korea struggles to make its R & D work: Country's conformist culture, lack of innovative thinking and pressure for quick returns are holding it back. *Financial Times*. Retrieved from https://www.ft.com/content/99450bd8-ba71-11e7-bff8-f9946607a6ba.

Sriraman, B., & Dickman, B. (2017). Mathematical pathologies as pathways into creativity. *International Journal on Mathematics Education (ZDM), 49*, 137–145. https://doi.org/10.1007/s11858-016-0822-8

Sternberg, R. J., & Kaufman, J. C. (2010). Constraints on creativity: Obvious and not so obvious. In J. C. Kaufman & R. J. Sternberg (Eds.), *The Cambridge Handbook of Creativity* (pp. 467–482). New York, NY: Cambridge University Press. https://doi.org/10.1017/CBO9780511763205.029

Suen, H. K., & Yu, L. (2006). Chronic consequences of high-stakes testing? Lessons from the Chinese civil service exam. *Comparative Education Review, 50*, 46–65. https://doi.org/10.1086/498328

Sung, Y.-T., Chao, T.-Y., & Tseng, F.-L. (2016). Reexamining the relationship between test anxiety and learning achievement: An individual-differences perspective. *Contemporary Educational Psychology, 46*, 241–252. https://doi.org/10.1016/j.cedpsych.2016.07.001

Tabach, M., & Friedlander, A. (2013). School mathematics and creativity at the elementary and middle-grade levels: How are they related. *Mathematics Education, 45*, 227–238. https://doi.org/10.1007/s11858-012-0471-5

Tadmor, C. T., Galinsky, A. D., & Maddux, W. W. (2012). Getting the most out of living abroad: Biculturalism and integrative complexity as key drivers of creative and professional success. *Journal of Personality and Social Psychology, 103*, 520–542. https://doi.org/10.1037/a0029360

Tam, K. (2013). Concepts and measures related to connection to nature: Similarities and differences. *Journal of Environmental Psychology, 34*, 64–78. https://doi.org/10.1016/j.jenvp.2013.01.004

Tamdogon, O. G. (2006). Creativity in education: Clearness in perception, vigorousness in curiosity. *Education for Information, 24*, 139–151. https://doi.org/10.3233/EFI-2006-242-303

Tan, P., Morgan, S., & Zagheni, E. (2016). A case for "reversed one-child" policies in Japan and South Korea? Examining the link between education costs and lowest-low fertility. *Population Research and Policy Review, 35*, 327–350. https://doi.org/10.1007/s11113-016-9390-4

Taylor, M. Z., & Wilson, S. (2012). Does culture still matter? The effects of individualism on national innovation rates. *Journal of Business Venturing, 27*, 234–247. https://doi.org/10.1016/j.jbusvent.2010.10.001

Tellis, G. J., Prabhu, J. C., & Chandy, R. K. (2009). Radical innovation across nations: The preeminence of corporate culture. *Journal of Marketing, 73*(1), 3–23. https://doi.org/10.1509/jmkg.73.1.3

Thrash, T. M., Maruskin, L. A., Cassidy, S. E., Fryer, J. W., & Ryan, R. M. (2010). Mediating between the muse and the masses: Inspiration and the actualization of creative ideas. *Journal of Personality and Social Psychology, 98*, 469–487. https://doi.org/10.1037/a0017907

Torrance, E. P., & Safter, H. T. (1999). Making the creative leap beyond. Buffalo, NY: Creative Education Foundation Press.

Torrance, E. P. (2000). *Research review for the Torrance tests of creative thinking figural and verbal forms A & B*. Bensenville, IL: Scholastic Testing Services.

Torrance, E. P. (2002). *The manifesto: A guide to developing a creative career*. West Westport, CT: Ablex.

Treffinger, D. J., Young, G. C., Selby, E. C., & Shepardson, C. (2002). *Assessing creativity: A guide for educators*. Sarasota, FL: Center for Creative Learning.

Walsh, C. (2013). *Jobs, Einstein, and Franklin: Isaacson deconstructs their genius and dedication to larger goals*. Retrieved from http://news.harvard.edu/gazette/stroy/2013/04/jobs einstein-and-franklin/

Wang, L. C. (2015). The effect of high-stakes testing on suicidal ideation of teenagers with reference-dependent preferences. *Journal of Population Economics, 29*, 345–364. https://doi.org/10.2139/ssrn.2189268

Warne, R. T., Anderson, B., & Johnson, A. O. (2013). The impact of race and ethnicity on the identification process for giftedness in Utah. *Journal for the Education of the Gifted, 36*, 487–508. https://doi.org/10.1177/0162353213506065

Wiederkehr, V., Bonnot, V., Krauth-Gruber, S., & Darnon, C. (2015). Belief in school meritocracy as a system-justifying tool for low status students. *Frontiers in Psychology, 6*(1053), 1–10. https://doi.org/10.3389/fpsyg.2015.01053

Winner, E. (2003). Creativity and talent. In M. H. Bornstein, L. Davidson, C. L. M. Keyes, & K. A. Moore (Eds.), *Well-being: Positive development across the life course* (pp. 371–380). Mahwah, NJ: Erlbaum.

Won, S. J., & Han, S. (2010). Out-of-school activities and achievement among middle school students in the U.S. and South Korea. *Journal of Advanced Academics, 21*, 628–661. https://doi.org/10.1177/1932202X1002100404

Yang, S., & Shin, C. S. (2008). Parental attitudes towards education: What matters for children's Well-being? *Children and Youth Services Review, 30*, 1328–1335. https://doi.org/10.1016/j.childyouth.2008.03.015

Yeo, J. S. (2016). Gifted education to help students reach their full potential. Retrieved from http://www.koreaherald.com/view.php?ud=20160108000828

Yonngong. (2015). *Suicide No. 1 cause of death for S. Korean teens, youths.* Retrieved from http://english.yonhapnews.co.kr/national/2015/04/28/11/0302000000AEN20150428004700320F.html

Yuan-kang, W. (2009). The irrelevance of Confucian culture in Chinese military policy: Song–Liao war and peace (960–1005). *Chinese Journal of International Politics, 2*, 489–538. https://doi.org/10.1093/cjip/pop008

Zhao, Y., Hoge, J., Choi, J., & Lee, S. (2007). Comparison of social studies education in the united States, China, and South Korea. *International Journal of Social Education, 21*(2), 91–122. Retrieved from https://files.eric.ed.gov/fulltext/EJ782141.pdf

Zhong, C.-B., Dijksterhuis, A., & Galinsky, A. D. (2008). The merits of unconscious thought in creativity. *Psychological Science, 19*, 912–918. https://doi.org/10.1111/j.1467-9280.2008.02176.x

K. H. Kim, PhD, is a professor at the College of William & Mary, USA. She taught English in South Korea for 12 years before earning her PhD from the University of Georgia. Her book, *The Creativity Challenge: How We Can Recapture American Innovation* is a culmination of her research. She co-edited *Creatively Gifted Students Are Not Like Other Gifted Students.* She serves as the co-editor of the *World Journal of Behavioral Science* and is on the editorial board of: (1) *Creativity Research Journal*; (2) *Psychology of Aesthetics, Creativity, and the Arts*; and (3) *Open Psychology.* Her research titled 'The Creativity Crisis' was the subject of a 2010 *Newsweek* cover story, which has caused widespread concern. Her research has been recognised by research organisations such as APA's *Berlyne Award*, ACA's *Paul Torrance Award*, NAGC's *Early Scholar Award* and others.

Jeongkyu Lee, PhD, is Director of the Division of Management and Planning, the Korea Foundation for the Advancement of Science & Creativity (KOFAC). He graduated from the Korea Military Academy before earning his PhD from Tsukuba University, Japan. He is one of the most influential policymakers and advocators of gifted education and creativity in South Korea. He is the incoming (2020–2022) President of both the Korean Society for the Gifted and Talented and the Korean Society for Creativity Education. He serves as a columnist for the *Digital Times, Asia Economy Daily,* and *Healthday News.* He is the author of the *Current Trends and Controversies in the Study of Creativity,* and co-author of *Understanding and Practice of Creativity* and the *Introduction to the Latest Gifted Education.*

Trends and Challenges of Creativity Development Among Selected Asian Countries and Regions: China, Hong Kong/ Macau, Japan, Malaysia, and South Korea

49

Bonnie Cramond, Kyung Hee Kim, T. W. Chiang, Takeo Higuchi, Takuya Iwata, Min Ma, and Ananda Kumar Palaniappan

Contents

B. Cramond (✉)
The University of Georgia, Athens, GA, USA
e-mail: bcramond@uga.edu

K. H. Kim
The College of William & Mary, Williamsburg, VA, USA
e-mail: kkim@wm.edu

T. W. Chiang
Gaterac Limited, Sheung Wan, Hong Kong, China
e-mail: twchiang@gaterac.com.hk

T. Higuchi
Idea-Marathon Institute (IMS Institute), Tokyo, Japan
e-mail: info@idea-marathon.net

T. Iwata
The University of Georgia, Athens, GA, USA

NIC International College, Osaka, Japan
e-mail: takuya.iwata11@gmail.com

M. Ma
Central University of Finance and Economics, Beijing, China
e-mail: catherine.mamin@gmail.com; mamin_psych@163.com

A. K. Palaniappan
Tunku Abdul Rahman University College, Kuala Lumpur, Malaysia
e-mail: ananda4989@yahoo.com

© Springer Nature Singapore Pte Ltd. 2021
S. R. Smith (ed.), *Handbook of Giftedness and Talent Development in the Asia-Pacific*,
Springer International Handbooks of Education,
https://doi.org/10.1007/978-981-13-3041-4_51

Abstract

In this chapter, the authors present scholarly yet practical comparisons of the perspectives of creativity in several Asian countries and territories from the viewpoints of scholars from those areas: China, Hong Kong/Macau, Japan, Malaysia and South Korea. The scholars considered each place's views of creativity in responding to the following questions: (a) "What is creativity and/or the public's perception of creativity?" (b) "In which field is creativity valued?" (c) "What do people see as characteristics of creative people?" and (d) "What is the place for creativity in education?" which includes the sub-questions: What assessments are used to measure creativity? Is there any official government agency that promotes creativity? What methods are used to encourage creativity? These conceptualisations were balanced by understanding current research and literature on creativity, assessing commonalities and differences in the views, and drawing upon cultural influences on those views.

Keywords

Creativity · Asian · Culture · Talent · Assessment

Introduction

The aims in this chapter are to:

1. Explore varying Asia-Pacific academics' perceptions of creativity.
2. Examine perceptions of what creativity fields are valued.
3. Identify some characteristics of creative people.
4. Relate assessment for creativity with the place of creativity in education.
5. Ascertain some official government agencies that promote creativity.
6. Indicate the methods that are used to encourage creativity.

What is creativity? Who is creative? Can and should creativity be nurtured, and if so, how can it be? These questions are at the root of investigations into the nature and value of creativity. The answers are affected by culture, as indicated in the following reports. For the purpose of this chapter, creativity is defined as the process of making something useful and unique, and the successful outcome of this process is defined as an innovation (Kim, 2016, 2017, 2018).

The contrast between the views of creativity in Eastern and Western cultures has been observed over the years and some differences have been noted. One view has indicated that Eastern culture is largely based on Confucianism and collectivism, while Western culture tends to value individualism (Kharkhurin & Motalleebi, 2008; Kim, 2016; Kim, Lee, Chae, Anderson, & Laurence, 2011; Niu & Sternberg, 2006). As evidence of this, studies indicated that people from individualist societies have produced more innovations than people from collectivist societies have (Chua, Roth, & Lemoine, 2015; Gelfand et al., 2011; Kurman, Liem, Ivancovsky, Morio, & Lee, 2015; Rinne, Steel, & Fairweather, 2012, 2013; Shane, 1992, 1993; Tellis, Prabhu, & Chandy, 2009). Related to the contrasting values of collectivism versus individualism is the notion that Western societies emphasise novelty, whereas Eastern societies tend to emphasise usefulness in new ideas (Morris & Leung, 2010). This may be interpreted that Western creativity is more revolutionary or radical, and Eastern creativity is more imitative or incremental (Simonton, 2009). As an extension of the Western emphasis on individuality and innovation, Simonton and Ting (2010) have observed that mental illness is more often associated with artistic creativity in the West than in the East, probably because of the emphasis on Western artists to be unique. Morris and Leung (2010) presented several examples in science and art as indicative of less innovation in Eastern cultures, but then, listed counterexamples of high creativity exhibited by individuals from the East. They posited that "many differences can be explained in terms of the model that creativity means a solution that is both novel/original and useful/appropriate, yet that Western social norms prioritise novelty whereas Eastern norms prioritise usefulness – an account which predicts cultural differences would arise in contexts that activate social norms" (p. 313). Thus, they viewed Eastern creativity as more incremental rather than innovative. They concluded that there are differences in Eastern and Western productivity and influences on creativity, but these influences are complex and change with time and society.

Another view is that the Eastern tradition of creativity is more focused on personal fulfilment, or another state of consciousness, rather than on products (Lubart, 1999). This view maintains that creativity is facilitated through Eastern practices like meditation (Horan, 2009) rather than those that promote innovative ideation. According to Lubart, "creativity is related to meditation because it helps one to see the true nature of the self, an object, or an event" (1999, p. 340). Lubart (1999) further compared this ethereal view of creativity to humanistic psychology's conception of self-actualisation (Maslow, 1962; Sarnoff & Cole, 1983). In other words, the creative product is the refinement of the self rather than an external object. In fact, in discussing his ideas about self-actualisation, Maslow (1962) cited Taoist philosophy.

However, this presents a conundrum: on the one hand, Eastern societies are seen as more collective with the emphasis on the group rather than the individual (Kharkhurin & Motalleebi, 2008; Kim, 2004, 2007, 2009, 2016; Kim et al., 2011; Niu & Sternberg, 2006), but, on the other hand, Eastern creative practices, such as meditation, are seen as facilitative of self-actualisation with an emphasis on personal growth (Maslow, 1959, 1962). So, another cultural difference may be for whom the creativity is valuable. Is it valuable as a benefit to the society, as for the medical, quality-of-life improvements, economic benefits, or world ranking of the society? Or, is it valuable for the health and well-being of the creator? Or both? The relative emphasis on societal recognition and value vis-à-vis personal value may differ by culture too (Morris & Leung, 2010).

Still another difference in views of creativity comes from the assumption that creativity is limited to either artistic expression or product innovation. For definition purposes, this bifurcated view has been defined as either expressive or adaptive creativity (Cramond, 2002; Cramond et al., 2014). Expressive creativity is the type that is used to communicate the creator's emotional and aesthetic senses, as in the arts, and judged by its originality and value in expressing feeling. In contrast, adaptive creativity is innovative; it addresses a worthwhile problem and results in a novel and appropriate solution.

Although this contrast may be meaningful in delineating different types of creativity, in reality, the creative process and product may not be so clearly defined. Robert and Michelle Root-Bernstein (2013), who interviewed top scientists and artists about their creativity, concluded that creative thinking is a universal process that is expressed in different modes: language, mathematics, images, and the like. They agreed with Koestler (1964) that science and art use similar methods to derive their results. Still, the emphasis on the expressive or adaptive creativity may be different in different cultures.

In order to examine the emphasis in several Asian cultures of these different views of creativity, scholars from several Asian countries were invited to respond to questions about how creativity is seen and encouraged in their countries.

Questions and Reflections About Creativity

Scholars from different Asian countries and two territories presented scholarly yet practical comparisons of the view of creativity in China (by Ma), Hong Kong/Macau (by Chiang [although technically part of The People's Republic of China, under the 'one country, two systems' policy, these two territories retain separate governments and cultures for the time being]), Japan (by Higuchi and Iwata), Malaysia (by Palaniappan) and South Korea (by Kim). The scholars answered five broad questions related to creativity development in their respective lands:

1. What is creativity and/or the public's perception of creativity?
2. In which fields is creativity valued (e.g., business, personal relations, education, and the like)?

3. What do people see as the characteristics of creative people?
4. What is the place for creativity in education, specifically, what assessments are used to measure creativity?
5. What official government agencies promote creativity, and what methods are used to encourage creativity?

What Is Creativity and/or the Public Perceptions of Creativity?

In China. The research domains of creativity have become increasingly diversified, such as studying the law of growth of creative persons, talented and gifted children, the brain mechanism of insight, the theory of divergent thinking, cross-cultural research on creativity, scientific creativity and cultivation modes used to encourage creativity, and the model of the creative process (Hu, 2016). In 2013, China announced the "Decision of the Chinese Communist Party Central Committee on Major Issues Pertaining to Deepening Reform of the Cultural System and Promoting the Great Development and Flourishing of Socialist Culture" (USC US-China Institute, 2013, para. 1), which allocated resources to the development of Chinese culture, including the arts, to promote Chinese culture and ward off cultural encroachment from both the West and other Asian countries (ChinaScope, 2019). That said, like most other nations, China perceives innovation as a key to economic success and world competitiveness. Accordingly, in 2006 the Chinese government developed the medium- to long-term plan for the development of science and technology (Springut, Schlaikjer, & Chen, 2011), which set forth a plan to develop China into an innovative society by 2020 and a world leader in science and technology by 2050. However, some researchers, both outside and inside China, question whether the methods that China are using to encourage creativity in business (Abrami, Kirby, & McFarlan, 2014) and the arts (Weiwei, 2012) will be fruitful because of the strict control the government has exercised over the allocation of funds. Yet, even these criticisms reflect a difference in the ways some view creativity and its encouragement.

In Hong Kong/Macau. The input from both the western and eastern cultures shaped the unique cultures of Hong Kong and Macau. As former colonies of the west, Hong Kong and Macau are places of cultural contact between the east and the west. Before its reversion to China in 1997, western values in Hong Kong were only adopted in a selective manner while maintaining a strong tradition of Chinese socialisation practices (Lau & Kuan, 1988). This adoption is similar in Macau, although limited literature can be located. Like most Asians who are collectivists, an individual is perceived as an element of society and is obligated to keep the society in harmony by cooperation, acceptance, compromise, and conformity (Dunn, Zhang, & Ripple, 1988; Kim, 2004, 2007, 2009, 2016; Smith & Bond, 1993). Parents and teachers deliver clear messages on how to behave properly or what is good and bad to their children or students (Rudowicz, Kitto, & Lok, 1994). However, values of collectivism, hard work, and respect for authority are often perceived as promoting submissiveness and conventionalism that are rarely conducive to creative thinking (e.g., Bond, 1991; Kim, 2016; Kim et al., 2011; Liu, 1990; Ng, 2001).

The increasing contact with the Mainland Chinese society after their reversion to China increases the *Eastern* cultural components in both the Hong Kong and Macau societies. However, globalisation also facilitates cultural exchange between the East and the West, and the Eastern and Western cultures become less distinguishable. Following the international trends on placing great emphasis on creativity, the public of both Hong Kong and Macau acknowledge the significance of creativity for the development of their societies.

In Japan. After World War II, Japan had great motivation to rebuild its economy and regain world stature and thus began what has been called the *Japanese Economic Miracle* (Takada, 1999) with the development of companies such as Toyota, Sony, Honda, and Nintendo and their resulting innovations. Japan, initially a student of Western business practices, soon became a world leader. However, the pendulum swung back in the 1990s when the West again gained prominence in the Information Age. Japanese business practices that had been seen as facilitative of innovation began to be viewed as inflexible and inefficient (Crawford, 1998). This change has affected the way that young people in Japan see their own creativity. According to a recent Adobe survey (2017), only 8% of Japanese children in Generation Z (ages 12–18) think that they are creative, as compared to 47% in the USA. However, the change may also be reflective of Japan's method of product development, which has been called more incremental than explosive.

In some fields in Japan, creativity is incremental. For instance, its innovations in the 1980s and 1990s have primarily been continuous improvement in existing products and services that led to Japan's 1980s and 1990s success in the automobile industry and high-technology industries (Herbig & Palumbo, 1996). Chandrasekaran and Tellis (2008) indicated that no other countries can beat Japan for the time it takes for new versions of products to launch. Nagaoka and Walsh (2009) also found that 66% of Japanese inventions result from projects with incremental objectives in Japan. Whereas in the USA this figure is 48%. In addition, inventions result less frequently from projects with serendipitous outcomes in Japan (8%) as compared to the USA (24%).

In Malaysia. As in most Asian collectivistic societies, there is a high emphasis on academic achievement from the early years to tertiary education in Malaysia (e.g., King, 2016). This is evidenced by the fact that Malaysia was ranked 63 among 139 countries in the *Global Creativity Index 2015* (Florida, Mellandar, & King, 2015). Despite this low ranking, the importance of creativity has always been in the minds of Malaysian educators and parents but was rarely given its due emphasis until quite recently when teachers were trained to incorporate thinking skills in their classrooms and students were also assessed on these skills in most public examinations (Andin, Ambotang, & Mosin, 2015). The importance of creativity in Malaysia has mostly been on the final creative outcomes—the product component in the 4P's model proposed by Rhodes (1961)—rather than on the creative process (process) or creative attitudes/personalities (person), or the environment (press). This is evident from the number of programs (e.g., Malaysian Global Innovation & Creativity Centre [MaGIC], 2018) and exhibitions (e.g., Arts and Creativity Exhibition [ACE], 2018) organised that value creativity.

In South Korea. Creativity is the process of making something unique *and* useful, which can lead to a successful outcome that is called innovation (Kim, 2016). Like most Asians who are collectivists and believe that the group's interests override the individuals, Korean people tend to value usefulness and fitting in with the group more than being unique (Kim, 2016). Since 2002, the goal of Korean education is to produce innovators who can lead the world into the twenty-first century (The Korea Ministry of Education, 2016). Korean education specifically aims to produce individuals who are capable of: (a) facing new challenges; (b) creating new values; (c) pioneering a career path; and (d) contributing to community. However, Korean education has been product-focused, which focuses on the creative *outcomes*, rather than process- and person-focused, which puts emphasis on the creative *process* of fulfilling each student's individualised potential through their creative attitudes and thinking skills. Additionally, like most Asians, Korean people tend to emphasise harmonious relationships, conformity and being liked by others more than individualistic values, such as independence, personal choice, self-expression, and uniqueness that are common values of creative individuals (Chun, 2013; Herbig & Jacobs, 1997; Kim, 2016; Kim et al., 2011; Mack-Cozzo, 2002; Rudowicz & Yue, 2000).

In Which Field(s) Is Creativity Valued (e.g., Business, Personal Relations, Education, and the Like)?

In China. The Chinese people have a long history of creativity in a wide variety of fields. From art and architecture to mathematics, medicine, military technology, science, and philosophy, the Chinese are credited with many important world contributions, such as acupuncture, calligraphy, the compass, gunpowder, the Great Wall, kites, paper, pasta, Taoism, and the terracotta warriors, for example. However, these famous innovations occurred a long time ago. In recent years, some have seen the Chinese as more limited in creativity in spite of the government's use of its wealth and political power to emphasise innovation in business and the resurgence of institutions of higher education (Abrami et al., 2014). Only time will tell if this investment in industrial innovation and research in universities will pay off. However, it appears that like many modern societies, the Chinese are emphasising innovation in business and research rather than in the arts.

In Hong Kong/Macau. In response to competition from other Chinese cities, such as Shanghai, and Asian countries, such as Singapore, and to contribute to the rise of the creative economy (Howkins, 2001), the Hong Kong government established the *Culture and Heritage Commission* in 2000 to develop the local creative economy. The *Home Affairs Bureau* (2004) stated that the policy in promoting creative industries was to: (a) improve the business environment; (b) safeguard a free economy; (c) induce local and overseas business investments; and (d) forge partnerships between creative talents and entrepreneurs. Modelled after Florida's (2002) Creativity Index, the *Home Affairs Bureau* (2005) commissioned the *Centre for Cultural Policy Research of the University of Hong Kong* to devise a framework for a creativity index to compare its creative vitality with its neighbours. Florida's index (2002), which ranks countries based on their creativity and economic competitiveness, is in large part determined by the country's talent, technology, and tolerance. In other words, countries that attract and keep talented individuals have advanced technology, are tolerant of diverse lifestyles, and are the most likely to encourage innovation.

Hong Kong's former chief executive pointed out that the development of creative industries must be accelerated to maintain the edge of Hong Kong (Tsang, 2007). However, critics claimed that the government took creativity as a marketing strategy, rather than a legitimate cultural capital. Hong Kong emphasised products that were *financed* in Hong Kong rather than those *produced* in Hong Kong (Chu, 2011), indicating that the role of Hong Kong is a financial centre rather than a base for local creative industries. Ultimately, the conflicting policies and rationales in promoting creativity led to little growth in Hong Kong's creative achievements. In fact, Hong Kong's ranking in the Global Innovation Index has dropped since 2015 (Bernard, Dutta, Escalona Reynoso, Lanvin, & Wunsch-Vincent, 2015; Dutta, Lanvin, & Wunsch-Vincent, 2016, 2017, 2018). It wasn't, until a new indicator—that is school life expectancy—was added in 2018 that Hong Kong had risen in rankings again and the weak indicators included expenditure on education and some indicators associated with research and development and information and communication technologies (Bernard et al., 2015; Dutta et al., 2016, 2017, 2018), which evidence the critics' claim on Hong Kong's weak base for local creative industries. Although limited literature has been located about the development of creativity in Macau, traces of local creative activities were still evident.

In Japan. In the postindustrial economy, many fields in Japan have called for creative and innovative individuals. There has been a need for innovative software writers, scientists, entrepreneurs, and political leaders (Eisenstodt, 1994). If one asks which field of creativity is most valued in Japan, the answer is the business industry. After the invasion led by Admiral Perry in 1853 and even more so in response to their loss in the Second World War, Japan looked to make their education and society competitive worldwide (Organisation for Economic Cooperation and Development [OECD], 2011). They saw industry and technology as the most obvious areas of international competition in the modern age (OECD, 2011) and have been very competitive in those fields (Schwarz-Geschka, 1994). Since 1992, the Japanese 18-year-old population has been decreasing (Central Council for Education, 2012). At the same time, due to the changing landscape of corporations in the global economy, industry in Japan has started calling for a new, more highly trained and skilled workforce with graduates possessing the characteristics of autonomy, persuasiveness, creativity, and a spirit of challenge (Negishi, 1993). With the steadily declining 18-year-old population, companies have had trouble recruiting students who fulfill the needs of industry. A graduate with creativity and other skills is highly valued (Doyon, 2001).

Still, there are cultural traditions, such as 'Omotenashi', which is the general expression of Japanese hearty hospitality arrangements and attitudes (Willis, 2019). The Japanese believe Omotenashi is a kind of creative arrangement or soft creativity. This, along with other traditions, such as hand craftsmanship, are sources of great pride.

In Malaysia. The increase in the globalisation and internationalisation of business as well as the innovations in digital technology, especially with Web 2.0 (Parveen, Jaafar, & Ainin, 2015), have showcased that creativity is crucial for building the creative economy (Gilmore & Comunian, 2016). Businesses, such as small- and medium-sized companies that sell products like birthday cakes and custom-made t-shirts, are increasingly going digital with their e-commerce ventures. Thus, creativity plays an important role on how media is used in marketing, sales, delivery and in ensuring customer satisfaction (Hassell, 2016). Many businesses are creatively using social media, such as *Facebook, YouTube, Twitter*, and *Instagram*, in all aspects of businesses. Air Asia (a Malaysian airline), voted the best low-cost airline in the world for the past nine years, has harnessed the full potential of social media in all aspects of its business (Air Asia, 2017).

In South Korea. Creativity has been valued mainly in science and technology. Since former President Park Geun-hye's inauguration in 2013, the Korean government used *the creative economy centred on job creation* as a core philosophy to secure national economic growth. The Korean government restructured the governance to promote leadership on the creative economy and departmental cooperation while placing an emphasis on the economy being driven by the private sector. The government's six strategies as an action plan for the creative economy include (Cha, 2015):

- Cultivate the culture in which people and government work together.
- Cultivate the ecosystem in which creativity is rewarded fairly and starting a new company is easy.
- Increase the competitiveness of science and technology as the basis of the economy.
- Increase the competitiveness of the venture and small- and medium-sized companies.
- Develop the growth engine for new products and new markets.
- Train creative talent.

As a result, Korean education has aimed to foster creativity in students, especially in gifted students in *Science, Technology, Engineering, and Mathematics* (STEM) fields (Jung & Mah, 2014; The Korea Foundation for the Advancement of Science & Creativity [KOFAC], 2018). For example, Korean education has created STEM-specialised high schools for gifted students and invention gifted education programs (Choi, 2014; Lee, 2016).

What Do People See as Characteristics of Creative People?

In Hong Kong/Macau. Since 1997, Hong Kong has placed a significant emphasis on defining its international visibility by packaging itself as *Asia's world city* (Chu, 2011). One of the means to achieve this was the educational reform in 2000. The Hong Kong government has named creativity as one of the three most significant skills in the education reform since 2000 with the hope to nurture a large pool of creative talents for local creative industries (Curriculum Development Council, 2001). Cheung and Lau (2013) reported a growth in creative thinking among students in Hong Kong before and after the education reform. However, the test-centric education in Hong Kong encourages teaching for rote learning and memorisation to prepare students for high-stakes tests (Cheung, 2012). Additionally, Hong Kong teachers' beliefs in creative students tend to be from their gut feelings rather than empirical research findings, and their knowledge, training, and level of confidence in creative practice are inadequate (Cheng, 2010). Teachers tend to believe that creativity is dependent on birth order, effort, health, and logical thinking (Quek, Ho, & Soh, 2008). Moreover, teacher education and professional development programs in Hong Kong do not adequately increase teachers' understandings of creativity (Cheung & Mok, 2013). Because teachers should be trained in thinking and teaching creatively before they can value and nurture the same creative thinking skills in their classrooms (Abdallah, 1996; Hoseeini & Watt, 2010), a modification in teacher training programs should be accompanied with the educational reform.

In Japan. Japanese people see creative people as extraordinary, special, and chosen people (Adobe Systems, 2017; Semmler, Uchinokura, & Pietzner, 2018). Many people, as in other countries the world over, believe that creative people are born that way, but, reflecting the Japanese value of education, they see the creative as those who graduate from select universities and become Nobel Prize winners or entrepreneurs. Also, they tend not to see themselves as creative and inventive in comparison to those in other developed countries, like the USA, the UK, Australia, and Germany (Adobe Systems, 2017), despite the findings from the *Program for International Student Assessment* (PISA) that Japanese students score the highest in creative problem-solving among East Asian countries (OECD, 2014).

In Malaysia. Malaysia has produced a number of internationally renowned individuals known for their creativity. For example, Jimmy Choo (who has been commissioned by the Queen of England to design her shoes, transformed his business into an international brand after learning the trade of handcrafting shoes from his father), Tony Fernandes (who won an award from the Queen of England for the low-cost airline, Air Asia), P. Ramlee (who excelled not only as an actor but also as a songwriter and singer), Mohammad Nor Khalid (who is known by his moniker Lat, is a cartoonist who began drawing cartoons from age 13) and A. Samad Said (who is a poet and novelist). What are common among these creative individuals include their passion for their work and willingness to break away from the norm. Although these creative attitudes have been recognised as critical for innovation, they are not emphasised in schools or the workplace. Efforts must be made to encourage these creative attitudes in individuals starting in their early years.

In South Korea. Korean society values creativity that leads to innovation, but it does not necessarily value a creative person's characteristics due to the culture's focus on conformity. Thus, the society inhibits original thoughts or expressions in school and at work. Since 2009, the Department of Education promoted new education, called *creativity and character education*, in which creativity is valued mainly within morals. The need for the new forms of education has evolved from the suggestion that one of the causes of the *recent* government officials' corruption and cheating originated from students' cutthroat competition on high-stakes tests that is commonly called *exam hell* in Asian societies (Chun, 2013; Kim, 2004, 2005, 2007, 2009, 2016, in press-a; Mack-Cozzo, 2002; Marginson, 2011; Suen & Yu, 2006; Wollam, 1992; Yang & Shin, 2008). Yet corruption and cheating in Korea are not new, and Korea has always suffered from these since the beginning of high-stakes testing, not because of individuals' selfishness, but perhaps because of their cultural emphasis on filial piety, in-group mentality, and respect for authority. However, Korean educators do not even attempt to stop exam hell because they assume high-stakes testing is inevitable in education. Any attempts to limit such testing have had limited and short-term impacts, probably due to the entrenchment of the practice in the minds of many people and the lack of widespread and long-term policies (Lee et al., 2010). Instead, the new education emphasises self-discipline, consideration of others and filial piety that require conformity and respect for authority (Lee et al., 2011). Developing creativity within such an emphasis on culturally specific morals is an oxymoron because creativity requires questioning authority and thinking in big-picture ways beyond filial piety and in-group mentality (Kim, 2016), although this view may be changing among the younger generation.

What Is the Place of Creativity in Education? What Assessments Are Used to Measure Creativity? Is There Any Official Government Agency that Promotes Creativity? What Methods Are Used to Encourage Creativity?

In China. Research centres and agencies on creativity have begun to emerge one after another. An earlier research and promotion agency was the *Research Center for Supernormal Children*, which is affiliated with the *Institute of Psychology of the Chinese Academy of Sciences* (CAS) and formally established in 1994 (Shi, 2017). A wide range of scientific studies about gifted children have been carried out by this centre, such as the development of evaluation of cognitive abilities and personal characteristics of gifted children; the comparative studies on cognition, memory, thinking styles, observation ability, and personality between gifted and other children; the development of diversified modes of gifted education; and the in-depth investigation of influencing factors on the development of gifted children (Duan, Shi, & Zhou, 2010; Hu, 2016; Hu & Adey, 2002; Luo, 2004; Ma & Van Oystaeyen, 2016; Shi & Li, 2018).

In 2014, a collaborative group for the study of Chinese creativity was set up in the Institute of Psychology of CAS. This work group still brings together domestic experts and organises an annual national conference on creativity. A series of research reports on creativity in China have being compiled by this work group (Hu, 2016). These research reports cover a wide range of domains, including the physical mechanism of creativity as well as the relationships between creativity and the development of human beings, didactics, organisation management, and social culture.

In the same year, the *Research Center of Teenager Innovative Thinking Education of the Chinese Society of Education* was officially authorised to begin. First, many studies and academic exchanges have been carried out based on the theoretical and practical issues of youth creative thinking education. Second, this centre develops many courses and practical activities related to creative thinking, and these courses and activities are also evaluated and promoted. Third, the centre also supplies the services of consultation and training, which are helpful for decision-making based on scientific analyses, information feedback, and professional suggestions.

A series of psychometric scales of creativity developed in the western culture have been widely used in China, such as the *Torrance Tests of Creative Thinking* (Torrance, 1990), *Consensual Assessment Technique* (Amabile, 1982), and others. Chinese researchers also have developed a series of scales for the assessment of creativity, for example, the *Scientific Creativity Test for Adolescents*, the *Technological Creativity Test*, the *Designed Scientific Creativity Test*, the *Creative Personality Scale* for the middle school student, an assessment model of creativity for a technology group, a group creativity assessment based on a mathematical model, an engineering talent creativity scale, and a *Chinese Remote Association Test* (Hu, 2001, 2016; Hu & Adey, 2002).

In Hong Kong/Macau. Besides the educational reform, attempting to be Asia's world city, the Hong Kong government also established the *Culture and Heritage Commission* in 2000 to develop the local creative economy. The *Department for Promoting Cultural and Creative Industries* was established in 2010 to assist in the elaboration of policies in support of the development of the cultural and creative industries. In Macau, some non-governmental organisations, such as the *Macau Creative Industry Association, Macau Cultural Association and Creative Industries Association*, were also set up to coordinate and initiate various creative development not only in the Macau region, but also mainland China, Taiwan and Hong Kong.

Recently, the Macau government has taken the lead to create measuring tools on creativity, and the Macau versions of the *Torrance Tests of Creative Thinking* (Chiang, 2016a, 2016b) were developed, and the Macau version of the *Thinking Creatively in Action and Movement* is also ready for implementation (Chiang, 2018a). With all of these tools ready, the government will set up formal identification procedures of highly creative students and improve the understanding of creativity by Macau teachers. In contrast, the Hong Kong government has relied on school-based management and free market policy significantly. Although an official definition of gifted students was enacted in 1990 (Education Commission, 1990), 28 years later, there is only one standardised tool, the *Wechsler Intelligence Scale for Children*, Fourth Edition, for the assessment of intellectually gifted students in Hong Kong. The Chinese version of the *Wallach-Kogan Creativity Tests* was developed in 2004 for students from grade one to grade nine (Cheung, Lau, Chan, & Wu, 2004). Yet, this tool is not used for official assessment, nor is it well-marketed in schools or to the public. Fourteen years later, the Hong Kong version of the *Thinking Creatively in Action and Movement* was developed (Chiang, 2018b) by an entrepreneur, instead of by the government.

When compared to Hong Kong, the Macau government's investment undoubt-edly increased educators' interests in creativity, thus enhancing creativity develop-ment in education. For instance, some schools in Macau have actively trained their teachers in using the *Torrance Tests of Creative Thinking* to implement school-based education programs for creativity. The development as well as the conceptions of creativity in a region is unavoidably affected by its creative climate, such as cultural background, policies, resource allocations, and education (Kim, 2016). The Macau government's active involvement in creativity education resulted in a change in the conceptions of creativity and a rapid leap in creative activities in the region, while the Hong Kong government's non-intervention policy resulted in a market-driven or user-driven phenomenon of creative activities.

In Japan. Higher education is considered one of the places for nurturing crea-tivity in Japanese students, and a number of different parties in Japan have been discussing higher education reform for several decades in order for its university graduates to survive and exploit their potential and talents in the twenty-first century. In addition, a decline in Japanese businesses has resulted in a decline in budgets for employee training as has been done before. Therefore, they look to universities to give more creativity training through active learning (Ito, 2016), design thinking (Brown, 2008) and the Idea-Marathon System (Higuchi, 2012).

The common view, however, has been that university life is a four-year morato-rium or 'leisure land' between 'examination hell' and a lifetime of regimented employment (Doyon, 2001). Students who have been through 'examination hell' are exhausted both mentally and physically and feel entitled to a period of relaxation, enjoyment, and diversion in their university years (Sugimoto, 1997).

Because there is such strict regimentation in the primary and secondary schools, this is seen as a barrier to the development of creativity in students (Hayakawa, 2004). Even when more creative education methods are encouraged, it is difficult to change such long held traditions, and there is concern that lessening of the stringency would result in a decrease in standards (Hayakawa, 2004). In order to tackle the sharp contrast between stringent primary and secondary schools and less intense higher education institutions, Japan needs to aim for universities in Japan to be places where students acquire a full range of skills: cognitive, ethical, social, creative, and conceptual learning (Central Council for Education, 2012).

Ogawa, Kuehn-Ebert, and DeVito (1991) indicated that there are no existing assessments or instruments to measure creativity in Japan, and one needs to adapt other measurement tools created and developed outside of Japan.

In Malaysia. Higher-order thinking skills, including creativity and problem-solving, were slowly introduced into the Malaysian school curriculum towards the end of the 1990s. The initial efforts were sporadic and did not produce any major changes in the quality of student outcomes. However, during the past five years, more concerted efforts have been initiated to not only incorporate higher-order thinking skills, but these skills were also tested in examinations (Ministry of Education Malaysia, 2013). Because Asian schools are very academic-focused, some educators have made efforts to rethink their approaches for teaching creativity. Some parents also emphasise giving extra-tuition classes to their children on those thinking skills. Schools organise art, poetry, drama, and song-writing competitions to encourage creativity in the arts (Ling, Puteh, & Toran, 2012).

There have been several events contributing to the government's emphasis on creativity, especially in disciplines and vocations that place a high premium on it. The foremost creativity event is the internationally known exhibition, the *International Invention, Innovation and Technology Exhibition* (ITEX, 2018), organised by the *Malaysian Invention and Design Society* (MINDS, 2018). The ITEX showcases unique inventions in various industries from around the world. The MINDS was founded in 1986 to provide an avenue for individuals, universities, and companies to exhibit their innovations. The awards of top prizes during this yearly international exhibition of all unique and useful products are also testimonies to the emphasis that both educational institutions and business enterprises in Malaysia are placing on enhancing creativity and rewarding creative products. Another important development in creative promotion is the formation of the *Malaysian Global Innovation and Creativity Centre* launched by then US President, Barack Obama, and the former Malaysian Prime Minister, Najib Razak, in 2014 to promote creativity, especially in entrepreneurship (MaGIC, 2018).

However, commercial organisations and firms still lag behind in encouraging creativity among their employees. Although there are occasional workshops and seminars organised by employers for their employees, these are usually undertaken to fulfill the training requirements imposed by the government. Moreover, what is valued and rewarded in a society or culture is what is incorporated into the attitudes and thinking of an individual. Although the Malaysian initiatives value environmental factors (i.e., press [Rhodes, 1961] or creative climate [Kim, 2016]) that impact creativity, they are mainly focused on the final creative outcomes (i.e., innovations), which are product-focused, rather than process- and person-focused. More concerted efforts need to be considered as a part of the creative process, and such efforts should nurture individuals' creative attitudes and develop their creative thinking skills in schools and the workplaces to be competitive in this era of the digital environment (Acedo & Cano, 2016; Kim, 2016).

There are many instruments or inventories that have been used to assess creativity. Those used in academic research were mostly based on western cultural values or principles, and translated versions of the western instruments are still used, which include the *Torrance Tests of Creative Thinking: Figural* (Torrance, 1990) and the *Khatena-Torrance Tests of Creative Thinking* (Khatena & Torrance, 1998). Malaysian scholars have also developed measures of creativity using biographical characteristics of individuals or online assessment, such as the *creativity assessment system*, which was based on Torrance's (1974) concepts and dimensions (Palaniappan, 2012).

In South Korea. The Korean Ministry of Education created the *Korea Foundation for the Advancement of Science and Creativity* in 2010 to foster both creativity and character in students, especially in *Science, Technology, Engineering, and Mathematics* (STEM; KOFAC, 2018) by:

- Cultivating a culture of generating and implementing new ideas.
- Developing an online platform to share information.

- Providing entrepreneurs with consulting services to commercialise their products.
- Promoting stories of innovation and celebrating outstanding creative achievements to cultivating a culture of innovation.
- Building science museums, libraries, and community centres to provide resources that support creativity.
- Supporting teachers' professional development and networking.
- Providing new models of curricula for preservice-teacher education.

Moreover, the KOFAC (2011) started *Crezone*, which is a website that offers information and programs for teachers and parents to foster students' creativity and character development (KOFAC, 2018).

Creativity centres in major universities across the country have been created to identify and support students with creative potential. The *Korea Invention Promotion Association* (KIPA) has identified and helped those who have potential to become creative entrepreneurs like Bill Gates and Larry Page and Sergey Brin (KIPA, 2018). The *Torrance Tests of Creative Thinking* and performance assessments have been used often to measure students' creativity (Lee, 2016). With 12 major Korean corporations, KIPA has also identified students who have creative ideas and provided them with mentorships to patent and/or implement their ideas (KIPA, 2018). Finally, KIPA has identified and trained gifted students to become inventors, and their teachers help the students towards pipelines for STEM careers. The students have participated in many official invention contests.

Koreans have boasted having one of the world's most highly educated workforces and students' have high international test scores. However, Korea's focus on short-term results and test scores force students to learn by rote memorisation and be extremely competitive. Although Korean creativity education is product-focused, students, even those who are in gifted programs that are specifically focused on inventions, have difficulty in thinking imaginatively or developing their ideas. Students are provided with a *narrow* framework or fragmented set of activities that are focused on generating new ideas or products. Because students are not provided with many opportunities to think about inventions in their own lives nor in areas other than science or technology, most students try to invent something by only adding miscellaneous functions to it (Lee, 2016). Students' performance, progress, and achievements are judged only by test scores or other measurable results in a short-term period. However, identifying students' areas of interest and talents and developing their expertise take a long time. This requires comprehensive, systematic, and continuous education *processes* facilitated by teachers who have the appropriate expertise in order for students to invent something worthwhile (Kim, 2016; Lee, 2016).

There is evidence that the Korean government has been attempting to increase creativity in education for the past 20 years through "flexibility in the national curriculum, developing teachers' creativity by improving teacher education and establishing supporting systems such as online information websites and teaching and learning materials" (So, Hu, & Park, 2017, p. 77). In spite of these efforts, So et al. (2017) concluded that there has not been a real change in creativity in schools.

Implications: Some East Asian Trends and Challenges of Creativity Development

In conclusion, we can see that native scholars viewing creativity in several Asian countries and territories have answered the questions posed to them with several similarities and a few differences.

What Is Creativity and/or the Public's Perception of Creativity?

Scholars' perspectives about creativity in China, Hong Kong/Macau, Japan, Malaysia, and South Korea were presented to define creativity and share general perceptions about creativity in their respective societies of expertise. They all saw a conflict between the traditional Eastern value of collectivism and the Western value of individualism. They all reported great influence from the West and Internationalism, and some indicated historical and more recent pushbacks to retain traditional values and practices, especially in Japan, Hong Kong and Macau. Japan sought Western know-how after it was invaded and forced into unfavourable trade agreements with the USA in the 1800s. Then, in 1890, 'the Imperial Rescript of Education' was issued in reaction to the public fear of losing traditional Japanese values (OECD, 2011). 'Ever since the rescript was issued, Japanese education policy has been anchored at one end by benchmarking Japan against the world's best education systems and, at the other end, by a firm grounding in traditional Japanese values' (OECD, 2011, p. 139). Although again influenced by the West after World War II, Japan took some aspects of Western education that they found beneficial, such as compulsory education for nine years, but retained the collectivist tradition of holding teachers and parents accountable for a student's behaviour, even outside of school (OECD, 2011). Hong Kong and Macau, having been European colonies, undoubtedly experienced more conflict and blending of values earlier than Mainland China, South Korea or Malaysia. However, with the recent move to become one with China, they have been greatly influenced by traditional Chinese values.

In Which Fields Is Creativity Valued (e.g., Business, Personal Relations, Education, and the Like)?

The scholars similarly reported the importance of creativity in the field of business and to promote economic growth. Additionally, government initiatives in these societies promoted creative industries as a marketing strategy, rather than promoting creativity as a culturally valued characteristic. These governments put specific strategies in place to boost economic growth by developing creativity within their respective countries. In these societies, creativity tends to be celebrated for creative individuals' accomplishments of creative products focused on innovation. Creativity serves a tangible purpose and is not typically celebrated without a tangibly creative product. Equating creativity to production of inventions communicates the importance of the external rewards and recognitions, rather than intrinsic desires and motivations as a result of creativity. Creativity in these countries also serves a societal purpose, specifically for economic development and competition with other global powers, rather than for the purpose of the development of an individual's creativity. Interestingly, while creativity in some forms may be supported in education, there does not seem to be a large focus on creative development in schools. Therefore, creativity in education may not be valued in these cultures as much as in business, industry, or technology.

What Do People See as the Characteristics of Creative People?

The scholars seemed to agree that the term creativity contains culturally specific values, and the ways in which various Asian countries speak of, demonstrate, and celebrate creativity relate to cultural and environmental contexts, which Kim (2016) calls 'creative climates'. They similarly reported that these societies emphasise harmony and conformity over independence and nonconformity, which reflect Confucian values and norms. Because of the importance of collectivistic values, a celebration of an individual's unique thoughts and expressions go against the expectation of fitting in with the status quo. However, independence and nonconformity are critical attitudes that are common among creative individuals and are necessary for innovation (Kim, 2016).

What Is the Place for Creativity in Education, Specifically, What Assessments Are Used to Measure Creativity?

Creativity has been valued and promoted in each society discussed in this chapter but in different ways. In some cases, creativity is encouraged contextually, such as training teachers to teach in ways that nurture creativity among their students. In some cases, initiatives are in place to encourage the development of inventions and inventive students. Individuals are celebrated for their creative achievements, and they report that the education curricula have attempted to incorporate creative teaching practices. However, creativity has not been specifically encouraged in education because high-stakes testing pressures have remained the same in these selected societies. This competitive nature of testing for the purpose of success promotes pedagogy related to rote memorisation. Moreover, despite the governments' attempt to promote creativity for each of their societies, the values of filial piety and respect for authority are more greatly valued than individual strengths or uniqueness.

Gifted students and creativity. All the participating authors from the Asian countries in this chapter reported that gifted students were identified and their needs met in some ways in their education system. Generally, those needs are met in regular schools, in special schools, or in community-based enrichment programs, resulting in fragmented curricula and a test-centric education environment. What is not clear is whether gifted students' creativity for innovation was specifically focused on or developed within these contexts or programs. For example, in practice, Malaysian schools tend to focus more on creative thinking development or problem-solving, which are only small components of creativity for innovation (Hu, 2016; Shi, 2017; Shi & Li, 2018). While in Korea, creativity in STEM seems to be the greatest focus for gifted students, STEM-focused high schools for gifted students specialise in creating inventions (Choi, 2014; Lee, 2016). In contrast, Malaysia promotes creativity through entrepreneurialism and in the arts (Ling et al., 2012; MaGIC, 2018).

The challenges of teachers accurately identifying creatively gifted students and addressing their specific academic needs in these cultural contexts were prominent in this review. That is, given that teachers may or may not have the required expertise, it is still a systematic, complex, and time-consuming educational process for teachers to identify gifted students' areas of interests and develop their creativity for inventions or innovations to ensue (Kim, 2016; Lee, 2016), but these processes are in their infancy it seems. For example, the Hong Kong/Macau government has only just acquired the TTCT and developed a formal identification process as well as provided teacher development on identifying creatively gifted students (Chiang, 2016a, 2016b, 2018a). Similarly, to measure creativity among individuals, all of these societies use translated versions of the TTCT, and most of the countries have also developed their own respective assessments to measure creativity and identify gifted students in education programs.

What Official Government Agencies Promote Creativity and What Methods Are Used to Encourage Creativity?

All respondents reported that their countries or territories are emphasising creativity, usually in education, but most evidently in industry and technology. Various gifted education programs to train creative thinking and incentivise innovation are used in the different areas with differing success.

The country that has been the most successful at innovation, according to the Bloomberg Innovation Rankings (Jamrisko & Lu, 2018), is South Korea—not only the most successful in Asia, but the most successful worldwide for the last several years. DeGraff (2016) theorised that this is because South Korea, like other high-ranking countries, has a "welfare state model, where the government itself is an investor in creative initiatives. This is essentially federal match-making; the government gives start-ups capital and connects them with universities and research labs" (DeGraff, 2016, para., 8). Whether other Asian countries will be able to raise their rankings with similar procedures remains to be seen.

Conclusion

There is a diverse range of research regarding gifted students and creativity, for example, in China, centres of creativity have been developed to explore giftedness and creativity, while in Korea, foundations have been developed to support research in creativity. Additionally, there are a number of research studies comparing creativity in the East and West in which East-West differences in creativity are seen as dichotomous (Kim, 2005; Morris & Leung, 2010; Niu & Sternberg, 2002; Ogawa et al., 1991; Weiner, 2000). However, each culture within these areas plays an integral role in the perceptions of creativity (Kaufman & Sternberg, 2006; Weiner, 2000), and the development of creativity or the public perceptions of creativity can be differentiated among East Asian countries.

Kim's (2016) *Climates, Attitudes, and Thinking Skills* (CATs) model identifies the three steps that are required for innovation, which are the same for the facilitation of creative expression: first, cultivate creative *climates*; second, nurture creative *attitudes* that notable innovators exhibit in common; and third, develop *thinking* skills to achieve innovation. The commonalities from the scholars' perspectives about creativity in Korea, Malaysia, China, and Hong Kong/Macau suggest that they value creativity and innovation. However, these places may not recognise the important role that creative climates play in innovation. In this review, it was suggested these societies can cultivate creative climates by: (a) considering alternatives to high-stakes testing that can still provide equitable ways for students to achieve academic, personal/social, college, and career success and (b) promoting systemic changes in education programs and policies through government- and locally-funded programs. Additionally, these societies can be process- and person-focused, as well as product-focused. This means that instead of just emphasising innovations, which are the tangible outcomes of creative processes, countries that wish to stimulate creativity can: (a) nurture creative attitudes, such as independence and nonconformity and (b) develop creative thinking skills in individual students by promoting opportunities that recognise and celebrate their creative attitudes, behaviours, and thoughts.

This discussion has largely centred on creativity as innovation in business and technology because that is the emphasis that the scholars reflected from their societies. However, all contributing cultures reported some focus on different aspects of creativity development in education, but this may not specifically be for gifted students. Undoubtedly, all of the academics from the varying cultures indicated that they have had great influence worldwide in the arts, but that would be another chapter.

Cross-References

► Creative and Gifted Education in Korea: Using the CATs Model to Illustrate How Creativity Can Grow into Innovation
► Creativity Talent Development: Fostering Creativity in Schools

▶ Diverse Dimensions of Gifted Education: Part V Introduction
▶ Engaging Gifted Students in Solving Real Problems Creatively: Implementing the Real Engagement in Active Problem-Solving (REAPS) Teaching/Learning Model in Australasian and Pacific Rim Contexts
▶ Exploring Diverse Perceptions of Wise Persons: Wisdom in Gifted Education
▶ Fostering and Developing Talent in Mentorship Programs: The Mentor's Perspectives
▶ Gifted Education in the Asia-Pacific: From the Past for the Future – An Introduction
▶ Leadership Development of Gifted Adolescents from a Korean Multicultural Lens
▶ Some Implications for the Future of Gifted Education in the Asia-Pacific
▶ The Career Decisions of Gifted Students: An Asian-Pacific Perspective
▶ The Predictors of the Decisions by Gifted Students to Pursue STEM Careers: The Case of Brazilian International Students in Australia
▶ Transitioning to Career: Talented Musicians' Identity Development
▶ Using the Idea-Marathon System (IMS) in University Education and Creativity Development

References

Abdallah, A. (1996). Fostering creativity in student teachers. *Community Review, 14*, 52–58.

Abrami, R. M., Kirby, W. C., & McFarlan, F. W. (2014). Why China can't innovate. *Harvard Business Review*. Retrieved from https://hbr.org/2014/03/why-china-cant-innovate

Acedo, S. O., & Cano, L. C. (2016). The ECO European Project: A new MOOC dimension based on an intercreativity environment. *The Turkish Online Journal of Educational Technology, 15*(1), 117–125. Retrieved from http://www.tojet.net/articles/v15i1/15112.pdf

Adobe Systems (Firm). (2017). *Gen Z in the classroom: Creating the future*. Retrieved from: http://www.adobeeducate.com/genz/

Air Asia. (2017). *Air Asia named world's best low-cost airline for 9th consecutive time*. Retrieved from https://www.thestar.com.my/news/nation/2017/06/21/airasia-named-worlds-best-low-cost-airline/

Amabile, T. M. (1982). The social psychology of creativity: A consensual assessment technique. *Journal of Personality and Social Psychology, 43*(5), 997–1013. https://doi.org/10.1037/0022-3514.43.5.997

Andin, C., Ambotang, A. S., & Mosin, M. (2015). Teaching thinking skills in teacher education. *International Journal for Educational Studies, 8*(1), 31–44.

Arts and Creativity Exhibition (ACE). (2018). Retrieved from http://www.minds.com.my/index.php/ace

Bernard, A. L., Dutta, S., Escalona Reynoso, R., Lanvin, B., & Wunsch-Vincent, S. (Eds.). (2015). *The global innovation index 2018: Effective innovation policies for development*. Cornell University, INSEAD, & WIPO. Retrieved from https://www.globalinnovationindex.org/userfiles/file/reportpdf/GII-2015-v5.pdf

Bond, M. H. (1991). *Beyond the Chinese face*. Hong Kong, China: Oxford University Press.

Brown, T. (2008, June). Design thinking. *Harvard Business Review*. Retrieved from https://hbr.org/2008/06/design-thinking

Bureau, H. A. (2004). *Culture and heritage commission policy recommendation report: Government response*. Hong Kong, China: Hong Kong SAR Government.

Central Council for Education. (2012). *Summary of report: Towards a qualitative transformation of university education for building a new future – Universities fostering lifelong learning and the ability to think independently and proactively.* Retrieved from http://www.mext.go.jp/en/publi cation/report/title01/detail01/__icsFiles/afieldfile/2016/12/06/1380275_001.pdf.

Cha, D. W. (2015). Building a creative economy: The creative economy of the Park Geun-Hye administration. In *Korea's economy* (Vol. 30, pp. 35–46). The Korea Economic Institute of America.

Chan, D. W., & Chan, L. K. (1999). Implicit theories of creativity: Teachers' perception of student characteristics in Hong Kong. *Creativity Research Journal, 12*(3), 185–195. https://doi.org/ 10.1207/s15326934crj1203_3

Chandrasekaran, D., & Tellis, G. (2008). Global takeoff of new products: Culture, wealth, or vanishing differences? *Marketing Science, 27*(5), 844–860. https://doi.org/10.1287/ mksc.1070.0329

Cheng, V. M. Y. (2010). Tensions and dilemmas of teachers in creativity reform in a Chinese context. *Thinking Skills and Creativity, 5*(3), 120–137. https://doi.org/10.1016/j.tsc.2010.09.005

Cheung, P. C., & Lau, S. (2013). A tale of two generations: Creativity growth and gender differences over a period of education and curriculum reforms. *Creativity Research Journal, 25*(4), 463–471. https://doi.org/10.1080/10400419.2013.843916

Cheung, P. C., Lau, S., Chan, D. W., & Wu, W. Y. H. (2004). Creative potential of school children in Hong Kong: Norms of the Wallach-Kogan creativity tests and their implications. *Creativity Research Journal, 16,* 69–78. https://doi.org/10.1207/s15326934crj1601_7

Cheung, R. H. P. (2012). Teaching for creativity: Examining the beliefs of early childhood teachers and their influence on teaching practices. *Australasian Journal of Early Childhood, 37*(3), 43–51. https://doi.org/10.1177/183693911203700307

Cheung, R. H. P., & Mok, M. M. C. (2013). A study of early childhood teachers' conceptions of creativity in Hong Kong. *Educational Psychology, 33,* 119–133. https://doi.org/10.1080/ 01443410.2012.735645

Chiang, T. W. (2016a). *The Torrance tests of creative thinking, Macao version, Figural version.* Hong Kong, China: Gaterac Limited.

Chiang, T. W. (2016b). *The Torrance tests of creative thinking, Macao version, Verbal version.* Hong Kong, China: Gaterac Limited.

Chiang, T. W. (2018a). *Thinking creatively in action & movement, Macao version.* Hong Kong, China: Gaterac Limited.

Chiang, T. W. (2018b). *Thinking creatively in action and movement, Hong Kong version.* Hong Kong, China: Gaterac Limited.

ChinaScope. (2019). *Cummunist China's cultural invastion of the world* (ChinaScope analysis series). Retrieved from http://chinascope.org/wp-content/uploads/2019/04/CSA20190415_ CCPCulturalInvasionStrategy.pdf

Choi, K. M. (2014). Opportunities to explore for gifted STEM students in Korea: From admissions criteria to curriculum. *Theory Into Practice, 53*(1), 25–32. https://doi.org/10.1080/ 00405841.2014.862117

Chu, Y. W. S. (2011). Brand Hong Kong: Asia's world city as method? *Visual Anthropology, 24,* 46–58. https://doi.org/10.1080/08949468.2011.525484

Chua, R. Y., Roth, Y., & Lemoine, J.-F. (2015). The impact of culture on creativity how cultural tightness and cultural distance affect global innovation crowdsourcing work. *Administrative Science Quarterly, 60,* 189–227. https://doi.org/10.1177/0001839214563595

Chun, A. (2013). De-societalizing the school: On the hegemonic making of moral persons (citizenship) and its disciplinary regimes. *Critique of Anthropology, 33,* 146–167. https://doi.org/ 10.1177/0308275X13478222

Cramond, B. (2002). The study of creativity in the future. In A. G. Alienikov (Ed.), *The future of creativity* (pp. 83–86). Bensenville, IL: Scholastic Testing Service.

Cramond, B., Sumners, S., & (in alphabetical order) An, D. G., Catalana, S. M., Ecke, L., Sricharoen, N., Paek, S., Park, H., Turkman, B., & Turkman, S. (2014). Cultivating creative thinking. In F. A. Karnes & S. M. Bean (Eds.) *Methods and materials for teaching the gifted* (4th ed.). Waco, TX: Prufrock.

Crawford, R. J. (1998, January-February). Reinterpreting the Japanese economic miracle. *Harvard Business Review.* Retrieved from https://hbr.org/1998/01/reinterpreting-the-japanese-economic-miracle

Curriculum Development Council. (2001). *Learning to learn: Life-long learning and whole-person development*. Hong Kong, China: Curriculum Development Council.

DeGraff, J. (2016, January 4). *This is how America can become the world's most creative country*. Inc. Retrieved from https://www.inc.com/jeff-degraff/what-s-wrong-with-america-s-business-model-for-innovation-and-entrepreneurship.html

Doyon, P. (2001). A review of higher education reform in modern Japan. *Higher Education, 41*, 443–470. Retrieved from https://link.springer.com/article/10.1023/A:1017502308832

Duan, X., Shi, J., & Zhou, D. (2010). Developmental changes in processing speed: Influence of accelerated education for gifted children. *The Gifted Child Quarterly, 54*, 85–91. https://doi.org/10.1177/0016986209355971

Dunn, J. A., Zhang, X. Y., & Ripple, R. E. (1988). Comparative study of Chinese and American performance on divergent thinking tasks. *New Horizons, 29*, 7–20.

Dutta, S., Lanvin, B., & Wunsch-Vincent, S. (Eds.). (2016). *The global innovation index 2018: Winning with global innovation*. Cornell University, INSEAD, & WIPO. Retrieved from http://www.wipo.int/edocs/pubdocs/en/wipo_pub_gii_2016.pdf

Dutta, S., Lanvin, B., & Wunsch-Vincent, S. (Eds.). (2017). *The global innovation index 2018: Innovation feeding the world*. Cornell University, INSEAD, & WIPO. Retrieved from http://www.wipo.int/edocs/pubdocs/en/wipo_pub_gii_2017.pdf

Dutta, S., Lanvin, B., & Wunsch-Vincent, S. (Eds.). (2018). *The global innovation index 2018: Energizing the world with innovation*. Cornell University, INSEAD, & WIPO. Retrieved from http://www.wipo.int/edocs/pubdocs/en/wipo_pub_gii_2018.pdf

Education Commission. (1990). *Education commission report No. 4*. Hong Kong, China: Hong Kong SAR Government.

Eisenstodt, G. (1994). Learning *shokku* (higher education reform in Japan). *Forbes, 153*(3), 59–61.

Florida, R. (2002). *The rise of the creative class: And how it's transforming work, leisure, community and everyday life*. New York, NY: Basic Books.

Florida, R., Mellandar, C., & King, K. (2015). *The global creativity index 2015*. Toronto, ON: Martin Prosperity Institute, University of Toronto.

Gelfand, M. J., Raver, J. L., Nishii, L., Leslie, L. M., Lun, J., Lim, B. Duan, C. L., . . . Yamaguchi, S. (2011). Differences between tight and loose cultures: A 33-nation study. *Science, 332*, 1100–1104. https://doi.org/10.1126/science.1197754

Gilmore, A., & Comunian, R. (2016). Beyond the campus: Higher education, cultural policy & the creative economy. *International Journal of Cultural Policy, 22*(1), 1–9. https://doi.org/10.1080/10286632.2015.1101089

Hassell, B. (2016, November). *Creative employees improve customer satisfaction*. Retrieved from https://www.clomedia.com/2016/11/09/creative-employees-improve-customer-satisfaction/.

Hayakawa, M. (2004, June). *Japanese creativity and the current educational reform*. (Asia Program Special Report. No. 121). Washington, DC: Woodrow Wilson International Center for Scholars. Retrieved from https://www.wilsoncenter.org/sites/default/files/asiarpt121.pdf

Herbig, P., & Jacobs, L. (1997). A historical perspective of Japanese innovation. *Management Decision, 35*, 760–778.

Herbig, P., & Palumbo, F. (1996). Innovation: Japanese style. *Industrial Management & Data Systems, 96*(5), 11–20.

Higuchi, T. (2012). *Idea-marathon system*. Retrieved from https://www.ue.katowice.pl/fileadmin/user_upload/WIiK/katedry/kat-badan-operacyjnych/2012-09-08_IMSEn11.pdf

Home Affairs Bureau. (2005). *A study on creativity index*. Hong Kong, China: Hong Kong SAR Government.

Horan, R. (2009). The neuropsychological connection between creativity & meditation. *Creativity Research Journal, 21*, 199–222. https://doi.org/10.1080/10400410902858691

Hosseini, A. S., & Watt, A. P. (2010). The effect of a teacher professional development in facilitating students' creativity. *Educational Research Review, 5*, 432–438.

Howkins, J. (2001). *The creative economy: How people make money from ideas*. London, England: Penguin.

Hu, W. (2001). *The development of adolescents' scientific creativity*. Dissertation of Beijing Normal University. [in Chinese].

Hu, W. (2016). *Progress report of creativity research in China*. Xi'an, China: Shanxi Normal University Press. [in Chinese].

Hu, W., & Adey, P. (2002). A scientific creativity test for secondary school students. *International Journal of Science Education, 24*(4), 389–403. https://doi.org/10.1080/09500690110098912

International Invention, Innovation, & Technology Exhibition (ITEX). (2018). Retrieved from http://pyrolysis-technology.com/index.php/achievements/international-exhibition/international-invention-innovation-technology-exhibition-itex/

Ito, H. (2017). Rethinking active learning in the context of Japanese higher education. *Cogent Education. 4*. https://doi.org/10.1080/2331186X.2017.129818

Jamrisko, M., & Lu, W. (2018, January 22). The U.S. drops out of the top 10 in innovation ranking. *Bloomberg News*. Retrieved from https://www.bloomberg.com/news/articles/2018-01-22/south-korea-tops-global-innovation-ranking-again-as-u-s-falls

Jung, H., & Mah, J. S. (2014). The role of the government in science and technology education of Korea. *Science, Technology and Society, 19*, 199–227. https://doi.org/10.1177/0971721814529877

Kaufman, J. C., & Sternberg, R. J. (Eds.). (2006). *The international handbook of creativity*. New York, NY: Cambridge University Press.

Kharkhurin, A. V., & Motalleebi, S. N. S. (2008). The Impact of culture on the creative potential of American, Russian, and Iranian college Students. *Creativity Research Journal, 20*, 404–411. https://doi.org/10.1080/10400410802391835

Khatena, J., & Torrance, E. P. (1998). *Khatena-Torrance creative perception inventory: Instruction manual*. Bensenville, IL: Scholastic Testing Service. (Originally published by Stoelting, 1976).

Kim, K. H. (2004). *Cultural influence on creativity: The relationship between creativity and Confucianism* (Unpublished Doctoral Dissertation). The University of Georgia, Athens, GA.

Kim, K. H. (2005). Learning from each other: Creativity in East Asian and American education. *Creativity Research Journal, 17*, 337–347. https://doi.org/10.1207/s15326934crj1704_5

Kim, K. H. (2007). Exploring the interactions between Asian culture (Confucianism) and creativity. *Journal of Creative Behavior, 41*, 28–54. https://doi.org/10.1002/j.2162-6057.2007.tb01280.x

Kim, K. H. (2009). Cultural influence on creativity: The relationship between Asian culture (Confucianism) and creativity among Korean educators. *Journal of Creative Behavior, 43*, 73–93. https://doi.org/10.1002/j.2162-6057.2007.tb01280.x

Kim, K. H. (2016). *The creativity challenge: How we can recapture American innovation*. Amherst, NJ: Prometheus Books.

Kim, K. H. (2017). The Torrance tests of creative thinking figural or verbal: Which one should we use? *Creativity: Theories-Research-Applications, 4*, 302–321. https://doi.org/10.1515/ctra-2017-0015

Kim, K. H. (2018). How can parents and teachers cultivate creative climates for children to become innovators? *Childhood Education, 94*(2), 10–17. https://doi.org/10.1080/00094056.2018.1451685

Kim, K. H., Lee, H. E., Chae, K.-B., Anderson, L., & Laurence, C. (2011). Creativity and Confucianism among American and Korean educators. *Creativity Research Journal, 23*, 357–371. https://doi.org/10.1080/10400419.2011.621853

King, R. B. (2016). Is a performance-avoidance achievement goal always maladaptive? Not necessarily for collectivists. *Personality and Individual Differences, 99*, 190–195. https://doi.org/10.1016/j.paid.2016.04.093

Koestler, A. J. (1964). *The act of creation*. New York, NY: Hutchinson & Co..

Kurman, J., Liem, G. A., Ivancovsky, T., Morio, H., & Lee, J. (2015). Regulatory focus as an explanatory variable for cross-cultural differences in achievement-related behavior. *Journal of Cross-Cultural Psychology, 46*, 171–190. https://doi.org/10.1177/0022022114558090

Lau, S. K., & Kuan, H. C. (1988). *The ethos of the Hong Kong Chinese*. Hong Kong, China: The Chinese University Press.

Lee, C. J., Lee, H., & Jang, H-M. (2010). The history of policy responses to shadow education In South Korea: Implications for the next cycle of policy responses. *Asia Pacific Education Review, 11*, 97–108. https://doi.org/10.1007/s12564-009-9064-6

Lee, M. J., Jin, Y. N., Seo, M. C., Kim, J. W., Kim, B. J., Park, H. J., & Lee, J. Y. (2011). *Character education through curriculum and creative experiential activities*. Seoul, Korea: The Korea Institute for Curriculum and Evaluation.

Lee, S. (2016). Identifying and developing inventive talent in the Republic of Korea. *Gifted Child Today, 39*, 40–50. https://doi.org/10.1177/1076217515613384

Ling, K. P., Puteh, S. N., & Toran, H. (2012, June). *Using visual art activities for creativity development in early childhood education*. Paper presented at the 4th National Early Childhood Intervention Council (NECIC), Sibu, Malaysia.

Liu, I. M. (1990). Chinese cognition. In M. H. Bond (Ed.), *The psychology of the Chinese people* (pp. 73–105). Hong Kong, China: Oxford University Press.

Lubart, T. (1999). Creativity across cultures. In R. J. Sternberg (Ed.), *Handbook of creativity* (pp. 339–350). Cambridge, England: Cambridge University Press.

Luo, J. (2004). Neural correlates of insight. *Acta Psychologica Sinica, 36*, 219–234. Retrieved from http://journal.psych.ac.cn/xlxb/EN/Y2004/V36/I02/219

Ma, M., & Van Oystaeyen, F. (2016). A measurable model of the creative process in the context of a learning process. *Journal of Education and Training Studies, 4*(1), 180–191. https://doi.org/10.11114/jets.v4i1.1152

Mack-Cozzo, J. B. (2002). If you think we have problems . . . Japan's inferior university system. *The American Enterprise, 13*(6), 46–47.

Malaysian Global Innovation & Creativity Centre (MaGIC). (2018). Retrieved from https://mymagic.my/

Malaysian Invention and Design Society (MINDS). (2018). Retrieved from http://www.arts.com.my/arts-guide/culture-history/malaysian-invention-design-society

Marginson, S. (2011). Higher education in East Asia and Singapore: Rise of the Confucian model. *Higher Education, 61*, 587–611.

Maslow, A. H. (1959). Cognition of being in the peak experiences. *The Journal of Genetic Psychology, 94*, 43–66. https://doi.org/10.1080/00221325.1959.10532434

Maslow, A. H. (1962). *Perceiving, behaving, becoming. A new focus for education.* (1962 yearbook of the Association for Supervision and Curriculum Development). Washington, DC: National Education Association.

McCreedy, A. (2004, June). *The "Creativity Problem" and the future of the Japanese workforce.* (Asia Program Special Report. No. 121). Washington, DC: Woodrow Wilson International Center for Scholars. Retrieved from https://www.wilsoncenter.org/sites/default/files/asiarpt121.pdf

Ministry of Education Malaysia. (2013). *Malaysia education blueprint 2013–2025 (Preschool to post-secondary education).* Putrajaya, Kuala Lumpur: Ministry of Education Malaysia.

Morris, M., & Leung, K. (2010). Creativity East and West: Perspectives and parallels. *Management and Organization Review, 6*, 313–327. https://doi.org/10.1111/j.1740-8784.2010.00193.x

Nagaoka, S., & Walsh, J. P. (2009). *Commercialization and other uses of patents in Japan and the US: Major findings from the RIETI-Georgia Tech inventor survey*. Research Institute of Economy, Trade and Industry (RIETI). Retrieved from https://www.rieti.go.jp/jp/publications/dp/09e011.pdf

Negishi, H. (1993). Sengo Nippon no gakkô kyôiku to kigyô [Japanese formal education and industry after World War 2]. *Asahi Daigaku Keiei Gakkai Keiei Ronshû, 8*(2), 99–109.

Ng, A. K. (2001). *Why Asians are less creative than Westerners*. Singapore, Singapore: Prentice Hall.

Niu, W., & Sternberg, R. J. (2002). Contemporary studies on the concept of creativity: The East and the West. *The Journal of Creative Behavior, 36*(4), 269–288. https://doi.org/10.1002/j.2162-6057.2002.tb01069.x

Niu, W., & Sternberg, R. J. (2006). The philosophical roots of Western and Eastern conceptions of creativity. *Journal of Theoretical and Philosophical Psychology, 26*, 18–38. https://doi.org/10.1037/h0091265

Ogawa, M., Kuehn-Ebert, C., & DeVito, A. (1991). Differences in creative thinking between Japanese and American fifth grade children. *Ibaraki University Faculty of Education Bulletin, 40*, 53–59.

Organisation for Economic Cooperation and Development (OECD). (2011). Japan: A Story of sustained excellence. In *Strong performers and successful reformers in education: Lessons from PISA for the United States*. Paris, France: OECD. http://www.oecd.org/japan/46581091.pdf

Organisation for Economic Cooperation and Development (OECD). (2014). *Program for international student assessment (PISA), results from PISA 2012 problem solving: Japan.* Retrieved from http://www.oecd.org/japan/PISA-2012-PS-results-eng-JAPAN.pdf

Palaniappan, A. K. (2012). Web-based creativity assessment system. *International Journal of Information and Education Technology, 2*(3), 255–258. https://doi.org/10.7763/IJIET.2012.V2.123

Parveen, F., Jaafar, N. I., & Ainin, S. (2015). Social media usage and organizational performance: Reflections of Malaysian social media managers. *Telematics and Informatics, 32*, 67–78. https://doi.org/10.1016/j.tele.2014.03.001

Quek, K. S., Ho, K. K., & Soh, K. C. (2008). Implicit theories of creativity: A comparison of student-teachers in Hong Kong and Singapore. *Compare, 38*(1), 71–86. https://doi.org/10.1080/03057920701419959

Rhodes, J. M. (1961). An analysis of creativity. *Phi Delta Kappan, 42*, 302–310.

Rinne, T., Steel, G. D., & Fairweather, J. (2012). Hofstede and Shane revisited the role of power distance and individualism in national-level innovation success. *Cross-Cultural Research, 46*, 91–108. https://doi.org/10.1177/1069397111423898

Rinne, T., Steel, G. D., & Fairweather, J. (2013). The role of Hofstede's individualism in national-level creativity. *Creativity Research Journal, 25*, 129–136. https://doi.org/10.1080/10400419.2013.752293

Root-Bernstein, R. S., & Root-Bernstein, M. M. (1999). *Sparks of genius: The thirteen thinking tools of the world's most creative people.* New York, NY: Houghton Mifflin.

Rudowicz, E., Kitto, J., & Lok, D. (1994). Creativity and Chinese socialization practices: A study of Hong Kong Chinese primary school children. *Australasian Journal of Gifted Education, 3*(1), 4–8.

Rudowicz, E., & Yue, X.-d. (2000). Compatibility of Chinese and creative personalities. *Creativity Research Journal, 14*, 387–394. https://doi.org/10.1207/S15326934CRJ1434_9

Sarnoff, D. P., & Cole, H. P. (1983). Creativity and personal growth. *Journal of Creative Behavior, 17*, 95–102. https://doi.org/10.1002/j.2162-6057.1983.tb00979.x

Schwarz-Geschka, M. (1994). Creativity in Japanese society. *Creativity and Innovation Management, 3*, 229–232. https://doi.org/10.1111/j.1467-8691.1994.tb00181.x

Semmler, L., Uchinokura, S., & Pietzner, V. (2018). Comparison of German and Japanese student teachers' views on creativity in chemistry class. *Asia-Pacific Science Education, 4*(1), 9. https://doi.org/10.1186/s41029-018-0025-4

Shane, S. (1992). Why do some societies invent more than others? *Journal of Business Venturing, 7*, 29–46. https://doi.org/10.1016/0883-9026(92)90033-N

Shane, S. (1993). Cultural influences of national rates of innovation. *Journal of Business Venturing, 8*, 59–73. https://doi.org/10.1016/0883-9026(93)90011-S

Shi, J. (2017, April). *Research center for supernormal children.* Institute of Psychology, Chinese Academy of Science. Retrieved from http://cngifted.psych.ac.cn/

Shi, J., & Li, P. (2018). New century gifted education in Mainland China. In B. Wallace, D. A. Sisk, & J. Senior (Eds.), *The Sage handbook of gifted and talented education* (pp. 446–455). London, England: Sage.

Simonton, D. K. (2009). *Genius 101: The psych 101 series.* New York, NY: Springer.

Simonton, D. K., & Ting, S.-S. (2010). Creativity in eastern and western civilizations: The lessons of historiometry. *Management and Organization Review, 6*, 329–350. https://doi.org/10.1111/j.1740-8784.2010.00188.x

Smith, P. B., & Bond, M. H. (1993). *Social psychology across cultures.* New York, NY: Harvester Wheatsheaf.

Springut, M., Schlaikjer, S., & Chen, D. (2011). *China's program for science and technology modernization.* Prepared for the US-China Economic and Security Review Commission. Arlington, VA: CENTRA Technology, Inc. Retrieved from http://sites.utexas.edu/chinaecon/files/2015/06/USCC_Chinas-Program-for-ST.pdf

Suen, H. K., & Yu, L. (2006). Chronic consequences of high-stakes testing? Lessons from the Chinese civil service exam. *Comparative Education Review, 50*, 46–65. https://doi.org/10.1086/498328

Sugimoto, Y. (1997). *An introduction to Japanese society.* Cambridge, England/New York, NY/Melbourne, Vic: Cambridge University Press.

Takada, M. (1999). *Japan's economic miracle: Underlying factors and strategies for the growth.* Retrieved from https://www.lehigh.edu/~rfw1/courses/1999/spring/ir163/Papers/pdf/mat5.pdf

Tellis, G. J., Prabhu, J. C., & Chandy, R. K. (2009). Radical innovation across nations: The preeminence of corporate culture. *Journal of Marketing, 73*(1), 3–23. https://doi.org/10.1509/jmkg.73.1.3

The Korea Foundation for the Advancement of Science & Creativity. (KOFAC). (2011). *Crezone.* Retrieved from https://www.crezone.net/

The Korea Foundation for the Advancement of Science & Creativity. (KOFAC). (2018). *What we do.* Retrieved from https://www.kofac.re.kr/?page_id=1784

The Korea Invention Promotion Association (KIPA). (2018). *About.* Retrieved from http://www.kipa.org/kipa/intro/kw_0101_01.jsp

The Korea Ministry of Education. (2016). *The Korea Ministry of Education.* Retrieved from http://english.moe.go.kr/sub/info.do?m=020101&s=english

Torrance, E. P. (1974). *Torrance tests of creative thinking.* Lexington, MS: Personal Press/Ginn.

Torrance, E. P. (1981). *Thinking creatively in action and movement.* Bensenville, IL: Scholastic Testing Service.

Torrance, E. P. (1990). *Torrance tests of creative thinking: Norms-technical manual.* Bensenville, IL: Scholastic Testing Service. (Originally published by Personnel Press, 1966).

Tsang, D. (2007). *The 2007–08 policy address.* Hong Kong, China: Hong Kong SAR.

USC US-China Institute. (2011). *Decision of the CPC Central Committee on major issues pertaining to deepening reform of the cultural system and promoting the great development and flourishing of socialist culture.* 18th National Congress of the Communist Party of China. University of Southern California (USC). Translation retrieved from http://www.cctb.net/bygz/wxfy/201111/W020111121519527826615.pdf

Weiner, R. P. (2000). *Creativity and beyond: Cultures, values, and change.* Albany, NY: SUNY Press.

Weiwei, A. (2012, September 10). Ai Weiwei: 'China's art world does not exist.' *The Guardian.* https://www.theguardian.com/artanddesign/2012/sep/10/ai-weiwei-china-art-world

Willis, P. (2019). Omotenashi-CX: Customer experience consultancy: ELearn. Retrieved from https://omotenashi-cx.com/what-is-omotenashi

Wollam, J. (1992). Equality versus excellence: The South Korean dilemma in gifted education. *Roeper Review, 14,* 212–217. https://doi.org/10.1080/02783199209553433

Yang, S., & Shin, C. S. (2008). Parental attitudes towards education: What matters for children's well-being? *Children and Youth Services Review, 30,* 1328–1335. https://doi.org/10.1016/j.childyouth.2008.03.015

Bonnie Cramond, PhD, is a Professor of Educational Psychology; is one of the six thought leaders with the National Innovation Collaborative; is on the boards of the American Creativity Association, the Future Problem Solving International, the Global Center for Gifted and Talented Children and the Japan International Creativity Society and is on the review board for several journals. Dr. Cramond has been the Director of the Torrance Center for Creativity and Talent Development, a board member of the National Association for Gifted Children; editor of the *Journal of Secondary Education* and has published numerous articles, chapters and a book. A national and international speaker, she gave a TEDx talk on creativity.

Kyung Hee Kim taught English in South Korea for 10 years before earning her PhD from the University of Georgia. Her book, *The Creativity Challenge: How We Can Recapture American Innovation,* is a culmination of her research. She co-edited *Creatively Gifted Students Are Not Like Other Gifted Students.* Dr. Kim serves as the co-editor of the *World Journal of Behavioral Science* and is on the editorial board of *Creativity Research Journal* and *Psychology of Aesthetics, Creativity, and the Arts.* Her research titled 'The Creativity Crisis' was the subject of a 2010 *Newsweek* cover story, which has caused widespread concern. Her research has been recognised by research organisations such as APA's *Berlyne Award*, ACA's *Paul Torrance Award*, NAGC's *Early Scholar Award* and *Hollingworth Award*, and others.

T. W. Chiang is the Director of an education research and consultation organisation, Gaterac Limited, and is a consultant of schools, the Macau government, and a lecturer of a variety of courses conducted by the government and various tertiary institutions in Hong Kong and Macau. Dr. Chiang has published the *Torrance Test of Creative Thinking* (TTCT, Torrance 1979), Macau version (Chiang, 2016a, b), *Thinking Creatively in Action and Movement* (TCAM, Torrance, 1981), Hong Kong version (Chiang, 2018b) and Macau version (Chiang, 2018a), and articles on giftedness. Dr. Chiang is particularly interested in the identification and nurturance of giftedness, creativity, and twice exceptionality. She is a former primary, secondary, and special school teacher, and was also a Hong Kong government officer of the Gifted Education Section who engaged in policy making, research, curriculum development, and teacher training.

Takeo Higuchi graduated from Osaka University of Foreign Studies, and joined Mitsui & Co., Ltd, Tokyo, Japan. He was stationed in Lagos, Nigeria (3.5 years); Riyadh, Saudi Arabia (8.5 years); Hanoi, Vietnam (2 Years) and Kathmandu, Nepal (4.5 years) with his family. He started Idea-Marathon™ in 1984 and established the Idea-Marathon Institute in 2004 after he retired. He joined the *Japan Advanced Institute of Science and Technology* (JAIST), Study of Knowledge Science, doctoral course in 2011. He graduated with a PhD in 2014. He specialises in human resources and ability development. Higuchi belongs to Japan Creativity Society (JCS) as the chairman of the council and also a member of Knowledge, Information and Creativity Support System (KICSS).

Takuya Iwata is the Student Recruitment Coordinator at NIC International College in Japan.

Min Ma is an Assistant Professor of the Department of Psychology at the Central University of Finance and Economics in China. Dr. Ma has been a Visiting Scholar at the Torrance Center for Creativity and Talent Development at the University of Georgia, and she also has visited the Centre of Cognitive Science at the University of Kaiserslautern. She teaches classes on social psychology and abnormal psychology. Dr. Ma's primary focus of research is exploring the transformational process and transformational abilities in the context of the creative process. Other research areas include models of creative process, perfectionism, materialism, life meaning, and collective intelligence.

Ananda Kumar Palaniappan, PhD, is an Educational Psychologist at the Faculty of Social Science and Humanities, Tunku Abdul Rahman University College, Malaysia, and at the Faculty of Education, University of Malaya. Dr. Palaniappan obtained his Doctorate in Creativity from the University of Malaya in 1994. He specialises in creative and innovative thinking, organisational creativity, and creative problem solving. Dr. Ananda also lectures in research methods, statistics, educational assessments, and has been conducting SPSS and AMOS workshops since 1995 for both academic and non-academic researchers in both public and private organisations. He has researched and published internationally on creativity and the validation of several instruments. He has published in many international journals, including *Perceptual and Motor Skills*, *Journal of Psychology* and *Asia-Pacific Journal of Public Health*. Dr. Ananda Kumar Palaniappan is a member of *American Psychological Association* (APA), *American Creativity Association* (ACA) and *International Association of Cross-Cultural Psychology* (IACCP).

Using the Idea-Marathon System (IMS) in University Education and Creativity Development

50

Takeo Higuchi, Shozo Saegusa, and Daehyun Kim

Contents

T. Higuchi
Idea-Marathon Institute (IMS Institute), Tokyo, Japan
e-mail: info@idea-marathon.net

S. Saegusa
Shujitsu University, Okayama, Japan
e-mail: shosaegu@shujitsu.ac.jp

D. Kim (✉)
Torrance Center for Creativity and Talent Development, University of Georgia, Athens, GA, USA
e-mail: daehyun@uga.edu

© Springer Nature Singapore Pte Ltd. 2021   1135
S. R. Smith (ed.), *Handbook of Giftedness and Talent Development in the Asia-Pacific*,
Springer International Handbooks of Education,
https://doi.org/10.1007/978-981-13-3041-4_52

Abstract

The *Idea-Marathon System* (IMS) can be used to develop creativity by fusing self-reflection, idea generation, and journal writing. As a person reflects on ideas and circumstances, he or she maintains a rigorous written record by enumerating ideas and drawing associated visuals. This particular method of self-reflection was created by Takeo Higuchi when he worked for a trading company. After retiring in 2004, Higuchi carried out several studies in Japan with participants from research institutes and industrial companies. Higuchi used the *Torrance Tests of Creative Thinking* (TTCT; Torrance, 1966/1974) to evaluate the use of the Idea-Marathon System. Moreover, through Higuchi's experiments with participants at various educational institutions, he assessed that the IMS can be useful way for students to capture their creative ideas. Higuchi also found that the IMS journals may help students to develop both creativity and good study habits. In this chapter, the measurement of creativity is discussed based on Higuchi's dissertation when he conducted research in Kobe University. Also discussed in this chapter, is the IMS application used by Saegusa who introduced the topic 'Thinking Ways to Creativity' to a freshmen class in Business Administration at Shujitsu University, Okayama, Japan. In 2016, Higuchi and Saegusa investigated the effects of the IMS by considering variables such as creativity, curiosity, intellectual interest, love of learning, and better cooperation among groups. The investigators introduced the IMS method to undergraduate students enrolled in an 'Introduction to Thinking Methodology' course during 2016 and 2017, with continuing studies in 2018. Throughout the initial two-year collaboration, the investigators' found in their evaluations that the IMS impacted the freshmen participants not only in the number of ideas generated, but also in a final performance assessment. It was also found that faculty support (i.e., weekly communication cards with students) was extremely important for students in order to maintain their motivation for the IMS writing regimen. To determine the impact of the IMS on student performance, a quantitative assessment of students' creativity was used along with an evaluation survey. The goals of these evaluations were to have students use the IMS method as a useful career tool to help their innate creative talents grow by engaging in self-reflection and encouraging written and visual expression.

Keywords

Idea-Marathon System (IMS) · Torrance Tests of Creative Thinking (TTCT) · Continuity power · Creativity · Self-reflection · Written and visual expression

The aims in this chapter are to:
1. Answer the question: What is the *Idea-Marathon System* (IMS)?
2. Reiterate the practical applications of the IMS in Japan.
3. Provide an overview of the impact of the IMS on creativity at Kobe University.
4. Outline the Group Idea-Marathon course for early university students at Shujitsu University.
5. Include some recommendations for progressing forward with the IMS.

Introduction

The curriculum of most universities in Japan is based on a one-way knowledge-delivery method, that is, lecturing, which is a knowledge-memory pedagogy that does not fully engage students' interests and intellectual curiosity (Ministry of Education, Culture, Sports, Science &Technology, 2017a, 2017b). In order to adjust to the needs of a global age, educators, researchers, and politicians realise that the present educational system in Japan needs to emphasise creative development and problem-solving (Sumida, 2013; Todd & Shinzato, 1999). Indeed, creativity is needed at all social levels to accommodate the challenges of a global age (Florida, 2005; Runco, 2014).

It is hard to define or assess creativity (Sternberg, 2018). Creativity can only be captured by embracing several aspects that include a person's creative characteristics, creative processes, creative environments, as well as creative products and achievements (Runco & Kim, 2011, 2013). In general, creativity is the ability to seek and identify solutions or choices within a variety of problem settings or endeavours (Torrance, 1988), the outcomes of which can be entrepreneurial innovations (Shavinina, 2009).

In a global age, students are expected to acquire skills such as: critical thinking, problem solving, collaboration, adaptability, accessing and analysing information, and imagination that lead to the development of their creativity (Bidshahri, 2017; Saavedra & Opfer, 2012; Shavinina, 2009; Trilling & Fadel, 2009). These creative skills are often acquired very quickly and more adeptly by gifted students who have the advanced capacity required to become the future leaders in our global age (Shavinina, 2009; Smith, 2017). Hence, it is apposite to provide the creativity training that enables the development of these particular skills which are supportive of talent development (Todd & Shinzato, 1999). For example, if students are encouraged by teachers to start looking for various creative solutions to the challenges that confront them, their studying style can become more positive, active, and enthusiastic. However, teaching creativity is essential for students to help them find and explore multiple possibilities as problem solvers (Lin, 2011; Renzulli, 2012; Shavinina, 2009; Torrance, 1963; Torrance, Murdock, & Fletcher, 1996).

Developing creativity has been one of the major focal points of studies related to giftedness and gifted education for several decades (Treffinger, 2004). Researchers and educators believe that favorable educational environments can develop the creative potential of gifted students (Smith, 2017; Torrance, 1963) and that creative thinking can be enhanced by providing safe psychological environments

(Davis, 2003, 2004; Schack, 2004), appropriate rewards, and a balance between stimulation and reflection (Cramond, 2005). That is, creativity can be both taught and learned, but consistent support by a more expert person can be needed to maintain students' motivation for creating (Cramond, 2005; Csikszentmihalyi, 1988; Prabhu, Sutton, & Sauser, 2008).

Japanese educational institutions, organisations, companies, industries, and laboratories have been searching for better creativity training methods (Higuchi, 2008a). *Active Learning* (AL) is one strategy that appears to have promise for supporting creativity development (Nishiura & Kunifuji, 2016). AL will be explained in this chapter and the research will be extrapolated that has led to the development of the Idea-Marathon System. Next, the application of the IMS will be discussed with view to exampling its usage in a variety of university contexts. Finally, the chapter concludes with practical and research implications for the future.

Active Learning (AL): A Teaching Strategy for Creativity Development

Active Learning (AL) is a teaching strategy that involves the intensive use of activities rather than lectures to enhance students' creativity development during engaged learning processes (Freeman et al., 2014). There are a variety of methods of AL, such as using visualisation, writing, role plays, discussion, debates, online quizzes, or Cooperative Learning (CL) tasks, such as jigsaw or think-pair-share intermittently during lectures (Higuchi, 2018; Kobayashi, Suzuki, & Suzuki, 2015). AL has been found to be very conducive to student achievement (e.g., Cherney, 2008; Freeman et al., 2014).

The Active Learning teaching strategy has been accepted in Japan and its usage is spreading rapidly among many universities and high schools (Kawamoto, 2016; Kobayashi et al., 2015; Matsushita, 2015). For example, Kawamoto (2016), a specialist of Higher Education with the Ministry of Education, Culture, Sports, Science, and Technology (MEXT) has been trying to increase creativity levels of university students in Japan through the implementation of various AL methods (Kawamoto, 2016; Kobayashi et al., 2015). Kawamoto works with students from Tokyo University (Brand Design Studio), Rikkyo University (Business Leadership Program-BLP), Doshisha University (Project Based Seminar), and the University of Electro-Communications 'Career Design' (Kawamoto, 2016). However, whether the creativity training that the students received has been useful has not been formally assessed.

Additionally, teachers have tried various AL methods to stimulate students' creativity, but are uncertain if their efforts have been effective (Kobayashi et al., 2015). This uncertainty may be due to the lack of creativity standards and methods for assessing creativity, particularly the ability to measure creativity quantitatively. As a result, most educational programs in Japan have never been critically assessed for creativity in problem solving as a student outcome (MEXT, 2017).

Since 2015, Active Learning has been a new teaching strategy in Japan. Consequently, it is important for such a new teaching strategy to be evaluated (Matsushita & Ishii, 2016). Multiple approaches for assessing AL have been developed (Matsushita, 2015). For example, when we train students to pick up a new intellectual habit we can design the program so that two instructors are involved. Both of the instructors can assume teaching and assessment responsibilities. The program can be designed so that both qualitative and quantitative data are generated. Students can be asked to complete a certain number of tasks and they can be interviewed at different stages in the program. Matsushita and Ishii (2016) explained that there are various kinds of AL evaluation, depending on the purpose of the learning activity. University students pursue different subject areas and their reactions are all unique, so it is necessary to develop teaching methods and evaluations that are appropriate for the learning of the IMS, which uses an AL teaching process across different subject areas.

What Is the Idea-Marathon System (IMS)?

In 1984, when Takeo Higuchi was stationed overseas as a representative of a Japanese trading company, he started to develop his theory of the IMS. Based on theories of creativity and the needs of educational systems, the IMS is a useful teaching method for encouraging creativity (Higuchi, 2008a). The IMS uses specific Active Learning (AL) teaching strategies, that is, the IMS involves students writing and illustrating thoughts into a notebook every day. He called this method the *Idea-Marathon System* (IMS) because a daily routine requires discipline and perseverance. A person must train his or her body and mind to maintain a daily routine. It takes effort to write each day like a runner who schedules and plans daily for a marathon. A person can capture their stream of consciousness, but at the same time search for ideas about business, life, and family (Higuchi, 1992). When Higuchi proposed the *Idea-Marathon System* (IMS) in 2014, which many researchers and practitioners unconsciously practice daily, he had a particular method in mind that focused on ideas and their visual representation.

The main purpose of introducing the IMS to university students is to give them confidence in their creativity. Concepts, ideas, beliefs, and emotions stream across our minds, so the IMS is a method for recognising the importance of ideas, as it provides a way to capture ideas through the processes of writing and visualisation. Moreover, a written record allows for reviewing, discussing, and taking action to realise the possibilities that these ideas present. Therefore, our research is directed towards understanding how to support and encourage students to use the IMS every day (Higuchi, 2014).

Creativity can bring economic success to individuals and it can create a greater good for the international community. Subotnik, Olszewski-Kubilius, and Worrell (2012) asserted that one of the most important goals of gifted education is to create an avenue for creativity. By preparing individuals for excellence, schools provide the appropriate support to the gifted so that society can benefit from their creative contributions (Shavinina, 2009). The world needs more geniuses to solve the serious problems humankind faces (Sumida, 2013). Methods can be developed to identify the gifted and not rely solely on paper and pencil tests. Indeed, new methods of pedagogy and simultaneously new methods of assessment and evaluation can be provided.

We cannot afford to let talent go unrecognised (Sumida, 2013). Many students go out into society without awareness of their hidden talents. They may have only fixed ways of thinking that have been institutionalised and repeated throughout history (Higuchi, 2018). The IMS helps students realise their interests and talents and consequently, the social and intellectual endeavours they wish to pursue. Therefore, we propose here that since the IMS addresses a person's cognitive facility, it should be a component of the liberal arts curriculum in universities.

The IMS is a method of practice that can be taught to gifted students to assist them with their self-evaluation of their own learning processes, that is, looking inwards for ideas. Moreover, it can help to determine what appropriate ideas are and to support gifted students to think independently and consistently every day (Higuchi, 2014). Group discussions about the IMS can also help to encourage students to explore and discover *various tasks every day*. Additionally, the IMS is a process in which students not only write down their ideas every day but also review them daily.

The particular method of writing down ones' own reflections about routine tasks has proven to be an effective form of idea generation for many companies, universities, and laboratories (Higuchi, 1998, 2008b, 2011, 2014, 2016; Higuchi, Yuizono, Miyata, Sakurai, & Kawaji, 2013; Kawaji, 2011). For example, from 2005 until 2009, the 400 employees of *Japanet-Takata*, the largest TV shopping company, have created millions of written ideas. Other companies, such as 300 researchers from *Asahibeer*, used the IMS from 2010 till 2017. Four subsidiary companies of *Hitachi Ltd.* used the IMS from 2013 till 2016. Since 2015, all newly employed staff of the *Fujitsu-PFU Company* have utilised the IMS, while the *Morinaga Confectionary Company* has used the IMS since 2016. Universities that have adopted the IMS are the *University of Electro-Communications, Osaka Institute of Technology, Shujitsu University, Kobe University, Wakayama University, Fukui University* and *Japan Advanced Institute of Science and Technology*.

Basic Rules Underpinning the IMS

The IMS method is very simple with the following basic rules:

1. Reflect on ideas daily and write your thoughts down immediately in a notebook: note the date, number the ideas, and consider ideas from your personal and professional life.
2. Draw as many pictures as possible.
3. Discuss your ideas with other people.
4. Accumulate, review, and select the best ideas out of your idea inventory and try to implement them.

These four rules represent the underlying principles for the Idea-Marathon System that was developed by Higuchi (1998, 2015, 2018). Whenever ideas are generated in the mind, they may vanish unless they are written down or illustrated in some form, for example, in a notebook. It is important to create pictures and to date and number the ideas. Drawing pictures with ideas in the notebook can help create a clearer understanding of the ideas, not only for the idea creator but also for the classmates and teachers. Through those drawings, classmates or teachers can easily understand that the ideas written are unique and the student may be gifted. The date and serial numbers of the ideas written in the Idea-Marathon notebooks makes it easy to identify the ideas later (Higuchi, 2014).

Designated Targets of the IMS Daily Activities

The four rules or processes are based on Higuchi's own experiences. He claims that by using the ideational AL process of thinking and writing within the IMS on a daily basis an individual will be able to do the following: (a) establish the habit of daily writing; (b) strengthen the diversity and originality of their thinking; (c) enhance curiosity; (d) deepen their thinking and writing by reviewing; (e) obtain better ideas through critical review; (f) share good ideas among IMS users; (g) review, improve, revise, value, and implement ideas; and finally (h) establish concentration and creativity confidence.

Applications for the IMS in Japan

After Higuchi retired in 2004, he initiated research with various universities on the creativity effects of the IMS on students. In addition, he continued to lead creative ability workshops for companies and research institutes in Japan. Higuchi also suggested that university faculties apply the IMS in their laboratories and lecture settings.

Since 2004, the IMS has been introduced into several universities, where many positive evaluation comments have been received from students. One student mentioned that he should have received the IMS lecture in his freshman year instead of his senior year. Furthermore, the IMS was introduced to several laboratories where the researchers used their notebooks to share ideas. For example, Professor Fujigaki has been using the IMS for four years with his Fukui university students. Also, individually, Professor Fujigaki got the first inspiration of 3D scanners from his written idea in an IMS notebook (i.e., The idea number '1830' from Professor Fujigaki's personal Idea Marathon Notebook, July 31, 2018). The universities and laboratories where the IMS has been applied are listed in Table 1.

Table 1 Universities and laboratories where the IMS is applied

Name of Institution	Application Period
Osaka Institute of Technology, Osaka Japan	2006–2009
University of Electro-Communications, Tokyo, Japan	2007–2015
Tsukuba University	2008–2009
Otemae University	2010
Japan Advanced Institute of Science and Technology (JAIST), Ishikawa, Japan	2009–2012
Shujitsu University	2016–Present
Professor Yoshino Laboratory in Wakayama University	2008–Present
Professor Fujigaki Laboratory in Fukui University	2015–Present
Professor Otsu Laboratory in Fukui University	2016–Present
Professor T. Mochida Laboratory in Kobe University	2016–Present
Professor Kazumori Miyata in Japan Advanced Institute of Science and Technology (JAIST)	2007–2014

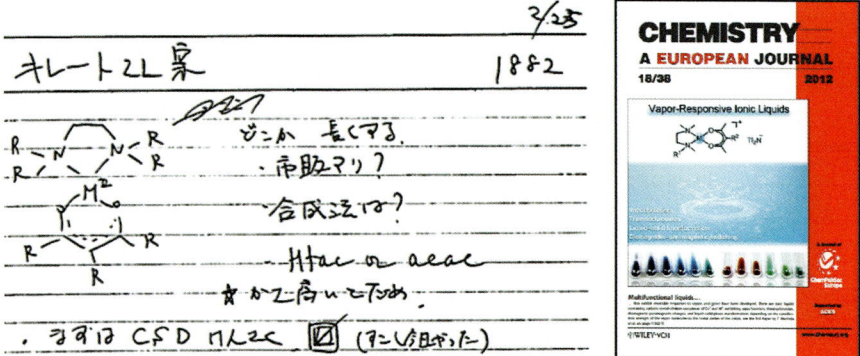

Fig. 1 Development of functional liquids (Saegusa & Higuchi, 2017b)

Kobe University

Professor Mochida who works for a laboratory at Kobe University has been keeping his own Idea-Marathon notebooks since 2006 (i.e., Research Manual of Mochida Research Office, from Professor Mochida's personal Idea Marathon Notebook, Mochida, 2014). He had an idea for a new chemical material called *Functional Liquid* on February 15, 2011, and wrote down the idea in his notebook (Idea No. 1882). He started to develop this idea the following month and produced the material in his laboratory. His invention was published in a European chemistry journal in the following year (Inagaki & Mochida, 2012; Fig. 1).

Japan Advanced Institute of Science and Technology (JAIST)

Professor Kazunori Miyata of JAIST had been looking for a new student group-work system to help create plans and proposals for a virtual reality contest called

International Collegiate Virtual Reality Contest (IVRC) in Japan. That system needed to help students develop creativity skills quickly for the generation of unique ideas within a limited time. He selected the IMS in 2009 for the competition's preparation period. Since 2010, by selecting the best out of many ideas through IMS accumulation, Miyata's students started earning many awards at IVRC (Miyata, Umemoto, & Higuchi, 2010). One of the ideas, *Landscape Bartender*, was created by Noda et al. (2008) and they credited the IMS with helping them create an award-winning project.

Measuring the IMS Impact

From 2012 to 2014, Higuchi applied the Torrance Tests of Creative Thinking (Torrance, 1966/1974) as pre- and post-tests to students at certain universities using IMS for three months of his dissertation research (Higuchi, 2014). The results of these tests showed significant quantitative improvement in several creativity factors for the IMS practising students, compared to the control group. It was reported that once students realised their creativity confidence, they started to apply the IMS to their other courses, using their note taking, asking questions, reporting content creatively, and inventing new products. Most of these participants became more positive in their thinking. As a result of these attempts and reactions from the students, Higuchi found that the IMS had a qualitatively large impact on students' ability to generate creative ideas (Kato et al., 2008). For example, one outcome of the IMS process that was created by Kato (2017), is the *Cooking Simulator*.

The IMS Use at Shujitsu University: Four-Month Trial

The IMS has become a featured lecture topic at Shujitsu University. All the students in one undergraduate department at the University used the IMS for the first time in 2016 (Saegusa & Higuchi, 2016). Nearly all of the 84 undergraduate students wrote down their thoughts every day; this was possibly their first attempt at sustained journal writing. This journal experience was carried out in 2016 and 2017. The goal was 99 ideas in 99 days for each student. One student wrote 330 ideas within 100 days. For 84 students, the total number of recorded ideas was 10,850 in 2016 and, for 96 students, 14,000 ideas were produced in 2017 (Saegusa & Higuchi, 2017a). It was necessary for teachers to provide responses and encouragement on a daily basis; thus, it was a labour intensive experience to keep student motivation high (Saegusa & Higuchi, 2017a, 2017b). Furthermore, there remains the question of delivery, that is, can we encourage creativity by bringing many students together in a large hall and still maintain an *Active Learning* experience?

Some literature suggests that intellectual habituation requires at least three months of daily practice (Lally, Van Jaarsveld, Potts, & Wardle, 2010). Therefore, our goal was to make the IMS an intellectual activity that lasted for four months, hoping that this period of time would be sufficient for students to become comfortable with the daily practice of writing their ideas with corresponding illustrations in their notebooks. Their teacher continued to check and record the number of ideas written weekly per student and honored excellent performance and encouraged mutual friendship and respect between the students (Saegusa & Higuchi, 2017a). The need to examine what types of support the teacher or leader needs, added another aspect to our research project. The teacher-leader must be supportive and able to find ways to promote AL practices without failing students due to negative influences within the group. Through our coaching and lecturing experiences, we found that creativity as well as other outcomes were produced from introducing the IMS to university students, hence, we decided to find out how the IMS might influence students over the course of a semester.

The Shujitsu University trial aimed to explore the outcomes of mastering the IMS which are generally expected to be: (a) reinforcing self-confidence in one's creativity; (b) making journal writing a natural habit; and (c) improving concentration and motivation.

Basic Principles of the IMS Usage at Universities

The IMS method from the teaching perspective consists of two parts, that is: (a) motivation and (b) a continuing support system.

(a) **Motivation: Inspiring lectures and workshops**. At the IMS Orientation in the first lecture of the semester, all participating students were handed a new notebook and given an orientation by Higuchi. He recommended that students think about common tasks. The students immediately started writing their ideas into their notebooks with the goal of continuing to do so daily for the duration of the four-month course.

(b) **IMS continuation-support system for all participants via the Internet**. Starting the IMS is easy, but daily continuation of IMS is not so easy. Most students will become unmotivated and stop using the IMS if not properly and regularly supported during the first three months, which is known as the minimum period to establish a new habit (Lally et al., 2010). Usually, a new habit or custom to do anything daily is difficult to establish even if students understand the benefits of the new habit. Without proper support to continue, students will forget to enter their ideas into their journals. The IMS method with a continual support system has been in the curriculum in one school for adults in Tokyo since 2006. In 2011, however, the researchers did not apply this support system. The first author, Takeo Higuchi, made Figures 2 and 3 from his own records about the participants during the three months of the IMS participation. The horizontal line shows the period and the vertical line shows the number of ideas which each participant created. Hence, after three months, only four people continued the IMS (see Fig. 2).

In 2013, we resumed a full IMS continuation-support system by checking the participants' total number of ideas every two weeks. In 2013, all participants

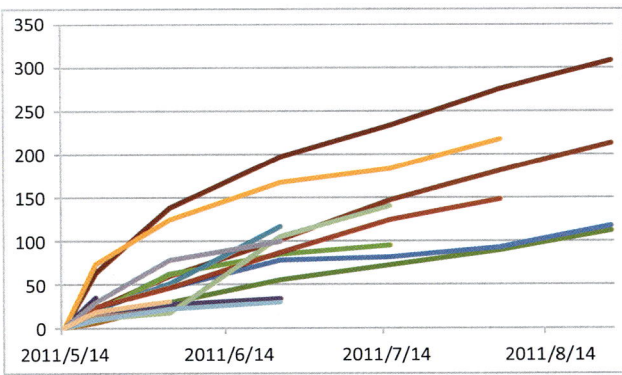

Fig. 2 IMS without continuation-support system for 3 months (24 students in the adult school in 2011) (Saegusa & Higuchi, 2017b)

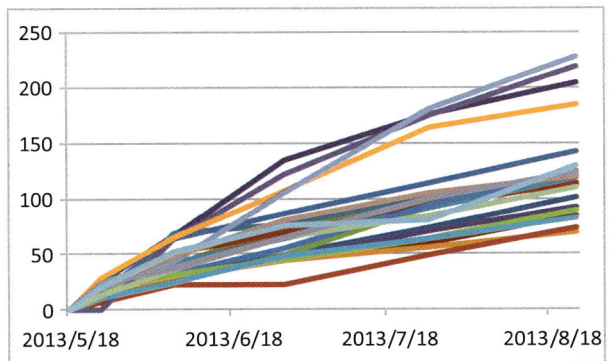

Fig. 3 IMS with continuation-support system for three months (23 students in the adult school in 2013) (Saegusa & Higuchi, 2017b)

completed the first three months (see Fig. 3). To motivate students and to prevent participants from neglecting their journal entries, it was found to be essential to maintain an IMS continuation-support system. The main reasons for students stopping were: (a) just forgetting to do the IMS; (b) tired of thinking, that is, physically fatigued; or (c) mentally frustrated from using their imagination. Students also had trouble choosing a subject or a domain from which to create new ideas. Though the IMS is designed to create ideas from any subject areas, the IMS beginners do not easily choose a new subject (Saegusa & Higuchi, 2016, 2017a, b).

The IMS Project at Shujitsu University

We started a joint research project in 2015 to assess whether the IMS is not only a method enabling students to be more creative, but also a method for study skill development that comes with a designated collaborative setting. Then in 2016, we started to apply the IMS to students enrolled in Saegusa's 'Introduction to Thinking Methodology' course at Shujitsu University, which lasted for four months. New notebooks were distributed to all students during the second lecture with the orientation of the IMS given by Higuchi. This course was for all freshmen in the Business Administration Department of Shujitsu University. The IMS requirements were applied for 14 weeks out of 15 weeks in 2016 and 2017. Students' ideas were counted every two weeks in 2016 and every week in 2017. By the end of the semester, students continued to use the IMS strategies and methods. After the IMS introductory lecture, as shown in Figure 3, students' ideas were counted (self-reported) every week; 14 times during the four-month period. The researchers decided not to inspect or interfere with the participants' personal journals because they did not want the students constrained. Not all ideas are important or appropriate, but the process of generating ideas was the foundational goal. We respected the spirit of students' self-assertions. We accepted the number of ideas in each group, which were checked by their group leaders. They brought the notebooks to class every week and showed and checked each other's work where appropriate. Students looked inside each other's notebooks; however, the researchers refrained from reading individual entries. All the students' numbered ideas were sent electronically to Higuchi every week for analysis. Higuchi sent encouraging comments to each student via the Internet and copied Saegusa. Saegusa, upon receipt of copies from Higuchi, advised or mentored the students in his office if they missed the assignments. Both Higuchi and Saegusa played an active supportive role to help motivate students to use the IMS process or recording ideas daily.

Dual Support System to Maintain Motivation

In 2017, this dual support system developed with Higuchi as the *Outside Teacher* communicating with students and Saegusa via the Internet and with Saegusa as the *Inside Teacher,* lecturing students and communicating with students via class and face-to-face meetings. Upon the completion of the IMS by all students, they decided to conduct an analysis. We had more confidence to encourage students to complete the IMS throughout the 14 weeks of the semester using this dual support system as a motivational process. For students with fewer ideas written down, both Inside and Outside Teachers cooperated so that the Outside Teacher would appeal to those students through the Internet. An actual continuation-support example follows (original is in Japanese):

> It is already two months since you started the IMS. You have been doing well. But it seems that the condition of the idea creation during these two weeks is decreasing a little. The number of ideas was a little less than the number of days in this period. This is the worst thing when young people like you do not try to use your brains to produce original, wonderful, beautiful thoughts.
>
> It's sad! The true ability you have is greater than you think. Don't let yourself be defeated by your own idleness. I believe that you can continue to think and recall various wonderful ideas.

It is now two months since you started. And it is in one more month that habitualisation will be established. Well, have you ever felt that you can think of something daily if you challenge yourself enough and use your strong will? Hang in there, and just think about it this weekend, even early in the mornings on weekdays, please write your ideas down. There is a shining future on the other side.

Special task:

1. You write 5 things you think that are very funny. Write 5.
2. What do you have to do now (other than college reports)? Write 5.
3. Now write 5 items you want to buy.
4. Now, write 5 things you want to start.
5. Now write 5 bad habits you want to stop.

The hints to think about this week:

(1) Usage of cherry blossom petals.
(2) New cocktail of Japanese liqueur.
(3) New cold-proof goods.
(4) Think of any food even if you don't get fat eating any amount of food.
(5) In gymnastics for health and diet, what kind of gymnastics that you plan to start.
(6) How to prevent fraud.
(7) Think of the differences between Western and Oriental cultures.
(8) Think of a new design, function table.
(9) Effective utilisation of an eyeglass case.
(10) New cooking with chocolate.
(11) Seasoning added to a cup of fried noodles.
(12) What if you have a reading club among the family.

Please continue your hard work.
Dr. Takeo Higuchi (knowledge science)
Idea Marathon Institute

The Inside Teacher Saegusa talked with and encouraged these students several times in his office and in class. The group activity strategy for the AL method also helped to inspire, motivate, and support students who submitted fewer ideas. Saegusa advised the hesitating and struggling students with statements such as "As you are proving to be actually creative, be confident and try to write more ideas in the notebooks". The researchers stayed positive and encouraging so that all students maintained motivation and continued to think and write until the end of the semester. Due to this dual support system, we encouraged confidence in at least a half-dozen unmotivated, hesitating, and struggling students to increase their creative ideas, hence increasing the overall numbers of ideas.

Cumulative Number of Ideas by Each Student

The lines on the graph in Figure 4 reflect the continuing IMS and show that the number of ideas increased for 97 individuals every week (from the 1st IMS week to the 14th IMS week), while the red bold line indicates the minimum number of ideas based on the calculation of one idea per day from the start date (i.e., Target line).

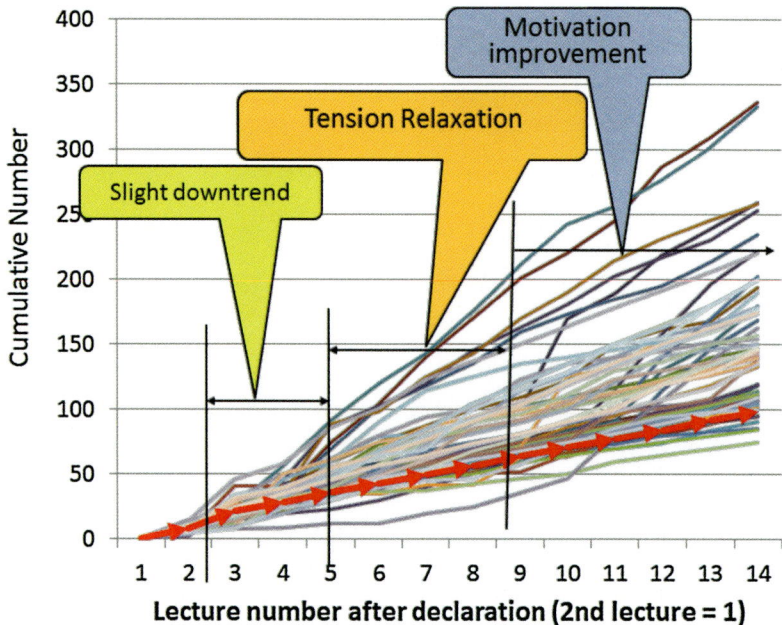

Fig. 4 Graph of number of ideas of all participants in the course [IMS's 1st week means 'one week after starting IMS' which is the 2nd week of course. Therefore, 14th week of IMS means 15th week of final lecture] (arrow in red is target line; Saegusa & Higuchi, 2017b)

In summary, the key points are: (a) no student stopped using the IMS and (b) only a few students were below the target line, but they started to improve after 10 weeks. In this course, the target number of ideas for the semester was expressed as 99 ideas within 99 days. The results revealed an average of 130 written ideas per student. By the 14 weeks, the evaluations suggested three trends: (a) a slight downtrend in the number of ideas; (b) that tension seemed to relax; and (c) that motivation seemed to improve (Saegusa & Higuchi, 2017b).

Graph of Differentiating Increments of Ideas Each Week

From the differentiating increments in the number of ideas of all participating students up to the 13th week, we observed three peaks where students tried harder at thinking of ideas and recording ideas, as shown in Figure 5. After a slight down trend, the first peak occurred three weeks from the beginning. Then at the 8th and 10th weeks, there were wider simultaneous peaks seen among many students.

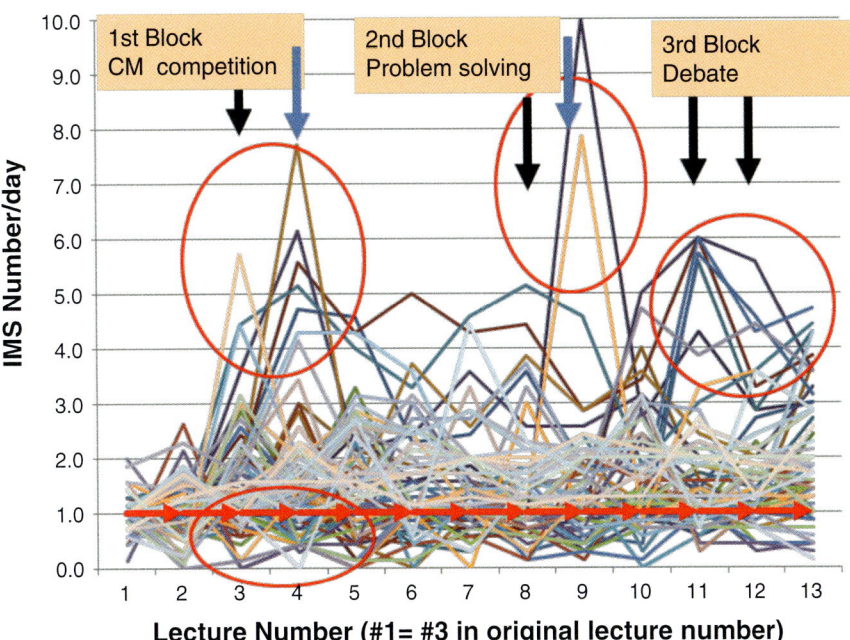

Fig. 5 Magnification of Difference from Target Line (Saegusa & Higuchi, 2017a)

Applications of the IMS for Students

For undergraduate students, we explained that they can apply the IMS to: (a) find a theme for their report papers and graduation theses and (b) improve their creative power to make their lives more valuable and interesting. In Saegusa's course, the group leaders recorded the number of ideas for their group members and reported the data to Saegusa (Inside Teacher) every week. Saegusa emailed the entire list of idea numbers to Higuchi (Outside Teacher) on the same day of the lectures, Thursdays. Upon receipt of all the idea numbers each week, Higuchi worked to analyse the changing pattern and tendency of the idea increments of all students and began sending individual comments and advice directly to all students via email texts. This procedure of sending specific comments to each student was not easy and is very time-consuming but quite powerful.

Continuation-Support System Involving Human Interaction

Providing advice and personal comments to students is appealing to students and has become the active teaching method, involving:

1. Sending comments concerning the total number of individual ideas each week to all students via e-mail and copying Saegusa (Higuchi).
2. Saegusa writing comments on the communication card or reports on which students wrote what they learned that week (Saegusa).
3. Direct verbal encouragement regarding the IMS in class each week (Saegusa).
4. Providing face-to-face advice in the professor's office to students who had fewer numbers of ideas (Saegusa).
5. Providing personal encouragement using email and copying Higuchi (Saegusa).
6. Emailing a weekly newsletter with hints for creating ideas to all students and copying Saegusa (Higuchi).
7. The researchers discussing the personal-encouragement plans via e-mail, focusing on struggling students, stopping indicators and other factors (Saegusa and Higuchi).
8. After Higuchi gave personal advice to a student, Saegusa immediately followed through by adding his support to this student via e-mail, as a coordinated movement (Higuchi and Saegusa).

Therefore, this IMS continuation-support system became an essential part of the IMS that is now delivered at universities and in corporate settings.

Relationships Between Students' Grades, C-Card Grades, and Number of Ideas

Every week at the end of class, Saegusa requested students to submit their C-cards (Communication Card) on which students wrote their opinions, impressions, proposals, and reflections about the class. On each C-card, Saegusa wrote a comment as feedback. The importance of writing is often mentioned in various active learning activities (Bonwell & Eison, 1991). Bonwell and Eison (1991) stressed the importance of writing in class, but Higuchi and Saegusa advised students to think and write always and on any occasion. We don't know when ideas are going to come to our minds.

Correlations among variables: Number of ideas, C-Card grades and final grades. In 2017, Higuchi and Saegusa devised a plan to analyse features of the IMS model for creativity generation. T-tests for significance of means of individual variables were conducted and correlation coefficients between variables were calculated. Several correlations were investigated: (a) the number of ideas generated by individual students; (b) the weekly report (C-Card) grades; and (c) the final course grades. The strong relationship between the C-card grade and final grade is shown in Figure 6. The C-card grade shows how seriously the student was taking the lecture on that day. The final grade is the grade decided by Saegusa at the end of the semester according to the syllabus. Saegusa found improvement in study motivation from the C-card grades by students with more written ideas.

Relationship between students' final grades and the number of ideas. At the end of the semester, many students remained at around the target idea line of 99

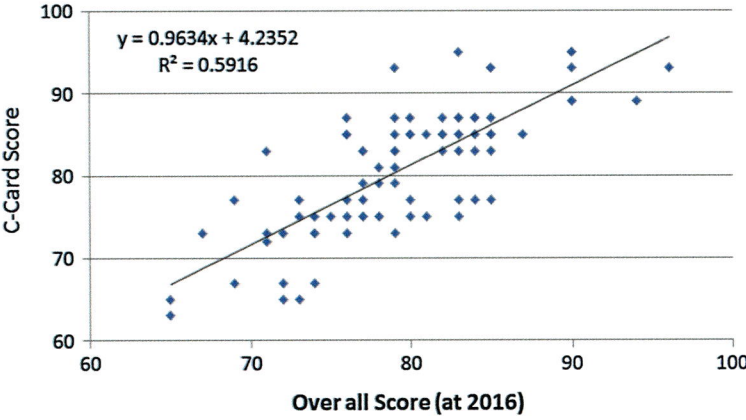

Fig. 6 Relation between C-card score and final score (Saegusa & Higuchi, 2016)

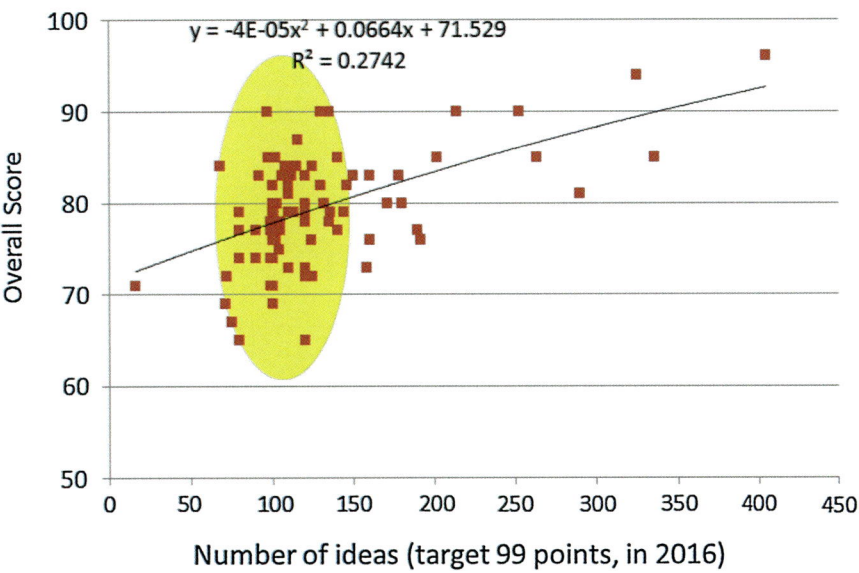

Fig. 7 Relationship between final grades of all students and the number of ideas (Saegusa & Higuchi, 2016)

ideas. Figure 7 shows a reasonable relationship between the final grades of all students and the number of ideas generated. Notably, some students whose number of ideas were at first below the target line, rapidly recovered and increased in the middle, possibly due to the dual support system.

Students' efforts to continue the IMS. The effort by struggling students to catch up to the minimum number of ideas according to the data is shown in Figure 8. Higuchi and Saegusa recommended that, "the students think and describe one idea per day, every day". The researchers needed to check, evaluate, and encourage student activity based on the number of ideas they generated. The data collected was divided into three zones. This was based on the number of ideas generated by the participants, that are: (a) under one idea per day is marked as the red zone; (b) 1–1.4 ideas are marked as the yellow zone; and (c) over 1.4 ideas are marked as the blue zone. The target was one idea per day, every day. We decided to use 140% of the target line as the cut off mark. We had no strong reason for using 1.4, other than those participants under one idea definitely needed encouragement, and those close to the mark needed to 'keep up the good work'. Consequently, we encouraged the students in the red zone to try harder by trying to connect with something they had seen or experienced; similarly, the students in the yellow zone were also encouraged. So, the number 1.4 is an indicator of where to focus encouragement.

The first problem regarding the students who had low performance indicators for the IMS model appeared around the 4th week. There was no class in the second week since it was a national holiday. Therefore, participants forgot to write in their IMS notebooks. There is a tendency that once a participant stops the IMS for any reason,

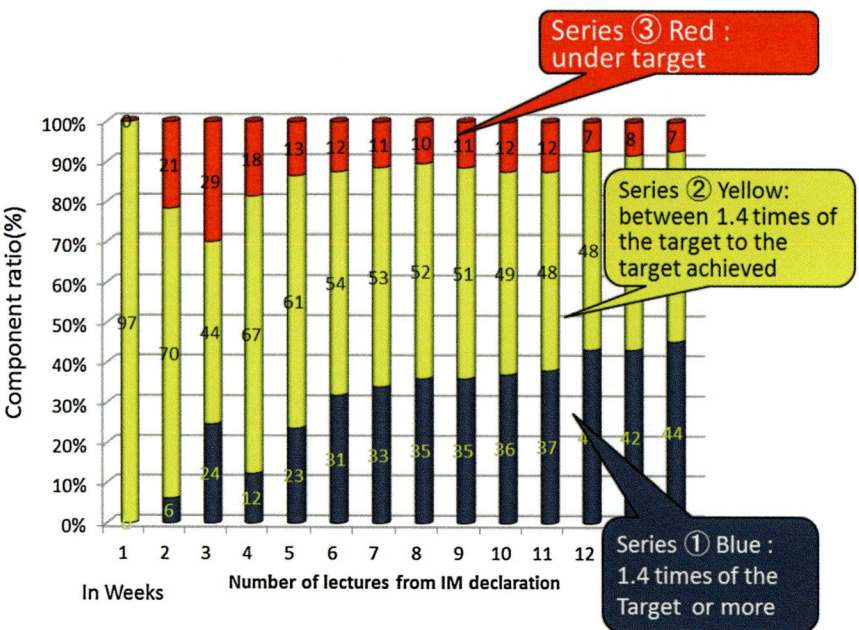

Fig. 8 Breakdown of Number of Students: The weekly change in the number of students categorised into three groups: (1) achieving more than 140% of the target (high, series 1 blue); (2) achieving more than the target but less than 140% of the target (mid, series 2 yellow); and (3) achieving less than the target (low, series 3 red; Saegusa & Higuchi, 2017b)

they are going to justify that decision in their mind. Such justification can be a serious problem since the IMS model is based on daily participation. We did remind the students not to forget to complete the IMS regime during the holidays.

Results of Students' Opinions at the End of the Class (14th Week) for 2016 and 2017

In the results of questionnaires (lowest 1; highest 5), it was suggested that the students' opinions of the IMS were quite high, and they appreciated their achievements, as indicated in Figure 9.

Specific Student Comments Regarding the IMS (July 2017)

1. My use of the IMS gave me confidence in my ability to think creatively. I like the process of reflective journal writing. I will use my IMS to tackle future problems (Student X, 2016).
2. At first, I did not expect any change, but through the course, I was able to get into the habit of 'I must use IMS', which led to an increase in continuing power (Student H, 2016).
3. It was easy for me as I could use it without any problem (Student J, 2016).
4. I wrote my ideas in my notebook, thus, I got useful ideas (Student S, 2016).
5. I was able to continue because it requires a small amount of time every day. Many hints of all sorts can be used in various situations of daily life (Student G, 2016).
6. We can use the method of the IMS for other classes (Student I, 2016).

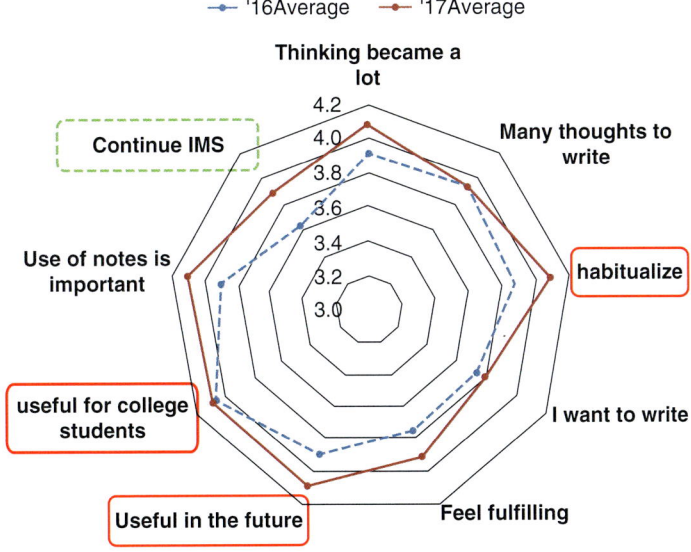

Fig. 9 Students' opinions regarding IMS at end of semester (Saegusa & Higuchi, 2017b)

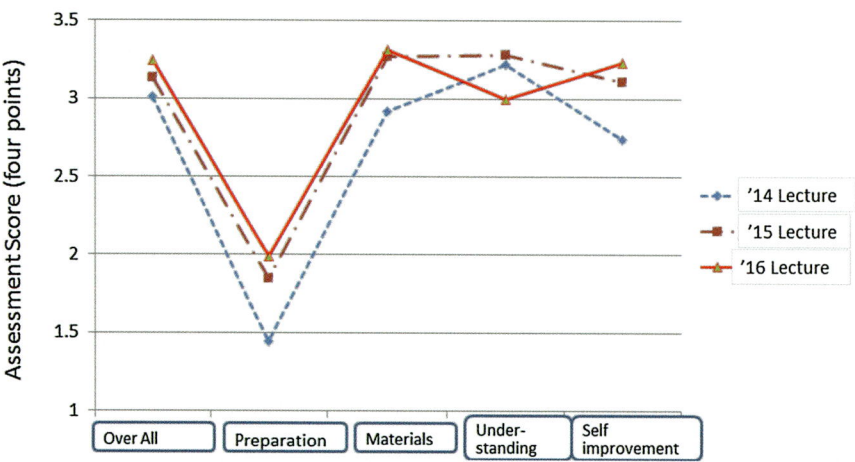

Fig. 10 Students' evaluation of a course without IMS (2014, 2015) and with IMS (2016) (Overall Score: 2014: 3.01 ⇒ 2015: 3.13 ⇒ 2016: 3.24) (Saegusa & Higuchi, 2017b)

Table 2 Students' Idea Numbers' Comparison for 99 days on 2016 and 2017 (Source: By author's own)

Year	Total idea number	Students number	Average number of ideas per one student
2016	10,850	84	129.0
2017	13,893	96	141.2

Students' evaluations regarding a course without the IMS (in 2014 and 2015) and with the IMS (2016). At the end of the semester, the university asked students to complete course evaluation questionnaires with nine questions. A four-point scale is used with one representing the lowest rating and four the highest rating. Figure 10 captures the responses to five of the nine questions. The descriptive data indicates that an approximate 3% difference exists among the three years reported 2014, 2015, and 2016. For the five questions selected, four questions indicated that the IMS had a positive effect. One question, 'Understanding', captured a negative effect, which is a problem that would benefit from future research (see Fig. 10).

Total number of ideas generated by students (and ideas by one person) between 2016 and 2017. Finally, the outcome of continuing support on the total idea numbers differed between 2016 and 2017 as in Table 2 the dual support system, including close contacts and weekly comments resulted in an almost 10% increase in the number of ideas from 2016 to 2017.

Implications of Using the IMS

Studying the evaluation data for 2017, it is not clear if the IMS had a positive impact on student achievement. It is assumed that the number and quality of ideas a student generated were indicators of their creative ability. Consequently, because of the mental ability to generate ideas these students should also be high achievers throughout their course work. Figure 4 reveals that some students suddenly became very serious about doing the IMS around week 8. We estimated that the sudden increase in idea numbers indicated that it takes time to create self-confidence and appreciation for the IMS process. Our interpretation is that students are learning to be creative at around the middle of semester (around week 8). This conclusion is supported by the students' comments provided earlier in the chapter. Gathering extensive achievement data on students who were taught the IMS and a control group of students who did not learn IMS would allow an opportunity to match participants and examine more closely the effects of IMS.

Prerequisite Conditions for Introducing the IMS into University Classes

Based on the first author's experience, the conditions for the best application of the IMS follow:

1. All students in the same department should start to use the IMS at the same time. If some students are doing the IMS and others are not in a class, those people who are doing the IMS are liable to be advised to stop the IMS by people who are not doing the IMS.
2. A freshmen class is desirable, as they can use the IMS throughout their university career and after graduation.
3. The course should last for at least three months (the longest period is 12 months).
4. The professors, teachers, lecturers, and teaching assistants in charge of the class should also be participants. They can say to the students, 'As I can do it easily, why not you?'

The IMS's Three-Month Propensity for Decrease and Increase in Number of Ideas

The following provides some implications surrounding the three-month timeframe of the implementation of the IMS with high achieving Japanese university students. The observations were made from our experience of the IMS in class in 2017 (see Fig. 8):

1. The number of students with less than the target idea number increased until the third week from the starting point. The following may have contributed to fewer targeted ideas:
   (a) Many students were getting bored or tired of doing the IMS by around the third week.
   (b) Initial motivation energy expired at around the third week.
   (c) Many students may be at a loss of finding an idea to think about daily.
   (d) They got tired from endless daily work.
   (e) Long holidays of one week started on the week which interrupted the IMS.

2. Then the students' numbers with less than the target idea number started to decrease by the ninth week. The following may have contributed to this decrease:

   1. After the holidays, the Inside Teacher (the second author) started to levy homework of getting new ideas for University's souvenirs or momentos, for which all the students started to apply the IMS for this homework.
   2. Students were getting used to using the IMS to create daily ideas according to the weekly supply of thinking hints from the outside teacher (the first author).
   3. Students with less numbers of ideas increased ideas in the 10th and 11th weeks.

The 10th and 11th weeks were the start of the third portion of this class for the debating program, during which students did not apply the IMS due to the debating preparation.

The IMS's Three-Month Propensity for Continuation

The students who recorded more than 140% of the target number of ideas during the course increased from the 1st week to the 6th week, but slowed from the 7th week to the 9th week, as shown in Figure 8.

In the IMS, during the first three weeks, students may struggle to get ideas from their past memory. Many students, through every day living, were unconsciously creating various devices or ideas in their minds, but they never wrote these ideas in the notebooks. When one starts writing down ideas, old ideas come to mind. Around the three-week mark, participants were strongly encouraged to try harder and come up with new ideas. It is necessary to create a breakthrough that may change one's old ways of thinking about idea generation. For example, one must do new things, go on a fresh trip, see various things, talk with friends, or go to the library to get new ideas. These students may struggle for a while in this state for 2–3 months. With the IMS, there is a strong possibility that a second change in thinking will occur around three months. Therefore, around the 10th week, students found a different way of thinking. The number of ideas of these students, whose thinking appeared to change, started increasing after the 10th week. We have our hypothesis that, after three months of the IMS, more students will continue the IMS on their own.

Conclusion

First, if students are supported regularly and continuously by teachers or coaches or mentors, they seem to be more willing to create and write more ideas (see Fig. 4). The average number of ideas per person in 2017 was 141.24 ideas within 99 days, while the average number in 2016 was 129.01 ideas within 99 days. Students' willpower seemed to be stronger in 2017, though the change in 2017 was the density of continuing support by the dual support system, which occurred every week in 2017, while it was every three weeks in 2016.

Second, three indicators for the IMS model were suggested: (a) individual total ideas, (b) score of communication cards, and (c) final grade scores seem to be mutually related. It is not clear if the total number of ideas and high C-card grades lead to a high final grade. Saegusa believes these scores are interlocking, but also feels that students' achievements may also be linked to their stronger enthusiasm in 2017.

Third, through 14 lectures, it was found that students' motivation for the IMS fluctuated at week three and at the third month, which suggests that consistent delivery and careful support are needed for students to persist with the IMS process. We believe that the integration of the *Idea-Marathon System* (IMS) within a university course may improve a students' willpower and contribute to the integrity of the course. However, these hypotheses are yet to be researched.

Future Work

The following plans for the 2019 semester of Saegusa's course were suggested from the evaluations:

1. Student assistants (SA) selected from the past successful IMS participants will be introduced.
2. Pre- and post-tests will be conducted to measure creativity.
3. A follow-up plan for freshmen will be created to see if they are continuing to use the IMS after the semester.
4. A 'Genius Talent Search' will be initiated through the dean of students/student affairs office. This contest is similar to other popular contests and cultural events. One of the goals for the IMS in a university setting is to create a public challenge among the students of the various academic disciplines. The principles and processes of the IMS will be made available. Students will be encouraged to write journals and generate ideas and pictures for 99 days. At the end of the semester, a panel of teachers, friends, and parents will judge the contestants' ideas, innovations, or creations. The place winners will receive recognition and cash prizes.

Higuchi has a hypothesis that, by using the IMS, families, friends, teachers, and students themselves may be able to discover talent or genius-level talent from the students' IMS notebooks, but an in-depth research project will be needed to investigate this. Historically, geniuses were found based on their demonstration of outstanding cleverness. Many gave up going to school as they were extremely poor. However, a few were picked up by feudal lords and sent to churches, temples, or schools. In case of scientific or other academic studies, they must have been given a certain level of education before their unique genius ideas emerged. These young geniuses started to write or draw something splendid or outstanding, which caught the eye of the public. However, by the stage that their outstanding products appeared, many were left buried in history without any public appreciation, as they were not given any elemental education. No genius can write without learning to write first. These lucky geniuses were very few out of the many talented but uneducated or talented and educated but not expressive in writing (Higuchi, 2014). Through these historical passages, we come to the necessity of encouraging all freshmen to start thinking of and immediately writing ideas into their notebooks, which is the concept of the *group IMS*. Students will need to master the IMS when they are new, to spend more time thinking during their university days and to see if they can have a positive impact on their post-graduation work.

Again, we hope that all students will discover their true specialty areas, devote themselves, learn further, and demonstrate advanced talent during their 4-year university career. We need to keep supporting students who learned the IMS in the first year with our IMS continuation-support system. In the future, we can carry out intellectual reform of students overseas by using the IMS in collaborative research partnerships and practice.

Broadly speaking, using the IMS has the potential to advance the recognition of gifted students. If students continue to embrace the practice of writing ideas and drawing pictures in notebooks, they have a method for capturing the creativity of their mind and visually representing their creativity. Many problems need creative solutions. The international community can embrace constructive active learning teaching methods, such as the IMS, in order to address global issues like ethnic conflict, pandemics, and global warming.

Cross-References

► A Model for Growing Teacher Talent Scouts: Decreasing Underrepresentation of Gifted Students
► Australian Teachers Who Made a Difference: Secondary Gifted Student Perceptions of Teaching and Teacher Effectiveness
► Bricolage and the Evolution of Giftedness and Talent in Taiwan
► Creative and Gifted Education in Korea: Using the CATs Model to Illustrate How Creativity Can Grow into Innovation
► Creativity Talent Development: Fostering Creativity in Schools
► Diverse Dimensions of Gifted Education: Part V Introduction
► Engaging Gifted Students in Solving Real Problems Creatively: Implementing the Real Engagement in Active Problem-Solving (REAPS) Teaching/Learning Model in Australasian and Pacific Rim Contexts
► Fostering and Developing Talent in Mentorship Programs: The Mentor's Perspectives
► Gifted Education in the Asia-Pacific: From the Past for the Future – An Introduction
► Sociocultural Perspectives on the Talent Development Megamodel
► Some Implications for the Future of Gifted Education in the Asia-Pacific
► The Career Decisions of Gifted Students: An Asian-Pacific Perspective
► Trends and Challenges of Creativity Development Among Selected Asian Countries and Regions: China, Hong Kong/Macau, Japan, Malaysia, and South Korea

References

Bidshahri, R. (2017, July 4). *7 Critical skills for the jobs of the future.* Retrieved from https://singularityhub.com/2017/07/04/7-critical-skills-for-the-jobs-of-the-future/#sm.0001j8z4vh10jheebzi3hi5t221eh

Bonwell, C. C., & Eison, J. A. (1991) *Active learning: Creating excitement in the classroom* (ASHE-ERIC higher education reports no. 1). Washington, DC: George Washington University.

Cherney, I. D. (2008). The effects of active learning on students' memories for course content. *Active Learning in Higher Education, 9*(2), 152–171. https://doi.org/10.1177/1469787408090841

Cramond, B. (2005). Developing creative thinking. In F. A. Karnes & S. M. Bean (Eds.), *Methods and materials for teaching the gifted* (pp. 313–351). Waco, TX: Prufrock Press, Inc.

Csikszentmihalyi, M. (1988). Society, culture, and person: A systems view of creativity. In R. J. Sternberg (Ed.), *The nature of creativity* (pp. 325–339). New York, NY: Cambridge University Press.

Davis, G. A. (2003). Identifying creative students, teaching for creative growth. In N. Colangelo & G. A. Davis (Eds.), *Handbook of gifted education* (pp. 311–324). Boston, MA: Allyn and Bacon.

Davis, G. A. (2004). Objectives and activities for teaching creative thinking. In D. J. Treffinger & S. M. Reis (Eds.), *Creativity and giftedness* (pp. 97–104). Thousand Oaks, CA: Corwin Press.

Florida, R. (2005). *The flight of the creative class.* New York, NY: Harper Collins.

Freeman, S., Eddy, S. L., McDonough, M., Smith, M. K., Okoroafor, N., Jordt, H., & Wenderoth, M. P. (2014). Active learning increases student performance in science, engineering, and mathematics. *Proceedings of the National Academy of Sciences, 111,* 8410–8415. Idea No. 1,830, July 31, 2018. https://doi.org/10.1073/pnas.1319030111

Higuchi, T. (1992). *You can get affluent ideas from this book.* Tokyo, Japan: Diamond Inc.

Higuchi, T. (1998). *How to create affluent ideas.* Tokyo, Japan: Toyo Keizai Shinpo Sha.

Higuchi, T. (2008a). *Group Idea-Marathon.* Tokyo, Japan: Just System.

Higuchi, T. (2008b). *Power to start with one note: Continue to give power: An idea marathon idea that both life and work goes well.* Tokyo, Japan: Kou-Shobo.

Higuchi, T. (2011). *Notebook technique for workers.* Tokyo, Japan: Toyo Keizai Inc.

Higuchi, T. (2014). *Enhancement effects of the Idea-Marathon system on creativity* (Unpublished doctoral dissertation). Japan Advanced Institute of Science and Technology (JAIST), Ishikawa, Japan.

Higuchi, T. (2015, November). *Application of the Idea-Marathon principle for ignition and fostering creativity of the pre-school children.* Paper presented at the Knowledge Information and Creativity Support System (KICSS), Phuket, Thailand.

Higuchi, T. (2016). Practice of the two-storied active learning structure in universities establishing a habit of thinking and immediate writing as the intellectual basis of active learning. *Journal of Japan Creativity Society, 20,* 36–39.

Higuchi, T. (2018). Idea-Marathon – Visualizing your thinking: The strongest notebook technology, 34 years of continued achievement. Tokyo, Japan: Amazon Digital Services LLC.

Higuchi, T., Yuizono, T., Miyata, K., Sakurai, K., & Kawaji, T. (2013). Creativity effects of the Idea-Marathon system (IMS): Torrance tests of creative thinking (TTCT) figural tests for college students. In A. M. J. Skulimowski & J. Kacprzyk (Eds.), *Knowledge, information and creativity support systems: Recent trends, advances and solutions* (pp. 185–200). New York, NY: Springer International Publishing.

Inagaki, T., & Mochida, T. (2012). Reactive half-metallocenium ionic liquids that undergo solvent-less ligand exchange. *Chemistry: A European Journal, 18*(26), 8070–8075. https://doi.org/10.1002/chem.201200157

Kato, F. (2017). Cooking simulator. *Open Lab Review.* Retrieved from https://bake-openlab.com/cooperator/kato-fumihiro

Kato, F., Shiina, M., Tokizaki, T., Mitake, H., Aoki, T., & Hasegawa, S. (2008). Culinary art designer. *Proceedings of the International Conference on Advances in Computer Entertainment Technology,* 398. https://doi.org/10.1145/1501750.1501847

Kawaji, T. (2011). Effect of creativity in Idea-Marathon system. *Proceedings of the Japan Creativity Society, 33*, 24–27. (in Japanese).

Kawamoto, T. (2016, October). *What is Active Learning we need today.* Paper presented at the Japan Creativity Society, Tokyo, Japan.

Kobayashi, A., Suzuki, T., & Suzuki, E. (2015). *Active learning practice.* Tokyo, Japan: Sangyo Noritzu University Press.

Lally, P., Van Jaarsveld, C. H. M., Potts, H. W. W., & Wardle, J. (2010). How are habits formed? Modelling habit formation in the real word. *European Journal of Social Psychology, 40*, 998–1009. https://doi.org/10.1002/ejsp.674

Lin, Y.-S. (2011). Fostering creativity through education: A conceptual framework of creative pedagogy. *Creative Education, 2*, 149–155. https://doi.org/10.4236/ce.2011.23021

Matsushita, K. (2015). *Deep active learning.* Tokyo, Japan: Keisou Shobo.

Matsushita, K., & Ishii, T. (2016). *Evaluation of active learning.* Tokyo, Japan: Toshindo.

Ministry of Education, Culture, Sports, Science and Technology. (2017a). *Japanese Government Policies in Education, Science, Sports, and Culture 1997.* Retrieved from http://www.mext.go.jp/b_menu/hakusho/html/hpae199701/hpae199701_1_002.htm

Ministry of Education, Culture, Sports, Science and Technology. (2017b). *On integrated reforms in high school and university education and university entrance examination aimed at realizing a high school and university articulation system appropriate for a new era.* Report by author. Retrieved from http://www.mext.go.jp/en/news/topics/detail/1372628.htm

Miyata, K., Umemoto, K., & Higuchi, T. (2010). An educational framework for creating VR application through group work. *Computers & Graphics, 34*, 811–819. https://doi.org/10.1016/j.cag.2010.08.007

Mochida, T. (2014). *Research manual of Mochida Research Office,* (p. 5). Kobe, Japan: University of Kobe

Nishiura, K., & Kunifuji, S. (2016). Establishment of SIG and the latest trend to creative education of AL: Active learning. *Journal of Japan Creativity Society, 20*, 1–3.

Noda, T., Nomura, K., Komuro, N., Chen, Y., Tao, Z., & Miyata, K. (2008). *Landscape Bartender: Landscape image generation system using analogy of cocktail.* Retrieved from https://www.youtube.com/watch?v=Z_1YyHDnWxI

Prabhu, V., Sutton, C., & Sauser, W. (2008). Creativity and certain personality traits: Understanding the mediating effect of intrinsic motivation. *Creativity Research Journal, 20*, 53–66. https://doi.org/10.1080/10400410701841955

Renzulli, J. S. (2012). Reexamining the role of gifted education and talent development for the 21st century: A four-part theoretical approach. *Gifted Child Quarterly, 56*, 150–159. https://doi.org/10.1177/0016986212444901

Runco, M. A. (2014). *Creativity: Theories and themes: Research, development, and practice.* New York, NY: Academic Press.

Runco, M. A., & Kim, D. (2011). Creativity complex. In M. A. Runco & S. Pritzker (Eds.), *Encyclopedia of creativity* (2nd ed., pp. 292–295). San Diego, CA: Elsevier.

Runco, M. A., & Kim, D. (2013). Four Ps of creativity and recent updates. In E. G. Carayannis (Ed.), *Encyclopedia of creativity, invention, innovation, and entrepreneurship* (pp. 755–759). New York, NY: Springer.

Saavedra, A. R., & Opfer, V. D. (2012). Learning 21st-century skills requires 21st-century teaching. *Phi Delta Kappan, 94*, 8–13. https://doi.org/10.1177/003172171209400203

Saegusa, S., & Higuchi, T. (2016). *Strengthening thought and idea in first year's education: Practice of active learning with IMS introduced.* Paper presented at the 38th Academic Lecture Meeting of the Japan Creativity Society, Tokyo, Japan.

Saegusa, S., & Higuchi, T. (2017a). Strengthening of thinking and imagination during the first year education (2nd report): Promotion and continued enhancement of independent IMS idea through internal and external collaborations with teachers. *Proceedings of the Japan Creativity Society, 39*, 9–12. (in Japanese).

Saegusa, S., & Higuchi, T. (2017b). *Active learning & teaching education method for University freshmen*. Paper presented at the 12th International Conference on Knowledge, Information and Creativity Support Systems (KICSS), Nagoya, Japan.

Schack, G. D. (2004). Effects of a creative problem-solving curriculum on students of varying abilities. In D. J. Treinger & S. M. Reis (Eds.), *Creativity and giftedness* (pp. 125–140). Thousand Oaks, CA: Corwin Press.

Shavinina, L. V. (2009). On giftedness and the economy: The impact of talented individuals on the global economy. In L. V. Shavinina (Ed.), *International handbook on giftedness* (pp. 1181–1202). Dordrecht, Netherlands: Springer Science.

Smith, S. R. (2017). Model of dynamic differentiation (MoDD): Innovation education for talent development. In T. S. Yamin, K. W. McCluskey, T. Lubart, D. Ambrose, K. C. McCluskey, & S. Linke (Eds.), *Innovation education* (pp. 41–66). Ulm, Germany: The International Centre for Innovation in Education (ICIE).

Sternberg, R. J. (2018). What's wrong with creativity testing? *Journal of Creative Behavior*, 1–17.

Subotnik, R. F., Olszewski-Kubilius, P., & Worrell, F. C. (2012). A proposed direction forward for gifted education based on psychological science. *Gifted Child Quarterly, 56*, 176–188. https://doi.org/10.1177/0016986212456079

Sumida, M. (2013). Emerging trends in Japan in the education of the gifted: A focus on science education. *Journal for the Education of the Gifted, 36*(3), 277–289. https://doi.org/10.1177/0162353213493534

Todd, S. M., & Shinzato, S. (1999). Thinking for the future: Developing higher-level thinking and creativity for students in Japan and elsewhere. *Childhood Education, 75*, 342–345. https://doi.org/10.1080/00094056.1999.10522054

Torrance, E. P. (1963). *Education and the creative potential*. Minneapolis, MN: The University of Minnesota Press.

Torrance, E. P. (1966/1974). *The Torrance tests of creative thinking-norms-technical manual research edition-verbal tests, forms A and B- figural tests, forms A and B.* Princeton, NJ: Personnel Press.

Torrance, E. P. (1988). The nature of creativity as manifest in its testing. In R. J. Sternberg (Ed.), *The nature of creativity* (pp. 43–73). New York, NY: Cambridge University Press.

Torrance, E. P., Murdock, M., & Fletcher, D. C. (1996). *Creative problem solving through role playing*. Pretoria, Republic of South Africa: Benedict Books.

Treffinger, D. J. (2004). Introduction to creativity and giftedness: Three decades of inquiry and development. In D. J. Treffinger & S. M. Reis (Eds.), *Creativity and giftedness* (pp. xxiii–xxxxx). Thousand Oaks, CA: Corwin Press.

Trilling, B., & Fadel, C. (2009). *21st century skills: Learning for life in our times*. New York, NY: Wiley.

Takeo Higuchi is an education and ability development consultant for universities and companies in Tokyo, Japan, the founder of the *Idea-Marathon System*, and the ex-chairman of the counsellor of Japan Creativity Society, Tokyo, Japan

Shozo Saegusa is a professor of Faculty of Business Administration, Shujitsu University, Okayama, Japan. He is also a Hiroshima university Professor Emeritus. His research interest is to educate young people and engineers with high creativity and innovation and regional activation.

Daehyun Kim is a full-time Research Professional in the *Torrance Center for Creativity and Talent Development* at the University of Georgia. Her research interests include creativity assessment and sociocultural factors influencing creativity such as bilingualism and multicultural experience.

Rural Adolescent Gifted Girls: Exploring the Impact of Popular Culture on Their Talent Development

51

Denise Wood

Contents

Abstract

Adolescents experience an abundance of popular culture in their lives that provides them with information, role models, and advice about career options, lifestyle, and aspirations. The impact of popular culture on all girls is well documented in the literature which suggests that it is a powerful influence on their lives. Understanding the relationship that adolescent gifted girls in rural settings have with popular culture, and its impact on their talent development, can ensure that the lived experiences of these girls afford them the opportunity to achieve to their potential. An outline of a model of talent development that evolved from a study of adolescent gifted girls in a rural context in Australia is provided in this chapter. Informed by the *Differentiated Model of Giftedness and*

D. Wood (✉)
Charles Sturt University, Bathurst, NSW, Australia
e-mail: dwood@csu.edu.au

© Springer Nature Singapore Pte Ltd. 2021
S. R. Smith (ed.), *Handbook of Giftedness and Talent Development in the Asia-Pacific*,
Springer International Handbooks of Education,
https://doi.org/10.1007/978-981-13-3041-4_54

1163

Talent (Gagné, 2009) and gender-specific talent development models (e.g., Kerr & Larson, 2007; Noble et al., 1999; Reis, 1998), the model identifies important influences on the aspirations of adolescent gifted girls, and unlike the earlier models, includes popular culture as a key influence on adolescent gifted girls. A process for supporting gifted girls as they navigate their world, establish their identity, and work towards achieving their potential is introduced. Suggestions are outlined for approaches and activities to support rural adolescent gifted girls to explore their giftedness and achieve their talent potential. An alternate view of eminence showing the recognition of the local domain as a venue for talent performance is elaborated. Through this alternate view of eminence, which is not simply about fame, rural adolescent gifted girls will have ways to remain connected to their rural contexts while concomitantly achieving their potential.

Keywords

Adolescent gifted girls · Rural · Popular culture · Talent development

The aims in this chapter are to:
1. Outline the challenges for gifted girls living in rural contexts.
2. Describe a research study that explores the lived experience of gifted girls as they engage with popular culture.
3. Outline a model that can inform programs that support rural adolescent gifted girls to achieve their talent potential.
4. Describe ways of implementing the model.
5. Provide some recommendations for future research.

Introduction

The focus in this chapter emphasises the influences popular culture has on gifted girls in rural contexts. A description is provided of an example research study (Wood, 2015) that used case study methods to explore the lived experiences of rural adolescent gifted girls, in seeking to discern the impact popular culture had on their talent development. Findings from the research indicated that popular culture can be a disruption to talent development for gifted rural adolescent girls, as well as a potential supporting influence. A model of talent development is described that provides a framework for the support of rural adolescent gifted girls. The chapter then describes the place of popular culture within a set of component factors that interact within the model to support talent development and introduces an interpretation of eminence in terms of gifted young people's achievements. Finally, for educators and other stakeholders who are engaged in supporting gifted girls' achievement of talent potential, specific activities and skills that can support the talent development of rural adolescent gifted girls are recommended.

The experiences of gifted or eminent women, and their recollections of important events and influences during their adolescence have been articulated in significant research (Kerr & Larson, 2007; Kronborg, 2010; Noble, 1992; Reis, 1995). Historically, though, adolescent gifted girls were described as an understudied subgroup of the gifted population (Reis, 1995; Noble, 1992) resulting in less than full understanding of the actual lived experiences of adolescent gifted girls. Australian adolescent gifted girls, particularly those in rural areas, are even more invisible in the literature on gifted young people (Wood, 2015). Their choices and aspirations are dependent on their environment which, in Australia, tends to continue to uphold traditional views about women and academic achievement (Eddles-Hirsch, 2006; Galitis, 2009; Lea-Wood, 2004). Despite feminism creating a context where it is possible for girls to aspire to enter diverse careers, to challenge themselves in rigorous study, and to consider options that include leadership, creative pursuits, science, and medicine alongside the more traditional occupational choices, marriage, and parenthood, this is not always the lived experience of adolescent gifted girls in rural settings. The influences on their lives can disrupt their aspirations or support their talent development (Maltby & Devlin, 2000; O'Quinn, 1999; Walshaw, 2006; Willard-Holt, 2008). They learn about the possibilities for their future achievements from information in either their immediate environment or in the mediated world of popular culture (Ward & Harrison, 2005; Wohlwend, 2009).

Popular culture is a generic term that applies to constructed texts, images, music, and cultural artefacts with purposes that span the extent of human life. It has been described as a tool to control social development and beliefs to maintain social order and to set roles and customs (Fishwick, 1985; Harris, 2004) and conversely, as a tool to breakdown and challenge social order (Fishwick, 1985). Popular culture represents the world through the eyes of an agent of construction, bringing to life their particular perspective, and as such can exaggerate or distort reality and show a biased view of the world (Wood, 2015).

The current artefacts of popular culture include items in visual, print, and social media: movies, music videos, popular literature, magazines, radio, images, websites, and online networks. Popular culture is an omniscient presence in the lives of adolescents (Wood & Vialle, 2015; Wood, 2015), providing them with information, role models, ways of being, and entertainment (Harris, 2004; Kearney, 2006; Nash, 2006). Adolescent girls have been recognised as key consumers of popular culture, and its impact on their view of the world and their aspirations for their future lives has been described in the literature (Charles, 2010; Cheu, 2007; Harris, 2004; Kearney, 2006). Adolescent gifted girls in rural contexts are able to access all forms of popular culture in their daily lives, engaging with the information presented in visual, audio, print, and multi-modal forms. In this chapter, their relationship with popular culture and its influence on their aspirations and their perception of giftedness and talent are explored.

The chapter opens with an exploration of the key topics for the research study described, bringing to the attention of the reader a summary of Australian and international literature that focuses on popular culture and girls, gifted girls in rural settings, and talent development. The example study that forms the basis of the chapter is then introduced. The second half of the chapter considers the application of a model of talent development and the implications for educators and those who support gifted girls.

Popular Culture and Girls

Popular culture reflects the human need to describe how people live and what they do by creating a narrative that becomes a commentary on the collective values and beliefs of groups of people. As such it is a source of information, role modelling, and instruction about daily life (Cheu, 2007; Driscoll, 2002; Gaerlan-Price, 2015; Harris, 2004). For rural adolescent gifted girls, popular culture sources include mainstream offerings such as television, magazines, music videos or film, film and movies, documentaries, newspapers, radio, and online media including social media sites and interactive webpages.

When engaging with popular culture, girls are able to gather information about 'being' (Harris, 2004). They learn about appearance, fashion, behaviours, and relationships. They see their favourite characters living out their lives—shopping, socialising, playing sport, discovering themselves, or being with others. It gives them information in diverse forms, in fiction and in reality and in segments that show disconnected and edited parts of life creating a patchwork of mediated living that is manipulated to deliver the view of the producer (Hamilton, 2008; Wood, 2015). They are encouraged to purchase products that will allow them to live in the way they see their idols living (Hamilton, 2008; Johnson, 2007) and to use the images to make choices about their appearance and clothing. Kearney (2006), expressed concern at the lack of information about technology and complex careers in the content of magazines available for young girls. Rather, the images and text outline ways of dressing and behaving while at work to impress or to attract the opposite gender.

The relationship that adolescent girls have with popular culture is abundantly described and reviewed in the literature (e.g., Fritzsche, 2004; Gaerlan-Price, 2015; Harris, 2004; Kearney, 2006; Tiggemann & McGill, 2004). Multiple examples of the impact of popular culture on identity (Duits, 2010; Fritzsche, 2004), body image (Tiggemann & Slater, 2003), aspirations (Harris, 2004; Kearney, 2006), and career options (Tally, 2007) have been provided in the literature over an extended period of time. From the mid-twentieth century, it was clear that young girls were a focus of the content and the storylines, and they were able to identify with characters who lived lives that were novel, adventurous, and fantasy-driven (Nash, 2006). As young women entered the workforce and had greater freedom and money, the cinema provided them with opportunities to engage with popular culture. Women's magazines presented idealised lives, and instructions for fashion, lifestyle, and cooking. Young girls saw new ways of being through the content in these media sources (Fritzsche, 2004; Harris, 2004; Nash, 2006).

During the 1980s and 1990s new role models showcased young girls who were sassy, confident, and aggressive, and the concept of *girlpower* emerged as a trait for young women (Harris, 2004). Music groups such as the Spice Girls dressed and behaved in ways that broke traditional ways of being. Buffy the Vampire Slayer beat down vampires and monsters, while maintaining an appearance of femininity and neatness. In contrast, Disney princesses continued to present an image of beauty that was stereotyped—fair of face, long hair, slimness, and traditional beauty. Princesses remained an influence on younger girls, supported by products that invited girls to participate in fantasy play and continue the storylines for themselves (Cheu, 2007) and that messaged the importance of preparing oneself for a prince (Cheu, 2007; Wohlwend, 2009). Historically popular culture both provided girls with options and diverse examples of being a girl (Harris, 2004) and reinforced traditional stereotypes of appearance and behaviour (Fabrianesi, Jones, & Reid, 2008).

There is evidence that the role models that influence social expectations for girls are changing. For example, a poll taken in Britain in 2010 found that 88% of 18–24 year olds and 66% of the wider British population were still not able to name a famous female scientist (State News Service, August 2010). However, overall scientists were seen as more favourable role models than popular culture icons for girls to aspire to imitate, along with doctors, lawyers, teachers, and elite athletes. Role models form part of identity formation for adolescents as they strive to establish their identity separate from their family, while aligning themselves with peers. Role models from popular culture have a part to play in providing adolescent girls with ideas for their future (Maxwell, 2007). Fabrianesi et al. (2008) noted the frequency of forensic scientists, crime solvers, medical positions, journalism, and fashion industries in the popular culture world; they further described them as often highly competitive, single-minded, and physically presented in stereotyped ways. Fandom (Fritzsche, 2004) has been a term used to describe the way that girls engage with real and fictional identities from popular culture, building their admiration into a parasocial relationship.

In a parasocial relationship, a role model offers vicarious affirmation and support for choices and behaviours (Theran, Newberg, & Gleason, 2010). Their study with 107 adolescent girls between 14 and 17 years of age identified that 97% of the girls could identify a female role model in popular culture who they admired and connected with. The role models provided cues for behaviour for the girls, who also acknowledged that they recognised the difference between the real identity and their media character. While some of the girls attempted to connect with their idol, most found that talking with their friends about their idols was part of the connection. Theran et al. (2010) concluded that parasocial relationships are for the most part normative in adolescent girls, reinforcing the place popular culture has in continuing to provide role models for adolescent girls.

Popular culture presents and reinforces messages to young girls about thin-ness, beauty, and identity. Key messages about thin-ness and beauty are presented through the images and information available for all girls (Fabrianesi et al., 2008; Grabe, Ward, & Hyde, 2008; Harper & Tiggemann, 2007). Grabe et al. (2008) found that exposure to thin women in popular culture impacted on the self-image of young women, and this supported findings in a study by Gilbert, Keery, and Thompson (2005) where Fijian girls were exposed to television for the first time, and quickly became obsessed with diet and appearance. In a number of Australian studies Tiggemann and others have shown connections between self-image, body dissatisfaction, and poor body image after interaction with popular culture, including music, television, magazines, and movies (Harper & Tiggemann, 2007; Tiggemann, 2005; Tiggemann & Slater, 2003).

Popular culture is replete with images of famous individuals, their lifestyles, their fashion, their philosophies of life, and their advice on everything from appearance to household appliances (Charles, 2010; Duits, 2010; Hylmo, 2006). These role models contribute to the development of identity, as young girls establish who they are and who they will be (Cheu, 2007; Kearney, 2006; Meyer, 2003). Meyer (2003) described the connections that adolescents felt with characters, both real and fictional, they met through popular culture, and highlighted the diversity of values, ethics, and life choices that were available for young people. Fabrianesi et al. (2008) confirmed earlier work by McRobbie and McCabe (1981) where there was concern that the information provided about intimate details of the lives of celebrities provides a pseudo-intimacy, whereby young girls developed a (false) close relationship with the stars, aspiring to live as they did, and shaped their identity to mirror their lives.

Conversely, such constant exposure to all facets of the lives of famous individuals provides a wider range of vicarious options for young girls, but the risk is developing a tendency to be highly self-critical. Theran et al. (2010) identified the patterns of behaviour in adolescent girls where they had parasocial interactions with idols from popular culture. Parasocial interactions are one-sided relationships formed when an individual becomes consumed with a character or identity in media. In a study of 107 adolescent girls, 94% of the girls described a form of parasocial interaction with a popular culture identity, ranging from 'normal' admiration and interest to obsessive imagined relationships where the outcome was a negative self-image based on a failure to become like the idol. The standard of appearance set by the manufactured perfection of images in popular culture was detrimental to the self-confidence of some girls who then substituted the vicarious interaction for healthy 'real' relationships.

In other studies (e.g., Charles, 2010; Hobbs, Broder, Pope, & Rowe, 2006), the strength of the impact of popular culture on girls' sense of self, body image, and overall well-being were questioned. In these studies, it is suggested that young girls have a sense of critical awareness of the messages popular culture deliver and are able to discern the constructed nature of the medium, clearly articulating their knowledge of manipulation and image construction, and making it evident that they are able to differentiate between the real world and the fantasy world of popular culture. There are many variables within a girl's life that influence their image, of self, including family, context, experience, and peers (Harper & Tiggemann, 2007; Hobbs et al., 2006; Holmstron, 2004).

Gifted Girls in Rural Settings

Lawrence (2009) undertook a comprehensive literature review of the published research focused on gifted students in rural settings. She found that, in the literature from the United States of America (USA), there were multiple small studies that considered gifted students in particular rural contexts, resulting in a fragmented understanding of the situation. Across the literature, rurality was ill-defined and diverse. However, Lawrence concluded that living in a rural context was qualitatively different for gifted adolescents. More recent literature confirms this remains an issue when attempting to understand the needs of gifted students (Colangelo, Assouline, Baldus, Ihrig, & New, 2006; Howley, 2009; Howley, Rhodes, & Beall, 2009; Stambaugh, 2015). Disadvantages have been related to isolation, poverty, poor attitudes towards achievement and limited role models for high levels of or diverse approaches to academic achievement. Further disadvantages were reported as lack of critical mass of like-minded peers, inconsistent experience and knowledge of teachers, poor identification processes, and lack of resources, including technology connectivity (Colangelo et al., 2006).

In the literature, there is little evidence of Australian research focused on gifted students in rural areas. As early as 1995, Bailey, Knight, and Riley (1995) wrote about the significant disadvantage experienced by gifted students in rural contexts, identifying that ambivalence towards academic achievement, gender stereotyping, powerful egalitarian attitudes, and distance were factors in this disadvantage. More recent literature, including work from New Zealand, reports similar concerns (Lea-Wood, 2004; Sanders & Munford, 2008; Walshaw, 2006). Identification of giftedness may be a challenge in rural areas as gifted young people have diverse experiences and diverse skills beyond academic achievement that demonstrate their ability (Laura & Smith, 2009; Pendarvis & Wood, 2009). Rural students may be more influenced by their families (James, Krause, & Jennings, 2010; Walshaw, 2006) in terms of their choices, and this familial influence may be exacerbated by the limited access they have to role models and diverse occupations and options (Alloway & Dalley-Trim, 2009; Schmitt-Wilson & Welsh, 2012). In Australian settings, technology access is not consistent (Bannister, Cornish, Bannister-Tyrrell, & Gregory, 2015) and gifted adolescents may have limited knowledge of career or further education opportunities (James et al., 2010; Wilson, Lyons, & Quinn, 2013) that then restrain them from taking up career options.

Living in a rural context also has been seen to have advantages for gifted students. Leadership opportunities are more accessible for young people in smaller communities, both in school and in the wider community (Grant, Battle, & Heggoy, 2000), where they have more prospects to learn skills of communication, self-perception, organisation, and problem solving in authentic settings. Interactions with people from across the community can offer chances for different learning styles and can lead to mentoring in diverse ways. There is greater opportunity to see science in action (Laura & Smith, 2009) and to be involved in multiple authentic activities that have a real impact on the community (Colangelo et al., 2006; Stambaugh, 2015). In smaller schools, gifted students, whether identified or not, are able to access accelerated content and may, in an unplanned intervention, experience learning at their own level of need (Cornish, 2010).

Adolescent gifted girls in rural settings have not been the key focus of the literature, internationally nor in Australia, leaving a gap in what is understood about their aspirational development, or their understanding of the implications for their talent development. O'Quinn (1999) identified that for many girls, leaving home for education created a conflict of lifestyle and interest, and while some gifted girls managed the conflict, others returned to their rural setting, and may not have had the opportunity to achieve their talent potential. Lea-Wood's 2004 study of Australian adolescent gifted girls in regional areas indicated the strength of family influences on young girls' choices. Given that in rural settings there tended to be a more conservative view of gender-appropriate achievement (Alloway & Dalley-Trim, 2009; Montgomery, 2004), Lea-Wood's study could be seen as an indication that, for gifted rural girls, there is less support for aspiring for something different. Overall, the literature suggests that the talent development of gifted rural adolescent girls is impacted on by their environmental setting, which may constrain their potential achievements. In the next section of the chapter, the processes and models of talent development are described to provide insight into suggested ways to support adolescent gifted girls to develop their talent.

Talent Development for Rural Gifted Girls

Models of talent development illustrate the influences, processes, and factors that contribute to the development of talent. Gagné (2009) described talent development as a confluence of catalysts, and a developmental process that, over time, influence the transformation of gifted behaviours into talented performance. The catalysts are both external to the individual and within the individual, and dynamically work together over a period of time, through practice, investment, and maturation to evidence behaviour that is within the top 10% of the population. Gagné defined the intrapersonal catalysts as the drivers of aspirational thinking and goal setting, which lead to successful talent actualisation. This developmental model of gifted-ness and talent has influenced education policies across Australian education systems for more than a decade (Henderson & Jarvis, 2016), providing a framework for better understanding of the needs of gifted students in school settings, and suggesting an approach for the development of programs to support talent development. As a model of talent development, it is valuable in providing a breakdown of the influences and opportunities that impact on the development of talent. The DMGT is gender neutral and, while it includes environmental catalysts that are external to the individual, it does not explicitly indicate that popular culture could be a powerful influence on the development of talent.

Women's talent development has been described in gender-specific models which reference retrospective studies, gathering reflections and narratives of lived experiences from eminent women. Over 25 years, Reis (1998) studied the barriers women experienced as they strove to reach their potential. A sense of personal purpose and drive related to a talent area that held societal worth was a key facet of talent development in the model Reis devised. Also, over an extended period of time in the 1980s, Kerr, with others, undertook studies with multiple women from a number of career domains, gleaning details of their early lives, their family life and their education experiences. In 2007, Kerr and Larson proposed a model of talent development that described the importance of personality and sense of personal identity—independence, responsibility, passion, and curiosity—in the process, as well as family support for career choices and resistance of stereotypical expectations. Also, emphasising the impact of unique personal traits as key to talent development, Moon (2003) described a female-oriented model, where disposition was described as an influence on talent development and the developmental process was described as a personal trajectory leading to both a high level of performance and a high level of life satisfaction.

The Model of Adult Female Talent Development (MAFTD) described by Noble, Subotnik, and Arnold (1999) from retrospective studies of eminent women similarly included the import of personal facets of personality and opportunity. Developed from a synthesis of studies by a range of female researchers (for detail of the development of the model, see Burton, VanHeest, Rallis, & Reis, 2006; Kronborg, 2010), the model comprised of three core elements: foundations, filters, and spheres of influence. Foundational elements to women's talent development included demographic and individual characteristics. These foundations are then filtered as a result of interactions, opportunities, and contexts, highlighting the individuality of talent development. Finally, talent is actualised through the spheres of influence, which relate to eminence. Talented women who achieve eminence become leaders or change agents in their field—the public domain. At actualisation there is also a personal/local domain, defined as the fulfilment of personal or community relationships and achievements (Burton et al., 2006). Noble et al. (1999) defined the end result of the talent development process as being either in the public domain (eminence) or in the private domain (interpreted here as local eminence).

In 2010, Kronborg described and expanded the MAFTD based on her earlier study of eminent Australian women. Kronborg undertook a retrospective, interview-based study of ten eminent Australian women from across a diverse range of career fields. Here analysis of the qualitative data added depth to the MAFTD in all three elements. Foundational family factors included the protective capacity of the family of origin, whereby either parent provided encouragement, support, and a buffer against stereotyped societal expectations. Individual characteristics that included persistence and resilience further expanded on the foundations of the MAFTD. The set of filters and catalysts includes influences (allies) from outside the family, opportunities in school and outside of school, passion, motivation, and identity factors including a feeling of being different. The final component describes the domains where talent is played out, or the fields of influence or domains of personal or public life that the talented woman will have impact on. Kronborg noted that all of the women in her study had achieved both personal actualisation in fields of endeavour that are traditionally masculine, and also public recognition in their fields. This Australian model, while expanding the MAFTD (Noble et al., 1999), also reflects elements in female talent development models described by Reis (1998) and Kerr and Larson (2007) and confirms that the earlier international models also illustrated the talent development of Australian women.

In 2015, Tweedale and Kronborg further explored Kronborg's model with adolescent girls (sample of six) in a New Zealand setting. This work confirmed that the model reflected the lived experience of adolescent gifted girls, finding a number of influences on girls' lives that impacted on their motivation and aspiration to work towards achieving their talent potential. The participants identified relational influences that played a part in providing guidance or who were role models, who supported the visualisation of future pathways. These influences included parents and extended family members, friends, peers, and teachers. The six participants attended the research site school, were aged from 17 to 20 years old and had already demonstrated considerable achievement in academic areas. They came from highly educated families, with parents who understood the value of education. The study did not indicate if these girls were rural based, or from metropolitan contexts.

Placing a gender lens across the concept of talent development allowed Kerr and Multon (2015) to define gendered behaviours that they consider play a part in talent development as an expansion to the MAFTD. They examined the impact of gender role, gender identity, and gender relations on the elements of the model, finding that the expectations and encouragement to achieve their talent potential placed on girls can be mitigated by societal expectations and more. Talent development may be impeded by role expectations, perceived capacity to do well in STEM areas, distractions from multiple extracurricular activities, home responsibilities, performance anxieties, and fear of risk taking. A further consideration is to understand the concept of *distance from privilege*, which is defined as the distance an individual has to travel to reach the centre of power in any domain (Kerr & Multon, 2015, p. 183). This was also explored in 2003 by Ambrose who described trajectories of talent development that included barriers that would impact on aspirational goals for individuals. He defined a number of barriers that would limit aspiration including milieu, opportunity, and gender.

The perceptions girls have of their future career trajectory, relationships, and opportunities have been described in the literature from Australia and internationally as changing (e.g., Duits, 2010; Eccles, 2011; Eddles-Hirsch, 2006; Hylmo, 2006; Kerr & Sodano, 2003). Gifted girls were described as under increased stress to achieve, experiencing greater expectations to take up multiple opportunities, and to be successful in their chosen area of work (Eccles, 2011; Eddles-Hirsch, 2006; Maxwell, 2007). Based on the retrospective view of talent development expressed in all the models described, the literature suggests that successful talent development for adolescent gifted girls is dependent on both strong intrapersonal characteristics—motivation, persistence, passion, resilience—and supportive environmental features, including milieu, family attributes, community support, opportunities, and context.

None of the earlier models explicitly described the place popular culture has in informing and driving talent development in adolescent girls, and yet the literature shows it is a key influence on the development of identity in all girls, influencing their understanding of what it is to be a girl (Harris, 2004; Kearney, 2006; Renold & Allan, 2006; Robbins, 2006; Wood, 2015). The literature suggests that popular culture has power over the thinking of young girls (Harris, 2004; Pipher, 1994) and that it emphasises a world of fame (Fabrianesi et al., 2008; Robbins, 2006; Wood, 2015). Adolescents spend many hours engaging with popular culture from a diverse range of media sources that provide multiple perspectives, patched together into what becomes a unified vision of life (Wood, 2015). Exploring the impact of popular culture on talent development for adolescent girls, in an Australian rural context, was the focus of the study that led to the model described and explored in this chapter.

Narratives of Lived Experiences of Rural Gifted Girls: Data Collection and Analysis

Using feminist case study methodology to provide a detailed rich narrative of lived experiences, Wood (2015) worked with adolescent gifted girls in rural settings to explore their engagement with popular culture and their reflections on how it influenced their identity as gifted and their subsequent talent development. The study was designed as a multiple case study, with a central case (rural adolescent gifted girls currently in secondary school) and two embedded cases (rural adolescent gifted girls at two different stages of development). In total there were 31 participants in the central case, with the two case study groups comprising 13 girls in Year 7/8 and 18 girls in Years 10/11. The participants were drawn from two regional secondary schools in New South Wales, Australia, with a cohort of each age group in each school. Neither school had a formal process for identifying gifted students. The selection of girls was made using their most recent results in standardised testing that was used across Years 7 and 9 at the time (the English Language and Literacy Assessment and the Secondary Numeracy Assessment Program), in-school grading and reporting, teacher identification and earlier primary school experiences in gifted programs. This method of identification had been previously used when a more formal method of identification was not available (Vialle, Heaven, & Ciarrochi, 2007; Bannister et al., 2015). Triangulation of the testing results led to the group of girls who were invited to participate in the research.

Using the DMGT (Gagné, 2009) as a theoretical framework to shape the approach, the study comprised a number of data generation strategies over two years. Potential ethics issues were identified around relationships, personal narrative, safety within the groups, and support for any personal issues that emerged. They were addressed through a process of meetings and information sheets for both girls and their parents. All groups and interviews were held during the school day, on school premises, and a counsellor was available if needed. All names were removed from data, and at all times an individual girl could choose to leave. The girls met with Wood on four occasions across the first year of the study in focus groups (16 focus groups in all). Each of the girls was provided with a journal that included free pages and a log chart to track their engagement with popular culture, their responses to what they saw or read and the time they were engaged. Eleven of the journals were returned for analysis. Each participant completed a timeline exercise identifying their life goals, their aspirations, and an indication of when they would achieve their goals. Further data was generated through a profile survey that offered the opportunity to identify factual data including: family size and profile; and preferences in terms of literature, music and film, hobbies or other interests. Eight months after the completion of the focus group stage, 18 girls met in small groups for semi-structured interviews to review the narrative constructed from the analysis of the data and add any further reflections and insights into the impact of popular culture on their talent development. Through analysis of the transcripts and artefacts that emerged from the various sources of data, a narrative of the lived experiences of rural adolescent gifted girls as they engaged with some forms of popular culture emerged.

Analysis was undertaken using constructivist grounded theory methods (Charmaz, 2006; Strauss & Corbin, 1990) and a process of triangulation across the sources of data. Focus group data was transcribed after each group, and emerging themes were identified, initially within each case study group and then across the whole study and written into a narrative that defined the core themes. The narratives were checked with the participants in the interviews, and the data generated in the interviews was then aligned with the earlier data. The timelines and profile surveys, and the journal entries and logs were then triangulated with all other data to consolidate the themes that emerged.

As a starting point, and to establish a common understanding, the girls were asked to define popular culture. A selection of their responses is included in Table 1 against the earlier definitions of popular culture (p. 3) and reflects the diversity and nebulousness of the concept. Central to the lists is the sense that popular culture is for and about the audience and that it was present in the everyday lives of the participants.

Table 1 Responses to the question: How do you define popular culture?

Themes connected to definitions in the literature	Response from Year 7/8 participants	Responses from Year 10/11 participants
Popular culture is items of constructed artefacts.	Music and other people's cultures and readings. . .. *CDs and magazines and stuff.* Music and the computer and technology. *It's Japanese comics . . ..* Playstation. . . *DS machine. . ..* Camera. . .laptop . . .comic book///book.	Today's commercial world – say billboards, magazines, TV, movies. *Music, clothes and stuff.* The latest thing. . .fashion. Imagery and magazines, stuff.
Popular culture aims to maintain social order and to set roles and customs.	You can find it all over the world. . .. *Something we are interested in and want to do.*	Mainstream society and what's popular. *Trends.* Trends, relationships and everything. *Just stuff that's popular to our age group . . .what's cool and what's not.*
Popular culture is a tool to breakdown and challenge social order.		Celebrities having an effect on us.
Popular culture tells the stories of ordinary human lives.	Stuff that's important to Australia and teenagers are interested in *The things other people do.*	Celebrity gossip.

During the focus group and interview sessions, it became evident that the main sources of popular culture they engaged with were television, music, magazines, and movies. This meant that, in this study, popular culture is defined as artefacts from these main sources. While the girls interacted online it was not as important a source of social or cultural information as may have been expected. Some girls did not have strong Internet connectivity to their homes, or unsupervised access to online content. This may have impacted on their view of it as popular culture. When they discussed the impact of popular culture on their identity or talent development, they referenced television, movies, magazines, and music videos. They understood popular culture to be constructed for certain purposes, and that it was controlled by those who made it and who paid for it. They knew that images were manipulated according to the intended audience. They knew the content was written to give an idea or approach. But even as they thought critically about it, there was evidence that it influenced their lives, particularly in the way they dressed and current trends in fashion, language, and people of interest.

The following sections outline some of the concepts and responses the girls had to the images and messages in their sources of popular culture and its presentation of giftedness or talent.

Giftedness in Popular Culture: Some Findings

In this section of the chapter, the responses the girls had to the presentation of giftedness within popular culture and its influence on their lives in terms of their giftedness are recounted. They were able to describe that popular culture was a key influence in their lives, even if they were not fully aware of it, as indicated in the following conversation:

> P: . . . it is just part of our lives; we go home and switch on the TV or read a magazine or something and just don't even realise. . . [the influence it may have on thinking] (Interview, years 10/11)

They were asked to talk about the way they saw intelligence, talent, or giftedness portrayed in popular culture. Both fictional (e.g., Lisa Simpson, Temperance Brennan) and real characters (e.g., Coco Chanel, Julia Gillard, Jessica Mauboy) were included in the examples they gave of women they saw as gifted or talented. They felt that the drive to achieve talent was dependent on the individual being able to act on their own behalf, and that it required independence and persistence to achieve potential. The following excerpts highlight the drive they believed was needed to achieve talent:

> P: you've got to do it yourself, you've got to find it somehow and do it. I'm referring to 'The Simpsons', like Lisa, she found it and is using it.
> P: I saw Coco Chanel . . .she's very intelligent, it was amazing . . .she wasn't at all beautiful, she was pretty plain. The way they portrayed her personality was what made her, you could sense she was intelligent and an incredible woman. (Excerpts from focus group conversations, years 10/11)

There were other ways popular culture presented gifted girls or women. One of the concerns the girls expressed was the way clever females were portrayed as problem solvers, or helpers who were not the main character, but who were called upon to correct errors, or to solve a problem. They were often presented as plain girls who were not socially popular but who were pragmatic, quirky, and isolated individuals used by others in myriad ways. Sometimes female characters were in roles connected with high levels of intelligence, such as medical careers, or science fields, but it was their appearance and sexuality that was the focus in the show or movie. The participants explained this as an outcome of how, in their view, gifted women who did not fit social expectations for appearance would not attract an audience, as can be seen in the following excerpts:

> P: if they were just smart, then . . .you don't really want to watch.
> P: they are also portrayed as people who don't have many friends, sometimes. . .outcasts because they are intelligent. . .people can't understand that women can be really successful and have money and be able to do those things. . .
> P: . . .they seem to portray women, if they are intelligent, they are really shut off to the world . . ..they are ice cold. . . (Excerpts from focus groups, years 10/11)

The older girls were able to recognise indications of giftedness or talent in the content of popular culture that they engaged with. Indications included women who: had made a difference in a context or in the world; or were able to create new music, new solutions; or spoke out about issues in the world context. They saw gifted women shown mainly as minor characters, lonely women, mean women, or women, who were 'useful' and quirky, rather than popular. They did not see intelligence being portrayed as positive and in a telling comment, felt that the popular culture delivered a message that they should "use [their] intelligence to plot against each other rather than aspire to be smarter or go onto uni . . . it's telling us just to play it against each other and not be very nice" (Interview, Year 10/11).

The younger girls felt that giftedness was portrayed poorly in popular culture. They talked about gifted characters being individuals who solve problems (e.g., Betty in Ugly Betty), created humour in a serious (fictional) setting (e.g., Lisa Simpson), or who had skills that were needed by others (e.g., Abbie Sciuto in NCIS, Penelope Garcia, in Criminal Minds), but who were portrayed as nerds, or geeks. Their comments, as shown below, showed this:

> P: most of the time the person that's like the nerd is usually the smart one
> P: cause you have like your hero kind of thing . . .your main character and he'll have some friend who's like a scientist . . .he gives all the information . . .
> P: there's that side person like the scientist who knows everything
> P: in the cartoons. . .the smart A grade student . . .mostly have glasses and look like geeks.
> P: I've seen a fair amount of movies that have had dorkier kind of girls, that are really smart . . . (Excerpts from focus groups, years 7/8)

They recognised the power of stereotyped images in popular culture when commenting:

Popular culture, it reflects women looking good . . .if they try and advertise something they usually use someone that doesn't necessarily have to be smart but looks good and skinny. (Excerpt from interview, years 7/8)

Responding to Popular Culture

Across the two age groups, the girls responded to popular culture in consistent ways. Most simply, the responses encapsulated: being non-critically engaging with the content; being entertained; and following characters or storylines that provided topics for shared conversations with peers. These responses were particularly so with the younger cohort who believed what they read or saw and discussed at length the lives of celebrities and characters, sometimes comparing their own lives and seeing similarities in their own environments. The younger girls also responded emotively, expressing empathy for celebrities who were constantly in the media, concerned for the lack of privacy in their lives, and showing emotional responses to some issues and messaging. They responded critically to the manipulation of images and messages, and to advertisements that represented women as objects used to enhance products. They were vulnerable to the messages displayed in popular culture about appearance and behaviours, while concurrently showing the capacity to be critically aware of them:

You sort of realise how manipulative it can be . . .. Do you get sucked into it? . . . Yes, absolutely.
You can sit there and eat a McDonalds meal and then . . . flick through a trashy magazine and . . . you see beautiful people and you're kind of like . . . shouldn't have eaten that meal. . .'
You're sort of like 'I can defy it as much as I want (responding to messages in popular culture) but you feel like left out if you don't. (Excerpt focus groups, years 10/11)

The ambiguity of their responses was evident to the researcher, but not necessarily to the participants. The younger girls could see others being influenced by popular culture, and felt they were not going to be influenced, as evidenced in the following excerpts:

For some girls, who idolise people like Britney Spears and Lindsay Lohan . . .will think 'Oh, it's cool coz they're doing it so let's do it' and for some people like us we just think 'no'
You see them and they're all so skinny and they've got all the perfect legs and hair and then they go, 'Oh, I'm so fat I've got to . . . not eat so I get as skinny as her. . . . to some people with low self-esteem it does (impact their behaviour). (Excerpt focus groups, years 7/8)

In the context of talent development, the persistent images of gifted women did not appear to provide the participants with a positive perspective on giftedness, nor did it portray the effort and work that may go into talent development. The emerging themes illustrated how the participants saw gifted or talented women in popular culture and are described in Table 2.

Table 2 Themes evident in the data and support in the literature

Themes	Concepts within theme	Supporting literature
Women must be beautiful.	Beauty is about thinness and physical appearance: long hair, white teeth, thin body and clear skin. Women need to prioritise their beauty routines and ensure they meet expectations at all times.	Charles, 2010; Cheu, 2007; Harris, 2004; Signorelli, 1997; Tiggemann & Slater, 2003; Wohlwend, 2009.
Women are manipulative.	Success is not about caring, collaborating or ethical behaviour as long as your goal is achieved. Aggressive behaviour towards others is acceptable. Power over others and competition is appropriate. People are to be used for own means.	Cheu, 2007; Duits, 2010.
Women need a relationship to be successful.	Having a relationship with the opposite gender is essential for success. Instructions for how to meet, keep and manage your partner provide guidelines about appearance and behaviours. If necessary, a girl hides her real self and adapts to be attractive. A career is a pathway to a relationship.	Fabrianesi et al., 2008; Hamilton, 2008; Kearney, 2006.
Clever women are odd or nasty.	Clever women are not traditionally beautiful, and present as quirky, and unattractive. They are pragmatic and solve problems.	Charles, 2010; Cheu, 2007; Harris, 2004.
Effort is not needed to be successful.	Success does not involve hard work. School and higher education are places for social interaction, being seen and looking at others. While women can be successful in a range of careers, the pathway to achieving success is not made clear. Effort is not something to talk about. Girls who comply in the classroom have an easier time during school.	Fabrianesi, et al., 2008; Hamilton, 2008; Harris, 2004; Kearney, 2006.

Within popular culture it was suggested to these girls that successful women were also stereotypically beautiful (see Table 2). A second theme was that talented women were manipulative, especially when in leadership roles, using others to achieve their own agendas, and showing aggressive behaviours to those around them (see Table 2). A third common theme discerned by the girls was that a key task for girls and women is to prepare for a romantic relationship (see Table 2). Capable and clever girls changed their style, behaviours, and aspirations to align themselves with an individual they identified as important. Other relationships were also important, including mentors, who were sometimes older women or teachers. Family relationships were present and important in many television shows and movies. A fourth theme described in the data focused on clever women. Clever women were not presented in a positive light. They were nasty, amoral, and used power to control others. These women did not show caring behaviours to others or use collaborative approaches to work tasks.

The final theme relevant to this chapter is that of women and effort. In much of popular culture, the participants felt that success was made to look easy, with effort not being required to achieve life goals, to learn, or to become successful. School was not about challenge but rather about social activity. They noted that they did not often see girls having to put in effort to work or being required to persevere with academic tasks.

While the study demonstrated that popular culture does have a pervasive presence in the lives of adolescent gifted girls in rural settings, influencing their daily lives and decisions, the data also provided insight into other influences on adolescent gifted girls during their secondary school years. The participants identified popular culture as having an impact on how they saw themselves, their futures, and their ability, but they also identified other sources of influence that were important in guiding their choices. Their description of influences supporting the development of their identity and their talent in their lives aligned with the influences identified by Tweedale and Kronborg (2015) and can be seen in Figure 1.

Many of these girls had allies within the family (Kronborg, 2010) and felt supported to achieve their goals. They felt it was important that the family supported their interests in sport, dance, and creative activities and in being exposed to other contexts and experiences. They came from diverse family groups, and while not all their parents had further education, they supported the girls in doing well. Some girls

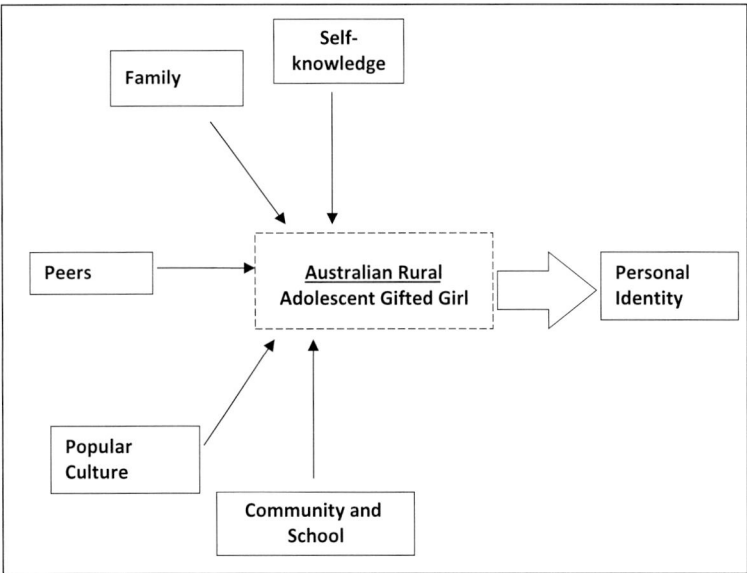

Fig. 1 The influences on the formation of personal identity for rural gifted adolescent girls (Wood, 2015)

had allies outside of the family of origin (Kronborg, 2010), including family friends, teachers, coaches or community identities who provided them with support in different ways. They also understood the strength they had in themselves to set goals and achieve them, and the importance of believing in oneself.

Popular Culture and Talent Development

The study found that popular culture was both a disruption and a support of talent development for rural adolescent gifted girls (Fig. 2).

A disruption is something that interrupts a process. From the themes that emerged from the data (see Table 2) and the sources of influence (see Fig. 2) it has been discerned that popular culture can potentially interrupt the process of talent development. The content of popular culture that the girls experienced in their daily lives did not showcase talent in terms of personal characteristics, persistent rigorous work, or meeting challenges of learning or skill development. Few characters in popular culture appear to engage in serious academic learning or effort, or discussion of serious life issues. The role models provided were women who showed a stereotypical image of beauty and judged others by the same standards. Those who were identified as gifted or talented often had a quirkiness that belied their ability and were in roles that were about solving problems or dealing with difficulties. They were put down and mocked by other characters, and often demonstrated low self-esteem. Popular culture can be described as a disruption to talent development when

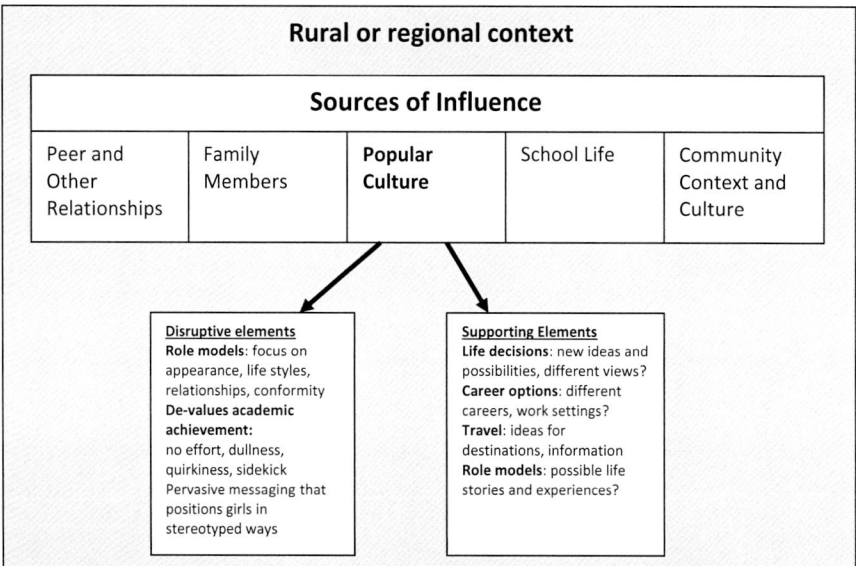

Fig. 2 The sources of influence on the development of a girl's talent development, defining the elements of popular culture that disrupt or support talent development (Wood, 2015)

it reinforces the loss of self-esteem and confidence that is consistent among young girls during this time of their lives (Capper et al., 2009; Chan, 2001; Harter, 2006; Reis, 2002).

In the study, it was also identified that popular culture could be recognised as a support to talent development through its capacity to provide rural girls with exposure to different locations, different career options, diverse role models, and opportunities to learn about options (see Fig. 2). In the lives of the girls in the study, popular culture sparked an interest in travel and provided insights about other settings, religions, or lifestyles. It did offer female role models who had achieved and continued to be successful, and whose lives were presented in the narratives to highlight how they succeeded.

A Model of Talent Development Inclusive of Gifted Girls in Rural Contexts

An earlier section of the chapter discussed a number of models that describe processes of talent development. The models outlined a range of factors that interact to achieve successful talent development and show a developmental sequence from gifted behaviours to talented performance. Gagné (2009) described a number of catalysts that can impact on the developmental process, filtering experiences through a set of intrapersonal catalysts that determine how an individual will experience opportunities. Others (Kerr & Larson, 2007; Kronborg, 2010; Noble et al., 1999; Reis, 2002) have written about specific gender factors that contribute to talent development in women, deriving the models largely from retrospective studies with successful, eminent women in a range of fields of endeavour. None of these models explicitly showed where popular culture fits as an influence, and yet, as shown in this study, it is a force in the lives of adolescent gifted girls. The model shown in Figure 3 evolved through the analysis of the case study data based on the responses and lived experiences of the participants. Figure 3 shows the initial frame of the model, and Figure 4 the final version. This section of the chapter will outline its evolution and describe how it explained talent development as interpreted from the data of the study.

In the initial figure, the connections between this model and earlier descriptions of talent development can be identified. Consistent among talent development models is the sense of a process, a period of time when there is ongoing development influenced by a number of factors or inputs. Each individual has a unique pattern of interactions between these factors, depending on their context and their personality. Gagné (2009) recognised that the individuality of each person changed the way the sources of influence were interpreted and acted on, seeing the intrapersonal catalysts as filters for the environmental catalysts. Noble et al. (1999) and Kronborg (2010) identified a key element of talent development as being filters, to create an individual response to opportunities, events, and milieu. Kerr and Multon (2015) identified the way that gender can act as a filter on opportunity and support. Possible filtering of experience was clearly evident in the data across the case studies. For

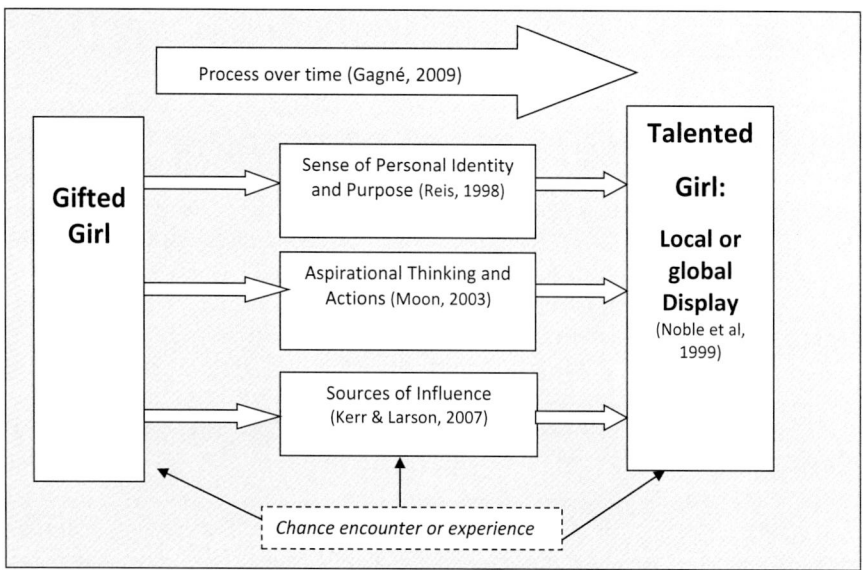

Fig. 3 Initial framework of the talent development model, showing its derivation from literature sources (Wood, 2015)

example, girls in the same school experienced: popular culture differently; friends differently; their community differently; and had different levels of drive even when they had similar aspirations. Such individuality is vital to consider because gifted learners are diverse, and it is important to recognise the impact of an individual's sense of self and purpose on his or her personal trajectory of talent development (Ambrose, 2003; Moon, 2003; Reis, 2002).

As a response to this, the relationship between popular culture and two other influences on adolescent gifted girls are acknowledged in Figure 4 and the relationship between them is illustrated, including the filtering of the interactions through the sense of self that leads to talent development. The concept of chance remains evident in the model to represent the unexpected real or mediated experiences, people, or opportunities that can happen for any girl, or group of girls. Gagné (2009) asserted that, while informed planning and preparation is an important part of the talent development process, chance encounters remain a valuable possibility.

The model shown in Figure 4 is set in the life stage of adolescence and, because of the location of the study, the rural context, shown by the foundation box that holds the components.

The model represents a trajectory of talent development when considering the influences on an individual, moving from the identification of giftedness to evidence of successful talent development. It contributes to the developmental process that includes practice, investment, time, and maturation (Gagné, 2009). In the context of the DMGT (Gagné, 2009) that framed the analysis of the data, the model provides greater detail about the environmental and intrapersonal

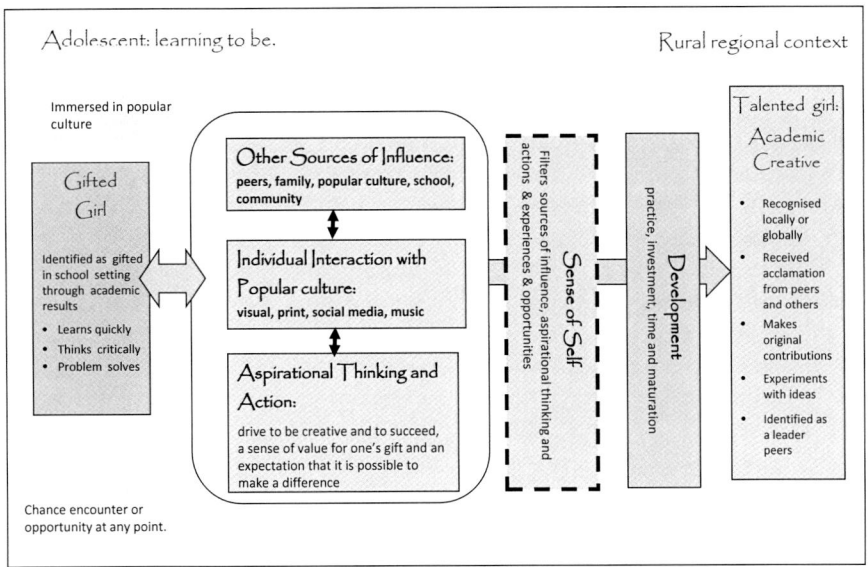

Fig. 4 Wood Talent Development Model for adolescent girls in rural settings. (Adapted from Wood, 2015)

catalysts, describing the place that popular culture has in these elements. Popular culture both surrounds the gifted girl and takes its place as one of a set of dynamic catalysts that form part of the developmental process. People, places, experiences, and opportunities influence the way a girl perceives her abilities and her future. Aspirational thinking and actions include the drive to be creative and to succeed, a sense of value for one's gift and an expectation that it is possible to make a difference. The responses that a gifted girl has to popular culture, as well as to other influences, contribute then to the process of development and are filtered through a sense of self to result in talented performance. The sense of self that a gifted girl establishes throughout her adolescence is acknowledged in all talent development models as a vital force in talent development. Through the analysis of the data for this study, it became clear that the sense of self, which emerges from a range of interactions with sources of influence, acts as a filter for all the sources of influence and has been placed at the end of the process, feeding into the development process, prior to talent actualisation, to illustrate this.

Finally, the talented girl emerges. Her successful development is recognised in either her local setting or in a global setting, when her products or actions result in recognition and acclamation, when she is identified as a leader or when her original contributions to an area of need makes a difference. In most talent development models, the achievement of talent actualisation is recognised as eminence. Eminence is a state of being that is attributed to women in much later life. By definition it has been identified by actions and impact that are widespread and transformational, contributing to the good of humankind, and extreme fame (Kronborg, 2010).

Kronborg's 2010 study participants were chosen because they fit this definition of eminence in Australian society, and had been written about in Australian media, having made a difference in their field of endeavour.

In this model of talent development, the final stage defines talented performance as being displayed in either a local or a global context. Noble et al. (1999) described two domains of talent performance: public or private. This interpretation has been taken up in this model, because eminence in its traditional definition may be out of reach for adolescent gifted girls and therefore not a state of being they will aspire to. However, a gifted rural adolescent girl, or woman, may, through her actions and her being, transform her local community, or impact on the rural context to make a difference to the wider community. Eminence at a local level may be described as advocacy for communities, contributions to local culture and development, leadership in industry, business or cultural endeavours, or acclaim and recognition for achievements, and is as important in the ongoing development in rural locations as the fame and celebrity presented in popular culture. In this model, the public and private domains (Noble et al., 1999) have been interpreted as global and local, allowing for the acclamation of talent demonstrated and applied within local communities or districts. In Australia, where rural and regional communities are vital components of the culture and society, seeking and applauding those who make a difference offers adolescent gifted girls new options for their futures.

Using the Talent Development Model: Implications for Practice

This section of the chapter presents a number of suggestions for applying the model to support the talent development of adolescent rural gifted girls as they negotiate a world replete with popular culture to find their identity, and their domain of talent. The model suggests that gifted girls need to be identified as gifted individuals as part of the talent development process. For most girls, their identification will come through their school setting, where their academic achievement can be monitored and recorded. However, there is the need to use multiple sources of evidence (Montgomery, 2004; Pendarvis & Wood, 2009), and this may include activity in the community, extracurricular activity, and achievements in music or sport. Collecting evidence of higher order thinking, problem solving, attempting new strategies and high levels of curiosity about the environment and the wider world will be useful in building a profile of the individual.

A benefit of living in a rural community is that there is a greater chance of recognition by a range of adults and peers in the community through a variety of connections (Colangelo et al., 2006). This can provide access to information about diverse extracurricular activities. A portfolio approach, whereby information and evidence are kept over an extended period of time will allow for ongoing observation and record keeping. Because in rural schools there may be long-term relationships with teachers and other staff (Colangelo et al., 2006), the portfolio can provide valuable insights into the interests and developing skills of the girl. Identifying a girl as gifted can contribute to her sense of self and offer her freedom to show her abilities (Mendez, 2000), which can make a difference to classroom outcomes. Seeking ways of enabling gifted girls to be confident in their own abilities is a starting point towards talent actualisation (Burton et al., 2006; Kerr & Multon, 2015).

The second component of the model groups together three interactive factors that play a part in the gifted girl reaching her potential, acting as catalysts for development and influencing the choices she makes towards talent achievement. The model suggests that these factors are core to ongoing development, which are in common with the talent development literature on women (e.g., Kronborg, 2010; Noble et al., 1999; Reis, 2002; Tweedale & Kronborg, 2015). They contribute to the development of a sense of identity, which in turn builds the sense of self and finally the demonstration of talent (Moon, 2003). Gifted girls experience multiple sources of influence in their lives (e.g., Eccles, 2011; Eddles-Hirsch, 2006; Maxwell, 2007; Tweedale & Kronborg, 2015; Willard-Holt, 2008), and, in the model, it is recognised that each contributes in different ways. Families, including the extended family, are role models, supporters, challengers, and advisors whose life experiences show ways of being that girls can imitate or move away from (e.g., Kerr & Sodano, 2003; Kronborg, 2010; Sanders & Munford, 2008; Walshaw, 2006). Classroom teachers provide another source of information and reaction. Their classroom interactions, including the questions they ask, the discipline they use, the manner in which they respond to a student, and their feedback on work or behaviour, influence how the student perceives herself, and what she believes about her capacity to complete academic work (Mendez, 2000). Classrooms are not gender-free, and in some instances, girls may be constrained in their actions by the responses of the teacher (Kerr & Multon, 2015; Renold & Allan, 2006). The way a classroom environment offers rewards, provides access to resources, and makes use of technology can deliver strong messages about what girls can do and aspire to (Maxwell, 2007).

Further, and in particular in rural settings, there will be a greater interaction between young people and the local community (Stambaugh, 2015). Mentors for traditional occupations may be easily accessible, engagement in real world activities, and problem solving may be part of a school day (Stambaugh, 2015). As a source of influence, the community itself can offer perspectives on the future, opportunities for leadership and for relationships that extend learning and a sense of familiarity that may allow for curiosity and exploration (Colangelo et al., 2006). Peers are recognised as a source of influence on young people, and in a rural context this may be a challenge, as a lack of like minds may result in gifted girls changing their aspirations to fit in, and not seeing their talent as appropriate (James et al., 2010; Lea-Wood, 2004). The various sources of influence are important as the gifted girl considers who she is, and what is possible for her in future life (Reis, 2002). However, the model identifies that the interactions adolescent gifted rural girls have with popular culture can influence her aspirational thinking and her sense of self.

Popular culture has an impact on the way an individual perceives herself physically (Tiggemann & McGill, 2004; Tiggemann & Slater, 2003), and in terms of her ability (Fabrianesi et al., 2008; Fritzsche, 2004; Renold & Allan, 2006). Each girl will interact with the various sources of popular culture in a unique way and needs to have the skills to recognise when truth is being manipulated or when the messages being delivered are not the only message. Skills of critical thinking and analysis—enabling the questioning and challenging of the messages presented in popular culture—are essential for adolescent gifted girls so that they are enabled to manage the multiple concepts and ideas presented (Harris, 2004; Kearney, 2006). Activities that deconstruct the production of popular culture, that break down images, and consider the way they have been manipulated to create the final image, empower girls to understand the process (Kearney, 2006). Creating media builds a deeper understanding of the way popular culture can be designed to tell stories and can also provide the opportunity to understand the power the construction of popular culture gives to the producer (Kearney, 2006). Strategically, rural adolescent gifted girls could be given the task of telling the stories of others through media, thus learning about new role models while also building an understanding of the power of media.

Finally, the girl is a source of influence for herself. Aspirational thinking and action drive positive self-confidence, and lead to the setting of goals, achievement of the same, a willingness to explore, and a sense of value (Kerr & Multon, 2015; Tweedale & Kronborg, 2015). If girls are encouraged to explore their passions, to reflect on their achievements and skills and to articulate their needs and ideas, they will be able to plan for their future (Tweedale & Kronborg, 2015). Activities that involve journaling, thinking skills, learning about diverse role models and women who have overcome the challenge to achieve provide rich material for future goal setting. Career information that is non-traditional and non-stereotyped, that highlights the work and effort as well as the possible fame and recognition, can provide different perspectives from those of family and friends (Kerr & Sodano, 2003; Maxwell, 2007; Wood, 2017) and open possibilities not evident in a rural community. Knowing why women took certain pathways, understanding the challenges and difficulties, and seeing successful women in diverse settings may inform rural adolescent gifted girls of the possibilities.

In the model, the suggestion is when the three influences (individual interactions with popular culture, aspirational thinking and action, and interactions with other people and places) are balanced within the life of a girl, they offer the support she needs to counteract the impact of popular culture on her vision of how a girl can be, or what she can do. When they are in balance, as indicated in the model diagram, she can more fully understand herself, her abilities, and her future potential. Managing the different pieces of information, and the diverse examples she will find around her and in popular culture will enable her to build a strong sense of self, form realistic goals, and have the volition to achieve them. Activities that provide skill development in goal setting, writing about personal responses, seeking different perspectives, and challenging the truth evident in popular culture will enable the gifted girl to reach talent potential.

The model then shows that the talented girl emerges, transforming her local environment, making a difference to her context, contributing to change, and development or inspiring others to action. Whatever area of human endeavour her talent falls into will be the focus of her attention and work. Over time this may change, but in this model it is recognised that talented performance can be evident at any age, and that the setting for the performance can be either local or global.

Implications for Research

In this chapter, a model describing a conceptual vision of the way talent development may be shaped through the presence of popular culture in the lives of rural adolescent gifted girls has been presented. Framed initially in the DMGT (Gagné, 2009), it incorporates elements of a range of other models, and introduces popular culture as an explicit consideration. The model needs further development, through testing its validity with other groups of girls in other rural settings, because of the diversity of rural contexts (Stambaugh, 2015), and to explore more deeply the relationship gifted rural adolescent girls have with popular culture.

It is imperative that in Australia there is also further research into the lived experiences of gifted girls, and gifted boys, in rural communities, to better understand what can be offered in their communities and schools to best nurture their talent.

Conclusion

In this chapter, an examination of the literature enabled the exploration of the way that popular culture may impact on talent development of gifted rural adolescent girls. A research study that used case study methods to explore the lived experiences of adolescent gifted girls in rural contexts was exampled. The study examined popular culture artefacts, such as visual, print, and music media. From the study, a model was developed that explained how the impact of popular culture could be included in a description of talent development. In the final section, the use of the model as a framework for developing programs was discussed.

Popular culture contributes to the development of talent and should be acknowledged as an influence on the talent development of rural adolescent gifted girls. While ever popular culture remains a pervasive presence in the lives of adolescents, it is valid to consider it as both a disruptive and a supportive influence on talent development. Gifted rural adolescent girls live in a world where popular culture provides information, concepts, and models that stretch beyond the confines of a rural community. Their talent may take them to global settings and provide them with opportunities to influence others on a large scale, but it may also have an outcome of eminence in the local domain that results in transformational change for the future. Either contextual outcome supports rural adolescent gifted girls to achieve their potential.

Cross-References

References

Alloway, N., & Dalley-Trim, L. (2009). 'High and dry' in rural Australia: Obstacles to student aspirations and expectations. *Rural Society, 19*(1), 49–59. https://doi.org/10.5172/rsj.351.19.1.49

Ambrose, D. (2003). Barriers to aspiration development and self-fulfilment: Interdisciplinary insights for talent discovery. *The Gifted Child Quarterly, 47*(4), 282–294. https://doi.org/10.1177/001698620304700405

Bailey, S., Knight, B. A., & Riley, D. (1995). Addressing the needs of the gifted in rural areas: The Armidale Catholic Schools Office project. *Education in Rural Australia, 5*(2), 1–13.

Bannister, B., Cornish, L., Bannister-Tyrrell, M., & Gregory, S. (2015). Creative use of digital technologies: Keeping the best and brightest in the bush. *Australian and International Journal of Rural Education, 25*(1), 52–65.

Burton, L. J., VanHeest, J. L., Rallis, S. F., & Reis, S. M. (2006). Going for gold: Understanding talent development through the lived experiences of us female Olympians. *Journal of Adult Development, 13*, 124–136. https://doi.org/10.1007/s10804-007-9021

Capper, M. R., Foust, R. C., Callahan, C. M., & Albaugh, S. B. (2009). Grade and gender difference in gifted students' self-Concepts. *Journal for the Education of the Gifted, 32*(3), 340–367. https://doi.org/10.4219/jeg-2009-862

Chan, D. W. (2001). Global and specific self-concepts of gifted adolescents in Hong Kong. *Journal for the Education of the Gifted, 24*(4), 344–364. https://doi.org/10.1177/016235320102400404

Charles, C. (2010). Raunch culture goes to school: Young women, normative femininities and elite education. *Media International Australia, 135*, 61–70. https://doi.org/10.1177/1329878X1013500109

Charmaz, K. (2006). *Constructing grounded theory: A practical guide through qualitative analysis.* Thousand Oaks, CA: Sage.

Cheu, H. F. (2007). Disney and Girlhood. In C. A. Mitchell, & J. Reid-Walsh, *Girl culture: An encyclopedia* (two Vols.) (pp. 48–56). Westport, CT: Greenwood Publishing Group.

Colangelo, N., Assouline, S., Baldus, C., Ihrig, D., & New, J. (2006). *Gifted in rural America: Faces of diversity.* Iowa City, IA: The University of Iowa.

Cornish, L. (2010). Multiage classes: What's in a name? *Journal of Multiage Education, 4*(2), 7–11.

Driscoll, C. (2002). *Girls: Feminine adolescence in popular culture and cultural theory.* New York, NY: Columbia University Press.

Duits, L. (2010). The importance of popular media in everyday girl culture. *European Journal of Communication, 25*(3), 243–257. https://doi.org/10.1177/0267323110373461

Eccles, J. S. (2011). Understanding women's achievement choices: Looking back and looking forward. *Psychology of Women Quarterly, 35*(3), 510–516. https://doi.org/10.1177/0361684311414829. http://pwq.sagepub.com

Eddles-Hirsch, K. (2006). If only they would listen: The lifeworld of academically advanced elementary students. *Australasian Journal of Gifted Education, 15*(1), 5–15.

Fabrianesi, B., Jones, S. C., & Reid, A. (2008). Are pre-adolescent girls' magazines providing age-appropriate role models? *Health Education, 108*(6), 437–449.

Fishwick, M. W. (1985). *Seven pillars of popular culture.* Westport, CT: Greenwood Press.

Fritzsche, B. (2004). Spicy strategies: Pop feminist and other empowerments in girl culture. In A. Harris & A. (Eds.), *All about the girl: Culture, power, and identity* (pp. 155–162). New York, NY: Routledge.

Gaerlan-Price, E. (2015). Meet, prey, like: A study of gifted girls' interactions with social media. APEX: *The New Zealand Journal of Gifted Education, 19*(1). Retrieved from www.giftedchildren.org.nz/apex

Gagné, F. (2009). Building gifts into talents: Detailed overview of the DMGT 2.0. In B. MacFarlane & T. Stambaugh (Eds.), *Leading change in gifted education: The festschrift of Dr. Joyce VanTassel-Baska* (pp. 61–80). Waco, TX: Prufrock Press.

Galitis, I. (2009). *A case study of gifted education in an Australian primary school: Teacher attitudes, professional discourses, and gender* (PhD thesis, Education). The University of Melbourne. Retrieved from http://hdl.handle.net/11343/35180

Gilbert, S. C., Keery, H., & Thompson, J. K. (2005). The media's role in body image and eating disorders. In E. Cole & J. H. Daniels (Eds.), *Featuring females: Feminist analyses of media* (pp. 41–56). Washington, DC: Psychology of women book series, American Psychological Association.

Grabe, S., Ward, L. M., & Hyde, J. S. (2008). The role of the media in body image concerns among women: A meta-analysis of experimental and correlational studies. *Psychological Bulletin, 134*(3), 460–476. https://doi.org/10.1037/0033-2909.134.3.460

Grant, D. F., Battle, D. A., & Heggoy, S. J. (2000). The journey through college of seven gifted females: Influences on their career related decisions. *Roeper Review, 22*(4), 251–261. https://doi.org/10.1080/02783190009554047

Hamilton, M. (2008). *What's happening to our girls?* Melbourne, VIC: Viking Penguin group.

Harper, B., & Tiggemann, M. (2007). The effect of thin ideal media images on women's self-objectification, mood, and body image. *Sex Roles, 58*(9), 649–657. https://doi.org/10.1007/s11199-007-9379-x

Harris, A. (2004). *Future girl. Young women in the twenty-first century.* New York, NY: Routledge.

Harter, S. (2006). The self. In W. Damon & N. Eisenberg (Eds.), *Handbook of child psychology: Vol. 3. Social, emotional, and personality development* (6th ed., pp. 505–570). New York, NY: Wiley.

Henderson, L., & Jarvis, J. (2016). The gifted dimension of the Australian Professional Standards for teachers: Implications for professional learning. *Australian Journal of Teacher Education, 41*(8). https://doi.org/10.14221/ajte.2016v41n8.4

Hobbs, R., Broder, S., Pope, H., & Rowe, J. (2006). How adolescent girls interpret weight-loss advertising. *Health Education Research, 21*(5), 719–730. https://doi.org/10.1093/her/cyl077

Holmstron, A. J. (2004). The effects of the media on body image: A meta-analysis. *Journal of Broadcasting & Electronic Media, 48*(2), 196–217. https://doi.org/10.1207/s15506878jobem 4802_3

Howley, A., Rhodes, M., & Beall, J. (2009). Challenges facing rural schools: Implications for gifted students. *Journal for the Education of the Gifted, 32*(4), 515–536. https://doi.org/10.1177/016235320903200404

Howley, C. (2009). The meaning of rural difference for bright rednecks. *Journal for the Education of the Gifted, 32*(4), 537–564, https://doi.org/10.1177/016235320903200405

Hylmo, A. (2006). Girls on Film: An examination of gendered vocational socialisation messages found in motion pictures targeting teenage girls. *Western Journal of Communication, 70*(3), 167–185. https://doi.org/10.1080/10570310600843488

James, R., Krause, K., & Jennings, C. (2010). *The first year experience in Australian universities: Findings from 1994 to 2009.* Melbourne, VIC: Centre for the Study of Higher Education, The University of Melbourne.

Johnson, N. R. (2007). Romance in teen publications. In C. A. Mitchell & J. Reid-Walsh (Eds.), *Girl culture: An encyclopaedia* [two Vols.], (pp. 57–63). Westport, CT: Greenwood Publishing Group.

Kearney, M. C. (2006). *Girls make media.* New York, NY: Routledge.

Kerr, B. A., & Larson, A. (2007). How gifted girls become eminent women. In S. Lopez (Ed.), *Positive psychology perspectives.* New York, NY: Praeger.

Kerr, B. A., & Multon, K. D. (2015). The development of gender identity, gender roles, and gender relations in gifted students. *Journal of Counseling & Development, 93*, 183–191.

Kerr, B. A., & Sodano, S. (2003). Career assessment with intellectually gifted students. *Journal of Career Assessment, 11*(2), 168–186. https://doi.org/10.1177/1069072703011002004

Kronborg, L. (2010). What contributes to talent development in eminent women? *Gifted and Talented International, 25*(2), 11–27. https://doi.org/10.1080/15332276.2010.11673567

Laura, R., & Smith, S. (2009). The re-enchantment of science education: Towards a new vision of engaging rural gifted children in science. In T. Lyons, J-Y Choi & G. McPhan (Eds.), *Symposium proceedings, international symposium for innovation in rural education (ISSFIRE): Improving equity in rural education* (pp. 153–166). UNE: Armidale, N.S.W. Australia.

Lawrence, B. K. (2009). Rural gifted education: A comprehensive literature review. *Journal for the Education of the Gifted, 32*(4), 461–494. https://doi.org/10.1177/016235320903200402

Lea-Wood, S. S. (2004). *Factors influencing the vocational decisions making of higher ability adolescent girls* (Doctoral thesis). University of Melbourne, Melbourne, VIC.

Maltby, F., & Devlin, M. (2000). Breaking through the glass ceiling without bruising: The breakthrough programme for high ability girls. *Gifted Education International, 14*, 112–124. https://doi.org/10.1177/026142940001400202

Maxwell, M. (2007). Career counselling is personal counselling: A constructivist approach to nurturing the development of gifted female adolescents. *Career Development Quarterly, 55*(3), 206–224.

McRobbie, A., & McCabe, T. (1981). *Feminism for girls: An adventure story.* London, England: Routledge.

Mendez, L. M. R. (2000). Gender roles and achievement-related choices: A comparison of early adolescent girls in gifted and general education programs. *Journal for the Education of the Gifted, 24*(2), 149–169.

Meyer, M. D. E. (2003). "It's me. I'm it.": Defining adolescent sexual identity through relational dialectics in Dawson's Creek. *Communication Quarterly, 51*(3), 262–276. https://doi.org/10.1080/01463370309370156

Montgomery, D. (2004). Broadening perspectives to meet the needs of gifted learners in rural schools. *Rural Special Education Quarterly, 23*(1), 3–16. https://doi.org/10.1177/875687050402300102

Moon, S. M. (2003). Personal talent. *High Ability Studies, 14*(1), 5–21. https://doi.org/10.1080/13032000093490

Nash, I. (2006). *American sweethearts: Teenage girls in twentieth century popular culture*. Bloomington, IN: Indiana University Press.

Noble, K. D. (1992). Living out the promise of high potential: Perceptions of 100 gifted women. *California Association for the Gifted*. September, 18–28.

Noble, K. D., Subotnik, R. F., & Arnold, K. D. (1999). To thine own self be true: A new model of female talent development. *The Gifted Child Quarterly, 43*(4), 140–149. https://doi.org/10.1177/001698629904300302

O'Quinn, M. D. (1999). Getting above our raising: A case study of women from the coalfields of southwest Virginia and eastern Kentucky. *Journal of Research in Rural Education, 15*(3), 181–189.

Pendarvis, E., & Wood, E. W. (2009). Eligibility of historically underrepresented students referred for gifted education in a rural school district: A case study. *Journal for the Education of the Gifted, 32*(4), 495–514. https://doi.org/10.1177/016235320903200403

Pipher, M. (1994). *Reviving Ophelia: Saving the selves of adolescent girls*. New York, NY: Riverhead Books.

Reis, S. M. (1995). Older women's reflections on eminence: Obstacles and opportunities. *Roeper Review, 18*(1), 66–73. https://doi.org/10.1080/02783199509553700

Reis, S. M. (1998). *Work left undone*. Mansfield Centre, CT: Creative Learning Press, Inc.

Reis, S. M. (2002). Internal barriers, personal issues, and decisions faced by gifted and talented females. *Gifted Child Today, 25*(1), 14–28. https://doi.org/10.4219/gct-2002-50

Renold, E., & Allan, A. (2006). Bright and beautiful: High achieving girls: Ambivalent femininities and the feminisation of success in the primary school. *Discourse: Studies in the Cultural Politics of Education, 27*(4), 457–473. https://doi.org/10.1080/01596300600988606

Robbins, A. (2006). *The overachievers: The secret lives of driven kids*. New York, NY: Hyperion.

Sanders, J., & Munford, R. (2008). Losing self to the future? Young women's strategic responses to adulthood transitions. *Journal of Youth Studies, 11*(3), 331–346. https://doi.org/10.1080/13676260801946480

Schmitt-Wilson, S., & Welsh, M. C. (2012). Vocational knowledge in rural children: A study of individual differences and predictors of occupational aspirations and expectations. *Learning and Individual Differences, 22*(6), 862–867. https://doi.org/10.1016/j.lindif.2012.06.003

Signorelli, N. (1997). *Reflections of girls in the media: A content analysis. A study of television shows and commercials, movies, music videos and teen magazine articles and ads*. Oakland, CA/Children Now and Menlo Park, CA: Henry J. Kaiser Family Foundation.

Stambaugh, T. (2015). Concluding thoughts and voices from gifted individuals in rural areas. In T. Stambaugh & S. M. Wood (Eds.), *A framework for bridging gifted education and rural classrooms: Serving students in rural settings*. Waco, TX: Prufrock Press Inc.

States News Service. (2010, August 26). Scientists trump popstars as role models for girls. *Expanded Academic ASAP*. Retrieved from http://link.galegroup.com/apps/doc/A235639884/EAIM?u=csu_au&sid=EAIM&xid=4e59f12a. Accessed 6 Oct 2018.

Strauss, A., & Corbin, J. (1990). *Basics of qualitative research: Grounded theory procedures and techniques*. Newbury Park, CA: Sage.

Tally, M. (2007). Representations of girls and young women in film: An entry point to studying girl culture. In C. Mitchell & J. Reid-Walsh (Eds.), *Girl culture: An encyclopedia* [2 Vols.] (pp. 108–115). Retrieved from http://www.eblib.com

Theran, S. A., Newberg, E. M., & Gleason, T. R. (2010). Adolescent girls' parasocial interactions with media figures. *The Journal of Genetic Psychology, 171*(3), 270–277. https://doi.org/10.1080/00221325.2010.483700

Tiggemann, M. (2005). Television and adolescent body image: The role of program content and viewing motivation. *Journal of Social and Clinical Psychology, 24*(3), 361–381. https://doi.org/10.1521/jscp.24.3.361.65623

Tiggemann, M., & McGill, B. (2004). The role of social comparison in the effect of magazine advertisements on women's mood and body dissatisfaction. *Journal of Social and Clinical Psychology, 23*(1), 23–44. https://doi.org/10.1521/jscp.23.1.23.26991

Tiggemann, M., & Slater, A. (2003). Thin ideals in music television: A source of social comparison and body dissatisfaction. *International Journal of Eating Disorders, 35*(1), 48–58. https://doi. org/10.1002/eat.10214

Tweedale, C., & Kronborg, L. (2015). What contributes to gifted adolescent females' talent development at a high achieving secondary girls' school? *Gifted and Talented International, 30*(1–2), 6–18. https://doi.org/10.1080/15332276.2015.1137450

Vialle, W., Heaven, P. C. L., & Ciarrochi, J. (2007). On being gifted, but sad and misunderstood: Social, emotional and academic outcomes of gifted students in the Wollongong Youth study. *Educational Research and Evaluation, 13*(6), 569–586. https://doi.org/10.1080/ 13803610701786046

Walshaw, M. (2006). Girls' workplace destinations in a changed social landscape: Girls and their mothers talk. *British Journal of Sociology of Education, 27*, 555–567. https://doi.org/10.1080/ 01425690600958741

Ward, L. M., & Harrison, K. (2005). The impact of media use on girls' beliefs about gender roles, their bodies, and sexual relationships: A research synthesis. In J. H. Daniel & E. Cole (Eds.), *Featuring females: Feminist analyses of media* (pp. 3–23). Washington, DC: American Psychological Association.

Willard-Holt, C. (2008). 'You could be doing brain surgery': Gifted girls becoming teachers. *The Gifted Child Quarterly, 52*, 313–324. https://doi.org/10.1177/00169208321807

Wilson, S., Lyons, T., & Quinn, F. (2013). 'Should I stay or should I go?' Rural and remote students in first year university STEM courses. *Australian and International Journal of Rural Education, 23*(2), 77–88.

Wohlwend, K. E. (2009). Damsels in discourse: Girls consuming and producing identity texts through Disney princess play. *Reading Research Quarterly, 44*(1), 57–83. https://doi.org/ 10.1598/RRQ.44.1.3

Wood, D. (2015). *Beauty or brains? The impact of popular culture on the development of adolescent rural gifted girls' identity and subsequent talent development* (Unpublished doctoral dissertation). University of Wollongong, Wollongong, NSW.

Wood, D. (2017). Into the world: Supporting the career aspirations of adolescent rural gifted girls. *Vision, 28*(2), 22–24.

Wood, D., & Vialle, W. (2015). Popular culture: A support or a disruption to talent development in the lives of rural adolescent gifted girls? *Australasian Journal of Gifted Education, 24*(1), 13–22.

Denise Wood, PhD, has been an advocate for, and teacher of, gifted students for more than 30 years, in rural NSW in Australia. She has worked with gifted students in classrooms and in a range of provisions, from a fulltime classroom to smaller part-time programs. Currently in the higher education sector, Denise has written and presented subjects focused on gifted education in undergraduate and postgraduate teacher education programs and presented programs of professional learning to classroom teachers across regional NSW. Her research interests include the support for gifted students throughout their schooling, and in particular, rural adolescent gifted girls and rural gifted women, and their talent development, building on the findings from her thesis.

A Model for Growing Teacher Talent Scouts: Decreasing Underrepresentation of Gifted Students

52

Julie Dingle Swanson, Lara Walker Russell, and Lindsey Anderson

Contents

Abstract

Underrepresentation of some talented students of promise has been an intractable issue in US public schools (Boothe & Stanley, 2004: Ford, 1995). Because giftedness as a concept is culturally bound, it is no surprise that the values of a culture contribute to the identification of who the gifted and talented are as well as the special educational services they receive. Access for high-ability students to programs and classes can positively impact an individual's future education and professional opportunities. Teacher development as an approach for opening access and opportunity and growing diverse learners' academic potential is addressed in this chapter. An overview of theories, models, and effective practices shown to develop teachers' knowledge and skills to recognise and grow emergent talent of students from diverse backgrounds (Olszewski-Kubilius & Clarenbach, 2012;

J. D. Swanson (✉)
College of Charleston, Charleston, SC, USA
e-mail: swansonj@cofc.edu

L. W. Russell, · L. Anderson
Javits Project, College of Charleston, Charleston, SC, USA
e-mail: lara_russell@charleston.k12.sc.us; lindsey_anderson@charleston.k12.sc.us

© Springer Nature Singapore Pte Ltd. 2021   1193
S. R. Smith (ed.), *Handbook of Giftedness and Talent Development in the Asia-Pacific*,
Springer International Handbooks of Education,
https://doi.org/10.1007/978-981-13-3041-4_55

Subotnik, Olszewski-Kubilius, & Worrell, 2011) provides grounding in what is known. The overview connects talent development to key research in educational psychology, for example, motivation, persistence, and grit (Duckworth, 2016; Dweck, 2007). Exemplars of successful teacher-focused programs and projects (Coleman, Coltrane, Harradine, & Timmons, 2007: Gavin, Casa, Adelson, Carrolll, & Sheffield, 2009; VanTassel-Baska & Stambaugh, 2007) that raise rigor and challenge for all students via advanced curriculum and instruction translate theory into practice. The model of talent development that emerges consists of three primary components: cultural influences (Gay, 2000; Ladson-Billings, 2009), psychology of learning (e.g., Duckworth, 2016; Dweck, 2007), and powerful curriculum and instruction that utilises the *Integrated Curriculum Model* (VanTassel-Baska, 2013) with student-driven inquiry (Gavin, Casa, Adelson, Carrolll, & Sheffield, 2009). Research-based approaches (Swanson, Brock, & Kessler, 2018) used to advance professional learning of teachers, including whole group, small group, fidelity observations, and differentiated teacher learning, are shared. The chapter concludes with a discussion of a framework for growing student talent through focused teacher development and the implications for adoption of such a framework in the field, and potential directions for further research.

Keywords

Teacher development · Talent · Talent development · Culturally and linguistically diverse (CLD) gifted · Curriculum and instruction

The aims in this chapter are to:
1. Describe a teacher-focused approach to addressing underrepresentation of gifted students.
2. Explain how a responsive model for teacher learning, using data and trends to inform professional development, effectively shifts teacher beliefs about students.
3. Build understanding of combining non-cognitive factors in student learning, responsive teaching and powerful curriculum and instruction as a tapestry that is woven to engage and challenge gifted students.
4. Use the model for Talent Development Academy to exemplify under what conditions innovation takes root.
5. Underscore the importance of ongoing and sustained teacher learning, in varied forms, that includes coaching and demonstration.

Introduction

Sandy Jamison, a teacher in a rural school serving 99% of students of colour from low-income households, offered the following statement about her class of grade 1 and 2 students. Ms. Jamison said, "these kids are becoming students I don't recognise". When asked to explain this rather puzzling statement, she replied, "they are thinking and expressing ideas and seeing connections I had no idea they had in their heads. I did not think they could do this" (S. Jamison, February 11, 2017, personal communication). What was the 'this' to which she was referring in her startling comment? The 'this' was using a set of purposefully crafted, high-level, advanced novel study guides called *Navigators* that tapped into deep and conceptual thinking of her students. She used a picture book called *If A Bus Could Talk* by Faith Ringgold. In the picture book, the bus 'tells' the story of the US civil rights movement of the 1960s, starting with the story of Rosa Parks' refusal to go to the back of the bus and going further into the efforts to challenge racial segregation and inequity. The teacher in this anecdote, a part of a Javits-funded project called the *Talent Development Academy Project*, was relating her reaction to abilities she saw in her students as she used these powerful teaching strategies. Up until this point, these students' abilities had been invisible to her. Use of a culturally relevant literary selection combined with student engagement in analysis and discussion through carefully crafted questions (Hammond, 2015) revealed talents in her students that astonished her (S. Jamison, February 11, 2017, personal communication).

Talent spotting and development is not quite as easy as it would seem. Clearly, underrepresentation in gifted programs of some talented students of promise has been a long-term issue in US public schools (Boothe & Stanley, 2004; Ford, 1995). Underrepresented students tend to be from low-income households, often are students of colour, and include many students who may be culturally different (Ford, 2013; Olszewski-Kubilius & Clarenbach, 2014). Giftedness as a concept is culturally bound, so it is no surprise that the values of a culture determine who the gifted and talented are as well as the special educational services they receive (Kaufman & Sternberg, 2008). Because specialised programs for high-ability students open up opportunities in education, exploring how to open up more access to high-level learning found in gifted education programs holds promise.

The opening story of Ms. Jamison suddenly seeing her students' abilities is meant to underscore the significance of teacher learning and understanding in the important task of talent spotting. Talent spotting, used interchangeably with talent scouting, is defined as the teacher planning for high-end instructional strategies that elevate the demand for student learning in tandem with teacher observation for students who demonstrate critical thinking, creative thinking, or problem-solving abilities that were previously not evident. Talent spotting allows students to show talent and ability in their response to learning. Ms. Jamison's vignette offers the reader a glimpse into the model of talent spotting and development focused on teacher learning. A model for the *Talent Development Academy* is explicated in this chapter, and teacher development is highlighted as an approach for opening access and opportunity and growing diverse learners' academic potential. The *Talent Development Academy* (TDA) is the name of a research and school demonstration project that set out to reshape schools in a way that relies on talent spotting as a pathway for underrepresented gifted students to develop their potential. The story of the TDA is told in this chapter. This Javits-funded project, which began in 2014, the partnership with selected public elementary schools serving low-income students and the effort to grow the partner schools into Talent Development Academies (TDAs) are reiterated here. The US Congress passed the Jacob K. Javits Gifted and Talented Education Act (Javits) in 1988, with its purpose to provide funding that supported research and demonstration projects for under-served gifted and talented students (Jacob K. Javits Gifted and Talented Students Education Act of 1988, 1988). The model that has emerged from the partnership with committed schools, teachers and their principals presents an innovative approach showing success in shifting teacher beliefs and perceptions about who the talented and gifted are and one way to open up access and opportunity to more students from underrepresented groups.

Grounding in the Literature

In the gifted education field, much time and effort has been invested in the identification of underrepresented students (e.g., Swanson, 2006). Fewer efforts focus on effective curricular interventions targeting *Culturally and Linguistically Diverse* (CLD) gifted learners (VanTassel-Baska & Stambaugh, 2007). Reconceptualising a different approach to address the academic and educational needs of the low-income students, moving from a deficit approach to building on students' strengths, that is, a talent-based approach (Subotnik, Olszewski-Kubilius, & Worrell, 2011), is this project's intention. At a 2017 symposium held at the National Association for Gifted Children annual meeting, the complexity of the issue of under-developed talent was discussed and illustrated. Under-developed talent differs from under-achievement in that it is related to the lack of access and opportunity that culturally and linguistically diverse gifted learners have to gifted education (Ford, 2013). The symposium (Robinson & Stambaugh, 2017, November) addressed the current state of what is known about low-income learners and successful efforts to open up educational access and opportunity. The symposium included deep discussion of: (a) identification as a means to serving underrepresented youth (e.g., Erwin & Worrell, 2012); (b) using curriculum as a springboard for talent spotting and growth (e.g., Little, Adelson, Kearney, Cash, & O'Brien, 2018; Robinson, Adelson, Kidd, & Cunningham, 2017); (c) effective programming to bridge key transitions for students from low-income backgrounds (e.g., Olszewski-Kubilius, 2010); and (d) key influences on talent development, for example, psychosocial factors, geographical factors, and factors related to race and language (e.g., Stambaugh, 2010b; Worrell, 2010). Acknowledging the complexity of the issue of underrepresentation, the work described in this chapter is not a comprehensive solution that solves all related problems. Rather, the Talent Development Academy project addresses curriculum and instruction as a platform for talent spotting and development as well as key influences on talent development, specifically psychosocial influences and cultural influences.

Talent development—as a pathway to opening up opportunity and access—is an issue of interest to many in the Asia-Pacific region as many countries have groups of students, that is, from indigenous populations, lower-level economic groups, immigrant, English language learners, and other ethnic sub-groups that have untapped potential (e.g., Guenther, 2011; Harslett, 1996; Liu, 2011). For example, in Chinese education (Zhang et al., 2015), talent is defined as a personal skill or special gift. Wu's research (2005) suggests an emphasis in China on talent development rather than innate abilities when considering a definition of what giftedness is. Australia's gifted education community draws mainly on the *Differentiated Model of Giftedness and Talent* by Gagné (2003), but also on theoretical constructs, such as Renzulli (2005), and Tannenbaum (2003) in how giftedness and talent are defined, so discussion of the concept of talent development holds relevance beyond the USA in other Asia-Pacific region countries.

Teachers are the most influential factor when it comes to student achievement (Rand, 2017), so teachers and their understandings are a conduit by which access and opportunity may be positively impacted. Because effective teachers impact how much students learn (Whitcomb, Borko, & Liston, 2009), the Talent Development Academy model is built around work with teachers to grow and develop their understanding of rigorous and challenging, conceptual curriculum (Swanson, 2010), how to scaffold student learning (Stambaugh & Chandler, 2012), and how to positively influence non-cognitive factors in student learning (e.g., Duckworth, 2013; Yeager & Dweck, 2012). The Talent Development Model ties closely to previous Javits projects and what has been learned (Swanson, 2016), with the foundation of the model building on the work of others (Bracken, VanTassel-Baska, Brown, & Feng, 2007; Coleman, Coltrane, Harradine, & Timmons, 2007; Gavin, Casa, Adelson, Carroll, & Sheffield, 2009; Kim et al., 2012; VanTassel-Baska & Stambaugh, 2007).

In the early development of this project, the principal investigator and partners made a conscious decision to use curricula and strategies that already had a track record of success in use with low income and English language learners who have not had access to rich, challenging learning (Bracken et al., 2007; Coleman et al., 2007; Gavin et al., 2009; Kim et al., 2012; VanTassel-Baska & Stambaugh, 2007). By integrating evidence-based, published curriculum and effective strategies into the teachers' repertoire, through ongoing sustained training, coaching, and support teachers have grown into more effective talent developers and spotters (Swanson, Brock, & Kessler, 2018). Academic foci for the TDA teacher learning are English/Language Arts (ELA), Mathematics, and Science. As the basis for teacher development, project staff utilise curriculum and strategies developed in previous Javits projects, all used with high-poverty students and with published efficacy studies (e.g., Bracken et al., 2007; Coleman et al., 2007; Gavin et al., 2009; Kim et al., 2012; VanTassel-Baska & Stambaugh, 2007). Table 1 shows the academic focus for teacher development in this project.

Both Project Athena (ELA) and Project Clarion (Science) came from research and development work led by Joyce VanTassel-Baska (Kim et al., 2012; VanTassel-Baska, Bracken, Feng, & Brown, 2009) at the Center for Gifted Education at The College of William and Mary. The science and literacy lessons from the project, Using Science, Talents, and Abilities to Recognise Students~Promoting Learning for Underrepresented Students (U~Stars Plus) led by Mary Ruth Coleman

Table 1 Academic foci of Talent Development Academy model

Academic content	Innovative curriculum and strategies used	Grade levels
Language arts and literacy	Project Athena: William and Mary Units developed for high-ability learners.	3, 4, 5
	Jacobs Ladders and Navigators as scaffolds to higher levels.	K–5
	Project U~Stars Plus: High interest, challenging literacy activities based on enrichment and extensions.	K–5
Science	Project Clarion: William and Mary Science Units with problem-based learning and inquiry-based activities.	K–5
	Project U~Stars Plus: High interest, challenging science activities based on enrichment and extensions.	K–5
Mathematics	Project Clarion: Math units that utilise problem-based learning and inquiry.	K–3
	Project M^2 and M^3: Math units developed for mathematically promising learners with mathematical habits of mind embedded.	3, 4, 5

(Coleman et al., 2007) from the University of North Carolina at Chapel Hill, served as an additional curricular resource. The mathematics content was based on Mentoring Mathematical Minds, a project led by Kathy Gavin (Gavin et al., 2009) out of the University of Connecticut. The published efficacy studies provide the evidence-base for the use of the curricula and instructional strategies.

A Model for Talent Development

Alongside the research-based, high-end curricula and strategies, the Talent Development Academy model includes psychosocial aspects. The emerging model of teacher development consists of these primary components: powerful curriculum and instruction that utilises the *Integrated Curriculum Model* (VanTassel-Baska, 2013) with student-driven inquiry (Gavin et al., 2009), cultural influences (Gay, 2000, 2010; Ladson-Billings, 2009), and the psychology of learning (e.g., Duckworth, 2016; Dweck, 2007). Partnering with a local school district and using external funding provided by Javits for this research and demonstration project, the principal investigator and staff worked with selected Title I schools to create Talent Development Academies (TDAs). As stated earlier, partner schools becoming TDAs serve K–5 students from low-income backgrounds. In the intervention, teachers learn to use curriculum and strategies developed for high-ability learners, whole school, with K–5 students. The goal of becoming a TDA is to impact teacher beliefs and perceptions about who the talented and gifted are and to open access and opportunity to more students. Figure 1 summarises the model that we will now describe.

The 'who' in this TDA model are elementary schools that serve mainly students from under-resourced households. The rationale for partnering with this group of schools demonstrates that talent spotting, that is, teaching teachers to recognise and grow hard-to-see student potential, is possible in schools where students may be

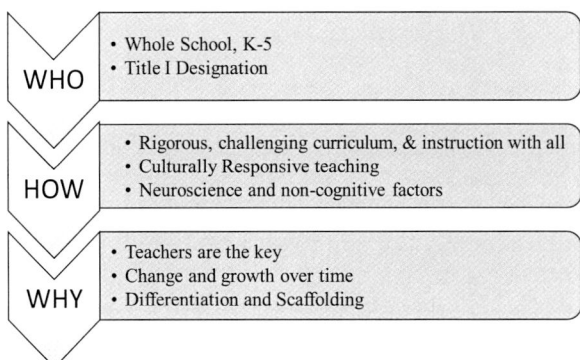

Fig. 1 A model for talent development academy

viewed through a deficit lens. The TDAs' goal of shifting teacher beliefs by demonstrating that all students have talent and ability to think and reason, given a conducive learning environment, is based on the assumption that teachers may not believe that all students can learn at high levels. Participating schools selected from an applicant pool met the following criteria. The school was: (a) designated as Title I, meaning that the school serves primarily low-income students; (b) had evidence of commitment from the principal and majority of staff to participate in this innovation; (c) included grades kindergarten through five; (d) served approximately 300 or more students; and (e) had compatible innovations underway, meaning that other ongoing innovations would mesh well with TDA innovations. The TDA model relies on whole school participation.

The 'how' of this model includes the three fundamental components described above. The first component is the use of rigorous and engaging curriculum and instruction with all K–5 students. In the TDA model, teachers learn how to use the thinking models embedded in the academic content (see Table 1). The evidenced-base and proven track record of the curricula and strategies with CLD students (Bracken et al., 2007; Coleman et al., 2007; Gavin et al., 2009; Kim et al., 2012; VanTassel-Baska & Stambaugh, 2007) is a strength. Teaching teachers how to use these strategies and curricula with their students is one step in supporting teachers as their school becomes a place where talent scouting and spotting is possible (Darling-Hammond, Hyler, & Gardner, 2017; Dixon, Yssel, McConnell, & Hardin, 2014; Swanson, 2010). Use of rich, engaging and challenging strategies and high-level curricula enables student talent to bubble up and become observable (Horn, 2014; Olszewski-Kubilius, Subotnik, Worrell, & Thomson, 2018; Stambaugh & Chandler, 2012). The opening story of Ms. Jamison's 'aha' moment is an example of a teacher seeing talent that previously had been invisible to her (Guskey, 2000).

The second component of the 'how' of this model is culturally relevant teaching. Teachers learning to talent spot revisit the importance of building a learning environment where respect, care and support are present (Noddings, 2005). Teachers practice empowering pedagogy, grounded in the culture of the student, and utilise instructional approaches matched to their students (e.g., Gay, 2010; Hammond, 2015; Ladson-Billings, 2009). The third component of the 'how' is teacher learning focused on neuroscience and non-cognitive factors (Duckworth, 2016; Dweck, 2010). Knowing how the brain works and how students learn (Carraway, 2014; Giedd et al., 1999) is essential in talent development. Food, water, and sleep, for example, are critical to a properly functioning brain (Popkin, D'Anci, & Rosenberg, 2010; Sadeh, Gruber, & Raviv, 2003). Exploration of non-cognitive factors such as motivation, persistence, and grit (Duckworth, 2016; Dweck, 2010) provide teacher talent scouts with important tools in coaching students.

In the TDA model, the focus is on teachers, their development, and their learning, with teacher change and growth expected over time. Sustained, ongoing, and responsive teacher support and development are the hallmarks of this work. Teacher development is planned with responsiveness, not according to a linear step-by-step recipe for success (Darling-Hammond et al., 2017). The teacher learning starts with building conceptual understanding of talent development, then moves to specific instructional strategies and curricular approaches that allow teachers to become stronger talent spotters and developers over time (Stambaugh & Chandler, 2012).

The next section elaborates further on how the responsive teacher development has unfolded as schools evolve into Talent Development Academies.

Growing Teacher Talent. Research-based approaches (Borko, 2004; Darling-Hammond et al., 2017; Guskey & Yoon, 2009; Swanson et al., 2018) used to advance teacher development, including whole group, small group, fidelity observations, and differentiated teacher development comprise the basis for professional learning in the TDA schools. Project leaders who design the professional learning include higher education faculty with expertise in educational psychology, neuroscience, and culturally responsive teaching. These experts partner with *Teachers In Residence* (TIRs) on loan from the local school district where the TDA project is based. The TIRs have content expertise in language arts, mathematics, and science, as well as in-depth of knowledge of gifted education practices, specifically the Integrated Curriculum Model (VanTassel-Baska, 2013), the William and Mary ELA and Science units (e.g., Kim et al., 2012; VanTassel-Baska et al., 2009), and the *Mentoring Young Mathematicians* (M^2) and the *Mentoring Mathematical Minds* (M^3) units (e.g., Gavin et al., 2009). These partners collaboratively design ways to grow teachers into talent spotters and developers, with the goal of seeing student strengths and abilities instead of student deficits.

One Size Does Not Fit All. In order to grow teachers into talent scouts and developers, their learning experiences must be designed developmentally. When teachers have first-hand opportunities to be thinkers and learners, they start to re-conceptualise who their learners are (Buczynski & Hansen, 2010; Darling-Hammond et al., 2017; Guskey, 2002; Guskey & Yoon, 2009; Trotter, 2006; Whitcomb et al., 2009). Teachers see students in a different light when they, themselves, begin acting differently in the classroom. "They believe it works because they have seen it work, and that experience shapes their attitudes and beliefs" (Guskey, 2002, p. 383). This acting differently requires a behavioural shift wherein teachers see their students as capable thinkers and learners. The shift has to do with a growth orientation (Dweck, 2007) towards learning, rather than a fixed mindset. In some instances, teachers embrace and believe that advanced reasoning, critical thinking, and creative production are possible by all students. In other instances, teachers must take a leap of faith and use high-level strategies and curricula with their students, until they see for themselves that their students, given access to scaffolds and interesting curriculum, are indeed talented. The teacher's behavioural shift is predicated on a shift in thinking and ultimately, a shift in their beliefs about what students can and cannot do. Cognisant that the prescriptive, one-size-fits-all teacher development prevalent in schools does not lead to changing teacher beliefs about students, this model creates deep, responsive learning opportunities for teacher development much like the opportunities they are later asked to create for their students (Borko, 2004; Buczynski & Hansen, 2010; Darling-Hammond et al., 2017; Trotter, 2006; Whitcomb et al., 2009).

The TDA project personnel create authentic, research-based opportunities for inquiry and discussion informed by teachers' needs, interests, and strengths. For example, in the first summer session together, teachers were introduced to the basics of neuroscience, brain-based learning and research-based approaches to motivation. Table 2 summarises the teacher development phases of the TDA model. During the TDA's first year of implementation, the project's development phases were varied, including an initial whole-group summer immersion in Talent Development; ongoing, individualised, school-based coaching and demonstration once school began in fall; and quarterly whole-group, after-school sessions based on teachers' needs and interests drawn from formative assessments. In year two, teachers participated in a second summer institute crafted around their interests and needs. A similar pattern of teacher development was followed during the second school year, with the addition of observational checks for fidelity and individualised follow-up. Each phase of development, save the first, was informed by where teachers were in terms of their growth and development and where they wanted to go next relative to the TDA goals.

Phase 1: Summer immersion. In the first year of a school's journey to become a Talent Development Academy, teachers as a whole group were introduced to the concept of Talent Development. This first phase of professional learning sought to provide teachers with seminal background information to ground the project and give teachers opportunities to delve more deeply into the TDA's three components via first-hand exploration, discussion, and inquiry. Equally important, the summer institute provided the TDA TIRs the opportunity to begin building relationships with

Table 2 Phases of teacher development

Phase	Grouping	Format
1	Whole group	Summer immersion
2	Individualised	School-based Coaching and demonstration
3	Whole group	Quarterly meetings, after school
4	Individualised	Fidelity observations
5	Small group	Differentiated learning based on needs and interests

the teachers with whom they would be working, paving the way for the more responsive professional development journey ahead.

Following an overview of school-based research leading up to TDA (Swanson, 1995, 2006) and the research base for project curricula (e.g., Bracken et al., 2007; Coleman et al., 2007; Gavin et al., 2009; Kim et al., 2012; VanTassel-Baska & Stambaugh, 2007), teachers were introduced to theoretical frameworks in which the TDAs' rationale is grounded (Gagné, 2003; Stambaugh, 2010a).

Teachers explored the psychology of learning and the cultural influences on Talent Development via presentations by an educational psychologist. Those presentations were paired with first-hand accounts to exemplify and substantiate the content. For example, after learning about the neuroscience of learning and exploring key tenets to motivation, talent scouts heard from a panel of culturally and linguistically diverse individuals whose talents had been identified, nurtured, and developed. New TDA teachers were able to hear from experienced TDA teacher panels on insights gained from experiences with the TDA curricula and strategies.

Other sessions during the summer immersion provided teachers with the opportunities to re-conceptualise ELA and mathematics instruction using an inquiry-based approach to learning. Using the thinking models embedded in the William and Mary ELA units (VanTassel-Baska, 2013) and M^3 units (Gavin et al., 2009), teachers acted as learners—discussing, analysing, and grappling with open-ended mathematics problems and rich, advanced literature. Stambaugh's model for curriculum development for culturally and linguistically diverse learners (Stambaugh & Chandler, 2012; Stambaugh, 2010a) served as a scaffold to assist teachers in linking the thinking models back to the three components of TDA. By the end of the summer immersion, teachers created a goal for themselves to try out one or more of the thinking models in their classrooms. This goal then served as the first-step in teacher's individual development and provided an opening for more individualised coaching and mentoring once the school year began (Karnes & Shaunessy, 2004; Trotter, 2006; Whitcomb et al., 2009). Meeting one-on-one with teachers, growing them from where they are, showing them through mentoring and modelling is highly effective in teacher development (Darling-Hammond et al., 2017; Guskey, 2002).

Phase 2: School-based coaching and demonstration. In the USA, teacher coaches are expert teachers who mentor other teachers, modelling instructional strategies in peer teachers' classes, demonstrating with real students in real class-rooms how to implement, for example, inquiry-based instruction. The terms 'coaching' and 'demonstration' refer to one form of school-based teacher develop-ment used by the TIRs that relies on mentoring and modelling for teachers. Working from the goals teachers created during the summer in the content areas with which they felt most comfortable, the TDA TIRs established on-site opportunities to meet with teachers, co-teach and co-plan lessons using the thinking models or talent development strategies like engaged dialogue (Borko, 2004; Darling-Hammond et al., 2017; Gavin et al., 2009; Karnes & Shaunessy, 2004; Trotter, 2006). When teachers were uncomfortable trying a strategy or thinking model on their own, the TIRs led demonstration lessons, providing classroom teachers the opportunities for purposeful observation, for example, spotting student talents using *TOPS: Teachers Observing Potential in Students* (Coleman, Shah-Coltrane, & Harrison, 2010) or observing for key fidelity indicators like open-endedness or redirecting via strategic discussion. On-site classroom visits by TIRs were followed by debriefing sessions to encourage teachers to discuss observations related to their students' talents, levels of engagement, and achievement. To maximise teacher buy-in, sustainability, and growth, the TIRs met teachers where they were in terms of readiness levels and motivation to innovate.

Within the first school year, teachers took part in a day-long ELA (William and Mary ELA units) or mathematics (M^2/M^3) professional development in which they learned how to teach a specific curriculum unit corresponding to their grade level. These curricula (the content, skills, and understandings) then became the fodder around which the TIR coaching sessions took place.

To track teachers' individual growth, the TIRs maintained logs and anecdotal notes for each teacher. In addition to tracking teachers' progress, the logs were used as an informal gauge for buy-in and formative progress, providing TDA staff with data on trends within and across grades and schools. These trends, especially those highlighting teacher learning needs across schools became the stepping stones for the next phase of teacher learning.

Phase 3: Whole-group sessions. Using the trends identified in the school-based, one-on-one coaching work, TIRs crafted four, whole-group after-school professional learning sessions lasting an hour to an hour and a half. These whole-group sessions provided the TDA TIRs and teachers with the opportunities to explore more deeply areas of needs, interests, and strengths. Topics ranged from understanding hidden biases to choice sessions in which teachers selected sessions in areas with which they were unfamiliar. When possible, these mini sessions were led by teachers and became a way to highlight teachers' talents, allowing them to showcase and share their talents with peers.

By the second summer, having attempted a variety of thinking models, strategies, and advanced curricula, the TDA teachers were ready to dig deeper. Building on the foundation laid in motivation theory and the neuroscience of learning, teachers went further into the psychology of learning, exploring how to give strategic feedback to promote student growth. Where teachers in their first summer had been exposed to the building blocks of the Integrated Curriculum Model (VanTassel-Baska, 2013), engaged dialogue (Gavin et al., 2009), and thinking models and strategies, they were now ready to delve into curricular approaches that they can incorporate within the units and within their everyday instruction to facilitate talent spotting. In order to further accommodate teachers' individual growth areas, the second summer was conducted conference style with teachers electing to join the sessions of their choice.

Moving to Differentiated Professional Learning

Phase 4: Fidelity observations. In the second year of the project, after nearly two years of engagement in varied professional learning opportunities, the majority of teachers confirmed their use of the thinking models and curriculum. At this point in the teacher learning, the TDA TIRs in consultation with the principal investigator determined the time had come to conduct fidelity checks designed to measure how well the teachers were implementing the TDA project's instructional strategies. Fidelity observations, created for each of the William and Mary thinking models and for the engaged dialogue model used in the mathematics curriculum, were scheduled with teachers. The scheduled observations allowed teachers autonomy to choose the content area and lesson to be observed for fidelity of implementation. So, if TIRs were asked to come in and observe a lesson using the literature web, the TIRs would mark yes or no for whether the teacher: (a) used all elements of the literature web; (b) employed the web as a tool for literary analysis; (c) extended and deepened the discussion and analysis of text through use of the web; and (d) demonstrated neutrality in leading the discussion. Table 3 shows an example of a fidelity check, a simple tool observers used to gauge fidelity of implementation of a literature web.

The TIRs conducted scheduled classroom observations using fidelity observations as formative assessment of all TDA teachers to determine where they were on a continuum of learning. The observations, which were followed by debriefing with teachers, enabled teachers to see their specific strengths and weaknesses in implementation. Further, observations provided concrete evidence of the degree to which each teacher was adopting TDA practices and strategies. The teacher's level of adoption was recorded in a continuum, with teachers grouped on the basis of the fidelity observation as low adopters, high adopters, and teachers falling in between those ends of the continuum. Low adopters were teachers who either actively resisted using any of the TDA strategies or used only selected parts. Teachers who fell in the middle met some or many of the fidelity components. Teachers who were high adopters met the fidelity check and additionally made adaptations based on students' needs, for example, added relevant resources utilised, added scaffolds, and/ or added modelling.

Phase 5: Grouping based on differentiated needs. Because the TDA's goal is to use a responsive development model, the continuum of teacher adoption created areas of focus for upcoming professional development sessions. The analysis of

Table 3 Literature web fidelity check

Teaching attribute	Y	N	Comments/ notes
1. Do you encourage students to discuss all five elements of the literature web (i.e., *feelings, key words, ideas, images/symbols* and *structure)?*			
2. Do you encourage students to build textual understanding by linking web elements back to the text?			
3. Do you use literature web as a springboard for deepening discussion and/or writing?			
4. Do you exhibit openness and neutrality in your instructional approach with the model?			
Additional comments/notes:			

where teachers fell on this adoption continuum illustrated the need for a differentiated approach to professional learning. For the low adopter group, those who lacked or showed minimal fidelity, a common learning need was understanding the lesson's objectives. Teachers who exhibited fidelity did well with the thinking model, but an identified need in this group was to include more practice to extend their instruction beyond prescriptive teaching. The third group, the high adopters, executed the curriculum with great success, building in scaffolds, acknowledging students' talents, and showed a readiness to go further in exploring other ways to personalise student learning. Because the project has two TIRs who lead the development and because three groups of TDA teachers needed development, a virtual, online professional learning session was designed as the delivery mode for the differentiated teacher development.

The program *VoiceThread* was used to design the online professional learning sessions based on the fidelity observations and where teachers fell on a continuum of adoption. Using the observed level of development, three differentiated sessions were designed. Because the teachers exhibiting minimal fidelity appeared to lack understanding of lessons within a unit, their session led them through the basics of how to unpack a rigorous and challenging lesson. Teachers in this group learned to understand the ways in which a lesson's objectives were addressed by studying, previewing, and carefully exploring the lesson prior to instruction. Teachers learned how to anticipate student misconceptions, identify areas where scaffolding may be needed, and experience how to prepare in advance for a more rigorous lesson.

The second differentiated session targeted teachers who showed fidelity with the thinking models yet were not modifying the curriculum for individual student needs. In this session, teachers explored ways to adapt lessons to strengthen the relevance for students. The how and why of cultural relevance in teaching along with specific approaches to boost relevance were the explicit foci for teachers in this session. The third differentiated session, designed for the highest adopters, prepared teachers for the next tier of development—instructional differentiation based on student readiness (Tomlinson, 2014). Teachers in this group analysed students' readiness levels using pre-assessment data. Through analysis of a lesson's task demands and student readiness based on pre-assessment, teachers created readiness-based student groups for an upcoming lesson. Additionally, teachers created additional scaffolds for students who needed them, as well as accelerated features for students ready to move forward. Essentially, teachers were learning the initial steps for flexible, readiness-based differentiation, intended to spur a more responsive approach to talent development.

The responsive approach to teacher development in the TDA started with the whole-group introduction to build common understanding of the underlying principles. From the whole-group work, the TDA staff worked closely with teachers to build relationships, trust, and collaborative work around a set of common goals. As those relationships and understandings of where teachers were in their learning evolved, more small group learning, more advanced learning and more teacher-led learning based on interest was possible. Using the platform of fidelity observations to see teacher talent development work in the classroom, the TIRs were then ready to shape learning in more differentiated ways (Tomlinson, 2014). What one sees in this model of growing teacher talent is support over time, with ongoing and informal assessment of teacher growth (Swanson et al., 2018).

Research and Practice: Implications and Future Directions

This project is a work in progress. A partnership between a university-based group of educators and school-based educators means finding common ground, that is, areas for agreement. Partnerships also mean that figuring out how to make teaching and learning innovation work in real classrooms with real teachers and students is a must. This creative and collaborative process has been interesting and challenging, especially given that school districts are typically more prescriptive and directive in innovation. The TDA staff endeavoured to work in organic and responsive ways to retool the TDA schools into places where talent spotting and development is the norm. Project data indicated that teacher perceptions and beliefs can change. More teacher engagement with the TDA professional learning opportunities has a positive correlation to a positive impact on teachers' beliefs and practices (Swanson et al., 2018). Swanson et al.'s findings show evidence that individualised face-to-face professional development results in increased teacher growth.

After two years of ongoing and sustained work, teachers reported greater efficacy in classroom management. Data indicated that teachers are observing more potential in students in terms of students' advanced skills, strong interests, reasoning/problem-solving, and social perceptiveness. Teacher perceptions of the importance of their students' talent development has increased significantly. Results in student talent spotting are evident in the fact that the rate of grade 3–5 nominations for the gifted and talented program grew to one in every three students in two TDA schools. One TDA school's gifted, and talented program nominations more than tripled in number. Identifiable grade 2–5 students increased in another TDA school, from 6.5% to 6.9%.

Clearly, this responsive teacher development is impacting practice. Observers blind to the project's goals, using the William and Mary *Classroom Observation Scale-Revised* (VanTassel-Baska et al., 2005) found gains in teachers' and students' behaviours across several dimensions, for example, evidence of individual accommodations, problem finding and solving, and use of creative and critical thinking strategies. Using the *Classroom Assessment Scoring System* (Pianta, Karen, Paro, & Hamre, 2008), blind observers reported significant gains in classroom organisation and a trending towards significance for instructional support.

Student outcomes related to achievement are to be assessed at the end of this project's funding, to determine long-term impact, if any, on student achievement gains in targeted areas. Leadership at the school and district level to support teacher innovation is essential. Additional research on how leadership impacts innovation and supports teachers in using innovative practice is a recommendation for future research. Further, research into supports and encouragement for teacher growth in innovation is needed. When teachers are learning to push student thinking, when they are practising shifting to inquiry-based instruction, they need ongoing support and encouragement from their building level administrator. Innovation of practice requires time for professional learning, curricular materials that support diverse student learning, and understanding that teacher learning takes time and practice. A case study examining teachers who are high adoptors of innovation and teachers who are resisters of innovation is currently underway (Swanson, Van Sickle, & Gutshall, 2018).

Conclusion

The issue of under-developed talent is one found in many countries in the Asia-Pacific rim, and the TDA model offers approaches applicable in many settings to allow for spotting and developing the talent in high-ability students from under-represented, culturally, or linguistically diverse groups. The rationale for using a talent spotting model is that it offers a different pathway to reveal and develop hard-to-see abilities that diverse students bring to the classroom. In this chapter, this model of responsive teacher development that was designed to provide teachers with instructional and curricular strategies to become talent spotters and developers of culturally and linguistically diverse high-ability students is set forth. The TDA model consists of three main components: rigorous, challenging curriculum and differentiated instruction with all students (Coleman et al., 2007; Gavin et al., 2009; VanTassel-Baska & Stambaugh, 2007); consistent use of culturally responsive teaching (Gay, 2010; Ladson-Billings, 2009); and application by teachers of neuroscience and non-cognitive influences as regular classroom practice (e.g., Duckworth, 2016; Dweck, 2007). While growing teacher talent in the TDA model is not a simple solution that addresses all issues related to who gets access, there are important considerations for schools interested in the implementation of a talent development approach that supports diversely gifted students.

The TDA model relies on school-wide buy-in and participation. Because teacher learning and growth is key, the TIRs are a critical part of the support for teacher learning in the TDA model. Having a peer teacher coaching and demonstrating, who can work side-by-side with the classroom teacher, with the students in real time and in real settings, is an absolute must in this model. The relationships that grow from this shared work build trust and allow for the responsiveness to teacher learning based on need. Teaching and learning is messy and organic, so responsiveness, not a recipe, works well in a growth-oriented mindset. By approaching professional development in the phases described in this chapter, moving from whole group to small group to individual, teacher attitudes and beliefs change (Swanson et al., 2018) and, in this TDA model, open up access and opportunity to grow diverse learners' academic potential.

The Talent Development Academy model is grounded in evidence-based practices with CLD learners (e.g., Swanson, 2016), culturally responsive teaching (Gay, 2010; Ladson-Billings, 2009), and neuroscience and non-cognitive factors (Dweck, 2010; Yaeger & Dweck, 2012). The model is drawn from results of a Javits-funded project in the USA with five schools (Swanson et al., 2018). The chapter opened with the story of Sandy Jamison, a teacher in one of those schools, who saw that her students were deep thinkers who like to ponder questions of consequence. Her 'aha moment' came after her experiences and professional learning as part of the TDA model for teacher development, that is, the use of instructional strategies that elevate thinking, challenge students in relevant ways, and engage students through authentic, meaningful learning. The 'invisible' abilities of her students 'bubbled up' and became visible to her when she used the rich and engaging curriculum, allowing her to spot talent in her students. Talent spotting, that is, seeing the abilities that students have, changes teachers' perceptions of students (Swanson et al., 2018). Teacher beliefs create a gate to which students get access and opportunity to high-level learning, so opening up the gate, that is, offering powerful learning to all students, is a key aspect of the TDA model. It is argued in this chapter that, through the use of a TDA model, teachers have the space to grow their instructional tools and knowledge and become better equipped to see their students' talents. The TDA model offers one approach to opening up the gate for under-served students.

Cross-References

▸ Attuned Pedagogy: The Artistry of Differentiated Instruction from a Taiwanese Cultural Perspective
▸ Australian Teachers Who Made a Difference: Secondary Gifted Student Perceptions of Teaching and Teacher Effectiveness
▸ Creativity Talent Development: Fostering Creativity in Schools
▸ Differentiation of Instruction for Gifted Learners: Collated Evaluative Studies of Teacher Classroom Practices
▸ Diverse Dimensions of Gifted Education: Part V Introduction
▸ Gifted Education in the Asia-Pacific: From the Past for the Future – An Introduction
▸ Identifying Gifted Learning in the Regular Classroom: Seeking Intuitive Theories
▸ Identifying Underrepresented Gifted Students: A Developmental Process
▸ Innovative Practices to Support High-Achieving Deprived Young Scholars in an Ethnic-Linguistic Diverse Latin American Country
▸ Motivational Issues in Gifted Education: Understanding the Role of Students' Attribution and Control Beliefs, Self-Worth Protection and Growth Orientation
▸ Sociocultural Perspectives on the Talent Development Megamodel
▸ Some Implications for the Future of Gifted Education in the Asia-Pacific
▸ Teaching Gifted Education to Pre-service Teachers: Lessons Learned

Acknowledgments Funding for this work comes from the US Jacob Javits Gifted and Talented Education Act, Grant Award Number S206A140029.

References

Boothe, D., & Stanley, J. C. (Eds.). (2004). *In the eyes of the beholder: Critical issues for diversity in gifted education*. Waco, TX: Prufrock Press.
Borko, H. (2004). Professional development and teacher learning: Mapping the terrain. *Educational Researcher, 33*(8), 3–15. https://doi.org/10.3102/0013189X033008003

Bracken, B. A., VanTassel-Baska, J., Brown, E. F., & Feng, A. (2007). Project Athena: A tale of two studies. In J. VanTassel-Baska & T. Stambaugh (Eds.), *Overlooked gems: A national perspective on low-income promising learners* (pp. 63–67). Washington, DC: National Association for Gifted Children.

Buczynski, S., & Hansen, C. B. (2010). Impact of professional development on teacher practice: Uncovering connections. *Teaching and Teacher Education: An International Journal of Research and Studies, 26*(3), 599–607.

Carraway, K. (2014). *Transforming your teaching: Practical strategies informed by cognitive neuroscience*. New York, NY: W.W. Norton & Company.

Coleman, M. R., Coltrane, S. S., Harradine, C., & Timmons, L. A. (2007). Impact of poverty on promising learners, their teachers, and their schools. *Journal of Urban Education: Focus on Enrichment, 6*, 59–67.

Coleman, M. R., Shah-Coltrane, S. S., & Harrison, A. (2010). *Teacher's observation of potential in students*. Arlington, VA: Council for Exceptional Children.

Darling-Hammond, L., Hyler, M. E., & Gardner, M. (2017). *Effective teacher professional development*. Palo Alto, CA: Learning Policy Institute.

Dixon, F., Yssel, N., McConnell, J., & Hardin, T. (2014). Differentiated instruction, professional development, and teacher efficacy. *Journal for the Education of the Gifted, 37*(2), 111–127. https://doi.org/10.1177/0162353214529042

Duckworth, A. (2016). *Grit: The power of passion and perseverance*. New York, NY: Scribner.

Duckworth, A. L. (2013, April). *Grit: The power of passion and perseverance*. Retrieved from https://www.ted.com/talks/angela_lee_duckworth_grit_the_power_of_passion_and_perseverance.

Dweck, C. (2007). *Mindset: The new psychology of success*. New York, NY: Ballentine.

Dweck, C. S. (2010). Even geniuses work hard. *Educational Leadership, 68*(1), 16–20.

Erwin, J. O., & Worrell, F. C. (2012). Assessment practices and the underrepresentation of minority students in gifted and talented education. *Journal of Psychoeducational Assessment, 30*(1), 74–87.

Ford, D. Y. (1995). Desegregating gifted education: A need unmet. *Journal of Negro Education, 64*, 52–62. Retrieved from https://www.jstor.org/stable/2967284

Ford, D. Y. (2013). *Recruiting and retaining culturally different students in gifted education*. Waco, TX: Prufrock Press.

Gagné, F. (2003). Transforming gifts into talents: The DMGT as a developmental theory. In N. Colangelo & G. A. Davis (Eds.), *Handbook of gifted education* (3rd ed., pp. 60–74). Boston, MA: Allyn & Bacon.

Gavin, M. K., Casa, T. M., Adelson, J. L., Carroll, S. R., & Sheffield, L. J. (2009). The impact of advanced curriculum on the achievement of mathematically promising elementary students. *The Gifted Child Quarterly, 53*(3), 188–202. https://doi.org/10.1177/0016986 209334964

Gay, G. (2000). *Culturally responsive teaching*. New York, NY: Teachers College Press.

Gay, G. (2010). *Culturally responsive teaching: Theory, research and practice*. New York, NY: Teachers College Press.

Giedd, J. N., Blumenthal, J., Jeffries, N.O., Castellanos, F. X., Liu, H., Zijdenbos, A., . . ., & Rapoport, J. L. (1999). Brain development during childhood and adolescence: A longitudinal MRI study. *Nature Neuroscience, 2*, 861–863. https://doi.org/10.1038/13158

Guenther, Z. C. (2011). Commentary on F. Gagné: Academic talent development and the equity issue in gifted education: Ethnic and socio-economic discrimination – Which prevails? *Talent Development and Excellence, 3*(1), 63–65.

Guskey, T. R. (2000). *Evaluating professional development*. Thousand Oaks, CA: Corwin Press.

Guskey, T. R. (2002). Professional development and teacher change. *Teachers and Teaching: Theory and Practice, 8*(3/4), 381–391. https://doi.org/10.1080/135406002100000512

Guskey, T. R., & Yoon, K. S. (2009). What works in professional development. *Phi Delta Kappan, 90*(7), 495–500. https://doi.org/10.1177/003172170909000709

Hammond, Z. L. (2015). *Culturally responsive teaching and the brain: Promoting authentic engagement and rigor among culturally and linguistically diverse students*. Thousand Oaks, CA: Sage.

Harslett, M. (1996). The concept of giftedness from an aboriginal cultural perspective. *Gifted Education International, 11*(2), 100–106. https://doi.org/10.1177/026142949601100207

Horn, C. (2014). The young scholars model. In C. M. Adams & K. M. Chandler (Eds.), *Effective program models for gifted students from underserved populations*. Waco, TX: Prufrock Press.

Jacob K. (1988). Javits Gifted and Talented Students Education Act of 1988, Pub. L. No. 100–297, §1001, 102, Stat. 237.

Karnes, F. A., & Shaunessy, E. (2004). The application of an individual professional development plan to gifted education. *Gifted Child Today, 27*(3), 60–64.

Kaufman, S. B., & Sternberg, R. J. (2008). Conceptions of giftedness. In S. I. Pfeiffer (Ed.), *Handbook of giftedness in children: Psychoeducational theory, research, and best practices* (pp. 71–91). Boston, MA: Springer.

Kim, K. H., VanTassel-Baska, J., Bracken, B. A., Feng, A., Stambaugh, T., & Bland, L. (2012). Project Clarion: Three years of science instruction in title I schools among K–third grade students. *Research in Science Education, 42*(5), 813–829. https://doi.org/10.1007/s11165-011-9218-5

Ladson-Billings, G. (2009). *The dreamkeepers: Successful teachers of African-American children*. San Francisco, CA: Jossey-Bass.

Little, C. A., Adelson, J. L., Kearney, K. L., Cash, K., & O'Brien, R. L. (2018). Early opportunities to strengthen academic readiness: Effects of summer learning on mathematics achievement. *The Gifted Child Quarterly, 62*, 83–95. https://doi.org/10.1177/0016986217738052

Liu, Q. (2011). Commentary on F. Gagné: Academic talent development and the equity issue in gifted education equality of access in academic talent development programs: The more appropriate method and criteria. *Talent Development and Excellence, 3*(1), 83–84.

Noddings, N. (2005). *The challenge to care in schools: An alternative approach to education* (2nd ed.). New York, NY: Teachers College Press.

Olszewski-Kubilius, P. (2010). Working with academically gifted students in urban settings: Issues and lessons learned. In J. VanTassel-Baska (Ed.), *Patterns and profiles of promising learners from poverty* (pp. 85–106). Waco, TX: Prufrock Press.

Olszewski-Kubilius, P., & Clarenbach, J. (2014). Closing the opportunity gap: Program factors contributing to academic success in culturally different youth. *Gifted Child Today, 37*, 103–110. https://doi.org/10.1177/1076217514520630

Olszewski-Kubilius, P., Subotnik, R. F., Worrell, F. C., & Thomson, D. (2018). Talent development as a framework for delivery of services to gifted children. In J. L. Roberts, T. F. Inman, & J. H. Robins (Eds.), *Introduction to gifted education* (pp. 277–297). Waco, TX: Prufrock Press.

Pianta, R. C., Karen, M., Paro, L., & Hamre, B. K. (2008). *Classroom assessment scoring system (CLASS) manual, K–3*. Baltimore, MD: Paul H. Brookes.

Popkin, B. M., D'Anci, K. E., & Rosenberg, I. H. (2010). Water, hydration, and health. *Nutrition Reviews, 68*(8), 439–458. https://doi.org/10.1111/j.1753-4887.2010.00304.x

Rand. (2017). Teachers matter: Understanding teachers' impact on student achievement. Retrieved from https://www.rand.org/education/projects/measuring-teacher-effectiveness/teachers-matter.html

Renzulli, J. S. (2005). The three-ring conception of giftedness: A developmental model for promoting productivity. In R. J. Sternberg & J. Davidson (Eds.), *Conceptions of giftedness* (2nd ed., pp. 217–245). Boston, MA: Cambridge University Press.

Robinson, A., Adelson, J. L., Kidd, K. A., & Cunningham, C. M. (2017). A talent for tinkering: Developing talents in children from low-income households through engineering curriculum. *The Gifted Child Quarterly, 62*(1), 130–144. https://doi.org/10.1177/0016986217738049

Robinson, A., & Stambaugh, T. (2017, November). State of the states: What matters when identifying and serving gifted students from low income backgrounds? In A. Robinson & T. Stambaugh (Chairs), *What works: Identifying and serving gifted learners from low income households*. Symposium conducted at the annual meeting of the National Association of Gifted Children in Charlotte, NC.

Sadeh, A., Gruber, R., & Raviv, A. (2003). The effects of sleep restriction/extension on school-age children: What a difference an hour makes. *Child Development, 74*, 444–455. https://doi.org/10.1111/1467-8624.7402008

Stambaugh, T. (2010a). *Curriculum and instructional strategies for promising students of poverty [webinar]*. Washington, DC: National Association for Gifted Children.

Stambaugh, T. (2010b). The education of promising students in rural areas: What do we know and what can we do? In J. VanTassel-Baska (Ed.), *Patterns and profiles of promising learners from poverty* (pp. 59–84). Waco, TX: Prufrock Press.

Stambaugh, T., & Chandler, K. L. (2012). *Effective curriculum for underserved gifted students.* Waco, TX: Prufrock Press.

Subotnik, R. F., Olszewski-Kubilius, P., & Worrell, F. C. (2011). Rethinking giftedness and gifted education. *Psychological Science in the Public Interest, 12*(1), 3–54. https://doi.org/10.1177/1529100611418056

Swanson, J. D. (1995). Gifted African-American children in rural schools: Searching for the answers. *Roeper Review, 17*(4), 261–266. https://doi.org/10.1080/02783199509553678

Swanson, J. D. (2006). Breaking through assumptions about low income, minority gifted students. *The Gifted Child Quarterly, 50*(1), 11–25. https://doi.org/10.1177/001698620605000103

Swanson, J. D. (2010). Teacher development to work effectively with diverse gifted learners. In J. VanTassel-Baska (Ed.), *Patterns and profiles of promising learners from poverty* (pp. 219–243). Waco, TX: Prufrock.

Swanson, J. D. (2016). Drawing upon lessons learned: Effective curriculum and instruction for culturally and linguistically diverse gifted learners. *The Gifted Child Quarterly, 60*(3), 172–191. https://doi.org/10.1177/0016986216642016

Swanson, J. D., Brock, L., & Kessler, L. (2018). Talent development academies: Providing access and opportunity to advanced learning for Title I students. Manuscript in preparation.

Tannenbaum, A. J. (2003). Nature and nurture of giftedness. In N. Colangelo & G. A. Davis (Eds.), *Handbook of gifted education* (3rd ed., pp. 45–59). Boston, MA: Allyn & Bacon.

Tomlinson, C. A. (2014). *The differentiated classroom* (2nd ed.). Reston, VA: Association for Supervision and Curriculum Development.

Trotter, Y. D. (2006). Adult learning theories: Impacting professional development programs. *Delta Kappa Gamma Bulletin, 72*(2), 8–13.

VanTassel-Baska, J. (2013). The integrated curriculum model. In C. Callahan & H. L. Hertberg-Davis (Eds.), *Fundamentals of gifted education considering multiple perspectives* (pp. 315–326). New York, NY: Routledge.

VanTassel-Baska, J., Avery, L., Struck, J., Feng, A. X., Bracken, B., Drummond, D., & Quek, C. (2005). *Classroom observation scale-revised*. Williamsburg, VA: Center for Gifted Education.

VanTassel-Baska, J., Bracken, B., Feng, A., & Brown, E. (2009). A longitudinal study of reading comprehension and reasoning ability of students in elementary Title I schools. *Journal for the Education of the Gifted, 33*, 7–37.

VanTassel-Baska, J., & Stambaugh, T. (Eds.). (2007). *Overlooked gems: A national perspective on low-income promising learners*. Washington, DC: National Association for Gifted Children.

Whitcomb, J., Borko, H., & Liston, D. (2009). Growing talent: Promising professional development models and practices. *Journal of Teacher Education, 60*, 207–212. https://doi.org/10.1177/0022487109337280

Worrell, F. C. (2010). Psychosocial stressors in the development of gifted learners with atypical profiles. In J. VanTassel-Baska (Ed.), *Patterns and profiles of promising learners from poverty* (pp. 33–58). Waco, TX: Prufrock Press.

Wu, E. H. (2005). Factors that contribute to talented performance: A theoretical model from a Chinese perspective. *The Gifted Child Quarterly, 49*(3), 231–246. https://doi.org/10.1177/001698620504900305

Yeager, D. S., & Dweck, C. S. (2012). Mindsets that promote resilience: When students believe that personal characteristics can be developed. *Educational Psychologist, 47*, 302–314. https://doi.org/10.1080/00461520.2012.722805

Zhang, Y., Zhang, D., Jiang, Y., Sun, W., Wang, Y., Chen, W., et al. (2015). Association between physical activity and teacher-reported academic performance among fifth-graders in Shanghai: A quantile regression. *PLoS One, 10*(3), e0115483. https://doi.org/10.1371/journal.pone.0115483

Julie Dingle Swanson has taught in and coordinated K–12 gifted programs and directed federal projects focused on high-poverty gifted students. Dr Swanson is a professor at the Teacher Education Department, College of Charleston, who teaches in and directs the Gifted and Talented Education Certificate Program. Swanson is active in gifted education leadership at state and national levels as past president of the SC NAGC Affiliate and member of the Center for Gifted Education at The College of William and Mary's National Advisory Board. She received several state and federal grants impacting gifted students and teachers and has authored articles, book chapters, and books.

Lara Walker Russell serves as Teacher in Residence for a university-based Javits project as well as a Gifted and Talented Lead Teacher in a local district. She holds a bachelor's degree in English, a master's degree in secondary education with a concentration in English Education, and a doctorate in curriculum and instruction. She is an adjunct instructor in Teacher Education at the College of Charleston. She has also taught elementary, middle, and high school Title I gifted children and served in the Peace Corps. Her professional interests include promising learners from poverty, teacher development and curriculum and instruction for underrepresented gifted learners.

Lindsey Anderson holds a BS Degree in Elementary Education and is endorsed in Gifted and Talented Education. She has taught grades 2–6 as a gifted education teacher in suburban and rural schools. Her experience in teaching in gifted and talented programs and her commitment to and passion for teaching students from low income and culturally diverse backgrounds led to her selection as teacher in residence for the university-based Javits project, Talent Development Academies. Her professional interests include school culture within schools serving low-income students and teacher development focused on gifts and talents of diverse students.

Educational Contexts, Transitions, and Community Engagement

Educational Contexts, Transitions and Community Engagement: Part VI Introduction

Selena Gallagher

Contents

Abstract

Giftedness is found in all environments; it cuts across geographical and cultural boundaries and is not bound by race, class, or social context. In Part VI, giftedness as it is manifested across a number of different educational contexts, including different levels of traditional schooling, homeschooling, and international schooling will be examined. The transitions between contexts, particularly the school to career transition, which can be particularly fraught for gifted individuals will also be addressed. Additionally, some discussion will be provided on the role of the educator and the unique rewards and challenges of working with gifted populations in a variety of contexts.

Keywords

Giftedness · Diverse educational contexts · International schools · Traditional schooling · Homeschooling · Transitions · Careers

The authors of the chapters in this section challenge our assumptions about gifted education. As the context changes, so too do the needs and nature of the gifted

S. Gallagher (✉)
Cairo American College, Cairo, Egypt
e-mail: selena.gallag@gmail.com

© Springer Nature Singapore Pte Ltd. 2021   1215
S. R. Smith (ed.), *Handbook of Giftedness and Talent Development in the Asia-Pacific*,
Springer International Handbooks of Education,
https://doi.org/10.1007/978-981-13-3041-4_80

students within them. Responses or solutions which may be readily available in mainstream dominant contexts may not be available or may not apply in a different one. Whether examining leadership perspectives of Korean college students, career choices of talented musicians, or the experiences of homeschooled students in Chile, the authors in Part VI each highlight the unique pattern of strengths and challenges that come with each diverse context.

Introductions to the Individual Chapters

Leadership potential is often included in definitions of giftedness, and our gifted students of today are frequently assumed to be our future leaders of tomorrow. In their ▶ Chap. 55, "Leadership Development of Gifted Adolescents from a Korean Multicultural Lens," Seon-Young Lee, Yun-Kyoung Kim, and Eunjoo Boo explore the views of leadership from the perspective of Korean college students and their teachers, exploring potential differences between mainstream Western conceptions of leadership and those exhibited by these gifted Asian students. They map the students' and teachers' perspectives against a model which addresses five cultural dimensions of leadership and make cautious interpretations, including a list of potential implications for leadership education in the classroom.

In ▶ Chap. 56, "Rural voices: Identifying the Perceptions, Practices, and Experiences of Gifted Pedagogy in Australian Rural and Regional Schools," Michelle Bannister-Tyrrell and Denise Wood examine the impact of geographical location on the experiences of gifted students and their teachers. While there are many challenges inherent in growing up gifted in a rural location, such as isolation, lack of community resources or support, poverty, and technology access, the authors also seek to explore the advantages of a rural context that might be leveraged for the benefit of gifted learners. These can include the flexibility that comes from a smaller school, the opportunity for meaningful connections amongst the community, access to the natural environment and a strong sense of place. Advances in technology have done much to mitigate the effects of living far from an urban centre, but these authors caution that it is far from a magic bullet. They draw attention to the pressing need to provide more support to the teachers of gifted students in these contexts, who may be far more disadvantaged than their urban peers when it comes to access to resources and professional learning.

Moving away from the mainstream school context altogether, Maria Leonor Conejeros-Solar and Susen Smith shed some light on the under-researched area of gifted students who are educated at home. In their ▶ Chap. 57, "Homeschooling the Gifted: What Do We Know from the Australian, Chilean, and US Context?" the authors examine homeschooling in the varied contexts of three diverse Asia-Pacific rim countries. Through a comprehensive review of the broader homeschooling literature in general, particularly as it pertains to the Unites States, and the more limited gifted homeschooling literature, the authors consider what factors might lead families to choose to educate their gifted or twice-exceptional children at home. While there were exceptions, the majority of families opted for homeschooling as a response to an unsatisfactory experience within a traditional school system, demonstrating that lack of fit is still a significant problem for gifted students across many different contexts.

The context addressed in Selena Gallagher's chapter is that of the growing sector of international education. ▶ Chapter 58, "Highly Able Students in International Schools," presents an overview of the many diverse environments found in international schools worldwide and considers the experiences of gifted students within these schools, along with the potential challenges and benefits of such environments. In acknowledging the extreme diversity of both curricula and cohort, a flexible talent development approach is proposed as a response to the needs of gifted students in international schools, whether they are expatriate 'third culture kids' or host country nationals.

Taking a group of gifted Brazilian students studying in STEM fields at Australian universities as the sample, Jae Yup Jung, Tay Koo, Peta Hay, and Susen Smith investigated the range of factors that influenced gifted students' decisions to pursue STEM careers. ▶ Chapter 59, "The Predictors of the Decisions by Gifted Students to Pursue STEM Careers: The Case of Brazilian International Students in Australia," draws on the broader literature examining the career decisions of gifted students in general and explores how two theories of career development may contribute to our understanding of these gifted international students. Contrary to existing literature, gender did not emerge as a significant factor for this cohort, whereas the desire for intellectual stimulation appeared to be a strong predictor of the decision to pursue a STEM career.

Similarly, life after high school is the focus of Jae Yup Jung's ▶ Chap. 60, "The Career Decisions of Gifted Students: An Asian-Pacific Perspective." He explores the differences and similarities between the career aspirations of gifted students in a number of countries in the region, in particular China, Korea, Japan, Vietnam, and Turkey, and their gifted peers in Western societies. In keeping with Confucianist philosophies that are predominant in the region, the families of gifted students exert great influence over their children's lives and decisions, and the author explores the implications of this for their eventual career destinations. With one eye on the future, Jung also speculates about the changing nature of the work environment and how this might impact the career decisions of gifted students in the region.

Career decisions are also a focus of Jennifer Rowley's chapter, as she examines the process of identity development of talented musicians as they prepare to complete their undergraduate music education in her ▶ Chap. 61, "Transitioning to Career: Talented Musicians' Identity Development." These talented students are in the unique position of being expert learners at the same time as being novice professionals, and Rowley details a case study which focuses on the space between these two positions. Through reflections on participation in workplace internships, these talented musicians begin to develop a sense of their future professional selves.

After considering the experiences of gifted students in a range of different educational contexts and transition points, the next three chapters examine the role of the educator in guiding gifted students on their journeys through the educational landscape. Turning to the higher education context, Margaret Plunkett and Leonie

Kronborg examine the impact of including gifted education in pre-service teacher education programs in ► Chap. 62, "Teaching Gifted Education to Pre-service Teachers: Lessons Learned." While most teachers enter the profession without having completed any studies of gifted learners and their needs, a large body of research points to the importance of this prior experience for enhancing attitudes and practices that in turn support the provision of appropriate educational experiences for these learners. By closely examining an Australian case study of gifted education at the pre-service level, these authors report the implications for the attitudes and beliefs of future teachers and draws some conclusions about this practice.

What makes for an effective teacher of gifted students? What traits or characteristics are considered to be most important in effective teachers by gifted students themselves? These are the questions that Karen Rogers addresses in her ► Chap. 63, "Australian Teachers Who Made a Difference: Secondary Gifted Student Perceptions of Teaching and Teacher Effectiveness." Drawing on research with an entire selective secondary school in Australia, Rogers teases out which characteristics are most desirable in teachers who wish to work with this population of high-ability learners, finding that while some of the most desirable characteristics are inherent personality traits, others are teaching moves that could be sought out in a judicious recruiting process or supported with appropriate professional development.

The vast majority of gifted children in Australia are educated in mainstream educational settings, and a key person involved in advocating for these students are the Gifted Education Coordinators in their schools. In their ► Chap. 54, "More Than Passion: The Role of the Gifted Education Coordinator in Australasian Schools". Lesley Henderson and Jane Jarvis explore this complex and multi-faceted role, considering how this position is defined, what responsibilities go along with it, who fulfils this role, and some of the particular challenges associated with occupying this often ill-defined space between teaching and administration. Passion seems to be a unifying factor, with many coordinators finding that their inherent interest in this population of learners helps them to deal with some of the many frustrations that come along with the position, such as an ambiguous role and the constant pressures of time and resources.

Conclusion

When it comes to research, much like in gifted education, one size does not fit all. The majority of the research literature into gifted education comes from the dominant culture in the United States, with fewer contributions from the United Kingdom, Australia, and internationally. Readers may sometimes find that the classrooms described in the research studies bear little resemblance to the situations in which they are working. The chapters in Part VI, and indeed in this handbook, help to fill some of the gaps in the incredibly diverse landscape of international gifted education and talent development, particularly in the Asia-Pacific rim region, but there is still a long way to go. Many of the authors in this section could be considered pioneers, seeking to shed light on areas where there is very little existing research.

Extrapolating instead from the general education literature, such as that around leadership, homeschooling, or international curricula, these chapters are taking the first steps into expanding our understanding of gifted learners in new directions.

Giftedness, and responses to it, are arguably highly context-specific, and using national perspectives for comparison to local contexts and different cultures will likely result in significant mismatches (Peters, Matthews, McBee, & McCoach, 2014). More research into less traditional educational contexts would help to provide a richer picture of the lived experience of more of our gifted young people. Several chapters in this section focus on gifted students at college and their future career decisions, but there is a gap here when considering how they got there and what factors influenced their path to post-school contexts. There are chapters centred on the role of educators in the lives of young gifted students, but a lack of research into the role of parents and other forms of community engagement. Community members can play a key role as talent scouts and investigating ways to increase the community's capacity to enhance the talent development process could prove worthwhile (Kay, 2019). These three areas would all help to enrich our understanding of highly able learners and would be useful directions for future research.

References

Kay, S. I. (2019). *On human potential: Nurturing talents and cultivating expertise*. Lanham, MD: Rowman & Littlefield.
Peters, S. J., Matthews, M. S., McBee, M. T., & McCoach, D. B. (2014). *Beyond gifted education: Designing and implementing advanced academic programs*. Waco, TX: Prufrock Press.

Selena Gallagher completed her PhD in gifted education through the University of New England, Australia, and has worked with highly able students in Australia, the United Kingdom, China, Thailand, and Egypt. She is involved in working with international schools to develop and implement gifted education and talent development programs. Her professional and research interests include acceleration and ability grouping as a response to advanced academic ability, the adoption of a talent development philosophy as a whole-school approach to the needs of highly able students, the intersection of giftedness and growth mindset, and expanded conceptions of giftedness.

More than Passion: The Role of the Gifted Education Coordinator in Australasian Schools

54

Lesley Henderson and Jane Jarvis

Contents

Abstract

Many schools in Australia and New Zealand appoint a dedicated coordinator to take responsibility for the education of gifted or academically advanced students, although the exact number is unknown and may represent a minority of all schools. This coordination role can be complex, with potential responsibilities including: educating and supporting teachers about gifted students; designing and implementing provisions for gifted students; and negotiating with school leaders,

L. Henderson (✉) · J. Jarvis
Flinders University, Adelaide, SA, Australia
e-mail: lesley.henderson@flinders.edu.au; jane.jarvis@flinders.edu.au

© Springer Nature Singapore Pte Ltd. 2021
S. R. Smith (ed.), *Handbook of Giftedness and Talent Development in the Asia-Pacific*,
Springer International Handbooks of Education,
https://doi.org/10.1007/978-981-13-3041-4_60

parents and others. However, very little research has examined the role of the gifted education coordinator in mainstream schools or explored its specific opportunities and challenges. In this chapter, findings from survey research in one Australian state that examined the experiences of 40 gifted education coordinators across government, independent, and Catholic schools are presented. While the context and generalisability of this research may be limited, the discussion is framed in relation to the broader literature about educational leadership, gifted programs, and professional learning to improve outcomes for gifted students. Findings suggest that gifted education coordinators may be passionate and derive satisfaction from their engagement with gifted students, but they may also be challenged by a lack of perceived time, resources, and recognition for their work and can struggle to define their role and balance a broad range of responsibilities. Implications are highlighted for professional learning and further research.

Keywords

Gifted education coordinator · Educational leadership · Professional learning

The aims in this chapter are to:
1. Consider the importance of coordinated leadership for gifted education within schools, with a focus on the role of gifted education coordinators.
2. Present the findings of research into the experiences of gifted education coordinators in one Australian state.
3. Propose a descriptive model of the gifted education coordinator's role in mainstream school settings.
4. Highlight the need for further research into effective, school-based leadership for gifted education in Australasia, with a focus on the gifted education coordinator or its equivalent.

Introduction

The role of the *Gifted Education Coordinator* (GEC) in mainstream Australasian schools, with a particular focus on the Australian context, is explored in this chapter. Although pivotal to the effectiveness of programs and services for academically gifted students, this educational leadership role has received strikingly little attention in the research literature or in discussions of policy. In Australia, gifted education is neither mandated nor federally funded, and approaches to the identification and education of gifted or academically advanced students vary between states and territories, systems, and schools (Walsh & Jolly, 2018). There is no national definition of giftedness, although approaches to gifted education (or 'gifted and talented education') in schools typically address the intellectual or academic domain, and identification methods emphasise IQ or achievement scores, often applied in combination with other measures (Jung & Hay, 2018). Program models across the country range from selective academic schools and programs, to classroom withdrawal programs, to early university entrance, and other forms of acceleration (Gross, Urquhart, Doyle, Juratowitch, & Matheson, 2011; Jarvis & Henderson, 2012; Jung, Young, & Gross, 2015). These efforts occur in the context of a well-documented cultural concern with egalitarianism, which has been associated with active resistance among some educators to both the terminology and concepts associated with the education of academically gifted students (Geake & Gross, 2008; Lassig, 2009). In this respect, similarities can be drawn to other Australasian countries, such as New Zealand (NZ), in which approaches to the education of gifted students have been inconsistent, sometimes challenged on egalitarian grounds, and lacking a strong federal mandate (Moltzen, Jolly, & Jarvis, 2018).

In the absence of a federal mandate or definition of giftedness, and in the context of varied practices across schools and systems, the work of school-based leaders in the area of gifted education also varies. In schools that do employ a dedicated GEC, the exact nature and title of the role is highly context-specific, with a commitment ranging from full-time responsibility for a well-defined program to a nominal designation within a much broader leadership or teaching position. In some cases, the responsibilities of the role might be well defined and clearly articulated in a job description. In others, a coordinator might be required to carve out a new role to suit the school's evolving needs. In this chapter, the term gifted education coordinator refers to the staff member within a school who is the key person assigned responsibility for gifted or academically advanced students and specialised aspects of their education, regardless of the specific duties or time allocation associated with the position. While a range of alternative terms may be used in practice (such as the term 'Gifted And Talented Education [GATE] coordinator' in NZ), GEC will be considered inclusive of all titles that may be assigned to this school-based leadership role. Given the centrality of the GEC's role within many models of gifted education, especially in mainstream settings, it is worth exploring how individuals understand and negotiate its complexity and unique leadership challenges.

Ideally, gifted education should not be considered in isolation from general education, but as an integral component of a comprehensive, inclusive approach to enacting goals of equity and excellence for all learners (Jarvis & Henderson, 2014). Regardless of how giftedness is conceptualised and defined, the majority of Australian students identified as gifted are educated in mainstream classrooms for most or all of their time at school (Fraser-Seeto, Howard, & Woodcock, 2015). It follows that the vast majority of Australian teachers are effectively teachers of gifted students, and all teachers require knowledge, skills, and understanding about gifted students and how they learn (Henderson & Jarvis, 2016; Plunkett & Kronborg, 2011). Furthermore, effective teaching of gifted students is supported by coordinated efforts across multiple levels of a school, shaped by a shared ethos (Robinson & Campbell, 2010). It can be argued that the GEC must simultaneously bolster the foundations of flexible, responsive teaching at the classroom level and negotiate ways to build on these across the school to be effective in creating opportunities for diverse gifted students to thrive (Henderson & Riley, 2018). By its very nature, this is a complex role, and arguably one with implications for achieving a more inclusive and socially just educational system. Being cognisant of how GECs understand their roles and experience this complexity is an important step in fostering effective school-based leadership for gifted education.

In this chapter, the nature of the GEC's role will be examined, with reference in particular to a South Australian research study that explored the experiences of GECs across government, independent, and Catholic schools. The findings of that study are discussed with the wider research literature in terms of the broader implications for policy, practice, and future research in the Australasian context.

Defining the Role of the Gifted Education Coordinator

Drawing on the USA's context of gifted education, Borland (1989) regarded both the title and the role of the GEC as problematic, suggesting that:

> The title of coordinator often has no meaning with regard to the administrative structure of the schools or school district. It is simply a token designation given to someone who has the status and power of a teacher but is expected to do the job of a program administrator. When the title is appended to the word teacher as in teacher/coordinator, it usually implies that the individual in question is expected to perform all of the administrative and instructional duties of the program. Moreover, although the coordinator or teacher/coordinator is expected to perform administrative functions, he or she is rarely assigned the administrative status necessary to carry out some of these functions. This is especially problematic when such duties require working with other teachers. Whereas an administrator can compel the (perhaps grudging) compliance of teachers with program requirements, a coordinator or teacher/coordinator must rely on powers of persuasion that are sometimes inadequate to the task. This places one in an awkward position and severely hampers one's effectiveness. (p. 167)

There has been limited Australasian research on the GEC's role in schools; therefore, little is known about how the tension between teaching status and coordination responsibilities is negotiated in particular school settings. A notable exception is an unpublished doctoral thesis by Downey (1999) that explored the role (responsibilities and time allocation of role; satisfaction; relationships; and support; education of coordinator) of 107 Gifted and Talented (GAT) Coordinators in independent secondary schools in New South Wales (NSW). Consistent with Borland's (1989) assertion, this research found that the majority (73%) of participants were assigned the role of GEC in the absence of any clearly defined job description. The perceived lack of adequate time allocation and the absence of a formal job title and salary allocation (i.e., a lack of administrative recognition for the role) were associated with higher levels of frustration and dissatisfaction among coordinators. The majority (79%) felt that their role was not sufficiently valued nor appreciated, most (54%) felt 'on their own' as they worked on behalf of gifted students, and 70% felt that they had to rely on persuasion rather than authority in order to accomplish their responsibilities. This research paints a picture of GECs working in relative isolation and with little perceived administrative support to define and enact their own roles and responsibilities. As noted by the author however, these findings should be interpreted in the context of the relatively recent introduction of GECs in schools, which had commenced in the 1980s and increased markedly throughout the 1990s (Downey, 1999). Although this research is now almost two decades old, there are no replication studies with which to compare the findings.

A more recent NSW study by Gruppetta (2005) involved case study research with seven GECs from two secondary and five primary schools classified as socio-economically disadvantaged. Coordinators were defined as "teachers nominated to act as coordinators and liaison support for the school within their local region in order to ensure the collaborative development of appropriate programs for gifted and talented students" (New South Wales Department of Education, Training, & Development [DET], 1991, cited by Gruppetta, 2005, p. 132). Data sources included interviews, journal entries, and observations over the course of a series of professional learning workshops. However, the only published findings were concerned with coordinators' notable deficit view in relation to students in their schools, reflected in the common belief that gifted students were unlikely to be found among such socio-economically disadvantaged cohorts for whom educational achievement was not valued. Thus, the research did not shed further light on the experience of defining and performing the role of a GEC or the tensions inherent in negotiating school-based leadership for gifted education.

In NSW as in other jurisdictions, the definition and nature of the GEC role at the individual school level is determined through negotiation with the school principal; however, the state's policy implementation guidelines (2004) suggest a long list of potential responsibilities, including:

- Developing school policy.
- Serving as chairperson of the school's gifted and talented committee.
- Organising identification programs.
- Developing and evaluating programs.
- Contributing to the professional learning of teachers.
- Training staff in cultural education.
- Serving on the Professional Learning Team.
- Serving on the Learning Support Team.
- Monitoring and tracking gifted students.
- Liaising with parents/caregivers.
- Attending conferences.
- Disseminating information.
- Mentoring.
- Counselling. (New South Wales DET, 2004, pp. 9–10)

This list delineates a broad range of potential tasks that may be involved in supporting gifted and academically advanced students. The workload implications are immense if one person is expected to perform all responsibilities on the list. Some responsibilities, such as identification and counselling of gifted or academically advanced students, require specialised knowledge and skills. Others, such as leading professional learning for teachers and developing school-wide programs, rely on both specific knowledge and leadership skills. This list of responsibilities, then, may serve to highlight the complexity and extent of the role, and by implication the need for strong background knowledge in both gifted education and educational leadership. It may also be indicative of the nature of the knowledge and skills that should be included in professional learning programs to prepare and support GECs to be effective in their role.

In New Zealand, the Ministry of Education has provided a series of online resources to guide schools and teachers to implement Gifted and Talented Education (GATE) programs, and these include a list of roles and responsibilities for GATE coordinators that is based on the work of Cathcart (2010). While the NZ list includes many similar responsibilities to the NSW DET document, there is additional focus on providing coaching and in-class support to teachers and facilitating differentiated teaching practices across the school (Ministry of Education, n.d.). Both the NSW list and the NZ list of responsibilities suggest that an effective GEC should possess multifaceted expertise, ranging from program design, development, and evaluation to assessment, budgeting, well-being support, public relations, and staff development. While some of these are arguably integral to all teaching roles, others are far more specialised.

In a research study based in California, one school-based GEC referred to her role as "the dreamkeeper" (Jensen, 1986, p. 13). This coordinator saw her role as maintaining a clear vision for gifted programs at the same time as investing time, effort, and passion into maintaining the programs. Downey's (1999) study similarly identified a high degree of passion and commitment among GECs, which often served to balance out the frustrations of the job. However, this idealism and commitment does not appear on lists of task-driven responsibilities and highlights the need to explore further the personal characteristics and leadership qualities that effective GECs bring to the role.

Educating Teachers and Leaders for Gifted Education

Downey's (1999) doctoral research found that the majority of GECs (63%) did not have any tertiary qualifications in gifted education and 43% had engaged in less than five days of in-service professional learning in this area. Shorter engagement with professional learning in gifted education was associated with higher perceived conflict, feelings of inadequacy, and role ambiguity. The Senate Inquiry into the education of gifted students in Australia (Collins, 2001) noted that professional learning about gifted education was critical to successful outcomes for gifted students, noting "the bad effects when coordinators are untrained and unsupported in the school" (p. 88). The Senate Inquiry also noted that most teachers graduate with little or no knowledge or skills specifically relating to gifted education, despite the presence of gifted students in all school populations. Plunkett and Harvey (1995, p. 20) found that specialist training in gifted education was essential and that "interest alone is not enough to make a difference in the confidence of teachers in dealing with gifted and talented children". There is a recognised need within the literature for teachers to undertake professional learning about gifted education in order to understand, identify, and provide for gifted students (Henderson & Jarvis, 2016; Lassig, 2009; Plunkett & Kronborg, 2011). In the view of the Australian Senate Committee (Collins, 2001):

> Teachers need appropriate training to handle gifted children. They need training to identify giftedness, and to differentiate the curriculum suitably, especially in comprehensive classes. Exposure to gifted education issues is important to dispel misconceptions and negative attitudes that arise from lack of training and lack of confidence. (p. 79)

Almost 20 years later, the specific preparation of Australia's pre-service and practising teachers to work with gifted students remains highly inconsistent (Kronborg & Plunkett, 2013; Walsh & Jolly, 2018). Commentators have pointed to the lack of adequate growth among Australia's highest achieving students in standardised literacy and numeracy assessments to argue that teachers are failing to support learning among academically advanced students (Griffin, 2013; Masters, 2015). There is a documented lack of knowledge and confidence related to recognising and teaching gifted or highly able students among mainstream teachers (Fraser-Seeto et al., 2015; Griffin et al., 2013).

In the absence of mandated pre-service studies in gifted education, it is important to prioritise in-service professional learning or postgraduate university studies in gifted education to provide the requisite knowledge, skills, and understandings for teachers and coordinators. Some teachers develop a passion for gifted education and seek out professional learning in order to be effective teachers for gifted students. Others may be more reluctant or resistant, owing to well-documented negative attitudes to and misconceptions about giftedness (Geake & Gross, 2008; Lassig, 2009). Without the school principal or leadership team prioritising gifted education, including professional learning about gifted education, programs, and teaching practices are not likely to be comprehensive or effective, and having a knowledge-able GEC seems like a non-negotiable first step.

Leadership for Gifted Education

Henderson and Riley (2018) highlighted the significance of the GEC's role in the development, implementation, and evaluation of schools' gifted programs in Australia and NZ. This is supported by Riley and Moltzen's (2010) NZ research, which established that, "enablers to meeting (gifted) programme objectives and evidencing growth in outcomes include having a passionate, committed programme director with knowledge and skills in gifted and talented education" (p. iii). Gifted education knowledge combined with a passion for making a difference for gifted students are acknowledged in Hurford's (2013) research findings as critical to the GEC's role, but specific leadership skills are also essential. Hurford's (2013) case study of six GECs in NZ schools found a link between their leadership and gifted students' learning outcomes, concluding that:

> Findings show the responses from participants highlighted the important connection between leadership and learning. Knowledge and passion to do their best for gifted and talented students, although important, was not sufficient. The leadership actions and support provided by others in their setting and beyond their setting were likewise needed. (p. iv)

Hurford (2013) referred to the importance of supportive 'others' in the school setting, and this category can include the school principal. While there is scant research specifically relating to the GEC, some studies have explored the principal's role in leadership for gifted education within schools. There is strong agreement within the literature that school-based leadership in support of gifted education is significant in achieving successful outcomes for gifted students. For example, based on two case studies of US principals, Weber, Colarulli-Daniels, and Leinhauser (2003) investigated the desirable characteristics, skills, and competencies of principals to be effective in supporting gifted education. Findings highlighted the critical role of the principal as instructional leader, in ensuring that teachers understood and had the skills to enact a shared vision of effective learning for every student, including those with advanced academic abilities. McDonald's (2014) doctoral thesis investigated the principal's role as stakeholder or gatekeeper, facilitating or restricting educational opportunities for gifted students in Ohio; principals in this study identified a need for access to high-quality professional learning opportunities about gifted education, to help them better understand issues relating to gifted students and provide appropriate leadership for this area of practice.

Lewis, Cruziero, and Hall (2007) interviewed principals known to be supportive of gifted education in Scotland, and these leaders raised particular issues related to educating gifted students in remote and rural contexts. In Scotland, research undertaken by the *Scottish Network for Able Pupils* (SNAP) examined school leadership for highly able students and suggested that there was little clarity about how schools managed learning for their highly able students, nor consistency across the sample. This seems consistent with a report for the Sutton Trust in the United Kingdom, which noted that, "the policy and provision for the highly able is littered by a hotch-potch of abandoned initiatives and unclear priorities" (Lampl, 2012). A cross-cultural study of head teachers in the United States, Scotland, and Ireland highlighted the crucial role that principals play in all settings as models of good practice and in supporting teachers to engage in professional learning aimed at improving outcomes for gifted students (Stack, Sutherland, O'Reilly, & Chandler, 2014).

In South Africa, Oswald and de Villiers (2013) interviewed principals and classroom teachers in public primary schools to explore the influence of those educators proximally involved in the education of gifted learners. Their findings highlighted that leadership responsibility for gifted education stretches beyond the teacher and principal to the broader education system, and they cited the importance of explicitly reflecting the needs of gifted students in a comprehensive educational agenda:

Gifted learners were most often those who were not receiving appropriate education and support and data suggested that a particular drive for the inclusion of gifted learners was absent in the agenda of education authorities. (p. 1)

In Australia, Long, Barnett, and Rogers (2015) investigated the role of the school principal in implementing the 2004 NSW state policy for gifted and talented students. Their findings suggested that the influence of principals on gifted education is both direct (through their decisions about the scope of programs) and indirect (through their relationships with teachers, which impacts the quality of programs). On the other hand, the knowledge, attitudes, and self-efficacy of teachers directly influence the quality of gifted education in schools. These findings highlight the multifaceted nature of leadership for gifted education, which must address a range of purposes and should be considered across different levels of a system (Henderson & Riley, 2018). A study of staff development programs designed to improve teachers' use of differentiation strategies for gifted students similarly found that different aspects of leadership were required to serve different functions (Brighton, Hertberg, Moon, Tomlinson, & Callahan, 2005). These researchers noted that:

To provide teachers with the on-going, informed support that they need, the on-site presence of an individual combining both power and knowledge of the initiative is necessary. On-site coaches provide one source of impetus and guidance for change, but a principal who is thoroughly trained in the initiative is most likely a key factor in effective approaches to supporting and encouraging teacher change—this individual has both the power of account-ability and the power of knowledge, the ability to be both a light source and a heat source for teachers engaged in the change process. (p. 348)

While the principal's role in allocating priority, resources, and personnel to professional learning about giftedness is essential, it is rarely the principal who delivers the professional learning program about gifted education. Instead, it is likely to be the GEC who engages with gifted students directly and indirectly, and with teachers and other staff through the provision of professional learning about gifted education, which might also include coaching or in-class support. In terms of Brighton et al.'s (2005) terminology, this might be the staff member who can act as a 'light source' for gifted education at a school, through their knowledge and passion. However, whether the GEC can also be a 'heat source' depends on the nature of their leadership role and capacity to hold teachers accountable for engaging in specific practices. This is likely to be context-dependent and, in some cases, might be a source of tension as the GEC attempts to effect change in isolation and without a recognised position of authority.

The GEC's role is undoubtedly crucial to positive outcomes for gifted students, but as one interdependent 'cog' in a multifaceted system of leadership, much is likely to depend on the setting in which the GEC works, the model of gifted education that is applied in that setting, and his or her skill in negotiating an effective role within the local system. There is a need for research into the nature and experience of the GEC's role in schools. How do GECs define their own leadership roles and set priorities? Who chooses to take on the role, and why? What do GECs see as facilitating, and perhaps impeding, their efforts on behalf of gifted students?

The following section reports on one research study which sought to address some of those questions and provide a brief snapshot of the GEC's role.

The Role of the Gifted Education Coordinator: An Australian Study

Many of the issues raised in the previous section are exemplified by the findings of a survey study conducted in South Australian schools. As part of a larger study of gifted education practices (Jarvis & Henderson, 2012), a section in the survey was specifically devoted to the experiences of the GEC, defined as the staff member nominated as having responsibility for gifted or academically advanced learners at their school. The aim was to examine the self-reported experiences of these individuals, who were working to address the needs of gifted or advanced learners through a range of school-based practices. A summary of the research and key findings relevant to the GEC's role are provided in the following sections, followed by a discussion that considers these findings in terms of their broader implications for leadership in gifted education across the region.

Research Method

Participants in the study of the GEC's role were 40 school educators who self-identified as having responsibility for gifted education or its equivalent in their school. These participants were drawn from a larger sample of 71 respondents to an anonymous online survey that was distributed to all schools (government, independent, and Catholic) in one Australian state in 2011. Detailed methods for school recruitment and data collection are reported elsewhere (Jarvis & Henderson, 2012), together with the survey findings related to programmatic approaches to the education of gifted or advanced students.

In the same survey that was employed in the study of gifted education practices, participants were asked to indicate whether their school had an allocated staff member responsible for services and programs for gifted or academically advanced students (even if that was not his or her primary role), and those who responded in the affirmative were directed to a set of 19 closed and open-ended items specifically related to the role of the GEC or equivalent. These questions related to the education and experience of the GEC, the structure and responsibilities of the role, and its perceived rewards and challenges. The number of participants who responded to each of these 19 items varied from 33–39, so it is more meaningful to refer to percentages of participants in the following analyses. Of the primary schools in the larger sample, 52% reported having a GEC, compared with 83% of the K–12 schools and 85% of the secondary schools. Since the schools that responded had at least one staff member willing to complete a survey about gifted education, it should be acknowledged that the results might not be representative of all schools in the state, and nor can these results be generalised across all contexts. Rather, the intention is to offer a snapshot of the work of GECs and provide an important stimulus to professional conversations within all educational contexts about how the leadership role might be structured to effect positive outcomes for gifted students.

Summary of Findings

The Gifted Education Coordinator: Experience and Education

The majority of participants were experienced educators in terms of years of teaching experience, with over 96% having taught for at least six years. A majority of primary (73.3%) and K–12 (75%) participants had been teaching for more than 15 years. Only one secondary coordinator was an early career teacher (first three years of teaching). None of the participants had a full-time position as coordinator of gifted education. 45.5% ($n = 15$) were classroom teachers with additional responsibility for gifted education and another 45.5% ($n = 15$), were coordinators of special education (sometimes termed inclusive or adaptive education, depending on the setting) with primary responsibility for students with disabilities or other identified special needs. The other 9% of participants ($n = 3$) were in a deputy principal role with the responsibility for curriculum and learning.

When asked why they chose to coordinate gifted education in their school, 36% reported that this responsibility was a component of a broader role, such as that of special education coordinator. However, participants could identify more than one reason for taking on the role, and the most prevalent reasons included being passionate about gifted education (53.4%), wanting to make a difference for the students who were under-challenged or underachieving (66.1%) and being interested in gifted education and wanting to find out more (38.9%). This suggests that the majority of GECs valued and were personally invested in the role. One participant elaborated on their response by saying, "I would pursue this as a volunteer. This is my passion and hobby. I am just so blessed to be paid to work with gifted children". Other reasons included wanting to work with individual students (25%) or with teachers in a coaching role (19%) or taking on the role because nobody else was willing to do so (13.9%). A couple of participants were attracted by the opportunity to move out of classroom teaching or to build up their administrative/leadership experience.

In addition to their teaching qualifications and general teaching experience, participants were asked to describe what professional learning they had undertaken in gifted education. While none of the GECs had a doctorate in gifted education, just over a third (36%) had completed either a graduate certificate or a master's degree in gifted education. Most had attended gifted education conferences and engaged with personal reading to enhance their knowledge and understanding of gifted education, although the extent and quality of the personal reading and the number of conference days they attended and conference papers presented were not specified.

Participants were asked to rank (from a list of 17 options), in order of priority, five areas in which they would like to pursue further professional development related to their role. Table 1 presents these professional learning priorities for GECs who had

Table 1 Top 5 professional learning priorities identified by gifted education coordinators with different levels of experience in the role, in ranked order

Years of experience as GEC		
0–3 ($n = 20$)	4–7 ($n = 9$)	>7 ($n = 8$)
1 Strategies for teaching gifted students	1 Designing defensible programs and services for gifted students	=1 Designing professional learning workshops in gifted education
2 Differentiating existing curriculum for gifted students	2 Differentiating existing curriculum for gifted students	=1 Strategies for coaching and collaborating with classroom teachers
3 Strategies for coaching and collaborating with classroom teachers	3 Strategies for coaching and collaborating with classroom teachers	3 Strategies for teaching gifted students
4 Teaching higher-order thinking skills	4 Advocating effectively for gifted students	=4 Differentiating existing curriculum for gifted students
=5 Designing professional learning workshops in gifted education =5 Developing leadership skills related to gifted education	5 Understanding giftedness and gifted students	=4 Developing creative potential in gifted students

been in the GEC role for less than three years, those with 4–7 years of experience in the role and those with more than seven years' experience. For all three groups, the top five priorities included a mix of developing knowledge and skills of practices for working with gifted students and developing knowledge and skills related to broader leadership responsibilities. For the least experienced coordinators, the top priority was to learn strategies for teaching gifted students, and each of the top five priorities related to working directly with students or teachers. Both of the more experienced groups gave highest priority to developing knowledge and skills related to their broader leadership responsibilities (i.e., program design; coaching and collaboration with teachers; designing professional learning). Differentiating existing curriculum for gifted students and strategies for coaching and collaborating with classroom teachers appeared among the top five priorities for all three groups. These findings might represent priorities dictated by the nature of gifted education practices offered at the school or could reflect personal learning goals based on each GEC's perceived level of knowledge and confidence. Further research could examine the way GECs develop and expand their understanding of the role and its possibilities over time, and the common professional learning priorities for GECs at different stages of their tenure.

The Nature of the Gifted Education Coordinator Role

A series of survey items invited participants to define the scope and responsibility of their coordination role related to gifted or academically advanced students.

About 40% of participants had been provided with a written description of their coordination role related to gifted students, while 60% had received nothing in writing. Most participants (53.2%) reported a workload allocation of less than 0.1 for this role, which equates to a half a day per week. Another 30% reported a 0.2 allocation, equivalent to one-day-per-week. In other words, 83% of GECs were paid the equivalent of one day or less per week to complete all tasks associated with this role. For most (60%) who had received no role description or specified list of responsibilities, determining what tasks they could achieve and prioritising those tasks was an added challenge. In open-ended follow-up responses, many of the GECs expressed frustration at the lack of time they had to engage with the role to the extent they would prefer. One deputy principal noted that "I don't believe I am doing the role justice as it is just a part of the DP role I undertake and is often left to get to 'one day'". Some of the special education coordinators with added responsibility for gifted students admitted that students with learning difficulties and disabilities tend to take priority over gifted students (e.g., "Unfortunately for the gifted students I place a higher importance on the children with learning difficulties"). The data suggested that many GECs perceive gifted education as desirable, but not their primary priority, and therefore, it receives less than adequate attention in the context of limited time, unclear job descriptions, and competing responsibilities.

When asked to select from a list which tasks were involved in their coordination role, participants on average identified approximately five core tasks. In order from the most commonly identified, specific tasks included: supporting teachers of gifted students (77.8%); coordinating the identification of gifted students or the selection of students for advanced classes (72.2%); directly identifying students as gifted or selecting students for advanced classes/opportunities (58.3%); coordinating or providing out-of-school or extracurricular opportunities for gifted students (58.3%); teaching gifted students in a withdrawal class (52.8%); supporting parents of gifted students (50%); providing professional development for teachers related to the education of gifted learners (47.2%); and working with gifted students in the regular classroom (38.9%).

Beyond the survey options provided, some participants identified additional responsibilities including: writing a gifted education policy; advising teachers and administrators about the needs of gifted students; collaborating with the wider community and coordinators from other schools; and supporting students to attend external events such as academic competitions. Some activities involved in the GEC's role may be infrequent (such as writing a policy), while others may necessitate a regular allocation of time (such as teaching gifted students in a regular withdrawal class). Activities such as supporting parents of gifted children may involve a planned program of regular information and support sessions or could entail interacting with parents in response to a specific query or concern. These nuances require further investigation, such as through further case study research. Overall, the data painted a picture of a multifaceted role that entails leadership at different levels, in the context of very limited time.

The Experience of Being a Gifted Education Coordinator

Participants were also asked what they found most satisfying about coordinating gifted education at their school. While one participant suggested that there was "nothing at the moment" that they found satisfying, the vast majority (23 responses out of 25) described the pleasure they gained from working with the gifted students as the most satisfying aspect of their role. The "passion of kids when they are switched on" and "the students' enthusiasm" appear to be rewarding and motivating factors for these educators, who enjoy "the buzz and energy I see in the students and their desire to come to school and learn"; "the absolute display of pleasure, excitement and satisfaction of students when they feel their needs are being met"; and "seeing kids achieve, engaged, and happy to learn". It appears that these GECs are rewarded for their efforts by the students' engagement and achievement, and, because they feel that they are making a tangible difference for these students, they are affirmed and sustained in their hard work and are prepared to commit unpaid time to the role. One participant explained that "[the students] stretch my mind as well", suggesting that there is reciprocity of relationship and engagement. Two responses mentioned the satisfaction derived from working with teachers ("Working with the students is fantastic—I also love it when the teacher gets on board") or contributing to progress at the broader school level (e.g., "seeing ideas adopted into Faculties that have come through the gifted and talented program and realising that a difference is made by the effort put in. Seeing the changes made in school structure").

The satisfaction from working with students appears to be balanced against frustrations commonly experienced by these GECs in other aspects of their role. Half ($n = 13$) of the responses to a question about the least satisfying aspect of the role reflected disappointment that the GEC role is not valued by other staff, or the difficulty of working with resistant or negative teachers. As one participant explained, "I feel like a person swept away in a current as I try to seek and deliver programs which are supported from the top but the staff (like most schools) are not inclined to value", while another described the challenge of working with some staff members "because of their general lack of sensitivity to gifted students and not wanting to acknowledge this group does exist". This sentiment was borne out in responses to an item asking participants to identify the three most significant challenges in their work. The challenge posed by a general lack of understanding of gifted students' needs among broader staff groups, and resistance to making special provisions for these students, was ranked among the top two challenges of the role in 25 out of 28 responses to this item. Responses suggested that some GECs must fight against "indifference, rudeness, and white-anting" from their colleagues as they attempt to provide for gifted students and that "raising the profile of gifted education in the school" is an ongoing challenge. It would seem that gifted education is not always valued as a legitimate educational response to a group of students with special learning needs. No participant reported working with classroom teachers or colleagues as one of the most satisfying aspects of their role, but "dealing with teachers" featured strongly in lists of the most challenging aspects.

In terms of the least satisfying aspect of the GEC role, half ($n = 13$) of responses described administrative challenges, including limited time allocation, lack of resourcing, and increasing paperwork associated with the role. The lack of allocated time, given the range of tasks required, also emerged as the most frequently identified challenge of the role, with 26 out of 28 responses nominating lack of time, funding, and/or administrative support among their top three challenges. Typical responses in this category reflected the difficulty posed by "lack of funds, lack of time" or by "keeping up with all the requirements in the allocated time, even with working above and beyond formal responsibilities". Beyond the most commonly cited challenges of working with teachers, encouraging staff to value gifted education and dealing with the limitations of time, budget, and other resources, a smaller number of responses pointed to the challenge of GECs developing and maintaining their own skills ("keeping abreast of all contemporary available resources"; "finding appropriate PD") supporting parents of gifted students, designing and implementing quality programs and practices ("developing a defensible program and range of services that really meet the needs of gifted students at my school"; "knowing the most effective strategies for these students with their wide range of individual needs") developing a school policy and working within the perceived limitations of age-based curriculum, assessment, and reporting practices ("meeting the needs of my gifted students within the confines and restrictions of the school program and paradigm").

Discussion

The findings from this survey study of GECs across 40 schools paint a picture of the role as complex, multifaceted, and often challenging, but highly satisfying in terms of engagement with students who clearly seem to appreciate and benefit from targeted learning opportunities. Context matters and not all GECs in the study expressed the same motivations for taking on the role or the same knowledge base, goals, or experiences of being a coordinator. Even so, the findings that these GECs typically reported being very motivated and passionate, derived much satisfaction from their perceived impact and engagement with students, felt that their role was insufficiently valued, received inadequate administrative support, and felt frustrated by resistance from other teachers are highly consistent with Downey's (1999) research several decades ago in a different state.

It should be noted that this study did not include measures of effectiveness in terms of the impact of the GEC's work on staff teaching practices or student outcomes. It is also acknowledged that this relatively small study offers one snapshot of the nature and experience of coordinating gifted education within one Australian state. These limitations notwithstanding, the findings prompt broader consideration of the role of school-based leadership for gifted education, and how designated GECs might best be selected and supported to progress the agenda of gifted education both within and beyond their local schools. Some of these broader issues, which have implications across diverse settings, are discussed in the following sections.

The Gifted Education Coordinator as Leader

Figure 1 represents the nature of the GEC's role at the nexus between teaching and leadership. Many of the tasks identified in this research and elsewhere as being part of the GEC's role require strong leadership skills. These include developing policy, designing and evaluating whole-school programs, negotiating budgets and resources, and supporting pedagogical change. Our research suggests that while this position in schools is sometimes undertaken by a staff member who is primarily a teacher, in other cases, it is subsumed within a specific leadership position, such as coordinator of special education or deputy principal. Depending upon how the role is negotiated at each site, it is likely to integrate elements of both teaching and leadership, and to involve work with other teachers as well as school leaders; this raises questions as to whether GECs see themselves primarily as teachers or as educational leaders, and how they go about negotiating this dual identity. For some GECs, taking on the role may necessitate an important shift in perspective from that of teacher of students to that of pedagogical leader of staff. Considering the balance between teaching and leading is significant in terms of the extent to which a GEC can influence whole-school practices, rather than simply making a difference for identified gifted students within a defined program. Case study research in the United Kingdom has highlighted the importance of leadership for gifted education across multiple levels of a school system, with all levels working towards a shared purpose related to student outcomes (Robinson & Campbell, 2010). The extent to which

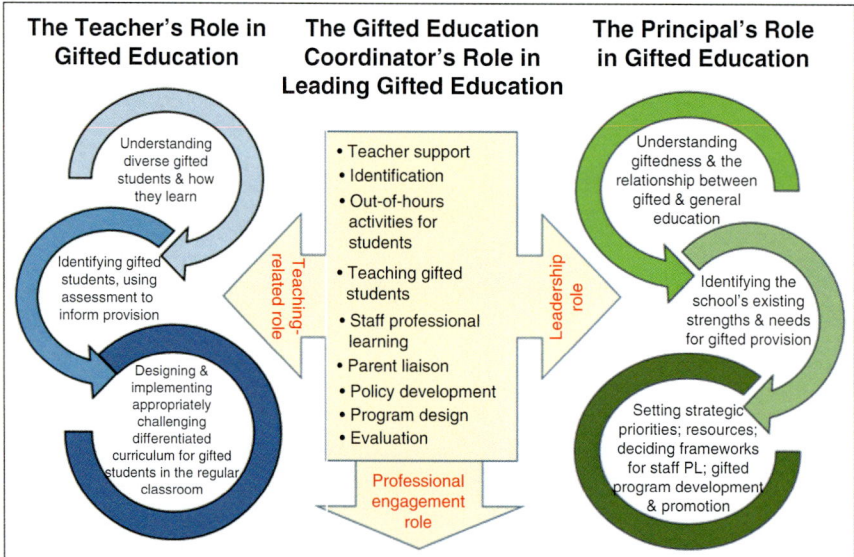

Fig. 1 Model summarising the gifted education coordinator's role in relationship to teaching and leadership

GEC is seen as a valued leadership role with 'clout' may vary across settings, providing different opportunities and challenges for influencing school-wide practices (Smithers & Robinson, 2012). As both a teacher and a leader, the GEC has a critical role at the interface between classroom practice and broader systemic processes and goals. As represented in Figure 1, taking on the role may also place the GEC in the position of advocate for gifted learners, and often entails professional engagement outside of the school and with a broader field of research and practice.

The Gifted Education Coordinator's Role in Whole-School Improvement

An interesting finding from this study was that GECs with different levels of experience identified differentiating the curriculum for gifted students and learning to coach and collaborate effectively with classroom teachers as among their top professional learning priorities. In the larger study reported in Jarvis and Henderson (2012), it was reported that in 86% of the participating schools, providing differentiated curriculum for gifted students within the regular classroom was one (or, in some cases, the only) component of the school's approach to gifted education. Yet in the vast majority (80%) of these same schools, participants reported that fewer than a third of staff had engaged in any professional learning related to understanding or teaching gifted students (Jarvis & Henderson, 2012). These findings suggest that for GECs in many of these school settings, the job entails working with teachers who are expected to design and differentiate learning experiences for gifted students, but may not have the knowledge and skills to do so. Considered in this light, it makes sense that bolstering their own differentiation skills and learning to collaborate effectively with classroom teachers were identified by GECs as high priorities for their own professional learning, especially since working with staff who may be reluctant or resistant was reported as a key challenge of the role. With the vast majority of Australia's gifted students being educated in mainstream classrooms (Walsh & Jolly, 2018), and given the well-documented lack of gifted education content in initial teacher education courses (Kronborg & Plunkett, 2013), these findings are likely to be consistent beyond state borders and in similar international contexts. Further research could confirm this assumption, while also exploring more deeply the experiences, specific challenges and professional learning needs of GECs as they support the capacity of general classroom teachers to work with gifted or academically advanced learners.

It can be argued that high-quality, appropriately challenging curriculum, supported by effective differentiated instruction, is the mainstay of inclusive education for all students, and is the critical foundation of any approach to gifted education (Callahan, Moon, Oh, Azano, & Hailey, 2015; Jarvis, 2018). Moreover, many practices and models that originated in the field of gifted education, such as higher-order thinking and problem-solving skills, have been adopted into mainstream approaches based on their perceived benefits for a broader range of learners (e.g., Hertberg-Davis & Callahan, 2013; Hockett, 2009; Renzulli, 2012). Through their work supporting, coaching, and providing professional learning opportunities for classroom teachers, GECs may be well-placed to contribute to whole-school change that could benefit both gifted students and students across the full range of ability. However, these efforts are likely to result in frustration rather than success if the GEC is working in isolation rather than as part of a coordinated, whole-school approach, or if school leaders unde-restimate the complexity of genuine change towards more inclusive teaching practices. VanTassel-Baska (2017) cautions against simply expecting teachers to differentiate effectively for gifted students in mainstream classrooms, obs-erving that:

> Monitoring the work of curriculum differentiation is a full-time job, not one to be left to chance or to the vagaries of busy administrators whose attention to the gifted program is scant. (p. 63)

Research has supported the notion that effective school-based leadership for differentiation is based on shared understandings of desired practices, grounded in the broader mission and vision of the school and fostered by multiple levels and forms of leadership across the setting (Henderson & Riley, 2018; Jarvis, Bell, & Sharp, 2016; Tait, 2018). Effective leadership for differentiation is multifaceted and includes providing the time for collaboration, resources, instructional support, and accountability for teachers to change their practices (Puzio, Newcomer, & Goff, 2015; Tomlinson, Brimijoin, & Narvaez, 2008). Within school structures, staff at a 'middle management' level are often in a good position to engage directly with teachers through mentoring and coaching in order to lead contextualised professional learning efforts, while also assuming a leadership role with an accountability component (Frankling, Jarvis, & Bell, 2017; Sharp, Jarvis, & McMillan, 2018). With specialist knowledge and skills, the motivating interest and passion, and an appropriate allocation of time, the GEC could assume this leadership role in the context of a coordinated, supported whole-school approach to more inclusive practice, including for gifted students. Without these elements in place, it is perhaps not surprising that GECs might prioritise the highly satisfying work of directly teaching appreciative students over engaging with resistant teachers.

Research and Practice: Implications and Future Directions

For GECs working in diverse mainstream schools, it seems reasonable to suggest that a clear delineation of responsibilities and description of the role should form the basis for directing and evaluating one's efforts, including in leadership. In lieu of a detailed description, it is likely that GECs might require support to shape effective, contextually appropriate ways of working over time. However, consistent with previous research (e.g., Downey, 1999), the study reported in this chapter found that most GECs (60%) were not provided with a formal role description. GECs in this study identified multiple tasks considered part of the role, and many reflected on the challenge of completing expected and desired tasks in the context of limited time, resources, and perceived support from colleagues. Considering that about two-thirds of the GECs in this study had not undertaken postgraduate studies in gifted education, and most teachers they worked with had completed very little professional learning related to working with gifted students (Jarvis & Henderson, 2012), it is easy to imagine why being passionate has its limits in fostering effective practices for gifted or advanced learners.

Gifted education coordinators from 40 schools in one Australian state were included in this study, but most gifted students across the country are educated in mainstream schools staffed by teachers with similarly limited pre-service education related to gifted students. In addition, Australia shares with other Australasian nations a lack of consistently federally funded and mandated gifted education, which has resulted in varied definitions, identification practices, and program models that are often left to school-based educators to define, develop, and implement. Therefore, the findings may be applicable across mainstream contexts, but further research is needed to confirm this assumption. In particular, future research should focus not only on the nature, scope, and challenges of the coordinator's role, but on the ways that effective coordinators seek to balance multiple responsibilities and overcome challenges related to their work and the school and system-level supports that help them achieve such a balance.

Beyond an understanding of the GEC role in different contexts, it is also important to consider the personal characteristics of an educator likely to be effective as a GEC. In-depth investigations of the personal qualities of successful GECs in different contexts, including their values, motivations, and specific expertise, and longitudinal studies of their effectiveness could be the subjects of further research. Findings from such research could help to guide recruitment, professional preparation, and ongoing support for GECs.

It is interesting to note that most of the GECs in the state study were experienced teachers. Armstrong (2010) suggested that experienced teachers may seek new challenges that take them out of the classroom, particularly if they see an opportunity to exert greater influence for more students. In this study, participants described a range of motivations for taking on the role of GEC, including to build leadership experience, out of passion for working with gifted students, or by default where coordination for gifted education was a component of a larger role. Newton, Riveros, and da Costa (2013) found that, teachers may be reluctant to become leaders, and relinquish their classroom teaching role. The Institute of Educational Leadership in the United States (2001, p. 8) found that, "as a matter of personal choice rooted in their own personalities and value systems, teachers crave neither the limelight of public attention nor the responsibilities and headaches of leadership of any kind outside their classroom fiefs". Further research could help educators to understand what motivates teachers to undertake leadership roles and how they might best be supported in their transition from the classroom to positions of leadership.

Conclusion

It is widely accepted that gifted students, whatever the definition, can be found in every cultural, geographic, and socio-economic milieu. Any effort to advance an education system with principles of equity and excellence at its core must consider the learning needs of these students, and it is a professional expectation that all teachers will differentiate the curriculum for learners across the full range of abilities, including those with advanced academic potential or exhibiting high academic performance. In mainstream Australian schools, as in other Australasian nations, the GEC is frequently the school-based staff member responsible for leading efforts to identify and provide for gifted or advanced students, in the classroom and beyond. The GEC might be passionate or reluctant, and may or may not have the knowledge, skills, and support to define and implement their role effectively. Yet, despite the central role of the coordinator in gifted education efforts, relatively little is known about its nature, scope, and specific challenges. In this chapter, the finding from one small, exploratory study has been reported that sheds some light on this important role. These findings suggest that across different types of schools, with different definitions and program models related to gifted students, there is remarkable consistency in the experiences, pressures, and professional learning priorities reported by coordinators. There is a need for further research to generalise and expand these findings with a view to fostering effective preparation and support for GECs across contexts. In particular, more case study research across different settings could provide a more in-depth understanding of how this role works in practice.

One implication of this discussion is that there appears to be a need to clearly define and position the GEC role within schools, and to consider the appropriate allocation of resources to ensure that the GEC is able to be effective. This study highlighted some of the professional learning priorities of GECs. Further research and consultation could assist in the development of resources that delineate the specific expertise (rather than only the specific tasks or responsibilities) required across different areas of the coordinator's practice, and this could serve as a tool to guide personal development and professional evaluation. A focus on raising the profile and demonstrating the value of the GEC's work is also indicated.

While the focus has been on the role of the GEC in this chapter, it is important to understand that the successful achievement and positive well-being of academically gifted and highly able students are not the sole responsibility of one individual. One person's passion, expertise, and effort can provide a powerful force for change, but whole-school commitment to an appropriate education for all students, including gifted students, demands a shared vision. Understanding the purpose, place, and possibilities of the gifted education coordinator is one element in a broader agenda of inclusive education for gifted students.

Cross-References

- ► Australian Teachers Who Made a Difference: Secondary Gifted Student Perceptions of Teaching and Teacher Effectiveness
- ► Being of Like-Mind: Giftedness in the New Zealand Context
- ► Differentiation of Instruction for Gifted Learners: Collated Evaluative Studies of Teacher Classroom Practices
- ► Educational Contexts, Transitions and Community Engagement: Part VI Introduction
- ► Fostering and Developing Talent in Mentorship Programs: The Mentor's Perspectives
- ► Gifted Education in the Asia-Pacific: From the Past for the Future – An Introduction
- ► Rural Voices: Identifying the Perceptions, Practices, and Experiences of Gifted Pedagogy in Australian Rural and Regional Schools
- ► Some Implications for the Future of Gifted Education in the Asia-Pacific
- ► Supporting Australian Gifted Indigenous Students' Academic Potential in Rural Settings
- ► Teaching Gifted Education to Pre-service Teachers: Lessons Learned
- ► Teachers' Knowledge and Understandings of Twice Exceptionality Across Australia
- ► Towards Exceptionality: The Current Status and Future Prospects of Australian Gifted Education

Acknowledgment The research reported in this chapter was funded by a Flinders University Faculty Project Grant.

References

Armstrong, D. (2010). Rites of passage: Coercion, compliance, and complicity in the socialization of new vice-principals. *Teachers College Record, 112*(3), 685–722.

Borland, J. (1989). *Planning and implementing programs for the gifted.* New York, NY: Teachers College Press.

Brighton, C. M., Hertberg, H. L., Moon, T. R., Tomlinson, C. A., & Callahan, C. M. (2005). *The feasibility of high-end learning in a diverse middle school* (RM05210). Storrs, CT: National Research Center on the Gifted and Talented.

Callahan, C. M., Moon, T. R., Oh, S., Azano, A. P., & Hailey, E. P. (2015). What works in gifted education: Documenting the effects of an integrated curricular/instructional model for gifted students. *American Education Research Journal, 52,* 137–167. https://doi.org/10.3102/0002831214549448

Cathcart, R. (2010). *Gifted programming made practical.* NZ: Essential Resources.

Collins, J. (Chair). (2001). *The education of gifted and talented children.* Canberra, ACT: Senate Employment Workplace Relations Small Business and Education Reference Committee.

Downey, P. (1999). *An analysis of perceived problems facing coordinators of gifted education in NSW independent secondary schools* (Unpublished doctoral dissertation). University of New South Wales, Australia.

Frankling, T., Jarvis, J. M., & Bell, M. R. (2017). Leading secondary teachers' understandings and practices of differentiation through professional learning. *Leading and Managing, 23*(2), 72–86.

Fraser-Seeto, K. T., Howard, S. J., & Woodcock, S. (2015). An investigation of teachers' awareness and willingness to engage with a self-directed professional development package on gifted and talented education. *Australian Journal of Teacher Education, 40*(1), 1–14. https://doi.org/10.14221/ajte.2015v40n1.1

Geake, J. G., & Gross, M. U. M. (2008). Teachers' negative affect towards academically gifted students: An evolutionary psychological study. *The Gifted Child Quarterly, 52*, 217–231. https://doi.org/10.1177/0016986208319704

Griffin, P. (2013). Submission 20. *The effectiveness of the National Assessment Program: Literacy and Numeracy.* Education and Employment References Committee. Retrieved from http://www.aph.gov.au/Parliamentary_Business/Committees/Senate/Education_and_Employment/Naplan13/Submissions

Griffin, P., Care, E., Francis, M., Hutchinson, D., Arratia-Martinez, A., & McCabe, C. (2013). *Assessment and learning partnerships: The influence of teaching practices on student achievement.* Melbourne, Victoria: Assessment Research Centre.

Gross, M. U. M., Urquhart, R., Doyle, J., Juratowitch, M., & Matheson, G. (2011). *Releasing the brakes for high-ability learners.* Sydney, Australia. Retrieved from https://education.arts.unsw.edu.au/media/EDUCFile/Releasing_the_Brakes_Overview_A4__Nov2011.pdf

Gruppetta, M. (2005). Investigating the role and experiences of gifted and talented coordinators. *Gifted Education International, 19*(2), 132–141. https://doi.org/10.1177/026142940501900207

Henderson, L., & Riley, T. (2018). School programs and strategies for gifted learners. In J. L. Jolly & J. M. Jarvis (Eds.), *Exploring gifted education: Australian and New Zealand perspectives* (pp. 112–131). Abingdon, UK: Routledge.

Henderson, L. C., & Jarvis, J. M. (2016). The gifted dimension of the Australian professional standards for teachers: Implications for professional learning. *Australian Journal of Teacher Education, 41*(8), 60–83. http://dx.doi.org/10.14221/ajte.2016v41n8.4

Hertberg-Davis, H. L., & Callahan, C. M. (2013). *Fundamentals of gifted education: Considering multiple perspectives.* New York, NY: Routledge.

Hockett, J. A. (2009). Curriculum for highly able learners that conforms to general education and gifted education quality indicators. *Journal for the Education of the Gifted, 32*, 394–440. https://doi.org/10.4219/jeg-2009-857

Hurford, L. H. M. (2013). 'Holding the torch' *for gifted and talented students in New Zealand primary schools: Insights from gifted and talented coordinators* (Unpublished master's thesis). University of Canterbury, Christchurch, New Zealand.

Institute for Educational Leadership. (2001). *Leadership for student learning: Redefining the teacher as leader.* Washington, DC: Author.

Jarvis, J. M. (2018). Designing and adapting curriculum for academically gifted students. In J. L. Jolly & J. M. Jarvis (Eds.), *Exploring gifted education: Australian and New Zealand perspectives* (pp. 95–111). Abingdon, UK: Routledge.

Jarvis, J. M., Bell, M. R., & Sharp, K. (2016). Leadership for differentiation: An appreciative inquiry of how educational leadership shapes pedagogical change. *Leading and Managing, 22*(1), 75–91.

Jarvis, J. M., & Henderson, L. C. (2012). Current practices in the education of gifted and advanced learners in south Australian schools. *Australasian Journal of Gifted Education, 21*(1), 5–22. https://doi.org/10.21505/ajge.2015.0018

Jarvis, J. M., & Henderson, L. C. (2014). Defining a coordinated approach to gifted education. *Australasian Journal of Gifted Education, 23*(1), 5–14.

Jensen, A. L. (1986). Greater than the parts: Shared decision making. *Roeper Review, 9*(1), 10–13. https://doi.org/10.1080/02783198609552994

Jung, J. Y., Young, M., & Gross, M. U. M. (2015). Early college entrance in Australia. *Roeper Review, 37*(1), 19–28. https://doi.org/10.1080/02783193.2014.976323

Jung, J., & Hay, P. (2018). Identification of gifted and twice-exceptional students. In J. Jolly & J. Jarvis (Eds.) Exploring gifted education: Australian and New Zealand perspectives (pp. 12–31). Oxon, UK: Routledge.

Kronborg, L. G., & Plunkett, M. M. (2013). Responding to professional learning: How effective teachers differentiate teaching and learning strategies to engage highly able adolescents. *Australasian Journal of Gifted Education, 22*(2), 52–63.

Lampl, P. (2012). Foreword. In A. Smithers & P. Robinson (Eds.), *Educating the highly able*. Buckingham, UK: Sutton Trust. Retrieved from https://www.suttontrust.com/wp-content/uploads/2012/07/Educating-the-Highly-Able-Report-1.pdf

Lassig, C. J. (2009). Teachers' attitudes towards the gifted: The importance of professional development and school culture. *Australasian Journal of Gifted Education, 18*(2), 32–42. https://doi.org/10.21505/ajge.2015.0012

Lewis, J., Cruzeiro, P., & Hall, C. (2007). Impact of two elementary school principals' leadership on gifted education in their buildings. *Gifted Child Today, 30*(2), 56–62. Retrieved from https://files.eric.ed.gov/fulltext/EJ756555.pdf

Long, L., Barnett, K., & Rogers, K. B. (2015). Exploring the relationship between principal, policy and gifted program scope and quality. *Journal for the Education of the Gifted, 38*, 118–140. https://doi.org/10.1177/0162353215578279

Masters, G. (2015, March). Understanding and addressing the learning needs of our highest-performing students. Keynote paper presented at the joint conference of the Australian Association for the Education of the Gifted and Talented and The International Research Association for Talent Development and Excellence, Brisbane, Australia.

McDonald, J. A. (2014). *Stakeholder or gatekeeper: The role of the principal in gifted education* (Unpublished doctoral thesis). Bowling Green State University, Bowling Green, OH.

Ministry of Education. (n.d.). *Responsibilities of the GATE Coordinator*. Retrieved from http://gifted.tki.org.nz/For-schools-and-teachers/Role-of-the-GATE-Coordinator/Responsibilities-of-the-GATE-Coordinator

Moltzen, R., Jolly, J., & Jarvis, J. (2018). Framing gifted education. In J. Jolly & J. Jarvis (Eds.) Exploring gifted education: Australian and New Zealand perspectives (pp. 5–11). Oxon, UK: Routledge.

New South Wales Department of Education and Training (NSW DET). (2004). *Policy and implementation strategies for the education of gifted and talented students* (Revised 2004). Sydney, Australia: DET Curriculum K–12 Directorate.

Newton, P., Riveros, G., & da Costa, J. (2013). The influence of teacher leadership in the career advancement of schoolteachers: A case study. *Journal of Educational Administration and Foundations, 23*(2), 105–117.

Oswald, M., & de Villiers, J. (2013). Including the gifted learner: Perceptions of South African teachers and principals. *South African Journal of Education, 33*(1), 1–21. Retrieved from http://www.scielo.org.za/scielo.php?script=sci_arttext&pid=S0256-01002013000100004

Plunkett, M., & Harvey, D. (1995). Teaching the gifted: Is interest alone enough? *Australasian Journal of Gifted Education, 4*(1), 16–21.

Plunkett, M., & Kronborg, L. (2011). Learning to be a teacher of the gifted: The importance of examining opinions and challenging misconceptions. *Gifted and Talented International, 26*, 31–46. https://doi.org/10.1080/15332276.2011.11673587

Puzio, K., Newcomer, S. N., & Goff, P. (2015). Supporting literacy differentiation: The principal's role in a community of practice. *Literacy Research and Instruction, 54*(2), 135–162. https://doi.org/10.1080/19388071.2014.997944

Renzulli, J. S. (2012). Re-examining the role of gifted education and talent development for the 21st Century: A four-part theoretical approach. *The Gifted Child Quarterly, 56*, 150–159. https://doi.org/10.1177/0016986212444901

Riley, T. & Moltzen, R. (2010). Enhancing and igniting talent development initiatives: Research to determine effectiveness. *Report prepared for the Ministry of Education, New Zealand*. ISBN: 978-0-478-34231-4.

Robinson, W. & Campbell, J. (2010). *Effective teaching in gifted education: Using a whole school approach*. London, UK: Routledge.

Sharp, K., Jarvis, J. M., & McMillan, J. M. (2018). Leadership for differentiated instruction: Teachers' engagement with on-site professional learning at an Australian secondary school. *International Journal of Inclusive Education*. https://doi.org/10.1080/13603116.2018.1492639. Advance online publication.

Smithers, A., & Robinson, P. (2012). *Educating the highly able*. Buckingham, UK: Sutton trust. Retrieved from https://www.suttontrust.com/wp-content/uploads/2012/07/Educating-the-Highly-Able-Report-1.pdf

Stack, N., Sutherland, M., O'Reilly, C., & Chandler, K. (2014, September). *The role of the school principal in gifted education*. Paper presented at the conference of the European Council for High Ability, Ljubljana.

Tait, D. (2018). To research and deliver a direct and positive impact on high potential students across Australia – USA, Singapore. Churchill Fellow Report. Retrieved from https://www.churchilltrust.com.au/fellows/detail/4173/Desilee+Tait

Tomlinson, C. A., Brimijoin, K., & Narvaez, L. (2008). *The differentiated school: Making revolutionary changes in teaching and learning*. Alexandria, VA: Association for Supervision and Curriculum Development.

VanTassel-Baska, J. (2017). Curriculum issues: What makes differentiated curriculum work? *Gifted Child Today, 40*(1), 62–63. https://doi.org/10.1177/1076217516675905

Walsh, R. L., & Jolly, J. L. (2018). Gifted education in the Australian context. *Gifted Child Today, 41*(2), 81–88. https://doi.org/10.1177/1076217517750702

Weber, C., Colarulli-Daniels, R., & Leinhauser, J. (2003). A tale of two principals. *Gifted Child Today, 26*(4), 55–65. https://doi.org/10.4219/gct-2003-112

Lesley Henderson is a lecturer in the College of Education, Psychology, & Social Work at Flinders University in South Australia, where she coordinates the Gifted Education specialisation. Her research interests include teaching and learning, professional learning, leadership for gifted education, design thinking and creativity, curriculum, thinking skills, and ethics.

Jane Jarvis is a senior lecturer in the College of Education, Psychology, and Social Work at Flinders University in South Australia. She received her PhD in Educational Psychology/Gifted Education from the University of Virginia and has worked in gifted education as a teacher, counsellor, and consultant. She has also worked in special education and disability services in Australia and the United States. Jane's teaching and research interests include curriculum design, differentiation, and inclusive educational practices, and she works with schools across Australia and overseas on differentiating instruction for diverse learners.

Leadership Development of Gifted Adolescents from a Korean Multicultural Lens

55

Seon-Young Lee, Yun-Kyoung Kim, and Eunjoo Boo

Contents

Abstract

This chapter is about leadership education for gifted students based on multicultural perspectives about leaders and leadership. Leadership has been identified as one form of giftedness since the Marland report (1972), and there is an increased demand for gifted populations taking the leading role in the global society (Lee, 2015; Lee & Olszewski–Kubilius, 2016). However, it is not clearly stated what kind of leadership is expected for the future world and what leadership roles are anticipated for gifted students. Since leadership and leaders' roles vary over time

S.-Y. Lee (✉) · Y.-K. Kim · E. Boo
Seoul National University, Seoul, South Korea
e-mail: seonylee@snu.ac.kr; acrosstheuniverse222@gmail.com; eunjoo.boo@gmail.com

© Springer Nature Singapore Pte Ltd. 2021   1245
S. R. Smith (ed.), *Handbook of Giftedness and Talent Development in the Asia-Pacific*,
Springer International Handbooks of Education,
https://doi.org/10.1007/978-981-13-3041-4_61

and according to circumstances, leadership and leaders must be understood in a multifaceted manner. Only a few studies, however, have dealt with sociocultural issues in conceptualising leadership and encouraging leadership development for gifted students. The majority of the literature has documented perceptions about leadership from a Western perspective and lives of leading eminent people in Western societies. These are major limitations of leadership studies, which lead to a skewed view of leadership deemed the by-product of the Western cultures (Den Hartog & Dickson, 2012). This chapter consists of two parts. First, we review the conception of leadership, types of leadership and leaders, and leadership development from multicultural perspectives by addressing the issues of cultural dimensions of leadership. Second, using pilot study data garnered from a group of Korean gifted students and teachers, gifted students' and teachers' perceptions about leaders and leadership development are summarised.

Keywords

Leadership · Leaders · Gifted students · Multicultural perspectives · Cultural dimensions · Leadership education

The aims in this chapter are to:
1. Introduce a multicultural model of leadership that involves five cultural dimensions.
2. Examine how gifted students and teachers in South Korea, one of the collectivistic nations, perceive leadership and leaders' roles.
3. Identify gifted students' and teachers' beliefs in gifted students' responsibility to take a leadership role.
4. Suggest educational guidance for schools to develop leadership of gifted and talented students in the classroom.

Introduction

Leadership has been one of the major issues in gifted education for over half a century since the well-known Marland report (Marland, 1972) addressed leadership as one of the domains and/or abilities of giftedness. Despite the early awareness of leadership perceived as one form of giftedness and the potential of gifted students, there are few educational programs designed to enhance gifted students' leadership. A heightened demand for leaders who are capable of coping with challenges, thinking critically and solving problems creatively is inevitable, and gifted students may be the ones who are able to perform these roles (Lee, 2015; Lee & Olszewski-Kubilius, 2016).

A growing expectation of gifted populations to take leadership roles makes us wonder if gifted students are prepared to become leaders for the future world.

Leadership is prone to vary according to the social and cultural context (Dorfman, 2003; Hofstede, 2001; House, Wright, & Aditya, 1997; Smith, 1997), and thus, leaders must take different roles by meeting the needs of the society. Only a few studies, however, have dealt with sociocultural issues in conceptualising leadership and encouraging the leadership development of gifted students (e.g., Chan, 2000; Feldhusen & Kennedy, 1988a). The majority of the research literature has documented perceptions about leadership from a Western perspective and lives of eminent leaders in Western societies (e.g., Feldhusen & Kennedy, 1988b; Karnes & Meriweather, 1988; Karnes, Riley, & McGinnis, 1996). These are major limitations of leadership studies, which result in a skewed view of leadership that is the by-product of Western culture (Den Hartog & Dickson, 2012).

Leadership is conceived as a multifaceted concept and typically discussed threefold: Intrapersonal leadership, interpersonal leadership, and a hybrid of intrapersonal and interpersonal leadership. A number of definitions address the intrapersonal nature of leadership that is mainly based on psychological traits and personality characteristics of well-respected leaders (e.g., Bono, Shen, & Yoon, 2014; Judge, Bono, Ilies, & Gerhardt, 2002). Particularly, some of the big five traits, such as openness to experience, conscientiousness, extraversion, and agreeableness are often referred to as the characteristics of effective leaders (Bono & Judge, 2004; Judge et al., 2002). For example, the extraverted leader tends to express his or her compelling visions and is good at convincing other people to believe that she/he is a competent leader (Hogan, Curphy, & Hogan, 1994). Leaders high in conscientiousness are likely to have a clear plan for the future, know how to set goals to achieve the plan, and persist in carrying it out (Bono et al., 2014). Judge, Thoresen, Pucik, and Welbourne (1999) reported that openness to experience predicted leadership in part because individuals high on this trait were analytic and capable of solving problems and coping with challenges. Also, in Bono, Shen, and Yoon's (2014) study, a positive correlation was found between extraversion and transformational leadership behaviours, while a negative correlation was found between neuroticism and the leadership behaviours (also see Bono & Judge, 2004).

Interpersonal leadership pays great attention to the process of interactions among people, solving problems, and making decisions in a group (Bass & Stogdill, 1990; Chemers, 2002; Hollander, 1992; Yukl, 2006). Abilities to influence, motivate, and convince other people to accomplish shared goals in a group are not only crucial in defining leadership, but also contribute to the success of the organisation to which one belongs (Hackman & Johnson, 2004; Northouse, 2006). Leaders with the interpersonal leadership style are capable of optimising group performances. Interpersonal leaders encourage group members to build teamwork (Chemers, 2002), inspire mutual efforts (Yukl, 2002), and provide directions and emotional support to achieve the collective goal. Researchers are aware that having excellent communication skills are also important for leaders, particularly for young leaders (Conner & Strobel, 2007; van Linden & Fertman, 1998).

Specifically, advanced oral and written communication skills are suggested as the two most needed skills for leaders (Ricketts & Rudd, 2002), because they enable leaders to build favourable relationships with other people (Boyd, Herring, & Briers, 1992; Thomas, 1992) and facilitate decision-making procedures among group members (Gilley, McMillan, & Gilley, 2009). Also, individuals with interpersonal leadership are good at managing diversity in a group (Hogan & Warrenfeltz, 2003).

A hybrid perspective emphasises balancing both intrapersonal and interpersonal leadership styles (Bass & Stogdill, 1990; Conner & Strobel, 2007). If interpersonal leadership focuses on how to communicate with people and convince them to follow the leader's vision, in a hybrid leadership, issues on 'how' to make an influence on people and 'why' they are influenced by the leader are equally important (Lee & Olszewski-Kubilius, 2016). Examples of this kind of leadership are charismatic, transformational, and transactional leadership, which are in fact well-cited modes of leadership in the literature. Each of the types of leadership is formed on the basis of the leader's personality characteristics and his/her relationships with other people (McGregor, 1987; van Knippenberg, van Knippenberg, De Cremer, & Hogg, 2004).

In summary, intrapersonal, interpersonal, and a hybrid of both styles of leadership identify leaders according to the leader's characteristics, competencies, and relationships with his/her followers. One dearth of research is about cultural diversity in conceptualising leadership and identifying leaders' characteristics and roles from gifted students' and/or educators' perspectives. Leadership connotes different meanings and values according to culture. For example, leadership has a positive tone in English, such as heroic images of individuals of high ability, while the German translation of a leader embodies a somewhat negative meaning related to dictatorship (Den Hartog & Koopman, 2001). Such differences originate from distinctive beliefs and values inherent in leadership, which varies according to the sociocultural context. Also, leadership has not been one of the central themes in research on gifted education, although it was first included as a gifted domain/ability in identifying gifted and talented students in the early 1970s.

With the aforementioned problems in mind, this chapter reviews the conception of leadership and characteristics of leaders and introduces a model of cultural diversity in leadership by elaborating how cultures are likely to influence theories and practices in leadership studies. The authors used empirical data from a pilot study involving a group of gifted college students and teachers in South Korea and summarised their perceptions about leaders, gifted students' possibilities to be leaders and leadership development. The students' and teachers' beliefs in leadership and leadership development were also discussed according to the Hofstede model (Hofstede, 1980, 2001) of cultural dimensions. Finally, the authors proposed 12 educational principles for leadership education for gifted students. The principles endorse theories and practices for leadership development that can be applied in the classroom.

Explaining Leadership from Multicultural Perspectives

Generally, leadership is defined as an individual's ability to influence, motivate, and enable other people in order to accomplish the success of the organisation to which one belongs (House, Hanges, Javidan, Dorfman, & Gupta, 2004). In a review of numerous definitions of leadership, Yammarino (2013) concluded that leadership is a multi-level (e.g., person, dyad, group collective) leader–follower interaction process that occurs in a particular situation where a leader and followers are willing to share a purpose and accomplish goals together. Although researchers suggested different views on leadership, leadership generally embraces an interplay between conflict and power among people (see Alvesson & Spicer, 2014; Huckaby & Sperling, 1981; Hughes, Ginnett, & Curphy, 1993; Smith, Wang, & Leung, 1997). It is also a purposeful, collaborative, and value-laden process of influencing people and aims to make positive changes for society (Komives, Lucas, & McMahon, 2009).

Den Hartog and Dickson (2012) claimed that cultural values determine leadership and leaders' roles because they influence people's mode of thinking and expectations of the society. All these assertions suggest that leadership ought to be comprehended with a purpose, values, and cultures that affect one's beliefs, ethics, and behaviours (Adler, 2002). Therefore, identifying how a culture has an influence on forming values and practices for leadership enables one to better understand what aspects of leadership are needed for a future leader, particularly for gifted students who have the potential to become leaders in adulthood.

An increased awareness of the importance of cultures and collective values on leadership has inspired researchers to consider cultural matters in defining leadership. Although not many, some researchers have suggested cultural elements in accounting for leadership differences among nations. For example, some of the well-cited works about leadership and cultures (e.g., Hofstede, 1980; Hofstede & McCrae, 2004; Inkeles, 1997; Inkeles & Levinson, 1969) discussed leadership in terms of issues in relation to authority, the conception of self, and a primary conflict, and its resolution, which are the three major problems that every nation ought to deal with to sustain the society (Hofstede, 1980; Hofstede & McCrae, 2004; Inkeles, 1997; Inkeles & Levinson, 1969). In relation to authority, this is the level of dependence on an individual of superior power, while the conception of self is explained by the balance between personal goals and dependence on the society, and between ego and social values. A primary conflict is related to the ways of resolving dilemmas. All these problems are linked to leadership in that a relation to authority determines a distance to power, and a desire to avoid uncertainty motivates the leader to resolve a primary conflict (see Ashkanasy, Wilderom, & Peterson, 2000 for a summary).

Inkeles and Levinson (1969) also claimed that issues on individualism versus collectivism, and masculinity versus femininity form one's conception of self, and thus, balancing personal and collective goals and values is quintessential to placing oneself appropriately into one's society. Franke, Hofstede, and Bond

(Franke, Hofstede, & Bond, 1991) adapted these three modes of national cultures and proposed a leadership model in terms of: (a) individualism versus collectivism, (b) masculinity versus femininity, (c) uncertainty avoidance, (d) power distance, and (e) future orientation. From 1967 to 1973, Hofstede estimated a reliability of the model using data on a series of organisational attitude surveys conducted by IBM and its subsidiaries in 71 nations (see Hofstede & McCrae, 2004). Research supported that Hofstede's leadership model is instrumental in accounting for the relationship between cultural themes and leadership practices, particularly in coping with challenges within society (House et al., 2004).

Roles of Leaders Based on the Five Cultural Dimensions of the Hofstede Model

In the following, we summarise the conceptions of leadership and expected roles of leaders based on the five cultural dimensions of the Hofstede model.

Individualism versus collectivism. According to Hofstede (1980, 2001), the degree to which one belongs to a group can be viewed as either individualistic or collectivistic (Hofstede & McCrae, 2004). In an individualistic society, self-interest is centred, and privacy and freedom are highly valued. Leaders must be aware of one's needs, be open-minded to accept one's unique talents, and facilitate individualism (Lee & Liu, 2012). In contrast, individuals in a collectivistic society are integrated into a tight-knit group, and harmony and conformity are highly appreciated among group members. Leaders should be capable of maintaining strong in-group bonds through rules and regulations that protect the group members (Goncalo & Staw, 2006).

Masculinity versus femininity. The second cultural dimension is about the distribution of emotional roles between genders called masculinity versus femininity (Hofstede & McCrae, 2004). Assuming that men and women have different values and that differences in values between the genders vary according to the societal context (e.g., women's values vary less than men's values), leadership in this dimension identifies different roles for leaders (Den Hartog, 2004; Hofstede & McCrae, 2004). The masculine society expects to have a leader who is a successful achiever and a 'superman' who behaves in an assertive, aggressive, competitive and decisive manner. Conversely, leaders in the feminine society are modest, tender, and likely to stay invisible are good at building and maintaining interpersonal relationships and are caring for people. They would seek communion with their followers and facilitate collaboration among group members (Den Hartog, 2004; Evetts, 2014; Hofstede & McCrae, 2004).

Avoidance versus acceptance of uncertainty. Avoidance versus acceptance of uncertainty is related to the level of tolerance for ambiguity in unstructured situations (Hofstede & McCrae, 2004). Hofstede's (1983) construct of uncertainty avoidance at the workplace consists of three factors, such as rule orientation, employment stability, and nervousness or stress at work. An uncertainty-avoiding society minimises facing possible unstructured situations by applying laws and rules (Hofstede & McCrae, 2004). Safety, security, and a strong belief in truths are well respected, and thus, leaders are apt to be controlling and authoritative to protect the society. However, individuals in an uncertainty-accepting society are highly tolerant of different points of view among group members and are less likely to depend on rules and regulations. An uncertainty-accepting society is eager to have a leader who is open-minded and willing to take risks, respects differences and diversity and promotes change and innovation (Furmańczyk, 2010).

High versus low power distance. High versus low power distance refers to the level of social acceptance of power that is equally distributed among people (Hofstede, 1980, 2001). It identifies the distance between the leader and his/her subordinates and the amount of authority given by a person in power. People in the high-power distanced society respect the social hierarchy, desire to have a leader who is capable of making autocratic decisions, and would obey their leaders (Bu, Craig, & Peng, 2001). By contrast, in the low-power distanced society, individuals look for democratic, horizontal, and consulting relationships with their leaders and are encouraged to speak out when making decisions (Hofstede, 2001).

Long-term versus short-term orientation. The final dimension is about a future orientation (Hofstede, 2001, 2006), which explains if a group promotes future oriented behaviours, such as planning and delaying gratification (House et al., 2004). A long-term future-oriented society emphasises hard work and efforts and inspires a feeling of hope about the future. Forward-thinking, long-term leaders pursue future-oriented goals and take actions to accomplish the chosen goals. A society oriented towards a short-term future urges individuals to follow tradition and convention, and pursue immediate rewards. Leaders who plan short-term are good at preserving traditional societal values and norms to maintain the status quo (Hofstede, 2001, 2006).

As presented, the perceived leadership and leaders' roles vary according to sociocultural circumstances. Sociocultural norms and values identify the conception of leadership and determine leaders' roles and commitments. For decades, research has suggested that generally Western societies encourage positive and advanced leadership practices more than do Eastern societies where the idea of paternalism and collectivism dominates across the nations (Aycan, 2004). There is also an impression that leadership is a by-product of the Western cultures where individualism guides whole societies (Ailon, 2008). Given that leadership involves a wide array of decision-making processes based on distinctive modes of forming and maintaining relationships with people, which vary by time and according to circumstances, leadership and leaders need to incorporate both the Eastern and Western cultural values and people. Specifically, for gifted students who have the potential to be leaders in a global society, understanding leadership and leaders from a multicultural perspective is a prerequisite.

Gifted Students' and Teachers' Perceptions About Leaders and Leadership Development: Some Findings from a Pilot Study

This section presents some of the results from a small pilot study that examined Korean gifted students' and teachers' perceptions about leaders and leadership development. Given that few studies have dealt with leadership involving gifted populations from different nations, we hope that results from this study help others to design and implement comparative research studies about leadership according to gifted students' and teachers' perspectives.

A two-hour focus group interview was conducted with eight gifted college students, and an email survey was administered to six teachers in South Korea. Using the same questions, both the interview and survey examined how gifted students and teachers perceived good leaders and leadership, and if they believed in the possibility of gifted students becoming leaders in a global society. Examples of the interview and survey questions were:

- Who are the good leaders around you and why?
- What kind of student do you think is a person of excellent leadership?
- Who will be ideal leaders for future societies?
- What leadership characteristics are expected for the future leader?
- Are academically gifted students more likely to become leaders when they grow up than their non-gifted counterparts?
- Do you have the same expectations of leadership and leadership development for gifted students versus non-gifted students?
- Are leaders born or made?
- Should academically gifted students develop their leadership potential for society?
- What skills are needed to be raised via leadership development programs and why?

A major reason for including the Korean sample was to compare their responses with those documented in the literature regarding leadership that mostly involved students and teachers from Western countries (e.g., Lonner, 2016; Markus & Kitayama, 1991). Having data from South Korea, a nation where collective values are pervasive across the society, would contribute to adding comparative results to the literature and help to better understand the multifaceted and/or cultural aspects of leadership. In addition, gifted education in South Korea has grown fast with the support of the Korean government, and raising global leaders is identified as one of the major goals of gifted education (Hong & Yoo, 2016; Shin & Jang, 2017). Hence, it is worth examining what gifted students and teachers in South Korea believe regarding leadership and leadership development of gifted students.

Interview participants were eight college students who attended the most academically prestigious university in South Korea. They were contacted by the research team via email using a university online recruitment program for research participants and were selected as academically gifted college students proven by superior academic performance that allowed them to get into the university. They majored in education, business, engineering, or music, and responded to ten questions about what they believed about leadership, the good characteristics of efficient leaders and gifted students' possibilities to be leaders. The students also spoke about their own leadership experiences before entering college.

Six secondary school teachers responded to an email survey that consisted of the same questions used for the university students. They were science, mathematics, or English teachers at gifted science and mathematics schools in South Korea and had an average of ten years of teaching experience in public schools. Three of them took gifted courses at the same university and majored in science education with a focus on gifted education. The other three participated in the survey following a recommendation by the first group of teachers. All of the teachers were teaching gifted students at the time of the data collection.

Because the interview and the survey intended to examine students' and teachers' implicit beliefs in leadership and leadership education, there was no premise about leadership for this pilot study. Both interview and survey data were analysed following the systematic coding procedure for content analysis (Freitas, Oliveira, Jenkins, & Popjoy, 1998). Keywords were extracted from original responses and were clustered into subcategories to engender major themes that embraced the student and teacher perspectives about leadership. In the following, a summary of results is presented according to three core themes generated from the interview and survey data. The themes were *leaders*, *gifted students' potential to be leaders*, and *leadership development and education*.

Leaders

Gifted college students mentioned leaders' interpersonal skills and intrapersonal traits as almost equally important for a good leader. They strongly believed that having advanced problem-solving ability ($n = 7$) and good communication skills ($n = 6$) enables one to convince other people and become an efficient national leader. Student #7 (2017) addressed the importance of finding the best or better solutions. She said, "I think the problem-solving skill matters the most. Leaders must be able to find the best or better solution to make a good judgment". At the same time, the students were highly aware that listening to other voices and being open-minded and trustworthy were crucial for future leaders. Student #5 (2017) claimed that good leaders give suggestions in a cooperative and strategic manner. She emphasised being open-minded and non-judgemental for leaders in Korea and said:

> Our society needs a leader who is open to different opinions. Leaders today must have expertise in technology but also accept difference and diversity to get to a final conclusion. A good leader inspires people to express what they think and feel before s/he offered his/her vision and goal. We willingly participate in the decision-making procedure if the leader does not judge our opinions.

Student #2 (2017) agreed that leaders should listen to other people and understand the diverse needs of their followers. She added, "There are many leaders who ignore others' opinions and simply make decisions of their own. It really discourages us from getting involved in and taking actions to social matters".

The majority ($n = 5$) of the Korean gifted teachers believed that for leaders, interpersonal abilities were more important than intrapersonal traits. They addressed abilities to get along with other people, understand differences, and stimulate one's autonomy as ideal characteristics of a future leader. The following quotation denotes the teachers' belief in the leader's interpersonal abilities:

> I believe that good leaders are someone who have great interpersonal skills. They understand the feelings of others and communicate well, so they can play a mediating role in facilitating collaboration between group members. (Teacher #1, 2017)

Another ability the teachers perceived as crucial for leaders was advanced problem-solving skills. Four teachers addressed problem-solving skills needed for a national leader. Teacher # 2's (2017) comments explained the reason for choosing problem-solving skills over others. "Excellent problem-solving ability is required for effective leadership in Korea. Leaders are not those who solve problems immediately, but rather choose one best solution after searching for comprehensive information and others' opinions."

As for an image of student leaders in class or school specifically, the students responded that a good student leader must have advanced cognitive ability, particularly having insight and creativity ($n = 4$), and a sense of responsibility and independence ($n = 2$). Student #4 (2017) recollected a friend and praised her insightful decision-making ability while serving as a class leader. She said:

> One of my friends was a good leader because she independently made a decision and made it work out. Such intuition, autonomy, or possibly independence enabled her to build leadership. I truly wanted to learn such an active and sometimes aggressive problem-solving ability.

Other responses included having an ability to bring people together ($n = 1$) and a strong task commitment ($n = 1$).

Overwhelmingly, the teachers expected leaders in class to get along and interact well with their peers. They particularly expected their class leaders to show respect for other classmates and divide up the group work fairly but efficiently when taking a leadership role ($n = 5$). They did not mention academic competence (e.g., good grades), creativity, or the intellectual ability of the student leader.

Gifted Students' Potential to Be Leaders

Both the students and teachers responded to a question asking if gifted students have a greater potential to be a global leader compared to their non-gifted counterparts. Data showed both believed in gifted students' higher possibility to become leaders in adulthood, but the reasons behind their beliefs were somewhat different. The students expressed their mixed feelings about gifted students becoming leaders. All acknowledged that they had observed expectations from other people to take a leadership role as a gifted student. However, half ($n = 4$) of them did not accept that they ought to be in a leadership position or be a leader due to their academic superiority. They believed that leadership comes from one's own will, and thus, none can force gifted students to take responsibility for society, simply because they are gifted. Two students were even suspicious about gifted students' potential to be a 'good' leader. Reasons were mainly from their belief in leadership that requires different abilities and personality characteristics from academic competence. Their comments were: "I think an academically gifted student is not likely be a good leader because when solving a problem, collaboration is more important than intellectual ability (Student #1, 2017)."

> Leadership is largely formed by one's personality. For example, an introverted person may not want to take a leader's position. I don't know the reason why a person of high academic ability is expected to be a great leader. (Student #7, 2017)

On the contrary, higher social expectations and greater educational opportunities given to gifted students than to their non-gifted counterparts ($n = 5$) were the two most visible reasons cited by the teachers. Yet, some teachers warned that giftedness per se does not warrant future leadership. For example, Teacher #4 (2017) said:

> When you are young, you tend to think that students with high academic records are gifted leaders. But these students must learn that practical ability related to problem solving and goal setting is more important than superior academic performance in being a leader.

In addition, four teachers asserted that although gifted students are likely to become leaders of future society, they must be well prepared to take a leadership role. "Surely, gifted students are likely to lead others and society when they grow up, but need to develop service-mindedness and persistence first to be a pioneer in the future", said Teacher #3 (2017).

Leadership Development and Education

Issues regarding whether leaders are supposed to be born or nurtured were discussed. Our gifted students responded that a leader is likely to be created by a society when the society grants adequate guidance and opportunities to the leader ($n = 5$). The following comment by student #1 (2017) was a good example supporting this assertion:

> I think one can be a good leader if one tries hard. We are hugely influenced by the environment, and it is important that society provides us with sufficient opportunities to discover our potential and strengths. I strongly believe that hard work can make a great leader.

Four of the six teachers said that leaders may be born or nurtured, but should attain interpersonal and problem-solving skills to meet the social needs. They addressed extraversion, sociability, and talents in a certain domain as attributes that leaders are supposed to be born with, while respect for other people, listening to others, empathy, and information-processing skills were referred to as the characteristics and/or abilities that leaders must develop. For example, teacher #2 emphasised the developmental aspect of leadership skills:

> People are born with some intrapersonal traits like extroversion and getting along with others. But there are leadership abilities, such as listening to others' opinions, choosing adequate information, showing respect to other people, etc., that can be trained. Requested leadership differs according to social circumstances because one faces a variety of problems daily. (Teacher #2, 2017).

The students and teachers suggested a specialised program for leadership development for gifted students. Overall, the students stated that leadership education must be designed to help gifted students to enhance their cognitive abilities. In particular, programs and activities that stimulate problem solving, logical thinking, and critical thinking skills were suggested for leadership education. Six students also expressed their desire to have a mentor or a role model whom they can look up to as a potential leader. Unlike the students, the teachers referred to non-cognitive skills related to communication, conflict management, and group cohesiveness as the examples of leadership ability that the program should consider specifically for gifted students' leadership development. Teacher #5 (2017) said that:

> Leadership qualities, such as conflict management, communication skills, task allocation, and caring for others ought to be developed. Those are hardly trained through lectures or reading in class. Practical experiences are absolutely needed.

Applicability of the Cultural Dimensions to the Pilot Study Results and Implications for Research

The major findings of the pilot study were summarised threefold. First, among the Korean gifted students, communication and problem-solving skills were the two most cited abilities expected of an efficient leader. Similar results were reported in a study conducted in the US that revealed critical reasoning ability, creative problem-solving skills, and communication skills to be the crucial leadership traits of gifted students perceived by their teachers (Adams-Green, 2016). These attributes were also similar to the ones found among extraverted leaders (Hogan et al., 1994) and leaders with the interpersonal leadership style (Bass & Stogdill, 1990; Chemers, 2002; Conner & Strobel, 2007; van Linden & Fertman, 1998; Yukl, 2006) documented in the previous literature from Western societies. In contrast, the teachers perceived abilities to get along with others, respecting differences, and stimulating autonomy as the leader's core characteristics, which were reported to be the characteristics of many leaders who show a balance of intrapersonal and interpersonal leadership (McGregor, 1987; van Knippenberg et al., 2004).

Second, both students and teachers believed that gifted students are likely to be a leader of a future world, but they differed regarding issues on gifted students' obligations to take leadership roles. Compared to the students who did not believe that academic giftedness necessarily leads to leadership nor in securing a leadership role, the teachers were aware that high expectations and better educational opportunities granted to gifted students would increase their chance to become leaders. This result was slightly different from a study conducted in South Korea that reported both gifted students' and teachers' strong beliefs in gifted students' potential to become future leaders and also their responsibility to take leadership roles (Lee et al., 2018). Few studies in fact dealt with gifted students' obligations to take leadership roles because of their academic giftedness. Thus, this pilot study result cannot be generalised and needs to be strengthened by studies involving a larger size of research participants.

Third, the students endorsed that leaders are raised more than born, while the teachers deemed that leaders are either born or nurtured but ought to be directed. Despite the differences, both claimed that leadership education through a well-designed educational program would help to raise a future leader.

Although responses did not fully mirror a dichotomy of perceptions about leadership, we attempted to diagnose students' and teachers' views according to the five cultural dimensions suggested by Hofstede (1980, 2001). First, the students' responses were more individualistic than collectivistic in portraying ideal leadership and leaders, while it was the opposite for the teachers. While the students referred to problem solving and communication skills as the crucial competencies of leaders, the teachers addressed interpersonal abilities and group cohesiveness as key qualifications for leaders. This was similar to the results involving American teachers that identified abilities to have good interaction and social skills, empathetic listening skills, and support for group members as the key leadership attributes the teachers expected of gifted students (Adams-Green, 2016).

Second, both groups conceived the feminine mode of leadership as the promising one, thereby expressing the importance of getting on well with other people, listening to different voices, caring about others' feelings, and showing empathy. The students and teachers were likely to believe that efficient leadership is formed on the basis of relationships with other people, and thus, having good interpersonal relationships, which is often perceived as the leader's qualification in the feminine society (Boyd et al., 1992; Den Hartog, 2004; Evetts, 2014; Hofstede & McCrae, 2004; Thomas, 1992), is anticipated for prospective leaders.

Third, acceptance of uncertainty compared to avoidance of uncertainty was another cultural dimension which students and teachers relied on while imagining visions for future leadership. Instead of complying with rules and authority, they expected global leaders to be open-minded (Judge et al., 1999) and have respect for diversity (Hogan & Warrenfeltz, 2003).

Fourth, the students were more tilted toward the dimension of the high-powered distanced leader than that of the low-powered distanced leader. They addressed leaders' intuition, independence, autonomy, and responsibility as the major qualifications. By contrast, the teachers preferred a leader who plays a role as an efficient moderator and/or facilitator in resolving conflicts. A study conducted in Australia showed that preservice teachers with the low-powered distanced orientation did not perceive gifted programs as a challenge to the status quo, but were likely to accept gifted service in a system (Jung, 2014). The study did not compare gifted teachers' and students' responses, and thus, did not report differences found between the students and teachers in their preferences for high-powered versus low-powered distance orientated leadership. Yet, our results recap the students' inclination to point out individualistic characteristics in envisaging competent leaders compared to the teachers who addressed collectivistic beliefs in portraying the leaders (also see Adams-Green, 2016).

Finally, although the dimension of long-term versus short-term orientations did not echo in either the students' or teachers' opinions as much as the other dimensions did, the long-term orientation is likely to account for their perceptions about leadership. Both believed in developing and nurturing the nature of leadership, and some further mentioned service-mindedness, practical ability, and goal setting as needed skills to prepare for future leadership (see Fig. 1 for summary).

In summary, the Korean students and teachers anticipated interpersonal leadership and/or a hybrid of interpersonal and intrapersonal leadership for leaders. The students believed in the leader's intrapersonal abilities, particularly problem solving and communication skills, independence, and intuition as the core qualifications to be the leader, while the teachers were highly aware of group values, goals, and collaborative conflict resolutions in identifying leaders' characteristics. Yet, all these attributes were documented in the studies conducted in Western societies as the quintessential calibre of leaders. Despite some differences found between the students and teachers, our results did not differ substantially from the

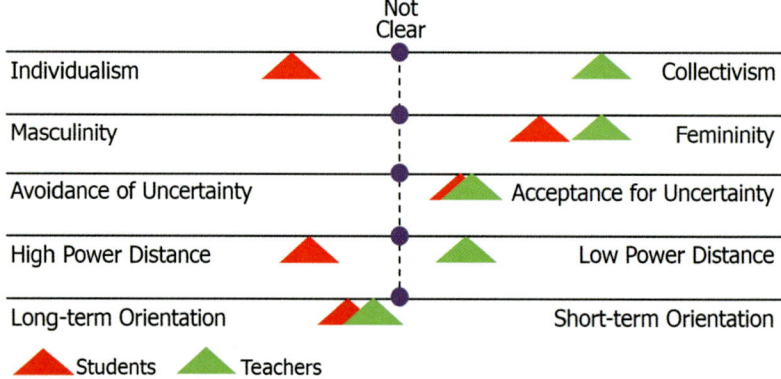

Fig. 1 Students' and teachers' views of leadership according to the Hofstede model.

results of the previous research, particularly in terms of beliefs in leaders' qualifications and leadership roles. For example, as documented in the previous literature: good communication and problem-solving skills (Adams-Green, 2016; Bass & Stogdill, 1990; Chemers, 2002; Conner & Strobel, 2007; van Linden & Fertman, 1998; Yukl, 2006), advanced interpersonal abilities (Adams-Green, 2016; Boyd et al., 1992, Den Hartog, 2004; Evetts, 2014; Hofstede & McCrae, 2004; Thomas, 1992), extroversion (Hogan et al., 1994), open-mindedness (Judge et al., 1999), and respect for diversity (Hogan & Warrenfeltz, 2003) were identified as major qualifications for leaders among our sample. Providing visions of the future with balanced intrapersonal and interpersonal leadership (McGregor, 1987; van Knippenberg et al., 2004) was also expected for effective leaders. This pilot study is one of the few attempts that raises awareness of cultural matters in understanding one's perceptions of leaders, leadership, and leadership practices. We suggest that further studies involving a larger sample of diverse cultural backgrounds and stronger methodology are need to support the multicultural model of leadership, and elaborate on how cultural values and context influence leadership education for all students, including the gifted.

Implications for Leadership Education in the Classroom

While the findings cannot be generalised to other contexts, the authors suggest the following for leadership practices that can be applied in the classroom. The list consists of 12 statements regarding beliefs in leadership, leaders, and leadership education derived from the pilot study.

1. There are different types of leadership.
2. Leadership varies according to the sociocultural context.
3. Advanced problem-solving ability and communication skills are prerequisites for leaders.
4. Leaders should have good interpersonal abilities.
5. Open-mindedness, respect for diversity and differences, and collaborations with other people are expected of good leaders.
6. Giftedness or academic excellence per se do not necessarily result in effective leadership.
7. Leaders are more likely to be nurtured than to be born.
8. Leadership may be developed with the help of a well-designed leadership program.
9. Leadership education needs to involve developing cognitive abilities, such as problem solving, logical thinking, and critical thinking skills.
10. Conflict management, communication, task allocation skills, and empathy are other leadership qualities that ought to be nurtured via leadership programs.
11. Mentoring is one mode of effective leadership education for gifted students.
12. The greater the societal expectations and leadership education are granted to gifted students, the better the gifted have opportunities to become leaders.

Conclusion

The first part of this chapter reviewed previous studies on leaders and leadership development and introduced multicultural perspectives about leadership according to the five cultural dimensions suggested by Hofstede and colleagues (Franke, Hofstede, & Bond, 1991; Hofstede & McCrae, 2004). The proposed leadership model was discussed in terms of: (a) individualism versus collectivism, (b) masculinity versus femininity, (c) uncertainty avoidance, (d) power distance, and (e) future orientation. Expected roles for future leaders were also summarised according to each dimension. Hofstede's model extends the type and scope of leaders by identifying the theoretical conceptions of leadership using cultural elements. On the other hand, major reported criticisms of the model have to do with the assumption of equating nation with culture (Baskerville, 2003), which contributes to dismissing difference and diversity within the culture; the quantification of culture is exemplified by cultural dimensions (Kirkman, Lowe, & Gibson, 2006; Sivakumar & Nakata, 2001) and the Western and male central views of leadership (Ailon, 2008; Ferguson, 1994). Hence, the model has limitations to account for a bi-cultural phenomenon in a nation (Baskerville, 2003) and cross-cultural integrations (Westwood & Low, 2003). The dearth of empirical data supporting the multicultural perspective of leaders and leadership in relation to gifted education also leaves the use of this suggested model in abeyance.

The second part of this chapter presented results from a pilot study that the authors have conducted with gifted students and teachers in South Korea. Because leadership in Western countries occupied most of the literature on leadership studies, we intended to present voices from people in an Eastern nation although one nation cannot represent all Eastern perspectives. From our sample, students' views of leadership (marginally) leant towards individualistic, feminine, accepting uncertainty, a high-powered distance leadership, and the long-term orientation modes. Among teachers, collectivistic, feminine, accepting uncertainty, a low-powered distance, and the long-term orientation modes were slightly perceptible than each of the opposite manners. As indicated, the students and teachers showed similarities and also differences in their perceptions about leadership and expectations of leaders. We are aware that the differences between the students and teachers may discourage gifted students from developing and fulfilling their potential strengths as future leaders (Milner & Ford, 2007). Given that the results came from part of a pilot study involving a small number of research participants, caution is needed when interpreting the findings, however. Further, the diagnosis of the students' and teachers' responses according to the cultural dimensions ought to be substantiated with other supportive data involving research participants from diverse cultures.

In conclusion, leadership education in the classroom begins with teachers' understanding the nature of leadership and believing in leadership development. A fast-moving society needs a leader who confronts unpredictability, diversity, and conflicts in everyday life, and is well equipped to become a leader in a global society. In this regard, educators should be aware of the importance of nurturing leaders who are capable of handling and resolving global leadership issues and embracing people's needs from diverse countries. Gifted students are the ones who have the great potential to fulfil the roles of global leaders.

Cross-References

▶ Creative and Gifted Education in Korea: Using the CATs Model to Illustrate How Creativity Can Grow into Innovation
▶ Educational Contexts, Transitions and Community Engagement: Part VI Introduction
▶ Engaging Gifted Students in Solving Real Problems Creatively: Implementing the Real Engagement in Active Problem-Solving (REAPS) Teaching/Learning Model in Australasian and Pacific Rim Contexts
▶ Exploring Diverse Perceptions of Wise Persons: Wisdom in Gifted Education
▶ Fostering and Developing Talent in Mentorship Programs: The Mentor's Perspectives
▶ Gifted Education in the Asia-Pacific: From the Past for the Future – An Introduction
▶ In Search of an Explanation for an Approach-Avoidance Pattern in East Asia: The Role of Cultural Values in Gifted Education
▶ Sociocultural Perspectives on the Talent Development Megamodel
▶ Some Implications for the Future of Gifted Education in the Asia-Pacific
▶ STEAM in Gifted Education in Korea
▶ The Lives and Achievements of Four Extraordinary Australians: A Master, a Maker, an Introspector, and an Influencer
▶ Trends and Challenges of Creativity Development Among Selected Asian Countries and Regions: China, Hong Kong/Macau, Japan, Malaysia, and South Korea

Acknowledgments This work was supported by Global Research Network program through the Ministry of Education of the Republic of Korea and the National Research Foundation of Korea (NRF-2016S1A2A2912130).

References

Adams-Green, S. D. (2016). Teacher perceptions of leadership potential of gifted and talented students (Doctoral dissertation). Retrieved from ProQuest Dissertations Publishing. (Accession No. 10158882)

Adler, N. J. (2002). *International dimensions of organizational behavior* (4th ed.). Cincinnati, OH: South-Western College Publishing.

Ailon, G. (2008). Mirror, mirror on the wall: Culture's consequences in a value test of its own design. *Academy of Management Review, 33*(4), 885–904. https://doi.org/10.5465/AMR.2008.34421995

Alvesson, M., & Spicer, A. (2014). Critical perspectives on leadership. In D. Day (Ed.), *The oxford handbook of leadership and organizations*. New York, NY: Oxford University Press.

Ashkanasy, N. M., Wilderom, C. P., & Peterson, M. F. (2000). *Handbook of organizational culture and climate*. Thousand Oaks, CA: Sage.

Aycan, Z. (2004). Key success factors for women in management in Turkey. *Applied Psychology,* *53*(3), 453–477. https://doi.org/10.1111/j.1464-0597.2004.00180.x

Baskerville, R. F. (2003). Hofstede never studied culture. *Accounting, Organizations and Society,* *28*(1), 1–14.

Bass, B. M., & Stogdill, R. M. (1990). *Bass & Stogdill's handbook of leadership: Theory, research, and managerial applications*. New York, NY: Simon and Schuster.

Bono, J. E., & Judge, T. A. (2004). Personality and transformational and transactional leadership: A meta-analysis. *Journal of Applied Psychology, 89*(5), 901–910. https://doi.org/10.1037/0021-9010.89.5.901

Bono, J. E., Shen, W., & Yoon, D. J. (2014). Personality and leadership: Looking back, looking ahead. In D. Day (Ed.), *The oxford handbook of leadership and organizations* (pp. 199–220). New York, NY: Oxford University Press.

Boyd, B. L., Herring, D. R., & Briers, G. E. (1992). Developing life skills in youth. *Leadership,* *4*(38), 6–80.

Bu, N., Craig, T. J., & Peng, T. K. (2001). Acceptance of supervisory direction in typical workplace situations: A comparison of US, Taiwanese and PRC employees. *International Journal of Cross Cultural Management, 1*(2), 131–152. https://doi.org/10.1177/147059580112001

Chan, D. W. (2000). Developing the creative leadership training program for gifted and talented students in Hong Kong. *Roeper Review, 22*(2), 94–97. https://doi.org/10.1080/02783190009554009

Chemers, M. M. (2002). Metacognitive, social, and emotional intelligence of transformational leadership: Efficacy and effectiveness. In R. E. Riggio, S. E. Murphy, & F. J. Pirozzolo (Eds.), *Multiple intelligences and leadership* (pp. 139–160). Mahwah, NJ: Lawrence Erlbaum Associates.

Conner, J. O., & Strobel, K. (2007). Leadership development: An examination of individual and programmatic growth. *Journal of Adolescent Research, 22*(3), 275–297. https://doi.org/10.1177/0743558407299698

Den Hartog, D. N. (2004). Assertiveness. In R. J. House, P. J. Hanges, M. Javidan, P. W. Dorfman, & V. Gupta (Eds.), *Culture, leadership, and organizations: The GLOBE study of 62 societies* (pp. 395–436). Thousand Oaks, CA: Sage.

Den Hartog, D. N., & Dickson, M. (2012). Leadership and culture. In D. Day & J. Antonakis (Eds.), *The nature of leadership* (pp. 393–436). Thousand Oaks, CA: Sage.

Den Hartog, D. N., & Koopman, P. L. (2001). Leadership in organizations. In N. Anderson, D. S. Ones, H. Kepir-Sinangil, & C. Viswesvaran (Eds.), *International handbook of industrial, work and organizational psychology* (Vol. 2, pp. 166–187). London, England: Sage.

Dorfman, P. W. (2003). International and cross-cultural leadership research. In B. J. Punnett & O. Shenkar (Eds.), *Handbook for international management research* (2nd ed., pp. 265–347). Ann Arbor, Michigan: University of Michigan.

Evetts, J. (2014). The concept of professionalism: Professional work, professional practice and learning. In S. Billett, C. Harteis, & H. Gruber (Eds.), *International handbook of research in professional and practice-based learning* (pp. 29–56). Dordrecht, Netherlands: Springer.

Feldhusen, J. F., & Kennedy, D. M. (1988a). Preparing gifted youth for leadership roles in a rapidly changing society. *Roeper Review, 10*, 226–230. https://doi.org/10.1080/02783198809553135

Feldhusen, J. F., & Kennedy, D. M. (1988b). Observing the nature and emergence of leadership talent among gifted youth. *Gifted Child Today, 11*(6), 2–7. https://doi.org/10.1177/107621758801100602

Ferguson, K. E. (1994). On bringing more theory, more voices and more politics to the study of organizations. *Organization, 1*(1), 81–99. https://doi.org/10.1177/135050849400100112

Franke, R. H., Hofstede, G. & Bond, M. (1991) Cultural roots of economic performance: A research note. *Strategic Management Journal* 12, 165–173. https://doi.org/10.1002/smj.4250120912

Freitas, H., Oliveira, M., Jenkins, M., & Popjoy, O. (1998). The focus group, a qualitative research method. *Journal of Education, 1*(1), 1–22.

Furmańczyk, J. (2010). The cross-cultural leadership aspect. *Journal of Intercultural Management,* *2*(2), 67–82.

Gilley, A., McMillan, H. S., & Gilley, J. W. (2009). Organizational change and characteristics of leadership effectiveness. *Journal of Leadership and Organizational Studies, 16*(1), 38–47. https://doi.org/10.1177/1548051809334191

Goncalo, J. A., & Staw, B. M. (2006). Individualism–collectivism and group creativity. *Organizational Behavior and Human Decision Processes, 100*(1), 96–109. https://doi.org/10.1016/j.obhdp.2005.11.003

Hackman, M. Z., & Johnson, C. E. (2004). *Leadership: A communication perspective.* Long Grove, Ill: Waveland Press.

Hofstede, G. (1980). Culture and organizations. *International Studies of Management and Organization, 10*(4), 15–41. https://doi.org/10.1080/00208825.1980.11656300

Hofstede, G. (1983). The cultural relativity of organizational practices and theories. *Journal of International Business Studies, 14*(2), 75–89. https://doi.org/10.1057/palgrave.jibs.8490867

Hofstede, G. (2006). What did GLOBE really measure? Researchers' minds versus respondents' minds. *Journal of International Business Studies, 37*(6), 882–896. https://doi.org/10.1057/palgrave.jibs.8400233

Hofstede, G., & McCrae, R. R. (2004). Personality and culture revisited: Linking traits and dimensions of culture. *Cross-Cultural Research, 38*(1), 52–88. https://doi.org/10.1177/1069397103259443

Hofstede, G. H. (2001). *Culture's consequences: Comparing values, behaviors, institutions, and organizations across nations* (2nd ed.). Thousand Oaks, CA: Sage.

Hogan, R., Curphy, G. J., & Hogan, J. (1994). What we know about leadership: Effectiveness and personality. *American Psychologist, 49*(6), 493–504. https://doi.org/10.1037/0003-066X.49.6.493

Hogan, R., & Warrenfeltz, R. (2003). Educating the modern manager. *Academy of Management Learning & Education, 2*(1), 74–84. https://doi.org/10.5465/AMLE.2003.9324043

Hollander, E. P. (1992). Leadership, followership, self, and others. *The Leadership Quarterly, 3*(1), 43–54. https://doi.org/10.1016/1048-9843(92)90005-Z

Hong, J., & Yoo, M. (2016). The effect of program for the gifted based on GI-STEAM model on leadership, creative personality, and learning flow of elementary gifted students. *Journal of Gifted/Talented Education, 26*(1), 77–99.

House, R. J., Hanges, P. J., Javidan, M., Dorfman, P. W., & Gupta, V. (2004). *Culture, leadership and organizations: The GLOBE study of 62 societies.* Thousand Oaks, CA: Sage.

House, R. J., Wright, N. S., & Aditya, R. N. (1997). Cross-cultural research on organizational leadership: A critical analysis and a proposed theory. In P. C. Earley & M. Erez (Eds.), *New perspective on international/organizational psychology* (pp. 535–625). San Francisco, CA: New Lexington Press.

Huckaby, W. O., & Sperling, H. B. (1981). Leadership giftedness: An idea whose time has not yet come. *Roeper Review, 3*(3), 19–22. https://doi.org/10.1080/02783198109552528

Hughes, R. L., Ginnett, R. C., & Curphy, G. J. (1993). *Leadership: Enhancing the lessons of experience.* Boston, MA: Irwin.

Inkeles, A. (1997). Continuity and change in popular values on the Pacific Rim. In J. D. Montgomery (Ed.), *Values in education: Social capital formation in Asia and the Pacific.* Hollis, NH: Hollis.

Inkeles, A., & Levinson, J. (1969). National character: The study of modal personality and sociocultural systems. In G. Lindzey & E. Aronson (Eds.), *Handbook of social psychology* (Vol. 4). Reading, MA: Addison-Wesley.

Judge, T. A., Bono, J. E., Ilies, R., & Gerhardt, M. W. (2002). Personality and leadership: A qualitative and quantitative review. *Journal of Applied Psychology, 87*(4), 765–780. https://doi.org/10.1037/0021-9010.87.4.765

Judge, T. A., Thoresen, C. J., Pucik, V., & Welbourne, T. M. (1999). Managerial coping with organizational change: A dispositional perspective. *Journal of Applied Psychology, 84*(1), 107–122. https://doi.org/10.1037//0021-9010.84.1.107

Jung, J. Y. (2014). Predictors of attitudes to gifted programs/provisions: Evidence from preservice educators. *The Gifted Child Quarterly, 58*(4), 247–258. https://doi.org/10.1177/0016986214547636

Karnes, F., Riley, T., & McGinnis, J. C. (1996). Perceptions of great leaders held by gifted youth. *Gifted Child Today, 19*(4), 14–50. https://doi.org/10.1177/107621759601900408

Karnes, F. A., & Meriweather, S. (1988). Teacher trainers' views on leadership. *Gifted Child Today, 11*(6), 8–10.

Kirkman, B. L., Lowe, K. B., & Gibson, C. B. (2006). A quarter century of culture's consequences: A review of empirical research incorporating Hofstede's cultural values framework. *Journal of International Business Studies, 37*(3), 285–320. https://doi.org/10.1057/palgrave.jibs.8400202

Komives, S. R., Lucas, N., & McMahon, T. R. (2009). *Exploring leadership: For college students who want to make a difference.* San Francisco, CA: Wiley.

Lee, S.-Y. (2015). Civic education as a means of talent dissemination for gifted students. *Asia Pacific Education Review, 16*(2), 307–316. https://doi.org/10.1007/s12564-015-9372-y

Lee, S.-Y., Kim, J. A., Kim, Y. K., Kim, E. S., Kim, S. Y., Kim, J. W., Kim, E. A., & Park, J. A. (2018). *Perceptions about gifted students' leadership development in terms of human capital and social capital.* Paper presented at the 2018 Conference of the Korean Society for the Gifted and Talented. Seoul, South Korea.

Lee, S.-Y., & Olszewski-Kubilius, P. (2016). Leadership development and gifted students. In R. J. Levesque (Ed.), *Encyclopedia of adolescence* (2nd ed., pp. 1–10). New York, NY: Springer.

Lee, Y. S., & Liu, W. K. (2012). Leadership behaviors and culture dimensions in the financial industry. *Journal of Applied Finance and Banking, 2*(2), 15–44. Retrieved from http://www.scienpress.com/Upload/JAFB%2fVol%202_2_2.pdf

Lonner, W. (2016). The introductory psychology text and cross-cultural psychology: Beyond Ekman, Whorf, and biased IQ tests. *Online Readings in Psychology and Culture, 11*(1), 4. https://doi.org/10.9707/2307-0919.1145

Markus, H. R., & Kitayama, S. (1991). Culture and the self: Implications for cognition, emotion, and motivation. *Psychological Review, 98*, 224–253. https://doi.org/10.1037/0033-295X.98.2.224

Marland, S. P. (1972). Education of the gifted and talented (Report to the Subcommittee on Education, Committee on Labor and Public Welfare, US Senate). Washington, DC: Government Printing Office. https://doi.org/10.1177/016235320402800105

McGregor, D. (1987). *The human side of Enterprise.* Harmondsworth, England: Penguin.

Milner, H. R., & Ford, D. Y. (2007). Cultural considerations in the underrepresentation of culturally diverse elementary students in gifted education. *Roeper Review, 29*(3), 166–173. https://doi.org/10.1080/02783190709554405

Northouse, P. (2006). *Leadership: Theory and practice* (4th ed.). London, England: Sage.

Ricketts, J. C., & Rudd, R. D. (2002). A comprehensive leadership education model to train, teach, and develop leadership in youth. *Journal of Career and Technical Education, 19*(1), 7–17. https://doi.org/10.21061/jcte.v19i1.655

Shin, N., & Jang, Y. J. (2017). Group creativity training for children: Lessons learned from two award-winning teams. *Journal of Creative Behavior, 51*(1), 5–19. https://doi.org/10.1002/jocb.82

Sivakumar, K., & Nakata, C. (2001). The stampede toward Hofstede's framework: Avoiding the sample design pit in cross-cultural research. *Journal of International Business Studies, 32*(3), 555–574. https://doi.org/10.1057/palgrave.jibs.8490984

Smith, P. B. (1997). Cross-cultural leadership: A path to the goal? In P. C. Earley & M. Erez (Eds.), *New perspectives on international industrial/organizational psychology.* San Francisco, CA: Jossey-Bass.

Smith, P. B., Wang, Z. M., & Leung, K. (1997). Leadership, decision-making and cultural context: Event management within Chinese joint ventures. *The Leadership Quarterly, 8*(4), 413–431. https://doi.org/10.1016/S1048-9843(97)90022-9

Thomas, K. W. (1992). Conflict and conflict management: Reflections and update. *Journal of Organizational Behavior, 13*(3), 265–274. https://doi.org/10.1002/job.4030130307

van Knippenberg, D., van Knippenberg, B., De Cremer, D., & Hogg, M. A. (2004). Leadership, self, and identity: A review and research agenda. *The Leadership Quarterly, 15*(6), 825–856. https://doi.org/10.1016/j.leaqua.2004.09.002

van Linden, J. A., & Fertman, C. I. (1998). *Youth leadership: A guide to understanding leadership development in adolescents*. San Francisco, CA: Jossey-Bass Publishers.

Westwood, R., & Low, D. R. (2003). The multicultural muse: Culture, creativity and innovation. *International Journal of Cross Cultural Management, 3*(2), 235–259. https://doi.org/10.1177/14705958030032006

Yammarino, F. (2013). Leadership: Past, present, and future. *Journal of Leadership and Organizational Studies, 20*(2), 149–155. https://doi.org/10.1177/1548051812471559

Yukl, G. A. (2002). *Leadership in organizations* (5th ed.). Upper Saddle River, NJ: Prentice Hall.

Yukl, G. A. (2006). *Leadership in organizations* (6th ed.). Englewood Cliffs, NJ: Prentice Hall.

Seon-Young Lee, PhD, is a professor in the Department of Education at Seoul National University in Seoul, South Korea. Previously, she was a faculty member of Yonsei University in South Korea and a research assistant professor at Northwestern University's Center for Talent Development. She is currently an executive editor of *Asia Pacific Education Review*, an editor of the *Journal of the Korean Society for the Gifted and Talented* and an associate editor of *Gifted Child Quarterly*. Seon-Young has conducted 100+ quantitative and qualitative studies involving gifted students with foci on their academic talent development and specialised gifted programs. Her research interests also encompass creativity, creative education, family and psychosocial and leadership development of gifted and creative populations. She received *the Gifted Child Quarterly Paper of the Year Award* for 2011.

Yun-Kyoung Kim is a doctoral student in educational psychology of the Department of Education at Seoul National University under the advice of Professor Seon-Young Lee. She has been teaching English in secondary schools since 2009. During her teaching career, she, as a principal investigator, led a government-funded project entitled *The Development of STEAM Project Learning Program*. From 2013 to 2014, she was on secondment at the Ministry of Education of South Korea and helped design policies on creative teaching and learning. Her research interests are in group creativity in the classroom and psychosocial development of gifted adolescents.

Eunjoo Boo is a high school teacher and a doctoral student studying educational psychology at Seoul National University. She participated in the Global Research Network project led by Professor Seon-Young Lee. Eunjoo has been teaching English in Korean public high schools since 2009. Bringing insights from her teaching career to educational research, she is trying to figure out how to nurture students' creativity and leadership by making small changes in the classroom. Her research interests encompass creative learning, gifted education, and leadership development.

Rural Voices: Identifying the Perceptions, Practices, and Experiences of Gifted Pedagogy in Australian Rural and Regional Schools

56

Michelle Bannister-Tyrrell and Denise Wood

Contents

M. Bannister-Tyrrell
School of Education, University of New England, Armidale, NSW, Australia
e-mail: mbannist@une.edu.au

D. Wood (✉)
Charles Sturt University, Bathurst, NSW, Australia
e-mail: dwood@csu.edu.au

© Springer Nature Singapore Pte Ltd. 2021   1267
S. R. Smith (ed.), *Handbook of Giftedness and Talent Development in the Asia-Pacific*,
Springer International Handbooks of Education,
https://doi.org/10.1007/978-981-13-3041-4_62

Abstract

The learning and teaching experiences of the teachers of gifted learners in rural and regional schools will be explored in this chapter. Rural gifted learners and their teachers are not represented well in the literature, either globally or locally. Also highlighted in the chapter will be the key findings about gifted learners and those who teach them that are consistent across the literature and a view of the Australian context through the voices of teachers of rural gifted learners. Some of the issues that rural and regional teachers face in supporting and assisting gifted and talented students, and the opportunities that rural and regional schools offer to support the teachers of gifted learners, will be explored. In this chapter, a picture of education for rural gifted students from the perspective of educators, who often have limited specialist training in teaching gifted students, will be provided. The impact of teacher perspectives on the provisions offered in rural and regional schools will be considered and suggestions for enhancing education settings for gifted students in rural contexts proposed.

Keywords

Gifted education · Gifted students · Rural education · Achievement · Opportunity gap

The aims in this chapter are to:
1. Explore the literature focused on rural gifted students and on teachers of the gifted in rural settings.
2. Report on the voices of teachers of gifted students in rural settings, outlining their perceptions and needs.
3. Recommend future approaches to support both gifted rural students and their classroom teachers.

Introduction

While significant research has been completed in the United Kingdom and in the United States of America with regard to gifted education in rural communities, relatively little comparable research has been completed within the Australian context. The experience of teaching rural gifted students in this country remains under-researched. According to Baxter, Hayes, and Gray (2011), "one in five (20%) Australians live in regional areas, one in 10 (9%) in outer regional areas and around one in 40 (2.3%) live in remote or very remote areas (1.5% remote and 0.8% very remote)". With a third of Australians living outside major cities in Australia, it can be assumed that gifted students are present in many rural schools and classrooms. The lack of recent research focused on the teaching of rural gifted students in Australia has not allowed the voices of their teachers to be heard. Local and international literature and some insights from a small Australian study focused on teachers and their experiences in teaching and supporting gifted and talented learners form the basis of this chapter. The chapter acknowledges the voices of rural teachers of the gifted and outlines suggestions to improve the opportunities for gifted students in rural settings to achieve their potential through addressing the perceptions, practices, and experiences of their teachers.

Definitions of Rural and Remote Contexts

Definitions of rurality and remoteness are developed based on population clustering and access to services. Consistently, rural is anything that is not urban (Australian Bureau of Statistics, 2018; Bayley & Goodyear, 2006; Puryear & Kettler, 2017; Stats NZ, 2017), and it is further refined by reference to the distance of a locality from a major urban centre and population numbers (National Rural Network for Gifted and Talented, 2010, p. 1). A key characteristic of rural environments identified in the literature is diversity. A review of the definitions of rural across current literature highlighted that each locality had different geography, demographics, industry, and culture, making it unique in terms of people and need (Kettler, Puryear, & Mullet, 2016). To contextualise rural in this chapter, the following definitions from the Australian Bureau of Statistics (ABS, 2018) are relevant:

> *Rural*: communities or areas which are not part of an urban area. The category of rural includes towns, villages, localities that have reasonable access to services including health, transport, communication and education.
> *Remote*: communities that are defined by their distance from and access to services such as health and education. The category of remote includes communities that are dispersed, with limited services.

In Australia, 26% of the 3.8 million school-aged students (Australian Bureau of Statistics, n.d.) attend schools that are categorised as rural or remote. Comparatively, 20% of school-aged students in England attend rural schools (Warwick, Dickenson, & Speakman, 2010). In Canada, 22% of the rural population is within school age, and in New Zealand (NZ), 2017 data showed that 20% of the population in rural demographic areas with a population up to 10,000 are school-aged children between 5 and 14 years of age (Stats NZ, 2017).

Gifted Education in Rural Contexts

The design of appropriate classroom teaching programs for gifted students in rural and regional schools is impacted by their location (VanTassel-Baska & Hubbard, 2016). Colloquially, there may be a deficit view of the rural context for gifted students (Howley, 2009), but the research literature describes opportunities and advantages that suggest the potential for rural contexts to engender positive learning experiences for gifted students. These include the size of the school, relationships with peers and teachers, connectedness to the community, and access to the natural environment (Azano, Callahan, Brodersen, & Caughey, 2017; Colangelo, Assouline, Baldus, Ihrig, & New, 2006; Howley, Rhodes, & Beall, 2009; Richards & Stambaugh, 2015).

Smaller School and Classroom Size

Smaller school numbers, and smaller class sizes in rural schools, affording the potential for individuals to have a stronger sense of place, are described as advantages of rural settings (Azano et al., 2017; Richards & Stambaugh, 2015). Greater chances of one-to-one learning opportunities and individualisation of teaching were identified by Colangelo, Assouline, and New (2001), alongside a greater sense of belonging and acceptance of difference, more diverse community engagement and, if distance allowed, chances to interact with other schools. A strong sense of school community offers concomitant opportunities for leadership and diverse intergenerational relationships that are qualitatively different to those of their urban peers (Howley et al., 2009; Richards & Stambaugh, 2015).

Community Connections

Students have the opportunity to work with members of the local community in mutually beneficial activities that include authentic problem-solving projects and diverse skill development (Colangelo et al., 2006). Gifted students can explore extra-curricular activities where their mentor or guide is someone within the local community, nurturing skills that go beyond the classroom (Howley et al., 2009). In a small community, students may have a greater number of such opportunities than in an urban school (Colangelo et al., 2006).

The Natural Environment

Gifted rural students have increased accessibility to the natural environment, including greater freedom to be outside and to engage with the natural sciences (Colangelo et al., 2006; Laura & Smith, 2009; Stambaugh, 2015). Similarly, Howley et al. (2009) also described the opportunity to connect with the natural world, in experiences that offer diversity of content and interest.

Disadvantages of Living in Rural Contexts

The literature also describes disadvantages of living in rural contexts that may impact on the opportunities of gifted students in a rural education setting. These include geographic isolation, lack of community support for talent development, poverty, and access to technology.

Isolation from Enrichment Opportunities and Community Support

Gifted students in rural or regional settings may experience limited access to cultural resources including art galleries, museums, and libraries that support the development of talent across the domains of activity, as a result of geographic isolation. Rural settings have limited easy access to the extra-curricular opportunities that supplement school education (Colangelo et al., 2001; Olszewski-Kubilius, Corwith, & Calvert, 2015). The costs of travel can inhibit access to experiences, and students may not be confident to leave their home town (Azano et al., 2017; Warwick et al., 2010). Networks that bring gifted students together in relationships of like minds are constrained by the costs of travel and limited time, although the constraints can be mitigated using technology and innovative planning of events (Olszewski-Kubilius et al., 2015). Colangelo, Assouline, and Gross (2004) include dual enrolment in higher education and the utilisation of higher education facilities as strategies to accelerate learning for gifted students, but distance and travel costs potentially isolate rural gifted students from such opportunities. The community can provide mentors and experts that extend the school learning for gifted students across talent domains (Olszewski-Kubilius et al., 2015). However, in some regional communities, there is a lack of community support for the development of talent because of a fear of losing young people to urban centres (Glendenning, 1998; Howley, 2009; Lamb & Daniels, 1993; Lawrence, 2009). Gifted students may be encouraged to remain locally rather than explore different career or education avenues, to lower their educational aspirations; they may not be provided diverse career information and role models (Howley, 2009; Warwick et al., 2010).

Poverty and 'Brain-Drain'

In many rural communities, poverty is a concern, not only because it may result in lower income, declining health, and lower educational attainments (Richards & Stambaugh, 2015), but also because it further limits the opportunities for wider experience and opportunities (Azano et al., 2017). Gifted students from low-income home environments may require extra support for the development of psychosocial characteristics, such as self-concept or confidence, as well as scaffolding the development of core academic skills before they are able to successfully engage in challenging learning experiences, due to limited resources in the home and family environment (Azano et al., 2017; Burney & Cross, 2006). It is suggested that when a rural community is struggling economically, there is an increased fear of the loss of talented individuals to urban settings, and a concomitant lowering of aspirations for young people to encourage them to remain locally (Lawrence, 2009; Paul & Seward, 2016). Paul and Seward (2016) describe the concept of 'brain-drain', as the loss of bright students who leave a rural community for education or employment. Gifted individuals seek challenging occupations that are more accessible in urban settings, tempted by the higher earning capacity and the greater celebration of advanced learning and experience (Paul & Seward, 2016). Paul and Seward proposed a model that encourages the development of skills of adaptability, and resilience in young gifted people in rural areas, to support them to see how their talents can contribute to community growth and development, and to support rural schools to better understand their role in overcoming both brain-drain and the effects of poverty in communities.

Access to Technology

Technology is a tool in classrooms in all contexts and is identified as a tool for the motivation and engagement of students, although Housand and Housand (2012) suggest that it is not the tool itself that is motivating as much as the authentic opportunities it allows for students. Their analysis of the characteristics of technology in learning settings identified the following as key motivating features in technology-supported learning experiences: control and autonomy, challenge, collaboration, curiosity, and recognition. They identified online resources and activities that provide rural gifted students with chances to learn from experts, to communicate with like minds, to share in discovery or exploration, and to solve real problems in the online environment within their local school. The learning opportunities afforded by technology suggest that it is a valuable tool for supporting gifted students in rural settings, helping them to overcome distance and encouraging interaction, providing advanced learning, and enabling access to experts and role models. In a comprehensive review of technology use in gifted education, Periathiruvadi and Rinn (2012) reached similar conclusions, finding that technology afforded benefits for both gifted learners (access to advanced knowledge, connections with others, platforms for creating content) and their teachers (resources, support, information). While the context of the studies they reviewed was not necessarily rural, these affordances potentially mitigate some of the perceived disadvantages for gifted rural students.

Rural Gifted Education in Australia

Australian research into gifted education has long recognised that giftedness crosses all socio-economic and cultural boundaries (Braggett, 1985; Merrotsy, 2011; Vialle, 2011). However, Australian rural gifted students still appear to remain hidden from view, with only the efforts of a small group of researchers in this country examining the status quo and reporting on cultural programs, teacher preparedness, identification, and provision (e.g., Fraser-Seeto, 2013; Plunkett, 2012; Thraves & Bannister-Tyrrell, 2017; Wood, 2015; Wood & Zundans-Fraser, 2012). Australian researcher Margaret Plunkett (2012) recounted the positives her own children experienced being educated in small schools: "I found my children were very well catered for in the small school they attended, as they were able to work at whatever level they were capable and were not restricted by chronology" (p. 38) and "nonetheless, my children have all been successful in their chosen fields" (p. 39). Peer friendships in rural settings span multiple grades, offering opportunities to find 'like minds' (Wood & Zundans-Fraser, 2012). A group of gifted adolescent girls in a study in a rural setting (Wood, 2015) voiced similar advantages, including the freedom to be outside and move, the connection with others and the opportunity it gave them to be different (Wood, 2015).

Rural Disadvantage

While the above rendered some advantages of rurality for Australian gifted students, there were also some disadvantages reiterated in the literature. For example, Bailey, Knight and Riley (1995) described Australian gifted rural students as disadvantaged and suggested that rural school settings were unable to provide the necessary rigour, experiences, and opportunities these students required. They attributed the lack of adequate services as primarily due to isolation, lack of specific training in gifted education for teachers, and limited access to advanced educational programs. Findings of the Senate Review into Gifted Education (2001) confirmed that the disadvantage was still evident nearly a decade later and the findings persist (Alloway & Dalley-Trim, 2009; Wood & Zundans-Fraser, 2012). In Australian rural contexts: gifted students may not find school education challenging (Wilson, Lyons, & Quinn, 2013); they may find school a socially isolating experience (Laura & Smith, 2009); and they may not develop strong learning-to-learn skills because they are not challenged (Wood & Zundans-Fraser, 2012). Gifted students themselves noted a lack of expert teachers, restricted options in terms of study choices, technology glitches, and a lack of academic peer stimulation as some of the limits on their learning experiences (Alloway & Dalley-Trim, 2009).

Schirmer (2016) found that one of the greatest concerns for people living in regional and rural areas within Australia was a lack of 'critical infrastructure, including telecommunications' with residents feeling underserviced. Only 37% of rural and regional Australians felt they had good access to high-speed Internet in 2015 (Schirmer, 2016). The *Rural and Remote Education Advisory Council* (RREAC, n.d.) found that "technology has the potential to contribute to the overall improved quality of teachers, attraction and retention, student achievement and community development/sustainability" (p. 1). The challenge of poor access is exacerbated when teachers do not realise that students do not have the access required to complete homework tasks nor to utilise online resources (Ewing, 2016). Access to technology is a very real problem that many teachers still experience in New South Wales. Technology has been described as a resource for rural gifted students and their teachers (Housand & Housand, 2012; Periathiruvadi & Rinn, 2012), providing opportunities for professional learning, for interactions and shared experiences and breaking down the tyranny of distance in terms of access to resources and like minds. In the light of the work of Periathiruvadi and Rinn (2012) and Housand and Housand (2012), it is clear that technology can mitigate some of the disadvantages of rural locations for teachers of rural gifted students and be a source of support for teachers of rural gifted students.

Australian state and federal government research reiterated similar issues. In 2013, the New South Wales (NSW) Department of Education published the Rural and Remote Education Blueprint for Action, which summarised the disadvantages for rural schools, teachers, and gifted students as the following:

- Difficulty in offering students a broad curriculum.
- Difficulty in sharing curriculum resources and collaborating with other teachers because of distance, as well as technological and school organisational limitations.
- Less opportunity to participate in cultural and sporting programs because of distance and the cost of travel.
- Difficulty accessing a specialist curriculum.
- Limited exposure to a broad range of career options and fewer career role models.
- Difficulty developing links with universities that build student engagement in science, mathematics and agriculture. (NSW Department of Education and Communities, 2013, p. 1)

Opportunity and Achievement Gap

In 2016, ABC reporters Leigo and Cansdale discussed the results of recent National Assessment Program—Literacy and Numeracy (NAPLAN) results with Pete Goss for the Grattan Institute. Goss and Sonnemann (2016) claimed, "disadvantage in schools was a pattern that played out geographically" (Leigo & Cansdale, 2016, para 3). They also stated that parents within regional and remote areas may have higher levels of unemployment as "some regional and remote towns are doing it really tough and living in a stressful environment" (Leigo & Cansdale, 2016, para 4). The report reflected a recent analysis by the Grattan Institute (Goss & Sonnemann, 2016), where research into rural education found the following issues:

> The findings for disadvantaged students are even more concerning when we take into account student capability... Students who display similar potential in Year 3 have very different growth trajectories depending on their parents' education level ... High achievers from disadvantaged families have the greatest lost potential, losing one year and nine months between Year 3 and 9. In fact, bright students from poor backgrounds make less progress in total (5 years 10 months) than lower achievers with highly educated parents (6 years 6 months) between Year 3 and Year 9. PISA data shows that in terms of giving students of

low education backgrounds the support to become high achievers Australia has slipped backwards slightly. (Goss & Sonnemann, 2016, pp. 27–28)

Advantage or Disadvantage?

The Grattan Institute report describes themes consistent with the literature discussed earlier with regard to the specific educational learning needs of gifted students in rural schools. Isolation in terms of geography, opportunity, inspiration, and challenge may mean they do not realise their potential, nor experience learning that requires concentrated attention and effort. A lack of community role models and diverse career examples, and the attitude in the community toward gaining education or achievement in diverse careers, may limit the future thinking of gifted students in rural settings. However, it is important to consider the identified advantages for gifted students in rural settings, including a sense of place, opportunity, and community encouragement, and acknowledge what these advantages offer, and how they stimulate and support gifted achievement (Goss & Sonnemann, 2016). Classroom teachers may play a key role in addressing the challenges and providing opportunities that broaden experience and offer different perspectives, if they have the training and support that enables them to understand the needs of gifted students and to plan appropriate learning experiences.

Teachers of the Gifted in Rural Settings

For teachers of gifted students in rural settings, there are the added complexities of living and teaching in a rural community. Gallagher, Smith, and Merrotsy (2011) described the experience of six teachers of gifted students in rural schools. The teachers had varying years of experience and were purposively selected because they had recently taught a gifted student. None had specific training in gifted education, although some had undertaken in-service professional development such as workshops or conferences. Their initial reaction to teaching a gifted child was panic despite the fact that afterwards they could recognise changes in their understanding and their efficacy towards gifted education. They identified their greatest needs as being resources, networking, further training, and support for planning and preparation.

Geographic isolation, limited resources, community attitudes, and familial reservations about different learning experiences and future aspirations have all been described as problematic for teachers and gifted students in rural schools (Alloway & Dalley-Trim, 2009; Arnold, 1991; Colangelo et al., 2001; Howley, 2009; Howley, et al., 2009; Lawrence, 2009). When reviewing three different programs in rural schools, Wood and Zundans-Fraser (2012) found that educators required additional support such as networking, sharing experiences, and working collegially to address the challenges for gifted learners.

Teaching in Rural Settings

Classroom teachers in rural schools experience different teaching opportunities because of school size and community context. Nye's (2014) research shows that there are positive aspects to teaching in rural schools that align with the effective practices to meet the learning needs of gifted learners as described earlier. In rural and regional communities, professional identity is reinforced by community acceptance and support for teachers. There is a feeling of a supportive community, less discipline problems, and a positive local community, including lifestyle, "with the country being perceived as quieter, safer and child-and-family friendly" (Jenkins, Reitano, & Taylor, 2011, p. 73). There are greater opportunities for leadership (Jenkins et al., 2011) and for high job satisfaction (p. 73), because of the small size of schools and connectedness across schools. Teachers are able to establish longer-term relationships with learners (Colangelo et al., 2001) and explore ways that the classroom context can provide opportunities for flexible learning experiences.

Multi-grade classrooms, with smaller numbers, support the planning for differentiated learning across multiple grade levels and enable teachers to plan for individual students across the span of the curriculum. Provided the teacher understands the learning needs of gifted students, they can provide a developmentally appropriate curriculum that can meet the individual student's learning needs (Cornish, 2010). These classroom structures have clear advantages for students of high potential (gifted) and high performance (talented), as they are not lock-stepped as they may otherwise be in a larger classroom. In this way, the accelerated learning opportunities that are widely described as best practice for gifted learners (Colangelo, et al., 2006; VanTassel Baska & Hubbard, 2016) are available to students in small schools. The close connections with the community offer opportunities for effective pedagogies, such as authentic problem-based and place-based learning, which are recommended curriculum practice for gifted learners (Donovan, 2016; Kettler, Puryear, & Mullet, 2016). These pedagogies nurture independent learning, as well as collaboration across diverse groupings of learners and serve to connect students to the needs of their community (Bartholomaeus, 2013) supporting them to identify ways to contribute to that community and to utilise their ability in making change (Donovan, 2016). Place-based activities offer opportunities for teachers and students to work together to produce knowledge that is relevant to their context and to produce knowledge that may solve real problems in their community (Smith, 2002). The advantage of this type of learning is that it connects both learner and teacher with the community and makes learning more meaningful. As Bartholomaeus (2013) states, it is an "opportunity for students to build an understanding of the local place where they live, and opportunities for students to participate in working for change" (p. 103).

Professional Development for Rural Teachers of the Gifted

Gifted students have distinct educational needs that can be addressed with pedagogical strategies, such as: the development of higher order thinking skills; the development of creative and critical thinking skills; research capacity such as investigating real-world issues; specialist or advanced discipline content; acceleration; inquiry and independent learning techniques; and self-paced learning opportunities (Aamidor, 2007; Azano et al., 2017; VanTassel-Baska & Hubbard, 2016). In the context of Gagné's (2009) *Differentiated Model of Giftedness and Talent* (DMGT), classroom teachers can be described as environmental catalysts for the development of talent. There is a clear link between professional learning focused on gifted students and more positive attitudes towards gifted students (Geake & Gross, 2008). The capacity of classroom teachers to identify gifted students, introduce specific interventions and understand the pedagogical approaches that support the specific learning needs of rural gifted students impacts on the successful achievement of those gifted students (Aamidor, 2007; Azano et al., 2017; VanTassel-Baska & Hubbard, 2016).

The importance of professional learning for improving outcomes for gifted students in the Australian context is described by Geake and Gross (2008), Lassig (2015), and Plunkett (2012). Jenkins et al. (2011) state that rural teachers need more professional learning to remain current about recent research. Geographic isolation, limited resources, community attitudes, and familial reservations about different learning experiences and future aspirations have all been described as problematic for teachers of gifted students in rural schools (Alloway & Dalley-Trim, 2009; Arnold, 1991; Colangelo et al., 2001; Howley, 2009, Howley et al., 2009; Lawrence, 2009). Edinger (2017) identified the need for resourcing to overcome access issues to assist teachers in understanding best practices and lead to change in teachers' pedagogical practice (p. 310).

Recent statistical evidence identifies an ongoing gap in national and international academic test results between rural and urban students (Thomson, De Bortoli, & Buckley, 2013), and the expertise of classroom teachers to understand and provide for gifted learners is inconsistent at best, and lacking at worst (Henderson & Jarvis, 2016; Rowley, 2012). Consequently, there is clearly a need for research into how we can more effectively support gifted rural students and their teachers. The voices of teachers in rural settings will provide an indicator of what is required to best support them in their provision of valid and challenging learning for gifted students.

Teaching Gifted Students in the Rural Australian Context

All teacher education courses in Australian universities must provide evidence that their programs address the teacher education content standards (Australian Institute for Teaching and School Leadership (AITSL), 2011). The graduating teacher education content standards (AITSL, 2011) acknowledge the range of learning needs across the full cohort of school-aged students in Standard 1, Criteria 1.5, as cited below:

Standard 1: Know your students and how they learn
Criterion 1.5: Differentiate teaching to meet the specific learning needs of students across the full range of abilities. (AITSL, 2011, p. 8)

Table 1 The Australian Professional Standards for Teachers (AITSL, 2011)

Domain of teaching:	Standards:
Professional knowledge	1. Know students and how they learn. 2. Know the content and how to teach it.
Professional practice	3. Plan for and implement effective teaching and learning. 4. Create and maintain supportive and safe learning environments. 5. Assess, provide feedback and report on student learning.
Professional engagement	6. Engage in professional learning. 7. Engage professionally with colleagues, parents/carers and the community.

Each of the seven standards (see Table 1) describes aspects of quality teaching that inform the practice of graduating teachers, practising classroom teachers, and lead teachers in schools.

Since 2004, these standards have informed the development of initial teacher education courses. While mention is made of differentiated levels of ability in academic learning, there is no specific use of the term gifted or talented in any of the standards. Henderson and Jarvis (2016) argue that such generalised statements do not provide assurance that teachers will know how to support gifted students in their classrooms. They suggest a set of elaborations that would better inform classroom practice with regard to gifted students. The elaborations describe explicit learning needs and characteristics based on literature from both Australia and overseas. The example below shows the elaboration suggested for Criterion 1.5.

Standard 1: Know your students and how they learn.
Criterion 1.5: Differentiate teaching to meet the specific learning needs of students across the full range of abilities.
Elaboration: Differentiating curriculum and instruction for diverse learners must include consistent appropriately challenging opportunities for advanced learners. Teachers need to understand the philosophy, principles and practices of differentiation in order to effectively implement this approach (Tomlinson & Jarvis, 2009). A key factor in differentiation is the use of diagnostic and pre-assessment to determine students' learning needs, interests, readiness, and learning profiles. (Henderson & Jarvis, 2016, p. 66)

Guiding the understanding of definitions of 'giftedness' and 'talent' within Australia, the *Australian Curriculum Assessment and Reporting Authority* (ACARA) acknowledged and promoted Gagné's (2009) DMGT (2.0) as an effective model for all Australian schools to use when developing learning opportunities for their gifted and talented students. Gagné articulated a definition that differentiated the terms 'giftedness' and 'talent' as:

GIFTEDNESS designates the possession and use of outstanding natural abilities, called aptitudes in at least one ability domain, to a degree that places an individual at least among the top 10% of age peers.
TALENT designates the outstanding mastery of systematically developed abilities, called competencies (knowledge and skills), in at least one field of human activity to a degree that

places an individual at least among the top 10% of age peers who are or have been active in that field. (Gagné, 2009, p. 1)

Henderson and Jarvis (2016) describe Gagné's model as a framework that has limits in terms of explicit guidance for classroom practice, even as it indicates the diversity of talent potential and the nature of the influences and catalysts that impact on talent development in classrooms. However, the definition aligns with the principles of ACARA, and the model itself indicates that schools and classrooms (and therefore classroom teachers) are environmental catalysts in the development of talent with the potential to either support or disrupt the successful development of talented behaviours. This reinforces the important role of teachers in the education of our gifted learners. The Australian Curriculum states, "gifted and talented students are entitled to rigorous, relevant, and engaging learning opportunities drawn from the Curriculum and aligned with their individual learning needs, strengths, interests, and goals" (australiancurriculum.edu.au/resources/student-diversity/gifted-and-talented-students, 2019). It can be assumed that this definition applies to all gifted students, whether they reside in urban or rural settings. Educators in the bush are far from the centre of decisions, and their voices may be silenced by prevailing attitudes about those in rural settings (Bannister et al., 2015; Miller, Graham, & Al-Awiwe, 2014). It is their voices that can prepare new teachers for their teaching experiences and support them as they enter rural education settings.

Initial teacher education establishes teacher understandings and knowledge of diverse needs of students as it prepares teachers for entry into the field and in-service professional learning extends and deepens understandings of practice and student needs. Despite the findings of two Senate Inquiries (1988, 2001) recommending that units in gifted education should be compulsory to all pre-service teachers, currently only three universities within NSW offer such core units, two in their Bachelor of Primary degrees and one in their Bachelor of Secondary degree. Recently, Rowan and Townend (2016) described the experiences of early career teachers with regard to both gifted and twice-exceptional students. While their research made it clear that early career teachers were anxious about the teaching of students with diverse abilities overall, it also highlighted that early career teachers felt that they were unprepared in terms of the knowledge and skills needed to teach gifted students well. There is evidence that experienced teachers also have a variety of responses to gifted students, which may be due to a lack of understanding or confidence in providing appropriate learning for gifted students (Lassig, 2015; Rowley, 2012).

Historically, studies (Cooper, 1999; Gross, 1994) showed a link between professional learning focused on gifted students and a more positive attitude towards gifted students. Currently, the importance of professional learning in providing classroom teachers with understanding and skills about giftedness, gifted learners, and the lived experience of gifted children and young people was reinforced by Lassig (2015). Plunkett (2012) identified that changing attitudes toward gifted students required more than professional learning. Teachers retained misconceptions about giftedness unless the professional learning included some specialised knowledge or study about giftedness, including explicit content about the learning needs of gifted students.

These findings focused on all classroom teachers and did not factor in the experiences of teaching in rural settings. Hence, it is important to consider the impact a rural setting may have on the teachers who are placed in rural, regional, or remote schools.

Seeking the Voices of Teachers of Gifted Students in Rural Contexts: Method

In 2016, an online pilot survey for teachers in rural, regional, remote, and very remote schools in New South Wales was developed by the authors to discern the voices of classroom teachers in these provincial settings. The size of the communities served included communities with a population of less than 1000, ranging from 100 to 700 in population. The survey sought to identify the perceptions rural teachers held of gifted education and gifted students, the perceived advantages and disadvantages they saw for gifted students in rural contexts, and the resources they felt would support effective teaching of gifted students. The respondents held diverse roles within schools, including the role of teaching principal. Other roles included teaching executive, teacher librarians, subject coordinators, support teachers, distance education teachers, and specialist teachers of gifted students. All participants were provided with Gagné's definitions of 'giftedness' and 'talent' for reference.

The questions asked of the participants were about their attitudes towards and level of confidence with the identification of gifted students and their attitudes and confidence in working with gifted and talented students. They were asked to share both positive and challenging issues in providing for their gifted and talented students within their schools. Participants were also asked about their confidence in identifying students who may be underachieving, from a minority cultural group, as well as issues they identified surrounding differentiation. Finally, after demographic information, a further question was asked inviting participants to share other relevant information about rural gifted and talented students.

Adopting a *raw data grid* (Mutch, 2013), the researchers transferred the data collected from the surveys onto an Excel spreadsheet. The raw data grid was interrogated by each researcher individually to find themes across the qualitative data.

The second stage involved coding and transferring the 94 survey responses into the first page of the Excel spreadsheet. The researchers then separately analysed the thematic themes from the transcriptions. Many responses contained multiple themes, and each of these was highlighted and placed within the spreadsheet across the identified themes within each response.

Co-coding procedures began with reflective dialogue between the researchers discussing possible themes based on the literature (Whitebread et al., 2008). The level of inter-rater agreement between the researchers was calculated at 96% (Whitebread et al., 2008). The final 4% were discussed between the researchers and absolute agreement was achieved (Whitebread et al., 2008). Finally, the researchers compared the themes identified and then the responses were placed under each theme until agreement was attained for all themes and the classification of all responses by participants were included.

Some findings are shared below with comparisons to the wider research literature.

Hearing the Voices of Teachers: Some Findings and Discussion

The voices of teachers in rural, regional, or remote contexts across NSW provided a valuable picture of how classroom teachers perceived the experience of teaching gifted students in rural classrooms. By reporting the comments from teachers directly, a clear picture of their perceptions and experiences emerged that reflected findings described in the literature.

The challenges of differentiating for various ability levels (VanTassel Baska & Hubbard, 2016), including the access to advanced learning materials, are described in Box 1.

Box 1 Differentiating Learning and Advanced Learning Materials

Respondent 1.04: *Acceleration works for most students that I have dealt with. Extension has not as it seems to be more of the same. We need to be able to connect students so they can see they are not alone, gifted and talented camps, perhaps like drama and band camps may be an option, with specialist staff.*

Respondent 1.08: *In a small rural school, there is a very small cohort anyway and an even smaller cohort of G&T. This makes it difficult to design programs that will fit the different needs and interests of the students particularly if it is to include group work.*

Respondent 1.24: *Differentiation is often difficult due to the small cohorts meaning there is a wide range of ability levels within the one class. We have staged GaT classes, which largely overcomes this. The variety of classes that need to be taught restricts how many GaT classes a teacher can be involved in, even if it is their passion.*

Respondent 1.01: *Often the gifted kids miss out on extension because there is so much time spent on those who experience difficulties with their learning and they also need to benefit from differentiation. Just because kids are poor doesn't mean they are not gifted or talented. Often there is a perception in low SES communities that their kids can't perform at high levels and they don't have the resources to send the student.*

The teachers noted the difficulties of designing differentiated learning where there are only small numbers, even when they were aware of a variety of the approaches recommended by VanTassel Baska and Hubbard (2016). While Cornish (2010) argued that the small numbers meant that individuals could be identified and offered individual programming, the importance of collegial networking for support with best practice for gifted students in terms of differentiation was identified by VanTassel Baska and Hubbard (2016) and Wood and Zundans-Fraser (2012) as key to successful classroom practice. Balancing the needs of all students in classrooms where there are multiple grade levels and ability levels is made more complex in multi-stage classrooms (Cornish, 2010). Wood and Zundans-Fraser talked about the need for gifted students to meet and work with others and these teachers' voices also note that, in their experience, this is something rural gifted students may miss out on.

Other teachers described the importance of, and difficulties with, technology (Box 2). Technology was described by Housand and Housand (2012) as a valuable resource for gifted students in rural classrooms as it provided them with access to diverse mentors, advanced content, and connections with peers and experts. The different uses of technology and the problems of connection and access are described in the comments in Box 2. Respondent 1.07 expressed concern that the social/emotional needs of isolated gifted children may not be met by technology, although Periathiruvadi and Rinn (2012) were able to demonstrate that gifted students were able to make and maintain connections with remote peers through classroom applications of social media tools.

Box 2 Technology in the Classroom for Gifted Students

Respondent 1.12: *If the NBN (National Broadband Network) was here - we could have a lot more opportunities for G&T interactive activities for students to be exposed to.*

Respondent 1.07: *The current Virtual High School (Aurora College) being run for country students from the city doesn't work. The previous incarnation, Xsel, based in Dubbo was far better. There needs to be far more emphasis on the social/emotional needs of GaT students, based on a model where country teachers with a passion for country students come together in an environment where the students, teachers, and parents can all thrive.*

Respondent 1.05: *Access to technology that works is difficult since teachers are responsible for maintenance. We need a designated computer coordinator who has time to maintain the complex system.*

Respondent 1.03: *Crappy slow Internet connection constantly drops out.*

Respondent 1.04: *Challenges re technology and costs for schools to access extra activities/programs/texts and resources to support students who are gifted.*

Other teachers noted, as Azano et al. (2017) also described, the impact poverty can have on what can be offered for students, and what students and their families can afford (see Box 3). Providing opportunities for social interaction was noted to be costly and limiting due to the expense of travel and the reality of geographical isolation. Richards and Stambaugh (2015) described the importance of understanding the support gifted students from lower socio-economic groups needed to achieve their potential. The comments from teachers in schools highlight this finding, as they noted the impact on a student's capacity to travel or engage in programs outside of school. Distance was identified as a factor in cost when supporting gifted students (Alloway & Dalley-Trim, 2009; Arnold, 1991; Colangelo et al., 2001; Howley, 2009; Howley, et al., 2009) and mentioned often by the teachers of gifted students.

Box 3 Challenges with Financial Load

Respondent 1.60: *Students have to do far more travelling to remain competitive with city students with similar abilities. There is (sic) always costs involved, and this presumes that students have access to adequate technology.*

Respondent 1.23: *Distance implies travel costs which some students cannot meet. Schools can help out with some of the cost, but students are disadvantaged by distance. We can't afford to spend large amounts of our Science budget on new technology and devices, especially when new Nat Curriculum texts are needed for G&T, mainstream, reading support, and life skills classes. Lack of competition is an issue.*

Respondent 1.25: *Due to the remoteness of rural schools it is a big cost to be involved in many activities due to the cost or availability of transport. Also, the cost of program for example our school is involved in a Webcats writing program at a cost of $250 a student, plus two release casual days plus private transport cost by a teacher.*

Respondent 1.28: *In a rural and remote location the travel factor can be prohibitive. [I]n other circumstances, low socio-economic constraints inhibit access to GAT opportunities. We have a very small sample of GAT students in my school and in my area of expertise (CAPA Drama)*

Respondent 1.05: *Financial constraints come from what we can provide for the students and accessing time for planning and unit development.*

Respondent 1.32: *Capacity to find the materials and information that may be the most beneficial. Being rural and remote from most resources is a strain on school resources & ability to cover absent teachers.*

Access to professional learning is described as a need by many of the teacher voices (Box 4). Both Lassig (2015) and Rowley (2012) stressed the importance of professional learning focused on the needs of Australian gifted students. Whether professional learning opportunities are online (Edinger, 2017) or face-to-face (VanTassel Baska & Hubbard 2016), the upskilling of classroom teachers to provide quality learning for gifted students is identified as essential in the provision of programs, and this is echoed in the comments focused on the need to understand gifted students and the pedagogies of teaching them. Overcoming the challenges of distance and access is identified by the teachers as a major challenge for their professional development, reinforcing the points made by Alloway and Dalley-Trim (2009), Colangelo et al. (2001), and Howley et al. (2009).

Box 4 Accessing Professional Learning

Respondent 1.05: *Recent graduate teachers have indicated that they do not receive any education in G&T. A recent survey indicated that the entire staff require TPL.*

Respondent 1.07: *I have been in the position of teaching a gifted and talented stage 3 class for less than a year. I have found it difficult to access affordable professional development that will enhance my teaching practice. I am trying to learn the underpinning pedagogy of teaching gifted and talented [students] but reliable sources are in short supply. This is made more difficult because my school has no money.*

Respondent 1.16: *Hi quality, targeted professional learning on the North Coast is very rare. When it is available it is usually in Sydney and this is far too expensive for staff to attend. Staff then have the added financial and time burden of travelling significant distances to access professional learning that staff in the city take for granted. Many schools also will not pay for either flights or accommodation.*

Respondent 1.01: *Living in a remote area makes it difficult and expensive to access professional development. Travel to Sydney where most of the courses are entails airfare, accommodation as well as time away from teaching. More support from professionals in all KLA areas from universities would be highly appreciated!!!!!*

Respondent 1.34: *High-quality professional learning that doesn't cost a fortune and is conducted in rural areas would be fantastic. Many gifted and/or talented students are not those from high-income families but rather from low. This means that they don't have the resources to send their children to various activities to extend them. Sometimes they don't see the value either because of their lack of education.*

Respondent 1.49: *In relation to professional development, most courses are in Sydney, a 5-hour drive, and all travel and accommodation costs are up to the teacher to pay. This makes professional development near impossible.*

Respondent 1.36: *We have to do 50 hours of PD, and there are no courses nearby; they are all in Sydney. We are much closer to Brisbane than Sydney, but there are no NSW Institute of Teachers-approved courses there.*

Coming through in the comments from the teachers is the concern that often, gifted students do not stay in rural schools and that they leave for greater stimulation or experience in larger and well-equipped schools. This was noted by Paul and Seward (2016) as a concern in rural communities when students finished school, but the teachers in this study noticed it within the school years. The effect of decreasing numbers on opportunities, relationships, and provisions is acknowledged as an issue for rural settings (Aamidor, 2007; Lawrence, 2009). Even though the literature provides suggestions for creating diverse opportunities to extend student learning (e.g., Richards & Stambaugh, 2015; VanTassel Baska & Hubbard, 2016), the voices of the teachers indicate that for them, it is an issue (Box 5).

Box 5 The Impact of Small Student Numbers.

Respondent 1.32: *Many capable students are removed from the local environment very quickly. So, it skews the local high school down.*

Respondent 1.02: *Dwindling student numbers in small rural schools escalate the range of abilities in classrooms. One entire year group may be in one classroom. Compounding this with the increasing social issues, family make-up, transient pop, rural 'water issues', farming decline etc. results in a demography of students quite unlike even 5–10 years ago. Travel and accommodation costs are a constant burden! Limits exposure.*

Respondent 1.11: *Often in rural settings, school size dictates the necessity of varying ability levels in one class. This is evident even in streamed class settings where a higher ability class will consist of a very broad mixture of student abilities.*

In Box 6, the perceptions of teaching gifted students in the rural classroom are described. There is a sense of needing more support and of concern that the diverse needs of the students are important to meet. The literature reviewed earlier in the chapter raised a number of challenges (e.g., distance, isolation, rigorous learning, advanced materials) that had been perceived for gifted students and their teachers (e.g., Colangelo et al., 2001, 2006; VanTassel Baska & Hubbard, 2016) and can be recognised in the comments from these teachers. There was also literature that presented a non-deficit view of rural environments for gifted students (e.g., Richards & Stambaugh, 2015) that is not as clearly expressed by these teachers whose daily work involves consistent planning for gifted students. For these participating classroom teachers, the difficulties appear to be more pressing.

Box 6 Perceptions of Teaching Gifted Students in the Rural Classroom

Respondent 1.21: *The growing workload for teachers is increasing. Students are more and more involved in other activities, which impinge on learning time. The current changes and demands on teachers' time, without much support, are overwhelming.*

Respondent 1.04: *High learning difficulties and behaviour needs in stage classrooms can absorb higher-order learning opportunities—as I type this it sounds a cop-out comment, but I am certain I am not alone in this thought. We are beginning to collaborate more at school, with attention to differentiated*

(continued)

Box 6 (continued)

learning and how to address these needs. We are getting there and not giving up. Programming time important.

Respondent 1.60: *Gifted and Talented Programs no longer seem to be a focus for the DET as they were say 10 years ago. The decline in the socio-economics [status] of the general population and [the fact that] that children's experiences before school are decreasing, and development delay, learning difficulties, and other support need to take priority.*

The participating teachers provided a list of tools and approaches used to identify gifted students. Objective measures used included IQ results by a professional, standardised tests, such as NAPLAN competitions and school results. Subjective measures mentioned included nomination by teachers, parent nomination, or self-nomination. Through the teacher voices represented in Box 7, insights into teacher experiences when identifying gifted and talented students were evidenced. Identifying gifted students in rural contexts requires a range of tools that address the diverse experiences of the rural gifted (Aamidor, 2007). In some instances, teachers may not realise a student is gifted (Gallagher et al., 2011), and their reaction to them may be negative (Geake & Gross, 2008) or non-accepting (Lassig, 2015; Rowley, 2012). The comments in the data here emphasises that teachers are not confident to identify gifted students and recognise that this means gifted students may be missed.

Box 7 Identifying Gifted and Talented Students

Respondent 1.21: *I feel that many teachers just don't know how to correctly identify their G&T students or how to differentiate learning.*

Respondent 5.09: *Do not know where to start—new teachers are not understanding how to identify and discuss.*

Respondent 5.05: *Cohort size too small to develop comparative data.*

Respondent 5.02: *Assessment tools can be limited in reliability. Experience, observation and demonstrations can be more effective in identification.*

Respondent 5.07: *Standardised testing only measures a very small range of students potential/giftedness/talent.*

Respondent 5.15: *NAPLAN results come in too late in the year to make a difference in that academic year.*

Respondent 5.13: *Teachers interpret the criteria differently and tend to nominate too many children as G&T based on inappropriate assumptions, e.g., they spell well or use good punctuation and grammar. Many parents believe that their children are exceptional and that teachers just don't recognise the talent. I have only ever referred three students, in 30 years, to a school counsellor that I believed had exceptional abilities. Two out of the three*

(continued)

Box 7 (continued)

were diagnosed as gifted. The last student was not, according to IQ testing; however, he recently scored in the top 3% in Australia in ICAS Science receiving a Distinction—and he is only 8 years old. So, who knows! Also, there is some debate about the 'worthwhileness' of officially identifying students via *testing—what will the student gain? I tried to create and run a G&T database of students at school but just couldn't maintain it.*

The voices of the teachers considered that rural locations may be positive environments for gifted students by expressing benefits that included safety, opportunities for accelerated learning in smaller schools, reduced class sizes, and diversity in the learning environment. Richards and Stambaugh (2015) support this sentiment in their discussion; they posit that a deficit view of rural education for gifted students was not helpful. VanTassel Baska and Hubbard (2016) also list a number of approaches that they believe will provide the support gifted students should have in their rural education context (e.g., metacognitive skills, inquiry skills, extracurricular opportunities) and teacher professional development that support a non-deficit view of rural education. Similarly, Goss and Sonnemann (2016) identify that, in Australia, rural contexts should not be considered a deficit for high-ability learners, despite evidence currently showing that the achievement of gifted students is a concern. A final voice summarises the overall perceptions evidenced in the responses across the survey questions:

> *Gifted rural students are quite disadvantaged and I doubt whether this is actually recognised by the wider academic community. Talented students from small rural areas, however, are extremely resourceful, motivated, and willing to do whatever it takes to achieve. (Participant 1.60 response)*

Acting on the Voices: Responding to the Perceptions of Rural Teachers of the Gifted

While rural living is described as a positive experience, teachers and gifted students growing up in these locations are faced with challenges not experienced by those living in or close to major cities. The voices of teachers reiterated the findings in the literature that were discussed earlier in the chapter. Issues of remoteness (Wood & Zundans-Fraser, 2012), lack of technology access (Schirmer, 2016), the under-identification of gifted students (Alloway & Dalley-Trim, 2009), and limited professional learning for teachers (Colangelo et al., 2006; VanTassel Baska & Hubbard, 2016) remain problems in need of solutions. Goss and Sonnemann (2016) reported a slide in achievement of high-end learners in rural Australian schools that the teachers who responded to the survey also noted.

The teachers teaching in rural and/or remote schools voiced an awareness that gifted students need differentiated learning experiences and support to develop their talent. In line with the literature, they articulated specific gaps in support that included their own ongoing teaching development (Lassig, 2015; Rowley, 2012), the need for better resourcing to provide advanced materials, the impact of the smaller numbers in rural contexts on the capacity to provide diverse opportunities for students (Aamidor, 2007) and support to identify and provide challenging learning for their gifted students (VanTassel Baska & Hubberd, 2016). Schools were able to offer opportunities, but were also limited by teacher experience and isolation (Alloway & Dalley-Trim, 2009), small numbers for students to connect with, and the impact of distance on the chance experiences of meeting other like minds (Wood & Zundans-Fraser, 2012).

In keeping with the literature that described the inclusion of training in gifted education in pre-service teacher education (Henderson & Jarvis, 2016), only 20% of the teachers who responded had any formal training in gifted education. Hence, teachers concurred with the literature that strongly identified a need for greater professional development in specific areas, such as support that explicitly addresses identification, enrichment, and best practice pedagogies for teaching gifted students (Lassig, 2015; Rowley, 2012; VanTassel Baska & Hubberd, 2016).

Conclusion

In this chapter, the discussion was focused on rural gifted students and on teachers of the gifted in rural and regional settings. A small pilot study was used to gauge teachers' perceptions of a variety of issues they are faced with when teaching gifted students. While it is recognised that there are limitations to this small study and that the findings cannot be generalised to other contexts, the implications are that more studies are needed to amplify the voices of rural gifted students and their teachers, especially in the unique context of rural gifted education.

The rural teachers in this study voiced the realities of teaching gifted students in rural contexts and indicated the challenges that included knowing how to provide for gifted students and having access to the resources needed while also providing for other learners in the classroom. The responses of the participants elaborated their perceptions and described how teachers feel in their classrooms, acknowledging some of the issues they experienced. The literature is echoed through the voices of teachers in schools across rural NSW. A compelling argument has been presented for ensuring that pre-service teachers, and teachers currently in schools, are supported in their understanding of gifted students and effective pedagogical approaches, to provide appropriate learning experiences for gifted students, in their rural contexts.

While a rural environment presents challenges, we are suggesting the voices of teachers in rural settings tell us that teaching gifted students in rural contexts requires them to have the ability to recognise the strengths of a rural setting and utilise these strengths to create learning environments where gifted students can thrive and can understand their potential. This may mean offering place-based, problem-oriented learning that is authentic and impacts constructively on the local environment. Supporting talent development may mean connecting gifted learners through innovative online opportunities that give them a network of like minds. For teachers to support the talent development process, it does mean that teachers need to develop a deeper understanding of the learning needs of gifted learners to enable the planning of differentiated learning experiences in mainstream classrooms. It means that it is important to support teachers in this process by ensuring more access to professional learning and increased networks for teachers to share practice and solve problems collaboratively.

Gifted learners in rural settings have the potential to make a difference in their local community and beyond. Their teachers want to identify them and design learning that is challenging and enriching for them. Supporting the teachers of gifted students in rural settings to understand giftedness and talent development will better equip them to create positive learning environments for talent development, nurturing giftedness into observable talented performance for gifted rural students.

Cross-References

▶ Australian Teachers Who Made a Difference: Secondary Gifted Student Perceptions of Teaching and Teacher Effectiveness
▶ Differentiation of Instruction for Gifted Learners: Collated Evaluative Studies of Teacher Classroom Practices
▶ Educational Contexts, Transitions and Community Engagement: Part VI Introduction
▶ Engaging Gifted Students in Solving Real Problems Creatively: Implementing the Real Engagement in Active Problem-Solving (REAPS) Teaching/Learning Model in Australasian and Pacific Rim Contexts
▶ Fostering and Developing Talent in Mentorship Programs: The Mentor's Perspectives
▶ Gifted Education in the Asia-Pacific: From the Past for the Future – An Introduction
▶ Identifying Underrepresented Gifted Students: A Developmental Process
▶ Learning from International Research Informs Academic Acceleration in Australasia: A Case for Consistent Policy
▶ Place-Based Gifted Education in Rural Schools
▶ Rural Adolescent Gifted Girls: Exploring the Impact of Popular Culture on Their Talent Development
▶ Some Implications for the Future of Gifted Education in the Asia-Pacific
▶ Supporting Australian Gifted Indigenous Students' Academic Potential in Rural Settings
▶ Teaching Gifted Education to Pre-service Teachers: Lessons Learned

References

Aamidor, S. (2007). Identification and intervention for rural, low-income, gifted students: A follow-up study. *Gifted Children, 2*, 2–5. Retrieved from https://pdfs.semanticscholar.org/8044/071265d41920cf3a3ea104b127d545906515.pdf
Alloway, N., & Dalley-Trim, L. (2009). 'High and dry' in rural Australia: Obstacles to student aspirations and expectations. *Rural Society, 19*(1), 49–59. https://doi.org/10.5172/rsj.351.19.1.49

Arnold, P. (1991). Review of contemporary issues for rural schools. *Education in Rural Australia, 11*(1), 31–42.

Australian Bureau of Statistics. (2018). Retrieved from http://search.abs.gov.au/s/search.html?collection=abs&form=simple&profile=_default&query=+rural+schools+2016

Australian Bureau of Statistics. (n.d.). Retrieved from http://www.abs.gov.au/AUSSTATS/abs@.nsf/DetailsPage/4221.02016?OpenDocument

Australian Institute for Teaching & School Leadership (AITSL). (2011). *Professional standards for teachers*. Carlton South, VIC: Education Services Australia.

Azano, A. P., Callahan, C. M., Brodersen, A. V., & Caughey, M. (2017). Responding to the challenges of gifted education in rural communities. *Global Education Review, 4*(1), 62–77.

Bailey, S., Knight, B. A., & Riley, D. (1995). Addressing the needs of the gifted in rural areas: The Armidale Catholic Schools Project. *Education in Rural Australia, 5*(2), 1–13.

Bannister, B., Cornish, L., Bannister-Tyrrell, M., & Gregory, S. (2015). Creative use of digital technologies: Keeping the best and brightest in the bush. *Australian and International Journal of Rural Education, 25*(1), 52–65.

Bartholomaeus, P. (2013). Educating for sustainable rural futures. *Australian and International Journal of Rural Education, 23*(2), 101–113.

Baxter, J., Hayes, A., & Gray, M. (2011, March). Families in regional, rural and remote Australia. Retrieved from https://aifs.gov.au/publications/families-regional-rural-and-remote-australia

Bayley, A., & Goodyear, R. (2006). New Zealand: An urban/rural profile update. *Product Development and Publishing Services Division of Statistics New Zealand*. Retrieved from http://archive.stats.govt.nz/browse_for_stats/Maps_and_geography/Geographic-areas/urban-rural-profile-update.aspx

Braggett, E. J. (1985). *Education of gifted and talented children from populations with special needs: A discussion paper*. Canberra, ACT: Commonwealth Schools Commission.

Burney, V. H., & Cross, T. L. (2006). Impoverished students with academic promise in rural settings: 10 lessons from Project Aspire. *Gifted Child Today, 29*(2), 14–21. https://doi.org/10.4219/gct-2006-200

Colangelo, N., Assouline, S. G., Baldus, C. M., Ihrig, D., & New, J. (2006). *Gifted in rural America: Faces of diversity*. Iowa City, IA: University of Iowa Press.

Colangelo, N., Assouline, S. G., & Gross, M. U. M. (Eds.). (2004). *A nation deceived: How schools hold back America's brightest students. Volume 1*. Iowa City, IA: The Connie Belin & Jacqueline N. Blank International Centre for Gifted Education and Talent Development.

Colangelo, N., Assouline, S. G., & New, J. (2001). *Gifted voices from rural America*. Iowa City, IA: The University of Iowa.

Cooper, S. M. (1999). *University teachers' attitudes towards giftedness, gifted students and special provision for the gifted*. Retrieved from http://ro.ecu.edu.au/theses_hons/832

Cornish, L. (2010). Multiage classes: What's in a name. *Journal of Multiage Education, 4*(2), 7–11. Retrieved from https://search.informit.com.au/documentSummary;dn=909066382893421;res=IELHSS

Donovan, E. (2016). Learning to embrace our stories: Using place-based education practices to inspire authentic writing. *Middle School Journal, 47*(4), 23–31. https://doi.org/10.1080/00940771.2016.1202657

Edinger, M. J. (2017). Online teacher professional development for gifted education: Examining the impact of a new pedagogical model. *Gifted Child Quarterly, 61*, 300–312. https://doi.org/10.1177/0016986217722616

Ewing, S. (2016, February). Australia's digital divide is narrowing but getting deeper. *The Conversation*. Retrieved from https://theconversation.com/australias-digial-divide-is-narrowing-but-getting-deeper-55232

Fraser-Seeto, K. (2013). Pre-service teacher training in gifted and talented education: An Australian perspective. *Journal of Student Engagement: Education Matters, 3*(1), 29–38. Retrieved from https://ro.uow.edu.au/cgi/viewcontent.cgi?article=1026&context=jseem

Gagné, F. (2009). Building gifts into talents: Detailed overview of the DMGT 2.0. In B. Macfarlane & T. Stambaugh (Eds.), *Leading change in gifted education: The festschrift of Dr. Joyce VanTassel Baska* (pp. 61–80). Waco, TX: Prufrock Press.

Gallagher, S., Smith, S. R., & Merrotsy, P. (2011). Teachers' perceptions of the socioemotional development of intellectually gifted primary aged students and their attitudes towards ability grouping and acceleration. *Gifted and Talented International, 26*(1–2), 11–24. https://doi.org/10.1080/15332276.2011.11673585

Geake, J. G., & Gross, M. U. M. (2008). Teachers' negative affect toward academically gifted students: An evolutionary psychological study. *The Gifted Child Quarterly, 52*, 217–231. https://doi.org/10.1177/0016986208319704

Glendenning, A. (1998). Family life, health and lifestyles in rural areas: The role of self-esteem. *Health Education, 2*(March), 59–68. https://doi.org/10.1108/09654289810199829

Goss, P., & Sonnemann, J. (2016, March). Widening gaps: What NAPLAN tells us about student progress. Retrieved from https://grattan.edu.au/report/widening-gaps/

Gross, M. U. M. (1994). Changing teacher attitudes towards gifted students through inservice training. *Gifted and Talented International, 8*(2), 15–21. https://doi.org/10.1080/15332276.1994.11672784

Henderson, L., & Jarvis, J. (2016). The gifted dimension of the Australian professional standards: Implications for professional learning. *Australian Journal of Teacher Education, 41*(8), 60–83.

Housand, B. C., & Housand, A. M. (2012). The role of technology in gifted students' motivation. *Psychology in the Schools, 49*, 706–715. https://doi.org/10.1002/pits.21629

Howley, A., Rhodes, M., & Beall, J. (2009). Challenges facing rural schools: Implications for gifted students. *Journal for the Education of the Gifted, 32*, 515–536. https://doi.org/10.1177/016235320903200404

Howley, C. (2009). The meaning of rural difference for bright rednecks. *Journal for the Education of the Gifted, 32*, 537–564. https://doi.org/10.1177/016235320903200405

Jarvis, J. M. (2009) Planning to unmask potential through responsive curriculum: The "Famous Five" Exercise. *Roeper Review, 31*(4), 234–241. https://doi.org/10.1080/02783190903177606

Jenkins, K., Reitano, P., & Taylor, N. (2011). Teachers in the bush: Supports, challenges, and professional learning. *Education in Rural Australia, 21*(2), 71–85. Retrieved from https://core.ac.uk/download/pdf/143850652.pdf

Kettler, T., Puryear, J. S., & Mullet, D. R. (2016). Defining rural in gifted education research: Methodological challenges and paths forward. *Journal of Advanced Academics, 27*, 245–265.

Lamb, J., & Daniels, R. (1993). Gifted girls in a rural community: Math attitudes and career options. *Exceptional Children, 59*(6), 513–517. https://doi.org/10.1177/001440299305900604

Lassig, C. (2015). Teachers' attitudes towards the gifted: The importance of professional development and school culture. *Australasian Journal of Gifted Education, 24*(2), 6–16. Retrieved from https://search-informit-com-au.ezproxy.csu.edu.au/fullText;dn=210156;res= AEIPT. ISSN: 1323-9686

Laura, R., & Smith, S. (2009). The reenchantment of science education: Towards a new vision of engaging rural gifted children in science. In T. Lyons, J.-Y. Choi, & G. McPhan (Eds.), *Symposium proceedings: International symposium for innovation in rural education (ISFIRE 2009): Improving equity in rural education* (pp. 153–166). Armidale, NSW: SiMERR National Centre, University of New England.

Lawrence, B. K. (2009). Rural gifted education: A comprehensive literature review. *Journal for the Education of the Gifted, 32*, 461–494. https://doi.org/10.1177/016235320903200402

Leigo, T., & Cansdale, D. (29 March, 2016). NAPLAN report reveals gap between city and country schools widening: Grattan Institute. Retrieved from http://www.abc.net.au/news/2016-03-29/naplan-report-reveals-divide-between-city-and-country-widens/7280916

Merrotsy, P. (2011). Teaching gifted aboriginal children. In N. Harrison (Ed.), *Teaching and learning in aboriginal education* (pp. 77–86). Melbourne, VIC: Oxford University Press.

Miller, J., Graham, L., & Al-Awiwe, A. (2014). Fast track, bush track: Late career female school leaders taking the slow road. *Australian and International Journal of Rural Education, 24*(1), 91–102.

Mutch, C. (2013). *Doing educational research: A practitioner's guide to getting started* (2nd ed.). Wellington, New Zealand: New Zealand Council for Educational research (NZCER Press).

NSW Department of Education and Communities. (2013). *Rural and remote education: A blueprint for action*. Retrieved from https://education.nsw.gov.au/teaching-and-learning/curriculum/rural-and-distance-education/media/documents/Rural-and-Remote-Education-Blueprint-accessible.pdf

Nye, A. (2014). Connections of place and generation: Women teachers in rural schools in NSW. *Australian and International Journal of Rural Education, 24*(3), 69–81.

Olszewski-Kubilius, P., Corwith, S., & Calvert, E. (2015). Serving rural gifted students through supplemental and out-of-school programming. In T. Stambaugh & S. M. Wood (Eds.), *Serving gifted students in rural settings*. Waco, TX: Prufrock Press.

Parliament of Australia (2001). The education of gifted and talented children. Canberra: Parliament of Australia.

Paul, K. A., & Seward, K. K. (2016). Place-based investment model of talent development: A proposed model for developing and reinvesting talents within the community. *Journal of Advanced Academics, 27*, 311–342. https://doi.org/10.1177/1932202X16669546

Periathiruvadi, S., & Rinn, A. N. (2012). Technology in gifted education. *Journal of Research on Technology in Education, 45*(2), 153–169. https://doi.org/10.1080/15391523.2012.10782601

Plunkett, M. (2012). Justice for rural gifted students. In S. Nikakis (Ed.), *Let the tall poppies flourish: Advocating to achieve educational justice for all gifted students*. Heidelberg, VIC: Heidelberg Press.

Puryear, J. S., & Kettler, T. (2017). Rural gifted education and the effect of proximity. *Gifted Child Quarterly, 61*, 143–152.

Richards, Z. J., & Stambaugh, T. (2015). National context of rural schools. In T. Stambaugh & S. M. Wood (Eds.), *Serving gifted students in rural settings*. Waco, TX: Prufrock Press.

Rowan, L., & Townend, G. (2016). Early career teachers' beliefs about their preparedness to teach: Implications for the professional development of teachers working with gifted and twice-exceptional students. *Cogent Education, 3*, 1242458. https://doi.org/10.1080/2331186X.2016.1242458

Rowley, J. (2012). Teaching strategies to facilitate learning for gifted and talented students. *Australasian Journal of Gifted Education, 17*(2), 36–42.

Rural and Remote Education Advisory Council. (n.d.) RREAC report. Retrieved from http://rreac.des.wa.gov.au/SiteCollectionDocuments/Future%20uses%20of%20technology%20in%20rural%20and%20remote%20schools.pdf

Schirmer, J. (2016). UC study finds regional Australians feeling good, but lack connections. Retrieved from https://www.canberra.edu.au/about-uc/media/media-releases/2016/june/uc-study-finds-regional-australians-feeling-good,-but-lack-connections

Smith, G. A. (2002). Going local. *Educational Leadership, 60*(1), 30–33.

Stambaugh, T. (2015). Concluding thoughts and voices from gifted individuals in rural areas. In T. Stambaugh & S. M. Wood (Eds.), *A framework for bridging gifted education and rural classrooms: Serving students in rural settings*. Waco, TX: Prufrock Press.

Stats NZ. (2016). *Defining urban and rural New Zealand*. Retrieved from http://archive.stats.govt.nz/browse_for_stats/Maps_and_geography/Geographic- areas/urban-rural-profile/defining-urban-rural-nz.aspx

Stats NZ. (2017). Retrieved from http://nzdotstat.stats.govt.nz/wbos/Index.aspx?DataSetCode=TABLECODE7541#

Thomson, S., De Bortoli, L., & Buckley, S. (2013). *PISA in brief: Highlights from the full Australian report: PISA 2012: How Australia measures up*. Retrieved from https://research.acer.edu.au/ozpisa/14

Thraves, G., & Bannister-Tyrrell, M. (2017). Australian aboriginal peoples and giftedness: A diverse issue in need of a diverse response. *TalentEd, 29*, 18–31.

VanTassel Baska, J., & Hubbard, G. F. (2016). Classroom based strategies for advanced learners in rural settings. *Journal of Advanced Academics, 27*(4), 285–310. https://doi.org/10.1177/1932202X16657645

Vialle, W. J. (2011). *Giftedness from an indigenous perspective*. Wollongong, NSW: AAEGT.

Warwick, I., Dickenson, M., & Speakman, R. (2010). *National rural network for gifted and talented education: Guidance for rural and isolated schools*. London, England: London Gifted & Talented.

Whitebread, D., Coltman, P., Pino Pasternak, D., Sangster, C., Grau, V., Bingham, S., . . . Demetriou, D. (2008). The development of two observational tools for assessing metacognition and self-regulated learning in young children. *Metacognition and Learning, 4*, 63–85.

Wilson, S., Lyons, T., & Quinn, F. (2013). "Should I stay or should I go?" Rural and remote students in first year STEM courses. *Australian and International Journal of Rural Education, 23*(2), 77–88.

Wood, D. (2015). *Beauty or brains? The impact of popular culture on the development of adolescent rural gifted girls' identity and subsequent talent development.* (Unpublished doctoral dissertation). University of Wollongong, Wollongong, NSW.

Wood, D., & Zundans-Fraser, L. (2012). Reaching out: Overcoming distance and supporting rural gifted students through educational opportunities. *The Australasian Journal of Gifted Education, 22*(1), 42–50.

Michelle Bannister-Tyrrell, PhD, was a senior lecturer and the Director of Program Impact and Innovation at the University of New England. After teaching in schools for more than three decades as both a primary and secondary teacher with gifted students, her research now includes under-identified gifted students such as rural, Indigenous, low socio-economic, and twice-exceptional students. Michelle has regularly presentsed her research at international, national, and state conferences. Her thesis was awarded the 2015 John Geake Outstanding Thesis Award presented at the AAEGT, and in 2014, she won the Beth Southwell Research Award for outstanding thesis from the NSW Institute for Education Research.

Denise Wood, PhD, has been an advocate for, and teacher of, gifted students for more than 30 years, in rural NSW in Australia. She has worked with gifted students in classrooms and in a range of provisions from a full-time classroom to smaller part-time programs. Currently in the higher education sector, Denise has written and presented subjects in gifted education in undergraduate and postgraduate teacher education programs and presented programs of professional learning to classroom teachers across regional NSW. Her research interests include the support for gifted students throughout their schooling, and, in particular, rural adolescent gifted girls and rural gifted women, and their talent development, building on the findings from her thesis.

Homeschooling the Gifted: What Do We Know from the Australian, Chilean, and US Context?

María Leonor Conejeros-Solar and Susen R. Smith

Contents

M. L. Conejeros-Solar (✉)
Escuela de Pedagogía, Pontificia Universidad Católica de Valparaíso, Viña del Mar, Chile
e-mail: leonor.conejeros@pucv.cl

S. R. Smith
GERRIC, School of Education, University of New South Wales, Sydney, NSW, Australia
e-mail: susen.smith@unsw.edu.au

© Crown 2021
S. R. Smith (ed.), *Handbook of Giftedness and Talent Development in the Asia-Pacific*,
Springer International Handbooks of Education,
https://doi.org/10.1007/978-981-13-3041-4_72

Abstract

The homeschooling movement has steadily developed in the last couple of decades, especially in the USA. In Australia and Chile, the movement is still growing as an alternative to school education. The social growth of homeschooling entails visions of support and criticism. Some consider it an approach to meet and foster children's interests and needs, and others consider it a private movement against public education and democratic societies. Motivations for homeschooling are mostly related to ideological and pedagogical conceptions in the way families approach homeschooling. In terms of research, in the last two decades, there's been a growth in peer-reviewed publications to better understand its motivations, implications, educational provisions, and outcomes. Homeschooling for gifted students in particular has little research, and the findings from the few studies that are available suggest that these families start homeschooling for different reasons compared to the general homeschool population. While research on homeschooling gifted students from the USA dominates, not much is heard about homeschooling research in Australia and even less is evident from the Chilean homeschooling experience. In this scenario, more research is needed about gifted homeschooling and the inner experiences these families and children face. In this chapter, findings are presented from a theoretical review in an effort to contribute to the understanding of this educational provision for gifted children and delve deeper into the options these families have in the context of Australia, Chile, and the USA.

Keywords

Gifted students · Homeschooling · Motivations · Socialisation · Provisions · Research

The aims in this chapter are to:

- Provide a theoretical understanding of the homeschooling educational modality in the American, Australian, and Chilean contexts.
- Identify the practices associated with the homeschooling modality and characteristics of students and families.
- Reiterate the legal status and regulations of homeschooling.
- Discuss curriculum provision in homeschooling.
- Discern motivations to homeschool gifted students.
- Explore concerns about socialisation and friendship building in homeschooling.

- Identify facilitators and difficulties that arise from the implementation of homeschooling for gifted students.
- Suggest future research and practice in homeschooling for gifted students.

Introduction

Homeschooling education can be defined as a form of educational provision for school-age children, between the ages 5 and 17, within the home setting. Consequently, parents decide not to send their children to a public or registered private school service and educate their children through a parent, family member, tutor, computer-related instruction, or a combination of services (D'Amato & Gundrum, 2017; King, 2018; Medlin, 2000).

Homeschooling for gifted students has become more of an option for families in the last two decades (Jolly & Matthews, 2017a) even though the homeschooling movement emerged in the 1970s as parents started to educate their children at home (Isenberg, 2007; Kunzman & Gaither, 2013). This educational modality has cultivated a series of social myths that include the thoughts that it produces social misfits or bad citizens, who may have difficulty entering college, with the main reason to homeschool being religious beliefs (Carpenter & Gann, 2015; Jolly & Matthews, 2018c; Romanowski, 2006).

As documented in previous studies on homeschooling, generally, parents' motivations to homeschool their children are based mainly on four broad reasons: (a) discontent with traditional school environments; (b) pedagogical and academic concerns; (c) religious values; and (d) family needs (Collom, 2005; Hanna, 2012; Jolly & Matthews, 2018c). In the case of Australia, Jackson and Allan (2010) found that families home educate their children basically for two reasons: first, negative views (real or perceived) associated with education in mainstream institutions and, second, the benefits (real or perceived) of educating their children in this modality. In the case of Chile, in a survey that included 67 homeschooling families in 2014, Aliaga (2017) found that when they were asked to prioritise between four types of reasons, the percentages obtained were the following: (a) pedagogical (33%), (b) ideological (31%), (c) psychological (21%), and (d) religious (15%).

In relation to families of gifted children, the limited empirical literature available (Jolly & Matthews, 2018a, 2017a; Jolly, Matthews, & Nester, 2013; Kula, 2018) suggests that these families often decide to homeschool only after numerous attempts to achieve effective education for their child in traditional schools (Jolly & Matthews, 2017b). In a previous study, Winstanley (2009) indicated that the reasons to homeschool varied from those of the general homeschool population and are more focused in pragmatic reasons rather than moral ones. The decision to homeschool gifted children appears to be precipitated by a combination of factors, and some of these include: (a) schools' lack of understanding of students who have both a learning disability and an advanced intellectual ability; (b) parents' perceptions of the difficulties their child has to face in a specific school environment related with an increased intensity of social and emotional issues; and (c) the teacher or school's inability or unwillingness to provide an accelerated curriculum (Jolly et al., 2013).

Research on gifted homeschoolers is still in the early stages of development and scarce, with most research from the US experience (Jolly & Matthews, 2017a, 2017b; Kula, 2018; Winstanley, 2009). Due to the lack of research in homeschooling the gifted in both Australia and Chile, research beyond the North American research needs to be undertaken to provide a more profound understanding of homeschooling as a form of educational choice for gifted families and their children in different regions of the world. Hence, in this chapter, we aim to contribute to the homeschooling literature with a theoretical review to narrow this gap with a focus in three Pacific Rim countries, Australia, Chile, and the USA, exploring the current homeschooling research literature and the emerging research literature across three disparate contexts.

Homeschooling Generally

The Homeschooling Movement

Homeschooling is as old as education and was the way in which parents and tutors educated the young population before the emergence of the public-school system that expanded from the nineteenth century into the twentieth century (Gaither, 2017a; King, 2018). The so-called homeschooling movement commenced in the late 1970s in the USA when an increasing number of families started to home educate motivated by a distrust in traditional education and inspired by the American school reformer and educator John Holt, who argued that children need to learn naturally and free from formal education (Jolly & Matthews, 2017a; Pell, 2018). By the 1980s, the dominant group was represented by conservative Christians (Jolly & Matthews, 2017a; Kula, 2018; Romanowski, 2006). Since then, homeschooling has diversified culturally, demographically, structurally, and geographically and spread globally (Gaither, 2009, 2017b; Jolly & Matthews, 2018c; Rothermel, 2015). This rebirth, in the words of Ray (2017a), "after about a century of quiescence has surprised many educators, sociologists, political scientists, historians, and theologians, and has captured the imagination and engagement of hundreds of thousands of families" (p. 86).

Gaither (2017a) explains that this increase in implementation has often been called the 'homeschooling movement', because the families involved have been engaged in legal and political actions to keep their children at home. This movement has been documented widely and strongly, mainly by researchers from the USA, even though homeschooling emerged in many parts of the world roughly at the same time. So, homeschooling can be considered a global movement in which different regions have developed their own legal policies and educational provisions (Gaither, 2017b).

Adherents' and Opponents' Perspectives of Homeschooling Education

Even though home education is a legal practice in all 50 US states and has become (King, 2018; Ray, 2017c) a solid educational alternative for a diverse range of children, whether they are gifted or not, some voices have been raised in concern about it. For example, it is suggested that homeschooling represents an individualistic positive conception of education, instead of a collective effort that is good for the education of the next generation (Brewer & Lubienski, 2017; Lubienski, 2000, 2003).

Others argue that homeschooling—as well as private schooling—fosters political intolerance and the unwillingness to be considerate of different viewpoints and beliefs that Cheng (2014) refutes based on a research study conducted with 304 undergraduate students who attended an evangelical Christian university and answered a content-controlled political-tolerance scale. The results suggested that a greater exposure to homeschooling—instead of a public school—is associated with more political tolerance. Despite these results, the author indicated that these findings are not sufficient to establish causal relationships, due to factors that were not possible to observe, like the motivations behind the reasons for choosing homeschooling, that could be leading to more political tolerance in these students.

Research Complexities on Homeschooling

Research on homeschooling is complex due to its diversity and limited access to related information and because the basic demographic data is unavailable (Gaither, 2017b; Kunzman & Gaither, 2013). Also, issues have emerged that are related with the anecdotal quality of the research that has already been conducted (Murphy 2014). A critique of the research conducted in the USA suggests homeschooling is politically motivated (Kunzman & Gaither, 2013). In this respect, Gaither (2017a) asserts that a large number of the studies have been developed and published independently with the support of the homeschooling advocacy organisation *Home School Legal Defense Association* (HSLDA), through his organisation the *National Home Education Research Institute* (NHERI). However, these studies present some design limitations and generalisations in their conclusions that need to be taken with care (Gaither, 2008; Kunzman & Gaither, 2013).

Another complexity exposed by Howell (2013) is that research in homeschooling is neglected by educational institutions because of a dominant educational research approach that is focused on quantitative analyses, data comparison, standardised settings, and large samples which could lead to little interest in its study. Howell suggested that instead of trying to find which educational mode is better than the other, more positive and useful outcomes for teachers and parents who home educate will be knowing the factors that affect motivation and learning in different educational contexts. Indeed, Gaither (2017b) points out that English-speaking countries like Australia, the UK, and bilingual Canada are the ones in which it is possible to find additional scholarship work besides the USA.

In light of the key issues raised above, the following sections provide overviews of North American, Australian, and Chilean homeschooling generally regarding: (a) legal status and regulations, (b) motivations, (c) concerns about socialisation and friendship building, and (d) curriculum provision.

Homeschooling in the USA

Reviewing the homeschooling movement in the USA is relevant because this country represents the main focus of theoretical and empirical research on this topic. Some consider this educational modality has reached certain maturity and is therefore a mandatory reference for researchers in other regions (Gaither, 2017b; Kunzman & Gaither, 2013).

While some suggest that the number of children who are being home educated in the USA has been growing steadily in the last 30 years (Gaither, 2017a; Ray, 2017c; Riley, 2015; Shepherd, 2015), others suggest a steep trajectory of growth of this education modality with undercalculated student numbers (e.g., Jolly & Matthews, 2018c). In the 2015 academic school year, approximately 2,200,000 US students did not attend public or private schools and were educated at home (Ray, 2017a). Brewer and Lubienski (2017) suggest that even though this practice has been growing and some of its advocates claim that homeschooling 'may be the fastest-growing form of education in the United States' (Ray, 2016, p. 1), it still remains a relatively small percentage of the educational practices, representing approximately 4% of all students.

The families in this modality do not receive public funding for their children's education since they are not attending public schools. This funding represents over $27 billion that American taxpayers do not have to spend (Ray, 2016). The cost of homeschooling then falls on the families as providers of educational resources (Hurlbutt, 2011; Hurlbutt-Eastman, 2017; Jolly et al., 2013). Another cost that is associated with homeschooling is that some parents are not able to continue with their work outside the home with the consequence of the loss of one of the family members' income and the subsequent precarisation and accommodation that this situation implies (Brewer & Lubienski, 2017).

Legal Status and Regulations Regarding Homeschooling in the USA

Since 1983, a legal defence association called the HSLDA, which is a Christian-based group, was established to protect the constitutional rights of parents to home educate their children and legalise this educational modality (Kolenc, 2017; Lagos, 2011). In 1993, homeschooling became legal in the USA; nevertheless, each one of the 50 states has its own unique homeschooling law (Gaither, 2017a; Kolenc, 2017). Within this diversity, it is possible to find lax, moderate, and extreme regulations.

For example, no notice of homeschool intention is needed in 11 states; parents' requirements of notification to local or state educational offices are needed in 15 states, while in the others, requirements are for homeschool curriculum approval by the state; home visits are undertaken by state officials; and present test scores or student progress is within the context of professionals' evaluations (Pell, 2018).

In this scenario, the way in which each state approaches homeschoolers' data collection also varies and could be done in a very haphazard fashion; only few states keep meticulous records (Gaither, 2017a). Related to this, a 2012 national survey about homeschooling in the USA by the *National Center for Education Statistics* of the Department of Education (NCES), found that "most homeschooled students were white (83 percent) and nonpoor (89 percent), lived in cities or suburban areas and rural areas" (Redford, Battle, & Bielick, 2016, p. ii). In relation to their parents' educational level, the higher percentage had vocational degrees or some college education, 23% of them had a high school degree, and 18% a graduate degree, while only 2% of the parents had less than a high school education degree (Redford et al., 2016). King (2018) argued that today homeschoolers are more diverse, with families belonging to different ethnic and racial backgrounds (African and Hispanic-Americans for example) and also coming from a wider geographic distribution.

Motivations for Homeschooling in the USA

One of the key works in the area of motivations that lead parents to decide to educate their children at home was the one developed by Jane Van Galen in the late 1980s. She established two differentiating categories of parents: the pedagogues and the ideologues, mainly by interviewing 23 parents from 16 homeschooling families (Van Galen, 1987, 1991). See Jolly and Matthews (2018c) for a detailed overview of Van Galen's theory of homeschooling.

The ideologue parents are characterised as being Christian fundamentalists and conservatives. They prioritise the transmission of their own values and beliefs and wish to strengthen family relationships that they think are diminished by the excessive time children spend in schools, and they express objection to public/private school teaching (Hanna, 2012; Lois, 2017; Van Galen, 1987, 1991). On the other hand, the pedagogues prioritise individuality and creativity in learning. They often share the conviction that children can develop their innate abilities in a holistic, unstructured, and natural way and have a lack of confidence in schools because of what they perceived as an inability to teach properly (Hanna, 2012; Lois, 2017; Van Galen, 1987, 1991). Like any bilateral categorisation—that is found in Van Galen's interpretation of homeschooling—it is insufficient to simply describe the wide diversity of motives that each family expresses, as they are usually multidimensional and related with their particular circumstances and context (Jolly et al., 2013; Murphy, Gaither, & Gleim, 2017). This is why other researchers have elaborated and expanded Van Galens's work, like Mayberry (1988), who identified four categories of parents, after analysing more than 500 surveys and 15 in-depth interviews. These were: (a) religious, (b) academic, (c) socio-relational, and (d) new-age parents. She explains that one way to understand this categorisation is to read it as a complement to the antecedent established by Van Galen. In this way, religious and new-age parents are linked to the notion of ideological parents, while academic and socio-relational parents are linked to the notion of pedagogical parents (Lois, 2017; Mayberry, 1988). Nemer, in 2002, suggested to transform Van Galen's typology into descriptors—ideological motivations and pedagogical motivations— that would fall into a continuum of motivations from low to high degree. Kunzman and Gaither (2013) in a review of 351 research articles pointed out that researchers have continued to use Van Galen's basic categories even though some have proposed new terminology when they found it inadequate, proving that her work is "remarkably resilient" (p. 13).

Related to survey results in this topic, the NCES (2012) survey, showed that the top reason (91%) for homeschooling identified by parents was their concerns about the school environment (safety, negative peer pressure). The second reason was a desire to provide moral instruction (77%), followed by dissatisfaction with academic instruction in schools (74%), and a desire to provide religious instruction (64%) (Redford et al., 2016). These results show that concerns about academic quality at schools are one of the primary reasons for homeschooling (Bielick, Chandler, & Broughman, 2001; Collom, 2005; Kula, 2018; Martin-Chang & Levesque, 2017), ahead of religious reasons, which was a major motivation three decades ago (Jolly & Matthews, 2018c; Kunzman & Gaither, 2013; Murphy et al., 2017).

Concerns About Socialisation and Friendship Building in US Homeschooling

One of the areas that arouse the most concern is the one related with socialisation, with stereotypical claims by outside viewers that homeschoolers lack enough contact with peers and public interactions, so students are socially isolated. Homeschooler advocates reply that they provided sufficient opportunities for social encounters outside the family, like extracurricular activities and group learning (Kunzman, 2017; Kunzman & Gaither, 2013; Murphy, 2014; Ray 2017b). Paradoxically, difficulties associated with socialisation are one of the reasons parents indicated their decision to homeschool (46%) when surveyed by the NCES (2012; Redford et al., 2016).

In a review conducted by Kunzman and Gaither (2013), they found 72 empirical studies on the issue of socialisation and homeschooling. Most of them focused on social interactions and evaluation of social skills through different methods, but the majority of studies relied on self-reporting by parents and/or students. The results point out that when comparing homeschoolers with schooled students in different social skills and participation in extracurricular activities for group interaction, both groups have similar outcomes. In another review of research on socialisation, Medlin (2013) synthesised that, when compared with children in conventional schools, results suggested that homeschoolers have "higher quality friendships and better relationships with their parents and other adults. They are happy, optimistic, and satisfied with their lives" (p. 284).

In relation to peer victimisation between homeschoolers and school students, data from small convenience samples didn't find differences (Green-Hennessy, 2014; Reavis & Zakriski, 2005). When social networks were compared, both groups seem to have a similar amount of intimate friends (Medlin, 2013; Reavis & Zakriski, 2005).

Researchers suggested that more empirical research with random and bigger samples is needed, to avoid favouring socially desirable responses on this issue (Green-Hennessy, 2014; Kunzman, 2017; Kunzman & Gaither, 2013; Medlin, 2013; Murphy, 2014).

Curriculum Provision in US Homeschooling

The homeschooling movement is based initially on the ideas of John Holt, an educator and writer who was searching throughout the 1970s for new ways to foster learning and growth in children. He was influenced by the ideas of Paul Goodman, a social and education critic, and Ivan Illich, a philosopher and activist (Farenga, 2010; Holt & Farenga, 2003; Pell, 2018). Holt didn't like the terms homeschooling or deschooling, "so he invented the word unschooling to better describe learning that does not have to occur at home and that does not resemble school" (Farenga, 2010, p. 216). Unschooling refers to child-directed learning that allows the child freedom to learn and explore what they want all the time without the disapproval from adults. Families work with the children's interests and abilities; they use learning opportunities instead of a standard curriculum. Some terms that are used interchangeably with unschooling are natural learning, self-directed learning, and child-led learning (English, 2013; Farenga, 2010; Haugh, 2014; Kula, 2018; Pell, 2018).

Within the homeschooling movement, it is possible to encounter categories that were created for different models or approaches for learning. In this context, there are broadly two streams, a traditional and a non-traditional educational philosophy or unschooling (Farenga, 2010; Hanna, 2012; Kula, 2018). A traditional approach accentuates structured curricula and obedience and compliance to authority; the non-traditional approach highlights the learner's autonomy and independence while encouraging the questioning of authority, which is considered a characteristic of the gifted child (Clark, 2013). Between these two streams, it is feasible to find eclectic homeschoolers (who use anything they think can work, combine other approaches, and can also involve part-time school attendance, distance education courses or e-learning, all of which would suit the learning needs of gifted children); classical homeschoolers (who include the study of classical literature, grammar, logic, and rhetorical thought, an approach that may benefit intellectually gifted learners in particular); and some other homeschooler groups who think of homeschooling as a way to teach arithmetic, reading, and writing and the values that are important for them that are depreciated at traditional schools. They can also follow a specific educational philosophy such as Montessori (i.e., focused on genuine everyday experiences, encourages learning at children's own pace which uses all the five senses, which aligns well with accelerating gifted learners) and

Waldorf/Steiner (which highlights children's imagination, fantasy, creative thinking, and analytical thinking and matches well with the learning needs of creatively gifted children) or the Charlotte Mason approach (which is rooted in the medieval university and trivium curriculum, which exposes children to different sources of knowledge and can parallel with gifted students' interests; Anthony & Burroughs, 2012; Bauer & Wise, 2016; Farenga, 2010; Kula, 2018).

Regarding academic achievement, research has found that structured homeschooling is associated with some positive achievements in relation to verbal skills predominantly (Green-Hennessy, 2014; Kunzman & Gaither, 2013; Martin-Chang, Gould, & Meuse, 2011). Even though it is not clear if the homeschooling itself was the cause of this outcome, it reflects high parental involvement that has been associated with good results (Barwegen, Falciani, Putnam, Reamer, & Star, 2004; Jolly & Matthews, 2017b; Kunzman & Gaither, 2013; Lubienski, Puckett, & Brewer, 2013; Ray, 2013). Another aspect consistently associated with positive achievement results and instructional quality for homeschoolers is parental educational background (Belfield, 2005; Kunzman, 2009; Kunzman & Gaither, 2013).

Furthermore, a longitudinal study was conducted by Hanna (2012) between 1998 and 2008 with 250 families in Pennsylvania regarding instruction, materials, and curricula used by the families. She found that, as children get older, the homeschooling experience is characterised by the search for more support in networks built with other families, co-operative instruction, and internet resources. For example, computer-related instruction to support student learning has increased in homeschooling as the technology has developed exponentially since the 1980s, become more readily available, and is a more economical resource to use (Jolly & Matthews, 2018c).

Additionally, Isenberg (2007) found that only 63% of homeschoolers continued to be homeschooled after the first year and that 15% from secular homes and 48% from religious ones remain homeschooled after six years. These results show a decrease in the growth of homeschooling as children age (Kunzman & Gaither, 2013).

Homeschooling in Australia

The homeschooling modality has a long history in this vast country—especially in rural and remote areas where access to schools is inhibited due to distance—and has become part of the educational options since the late 1970s (Jackson, 2017a).

In relation to research, there's a growing body of literature on various aspects of home education that come from academic projects, postgraduate- and honours-level studies, and demographic information research, such as motivations, students' perceptions, learning processes, academic success, students' competencies, social development, parents' management of the home education process, special needs, home education in rural areas, and legislative and legal aspects in all Australian states (Allan & Jackson, 2010; Jackson 2017a, 2017b; Select Committee on Home Schooling, Legislative Council, NSW Parliament, 2014).

One aspect that researchers in the area make clear is that the three decades of research carried out in the Australian context reveal different results—in relation to the practice and experience of home education—to the research carried out in the USA. In this sense, they warn researchers and academics about the need to consider these conceptual frameworks and results with caution and to not assume that it equates to home education in Australia or in other countries (Allan & Jackson, 2010; English, 2015; Jackson, 2017a, 2017b).

About the number of home educators, data related to the extent of registered students at a national level from all the states and territories between 2011and 2017 show that this educational modality has experienced a sustained growth of around 82%. The total number of registered home education students in 2017 was 19,004, whereas in mainstream education institutions, there were a total of 3,849,000 students (Chapman, 2017). Hence, it can be estimated that the number of homeschooled gifted students would be in the thousands. However, generally, the real number of homeschooled students remains unknown because some families do not formalise the registration of their children (Select Committee on Home Schooling, Legislative Council, NSW Parliament, 2014). Nonetheless, Allan and Jackson (2010) indicate that families who home educate can be found in rural, remote, suburban, and city locations and represent all types of families, inclusive of families with gifted children.

Legal Status and Regulations Regarding Homeschooling in Australia

Home education in Australia is a legal and accepted alternative to school education (Allan & Jackson, 2010; Harding, 2011; Jackson & Allan, 2010). There isn't a national regulation, which implies that the six states and two territories that make up the country have different regulations and procedures (Jackson & Allan, 2010). Allan and Jackson (2010) argue that, "a more consistent regulatory framework is needed across Australia. Such a framework should facilitate and encourage children who are being home educated, rather than police home educating families" (p. 55). Indeed, such a framework needs to include the varieties of educational approaches that home education families have been providing (Allan & Jackson, 2010; Jackson, 2014). Another aspect to consider is a national statutory definition of homeschooling, as only New South Wales, the Australian Capital Territory and Queensland provide one (Select Committee on Home Schooling, Legislative Council, NSW Parliament, 2014).

The term homeschooling is used for the majority of researchers in Australia, but most researchers from Victoria and Tasmania refer to it as home education to insist that this is not just about the school practice at home. Other terms used include unschooling and natural learning (Jackson, 2017a; Paine, 2018). Jackson (2017a) affirms that for many researchers "these distinctions have not been significant" (p. 347).

Since the work of Barratt-Peacock in the late 1990s, it is possible to observe tensions between regulations, legislatures, and families, especially in those states with more tight controls (Barratt-Peacock, 1997). This tension highlights that in Australia, its states and territorial governments do not agree with the idea that education in the case of homeschoolers is only the domain of the family, and that is why they have established their own register of regimes and, in some states, requirements of approval of education programs (Harding, 2011). The Australian-governing authorities agree with the idea that "parents had the right to determine the education of their children but also acknowledged the state's need to be assured that the children's right to an education was upheld through family practice" (Jackson, 2017a, p. 342).

Further discourse and research about this topic are still needed as a way to provide evidence and direction on behalf of the students' interests—especially as there is such a diverse range of students' needs currently being addressed in the homeschooling context, including diversely different gifted children (Allan & Jackson, 2010; Conejeros-Solar & Smith, 2019; Harding, 2011; Jackson, 2014; Jackson, 2017a; Liberto, 2016).

Motivations for Homeschooling in Australia

Australia is a country and continent surrounded by the Indian and Pacific Oceans with a land mass of 7,692 million kilometres, of which over half is considered rural or remote (Bureau of Rural Sciences, 2018). There are "five mainland remoteness categories based on road distances between locations and five different sized service centres, namely Major Cities, Inner Regional, Outer Regional, Remote Areas, and Very Remote Areas" (Halsey, 2017, p. 13). Hence, one would expect that specific motivators for homeschooling in the Australian context would be distance and isolation due to the enormity of the country and concerns expressed by home-schoolers, such as:

> Imagine you haven't seen another kid in three months. The mail plane arrives only every three weeks as you anxiously wait for it just to connect with the rest of the world. You have been flooded in for 12 weeks with nothing to do and nowhere to go, just water for kilometres and your imagination. Our students face challenges like these every day. It is hard to envision a future when you're living in severe isolation and finding it hard to connect with the world. (Anonymous, 2008, p. 78)

From the necessity to homeschool due to the remote location, extreme weather conditions or medical reasons, school of the air and virtual schooling have evolved in this context (Halsey, 2017). However, Jackson (2017a) asserts that different researchers give different reasons for homeschooling depending on the sample that was being used and that a good way to group these reasons is to consider the two major characteristics of the decisions as were described in the late 1990s by Hertzel (1997) and used in Australia in the work of Patrick (1999). These are the push and pull factors (negative experiences and positive entries, respectively) between traditional schools and home education. Croft (2013) adds that, instead of classifying types of motivations for homeschooling, it is more useful to assess the direction of the motivation. From this way of organising the motivational factors, Jackson and Allan (2010) indicated that the reasons families have to home educate fall into two categories that could be real or perceived: (a) negative aspects of traditional schools, like learning difficulties not catered for, especially for children with special needs, instruction or curriculum not meeting student's needs and/or interests such as for gifted students, large-sized classes, lower academic achievement, negative peer pressure or bullying that are often experienced by gifted students, low self-esteem, children's unhappiness with school and contrasting values between the school and home and (b) benefits of educating children at home, like broader curriculum and social experiences with a wider age range of people, holistic learning with greater connection with the real world, flexible learning to cater to the students' individual needs, low teacher-student ratio (one-to-one), values teaching, academic benefits, and tight family relations.

Conejeros-Solar and Smith's (2019) research on homeschooling in Australia found that parents considered there were many reasons for homeschooling their gifted child, but mainly the mismatch between the traditional school and their gifted children's learning needs turned them towards homeschooling. In regard to students with special needs, Kidd and Kaczmarek (2010), in a research study with ten mothers who homeschooled their children with *Autism Spectrum Disorder* (ASD), found that the reasons they wielded for homeschooling were mainly related to cognitive and educational challenges at school, lack of understanding of ASD by the teachers, and school stress and anxiety.

Concerns About Socialisation and Friendship Building in Australian Homeschooling

Jackson (2017a, 2017b) indicated that while there is no large research project in Australia specifically focused on the socialisation of children who are home educated, most of the research carried out partially addresses this topic. Generally, homeschooled students have positive and healthy social interactions, and they appreciate the social experiences they can get being at home with people of different ages. In this sense, their socialisation experiences are qualitatively different from their age peers at school and more similar to the experiences they can get in the adult world context (Allan & Jackson, 2010).

For those who reported that they had bad social experiences at school, being at home helped them to recover. Nonetheless, some homeschooled students would like to have more interaction opportunities with peers, even though special interest groups, home education network groups, and volunteer service opportunities, amongst others, are activities most of the families provide (Allan & Jackson, 2010; Croft, 2013; Jackson, 2017a, 2017b; Select Committee on Home Schooling, Legislative Council, NSW Parliament, 2014).

Curriculum Provision in Australian Homeschooling

The homeschooling families use a variety of educational approaches to learning (Select Committee on Home Schooling, Legislative Council, NSW Parliament, 2014). These approaches could be organised into a theoretical framework for homeschooling in which it is possible to find a gradation of three types of curriculum or family program: structured, eclectic (blended learning), and informal or unschooling or natural learning. These types may be used by families in a combination or continuum (Allan & Jackson, 2010; Croft, 2013; Jackson, 2017a).

Something that researchers have noticed is that homeschooling families tend to initially start with a more structured approach that follows the school model (mostly characterised by schedules, lesson plans, textbooks, and record keeping), but move to a more informal approach as they gain confidence and experience, especially in a long-term experience (English, 2013; Jackson, 2017a; Kidd & Kaczmarek, 2010; McDonald & Lopes, 2014).

Common methods that were described in Allan and Jackson's research (2010) included unit studies (focused on the child's interests and from that, linked with different subject areas), classical approach (Charlotte Mason, Montessori, Waldorf/Steiner, unschooling or natural learning), and eclectic approach (Croft, 2013; English, 2013; Select Committee on Home Schooling, Legislative Council, NSW Parliament, 2014).

Researchers point out that the broader curriculum, flexible learning to meet personal needs, holistic learning opportunities connected with the real world, and low student-teacher ratio are all positive benefits of home education in Australia (Allan & Jackson, 2010; Jackson & Allan, 2010, Jackson, 2017a, 2017b; Kidd & Kaczmarek, 2010).

Homeschooling in Chile

This South American country has a scarcity of research and formal publications in homeschooling. Only one published paper in a peer-reviewed journal and four theses were found, three of these from Master programs in Education. In regard to data collection, Aliaga (2017) stated that Chilean families have opted to de-school their children as an educational alternative in recent times. In relation to its prevalence, there is no official data available to account for this reality nor an official figure that allows us to know how many children and young people study outside the school context (Julio, 2016a; Poblete, 2016; Troncoso, 2015). The only approximate and informal data were published in an official newspaper in 2013; the information stated, after interviewing the director of a home education organisation, that it is estimated that the families in this modality are around a thousand (Sepulveda, 2013; Troncoso, 2015).

Legal Status and Regulations Regarding Homeschooling in Chile

There are no legal obstacles to home education in Chile (Aliaga, 2017; García, Barrera, & Alejandro, 2017). The Chilean Constitutional Policy (2017) establishes that parents have the preferential right and the duty to educate their children (Article 19 paragraph 10). The same article declares the freedom of teaching (paragraph 11). In respect to the General Educational Law 20370. Article 4 (Mineduc, 2009), 12 years of general education are mandatory in the country, but this is not restricted to school attendance (García et al., 2017).

A resource that is used for families that home educate is the validation of studies (Article 7, Exempt Decree 2272 of 2007). This validation means that people under 18 years old can take validation exams of Basic Education and/or Secondary Education if they don't have regular studies or their education has been interrupted (Mineduc, 2018a). To submit this annual evaluation, students need to be personally enrolled by their legal representatives or guardians. The Ministerial Regional Secretariats of Education will designate educational establishments as examining entities to validate studies of Basic and Secondary Education. These establishments will sign the record of grades, evaluation, and school promotion. The Decree Exempt 2272 (Mineduc, 2007) says that these establishments have to designate a coordinator for the examination process and set up the commissions with appropriate teachers to carry out the examination. This coordination has to be exercised by the establishment's director. Once the record of grades and promotion of students is complete, they are sent to the corresponding Regional Ministry of Education. To prepare for these exams, families need to use the official plans and programs of the Ministry of Education for the respective course or grade level; it is relevant to note that the Ministry of Education delivers these texts freely to the families. The validation exam from first to fourth year of General Basic Education consists of a global assessment, and for fifth year of General Basic Education to fourth year of High School, students need to undertake an exam for each course and sub-sector of learning or a global exam by level or cycle, which will include the subsectors of the General Training field (Mineduc, 2007). To be promoted, all pertinent learning sub-sectors to at least note 4.0 level (the note scale is 1–7), must be approved (Mineduc, 2018b).

This process, as reported in a qualitative research study with ten families from different regions of the country, generates uncertainty regarding the exams, because even though there is a regulation, the ignorance about it in many of the professionals and administration staff in the Ministerial Regional Secretariats of Education and in the schools causes social pressure and attrition in the mothers who educate at home (Poblete, 2016). Two important reasons for this are that homeschooling is an emergent modality that is still very unfamiliar (Aliaga, 2017; Julio, 2016a) and among the countries where home education is a legal option, Chile has minimal supervision (Cabo, 2012). The lack of supervision can be observed when families have to enrol every year for the validation exam. The registration process and the surrender to the exam experience will depend on their place of residence and the preparation and willingness of the educational establishment that is assigned for them. As these establishments have to create and apply for the annual examination, there isn't a standardised instrument by grade level or subject, so this aspect is complex because being based on the same National Curricular Bases, these evaluations present notable differences (Poblete, 2016).

In relation to some of the characteristics these families exhibit, Aliaga (2017), stated that in the survey he conducted in 2014 with a group of 67 families from different places in Chile, he found a high level of parental education in the group. Indeed, 74% of mothers had a higher education degree; the most representative professions were teachers, entrepreneurs, and engineers. Most parents were dedicated to their children's care, so they did not develop a remunerated activity, and only 21% of the group performed tasks in a dependent manner. In reference to fathers, 77% had a university degree and all of them worked. In regard to their geographical distribution, most of them lived in urban areas (78%).

Motivations for Homeschooling in Chile

In the few works carried out to date, some constants were observed. In the survey conducted by Aliaga (2017), the pedagogical reason appears as the most relevant with 33% of the total answers. In his words, this pedagogic motive could be understood as families who disagree with the school system, want a more personalised education in which their children could learn by discovering and where their way of learning is respected. Although the research developed by Julio (2016a) only considers one family as a case study, it also indicates that the main motivation is linked to the school ethos in its way of managing knowledge, its routines, its discipline, and in the belief that the school does not perform its task well. The study carried out by Troncoso (2015) who interviewed five families corroborates these findings. The parents expressed dissatisfaction with public, charter, and private education, distrust of teachers, and the feeling that the traditional school is not what they want for their children. In addition, they also manifest discontent with the academic quality of the education provided in these establishments.

The ideological (31%), psychological (21%), and religious (15%) reasons presented in Aliaga's survey (2017) are also present in the other studies. The ideological reasons indicated that education is a parent's task where more freedom, sharing more family time, and teaching more values are needed (Aliaga, 2017; Troncoso, 2015). The psychological reasons referred to an authentic parents' concern for the well-being of their sons and daughters and the avoidance of the hostile environment of the school or bullying (Julio, 2016b; Troncoso, 2015), two common motivations for homeschooling gifted students. The religious reasons are related with a desire to share and preserve with their children the Christian and moral principles that the family professes (Aliaga, 2017; Troncoso, 2015).

Poblete (2016) adds an interesting view that can be correlated with the reasons mentioned previously. She distinguishes at least two ways in which families decide to marginalise themselves from the traditional school system, first as part of a philosophy of life that has been thought of since before the birth of their children and, second, as a consequence of a negative school experience. The first view could be correlated with the ideological and religious reasons and the second one with the pedagogical and psychological ones. These two paths of non-schooling and deschooling could be understood, respectively, as a greater project, a conception of life and family and as the interruption or the withdrawal of the educational process from the school system, both of which are parallel ways into which families start homeschooling (Poblete, 2016).

Concerns About Socialisation and Friendship Building in Chilean Homeschooling

There isn't much reference to this topic in the Chilean research. Aliaga (2017) indicated through his survey that parents expressed that they provided their children with multiple socialisation opportunities and that their children show good skills and abilities to relate with people from different age groups. Indeed, with the global influence of technology, the different facebook groups, blogs, and organisations around them are considered communities that share learning and socialisation activities as well (Aliaga, 2017; Julio, 2016b; Poblete, 2016).

Curriculum Provision in Chilean Homeschooling

Poblete (2016) indicated that homeschooling in Chile is a hybrid between homeschooling and unschooling and that this combination, mixture, or absence of distinction between these concepts derives in practice that is redefined by its pro-tagonists as 'home education' and less frequently 'school at home' and 'natural learning'. In this context, families organise their educational provision in different ways: some create their own programs and activities; others are based in the Ministry of Education curriculum and books; and a third group uses virtual schools or the Waldorf/Steiner and Montessori approach (Aliaga, 2017; Poblete, 2016).

Regarding academic results, the only reference is the one that Aliaga (2017) provides from the survey, in which families expressed that all their children were approved for the national validation exam and that 86% of them achieved results in each category from good (5.0) to very good (7.0).

Homeschooling for the Gifted

Research on this specific group of homeschoolers is scarce in the North American context (Jolly & Matthews, 2017a; Jolly et al., 2013; Kula, 2018; Kunzman, 2009; Murphy et al., 2017). No empirical literature was found in this regard in the Australian nor Chilean contexts, while the only mentions in Australia were related with the need for research and prioritisation of this group (Jackson, 2017a, 2017b) and some reports and articles that reinforced motivations to homeschool (Croft,

2013; English, 2013; Jackson & Allan, 2010; Select Committee on Home Schooling, Legislative Council, NSW Parliament, 2014).

Researchers argue that the lack of systematic research and interest in this topic is surprising (Jolly & Matthews, 2017a, 2018a; Murphy et al., 2017). Winstanley (2009) explains that a reason could be related with the difficulty in defining this group because, in the home setting, assigning the label gifted is unnecessary and irrelevant as it is not related with provisions and funding activities as it is at schools.

A point of coincidence between academics is the need for research in this area, as a way to understand the experiences, choices, needs, best practices, socialisation, achievements, outcomes, and challenges of homeschooling families with gifted and twice-exceptional children (Jolly et al., 2013; Kula, 2018; Kunzman & Gaither, 2013; Ronksley-Pavia, Grootenboer, & Pendergast, 2019).

Representation of Gifted Children in Homeschooling

The occurrence of gifted children in the whole homeschool community is unknown. Gifted children are only one group of participants and a minority in this steadily growing homeschooled population (Jolly & Matthews, 2018a; Jolly et al., 2013). A reason Jolly and Matthews (2017a, 2017b) exposed is that in half of the US states gifted education is not mandatory. In this context, they estimated that if gifted children represent between 6% and 10% of the total school population (National Association for Gifted Children, n.d.), gifted students could be around 60,000–200,000 from a total homeschool population ranging from one to two million children.

Motivations for Homeschooling Gifted Students

The motivations that have been described by parents are linked in many cases with a dissatisfaction with mainstream schooling and how they are failing gifted students. This failure is associated with: the need of a more challenging and flexible curriculum; lack of teacher preparation to meet these learners' needs; teachers' lack of awareness of students with twice exceptionality; limited or non-existent provision for gifted and twice-exceptional students at the school; offering of educational options that do not consider the needs, interests, and characteristics of gifted children, like using gifted students to tutor other students, their need to accelerate, or participation in advanced classes, for example; dissatisfaction with the learning environment; and difficult social and emotional issues, like bullying and isolation (Freeman, 2001; Goodowens & Cannaday, 2018; Goodwin & Gustavson, 2009; Jolly & Matthews, 2018a, 2018b, 2018c; Jolly et al., 2013; Kula, 2018; Ronksley-Pavia et al., 2019; Winstanley, 2009). In a narrative-based Australian study, three of the eight student participants with twice exceptionalities expressed support for homeschooling as a way to address their emotional distress of not coping with general school and considered homeschooling as more interesting and of higher quality than general schooling (Ronksley-Pavia et al. (2019).

The scarce results of research available suggest that the motivations that lead these families to decide to marginalise themselves from the traditional school system is less of a deliberate choice and more of a last resort after other school options have been tried without success (Jolly & Matthews, 2017a, 2018a, 2018b; Rivero, 2002; Winstanley, 2009). In the words of Winstanley, "They are instead, making a pragmatic response to the situation they are in where schools cannot cope with their unusual children" (2009, p. 360). Is it then a forced decision that differentiates this group from the general homeschool population, more as Jolly and Matthews (2018a) express, a mismatch between services and needs than a philosophical disagreement with school goals. Parents want to stimulate and enhance the learning aspirations and curiosity of their gifted children, and they find that their progress in the traditional school environment has "stagnated or in some cases even regressed, in relation to the potential and learning expectations that their gifted identification status had implied" (Jolly, et al., 2013, p. 127).

Parents' Characteristics

In terms of parents' characteristics, the research shows that usually mothers have the primary responsibility of homeschooling, and this means they coordinate, organise and select curricular and extracurricular activities (Jolly & Matthews, 2018a). They have a range of educational backgrounds from high school diploma to university degrees (Ensign, 2000; Jolly & Matthews, 2018a; Kula, 2018).

An interesting aspect of these parents is that they engage in formal training and research when starting as a home educator (Hanna, 2012; Kula, 2018; Redford et al., 2016). This is not only restricted to parents who homeschool gifted children, but to the regular homeschoolers as well (Jolly et al., 2013).

Also, from the literature, it can be gleaned that for some parents who homeschool, they manage all the different tasks and responsibilities that this decision entails (i.e., caring of family, preparing lessons, meeting children's needs amongst others), which can be difficult, and they can experience emotional burden and burnout and feelings of frustration and isolation (Jolly et al., 2013; Kula, 2018; Kunzman & Gaither, 2013). Researchers provide suggestions to manage these difficulties when homeschooling a gifted student, for example, searching for external help, such as seeking experts, exploring online curricula, accessing homeschooling organisations, or undertaking outside courses (Jolly et al., 2013; Kula, 2018; Winstanley, 2009).

Kula (2018) affirms that homeschooling is not a panacea for all the families that are experiencing difficulties in traditional schools. Resources, time, parents' skills, knowledge, and energy are needed (Jolly et al., 2013). In the case of gifted children "who have uneven development and highly specific needs that do not fit traditional school systems" (Kula, 2018, p. 167), homeschooling can be a positive experience (Hurlbutt-Eastman, 2017; Winstanley, 2009).

Socialisation and Friendship Building of Homeschooled Gifted Students

Because of the particular characteristics of gifted children, sometimes finding intellectually engaging peers can be difficult in traditional schools and socialisation is
one of the reasons for school withdrawal (Clark, 2013; Gross, 2004; Winstanley,
2009). Homeschooling gives them the opportunity to build friendships that are based
on mutual interests in a relaxed context where they can express their abilities and
interests (Kula, 2018; Winstanley, 2009).

Jolly et al. (2013) called attention to the feeling of isolation as a cause of school
withdrawal and that some gifted students describe themselves as being outsiders.
In some cases, this feeling could continue or even intensify after leaving school. In
their research (Jolly et al. 2013), parents also reported this isolated feeling because
they cannot find empathetic peers in the wider homeschool parental community. This
disconnect is reported to be because of others' lack of understanding of their
children's giftedness and/or other motivations to homeschool not related with
religion (Jolly & Matthews, 2018a). These findings are also supported by the
longitudinal research of Gross on profoundly gifted students (2010).

While parents usually make efforts and seek opportunities to find intellectual and
social peers for their own children around the learning activities they provide for
them, Jolly and Matthews (2017a) suggest that parents give preference to learning
needs over social needs.

Curriculum Provision for Homeschooled Gifted Students

Jolly et al. (2013) indicated that every gifted homeschooling experience is different
and that parents approach learning in a very individual way that suits their children's
needs. In this scenario, the common experience will be the variability and flexibility
of styles, teaching methods, curricular offerings, learning venues, opportunities for
choice, and possible freedom that give parents a sense of control of the academic
future of their children, and they can change, adapt, or create the curriculum as
needed. All these different experiences allow parents the opportunity to differentiate
teaching to meet their children's unique learning and affective needs and to tailor
matters associated with their child's asynchronous development (Ensign, 2000; Jolly
et al., 2013; Kula, 2018).

The possibilities of this diverse pedagogical spectrum move between a more
structured approach (school at home) to an unschooling model (Rivero, 2002).
Others take advantage of the eclectic approach (Jolly et al., 2013; Winstanley,
2009). Kula (2018) mentions that this approach works well with gifted students
because it accommodates their uneven development in different subjects areas and
also helps with their need for more creative, experiential, and deeper learning. Jolly
and Matthews (2018a) indicated that unschooling doesn't seem to have many
followers among the gifted homeschooling population and that more empirical
data is needed on this topic.

Other approaches that are popular with the gifted homeschoolers group—like in general homeschooling—are the Charlotte Mason, Montessori, and Waldorf/Steiner approaches—described earlier in this chapter (Kula, 2018).

Some parents prepare beforehand for the transition to homeschooling and organise the educational provision, which makes it easier for the students (Winstanley, 2009). Between the different possibilities parents have, they can accelerate in an array of ways they like, vary the content, or even compact the curriculum, so their child can work faster through each grade or skip a grade.

In relation to pre-packaged curricula (textbooks), parents reported that the content was unchallenging and less flexible, or their children completed it more quickly than expected, so they often had to be accelerated faster through the curriculum chronologically earlier (Jolly & Matthews, 2018c). These difficulties for homeschooled gifted students were similar to the ones experienced by gifted students at schools with the school curriculum (Callahan, Moon, & Oh, 2014; Jolly & Matthews, 2018a).

Additionally, parents can seek supports within or outside the home, such as students working with tutors, using traditional subject-specific curriculum, accessing learning co-ops, videos or the Internet, posting lesson plans, using online academic programs for advanced learners, linking resources, and finding source material for homeschooling (Hanna, 2012; Jolly & Matthews, 2017a, 2018a, 2018c; Kunzman & Gaither, 2013). Indeed, as homeschooled gifted students age, more autonomous community-based options—such as dual enrolment, mentoring, competitions, internet programs, or virtual schooling—become relevant educational choices and supports (Jolly & Matthews, 2018c).

Research and Practice on Homeschooling Gifted Students: Implications and Future Directions

While there is a growing body of research on homeschooling that has some critics in relation to its methods and conclusions (Kunzman & Gaither, 2013; Medlin, 2013), in the area of gifted and twice-exceptional homeschooling, there are a scarcity and neglect that represent an almost unexplored topic area (Hurlbutt-Eastman, 2017; Jackson, 2014; Jolly & Matthews, 2017b, 2018a, 2018b; Kula 2018; Kunzman & Gaither, 2013; Winstanley, 2009). This shortage is more evident in Australia and Chile than the USA. Both Chile and Australia have limited trajectories in homeschooling research, but they are in a similar stage of development in relation to the pragmatics of gifted homeschooling. Steps forward include Australian researchers' highlighting twice-exceptional students' experiences with homeschooling and requests for research with gifted and twice-exceptional homeschooled students (Jackson 2014, 2017a, 2017b; Ronksley-Pavia et al., 2019).

It is urgent to prioritise research in this area in each of the countries of Australia, Chile, and the USA. Only in this way will they be able to provide support and guide families who have chosen to educate their children at home. Research in local contexts can provide rigorous evidence unique to those contexts to help them make informed decisions and learn from the experience of others (Jackson 2017a; Kula, 2018).

Advice from North American researchers suggests considering larger samples and creative approaches to work with the limitations in databases, for example, when working with the gifted homeschooling population (Jolly & Matthews, 2017b). Potential aspects for future studies are the number of students who can be identified as gifted or have high ability, underachievers, or twice-exceptional within the homeschooling population, relationships between schools and families, university enrolment (type of post-secondary institution, pursued majors, readiness comparison in relation to students from traditional schools), experiences of homeschooling gifted families and how to include these families in more effective conversations with general and gifted education about policy, advocacy, and research (Jolly & Matthews, 2018a; Kula, 2018). Another line of research suggested for homeschooling in general that may be positive for gifted homeschooling as well is comparative international research, which can expand homeschooling conceptions about curriculum, learning experiences, affective implications, regulations, and state involvement (Kunzman & Gaither, 2013).

Considering the extraordinary new context that the recent world-wide pandemic has caused, where millions more adults are now working from home and millions more children are now being educated at home, this new educational context engenders exploration. We raise many questions for possible research, for example:

- What are the differences between traditional schooling, long-standing homeschooling, different forms of home education, and parents newly educating gifted children digitally in different socially isolated contexts?
- What can parents who are new to educating their gifted children at home learn from those who have been homeschooling their children before the pandemic?
- Considering the diverse online teaching expertise of teachers, how can teachers bridge the digital divide between school and home to help parents effectively support the diverse needs of their children—including gifted children—within the new home educational context?
- How can parents be supported by educators in the parents' new role as fledgling teachers to their gifted children at home?
- How can parents, their children, teachers, and others now working from home or working externally to the home, balance family life and death, social distancing, and home educating their gifted children?
- What has been the role of home-schooled gifted children who are now eminent experts—for example, exceptional educators, researchers, scientists, medical personnel, inventors, innovators, Nobel Laureates, philanthropists, mathematicians, statisticians, leaders, prodigies, or other esteemed colleagues—in finding the solutions to the world-wide problem the pandemic has caused?

With so many questions that the new world order propagates, educators, researchers, advocates, and parents of gifted children, as well as eminent peoples themselves, now have even more incentives to explore and inform the possibilities for home educating in the future generally and, crucially, home educating gifted children for the future, specifically.

Conclusion

This chapter review sheds light on the topic of homeschooling generally and gifted homeschooling with an emphasis on three Pacific Rim countries: Australia, Chile, and the USA. The scarcity of researchers in gifted education who have pursued the research endeavour in this growing educational modality is puzzling. It is important to understand the relationship between gifted homeschoolers and public education and its implications in the long term for schools and society (Hanna, 2012). How to manage gifted children, parents, and societal interests in relation to homeschooling education is another issue that needs to be addressed (Kunzman & Gaither, 2013).

In relation to curricular approaches used in the different countries for both regular and gifted homeschoolers, the same variety of teaching and learning methods was found in each (Jackson, 2017a; Jolly et al., 2013; Kula, 2018; Kunzman & Gaither, 2013). Specifically, the emphasis was on acceleration and a focus on gifted students' interests and readiness to master content (Jolly & Matthews, 2018a; Kula, 2018).

In terms of motivations to homeschool gifted students, research indicated that most of the families tended to homeschool after many unsatisfactory attempts to stay within the school system (Jolly & Matthews, 2017a, 2018a, 2018c; Jolly et al., 2013; Winstanley, 2009). In this sense, school teachers could be more sensitive to the needs of gifted children to provide better support, guidance, and accompaniment to families and students who decide to leave school and for those who choose to return at some point. Jolly and Matthews (2018a) affirm that more attention and resources are needed at the school level to meet the needs of gifted students as a way to minimise the possibilities of school withdrawal as a consequence of indirect school push out. This is significant and a red light for the school system, a warning that questions the schooling model that in most cases expels gifted students without even noticing. All students should be valued regardless of their capacities and none should leave school because they did not fit in or because their learning needs were not respected as evidenced by irrelevant programming or provisions.

Cross-References

► Differentiation of Instruction for Gifted Learners: Collated Evaluative Studies of Teacher Classroom Practices
► Educational Contexts, Transitions and Community Engagement: Part VI Introduction
► Engaging Gifted Students in Solving Real Problems Creatively: Implementing the Real Engagement in Active Problem-Solving (REAPS) Teaching/Learning Model in Australasian and Pacific Rim Contexts

▶ Fostering and Developing Talent in Mentorship Programs: The Mentor's Perspectives

▶ Differentiation of Instruction for Gifted Learners: Collated Evaluative Studies of Teacher Classroom Practices

▶ Gifted Education in the Asia-Pacific: From the Past for the Future – An Introduction

▶ Implementing the DMGT's Constructs of Giftedness and Talent: What, Why, and How?

▶ Innovative Practices to Support High-Achieving Deprived Young Scholars in an Ethnic-Linguistic Diverse Latin American Country

▶ Learning from International Research Informs Academic Acceleration in Australasia: A Case for Consistent Policy

▶ Online Learning for Mathematically Talented Students: A Perspective from Hong Kong

▶ Some Implications for the Future of Gifted Education in the Asia-Pacific

▶ Why Is It So? Interest and Curiosity in Supporting Students Gifted in Science

Acknowledgments We gratefully acknowledge the Endeavour Research Fellowship Award from the Department of Education and Training of the Australian Government that funded this research, which was hosted by GERRIC, School of Education, UNSW, Australia.

References

Aliaga, L. (2017). Educación en el hogar en Chile. Informe de resultados de la Encuesta Nacional. *Educación, 26*(50), 7–27. https://doi.org/10.18800/educacion.201701.001

Allan, S., & Jackson, G. (2010). The what, whys and wherefores of home education and its regulation in Australia. *International Journal of Law & Education, 15*(1), 55–77. Retrieved from http://www5.austlii.edu.au/au/journals/IntJlLawEdu/2010/5.pdf

Anonymous. (2008). Connecting with my community: Katherine School of the Air. *Education in Rural Australia, 18*(1), 78.

Anthony, K. V., & Burroughs, S. (2012). Day to day operations of home school families: Selecting from a menu of educational choices to meet students' individual instructional needs. *International Education Studies, 5*(1), 3. https://doi.org/10.5539/ies.v5n1p3

Barratt-Peacock, J. (1997). *The why and how of Australian home education* (PhD Dissertation). La Trobe University, Melbourne, Australia. Published by Beverly Paine, Learning Books, Yankalilla, SA.

Barwegen, L. M., Falciani, N. K., Putnam, S. J., Reamer, M. B., & Star, E. E. (2004). Academic achievement of homeschool and public school students and student perception of parent involvement. *School Community Journal, 14*(1), 39–58. Retrieved from https://files.eric.ed.gov/fulltext/EJ794828.pdf

Bauer, S. W., & Wise, J. (2016). *The well-trained mind* (4th ed.). New York, NY: W. W. Norton.

Belfield, C. R. (2005). Home-schoolers: How well do they perform on the SAT for college admissions? In B. S. Cooper (Ed.), *Home schooling in full view: A reader* (pp. 167–178). Greenwich, CT: Information Age Publishing.

Bielick, S., Chandler, K., & Broughman, S. P. (2001). *Homeschooling in the United States: 1999 (NCES 2001–033)*. U.S. Department of Education. Washington, DC: National Center for Education Statistics. Retrieved from https://nces.ed.gov/pubs2001/2001033.pdf

Brewer, J., & Lubienski, C. (2017). Homeschooling in the United States: Examining the rationales for individualizing education. *Pro.posiçoes 28, 2*(83), 21–38. https://doi.org/10.1590/1980-6248-2016-0040

Bureau of Rural Sciences. (2018). *Research data Australia*. Australian National Data Service: Australian Government. Retrieved at https://researchdata.ands.org.au/bureau-rural-sciences-australian-government/680400

Cabo, C. (2012). *El Homeschooling en España: Descripción y análisis del fenómeno* (Doctoral dissertation). Universidad de Oviedo, Oviedo, España. Retrieved from https://www.tesisenred.net/bitstream/handle/10803/94200/UOV00100TCCG.pdf?sequence=5

Callahan, C. M., Moon, T. R., & Oh, S. (2014). *National surveys of gifted programs executive summary 2014*. Charlottesville, VA: National Research Center on the Gifted and Talented, University of Virginia. Retrieved from http://www.nagc.org/sites/default/files/key%20reports/2014%20Survey%20of%20GT%20programs%20Exec%20Summ.pdf

Carpenter, D., & Gann, C. (2015). Educational activities and the role of the parent in homeschool families with high school students. *Educational Review, 68*, 1–18. https://doi.org/10.1080/00131911.2015.1087971

Chapman, S. (2017). Growth 2011–2017. *Registered home educated students in Australia*. Southern Cross Educational Enterprise. Retrieved from http://accelerate.edu.au/wp-content/uploads/2018/04/Screen-Shot-2018-04-20-at-10.37.16-AM.png

Cheng, A. (2014). Does homeschooling or private schooling promote political intolerance? Evidence from a christian university. *Journal of School Choice, 8*(1), 49–68. https://doi.org/10.1080/15582159.2014.875411

Clark, B. (2013). *Growing up gifted: Developing the potential of children at school and at home* (8th ed.). Boston, MA: Pearson.

Collom, E. (2005). The ins and outs of homeschooling: The determinants of parental motivations and student achievement. *Education and Urban Society, 37*(3), 307–335. https://doi.org/10.1177/0013124504274190

Conejeros-Solar, M. L., & Smith, S. R. (2019). *Homeschooling the gifted: Experiences from the Australian and Chilean context*. Proposal presented at the World Council for Gifted and Talented Children Conference (WCGTC): A world of possibilities: Gifts, talents, and potential, Vanderbilt University, Nashville, TN.

Constitución política de la República de Chile (Revised 2017). *Artículo Nº 19*. Santiago, 17 de septiembre de 1980. Retrieved from https://www.camara.cl/camara/media/docs/constitucion_0517.pdf

Croft, K. E. (2013). *So you're a teacher, and you home educate? Why would you, and how does that work for you? Exploring motivations for, and implementation of, home education by qualified teachers in Australia* (Master thesis). Avondale College of Higher Education, Wahroonga, Australia. Retrieved from https://research.avondale.edu.au/cgi/viewcontent.cgi?article=1014&context=theses_masters_coursework

D'Amato, R. C., & Gundrum, C. (2017). Homeschooling (Homeschool education). In J. Kreutzer, J. DeLuca, & B. Caplan (Eds.), *Encyclopedia of clinical neuropsychology* (pp. 9151–9151). Cham, Switzerland: Springer International Publishing AG. https://doi.org/10.1007/978-3-319-56782-2_9151-1

English, R. (2013). The most private private education: Home education in Australia. *Homeschool Researcher, 29*(4), 1–7. Retrieved from http://eprints.qut.edu.au/61433/

English, R. (2015). Use your freedom of choice: Reasons for choosing homeschool in Australia. *Journal of Unschooling and Alternative Learning, 9*(17), 1–18. Retrieved from https://jual.nipissingu.ca/wp-content/uploads/sites/25/2014/06/v91171.pdf

Ensign, J. (2000). Defying the stereotypes of special education: Home school students. *Peabody Journal of Education, 75*(1–2), 147–158. https://doi.org/10.1080/0161956X.2000.9681939

Farenga, M. (2010). Homeschooling. In P. Peterson, E. Baker, & B. McGaw (Eds.), *International encyclopedia of education* (3rd ed., pp. 214–220). Amsterdam, The Netherlands: Elsevier. Primary and Secondary Education-Learning and Teaching in School Age Education. https://doi.org/10.1016/B978-0-08-044894-7.01078-2

Freeman, J. (2001). *Gifted children grown up*. London, England: David Fulton.

Gaither, M. (2008, September 30). Brian D. Ray and NHERI, part 1. Retrieved from http://gaither. wordpress.com/2008/09/30/brian-d-ray-and-nheri-part-1/

Gaither, M. (2009). Homeschooling in the USA: Past, present, and future. *Theory and Research in Education, 7*(3), 331–346. https://doi.org/10.1177/1477878509343741

Gaither, M. (2017a). Homeschooling in the United States: A review of select research topics. *Pro. posiçoes, 28, 2*(83), 213–241. https://doi.org/10.1590/1980-6248-2015-0171

Gaither, M. (2017b). Introduction to the Wiley handbook of home education. In M. Gaither (Ed.), *The Wiley handbook of home education* (1st ed., pp. 1–3). Malden, MA: Wiley.

García, E., Barrera, D., & Alejandro, W. (2017). Theories, practices, and environments of learning and home education in Latin America. In M. Gaither (Ed.), *The Wiley handbook of home education* (1st ed., pp. 362–394). Malden, MA: Wiley.

Goodowens, S., & Cannaday, J. (2018). Homeschooling/unschooling in gifted education: A parent's perspective. In J. Cannaday (Ed.), *Curriculum development for gifted education programs* (pp. 172–190). Hershey, PA: IGI Global. https://doi.org/10.4018/978-1-5225-3041-1. ch008

Goodwin, C. B., & Gustavson, M. (2009, Spring). Gifted homeschooling in the US. *NAGC Magazine,* 26–28. Retrieved from https://giftedhomeschoolers.org/articles/NAGCMagazi neSpring09.pdf

Green-Hennessy, S. (2014). Homeschooled adolescents in the United States: Developmental outcomes. *Journal of Adolescence, 37*, 441–449. https://doi.org/10.1016/j.adolescence.2014.03.007

Gross, M. U. M. (2004). *Exceptionally gifted children* (2nd ed.). London, England: Routledge Falmer.

Gross, M. U. M. (2010). *Miraca Gross in her own write: A lifetime in gifted education*. Sydney, NSW: UNSW, Sydney, GERRIC.

Halsey, J. (2017). *Independent review into regional, rural, and remote education* (Discussion paper). The Department of Education and Training, Australian Government: Commonwealth of Australia.

Hanna, L. (2012). Homeschooling education: Longitudinal study of methods, materials, and curricula. *Education and Urban Society, 44*(5), 609–631. https://doi.org/10.1177/0013124511404886

Harding, T. J. A. (2011). *A study of parents' conceptions of their roles as home educators of their children* (Doctoral dissertation). Queensland University of Technology, Brisbane, QLD, Australia. Retrieved from https://eprints.qut.edu.au/40931/1/Terrence_Harding_Thesis.pdf

Haugh, B. (2014). Hesitation to resolution: Our homeschooling narrative. *Journal of Unschooling and Alternative Learning, 8*(16), 1–12. Retrieved from https://jual.nipissingu.ca/wp-content/uploads/sites/25/2014/06/v82161.pdf

Hertzel, J. (1997). Literacy in the homeschool setting. In P. H. Dreyer (Ed.), *Literacy: Building on what we know* (pp. 61–81). Claremont, CA: Claremont Reading Co.

Holt, J., & Farenga, P. (2003). *Teach your own: The John Holt book of home schooling*. Cambridge, MA: Perseus Publishing.

Howell, C. (2013). Hostility or indifference? The marginalization of homeschooling in the education profession. *Peabody Journal of Education, 88*(3), 355–364. https://doi.org/10.1080/0161956X.2013.798510

Hurlbutt, K. (2011). Experiences of parents who homeschool their children with autism spectrum disorders. *Focus on Autism and Other Developmental Disabilities, 26*(4), 239–249. https://doi.org/10.1177/1088357611421170

Hurlbutt-Eastman, K. (2017). Teaching the child with exceptional needs at home. In M. Gaither (Ed.), *The Wiley handbook of home education* (1st ed., pp. 222–245). Malden, MA: Wiley.

Isenberg, E. J. (2007). What we have learned about homeschooling? *Peabody Journal of Education, 82*, 387–409. https://doi.org/10.1080/01619560701312996

Jackson, G. (2014). *Australian research on home education: And how it can inform legislation and regulation*. Invited submission (0412) to the Select Committee on Home Schooling, 142.16. Legislative Council of New South Wales. Parliament House, Sydney, NSW. Retrieved from https://www.parliament.nsw.gov.au/lcdocs/submissions/50267/0142%20Ms%20Glenda%20Jackson%20(PHD).pdf

Jackson, G., & Allan, S. (2010). Fundamental elements in examining a child's right to education: A study of home education, research, and regulation in Australia. *International Electronic Journal of Elementary Education, 2*(3), 349–364. Retrieved from https://www.iejee.com/index.php/IEJEE/article/view/244

Jackson, G. M. (2017a). Common themes in Australian and New Zealand home education research. In M. Gaither (Ed.), *The Wiley handbook of home education* (1st ed., pp. 329–361). Malden, MA: Wiley.

Jackson, G. M. (2017b). *Summary of Australian research on home education*. Australian Home Education Advisory Service. Retrieved from https://home-ed.vic.edu.au/wp-content/uploads/2017/02/SUMMARY-OF-AUSTRALIAN-RESEARCH-ON-HOME-EDUCATION-Feb-2017-1.pdf

Jolly, J. L., & Matthews, M. S. (2017a). The chronicles of homeschooling gifted learners. *Journal of School Choice*, 1–23. https://doi.org/10.1080/15582159.2017.1354644

Jolly, J. L., & Matthews, M. S. (2017b). Why we blog: Homeschooling mothers of gifted children. *Roeper Review, 39*, 112–120. https://doi.org/10.1080/02783193.2017.1289579

Jolly, J. L., & Matthews, M. S. (2018a). Homeschooling: An alternative approach for gifted and talented learners? In C. Callahan & H. Hertberg-Davis (Eds.), *Fundamentals of gifted education: Considering multiple perspectives* (pp. 467–476). New York, NY: Routledge.

Jolly, J. L., & Matthews, M. S. (2018b). The chronicles of homeschooling gifted learners. *Journal of School Choice, 12*(1), 123–145. https://doi.org/10.1080/15582159.2017.1354644

Jolly, J. L., & Matthews, M. S. (2018c). The shifting landscape of the homeschooling continuum. *Educational Review, 12*(1), 123–145. https://doi.org/10.1080/00131911.2018.1552661

Jolly, J. L., Matthews, M. S., & Nester, J. (2013). Homeschooling the gifted: A parent's perspective. *Gifted Child Quarterly, 57*, 121–134. https://doi.org/10.1177/0016986212469999

Julio, C. (2016a). *Sobre la Experiencia de Educar sin Escuela en Chile hoy* (Undergraduate dissertation). Universidad Metropolitana de Ciencias de la Educación, Santiago, Chile. Retrieved from https://www.researchgate.net/publication/316493480_Sobre_la_experiencia_de_Educar_sin_Escuela_en_Chile_hoy

Julio, C. (2016b). *Revisitando a Iván Illich. Sobre algunas experiencias de desescolarización en Chile hoy: el Grupo Monte Tabor* (Master dissertation) Universidad Arcis, Santiago, Chile. Retrieved from https://www.researchgate.net/publication/316473221

Kidd, T., & Kaczmarek, E. (2010). The experiences of mothers home educating their children with autism spectrum disorder. *Issues in Educational Research, 20*(3), 257–275. Retrieved from http://www.iier.org.au/iier20/kidd.pdf

King, S. (2018). Homeschooling as social policy. In A. Farazmand (Ed.), *Global encyclopedia of public administration, public policy, and governance* (pp. 3099–3105). Cham, Switzerland: Springer International Publishing AG. https://doi.org/10.1007/978-3-319-20928-9

Kolenc, A. (2017). Legal issues in homeschooling. In M. Gaither (Ed.), *The Wiley handbook of home education* (1st ed., pp. 59–85). Malden, MA: Wiley.

Kula, S. (2018). Homeschooling gifted students: Considerations for research and practice. In J. Cannaday (Ed.), *Curriculum development for gifted education programs* (pp. 151–171). Hershey, PA: IGI Global. https://doi.org/10.4018/978-1-5225-3041-1.ch007

Kunzman, R. (2009). Understanding homeschooling a better approach to regulation. *Theory and Research in Education, 7*(3), 311–330. https://doi.org/10.1177/1477878509343740

Kunzman, R. (2017). Homeschooler socialisation. Skills, values, and citizenship. In M. Gaither (Ed.), *The Wiley handbook of home education* (1st ed., pp. 136–156). Malden, MA: Wiley.

Kunzman, R., & Gaither, M. (2013). Homeschooling: A comprehensive survey of the research. *Other Education, 2*(1), 4–59. Retrieved from https://www.othereducation.org/index.php/OE/article/view/10

Lagos, J. A. (2011). *Parental education rights in the United States and Canada: Homeschooling and its legal protection* (PhD Dissertation). Pontificia Universitas Sanctae Crucis Facultas Iuris Canonici, Rome, Italy. Retrieved from http://bibliotecanonica.net/docsag/btcagz.pdf

Liberto, G. (2016). Child-led and interest-inspired learning, home education, learning differences, and the impact of regulation. *Cogent Education, 3*, 1–10. https://doi.org/10.1080/2331186X.2016.1194734, 1194734.

Lois, J. (2017). Homeschooling motherhood. In M. Gaither (Ed.), *The Wiley handbook of home education* (1st ed., pp. 186–206). Malden, MA: Wiley.

Lubienski, C. (2000). Whither the common good? A critique of homeschooling. *Peabody Journal of Education, 75*(1–2), 207–232. https://doi.org/10.1080/0161956X.2000.9681942

Lubienski, C. (2003). A critical view of home education. *Evaluation and Research in Education, 17*, 167–178. https://doi.org/10.1080/09500790308668300

Lubienski, C., Puckett, T., & Brewer, T. J. (2013). Does homeschooling "work"? A critique of the empirical claims and agenda of advocacy organizations. *Peabody Journal of Education, 88*, 378–392. https://doi.org/10.1080/0161956X.2013.798516

Martin-Chang, S., Gould, O. N., & Meuse, R. E. (2011). The impact of home schooling on academic achievement: Evidence from homeschooled and traditionally schooled children. *Canadian Journal of Behavioural Science, 43*, 195–202. https://doi.org/10.1037/a0022697

Martin-Chang, S., & Levesque, K. (2017). Academic achievement making an informed choice about homeschooling. In M. Gaither (Ed.), *The Wiley Handbook of Home Education* (1st ed., pp. 121–134). Malden, MA: Wiley.

Mayberry, M. (1988). Characteristics and attitudes of families who home school. *Education and Urban Society, 21*(1), 32–41. https://doi.org/10.1177/0013124588021001004

McDonald, J., & Lopes, E. (2014). How parents home educate their children with an autism spectrum disorder with the support of the Schools of Isolated and Distance Education. *International Journal of Inclusive Education, 18*(1), 1–17. https://doi.org/10.1080/13603116.2012.751634

Medlin, R. G. (2000). Home schooling and the question of socialisation. *Peabody Journal of Education, 7*(1–2), 107–133. Retrieved from http://www.tandfonline.com/doi/abs/10.1080/0161956X.2000.9681937

Medlin, R. G. (2013). Homeschooling and the question of socialization revisited. *Peabody Journal of Education, 88*(3), 284–297.

Mineduc. (2007). *Decreto 2272 EXENTO. Aprueba procedimientos para el reconocimiento de estudios de Enseñanza Básica y Enseñanza Media Humanístico-Científica y Técnico-Profesional y de Modalidad Educación de Adultos y de Educación* Especial. Retrieved from https://www.leychile.cl/Navegar?idNorma=267943

Mineduc. (2009). *Ley General de Educación* No. 20.370. Santiago, 12 de septiembre de 2009. Retrieved from https://www.leychile.cl/Navegar?idNorma=1006043

Mineduc. (2018a). *Exámenes Libres-Menores de 18 años*. Portal de Atención Ciudadana del Ministerio de Educación del Gobierno de Chile. Retrieved from https://www.ayudamineduc.cl/ficha/examenes-libres-menores-de-18-anos-11

Mineduc. (2018b). *Normativa de Evaluación y Promoción Educación Básica*. Retrieved from https://www.ayudamineduc.cl/ficha/normativa-de-evaluacion-y-promocion-educacion-basica

Murphy, J. (2014). The social and educational outcomes of homeschooling. *Sociological Spectrum, 34*(1), 244–272. https://doi.org/10.1080/02732173.2014895640

Murphy, J., Gaither, M., & Gleim, C. E. (2017). The calculus of departure. In M. Gaither (Ed.), *The Wiley handbook of home education* (1st ed., pp. 86–120). Malden, MA: Wiley.

National Association for Gifted Children. (n.d.). What is giftedness? Retrieved from https://www.nagc.org/resources-publications/resources/what-giftedness

Nemer, K. M. (2002). *Understudied education: Toward building a homeschooling research agenda*. New York, NY: National Center for the Study of Privatization in Education. Retrieved from https://files.eric.ed.gov/fulltext/ED480142.pdf

Paine, B. (2018). *What is unschooling?* The educating parent. Retrieved from http://homeschoolaustralia.com/articles/unschoolingindex.html

Patrick, K. (1999). *Enhancing community awareness of home-schooling as a viable educational option* (Honours thesis). Avondale College, Cooranbong, NSW.

Pell, B. (2018). Homeschooling. In B. B. Frey (Ed.), *The SAGE encyclopedia of educational research, measurement, and evaluation* (pp. 792–793). Thousand Oaks, CA: Sage. https://doi.org/10.4135/9781506326139.n312

Poblete, V. (2016). *Uso de las Tecnologías de la Información y la Comunicación en el Homeschooling desde las significaciones socioculturales de los padres: Un estudio interpretativo en el contexto de la Educación Básica* (Master dissertation). Universidad de Chile, Santiago, Chile. Retrieved from http://repositorio.uchile.cl/handle/2250/150973

Ray, B. (2013). Homeschooling associated with beneficial learner and societal outcomes but educators do not promote it. *Peabody Journal of Education, 88*, 324–341. https://doi.org/10.1080/0161956X.2013.798508

Ray, B. (2016). *Research facts on homeschooling*. National Home Education Research Institute. Retrieved from http://www.nheri.org/ResearchFacts.pdf

Ray, B. (2017a). A review of research on homeschooling and what might educators learn? *Pro. posiçoes 28, 2*(83), 85–103. https://doi.org/10.1590/1980-6248-2016-0009

Ray, B. (2017b). A systematic review of the empirical research on selected aspects of homeschooling as a school choice. *Journal of School Choice, 11*(4), 604–621. https://doi.org/10.1080/15582159.2017.1395638

Ray, B. (2017c). A description and brief history of home schooling in America. In R. A. Fox & N. K. Buchanan (Eds.), *The Wiley handbook of school choice* (1st ed., pp. 329–343). Malden, MA: Wiley.

Reavis, R., & Zakriski, A. (2005). Are home-schooled children socially at-risk or socially protected? *The Brown University Child and Adolescent Behavior Letter, 21*(9), 4–5. https://doi.org/10.1002/cbl.20003

Redford, J., Battle, D., & Bielick, S. (2016). *Homeschooling in the United States: 2012* (NCES 2016–096). National Center for Education Statistics, Institute of Education. Retrieved from https://files.eric.ed.gov/fulltext/ED569947.pdf

Riley, G. (2015). Differences in competence, autonomy, and relatedness between home educated and traditionally educated young adults. *International Social Science Review, 90*(2), 1–29. Retrieved from http://digitalcommons.northgeorgia.edu/issr/vol90/iss2/2

Rivero, L. (2002). Progressive digressions: Home schooling for self-actualization. *Roeper Review, 24*(4), 197–202. https://doi.org/10.1080/02783190209554180

Romanowski, M. (2006). Revisiting the common myths about homeschooling. *Clearing House: A Journal of Educational Strategies, Issues, and Ideas, 79*, 125–139. https://doi.org/10.3200/TCHS.79.3.125-129

Ronksley-Pavia, M., Grootenboer, P., & Pendergast, D. (2019). Privileging the voices of twice-exceptional children: An exploration of lived experiences and stigma narratives. *Journal for the Education of the Gifted, 42*(1), 4–34. https://doi.org/10.1177/0162353218816384

Rothermel, P. (2015). *International perspectives on home education: Do we still need schools?* London, England: Palgrave Macmillan.

Select Committee on Home Schooling. (2014). *Home schooling in NSW* [Sydney, N.S.W.]. BOSTES Inquiry report. Parliament. Legislative Council. (Report; no 1). Retrieved from https://www.parliament.nsw.gov.au/lcdocs/inquiries/2128/141203%20Final%20Report.pdf

Sepúlveda, P. (2013, March 11). Padres cuentan por qué eligieron no enviar a sus hijos al colegio y educarlos en casa. *El Mercurio*. Retrieved from https://www.emol.com/noticias/nacional/2013/03/08/587536/ninos-que-estudian-en-la-casa-fin-de-semana.html

Shepherd, G. (2015). Homeschooling's harms: Lessons from economics. *Akron Law Review, 49*(2/5), 1–33. Retrieved from http://ideaexchange.uakron.edu/akronlawreview/vol49/iss2/5

Troncoso, D. (2015). *Perspectivas teóricas y parentales del concepto de Educación en el Hogar* (Master dissertation). Universidade Do Porto, Porto, Portugal. Retrieved from https://sigarra.up.pt/fpceup/en/PUB_GERAL.PUB_VIEW?pi_pub_base_id=120001

Van Galen, J. A. (1987). Explaining home education: Parents' accounts of their decisions to teach their own children. *The Urban Review, 19*(3), 161–177. Retrieved from https://link.springer.com/article/10.1007/BF01111877

Van Galen, J. A. (1991). *Home schooling: Political, historical, and pedagogical perspectives.* Norwood, NJ: Ablex Publishers.

Winstanley, C. (2009). Too cool for school? Gifted children and homeschooling. *Theory and Research in Education, 7*(3), 347–362. https://doi.org/10.1177/1477878509343736

María Leonor Conejeros-Solar is a professor, psychologist, and doctor in Education at the School of Pedagogy of the Pontificia Universidad Católica de Valparaíso. Among her duties, she has served as the director of the Academically Talented Education Program BETA in the same university. Her main research interests are academically talented students from underprivileged socio-economic backgrounds, gifted college students, provisions and socio-emotional issues of gifted and twice-exceptional students, and gifted homeschooling. She has published several articles and book chapters.

Susen R. Smith, PhD, is a GERRIC senior research fellow and senior lecturer in Gifted and Special Education at the School of Education, UNSW, Australia. Over three decades, she has held many leadership, consultancy and educator roles from early childhood through to tertiary. Susen's research interests include differentiating curriculum and pedagogy for underachieving gifted students, indigenous students, and twice-exceptional students, and emotional learning, and she developed the *Model of Dynamic Differentiation (MoDD)*. She has been a visiting scholar at Columbia University and CUNY, USA; Imperial College London, UK; the National Taipei University of Education, Taiwan; and the Hong Kong University of Education, China, guest editor of the *Australasian Journal of Gifted Education (AJGE)* and on editorial review boards, such as the *Gifted Child Quarterly*, published in top international journals in the field, for example, *Roeper Review*, and has keynoted nationally and internationally.

Highly Able Students in International Schools

58

Selena Gallagher

Contents

Abstract

Almost five million children attend international schools around the world, many of which attract a highly motivated and highly competitive student body of both local and expatriate children. Despite this, the majority of international schools do not offer any specific programming or services for gifted or highly able students, and there is very little research on how these students fare in international schools. In this chapter, an overview of international education worldwide will first be presented, and then an insight into the unique context provided by these schools, as well as considering the strengths and challenges inherent in these schools for highly able students, will be provided. Some attributes of international school students and some potential issues or barriers that may prevent a 'national' approach to gifted education being successfully transplanted into an international environment will be discussed. It will then be proposed in the chapter that a talent development approach is a model for meeting the needs of highly able students in international schools, drawing on

S. Gallagher (✉)
Cairo American College, Cairo, Egypt
e-mail: selena.gallag@gmail.com

© Springer Nature Singapore Pte Ltd. 2021   1325
S. R. Smith (ed.), *Handbook of Giftedness and Talent Development in the Asia-Pacific*,
Springer International Handbooks of Education,
https://doi.org/10.1007/978-981-13-3041-4_63

theory, the research literature and practical examples of talent development in action. Finally, some recommendations for implementation suitable for an international school environment and research will be suggested.

Keywords

International school · International Baccalaureate · Talent development · Asia · Third culture kids

The aims in this chapter are to:
1. Present an overview of the historical and current context of international schools, their students and curricula.
2. Review the status of highly able learners in international schools.
3. Advocate for a talent development approach in meeting the needs of highly able learners in international schools.
4. Present suggestions for capitalising on the strengths of the international school environment for the benefit of highly able learners.

Introduction

Over the past century, the field of international education has sprung into existence and experienced exponential growth. Despite the numbers of students attending these schools and the economic value of this sector, it remains a relatively under-researched field. Consequently, little is known about the experiences of highly able students in these schools. While many international schools may follow a British or American curriculum, the diversity of cohorts, culture, and classroom practices may limit the applicability of gifted identification and service provisions 'imported' from their national counterparts. However, the evolution of the field of gifted education and the movement towards a more inclusive talent development approach presents an opportunity on which international schools can capitalise in order to better meet the needs of this underserved population.

Overview of International Education

Globally, almost five million children currently study in more than eight thousand international schools around the world, paying more than US$43 billion in fees annually. This represents a growth of around 45% in just the last 5 years, and by 2026, the numbers of K–12 students in international schools is expected to rise to 8.75 million in over 16,000 schools, generating fee revenue of US$89 billion (John Catt, 2016). International schools can be found all over the world, including in English-speaking countries, such as Australia, the United Kingdom, and the United States, but Asia is the fastest growing region, with over 54% of international schools and over 60% of international school students. More than 20 cities in the world are host to at least 50 international schools, including Bangkok, Beijing, Shanghai, Singapore, and Tokyo (International Schools Research, 2016a).

International education can trace its roots to 1926 and the establishment of both the International School of Geneva and Yokohama International School. Both schools were established to meet the demand from 'foreign' parents working in those cities, and the driving force behind the growth of international schools since then has been largely to cater to the children of expatriate diplomats and professionals who wanted to ensure a 'Western' style education for their children during their overseas posting (Hayden & Thompson, 2008). In many cases, parents were instrumental in setting up these overseas schools, which operate outside the national education system of the host country, and parents may continue to serve an influential role in many schools today, serving as board members or trustees. While expats continue to be an important demographic for international schools, the recent rapid growth has been due to increasing numbers of host country nationals who have chosen to send their children to international schools, preparing them for future admission to Western colleges and universities. Today, around 80% of students in international schools are host country nationals (Hayden & Thompson, 2008).

The extensive network of international schools globally is typified by their almost exclusive use of English as the medium of instruction. Beyond that commonality, however, there is incredible diversity. They are essentially private schools and while there are a number of different accrediting organisations, there is no single overarching system of standards or regulations with which schools must comply. Schools may closely follow a US or British curriculum or that of another Western English-speaking nation such as Canada, Australia, or New Zealand; they may offer an 'international' curriculum, such as the programs developed by the International Baccalaureate Organisation (IBO); or they may design their own curriculum drawing on favoured practices and standards from a number of different sources. They may have a school population made up of students from more than 50 different nationalities, or they may be dominated by one or two nationalities. Some countries impose restrictions on host country students attending international schools; others do not. Schools may be highly selective or open to any student who can pay the fees. They may operate as a not-for-profit educational foundation or be owned and operated as a business. They may be a 'franchise' of an established elite private school, such as Harrow or Dulwich College; belong to a network of schools such as Nord Anglia or Cognita; or, be individual entities and be completely independent.

Students in International Schools. While there is also considerable diversity among the student population in most international schools, they do share a few similar characteristics. Whether the globally mobile child of an expat professional or the child of wealthy host country nationals, students at international schools tend to be economically advantaged. They tend to be the children of highly educated and successful parents. Unlike schools in a national system, virtually all students will be expected to go on to higher education following their graduation from high school. Indeed, securing an edge in admissions to highly selective Western colleges and universities is one reason why an international education is so attractive to the wealthy elite of the host country. Given these circumstances, it may be the case that the level of ability of the student population does not follow the typical bell curve, but is skewed towards the right, meaning there may be many more gifted children than would typically be found in a national school system.

Children, who spend a significant portion of their formative years living outside of their country of origin, or passport country, are known as *Third Culture Kids* (TCK; Useem & Useem, 1967). Because they have been exposed to one or more different cultures before they have formed their own cultural identity, they take on a 'third' culture, not that of their home or host country, but an amalgamation of many different cultural experiences they share with other TCKs. Some benefits of this experience can be an expanded worldview, greater cultural awareness and sensitivity, increased levels of interpersonal skills and higher levels of overall adjustment (Sheard, 2008). As previously discussed, they also tend to be economically advantaged. Perhaps not surprisingly then, TCKs graduate college at four times the rate of non-TCKs and are more likely to graduate with honours (Useem & Cottrell, 1999). While there can be some adjustment difficulties associated with transitioning back into the 'home' culture, for the most part, TCKs are successful in higher education. Given the nature of the international school population, there is considerable overlap between the phenomenon of TCKs and that of giftedness, with many students owning both labels.

While the diversity of international schools means it is impossible to generalise, what then is the status of gifted education in these environments, populated by economically advantaged TCKs and host country students, with average IQs skewed to the right of the typical distribution? For the most part, it seems formal recognition and attention to the needs of highly able students in international schools is a relatively recent phenomenon.

Curriculum and Services for Highly Able Students. *Next Frontier Inclusion* (NFI) is an organisation dedicated to the advocacy of students with special needs in international schools. In January 2016, NFI collaborated with International Schools Consultancy to conduct a survey of over 8,000 international schools around the world regarding their inclusion practices and 584 schools responded. One particularly interesting finding was that of the schools which responded to the survey, 84% said that they enrol children with gifts and talents, but only 35% of schools said that they are satisfied with their provision for this group of learners (International Schools Consultancy Research, 2016b). Reporting on these findings, the Director of NFI, Bill Powell (cited in International Schools Consultancy Research, 2016b), said:

> There is a disconnect here. Many times, school leaders use finances as a reason to exclude children with special educational needs. They'll say: 'We don't have the programme for you, so it would be wrong for us to take you into our school'. But on the flip side of this, some of these schools are accepting children with high academic gifts and talents, even though they admit they are not happy with the provision they provide. That's a significant ethical consideration that this survey has highlighted. (p. 3)

Given that the schools most likely to have responded to the survey are those with the greatest awareness or interest in the inclusion of special populations, the current situation for highly able learners in international schools seems to be somewhat problematic. If pressed, educators in many international schools will claim they meet the needs of their gifted students simply by virtue of their academically rigorous and culturally rich environment. In their booklet, 'Transitioning to an overseas assignment with a child with special needs: Guidance for Parents Supporting a Gifted Child in the Foreign Service' the United States Department of State (n.d.) advises:

> It is often just as difficult to secure accommodations for your gifted child as for a child with a learning disability, although securing admission will be easier. Just as in independent schools in the United States, very few overseas schools have special programs for gifted children. Many schools believe that their curriculum is sufficiently demanding for any student, particularly the highly selective schools and those that offer Advanced Placement classes and/or the International Baccalaureate programs. (para. 1)

In national systems, the *International Baccalaureate Diploma Program* (IBDP) is often promoted as a suitable curriculum for gifted students at the high school level (Gross, Urquhart, Doyle, Juratowitch, & Matheson, 2011; Hertberg-Davis & Callahan, 2008; National Association for Gifted Children [NAGC], 2004). The *International Baccalaureate Organisation* (IBO) is a non-profit educational foundation that was established in 1968 with a mission to create a better world through education (IBOa, n.d.-a). The *Diploma Program* (DP) was originally developed by teachers at the International School of Geneva and has become well established as an academically challenging and rigorous university preparation program that encourages students to develop depth and breadth of knowledge and to think critically and ethically about the world (IBOb, n.d.-b). The IB Diploma is widely offered in international schools, although it has become increasingly popular around the world and is now taken by more students in national systems than by students in international schools (Hayden & Thompson, 2008). However, it was never developed explicitly as an advanced curriculum for highly able learners, and while it may be offered as a selective program in many national system schools, it is the default option for many students in international schools.

Research on the use of the IB Diploma with gifted students is limited, and what research exists generally focuses on schools in the United States, or, to a lesser extent, in Australia or the UK (Doherty, 2013; Hertberg-Davis, Callahan, & Kyburg, 2006; Shaunessy, Suldo, Hardesty, & Shaffer, 2006; Vanderbrook, 2006). This means that findings must be treated with caution. In particular, one of the main benefits associated with the IB program in US schools, where the program is generally offered as a selective option for highly able or highly motivated students, is the opportunity to study with intellectual peers (Hertberg-Davis et al., 2006; Shaunessy et al., 2006). However, in an international school where the majority of students of all abilities take IB courses, there may be much less homogeneity among the student cohort, and this benefit may be mitigated.

There is no doubt that the IB Diploma curriculum is challenging and rigorous. However, there are some issues that may arise when using this curriculum with highly able learners. Firstly, the IBDP is designed for breadth. Students take six different courses from six different subject groups—typically three at Standard Level and three at Higher Level—alongside the three core components of Theory of Knowledge, Extended Essay and Creativity, Action and Service. The focus on breadth means talented students who wish to focus more in depth on one specialised area, such as STEM or the Arts, are unable to do so within the constraints of the Diploma. There is limited flexibility, in that students who wish to take one additional science or foreign language course, may do so, at the expense of one course in the arts subject group. There is no provision for students who wish to take an additional arts subject. Consequently, the IBO promotes well roundedness and breadth, but it seems the arts are not valued as highly as the other five subject groups. In a case study of schools in Australia offering the IB Diploma, Doherty (2013) found that the most often cited reason for students opting out of the IBDP was the flexibility and choice offered in the locally available alternative curriculum.

Furthermore, the rigid requirements of the IBDP make subject acceleration difficult. In order to qualify as part of the Diploma, all six subjects must generally be assessed during the same exam period, at the end of two years of study. There is one exception, where students may be assessed on an 'Anticipated' subject one year early; however, this subject can only be taken at Standard Level and not at a Higher Level, making it unsuitable as a response to advanced ability in a particular subject. The IBDP may therefore be a better fit for gifted students who are equally advanced across multiple subject areas, rather than those who show exceptional talent in only one or two areas. Similarly, moderately gifted students may cope better with the 'one-size-fits-all' approach of the Diploma (Hertberg-Davis et al., 2006) than highly or profoundly gifted students, who are more likely to need significant accelerative opportunities or who may resist the need for conformity. International schools that offer the British curriculum in the final years of high school may have more flexibility to respond to the need for academic acceleration and subject specialisation.

In qualitative studies of gifted students taking the IB in US high schools, most students reported feeling genuinely challenged for the first time in their school career (Hertberg-Davis & Callahan, 2008; Vanderbrook, 2006). They relished the qualitative differences to their other regular high school classes, such as the ability to go deeper and the increased emphasis on thinking, but they did not enjoy the quantitative differences, with many reportedly feeling overwhelmed by the volume of work and the preoccupation with exams. They enjoyed the emotional support of their peers and the feeling that they were 'all in it together', but some students were dissatisfied with the 'lecture-heavy' teaching style in some of their classes, or still felt unchallenged in areas where they had already shown mastery (Vanderbrook, 2006). Studies have found little differentiation is provided in IB courses, with teachers strongly focused on the content demands and end-of-course exams, rather than with any academic diversity amongst their students (Hertberg-Davis et al., 2006). Increased levels of stress and anxiety have also been reported amongst high school students taking IB and AP courses compared to the general high school population (Suldo, Shaunessy-Dedrick, Ferron, & Dedrick, 2018), with sleep deprivation seen as a necessary sacrifice for success in the program (Foust, Hertberg-Davis, & Callahan, 2008).

In the primary years of schooling, the International Baccalaureate has developed the *Primary Years Program* (PYP), a transdisciplinary, inquiry-based curriculum that focuses on developing international-mindedness and conceptual understanding (IBOd, n.d.-d). Introduced in 1997, it has not yet developed the reach of the Diploma Program, but is currently offered in around 1500 schools worldwide, many of which are international schools. It has been suggested that the PYP, while a curriculum for all students, is uniquely suitable for gifted primary-aged students, because of its focus on concept-based, thematic units and the emphasis on student-directed inquiry learning (Carber & Reis, 2004). The structure of the PYP may support the needs of gifted learners by providing open-ended conceptual units of study rather than being bound by specific grade-level expectations and is compatible with other approaches to meeting the needs of this population, such as cluster grouping (Rogers, 2007).

The IB *Middle Years Program* (MYP) was introduced in 1994 and aims to bridge the gap between the holistic, transdisciplinary PYP and the rigorous university preparation of the Diploma (IBOc, n.d.-c). Some US middle schools are promoting the MYP as an inclusive yet challenging curriculum that will support the emergence of gifted behaviours in a wider range of students than those typically served in gifted programs (Olszewski-Kubilius & Clarenbach, 2012). Less popular than the Diploma Program and the PYP, the MYP is still valued for its holistic approach and focus on global citizenship, and there is considerable flexibility in how individual schools may enact the curriculum locally (Wright, Lee, Tang, & Chak Pong Tsui, 2016).

Besides the International Baccalaureate programs, other curricula in use in international schools globally include: the *International Primary Curriculum* (IPC), the *International General Certificate of Secondary Education* (IGCSE), *Advanced Placement* (AP), and national or state curricula from England, Australia, Canada, and the United States, including the Common Core State Standards. Many schools take a 'mix and match' approach, offering different types of curriculum at different stages of schooling, depending on their individual context and mission (Hayden & Thompson, 2008). There will also be considerable diversity in how a particular curriculum is implemented from school to school.

Benefits and Challenges

Operating outside the realm of national systems offers some unique benefits and challenges for schools when it comes to the provision for highly able learners. On the one hand, schools are freed from onerous burdens of state-mandated definitions and programs and have the flexibility to design their own unique approach to suit their particular context. On the other hand, without some kind of mandated expectation, deliberate and purposeful provision for highly able learners may not be considered a priority at all, and without a dedicated advocate on staff, it may simply not happen.

Teachers and administrators in international schools generally come from English-speaking countries such as the United Kingdom and the United States, with fewer numbers from Australia, New Zealand, and Canada. The education of gifted students is not a frequent inclusion in most teacher preparation programs in these countries (NAGC, 2015; Riley & Sturgess, 2005; Taylor & Milton, 2006) and so the awareness of the highly able learner's characteristics and needs may be similar to that found in national systems. Despite the promotion of the IB Diploma as a suitable curriculum for gifted students, the IBO does not encourage or require Diploma teachers to undertake any specific training in the learning needs of highly able students (Vanderbrook, 2006).

One idiosyncratic feature of international schools is the relatively frequent turnover of staff. In a survey of 25 international schools accredited by US organisations, Hawley (1994) found that the average length of tenure of an international school head was 2.8 years. A more recent study of 83 international school administrators found an average tenure of 3.7 years (Benson, 2011), while another study found the average teacher turnover rate in international schools was 17% per year (Mancuso, Roberts, & White, 2010). Many teachers and principals do stay in schools for much longer than this, but frequent faculty and administrative changes can make it difficult to establish a program or provision and to ensure continuity. However, this frequent turnover ensures that change is a constant feature of international schools, which may present an opportunity for innovative leaders to introduce new approaches or policies (Gillespie, 2017). Likewise, international school students are also particularly mobile and this may also present challenges, as well as opportunities. For example, some schools or systems may cover particular topics in a different sequence, leading to gaps in knowledge that may exclude some highly able learners from advanced opportunities, or conversely, they may be expected to repeat a topic that has already been thoroughly mastered. Students may be faced with adapting not only to different curricula, but also to very different styles of teaching, such as that encountered when moving from a more traditional, prescriptive knowledge-based system, to one in which open-ended inquiry and questioning is encouraged.

Educators have long found tensions with providing programs for highly able students, and the international school context is no exception. The political tensions inherent in discussing the concept of giftedness have held back international school educators in particular, in making these first steps. There is virtually no research in existence on giftedness in international schools, and research from the dominant US perspective may make assumptions about classroom practices that seem far removed from the reality of the international school classroom (Hertzog, 2017). School leaders are wary of alienating their parent community and may fear charges of elitism (Gallagher & Curtain, 2017). Cultural differences in the way intelligence is perceived may also play a role. Contrary to the popular myth of the Tiger Mother (Chua, 2011), many Asian parents are extremely humble when it comes to discussing their children's talents. The Asian conception of intelligence tends to follow the belief that success comes only through hard work and effort, and there is no such thing as innate ability (Juang, Qin, & Park, 2013; Ripley, 2013). Combined with a deep respect for education and educators, these parents may be particularly unwilling to put themselves in the role of advocate.

Taking a Talent Development Approach. The way forward for international schools is to celebrate their uniqueness and to accept that, just as a 'one-size-fits-all' education typically fits no-one, a 'one-size-fits-all' gifted education program imported from their home country will not meet the needs of their diverse cohort in an international context. The field in general has started to move away from traditional notions of gifted education and towards a broader, more flexible and inclusive talent development perspective (Olszewski-Kubilius, 2012; Subotnik, Stoeger, & Olszewski-Kubilius, 2017), and nowhere is this more applicable than in the richly diverse environments of international schools.

Talent development as a concept was foregrounded by the work of Benjamin Bloom (1985) with talented artists, scientists, and athletes. Talent development offers an inclusive way to think about and work with students of high ability, because rather than conceptualising high ability solely in terms of innate intelligence, talent development proposes that giftedness is a state that an individual grows into and develops over time, given the appropriate opportunities, support, and effort (Olszewski-Kubilius, 2012). This perspective aligns with more recent thinking about growth mindset (Dweck, 2008) and the malleability of the brain, and it recognises the importance of non-cognitive factors in transforming potential into achievement (Olszewski-Kubilius & Thompson, 2015; Subotnik, 2015). While students may demonstrate exceptional potential in general ability in the early years of school, domain-specific ability becomes more important over time, with the understanding that exceptional ability may take varying degrees of time and diverse pathways to become transformed into exceptional achievement, depending on the specific knowledge or performance domain involved.

The talent development approach does not emphasise the identification and labelling of a select group of students based on a generic list of criteria or on the basis of an IQ test. Instead, the emphasis is on identifying students who have a mismatch between their level of academic need and their currently provided level of curriculum and instruction. This is particularly important in the international school context as giftedness, from a talent development perspective, is a system involving both an individual and their environment, making the context critical to the development of any policies or programs (Subotnik et al., 2017). Where a school is highly selective or populated with the children of many highly educated locals and expats, the IQ distribution of the student body is likely to be skewed towards the higher end. In some cases, identification processes that rely on IQ cut scores may end up identifying half the school population. On the other hand, even native English speaking children may lack the shared cultural capital required to score well on IQ tests if they have spent their formative years away from their home country. In either case, rather than focus on arbitrary scores or labels, the primary concern should always be the academic needs of the student and the degree to which a student *fits* with their current educational environment.

Expat students may arrive at an international school with a gifted label from their national system and a history of participation in different forms of gifted programming. The label, and the underlying information that goes with it, will be helpful to the new school in forming a picture of the new student, but may not necessarily confer any special status in the new environment. Services that were required because of a mismatch in the previous environment may not be necessary in the new one. A gifted student in a PYP classroom may require only minor adjustments to the curriculum or environment (Carber & Reis, 2004), whereas a gifted learner enrolled in a school using the UK National Curriculum or the Common Core State Standards may require more substantial accommodations.

Ideally, admissions teams will include an educator who is knowledgeable and experienced with highly able learners. Appropriate placement decisions can alleviate many potential problems later on. The frequent mobility of highly able expat TCKs can provide an opportunity to align their current level of academic functioning with an appropriate educational fit, especially when moving between systems with different calendars. For example, a student moving from a Southern hemisphere school calendar to a Northern hemisphere calendar will face a choice of having to repeat one semester, or to advance one semester. Schools will often advocate a conservative approach, wary of 'gaps' arising from the switch in curricula, but for a highly able learner this may present an opportunity to find a more challenging educational fit. It is important that such decisions are made with a basis of knowledge of the research on academic acceleration (Dare, Smith, & Nowecki, 2016).

All children learn best in a challenging, enriched environment. The starting point for international schools is to ensure that a rigorous, academically challenging curriculum is in place for all learners (Olszewski-Kubilius & Thompson, 2015). If the average ability level of the entire cohort is skewed one standard deviation to the right, then the grade-level curriculum should be similarly skewed. An inclusive, responsive classroom is one where all students are supported to work in their Zone of Proximal Development, to be challenged and stretched to reach mastery, and to be empowered in fostering a growth mindset (Smith, 2017). Most international schools are uniquely placed to be able to choose the most appropriate curriculum for their particular context and mission. Many are extremely well resourced in terms of technology, facilities, and faculties, and their legislative freedom allows them to be innovative and to experiment with their curriculum design and delivery.

From this foundation of challenge and enrichment for all, a talent development approach to meeting the needs of the highly able should allow schools to identify those students with a mismatch between their level of readiness and their current educational placement, regardless of any labels which may or may not apply, and to provide a menu of services with which to address that mismatch. All talent development starts with exposure to a challenging curriculum and a diverse array of enrichment opportunities, allowing for emergent talents to be identified and strengthened (Olszewski-Kubilius & Thompson, 2015; Subotnik, 2015).

Rather than starting with identification and then providing programming, the talent development approach begins with exposing all students to an enriched curriculum, and then identifying students who may benefit from additional services (Olszewski-Kubilius & Clarenbach, 2012). As more formal identification becomes necessary, it should be based on domain-specific abilities and achievement, rather than general ability. Research has shown that by middle school, domain-specific abilities are a better indicator of adult accomplishments than are measures of general intelligence (Subotnik et al., 2017).

Some highly able children may do well academically in the regular international school classroom, with appropriate differentiation and enrichment. Others may need acceleration, either in their area of greatest need or through whole grade level advancement. Academic and social and emotional development may best be supported by placement in a self-contained gifted class, within a cluster group of similarly able children in a regular classroom or in a placement with older peers. In this inclusive approach, the door is always kept open for late bloomers or for domains in which talent typically develops later (Subotnik, 2015). As always, the *need,* not the label, should be the guide. An example of a Talent Development Framework can be seen in Figure 1.

In this framework, it is the support services that are classified, not the students, with the opportunities becoming gradually more selective as the need for more advanced expertise grows (Treffinger et al., 2004). As talent is developmental, the nature of the support required at different stages will necessarily change (Dai, 2017). Any student may benefit from the services offered at Levels 1 and 2, and so formal identification is not necessary for a student to take advantage of them. For Level 3 services onwards, specific selection criteria apply in order to ensure the best match between the academic opportunity provided and the students most likely to benefit from them. Just as giftedness develops from exceptional potential to domain-specific achievement, the services provided also become more specialised over time. As such, the selection criteria should also reflect the demands of the specific domain (Subotnik, Worrell, & Olszewski-Kubilius, 2017). The key tenets of a talent development approach are inclusivity, flexibility, and responsiveness, so it is vital that a range of services is available, depending on student need and the local context.

Implementing change designed to meet the needs of highly able learners can be fraught with misconceptions, emotional baggage, and conflicting values. International school leaders should be guided by their individual school context when developing policies that support the needs of highly able learners in their own schools (Gallagher & Curtain, 2017). However, developing a school policy should include an opportunity to examine inherent biases and deeply held beliefs, and to construct a philosophical statement that the leadership team can support. Using the school's existing mission statement as a starting point will ensure consistency with the school context and culture. Political tension can be alleviated when schools develop robust practices that have a strong foundation in equity and inclusion, that are supported by research, and that align with the school's mission and vision.

International schools will have success in easing tension and concerns around meeting the needs of their highly able learners by developing a policy or approach that has more or less emphasis on particular provisions or programs. See Table 1.

LEVEL 1 – TALENT DEVELOPMENT FOR ALL STUDENTS

Differentiated and challenging content and process for all students
Occurs in the regular classroom every day
Provides foundational skills and explicit tools of metacognition
Exposure to a diverse array of subjects, topics and talent opportunities

Examples: Differentiated instruction, including preassessment and instructional compacting, field trips, guest speakers, creativity challenges, mindfulness training

LEVEL 2 – TALENT DEVELOPMENT FOR MANY STUDENTS

Invitational opportunities—'everyone might; not everyone will'
Open enrolment—students may self-select or be nominated by parent or teacher
Exploration of possible strengths, talents or interests

Examples: after-school activities & clubs, science fairs, competitions, some performing arts opportunities, non-selective sports & music programs, leadership opportunities

LEVEL 3 – TALENT DEVELOPMENT FOR SOME STUDENTS

Responds to needs based on demonstrated strengths, talents and interests
Student selection based on readiness and likely success in specific activity
Specific criteria for participation—evidence of achievement or ability in specific content area

Examples: Advanced courses, placement in cluster group or telescoped curriculum group, selective sports teams, audition-based performing arts activities, some criteria-based competitions

LEVEL FOUR – TALENT DEVELOPMENT FOR A FEW STUDENTS

High-level, individualised services constructed for a particular student in response to strengthening expertise in one or more specific content areas
Supported by Child Study Team or similar

Examples: Whole grade or subject acceleration, online courses, mentorships, personalized or non-traditional pathways

Adapted from Treffinger, Young, Nassab, & Wittig (2004).

Fig. 1 Talent Development Framework

Case Study: Talent Development in Practice. At the International School of the Pacific (pseudonym), it is the practice of the admissions team to flag any highly able learners during the admissions process and refer the files to the highly able student support team. Such was the case with Kaylin, who was moving with her family from the United States, where she had been enrolled in an accelerated

Table 1 Developing defensible talent development policies

More emphasis on	Less emphasis on
Identifying who needs additional challenge.	Identifying who is gifted.
Providing inclusive opportunities for appropriate challenge for all learners, including the highly able.	Providing exclusive opportunities for challenge for a specific group of students.
Ensuring multiple opportunities for student need to be identified or recognised.	Using a one-off screening tool or identification process.
Providing a range of different services to focus on different needs.	Providing a 'one size fits all' program.
Providing scheduling and grouping structures and support so student needs can be met in the regular classroom as much as possible.	Relying heavily on pull-out models of support.
Shared responsibility of all teachers.	Responsibility of the 'gifted support' teacher.
Professional development for all teachers to support high-end differentiation.	Professional development only for the 'gifted support' teacher.

(Gallagher & Curtain, 2017)

program in a local selective school. Reports submitted during the application process indicated that Kaylin was currently working at least one year ahead of her current grade level across all subject areas, and was several grades advanced in mathematics. Although age-appropriate for grade six, after discussion with the parents and a more comprehensive data-gathering process, the team made the decision to offer Kaylin a place in grade seven. This represented a one-year grade skip. Further assessments with locally normed mathematics tests determined that an appropriate mathematics placement would be a high school class, mostly populated by grade ten students.

Taking a high school mathematics class involved some trade-offs for Kaylin's middle school schedule, but after discussions with the family, Kaylin and her parents decided to proceed. Starting the educational planning early, during the admissions process, meant that Kaylin's transition to ISP was much smoother than it might have been, had the team waited. Kaylin quickly settled in to grade seven, excelling academically and forming a close circle of friends, who considered her modified schedule to be unremarkable. For the first few weeks, she was something of a novelty in her tenth grade mathematics class, but she quickly earned the respect of her peers for her quiet determination and became a valued partner or group participant.

Besides her whole-grade and subject acceleration, the student support team also steered Kaylin towards some targeted extra-curricular opportunities to provide additional challenge and enrichment in her other areas of strength. They also provided her parents with information about community resources that would enable Kaylin to further develop her talents in soccer, her other main passion.

Kaylin has continued to thrive, both academically and socially. She is now on track to complete IB Higher Level Mathematics by the end of grade nine. A plan is in place that will allow her to continue on to IB Further Mathematics, followed by an individual pathway of university-level mathematics, accessed online and supported by a local mentor.

Implications and Future Directions

Once a local policy has been established, schools can begin the process of designing or expanding a menu of services that will help to meet the needs of their highly able learners. As well as developing procedures to support acceleration and a variety of different grouping practices to support advanced academic needs, schools may also like to:

- Take advantage of curricular flexibility to incorporate project-based learning (PBL) opportunities across the school. This can range from relatively short-term projects in primary classrooms, to designing entire high school courses around the principles of PBL. One international school in China has taken the concept of '20% time' literally, allocating one-day-per-week for students in primary classrooms to work on individual projects.
- Capitalise on the enhanced sense of justice common to many gifted students and find the time to include service-learning opportunities in the curriculum. Like project-based learning, service learning helps to meet the needs of highly able students for meaningful, open-ended, differentiated learning experiences. "Service is a *need* of the gifted. I have found tremendous moral sensitivity in the gifted population, a desire to help others and a desire for their lives to be meaningful. When gifted children find their paths of service, they experience a deep sense of fulfilment, as if there is some reason that they are here" (Silverman, 1994). Despite the background of economic advantage inherent in international schools, most have a plethora of service learning opportunities on their doorsteps.
- Audit the enrichment opportunities already available and look for ways to fill in the gaps. Some international schools have rich after-school sports and arts programs, but there are fewer opportunities for academic enrichment. Look for what is missing and encourage interested faculty to offer something in their own area of passion. In investigating what contributed to exceptional achievement and productivity in STEM careers, researchers found that early exposure to a consistent and sufficient 'dose' of talent development opportunities, both in and out of school, was of primary importance (Wai, Lubinski, Benbow, & Steiger, 2010). These included talent searches, summer programs, competitions and science fairs, scientific research, and writing opportunities. The greater the 'dose', the greater the impact on future STEM accomplishments, including PhDs, patents, and publications.
- Investigate competitions as a source of enrichment and powerful learning. Competition can present an effective way for students to learn about losing *and* about winning—graciously. "With experience, people learn that winning and losing are just short-term consequences to the long-term goal: improvement" (Bronson & Merryman, 2013, p. 239). There are many competitions that are open to students in international schools, including international programs like the Google Science Fair, the Intel International Science and Engineering Fair, the Scholastic Art and Writing Awards, Mathematical Olympiad, Mathematics Counts, and Mathematics League. The World Scholar's Cup is a global multidisciplinary academic competition popular with international schools, and programs like Tournament of Minds are expanding internationally. There may

also be regional competitions that offer students the benefit of interacting with other like-minded competitors.

- Introduce a mentoring program and take advantage of the rich untapped resource of talented parents that is common to most international schools. A mentorship involves a supportive relationship in which an experienced guide facilitates the learning and understanding of a student with a keen interest and strength in a particular area, in which the guide has expertise. Mentors are positive role models and may provide insight into the pathways to high achievement as well as give practical support to a student's learning.
- Organise or join a local network of international schools with the purpose of sharing ideas, expertise, and resources among highly able learners. Many international schools are already members of interscholastic sporting organisations. Find out what opportunities exist for shared academic pursuits and look for ways to expand them.
- Lobby the International Baccalaureate Organisation to increase the flexibility of the IB Diploma and to educate university admissions departments of the potential for highly able students to follow a non-standard IB pathway.

Further research is called for on how to develop talent in advanced learners within the unique international school contexts. All of the above pedagogic recommendations also lend themselves to evaluation and to research in relation to highly able learners, for example, policy development, project-based learning, mentoring, enrichment, competitions, acceleration, grouping, and the talent development approach.

Conclusion

Despite the claims of some international schools, it would be naïve to suggest that the academic needs of all students can be met simply by providing access to a rich curriculum and learning environment. However, it would also be unwise to attempt to transplant a gifted education program from a national system to an international school. Definitions, policies, and practices designed for one particular system may have limited applicability in the complex context of an international school. Assumptions of a state or national system, such as access to magnet schools, university campuses, or weekend enrichment courses, are unlikely to translate to the international location. Nonetheless, international schools can capitalise on the flexibility that is inherent in their independence and strive to be truly innovative in their approach to individual differences. Taking a talent development perspective may help international schools to develop a menu of context-specific services for meeting the needs of their highly able learners that are rigorous, sustainable, defensible, and effective.

Cross-References

▶ Gifted Education in the Asia-Pacific: From the Past for the Future – An Introduction
▶ Sociocultural Perspectives on the Talent Development Megamodel
▶ Some Implications for the Future of Gifted Education in the Asia-Pacific

References

Benson, J. (2011). An investigation of chief administrator turnover in international schools. *Journal of Research in International Education., 10*(1), 87–103. https://doi.org/10.1177/1475240911398779

Bloom, B. (1985). *Developing talent in young people*. New York, NY: Ballantine.

Bronson, P., & Merryman, A. (2013). *Top dog: The science of winning and losing*. New York, NY: Twelve.

Carber, S., & Reis, S. (2004). Commonalities in IB practice and the schoolwide enrichment model. *Journal of Research in International Education., 3*(3), 339–359. https://doi.org/10.1177/1475240904047359

Chua, A. (2011). *Battle hymn of the tiger mother*. New York, NY: Penguin Press.

Dai, D. (2017). Envisioning a new foundation for gifted education: Evolving complexity theory (ECT) of talent development. *Gifted Child Quarterly, 6*(13), 172–182. https://doi.org/10.1177/0016986217701837

Dare, L., Smith, S. R., & Nowecki, E. (2016). Parents' experiences of grade-based acceleration: Successes, struggles, and subsequent needs. *Australasian Journal of Gifted Education, 25*(2), 6–21. https://doi.org/10.21505/ajge.2016.0012

Doherty, C. (2013). Making a point of difference: The globalised ecology of the international baccalaureate diploma in Australian schools. *Globalisation, Societies and Education, 11*(3), 379–397. https://doi.org/10.1080/14767724.2012.761809

Dweck, C. (2008). *Mindsets: The new psychology of success*. New York, NY: Ballantine.

Foust, R. C., Hertberg-Davis, H., & Callahan, C. M. (2008). "Having it all" at sleep's expense: The forced choice of participants in advanced placement courses and international baccalaureate programs. *Roeper Review, 30*(2), 121–129. https://doi.org/10.1080/02783190801955293

Gallagher, S., & Curtain, T. (2017). *Serve the need, not the label: Highly able students in international schools*. Charleston, SC: CreateSpace.

Gillespie, S. N. (2017). *The role of leadership in changing the culture of an international school to be inclusive of students with special learning needs* (Unpublished doctoral dissertation). Minneapolis, MN: Walden University.

Gross, M. U. M., Urquhart, R., Doyle, J., Juratowitch, M., & Matheson, G. (2011). *Releasing the brakes for high ability learners: Administrator, teacher and parent attitudes and beliefs that block or assist the implementation of school policies on academic acceleration*. Sydney, Australia: University of New South Wales.

Hawley, D. B. (1994). How long do international school heads survive? A research analysis (part 1). *International Schools Journal, 14*(1), 8–21.

Hayden, M., & Thompson, J. (2008). *International schools: Growth and influence*. Paris, France: UNESCO International Institute for Educational Planning.

Hertberg-Davis, H., & Callahan, C. M. (2008). A narrow escape: Gifted students' perceptions of Advanced Placement and International Baccalaureate programs. *Gifted Child Quarterly, 52*(3), 199–216. https://doi.org/10.1177/0016986208319705

Hertberg-Davis, H., Callahan, C. M., & Kyburg, R. M. (2006). *Advanced placement and international baccalaureate programs: A "fit" for gifted learners? (RM06222)*. Storrs, CT: The National Research Center on the Gifted and Talented, University of Connecticut.

Hertzog, N. (2017). Designing the learning context in school for talent development. *Gifted Child Quarterly, 61*(3), 219–228. https://doi.org/10.1177/0016986217705712

International Baccalaureate Organisation. (n.d.-a, IBOa). About the IB. Retrieved from https://www.ibo.org/about-the-ib/

International Baccalaureate Organisation. (n.d.-b, IBOb). Diploma programme. Retrieved from https://www.ibo.org/diploma-programme/

International Baccalaureate Organisation. (n.d.-c, IBOc). Middle years programme. Retrieved from https://www.ibo.org/middle-years-programme/

International Baccalaureate Organisation. (n.d.-d, IBOd). Primary years programme. Retrieved from https://www.ibo.org/primary-years-programme/

International Schools Consultancy Research. (2016a). *Demand for international education continues to expand globally.* Retrieved from https://www.iscresearch.com

International Schools Consultancy Research. (2016b). *Research survey: Inclusion in international schools and those offering international curricula*. Retrieved from https://www.iscresearch.com

John Catt Ltd. (2016). *Report reveals rapid rise in international schools*. Retrieved from http://www.internationalschoolsearch.com/news/report-reveals-rapid-rise-in-international-schools

Juang, L. P., Qin, D. B., & Park, I. J. K. (2013). Deconstructing the myth of the "tiger mother": An introduction to the special issue on tiger parenting, Asian–heritage families, and child/adolescent wellbeing. *Asian American Journal of Psychology., 4*(1), 1–6. https://doi.org/10.1037/a0032136

Mancuso, S. V., Roberts, L., & White, G. P. (2010). Teacher retention in international schools: The key role of school leadership. *Journal of Research in International Education, 9*(3), 306–323. https://doi.org/10.1177/1475240910388928

National Association for Gifted Children [NAGC]. (2004). *Acceleration position statement*. Washington, DC: National Association for Gifted Children.

National Association for Gifted Children [NAGC]. (2015). *2014–2015 state of the states in gifted education: Policy and practice data*. Washington, DC: National Association for Gifted Children & The Council of State Directors of Programs for the Gifted.

Olszewski-Kubilius, P. (2012). Building on the best of gifted education with programming for talent development. *The Catalyst, 1*(2), 1–6.

Olszewski-Kubilius, P., & Clarenbach, J. (2012). *Unlocking emergent talent: Supporting high achievement of low-income, high ability students*. Washington, DC: National Association for Gifted Children.

Olszewski-Kubilius, P., & Thompson, D. (2015). Talent development as a framework for gifted education. *Gifted Child Today., 38*(1), 49–59. https://doi.org/10.1177/1076217514556531

Riley, T., & Sturgess, A. (2005). Professional development to support gifted and talented education in New Zealand. *Australasian Journal of Gifted Education, 14*(1), 36–49.

Ripley, A. (2013). *The smartest kids in the world: And how they got that way*. New York, NY: Simon & Schuster.

Rogers, K. (2007). Lessons learned about educating the gifted and talented: A synthesis of the research on educational practice. *Gifted Child Quarterly, 51*(4), 382–396. https://doi.org/10.1177/0016986207306324

Shaunessy, E., Suldo, S. M., Hardesty, R. B., & Shaffer, E. J. (2006). School functioning and psychological well-being of International Baccalaureate and General Education students. *The Journal of Secondary Gifted Education, 17*(2), 76–89. https://doi.org/10.4219/jsge-2006-683

Sheard, W. (2008). Lessons from our kissing cousins: Third culture kids and gifted children. *Roeper Review, 30*(1), 31–38. https://doi.org/10.1080/02783190701836437

Silverman, L. (1994). The moral sensitivity of gifted children and the evolution of society. *Roeper Review, 17*, 110–116. https://doi.org/10.1080/02783199409553636

Smith, S. R. (2017). Responding to the unique social and emotional learning needs of gifted Australian students. In E. Frydenberg, A. Martin, & R. Collie (Eds.), *Social and emotional learning in Australia and the Asia-Pacific* (pp. 147–166). Singapore: Springer.

Subotnik, R. (2015). Psychosocial strength training: The missing piece in talent development. *Gifted Child Today, 38*(1), 41–48. https://doi.org/10.1177/1076217514556530

Subotnik, R., Stoeger, H., & Olszewski-Kubilius, P. (2017). Talent development research, policy and practice in Europe and the United States: Outcomes from a summit of international

researchers. *Gifted   Child   Quarterly,   61*(3),   262–269.   https://doi.org/10.1177/
0016986217701839

Subotnik, R., Worrell, F. C., & Olszewski-Kubilius, P. (2017). The 15-minute audition: Translating
a proof of concept into a domain-specific screening device for mathematical talent. *Gifted
Quarterly, 61*(3), 164–171. https://doi.org/10.1177/0016986217701835

Suldo, S. M., Shaunessy-Dedrick, E., Ferron, J., & Dedrick, R. F. (2018). Predictors of success
among high school students in advanced placement and International Baccalaureate programs.
Gifted Child Quarterly, 62(4), 350–373. https://doi.org/10.1177/0016986218758443

Taylor, T., & Milton, M. (2006). Preparation for teaching gifted students: An investigation into
university courses in Australia. *Australasian Journal of Gifted Education., 15*(1), 25–31.

Treffinger, D. J., Young, G. C., Nassab, C. A., & Wittig, C. V. (2004). *Enhancing and expanding
gifted programs: The levels of service approach*. Waco, TX: Prufrock Press.

United States Department of State. (n.d.). *Transitioning to an overseas assignment with a child with
special needs: Guidance for parents supporting a gifted child in the foreign service*. Retrieved
from https://www.state.gov/m/a/os/208865.htm

Useem, H. R., & Cottrell, A. B. (1999). *TCKs four times more likely to earn bachelor's degrees*.
TCKWorld. Retrieved from http://www.tckworld.com/useem/art2.html

Useem, J., & Useem, H. R. (1967). The interfaces of a binational third culture: A study of the
American community in India. *Journal of Social Issues, 23*(1), 130–143. https://doi.org/
10.1111/j.1540-4560.1967.tb00567.x

Vanderbrook, C. M. (2006). Intellectually gifted females and their perspectives of lived experience
in the AP and IB programs. *The Journal of Secondary Gifted Education, 17*(3), 5–20. Retrieved
from https://files.eric.ed.gov/fulltext/EJ746051.pdf

Wai, J., Lubinski, D., Benbow, C. P., & Steiger, J. H. (2010). Accomplishment in Science,
Technology, Engineering and Mathematics (STEM) and its relation to STEM educational
dose: A 25-year longitudinal study. *Journal of Educational Psychology, 102*(4), 860–871.
https://doi.org/10.1037/a0019454

Wright, E., Lee, M., Tang, H., & Chak Pong Tsui, G. (2016). Why offer the International
Baccalaureate Middle Years Program? A comparison between schools in Asia-Pacific and
other regions. *Journal of Research in International Education, 15*(1), 3–17. https://doi.org/
10.1177/1475240916635896

Selena Gallagher, who completed her PhD in gifted education through the University of New
England, Australia, and has worked with highly able students in Australia, the United Kingdom,
China, Thailand, and Egypt. Dr Gallagher is involved in working with international schools to
develop and implement gifted education and talent development programs. Her professional and
research interests include acceleration and ability grouping as a response to advanced academic
ability, the adoption of a talent development philosophy as a whole-school approach to the needs of
highly able students, the intersection of giftedness and growth mindset, and expanded conceptions
of giftedness.

The Predictors of the Decisions by Gifted Students to Pursue STEM Careers: The Case of Brazilian International Students in Australia

59

Jae Yup Jung, Tay T. R. Koo, Peta K. Hay, and Susen R. Smith

Contents

Abstract

A review of the current research on the major predictors of the decisions made by gifted students to pursue careers in *Science, Technology, Engineering, and*

J. Y. Jung (✉) · P. K. Hay
GERRIC/School of Education, The University of New South Wales, Sydney, NSW, Australia
e-mail: jae.jung@unsw.edu.au; p.hay@unsw.edu.au

T. T. R. Koo
The University of New South Wales, Sydney, NSW, Australia
e-mail: t.koo@unsw.edu.au

S. R. Smith
GERRIC, School of Education, The University of New South Wales, Sydney, NSW, Australia
e-mail: susen.smith@unsw.edu.au

© Crown 2021
S. R. Smith (ed.), *Handbook of Giftedness and Talent Development in the Asia-Pacific*,
Springer International Handbooks of Education,
https://doi.org/10.1007/978-981-13-3041-4_71

Mathematics (STEM) areas is presented in this chapter. After a discussion of the main findings of the *Study of Mathematically Precocious Youth*, elements of the emerging literature on the STEM career decisions of adolescents and the career decisions of gifted students in general are introduced. Thereafter, two theories that may be among the most relevant to understanding the STEM career decisions of gifted students—the theory of circumscription and compromise and the theory of work adjustment—are outlined. As an illustrative example, the findings of a two-stage mixed methods study on the predictors of the STEM career decisions of gifted Brazilian international students who have studied in Australia are reported. The chapter concludes with a number of suggestions for future research and practice.

Keywords

Career decision · Career choice · Gifted · STEM · Brazil · Australia · Asia · Asia-Pacific · International students

The aims in this chapter are to:
1. Provide an overview of the major predictors of the STEM career decisions of gifted students.
2. Outline the career theories that may be most relevant and useful in understanding the STEM career decisions of gifted students.
3. Elaborate on the major predictors of the STEM career decisions of gifted Brazilian international students who have studied in Australia.
4. Outline areas for future research and practice on the STEM career decisions of gifted students.

Introduction

Around the world, there appears to be a decreasing level of interest in the pursuit of careers in the fields of *Science, Technology, Engineering, and Mathematics* (STEM) by young people generally (Lyons, Cooksey, Panizzon, Parnell, & Pegg, 2006; Nugent et al., 2015; Osborne & Dillon, 2008). This is despite the fact that a wide consensus exists on the importance of such fields to allow for the support of national and global economies, and for the development of the scientific literacy that may be necessary for people to make informed decisions and to actively participate in civic and cultural life (National Academy of Sciences, 2010; Nugent et al., 2015). The focus in this chapter is on the career decisions in STEM fields of a group of young people—gifted students—who by the virtue of their exceptional abilities may have the greatest potential to make a substantial impact on the lives of others in society (Jung, 2012, 2019, in press a). In this chapter, gifted students have been defined as advanced learners with higher academic potential than their age peers (Gagné, 2009).

It is noted that the general lack of research in the area has meant that the chapter is informed not only by the select number of studies that have investigated the STEM career decisions of gifted students, but also by studies on the STEM career decisions of general adolescents, and the emerging literature on the career decisions of gifted students in general. As an illustrative example, the case is presented of the career decisions of gifted students from one part of the broad Asia-Pacific region (i.e., Brazil) who have undertaken studies at the tertiary level in STEM areas in another part of the Asia-Pacific region (i.e., Australia), as international exchange students.

Study of Mathematically Precocious Youth

The research that exists, at the present time, on the STEM career decisions of gifted students primarily relates to a number of longitudinal studies originating from the *Study of Mathematically Precocious Youth* that was instigated by Julian C. Stanley in 1971 to identify and develop talent for Science, Technology, Engineering, and Mathematics among intellectually gifted students (Lubinski & Benbow, 2006; Lubinski, Benbow, & Kell, 2014). Under this series of studies, longitudinal data were collected from five separate cohorts of gifted students in the United States, representing students in the top 3% of intellectual ability (i.e., students in the top 3% of ability approximately at age 12–13 for the first four cohorts and top first and second year postgraduate students in the fields of mathematics and science attending elite universities in the United States for the fifth cohort) across almost five decades (Lubinski & Benbow, 2006). These studies have generally suggested that the decisions by exceptionally gifted students to pursue careers in STEM fields may be predicted by their patterns of cognitive ability, gender, interests, values, and level of commitment (Lubinski & Benbow, 2006; Lubinski et al., 2014; Park, Lubinski, & Benbow, 2007).

Lubinski and Benbow (2006) suggest that among the most important predictors of the STEM career intentions of gifted students may be their comparative levels of verbal, mathematical, and spatial abilities. Specifically, higher levels of mathematical and spatial abilities in comparison to verbal abilities appear to be consistent with decisions to pursue future study and careers in areas such as engineering, mathematics and computer science, while higher levels of verbal abilities in comparison to mathematical/spatial abilities appear to be associated with later study and careers in the social sciences and the humanities (Lubinski & Benbow, 2006; Park et al., 2007). Interestingly, gender differences appear to exist in the patterns of comparative ability, with gifted male students more likely than gifted female students to exhibit higher levels of mathematical/spatial ability (Park et al., 2007). Such comparative ability patterns may be conducive to the time and effort that is devoted to the different activity domains by gifted students, irrespective of whether the relevant educational opportunities are provided to these students (Lubinski, Webb, Morelock, & Benbow, 2001). Nevertheless, the importance of non-ability factors in the pursuit of STEM careers is highlighted by the fact that approximately 25% of gifted students with higher levels of mathematics/spatial abilities *have not* been found to pursue STEM careers in later life, while approximately 33% of gifted students with higher levels of verbal abilities *have* been found to eventually pursue STEM careers (Lubinski et al., 2001).

Among the most important non-ability factors may be the areas of interest and values of gifted students. Again, gender differences have been identified, with gifted male students appearing to demonstrate a preference for 'things' and gifted female students indicating a preference to work with people (Lubinski & Benbow, 2006). This may be illustrated by the fact that 72% of male students and only 35% of female students in the fourth cohort of the Study of Mathematically Precocious Youth ranked 'theoretical' values as one of their top two dimensions in the Study of Values (Allport, Vernon, & Lindzey, 1960), while 16% of male students and 61% of female students in the same cohort ranked 'artistic' interests to be among the top two vocational dimensions under Holland's RIASEC taxonomy of occupational classifications (Achter, Lubinski, & Benbow, 1996; Harmon, Hansen, Borgen, & Hammer, 1994; Holland, 1997). Furthermore, Lubinski and Benbow (2006) observed that, "social interests and values were nearly three times as likely to be in the top two (dimensions) for females as for males, whereas males were four times as likely as females to rank realistic interests as one of their top two (dimensions)" (p. 328).

In recognition of the intellectually demanding and the time-consuming nature of many careers in STEM fields, Lubinski and Benbow (2006) have also highlighted the importance of a willingness to devote substantial amounts of time and effort to be an important predictor of STEM career outcomes. While some variation was noted among the Study of Mathematically Precocious Youth participants in the precise degree of commitment they would be willing to give, a gender difference was again identified, with gifted females comparatively less likely to demonstrate a willingness to work long hours than gifted males, possibly reflecting their greater willingness to sacrifice their career aspirations for the needs of their family (Lubinski & Benbow, 2006).

Whether it is related to differences in ability patterns, interests, values, or conative factors, the findings of the Study of Mathematically Precocious Youth studies clearly and collectively suggest that gifted male students may be much more likely than gifted female students to choose STEM careers. Interestingly, no mention is made in these studies of the desire to pursue careers due to common societal stereotypes about traditional gender roles, despite the fact that it has been frequently raised in the literature on the general career decisions of gifted students (Chen & Wong, 2013; Fiebig, 2008: Kerr & Sodano, 2003; Miller & Cummings, 2009).

Literature on STEM Careers and Gifted Student Career Decisions

In broad terms, the literature on the factors influencing the pursuit of STEM careers among adolescents and the literature on the career decisions of gifted students in general appear collectively to *reiterate* the importance of factors such as ability, interests, and values noted in the Study of Mathematically Precocious Youth as informing the STEM career decisions of gifted students. Simultaneously, the literature in the two areas has provided possible elaborations on these factors and has raised the possibility of the importance of other factors in the pursuit of STEM careers by gifted students.

Ability, Interests, and Values

Jung (2019) noted the joint and pivotal roles that abilities, interests, and values may play in the general career decisions of gifted students. These three intrapersonal factors have also been recognised by scholars to be among the major considerations in the formulation of intentions to pursue STEM careers by adolescents in the general population. Indeed, van Tuijl and van der Molen (2016) have suggested that the focus of studies in the area have been on these three factors, while Wang, Ye, and Degol (2017) have proposed that cognitive ability along with motivational beliefs (defined as ability self-concept, *interest*, utility *value*, and attainment *value*) may be major influences on STEM career decisions, with cognitive ability possibly setting "the stage for successful pursuit of STEM careers [while] interest and task value are likely to motivate youth to persist through these STEM pathways" (p. 1807).

With respect to ability, Wang et al. (2017) have suggested that mathematical/scientific abilities may not need to be exceptionally high to allow for the successful pursuit of STEM careers. Nevertheless, they proposed that low-level abilities in these domains may present barriers that may be difficult to overcome, while high-level abilities may increase the likelihood of pursuing STEM careers. Furthermore, reflecting the findings in the Study of Mathematically Precocious Youth (Lubinski & Benbow, 2006; Park et al., 2007), Wang et al. (2017) suggested that *relative* strengths in mathematical/scientific abilities in comparison to verbal abilities may be more important than *absolute* strengths in mathematics or science in the pursuit of STEM careers, due to the fact that the existence of relative strengths may allow for the capitalisation on one's strengths and the avoidance of one's weaknesses. Related to abilities, some scholars in the field of STEM careers have further suggested that *confidence* in one's ability in STEM areas, or self-efficacy in STEM areas, may be a major predictor of STEM-related activities, choice of STEM study areas, and the eventual pursuit of careers in STEM and related areas (Britner & Pajares, 2001; Nugent et al., 2015; Vedder-Weiss & Fortus, 2013).

In comparison, studies on the construct of *interest* in the literature on STEM careers and gifted student career decisions have tended to focus on the enjoyment and satisfaction that may be gained from such careers (DeBacker & Nelson, 1999; Jung, 2019; Nugent et al., 2015; Organisation for Economic Co-operation and Development, 2007; Steenbergen-Hu & Olszewski-Kubilius, 2017; Wang et al., 2017). Therefore, in recognition of the stereotypical views of STEM careers in society that may swing between "the two visions of a man in a white lab coat staring intelligently at some exotic glassware full of scientific-looking liquid, or of a wild-haired eccentric solving mile long equations but incapable of posting a letter" (Organisation for Economic Co-operation and Development, 2008, pp. 55–56) and common perceptions that such careers may be 'dry', 'boring', 'uncreative', 'inflexible', 'unsociable' and 'dangerous' (Akram, Iljaz, & Ikram, 2017; Archer et al., 2010; van Tuijl & van der Molen, 2016), students who select STEM careers may be those who are able to overcome such perceptions and appreciate the many positives of these careers, including the practicality of the experimental process, the joy of discovery, and the development of innovations.

Related to the construct of interest may be a desire for intellectual challenge and stimulation that has been repeatedly recognised to characterise the career decisions of gifted students in any domain (Emmett & Minor, 1993; Herr & Cramer, 1996). Indeed, Jung (2014, 2017) identified a strong and positive relationship between the valuing of interest/enjoyment in a future career and a desire for intellectual stimulation in the career decision-making processes of two cohorts of gifted students. The challenge factor may be a particularly important contributor to interest in careers in STEM fields due to their generally high level of difficulty and intellectual rigour (Archer et al., 2010; Christensen, Knezek, & Tyler-Wood, 2014; van Tuijl & van der Molen, 2016). For example, Archer et al. (2010) have proposed that a large number of students may be attracted to the difficult nature of science when observing that many students enjoy "the challenge of science as a 'complicated' subject that requires students to use their 'brains'" (p. 629). Similarly, Xu (2013) noted that the level of satisfaction with job challenge may be an important factor that determines the career choices of highly able students at university.

Family Influence, Prestige, and Income

Among the factors that were not identified in the Study of Mathematically Precocious Youth, the literature on STEM careers and the career decisions of gifted students *both* suggest that the expectations of family members and other members of society, the desire for prestigious and well-paying careers, and a desire for careers that allow for major contributions to society may be additionally important.

Generally, gifted students appear to be subject to high-level expectations from other members of society, and particularly their families, to be successful in their future careers (Jung, 2019, in press a). Wang and Degol (2013) have proposed that family members may be particularly influential due to the environment that is created at home, the values that are promoted and the experiences that are provided. Of note, the promotion by parents of the importance and value of STEM skills has been found to be related to an increased level of self-efficacy for STEM-related tasks (Nugent et al., 2015), while parental encouragement to study STEM fields has been identified to be associated with greater interest in STEM fields, the selection of advanced courses in STEM fields and plans for future employment in STEM fields (Simpkins, Fredericks, & Eccles, 2012; Wang et al., 2017). Relatedly, having parents working in a STEM field may contribute to an increased likelihood of entry into STEM fields due to probable role modelling effects and the possible adoption of pro-STEM values (van Tuijl & van der Molen, 2016; Wang & Degol, 2013; Wang et al., 2017). Unsurprisingly, Xu (2013) has pointed out that the influence of the family may be greatest prior to the commencement of tertiary studies, as "once enrolled in higher education institutions, students start at a new social environment with relatively equal opportunities and increased autonomy to access resources and information, and to build network supports" (p. 377).

Some of the characteristics of STEM careers that the families of gifted students—along with others in society—may have the highest expectations in may be related to the prestige, respect, and the remuneration offered in such careers (Jung, 2019, in press a). For example, Nugent et al. (2015) have identified income and prestige, along with self-satisfaction, to be among the most important determinants of interest in STEM careers, while Xu (2013) has suggested that the STEM career choices of university students may be predicted by the benefits of the available career options including 'pay rate' and 'job status'. Related to these factors, both Nugent et al. (2015) and Xu (2013) make reference to the importance of *career prospects* to family and societal perceptions about whether one has been successful in a career.

Theories Relevant to the STEM Career Decisions of Gifted Students

Among the existing career theories, a number of theories may have the potential to be useful in understanding the STEM career decisions of gifted students. Within the field of gifted education, the theory of work adjustment (Dawis & Lofquist, 1984; Lofquist & Dawis, 1991) and the theory of circumscription and compromise (Gottfredson, 1981, 2002, 2005) have been identified to be among the most relevant (Jung, 2019, in press a, in press b; Muratori & Smith, 2015), while scholars of STEM career decisions among general adolescents have tended to use a number of alternative theories including Holland's RIASEC taxonomy of occupational classifications (Holland, 1997), social cognitive career theory (Lent, Brown, & Hackett, 1994), and expectancy value theory (Eccles & Wigfield, 2002; Nugent et al., 2015; van Tuijl & van der Molen, 2016; Wang & Degol, 2013; Wigfield & Eccles, 2000).

Of these theories, the theory of circumscription and compromise has been recognised to be an 'optimal' theory in understanding the STEM career decisions of both general adolescents and gifted adolescents (Jung, 2019, in press a, in press b; Muratori & Smith, 2015; van Tuijl & van der Molen, 2016), while the theory of work adjustment has been used repeatedly in the Study of Mathematically Precocious Youth (Lubinski & Benbow, 2006; Lubinski et al., 2014; Park et al., 2007). Both these theories appear to have merit in understanding the STEM career decisions of gifted students.

Theory of Circumscription and Compromise

Under the theory of circumscription and compromise, Gottfredson (1981, 2002, 2005) has proposed that the career decision is preceded by a four-stage developmental process, during which 'unacceptable' career options may be progressively removed from consideration. The first two stages of this developmental process (i.e., ages 3–5 and 6–8 years) are conceptualised to involve the development of one's interests, skills, values, and goals with respect to one's future career, while the third stage (i.e., the circumscription stage at ages 9–13 years) is considered to be the stage whereby various career options start to be eliminated on the basis of factors including gender compatibility, prestige, and interest, along with the level of difficulty, income, and the expectations of others. The final stage (i.e., the compromise stage from age 14 onwards) is seen to be the stage at which the final career decision is made according to the accessibility of the remaining career options.

It is apparent that virtually *all* of the factors that have been identified to be predictive of the STEM career decisions of gifted students—ability, gender, interests, values, family influence, prestige, income, and level of commitment—form the basis for the elimination of career options under the theory of circumscription and compromise. Specifically, gender, prestige, and interests form the three main criteria for the elimination of careers in the circumscription stage of the theory, while ability level and income form two of the other criteria for elimination at this stage. Of the remaining two predictor variables, family influences may be considered to form an element of the 'expectations of others' in the circumscription stage, while a loose interpretation of 'accessibility' may mean that the level of commitment may be recognised to be a consideration in the final, compromise stage of the theory. The theory of circumscription and compromise generally appears to represent a very good fit for conceptualising the STEM career decisions for gifted students. Nevertheless, it must be recognised that it does not capture some of the subtle nuances associated with such decisions, including the importance of comparative cognitive abilities in the mathematical, spatial, and verbal domains, or the desire for intellectual challenge and stimulation.

The Theory of Work Adjustment

In comparison, the theory of work adjustment may be considered to be a modern 'trait and factor' theory that places a focus on the congruence between the characteristics of an individual and the career. The theory proposes that a simultaneous match between: (a) the mathematical/spatial/verbal abilities of the individual and the ability requirements of a career and (b) the needs/values of the individual and the working conditions offered in the career (e.g., income and prestige) may be predictive of an 'optimal' career decision (Dawis & Lofquist, 1984; Jung, 2019; Lofquist & Dawis, 1991). In the situation where more than one career satisfies this criterion, the theory suggests that other factors may also be considered, including vocational interests, personality traits, family expectations, socio-economic status, and the state of the labour market (Dawis, 2005; Jung, 2019). It is noted that a slightly adapted version of the theory of work adjustment was used in the Study of Mathematically Precocious Youth, as interest was considered to form an element of the 'needs/values' of individuals in making determinations about what constitutes an optimal career (Lubinski & Benbow, 2006; Lubinski et al., 2014; Park et al., 2007).

As for the theory of circumscription and compromise, many of the identified predictors of the STEM career decisions of gifted students have been acknowledged in the theory of work adjustment. Specifically, abilities, interests, values, family expectations, prestige, income, and level of commitment appear to form an element of either the 'matching' process between the characteristics of the individual and the career or the additional considerations when multiple careers satisfy the matching criteria. It is nevertheless noted that as for the theory of circumscription and compromise, the theory has some shortcomings, including its lack of clear recognition of gender considerations or a desire for intellectual stimulation and challenge. Moreover, acknowledgement needs to be given to the fact that while both the theory of circumscription and compromise and the theory of work adjustment may be useful in understanding the STEM career decisions of gifted students, neither theory was designed specifically for this purpose.

The Case of Gifted Brazilian International Students in Australia

As an example of the predictors of the STEM career decisions of gifted students, a study is presented of the predictors of the STEM career decisions of gifted Brazilian international students in Australia. According to Taube, Renn and Hohlt (2015), the context in Brazil is such that science and technology are considered to be important areas in the public interest that will be of benefit to society, although serious problems exist in STEM education in the country, such as a "lack of qualified teachers, lack of laboratories and other institutional conditions for conducive learning environments, extensive but widely ineffective mandatory curricula, and a focus on memorising and reiterating facts instead of experimenting and discovery orientated learning experiences" (p. 197). This may be reflected in the generally low level of educational attainment in Brazil in STEM areas, with the majority of the less than 20% of the population with higher education degrees having studied in areas such as the humanities, social sciences, and teaching (Cordeiro & Albuquerque, 2017; Schwartzman, 2015).

For those who do pursue study and careers in STEM areas in Brazil, some of the factors that have been recognised to be important may include self-fulfilment, an affinity for STEM subjects, perceived personal talent, career opportunities, social prestige, compensation, gender, and the meeting of family expectations, which are factors that largely coincide with the factors that have been identified to be predictive of STEM career decisions of young people in Australia, other parts of the Asia-Pacific region and around the world (Cordeiro & Albuquerque, 2017; Jung, 2019; Schwartzman, 2015; Taube et al., 2015; Varella, Ferreira, Pereira, Bussab, & Valentova, 2016). Nevertheless, the 'extrinsic' rather than the 'intrinsic' predictors appear to take on an added significance for the many of those from the less privileged backgrounds in Brazil (as is the case for those from many countries in the underdeveloped parts of the Asia-Pacific region), as STEM fields are often perceived to provide greater opportunities to climb the 'social ladder' (Cordeiro & Albuquerque, 2017; Taube et al., 2015).

Method

Study Participants

The participants of the study comprised a group of undergraduate university students from Brazil who were involved in a prestigious international STEM exchange program at a number of Australian universities. All participants in the exchange program, which was primarily funded by the Brazilian federal government, may be considered intellectually gifted as only the top students attending Brazilian universities, on the basis of academic merit, are eligible for participation (Ciência sem fronteiras, 2018).

Stage 1 Data Collection, Analysis, and Results

The first stage of the two-stage, mixed methods sequential exploratory study (Creswell & Plano Clark, 2007) involved the conduct of semi-structured interviews with 22 participants of the international STEM exchange program. Some examples of the questions that were asked during the interviews included: 'Have you given any thought to your future job or career?' and 'What specific/particular issues have you considered in thinking about your future career?' The average age of the participants, comprising 10 male students and 12 female students, was 21.05 years ($SD = 1.33$). The most common ancestries of the participants were Portuguese, Italian, German, Japanese, Indigenous, and/or Spanish. All participants were pursuing studies in STEM and related areas including civil/manufacturing/mechanical/industrial/naval/biomedical engineering (59%), architecture (14%), biology (9%), materials science (9%), medicine (5%), and international business (5%). Theoretical saturation was deemed to have been achieved after the 22nd participant was interviewed due to the lack of newly emergent data (Braun & Clark, 2006).

After transcription of the data collected from all 22 interviews, thematic analysis procedures (Joffe, 2012) were followed recursively and iteratively to extricate themes relating to the predictors of the STEM career intentions of the participating students. Specifically, after familiarisation with the interview data, codes (i.e., the most basic segments of the interview data) were generated and sorted into potential themes, and the emerging themes were reviewed, prior to the assignment of appropriate names to these themes (Braun & Clark, 2006; Joffe, 2012). At the conclusion of this process, nine themes (i.e., interest and enjoyment in STEM areas, academic success in STEM areas, family's favourable views towards STEM, social recognition and prestige, employment prospects, income, multipotentiality, intellectual stimulation, and societal importance) were identified as being potentially predictive of the STEM career decisions of the participating gifted Brazilian international students. These themes, along with illustrative participant quotes, are outlined in Table 1.

Stage 2 Data Collection, Analysis, and Results

The findings of the first stage of the study informed the development of a survey instrument to allow for a quantitative investigation of the statistically significant predictors of the STEM career intentions of gifted Brazilian international students in Australia. This survey comprised a selection of established scales with strong psychometric properties, which were either used in their original or adapted forms,

Table 1 Thematic analysis

Theme	Illustrative participant quotes
Interest and enjoyment in STEM areas	I liked exact things. (Participant #14) I always liked to know how things worked. In mechatronic engineering, you can have a general view of it because you learn a lot of mechanics. (Participant #21)
Academic success in STEM areas	I tried to find things I am good at, and I was good at geology, maths, and physics. So I put them together and decided to study mining engineering at university. (Participant #19) I am not good at human science (humanities) like writing, composition... (Participant #4)
Family's favourable views towards STEM	I needed an approval from my family. (Participant #17) I think I want to do something they (family) also want me to do, just because we think in a similar way. (Participant #13)
Social recognition and prestige	(Engineering) is a job with a lot of prestige in Brazil. (Participant #8) I really like (it) when other people are impressed about me doing engineering. (Participant #14)
Employment prospects	Because in manufacturing engineering, we have lots of opportunities, have different kinds of things to work with. (Participant #3) But I thought that the job market for journalism is not as big as that of engineering. (Participant #21)
Income	(STEM careers offer) enough (income) to have a comfortable house, and car, and be able to travel. (Participant #1) Engineering is very good to earn more money... I want to make money, as much as possible. (Participant #14)
Multipotentiality	Being good at both maths and writing... makes things a lot more complicated to make a career decision... But it's very good now (that I have made a decision to pursue a STEM career), because I need to write many reports... I think it will give me a lot of benefits in my future. (Participant #21)
Intellectual stimulation	You have to place yourself in a situation (where) you meet a challenge. (Participant #5) It's good for you because you push yourself to the limit and you can overcome obstacles. (Participant #8)
Societal importance	Sustainable development... Brazil wants to grow in a next few years. And if I can make that impact of this growth to a minimum, it would be very great. (Participant #8) I am working on a project building medical device for increasing people's life expectancy. (Participant #5)

to validly and reliably assess each of the nine themes that emerged from the first stage of the study:

(a) Interest/enjoyment in STEM areas: The intrinsic motivation scale in Noels, Clement and Pelletier (1999) and the occupational interest/enjoyment scale in Jung, McCormick, Gregory, and Barnett (2011).

(b) Academic success in STEM areas: The expectancy for occupational success scale in Jung et al. (2011) and the self and task perceptions questionnaire in Eccles and Wigfield (1995).

(c) Family's favourable views towards STEM: The family influence scales in Jung et al. (2011) and Jung (2014).

(d) Social recognition and prestige: The recognition scales in Jung and McCormick (2011a, 2011b) and Jung (2014).

(e) Employment prospects: The employment prospects scale in Tamayose, Madjidi, Schmieder-Ramirez, and Rice (2004); the job security scale in Kraimer, Wayne, Liden, and Sparrowe (2005); and participant responses relating to employment prospects in the first stage of the study.

(f) Income: The occupational income scales in Jung et al. (2011) and Jung (2014).

(g) Multipotentiality: The multipotentiality scale in Jung (2013).

(h) Intellectual stimulation: The intellectual stimulation scale in Jung (2014).

(i) Societal importance: Items used to assess attitudes towards occupations in science and technology in Kind, Jones, and Barmby (2007) and participant responses relating to societal importance in the first stage of the study.

In 2014, the survey instrument was administered to 471 former and current participants of the international STEM exchange program. Of the completed survey instruments, those completed by 374 of the participants who indicated an intention to pursue a STEM career in the future were analysed. This subset of the participants comprised 211 male students and 163 female students, had a mean age of 22.38 years ($SD = 2.36$) and were primarily of Portuguese, Italian, Japanese, German, Indigenous, Spanish, and/ or Chinese ancestry. They were pursuing studies in a number of STEM areas including electrical/civil/chemical/general/environmental/mining/aerospace/production/ manufacturing/computer/industrial/agricultural/telecommunications/biochemical engineering (59%), biology (6%), computer science/information technology (4%), pharmacy (3%), veterinary science (3%), and medicine (2%).

Initially, exploratory factor analysis was conducted on the completed survey data using principal axis factoring with direct oblimin rotation in IBM SPSS Statistics 20. Nevertheless, due to issues such as cross-loading, low communality values (i.e., below 0.20), non-significant loading (i.e., below 0.30), and the emergence of single/dual item 'factors', 31 problematic items needed to be progressively removed. The KMO measure of sampling adequacy (0.83) and Bartlett's test of sphericity (6133.58, $p < 0.00$) supported the appropriateness of exploratory factor analysis for the resulting data set. Kaiser's criterion and the scree plot criterion *both* indicated that eight factors (i.e., career intention, recognition, enjoyment/success in STEM, family influence, income, enjoyment/success in humanities, employment prospects, and intellectual stimulation) could be extracted from this data set (Field, 2013; Hair, Anderson, Tathan, & Black, 2010). Table 2 outlines the items that comprised each of the eight factors, the respective factor loadings, and the Cronbach alpha values of each factor, while Table 3 outlines the correlations between the eight factors.

In acknowledgement of the possible differences in the predictors of the STEM career intentions of gifted Brazilian international students depending on their period

Table 2 Final factor solution for career decisions in STEM

Factors/items.	Loading	Alpha
Career intention		0.85
I am committed to this job/occupation.	0.757	
My personal preference is to pursue this job/occupation.	0.746	
I have resolved to follow this occupational path.	0.671	
I intend to pursue this job/occupation.	0.628	
It is likely that I will pursue this job/occupation.	0.508	
It is good for me to pursue this job/occupation.	0.407	
Recognition		0.80
What matters most is how much recognition I will gain from other people from this job/occupation.	0.767	
To me, success means being noticed by others for my achievements in this job/occupation.	0.753	
It is very important for me to impress people around me through this job/occupation.	0.747	
I believe that there is no point in doing a good job if nobody else knows about it.	0.531	
I would like other people to find out how good I really am in this job/occupation.	0.504	
Enjoyment/success in STEM		0.79
Since I was young, I received good grades in maths or science.	0.862	
I was among the best students in maths or science in high school.	0.733	
Since I was very young, I loved maths or science.	0.709	
I am very good at maths or science.	0.621	
I get pleasure from working with numbers.	0.337	
Family influence		0.83
My family thinks that I should pursue this job/occupation.	−0.855	
My family thinks that it is a good idea for me to choose this job occupation.	−0.790	
My family wants me to pursue this job/occupation.	−0.738	
My family approves of this job/occupation.	−0.615	
My family influences me to pursue this job/occupation.	−0.557	
Members of my family give their backing for this job/occupation.	−0.455	
Income		0.77
What matters most is how much money I will make in this job/occupation.	−0.667	
I believe that you work to make money.	−0.654	
What I will be paid in this job/occupation is important to me.	−0.647	
The financial rewards will motivate me in this job/occupation.	−0.624	
One way of becoming rich is to get this job/occupation.	−0.489	
Enjoyment/success in humanities		0.82
I am not good at the humanities.	0.906	
I do not get satisfaction from working in the humanities.	0.728	
I think I am better at science-related things than humanities.	0.701	
Employment prospects		0.76
There is a large job market in this occupational area.	−0.847	
A lot of job opportunities exist in this field.	−0.827	

(continued)

Table 2 (continued)

Factors/items.	Loading	Alpha
I like my chances of getting a good job in this area.	−0.417	
Intellectual stimulation		0.80
This job/occupation will be mentally demanding.	−0.729	
This job/occupation will test the limits of my abilities.	−0.623	
I will need to work hard in this job/occupation.	−0.601	
This job/occupation will provide me with sufficient intellectual challenge.	−0.553	

Table 3 Factor correlations

	1	2	3	4	5	6	7	8
1. Career intention								
2. Recognition	0.06							
3. Enjoyment/success in STEM	0.17*	0.02						
4. Family influence	−0.24*	−0.26*	−0.12*					
5. Income	0.00	−0.29*	−0.08	0.23*				
6. Enjoyment/success in humanities	−0.02	0.14*	0.33*	−0.01	−0.27*			
7. Employment prospects	−0.28*	0.02	−0.23*	0.26*	0.34*	−0.19*		
8. Intellectual stimulation	−0.57*	0.06	−0.29*	0.12*	0.04	0.07	0.30*	

$^*p < .05$

of study in Australia, two multiple regression analyses were performed—one analysis for participants who had studied in Australia for three months or less ($n = 114$) and another analysis for participants who had, at the time of the survey completion, studied in Australia for a longer period of time (i.e., equivalent to at least one complete semester of university study; $n = 260$). For both sets of analyses, career intention was designated as the dependent variable, while the socio-demographic variables of the participants (i.e., gender, urban/rural home location, age, year of study), and the other seven factors that emerged from the exploratory factor analysis (i.e., recognition, enjoyment/success in STEM, family influence, income, enjoyment/success in humanities, employment prospects, and intellectual stimulation) were designated as independent variables. A mixed approach was used to enter the independent variables in both analyses, with the socio-demographic variables entered using the assumed temporal order under the hierarchical approach (i.e., gender was assumed to be determined prior to urban/rural home location, age, and year of study), while the remaining variables were thereafter entered using the stepwise approach. Prior to the acceptance of the final multiple regression models, data from 13 cases needed to be removed as they either represented outliers or influential cases (as measured using Cook's distance values, leverage values and Mahalanobis distance values; Field, 2013).

The finally accepted multiple regression models suggested that for those gifted Brazilian international students who had studied in Australia for less than three months

Table 4 Multiple regression model for gifted Brazilian international students who have studied in Australia for less than 3 months

Variable	R^2	ΔR^2	B	SE B	β
Gender	0.01	0.01	−0.15	0.17	−0.07
Population of residence	0.01	0.00	−0.08	0.29	−0.02
Age	0.05	0.04	0.07	0.05	0.13
Year of study	0.06	0.01	0.02	0.08	0.02
Intellectual stimulation	0.34	0.28*	−0.56	0.08	−0.54

*$p < .05$

Table 5 Multiple regression model for gifted Brazilian international students who have studied in Australia for more than 3 months

Variable	R^2	ΔR^2	B	SE B	β
Gender	0.00	0.00	−0.09	0.09	−0.05
Population of residence	0.02	0.02	−0.30	0.16	−0.10
Age	0.02	0.00	0.02	0.03	0.04
Year of study	0.02	0.00	0.05	0.05	0.05
Intellectual stimulation	0.32	0.30*	−0.51	0.05	−0.50
Employment prospects	0.35	0.03*	−0.16	0.06	−0.15
Income	0.37	0.02*	−0.14	0.05	−0.14

*$p < .05$

(refer Table 4), the only statistically significant predictor ($p < 0.05$) of STEM career intentions, accounting for 28% of the variance of STEM career intentions, was intellectual stimulation. In comparison, for those students who had studied in Australia for longer than three months (refer Table 5), three statistically significant predictors ($p < 0.05$) of STEM career intentions were identified, which collectively accounted for 35% of the variance of STEM career intentions. These were intellectual stimulation (30%), employment prospects (3%), and income (2%). The other potential predictor variables including gender, urban/rural home, location, age, year of study, recognition, enjoyment/success in STEM, family influence, and enjoyment/success in humanities were identified to make less important, and statistically non-significant, contributions to the variance of STEM career intentions of the gifted Brazilian international students.

Discussion

The mixed methods study provided a number of useful insights into the predictors of the STEM career decisions of gifted Brazilian international students who have studied in Australia. The findings of the first qualitative stage of the study largely verified the importance of predictors that have been recognised in the emerging international literature in the area to be salient to the STEM career decisions of gifted students. Specifically, interest/enjoyment in STEM areas, academic success in STEM areas, the family's favourable views towards STEM, social recognition and prestige, employment prospects, and income were each identified as themes that closely overlapped with factors such as interests, values, ability, family influence, prestige, and income (Jung, 2019; Lubinski & Benbow, 2006; Lubinski et al., 2014; Nugent et al., 2015; Park et al., 2007; Steenbergen-Hu & Olszewski-Kubilius, 2017; Tuijl & van der Molen, 2016; Wang et al., 2017). Furthermore, these predictive factors were recognised as being salient in the second stage of the study, although the possibility was raised that interest/enjoyment in STEM areas and academic success in STEM areas may represent different facets of the *one* factor due to the emergence of 'enjoyment/success in STEM areas' as a single factor during exploratory factor analysis. Nevertheless, a desire for intellectual stimulation, along with strong employment prospects, and high income for those who have studied in Australia for a substantial period of time, were identified to be most important in the prediction of the STEM career decisions of gifted Brazilian international students.

Essentially, the findings of the study provided nuanced information on the relative importance, or *rankings*, of the various factors that may predict the STEM career decisions of gifted Brazilian international students who have studied in Australia. That is, while the pool of factors that are considered may largely resemble the factors that the existing international literature suggests may be predictive of the STEM career decisions of gifted students (Jung, 2019; Lubinski & Benbow, 2006; Lubinski et al., 2014; Nugent et al., 2015; Park et al., 2007; Tuijl & van der Molen, 2016; Wang et al., 2017), along with the STEM career decisions of Brazilian students generally (Cordeiro & Albuquerque, 2017; Jung, 2019; Schwartzman, 2015; Taube et al., 2015; Varella et al., 2016), these students appear to concentrate on a narrow range of factors—intellectual stimulation, employment prospects, and income—with the highest priority given to intellectual stimulation. It is noteworthy that intellectual stimulation has been identified to be a more important predictor of STEM career intentions than other related factors, such as interest, enjoyment, and success in a career, which have traditionally been considered to be the most important predictors of the career decisions of both gifted and non-gifted students (Jung, 2014, 2017, 2019; Jung & McCormick, 2011a; Jung et al., 2011; Jung & Young, 2019). One possible explanation for this finding is that intellectual stimulation may be what gifted Brazilian international students consider to be interesting, enjoyable, and conducive to success in a career.

In comparison, a number of explanations may be possible for the finding that employment prospects and income, two extrinsic motivators of the career decision, may become important for gifted Brazilian international students after a substantial period of study in Australia. First of all, it is likely that these students will, possibly for the first time in their lives, be separated from their families who would have taken care of their many needs in collectivist Brazilian society (Hofstede, 2001; Taningco, Mathew, & Pachon, 2008). As a result, they may be given a good opportunity to 'fend for themselves' and to otherwise become more emotionally and financially independent of their families. It is indeed noteworthy that while family influence was identified to be a possible predictor of the STEM career decisions of these students, it was not one of the three 'critical' factors that may be given the most attention. Relatedly, the probable difficulties that these students may have faced in any attempts at securing part-time employment in a new culture and country during their studies may highlight to them the importance of the many practicalities of the career decision. Furthermore, it may be the case that, a longer duration of stay in Australia may have allowed these students to gain a greater understanding of the differences in the levels of wealth and rates of youth unemployment in Brazil and Australia (Jung & Young, 2019; Organisation for Economic Co-operation and Development, 2017, 2018), to increase the importance of income and employment prospects in the career decision (Cordeiro & Albuquerque, 2017; Taube et al., 2015). Finally, independent of studying and living abroad, the growing maturity of these students with age may allow them to gain a heightened appreciation of a multitude of non-intrinsic factors that may need to be considered in a mature career decision.

Of the various factors that have been recognised in the existing literature to be predictive of the STEM career decisions of gifted students, gender stood out as being a factor that was *not* demonstrated to be a meaningful critical or non-critical predictor of the STEM career decisions of the gifted Brazilian international students. None of the other commonly recognised predictors of STEM career intentions failed to be identified in this study. While this is inconsistent with expectations, along with the gendered patterns of career decision-making that have been commonly identified in Brazil, a different picture may emerge if the career decisions of these students *within* STEM fields are more closely examined (Varella et al., 2016). For example, it is possible that gifted female students may be more likely than gifted male students in Brazil to pursue STEM careers that involve high levels of human interaction (such as careers in health and biology) than low levels of human interaction (such as careers in fields such as physics or computer science; Kfouri, Moyses, & Moyses, 2013; Varella et al., 2016).

With respect to the theories that may be relevant to the STEM career decisions of gifted students, both the theory of circumscription and compromise and the theory of work adjustment appear *broadly* to be useful in understanding the STEM career decisions of gifted Brazilian international students. That is, both theories largely give acknowledgement to the pool of factors that represent non-critical predictors in the STEM career decision. In terms of the three critical predictors (i.e., intellectual stimulation, income, and employment prospects), the theory of circumscription and compromise may consider income to be one of the bases for the elimination of career options in the circumscription stage of the theory, while employment prospects may be recognised as a factor that influences the accessibility of career options in the compromise stage of the theory. In comparison, the theory of work adjustment may be considered to give acknowledgement to income in the process of matching the needs/values of the individual with the working conditions offered in a career, while employment prospects appear to be highly associated with one of the factors (i.e., state of the labour market) that may be considered when multiple careers satisfy the matching criteria for an 'optimal' career. Unfortunately, neither the theory of circumscription and compromise nor the theory of work adjustment gives explicit acknowledgement to intellectual stimulation, which was identified overwhelmingly to be the most important predictor of the STEM career decisions of the gifted Brazilian international students. Consequently, neither theory may be considered to be a perfect representation of the STEM career decisions of gifted Brazilian international students who have studied in Australia. Further research may be desirable to identify and/or develop a model or a theory that more accurately reflects the STEM career decisions of these students.

The findings of this study provide potentially useful information for career practitioners, educators, families, and other stakeholders in the STEM career decisions of gifted Brazilian international students who study abroad on how to optimally support these decisions. Specifically, it is apparent that any guidance or counselling for these students may need to have a focus on the intellectual stimulation, along with the positive employment prospects and high levels of income, which may be possible in careers in STEM areas. For example, these students could be connected to mentors or provided with case studies of successful individuals in any one of a multiple range of STEM career fields with plentiful job opportunities, substantial material rewards, and intellectual challenge. In the situation where the relevant governments, policymakers, or community representatives in Brazil wish to promote careers in STEM areas among its most capable adolescents (who will be offered opportunities to study in countries such as Australia), the focus of any promotional campaigns may again need to be on the three 'critical' factors in the STEM career decision (i.e., intellectual stimulation, employment prospects, and income).

Conclusion

The importance of Science, Technology, Engineering, and Mathematics for individual members of societies and for societies as a whole means that much greater attention is necessary on how people make decisions to pursue careers in these fields. In particular, greater attention may be necessary on how the most intellectually capable members of society who are about to make their career decisions (i.e., gifted students) actually go about making these decisions, due to their tremendous potential to make a lasting impact on others. Unfortunately, research in the area is only in its early stages. While knowledge currently exists on some of the major predictors of the STEM career decisions of gifted students (i.e., ability, gender, interests, values, family influence, prestige, income, intellectual stimulation, employment prospects, and commitment), the picture appears incomplete. For example, it is apparent from the investigation of the STEM career decisions of gifted Brazilian international students that there may be some variation in the pool of factors, and the relative importance of such factors, that may be predictive of STEM career intentions for gifted students in different societies. Furthermore, minimal knowledge appears to exist, at the present time, on the career decisions that may be made *within* the broad range of careers that lie in STEM fields, the cognitive decision-making *processes* associated with the pursuit of careers in STEM fields, and the many *difficulties* that may surround the pursuit of careers in STEM fields. Only with greater advances in knowledge in these areas may a clearer and a more complete understanding of the STEM career decisions of gifted students be possible, to allow for optimal support to be provided to gifted students with intentions to pursue STEM careers in the future.

Cross-References

▶ Educational Contexts, Transitions and Community Engagement: Part VI Introduction
▶ Fostering and Developing Talent in Mentorship Programs: The Mentor's Perspectives
▶ Gifted Education in the Asia-Pacific: From the Past for the Future – An Introduction
▶ How Do Teachers Meet the Academic Needs of High-Ability Students in Science?
▶ Innovative Practices to Support High-Achieving Deprived Young Scholars in an Ethnic-Linguistic Diverse Latin American Country
▶ Some Implications for the Future of Gifted Education in the Asia-Pacific
▶ STEAM in Gifted Education in Korea
▶ The Career Decisions of Gifted Students: An Asian-Pacific Perspective
▶ The Lives and Achievements of Four Extraordinary Australians: A Master, a Maker, an Introspector, and an Influencer
▶ Transitioning to Career: Talented Musicians' Identity Development

Acknowledgments   Work relating to parts of this chapter was funded by the Australian Federal Department of Foreign Affairs and Trade under the Council on Australia Latin America Relations (COALAR) Grants Program for a project titled 'Evaluating the impact of Australian education, cultural, and tourism experiences on the future career intentions of students in Brazil's Science without Borders Program'.

References

Achter, J. A., Lubinski, D., & Benbow, C. P. (1996). Multipotentiality among intellectually gifted: "It was never there and already it's vanishing". *Journal of Counseling Psychology, 43*, 65–76. https://doi.org/10.1037/0021-9010.75.1.77
Akram, T. M., Ijaz, A., & Ikram, H. (2017). Exploring the factors responsible for declining student interest in chemistry. *International Journal of Information and Education Technology, 7*, 88–94. https://doi.org/10.18178/ijiet.2017.7.2.847
Allport, G. W., Vernon, P. E., & Lindzey, G. (1960). *Manual for study of values* (3rd ed.). Boston, MA: Houghton Mifflin.
Archer, L., DeWitt, J., Osborne, J., Dillon, J., Willis, B., & Wong, B. (2010). 'Doing' science versus 'being' a scientist: Examining 10/11-year-old schoolchildren's constructions of science through the lens of identity. *Science Education, 94*, 617–639. https://doi.org/10.1002/sce.20399
Braun, V., & Clark, V. (2006). Using thematic analysis in psychology. *Qualitative Research in Psychology, 3*, 77–101. https://doi.org/10.1191/1478088706qp063oa
Britner, S. L., & Pajares, F. (2001). Self-efficacy beliefs, motivation, race, and gender in middle school science. *Journal of Women and Minorities in Science and Engineering, 7*, 1–15. https://doi.org/10.1615/JWomenMinorScienEng.v7.i4.10
Chen, C. P., & Wong, J. (2013). Career counseling for gifted students. *Australian Journal of Career Development, 22*, 121–129. https://doi.org/10.1177/1038416213507909
Christensen, R., Knezek, G., & Tyler-Wood, T. (2014). Student perceptions of science, technology, engineering and mathematics (STEM) content and careers. *Computers in Human Behavior, 34*, 173–186. https://doi.org/10.1016/j.chb.2014.01.046
Ciência sem fronteiras. (2018, October 27). *FAQ*. Retrieved from http://www.cienciasemfronteiras.gov.br/web/csf-eng/faq
Cordeiro, H. T., & de Albuquerque, L. G. (2017). Career profiles of generation Y and their potential influencers. *Brazilian Administration Review, 14*, 2–21. https://doi.org/10.1590/1807-7692bar2017170013

Creswell, J. W., & Plano Clark, V. (2007). *Designing and conducting mixed methods research.* Thousand Oaks, CA: Sage.

Dawis, R. V. (2005). The Minnesota theory of work adjustment. In S. D. Brown & R. W. Lent (Eds.), *Career development and counseling: Putting theory and research to work* (pp. 3–23). Hoboken, NJ: Wiley.

Dawis, R. V., & Lofquist, L. H. (1984). *A psychological theory of work adjustment.* Minneapolis, MN: University of Minnesota Press.

DeBacker, T. K., & Nelson, R. M. (1999). Variations on an expectancy-value model of motivation in science. *Contemporary Educational Psychology, 24,* 71–94. https://doi.org/10.1006/ceps.1998.0984

Eccles, J. S., & Wigfield, A. (1995). In the mind of the achiever: The structure of adolescents' academic achievement related-beliefs and self-perceptions. *Personality and Social Psychology Bulletin, 21,* 215–225. https://doi.org/10.1177/0146167295213003

Eccles, J. S., & Wigfield, A. (2002). Motivational beliefs, values, and goals. *Annual Review of Psychology, 53,* 109–132. https://doi.org/10.1146/annurev.psych.53.100901.135153

Emmett, J. D., & Minor, C. W. (1993). Career decision-making factors in gifted young adults. *Career Development Quarterly, 41,* 350–366. https://doi.org/10.1002/j.2161-0045.1993.tb00409.x

Fiebig, J. N. (2008). Gifted American and German adolescent women: A longitudinal examination of attachment, separation, gender roles, and career aspirations. *High Ability Studies, 19,* 67–81. https://doi.org/10.1080/13598130801980349

Field, A. (2013). *Discovering statistics using IBM SPSS statics* (4th ed.). Thousand Oaks, CA: Sage.

Gagné, F. (2009). Building gifts into talents: Detailed overview of the DMGT 2.0. In B. MacFarlane & T. Stambaugh (Eds.), *Leading change in gifted education: The festschrift of Dr. Joyce VanTassel-Baska* (pp. 61–80). Waco, TX: Prufrock Press.

Gottfredson, L. S. (1981). Circumscription and compromise: A developmental theory of occupational aspirations. *Journal of Counseling Psychology, 28,* 545–579. https://doi.org/10.1037/0022-0167.28.6.545

Gottfredson, L. S. (2002). Gottfredson's theory of circumscription, compromise, and self-creation. In D. Brown (Ed.), *Career choice and development* (4th ed., pp. 85–148). San Francisco, CA: Jossey-Bass.

Gottfredson, L. S. (2005). Applying Gottfredson's theory of circumscription and compromise in career guidance and counseling. In S. D. Brown & R. W. Lent (Eds.), *Career development and counseling: Putting theory and research to work* (pp. 71–100). New York, NY: Wiley.

Hair, J. F., Black, W. C., Babin, B. J., & Anderson, R. E. (2010). *Multivariate data analysis: A global perspective* (7th ed.). Upper Saddle River, NJ: Pearson.

Harmon, L. W., Hansen, J. C., Borgen, F. H., & Hammer, A. L. (1994). *Applications and technical guide for the Strong Interest Inventory.* Palo Alto, CA: Consulting Psychologists Press.

Herr, E. L., & Cramer, S. H. (1996). *Career guidance and counseling through the lifespan: Systematic approaches* (5th ed.). New York, NY: Harper Collins.

Hofstede, G. (2001). *Culture's consequences: Comparing values, behaviors, institutions, and organizations across nations* (2nd ed.). Thousand Oaks, CA: Sage.

Holland, J. L. (1997). *Making vocational choices: A theory of vocational personalities and work environments.* Odessa, FL: Psychological Assessment Resources.

Joffe, H. (2012). Thematic analysis. In D. Harper & A. R. Thompson (Eds.), *Qualitative research methods in mental health and psychotherapy: A guide for students and practitioners* (pp. 209–223). Chichester, UK: Wiley-Blackwell.

Jung, J. Y. (2012). Giftedness as a developmental construct that leads to eminence as adults: Ideas and implications from an occupational/career decision-making perspective. *The Gifted Child Quarterly, 56,* 189–193. https://doi.org/10.1177/0016986212456072

Jung, J. Y. (2013). The cognitive processes associated with occupational/career indecision: A model for gifted adolescents. *Journal for the Education of the Gifted, 36,* 433–460. https://doi.org/10.1177/0162353213506067

Jung, J. Y. (2014). Modeling the occupational/career decision-making processes of intellectually gifted adolescents: A competing models strategy. *Journal for the Education of the Gifted, 37*, 128–152. https://doi.org/10.1177/0162353214529045

Jung, J. Y. (2017). Occupational/career decision-making thought processes of adolescents of high intellectual ability. *Journal for the Education of the Gifted, 40*, 50–78. https://doi.org/10.1177/0162353217690040

Jung, J. Y. (2019). *The career decisions of gifted students and other high ability groups*. Oxon, UK: Routledge.

Jung, J. Y. (in press a). The career development of gifted students. In J. A. Athanasou & H. N. Perera (Eds.), *The international handbook of career guidance*. Dordrecht, The Netherlands: Springer.

Jung, J. Y. (in press b). The career decisions of gifted students: An Asian-Pacific perspective. In S. R. Smith (Ed.), *Handbook of giftedness and talent development in the Asia-Pacific*. Singapore, Singapore: Springer.

Jung, J. Y., & McCormick, J. (2011a). The occupational decision: A cultural and motivational perspective. *Journal of Career Assessment, 19*, 75–91. https://doi.org/10.1177/1069072710382616

Jung, J. Y., & McCormick, J. (2011b). Occupational decision-related processes for amotivated adolescents: Confirmation of a model. *Journal of Career Development, 38*, 275–292. https://doi.org/10.1177/0894845310367638

Jung, J. Y., McCormick, J., Gregory, G., & Barnett, K. (2011). Culture, motivation, and vocational decision-making of Australian senior high school students in private schools. *Australian Journal of Guidance and Counselling, 21*, 85–106. https://doi.org/10.1375/ajgc.21.1.85

Jung, J. Y., & Young, M. (2019). The occupational/career decision-making processes of intellectually gifted adolescents from economically disadvantaged backgrounds: A mixed methods perspective. *Gifted Child Quarterly, 63*, 36–57. https://doi.org/10.1177/0016986218804575

Kerr, B. A., & Sodano, S. (2003). Career assessment with intellectually gifted students. *Journal of Career Assessment, 11*, 168–186. https://doi.org/10.1177/1069072703011002004

Kfouri, M. G., Moyses, S. J., & Moyses, S. T. (2013). Women's motivation to become dentists in Brazil. *Journal of Dental Education, 77*, 810–816. https://doi.org/10.1002/j.0022-0337.2013.77.6.tb05533.x

Kind, P., Jones, K., & Barmby, P. (2007). Developing attitudes towards science measures. *International Journal of Science Education, 29*, 871–893. https://doi.org/10.1080/09500690600909091

Kraimer, M. L., Wayne, S. J., Liden, R. C., & Sparrowe, R. T. (2005). The role of job security in understanding the relationship between employees' perceptions of temporary workers and employees' performance. *Journal of Applied Psychology, 90*, 389–398. https://doi.org/10.1037/0021-9010.90.2.389

Lent, R. W., Brown, S. D., & Hackett, G. (1994). Toward a unifying social cognitive theory of career and academic interest, choice, and performance. *Journal of Vocational Behavior, 45*, 79–122. https://doi.org/10.1006/jvbe.1994.1027

Lofquist, L. H., & Dawis, R. V. (1991). *Essentials of person-environment-correspondence counseling*. Minneapolis, MN: University of Minnesota Press.

Lubinski, D., & Benbow, C. P. (2006). Study of Mathematically Precocious Youth after 35 years: Uncovering antecedents for the development of math–science expertise. *Perspectives on Psychological Science, 1*, 316–345. https://doi.org/10.1111/j.1745-6916.2006.00019.x

Lubinski, D., Benbow, C. P., & Kell, H. J. (2014). Life paths and accomplishments of mathematically precocious males and females four decades later. *Psychological Science, 25*, 2217–2232. https://doi.org/10.1177/0956797614551371

Lubinski, D., Webb, R. M., Morelock, M. J., & Benbow, C. P. (2001). Top 1 in 10,000: A 10 year follow-up of the profoundly gifted. *Journal of Applied Psychology, 7*, 718–729. https://doi.org/10.1037/0021-9010.86.4.718

Lyons, T., Cooksey, R., Panizzon, D., Parnell, A., & Pegg, J. (2006). *Science, ICT and mathematics education in rural and regional Australia: The SiMERR national survey*. Armidale, NSW: University of New England, National Centre of Science, ICT and Mathematics for Rural and Regional Australia.

Miller, K., & Cummings, G. (2009). Gifted and talented students' career aspirations and influences: A systematic review of the literature. *International Journal of Nursing Education Scholarship, 6*, 8. https://doi.org/10.2202/1548-923X.1667

Muratori, M. C., & Smith, C. K. (2015). Guiding the talent and career development of the gifted individual. *Journal of Counseling and Development, 93*, 173–182. https://doi.org/10.1002/j.1556-6676.2015.00193.x

National Academy of Sciences. (2010). *Rising above the gathering storm, revisited: Rapidly approaching category 5*. Washington, DC: National Academies Press.

Noels, K. A., Clement, R., & Pelletier, L. G. (1999). Perceptions of teachers' communicative style and students' intrinsic and extrinsic motivation. *Modern Language Journal, 83*, 23–34. https://doi.org/10.1111/0026-7902.00003

Nugent, G., Barker, B., Welch, G., Grandgenett, N., Wu, C., & Nelson, C. (2015). A model of factors contributing to STEM learning and career orientation. *International Journal of Science Education, 37*, 1067–1088. https://doi.org/10.1080/09500693.2015.1017863

Organisation for Economic Co-operation and Development. (2007). *Education at a glance 2007: OECD indicators*. Paris, France: OECD.

Organisation for Economic Co-operation and Development. (2008). *Encouraging student interest in science and technology studies*. Paris, France: OECD. https://doi.org/10.1787/9789264040892-en

Organisation for Economic Co-operation and Development. (2017). *OECD economic surveys: Australia*. Paris, France: OECD. Retrieved from www.oecd.org/australia/economic-survey-australia.htm

Organisation for Economic Co-operation and Development. (2018). *OECD economic surveys: Brazil*. Paris, France: OECD. Retrieved from OECD: www.oecd.org/brazil/economic-survey-brazil.htm

Osborne, J., & Dillon, J. (2008). *Science education in Europe: Critical reflections*. London, UK: Nuffield Foundation.

Park, G., Lubinski, D., & Benbow, C. P. (2007). Contrasting intellectual patterns predict creativity in the arts and sciences. *Psychological Science, 18*, 948–952. https://doi.org/10.1111/j.1467-9280.2007.02007.x

Schwartzman, S. (2015). Science culture in Brazilian society. In O. Renn, N. C. Karafyllis, A. Hohlt, & D. Taube (Eds.), *International science and technology education: Exploring culture, economy, and social perceptions* (pp. 134–153). Oxon, UK: The Berlin-Brandenburg Academy of Sciences and Humanities.

Simpkins, S. D., Fredricks, J. A., & Eccles, J. S. (2012). Charting the Eccles' expectancy-value model from mothers' beliefs in childhood to youths' activities in adolescence. *Developmental Psychology, 48*, 1019–1032. https://doi.org/10.1037/a0027468

Steenbergen-Hu, S., & Olszewski-Kubilius, P. (2017). Factors that contributed to gifted students' success on STEM pathways: The role of race, personal interests, and aspects of high school experience. *Journal for the Education of the Gifted, 40*, 99–134. https://doi.org/10.1177/0162353217701022

Tamayose, T., Madjidi, F., Schmieder-Ramirez, J., & Rice, G. (2004). Important factors when choosing a career in public health. *Californian Journal of Health Promotion, 2*, 65–73. https://doi.org/10.32398/cjhp.v2i1.584

Taningco, M. T. V., Mathew, A. B., & Pachon, H. P. (2008). *STEM professions: Opportunities and challenges for Latinos in science, technology, engineering, and mathematics*. Los Angeles, CA: University of Southern California.

Taube, D., Renn, O., & Hohlt, A. (2015). STEM education from a comparative transnational perspective: Results of a Delphi process. In O. Renn, N. C. Karafyllis, A. Hohlt, & D. Taube (Eds.), *International science and technology education: Exploring culture, economy, and social perceptions* (pp. 191–216). Oxon, UK: The Berlin-Brandenburg Academy of Sciences and Humanities.

van Tuijl, C., & van der Molen, J. H. W. (2016). Study choice and career development in STEM fields: An overview and integration of the research. *International Journal of Technology and Design Education, 26*, 159–183. https://doi.org/10.1007/s10798-015-9308-1

Varella, M. A. C., Ferreira, J. H. B. P., Pereira, K. J., Bussab, V. S. R., & Valentova, J. V. (2016). Empathizing, systemizing, and career choice in Brazil: Sex differences and individual variation among areas of study. *Personality and Individual Differences, 97*, 157–164. https://doi.org/10.1016/j.paid.2016.03.058

Vedder-Weiss, D., & Fortus, D. (2013). School, teacher, peers, and parents' goals emphases and adolescents' motivation to learn science in and out of school. *Journal of Research in Science Teaching, 50*, 952–988. https://doi.org/10.1002/tea.21103

Wang, M. T., & Degol, J. (2013). Motivational pathways to STEM career choices: Using expectancy-value perspective to understand individual and gender differences in STEM fields. *Developmental Review, 33*, 304–340. https://doi.org/10.1016/j.dr.2013.08.001

Wang, M. T., Ye, F., & Degol, J. L. (2017). Who chooses STEM careers? Using a relative cognitive strength and interest model to predict careers in science, technology, engineering, and mathematics. *Journal of Youth and Adolescence, 46*, 1805–1820. https://doi.org/10.1007/s10964-016-0618-8

Wigfield, A., & Eccles, J. S. (2000). Expectancy-value theory of achievement motivation. *Contemporary Educational Psychology, 25*, 68–81. https://doi.org/10.1006/ceps.1999.1015

Xu, Y. J. (2013). Career outcomes of STEM and non-STEM college graduates: Persistence in majored-field and influential factors in career choices. *Research in Higher Education, 54*, 349–382. https://doi.org/10.1007/s11162-012-9275-2

Jae Yup Jung, PhD, is an associate professor in the School of Education and the Director of GERRIC at the University of New South Wales, Australia. His research program incorporates various topics relating to gifted adolescents, with a particular focus on their career-related decisions. His research has been recognised with awards from the American Educational Research Association, the Mensa Education and Research Foundation/Mensa International and the Society for Vocational Psychology, and grants from the Australian Research Council and the Australian Department of Foreign Affairs and Trade. He is the editor of the *Australasian Journal of Gifted Education*, a member of the Executive Committee of the Asia-Pacific Federation on Giftedness (APFG), and a member of the Council of the Australian Association for the Education of the Gifted and Talented (AAEGT).

Tay T.R. Koo, PhD, serves as a lecturer in the School of Aviation at the University of New South Wales, Australia. His research involves the spatial and quantitative measurement of tourism, leisure, and visitor activities and their impact, including their interrelationship with aviation and mobility. He is interested in sustainable tourism as a broad range of activities involving travel beyond the usual place of residence for various purposes, including education, leisure, and business.

Peta K. Hay, PhD, is a lecturer in the School of Education and GERRIC at the University of New South Wales. She lectures in gifted education in undergraduate and postgraduate capacities and provides professional learning and support to teachers and schools across Australia. Her research interests include the socio-affective areas of giftedness, as well as the efficacy of school programming options for gifted students.

Susen R. Smith, PhD, is a GERRIC senior research fellow and senior lecturer in Gifted and Special Education at the School of Education and GERRIC, University of New South Wales, Australia. She has extensive experience as a teacher, curriculum consultant, and educational leader from early childhood to tertiary education and adult education. She has been an invited visiting scholar at Columbia University, City University New York, Hong Kong Institute of Education, National Taipei University of Education, and Imperial College London. Her specific research interests include ecological systems theory underpinning dynamically differentiating curriculum and pedagogy models and matrices for students with giftedness, indigeneity, underachievement, multi-exceptionalities, and learning difficulties. She is widely published in international journals and has keynoted at national and international conferences.

The Career Decisions of Gifted Students: An Asian-Pacific Perspective

Jae Yup Jung

Contents

Abstract

Drawing on the literature in multiple related areas, an overview is presented in this chapter of the major issues that may surround career decisions for gifted students in the Asia-Pacific region. After a discussion on the pervasive role of family influence reflecting cultural values in the region, coverage is given to the importance placed on extrinsic values such as prestige, economic returns, and stability in a career (and the lack of emphasis on intrinsic values such as interest

J. Y. Jung (✉)
GERRIC/School of Education, The University of New South Wales, Sydney, NSW, Australia
e-mail: jae.jung@unsw.edu.au

© Springer Nature Singapore Pte Ltd. 2021   1367
S. R. Smith (ed.), *Handbook of Giftedness and Talent Development in the Asia-Pacific*,
Springer International Handbooks of Education,
https://doi.org/10.1007/978-981-13-3041-4_65

and a desire for intellectual stimulation), along with gender role expectations and the experience of career indecision. Thereafter, the similarities and differences in the career aspirations of gifted students in the region with the career aspirations of gifted students in Western societies are explained. Following this, two career theories that may be useful in understanding the career decisions of this group—the theory of circumscription and compromise and the theory of work adjustment—are discussed. The chapter concludes with some speculative, but research-informed, thoughts on the future of the career decisions of gifted students in the region.

Keywords

Career decision · Career choice · Asia · Asia-Pacific · Low socio-economic status · Economic disadvantage

The aims in this chapter are to:
1. Outline the major issues surrounding the career decisions for gifted students in the Asia-Pacific region.
2. Outline the career aspirations of gifted students in the Asia-Pacific region.
3. Outline the career theories that may be relevant and useful in understanding and supporting the career decisions for gifted students in the Asia-Pacific region.
4. Discuss what the career decisions for gifted students in the Asia-Pacific region may be like in the future.

Introduction

The multiple issues surrounding the career decisions for gifted students in the Asia-Pacific region appear to be simultaneously similar *and* different to the issues surrounding the career decisions for gifted students in other parts of the world. In all likelihood, any similarities may be related to the fact that gifted students across the world may share common traits and characteristics associated with their abilities, regardless of the definitions of giftedness that are followed and the types of abilities that are valued. In comparison, any differences may stem from the differing environments, settings, contexts, societies, and cultures that gifted students from different parts of the world may live in. Unfortunately, due to the general paucity of research in the area, a clear picture is yet to emerge of the general features of the career decisions of gifted students in the region. Consequently, this chapter was informed not only by the existing literature in the area from a select number of Asia-Pacific countries (i.e., China, Japan, Korea, Turkey), but also by the literature in related areas including the career development of general adolescents in the Asia-Pacific region, giftedness in the Asia-Pacific region, and the career decisions and career decision-making processes of gifted students from different parts of the world.

Unsurprisingly, most of the research that has been conducted to date on the career decisions of gifted students relates to the career decisions of gifted students living in Western societies. Specifically, research has been conducted on the career decisions of gifted students in the United States and Canada (Achter, Lubinski, & Benbow, 1996; Emmett & Minor, 1993; Grant, Battle, & Heggoy, 2000; Greene, 2003, 2006; Kerr & Sodano, 2003; Stewart, 1999), Australia (Jung, 2013, 2014, 2017, 2019; Jung & Young, 2017, 2019; Watters, 2010), and a number of European countries (Fiebig, 2003, 2008; Vock, Köller, & Nagy, 2013). These studies have generally suggested that a number of issues may be important to the career decisions of gifted students, including:

(a) The areas of ability and interest (Achter, Lubinski, Benbow, & Eftekhar-i-Sanjani, 1999; Chen & Wong, 2013; Gottfredson, 2003; Grant et al., 2000; Jung, 2014; Lubinski & Benbow, 2000; Vock et al., 2013; Webb, Lubinski, & Benbow, 2002).
(b) Multipotentiality (or the existence of multiple areas of ability and interest; Greene, 2003, 2006; Gross, 2006; Jung, 2018; Kerr & Sodano, 2003; Leung, 1998; Maxwell, 2007; Rysiew, Shore, & Carson, 1994; Rysiew, Shore, & Leeb, 1999).
(c) Tendencies toward perfectionism (Chen & Wong, 2013; Greene, 2003, 2006; Jung, 2013, 2014, 2018; Kerr & Sodano, 2003; Maxwell, 2007; Stornelli, Flett, & Hewitt, 2009).
(d) A desire for intellectual stimulation and challenge (Emmett & Minor, 1993; Stewart, 1999).
(e) The high expectations of others in society, including expectations relating to prestige, income and the fulfilment of potential (Chen & Wong, 2013; Emmett & Minor, 1993; Fiebig, 2003; Grant et al., 2000; Kerr & Sodano, 2003; Leung, 1998; Miller & Cummings, 2009; Muratori & Smith, 2015; Sampson & Chason, 2008).
(f) Gender role (Chen & Wong, 2013; Jung, 2017; Kerr & Sodano, 2003; Vock et al., 2013).
(g) The difficulties in making a career decision (Emmett & Minor, 1993; Jung, 2013; Jung & Young, 2017).
(h) Superior access to career-related information (Chen & Wong, 2013; Kelly, 1992; Stewart, 1999).
(i) The early emergence of career-related interests (Greene, 2003, 2006; Matthews & Foster, 2005; Stewart, 1999).
(j) Career aspirations in a small range of unoriginal and traditional fields (Chen & Wong, 2013; Fiebig, 2008; Greene, 2006; Persson, 2009; Vock et al., 2013).

Many of the issues identified in the literature appear to be salient to the career decisions of gifted students in the Asia-Pacific region. Nevertheless, there appear to be some differences in their degree of salience.

Family Influence

Probably of *greater* salience to gifted students in the Asia-Pacific region than those in Western societies may be the high expectations of others, particularly the parents and families of gifted students, with respect to the career decision. For some countries in the region (e.g., China, Japan, Korea, and Vietnam), this may be reflective of the Confucian and related cultural values that are espoused in these countries, which emphasise filial piety, loyalty to family, and obedience to parents (Hou & Leung, 2011). Confucius was a Chinese philosopher who advocated a system encompassing human relationships, social structures, virtuous behaviour and work ethics (Fan, 2000) that proposed unequal relations among people, the need for righteousness and propriety in human relationships, a focus on the family unit, hard work, thrift, and perseverance (Hofstede, 2001; Hofstede & Bond, 1988; Huang & Gove, 2015; Jung, 2009). Although Confucian thinking, or Confucianism, may now be undergoing a degree of re-interpretation due to influences such as secularisation (i.e., decreasing influence of religion), localisation (i.e., adaptation of phenomenon to a particular society), and globalisation (i.e., increasing integration among societies), its key elements, including respect for the family, stress on hard work, diligence, possession of knowledge, and scholarly achievements (Chen, Ng, & Rao, 2005; Lim, 2003) continue to be noted by scholars in the field.

The influence of parents and other family members in the career decision may be similarly important in those countries of the Asia-Pacific region that do not espouse Confucian values, as most of these countries may be classified as being 'collectivist' (Hofstede, 2001; Singelis, Triandis, Bhawuk, & Gelfand, 1995; Triandis, 1995). In collectivist societies, people are considered to be part of one or more collectives, show a tendency to prioritise the goals of these collectives and are primarily motivated by the expectations that are communicated by these collectives. The collective of importance for gifted students in the region is likely to be their families, which may lead to the prioritisation of family views over personal views in the career decision, the formation of career intentions that are consistent with these family views and the implementation of such career intentions in the eventual career decisions.

Generally, the influence of the family appears to be a *pervasive* feature of the career decisions of gifted students across the large number of countries and societies in the Asia-Pacific region, with only some minor exceptions (Hou & Leung, 2011; Karibe et al., 2009; Lee & Sriraman, 2012; Ogurlu, Kaya, & Hizli, 2015).

Prestige, Economic Returns, and Stability

In broad terms, the careers that are encouraged by the families of gifted students in the Asia-Pacific region appear to be the professional-type careers that require substantial educational investment and are considered prestigious, are favourably recognised by other members of society, are well remunerated, and offer stability. While a number of scholars have suggested that gifted students living in Western cultures are also likely to aspire to such careers (Chen & Wong, 2013; Emmett & Minor, 1993; Kerr & Sodano, 2003), the preference given to these careers appears to be magnified in the region. For example, Hou and Leung (2011) have proposed that Chinese families consider prestige to be one of the most important factors in career selection, as reflected in the Chinese idiom "to expect our sons to be a dragon" (p. 357) which illustrates a desire by Chinese parents for their children to become accomplished and powerful adults. Similarly, Kim (2012) has noted that many Korean students make decisions about university study in preparation for a career decision, on the basis of social prestige and economic returns rather than on the basis of their areas of ability or personal interest. Outside of East Asia, Raychaudhuri and Jana (2016) have noted that prestige and respectability may be two of the most powerful factors in the career decisions among middle-class families in India. Similarly, Ogurlu et al. (2015) have suggested that gifted students in Turkey may be inclined toward careers that are considered prestigious and well paying, along with 'safe' careers that offer multiple job opportunities after the completion of one's education. Interestingly, the career decisions for gifted students in Japan may additionally be influenced by a desire to continue in the line of work of other members of the family (Karibe et al., 2009).

To some degree, the apparent focus on extrinsic and security values, rather than on intrinsic values, in the career decision, may reflect the cultural values of societies in the Asia-Pacific region (Chen et al., 2005; Hofstede, 2001; Hofstede & Bond, 1988; Huang & Gove, 2015; Jung, 2009; Lim, 2003). Nevertheless, it is also possible, particularly in the more underdeveloped parts of the region, that this may reflect a desire for survival, upward mobility, and a better life. Indeed, a number of similarities have been identified between the value placed on income and stability by gifted students in the region, and the importance of income and stability in the career decision-making processes of gifted students of low socio-economic status backgrounds. For example, income and stability have been identified to be major components of the model of the career decision-making processes of economically disadvantaged gifted students in Jung and Young (2019), with stability and an expectancy for success also recognised as being two of the five 'pivotal' factors in the career decision-making process. For such adolescents, financial security and survival may be among the most important considerations in the career decision, which may need to take priority over considerations such as interest or enjoyment (Blustein et al., 2002; Blustein, McWhirter, & Perry, 2005; Doyle, 2011; Gore, Holmes, Smith, Southgate, & Albright, 2015; Leitão, Guedes, Yamamoto, & Lopes, 2013; Mello, 2009).

Gender Role

In addition to family influence and a preference for prestigious, highly paid, and stable careers, gifted students in the Asia-Pacific region appear to make career decisions that are compatible with traditional societal views about gender role. The research that has been conducted to date on gifted students living in Western societies (Chen & Wong, 2013; Holland, 1997; Kerr & Sodano, 2003; Vock et al., 2013) has generally identified gender differences in the career decision, with gifted boys tending to pursue careers that are stereotypically considered 'masculine' in fields such as engineering and the physical sciences. In comparison, gifted girls have traditionally demonstrated a preference for careers that are considered 'feminine' in fields such as the health sciences.

The division of careers into 'masculine' and 'feminine' careers appears to be even more pronounced for gifted students in the Asia-Pacific region due to a greater level of gender inequality in the region. This may be manifested in socialisation practices with children, a clearer distinction between the roles of men (e.g., 'breadwinner') and women (e.g., family responsibilities), and the availability or non-availability of mentors and role models of the different genders in the various career fields. For example, Lee and Sriraman (2012) have suggested that Korean families may not always consider careers in STEM fields (i.e., Science, Technology, Engineering, and Mathematics) for gifted girls and even discourage such careers (while encouraging such careers for gifted boys) due to perceptions that such careers may be difficult to balance with married life and the raising of a family. Furthermore, common perceptions that females may be discriminated against in certain career fields that are dominated by men (e.g., science, engineering, and politics) may act as a deterrent for many gifted girls in pursuing careers in these fields (Lee & Sriraman, 2012). Instead, many gifted girls may find careers in fields where women are better represented, such as teaching, counselling, and nursing, to be more inviting (Kim, 2012). These are the very careers that gifted boys may be dissuaded from entering, due to possible threats to their masculine identity, concerns about discrimination from women, and the lack of male role models or mentors.

As in Western societies, where gifted girls are more likely than gifted boys to cross gender boundaries in the career decision (Leung, 1998; Vock et al., 2013), it may be the case that there are some differences between gifted boys and girls in the Asia-Pacific region in their willingness to pursue careers commonly associated with the opposite gender. As an example, Hou and Leung (2011) have suggested that despite the cultural sex-role tradition in Chinese society, the greater parental focus on the career decisions of boys as the traditional bearer of the family, may mean that girls may be subject to fewer restrictions, and consequently greater flexibility and autonomy, in their career decisions.

Career Indecision

Irrespective of the career decision that is eventually made, gifted students in the region appear likely to experience some level of difficulty with the career decision. The phenomenon of *career indecision*, which may be defined either as an inability to reach a career decision or the problems in making such a decision, has been widely researched in the field of vocational psychology (Gati, Krausz, & Osipow, 1996; Guay, Senécal, Gauthier, & Fernet, 2003; Leong & Chervinko, 1996). For many gifted students, this may be manifested in delays to the making of the career decision, frequent changes to the area of study or training, a sense of being 'stuck' in a career due to prior investments in education or training, or the making of a career decision after consideration of only a limited number of options (Di Fabio, Palazzeschi, Asulin-Peretz, & Gati, 2013; Emmett & Minor, 1993; White & Tracey, 2011). Typically, career indecision is seen as a *temporary* developmental stage that all students, including gifted and non-gifted students, may go through as a normal part of their career development (Jung, 2013).

In the Asia-Pacific region, the potential exists for career indecision to be a very serious issue for many gifted students, due to the expectations that are likely to be placed on these students by their families. First of all, it is possible that any *differences* in the career expectations of the family and the gifted student's personal preferences will lead to conflicts that may not be experienced by gifted students who are allowed to make autonomous career decisions (Hou & Leung, 2011). Furthermore, in the situation where parental or family expectations are *very high* (e.g., to allow for the pursuit of prestigious, well-remunerated, and stable careers), the gifted student may experience substantial anxiety and stress relating to the anticipated difficulty of fulfilling these expectations (Leung, Hou, Gati, & Li, 2011). Additional to such potential conflicts and difficulties be any *internal* conflicts that the gifted student himself or herself may experience relating to factors such as their capability in multiple career fields, or tensions between those careers that are compatible with the gifted student's areas of ability and those that are compatible with his/her areas of interest. Unfortunately, many gifted students in the region do not appear to have ready access to career counselling nor the necessary information and resources relating to the various career options, to support their career decisions (Kim, 2012).

For gifted students from the more underdeveloped parts of the region, some of the difficulties with the career decision may be related to their impoverished backgrounds. For example, a number of scholars who have investigated career indecision among adolescents of low socio-economic status have suggested that such adolescents may have a greater likelihood of uncertainty with the career decision, and relatedly, transitions from education to career that may not be very smooth (Furlong & Cartmel, 2004; Jung & Young, 2017; Yates, Harris, Sabates, & Staff, 2011). Complicating the career decision further may be other factors that have been identified to be related to economic disadvantage, such as low career expectations, the placement of excessive reliance on informal career-related information, and having limited career-related experiences (Diemer, 2007; Fouad & Kantamneni, 2008; Greenbank & Hepworth, 2008; Mello, 2009; Metheny & McWhirter, 2013).

Less Salient Issues in the Career Decision

Among the issues that are commonly recognised to influence the career decisions of gifted students in Western societies, the less salient issues for gifted students in the Asia-Pacific region may be the intrinsic factors related to the personal traits and characteristics of gifted students. These may include the areas of ability, the areas of interest, multipotentiality, perfectionistic tendencies, and a desire for intellectual stimulation and challenge (Hou & Leung, 2011; Karibe et al., 2009; Lee & Sriraman, 2012; Ogurlu et al., 2015). While gifted students in the region may have a *personal* desire to choose a 'perfect' career that is interesting, intellectually stimulating, and compatible with their area of high ability, the selection of a career on this basis may not be realistic or viable due to the substantially greater focus placed on factors such as prestige, income, and stability by their families (Hou & Leung, 2011; Jung & Young, 2019; Kim, 2012). Indeed, intrinsic factors such as interest, enjoyment, and intellectual stimulation may need to be considered as 'luxuries' that need to be ignored or at least relegated to secondary importance in the career decision (Chen & Wong, 2013; Emmett & Minor, 1993; Gottfredson, 2003; Grant et al., 2000; Jung, 2014; Stewart, 1999). Nevertheless, as such factors may continue to be personally important for gifted students in the region, it is possible that they instead form the basis for the selection of hobbies, other recreational pursuits or even secondary part-time 'careers'.

Career Aspirations

Generally, the career aspirations of gifted students in the Asia-Pacific region appear to be in a narrower range of fields than for gifted students in Western societies. This may be related to the strong influence of parents and families in the career decision, which may mean that parents and families set parameters for these students around the range of careers that may be considered acceptable and worthy of consideration (Hou & Leung, 2011; Karibe et al., 2009; Lee & Sriraman, 2012; Ogurlu et al., 2015). For example, Raychaudhuri and Jana (2016) have proposed that only three or four careers may be considered 'good' careers by middle-class families and communities in India, while Hou and Leung (2011) have suggested that some parents may effectively 'filter' the range of careers for their children in China. Similarly, research on the career aspirations of a related group, Asian Americans, have suggested that Asian American adolescents tend not to be open to the entire range of career options that are available to the rest of the adolescent population in the United States (Leong & Serafica, 1995; Leung, Ivey, & Suzuki, 1994).

Despite the narrowness of the range of career options given serious consideration by gifted students in the region, the actual *types* of careers that they aspire to may be fairly similar to the types of careers aspired to by gifted students in Western societies. A general consensus appears to exist that gifted students in Western societies are likely to aspire to unoriginal and traditional careers in the investigative and realistic realms (Holland, 1997) in fields such as engineering, the physical sciences, health, communications, and technology that are characterised by analytical, intellectual, and scholarly activities (Achter, Benbow, & Lubinski, 1997; Chen & Wong, 2013; Jung, 2017, 2019; Kerr & Sodano, 2003; Sparfeldt, 2007; Vock et al., 2013). Most of the emerging research on the career aspirations of gifted students in the Asia-Pacific region has reached a similar conclusion, with Hou and Leung (2011) and Ogurlu et al. (2015) noting the focus on careers in the investigative realm in China and Turkey.

In fact, after identifying a tendency by gifted students in Turkey to aspire to careers in engineering, medicine, design, science, defence, and law, Ogurlu et al. (2015) suggested that the career aspirations of gifted students in Turkey may not be substantially different to the career aspirations of gifted students in other parts of the world.

Interestingly, a greater focus appears to exist in some countries in the Asia-Pacific region (such as China) toward 'enterprising'-type careers (e.g., business and management) which involve substantial human interaction and leadership activities for economic gain, than in Western societies (Hou & Leung, 2011; Vock et al., 2013). One possible explanation for such career aspirations, particularly in the developing parts of the region, may be related to the increasing importance of business and management to the economies of these countries.

Relevant Career Theories

At the present time, multiple career theories exist and are used to understand and support the career decisions of adolescents around the world. These include the trait and factor theories that place a focus on matching an individual to a career (Brown, 2002; Holland, 1997), the career developmental theories that conceptualises the career decision to be the product of a developmental process (Hodkinson & Sparkes, 1997; Savickas, 2007), the social learning theories that view the career decision as arising from a variety of learning experiences (Krumboltz, 1979) and the postmodern theories which represent contemporary approaches to conceptualising the career decision (Savickas, 2002). Of the various career theories, two appear to have the greatest potential to be relevant in understanding and supporting the career decisions of gifted students in the Asia-Pacific region—Gottfredson's (1981, 2002, 2005) *theory of circumscription and compromise* and the *theory of work adjustment* (Dawis & Lofquist, 1984; Lofquist & Dawis, 1991). Both theories have been used previously in investigations of gifted students in Western societies (Achter & Lubinski, 2005; Jung, 2019; Muratori & Smith, 2015).

Theory of Circumscription and Compromise

Gottfredson's (1981, 2002, 2005) theory of circumscription and compromise proposes that the career decision may be arrived at after the progression by adolescents through four developmental phases:

(a) Phase 1: Familiarisation with the activities, conditions, rewards, stereotypes, and personalities of the people working in the various career fields.
(b) Phase 2: The development of interests, skills, values, and goals related to a career that is likely to be the product of one's genes, environment, culture, and experiences.

(c) Phase 3: The elimination of career options on the basis of gender role, prestige, and personal interests (along with the difficulty of the career, income, and education).

(d) Phase 4: The elimination of the remaining career options on the basis of accessibility (e.g., the availability of relevant education/training programs, the costs of relevant education/training programs, the availability of employment opportunities, and the level of support from parents).

While the theory was not developed specifically for gifted students in the Asia-Pacific region, it nevertheless gives acknowledgement to many of the factors that have been repeatedly identified to be salient to this group. In particular, the importance of factors such as prestige, gender role, and income are recognised in the third of the four phases in the theory. Additionally, while the recognition of the influence of parents or families is not substantial, any lack of parental support is acknowledged in the final phase of the theory as a factor that may restrict accessibility to one or more careers. Furthermore, the minimal attention given to factors such as a desire for intellectual stimulation, multipotentiality, and perfectionism in the theory is consistent with the lack of attention to intrinsic factors in the career decision for many gifted students in the region. Finally, the argument may be made that *compromise*, which may be considered to be a major component of the theory (as reflected in the name of the theory), may be a major component of the career decision-making process for many gifted students in the region, particularly as means to address any differences between a gifted student's personal views and the expectations of his/her family with respect to the career decision.

The Theory of Work Adjustment

The theory of work adjustment may also be considered relevant to the career decisions of gifted students in the Asia-Pacific region. To date, the theory has been used extensively to investigate the career decisions of multiple cohorts of highly gifted students in the *Study of Mathematically Precocious Youth* (Achter & Lubinski, 2005; Lubinski & Benbow, 2000; Makel, Kell, Lubinski, Putallaz, & Benbow, 2016). Under this theory, a career decision is seen to be made after "specifying important characteristics between the individual and the (work) environment and then attempting to find the best match or fit" (Swanson & Schneider, 2013, p. 29), with an optimal career decision being deemed when there is both: (a) a correspondence between the individual's abilities and the ability requirements of the career and (b) a correspondence between the rewards offered by the career and the individual's needs (Dawis, 2005; Jung, 2019; Swanson & Schneider, 2013). In the situation where multiple careers allow for the achievement of both forms of correspondence, factors other than abilities and rewards may be considered, including vocational interests, family expectations, family culture, family socio-economic status, personality traits, and the state of the labour market (Dawis, 2005; Jung, 2019).

As for the theory of circumscription and compromise, family influence is given some attention in the theory, as a consideration when multiple realistic career options exist. Moreover, the valuing of prestige, income, and stability appears to be compatible with the theory as they may qualify as individual 'needs' that are satisfied with corresponding career rewards. Nevertheless, neither gender role expectations nor career indecision has been given any meaningful acknowledgement in the theory. Specifically, gender role appears to be ignored, while only an oblique reference to career indecision exists in the following statement by Dawis (2005): "in choosing from among the finalist occupations, an individual must be aware of the trade-off nature of choice, the need to balance between advantages and disadvantages, and finally to decide on the basis of what is most important to the person" (p. 18).

Between the two theories, the theory of circumscription and compromise appears to be marginally more useful for, and applicable to, gifted students in the region, due to its recognition of a greater number of factors that have been commonly identified to be salient to the career decisions of these students.

The Future

In the future, gifted students in the region and around the world are likely to be faced with a very different work environment to the work environment of today. The new environment may be characterised by rapid developments in production, manufacturing, service, information, and communication technologies leading to an increasing displacement of labour intensive roles; a parallel increase in the number of new roles requiring complex, intellectual, and creative capabilities that cannot be automated; and an increasing internationalisation and globalisation of the workforce (Autor, 2015; Gittins, 2017; Herr, 2003; Jung, 2019; Storey, 2000; Störmer et al., 2014). Simultaneously, in an effort by organisations to become more flexible and adaptive to the changing environment, they may become increasingly reluctant to offer permanent roles, and may rely instead on greater numbers of temporary and part-time employees (Passaretta & Wolbers, 2019; Storey, 2000; Störmer et al., 2014). The consequence is that the nature of careers in the future may become substantially different to the careers commonly seen today, with a greater likelihood of discontinuity and a higher frequency of movements across organisations, occupations, and cultures (Chudzikowski, 2012).

The implications for gifted students in the Asia-Pacific region are many. First of all, it is possible that the increasing internationalisation and globalisation of the workforce, and relatedly, the increasing internationalisation of societies in the region, may lead to a greater acceptance of non-traditional values and approaches to thinking about the career decision. For example, the Confucian and collectivist values espoused in many societies in the region may become 'modernised' or 're-interpreted' to allow for a greater acknowledgement of the personal views of gifted students in the career decision and a corresponding reduction to the influence of family (Hou & Leung, 2011). Consequently, intrinsic factors in the career decision such as interest, enjoyment, and a desire for intellectual stimulation may become more important, while extrinsic factors such as prestige and income may decline in importance (Gore et al., 2015; Jung & Young, 2019; Leitão et al., 2013). Relatedly, the greater level of exposure by people in the region to non-traditional values may lead to a progressive reduction in gender inequality, and a greater general level of acceptance of gifted students crossing gender boundaries in the choice of their future careers (Hou & Leung, 2011; Lee & Sriraman, 2012). Therefore, in many ways, the career decisions of gifted students in the Asia-Pacific region in the future may come to more closely resemble the career decisions of gifted students in Western societies today, particularly in terms of the specific range of careers that are considered, and the gender compatibility of these careers.

As for gifted students in Western societies, the unique characteristics of gifted students in the region may mean they are at a considerable advantage in comparison to their non-gifted counterparts in the work environment of the future. First of all, their capabilities and interests in multiple areas may mean that they are better suited than non-gifted students to the new range of complex, intellectual, and creative careers that are likely to emerge (Chen & Wong, 2013; Emmett & Minor, 1993; Herr & Cramer, 1996; Jung, 2019; Storey, 2000; Störmer et al., 2014; Tang, 2003; Vock et al., 2013). Furthermore, the multipotentiality of these students may mean that they are better positioned than non-gifted students to continuously seek new positions, and to adapt to new work environments, that may require different sets of skills (Greene, 2006; Gross, 2006; Jung, 2018; Kerr & Sodano, 2003). In the situation where they are required to undergo retraining or re-education to adapt to any major technological developments, or even to the need to change career fields due to a lack of job opportunities or career obsolescence, gifted students may again be at an advantage due to their motivation and capacity for continuous learning (Jung, 2014, 2019, in press; Watts, 2000). While the cultural values of these students may mean that they prefer careers that are stable and secure, they may in fact be able to readily cope with the anticipated changes that the future may bring. Nevertheless, to maximise their chances of success, gifted students in the region may need to consciously and deliberately 'manage' their careers, through the continuous updating of their career and related skills (Herr, 2003; Savickas, 2003; Störmer et al., 2014; Verbruggen, 2010; Watts, 2000) and the development of strong and diverse professional networks that may give these students access to important contacts and information about the latest developments in the field (Jung, in press; Störmer et al., 2014; Sullivan, 1999).

Concluding Remarks

Gifted students in the Asia-Pacific region appear to be faced with a unique set of issues with the career decision relating to their personal traits and characteristics, and their cultural backgrounds that distinguish them from gifted students from other parts of the world. Unfortunately, most of the existing research literature relates to the career decisions of gifted students from Western societies, and a complete picture is yet to emerge of the career decisions of this Asian-Pacific group.

Moreover, the research that is emerging is concentrated in a small number of countries that may not be representative of the diversity or vastness of the region that spans multiple countries, cultures, and continents. In recognition of the enormous size of this group, their tremendous potential to contribute to the various career fields and their capacity to make a lasting impact on the work and non-work lives of others in society, urgent attention is necessary by scholars and practitioners in the area to better understand and support the career decisions of these highly capable students.

Cross-References

▶ Educational Contexts, Transitions and Community Engagement: Part VI Introduction
▶ Gifted Education in the Asia-Pacific: From the Past for the Future – An Introduction
▶ How Do Teachers Meet the Academic Needs of High-Ability Students in Science?
▶ In Search of an Explanation for an Approach-Avoidance Pattern in East Asia: The Role of Cultural Values in Gifted Education
▶ Innovative Practices to Support High-Achieving Deprived Young Scholars in an Ethnic-Linguistic Diverse Latin American Country
▶ Leadership Development of Gifted Adolescents from a Korean Multicultural Lens
▶ Some Implications for the Future of Gifted Education in the Asia-Pacific
▶ STEAM in Gifted Education in Korea
▶ The Predictors of the Decisions by Gifted Students to Pursue STEM Careers: The Case of Brazilian International Students in Australia
▶ Transitioning to Career: Talented Musicians' Identity Development
▶ Trends and Challenges of Creativity Development Among Selected Asian Countries and Regions: China, Hong Kong/Macau, Japan, Malaysia, and South Korea

Acknowledgment Work relating to parts of this chapter was funded by the Australian Research Council under the Discovery Early Career Researcher Award scheme (DE130100015).

References

Achter, J. A., Benbow, C. P., & Lubinski, D. (1997). Rethinking multipotentiality among the intellectually gifted: A critical review and recommendations. *The Gifted Child Quarterly, 41*, 5–15. https://doi.org/10.1177/001698629704100102
Achter, J. A., & Lubinski, D. (2005). Blending promise with passion: Best practices for counseling intellectually talented youth. In S. D. Brown & R. W. Lent (Eds.), *Career development and counseling: Putting theory and research to work* (pp. 600–624). Hoboken, NJ: Wiley.
Achter, J. A., Lubinski, D., & Benbow, C. P. (1996). Multipotentiality among the intellectually gifted: "It was never there and already it's vanishing". *Journal of Counseling Psychology, 43*, 56–76. https://doi.org/10.1037/0022-0167.43.1.65
Achter, J. A., Lubinski, D., Benbow, C. P., & Eftekhari-Sanjani, H. (1999). Assessing vocational preferences among gifted adolescents adds incremental validity to abilities: A discriminant analysis of educational outcomes over a 10-year interval. *Journal of Educational Psychology, 91*, 777–786. https://doi.org/10.1037/0022-0663.91.4.777

Autor, D. H. (2015). Why are there still so many jobs? The history and future of workplace automation. *The Journal of Economic Perspectives, 29*, 3–30. https://doi.org/10.1257/jep.29.3.3

Blustein, D. L., Chaves, A. P., Diemer, M. A., Gallagher, L. A., Marshall, K. G., Sirin, S., & Bhati, K. S. (2002). Voices of the forgotten half: The role of social class in the school-to-work transition. *Journal of Counseling Psychology, 48*, 311–323. https://doi.org/10.1037/0022-0167.49.3.311

Blustein, D. L., McWhirter, E. H., & Perry, J. C. (2005). An emancipatory communitarian approach to vocational development theory, research, and practice. *The Counseling Psychologist, 33*, 141–179. https://doi.org/10.1177/0011000004272268

Brown, D. (2002). *Career choice and development*. San Francisco, CA: Jossey-Bass.

Chen, C. P., & Wong, J. (2013). Career counseling for gifted students. *Australian Journal of Career Development, 22*, 121–129. https://doi.org/10.1177/1038416213507909

Chen, H. A., Ng, S., & Rao, A. R. (2005). Cultural differences in consumer impatience. *Journal of Marketing Research, 17*, 291–301. https://doi.org/10.1509/jmkr.2005.42.3.291

Chudzikowski, K. (2012). Career transitions and career success in the "new" career era. *Journal of Vocational Behavior, 81*, 298–306. https://doi.org/10.1016/j.jvb.2011.10.005

Dawis, R. V. (2005). The Minnesota theory of work adjustment. In S. D. Brown & R. W. Lent (Eds.), *Career development and counseling: Putting theory and research to work* (pp. 3–23). Hoboken, NJ: Wiley.

Dawis, R. V., & Lofquist, L. H. (1984). *A psychological theory of work adjustment*. Minneapolis, MN: University of Minnesota Press.

Di Fabio, A., Palazzeschi, L., Asulin-Peretz, L., & Gati, I. (2013). Career indecision versus indecisiveness: Associations with personality traits and emotional intelligence. *Journal of Career Assessment, 21*, 42–56. https://doi.org/10.1177/1069072712454698

Diemer, M. A. (2007). Parental and school influences upon the career development of poor youth of color. *Journal of Vocational Behavior, 70*, 502–524. https://doi.org/10.1016/j.jvb.2007.02.003

Doyle, E. (2011). Career development needs of low socioeconomic status university students. *Australian Journal of Career Development, 20*, 56–65. https://doi.org/10.1177/103841621102000309

Emmett, J. D., & Minor, C. W. (1993). Career decision-making factors in gifted young adults. *Career Development Quarterly, 41*, 350–366. https://doi.org/10.1002/j.2161-0045.1993.tb00409.x

Fan, Y. (2000). A classification of Chinese culture. *Cross Cultural Management, 7*, 3–10. https://doi.org/10.1108/13527600010797057

Fiebig, J. N. (2003). Gifted American and German early adolescent girls: Influences on career orientation and aspirations. *High Ability Studies, 14*, 165–183. https://doi.org/10.1080/1359813032000163898

Fiebig, J. N. (2008). Gifted American and German adolescent women: A longitudinal examination of attachment, separation, gender roles, and career aspirations. *High Ability Studies, 19*, 67–81. https://doi.org/10.1080/13598130801980349

Fouad, N. A., & Kantamneni, N. (2008). Contextual factors in vocational psychology: Intersections of individual, group, and societal dimensions. In S. D. Brown & R. W. Lent (Eds.), *Handbook of counseling psychology* (pp. 408–425). Hoboken, NJ: Wiley.

Furlong, A., & Cartmel, F. (2004). *Vulnerable young men in fragile labour markets: Employment, unemployment and the search for long-term security*. York, UK: Joseph Rowntree Foundation.

Gati, I., Krausz, M., & Osipow, S. H. (1996). A taxonomy of difficulties in career decision making. *Journal of Counseling Psychology, 43*, 510–526. https://doi.org/10.1037/0022-0167.43.4.510

Gittins, R. (2017, December 13). Robots aren't stealing jobs: Truth behind claim scaring pants off our graduates. Sydney Morning Herald. Retrieved from http://www.smh.com.au/comment/robots-arent-stealing-jobs-truth-behind-claim-scaring-pants-off-our-graduates-20171211-h02y18.html

Gore, J., Holmes, K., Smith, M., Southgate, E., & Albright, J. (2015). Socioeconomic status and the career aspirations of Australian school students: Testing enduring assumptions. *The Australian Educational Researcher, 42*, 155–177. https://doi.org/10.1007/s13384-015-0172-5

Gottfredson, L. S. (1981). Circumscription and compromise: A developmental theory of occupational aspirations. *Journal of Counseling Psychology, 28*, 545–579. https://doi.org/10.1037/0022-0167.28.6.545

Gottfredson, L. S. (2002). Gottfredson's theory of circumscription, compromise, and self-creation. In D. Brown (Ed.), *Career choice and development* (4th ed., pp. 85–148). San Francisco, CA: Jossey-Bass.

Gottfredson, L. S. (2003). The challenge and promise of cognitive career assessment. *Journal of Career Assessment, 11*, 115–135. https://doi.org/10.1177/1069072703011002001

Gottfredson, L. S. (2005). Applying Gottfredson's theory of circumscription and compromise in career guidance and counseling. In S. D. Brown & R. W. Lent (Eds.), *Career development and counseling: Putting theory and research to work* (pp. 71–100). New York, NY: Wiley.

Grant, D. F., Battle, D. A., & Heggoy, S. J. (2000). The journey through college of seven gifted females: Influences on their career related decisions. *Roeper Review, 22*, 251–260. https://doi.org/10.1080/02783190009554047

Greenbank, P., & Hepworth, S. (2008). *Working class students and the career decision-making process: A qualitative study.* Manchester, UK: HECSU.

Greene, M. J. (2003). Gifted adrift? Career counseling of the gifted and talented. *Roeper Review, 25*, 66–72. https://doi.org/10.1080/02783190309554201

Greene, M. J. (2006). Helping build lives: Career and life development of gifted and talented students. *Professional School Counseling, 10*, 34–42. https://doi.org/10.1177/2156759X0601001S05

Gross, M. U. M. (2006). Exceptionally gifted children: Long-term outcomes of academic acceleration and nonacceleration. *Journal for the Education of the Gifted, 29*, 404–429. https://doi.org/10.4219/jeg-2006-247

Guay, F., Senécal, C., Gauthier, L., & Fernet, C. (2003). Predicting career indecision: A self-determination theory perspective. *Journal of Counseling Psychology, 50*, 165–177. https://doi.org/10.1037/0022-0167.50.2.165

Herr, E. L. (2003). The future of career counseling as an instrument of public policy. *The Career Development Quarterly, 52*, 8–17. https://doi.org/10.1002/j.2161-0045.2003.tb00622.x

Herr, E. L., & Cramer, S. H. (1996). *Career guidance and counseling through the lifespan: Systematic approaches* (5th ed.). New York, NY: Harper Collins.

Hodkinson, P., & Sparkes, A. C. (1997). Careership: A sociological theory of career decision-making. *British Journal of Sociology of Education, 18*, 29–44. https://doi.org/10.1080/0142569970180102

Hofstede, G. (2001). *Culture's consequences: Comparing values, behaviours, institutions and organizations across nations* (2nd ed.). Thousand Oaks, CA: Sage.

Hofstede, G., & Bond, M. H. (1988). The Confucius connection: From cultural roots to economic growth. *Organizational Dynamics, 16*, 5–21. https://doi.org/10.1016/0090-2616(88)90009-5

Holland, J. L. (1997). *Making vocational choices: A theory of vocational personalities and work environments* (3rd ed.). Odessa, FL: Psychological Assessment Resources.

Hou, Z., & Leung, S. A. (2011). Vocational aspirations of Chinese high school students and their parents' expectations. *Journal of Vocational Behavior, 79*, 349–360. https://doi.org/10.1016/j.jvb.2011.05.008

Huang, G. H. C., & Gove, M. (2015). Confucianism, Chinese families, and academic achievement: Exploring how Confucianism and Asian descendant parenting practices influence children's academic achievement. In M. Khine (Ed.), *Science education in East Asia* (pp. 41–66). New York, NY: Springer. https://doi.org/10.1007/978-3-319-16390-1_3

Jung, J. Y. (2009). *Culture, motivation, and vocational decision-making of senior high school students* (Doctoral dissertation). Retrieved from http://unsworks.unsw.edu.au/fapi/datastream/unsworks:5596/SOURCE02?view=true

Jung, J. Y. (2013). The cognitive processes associated with occupational/career indecision: A model for gifted adolescents. *Journal for the Education of the Gifted, 36*, 433–460. https://doi.org/10.1177/0162353213506067

Jung, J. Y. (2014). Modeling the occupational/career decision-making processes of intellectually gifted adolescents: A competing models strategy. *Journal for the Education of the Gifted, 37*, 128–152. https://doi.org/10.1177/0162353214529045

Jung, J. Y. (2017). Occupational/career decision-making thought processes of adolescents of high intellectual ability. *Journal for the Education of the Gifted, 40*, 50–78. https://doi.org/10.1177/0162353217690040

Jung, J. Y. (2018). Occupational/career amotivation and indecision for gifted and talented adolescents: A cognitive decision-making process perspective. *Journal of Psychologists and Counsellors in Schools, 28*, 143–165. https://doi.org/10.1017/jgc.2016.33

Jung, J. Y. (2019). *The career decisions of gifted students and other high ability groups.* Oxon, UK: Routledge.

Jung, J. Y. (in press). The career development of gifted students. In J. A. Athanasou & H. N. Perera (Eds.), *International handbook of career guidance.* Dordrecht, The Netherlands: Springer.

Jung, J. Y., & Young, M. (2017). Occupational/career indecision for economically disadvantaged high school students of high intellectual ability: A mixed methods cognitive process model. *Psychology in the Schools, 54*, 718–735. https://doi.org/10.1002/pits.22023

Jung, J. Y., & Young, M. (2019). The occupational/career decision-making processes of intellectually gifted adolescents from economically disadvantaged backgrounds: A mixed methods perspective. *Gifted Child Quarterly, 63*, 36–57. https://doi.org/10.1177/0016986218804575

Karibe, H., Kawakami, T., Suzuki, A., Waita, S., Ogata, K., Aoyagi, K., et al. (2009). Career choice and attitudes towards dental education amongst dental students in Japan and Sweden. *European Journal of Dental Education, 13*, 80–86. https://doi.org/10.1111/j.1600-0579.2008.00543.x

Kelly, K. (1992). Career maturity of young gifted adolescents: A replication study. *Journal for the Education of the Gifted, 16*, 36–45. https://doi.org/10.1177/016235329201600105

Kerr, B. A., & Sodano, S. (2003). Career assessment with intellectually gifted students. *Journal of Career Assessment, 11*, 168–186. https://doi.org/10.1177/1069072703011002004

Kim, K. N. (2012). Trajectories of female student's career decision between high school and college: Organizationally separate but developmentally linked. *Asia Pacific Education Review, 13*, 349–562. https://doi.org/10.1007/s12564-012-9217-x

Krumboltz, J. D. (1979). A social learning theory of career decision making. In A. M. Mitchell, G. B. Jones, & J. D. Krumboltz (Eds.), *Social learning and career decision making* (pp. 19–49). Cranston, RI: Carroll.

Lee, K. H., & Sriraman, B. (2012). Gifted girls and nonmathematical aspirations: A longitudinal case study of two gifted Korean girls. *The Gifted Child Quarterly, 56*, 3–14. https://doi.org/10.1177/0016986211426899

Leitão, M., Guedes, Á., Yamamoto, M. E., & Lopes, F. D. A. (2013). Do people adjust career choices according to socioeconomic conditions? An evolutionary analysis of future discounting. *Psychology & Neuroscience, 6*, 383–390. https://doi.org/10.3922/j.psns.2013.3.16

Leong, F. T. L., & Chervinko, S. (1996). Construct validity of career indecision: Negative personality traits as predictors of career indecision. *Journal of Career Assessment, 4*, 315–329. https://doi.org/10.1177/106907279600400306

Leong, F. T. L., & Serafica, F. C. (1995). Career development of Asian Americans: A research area in need of a good theory. In F. T. L. Leong (Ed.), *Career development and vocational behavior of racial and ethnic minorities* (pp. 67–102). Hillsdale, NJ: Erlbaum.

Leung, A. S., Ivey, D., & Suzuki, L. (1994). Factors affecting the career aspirations of Asian Americans. *Journal of Counseling and Development, 72*, 404–410. https://doi.org/10.1002/j.1556-6676.1994.tb00958.x

Leung, S. A. (1998). Vocational identity and career choice congruence of gifted and talented high school students. *Counseling Psychology Quarterly, 11*, 325–335. https://doi.org/10.1080/09515079808254064

Leung, S. A., Hou, Z.-J., Gati, I., & Li, X. (2011). Effects of parental expectations and cultural-values orientation on career decision-making difficulties of Chinese university students. *Journal of Vocational Behavior, 78*, 11–20. https://doi.org/10.1016/j.jvb.2010.08.004

Lim, V. K. G. (2003). Money matters: An empirical investigation of money, face and Confucian work ethic. *Personality and Individual Differences, 35*, 953–970. https://doi.org/10.1016/S0191-8869(02)00311-2

Lofquist, L. H., & Dawis, R. V. (1991). *Essentials of person-environment-correspondence counseling.* Minneapolis, MN: University of Minnesota Press.

Lubinski, D., & Benbow, C. P. (2000). States of excellence. *American Psychologist, 55*, 137–150. https://doi.org/10.1037//0003-066X.55.1.137

Makel, M., Kell, H. J., Lubinski, D., Putallaz, M., & Benbow, C. P. (2016). When lightning strikes twice: Profoundly gifted, profoundly accomplished. *Psychological Science, 27*, 1004–1018. https://doi.org/10.1177/0956797616644735

Matthews, D. J., & Foster, J. F. (2005). Mystery to mastery: Shifting paradigms in gifted education. *Roeper Review, 28*, 64–69. https://doi.org/10.1080/02783190609554340

Maxwell, M. (2007). Career counseling is personal counseling: A constructivist approach to nurturing the development of gifted female adolescents. *The Career Development Quarterly, 55*, 206–224. https://doi.org/10.1002/j.2161-0045.2007.tb00078.x

Mello, Z. R. (2009). Racial/ethnic group and socioeconomic status variation in educational and occupational expectations from adolescence to adulthood. *Journal of Applied Developmental Psychology, 30*, 494–504. https://doi.org/10.1016/j.appdev.2008.12.029

Metheny, J., & McWhirter, E. H. (2013). Contributions of social status and family support to college students' career decision self-efficacy and outcome expectations. *Journal of Career Assessment, 21*, 378–394. https://doi.org/10.1177/1069072712475164

Miller, K., & Cummings, G. (2009). Gifted and talented students' career aspirations and influences: A systematic review of the literature. *International Journal of Nursing Education Scholarship, 6*, Article 8. https://doi.org/10.2202/1548-923X.1667

Muratori, M. C., & Smith, C. K. (2015). Guiding the talent and career development of the gifted individual. *Journal of Counseling and Development, 93*, 173–182. https://doi.org/10.1002/j.1556-6676.2015.00193.x

Ogurlu, U., Kaya, F., & Hizli, E. (2015). Career decisions of gifted students in Turkey. *Journal of European Education, 5*, 31–45.

Passaretta, G., & Wolbers, M. H. J. (2019). Temporary employment at labour market entry in Europe: Labour market dualism, transitions to secure employment and upward mobility. *Economic and Industrial Democracy, 40*, 382–408. https://doi.org/10.1177/0143831X16652946

Persson, R. S. (2009). Intellectually gifted individuals' career choices and work satisfaction: A descriptive study. *Gifted and Talented International, 24*, 11–23. https://doi.org/10.1080/15332276.2009.11674857

Raychaudhuri, S., & Jana, B. (2016). Factors influencing career choice of adolescent girls in Kolkata. *International Journal of Innovative Research and Advanced Studies, 3*, 281–290.

Rysiew, K. J., Shore, B. M., & Carson, A. D. (1994). Multipotentiality and overchoice syndrome: Clarifying common usage. *Gifted and Talented International, 9*, 41–46. https://doi.org/10.1080/15332276.1994.11672792

Rysiew, K. J., Shore, B. M., & Leeb, R. T. (1999). Multipotentiality, giftedness, and career choice: A review. *Journal of Counseling and Development, 77*, 423–430. https://doi.org/10.1002/j.1556-6676.1999.tb02469.x

Sampson, J. P., Jr., & Chason, A. K. (2008). Helping gifted and talented adolescents and young adults make informed and careful career choices. In S. I. Pfeiffer (Ed.), *Handbook of giftedness in children: Psychoeducational theory, research, and best practices* (pp. 327–346). New York, NY: Springer.

Savickas, M. L. (2002). Career construction: A developmental theory of vocational behaviour. In D. Brown & associates (Eds.), *Career choice and development* (4th ed., pp. 149–205). San Francisco, CA: Jossey-Bass.

Savickas, M. L. (2003). Special issue: Career counseling in the next decade. *The Career Development Quarterly, 52*, 87–96. https://doi.org/10.1002/j.2161-0045.2003.tb00631.x

Savickas, M. L. (2007). Occupational choice. In H. Gunz & M. Peiperl (Eds.), *Handbook of career studies* (pp. 79–96). Los Angeles, CA: Sage.

Singelis, T. M., Triandis, H. C., Bhawuk, D. P. S., & Gelfand, M. J. (1995). Horizontal and vertical dimensions of individualism and collectivism: A theoretical and measurement refinement. *Cross-Cultural Research, 29*, 240–275. https://doi.org/10.1177/106939719502900302

Sparfeldt, J. R. (2007). Vocational interests of gifted adolescents. *Personality and Individual Differences, 42*, 1011–1021. https://doi.org/10.1016/j.paid.2006.09.010

Stewart, J. B. (1999). Career counseling for the academically gifted student. *Canadian Journal of Counseling, 33*, 3–12. Retrieved from https://cjc-rcc.ucalgary.ca/article/view/58611

Storey, J. A. (2000). "Fracture lines" in the career environment. In A. Collin & R. A. Young (Eds.), *The future of career* (pp. 21–36). Cambridge, UK: Cambridge University Press.

Störmer, E., Patscha, C., Prendergast, J., Daheim, C., Rhisiart, M., Glover, P., & Beck, H. (2014). *The future of work: Jobs and skills in 2030*. London, UK: U. K. Commission for Employment and Skills.

Stornelli, D., Flett, G. L., & Hewitt, P. L. (2009). Perfectionism, achievement, and affect in children: A comparison of students from gifted, arts, and regular programmes. *Canadian Journal of School Psychology, 24*, 267–283. https://doi.org/10.1177/0829573509342392

Sullivan, S. E. (1999). The changing nature of careers: A review and research agenda. *Journal of Management, 25*, 457–484. https://doi.org/10.1177/014920639902500308

Swanson, J. L., & Schneider, M. (2013). Minnesota theory of work adjustment. In S. D. Brown & R. W. Lent (Eds.), *Career development and counseling: Putting theory and research to work* (2nd ed., pp. 29–53). Hoboken, NJ: Wiley.

Tang, M. (2003). Career counseling in the future: Constructing, collaborating, advocating. *The Career Development Quarterly, 52*, 61–69. https://doi.org/10.1002/j.2161-0045.2003.tb00628.x

Triandis, H. C. (1995). *Individualism and collectivism*. Boulder, CO: Westview.

Verbruggen, M. (2010). Career counseling in the new career era. *Review of Business and Economics, 55*, 2–22.

Vock, M., Köller, O., & Nagy, G. (2013). Vocational interests of intellectually gifted and highly achieving young adults. *British Journal of Educational Psychology, 83*, 305–328. https://doi.org/10.1111/j.2044-8279.2011.02063.x

Watters, J. J. (2010). Career decision making among gifted students: The mediation of teachers. *The Gifted Child Quarterly, 54*, 222–238. https://doi.org/10.1177/0016986210369255

Watts, A. G. (2000). The new career and public policy. In A. Collin & R. Young (Eds.), *The future of careers* (pp. 259–275). Cambridge, UK: Cambridge University Press.

Webb, R. M., Lubinski, D., & Benbow, C. P. (2002). Mathematically facile adolescents with math–science aspirations: New perspectives on their educational and vocational development. *Journal of Educational Psychology, 94*, 785–794. https://doi.org/10.1037/0022-0663.94.4.785

White, N. J., & Tracey, T. J. G. (2011). An examination of career indecision and application to dispositional authenticity. *Journal of Vocational Behavior, 78*, 219–224. https://doi.org/10.1016/j.jvb.2010.09.015

Yates, S., Harris, A., Sabates, R., & Staff, J. (2011). Early occupational aspirations and fractured transitions: A study of entry into "NEET" status in the UK. *Journal of Social Policy, 40*, 513–534. https://doi.org/10.1017/S0047279410000656

Jae Yup Jung, PhD, is an Associate Professor in the School of Education and the Director of GERRIC at The University of New South Wales, Australia. His research program incorporates various topics relating to gifted adolescents, with a particular focus on their career-related decisions. His research has been recognised with awards from the American Educational Research Association, the Mensa Education and Research Foundation/Mensa International, and the Society for Vocational Psychology, and grants from the Australian Research Council and the Australian Department of Foreign Affairs and Trade. He is the editor of the *Australasian Journal of Gifted Education*, a member of the Executive Committee of the *Asia-Pacific Federation on Giftedness* (APFG) and a member of the *Council of the Australian Association for the Education of the Gifted and Talented* (AAEGT).

Transitioning to Career: Talented Musicians' Identity Development

61

Jennifer Rowley

Contents

Abstract

Students who are actively involved in developing an understanding of their individual sense of self as a musician, whilst engaged in their formal tertiary music studies, are more successful than others in their future careers (Bennett, Rowley, Dunbar–Hall, Hitchcock, & Blom, 2016). However, formal studies often do not lead to a deep understanding of the potential professional world that is required of musicians across their career lifespan. Musician identity is a complex

J. Rowley (✉)
The University of Sydney, Sydney, NSW, Australia
e-mail: jennifer.rowley@sydney.edu.au

© Springer Nature Singapore Pte Ltd. 2021
S. R. Smith (ed.), *Handbook of Giftedness and Talent Development in the Asia-Pacific*,
Springer International Handbooks of Education,
https://doi.org/10.1007/978-981-13-3041-4_66

notion that comprises a sense of self or becoming. Talent development and musician identity are multifaceted ideas that may be understood from theoretical and practical perspectives and the intersection between the two will be explored in this chapter. To understand the manner in which talent development and musical identity are developed in practice, a lens of the *Comprehensive Model of Talent Development* (CMTD) is used (Gagné & McPherson, 2016). Talent development for musicians and musician identity are aspects that evolve out of the study across a musician's career lifespan. How music students experience the space between formal music study and work experiences and how, in turn, thinking is transformed accordingly for the development of a future work-ready career professional can impact curriculum design in higher education. Professional musicians' identity development will be explored by reporting how talent development is understood through a mentoring program and what musician identity means from the perspective of self-reflections of ten final year music students undertaking an internship placement. The theoretical paradigm of the focus in the chapter is housed within the *Sense of Self Model* (Rowley & Munday, 2014). Following this discussion, how career transition is perceived through the work experience of students will be reiterated. Student responses show that those who re-imagine what their musical world means and how their own capabilities, talents, gifts, and creativity can be utilised as leaders in the professional practice context are more successful.

Keywords

Musician identity · Transition to career · Future self · Talent development

The aims in this chapter are to:
1. Explore three theoretical frameworks (Gagné and McPherson's *Comprehensive Model of Talent Development* [CMTD], Kolb's *Experiential Learning Cycle* and Rowley and Munday's *Sense of Self Model*) highlighting research and practice directly related to tertiary music studies and gifted education.
2. Provide an account of one cohort of undergraduate music students' professional practice work experiences as evidence and understanding of the promotion of giftedness, talent development, creativity, musician career identity and optimal development of undergraduate music students as they transition to career professional.
3. Share a case study account of narratives of ten musically talented undergraduate students' musician career and identity awareness and development that can inform curriculum and other higher education practitioners.
4. Address the research question: How does the space between formal music study for talented musicians and professional practice work experiences transform thinking and provide flexibility for imagining a future musician career possible 'self'?

5. Share talented student responses that support creating guided online reflective written narratives reflecting on a *Work Integrated Learning* (WIL) placement experience that promoted professional career skills, such as leadership, a predisposition to sharing talent (e.g., mentoring), and expertise and learning practices with others in preparation for future career self.

6. Discuss the themes identified through the talented music student's writing and imagining of future 'self' within a domain of multiple identities, future leadership development, identified well-being and psychological qualities, individual abilities emerging as a result of professional practice (e.g., teaching music) and opportunities to explore talent domain through mentoring.

7. Conclude that well-scaffolded WIL through formal internship programs provides curriculum enhancement allowing talented undergraduate music students to re-imagine their future 'self' and to engage in the space between student and professional (e.g., autonomy, intrinsic motivation, self-efficacy).

Introduction

A conservatorium or conservatoire provides a range of music educational courses for talented students who compete to attend. Typically, one in ten who audition for an undergraduate music degree are accepted into conservatoire degree programs. Therefore, those who gain entry are 'talented' according to Gagné's definition of talent as they are performing in the top 10–15% of their age peers/population (Gagné, 1999). The educational contexts and developmental transitions that talented undergraduate music students experience before entering their specific professional role as music graduates are not always explicitly addressed in higher education. Most music students expect an orchestral or performance career at the conclusion of their undergraduate studies in a conservatoire only to realise that less than 1% are successful in this pursuit.

Evidence of a musician's career thinking and perceptions of their readiness for a music career are presented in the chapter through examining reflective written narratives about their future professional possible 'self' from ten talented music students. Through extrapolation of their narratives written during an elective unit of study (a formal internship program) it was revealed that this group of tertiary music students face challenges and experience moments of enlightenment about their musical talent and future musical and professional identity. Through a lens of the *Sense of Self Model* (Rowley & Munday, 2014) and the CMTD (Gagné & McPherson, 2016) as theoretical frameworks, it is determined that higher levels of thinking (synthesis and evaluation) are required to be prepared with a possible future self-image—or what you re-imagine you might look like in the future. Unpacking stories of the internship journey that included mentoring younger musicians and teaching music provides valuable data about the impact of the written assessment task of reflective writing on talent development. As a useful pedagogic tool, the ePortfolio is a curriculum innovation for internship programs.

An ePortfolio is an electronic portfolio which can also be referred to as an ifolio, online, or digital portfolio, and many other labels describing the digitalisation of written work. An ePortfolio provides a personal learning space for students to explore what they know about their discipline and allows them to showcase their musical talent, especially in how this can be synthesised and applied to the future possible career 'self'. What students discover is that they have to invest in an adaptation of skills, talents, knowledge, and competencies to be better prepared for the future professional life as a musician, which traditionally encompasses more than one job or role. Musicians are determined as having 'portfolio' careers as they often perform, teach, administrate, and practice (Bennett & Bridgstock, 2015). Therefore, a typical career lifespan of a musician is not as imagined when entering a talented musician program, such as an undergraduate music degree program in a conservatoire.

Factors Influencing Music Students' Transitions to the Music Career Profession

The background of this chapter is the act of reflective writing to contribute to experiential learning in the transitioning from talented music student to music career professional. It is traditional in the final stages of formal learning (such as an undergraduate music degree program) that students consider the next step of their life journey. Often the choice is to remain in formal studies (honours or postgraduate options) although many look to venturing out into the profession for which they have studied. It is posited, therefore that at this stage we could consider the talented student as 'expert' and yet their professional practice is explained as 'novice'. A formal internship or *Work Integrated Learning* (WIL) program offers a bridge (the space) to assist in the transition from expert student to early career professional (see Fig. 1 below).

Pre-professionals (in any discipline) are part of multiple work sites where they are expert learners at the same time as being novice professionals. Hence, the multiple communities of practice they belong to may look like a balancing of scales as depicted in Figure 1. These and other communities enable students to think and carefully consider their holistic development and identities in very different ways as they transition (Rowley et al., 2016). Through internships and practicums, professional experience placements and the like, students experience the 'space' between formal study and work experiences. The issue is how, in turn, students are equipped to adapt and transform their capabilities from a known state as student to a lesser-known state of professional practitioner (or in this case, professional musician). It was intentional in the reflections in this chapter that music students investigated the 'space' as the design of the assessment task (ePortfolio) was to reorientate learning for career relevance—as WIL experiences potentially are two-way learning because students notice the need for flexibility in the workplace and in their own thinking about self (Bennett, Richardson, & MacKinnon, 2016). As students begin to develop the creative skill of reorienting learning towards career relevance, they

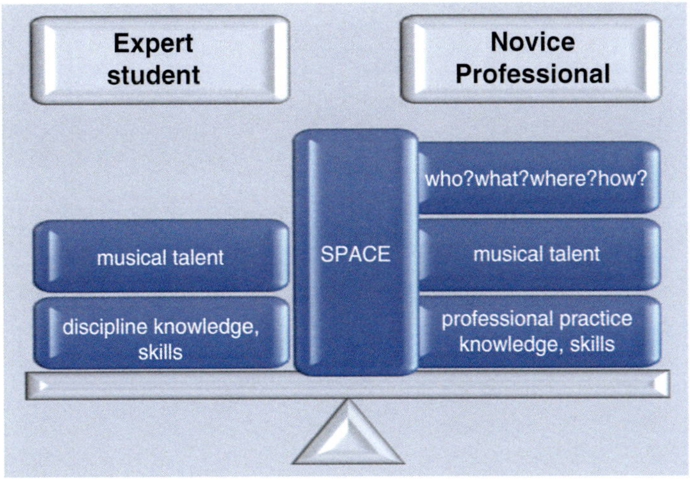

Fig. 1 The transitional 'space' between expert music student and novice music professional (Rowley, Bennett, & Reid, 2016)

operationalise the experiences and dialogue with the professionals they work with during the placement.

So, what does this space look like as talented students' transition to becoming a professional? The design and delivery of effective and positive career-related learning and support is predicated on understanding both students and the thinking of educators (Bennett, Richardson, & MacKinnon 2016). However, students often adjust their formal report of career intentions to align with the goal expectations of significant others. Who are these significant others? Peers? Teachers? Family? It is thought that there is a range of others (or catalysts) that impact development which the following sections explore further.

Reflective writing offers undergraduate music students a personal space to think critically about experiences and can be seen as useful in identity development as the reflection engages the individual in negotiating and constructing future musical lives and careers (Bennett, Richardson, & MacKinnon 2016). Ferm (2008) reports that a formalised reflection on an experience combined with learning, goals, and development are essential factors in developing musical identity. As Kolb (1984) details in his *Experiential Learning Model,* "learning is the process whereby knowledge is created through the transformation of experience" (p. 38) and therefore transformative thinking in ePortfolio creation encourages learning. Brooks and Rowley (2013) claim that an individual's identity evolves as you move through the experiential learning cycle and pose the argument that one is better able to assess capacities about oneself through reflective practice.

Although this chapter contains music student experiences, the themes emerging from students' reflective narratives reported here could be adapted across disciplines.

Literature Review

Theoretical Foundation of Talent Development and Musical Identity: Talented Students as Reflective Practitioners

Comprehensive Model of Talent Development or CMTD

Within the framework of the CMTD (Gagné & McPherson, 2016), it is apparent that a mix of catalysts promotes the dynamic interplay in the learning, training, and practice continuum for early career musicians during their professional development. The emergence of talent can be realised when there is a synergy between both the interpersonal and intrapersonal catalysts. Gagné and McPherson explored Gagné's original talent development (the *Differentiating Model of Giftedness and Talent* or DMGT) to determine the CMTD as a framework to analyse the phenomenon of musical prodigiousness.

The CMTD allows for defining an extreme level of talent (T component), the gifts (G component) that contribute to musical prodigiousness, as well as its typical developmental process (D component). The CMTD encourages two types of catalytic causal influences to be explored: intrapersonal characteristics (I component) and the environmental influences (E component; Gagné & McPherson, 2016).

Whilst it is clearly recognisable that the Gagné (2015) DMGT has been applied to music, the influences of interpersonal (E) and intrapersonal (I) catalysts are very much apparent as Gagné and McPherson (2016) have integrated the components into a dynamic developmental perspective to propose a tentative answer to the key question: "Which causal influences better 'explain' the early manifestation and development of musical prodigiousness?" or "what makes a difference?" (p. 11). They conclude that "talent emerges from a unique combination of complex interactions between multiple causal influences" (p. 93). The ePortfolio is a formal learning tool that promotes exploration of the what, how, and why the student in an internship classifies and curates their work experiences by writing about where they imagine the future possible 'self' to be after the completion of tertiary study (Rowley & Munday, 2014). These collation of work experiences in written narratives could be labelled within the CMTD as the causal influences in the development of musical prodigiousness.

The model presented in Figure 2 clearly exposes the importance of the developmental phase or the 'space' that is often filled by experiential learning, reflecting, and thinking about the how, what, and why of a future professional 'self'.

Sense of Self Model

The *Sense of Self Model* (Rowley & Munday, 2014) provides a theoretical framework for analysing responses taken from student-created self-reflections in their ePortfolios, which is the assessment component of undergraduate musicians' WIL internship program explored in this chapter. The model is adapted from Deci and Ryan's (2000) model of self-determination theory and is a learning theory of

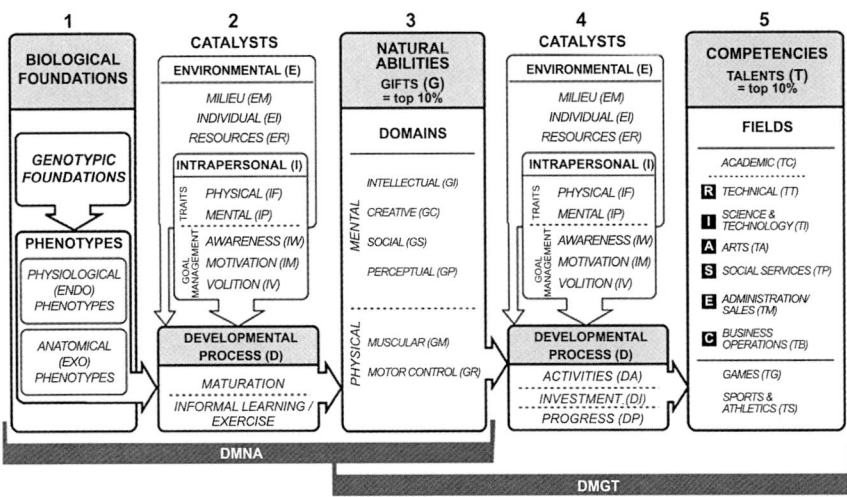

Fig 2 Gagné's *Integrative Model of Talent Development* (IMTD). (Reproduced from Françoys Gagné [2015], Fig. 3)

motivation and personality that addresses three universal, innate, and psychological needs: competence, autonomy, and psychological relatedness. The adaptation of the Deci and Ryan model shown below is grounded in social cognitive theory with many items drawn from or informed by the educational psychology literature including social cognitive self-management and decision-making relative to self and career (Lent, Brown, & Hackett, 1994); self- and academic self-efficacy (Bandura, 1993); self-esteem; professional identity construction related to academic work and future work; and emotional intelligence (Brackett & Mayer, 2003). These traits are encouraged by an individual's self-reflection on experiences during the placement, that is deliberately designed as WIL so the reflection is occurring during the practice and later as a recall on the experience and using previous knowledge to perform the tasks and/or to build new knowledge (see Fig. 3 below). Self-reflection by building a narrative through storying is beneficial to those in new experiences as it demands higher order thinking such as analysis (comparing and contrasting), synthesis (transfer of knowledge into new concepts), and evaluation of the experience as presented in Bloom's Taxonomy (Anderson & Krathwohl, 2001).

It is expected that the impact of creating the ePortfolio for determining 'self' sits in between 'nonself-determined' *Amotivation* and the *Extrinsic Motivation* where self-concept and self-image develop as a result of undergraduate music students digging deeper into the how, what, and why of the experience included in the portfolio written narrative and evidence. The model posits that 'ideal-self' (or in the case of the WIL experience explored in this chapter, 'future professional self') emerges as students curate and classify the knowledge and practice through self-reflection.

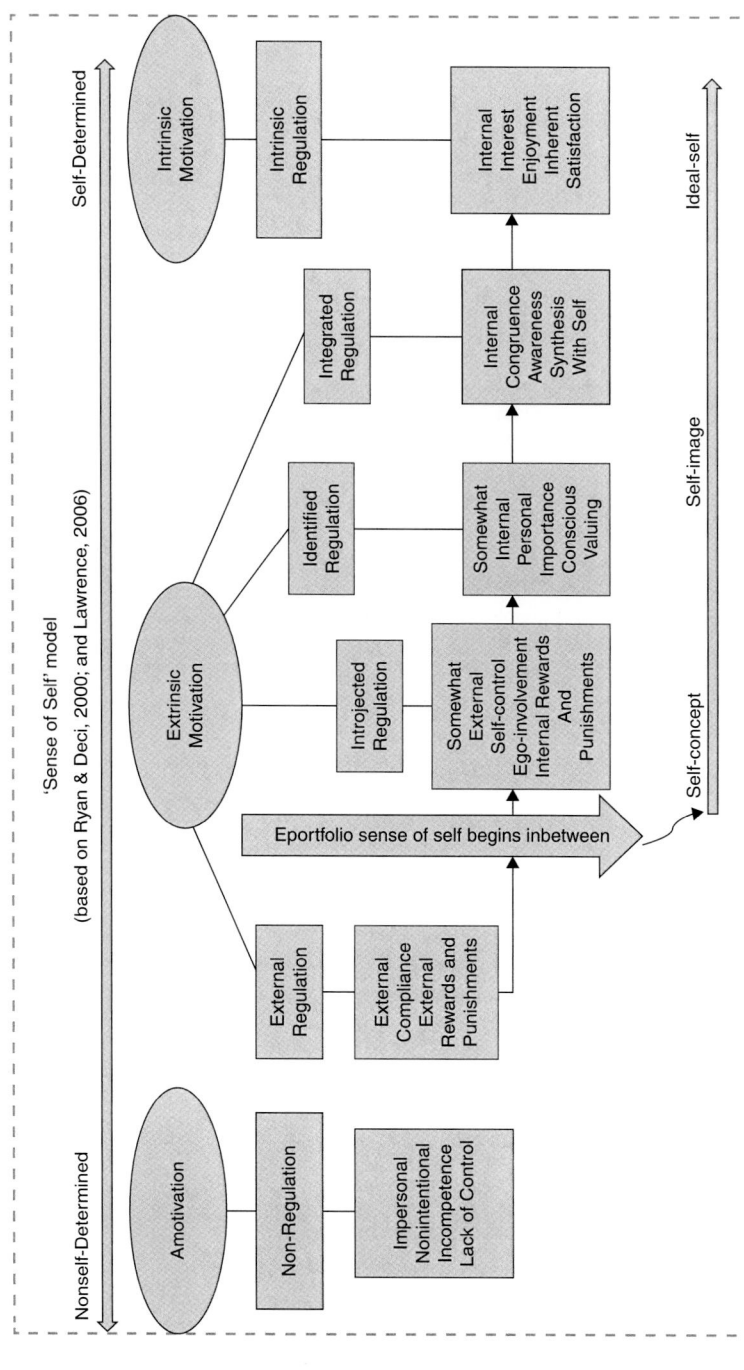

Fig. 3 *Sense of Self Model* (Rowley & Munday, 2014)

Talented Students as Reflective Practitioners

The above theoretical foundations lead students as *reflective practitioners* according to Schön (1995), who details a theory that shows reflection *in* action and reflection *on* action can positively impact a growth in a person's understanding of self as they develop a reflection *on* practice and *during* practice. Schön (1995) defines reflective practice as the practice by which professionals become aware of their implicit knowledge base and learn from their experience. The CMTD and *Sense of Self Models* can be operationalised through reflective writing of the internship experiences in an ePortfolio and, according to Schön (1995), those who engage in reflection build a capacity for lifelong learning through the reflective process. The ePortfolio encourages talented learners to write reflectively by telling the 'story' of learning and, in this chapter's case study, how talented music students' transition to the profession through a narrative of who they are becoming and what they are learning through the WIL experience. The process of writing reflectively entailed guided reflection on current and past selves, possible future selves and both personal and employment-related traits by the talented undergraduate music students. The contribution of the reflective ePortfolio to music talent development is paramount to the successful transition from student to professional. ePortfolios are predominantly being used in higher education and career development for those preparing for and working in professional employment. The collection and curation of evidence and artefacts to demonstrate understanding and acquisition of skills can be flexibly showcased for different audiences through a versatile ePortfolio platform, giving the creator the ability to present their 'selves' appropriately and specifically.

Musician Identity and Talent Development

It is noted by Jung (2012) that work by Subotnik et al. shows individual abilities as a necessary condition for outstanding achievement. In the case of talented musicians, high aspirations, 'identity', and higher expectation are influencers for career development. Professional 'identity' develops as a reaction to several catalysts that include experiential learning, multi-levelled mentoring, and reflection on (and in) knowledge and action (Schön, 1995). Bennett and Bridgstock (2015) ask how does this networked community enable the expert student (i.e., the talented student who is near to completing their undergraduate studies) to re-imagine what their career world might mean, and how their own capabilities, talents, and creativity might be utilised as future leaders in their field? Here we consider a student's individual learning that encompasses the development of 'self' with impact on career transition and transformation. A recommended strategy is to acknowledge the membership of a *Community of Practice* (CoP) that invites other expert students to share experiences and learning gained in the WIL. These are potential conversations that could be started with the designer of the WIL program in collaboration with students and host organisations so that the topic of career orientation is at the forefront of learning, professional practice experiences, and career preparation.

Most theories on talent development assume that a young artist has access to the resources required to advance in the discipline-specific domain (e.g., Bloom, 1985; Schön, 1995). According to Bloom (1985) talent development of young people is concerned with explicit and directed programs that provide opportunities to practise a craft within real-life situations. WIL experiences have the potential to provide a platform for talent development. The Gagné and McPherson (2016) model conceptualises talent development in that musical prodigies specifically acknowledge the role of significant others as salient. Thus, the motivation to pursue talent development within a music context needs structured learning experiences that include formal mentoring through masterclass and studio environments, for example, that allow for individualised and differentiated educational facilitation promoting excellence (Schön, 1995). The development of talent in music is often directed towards a life of a soloist and, therefore, may exclude many undertaking tertiary training (Bennett et al., 2016). By turning this around and including broader musician WIL experiences (learning experiences inside a work environment) towards a more inclusive model opens up a window for those who seek a musical career beyond that of the traditional orchestra or ensemble.

Associated Issues in Transitions of Talented Music Students

There are a variety of contributors to the development of musical talent. Alongside early music learning is the numerous contributors to musical talent development including training and deliberate practice. Included in this list is the motivation to develop musical expertise (Garces-Bacsal, 2014). As educators and practitioners, we have a responsibility to ensure environmental aspects (such as motivation) are available to all and are seen as positive in talented musicians' career development. Bennett and Bridgstock (2015) ask, "Does the notion of career emerge as a messy concept fraught with misunderstanding?" (p. 263). I think the answer is yes! Often entering a career is chaotic and it is fractured, clumsy, unknown with non-productive time and energy expended as the early career professional may lack work experiences or knowledge of their professional world. This chaotic transition is particularly apparent amongst new graduate students. To assist with the transition, higher music education needs clear goals and beneficial tools that provide access to the keys for successful transition from student to professional. ePortfolios are increasingly used in internships to help students curate WIL experiences by collecting and classifying evidence of skills developed during professional experience placements (Waikato & Lewis, 2014). This chapter puts forward the argument that unpacking the story of transitioning and exploring the 'space' can release the essential ingredients required in creating an individual's recipe for achieving personal musician career goals. Therefore, reorientating learning for career relevance is key to assisting in the development of talent, potentially career leadership, and professional identities in musicians.

Jung (2018) notes that today's career decisions appear complex because of globalisation, the greater range of new occupations, and influences such as technology, and societal values. Due to this change in employment and labour markets, gifted students have increased potential to transition into these careers.

Mentoring and Developing a Leadership Role

Rowley et al. (2016) proposed that the space between formal music study and internship work experiences has the potential to transform thinking and provide flexibility through compiling a self-reflection journal inside the ePortfolio. In the ePortfolio reflections of 10 penultimate and final year music students undertaking an internship placement, the talented students' narratives show how career is developed within a formal reflective practice learning space as students document and provide evidence of themselves as a work ready musician career professional. Much of what students write about during and after the WIL experience is often challenging as they move from an ideal to a realistic view of employment, career, and work possibilities they are being trained for in an undergraduate music degree. In fact, to re-imagine a musician's world that does not encompass a full-time orchestral or performance job can be confronting for many students. One of the positives in reviewing a personal career development journey is through a series of employability skills audits that encourage a valid view of where the gaps are in an individual's career preparation (see employability.com.au for an open access Student Profile tool). How their own capabilities, talents, gifts, and creativity can be utilised as potential/emerging leaders in the musical professional career practice context to become more successful in transitioning ready for work is revealed in the scaffolded self-reflection narratives. Therefore, through a method of analysis using exponents of complexity science, the dynamic is exposed so that a sense of self of who they are currently and who they strive to become is contained in the development of the self-reflective practitioner.

Traditionally mentor programs occur in the first year or years of professional undergraduate degree programs, having been designed to combat high attrition rates post graduation (as one example). Mentoring for talented musicians is part of how they learn within the studio learning environment context using the following principles: (a) skills development, (b) personal values, (c) ensemble behaviours, and (d) building self-efficacy in a notoriously difficult art form that also suffers from high attrition (Rowley et al., 2016). As a tool for developing musical talent in undergraduate students, as they move towards completion of their degree, students mentoring younger talented musicians can be effective in assisting musical career development (Yeo & Rowley, 2018). Students as mentors themselves need to understand the musical process involved and be able to adequately articulate that process to younger (less experienced but not less talented) mentees (Yeo & Rowley, 2018). There are relatively few studies on the mentoring of gifted musicians; however, there are many studies on the mentoring of beginning music teachers. Effective mentoring has to consider emotional well-being and specific needs of the mentee, by expanding the perceptions and values of those involved (Campbell & Brummett, 2007). As the case study presented in this chapter includes student experiences written in their ePortfolio of being mentored and some others write reflections from a three-way mentoring WIL program, it is appropriate to include mentoring in the theoretical foundations here.

Example Case Study: Research Methods: Data Collection and Analysis

Presented here are selected reflections as a case study, which is used as an example of talented student musicians' career preparation. The case study exemplar is part of a larger longitudinal research project from 2014 to 2017 (for detail on the longitudinal study, see Bennett et al., 2016; Rowley et al., 2016; Yeo & Rowley, 2018). Participant responses reported in this chapter were ten Australian undergraduate full-time music students at a Sydney (Australia) music conservatorium who were in a professional practice internship within a performance setting and enrolled in either composition, performance, musicology, or music teacher education degree programs. The students created reflective written portfolios with evidence of experience, practice, performance, and leadership opportunities, and learning in internship placements such as the Opera and Ballet Orchestra in Sydney, band camp in a NSW Regional Conservatorium and in an Opera production in Wollongong—all for the duration of 60–80 hours.

Using a Framework Thematic Analysis model (Ritchie, Lewis, McNaughton Nicholls, & Ormston, 2014), an observational case study provided all the responses that were refined through an open coding process that utilised reported principles of grounded theory (Creswell, 2014). From this initial review of the talented students' narratives in their ePortfolio assessment task, themes were generalised and classification was undertaken using one or two words to categorise similar dimensions and the inquiry of 'how' and 'why' a phenomenon occurs was viewed from multiple standpoints exploring meaning and similarities and/or differences between students' experiences. The written reflection or 'stories' and evidence found in the portfolio allowed adoption of a phenomenological perspective within a narrative framework as data were expressed in words, sounds, and images. Selective coding followed using a cross-sample analysis to establish similarities. By reading the students' portfolio reflections, taking into account the previous research literature, and observations gleaned during portfolio presentations, the method of triangulation, including space and within-method applications (Cohen, Manion, & Morrison, 2007), enabled a comparison within and between the experiences of the participants. Exploring student engagement through this lens provided insight into the transformative processes for developing a sense of 'professional' musician self. In their ePortfolio they described how their experiences of work informed the complexity of issues in their journey from talented musician and novice to the development of a sense of 'becoming' a professional musician.

The students were guided by key questions inside five categories (see below) and asked to complete the portfolio with evidence to support the narrative. The categories were: (a) summary of learning; (b) learning objectives and outcomes; (c) relating theory, policy, and practice; and (d) self-reflection and future learning areas. Three workshops were held with the students before and during the internship placement that focused on Kolb's (1984) *Experiential Learning Model,* Schön's (1995) reflective practitioner, and collecting, curating, and presenting learning outcomes of the WIL in the ePortfolio was an assessment task. The students' responses in this chapter are part of a larger study looking at career relevance established to test strategies, based on the notion of self-authorship (the narrative) investigating talented students' transitioning to work by aligning with a personal student identity to demonstrate a burgeoning professional musician identity.

Aligning Talented Students' Personal Identity When Transitioning to Professional Musician Identity: Results and Discussion

As an emerging approach to research, *complexity science* is a study of a system that is concerned with complex systems and problems that are dynamic, unpredictable, and multi-dimensional, which consist of a collection of interconnected relationships and parts (Byrne, 2001). It is not a single theory, but a collection of theories and conceptual tools from an array of disciplines (Paley & Eva, 2011). Within the context of exploring the 'space' between student and professional, complexity science is useful as it allows a view of what we are trying to understand in relation to an element of social inquiry. So, in a way, it is essential for re-interpreting data (such as the music students' reflections in their ePortfolio) to identify where and how change occurs.

The responses below are taken from the section of the online ePortfolio titled *Self-Reflection.* Allowing the talented students to be guided into thinking about their future possible self provides valuable data for curriculum planning in higher music education and talent development for musicians of all ages.

> I feel like, as music students, our main goal is to win an audition with a great orchestra. However, we rarely think about what comes after that. I think that the two require different skills. Winning an audition is based on the preparation of a set of excerpts which requires perfectionism and automatism because auditions are screened and nothing less than excellence will make it through to the next round. However, while orchestral playing still requires the highest level of technique, playing excerpts excellently doesn't guarantee that you will be an excellent ensemble player. Adrian told us that sometimes making good sound doesn't matter and playing a passage 'the hard way' is no good if we can't pull it off one hundred times: because that's at least how many times you'll play a passage in one season. (3rd year female, 2016)

> The outcomes of this internship are an array of more in depth observations about the music profession, from rehearsal attitudes and etiquette to the need for adequate physical recuperation time in a company with such extensive playing hours and seasons. (4th year female, 2017)

Making obvious connections between themselves as current experts as music student/learner and not fully developed or 'novice' professional was important to the development of sense of 'self'.

> My insight into Opera orchestra has shown me that there is no complacency in music and there is always room for creative improvement. For me, this means that my biggest area for future development is perseverance and constructive self-criticism because it is sometimes very easy to be overwhelmed by the amount of work that I need to do in order to develop and achieve my goals. (3rd year female, 2016)

> I hope to develop further skills, knowledge and experience in piano technique, piano teaching, accompanying and performing and share them. (3rd year male, 2017)

It is crystallising moments of self-realisation drawn to students' attention by peer feedback when they present their ePortfolio (as an assessment task) that students take back to their written narrative. Digging deeper into other areas of music study allows them to see multiple connections to their learning and musician career capacity building realisation.

> I am seriously considering if the performance path I'm on is the right thing for me because of the teaching experiences I had in the internship. It was great to share my musical knowledge with a group of enthusiastic and talented students. It's a wonderful feeling knowing you've inspired someone or a group of talented students to put on a good performance. (3rd year female, 2017)

> Showing the students that a music degree is more than just being really good at playing and performing all the time was very rewarding. (3rd year female, 2017)

The realisation by this student is affirmation of musician career lifespan expectations. They have not complained about the hard work, but used the challenge to feel positive about the future—thus exposing the emerging self-image and self-concept that leads to ideal self (as presented in the *Sense of Self Model* in Fig. 3). This reflection on WIL experiences as a musician skills audit has contributed to their knowledge as professional music learning development.

> Knowing that I'd had strong musical training gave me confidence to go outside my comfort zone and help tutor the talented group of young Violin 3's... something that I wouldn't normally do. (3rd year female, 2017)

> I gained real life exposure in the educational world, was shown the realities of planning, organisation and what goes on in the life of a touring professional musician, and also allowing us to network and pass on our knowledge to talented kids who young and eager to learn. (4th year male, 2016)

The ability of students to re-imagine what their musical world might mean beyond that of an orchestral or performance career path, and how their own capabilities and creativity might be utilised as future leaders of other talented musicians, is evidenced in their reflections on this challenging professional career practice experience.

> I was able to experience cross-generation responsibility of fostering talent and appreciating the arts by sharing and gaining knowledge with all involved. I think this was extremely valuable as is allowed myself to share all learnt throughout my performance experiences, it also gave me the chance to take a step back and learn from some extremely successful opera performers...we were able to reflect on our time and why this project emphasised the need to continue and produce more opportunities for our talented younger generation in accordance with the arts. (3rd year female, 2017)

> It became apparent that although I have some teaching experience some structured education in the science of teaching would be highly beneficial. I've enrolled in String Pedagogy for next year and I'm looking forward to improving my teaching skills...it opened my mind to the endless possibilities in the music industry and I look forward to exploring these options and finding my own path. (3rd year female, 2017)

The imagining of themselves as future career ready coupled with their confidence as expert students through ePortfolio process and thinking (Rowley et al., 2016) acts as a catalyst for their musician identity development. The following quotes from the talented students' responses are evidence that the WIL could contribute to the learning journey of talented and creative students for sustainable future careers.

> I am looking forward to developing more and more teaching techniques. I believe that a good teacher should have a thousand ways to explain a single thing, and working with different people and taking part in camps like this is a great way to build up experience and belief in yourself as a teacher. (3rd year female, 2017)

> Where has the internships taken me? To a land of new thoughts, and new career possibilities. Where have I taken myself? To a more positive, enduring, and inspired state of being. (4th year female, 2017)

Bringing together psychological influences, social, cultural, and environmental aspects of professional career 'self' preparation as is detailed in the CMTD (Gagné & McPherson, 2016), indicates a synergy between who the student musician is and who they are wanting to become. Building on previous ePortfolio research projects (e.g., see Bennett et al., 2016; Rowley & Bennett, 2013), talented students create narratives, curate evidence of learning, and use multimedia to help develop their musical identities and talent (e.g., self, professional, artistic, and the like) inside an ePortfolio as a personal learning space. This demonstrates the effectiveness of ePortfolio thinking (see eportfolio.com.au) and of the *Sense of Self Model* containing WIL and reflective personal narratives.

> Through this internship I was able to see the inner workings of this professional Opera team as it develops the whole performance from rehearsal stages to opening night. It is a collaboration on all levels and one I need to consider if I am up for it! The self-reflection allowed me to re-consider my original plans for an orchestra job. (4th year female, 2016)

> As a Musician who mainly thinks about performing, my teaching had always been something I enjoyed but not something I was aiming for in my career, my experience with other talented musicians who have done teaching is that they enjoy it to an extent but would rather

be playing. After talking to the local musicians and participating in the internship I can now envisage a satisfying career in music tuition. (4th year male, 2017)

For some students, there has been an imagining of musical identity beyond their original plans as they transition from talented student to professional. Exploring how identity is developed during the music students' WIL professional practice internship was seen by some students as inspirational. Read through these students' discovery of self:

I have had to develop my skills of communication, teamwork and problem-solving. Relating to people who are in some cases many times my age has been a challenge. But it is all for the music. Having that as the thing that unites us has been really rewarding. I have had to sustain conversations and interactions that I have not had much exposure to in the past. (3rd year male, 2017)

The discussion of how future leadership is evidenced in the experience of talented students who have undertaken internship programs within the music industry enabled some to bridge the gap between theory and practice; notice the need for flexibility and critical thinking in the workplace and in their own thinking about future self; and develop the creative skill of reorienting learning as their musician career relevance is realised. (3rd year male, 2017)

We all gained some valuable insight into what we can do after we finish studying—we could go overseas and study more, get a separate teaching degree, pursue a performing career and then move into teaching—all options which the NRC staff shared with us. This was by far my favourite learning experience and not one I expected to have. As a performance major our studies are very focused on performing and we are very contained as part of the university experience, we don't get much outside perspective and it was great to have this. (4th year female, 2017)

The [young Con] children's experience throughout Pagliacci Opera was nurtured and memorable—being able to have a person to talk to, look up to and assist. One of the highlights of the rehearsal period was after a particular session, the principal artists took time to sit with the student cast, and ask about our aspirations for the future. Hearing their journeys and opinions … provided a realistic idea of varying avenues of music and music education. (3rd year female, 2017)

Painting a picture of themselves as future professionals working in the music industry revealed new perspectives that may serve to inform higher education teachers in the preparation of undergraduates for a successful transition to work. The following are two excerpts from the talented student musicians who wrote about how they moved through multiple domains of the musicians' identity:

This internship has provided insight into careers of employed musicians and contact with professionals that has certainly given me much to think about for future improvement and learning. (4th year female, 2017)

We were part of a music experience that involves a cross-generation responsibility of the passing down of knowledge and values of music. The combination of amateur and professional performers not only improved and contributed to the musical sound and overall performance quality, but established an attitude of valuing performance opportunities as a fostering and sharing experience, not just for personal gain and individual promotion. (3rd year female, 2017)

How to develop a sense of self in a music professional practice context allowed students to explore the space between being a talented student musician and becoming a professional musician. This transition process enabled students to view the WIL as a creative contributor to the process of future musician 'work' (and employment).

I believe one can never know enough about pedagogy and teaching various levels of string playing. . . this was a great way to jump into the deep end of group teaching, and I am pleased to say I thoroughly enjoyed. . .and that I am more confident in teaching in group situations with children with lesser knowledge of the violin. (3rd year female, 2017)

The [young] students of Wollongong con were excellent and talented vocalists however, they lacked in theory and technique. This is normal as most students were between the ages of 9–16 and their voices are not fully developed. I took this as an opportunity to assist with the reading of the score, pronunciation of selected Italian words that were kept and help with rhythm. (4th year male, 2017)

That these students recognised their own talent and those they mentored along with the process of talent development was a strong indicator that they were successfully transitioning the space and moving through the possible steps from talented student to professional and, in fact, bridging the gap, filling the space, and balancing the scales (see Fig. 1).

The first is developing my skills in relating to people in positive and reflective ways. The second is giving me skills in creativity in new areas and understanding in relating my theoretical musical knowledge to the real world and people. Finally, the internship has broadened my horizons of potential when it comes to future career paths. (3rd year male, 2016)

This internship has shaped my whole year as a performance student and is turning out to be a huge stepping stone into the professional world, this internship has helped develop my goals as a musician and has helped me realise that I want to be a bassoonist in an orchestra. (2nd year female, 2017)

Considering the multiple dimensions presented in the talented student responses, the points begin with exploring the themes emerging from data which include that personal time is required to be a professional musician (intrinsic motivation was included in the sense of self model). The case study assists us to see that a Portfolio career is a reality for talented musicians over a career lifespan. The student comments reveal that they felt under-prepared in tertiary study for the real world (for example the time required in a real orchestral context in preparing for repertoire). Much of what was reported shows us that the value of this professional experience internship placement in gaining a reality check of future careers in the music industry provides a scaffold for transitioning to the profession.

As a tool for reflective practice, the ePortfolio assessment task provided musician career clarity by writing the narrative to realise positives and negatives of work of a professional musician career. Students reported that creating the ePortfolio of evidence was beneficial as the reflective process showed clear future directions.

So, in summary, the case study provides some evidence that there is the need to be proactive and to make things happen yourself and so developing a sense of self is essential because a musician's career life cycle exists and so learning never stops. That is, learning is cyclic and in future we could correlate the transition from talented student to expert professional to re-imagine what the individual musician's career life cycle looks like.

Implications and Future Directions for Practice and Research

First, we have the challenge of transitioning the talented musician learner/student to be career ready. Next, we have the space that is instrumental in providing essential ingredients for a successful launch into being career prepared. The process for successful transitioning includes developing an ideal professional musician self which could be achieved through engaging in portfolio writing according to a reflective cycle that aligns with Kolb's experiential learning cycle (Kolb, 1984) detailed in Figure 4.

In Figure 4, it is proposed that the *Concrete Experience* is a new experience or situation which is encountered and/or a reinterpretation of an existing experience. The *Reflective Observation* could be the actual documenting of the new experience and of particular importance are any inconsistencies between the experience and understanding, which would be noted in the writing of the experience (e.g., the student comments reported in the case study). The *Abstract Conceptualisation* presents how the reflection has the potential to give rise to a new idea or a modification of an existing abstract concept. Finally, the *Active Experimentation* purports that the learner applies the new knowledge and skills (e.g., what was learnt in the talented student musicians' WIL) to the world around them to see what results as far as future career thinking.

Given that tertiary educators are a primary source of career information for students (Bennett et al., 2016), these findings have particular significance from an educational perspective. Few educators see themselves as career educators per se and there is often little curricula space for such discussions, and evidence of the lack of discussion can perhaps be seen in student responses presented in the results. One interpretation could be that educators need to provide clearly defined and consistent pathways to understanding future 'ideal' professional selves. This busy mosaic of self-reflection fills the 'space' but may not be effective. The ePortfolio narratives reflecting on career preparation focus on reflecting, being digitally literate and responsible, networking, collaborating, organising content, synthesising, and creating. These are all good areas to start developing and we know from the literature that employers look for these skills in new graduates as future employees. Jung (2018)

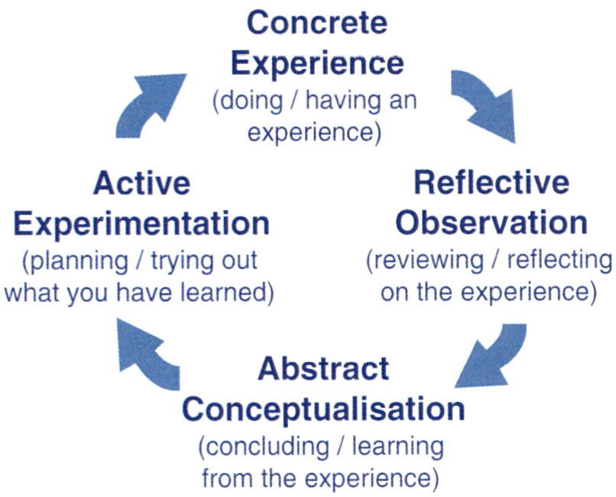

Fig. 4 Kolb's Experiential Learning Cycle (Kolb, 1984)

states that career decisions of the gifted and talented will impact significantly on the success of jobs that are yet to be created.

It is apparent that Subotnik et al.'s ideas on re-thinking giftedness (as presented in Jung, 2012) give our research community of practice an alternate approach to consider. Presenting us with a domain-specific nature of developmental trajectories (Jung, 2012) gives rise to an alignment to career-making theories. The greater the opportunities to interact professionally across different landscapes (environmental, physical, intellectual, and emotional), the more development of the future professional self can occur (Rowley & Bennett, 2013). Responses from this small cohort of students suggested that talented musician students on internship professional practice placements began to clarify their present selves and to envisage their possible future selves as emerging graduates beginning their musician careers. This highlights the networked *Community of Practice* context of musicians' identity which is more than likely no different to that of other disciplines (e.g., teachers, nurses, engineers). A career life cycle for musicians is one that is traditionally seen as a montage and one that contains many parts and it is challenging when one is beginning a professional career. Bennett and Bridgstock (2015) refer to a musician's professional life as a 'portfolio' career where the early career musician performs, teaches, administrates, for example, and perhaps for different organisations all at the same time. Many professional musicians report that this portfolio career continues throughout their working life. It was noted in the talented students' reflections that within the 'space', musicians appear to have multiple socially and culturally defined identities. These are endorsed through musical encounters, role models, and aspirations. Therefore, within this context, the CMTD is a valuable framework to reflect on the various intrapersonal and interpersonal catalysts at play in developing talent for future musician career success. The musician identity encapsulates shared understandings and practices in musical, social, and cultural terms.

Some information was provided here about constructive ways to transition the talented student to the professional and provides an exploration of how internship programs could impact future career relevance for talented tertiary music students. The alignment of career decisions is based on the reality of barriers to traditional career pathways. The process of reflective writing and creating an ePortfolio of evidence assisted the students to develop the more traditional employability skills, such as communication, problem-solving, critical thinking, and mentoring.

Conclusion

Students' experiences during a semester-long internship journey see self-reflections on their musicality, teaching, leadership, professional musician identity, talent development to career ready musicians and future 'self' and strategies for bridging the gap between theory and practice were all discussed in this chapter. Talented music students who engage in the ePortfolio learning process and reflective thinking gain skills that potentially contribute to lifelong learning and global citizenship. Rowley et al. (2016) argue that those students who do not engage in the WIL experience, the dialogue, and the reflective practice do in fact risk missing out on the benefit of being able to connect their own talent and study to their future, professional career 'possible' future self.

Talented student stories detailed in this chapter paint a portrait of what the future professional musician could resemble and reveal new perspectives to better inform the successful transition to work. Higher education teachers responsible for the preparation of undergraduates and a graduate world of work may benefit from insights into open and explicit discussions of career preparation. As the talented student musicians wrote about how they moved through multiple domains of identity, the students' reflections suggested that the curation of evidence (and the accompanying narrative) presented in their ePortfolio fosters experiential learning outcomes and talent development. The reflective writing assisted students' sense of becoming and deeper understanding of thinking required for successful future professional musician employment. Therefore, the argument was posed that reorienting tertiary music curriculum and learning for career relevance is important to enable the development of essential, transferable skills such as critical thinking, communication, teamwork, workplace negotiation, and problem-solving for talented young musicians.

The *Sense of Self Model* (Rowley & Munday, 2014) and the CMTD (Gagné & McPherson, 2016) enhanced understanding of *becoming* in a learning context where emphasis is on arts practice rather than professional musician identity formation. Transitioning to work for talented student musicians requires collaborative action from performing and creative arts organisations, the higher education provider, and the talented student.

Cross-References

▶ A Model for Growing Teacher Talent Scouts: Decreasing Underrepresentation of Gifted Students
▶ Australian Teachers Who Made a Difference: Secondary Gifted Student Perceptions of Teaching and Teacher Effectiveness
▶ Creativity Talent Development: Fostering Creativity in Schools
▶ Educational Contexts, Transitions and Community Engagement: Part VI Introduction
▶ Fostering and Developing Talent in Mentorship Programs: The Mentor's Perspectives
▶ Gifted Education in the Asia-Pacific: From the Past for the Future – An Introduction
▶ Implementing the DMGT's Constructs of Giftedness and Talent: What, Why, and How?
▶ Motivational Issues in Gifted Education: Understanding the Role of Students' Attribution and Control Beliefs, Self-Worth Protection and Growth Orientation
▶ Self-Regulated Learning for High-Ability and High-Achieving Students in Mixed-Ability Classrooms Throughout the Asia-Pacific
▶ Some Implications for the Future of Gifted Education in the Asia-Pacific
▶ The Career Decisions of Gifted Students: An Asian-Pacific Perspective
▶ Teaching Gifted Education to Pre-service Teachers: Lessons Learned
▶ The Lives and Achievements of Four Extraordinary Australians: A Master, a Maker, an Introspector, and an Influencer

Acknowledgments USYD Ethics approval 2017/652.

References

Anderson, L., & Krathwohl, D. (2001). *A taxonomy for learning, teaching, and assessing*. New York, NY: Longman.
Bandura, A. (1993). Perceived self-efficacy in cognitive development and functioning. *Educational Psychologist, 28*, 117–148. https://doi.org/10.1207/s15326985ep2802_3
Bennett, D., & Bridgstock, R. (2015). The urgent need for career preview: Student expectations and graduate realities in music and dance. *International Journal of Music Education, 33*(3), 263–277. https://doi.org/10.1177/0255761414558653
Bennett, D., Richardson, S., & MacKinnon, P. (2016). *Enacting strategies for graduate employability: How universities can best support students to develop generic skill Part A.* Canberra, ACT: Australian Government.
Bennett, D., Rowley, J., Dunbar-Hall, P., Hitchcock, M., & Blom, D. (2016). Electronic portfolios and learner identity: An ePortfolio case study in music and writing. *Journal of Further and Higher Education, 40*(1), 107–124. https://doi.org/10.1080/0309877X.2014.895306
Bloom, B. (1985). Talent development in young people. New York, NY: Ballantine.
Brackett, M. A., & Mayer, J. D. (2003). Convergent, discriminant, and incremental validity of competing measures of emotional intelligence. *Personality and Social Psychology, 29*, 1147–1156. https://doi.org/10.1177/0146167203254596

Brooks, W., & Rowley, J. (2013). Music students' perspectives on learning with technology [online]. In *Redefining the musical landscape: Inspired learning and innovation in music education – XIX National Conference Proceedings* (pp. 30–36). Parkville, VI: Australian Society for Music Education. Retrieved from http://search.informit.com.au/documentSummary;dn=713887583364631;res=IELHSS. ISBN: 9780980379235.

Byrne, D. (2001). *Complexity theory and the social sciences: An Introduction*. Routledge: Taylor & Francis e-Library. ISBN 0-203-00391-8

Campbell, M. R., & Brummett, V. M. (2007). Mentoring preservice teachers for development and growth of professional knowledge. *Music Educators Journal, 93*(3), 50–55. https://doi.org/10.1177/002743210709300320

Cohen, L., Manion, L., & Morrison, K. (2007). *Research methods in education* (6th ed.). London, England: Routledge. ISBN 0-203-02905-4 Master e-book.

Creswell, J. W. (2014). *Research design qualitative, quantitative and mixed methods approaches* (4th ed.). Thousand Oaks, CA: Sage.

Deci, E. L., & Ryan, R. M. (2000). The "what" and "why" of goal pursuits: Human needs and the self-determination of behavior. *Psychological Inquiry, 11*(4), 227–268. https://doi.org/10.1207/S15327965PLI1104_01

Ferm, C. (2008). Playing to teach music–embodiment and identity-making in musikdidaktik. *Music Education Research, 10*(3), 361–372. https://doi.org/10.1080/14613800802280100

Gagné, F. (1999). Gagné's differentiated model of giftedness and talent (DMGT). *Journal for the Education of the Gifted, 22*(2), 230–234. https://doi.org/10.1177/016235329902200209

Gagné, F. (2015). From genes to talent: The DMGT/CMTD perspective. *Revista de Educación, 368*, 30. Ministry of Education, Culture and Sport. General Tecnhicall Secretariat. https://doi.org/10.4438/1988–592X-RE-2015-368-289

Gagné, F., & McPherson, G. (2016). Analyzing musical prodigiousness using Gagné's Integrative Model of Talent Development. In G. E. McPherson (Ed.), *Musical prodigies: Interpretations from psychology, education, musicology and ethnomusicology* (pp. 3–114). Oxford, UK: Oxford University Press. ISBN-13: 9780199685851. Oxford Scholarship Online.

Garces-Bacsal, R. M. (2014). Alternative pathways to talent development in music: The narrative of an eminent Filipino singer-songwriter. *The Gifted Child Quarterly, 58*(3), 231–242. https://doi.org/10.1177/0016986214535627

Jung, J. Y. (2012). Giftedness as a developmental construct that leads to eminence as adults: Ideas and implications from an occupational/career decision-making perspective. *The Gifted Child Quarterly, 56*(4), 189–193. https://doi.org/10.1177/0016986212456072

Jung, J. Y. (2018). *The career decisions of gifted students and other high ability groups*. Abingdon, Oxon; New York, NY: Routledge.

Kolb, D. A. (1984). *Experiential learning: Experience as the source of learning and development* (Vol. 1). Englewood Cliffs, NJ: Prentice-Hall.

Lent, R. W., Brown, S. D., & Hackett, G. (1994). Toward a unifying social cognitive theory of career and academic interest, choice, and performance. *Journal of Vocational Behaviour, 45*(1), 79–122. https://doi.org/10.1006/jvbe.1994.1027

Paley, J., & Eva, G. (2011). Complexity theory as an approach to explanation in healthcare: A critical discussion. *Nursing Studies, 48*(2), 269–279. https://doi.org/10.1016/j.ijnurstu.2010.09.012

Ritchie, J., Lewis, J., McNaughton Nichols, C., & Ormston, R. (2014). *Qualitative research practice: A guide for social science students and researchers* (2nd ed.). Los Angeles: SAGE Publications Ltd.. ISBN-10: 1446209121.

Rowley, J., & Bennett, D. (2013). Technology, identity and the creative artist. *30th Australasian Society for Computers in Learning in Tertiary Education Conference: Electric Dreams (ASCILITE 2013)* (pp. 775–780). Sydney, NSW: Macquarie University.

Rowley, J., Bennett, D., & Reid, A. (2016). Leadership as a core creativity for musician identity. *32nd World Conference on Music Education (ISME 2016)*, Glasgow, Scotland: International Society of Music Education (ISME).

Rowley, J., & Munday, J. (2014). A 'sense of self' through reflective thinking in ePortfolios. *International Journal of Humanities Social Sciences and Education (IJHSSE)*, *1*(7), 78–85. ISSN 2349-0373.

Schön, D. (1995). *The reflective practitioner*. San Francisco: Jossey Banks.

Wakimoto, D. K., & Lewis, R. E. (2014). Graduate student perceptions of eportfolios: Uses for reflection, development, and assessment. *The Internet and Higher Education, 21*, 53–58. https://doi.org/10.1016/j.iheduc.2014.01.002

Yeo, N., & Rowley, J. (2018). Reflections on a three-way mentoring program using ePortfolios: I Pagliacci (Leoncavallo) under the Buddy Mentoring Program. *33rd World Conference on Music Education (ISME 2018)*, Prague, Czech Republic: International Society of Music Education (ISME).

Jennifer Rowley   is an Associate Professor who currently lectures Music Education at the Sydney Conservatorium of Music (SCM) at The University of Sydney and coordinates the professional placement program for SCM students into the Arts industry, regional conservatoriums and schools. She is particularly interested in the areas of identity development; gifted musicians' talent development; and the impact of the electronic Portfolio for fostering enhanced work readiness. Jennifer is committed to musician's professional learning and how individual cognitive, social, emotional, and behavioural needs of all learners can be met in a diverse range of educational settings.

Teaching Gifted Education to Pre-service Teachers: Lessons Learned

62

Margaret Plunkett and Leonie Kronborg

Contents

Abstract

In Australia, most teachers enter the profession without having completed any dedicated undergraduate studies pertaining to gifted education, yet many go on to teach gifted students in either mainstream or specialised educational settings.

M. Plunkett (✉)
School of Education, Federation University, Churchill, VIC, Australia
e-mail: Margaret.plunkett@federation.edu.au

L. Kronborg
Faculty of Education, Monash University, Clayton, VIC, Australia
e-mail: leonie.kronborg@monash.edu

© Springer Nature Singapore Pte Ltd. 2021
S. R. Smith (ed.), *Handbook of Giftedness and Talent Development in the Asia-Pacific*,
Springer International Handbooks of Education,
https://doi.org/10.1007/978-981-13-3041-4_67

Research suggests that specific education relating to giftedness enhances attitudes and practices that are conducive to appropriate provisioning for gifted students (Fraser-Seeto, 2013; Geake & Gross, 2008; Kronborg & Meyland, 2003; Lassig, 2009; Plunkett, 2002; Troxclair, 2013). This chapter examines the value of specifically covering giftedness in pre-service teacher education through highlighting the findings from a research project conducted over seven years (2008–2014) with 588 pre-service teachers who completed an elective unit in gifted education at a major Australian university. Participants reported a significant growth in awareness of the challenges associated with educating gifted students, highlighting the value of an evidence-based understanding of all the topics covered in the unit, with the vast majority strongly recommending gifted education as a compulsory part of all *Initial Teacher Education* (ITE) programs. The areas where attitudes underwent significant changes and some of the lessons learned about the potential role of ITE in preparing future teachers to confront the complexities associated with teaching gifted students will be outlined in this chapter.

Keywords

Initial teacher education · Teacher attitudes towards giftedness · Gifted education · Pre-service teachers

The aims in this chapter are to:
1. Outline the main body of literature relating to attitudes of teachers and particularly pre-service teachers towards giftedness and gifted education.
2. Highlight the importance of positive attitudes towards giftedness within the teaching profession, as this has been associated with appropriate responses/provisioning.
3. Detail findings about attitudinal change from a case study of almost 600 preservice teachers (PSTs) who completed a semester long elective in gifted education.
4. Reinforce the important role of *Initial Teacher Education* (ITE) in challenging and enhancing teachers' knowledge, attitudes, and beliefs related to gifted students.

Introduction

Despite the importance of teachers having positive and informed attitudes towards all aspects of teaching, the extant research does not support the efficacy of initial teacher education courses in changing ingrained misconceptions that can negatively impact student learning (Goddard & Evans, 2018; Hudson, Hudson, Lewis, & Watters, 2010; Kagan, 1992). Of course, the relationship between attitudes and behaviours is complex, but generally opinions or attitudes affect perceptions, which in turn influence behaviour (Bergman, 1998; Bohner & Wänke, 2002).

Within Australia, initial teacher education programs rarely offer specific units in gifted education, and if they are offered they tend to be electives rather than core units (Fraser-Seeto, Howard, & Woodcock, 2013; Kronborg, 2018a). An exemplar study of one elective pre-service teacher unit on gifted education in one large university in Australia is provided to inform the broader focus of this chapter, that is, pre-service teacher attitudes and beliefs about gifted students and gifted education. Reflective commentary provided by participants indicated that the elective unit was perceived as providing opportunities for critical examination of preconceived opinions and beliefs, resulting in reconsideration of a range of common misconceptions associated with teaching gifted students.

Why are Positive Teacher Attitudes Towards Giftedness Important?

A large body of literature exists on the topic of teacher attitudes towards giftedness (e.g., Cramond & Martin, 1987; Gagné & Nadeau, 1985; Geake & Gross, 2008; Kronborg & Plunkett, 2012; Plunkett, 2000, 2002; Plunkett & Kronborg, 2011). A number of other studies support the importance of teachers for gifted students particularly in terms of providing support (VanTassel-Baska, 1997), facilitating learning (McCoach & Siegle, 2007), identification for gifted services (Szymanski, Croft, & Godor, 2018), and helping gifted students to reach their potential (Mills, 2003; Smith & Chan, 1996). Fraser-Seeto, Howard, and Woodcock (2015) claim that, "when considering the unique characteristics and needs of gifted and talented students, it is clear that teachers play a central role in the academic success (or failure) of these students" (p. 2).

With a central role to play, it is therefore important that attitudes are supportive as they have been found to inform a teacher's philosophy, curriculum, and instruction (Adams & Pierce, 2004; Block & Hazelip, 1995; Polyzopoulou, Kokaridas, Patsiaouras, & Gari, 2014). Some studies have examined attitudes but not practices, nevertheless acknowledging the relationship between these (Szymanski et al., 2018). For instance, Adams and Pierce (2004) found that the attitudes and beliefs, of teachers influenced "how they design and implement learning experiences in the classroom" (p. 21). According to Fraser-Seeto (2013), teacher perceptions, beliefs, and attitudes towards gifted students have been found to be instrumental in ensuring appropriate educational provision. As a result of working with Belgian teachers to try to improve their responses to giftedness in the classroom, Vreys, Ndungbogun, Kieboom, and Venderickx (2018) concluded, "given the close relationship between beliefs and behaviour improving teachers' beliefs about gifted children and their educational needs is an essential step to alter teachers' attitudes toward the best practices for gifted children" (p. 18). Laine and Tirri (2016), in their study of Finnish teachers' approaches to gifted students, also found that lack of knowledge and uninformed beliefs can contribute to inappropriate educational provisions for this group of students.

A number of studies have also shown that attitudes of teachers towards gifted students are often not positive, especially amongst teachers without professional development/study in gifted education (Adams & Pierce, 2004; Geake & Gross, 2008; Lassig, 2009; Plunkett, 2000, 2002).

Attitude Formation and Change

Research into attitude formation suggests that it is not a straightforward process and both personal and environmental factors influence how attitudes are formed (Begin & Gagné, 1994; Bohner & Wänke, 2002). Stern and Keislar (1975) highlighted the importance of knowledge in terms of influencing cognitive beliefs, which underpin personal feelings and behaviours and therefore attitudes. Jung's (2014) study with 241 Australian *Pre-Service Teachers* (PSTs) examined predictors of attitudes towards gifted programs and provisions and found that power distance orientation, contact with gifted persons and age all had an impact on how PSTs viewed the value of specific provisions for gifted students.

Due to the complexity associated with attitude formation, the process of modifying attitudes can be a challenging task, especially if those attitudes have not been previously challenged (Fives & Buehl, 2008) or are deep-seated due to personal experience (Oppenheim, 1992). Block and Hazelip (1995) argued that many beliefs held by teachers are ingrained and need to be closely examined in order to be modified.

It can be assumed that such an opportunity for close examination and challenging of beliefs is provided via the extensive period of undergraduate education. However, early research into how pre-service teachers' general attitudes towards teaching changed over the course of their study suggest little change occurs (Finlayson & Cohen, 1967; Lortie, 1975; Tabachnick & Zeichner, 1984). Lortie (1975) argued that the dispositions brought to teaching by PSTs have a stronger influence on socialisation than their pre-service education. A review of 40 studies examining attitude changes to teaching also found that pre-service experience did not have an impact on attitudes based on personal experience (Kagan, 1992). It has been argued that this is due to the lack of opportunities afforded PSTs in their teaching courses to reflect on and assess their personal experiences and attitudes towards teaching, which is an important catalyst for change (Ross, 1988).

Current Understandings Regarding ITE and Attitudes Towards Giftedness

During initial teacher education, PSTs are beginning to develop the understandings that will underpin their practice. Obviously as they enter their own classrooms, their new teaching experience and professional learning will shape their ongoing development, but during the four or so years that they spend engaged in ITE, their learning and teaching 'philosophy' is being formed. According to Rowley (2012), "many professional educators rely heavily upon their pre-service teacher training to provide the resources for a lifetime of experiences in teaching" (p. 79). Moreover, this time is full of in-built reflection opportunities, and yet, most ITE courses have little or no content relating to giftedness or gifted education (Berman, Schultz, & Weber, 2012; Fraser-Seeto et al., 2013; Vreys et al., 2018). According to Troxclair (2013), who wrote of the US situation:

> historically, preservice teachers have had little exposure in their teacher training programs regarding the nature and needs of gifted learners, theories of gifted education, curriculum for those with advanced abilities, and teaching strategies to be used with gifted learners. (p. 58)

The lack of coverage of giftedness within ITE courses was also reported in the Victorian Parliamentary Inquiry (2012), and in two previous Australian Parliamentary Senate reviews (1988, 2001) into the education of gifted and talented children. The Victorian Parliamentary Inquiry (2012) found that ITE was inadequate, stating that, "the committee recognises that the current pre-service training does not adequately equip teachers to identify and cater for gifted children in Victorian schools" (p. 253). A further issue identified by Walsh and Jolly (2018) is that preservice training in gifted education in Australia is actually on the decline, with more emphasis now being placed on in-service education.

Yet both national and international studies acknowledge that teachers of the gifted are often "guided by beliefs that are not related to evidence-based practices" (Bain, Bliss, Choate, & Sager Brown, 2007, p. 451). Hudson et al. (2010) also argue that, "if the negative attitudes of preservice teachers about gifted students are unchallenged, they will retain these attitudes in professional practice" (p. 6).

However, when specific education relating to giftedness is introduced into the mix of both initial and in-service teacher education, there is evidence of more positive attitudes and, often, an extension into teaching practice (Adams & Pierce, 2004; Kronborg, 2018b; Vialle, 2012). According to Walsh and Jolly (2018), Australian research suggests that, "teacher attitudes toward gifted students are often negative but that training in the field has the effect of changing teacher attitudes" (p. 86). Other research highlights the importance of more field work and other opportunities to work with gifted students so that understanding can be put into practice (Almulla & Fateel, 2017; Brevik, Gunnulfsen, & Renzulli, 2017; Chamberlin & Chamberlin, 2010; Hudson et al., 2010; Jung, 2014). Incorporating practical applications of knowledge has also been highlighted as advantageous, particularly in relation to learning how to effectively differentiate teaching for individual student learning and achievement. According to Vreys et al. (2018), "...differentiation is a complex process, and teachers need to develop the necessary knowledge and skills in order to be able to implement proper challenging activities for gifted pupils" (pp. 18–19). Jung (2014) also advocated more exposure to gifted students if possible in professional experience in schools and a specific focus on learning how to differentiate the curriculum for mixed ability settings.

Measurement of attitudes adds another layer of complexity within this body of research, with numerous formats employed. A number of studies have used Gagné and Nadeau's (1985) survey to measure attitudes of either practising teachers or those studying to be teachers (Allodi & Rydelius, 2008: Krijan & Borić, 2015; Kronborg & Plunkett, 2012; Lassig, 2003; McCoach & Siegle, 2007; Plunkett & Kronborg, 2011; Troxclair, 2013; Watts, 2006). Although issues have been noted regarding internal reliability of this scale outside its original context (McCoach & Siegle, 2007), it does provide a comprehensive set of items to help measure teachers' opinions relating to giftedness and gifted education. For the purposes of the study examined below, the terms attitude and opinion were used synonymously (Bergman, 1998).

Exemplar Australian Study to Inform the Broader Research

In 2008, a new elective called 'Gifted Education' was offered at a large Australian university. Between 2008 and 2014, approximately 950 pre-service teachers undertaking degrees in primary and secondary education and a small number of practicing teachers who were upgrading their qualifications, completed the undergraduate unit across both metropolitan and regional campuses. The unit is still offered today, but this chapter focuses only on results for the cohort who completed the unit up to and including 2014, in line with the ethics approval timeframe for the project.

The unit introduced students to the theory and practice underpinning appropriate educational responses to high ability or gifted students, providing a framework for understanding giftedness and the practices associated with gifted education from a theoretical perspective. The assessment tasks provided opportunities for both critically reflective appraisal and practical application of new understandings. The unit provided an overview of current conceptualisations relating to giftedness and gifted behaviour and outlined a range of pedagogical and curricula responses found to be effective in meeting the specific educational and social needs of gifted students. A specific focus was the development of differentiated curricula suitable for engaging students of all ability levels and gifted students in particular. The main topics covered in the unit included: attitudes towards and changing conceptions of giftedness; characteristics and identification of giftedness; underachieving gifted; organisational provisions for gifted: grouping and acceleration; curricula provisions for gifted, differentiation; special gifted groups; and social/emotional aspects of giftedness.

Method Used in the Australian Study

A case study framework (Yin, 2003) within a mixed methods approach were employed in this exemplar study (Creswell & Plano Clark, 2011), where quantitative and qualitative data were compared and contrasted to form the results. The research question underpinning the study was: *In what ways do attitudes of PSTs change towards giftedness and the education of gifted students after completing a semester long unit on gifted education?*

As an introductory activity each semester, students in the elective were asked to complete a survey (online or in class) on their opinions and attitudes towards giftedness and gifted education. On completion of the unit 12–13 weeks later, students were again asked to complete the same survey to help them determine whether there had been either a shift or consolidation of their opinions. Students were then invited to provide their pre- and post-survey results as part of a final reflection on their journey of understanding in this unit. This was not part of the assessment and was totally voluntary. Ethics approval had been obtained for the conduct of the research for a period of seven years (one of which was retrospective). This chapter reports on data collected during the period between 2008 and 2014, where 588 (62%) of the 950 students completing the unit, responded to the pre- and post-surveys, with many providing written reflections on how and why they felt their opinions had changed.

The 588 participants were all enrolled in the elective unit and all provided both pre- and post-surveys. Demographic data was not collected except for gender, with 479 (81.5%) females and 109 males (18.5%) participating, which was reflective of the unit composition. Although exact numbers are not known, a small number of participants were also practicing teachers who were upgrading their qualifications. Of the 588 survey participants, almost half (283) also provided reflective journal entries summarising their perceptions of where and why attitudinal changes had occurred.

Survey Instrument for the Quantitative Data Component of the Australian Study

The survey instrument utilised was developed by Gagné and Nadeau (1985) entitled 'Opinions about the Gifted and Their Education'. The survey was developed to gain insight into opinions concerning the gifted and their education in six areas:

1. *Needs and Support*: needs of gifted children and support for special services.
2. *Resistance to objections*: objections based on ideology and priorities.
3. *Social Value*: social usefulness of gifted persons in society.
4. *Rejection*: isolation of gifted persons by others in the immediate environment.
5. *Ability Grouping*: attitudes towards special homogeneous groups, classes, and schools.
6. *School Acceleration*: attitudes towards accelerative enrichment.

As in previous research (McCoach & Siegle, 2007; Plunkett & Kronborg, 2011), there were issues with reliability analysis in this study, with the subscales not registering sufficient internal reliability at 0.07 or above (Nunnally, 1978), even with the revised subscales developed by McCoach and Siegle (2007). Therefore, as suggested by Gagné (1991), mean scores for each item were reported.

Reflective Commentary for the Qualitative Data Component of the Australian Study

The reflective journal entries used in this project provided an overview of differences in responses to the two surveys. Participants were asked to complete the second survey before examining their previous responses to the first survey. Data from the reflective journal entries were analysed using constant comparison (Patton, 1990) and inductive analysis (Lincoln & Guba, 1985; Denzin & Lincoln, 2005) to develop and consider emergent themes. Representative quotes were drawn from the entries, after repeated reading and re-reading of the data. This formed the first-order analysis, which showed thematic descriptions of understandings about changes to previous perceptions. In the first instance, descriptive codes were used to identify potentially interesting reflections. Further inferential coding resulted in identification of conceptual links which were used to develop new categories. This second order of analysis explored the patterns that emerged from insights of participants into how their attitudes had changed.

Findings from the Australian Study

Quantitative Data: Survey Responses

The 34 items in the survey utilised a five-point Likert scale for responses, ranging from one indicating strong disagreement to five which related to strong agreement. For descriptive analytical purposes, and as suggested by Gagné (1991), mean scores were classified as follows: between 4 and 5 indicated a high positive (HP) attitude; between 3.24 and 3.9 indicated a Positive (P) attitude; between 2.75 to 3.25 was interpreted as Ambivalent (A); between 2 to 2.74 was considered as Negative (N); and less than 2 classified as High Negative (HN). Seventeen of the items were negatively worded and thus, scores were reversed during analysis.

Table 1 outlines the pre- and post-mean scores for the sample with the associated standard deviations (SD), effect sizes calculated using Cohen's d and the classification ratings. In all instances except with Item 17, scores increased between pre- and post-administrations. All changes except for Item 17 were also statistically significant, with Item 31 significant at $p < 0.05$ and all the others significant at $p < 0.001$. In terms of effect sizes, it was interesting to see that all effect sizes for the subscales relating to ability grouping and acceleration were large. The only other subscale which had a noticeable pattern of influence was the first subscale on needs and support in which effect sizes were all moderate to high. Other high effect sizes were found in relation to Items 4 and 23.

In terms of the ratings, the second administration of the survey indicated that all except two items reflected mean scores that were either positive or highly positive (17 HP and 15 P). The two that remained ambivalent were Items 17 and 19, but 19 moved from negative in the first administration. This differed from the first

Table 1 Pre- and post-results for responses to Gagné and Nadeau's survey (N = 588)

Item No.	Item	Mean		SD		Cohen's d	Rating	
		Pre	Post	Pre	Post		Pre	Post
Subscale 1: Needs and support								
01	Our schools should offer special educational services for the gifted.	4.33	4.84	0.86	0.44	0.75	HP	HP
09	Gifted children are often bored in school.	4.01	4.55	0.93	0.83	0.61	HP	HP
11	The gifted waste their time in regular classes.	2.77	3.70	1.11	1.07	**0.85**	A	P
14	Specific educational needs of the gifted are too often ignored in schools.	4.06	4.72	0.51	0.89	**0.91**	HP	HP
15	The gifted need special attention in order to fully develop their talents.	3.95	4.63	0.89	0.68	**0.86**	P	HP
24	To progress, a society must develop talents of gifted individuals to a maximum.	3.46	4.14	1.06	0.96	0.67	P	HP
30	Since we invest supplementary funds for children with difficulties we should do same for the gifted.	4.10	4.63	0.89	0.68	0.67	HP	HP
32	The regular school program stifles the intellectual curiosity of gifted children.	3.39	4.17	0.95	0.91	**0.84**	P	HP
Subscale 2: Resistance to objections								
#03	Children with difficulties have the most need of special services.	3.06	3.89	1.2	1.3	0.66	A	P
#04	Special programs for the gifted have the drawback of creating elitism.	2.71	3.88	1.04	1.12	**1.08**	N	P
#05	Special educational services for the gifted are a mark of privilege.	3.48	4.17	1.15	1.05	0.63	P	HP
#12	We have a greater moral responsibility to give special help to children with difficulties than to gifted children.	3.5	4.06	1.25	1.12	0.47	P	HP
#16	Our schools are already adequate in meeting the needs of the gifted.	3.93	4.4	0.85	0.78	0.58	P	HP
#18	Parents have the major responsibility for helping gifted children develop talents.	3.15	3.34	1.13	1.13	0.17	A	P

(continued)

Table 1 (continued)

Item No.	Item	Mean		SD		Cohen's d	Rating	
		Pre	Post	Pre	Post		Pre	Post
#23	The gifted are already favoured in schools.	3.51	4.39	1.01	0.79	**0.97**	P	HP
#26	Taxpayers should not have to pay for special education for the minority of children who are gifted.	3.73	4.33	1.06	0.95	0.60	P	HP
#27	Average children are the major resource of our society so should be the focus of our attention.	3.52	4.05	1.1	0.97	0.51	P	HP
#28	Gifted children might become egotistical if given special attention.	3.37	4.17	1.15	0.95	0.76	P	HP
Subscale 3: Social value								
13	Gifted persons are a valuable resource for our society.	4.37	4.73	0.85	0.54	0.51	HP	HP
17+	I would very much like to be considered a gifted person.	2.95	2.92	1.15	1.23	0.02	A	A
#25	Offering special educational services to the gifted prepares future members of a dominant class.	3.35	3.61	1.09	1.18	0.23	P	P
33	Leaders of tomorrow's society will come mostly from the gifted of today.	2.64	3.31	1.08	1.08	0.62	N	P
Subscale 4: Rejection								
19	A child identified as gifted has more difficulty in making friends.	2.64	3.02	1.08	1.17	0.34	N	A
22	Some teachers feel their authority threatened by gifted children.	3.35	3.91	1.13	1.01	0.52	P	P
31 **	Often gifted children are rejected because of envy.	3.35	3.48	1.0	1.11	0.12	P	P
Subscale 5: Ability grouping								
02	Best way to meet needs of the gifted is special classes.	2.91	3.77	0.99	0.93	**0.89**	A	P
#06	When the gifted are put in special classes others feel devalued.	2.76	3.83	1.1	1.04	**1.0**	A	P
#20	Gifted children should be left in regular classes since they serve as an intellectual stimulant for others.	3.06	4.21	1.07	0.91	**1.16**	A	HP
#21	Separation into gifted and other groups increases labelling of children as strong–weak etc.	2.33	3.44	1.09	1.19	**0.97**	N	P

(continued)

Table 1 (continued)

Item No.	Item	Mean Pre	Post	SD Pre	Post	Cohen's d	Rating Pre	Post
Subscale 6: School acceleration								
#07	Most gifted children who skip a grade have difficulties in social adjustment to older students.	2.64	3.8	1.1	1.16	**1.0**	N	P
08	It is more damaging for a gifted child to waste time in class than to adapt to skipping a grade.	3.55	4.38	1.06	0.98	**0.81**	P	HP
#10	Children who skip a grade are usually pressured to do so by parents.	2.84	3.67	0.97	1.0	**0.84**	A	P
#29	When skipping a grade gifted students miss important ideas.	3.03	3.93	1.15	0.95	**0.85**	A	P
34	A greater number of gifted children should be allowed to skip a grade.	2.76	3.94	0.92	0.94	**1.3**	A	P

\# Scores reversed: negatively worded items, + not significant, ∗∗ $p < 0.05$. All other items significant at $p < 0.001$

administration of the survey where the pattern was much broader with mean responses resulting in 5 HP, 14 P, 10 A, and 5 N ratings. The shaded ratings in Table 1 illustrate where responses changed from ambivalent or negative to positive, with Item 20 jumping two categories from A to HP. Item 20 also had the second highest effect size. All ratings in Subscale 2 moved up a classification level.

Qualitative Data: Reflective Commentary

The qualitative data emerged from 283 reflective journal responses from participating students in relation to how they felt their understandings and opinions/attitudes had changed as a result of completing the elective. Table 2 outlines the main themes and subthemes that emerged from the reflective commentary provided by participants and the associated number of mentions. Percentages have also been listed to illustrate the percentage of participants who made reference to the ideas, with multiple references only listed once. Subthemes which had more than 200 references, thus representing more than 70% of participants, are highlighted in bold.

The areas concentrated on in the qualitative reflections did not always correspond directly to an area or topic covered in the survey, as many participants commented more generally on how they felt their perspectives and opinions in relation to educating gifted students had changed over the semester. The main themes can generally be linked with particular subscales of the survey, but definitely with topics covered in the unit.

Table 2 Themes emerging from final reflective journal entries of participants (N = 283)

Themes and subthemes			No of mentions
1. Giftedness as a complex construct	Definitions	No universal definition	128 (45%)
		Difference between gifted and talented	117 (41%)
		Asynchrony	109 (39%)
	Complicating factors	**Concept of underachieving gifted**	**239 (84%)**
		Twice exceptionality	**238 (84%)**
		Social emotional components of giftedness	**219 (77%)**
2. Efficacy of evidence-based practices	Ability grouping & acceleration	**Lack of evidence of social emotional problems with acceleration/ability grouping**	**209 (74%)**
		Need for and value of spending time with like-minds	176 (62%)
	Differentiation	**Gifted students not necessarily role models**	**203 (72%)**
		Complexity of and need for differentiation	178 (63%)
		Differentiation can assist every student	175 (62%)
3. Complexity of identification	Process	Need for multi-faceted approach	156 (55%)
		Understanding of IQ (benefits and limitations)	134 (47%)
		Value of parental input	126 (45%)
	Added complications	**Impact of underachievement**	**226 (80%)**
		Impact of twice exceptionality	**232 (82%)**
4. Equity issues	Equal opportunities	**Gifted need assistance**	**202 (71%)**
		Gifted just as deserving of assistance	**200 (71%)**
	Teacher education	**Absolute need for coverage of giftedness in teacher education**	**245 (87%)**
		Inequity in coverage of giftedness	134 (47%)
5. Catharsis and deeper understandings	Deeper self-awareness/ acceptance	Self-understanding	120 (42%)
		Acceptance of self	75 (27%)
	More informed awareness of others	Understanding of partners/siblings/ colleagues	95 (34%)
		Understanding of own children	65 (23%)
		Another lens to view behaviour	110 (39%)

Theme 1: Giftedness as a complex construct. This theme related to the references made in relation to developing understandings of what giftedness involves. Main comments included a growing awareness of lack of a universal definition or conception of giftedness, but acknowledgement of the value in differentiating between giftedness and talent. The concept of asynchrony in terms of development was also raised many times as something that made sense but was previously unknown. The two most common points raised within this

theme related to the idea of gifted students underachieving OR being twice exceptional. Even experienced teachers completing this course (in order to upgrade their Diploma qualifications) commented on how surprised they were when introduced to this body of literature, and how it made them reassess previous understandings of gifted students. The final factor in this theme related to the social emotional aspects associated with giftedness, which was covered at the end of the unit, and often had a profound impact on how giftedness was understood.

Many comments related to the complexity of giftedness, where the social emotional context had not been considered and the impact of lack, or even denial, of recognition of a student's giftedness and appropriate educational provision, are underestimated. Thus, changes in attitudes in relation to social-emotional aspects of giftedness were reflected in changes to responses in Subscales 1 and 2 of the survey. The following comments are chosen as representative of those related to this theme:

> As an experienced teacher, I felt I was reasonably well informed about giftedness. However, this unit has inspired me to critically look at how I go about teaching gifted individuals in every aspect of their education. I now understand the importance of not only supporting students academically but emotionally and socially … areas where I just didn't fully understand the impact of giftedness. (Nicky, 2010)

> I never needed to be converted from the other side, but did have my doubts about the authentic nature of gifted ed. I'd never really thought about how I'd cope in a class situation, and the reality of the number of gifted students and their potential capabilities does scare me as an educator yet excites me as a member of society. (Kayla, 2013)

There were also references to acknowledgement of a lack of awareness about the concepts of gifted underachievement and twice exceptionality, which can impact on identification of giftedness:

> It really blew me away when I started reading about twice exceptional kids and underachievers as I thought you won the lottery if you were gifted. (Angus, 2013)

> I had never considered the possibility of a gifted student underachieving, or of being learning disabled… Why aren't we introduced to this info in other classes? (Jacob, 2011)

Theme 2. Efficacy of evidence-based practices. This theme incorporated ability grouping, accelerative options, and curriculum differentiation. As with the survey results, noticeable changes in attitudes were noted by participants, particularly in relation to items included in Subscales 5 and 6. A lack of awareness of literature was reported, particularly regarding the positive impact of high ability grouping and acceleration, as illustrated in the following comments:

> Ability grouping is heavily criticised in a lot of our courses and I must admit it took a fair bit of convincing from the readings to get me to see how it might be good…at least for gifted kids…. but this view is certainly not a popular one. (Reagan, 2014)

I now believe that acceleration doesn't have the same degree of risk as I originally thought. (Karla, 2011)

An awareness of previous misconceptions about the need for gifted students to remain with same-aged peers and to provide role models was also acknowledged:

I always believed that gifted students were the great role models and that they sort of owed it to the less advantaged students to help them understand. (Paula, 2009)

I now understand why forcing gifted students to be friends with age peers can be quite damaging—as teachers we do so much in the mistaken belief that children belong with their age peers. The readings on social emotional factors really challenged my beliefs—I fought the literature to begin with but finally conceded. (David, 2011)

Participants also highlighted changes to understandings about the value of curriculum differentiation as a practice that can be very effective in meeting the academic needs of gifted students in mixed ability classrooms, which is the norm in Australia:

The main thing I've really changed my mind about is differentiation. I had no idea how complex it was, but how necessary. I have so often seen just different worksheets being passed off as differentiation but after having to complete the differentiated unit, I could see how little this is really understood in schools. I swear by it now! (Sam, 2008)

Having to create the differentiated unit of work, which I was fortunate enough to implement on prac., showed me how much difference it can make. (Marie, 2010)

Theme 3. Complexity of identification. Many participants remarked on how they had not really thought about identification of gifted students—assuming naively that comprehensive testing was used to identify these students and thus were shocked to realise that many gifted students never get identified:

I can't believe my naivety really . . . I assumed all schools tested for giftedness . . . but realise I haven't ever seen any evidence of this on my placements. (Jack, 2008)

The most common references in the reflections were in response to changed understandings in relation to the concepts of underachievement of gifted students and twice exceptionality, which had often not been considered as possibilities. These were noted as impacting on responses to items in subscales 1 and 2 in particular. There was also recognition of the impact these can have on the identification of giftedness:

Each time I thought I was beginning to understand how to identify giftedness, another complicating factor was introduced! I can't believe it's so complicated and why we never learnt any of this until just before leaving uni. (Kara, 2012)

The following reflection from an experienced teacher who was upgrading her qualifications shows that not only PSTs can undergo significant attitudinal change when confronted with new information:

> I have often wanted to cry as I immersed myself in the gifted literature, as I recognised little souls who I have totally misunderstood over the years. If only I'd known of the possibilities of twice exceptionality and underachievement, of the need for like-minded rather than age peers, of the search for acceptance that can lead to dumbing down and hiding of talents—it could have been a very different story. My heart aches for those who I have failed through a lack of awareness. Thank goodness, I can make a difference in the years I have left! (Anna, 2008)

Theme 4. Equity issues. The main points raised in this theme related to understanding the need for specific attention to giftedness as an equity issue (subscales 1 and 2) and the concomitant need for specific teacher education to support the first point becoming more likely:

> Whereas I previously thought giftedness wasn't well catered for and believed it should be, I didn't have anything other than anecdote and personal experience to back my beliefs. While I did have a few strong opinions before… I wouldn't have been able to defend my beliefs, which I now feel very comfortable doing. (Alex, 2011)

In relation to equity, more than 70% of participants in this section of the study mentioned the need for recognition of and provision for gifted students. Specific references to many of the items making up Subscale 2 featured in this section:

> Like so many of us, I believed the limited educational budget shouldn't be stretched in the direction of the gifted because they already performed so well. I thought schools catered very well for these students—it was a misconception that was highlighted and well rewarded throughout my degree. Now I can't believe how wrong this perception is and how much harm is done in the name of equity. (Jacqui, 2014)

The general consensus of the majority of participants was the need for coverage of gifted education to be a mandatory part of teacher education:

> Personally, I can't believe this [unit] isn't compulsory. I've learned more in it than in any other course in my four years… The differentiated unit was also the most useful assignment ever and I loved putting it into practice. I really feel sorry for the students who don't do this unit, as they won't have a clue about what to do with gifted kids. (Corinne, 2012)

Theme 5. Catharsis and deeper understandings. This theme related to the development of greater understandings in relation to self and others. Examples included reflections on the cathartic process of better self-understanding or being able to better understand students, partners, children, work colleagues, or peers:

> Before I began this unit, I considered myself a sensitive, sensible and intelligent teacher. During my progression, more often than not I was appalled at my ignorance. It has expanded

my beliefs and given me depth and insight in areas my vague perceptions told me were right but where I lacked knowledge to really understand and support in a classroom. (Jan, 2011)

I didn't realise how little I knew ... I now have far more understanding of the magnitude of emotional, psychological, physical and academic issues that gifted students face every day and can see that little Johnny's sensitivity, constant questioning and energetic and anti-social behaviour may well be an indication of something bigger that requires further investigation...and through this unit I now know where to turn for help! I have developed a greater understanding with regards to the misfounded belief that giftedness is the key to automatic success. (Gael, 2009)

The following comment provides insight into how one participant felt about how his knowledge and understandings had developed and enabled him as a future teacher:

This opportunity has certainly enabled me to approach my students in a more holistic manner, encouraged me to investigate more diverse teaching and learning methods, and has stimulated me to learn more about 'giftedness', and approach students with a diverse range of specialised individual needs in a more positive fashion. My ignorance and lack of understanding was my disabler, my new knowledge, resourcefulness and enthusiasm will be my enabler, and I will now look forward to, feel ready for, and even invite the teaching challenges that 'gifted' students will bring to my classroom. (Andy, 2009)

Summation of Results from the Australian Study

The data provided over the period of seven years illustrated that these PSTs and the few participants who were practicing teachers did not have an evidence-based understanding of giftedness or the practices that underpin gifted education. While the initial implementation of the survey indicated mixed attitudes ranging from negative to highly positive, the second administration demonstrated a significant change, with mean scores for all except two items rated as positive or highly positive. The effect sizes also demonstrated that participation in the unit had a moderate-to-high effect on many of the attitudes covered by the range of items but particularly in relation to needs and support, ability grouping, and acceleration. The written reflections provided meaningful additional support to the positive nature of attitudinal development achieved through completion of this single semester unit of study in gifted education.

Lessons Learned and Implications for Initial Teacher Education

Although the findings outlined in this chapter emanate from a single case study, they support other similar findings in relation to the value of specific education on giftedness (e.g., Lassig, 2009; Plunkett & Kronborg, 2011; Troxclair, 2013). According to Berman et al. (2012), "teacher education programs must include coursework and experiences focusing on the nature and needs of GT learners if we expect to meet these learners' needs in common classroom settings" (p. 24). Yet it appears that PSTs have little opportunity in their ITE courses to interrogate their understandings of and attitudes towards teaching gifted students. This was acknowledged in the Victorian Parliamentary inquiry (2012) and reiterated in the reflections provided by participants in this study and in other similar national and international studies. As research supports a link between attitudes towards giftedness and practices (Fraser-Seeto, 2013; Szymanski et al., 2018; Vreys et al., 2018), it would appear that opportunities for critiquing and concomitantly revising attitudes or beliefs based on misinformation or a lack of information, would be better to occur as early as possible, such as during initial teacher education.

However, if ITE is to be targeted as a place to introduce gifted education, a number of salient points that emerged from this study, need to be considered:

1. Little appears to be known about the complex task of changing attitudes. Lortie (1975) described the hundreds of hours which made up the 'apprenticeship of observation', but there does not appear to be any specific research that explicates how much time it takes to bring about a change in teacher attitudes towards giftedness. According to Darling-Hammond, Hyler, and Gardner (2017), in order for teacher professional learning to be effective, it needs to be of sustained duration to provide teachers with "adequate time to learn, practice, implement, and reflect upon new strategies that facilitate changes in their practice" (p. vi). This need for a sustained period of time would be equally applicable to professional learning in teacher education. The fact that the unit discussed in this chapter went for a full semester may also be of relevance, as it provided participants with time to reflect, which may not be possible in generic 'special needs' units where the topic of giftedness is only one of many covered over a semester, or in short PD courses generally offered at the in-service level. However, Berman et al. (2012), found that even a semester was not long enough to shift some preconceived notions.

   Also, in terms of ITE, a number of recent studies have attempted to evaluate attitudes across the training years, as a way of measuring attitudinal change, with Goddard and Evans (2018) finding that PSTs in their final year of their program were more likely to hold positive attitudes to diverse learners than in their first year. Thus, the time frame within ITE appears to be relevant, as participants in the study outlined in this chapter were mainly in their final year of their degree and therefore had more experience to reflect upon.

2. Other elements specified by Darling-Hammond et al. (2017) as important components of effective professional learning for teachers include: being content-focused; allowing time and opportunities for reflection; and incorporating models of effective practice. All of these elements were present in the unit discussed in this chapter. The PSTs were required to reflect on carefully selected evidence-based research literature in their reflective journals. They were also

introduced to a range of relevant content and curriculum models (e.g., Williams, Kaplan, and Maker), as a way of teaching important skills related to differentiation (Vreys et al., 2018), which PSTs then put into practice for their assessment task of developing differentiated curricula. As Berman et al. (2012) pointed out, "it is not enough to know about GT learners. Teachers must also identify GT learner needs and be able to skillfully implement instructional strategies to meet these needs" (p. 24). In the elective unit discussed in this chapter, assessment tasks required both reflection and practical application, both of which have been highlighted as necessary for professional learning (Darling-Hammond et al., 2017).

3. Although not formally integrated into the unit discussed in this chapter, exposure to gifted students through targeted placements at schools or even visits or stories from gifted students has been found to be a valuable experience for PSTs (Almulla & Fateel, 2017; Brevik et al., 2017; Chamberlin & Chamberlin, 2010; Hudson et al., 2010; Jung, 2014). It may be possible in some institutions to implement one of the recommendations from Jung (2014), to "encourage practicum placements in schools with high enrolments of gifted students (e.g., academically selective schools) for at least a part of the requirements of preservice training programs, to allow for greater exposure to gifted students" (pp. 255–6).

Conclusion

This chapter sought to provide insights into the value of specifically covering giftedness in ITE courses to help prepare future teachers to understand the complexities associated with teaching gifted students. Although the data presented were from one case study in Victoria, Australia, the teacher experience varied across the campuses from metropolitan to regional locations, and it is likely that parallels can be drawn with other Australian states and possibly other countries. The extant literature supports a relationship between knowledge, attitudes, and practice; thus it is important that teachers enter the profession with knowledge relating to giftedness and gifted education that is evidence-based and with a concomitant positive attitude towards meeting the needs of this group of students.

The results from the study presented in this chapter demonstrated that pre-service teacher attitudes can be changed in a positive direction through the dedicated study of giftedness and gifted education that incorporates evidence-based readings, extensive opportunities for reflection on developing knowledge and understandings and practical applications of these understandings. While the wider research reiterated that there is room for other strategies to be incorporated into ITE programs— such as more formalised opportunities for field experience with gifted students and support for working with these students while on placement—it appears there is a clear argument that initial teacher education can play a valuable role in helping to prepare future teachers of the gifted.

Cross-References

▶ Differentiation of Instruction for Gifted Learners: Collated Evaluative Studies of Teacher Classroom Practices
▶ Educational Contexts, Transitions and Community Engagement: Part VI Introduction
▶ Gifted Education in the Asia-Pacific: From the Past for the Future – An Introduction
▶ Learning from International Research Informs Academic Acceleration in Australasia: A Case for Consistent Policy
▶ Some Implications for the Future of Gifted Education in the Asia-Pacific
▶ Teachers' Knowledge and Understandings of Twice Exceptionality Across Australia

References

Adams, C. M., & Pierce, R. l. (2004). Attitudes of American and English pre-service teachers toward gifted learners. *Gifted and Talented International, 19*(1), 15–23. https://doi.org/10.1080/15332276.2004.11673028

Allodi, M. W., & Rydelius, P. A. (2008). The needs of gifted children in context: A study of Swedish teachers' knowledge and attitudes. Paper presented at the ECHA, Conference, Prague, online. Retrieved from https://www.academia.edu/254805/The_needs_of_gifted_children_in_context_a_study_of_Swedish_teachers_knowledge_and_attitudes

Almulla, E. K., & Fateel, M. J. (2017). Pre-service teachers perceptions of gifted students. *Journal of Teaching and Education, 6*(2), 53–70.

Bain, S. K., Bliss, S. L., Choate, S. M., & Sager Brown, K. (2007). Serving children who are gifted: Perceptions of undergraduates planning to become teachers. *Journal for the Education of the Gifted, 30*(4), 450–478. Retrieved from https://files.eric.ed.gov/fulltext/EJ769921.pdf

Begin, J., & Gagné, F. (1994). Predictors of a general attitude toward gifted education. *Journal for the Education of the Gifted, 18*, 74–86. https://doi.org/10.1177/016235329401800106

Bergman, M. M. (1998). A theoretical note on the differences between attitudes, opinions, and values. *Swiss Political Science Review, 4*(2), 81–83. https://doi.org/10.1002/j.1662-6370.1998.tb00239.x

Berman, K. M., Schultz, R. A., & Weber, C. L. (2012). A lack of awareness and emphasis in preservice teacher training: Preconceived beliefs about the gifted and talented. *Gifted Child Today, 35*(1), 19–26. https://doi.org/10.1177/1076217511428307

Block, J. H., & Hazelip, K. (Eds.). (1995). *Teachers' beliefs and belief systems*. Oxford, UK: Pergamon.

Bohner, G., & Wänke, M. (2002). *Attitudes and attitude change*. East Sussex, UK: Psychology Press.

Brevik, L. M., Gunnulfsen, A. E., & Renzulli, J. S. (2017). Student teachers' practice and experience with differentiated instruction for students with higher learning potential. *Teaching and Teacher Education, 71*(2018), 34–45. https://doi.org/10.1016/j.tate.2017.12.003

Chamberlin, M. T., & Chamberlin, S. A. (2010). Enhancing preservice teacher development: Field experiences with gifted students. *Journal for the Education of the Gifted, 33*(3), 381–416. https://doi.org/10.1177/016235321003300305

Cramond, B., & Martin, C. E. (1987). Inservice and preservice teachers' attitudes toward the academically brilliant. *Gifted Child Quarterly, 31*, 15–19. https://doi.org/10.1177/0016962870310103

Creswell, J., & Plano Clark, V. (2011). *Designing and conducting mixed methods research* (2nd ed.). Thousand Oaks, CA: Sage Publications.

Darling-Hammond, L., Hyler, M. E., & Gardner, M. (2017). *Effective teacher professional development.* Palo Alto, CA: Learning Policy Institute. Retrieved from https://learningpoli cyinstitute.org/product/teacher-prof-dev

Denzin, N. K. & Lincoln, Y. S. (Eds.). (2005). Handbook of Qualitative Research (3rd Edition). Thousand Oaks, CA: Sage Publications.

Finlayson, D., & Cohen, L. (1967). The teacher's role: A comparative study of the conceptions of college education students and head teachers. *British Journal of Educational Psychology, 37,* 22–31. https://doi.org/10.1111/j.2044-8279.1967.tb01897.x

Fives, H., & Buehl, M. M. (2008). What do teachers believe? Developing a framework for examining beliefs about teachers' knowledge and ability. *Contemporary Educational Psychology, 33*(2), 134–176. https://doi.org/10.1016/j.cedpsych.2008.01.001

Fraser-Seeto, K. (2013). Pre-service teacher training in gifted and talented education: An Australian perspective. *Journal of Student Engagement: Education Matters, 3*(1), 29–38. Retrieved from http://ro.uow.edu.au/jseem/vol3/iss1/5

Fraser-Seeto, K., Howard, S. J., & Woodcock, S. (2013). Preparation for teaching gifted students: An updated investigation into university offerings in New South Wales. *Australasian Journal of Gifted Education, 22*(2), 45–51. Retrieved from http://citeseerx.ist.psu.edu/viewdoc/download? doi=10.1.1.905.465&rep=rep1&type=pdf

Fraser-Seeto, K. T., Howard, S. J., & Woodcock, S. (2015). An investigation of teachers' awareness and willingness to engage with a self-directed professional development package on gifted and talented education. *Australian Journal of Teacher Education, 40*(1). https://doi.org/10.14221/ ajte.2015v40n1.1

Gagné, F. (1991). *Brief presentation of Gagné and Nadeau's attitude scale: Opinions about the gifted and their education.* Unpublished manuscript. University of Québec, Montreal: Canada.

Gagné, F., & Nadeau, L. (1985). Dimensions of attitudes towards giftedness. In A. H. Roldan (Ed.), *Gifted and talented children, youth, and adults: Their social perspective and culture* (pp. 148–170). Monroe, NJ: Trillium.

Geake, J. G., & Gross, M. U. M. (2008). Teachers' negative affect toward academically gifted students: An evolutionary psychological study. *Gifted Child Quarterly, 52,* 217–231. https://doi. org/10.1177/0016986208319704

Goddard, C., & Evans, D. (2018). Primary pre-service teachers' attitudes towards inclusion across the training years. *Australian Journal of Teacher Education, 43*(6), 122–142. http://dx.doi.org/ 10.14221/ajte.2018v43n6.8

Hudson, P., Hudson, S., Lewis, K., & Watters, J. J. (2010). Embedding gifted education in preservice teacher education: A collaborative school-university approach. *Australasian Journal of Gifted Education, 19*(2), 5–15.

Jung, J. Y. (2014). Predictors of attitudes to gifted programs/provisions: Evidence from preservice educators. *Gifted Child Quarterly, 58*(4), 247–258. http://dx.doi.org/10.1177/0016986214547636

Kagan, D. M. (1992). Implications of research on teacher belief. *Educational Psychologist, 27,* 65–90. https://doi.org/10.1207/s15326985ep2701_6

Krijan, I. P., & Borić, E. (2015). Teachers' attitudes towards gifted students and differences in attitudes regarding the years of teaching. *Croatian Journal of Education, 17*(1), 165–178. https://doi.org/10.15516/cje.v17i0.1490

Kronborg, L. (2018a). Gifted education in Australia and New Zealand. In S. Pfeiffer (Ed.-in-Chief), *APA handbook of giftedness and talent* (pp. 85–96). Washington, DC: American Psychological Association.

Kronborg, L. (2018b). Cultivating teachers to work with gifted students. In J. L. Jolly & J. M. Jarvis (Eds.), *Exploring gifted education: Australian and New Zealand perspectives* (pp. 83–94). Abingdon, Oxon: Routledge.

Kronborg, L., & Plunkett, M. (2012). Examining teacher attitudes and perceptions of competencies required in a new selective high school. *Australasian Journal of Gifted Education, 21*(2), 33–46.

Laine, S., & Tirri, K. (2016). How Finnish elementary school teachers meet the needs of their gifted students. *High Ability Studies, 27,* 149–164. https://doi.org/10.1080/13598139.2015.1108185

Lassig, C. (2003). *Teachers' attitudes towards intellectually gifted children and their education* (Masters' thesis, Griffith University, Queensland, Australia). Retrieved from http://eprints.qut.edu.au/14473/

Lassig, C. J. (2009). Teachers' attitudes towards the gifted: The importance of professional development and school culture. *Australasian Journal of Gifted Education, 18*(2), 32–42. https://doi.org/10.21505/ajge.2015.0012

Lincoln, Y. S., & Guba, E. G. (1985). Naturalistic Inquiry. Newbury Park, CA: Sage Publications.

Lortie, D. C. (1975). *School teacher.* Chicago, IL: University of Chicago Press.

McCoach, B., & Siegle, D. (2007). What predicts teachers' attitudes towards the gifted? *Gifted Child Quarterly, 51*, 246–255. https://doi.org/10.1177/0016986207302719

Mills, C. J. (2003). Characteristics of effective teachers of gifted students: Teacher background and personality styles of students. *Gifted Child Quarterly, 47*(4), 272–281. Retrieved from http://www.gifted.gr/documents/useful-documents/Effective_teacher.pdf

Nunnally, J. C. (1978). Psychometric theory (2nd ed.). New York: McGraw-Hill.

Oppenheim, A. N. (1992). *Questionnaire design, interviewing, and attitude measurement.* New York, NY: Pinter.

Parliament of the Commonwealth of Australia. (1988). *Report of the select committee on the education of the gifted and talented children.* Canberra, ACT: Australian Government Publishing Services.

Parliament of the Commonwealth of Australia. (2001). *The education of gifted children.* Retrieved from https://www.aph.gov.au/Parliamentary_Business/Committees/Senate/Education_Employment_and_Workplace_Relations/Completed_inquiries/1999-02/gifted/report/contents

Patton, M. (1990). Qualitative evaluation and research methods. Thousand Oaks, CA: Sage Publications.

Plunkett, M. (2000). Educating teachers to meet the needs of the gifted: An option or a necessity? *TalentEd, 18*(1), 9–16.

Plunkett, M. (2002). Impacting on teacher attitudes toward gifted students. In W. Vialle & J. Geake (Eds.), *The gifted enigma: A collection of articles.* Melbourne, Australia: Hawker Brownlow Education.

Plunkett, M., & Kronborg, L. (2011). Learning to be a teacher of the gifted: The importance of examining opinions and challenging misconceptions. *Gifted and Talented International, 26*(1/2), 31–46. https://doi.org/10.1080/15332276.2011.11673587

Polyzopoulou, K., Kokaridas, D., Patsiaouras, A., & Gari, A. (2014). Teachers' perceptions toward education of gifted children in Greek educational settings. *Journal of Physical Education and Sport, 14*(2), 211–221. https://doi.org/10.7752/jpes.2014.02033

Ross, E. W. (1988). Becoming a teacher: The development of preservice teacher perspective. *Action in Teacher Education, 10*, 101–109. https://doi.org/10.1080/01626620.1988.10519395

Rowley, J. L. (2012). Professional development needs of teachers to identify and cater for gifted students. *Australasian Journal of Gifted Education, 21*(2), 75–80. Retrieved from https://search.informit.com.au/documentSummary;dn=098757303683336;res=IELHSS

Smith, W., & Chan, L. K. S. (1996). Attitudes of secondary school teachers towards education of the gifted. *Australasian Journal of Gifted Education, 5*(2), 26–33. https://doi.org/10.21505/ajge.2015.0012

Stern, C., & Keislar, E. (1975). *Teacher attitude and attitude change; Vol.: Summary and analysis of recent research.* Washington, DC: National Institute of Education.

Szymanski, A., Croft, L., & Godor, B. (2018). Determining attitudes toward ability: A new tool for new understanding. *Journal of Advanced Academics, 29*(1), 29–55. https://doi.org/10.1177/1932202X17738989

Tabachnick, B. G., & Zeichner, K. M. (1984). The impact of the student teaching experience on the development of teacher perspectives. *Journal of Teacher Education, 35*, 28–36. https://doi.org/10.1177/002248718403500608

Troxclair, D. A. (2013). Preservice teacher attitudes towards giftedness. *Roeper Review, 35*(1), 58–64. https://doi.org/10.1080/02783193.2013.740603

VanTassel-Baska, J. (1997). Excellence as a standard for all education. *Roeper Review, 20*(1), 9–12. https://doi.org/10.1080/02783199709553843

Vialle, W. (2012). The role of school counsellors in fostering giftedness: The Australian experience. In A. Ziegler, C. Fischer, H. Stoeger, & M. Reutlinger (Eds.), *Gifted education as a life-long challenge* (pp. 265–278). Berlin, Germany: LIT-Verlag.

Victorian Parliamentary Education and Training Committee. (2012). *Parliamentary inquiry into the education of gifted and talented students. Parliamentary paper.* Melbourne, Australia: Victorian Government Printer.

Vreys, C., Ndungbogun, G. N., Kieboom, T., & Venderickx, K. (2018). Training effects on Belgian preschool and primary school teachers' attitudes towards the best practices for gifted children. *High Ability Studies, 29*(1), 3–22. https://doi.org/10.1080/13598139.2017.1312295

Walsh, R. L., & Jolly, J. L. (2018). Gifted education in the Australian context. *Gifted Child Today, 41*(2), 81–88. https://doi.org/10.1177/1076217517750702

Watts, G. (2006). Teacher attitudes to the acceleration of the gifted: A case study from New Zealand gifted and talented. *Journal of the National Association for Gifted Children, 10*(1), 11–19.

Yin, R. (2003). *Case study research: Design and methods* (3rd ed.). Thousand Oaks, CA: Sage.

Margaret Plunkett, PhD, is an Associate Professor who works in th School of Education at Federation University, Australia. Margaret has developed and taught courses in gifted education and has won a number of national teaching awards including the Pearson/ATEA Teacher Educator of the Year (2012) and an Australian Office of Learning and Teaching Citation (2014). Her research interests include giftedness, rural and alternative education, and teacher professional learning. Margaret is an elected Australian delegate on the World Council for Gifted and Talented Children, Associate Editor of the *Australasian Journal of Gifted Education* and on the Editorial Board of *Gifted and Talented International.*

Leonie Kronborg, PhD, is a Senior Lecturer and Coordinator of Gifted Education in post graduate and pre-service studies in the Faculty of Education, Monash University, Australia. Her research interests include teacher education, talent development, giftedness and gender. Leonie is a past president of the Australian Association for the Education of Gifted Children. Dr Kronborg is Vice President of the World Council for Gifted and Talented Children, Co-Editor of *Gifted and Talented International* and on the Editorial Boards of *Gifted Child Quarterly, Journal for Advanced Academics*, and the *Australasian Journal of Gifted Education.* Leonie gained the Dean's Award for Teaching Excellence in 2012 and the Monash University Vice-Chancellor's Award for Teaching Excellence in 2013.

Australian Teachers Who Made a Difference: Secondary Gifted Student Perceptions of Teaching and Teacher Effectiveness

63

Karen B. Rogers

Contents

Abstract

In this chapter, gifted students' perspectives of teacher effectiveness will be explored and supported by a case study of 900+ Australian selective school students. The intellectual, personal, and professional traits most described by gifted students of their 'most effective' and their 'least effective' teachers were identified using mixed methods survey research. These traits were later analysed to determine how to counsel teachers desiring to work in a selective school atmosphere. In some cases, these traits were something the teacher possessed naturally, but several were ones that could be supported with consistent professional development and learning within this school environment. The traits

K. B. Rogers (✉)
University of St. Thomas, Minneapolis, MN, USA
e-mail: KBROGERS@stthomas.edu

© Springer Nature Singapore Pte Ltd. 2021   1431
S. R. Smith (ed.), *Handbook of Giftedness and Talent Development in the Asia-Pacific*,
Springer International Handbooks of Education,
https://doi.org/10.1007/978-981-13-3041-4_68

identified also corresponded well with previous international research on teacher effectiveness and marked a distinctive difference from what might be regarded as teacher effectiveness for the general population of secondary learners. Some recommendations for future research and practice to further support gifted students will also be provided.

Keywords

Teaching effectiveness · Selective secondary schools · Giftedness · Intellectual teacher traits · Professional teaching traits · Personal teacher traits

The aims in this chapter are to:
1. Identify personal, intellectual, and professional teacher traits that are most effective in supporting the well-being and academic motivation of students with gifts and talents.
2. Make suggestions for the kind of professional learning that could be provided at the secondary level for teachers whose main responsibilities lie with 'bringing out the best' in gifted learners.
3. Recommend the kinds of teachers that might need 'counselling out' of working in selective school settings.
4. Describe the methodology of collecting data on selective school students in Australia or elsewhere in Australian, New Zealand, and Asian schools.
5. Recommend next steps in supporting gifted learners in selective school settings.

Introduction and Literature Review

Despite the current international trends toward ensuring that all students are meeting expectations set by national/international standards, the provision of foundational curricula, and consistent assessment of achievement outcomes, little is stated presently about the impact of instructional (i.e., teacher) quality upon student achievement (Chan, 2001; Cheung & Fai, 2011). In most cases, researchers have not consistently asked the students themselves, what is the most important thing if they are to learn what they are supposed to be learning (Bishop, 1968). Common sense and the literature tell us, moreover, that the quality of pedagogy plays a substantial role in bringing out the best in all students (Delisle, 1992; Zimmerman, 1991). Common sense and the literature would suggest that teachers can and do make a difference in the achievement of learners, and certainly retrospective studies of the 'Termites', that is Lewis Terman's 'Genetic Studies of Genius', the MacArthur Fellows and Australia's own Nobel Prize winners support this point, if only for those who possess gifts and talents.

In Lewis Terman's 9-volume *Genetic Studies of Genius*, 1,528 gifted learners were followed throughout their lives and surveyed at regular intervals about their success and failures and to what factors they attributed their personal outcomes. Among those with the highest rates of success professionally, both men and women, the impact of at least one teacher was mentioned in the adult retrospectives of these children who were identified in 1922 and followed by a team of researchers who continued long after Terman's death in 1956. In volumes 4–5, these 'Termites' used teacher descriptors such as motivating, enthusiastic, likely to make individual accommodations, supportive, as well as evidencing advanced intellectual capacity, a love for lifelong learning, and content expertise which were readily shared with these children while they were in school. For those who were less successful in higher education and careers, the negative influence of teachers from year 3 on were often recorded by the researchers as the reason for their lack of interest in school generally (Terman & Oden, 1947, 1968).

In the small amount of analysis conducted on the 'genius grant' recipients, also known as the MacArthur Fellows, the findings were summarised as the recipients being able to identify a mentor, family friend, or classroom teacher who guided them into the fields they ultimately combined in their own creative and notable ways (Hennessy, 2017). This formative book of insights on a large number of these recipients (the first 25 years of recipients) published by the MacArthur Foundation showed a strong pattern for these winners to attribute their development of a 'passion' to teachers or mentors in their own educational years. These educators modelled personal enthusiasm for a subject area as well as how to persist, be curious, and stay focused on learning all the foundations of this chosen field. Hennessy's recent analysis does little to recognise this first pattern, but focuses more on the personal characteristics that ultimately did lead to creative production in each of eight winners (of the over 1,000 winners since 1981) who have led or are leading nonprofit or for-profit organisations in education, technology, agriculture, disability advocacy, medicine, the environment, and music. It is implied that the persistence, the search for possible solutions to a problem or issue in their respective fields as well as the ultimate verification of solutions once found comes down to educational mentors who modelled openness, risk-taking, persistence, and resilience in the face of 'naysaying' and disbelief among their contemporaries.

In an exhibition observed by this author at the University of Technology at Sydney, several years ago, the 13 of Australia's 15 Nobel Laureates (not including the Australian contributions to the International Campaign to Abolish Nuclear Weapons Peace Prize in 2017) were displayed along with their backgrounds and their own words. A common theme among these 13 was that some time in their formative years, a teacher or mentor has evinced interest in the child's ability and helped to direct the child's learning to advanced levels not encountered in the regular school system. To corroborate this, the autobiographies of each of these Laureates were analysed. Specific mention of a primary teacher (n = 2), a secondary teacher (n = 3), or a university professor (n = 5) was found, indicating that the majority of this august group had 'found their path' with the guidance of a teacher/mentor along the way.

In general, it appears that teachers can make a 'difference', either positively or negatively in the areas of *academic success* (e.g., Cheung & Fai, 2011;

Nelson & Prindle, 1992; Stott & Hobden, 2016; Tirri, 2008; Whitlock & DuCette, 1989), *differentiating teaching or personalising learning for gifted students' needs* (e.g., Chandra Handa, 2019; Prior, 2011); *student contributions to designing and implementing accelerative programs* (e.g., Vialle, Ashton, Carlon, & Rankin, 2001); and *support for career/life direction* (Gentry, Peters, & Mann, 2007; Zimmerman, 1991), *psychological support* (e.g., Bishop, 1968; Siegle, Rubenstein, DaVia, & Mitchell, 2014), *social integration* (e.g., Heath, 1997; Hong, Greene, & Hartzell, 2011; Swanson, 2016) and as a *role model or exemplar* of what needs to be done if one is to become an 'effective' adult (e.g., Gentry, Steenbergen-Hu, & Choi, 2011; Seeley, 1979). Of note in this review of recent research, student sample sizes, when students have been asked to rate their teachers, are extremely small, and in most cases, the teacher characteristics and behaviours are reported by the teachers, rather than students (e.g., Chan, 2001; Cheung & Fai, 2011; Gentry et al., 2011; Houghton, 2014; VanTassel-Baska & Johnsen, 2007). This may beg the question about what, from the student perspective, makes for effective teaching?

If one reflects on one's own most and least effective teachers, the contrasts seem pretty much what we would expect: A teacher's attitudes toward giftedness and gifted learners substantially influences the pedagogy and quality of instruction provided to this population (Begin & Gagné, 1994). The best teachers, according to previous decades of research on teacher effectiveness with students with gifts and talents (Welsh, 2011): 'got out of the way' when content was already understood (Whitlock & Ducette, 1989); provided advanced access to content, concepts, and skills beyond age or year-level expectations when readiness was demonstrated (Nelson & Prindle, 1992); allowed ample individualisation and opportunities for independent learning (Vialle et al., 2001; Zimmerman, 1991); held high expectations for accomplishments and achievement (Landvogt, 2001; Vialle & Quigley, 2002); and were highly energetic and funny and absolutely loved to teach (Bernal, 1994; Chan, 2001). These teachers: did not raise their voices to anyone specific in class; did not pay more attention to 1–2 students and ignore the rest; did not spend a lot of classroom time 'managing' the administrative busy work of the job; did not give marks or grades that were undeserved; did *not* regularly go off on tangents; did not create 'projects' that involved longer periods of time but with little new learning occurring, did not act like the 'sage on the stage' in the classroom; *were* not disorganised; and likely did not teach repetitive whole group lessons when just a few students had not mastered specific skills yet (Vialle & Quigley, 2002). Attempts have, furthermore, been made in the past to identify the areas of competency a teacher must have, those that can be 'taught' (Roberts & Boggess, 2011), but in recent years, not much has been updated in this body of research (Roberts & Boggess, 2011; Rogers, 1989). The question, then, is *do the traits, the research and what our own retrospective experiences suggest still hold for teachers of gifted students today*? That was the purpose of this case study surveying one entire school of selective school students in one of the selective schools in the state of New South Wales that will be used as an exemplar.

Exemplar of One Entire School of Selective School Students: Method

Selective or partially selective schools in Australia are managed by the New South Wales Department of Education (NSW Department of Education, 2018a) and were created to cater for a range of gifted and talented students. For example, some selective schools are sports schools, while others are technology or creative arts based—that is, music or art—however, most are for academic achievers (NSW Department of Education, 2018b). "Selective high schools are unzoned so parents can apply regardless of where they live" (NSW Department of Education, 2018b, para. 2), and an entry test and internal committee assess whether a student can gain entry based on merit.

There is widespread research that supports gifted and talented students being grouped together for more effective learning (e.g., Rogers, 2002, 2007). Selective schools help gifted and talented students to learn by grouping them with other gifted and talented students, teaching them in specialised ways, and providing educational materials at the appropriate level (NSW Department of Education, 2018b, para. 2).

Opportunity Classes for Gifted and Talented Primary Students

These classes are situated within 76 Department of Education primary/elementary schools in NSW, Australia, and cater primarily to Years 5 and 6. They were created to support academically gifted students who need the opportunity to be grouped together with, learn with, and socialise with like-ability peers. Students in opportunity classes should be provided with learning and teaching that are specific to the unique academic and social needs of highly achieving gifted and talented students (NSW Department of Education, 2018b, para. 2). Parents apply when their eligible child is in Year/Grade 4, and this is for a two-year full-time placement for Year/Grade 5 and 6 that may or may not be in the primary school that the student is attending (NSW Department of Education, 2018c, para. 1–2). This background has been provided because it was expected that many of the responses this group of students provided would have been formed while they possibly were in opportunity classes.

Sample Selective School

In this exemplar, all selective school students, Years 7–12 in a highly ranked New South Wales selective school, were sampled on the same day and during the same hours of the day. Of the estimated 1,100 students in the school, the actual questionnaires were fully completed by 906 students, who provided their perspectives on the characteristics of teachers of the gifted in their schooling. The remainder were either absent on the day or did not wish to participate in the survey or did not fully complete the questionnaire itself. As indicated in Table 1, there was fairly representative

Table 1 Demographics of the participant sample

Year level	Number of females	Percentage of females	Number of males	Percentage of males	Total
7	57	38	90	62	147
8	60	37	99	63	159
9	56	34	107	66	163
10	57	39	88	61	145
11	65	41	92	59	157
12	59	44	75	56	134
Total	354	100	551	100	905[a]

[a]One student did not indicate year level or gender

participation at all year levels. Males outnumbered female participants in a 3:2 ratio, which reflected the overall population of this school.

Self-Reporting Questionnaire Used in This Study

The instrument was developed by the researcher and incorporated all research-based characteristics and behaviours of teachers mentioned in the gifted education literature (e.g., Bishop, 1968; Hong et al., 2011; Nelson & Prindle, 1992; Rogers, 2002; Whitlock & DuCette, 1989; Zimmerman, 1991) and described in the previous literature review and supported by the author's previous and extensive research (e.g., Rogers, 1989, 2002, 2007). The author may be contacted for a copy of the full questionnaire; only a part of the initial results are reported here.

Although the number of items was large and unwieldy, it was considered that, as a second goal of this study, the list might determine which characteristics would merit further study among other selective high schools. As such, the questionnaire contained 82 items clustered by the researcher as either teaching approaches/behaviours (e.g., compacts previously learned material), personal characteristics/behaviours (e.g., has sense of humor in line with the subject matter), or cognitive−/intelligence-related characteristics/behaviours (e.g., has strong subject matter expertise). Students were asked to rate on a 3-point Likert scale (3, very important; 2, important; 1, somewhat or not important) how important each item descriptor was. Additionally, they were asked to rate these same descriptors on a similar Likert scale as to how 'essential' each was to being an effective teacher. On the first page of the questionnaire, in additional to collecting demographic information on students, the students were asked to answer an open-ended question on what the characteristics were of the teacher they felt had been their 'most effective' (i.e., 'best') teacher and the circumstances that made that teacher the best or most effective. On the last page of this 6-page questionnaire, students were asked to describe the characteristics and circumstances that were of their 'least effective' teacher. In both questions students were cautioned not to identify teachers by name but just by behaviours and characteristics.

As this case study was a pilot for future solicitations of student perspectives on teachers, the instrument itself contained the listed characteristics that at least three of the following research studies reported. These seminal research studies included Bishop (1968), Heath (1997), Landvogt (2001), Nelson and Prindle (1992), Rogers (1989, 2002), and Zimmerman (1991).

Data Collection Procedure and Analyses

In 2007, the questionnaires were distributed in first period on a single morning at the school, under the supervision of the school front office. Packets with requisite numbers of questionnaires were provided to each classroom teacher with a protocol sheet attached to the front of the packet. As the questionnaires were completed, they were brought to the researcher on-site. Three classes were off campus that day. Those packets were mailed to the researcher within one week of the initial administration. The quantitative questionnaire data were then inputted into the Statistical Package for the Social Sciences (SPSS v.11) for analysis. It was found that 140 students did not complete the full questionnaire, made 'patterns' of their responses in a recognisably, predictive way or gave identical answers to a group of other students in the same classroom. These data were ultimately deleted from the spreadsheet when analyses were undertaken.

The quantitative data were analysed preliminarily using descriptives resulting in percentages, means, and standard deviations, while qualitative data were analysed through content analysis initially. While these analysis methods have limitations, for example, item-by-item quantitative analyses, means, standard deviations, or probability levels are not very helpful with the fine-grained survey statements, these preliminary analyses will lead to deeper exploratory and confirmatory factor analyses and correlations in the next phases of data analyses, which would make the data more accessible. Deeper analyses could inform future professional learning for teachers and teaching of gifted students in secondary selective schools (VanTassel-Baska & Johnsen, 2007).

Student Perceptions of Teacher Traits and Teaching Techniques: Quantitative Results and Discussion

General Demographic Information

Six hundred and ten students (67.3% of the sample) had formerly participated in opportunity classes or gifted programs before entering the selective school environment. Such participation would seem to indicate that the majority had experiences with teachers who were trying to cater for their giftedness. The students considered their best subject or favourite subject in school, which differed by gender for each year level. Table 2 displays these differences. Noted is that science was not ranked first by any of the subgroups and ranged from third place to eighth place. Ranked last consistently, however, as 'best' or 'favourite' subject were nonschool activities. In general, girls showed a greater variety in this respect, maintaining a better balance between mathematics and 'softer' studies than did boys. For the latter years of school, girls as well as boys were most likely to select mathematics as their favourite subject. Although this table may seem extraneous to the topic of this chapter, the patterns discerned may help to explain why a favourite subject could be attributed to what a student does 'best' in and/or how that subject has been taught.

Table 3 summarises the performance levels of this student sample. The mean mark across the entire group of 906 students was 83.88, with a standard deviation of 5.76, although the differences in marks were found for females and males by year level, the differences were insignificant. In general, females tended to get slightly higher marks overall than did males, but during Years 10–11, there was a slightly greater deviation in females' marks from the mean of their gender groups. Of note is that students were achieving at high levels regardless of gender or year, signifying, perhaps, that qualification for selective school participation was a valid process.

Tables 4 and 5 summarise students' perceptions of the effectiveness across all 82 behaviours and characteristics surveyed and interpret the degree of importance the students ascribed to this. As can be seen, there were 30 behaviours considered 'very important' by the group, of which 11 involved specific teaching approaches, 13 were about teacher personality and 6 dealt with the cognitive and intellectual traits of teachers. Among these 30, 12 differed from previous research on the general school population (Whitlock & DuCette, 1989), but agreed with previous research on gifted students' perceptions (Whitlock & DuCette, 1989). Of these 12, 3 were 'cognitive/intellectual, 5 were personality, and 4 were teaching behaviours'. In

Table 2 Differences in 'best' and 'favourite' subjects by year and gender

Year level	Female 'best' subject	Female 'favourite' subject	Male 'best' subject	Male 'favourite' subject
7	Maths (39%) English (35%)	Arts (21%) English (13%) Maths (13%)	Maths (46%) Sport (14%)	Sport (41%) WL (12%)
8	English (29%) WL (22%) Arts (17%)	Electives (22%) English (20%) Arts (20%)	SS (18%) Maths (17%) English (16%)	Sport (41%) SS (20%)
9	Arts (29%) maths (18%) English (16%)	Arts (32%) Sport (29%)	Maths (26%) English (19%)	Sport (24%) Electives (19%)
10	Maths (20%) WL (18%) Arts (18%)	Sport (26%) Electives (20%)	Maths (30%) English (21%)	Sport (26%) Electives (20%)
11	Maths (35%) English (28%)	Maths (16%) SS (16%)	Maths (38%) Electives (16%)	Maths (27%) Elective (17%)
12	English (30%) Maths (26%)	Maths (20%) English (20%)	Maths (46%) Electives (18%)	Maths (28%) Electives (25%)

SS social studies/history, WL world languages

Table 3 Student mean marks by year and gender

Year level	Female mean	Female SD	Male mean	Male SD
7	88.48	4.41	86.20	4.77
8	83.30	4.28	81.67	5.30
9	84.61	4.86	85.07	5.64
10	84.34	6.03	84.26	5.89
11	82.74	6.21	83.13	6.14
12	84.41	5.76	83.36	5.90

Table 4 Mean responses in 'very important' category

Item	Variable type	Mean	SD
Explains clearly	Teaching	2.70	0.51
Offers help when there are problems	Personal	2.70	0.52
Tries to make work interesting	Teaching	2.65	0.57
Defines new or unfamiliar terms	Teaching	2.63	0.53
Communicates effectively 'most of the time'[a]	Cognitive	2.62	0.53
Is friendly with students	Personal	2.61	0.56
Shows enthusiasm about subject 'taught'[a]	Teaching	2.58	0.56
Tries to do best in most situations	Personal	2.57	0.55
Creates a non-threatening learning environment	Teaching	2.57	0.61
Open-minded about people and ideas[a]	Personal	2.57	0.55
Levelheaded, patient, not easily upset[a]	Personal	2.56	0.55
In-depth knowledge of subject, expertise[a]	Cognitive	2.55	0.59
Covers content 'supposed', to cover[a]	Teaching	2.52	0.63
Admits own mistakes[a]	Personal	2.51	0.59
Appreciates individual differences among students[a]	Personal	2.50	0.60
Is accepting, nonjudgmental	Personal	2.50	0.58
Encourages student comments, questions[a]	Teaching	2.47	0.60
Well-organised	Teaching	2.47	0.63
Flexible in thinking, decision-making	Cognitive	2.47	0.56
Willing to work hard	Personal	2.46	0.59
Really likes students, relates positively	Personal	2.43	0.65
Explains in everyday language	Teaching	2.42	0.65
Really likes to teach	Teaching	2.41	0.65
Shows respect, personal interest in students[a]	Personal	2.41	0.62
Willing to spend extra time on planning teaching	Teaching	2.40	0.62
Interested in having students use their minds[a]	Cognitive	2.40	0.61
Understands what it means to teach	Cognitive	2.37	0.63
Praises students for good ideas, effort	Teaching	2.36	0.61
Sensitive to feelings, needs of students	Personal	2.35	0.64
Genuine interest in bright students[a]	Cognitive	2.34	0.62

[a]Indicates characteristics that *differ* from general literature on teacher effectiveness among the general population

Table 5 Mean responses for 'important' category

Item	Variable type	Mean	SD
Firm, but fair	Teaching	2.33	0.63
Encourages 'independence'[a]	Teaching	2.32	0.62
Challenges[a]	Cognitive	2.31	0.60
Keeps learning about subject[a]	Cognitive	2.30	0.67
Thinks creatively	Cognitive	2.30	0.65
Teaches in logical sequence	Teaching	2.29	0.71
Doesn't mind change	Personal	2.28	0.65
Self-confident	Personal	2.27	0.60
Smiles, laughs when teaching	Teaching	2.25	0.71
Repeats difficult ideas in different ways	Teaching	2.25	0.70
Is intelligent	Cognitive	2.24	0.67
Sees issues from different cultural perspectives	Cognitive	2.24	0.67
Asks high-level questions	Teaching	2.24	0.63
Provides activities according to student interests[a]	Teaching	2.23	0.69
Asks questions of the class as a whole	Teaching	2.23	0.64
Clearly indicates transitions to next topic	Teaching	2.23	0.67
Curious about learning more on the subject	Cognitive	2.21	0.66
Knows about a lot of things[a]	Cognitive	2.20	0.68
Values lifelong learning	Cognitive	2.20	0.71
Understands my need to feel I belong in class	Teaching	2.20	0.66
Understands how to challenge me	Teaching	2.19	0.58
Understands how I can feel secure in class	Teaching	2.18	0.67
Loves learning new things[a]	Cognitive	2.16	0.66
Speaks expressively	Teaching	2.16	0.68
Knows all students' names	Teaching	2.15	0.76
Tells jokes, humorous anecdotes	Teaching	2.15	0.74
Periodically summarises what has been learned	Teaching	2.12	0.62
Facilitates, rather than lectures[a]	Teaching	2.11	0.68
Voices expectations that I will succeed	Teaching	2.10	0.70
Uses headings to organise lessons	Teaching	2.10	0.69
Willing for contact outside of class	Teaching	2.09	0.75
Acts maturely with students and colleagues	Personal	2.08	0.71
Explains how topic fits into class, course	Teaching	2.04	0.70
Experiences in teaching students who are bright	Cognitive	2.04	0.72
Vivid imagination	Cognitive	2.01	0.75
Communicates importance of learning	Cognitive	1.98	0.73
Differentiates tasks for individual students[a]	Teaching	1.94	0.69
Differentiates questions asked of different students[a]	Teaching	1.93	0.66
Credits students with prior learning[a]	Teaching	1.91	0.72
Talks with students outside of class	Personal	1.91	0.71
Outlines lessons to be covered	Teaching	1.88	0.75
Is excited by motivated, bright learners[a]	Cognitive	1.88	0.70
Outside literary and cultural arts interests	Cognitive	1.88	0.75

(continued)

Table 5 (continued)

Item	Variable type	Mean	SD
Uses expressive gestures	Teaching	1.87	0.75
Has done gifted coursework[a]	Cognitive	1.86	0.74
Ensures no repetition of what is already mastered[a]	Teaching	1.83	0.76
Item	**Variable type**	**Mean**	**SD**
Gives overview of each lesson up front[a]	Teaching	1.75	0.69
Keeps fast presentation pace[a]	Teaching	1.71	0.67
Uses facial, arm gestures	Teaching	1.69	0.70

[a]Indicates characteristics that *differ* from general literature on teacher effectiveness among the general populations

summarising these differences, then, the gifted students tended to identify both specific teaching approaches and their teachers' cognitive characteristics as being of equal importance, with less emphasis placed on personality, unlike the preferences of students in mainstream schools, but they were more likely to rate the few personal characteristics they did select as 'very important'. Of interest, too, are the two characteristics they rated as 'unimportant' by the group as a whole: (a) moves about when teaching and (b) takes classes or courses in spare time. When means were compared among cognitive vs. personal vs. teaching approach, there was a significant difference in rating for personal characteristics ($M = 2.45$, $sd = 0.65$, 'very important') than for teaching approach ($M = 2.17$, $sd = 0.67$, 'important') and cognitive characteristics ($M = 2.19$, $sd = 0.66$, 'important'). In general, this same pattern has been found in previous research on general student populations (e.g., Shulman, 1986), but the individual characteristics that comprise these three categories differ substantially for the sample in this research.

A similar analysis was conducted about student ratings for how essential these behaviours and characteristics were in an effective teacher. The correlations conducted on the initial half of the data suggested a strong correlation ($r = 0.76$; $r_{teaching\ approach} = 0.76$; $r_{personality} = 0.79$; $r_{cognitive} = 0.72$); hence, these responses have not been reported further. Elimination of this distinction in future uses of the questionnaire is therefore recommended.

Across the sample, there were several significant ($p \leq 0.05$) gender-related differences in perceptions of what makes a teacher effective. These are summarised in Table 6. In general, girls tended to rate the mechanics of teaching more highly (e.g., *covers what is supposed to be covered*), while boys tended to perceive more about the person behind the teacher while in the act of teaching (e.g., *admits own mistakes or lack of knowledge*). Girls rated affective support strategies more favourably as well (e.g., *sensitive to feelings and needs of others*). Table 7 displays the actual differences girls and boys had regarding specific teacher behaviours, perhaps making the statistics of Table 6 a bit more comprehensible.

Tables 8 and 9 summarise the significant differences among different year levels of students in this study. Table 8 indicates the specific statistical differences among year-level perceptions, while Table 9 shows the general patterns of perceptions per

Table 6 Mean gender-related differences in teacher perceptions

Perception	Girls' mean	Girls' SD	Boys' mean	Boys' SD	P value
Very important ratings differences					
Explains concepts, ideas, procedures clearly	2.80	0.42	2.63	0.55	0.0001
Makes work interesting	2.74	0.49	2.60	0.61	0.0001
Offers to help students with problems	2.74	0.49	2.67	0.53	0.04
Defines new, unfamiliar terms	2.68	0.49	2.59	0.56	0.01
Open-minded about ideas, people	2.67	0.49	2.50	0.58	0.0001
Non-threatening learning environment	2.64	0.55	2.52	0.64	0.004
Covers content that is supposed to be covered	2.63	0.57	2.44	0.66	0.0001
Appreciates differences in students	2.62	0.54	2.42	0.62	0.0001
Accepting, nonjudgmental	2.60	0.53	2.44	0.61	0.0001
Willing to and does work hard at teaching	2.53	0.56	2.42	0.61	0.007
Willing to devote extra time, effort to teaching	2.47	0.57	2.36	0.65	0.01
Admits to mistakes or when does not know	2.45	0.55	2.54	0.61	0.0001
Sensitive to feelings, needs of others	2.45	0.60	2.28	0.65	0.0001
Firm, but fair	2.42	0.58	2.27	0.65	0.0001
Defines new, unfamiliar terms	2.35	0.67	2.19	0.73	0.001
Important ratings differences					
Sees issues from variety of cultural perspectives	2.33	0.20	2.19	0.70	0.002
Clearly indicates transitions to the next topic	2.29	0.67	2.18	0.67	0.02
Understands what I need to feel secure in class	2.28	0.63	2.12	0.69	0.0001
Uses headings to organise lessons	2.20	0.69	2.04	0.68	0.001
Facilitates learning	2.19	0.65	**2.52**	0.64	0.009
Differs activities according to individual interests	2.16	0.67	**2.28**	0.70	0.01
Knows a lot about a lot of things	2.11	0.66	**2.26**	0.69	0.001
Communicates importance of learning	2.06	0.71	1.93	0.73	0.01
Tells jokes or humorous anecdotes	2.03	0.72	**2.23**	0.75	0.0001
Has vivid imagination	1.94	0.73	**2.06**	0.76	0.02
Gives credit for prior learning	1.83	0.70	**1.96**	0.74	0.007
Has cultural, literary, arts interests outside of school	1.81	0.72	**1.92**	0.77	0.03
Ensures no one repeats what is already known	1.74	0.71	**1.90**	0.78	0.002
Not important ratings differences					
Keeps fast pace when presenting content	1.60	0.64	**1.79**	0.68	0.03
Takes courses in spare time	1.44	0.61	**1.58**	0.70	0.002

Boldfaced means indicate boys significantly higher on perception than girls

Table 7 Gender differences in teacher perceptions

Girls' higher ratings	Boys' higher ratings
Understands my need to feel safe in class	Tells jokes, anecdotes in class
Sees issues from different perspectives	Admits own mistakes, lack of knowledge
Firm, but fair	Vivid imagination
Sensitive to feelings, needs of others	Explains concepts clearly
Accepting, nonjudgmental	Keeps fast presentation pace
Smiles, laughs when teaching	Ensures no repetition of what already known
Defines new, unfamiliar terms	Gives credit for prior learning
Uses headings to organise lessons	Differentiates activities according to abilities
Clearly indicates transitions	Has outside literary, arts interests
Offers help to students with problems	Takes classes, courses on own time
Facilitates rather than lectures	Is willing, does work hard at teaching well
Creates non-threatening environment	Knows about a lot of things
Makes work interesting	
Covers the content that is supposed to be covered	
Communicates the important of learning	
Willing to devote extra time, effort	
Open-minded about ideas, people	
Appreciates individual differences	

year level. As can be seen, there were three patterns of difference by year (or possibly, developmental level): (a) Years 7–9 felt more strongly about the importance of a teaching characteristic or behaviour; (b) Years 11–12 felt more strongly or less strongly about the importance of a behaviour; and (c) Year 7 students rated a trait more strongly than other year levels. In general, the younger students tended to focus on specific personality or cognitive characteristics and on affective support provided in their classrooms, while the latter year, students focused on teaching approaches almost entirely and viewed personal traits as relatively less important. The younger students varied in their perspective of being recognised as individuals by their teachers, being provided affective support by the teachers, as well as on what the teacher does outside of school.

In looking for significant gender-by-year-level differences in preferences and perceptions of teacher effectiveness, the means for each category (C, Cognitive, vs. P, Personal, vs. T, Teaching) were calculated across all items in the questionnaire. As can be seen in Table 10, personality traits were rated more strongly by all year levels and both genders; even with those, the number of personal traits selected as 'very important' were considerably fewer in number than for cognitive and teaching behaviours. This might suggest that 'effective' teachers are judged first on their genuine liking and respect for and friendliness toward gifted students, their nonjudgmental and open-minded stance when dealing with gifted students, and their levelheadedness/patience. There were no significant gender-by-year interactions.

Table 8 Year-related differences in perceptions of teacher effectiveness

Perception	7–9 mean	7–9 SD	10–12 mean	10–12 SD	Year 7 mean	Year 7 SD	P value
Understands need to feel safe in class	2.25	0.58	2.14*	0.55	2.27	0.54	0.0001
Understands need to belong in class	2.30*	0.63	1.99	0.61	2.48*	0.52	0.0001
Tells jokes, anecdotes in class	2.22*	0.72	2.07*	0.70	2.32*	0.71	0.0001
Acts maturely with students, teachers	2.20	0.69	2.07*	0.70	2.24	0.68	0.004
Sensitive to student feelings, needs	2.49	0.57	2.20*	0.65	2.46	0.58	0.0001
Relates well to students, likes them	2.50	0.61	2.30*	0.68	2.61	0.59	0.0001
Gets excited when has bright students	1.89	0.69	1.79	0.64	2.01*	0.71	0.01
Has vivid imagination	2.15	0.74	1.80*	0.75	2.23	0.72	0.0001
Shows respect for students	2.50	0.59	2.30*	0.62	2.56	0.57	0.001
Is friendly with students	2.68	0.51	2.50*	0.58	2.70	0.53	0.004
Self-confident	2.25	0.58	2.22	0.56	2.38*	0.58	0.006
Praises students for good ideas, effort	2.42*	0.59	2.26	0.63	2.52*	0.58	0.0001
Knows names of all students	2.17	0.76	2.15	0.75	2.38*	0.70	0.0001
Differentiates tasks by ability	2.13	0.66	1.83*	0.68	2.26	0.61	0.0001
Smiles, laughs when teaching	2.35	0.72	2.13*	0.70	2.43	0.65	0.0001
Uses facial expressions in class	1.99	0.76	1.70*	0.70	2.05	0.75	0.0001
Speaks expressively	2.20	0.68	2.04*	0.68	2.29	0.66	0.02
Asks questions of whole class	2.30	0.65	2.14*	0.64	2.35	0.61	0.01
Explains subject in everyday language	2.50*	0.61	2.18	0.68	2.35	0.56	0.0001
Outlines lesson to be covered	1.88	0.73	1.80	0.73	2.08*	0.71	0.006
Explains how topic fits in course	1.91	0.71	2.30*	0.65	2.03	0.71	0.0001
Follows logical sequence in lessons	2.20	0.70	2.46*	0.69	2.20	0.68	0.001
Gives preliminary overview	1.85	0.71	1.64*	0.69	1.88	0.65	0.007
Clearly makes transitions to next topic	2.20	0.70	2.30	0.64	2.04*	0.72	0.02

(continued)

Table 8 (continued)

Perception	7–9 mean	7–9 SD	10–12 mean	10–12 SD	Year 7 mean	Year 7 SD	P value
Moves around while teaching	1.70	0.76	1.47	0.66	1.98*	0.70	0.0001
Moves among students while teaching	1.80*	0.72	1.47	0.66	1.98*	0.70	0.0001
Encourages comments and questions	2.55	0.58	2.40*	0.64	2.52	0.62	0.03
Fast presentation pace	1.75	0.70	1.52*	0.64	0.88	0.68	0.0001
Ensures lack of repetition	1.85*	0.78	1.62	0.65	2.04*	0.74	0.0001
Credit for prior learning	1.99	0.78	1.71*	0.64	2.10	0.72	0.0001
Willing for contact outside of class	2.00	0.78	2.29*	0.65	2.09	0.75	0.001
Differentiates according to student interests	2.38*	0.62	2.02	0.66	2.50*	0.59	0.0001
Encourages student independence	2.45*	0.58	2.21	0.62	2.50*	0.59	0.0001
Facilitates, not lectures	2.20	0.73	1.98*	0.68	2.23	0.62	0.004
Non-threatening learning environment	2.70	0.50	2.38*	0.72	2.74	0.49	0.0001
Voices high expectations for success	2.25*	0.65	1.89	0.66	2.35*	0.65	0.0001
Makes work interesting	2.72	0.52	2.61*	0.59	2.71	0.47	0.01
Covers content supposed to cover	2.42	0.65	2.77*	0.46	2.34	0.65	0.0001
Expresses the importance of learning	2.07*	0.71	1.82	0.72	2.26*	0.72	0.0001
Likes to teach bright students	2.52	0.63	2.30*	0.63	2.53	0.64	0.01
Lots of experience as a teacher	2.08	0.77	1.90	0.69	2.26*	0.70	0.0001
In-depth knowledge of subject	2.48	0.63	2.63*	0.48	2.44	0.65	0.04
Outside literary, arts, cultural interests	1.87	0.71	1.77	0.71	2.14*	0.76	0.001
Values lifelong learning	2.30	0.72	2.10*	0.73	2.34	0.66	0.005
Loves learning something new	2.20*	0.64	1.99	0.63	2.34*	0.66	0.0001
Thinks creatively	2.40	0.61	2.06*	0.66	2.44	0.63	0.0001
Flexible in thinking	2.53	0.53	2.36*	0.55	2.48	0.57	0.001
Has taken gifted courses	1.81	0.72	1.75	0.71	2.11*	0.76	0.0001
Knows about a lot of different things	2.25*	0.67	2.01	0.67	2.36*	0.69	0.0001
Doesn't mind making changes	2.35*	0.65	2.18	0.61	2.23*	0.69	0.001

$*p \leq 0.05$

Table 9 Summary of significant perception differences by school level ('younger' 7–9 vs. 'older' 10–12)

Younger > older	Older > younger	Year 7 > Years 8–12
Understands what I need to feel safe	Willing to have contact outside of class	Self-confident
Understands what I need to belong in class	Covers what is 'supposed' to be covered	Knows names of all students in class
Tells, jokes, anecdotes I understand	Has in-depth knowledge, subject expertise	Voices expectations for student success
Sensitive to feelings, needs of others	Acts maturely with students, colleagues	Stresses importance of learning
Really likes students	Outlines lesson to be covered	Has lots of experience teaching bright kids
Vivid imagination	Explains how topic fits into course	Has outside literary, arts, cultural interests
Shows respect, personal interest in kids	Follows logical sequence in lessons	Has taken gifted courses
Is friendly with students	Gives preliminary overview of topic	Moves about when teaching
Praises students for good effort, ideas		Expresses importance of learning
Differentiates tasks by ability		Makes transitions to next topic
Smiles, laughs when teaching		
Uses facial gestures in class		
Speaks expressively		
Asks questions of class as a whole		
Explains in everyday language		
Moves among students while teaching		
Little repetition of previous learning		
Encourages questions, comments		
Keeps fast presentation pace		
Gives credit for prior learning		
Encourages student independence		
Well-organised when presenting lessons		
Provides different tasks by interest		
Values lifelong learning		
Really likes to teach		
Facilitates, not lectures		
Creates non-threatening environment		

(continued)

Table 9 (continued)

Younger > older	Older > younger	Year 7 > Years 8–12
Tries to make work interesting		
Thinks creatively		
Flexible in thinking, decision-making		
Knows a lot about a lot of things		
Does not mind when things change		

Table 10 Gender by year mean perceptions

Year X gender	Cognitive M	Cognitive SD	Personal M	Personal SD	Teaching M	Teaching SD
Year 7 females	2.27	0.59	2.52*	0.51	2.26	0.62
Year 7 males	2.30	0.59	2.51*	0.51	2.26	0.62
Year 8 females	2.25	0.63	2.51*	0.50	2.28	0.67
Year 8 males	2.20	0.64	2.49*	0.54	2.16	0.68
Year 9 females	2.15	0.63	2.49*	0.53	2.16	0.67
Year 9 males	2.18	0.65	2.43*	0.58	2.17	0.71
Year 10 females	2.21	0.64	2.47*	0.52	2.18	0.68
Year 10 males	2.21	0.64	2.39*	0.59	2.09	0.68
Year 11 females	2.09	0.65	2.46*	0.53	2.14	0.69
Year 11 males	2.12	0.63	2.35*	0.56	2.09	0.67
Year 12 females	2.11	0.60	2.41*	0.52	2.14	0.66
Year 12 males	2.13	0.65	2.42*	0.56	2.09	0.68

M mean, *SD* standard deviation
*$p \leq 0.05$

Qualitative Results

The open-ended questions enabled students to describe the circumstances surrounding what made an effective teacher and what makes a teacher less effective. The students were quite verbal in this and very emphatic in stating their opinions. In general, the content analysis of remarks, usually resulting in specific descriptors or short phrases, showed remarkable consistency in themes from trait to trait and from behaviour to behaviour. Krippendorff's (2004) and Neuendof's (2011) methodologies of word frequencies and keyword in context were applied in aggregating these responses into themes. Because the questionnaire asked students to just use a word or phrase to describe their best and least effective teachers, no memorable sentences or descriptions were found that represented the open-ended descriptors as a whole. It would be recommended that perhaps future researchers would make this a part of this replicable questionnaire. Due to the length of it, students were not asked to write

Table 11 Content analysis of effective vs. ineffective teacher qualities

Effective teacher descriptors ($N = 600$)	Ineffective teacher descriptors ($N = 202$)
Kind, caring, friendly ($n = 116$)	Cannot teach, is disorganised ($n = 107$)
Funny, sense of humor ($n = 112$)	Can't be understood, does not stay on topic, poor language ($n = 85$)
Personal relationship with, interest in students ($n = 79$)	Is easily annoyed, unstable, impatient ($n = 77$)
Makes learning fun, motivating, gives learning choices ($n = 64$)	Violent, aggressive, unfriendly, mean ($n = 71$)
Enthusiastic about learning ($n = 38$)	Is racist, biased, sexist, prejudiced ($n = 65$)
Clear explanations, organised presentations ($n = 33$)	Is ignorant, stupid, doesn't know subject ($n = 63$)
Respectful of students ($n = 31$)	No enthusiasm for subject, teaching, is boring ($n = 61$)
Calm, patient ($n = 23$)	Very/overly strict, unfair ($n = 60$)
Clever, smart ($n = 22$)	Distances self from, picks on students, abuses power ($n = 59$)
Approachable ($n = 22$)	Does not like students, plays favourites, holds grudges ($n = 58$)
Easy going ($n = 21$)	Stubborn, inflexible, one-sided arguments ($n = 56$)
Challenges students ($n = 19$)	Easily angered, screams and yells ($n = 50$)
Teaches well ($n = 17$)	Wastes time in class, tangents, doesn't cover content well ($n = 40$)
Likes to teach, is engaging as teacher ($n = 15$)	Repeats self, no enjoyment in learning, teaches from text ($n = 34$)
Firm, but fair ($n = 14$)	Does not want to be here, not interested in subject ($n = 30$)

a paragraph or such for this survey. Table 11 delineates the parallel themes that emerged from the students' descriptors. As can be seen, students were more likely to describe how *not* to be an effective teacher with very clear-cut patterns, rather than how to be one. Interestingly, the personal characteristics were more likely to be mentioned of the effective teacher (e.g., funny, caring, approachable, easygoing) and the ineffective teachers as well (e.g., unfriendly, mean, biased, unstable, angry). Cognitive abilities of the teacher were more likely to be mentioned of the effective teacher, while inappropriate teaching strategies or approaches were more likely to be mentioned of the less effective teachers. The numbers next to each descriptor in the table indicate how many students mentioned the descriptor.

Conclusions and Discussion: Implications for Research and Practice

Although further studies of students who participate in selective high schools need to be conducted before generalisations of the response patterns found in this one school can be made, there were a few enduring understandings that correspond well with previous gifted literature on student perceptions of their most effective teachers. It is interesting that this topic that endured through the late 1970s through to the 1990s has not been as well researched in recent years. Perhaps it is the focus on what teachers teach and the assessment results they achieve that has hindered further studies of what students see as important in their teachers.

1. The personal traits of an 'effective' teacher carry more weight with gifted students even though they are less frequently mentioned as 'very important'. This pattern seems to change to more of a focus on a teacher's approach to teaching as students move beyond Years 7 and 8. To some extent, the inclination toward personal traits corresponds in part to both somewhat recent and fairly dated research for which comparisons have been made between gifted and regular students (e.g., Hong et al., 2011; Whitlock & DuCette, 1989).

2. Secondary students in this study felt they knew the difference between effective and ineffective teaching, both quantitatively and qualitatively. Clarity of explanations, provision of challenge, design of motivating and interest-provoking experiences discriminated the effective teacher from the ineffective one according to the perceptions of students in this study. This pattern corresponds with James Delisle's work from 1992 to the present (e.g., Delisle, 1992; Galbraith & Delisle, 2015).

3. The cognitive capabilities of the effective teacher were important, especially among the younger secondary students in this study: that a teacher knew his/her subject well, knew how to teach, was experienced as a teacher, could use language well, had an outside 'life' to teaching and recognised the individuality of abilities and interests and programmed for them were appreciated. To some extent this meshes with the previous work of several researchers mentioned in the literature review section of this chapter (e.g., Vialle et al., 2001; Zimmerman, 1991).

4. There were distinct differences between girls and boys in this study in what was perceived as an effective teacher. The girls tended to identify more strongly with the teachers' personal traits along with correct teaching behaviours than did the boys. The boys tended to think more highly of the teacher when he or she had a life outside of the classroom and was a more well-rounded human being. At this point in time, gender preference has not been directly researched, but will be a way to pursue this pattern of gender difference in future studies.

5. Although the entire sample did not choose to respond to the two qualitative questions about their most and least effective teachers, if one looks at the percentages among students who did respond, especially to their negative learning 'experiences', there is a need to look at teachers currently teaching in selective school environments to determine if the experiences described by this sample are more generalisable to other selective school environments. Too many students in this study had been subjected to teachers who did not treat them well or with respect as well as who could not 'teach' them effectively. This begs the question of what professional development is needed and will be effective in supporting teachers who work in the Australian selective school environment with students who are bright, motivated, and truly can learn more than they are being offered at present.

One further table may elucidate what this study suggests about what will be most supportive of preparing teachers in selective schools to ensure their students receive the most effective teachers possible. As Table 12 shows when parsing out the behaviours students were asked about, those behaviours that 'came naturally' to teachers are probably not ones we can expect to change in teachers once they are in a classroom and confronted with the day-to-day challenges in front of them. The best

Table 12 Teacher effectiveness strategy categorisation by previous experience and background

Behaviour	Natural cannot be taught	Is response to actual context and experiences	Is response through specific, strategic PD or preservice experiences
Covering the material supposed to be covered			X
Eliminating excess drill and review		X	
Compacting		X	
Adjusting instructional pace		X	
Providing immediate corrective feedback			X
Providing whole concept first, then break it down		X	
Making individual accommodations for some learners		X	
Organised and clear presentations	X		
Seeing gifted learner as unique individual	X		
Genuinely liking able students	X		
Patience and equanimity	X		
Sense of humor in line with the subject	X		
Enthusiasm for subject	X		
No overt biases with gender, race	X		
Trusting students to make good learning choices		X	
Expertise in specific academic area and ability to go deeply into that area			X
Self-directed in own learning	X		
High degree of intelligence	X		
Facilitator of learning		X	
Recognition of importance of intellectual development	X		
Highly developed teaching skill and knowledge			X
Using learning preferences to determine instructional strategies		X	

that can be done is to encourage teachers who apply to the selective schools to consider whether or not they have these character traits to a degree they feel confident they can work productively with students in these settings. In the second category, the responses to the actual learning context in which students have already mastered aspects of the subject or need to learn at a faster pace, that is, the gifted course training behaviours stressed in programs throughout Australian and Asian universities within such programs, are ones that can be reinforced through on-site professional learning and monitoring. The third column, that is, teachers who employ these strategies due to their preservice training, may suggest that a quick review of these approaches be considered for professional learning, especially when a teacher is newly recruited to the selective school system. Hence, just as it is important for educators to differentiate for gifted students within the selective schools, it will be equally important to consider the background and experiences recruited teachers will have when they come into this setting as well as how long they have been out there using or not using these strategies.

Based on these findings, administrators and educators in selective school environments might wish to consider the following recommendations for professional learning/development, hiring practices, and further study of the school population:

1. Select teachers with a very strong, deep background in their subject area, and do not allow them to teach in a content area that is not their major emphasis or area of passion. Certainly the research of Zimmerman (1991), Seeley (1979), and Heath (1997) support this recommendation.
2. Provide subject-area professional learning to update current subject knowledge levels. The professional literature in education as a whole iterates this theme consistently (e.g., Rogers, 1989, 2007; VanTassel-Baska & Johnsen, 2007).
3. Encourage teachers who do not love teaching to consider another occupation (or at least teaching at another school).
4. Provide professional learning 'reviews' to all teachers on appropriate class management techniques—not inappropriate ones such as arbitrary rules, behaviour modification, and management techniques, disrespect, unwillingness to engage with students and a dislike for gifted students. The work of Hong, Greene, and Hartell (2011), as well as the research of Whitlock and DuCette (1989), supports this recommendation in their comparisons of both teachers of regular students and of high-ability students.
5. Explore the issues of racism and sexism as they might exist in various selective school settings. This recommendation is based upon the open-ended responses a large number of the selective students surveyed in this study mentioned. Whether or not this is a growing issue in selective school participation needs to be uncovered.
6. Administer the questionnaire on a regular basis among different year levels of students in the selective school setting to ensure that professional development is being implemented by teachers and 'appreciated' or recognised by their students. A copy of this instrument can be obtained from the researcher.

Last Words

It is hoped that using this study as a way of getting at gifted students' perceptions of effective teachers does not make readers feel they must throw up their hands and 'chuck it all in'. More research needs to take place that takes students' perceptions of their educational setting and context into account, using a mixed methods approach. The work of Coleman, Micko, and Cross (2015) may lead the way for researchers to focus their work on student perceptions (or voice) regarding their teachers. The work of these researchers represents 25 years of research they have undertaken by observing and interviewing students in the school context, for the purpose of understanding their needs, their social and emotional behaviour, and their motivation to learn. The focus, unfortunately has not been on their teachers so much as the school setting and culture of learning. The model, however, taken up by this research team is one way the research represented here could be either replicated or expanded. It is unfortunate that this study and its fairly comprehensive questionnaire have not been used in previous or in current research studies. Instead, the questionnaire represented the latest, albeit somewhat dated, research on behaviours and characteristics gleaned from multiple studies. Hence, what was being asked of students had not been comprehensively asked in previous research, making it difficult to connect with most research out there on this topic on a final compendium of teacher characteristics. It is hoped that other researchers interested in this population, as well as researchers interested in the student population as a whole, will consider using this questionnaire so that comparisons can ultimately be made. This study was conducted in 2007, and no replications of it have taken place since that time. It is hoped that by reporting this previously unreported study now, other researchers will take this up and perhaps collaborate in studying whether or not perceptions have changed in the intervening years. It is suspected that things have not changed, but an update is due. The words of James Delisle may, it is hoped, provide comfort for those administrators and educators who try to take on all that is suggested here about teacher effectiveness with gifted students:

> It's a daunting task, being an educator, bearing the responsibility for shaping both the academics and attitudes of students. Accountability, as defined in today's schools, often measures the easy stuff: the math facts memorized, the commas placed correctly, the historical events sequenced. But the true measure of an educator's teaching performance is not so readily determined. No computer scanned bubble sheet measures how our students feel about learning, or their biases toward self and others. These indexes, the true value of learning and education, elude detection and measurement, sometimes for years...So brave educators wishing to enhance both students' self-concepts and their achievement must be content with not knowing the immediate or long-term impacts of their actions. (Delisle, 1992, p. 49–50)

Cross-References

▶ Attuned Pedagogy: The Artistry of Differentiated Instruction from a Taiwanese Cultural Perspective

▶ Australian Teachers Who Made a Difference: Secondary Gifted Student Perceptions of Teaching and Teacher Effectiveness

▶ A Model for Growing Teacher Talent Scouts: Decreasing Underrepresentation of Gifted Students

▶ Differentiation of Instruction for Gifted Learners: Collated Evaluative Studies of Teacher Classroom Practices

▶ Educational Contexts, Transitions and Community Engagement: Part VI Introduction

▶ Engaging Gifted Students in Solving Real Problems Creatively: Implementing the Real Engagement in Active Problem-Solving (REAPS) Teaching/Learning Model in Australasian and Pacific Rim Contexts

▶ Gifted Education in the Asia-Pacific: From the Past for the Future – An Introduction

▶ How Do Teachers Meet the Academic Needs of High-Ability Students in Science?

▶ Put Them Together and See How They Learn! Ability Grouping and Acceleration Effects on the Self-Esteem of Academically Gifted High School Students

▶ Self-Regulated Learning for High-Ability and High-Achieving Students in Mixed-Ability Classrooms Throughout the Asia-Pacific

▶ Some Implications for the Future of Gifted Education in the Asia-Pacific

▶ Teaching Gifted Education to Pre-service Teachers: Lessons Learned

▶ Teachers' Knowledge and Understandings of Twice Exceptionality Across Australia

References

Begin, J., & Gagné, F. (1994). Predictors of attitudes toward gifted education: A review of the literature and a blueprint for future research. *Journal for the Education of the Gifted, 17*, 161–179. https://doi.org/10.1177/016235329401700206

Bernal, E. M. (1994). *Finding and cultivating minority gifted/talent students.* ERIC Document Resource Report # ED391345. Washington, DC.

Bishop, W. E. (1968). Successful teachers of the gifted. *Exceptional Children, 34*, 317–325. https://doi.org/10.1177/001440296803400502

Chan, D. W. (2001). Characteristics and competencies of teachers of gifted learners: The Hong Kong teacher perspective. *Roeper Review, 23*, 32–41. https://doi.org/10.1080/13598130120084348

Chandra Handa, M. (2019). Leading differentiated learning for the gifted. *Roeper Review, 41*, 102–118. https://doi.org/10.1080/02783193.2019.1585213

Cheung, H. Y., & Fai, S. K. (2011). Competencies and characteristics for teaching gifted students: A comparative study of Beijing and Hong Kong teachers. *Gifted Child Quarterly, 55*, 139–148. https://doi.org/10.1177/0016986210397832

Coleman, L. J., Micko, K. J., & Cross, T. L. (2015). Twenty-five years of research on the lived experience of being gifted in school: Capturing the students' voices. *Journal for the Education of the Gifted, 38*(4), 358–376. https://doi.org/10.1177/0162353215607322

Delisle, J. R. (1992). *Guiding the social and emotional development of gifted youth. A practical guide for educators and counselors.* New York, NY: Longman.

Galbraith, J., & Delisle, J. (2015). *When gifted kids don't have all the answers.* Minneapolis, MN: Free Spirit Publishing.

Gentry, M., Peters, S., & Mann, R. (2007). Differences between general and talented students' perceptions of their career and technical education experiences compared to their traditional high school experiences. *Journal of Advanced Academics, 18*, 372–401. https://doi.org/10.4219/jaa-2007-496

Gentry, M., Steenbergen-Hu, S., & Choi, B.-Y. (2011). Student-identified exemplary teachers: Insights from talented teachers. *Gifted Child Quarterly, 55*, 111–125. https://doi.org/10.1177/0016986210397830

Heath, W. J. (1997). *What are the most effective characteristics of teachers of the gifted?* Unpublished document. Washington, DC: Educational Resources in Education (ERIC Document # ED411665).

Hennessy, L. (2017). *Activating creativity: Insights and wisdom of the MacArthur fellows.* Morrisville, NC: Lulu Press, Inc.

Hong, E., Greene, M., & Hartzell, S. (2011). Cognitive and motivational characteristics of elementary teachers in general education and in gifted programs. *Gifted Child Quarterly, 55*, 201–264. https://doi.org/10.1177/0016986211418107

Houghton, C. (2014). Capturing the pupil voice of secondary gifted and talented students who had attended an enrichment programme in their infant school. *Gifted Education International, 30*(1), 33–46. https://doi.org/10.1177/0261429413480421. gei.sagepub.com.

Krippendorff, K. (2004). *Content analysis: An introduction to its methodology* (2nd ed.). Thousand Oaks, CA: Sage.

Landvogt, J. (2001). The teaching life. *The Australian Journal of Teacher Education, 22*(2). https://doi.org/10.14221/afte.1997v22n2.4

Nelson, K. C., & Prindle, N. (1992). Gifted teacher competencies: Ratings of rural principals and teachers compared. *Journal for the Education of the Gifted, 15*, 357–369. https://doi.org/10.1177/016235329201500405

Neuendorf, K. A. (2011). *The content analysis guidebook.* Thousand Oaks, CA: Sage.

NSW Department of Education. (2018a). *Selective high schools and opportunity classes.* Retrieved from https://education.nsw.gov.au/public-schools/selective-high-schools-and-opportunity-classes/general-information

NSW Department of Education. (2018b). *Selective high schools and opportunity classes: What are selective schools?* Retrieved from https://education.nsw.gov.au/public-schools/selective-high-schools-and-opportunity-classes/year-7/what-are-selective-high-schools

NSW Department of Education. (2018c). *Selective high schools and opportunity classes: What are opportunity classes?* Retrieved from https://education.nsw.gov.au/public-schools/selective-high-schools-and-opportunity-classes/year-5/what-are-opportunity-classes

Prior, S. (2011). Student voice: What do students who are intellectually gifted say they experience and need in the inclusive classroom? *Gifted and Talented International, 26*(1–2), 121–129. Retrieved from https://doi.org/10.1080/15332276.2011.11673596

Roberts, J. L., & Boggess, J. R. (2011). *Teacher's survival guide: Gifted education.* Waco, TX: Prufrock Press.

Rogers, K. B. (1989). Training teachers of the gifted: What do they need to know? *Roeper Review, 11*, 145–151. https://doi.org/10.1080/02783198909553191

Rogers, K. B. (2002). Grouping the gifted and talented: Questions and answers. *Roeper Review, 16*(1), *24*(3), 103–107. https://doi.org/10.1080/02783190209554140

Rogers, K. B. (2007). Lessons learned about educating the gifted and talented: A synthesis of the research on educational practice. *Gifted Child Quarterly, 51*(4), 382–396. https://doi.org/10.1177/0016986207306324

Seeley, K. R. (1979). Competencies for teachers of gifted and talented children. *Journal for the Education of the Gifted, 3*, 7–13. https://doi.org/10.1177/01623532900300103

Shulman, L. S. (1986). Those who understand: Knowledge and growth in teaching. *Educational Researcher, 15*(2), 4–14. https://doi.org/10.3102/0013189X015002004

Siegle, D., Rubenstein, L., DaVia, L., & Mitchell, M. S. (2014). Honor students' perceptions of their high school experiences: The influence of teachers on student motivation. *Gifted Child Quarterly, 58*, 35–50. https://doi.org/10.1177/0016986213513496

Stott, A., & Hobden, P. A. (2016). Effective learning: A case study of the learning strategies used by a gifted high achiever in learning science. *Gifted Child Quarterly, 60*, 63–74. https://doi.org/10.1177/0016986215611961

Swanson, J. D. (2016). Drawing upon lessons learned: Effective curriculum and instruction for culturally and linguistically diverse gifted children. *Gifted Child Quarterly, 60*, 172–191. https://doi.org/10.1177/0016986216642016

Terman, L. M., & Oden, M. H. (Eds.). (1947). *The gifted child grows up: Twenty-five years' follow-up of a superior group* (Vol. Volume IV). Stanford, CA: Stanford University Press.

Terman, L. M., & Oden, M. H. (Eds.). (1968). *The fulfillment of promise: 40–year follow-up of the Terman gifted group* (Vol. Volume V). Stanford, CA: Stanford University Press.

Tirri, K. (2008). Who should teach gifted students? *Revista Espanola de Pedagogia, 240*, 315–324.

VanTassel-Baska, J., & Johnsen, S. K. (2007). Teacher education standards for the field of gifted education: A vision of coherence for personnel preparation in the 21st century. *Gifted Child Quarterly, 51*, 182–205.

Vialle, W., Ashton, T., Carlon, G., & Rankin, F. (2001). Acceleration: A coat of many colours. *Roeper Review, 24*(1), 14–19. https://doi.org/10.1080/02783190109554119

Vialle, W., & Quigley, S. (2002). *Selective students' views of the essential characteristics of effective teachers*. Brisbane, Australia: Association for active educational researchers' conference.

Welsh, M. (2011). Measuring Teacher Effectiveness in Gifted Education: Some Challenges and Suggestions. *Journal of Advanced Academics, 22*(5), 750–770. https://doi.org/10.1177/1932202X11424882

Whitlock, M. S., & DuCette, J. P. (1989). Outstanding and average teachers of the gifted: A comparative study. *Gifted Child Quarterly, 33*, 15–21. https://doi.org/10.1177/001698628903300103

Zimmerman, E. (1991). Rembrandt to Rembrandt: A case study of a memorable painting teacher of artistically talent 13–16 year-old students. *Roeper Review, 13*, 76–84. https://doi.org/10.1080/02783199109553315

Karen B. Rogers, PhD, is a Professor Emerita of Gifted Studies in the Special Education and Gifted Education Department at the College of Education, Leadership, and Counselling, University of St. Thomas in Minneapolis, Minnesota, USA. She is a Professorial Fellow at the University of Wollongong and an Honorary Professor at the University of New South Wales in Australia. Her lifelong passion for serving the needs of high potential learners has seen her associated with many prestigious organisations, including terms as President of The Association for the Gifted, Council for Exceptional Students (USA) and a role on the Board of Directors for the National Association for Gifted Children (USA). Currently she is also an advisor for the US Department of State Overseas Schools Committee and a 'Critical Friend' for both the Sydney and Newcastle-Maitland Archdioceses in Australia. Professor Rogers has engaged extensively in both research and research syntheses in a variety of areas in gifted education. She has expertise in gifted program development, evaluation, cognitive processing, creativity, and twice-exceptional education. She is a prolific author in the field and reviews manuscripts for all the major journals in gifted education (USA and Australia) and recently received the prestigious NAGC 2015 Distinguished Scholar Award.

Conclusion

Some Implications for the Future of Gifted Education in the Asia-Pacific

64

Susen R. Smith

Contents

S. R. Smith (✉)
GERRIC, School of Education, The University of New South Wales, Sydney, NSW, Australia
e-mail: Susen.smith@unsw.edu.au

© Crown 2021
S. R. Smith (ed.), *Handbook of Giftedness and Talent Development in the Asia-Pacific*,
Springer International Handbooks of Education,
https://doi.org/10.1007/978-981-13-3041-4_69

Abstract

In this handbook, innumerable achievements, issues, and concerns were considered about researching gifted education and educating gifted and talented students in the Asia-Pacific and rim nations. Not including the introductory and the concluding chapters, 62 chapters were divided amongst the six parts of the handbook, ranging from 8 to 13 chapters to a section. This large corpus of chapters makes for a diverse range of ideas, theories, discourse, research, content, and practical applications to nurture the talent development of gifted children, youth, and adults and support families, educators, researchers, mentors, and advocates. A number of issues and associated implications evolved from these six sections and some of these will be reiterated in this chapter. It is hoped that reading the chapters in this handbook will encourage even more scholarly reflection, interdisciplinary research, collaborative action, and some new directions to support talent development both within this region and beyond.

Keywords

Implications of teaching and learning · Research for gifted students · Talent development

Introduction

For the first time, researchers and educators from around all the Asia-Pacific and rim nations were invited to express their views and collaboratively report their research, discourse, and practice in a handbook. A comprehensive manuscript evolved from this invitation and innumerable issues and perspectives unique to the research and practice in these nations were raised, that both reiterated and built upon the international literature in the field. So, what are the implications that derived from the authors' submissions in this handbook from around the Asia-Pacific and rim nations? The authors in this handbook raised too many issues and implications to mention every one of them here. Hence, only some are summarised in the following, with some links made between foci and across countries and chapters.

Key Issues and Implications

As a field, some aims are to progress:
- From fragmented research and practice to collaborative multidisciplinary research and practice.
- From theoretical models to effective research and practice for talent development.
- Towards closing the gap between theoretical models and practical implementation.
- From underachievement and underrepresentation to talent development for diversity.

- From cognitive testing to spotting potential.
- From Eurocentric, Americentric, or Ethnocentric views to cultural sensitivity inclusive of Indigenous views.
- From conformity and meritocracy to creativity and innovation.
- Towards frameworks to support creativity development.
- From social and emotional characteristics to social and emotional learning.
- From curriculum models to research-based pedagogy models in practice.
- From differentiation or personalisation or attuned pedagogy?
- From exclusion to teaching developmentally and inclusively.
- Towards special education, gifted education, or talent development within general education?
- From an isolated field to multidisciplinary research and community collaboration.
- From career expectations to career choices.
- From misconceptions to positive attitudes and contextually supporting talent development.

From Fragmented Research and Practice to Collaborative Multidisciplinary Research and Practice

If there is one similarity across all of the Asia-Pacific countries, research that underscores effective gifted education practice is thriving due to the commitment of dedicated researchers, educators, families, mentors, and advocates (e.g., VanTassel-Baska & Brown, 2015). Unfortunately, another similarity is that research, programming, and provisions for gifted students are fragmented, inconsistent, and supported in waves of agreement and unsupported in troughs of disagreement. Fortunately, with this fragmentation, there are strengths in some areas of research and practice but, unfortunately, weaknesses in others, resulting in the disconnect between theory, research, and practice.

This fragmentation is reflected in the Asia-Pacific, as it is in other parts of the world (e.g., Ambrose, VanTassel-Baska, Coleman, & Cross, 2010; Lo & Porath, 2017). For example, the issue that many of the participants in gifted education research are biased convenience samples of *high achieving gifted* students was raised as a clear concern by authors in this handbook. These research samples can exclude certain gifted populations, such as those who are underachieving or underrepresented, as they are rarely identified as gifted or are usually excluded from classes or programs in which the convenience samples are selected. In her chapter in this handbook, Ballam (2021) suggests that research needs to be authentically reflected upon to alleviate self-bias and be contextually based and planned around the specific participants involved.

The international call continues for more rigorous empirical research with larger datasets and diverse participants across different contexts, with control groups from the general student population or similar selective schools, and these issues are very relevant in the Asia-Pacific context as well (e.g., Plucker & Callahan, 2014; VanTassel-Baska & Brown, 2015). It remains to be seen, however, if such large-scale investigations are possible, considering the huge amount of funds and resources required to complete such research projects.

Additionally, according to egalitarianism and the *inclusion* ideology, the gifted population is considered advantaged, special provisions can be considered elitist, and they are not viewed as a population *in need*. Hence, the type of research investigations totally focused on gifted education does not attract much funding in our part of the world. However, funding may eventuate if funding agents are sympathetic to the disadvantage that many gifted students can actually experience, such as indigeneity, twice-exceptionality, or low socio-economic background.

In the wider research, Ambrose (2015) has found that his work has benefitted from seeking answers from other disciplines. He raised a valuable issue, in that more consideration can be given to cross-disciplinary and interdisciplinary research and practice or the multidisciplinary approach where experts within different disciplines contribute to the one study. This multidisciplinary approach may encourage more collaboration between researchers and the wider community and enable collaborators to tap into additional and unique expertise, resources, and infrastructure across disciplines. Such collaborations can also reduce the research load, that is, use the research that's already been undertaken in other disciplines or other fields and see what models, pedagogies, or strategies can be applied in gifted education. Indeed, McCluskey (2017) suggests that rather than continue to delve into the perplexity of already answered questions in the field that may or may not continue to contribute to the quicksand of an isolated field, with little respect from the wider education community, there is the need to search for new answers to new issues within the current technological and cultural contexts. The call for a paradigm shift in the field to encompass this multidisciplinary approach going forward is echoed in this handbook and elsewhere (e.g., Lo & Porath, 2017; Plucker & Callahan, 2014; Wallace, Sisk, & Senior, 2018). Some ideas presented in this handbook may contribute to that endeavour.

From Theoretical Models to Effective Research and Practice for Talent Development

In this handbook, three models on the conceptions of giftedness and talent were represented by experts in the field. One model, the *DMGT*, came from a Canadian scholar (Gagné, 2013, 2021) and is used mainly in Australia, Canada, and the USA, another is from the USA, the *Megamodel of Talent Development* (Olszewski-Kubilius et al., 2021) which is used mainly in the USA, the third is from Germany/Asia, being the *Actiotope Model* (Phillipson & Ziegler, 2021), and is used more widely. This in itself presents a biased perspective towards the Americentric/Eurocentric views evident in these models that echo other models in the wider research. While Australasian perspectives were considered during the creation of one of the models and cross-cultural perspectives of the implementation of the megamodel was sought, Olszewski-Kubilius et al. (2021) reflected:

all the respondents emphasised the importance of broadening the model to include socio-cultural factors that influence talent development, including the socio-political context, values, and beliefs. These concerns challenge us to think more deeply about the utility of the megamodel and how to assist educators in translating the megamodel for practice in different national contexts.

Indeed, all the authors of all the current models can pursue this goal, especially in our context, as neither the South American perspectives nor the Indigenous sensitivities appeared to have had any specific representation in any of the conceptual models. South America, like elsewhere, experiences difficulties with researching, identifying, and educating gifted students (Wechsler, Muglia, Blumen, & Bendelman, 2018). Hence, more reflection and multicountry research on the implementation of the conceptual models derived from specific Asia-Pacific and rim countries' sociocultural perspectives are warranted.

Towards Closing the Gap Between Theoretical Models and Practical Implementation

There are still concerns that there is a huge gap between the theoretical models and the implementation of them within practice, for example, Gagné's DMGT in the Australian context (Bannister-Tyrrell, 2017; Gagné, 2013, 2021). Additionally, there are other models that have only emerging research to support their implementation in the Asia-Pacific, but are widely used in practice (e.g., Gardner's, 1999, *Multiple Intelligences*, though this is a conceptual framework of *intelligence* rather than of *giftedness*). Then there are other models again that have an impressive array of supportive research, but have not been applied much in the Asia-Pacific (e.g., Sternberg's *Triarchic Theory of Giftedness,* Sternberg, 1986) with little link with the sociocultural contexts within which they are attempting implementation, while there are some with a more sound research base that have been applied within the Asia-Pacific context (e.g., Renzulli's *Three Ring Conception of Giftedness,* Renzulli, 2005). There are benefits and concerns about each of the models (as there are of all models), but there are also beneficial similarities and differences between these models. So, these models can benefit from evaluation and exploration to determine the gaps within the models, but also the gaps in application of the models in relation to the sociocultural context to help lessen the gaps within practice.

From Underachievement and Underrepresentation to Talent Development for Diversity

Worldwide, the '*uns*' are prevalent in gifted education: *un*identified, *un*derachievement, *un*developed talent, *un*derserved, or *un*derrepresented in talent programs are widely acknowledged in the literature (e.g., Plucker & Callahan, 2014). Authors in this handbook also reiterated these concerns. For example, Korean and USA colleagues Cho, Mandracchia, and Yang (2021) and Peters et al. (2021) reinforced the concerns regarding underrepresentation of minorities in gifted education programs. Models, frameworks, and pedagogy for talent development are beneficial, but unless all student populations are considered, then the lofty ideals imparted in these pedagogical models can be marginalised. Furthermore, Peters et al. (2021) highlighted the hidden gifted, underachievers, and the underserved in the USA and implored that it is incumbent on the field to overcome underrepresentation by improving identification of and programming for previously invisible Asian-Pacific gifted students.

Swanson, Russell, and Anderson (2021), also from the USA, offer the *Talent Development Academy* (TDA) school-wide model as: a foundation for classroom teachers peer collaborating to model and differentiate the curriculum and instruction; provide noncognitive and neuroscience strategies; and use culturally sensitive teaching for identifying "and developing the talent in high-ability students from underrepresented, culturally, or linguistically diverse groups". Like Burns and Martin (2021), they embedded growth-orientation within teacher practice to support the growth of the academic potential of diverse learners (Swanson et al., 2021). These authors promote educating gifted students within the general school population with opportunities for acceleration, enrichment, and other strategies that support talent development. Greater equity to allow more underserved diversely gifted populations to partake more in enrichment gifted education programs is still being called for in the wider literature (e.g., McCluskey, Treffinger, Baker, & Wiebe, 2016).

Again from the USA, in Delisle's and Schultz' (2021) handbook chapter, they argued for the collaboration between significant others in a gifted underachiever student's life and called for interventions that cultivate underachievers' sense of self, integrity, and dignity for academic success to ensue. They portend the six A's of *A*utonomy, *A*ccess, *A*dvocacy, *A*lternatives, *A*spirations, and *A*pproachable educators, all of which resonate many ideals we aim for in educating all our children generally, but can be aims to support gifted underachievers more specifically.

From Cognitive Testing to Spotting Potential

The limitations of identification based solely on intelligence and cognitive testing are well researched (e.g., Phillipson & Phillipson, 2016). Alternative forms of assessment to identify underrepresented students were explored in this handbook. For example, in Australia, Munro (2021) suggested that concept mapping could be used as a form of identification—especially for gifted underachievers—enabling some discernment between students who are gifted in one domain or across several domains. "These tools can be used across the multiple domains and modified to match the learning profiles of particular cohorts. They have implications for formative assessment and the differentiation of pedagogy and curriculum." There has been controversy regarding the use of nominations in identification processes, with the nomination of high achievers rather than high-ability students. This may be a result of the bias of contributors to this process, heavy reliance on teacher-only nominations, lack of training on using nominations, and inappropriate nomination forms, all contributing to underrepresentation of minority groups (McBee, Peters, & Miller, 2016). Additionally, there have been calls for more research on different forms of nominations that would be most appropriate in the Asian-Pacific context. For example, in Zavala-Berbena and De la Torre García's (2021) handbook chapter, they suggested that a "self-nomination inventory may be a useful instrument to support the identification process of [Mexican] gifted and talented students". They linked the value of future research for educators to understanding the reasons students nominate or do not nominate, and the connection between the use of self-nominations with variables, such as the nominee's self-esteem and self-efficacy.

Curriculum Models inclusive of identification processes were also represented in the handbook. For example, Callahan and Azano (2021) presented the empirically validated *CLEAR* curriculum model and *Project PLACE* in their handbook chapter, with the focus on *spotting* potential within context rather than labouring on the limitations of out-of-reach resources for supporting diversely different gifted students. These authors also suggested an alternative identification process for rural schools embedded in place-based learning. Swanson and her colleagues (2021) also offered hope of a useful approach to identification of underachievers in the talent spotting process, within the *Talent Development Academy* model. Likewise, following Maker's DISCOVER (Maker & Schiever, 2010) and the *Real Engagement in Active Problem Solving* (REAPS) models allows gifted students to be *spotted* while undertaking creative problem-solving tasks (Maker & Wearne, 2021).

From Eurocentric, Americentric, or Ethnocentric Views to Cultural Sensitivity Inclusive of Indigenous Views

Sociocultural links and comparisons were evident throughout the handbook. For example, Park and Kim (2021) examined the concept of wisdom from the Korean cultural perspective, while Walton and Vialle (2021) discussed spirituality from the Australian view. Furthermore, from the Taiwanese perspective, Albanese, Yu, and Wu (2021) explored the differences between eastern and western views in their chapter and indicated the need for socioculturally informed understandings of gifted and talented education, educational philosophies, and research methodologies in Confucian-influenced societies. They reiterated that education is the foundation of creative responses to current and future concerns about society and the environment, stating that:

> Scholars, practitioners, and policymakers are indeed working hard to adapt to changing global and local challenges and opportunities. In Taiwan, rising socioeconomic inequality makes the need to reach diverse learners all the more imperative. Efforts to move away from exam-based achievement in traditional academic areas as primary criteria for the identification of ability and to open pathways to success and further development of gifts and talents must still reckon with meritocracy. As we argue in this chapter, policy intentions and the realities of practice are not yet, nor may they ever be, fully aligned. We offer an exploration of Taiwan as an example of how the engagement of educational reforms and initiatives with local sociocultural conditions is a crucial component of the outcomes of those efforts.

Furthermore, Lupkowski-Shoplik, Assouline, Wienkes, and Easter (2021) reinforced the importance of policy development, which is inclusive of the holistic needs of gifted students to span the gap between research and practice. Such effective policy can encourage the use of acceleration and other programming options that are more culturally relevant for highly able students.

There was also a focus on Indigenous peoples in the handbook, a student population that has been considered disadvantaged (McCluskey et al., 2016). For example, in her New Zealand chapter, Webber (2021) elaborated family, educators, and community collaboration. This is uppermost when all can nurture the gifted child "to ensure that they are aware of their mana tangata—their unique leadership potential, collective belonging, cultural connectedness, embedded achievement, and responsibilities to others". Steeped in a culturally-based model, Webber highlighted the plight of gifted Māori students and reinforced the importance of "connectedness to their racial-ethnic identity and their sense of *mana* (pride, status, and esteem)" for the development of their academic engagement and social-emotional well-being. To engage gifted students and their parents, researchers can respect cultural achievements and understandings by grounding studies in "Māori realities, knowledge, and epistemologies".

Then there's the recognition of the need to collaborate with multiple caregivers and significant others within specific cultural communities to achieve success for gifted Australian Indigenous students (Garvis, Windsor, & Pendergast, 2021). Like Webber (2021), these authors recommended building on current successes within the Aboriginal cultures. Specifically, these authors provided five steps towards acknowledging cultural understandings of Indigenous peoples and using pedagogies that are: culturally responsive, wonder-based, generative, place-based, and prioritise engaging gifted Indigenous students.

Interdisciplinary collaborations have been encouraged in the wider literature (e.g., Ambrose, 2015; McCluskey, 2018). However, care can be taken to avoid ethnocentric approaches by the well-meaning who provide support to the so-called disadvantaged based on the researcher or educator's own cultural beliefs, rather than respecting culture and taking guidance from those within the sociocultural context of the research or practice (McCluskey, 2018). For example, Townend, Hay, Jung, and Smith (2021) also reviewed the literature on Indigenous gifted students in Australia, but within a specific rural context. They aligned with Garvis et al. (2021), in that culturally responsive curriculum is needed to support gifted Indigenous students, but they also contended that the rural context provides unique opportunities for founding research-based interventions and culturally sensitive research in situ. The authors felt that greater funding to support culturally relevant identification procedures—such as dynamic assessment—and fairer distribution of resources with flexible provisions can help enhance talent potential in Australian Indigenous gifted students. However, funding ebbs and flows according to the political decision-makers of the time and usually there is limited, if any, funding for gifted education programs or research, though Indigenous programs and research can attract more funding support (e.g., Bicknell & Riley, 2013).

In her chapter in this handbook, Blumen (2021) examined the "challenges of gifted education in Peru that underline the advocacy efforts towards the indigenous population facing socioeconomic inequity ... from a developmental and cross-cultural approach". She aligned with her Australasian counterparts above, that culturally sensitive provisions are required for the Indigenous population. Blumen also concluded that research was needed to explore differences between the conceptions of the highly gifted culturally diverse ethnic-linguistic groups with acceleration, advanced placement, and home schooling as future programming options.

From Conformity and Meritocracy to Creativity and Innovation

The influence of the prioritisation of conformity, standardisation, performativity, and meritocracy over creativity development looms large in education today, regardless of whether teaching gifted students or not. From China, Dai and Zhao (2021) raised credentialism, conformity for achievement, and institutionalised pathways to success as inhibitors of creativity. In Australia, Lassig (2021) indicated the value of understanding and nurturing highly creative students' creative intelligence and engagement in learning by teaching for creativity. Here, scaffolding student learning is of note. She encouraged teachers to understand their own creativity and the different levels of creativity as these may impact the identification of creativity in their own students. There are also calls for teacher educators to teach creatively for creativity to emerge and for the directive to teach for creativity currently already in policies and curricula documents to be translated into practice. Lassig further suggested that researching the promoters and inhibiters of creativity development in varying sociocultural contexts would be worthwhile progressing forward. It is encouraging that a recent USA study found that there was a large focus on developing creativity skills in pull-out classes for gifted students; however, this is a focus that can be applied in the general classroom too (Long et al., 2019).

A multicountry collaboration by Cramond et al. (2021) examined trends and challenges in creativity developed in selected Asian countries. Some of the recommendations from their handbook chapter included: the need for "systematic changes in education programs and policies" that include the trilogy of person-, process-, and product-focused creativity; nurturing characteristics, such as autonomy and creative thinking skills; as well as facilitating creative attitudes for creative outcomes.

Like Albanese et al. (2021), Dai and Zhao (2021) implored the need to be aware of the differences between east and western cultures' values regarding PISA results and the link with innovation. They contended that there is the need to "educate our bright and talented minds to be more adaptive and innovative [which] is the main challenge facing educators for the twenty-first century". This education requires cultural sensitivity and cultural change that encompasses teaching for creativity, creativity development, interest-based choices, self-exploration, and entrepreneurship for nonconventional talent development.

Towards Frameworks to Support Creativity Development

For creativity development, Higuchi, Saegusa, and Kim (2021) reported the consistent use of a teacher dual-support system to scaffold students' drawing and writing about innovations in journals within the *Idea-Marathon System* (IMS) in a university course in Japan. They believe that real innovations derive from this process if it is consistent over four months and provided some successful examples. They also believe that talented students can be identified through the IMS process, but further research is required to support their hypotheses.

South Korean views of scaffolding creativity for innovation using a research-based model, the *C*limates, Attitudes, and *T*hinking skills (CATs) model were elaborated by Kim and Lee (2021) in their chapter in this handbook. The authors contended scaffolding creativity development results in innovation and the focus should be on the *4S* attitudes and climates connected to the four seasons metaphorically that are: *S*torm-related expertise based on interests; *S*oil-related critical thinking; *S*un- and *S*pace-related climates and attitudes of problem-solving; and all 4S's are related to creating a new innovation.

From Social and Emotional Characteristics to Social and Emotional Learning

It is well known in the literature that catering for the holistic needs of the gifted nurtures their social-emotional needs as well (Gross, 2010; Smith, 2017). Social and emotional development requires going beyond identifying mere characteristics to scaffolding to enable students to learn new skills relevant to specific social contexts. Hence, *Social-Emotional Learning* (SEL) processes are needed to guide social-emotional development.

In the handbook, a number of issues and implications arose, which were contextually mediated. For example, Stoeger, Balestrini, and Steinbach (2021) explored cross-cultural aspects of *Self-Regulated Learning* (SRL) for gifted students in the Asia-Pacific and recommended more collaborative research on mixed-cultural general classroom students' "cognitive, metacognitive, and motivational components of SRL" and their achievements.

Furthermore, Overexcitabilities (OE) are "inextricably bound to human potential, which is integral to human development" said Canadian scholar, Mendaglio (2021). His message is that researchers need to use the full *Theory of Positive Disintegration* (TPD) in their research as questionnaires alone are inadequate for assessing OEs and giftedness, unless they are designed within mixed-method studies founded fully on Dabrowski's (1964) TPD.

In the wider literature, Kanevsky (2011, 2019) also reinforced the need for scaffolding student learning contextually and not assuming the gifted child already knows how to undertake a task productively without support. However, scaffolding is rarely associated with gifted learners as they are misconceived as advantaged and not needing much support (Smith, 2017). The issue of scaffolding was raised by a number of authors in this handbook and is particularly pertinent for SEL, as gifted students still require support for social-emotional development. For example, Cho et al. (2021) used the acronym RED to *R*ecognise strengths, efforts and improvement, *E*xpect High, and *D*ifferentiation in the Korean context. Teachers can scaffold instructions, provide flexible grouping, complex content, challenging tasks, and metacognition for supporting language skills and overall academic achievement of potentially talented Els so high motivation, autonomy, and risk-taking evolve. The importance of the teacher/student relationship is paramount for the success of teaching and learning in this context (Hertzog, 2017). As New Zealander Ballam (2021) said, being in minority ethnicities and in low socio-economic contexts can inhibit Indigenous students' resilience development. She emphasised that if resilience is to be developed and enhanced then there is the need for 'caring and supportive relationships' in developing the students' 'sense of identity'. Gómez-Arízaga and Conejeros-Solar (2021) also reinforced the need for "meaningful and constructive peer and teacher relationships with 2e students", the respect for diversity, acceptance of difference, and the focus on student strengths which can influence the quality of the classroom climate needed to support Chilean twice-exceptional students. More specifically, in Blackburn and Townend's (2021) handbook chapter, they also reiterated the need to provide twice-exceptional ASD girls with support, which raised the gender issue. Wood (2021) also studied Australian gifted girls, but in a rural context and found that Australian rural adolescent gifted girls need opportunities to explore their own giftedness in order for their potential talent to be developed, so connectedness to their rural environment for place-based talent development is encouraged, which is similar to Garvis et al.'s (2021) recommendation for placed-based pedagogy in Aboriginal contexts and Callahan and Azano's (2021) recommendation for place-based learning in early childhood contexts. However, Wood incorporates popular culture more explicitly in her model conceptualising talent development, in line with Gagné's DMGT (Gagné, 2013). She calls for research on the disruptive and supportive impacts of popular culture on the education of diverse rural gifted girls to nurture talent development. This focus is timely, as the impact of popular culture has become more evident in society in general with the outcomes of social media on the Internet contributing to both constructive and negative outcomes. The devastating news stories on television or the Internet in particular can have a profound impact on sensitive young gifted youth who may feel more empathetically and express emotions more readily than their same-age typical peers (Smith & Laura, 2009). In contrast, the benefits of technological resources and online learning for gifted students are evident, particularly for developing self-efficacy, motivation, and self-regulation as suggested by Fung, Yuen, and Yuen (2021) from Hong Kong. In the wider research literature, Periathiruvadi and Rinn (2012) imparted that the use of technology and the Internet can be an individual creative outlet as well as provide differentiated learning opportunities, such as assessing interests and strengths, scaffolding self-regulation, undertaking inquiry-based project learning, and developing problem-based skills both within the general classroom and without. Such technological tools and programs allow flexibility in teaching and learning from which gifted students can benefit. However, Bannister-Tyrell and Wood (2021) caution reliance on online resources as the primary enrichment support for rural gifted students.

Nearly a century ago, Leta Hollingworth believed that both inherited natural abilities and nurturing the educational and familial environment contributed to enhancing talent potential. Consequentially, she worked tirelessly to develop curriculum and effective enrichment strategies using biographies of creative experts to scaffold the talent development of gifted children (VanTassel-Baska & Brown,

2015). In her handbook chapter, Diezmann (2021) chronicled the life and education of four extraordinary Australians as role models for gifted students. Scaffolding Singaporean students' interests through social justice passion projects inspired by *Picture Book Biographies* (PBBs) of eminent peoples can support the growth orientation of gifted students. Through the use of authentic visual narratives of those who have excelled, gifted students can come to the realisation that excellence requires hard work and resiliency (Garces-Bacsal, 2021). This connects with Australians Burns' and Martin's (2021) notion of growth orientation, which is also in line with Dweck's (2017) growth mindset theory. As such, the influence of growth orientation involves a greater exploration of growth goal setting and growth mindset and how these influence students' outcomes. Indeed, to support talent development, Burns and Martin recommended investigating both the predictors and the outcomes of gifted students' motivation for learning. They also imparted that, "future work may consider examining the antecedents of gifted students' motivation, such as the role of personal relationships and classroom climate, each of which are salient predictors of motivation in 'general' populations'.

As David Dai (2021) states in this handbook, "one of the purposes of gifted education is to prepare youth for solving pressing problems in the world." Young gifted visionaries, crusaders, philanthropists, entrepreneurs, inventors, innovators, pioneers, and activists who actioned their altruism in pre-teen and teenage years example some of these: Swedish *Greta Thunberg*, is a young environmental activist, who has the social gift of galvanising school students and adults globally for youth climate change for environmental sustainability; in 1995, 10-year-old American *Aubyn C. Burnside* used his empathy and innovation to co-found *Suitcases for Kids* to provide suitcases for foster children; Pakistani *Malala Yousafzai* escaped an assassination attempt, used her social advocacy to create the *Malala Fund* that advocates for women's rights, and is a role model for girls' education. She became the youngest Nobel prize winner in history; Fijian *Timoci Naulusala* uses his social-emotional gifts to crusade for climate change and subsequently, young people's security and well-being; Syrian *Bana Alabed* is a talented author who documented the atrocities of war in Aleppo, advocates for peace, and received the *Atlantic Council Freedom Award*; over a decade ago, African Zambian *Thandiwe Chama*, a gifted adolescent, was awarded the 2007 *International Children's Peace Prize* and still uses her social-emotional strengths to campaign for the rights of those living with HIV/AIDS; Indonesian Balinese 10-year-old *Melati Wijsen* and her 12-year-old sister *Isabel* used their social strengths to start a campaign for reducing plastics; American/Cuban *Emma González* co-founded *Never Again MSD* and has committed her life to decreasing gun violence; English *Siena Castellon* has autism and learning difficulties and is gifted intellectually and socially, is a neurodiversity advocate and anti-bullying activist, she created a website to mentor autistic students, is an author, created the #AlwaysBeKind Instagram campaign, and is a multi-award winner (e.g., *Points of Light, Diana Award, and British Citizen Youth Award, BBC Radio 1 Teen Hero Award*); Gifted in many ways, Indian West Bengali *Anoyara Khatun* campaigns to work with the *Save the Children* foundation to create children's advocacy groups to help stop child trafficking, labor exploitation, and child marriage; and, demonstrating his creativity and social giftedness, Dutch *Boyan Slat's* non-profit

Ocean Clean-up for plastic reduction originated when he was a teenager. There are many more children and adolescents using their gifts altruistically around the world. It is hoped that gifted research and education can assist them in their endeavors. As gifted adults strive to find peaceful, equitable, inclusive, and transformative outcomes through the *Black Lives Matter Movement* and solutions to the *Coronavirus* pandemic crisis, and other crises, again we acknowledge that education, equitable access to resources, and opportunities can allow gifted people to develop their creativity, social-emotional, and intellectual and other gifts for their own good and — if they so choose — for the good of humanity worldwide.

Socioculturally, socio-economically, and social-emotionally, I wish everyone well and safe during the unprecedented and uncertain times within which this handbook emerged. While this handbook was conceived well before the 2020 Black Lives Matter Movement or the COVID-19 Pandemic, both of which have gripped the global community in inconceivable ways, causing unparalleled and unexpected outcomes, the handbook was born within a global culture where inequities, discrimination, misogyny, chauvinism, despotism, racism, fanatism, ageism, sizeism, and many other forms of discriminatory "isms" are still rife. One reason for developing this handbook was to address many of these inequities in the education of gifted students and to celebrate the diverse students, parents, academics, educators, advocates, and the like who strive to respect cultural diversity, neurodiversity, and other differences in education. Those who are: living with open-heartedness not closed-mindedness; respecting and being kind to everyone, not bullying those conceived as weaker; peacefully expressing views and calling for attitudinal change not hostility; creating a safe, inclusive, and transformative future, not provoking divisiveness, hatred, and violence; or the giving of themselves to enhance life, not taking it for selfish individual self-aggrandisement; amongst many other polarising perspectives, are the inspirations for future leadership.

From the South Korean perspective, Lee, Kim, and Boo (2021) contended that teachers can prepare leaders of tomorrow to address today's and tomorrow's diverse global twenty-first-century concerns, such as the uncertainty of pandemics, the exponential growth of environmental destruction, the singularity of machine intelligence, the existential risk of overpopulation and civil unrest, the steep growth of cyber-bullying, the increased threat of terrorism, or increasing homelessness. The authors match the skills needed for leadership with those often cited as needed in the twenty-first century, such as problem-solving, critical and creative thinking, communication, open-mindedness, respect for diversity, collaboration, conflict management, and empathy and suggested that "a well-designed leadership program", role-modelling, and SEL mentoring can help develop these skills in gifted students.

From Curriculum Models to Research-Based Pedagogy Models in Practice

There are a number of curriculum and pedagogy models presented in the handbook and their applications have been applied differently in different sociocultural contexts, which are derived from diverse research. Some of them are well known and used intermittently; some are more strongly research-based, while others are not.

From Differentiation or Personalisation or Attuned Pedagogy?

Today there is still debate between differentiation and personalisation (e.g., Bevan-Brown, McGee, Ward, & MacIntyre, 2011; Yuen et al., 2018; VanTassel-Baska & Brown, 2015). While personalised learning appears to align closely with differentiated instruction, the broader definition of differentiation incorporates much more than differentiated instruction, such as differentiating teaching, learning, content, processes, products, assessment, resources, and outcomes individually and in different grouping contexts (e.g., Maker & Schiever, 2010; Reis & Renzulli, 2015; Smith, 2015; Tomlinson & Reis, 2004). Differentiation is not just using many different strategies miscellaneously, but differentiation is the careful planning of evidence-based curriculum, assessment, strategies, and programs for individual learning student needs within varying grouping contexts both within and outside the general classroom (Smith, 2015). Notably, VanTassel-Baska and Brown (2015) query whether differentiation is actually applied for gifted students and implore educators to use the effective practices—derived from the gifted education research and otherwise—that are relevant for all students in the general education context, inclusive of gifted students.

In Lu and Chen's (2021) chapter in this handbook they added another dimension to this debate, and that is *attuned pedagogy*. They suggested that the uniqueness of the individual, professional relationships, and matching the student needs with attuned personalised connections with their learning readiness, their discipline for learning, and their natural desire for achievement can initiate their talent potential. Though the Actiotope model is not mentioned in their chapter, *attuned pedagogy* aligns with Zeigler's Actiotope model, in that the focus is not on the gifted child, but contextually focused on mastering the social-cultural learning environment and seeking "wisdom based on professional knowledge and judgement", imagination, and diversity to enhance learning potential.

Several authors in this handbook discussed differentiation for talent development in their chapters (e.g., Cho et al., 2021; Maker & Wearne, 2021; Munro, 2021; Swanson et al., 2021; VanTassel-Baska, Hubbard, & Robbins, 2021). For example, Maker (1982) extended her original differentiation model with a recent Australian study (Maker & Wearne, 2021) and provided recommendations for identifying advanced problem-solving skills and differentiating for talent development using the REAPS model. Advantages of the REAPS model are that it has been researched within Australasian and Pacific rim contexts and can be applied within the general classroom with all students regardless of their level of ability.

There are many program models and curriculum approaches not mentioned in the handbook that have been validated by sound research, so educators have many choices to support effective practice for talent development (e.g., Gardner, 1999; Renzulli, 2005; Sternberg, 1986; Tomlinson et al., 2009; VanTassel-Baska & Brown, 2007, 2015). However, Grant and Morrissey (2021) recommend there is "a pressing research need to validate suitable curriculum and pedagogical approaches" in the Australian early childhood field. Indeed, there is a pressing need for evaluations across all the models and frameworks currently used! In regard to the effectiveness of these models, VanTassel-Baska and Brown's (2007) criteria can be applied to any new curriculum models or well-used models that have not been effectively evaluated. Additionally, more meta-analyses of programs and curriculum models may progress more rigorous support for gifted students in practice. These may be steps forward for validating the models currently used to frame assessment, curricula, and pedagogy in the Asia-Pacific and rim nations. Many of the models originally validated by the VanTassel-Baska and Brown assessment (e.g., *The Stanley Model of Talent Identification and Development, The Renzulli & Reis Schoolwide Enrichment Triad Model* [SEM], 2014, *Sternberg's Triarchic Componential Model,* 1986) have been used sporadically in the Asia-Pacific region, but VanTassel-Baska and Brown's evaluation criteria are yet to be applied to any of these models in this region since their seminal work on them was focused in the USA. Hence, care needs to be taken to ensure the appropriate sociocultural considerations of using the chosen models in the Asia-Pacific contexts more widely.

From Exclusion to Teaching Developmentally and Inclusively

Teaching developmentally is inclusive and holistic practice that entails supporting the academic, social, emotional, physical, cultural, and spiritual (Walton & Vialle, 2021) needs of all students at different levels of the educational continuum, such as students with special needs, typical grade students, and students with giftedness (Moltzen, 2006). In order to accomplish teaching developmentally according to learning readiness, Grant and Morrisey (2021) suggested the use of the sociocultural approach to curriculum and pedagogy, that is inclusive of gifted students in the general classroom, stating that this is one way to develop respect for various cultural beliefs and values.

Building on the work of June Maker and Carol Ann Tomlinson and other *Differentiation* gurus, in the wider research and practice, Kanevsky (2019) created *Possibilities for Learning*, an online resource to support the identification of gifted traits and strengths in relation to needed differentiated strategies. This online resource and many others available today, for example, Renzulli's and Reis's (2014), are beneficial to support the identification, programming, and provisions for diversely gifted students in the general education context. The benefits derive from going beyond labelling the gifted child, to focusing on their developmental readiness, strengths, behaviours, and needs matched with associated practical and differentiated support mechanisms. Maker's (Maker & Wearne, 2021) REAPS curriculum model is again relevant here as it focuses on teaching the student when developmentally appropriate.

Research has tried to include the perspectives of students when assessing programs and provisions (e.g., Coleman, Micko, & Cross, 2015). Kanevsky (2011) reinforced the value of engaging student voice in assessing the differentiated teaching they believed they needed for effective learning. In New Zealand, Riley (2021) also used student voice to report on ability grouping—a highly supported learning environment for gifted students (e.g., Steenbergen-Hu, Makel, & Olszewski-Kubilius, 2016)—reinforcing how important such a learning context is for developing a sense of belonging within socialisation. In Australian selective school contexts, Rogers (2021) explored gifted students' perspectives of effective teachers and provided some informative recommendations to support the talent development of gifted students in secondary schools. For example, gifted secondary students reported that effective teachers have strong content knowledge, need to update subject area knowledge with consistent professional learning, and can examine how to address classroom behaviour and bullying. Rogers is hopeful that the study exampled in her handbook chapter is replicated with different levels of cohorts and in varying educational contexts for gifted students.

Towards Special Education, Gifted Education, or Talent Development Within General Inclusive Education?

Experts support the 'talent development' approach (e.g., Plucker & Callahan, 2014). On the one hand, there is the view that gifted education should be an entity on its own, while on the other the view is that it should be a part of special, inclusive, and/or general education (e.g., Moltzen, 2006; Roda, 2015; Sánchez-Escobedo, Camelo-Lavadores, & Valdés-Cuerv, 2021). Hence, researchers have promoted research and practice that bridges the general, special, and gifted populations and inclusive contexts, to encourage a shared vision that incorporates multilevel, multimodel, and multi-disciplinary inclusive education for all (e.g., Renzulli & Reis, 2014; Sapon-Shevin, 2003; VanTassel-Baska & Brown, 2015). Building such bridges by combining gifted education research within general education inclusive practice may be of merit going forward, especially if access to funding is reliant in such a philosophy in practice.

From an Isolated Field to Multidisciplinary Research and Community Collaboration

Often, researchers, families, and educators of gifted students feel isolated in their context (Sapon-Shevin, 2003). Effective leadership can dissipate some isolation in practice (VanTassel-Baska & Brown, 2015). Furthermore, the field itself can be isolated. However, heeding Ambrose's (2015) suggestion for multidisciplinary research that was mentioned earlier and collaborative research partnerships exampled in the work of Cramond et al. (2021), Sánchez-Escobedo et al. (2021), and Olszewski-Kubilius et al. (2021) in chapters in this handbook can alleviate some of this isolation.

For families and educators, tapping into community resources and personnel can help support them in their endeavour to support gifted students. For example, in a chapter from Singapore, Garces-Bacsal (2021) suggested linking the use of inspiring narratives/biographies to encourage community-based initiatives or passion projects. Community-based projects can provide the opportunity for students to develop those interests and creative skills for the twenty-first century for future innovative and productive outcomes. Furthermore, undertaking community-based research enables linking with authentic service-based initiatives to enhance reflection on local contextual issues that may concern the gifted child and inform wider global solutions to the world's problems hinted at earlier. Many authors in this handbook promoted scaffolding (Cho et al., 2021; Garces-Bacsal, 2021), mentoring (Horsley & Moeed, 2021; Jung, Koo, Hay, & Smith, 2021; Tan, Tan, & Chia, 2021), goal setting (Burns & Martin, 2021), and counselling (Bakar & Brody, 2021) as additional collaborative ways to support talent development.

In the Singaporean context, Tan et al. (2021) reiterated the need for a community-based approach with: scientists as mentors sharing their professional expertise; mentor training to ensure understanding of gifted students' needs; planning; and student goal setting with monitoring and evaluation to ensure more success within the mentor/mentee relationship and in the outcomes. In New Zealand, Horsley and Moeed (2021) called for more research on the academic achievements of academically gifted students in science to investigate whether an interest-based curriculum and pedagogy with mentoring by inspirational role-models, autonomous learning, and practical learning tasks are enabling exceptional outcomes that may lead to eminence. In the handbook, Horsley's and Moeed's (2021) views are supported by Australian scholar Watters (2021), who adds the need for interest-based learning tasks inclusive of negotiation and choice, ability grouping with like-minded peers, and tapping into students' curiosity to engage student learning in science. Watters links these academic needs with the support of the development of the social-emotional well-being of gifted students, with *motivation* being one such construct of importance here that aligns with the wider research literature (e.g., Baker, 2018; Wright-Scott, 2018) as being needed for talent to develop.

From Career Expectations to Career Choices

There has been an increased interest in the career journeys of highly able students over the last decade or so. For example, in his handbook chapter, Jung (2021) examined the career-decisions of Asia-Pacific gifted students generally and concluded that the career decisions of gifted students in this region were different to others outside the region due to the influences of their cultural backgrounds and their individual characteristics. He implored further research on this under-researched group was warranted, mainly for sociocultural reasons and to support their future career decisions across cultural contexts. Building on this career-based research, Jung et al. (2021) also called for more research on the career decision-making processes of gifted Brazilian international university students studying in STEM subjects in Australia. Support for this gifted population is also needed on campus, for example, guidance, counselling, and mentoring on employment prospects with a view to exploring the inhibitors and promoters of career decisions associated with STEM subjects. Also, Korean and Australian colleagues, Ryu, Lee, Kim, Goundar, Lee, and Jung (2021) collaborated in their chapter and they indicated that STEM was extended to STEAM in Korea to include the Arts and to encourage more interest in STEM-related subjects and careers.

With a focus on the Arts more specifically, talent development in an Australian university level music course was the emphasis of Rowley's (2021) handbook chapter. This author specifically presented perceptions of transitions to music careers within students' work experience contexts. She found that engaging in dialogue and using reflective ePortfolios "on their musicality, teaching, leadership, professional musician identity, talent development to career ready musicians" enabled gifted musicians to project their expertise forward into their imagined successful future professional careers and enabled more success in actually achieving their career goals. A university course can re-orientate the "tertiary music curriculum and learning for career relevance … to enable the development of essential, transferable skills such as critical thinking, communication, teamwork, workplace negotiation. and problem-solving for talented young musicians". Rowley (2021) reinforced that the strategy could be applied across all disciplines making it a multi-dimensional teaching and learning approach to support career development and career choices.

From Misconceptions to Positive Attitudes and Contextually Supported Talent Development

Societal misconceptions that feed negative attitudes towards gifted students, gifted education, and the word 'gifted' in particular are rife everywhere (Smith, 2017), so much so, that the *Gifted Child Quarterly* (1982, 2009) has dedicated special editions to the issues around trying to demythologise gifted education. Perhaps it is time for another special edition on the matter? Generally, researchers and practitioners have tried to eradicate these myths or misconceptions by moving towards a talent development model and reducing the use of the word gifted to *highly able*, *supernormal*, or *talented*, but these myths still persist today. Many believe that the starting place to eradicating these myths and divisive attitudes is in teacher professional training.

In an Australian chapter, Plunkett and Kronborg (2021) assessed preservice teachers' perspectives about teaching gifted students in an *Initial Teacher Education* (ITE) program. They concluded that there is the need for these courses in all-undergraduate programs for future teachers to be made aware of the complexities of teaching gifted and talented students. The value of nurturing positive attitudes towards gifted children, reflections on practice, and in identifying research-based strategies and programs to support highly able learners were highlighted factors in their findings. Constructive attitudes can then be translated into effective practice if the practice is also research-based. From the USA, VanTassel-Baska, Hubbard, and Robbins (2021) reiterated the care needed in teacher preservice training programs when choosing and teaching research-based differentiation strategies, especially when differentiation practice is not as evident for gifted students in practice. They reinforced the value of using professional standards to guide planning and implementation of teaching and learning for gifted students. Still others believe in tackling in-service teacher attitudes themselves. For example, Wormald and Bannister-Tyrrell's (2021) nationwide Australian study found that in-service teachers did not even know what *twice-exceptional* meant!

Meanwhile, others examined the perspectives and roles of paraprofessionals who support talent development contextually. For example, in their handbook chapter Henderson and Jarvis (2021) researched *Australian Gifted Education Coordinators* (GEC) who considered their roles ill-defined and inhibitors to their role to be lack of recognition, few resources, and time constraints. The authors suggested that these issues could be addressed through a shared vision of a whole school approach that incorporates further professional learning to elevate the positive profile of the GEC. The provision of more adequate resourcing that matches the coordinator's expertise can enable the GEC to be a more effective change agent for students' talent development to ensue. In the USA, a study conducted by Long et al. (2019) found that there is still a huge reliance on GECs taking part-time pull-out programs for gifted learners that focus on project-based learning, critical thinking, and creativity skills rather than providing advanced academics that accelerate learning, but no mention of the coordinator's specific role or responsibilities was reported though.

Then others explored talent development in different school contexts. For example, Conejeros-Solar and Smith (2021) examined homeschooling for gifted children in Chile, Australia, and the USA. Parents have sought home education as an alternative educational context for their children due to harmful misconceptions and negative societal attitudes that have resulted in bullying and very unhappy students. Additionally, Gallagher (2021) explored the attributes, issues, and barriers to talent development in the Thai international schooling system. There is very little empirical research on either of these educational contexts. Gallagher suggested that localised policy and "taking a talent development perspective may help international schools to develop a menu of context-specific services for meeting the needs of their highly able learners that are rigorous, sustainable, defensible, and effective". Socio-culturally context-specific services can include the trilogy of provisions including acceleration, grouping, and enrichment with differentiated strategies, such as curricular flexibility, project-based learning, service-learning opportunities, community competitions, awards, science fairs, or mentoring with staff who have the interest, expertise, and willingness to provide the support needed. These approaches can be researched in different cultural and community contexts with different student populations and control groups for rigor, especially how international schooling or homeschooling enhances or inhibits talent development for diversely gifted students in different countries.

Conclusion

This concluding chapter reviewed some of the implications for research and practice according to the views of educators in many Asia-Pacific and rim countries. The astute scholar in the field will have identified the *familiar*, while also noticing the *new* within the authors' contributions. Effective practice that is evident in the international literature was reiterated, while providing original insights for trialling original research and practices both in the Asia-Pacific region and elsewhere. In several chapters in the handbook, preliminary studies were exampled so authors have either published results elsewhere or are encouraged to undertake deeper analyses and write up their results in more detail for journal publications and seek interdisciplinary collaborations that will inspire further research on the investigations initiated.

As authors, editors, and publisher we collaborated on this momentous task to share our vision for improved gifted education for talent development in the Asia-Pacific and rim parts of the world. We shared our perspectives, unique research, strategies, and programs that we hope will be built upon by the contributing authors and others who may be inspired by our work. Ultimately, we shared our passion for effective gifted education and provided some impetus for more constructive action to overcome underachievement and underrepresentation. In the foreword, Borland stated that, giftedness is not a universal construct, but "is profoundly shaped by the various cultures in which it is created, and that there is no such thing as giftedness divorced from a specific context". However, "few of our ways of thinking about giftedness take sociocultural contexts into consideration". Nearly two decades ago, Borland and colleagues (2003) also argued for a paradigm shift in gifted education, that reinforced the need for effective education for all, including gifted students. There have been many calls to *educational* arms over the years for a paradigm shift in gifted education, the most recent in Wallace et al. (2018) *SAGE Handbook of Gifted and Talented Education*. We would suggest that it is a call to *sociocultural* educational arms for a paradigm shift in education as a whole; so all students' education is included, inclusive of the holistic needs of highly able students world-wide. After all, our ultimate goal is to support the holistic, creative, and talent development of students whoever or wherever they may be.

References

Ambrose, D. (2015). Borrowing insights from other disciplines to strengthen the conceptual foundations for gifted education. *International Journal for Talent Development and Creativity, 3*(2), 33–57.

Ambrose, D., VanTassel-Baska, J., Coleman, L., & Cross, T. (2010). Gifted education as a porous fragmented discipline. *Journal for the Education of the Gifted, 33*(4), 453–478. Retrieved from https://files.eric.ed.gov/fulltext/EJ893880.pdf

Baker, G. (2018). *Gifted adolescent wellbeing: Case study of an Australian immersion.* Unpublished doctoral dissertation. Queensland University of Technology, Brisbane, QLD

Bannister-Tyrrell, M. (2017). Gagné's DMGT 2.0: A possible model of unification and shared understandings. *Australasian Journal of Gifted Education, 26*(2), 43–50. Retrieved from https://eric.ed.gov/?id=EJ1169281

Bevan-Brown, J., McGee, A., Ward, A., & MacIntyre, L. (2011). Personalising learning: A passing fad or a cornerstone of education? *New Zealand Journal of Educational Studies, 46*(2), 75–88. Retrieved from https://search.informit.com.au/documentSummary;dn=956593406382955; res=IELHSS. ISSN: 0028-8276.

Bicknell, B. & Riley, T. (2013). Gifted and talented education in New Zealand schools: A decade later. *APEX: The New Zealand Journal of Gifted Education, 18*(1), 1–16. Retrieved from https://researchcommons.waikato.ac.nz/handle/10289/8872

Borland, J. H. (Ed.) (2003). *Rethinking gifted education.* New York: Teachers College Press.

Coleman, L. J., Micko, K. J., & Cross, T. L. (2015). Twenty-five years of research on the lived experience of being gifted in school: Capturing the students' voices. *Journal for the Education of the Gifted, 38*(4), 358–376. https://doi.org/10.1177/0162353215607322

Dabrowski, K. (1964). *Positive disintegration* (p. 1964). Boston, MA: Little, Brown.

Dweck, C. (2017). The journey to children's mindsets and beyond. *Child Development Perspectives, 11*(2), 139–144. https://doi.org/10.1111/cdep.12225

Gagné, F. (2013). The DMGT: Changes within, beneath, and beyond. *Talent Development and Excellence, 5*(1), 5–19.

Gardner, H. (1999). *Intelligence reframed: Multiple intelligences for the 21st century.* New York, NY: Basic Books.

Gross, M. U. M. (2010). *In her own write: A lifetime in gifted education.* Sydney, NSW: Gifted Education Research/Resource and Information Centre, UNSW.

Hertzog, N. B. (2017). Designing the learning context in school for talent development. *The Gifted Child Quarterly, 61*, 219–228. https://doi.org/10.1177/0016986217705712

Kanevsky, L. S. (2011). Deferential differentiation: What types of differentiation do students want? *The Gifted Child Quarterly, 55*(4), 279–299. https://doi.org/10.1177/0016986211422098

Kanevsky, L. S. (2019). *Planning for and with highly able learners.* Retrieved from http://possibilitiesforlearning.com

Lo, C. O., & Porath, M. (2017). Paradigm shifts in gifted education: An examination vis-à-vis its historical situatedness and pedagogical sensibilities. *The Gifted Child Quarterly, 61*(4), 343–360. https://doi.org/10.1177/0016986217722840

Long, D., Hamilton, R., McCoach, B., Siegle, D., Gubbins, E. J., & Callahan, C. M. (2019). What really happens in gifted education: A portrait of three states. National Center for Research on Gifted Education (NCRGE) brief on gifted education curriculum and gifted achievement growth of gifted students in three states. Presented at the *annual meeting of the American Educational Research Association*, Toronto.

Maker, C. J. (1982). *Curriculum development for the gifted.* Rockville, MD: Aspen Systems Corporation.

Maker, C. J., & Schiever, S. W. (2010). *Curriculum development and teaching strategies for gifted learners* (3rd ed.). Austin, TX: Pro-Ed.

McBee, M. T., Peters, S. J., & Miller, E. M. (2016). The impact of the nomination stage on gifted program identification: A comprehensive psychometric analysis. *The Gifted Child Quarterly, 60*(4), 1–21. https://doi.org/10.1177/0016986216656256

McCluskey, K. W. (2017). Identification of the gifted redefined . . . with ethics and equity in mind. *Roeper Review, 39*(3), 195–198. https://doi.org/10.1080/02783193.2017.1318999

McCluskey, K. W. (2018). Gifted education: The future awaits. In B. Wallace, D. Sisk, & J. Senior (Eds.), *SAGE handbook of gifted and talented education* (pp. 553–565). New York, NY: Sage.

McCluskey, K. W., Treffinger, D. J., Baker, P. A., & Wiebe, A. C. (2016). *Lost prizes: Identifying and developing the talents of marginalized populations.* Winnipeg, MB: UW Faculty of Education Publishing.

Moltzen, R. (2006). Can 'inclusion' work for the gifted and talented? In C. M. M. Smith (Ed.), *Making Inclusion Work for More Gifted and Able Learners.* (pp. 41–55). New York: Routledge.

Periathiruvadi, S., & Rinn, A. N. (2012). Technology in gifted education: A review of best practices and empirical research. *Journal of Research on Technology in Education, 45*(2), 153–169. Retrieved from https://files.eric.ed.gov/fulltext/EJ991843.pdf

Phillipson, N. S., & Phillipson, S. (2016). Gifted Education in Asia: Problems and Prospects. In D. Y. Dai & C. C. Kuo (Eds.), *Chinese American education research and development association* (pp. 215–229). Charlotte, NC: Information Age Publishing.

Plucker, J. A., & Callahan, C. M. (2014). Research on giftedness and gifted education: Status of the field and considerations for the future. *Exceptional Children, 80*, 390–406. https://doi.org/10.1177/0014402914527244

Reis, S. M., & Renzulli, J. S. (2015). Five dimensions of differentiation. *Gifted Education Press Quarterly, 29*(3), 2–9. Retrieved from https://gifted.uconn.edu/wp-content/uploads/sites/961/2018/07/Five_Dimensions_of_Differentiation.pdf

Renzulli, J. S. (2005). The three-ring conception of giftedness: A developmental model for promoting creative productivity. In R. J. Sternberg & J. E. Davidson (Eds.), *Conceptions of giftedness* (2nd ed., pp. 246–279). New York, NY: Cambridge University Press.

Renzulli, J. S., & Reis, S. M. (2014). *The schoolwide enrichment model: A how-to guide for educational excellence* (3rd ed.). Waco, TX: Prufrock Press.

Roda, A. (2015). *Inequality in gifted and talented programs: Parental choices about status, school opportunity, and second-generation segregation.* New York, NY: Palgrove Macmillan.

Sapon-Shevin, M. E. (2003). Inclusion: A matter of social justice. *Educational Leadership, 61*(2), 25–28.

Smith, S. R. (2015). A dynamic differentiation framework for talent enhancement: Findings from syntheses and teachers' perspectives. *Australasian Journal of Gifted Education, 24*(1), 59–72.

Smith, S. R. (2017). Responding to the unique social and emotional learning needs of gifted Australian students. In E. Frydenberg, A. Martin, & R. Collie (Eds.), *Social and emotional learning in Australia and the Asia-Pacific: Perspectives, programmes, and approaches* (pp. 147–166). Singapore, Singapore: Springer.

Smith, S. R., & Laura, R. S. (2009). Repersonalizing educational ecologies to nurture the social and affective needs of gifted children. *Asia-Pacific Journal of Gifted and Talented Education, 1*(1), 23–40.

Steenbergen-Hu, S., Makel, M. C., & Olszewski-Kubilius, P. (2016). What one hundred years of research says about the effects of ability grouping and acceleration on K–12 students' academic achievement. *Review of Educational Research, 86*(4), 849–899. https://doi.org/10.3102/0034654316675417

Sternberg, R. J. (1986). A triarchic theory of intellectual giftedness. In R. J. Sternberg & J. E. Davidson (Eds.), *Conceptions of giftedness* (pp. 223–243). New York, NY: Cambridge University Press.

Tomlinson, C. A., Kaplan, S. N., Renzulli, J. S., Purcell, J., Leppien, J., Burns, D., . . . Imbeau, M. B. (2009). *The parallel curriculum model: A design to develop high potential and challenge high-ability learners* (2nd ed.). Thousand Oaks, CA: Corwin.

Tomlinson, C. A., & Reis, S. M. (Eds.). (2004). *Differentiation for gifted and talented students.* Thousand Oaks, CA: Corwin Press/SAGE.

VanTassel-Baska, J., & Brown, E. (2007). Towards best practice: An Analysis of the efficiency of curriculum models in gifted education. *The Gifted Child Quarterly, 51*(4), 342–358. https://doi.org/10.1177/0016986207306323

VanTassel-Baska, J., & Brown, E. (2015). An analysis of gifted education curriculum models. In F. Karnes & S. Bean (Eds.), *Methods and materials for the gifted* (4th ed., pp. 107–138). Waco, TX: Prufock Press.

Wallace, B., Sisk, D. A., & Senior, J. (Eds.). (2018). *The SAGE handbook of gifted and talented education.* New York, NY: Sage. https://doi.org/10.1080/02783193.2019.1553100

Wechsler, S. M., Blumen, S., & Bendelman, K. (2018). Challenges on the identification and development of giftedness in South America. In S. I. Pfeiffer (Ed.), *APA handbook of giftedness and talent* (pp. 97–112). Washington, DC: American Psychological Association.

Wright-Scott, K. (2018). *The social-emotional well-being of the gifted child and perceptions of parent and teacher social support.* Unpublished doctoral dissertation. Queensland University of Technology, Brisbane, QLD.

Yuen, M., Chan, S., Chan, C., Fung, D. C. L., Cheung, W. M., Kwan, T., & Leung, F. K. S. (2018). Differentiation in key learning areas for gifted students in regular classes: A project for primary school teachers in Hong Kong. *Gifted Education International, 34*(1), 36–46. https://doi.org/10.1177/0261429416649047

Susen R. Smith, PhD, is a GERRIC Senior Research Fellow and Senior Lecturer in Gifted and Special Education at the School of Education, University of NSW, Australia. She has extensive experience as a teacher, curriculum consultant, and educational leader from early childhood to tertiary education and adult education. She has been an invited visiting scholar to Columbia University, City University New York, the Hong Kong Institute of Education, National Taipei University of Education, Taiwan, and Imperial College London. Her specific research interests include ecological systems theory underpinning dynamically differentiated curriculum and pedagogy models and matrices for students with giftedness, indigeneity, underachievement, and multi-exceptionalities. She has published in international journals and has keynoted at national and international conferences, chaired the inaugural GERRIC Gifted Futures Forum, and is the inaugural editor of the first Asia-Pacific handbook on giftedness and talent development.

Index

© Springer Nature Singapore Pte Ltd. 2021
S. R. Smith (ed.), *Handbook of Giftedness and Talent Development in the Asia-Pacific*,
Springer International Handbooks of Education,
https://doi.org/10.1007/978-981-13-3041-4